THE HISTORY OF THE
UNIVERSITY OF OXFORD
VOLUME V

Scholars at a Lecture, January 1737. Henry Fisher of Jesus College agreed to be drawn for this satire. His text begins 'Datur Vacuum'. British Library: Paulson 143.

THE HISTORY

OF THE

UNIVERSITY OF OXFORD

GENERAL EDITOR · T. H. ASTON

VOLUME V

The Eighteenth Century

EDITED BY
L. S. SUTHERLAND AND
L. G. MITCHELL

CLARENDON PRESS · OXFORD
1986

Oxford University Press, Walton Street, Oxford OX2 6DP

Oxford New York Toronto
Delhi Bombay Calcutta Madras Karachi
Kuala Lumpur Singapore Hong Kong Tokyo
Nairobi Dar es Salaam Cape Town
Melbourne Auckland

and associated companies in
Beirut Berlin Ibadan Nicosia

Oxford is a trade mark of Oxford University Press

Published in the United States by
Oxford University Press, New York

British Library Cataloguing in Publication Data
The History of the University of Oxford.
Vol. 5: The Eighteenth Century
1. University of Oxford—History
I. Aston, T. H.   II. Sutherland, Dame, Lucy
III. Mitchell, L. G.
378.425'74'09   LF509
ISBN 0-19-951015-6

Typeset by Joshua Associates Limited, Oxford
Printed in Great Britain
at the University Printing House, Oxford
by David Stanford
Printer to the University

General Preface

It is to be doubted if any private institutions have been so fortunate in attracting the attention of antiquarians and historians as have the university and colleges of Oxford. As early as the beginning of the fourteenth century Henry Harclay compiled his *historiola*, and in the next century John Rous assembled facts relating to the history of Oxford as well as his important list of colleges and academical halls. From the sixteenth century we have for instance Miles Windsor, 'antiquae historiae Artifex' (Brian Twyne) and author of the brief *Academiarum totius Europae catalogus* (1586 etc.). Later we have an increasingly rich assemblage of works and collections on the university and its colleges. To select but a few from the scholars and artists who directed at least some of their attention this way: Brian Twyne, indefatigable antiquarian and archivist of both Corpus Christi College and the university and collector of much other information on town and gown, who wrote the first, if short, history of the university, his *Antiquitatis academiae oxoniensis apologia* (1608), not least for propagandist purposes in relation to the relative antiquity of Oxford and Cambridge; David Loggan, in the tradition of John Bereblock (1566) and Ralph Agas (1578), the most outstanding draughtsman ever to tackle both university and colleges, who published in 1675 his beautifully executed engravings which are an invaluable architectural presentation; Anthony Wood who compiled the first large-scale history; John Gutch who finely edited and expanded Wood's work in the late eighteenth century; and Rudolph Ackermann, in whose history (1814) various artists depicted not only the exterior but also the interior of university and college buildings, not to mention academic robes and founders of colleges.

In the last century or so the pace has quickened. For instance we have the first attempt to survey the history of all colleges in the unpretentious but none the less useful series of College Histories (1898–1903), not to mention other particular studies. More recently in the third volume of the *Victoria History of the County of Oxford* (1954) we have short studies of the history of the university and each of the colleges by various hands. Much more important have been the publications of the Oxford Historical Society beginning in 1884. Some of these have been monographs of a high standard, but the majority have been of source material bearing on the history of the university and its colleges and of institutions in the town or the town itself with all of which they had the closest connections.

Of the society's contributors one stands paramount, H. E. Salter, responsible alone or in collaboration for no less than thirty-five volumes. Then there is the relevant material in the Oxfordshire Record Society which began publication in 1919. Besides all this must be mentioned Strickland Gibson's *Statuta antiqua* (1931), a most masterly achievement even though subsequent work on the earliest volume of statutes, Registrum A, by himself and more prominently Graham Pollard, has altered the dating of many statutes and changed our understanding of the make-up of the volume as a whole; John Griffiths's edition of the Laudian code, with subsequent amendments, published in 1888; and the royal commission's edition, albeit far from definitive, of the *Statutes of the Colleges of Oxford* (1853). The result is that all the pre-1500 records of the university and much of later date are now available in scholarly print. In addition, on the side of biographical studies vital for social no less than personal and intellectual history, we have following on Foster's heroic if imperfect eight volumes covering the period 1500 to 1886 A. B. Emden's superb four volumes to 1540 not to mention sundry college registers.

But not surprisingly historians have recoiled from the monumental task of essaying an up-to-date version of Wood's history, save for Sir Henry Maxwell Lyte (1886) for the earlier centuries and Hastings Rashdall in the third volume of his *The Universities of Europe in the Middle Ages* (1895), subsequently (1936) and admirably edited by F. M. Powicke and A. B. Emden. It took an amateur, Sir Charles Mallet, boldly to attempt the overall task in his three-volume *History of the University of Oxford* (1924–7). For one man this was in many ways a remarkable achievement, but it is no discredit to Mallet to observe that it did not really meet the need. Nor, in fact, could that need be met by a single person or even by a small number, though V. H. H. Green published an interesting short history in 1974. After all, by about 1966–7 there had been published, according to E. H. Cordeaux's and D. H. Merry's *Bibliography of Printed Works relating to the University of Oxford* (1968), no less than 8,868 items, some slight of course but more or less all requiring at least some attention. And in addition to these specifically relating to the university are countless others which have at least something to say of relevance to its history and character: many biographies, literary output, ephemera and other material. And yet the very richness of the collections, published and unpublished, primary and secondary, the vital role of Oxford over the centuries, the importance of its institutional and social no less than its intellectual history and so on required and proposed the challenge for a truly comprehensive treatment on the grand scale. It was Lord Bullock who, towards the end of 1966, saw the need, pointed to the wealth of available material and to the fact that no individual scholar could undertake the necessary research for the authoritative account that was possible and required; it would have to be a co-operative effort. He took note of the fact also that the university was engaged on an extensive series of reforms which was a particularly appropriate time 'to put these reforms into a proper historical perspective [which] would be a declaration of confidence in ourselves as heirs of a great tradition which could not fail to make its impact at home and abroad' (memorandum to hebdomadal council, 17 October 1966, hebdomadal council papers, vol. 255, pages 279–80). The work was envisaged as a comprehensive history covering such aspects as the intellectual, the institutional, the social, the economic and the architectural character of the university in relation to national life and also its international role, with material on the colleges being included wherever this was relevant to the history of the university as such. Though to be launched by the university itself, the new History was in no way thought of as an 'official' one. Rather was it to be as scholarly and objective as possible and by no means to be written exclusively by scholars in Oxford.

It was Lord Bullock too who not only chaired the committee of inquiry into the proposal for a new and ambitious history but who steered it and its report through many discussions. Thus it was that the Project for the History of the University was launched in October 1968, among the most ambitious research projects in the humanities that the university has ever sponsored.

That the Project ever really materialized was, however, due not only to Lord Bullock's insight and skill as a negotiator, but to the financial generosity of various bodies. First, of course, the university itself. Then the university's higher studies fund. Thirdly the Nuffield Foundation with most handsome and continuing support. And finally, signalling the comprehensiveness at which the Project was aiming, the generality of the colleges which responded most warmly to the request for assistance. For this financial support we are deeply grateful. Beyond this we are indebted to bodies and persons who have supported the Project in various other ways. The colleges again, for instance, in the readiness with which they have given us access to their archives; and numerous individuals who will be thanked personally in the usual way in the editorial prefaces and chapters of the several volumes. Lastly we are deeply indebted to the Oxford University Press for shouldering the burden of publishing the new History. The new History will thus not only be co-operative in the sense that it is the work of many hands; it will also be so in the wide support on which it is founded.

T. H. A.

Preface

THIS volume, a monument to the memory of Dame Lucy Sutherland, has been made possible by the generosity of the Oxford colleges which have put their archives and libraries at our disposal and by the unstinting help given by their librarians and others for which we are deeply grateful. It is invidious to name any individual but our particular gratitude goes to Anne Whiteman of Lady Margaret Hall for her help in a variety of ways; to John Simmons, formerly librarian of All Souls; to John Wing of Christ Church library for whom nothing is ever too much trouble; to Vincent Quinn, formerly librarian of Balliol; to David Cox, emeritus fellow of University College and Christopher Pelling of the same college; to Tony Simcock of the Museum of the History of Science, Oxford; to Christopher Clayton and Penny Bowen; to John Stephens; to Philip Rotheram, who helped with the identification of the classical reading at Christ Church; to the staff of the Victoria County History of Oxfordshire; to Eileen Davies of the Bodleian law library; and to Rosamond Faith and Ralph Evans of the History of the University project. We should especially like to pay tribute to Ruth Vyse, assistant archivist of the university and to Richard Budgeon of the Bodleian Library who have both had excessive demands put upon them by us over the years. We thank the staff of the Bodleian Library for their courtesy.

We are indebted to scholars on both sides of the Atlantic but we should like to thank in particular the University of Kansas and the American Council of Learned Societies for making grants available to the late Robert Greaves, thus enabling him to work in England; and Richard Heitzenrater of Southern Methodist University for allowing us to use his transcripts of Benjamin Ingham's diary.

We are grateful to all owners and custodians of manuscripts and particularly to the marquess of Lansdowne for allowing us to quote from the letters of the first marquess, to the trustees of the Bowood Manuscript Collection, to all record offices and university libraries, to the late Mrs Beachcroft and her husband, to Mrs C. Harrison and Miss Elizabeth Wood and to the late W. N. Hargreaves-Mawdsley.

All contributors have been most patient with us over a number of years but in particular we should like to acknowledge the debt we owe to Ian Doolittle who at very short notice took over one of the most difficult chapters in the volume.

Finally, above all, our deepest thanks go to Mrs Valerie Jobling for her devotion and hard work in research and preparation of the volume from its inception, allied to her real interest in the eighteenth century and its values. Members of the university and persons connected with it have normally been identified in a footnote on their first mention in the volume, with their date of matriculation, college or colleges and last university or public appointment; if necessary, or to make a point, degrees have also been given. Where only the date of matriculation is known, however, identification has been confined to the index.

Unless otherwise stated the year has been taken to begin on 1 January.

L. G. M.

Contents

Plates

Figures

Acknowledgement is gratefully made to the Ashmolean Museum, Oxford, for assistance in the production of plates V and VI; to the Trustees of the British Museum for the frontispiece and plate XIV; to the Bodleian Library, Oxford, for plates I, II, III, XII, and XIII; to the warden and fellows of All Souls for plate IV; to the dean and students of Christ Church for plates of the Collections Books; and to H. M. Colvin, Esq., for figure 2 and plate XI.

Abbreviations

ASA	All Souls College archives
abp	archbishop
BA	bachelor of arts
BCA	Balliol College archives
BCL	bachelor of civil law
BD	bachelor of divinity
BL	British Library, London
Bloxam, *Reg. Magdalen*	J. R. Bloxam, *A Register of the Presidents, Fellows, Demies, Instructors in Grammar and in Music, Chaplains, Clerks, Choristers, and Other Members of Saint Mary Magdalen College in the University of Oxford, from the foundation of the College to the Present Time* (7 vols Oxford 1853–81, index vol. by W. D. Macray Oxford 1885); cf Macray, *Reg. Magdalen*
BM	bachelor of medicine
BMus	bachelor of music
bn	baron
BNC	Brasenose College
BNCA	Brasenose College archives
Bodl.	Bodleian Library, Oxford
bp	bishop
Brasenose Monographs	*Brasenose College Quatercentenary Monographs* (2 vols in 3 OHS lii–iv 1909)
Bray MSS	Exeter College archives, Bray MSS
bt	baronet
Building Accounts of the Radcliffe Camera	*The Building Accounts of the Radcliffe Camera*, ed. S. G. Gillam (OHS new ser. xiii 1958)
CA	Christ Church archives
Catalogue of Portraits	Mrs R. L. Poole, *Catalogue of Portraits in the Possession of the University, Colleges, and County of Oxford* (3 vols OHS lvii 1912, lxxxi–ii 1926)

CCC	Corpus Christi College (Oxford)
CCCA	Corpus Christi College (Oxford) archives
Ch. Ch.	Christ Church
Collectanea i	*Collectanea* 1st series, ed. C. R. L. Fletcher (OHS v 1885)
Collectanea iv	*Collectanea* 4th series (OHS xlvii 1905)
Costin, *St. John's*	W. C. Costin, *The History of St. John's College, Oxford, 1598–1860* (OHS new ser. xii 1958)
CSPD	*Calendar of State Papers, Domestic Series, preserved in the Public Record Office, 1547–1704* (92 vols London 1856–1972)
d.	duke
d	died
DCL	doctor of civil law
DD	doctor of divinity
DM	doctor of medicine
DMus	doctor of music
DNB	*The Dictionary of National Biography from the Earliest Times to 1900* (66 vols London 1885–1901, repr. in 22 vols London 1921–2)
e.	earl
ECA	Exeter College archives
Enactments in Parliament	*Enactments in Parliament specially concerning the Universities of Oxford and Cambridge and the Halls and Colleges therein and the Colleges of Winchester, Eton and Westminster*, ed. L. L. Shadwell (4 vols OHS lviii–lxi 1912)
Fowler, *Corpus*	T. Fowler, *The History of Corpus Christi College* (OHS xv 1893)
FRCP	fellow of the Royal College of Physicians
FRS	fellow of the Royal Society
Hearne, *Collections*	*Remarks and Collections of Thomas Hearne*, ed. C. E. Doble, D. W. Rannie, H. E. Salter *et al.* (11 vols OHS ii, vii, xiii, xxxiv, xlii–iii, xlviii, l, lxv, lxvii, lxxii 1884–1918)
HMC	Royal Commission on Historical Manuscripts
HMC *Bucks, MSS*	*The Manuscripts of the Earl of Buckinghamshire, the Earl of Lindsey, the Earl of Onslow, Lord Emly*

	Theodore J. Hare, Esq., and James Round, Esq., M.P. (HMC 38th series 1895 as part 9 of appendix to 14th report)
HMC *Carlisle MSS*	*The Manuscripts of the Earl of Carlisle, preserved at Castle Howard* (HMC 42nd series 1897 as pt 6 of appx to 15th report)
HMC *Downshire MSS*	*Report on the Manuscripts of the Marquis of Down-shire, preserved at Easthampstead Park, Berks.* (4 vols in 5 HMC 75th series 1924–[42])
HMC *Egmont Diary*	*Manuscripts of the Earl of Egmont: diary of the first earl of Egmont (Viscount Percival)* (3 vols 1920–3 in HMC 63rd series)
HMC *Egmont MSS*	*Report on the Manuscripts of the Earl of Egmont* (2 vols in 3 1905–9 in HMC 63rd series)
HMC *Fifth Report*	*Fifth Report of the Royal Commission on Historical Manuscripts* (HMC 4th series 1876)
HMC *Finch MSS*	*Report on the Manuscripts of Allan George Finch, Esq., of Burley-on-the-Hill, Rutland* (2 vols HMC 71st series 1913–22)
HMC *Fortescue MSS*	*The Manuscripts of J. B. Fortescue, Esq., preserved at Dropmore* (10 vols HMC 30th series 1892–1927, i–ii as appx 3 and 4 to 13th and 14th reports)
HMC *Fourteenth Report*	*Fourteenth Report of the Royal Commission on Histor-ical Manuscripts* (HMC 13th series 1896)
HMC *Kenyon MSS*	*The Manuscripts of Lord Kenyon* (HMC 35th series 1894 as pt 4 of appx to 14th report)
HMC *Leyborne-Popham MSS*	*Report on the Manuscripts of F. W. Leyborne-Popham, Esq., of Littlecote, Co. Wilts.* (HMC 51st series 1899)
HMC *Lonsdale MSS*	*The Manuscripts of the Earl of Lonsdale* (HMC 33rd series 1893 as pt 7 of appx to 13th report)
HMC *Ormonde MSS*	*The Manuscripts of the Marquis of Ormonde, pre-served at Kilkenny Castle* (HMC 36th series, 3 vols 1895–1909, i–ii as pt 7 of appx to 14th report, new ser. 8 vols 1902–20)
HMC *Portland MSS*	*The Manuscripts of his grace the Duke of Portland, preserved at Welbeck Abbey* (10 vols HMC 29th series 1891–1931, i–iv as pts 1–2 of appx to 13th report, pt 2 of appx to 14th report and pt 4 of appx to 15th report)
HMC *Seventh Report*	*Seventh Report of the Royal Commission on Historical Manuscripts* (HMC 6th series 1879)

HMC *Townshend MSS*	*The Manuscripts of the Marquess Townshend* (HMC 19th series 1887 as pt 4 of appx to 11th report)
HMC *Various MSS*	*Report on Manuscripts in Various Collections* (8 vols HMC 55th series 1901-14)
hon.	honorary
Hon.	Honourable
JCA	Jesus College (Oxford) archives
Laudian Code, ed. Griffiths	*Statutes of the University of Oxford codified in the year 1636 under the authority of Archbishop Laud, Chancellor of the University*, ed. J. Griffiths, intr. C. L. Shadwell (Oxford 1888); the numbered titles into which the statutes are divided and the numbered sections and chapters (§§) into which titles may be subdivided (most titles have chapters which are not grouped into sections, a few titles are not subdivided at all) are here designated respectively by upper-case roman, lower-case roman and arabic numbers (for example VII. ii. 3 represents title VII, section ii, chapter 3 and V. 2 represents title V. chapter 2)
LCM	Lincoln College muniment room
Letters of Radcliffe and James	*Letters of Richard Radcliffe and John James of Queen's College, Oxford, 1755-83*, ed. M. Evans (OHS ix 1888)
Linc.	Lincoln College
m.	matriculated
MA	master of arts
Macleane, *Pembroke*	D. Macleane, *A History of Pembroke College, Oxford* (OHS xxxiii 1897)
Macray, *Reg. Magdalen*	W. D. Macray, *A Register of the Members of St. Mary Magdalen College, Oxford, from the Foundation of the College* (new series, cf Bloxam, *Reg. Magdalen*) (8 vols London 1894-1915)
MCA	Magdalen College (Oxford) archives
MCR	Merton College records
Magd.	Magdalen College (Oxford)
Magdalen and James II	*Magdalen College and King James II 1686-1688*, ed. J. R. Bloxam (OHS vi 1886)
ML	licence to practise medicine
MSS Ballard	Oxford, Bodleian Library, Ballard MSS

NCA	New College archives
Newdigate MSS	Warwick, Warwick county record office, New-digate MSS
nd	no date given
np	no place of publication given
NS	dated by new style, with year taken to begin on 1 January (dates in this volume are new style unless otherwise stated; NS is added explicitly only in a few cases to avoid possible ambiguity)
OCA	Oriel College archives
OED	*A New English Dictionary on Historical Principles*, ed. J. A. H. Murray, W. A. Craigie, H. Bradley and C. T. Onions (A–Z 10 vols in 20 Oxford 1888–1928; introduction, supplement and bibliography Oxford 1933)
OHS	Oxford Historical Society
OS	dated by old style, with year taken to begin on 25 March (cf NS)
OUA	Oxford University archives
Salter, *Oxford City Properties*	H. E. Salter, *Oxford City Properties* (OHS lxxxiii 1926)
Oxford Council Acts 1701–1752	*Oxford Council Acts 1701–1752*, ed. M. G. Hobson (OHS new ser. x 1954)
Oxford Council Acts 1752–1801	*Oxford Council Acts 1752–1801*, ed. M. G. Hobson (OHS xv 1962)
Parker, *Early History of Oxford*	J. Parker, *The Early History of Oxford 727–1100* (OHS iii 1885)
PCA	Pembroke College (Oxford) archives
Pemb.	Pembroke College (Oxford)
Portland MSS	Nottingham University library, Portland MSS
priv.	privileged person, entitled to enjoy the privileges of the university
PRO	Public Record Office, London
prof.	professor
QCA	Queen's College (Oxford) archives
Reg. Exeter Coll.	C. W. Boase, *Register of the Rectors, Fellows, and other members on the Foundation of Exeter College, Oxford (Registrum collegii exoniensis)* (OHS xxvii 1894)

Reg. Univ. ii	*Register of the University of Oxford* ii *1571–1622*, ed. A. Clark (4 parts OHS x, xi, xii, xiv 1887–9)
Reminiscences of Oxford	*Reminiscences of Oxford by Oxford Men 1559–1850*, ed. L. M. Quiller Couch (OHS xxii 1892)
SEH	St Edmund Hall
SJM	St John's College (Oxford) muniments
Statutes, trans. Ward	*Oxford University Statutes*, trans. G. R. M. Ward (2 vols London 1845–51); titles, sections and chapters cited in the same form as for *Laudian Code*, ed. Griffiths
subs.	subscribed to the thirty-nine articles of the Church of England (on entering the university)
Surveys and Tokens	*Surveys and Tokens*, ed. H. E. Salter (OHS lxxv 1923)
TCA	Trinity College (Oxford) archives
The Flemings in Oxford	*The Flemings in Oxford*, ed. J. R. Magrath (3 vols OHS xliv 1903, lxii 1913, lxxix 1924)
Trin.	Trinity College (Oxford)
UCA	University College (Oxford) archives
Univ.	University College (Oxford)
VCH Cambs. iii	*A History of the County of Cambridge and the Isle of Ely* iii, ed. J. P. C. Roach (London 1959)
VCH Oxon. iii	*The Victoria History of the County of Oxford* iii, ed. H. E. Salter and M. D. Lobel (London 1954)
VCH Oxon. iv	*The Victoria History of the County of Oxford* iv, ed. A. Crossley (Oxford 1979)
visc.	Viscount
Wake MSS	Christ Church Library, Wake MSS
WCA	Worcester College archives
WCM	Wadham College muniments
Woodforde at Oxford	*Woodforde at Oxford 1759–1776*, ed. W. N. Hargreaves-Mawdsley (OHS new ser. xxi 1969)
Wood, *Life and Times*	*The Life and Times of Anthony Wood, Antiquary, of Oxford, 1632–1695, described by himself*, ed. A. Clark (4 vols OHS xix, xxi, xxvi, xxx 1891–5)

Introduction

L. G. MITCHELL

By LONG and hallowed tradition the description of Oxford University in the eighteenth century that has carried the greatest credibility has been that given by Edward Gibbon in his autobiography.[1] An impressionistic account of dissipated undergraduates failing to be taught or examined by college fellows sunk in port and prejudice has hardened into historical fact. The eighteenth-century university would appear as a sluggish stream meandering between overgrown meadows, contrasting sharply with the torrents of intellectual activity that came before and would follow after.

Gibbon can no longer be allowed to dominate the field. He came up to Oxford young, and was perhaps young for his age. As a result of these considerations he was, according to his contemporaries, a rather solitary undergraduate, with few friends or close associates. He was taken up by some gentlemen-commoners, slightly older than himself, who led him to the reading of Bossuet and to that conversion to Roman Catholicism which later so gravely embarrassed the historian of the Roman empire. When indifferent health is also taken into account, it is not surprising that Gibbon should have looked back on his Oxford days with undisguised hostility. No one is perhaps neutral in his observations on Oxford, but Gibbon was undoubtedly partial in his testimony.

If, however, the historian looks hard for Gibbon's Oxford, it can be found. No one would claim, though some did, that eighteenth-century Oxford could rival Leiden or Göttingen, Edinburgh or Glasgow as a centre of intellectual dynamism. As Oxford has always been worth a paragraph in London newspapers, so its critics can be found at all times and at all levels of society. Jane Austen, for example, early in *Sense and Sensibility* records a young man as boasting that

as there was no necessity for my having any profession at all, as I might be as dashing and expensive without a red coat on my back as with one, idleness was pronounced on the whole to be the most advantageous and honourable,

---

[1] *Miscellaneous Works of Edward Gibbon, Esquire*, ed. [John Holroyd,] Lord Sheffield (2 vols London 1796, 3rd vol. 1815, new edn in 5 vols London 1814) i; E. Gibbon, *Memoirs of My Life*, ed. G. A. Bonnard (London 1966).

and a young man of eighteen is not in general so earnestly bent on being busy as to resist the solicitations of his friends to do nothing. I was therefore entered at Oxford and have been properly idle ever since.[1]

In 1839, after the major reform projects of the early nineteenth century, a fellow of Lincoln could still complain that the 'standard tutorial capacity [was] too low to frighten even the diffident or lazy'.[2] Oxford has always had its critics, and it would be strange, given its prominence in national life, if it were not so.

In the eighteenth century there were special reasons for Oxford to attract the suspicion of the outside world. To the usual doubts about the purpose and value of academic life was added a widespread anticlericalism, associated with enlightened values, that made Oxford's clerical nature either amusingly irrelevant or sinister. The real, or theoretical, celibacy of Oxford tutors and the interpenetration of academic exercise and religious observance could not be taken seriously by increasingly secularized minds. Further, there was anxiety about the inevitable influence that Oxford could wield over impressionable minds, particularly if the university authorities were themselves believed to be tainted with unfortunate kinds of politics or social attitudes. Although the careers of Benjamin Kennicott, John Potter, Edmund Gibson and William Blackstone prove that poor men could still build a reputation on the basis of an Oxford education, the fact that the university as a whole was becoming more socially exclusive as the century wore on led to worries about what those future leaders of society were being taught. For the cartoonist and the pamphleteer therefore, anything reported about Oxford, particularly of a scandalous or sensationalist nature, was sure of an audience.

The necessity of revising this traditional picture was suggested by the late Dame Lucy Sutherland in her 1972 James Bryce Memorial Lecture.[3] While admitting that decline could be measured in some areas, she argued that such setbacks had to be put into perspective and set against gains, taking as her starting-point a conversation that Boswell had with Johnson when they both visited Oxford in 1768:

The tutors are anxious to have their pupils appear well in the college; the colleges are anxious to have their students appear well in the University. There are all opportunities of books and learned men; there are excellent rules of discipline in every college. I objected that the rules and indeed the whole system is very ill observed 'Why, Sir', said he, 'that is nothing against the institution. The members of an university may for a season be unmindful of their duty. I am arguing for the excellence of the institution.[4]

[1] J. Austen, *Sense and Sensibility* (3 vols London 1811) i, ch. 19.
[2] A. Heeson, *The Founding of the University of Durham* (Durham 1982), 6.
[3] L. S. Sutherland, *The University of Oxford in the Eighteenth Century: a reconsideration* (Oxford 1973).
[4] Ibid. 3.

The university did not mark time in the eighteenth century, and, although movement might be limited in scope, movement there undoubtedly was.

A reassessment of Oxford's role must start with a clear understanding of what contemporaries conceived the function of universities to be. For many, they were *intended* to be conservative rather than innovative. As one of the earliest contributors to this volume puts it, universities 'were the guardians of a body of traditional learning on which religious orthodoxy, political obedience and social order were thought to depend ... few imagined that a university ought to be concerned with pure research or disinterested scholarship'.[1] As long as the precepts of Aristotle and the ancients were unchallenged, and as long as Anglicanism retained its political monopoly, academics were simply required to receive a body of information from their forefathers and to hand it on intact to the next generation. Established theory was to be cherished, not challenged, and thereby the context for intellectual life became almost crystalline. It is in this sense that Oxford could be seen by contemporaries as contributing to social and political stability, cushioning the entry of young men into full adult responsibilities. To many foreign observers who were caught up in the values of the Enlightenment, this stance appeared criminally unadventurous, but it would not have seemed so to many Englishmen.

In particular Oxford and Cambridge were the trustees of orthodoxy in the church. Together, they trained the clergy of the Church of England, and provided the intellectual defences against Roman Catholicism, dissent and the kinds of unfortunate political options, with which these creeds were associated in the Anglican mind. Clerical dons were expected to instruct their pupils, many of whom owned advowsons, in sound religion. For contemporaries, Gibbon's flirtation with Catholicism was a more serious indication of Oxford failing than his strictures on Oxford's teaching and discipline. It was the hope of most fellows to move on to a parish, and livings could only be provided by their college or by patronage circles in Oxford. Only such a move made marriage a financial possibility, and it is not surprising that common-room betting books are much involved with the topic. As Oxford-finished clergy moved into the parishes of England, particularly in the south and west, Oxford's role in national life was guaranteed. Criticisms that the university had too strong a clerical bias would have seemed strange to those who saw in Oxford's clergymen an essential mainstay of the civil and religious establishment.

Against such a background, those reformers arguing for revisions of the curriculum or a more systematic approach to lecturing and examining were likely to encounter obstacles. Throughout the century the

[1] G. V. Bennett, 'University, Society and Church 1688–1714', p. 359 below.

teaching of new subjects, notoriously in the physical sciences, was based on a number of *ad hoc* arrangements or restricted to certain colleges, quite often dependent on the residence of a particular scholar. Such licensed lecturers were paid from the fees extracted from those attending, and, like as not, were also expected to provide their own equipment. Without established posts it proved almost impossible to sustain a tradition of scholarship in a subject, and therefore in fields outside the medieval curriculum there was a pattern of gifted individuals making valuable contributions which were not immediately taken up by a new Oxford generation. The unyielding nature of the curriculum was much criticized, particularly by foreign visitors, but its static nature was a function of the university on the English model. Reformers had to break the clerical mould of Oxford before major changes could be effected. The practice of requiring all those entering the university to subscribe to the thirty-nine articles on matriculation, reaffirmed in 1773, annually underlined the scale of the reformers' task.

Before considering the validity of those criticisms, one further point needs to be mentioned. For the greater part of the century Oxford lay under an anathema. Whig governments after 1714 saw the real or imaginary Jacobitism of Oxford as infecting young men with scabrous ideas. Anything that could be said to Oxford's disadvantage therefore received official sanction and favour. In sharp contrast to the whig orthodoxies of Cambridge, Oxford politics were seen in London as lying in alarming shadow. Fellows in whig colleges such as Exeter, Wadham and Merton were employed as spies to provide evidence of Oxford's disloyalty. One of the motives for founding regius professorships was the belief that the holders of these chairs would reinforce the whig presence in the university. Twice in the first half of the century direct government intervention was threatened, with proposals that ministers should nominate directly to fellowships. This proscription was eased by the accession of George III and ended by the election of Lord North as chancellor of the university in 1772. Until then critics of Oxford were in a real sense the spokesmen of government.

For obvious reasons, therefore, Oxford for much of the eighteenth century was an institution on the defensive. Endlessly attacked by the servants of Hanoverian kings, who were not thought by Oxford men to be the soundest of Anglicans, the university took refuge in a stolid defence of its customary functions. The price paid was high. So successful was the campaign to smear Oxford with Jacobitism that it became one of the reasons (rising costs and changing career prospects being others) why the numbers entering the university dropped significantly, reaching a nadir in the 1750s. With such a decline came the associated problems of lost fees and lost patronage opportunities. Much of the building work undertaken in this period was partly motivated by the desire to entice back to Oxford social groups who had been frightened by the reputation of the university that had been sedulously fostered by its critics. When evaluating the claims of such critics it is important to remember that their views might be inspired by political prejudice as much as by a desire for Oxford's health and prosperity as an academic institution.

This profound suspicion between Oxford and government involved the university in many embarrassments, but one in particular needs emphasizing. Under the terms of the Laudian statutes of 1636, which governed all aspects of the university's conduct, no changes of a major kind could be enacted without the sanction of the government. Oxford could not reform itself without making itself vulnerable to intervention by outside forces. Given the antipathy felt by successive whig administrations towards Oxford, it was extremely unlikely that the university would take such risks. The arguments in favour of a particular change or reform were lost in the difficulties of actually effecting it. Such a situation could not change until William Blackstone, in 1759, found a way of interpreting the statutes which allowed Oxford to initiate reforms without reference to London. Until then, however, what existed might be tolerated because the risks involved in any reform project were almost literally incalculable.

If this was the context in which criticisms of Oxford were made, it now becomes necessary to assess their validity. In 1809 Edward Copleston of Oriel had no doubts that his university had been greatly traduced: 'The world ought to be set right in a serious way as to the nature and system of our studies. I am convinced that as things are now managed, Oxford is the most efficient University in the world.'[1] Such a comment from a scholar of note deserves careful evaluation, even though it may contain an element of special pleading. Even so, the university had a European-wide reputation, and it would indeed be odd if the intellectual home of Halley, Blackstone, Kennicott, Lowth, Thwaites, Gaisford and William Jones was thought of as a backwater. Whatever English governments said of Oxford, Europeans took a different view. The wide-ranging correspondence of an Arthur Charlett makes this fact clear, and, as Bromley has recently pointed out, 'when Catherine II wished to send a dozen young Russians for study in the West, she chose Göttingen, Leiden and Oxford'.[2] Without wishing to claim that the eighteenth century was a period of outstanding intellectual activity therefore, some revision of the Gibbonian account is in order.

On the central questions of teaching and examining, continuity between periods of excellence, if nothing more, was maintained. Further,

[1] E. Copleston-R. Heber, 28 Nov. 1809, *The Heber Letters*, ed. R. Cholmondeley (London 1950), 228.
[2] J. S. Bromley, 'Britain and Europe in the eighteenth century', *History* lxvi (1981), 403.

if the university's supervision of these exercises was fitful and irregular, the colleges seem to have taken their responsibilities seriously in this respect. Eighteenth-century Oxford had as many good tutors as bad tutors. Alongside 'Jolly' Ward of University College must be set John Wesley, John Napleton, John Burton, Edward Bentham and Edward Copleston. Gibbon's own tutor Thomas Waldegrave was a conscientious man, who apparently tried hard to interest his pupils in intellectual matters. In refounding Hertford College, Richard Newton sanctioned statutes providing for the close, regular supervision of teaching and instruction. Undergraduates clearly responded to such men. The Christ Church collections books are an extraordinary testimony to the extent to which Oxford men pursued a systematic course of reading.

Some colleges were of course more lax than others. The level of intellectual excitement might rest precariously on the chance residence of a particular man. These, however, are constant factors within a collegiate university. Equally, there were undoubtedly undergraduates who passed their university days in dissipation. These came largely from the noblemen and gentlemen-commoners, who were not, until late in the century, expected to read in any regular way. Even at this social level, however, the dutiful undergraduate days of North and Shelburne should be remembered. William Windham's progress was reported to his mother in 1770 as follows: 'Twas a great Satisfaction to me to find him in such good health, and still greater to hear the excellent character given of him for sobriety and learning.'[1]

For the rest of the undergraduate population—the commoners, foundationers, battelers and servitors—university life was usually a step towards a career or the cutting of a figure in the world, and therefore needed to be taken with some seriousness. Lecturers, who often lived by the fees collected from their audiences, do not appear to have starved, and, as the chapters of this volume which deal with particular areas of study indicate, lectures were available, on a formal or informal basis, in most subjects. The interest taken in them could be extraordinary. In the 1750s, a decade which is generally regarded as representing the nadir of Oxford's intellectual development, nearly a third of the freshmen paid the necessary extra fees to be allowed to hear the chemistry lectures of James Bradley in the basement of the Ashmolean Museum. Blackstone's lectures on the common law seem to have been equally popular. For subjects within and without the traditional syllabus, therefore, there seems to have been a ready audience. For many undergraduates, being examined on the subject-matter of lectures was not the purpose of attending a university. But this convention did not necessarily mean that they were idle or lacking the wish to learn.

[1] R. W. Ketton-Cremer, *Felbrigg: the Story of a House* (London 1962), 163.

Alongside the traditional picture of dissolute undergraduates, unduly concerned with horses, drinking and play—the image fostered by hostile whig governments in London—must be set other Oxford careers. The letters of Charles Kirkpatrick Sharpe, for example, suggest a different approach to life. He came up to Christ Church in 1798 and his description of the college is wholly flattering. On 27 April 1799 he reported to his father:

We are all in a sad fuss here about Collections, which come on next week. Some sit up the whole night skimming the heads of chapters instead of the chapters themselves, while others scrawl compendiums which not the devil himself, far less the Dean, could read for his life. And all are quaking with the thoughts of the black tribunal at which they are to appear. Whenever I consider about it, my head shakes in the prettiest fashion imaginable.[1]

If there was always a firm intellectual base in Oxford, therefore, more and more people, as the century wore on, were anxious to build on it. Once the restrictions of the Laudian code of statutes had been lifted, reformers found new voice. In the last four decades of the century men such as Blackstone were able to initiate reforms, not least the better organization of the University Press, and, when the process of examining was systematized by the establishment of the honours school in 1801, the intellectual credibility of Oxford was no longer in doubt. Inevitably the fear engendered by the French revolution and its attendant wars retarded all projects for reform, but many of the changes accredited to the early nineteenth century had eighteenth-century roots. It would take time for the traditional assumptions about the purpose of a university to be overthrown, but by 1800 they had already been somewhat dented.

In judging the vitality of a university community many yardsticks must be used. The musical life of eighteenth-century Oxford was, for example, vivid, with the celebrated visits of Handel and Haydn merely highlighting a pattern of sustained interest. Equally, under the supervision of the Radcliffe trustees, the skyline of Oxford underwent a significant and glorious transformation with the building of the Camera and the Observatory. At a humbler level, close co-operation with the city authorities allowed major modifications to Oxford's street-system which are still evident. A major Oxford figure such as Dean Aldrich of Christ Church was at once scholar, architect, engraver and musician. Such energy could not go unrecorded, and the evidence provided by the chapters in this volume which deal with such matters forms a necessary complement to discussions of teaching and examining.

Eighteenth-century Oxford was therefore not the moribund institution that its critics depicted, even if it still fell short of the high standards

---

[1] *Letters from and to Charles Kirkpatrick Sharpe, Esq.* ed. A. Allardyce (2 vols Edinburgh and London 1888) i. 89.

claimed by its apologists. Then, as always, the reformer and the traditionalist, the conscientious and the less than conscientious, the religiously inclined and the secularly minded all jostled one another in the High and the Broad. If Oxford dazzled the world less than it had done before, its influence was still such as to inspire fear in the university's enemies. Throughout the years of proscription Oxford staved off interference in its affairs from outside and fulfilled its function of handing on a body of traditional knowledge to successive generations. In so doing the university contributed materially to the social and political equilibrium of eighteenth-century England. Many contemporaries would not have expected anything more.

The production of this volume is a final testimony to the achievement of its first editor, Dame Lucy Sutherland, in eighteenth-century studies. In the lecture referred to earlier she offered an assessment of Oxford in this period that it would be hard to improve upon:

When we come to sum up the eighteenth-century University as a whole we see weaknesses which are only too obvious, though also some less obvious strengths. It is not easy to summarize them in one statement. It was clearly not a period of notable intellectual activity; but neither was it one of complete intellectual inertia. It had inherited a formal academic structure badly in need of reform, and, despite many obstacles, it ultimately did a good deal to reform it, though built-in inertia, both social and intellectual, obviously remained. But it played its part in producing a conscientious and educated clergy: it maintained its independence, and it gave to many men, one way or another, the habits and interests of a liberal education. Dr Johnson had undoubtedly seen it in too rosy a light, but he was wiser than those who thought it incapable of regeneration.[1]

---

[1] Sutherland, *The University of Oxford in the Eighteenth Century*, 30.

I

Loyalist Oxford and the Revolution

G. V. BENNETT

IN THE later seventeenth century foreign travellers to Oxford waxed enthusiastic over the city's sweet setting in a broad, well-watered valley, its fine streets and buildings, and its richly stocked libraries. But to native Englishmen the university and its colleges stood not so much for quiet scholarship in incomparable surroundings as for the power and prestige of the Church of England and for a strident Stuart loyalism. Indeed, in the generation after the Restoration, Oxford came to be an essential pillar in the edifice of Charles II's political regime. It set forth and defended the distinctive political teachings of the restored monarchy and, at a time when other opinions were restricted by persecution and censorship, ceaselessly propagated its loyalist divinity in learned treatise, popular pamphlet and parochial sermon. With Cambridge it controlled the training of the clergy and progressively remodelled the Anglican priesthood into an army of political activists distributed throughout the countryside. While King Charles may well have resented the virtual monopoly of public office possessed by Anglican laymen, he can never have doubted the political usefulness of the clergy. In the exclusion crisis their firm support as writers, preachers and election-agents had been essential to his victory. Nor can he have failed to recognize that the ordinary parish priests took their lead in matters political and theological from the clergy of the universities, and from those of Oxford in particular. Only the distinguished body of London incumbents was listened to with equal respect. To a simple rector or vicar, living remotely in some country parish, Oxford must have seemed a veritable citadel of the church. The statutes of the university and the colleges ensured the predominance of the clergy in its academic life. Professorships, headships and fellowships were held by some four hundred clergymen, of whom no fewer than three hundred were ordinarily resident. The chapel of one great college was the cathedral church of the diocese, and to its services was added daily worship in twenty-three other colleges and halls. Week by week the opinions of the resident dons on both politics and theology were given forth from the university pulpit. Present fellows, old members and young aspirants to holy orders were caught up in a network of ecclesiastical patronage which centred in the colleges but extended out through the midlands and down into the south and the west. When Charles II died Oxford had become the key institution in a great political interest of men deeply concerned with the maintenance of an Anglican ascendancy in the life of the nation.

It was perhaps as the guardian of the regime's ideology that Oxford rendered its most characteristic service. In the seventeenth century ideas about kingship, law, society and the family were usually discussed in terms of Christian faith and were regarded as within the special province of the professional theologian. Arguments were won or lost by an appeal to scripture or turned on a claim to the more accurate interpretation of a proof-text. Now, after the wild excesses of the civil-war sects, there was a determination to confine theology to those who could be trusted to support the established order. Thus, as persecution silenced the opposition, the university theologians were encouraged to develop a new conservative scholarship. At Oxford John Fell, dean of Christ Church, was the leading figure in a patristic revival which sought to confound both Bellarmine and Baxter by demonstrating that Anglican church-order conformed closely to the pattern of primitive Christianity. His magnificent folio edition of the works of St Cyprian, which appeared in 1682, was designed to establish the Anglican view of episcopacy against the protagonists of popery and presbytery, and to make it 'impossible for them to continue their opinions, and be either Papists or Separatists'.[1] Perhaps more widely effective was the theologians' revival of the politics of divine kingship. If such teachings had a venerable lineage in the apologists for the Elizabethan church, they were now taken up again by men who felt a need to consolidate the social order and strengthen their institutions. The doctrine of passive obedience was, of course, more than a theory of monarchy; it stemmed from a profound belief, held by most contemporaries, that human society and its sanctions were basically religious in character, and that there was a moral requirement of obedience to a divinely sanctioned order. Indeed, it tended to the position that all the powers were ordained of God: not just kings but magistrates, landlords, parsons and parents. Thus each 30 January, the anniversary of the execution of Charles I, and each 29 May, the day of his son's return, the university pulpit thundered out the Anglican teaching on obedience: that rebellion was heinous and utterly sinful; that even if an unjust ruler's commands could not be actively obeyed he was to be offered the passive obedience of one prepared to endure all his punishments. No more fervent exponent of this divinity was to be found than William Jane

---

[1] S. A. Morison, *John Fell, the University Press and the 'Fell' Types* (Oxford 1967), 31-3, 48-52. John Fell (1625-86), Student Ch.Ch. 1637, dean 1660-86; vice-chancellor 1666-9; bp of Oxford 1676-86.

whom the crown appointed regius professor in 1680. If his theological learning was unremarkable and his ability to lecture notoriously defective, his mastery of the phraseology and scriptural exegesis of loyalism was complete. After the Rye House plot in 1683 he composed and guided through convocation a famous 'Judgment and Decree of the University of Oxford' which was to mark the highpoint of royalist rhetoric. It condemned '*certain* Pernicious Books *and* Damnable Doctrines Destructive to the Sacred Persons of Princes'. A comprehensive list was drawn up of points deemed destructive of civil order, and convocation affirmed that 'We decree, judge and declare all and every of these Propositions to be false, seditious and impious; and most of them to be also Heretical and Blasphemous, infamous to Christian Religion, and destructive of all Government in Church and State'.[1] The works, including those of Thomas Hobbes and John Milton, were forbidden to members of the university and ordered to be ceremonially burned. That evening at the bookburning in the schools quadrangle, as the 'marshal of beggars' cast the offending volumes into the flames, the undergraduates pressed around and, under the direction of Jane, 'gave severall hums whilst they were burning'.[2] With such credentials it is scarcely surprising that Oxford divines were much in demand for sermons before tory judges of assize, grand juries, sheriffs and mayors. From them at least one could be assured of the pure milk of the loyalist gospel.

An important aspect of the university's service to the political ascendancy lay in the education of its young recruits. Dean Fell was particularly concerned to attract the sons of tory magnates and gentlemen to Oxford, and at Christ Church he created the pattern of a university education for aristocrats on lines significantly different from that of aspirants to holy orders. Tutors were appointed to give instruction in the classics and polite letters, prizes were awarded to spur on flagging interest, and time was allowed for the pursuit of country sports. Special academic dress and privileges were given to those who matriculated in the rank of nobleman or gentleman-commoner, and it became usual for the sons of distinguished fathers to be presented for an honorary degree when they had completed a period of residence.[3] Christ Church, closely followed by other fashionable colleges, began to plan and build sets of new chambers to accommodate aristocratic youth in the style to which it was accustomed. Fell himself did not doubt that he was creating the future leadership of a ruling class which would be firmly attached to the church and which would see its own security in the defence of the Anglican

[1] *The Judgment and Decree of the University of Oxford Past in their Convocation July 21.1683* (Oxford 1683), 7. William Jane (1645-1707), m. Ch.Ch. 1660; regius prof. divinity 1680-1707; dean of Gloucester 1685; prolocutor lower house of convocation 1689.

[2] Wood, *Life and Times* iii. 61-3.

[3] Fell-R. Southwell, 4 Feb. 1679, HMC *Ormonde MSS* iv. 319.

cause. That such aspirations were shared by influential tories is clear. The duke of Ormonde, writing to Fell concerning the education of his grandson, Lord James Butler, set out his own ideal: he hoped that the young man 'may be confirmed and perfectly instructed in the religion professed, practised, and best taught in that University, wherein is comprehended the principles of honour, virtue and loyalty'.[1] By the end of Fell's reign at Christ Church there were as many as ten noblemen and thirty-six gentlemen-commoners usually in residence in this college alone.[2]

Not less significant was the universities' gradual reshaping of the clerical profession. In 1662, even after the passing of the act of uniformity, there remained in the ministry many who had served in the Cromwellian church and whose attitude to the new regime was at best equivocal. But in the 1670s and 1680s these survivors were, appointment by appointment, replaced by the new products of Oxford and Cambridge. In these years the ministry of the Church in England became almost wholly a graduate profession; and those without a degree, even if they had spent some time at a university, could expect to be employed only in the poorest livings or in the clerical proletariat of unbeneficed stipendiary curates.[3] Gradually the number of undergraduates from the lowest social origins was reduced by the decay of ancient grammar schools which could provide a classical education for the children of the poor. There was a perceptible rise in fees and the cost of living in colleges, while scholarships, originally intended for poor boys, were increasingly awarded to those who could bring pressure or influence to bear.[4] By the time of the Revolution the profession was being increasingly recruited from the younger sons of gentlemen and substantial yeomen. Undergraduates from an impoverished background still eked out an existence in the halls and cheaper colleges and left immediately on obtaining a bachelor's degree, but the general tone was towards higher social pretensions and an improved standard of living. There is ample testimony to the rise in the consumption of food and wine, and to

[1] Ormonde-Fell, 20 Jan. 1679, HMC, *Ormonde MSS* iv. 306. James Butler (1610-88), 1st d. of Ormonde; chancellor of the university 1669-88. James Butler (1665-1745), 2nd d. of Ormonde; m. Ch.Ch. 1679; chancellor of the university 1688-1714.   [2] Wood, *Life and Times* iii. 257.
[3] See J. H. Pruett, *The Parish Clergy under the Later Stuarts: the Leicestershire experience* (Urbana, Illinois 1978), 43, for a detailed study of one English county. In 1670 only 5 per cent of the parochial incumbents had no degree, and in 1714 only 3 per cent. For stipendiary curates the proportion was 16 per cent in 1671 and 9 per cent in 1700. Similar figures are shown in J. L. Salter, 'Warwickshire clergy, 1660-1714' (Birmingham Ph.D. thesis 1975), 50-3. The percentage of clergy known to have been non-graduates in the period 1660-79 was 12.53; in the period 1680-99 it had been reduced to 4.24; and in the period 1700-14 it was 3.90. In the Welsh dioceses, where benefices were small and remote, the proportion of graduates was much smaller. In the diocese of Bangor as late as the period 1689-1713 out of 136 men ordained deacon 38 had not been to a university and 59 had no degree: see A. I. Pryce, *The Diocese of Bangor during Three Centuries* (Cardiff 1929) for a digest of the episcopal registers.
[4] L. Stone, 'The size and composition of the Oxford student body 1580-1909' in L. Stone (ed.), *The University in Society* (2 vols Princeton 1975) i. 37-43.

the bibulous habits of both senior and junior members. Indeed, many noble and gentry families became distinctly anxious about exposing their impressionable offspring to the conspicuous expenditure and high living of the universities, and some even sent them to private academies kept by dissenters.[1] The fact remains, however, that, while poor clergy by no means disappeared, a leading section of the profession was being assimilated to the life-style of the gentry with whom they were becoming increasingly associated.[2] Certainly the presence in the same colleges of noblemen and gentlemen-commoners provided opportunities for important connections for both tutors and fellow-pupils.

It was to be expected that a body so fiercely partisan would seek to build up a strong working relationship with the government and court politicians. But the leading men in the university were painfully aware that the king himself was at best an unreliable friend. A man of dubious faith or none, and always surrounded by persistent Roman Catholic influences, Charles resented having to work with a political ascendancy which limited his choice of servants and confined his policies. And so, whenever circumstances seemed propitious, he moved towards an alternative strategy: a union of ambitious Catholics, aggrieved dissenters and certain compliant Anglicans into a new 'king's party' under the banner of a general religious toleration. It thus became the policy of Archbishop Sheldon and his successor, William Sancroft, to work in close alliance with those politicians at court who were firmly committed to the preservation of the Anglican monopoly. One of their most active supporters was John Fell who in 1676 added the bishopric of Oxford to his deanery of Christ Church. Fell's relentless campaigns against dissent in the diocese and his co-operation with local tory magnates and magistrates quickly established him as one of Sancroft's most trusted episcopal lieutenants.[3] And it was he who took the lead in attaching the university to the interest of certain prominent Anglican politicians engaged in the struggle for power around the king. In this the two university seats in parliament were of prime importance. Their holders had a prestige in the commons which was rivalled only by that of a knight of the shire for one of the largest counties. With the Cambridge members, the Oxford burgesses were accounted the special representatives in the house of the Anglican clergy and could speak with authority on ecclesiastical issues. The seats involved little electoral expenditure and there was a good chance of unopposed re-election. While it was true that many of the ordinary members of convocation preferred to have a resident academic,

[1] Ibid. 52-3.   [2] Ibid. 43-6.
[3] For Fell's support of Sancroft's policies see G. V. Bennett, 'The seven bishops: a reconsideration' in D. Baker (ed.), *Religious Motivation: biographical and sociological problems for the church historian* (Studies in Church History xv Oxford 1978), 269. For a visitation charge of 1685 setting out his aims see Bodl. MS Tanner 31, fo 156; see also Fell-Sancroft, 26 June 1683, MS Tanner 34, fo 55.

usually one of the civil lawyers who could be relied upon to pay close attention to parliamentary business which affected university interests, it was generally accepted that at least one of the seats should be held by an Anglican politician of ministerial calibre.[1]

In fact the connections with prominent courtiers formed in this era were to prove remarkably durable, and were to sustain the university's toryism even into the reign of Queen Anne. The most important was undoubtedly that with the Hyde family, and principally with Laurence Hyde, from 1682 first earl of Rochester.[2] In 1661, at the tender age of 20, he had been elected burgess on the recommendation of his father, the great earl of Clarendon, chancellor of the university.[3] Hyde's member-ship of the cavalier parliament was not particularly distinguished and he was even accused of neglecting the university's business, but by the time of the exclusion crisis he had emerged as a major court politician and the head of the party which supported the cause of James, duke of York.[4] By 1681 he, his brother the second earl of Clarendon,[5] and Archbishop Sancroft were the principal architects of the great Anglican-tory reac-tion. As a member of the commission for ecclesiastical promotions he saw to it that only committed loyalists were appointed to bishoprics and deaneries, and his friends at Oxford received a veritable shower of preferments.[6] Men like Henry Aldrich[7] and William Jane at Christ Church were to look back on this as the golden age of toryism. As lord treasurer from 1685 to 1687 Rochester was the dominant figure in Oxford politics, and he and his brother were frequent visitors to the city and to the deanery at Christ Church. Only slightly less important was the interest of the Finch family. In 1661 Hyde's partner as university member had been Heneage Finch, a brilliant lawyer who quickly estab-lished himself as the ablest court spokesman in the commons.[8] As lord keeper in 1673 and lord chancellor two years later he used the immense ecclesiastical patronage of the seals to build up an impressive group among the senior clergy who looked to him and to his son, Daniel Finch, as their patrons and mentors. Daniel Finch, who succeeded as second earl of Nottingham in 1682, was a devoted Anglican churchman, though

[1] M. B. Rex, *University Representation in England 1604-1690* (London 1954).
[2] Laurence Hyde (1641-1711); MP Oxford Univ. 1661-79.
[3] Edward Hyde (1609-74), 1st e. of Clarendon, m. Magdalen Hall 1623; chancellor of the univer-sity 1660-7; high steward of Cambridge borough 1660-70.
[4] Rex, 236, 241-3.
[5] Henry Hyde (1638-1709), 2nd e. of Clarendon; MA by diploma 1661; high steward of the uni-versity 1686-1709.
[6] R. Beddard, 'The commission for ecclesiastical promotions, 1681-84: an instrument of tory reac-tion', *Historical Journal* x (1967).
[7] Henry Aldrich (1647-1710), m. Ch. Ch. 1662, dean 1689-1710; vice-chancellor 1692-5.
[8] Heneage Finch (1621-82), 1st e. of Nottingham; m. Ch. Ch. 1636; MP Oxford Univ. 1661-73.

his followers were more inclined to work for a reconciliation of moderate dissenters within the national church than to continue the persecution to which the 'thorough' tories were increasingly committed.[1] The lord chancellor had many friends in Oxford and when in 1679 he pressed that his second son, also Heneage Finch, should be elected burgess, there was an immediate and energetic campaign on his behalf, led by the duke of Ormonde and Bishop Fell, and orchestrated by Humphrey Prideaux of Christ Church.[2] As solicitor general the younger Finch was to be one of the chief instruments of the tory reaction, superintending the surrender of borough charters and prosecuting whig leaders like Lord Russell with relentless zeal. As university burgess and later as elder statesman Heneage Finch was to represent the tory interest in Oxford for over thirty years.

An influence which remained surprisingly powerful was that of Thomas Thynne, burgess from 1674 to 1678.[3] As Viscount Weymouth from 1682 he was to hold office in various ministries, even down to 1714, but he was hardly to be accounted a party leader, and for the most part followed obediently after the Hydes and the Finches. His reputation seems to have been derived from his great wealth, his consistently extreme tory opinions and his strict observance of all the niceties of Laudian piety. At Oxford as burgess he had provided lavish entertainments for his constituents, and after the Revolution he cultivated within the university the role of a patron of learning which had many of the younger dons competing for his attention. Even grave heads of houses enjoyed his magnificent hospitality at Longleat, where the deprived Bishop Ken was living in honoured retirement.[4] The elaborate deference paid to Weymouth's advice and opinions seems quite disproportionate to his actual political stature until his character as the would-be Maecenas of Oxford letters is remembered. The most considerable local magnate was James Bertie, Lord Norreys, from 1682 first earl of Abingdon. As lord lieutenant of Oxfordshire he earned the plaudits of the university by bullying the city of Oxford into surrendering its charter and by turning whig supporters out of the magistracy.[5] Although he worked closely with

---

[1] See H. Horwitz, *Revolution Politicks: the career of Daniel Finch, second earl of Nottingham, 1647-1730* (Cambridge 1968) for an account of the Finch clerical connection. Daniel Finch (1647-1730), 2nd e. of Nottingham, from 1729 7th e. of Winchilsea; m. Ch.Ch. 1662.

[2] Rex, *University Representation* 266-72. For the campaign on Finch's behalf see HMC *Ormonde MSS* iv. 310-25 *passim*; *Letters of Humphrey Prideaux, sometime Dean of Norwich, to John Ellis, sometime Under-Secretary of State, 1674-1722,* ed. E. M. Thompson (Camden Soc. new ser. xv 1875), 65-6; HMC *Egmont MSS* ii. 78-80; Wood, *Life and Times* ii. 440-4. Heneage Finch (1647-1719), from 1714 1st e. of Aylesford; m. Ch.Ch. 1664; MP Oxford Univ. 1679-98, 1701-3.

[3] Thomas Thynne (1640-1714), from 1682 1st Visc. Weymouth; m. Ch.Ch. 1657; MP Oxford Univ. 1674-8.

[4] Thomas Ken (1637-1711), subs. Hart Hall 1657; fellow New College 1657; bp of Bath and Wells 1685-91.

[5] T. Clarges-Abingdon, 19 July 1684, Bodl. MS Top. Oxon. c. 325, fo 35.

Bishop Fell in the campaign against dissent and was much cried up by the undergraduates at election-time, his political influence with the heads of houses was ruined by his constantly espousing the cause of the city in its attempts to reduce the university's privileges. Surprisingly ineffective was the part played by James Butler, first duke of Ormonde and chancellor since 1669. Ormonde was the beau ideal of a cavalier and a faithful son of the church but his chequered political career and his preoccupation with Irish affairs meant that he was never able to give sufficiently close attention to the climate of Oxford opinion. His interventions had an air of princely grandeur but were frequently inept enough for convocation to take the liberty of ignoring them.[1] What the university desired was political patrons who were at the centre of royal power.

This close association with tory men and measures made it all the more shattering when, in the summer of 1686, James II abandoned his 'old friends', reversed his policies and began to exert the royal authority to destroy the Anglican ascendancy. It is wholly improbable that he wished to establish a military despotism and impose Catholicism by force on a fiercely protestant nation. His aim was more limited: to achieve civil and religious emancipation for the small minority of his Roman Catholic co-religionists by a process of political manœuvre and manipulation, and by the exercise of direct royal pressure on recalcitrant Anglicans.[2] James had so absolute a belief in the rightness of the Roman case that he was sure that men would freely embrace it if it were openly taught and explained, and if no disabilities were attached to those who were converted. The universities had thus an important part to play in this strategy, and he wished to create within each a body of Catholic professors, heads and fellows who would publish, lecture and preach, and at the same time make Roman worship available to all who wished to attend it. But, in view of the Anglican character of the universities, entrenched in acts of parliament and local statutes, this involved a stretching of the prerogative well beyond its usually accepted limits. Much depended on how far the universities were ready to comply with royal instructions and menaces.

In Oxford the first responses to the king's moves were favourable enough to encourage him to go further. It was perhaps understandable that little objection should be raised when the master of University College, Obadiah Walker, pleaded a royal dispensation to withdraw from Anglican worship and have mass said in his lodgings.[3] University

---

[1] For a recommendation which was ignored see Ormonde-Fell, 23 July 1679, HMC *Ormonde MSS* v. 160-1; Rex, 280-2.

[2] For James's policy and the reaction to it see J. Miller, *Popery and Politics in England, 1660-1688* (Cambridge 1973), chs. 10-12; Bennett, 'The seven bishops'.

[3] Obadiah Walker (1617-99), m. Univ. 1633, master 1676-89.

College was small and poor, and Walker had been an Anglican priest when elected. It was quite another thing for the canons of Christ Church to receive and install as dean a man who was clearly disqualified. When in July 1686 Bishop Fell died, there was ample warning that the court intended that one of Walker's disciples, John Massey, a young fellow of Merton, should be Fell's successor.[1] Massey was a mere MA who had progressed no further than deacon's orders, but in December he arrived at Christ Church with letters patent and a royal dispensation 'from coming to prayers, receiving the sacrament, taking of all oathes, and other duties belonging to him as deane'.[2] It was obvious that he was a Roman Catholic and that his installation as dean of an Anglican cathedral was both illegal and uncanonical. It may well be that the chapter acted on the advice of their patron, Lord Rochester, who was still lord treasurer and a member of the ecclesiastical commission of 1686, but their compliance was bitterly resented by loyalist churchmen. For George Hickes, the doughty dean of Worcester, it was a 'temptation to others to forsake our religion in hopes of preferment' and could only proceed from 'fear, and flattery'.[3] When Massey set up a Roman chapel in Canterbury quadrangle the canons' poor spirit led to a collapse of discipline in the college. Undergraduates treated the new dean with open insolence and crowded into his services to jeer and interrupt.[4] Soon the valuable noblemen and gentlemen-commoners were being ordered home by their alarmed parents. Only one canon, Aldrich, emerged with any credit, and even his opposition was clandestine. When Walker began to print a series of Roman propaganda tracts Aldrich organized a group of the ablest Christ Church Students to compose instant replies.[5]

Resistance began to consolidate, however, with the widespread dismissals of tories from their places in local government and with James's declaration of indulgence of 4 April 1687. Professor Jane even roused himself to persuade the clergy of the diocese of Oxford to refuse absolutely an address of thanks for the king's declaration.[6] But the most serious opposition came from the fellows of Magdalen.[7] When their

---

[1] Wood, *Life and Times* iii. 197-8. John Massey (1651-1716), m. Magd. 1669; fellow Merton 1672; dean Ch.Ch. 1686-8.   [2] Ibid. 201.

[3] Hickes-Charlett, 3 Jan. 1687, MS Ballard 12, fo 19. George Hickes (1642-1715), m. St John's 1659; BA Magd. 1662; fellow Linc. 1664-80; dean of Worcester 1683-91.

[4] Wood, *Life and Times* iii. 201, 244.

[5] See W. G. Hiscock, *Henry Aldrich of Christ Church, 1648-1710* (Oxford 1960); G. V. Bennett, *The Tory Crisis in Church and State, 1688-1730* (Oxford 1975), 27-30.

[6] For the order in council, dated 20 Jan. 1687, dismissing Sir Robert Dashwood (1662-1734, 1st bt; m. Trin. 1679), Sir Thomas Clarges (d. 1695, of Wadham 1689; MP Oxford Univ. 1688-95), his son Sir Walter Clarges (1653-1706, 1st bt; m. Merton 1671) and other tory gentlemen from the city corporation of Oxford see Bodl. MS Top. Oxon. c. 325, fo 63. For Jane's passionate speech see T. Castillion–Bp Turner, 1 June [1687], Bodl. MS Rawl. lett. 94, fo 290.

[7] *Magdalen and James II*, OHS vi. For a detailed account of events at Magdalen see the diary of Thomas Smith (1638-1710, m. Queen's 1661; fellow Magd. 1666-92; Cottonian Librarian), Bodl. MS Smith 141.

president, Henry Clerke, died in March they had the courage deliberately to ignore a royal *mandamus* instructing them to elect a Cambridge graduate, Anthony Farmer, who was recommended by Obadiah Walker but was of notoriously defective moral character. On 15 April they proceeded formally to choose John Hough, fellow of the college and chaplain to the duke of Ormonde; and to this perfectly legal election they remained committed in spite of all that the ecclesiastical commission could do. Even when Hough was declared deposed and the king appointed Samuel Parker, bishop of Oxford, by letters under the privy seal, the college refused to recognize the legality of the appointment.[1] Magdalen now provided a textbook case of passive obedience: the fellows asserted their legal rights, refused active obedience to an unlawful command, passively incurred deprivation, and thus step by step pushed the crown into action which was even more obviously illegal. The contrast between their resistance and the craven submission at Christ Church was noted on all sides.[2] In September the king paid a state visit to Oxford with the clear intention of impressing upon the university his determination that all places were to be open to Roman Catholics. On 3 September he was received at the gate of Christ Church by the canons headed by their Roman convert dean.[3] But the next day, when he summoned the fellows of Magdalen before him, there was quite a different scene. Though they were berated and angrily commanded to repair instantly to their chapel and elect the bishop of Oxford, they steadily refused to abandon their properly elected president.[4] When in November twenty-five of the fellows were expelled for their continuing contumacy the ecclesiastical commissioners were committed to the perilous course of depriving men of their legal freeholds for refusing to act illegally. By March 1688 virtually all the Anglican members of the college had been ejected, and the buildings were occupied by a set of Roman Catholic fellows and demies with a titular bishop, Bonaventure Giffard, as president. Anglican services in the chapel were discontinued and mass publicly celebrated. It is difficult to overestimate the shock and anger which these events caused, not least among those bishops and clergy who had been educated at Oxford.[5]

[1] Henry Clerke (1622-87), m. Magdalen Hall 1638; demy Magd. 1639-42, fellow 1642-67, president 1672-87. John Hough (1651-1743), m. Magd. 1669, demy 1669-74, president 1687 and 1688-1701; bp of Oxford 1690-9, Lichfield and Coventry 1699-1717, Worcester 1717-43. Samuel Parker (1640-88), m. Wadham 1657; MA Trin. 1663; president Magd. 1687-8; bp of Oxford 1686-8.

[2] See J. Laughton-Charlett, 18 Apr. 1687, MS Ballard 23, fo 22 for a vehement criticism from Cambridge: Laughton asserted that the canons had 'by their half Compliance somewhat prejudiced if not betray'd (in part) the merits of the Cause'.

[3] The canons' chief concern was that their admitting Massey without his taking the oath of supremacy might render them liable to prosecution: see Aldrich-St John Brodrick, 16 Jan. 1687, Surrey Record Office, Guildford Muniment Room, Midleton MS 1248/1/217.

[4] [E. Bernard]-T. Smith, 4 [Sept.] 1687, Bodl. MS Smith 47, fo 46.

[5] Ken-Wake, 12 Aug., 28 Dec. 1687, Wake MS 17, fos 21, 25; M. Cartier-T. Smith, 5 Apr. 1688, Bodl. MS Smith 48, fo 45. For the anger at Oxford against Samuel Parker, the bishop, see

In spite of the determined stand at Magdalen, however, the rest of the university remained remarkably quiet. With a large contingent of the royal army quartered in Oxford, much of the overt protest was left to the hooligan tactics of undergraduates who kept up a continual campaign of harassment against Walker, Massey and the new fellows of Magdalen. Gilbert Ironside, warden of Wadham, who became vice-chancellor in 1687, acted with extreme caution. He allowed the Roman heads of colleges to sit on the hebdomadal board, and even visited Bishop Giffard in the lodgings at Magdalen.[1] But still more remarkable was the silence of the tory politicians. Indeed, that veteran country tory, Sir Thomas Clarges, who had fought for church and squirearchy in half a dozen parliaments, had to put pressure on Lords Abingdon, Weymouth and Nottingham to provide some financial relief for the deprived fellows of Magdalen.[2] And when on 13 June a *quo warranto* was issued against the privileges of the university, the vice-chancellor found Ormonde and Clarendon unhappily ineffective in getting the writ withdrawn or its intention made clear.[3] But if Oxford did virtually nothing actively to oppose James, it was soon clear that he had dissipated the fervent loyalty of only two years earlier. When in June news came of the death of Ormonde, convocation at once met and elected his young grandson as chancellor before the king had a chance to send down a royal *mandamus* in favour of George Jeffreys. When in September news arrived of Dutch preparations for an invasion, and the royal garrison marched away, the university failed to rally to the king's cause. Anthony Wood, that caustic recorder of the mutability of mankind, noted the contrast between the many companies which Lord Abingdon had enlisted from the undergraduates at the time of Monmouth's rebellion and the fact that now 'no man stirs'.[4] None of James's frantic reversals of his measures produced any change. At the end of October the bishop of Winchester[5] came to restore the fellows of Magdalen, and Walker and Massey dismantled their chapels and crept quietly away.[5] When the whig Lord Lovelace entered the city on 5 December to seize it for the prince of Orange, he and his troops were welcomed by citizens and scholars alike. Indeed,

Smalridge-J. Harrington [Apr. 1688], BL Add. MS 36707, fo 20. Bonaventure Giffard (1642-1734), president Magd. Mar.-Oct. 1688.

[1] Gilbert Ironside (1632-1701), m. Wadham 1650, warden 1665-89; vice-chancellor 1687-9; bp of Bristol 1689-91, Hereford 1691-1701.

[2] T. Clarges-'Mr Moore', 23 Nov. 1687, Bodl. MS Top. Oxon. c. 325, fo 71.

[3] See Bodl. MS Carte 131B, fo 242 (for the writ) and Ironside-Ormonde, 18 June 1688, ibid. fo 234. The purpose of the inquiry seems to have been to prevent the publication of anti-Roman books by threatening the privileges of the University Press.

[4] Wood, *Life and Times* iii. 281 (6 Nov. 1688).

[5] Ibid. 282, 285; *The Flemings in Oxford* ii. 233. For a full account of the restoration at Magdalen see F. Atterbury-St John Brodrick, 26 Oct. 1688, Surrey Record Office, Guildford Muniment Room, Midleton MS 1248/1/211. Peter Mews (1619-1706), m. St John's 1637, president 1667-73; vice-chancellor 1669-73; bp of Bath and Wells 1672-84, Winchester 1684-1706.

the vice-chancellor went out to Abingdon to greet the prince on his journey to London and place 'all the university plate' at his disposal.[1]

King James's flight into exile did not, however, end the university's crisis, and 1689 was to see a veritable shaking of the foundations upon which the politics of Restoration Oxford had been raised. It was soon apparent that there were many, including even some bishops, who wanted to make William of Orange king. A convention was summoned for 22 January, and early returns indicated that there would be in it a powerful party of former exclusionists who wanted to depose James. All attention in Oxford was now taken up with an agonized debate on the succession. No public lectures were given as senior and junior members in common rooms and coffee-houses pored over the dozens of pamphlets in which 'Williamite' and 'Jacobite' argued the question of allegiance. Would it really be possible for the Oxford divines to disavow what they had preached for a generation? Would not the deposition of an anointed king be a prime example of that rebellion which the Oxford decree of 1683 had condemned in such unequivocal terms?[2] It seemed essential to procure a settlement which, even if it incapacitated James, at least had some kind of consistency with loyalist theory.[3] A heavy burden of the university's hopes and fears thus rested on the two men whom convocation on 7 January chose to represent them in the convention. Heneage Finch and Sir Thomas Clarges were both leading parliamentarians, wholly committed to the Anglican cause. Finch had been university burgess in the first exclusion parliament and had recently earned acclaim as one of the counsel defending the seven bishops. Clarges was an even more experienced and formidable speaker in the commons. Although a man of humble origins who had begun his career as an apothecary, he had gained a popular reputation as an earnest defender of church and parliament against royal encroachments.[4] Both men had been pitched upon as early as the previous September when it was thought that they would lead the Anglican party in the parliament which James had summoned to repeal the penal laws.[5] Clarges had been virtually acting as burgess since April 1687, paying frequent visits to Oxford, consulting with heads on ways of resisting James, and trying to rouse the tory grandees to some common action on behalf of the victims of the ecclesiastical commission.[6]

[1] Wood, *Life and Times* iii. 286; *The Flemings in Oxford* ii. 243.
[2] A. Campion-Charlett, 5 Jan. 1689, MS Ballard 30, fo 24.
[3] T. Newey-J. Harrington, 27 Jan. 1689, BL Add. MS 36707, fo 56.
[4] For Finch and Clarges see Rex, *University Representation,* 311-19.
[5] H. Fleming-D. Fleming, 20 Sept. 1688, *The Flemings in Oxford* ii. 224.
[6] Clarges-Weymouth, 23 Apr. 1687, Longleat House, Thynne MS xii, fo 275.

When the convention met, the two Oxford members made a heroic effort to serve their constituents. In an angry and protracted debate on 28 January they, with Sir Robert Sawyer of Cambridge University, were the most cogent of all the fourteen speakers who endeavoured to stem the tide of opinion running in favour of William becoming king.[1] Finch, as a lawyer, protested the legal impossibility of deposing a king, the very notion of which would alter the constitution into the form of an elective commonwealth. Clarges adopted the more subtle argument that the house should confine itself to implementing William's own aims as publicly stated in his declaration and not move on to doing something which he had solemnly disavowed. But the majority in the commons was adamant, and the day ended with the famous resolution that James had 'abdicated' the government and that the throne was thereby 'vacant'. In the lords the loyalist cause had greater support, and most of the university's friends voted for a regency which would allow William to govern while preserving the bare title of king for James. The final outcome was, however, stark. William made it clear that he would not be a regent, and Mary let it be known that she would not reign alone if offered the crown as the next heir. There was therefore nothing which the lords could do but concur in the commons' resolution of 28 January, and invite William and Mary to accept the throne jointly as king and queen.[2] There was to be only one concession for tender loyalist consciences. According to a form proposed by Lord Nottingham, the new oaths required only a promise to 'bear faith and true allegiance' to William and Mary; the new rulers did not have to be acknowledged as 'lawful and right'. But it was enacted that the oaths were to be taken by all incumbent clergy and by all university officers and heads and fellows of colleges by 1 August on pain of suspension, and by the following 1 February on pain of deprivation.

Surviving diaries and correspondence testify to the agonies of mind suffered by Oxford men in the following months. Prideaux, former Student of Christ Church, saw only the prospect of a total disruption: the oaths were such that 'many thousands among us thinke we cannot take with a good conscience, considering the oath already taken to the late King; the consequence of which will be, the turning out of us all'.[3] When the time came for the proclamation of the new sovereigns the clergy had to decide whether to include their names in the public prayers. Many, like White Kennett of St Edmund Hall, decided to pray

[1] For the best account of the debate see 'A Jornall of the Convention at Westminster begun the 22 of January 1688/9', ed. L. G. Schwoerer, *Bull. Inst. Hist. Research* xlix (1976); Clarges-Tenison, 17 Jan. 1689, London, Lambeth Palace Library, MS 930, no. 7. Tenison, then vicar of St Martin-in-the-Fields, had omitted the prayer for James II.
[2] H. Horwitz, *Parliament, Policy and Politics in the Reign of William III* (Manchester 1977), 6-14.
[3] Prideaux-Mrs A. Coffin, 11 Feb. 1689, HMC *5th Report*, 373.

only for a king and queen without actually naming them.[1] In Oxford on 14 February town and gown together celebrated their deliverance from popery but two days later when the mayor solemnly proclaimed William and Mary at Carfax, while the citizens cheered and the conduit ran with wine, there was no sign of the vice-chancellor and the response of the university appeared tepid.[2] When news came that Archbishop Sancroft and five of his episcopal brethren, the earl of Clarendon and other venerable figures of the old tory ascendancy had refused the oaths in parliament, there was a widespread fear that Oxford was on the verge of disaster. 'I am afraid that your University Politics are going downwind', wrote one country parson, 'You cannot, I warrant you, abate an Ace of your rigid obsolete Loyalty'.[3]

That no such disruption did occur was due in large measure to the firm conduct of the vice-chancellor, Gilbert Ironside. In spite of the continued presence of over two thousand soldiers in the city, proctorial discipline was gradually re-established and the last effects of the Catholic campaign were removed. On 4 February Ironside presided over a meeting of the visitors of University College which formally deposed Obadiah Walker and opened the way for the election of a new master.[4] And at the beginning of April news came that King William had appointed Aldrich to be the new dean of Christ Church.[5] Nothing had a more reassuring effect than knowledge that the affairs of the college and the cathedral were to be in the hands of a man who was known to be both a tory and a rigid Anglican churchman. This, taken with the information that Rochester, Nottingham, Abingdon, Clarges and Heneage Finch had all taken the oaths, served to fix the resolution of most dons and their country correspondents. At the end of May Ironside was still cautious: he was worried about the circulation of Jacobite pamphlets and sufficiently apprehensive about demonstrations in the Sheldonian to ask the chancellor to cancel the Act.[6] But, in fact, Oxford politics were steadily returning to normal. Most members of the university simply refused to admit that in taking the oaths they were making any break

[1] Kennett-F. Peck, n.d., but in reply to a letter of 20 Feb. 1689, BL Lansdowne MS 960, fos 15-16. White Kennett (1660-1728), m. SEH 1678; bp of Peterborough 1718-28.

[2] G. Fleming-D. Fleming, 19 Feb. 1689, *The Flemings in Oxford* ii. 248; Cartier-T. Smith, 5 Mar. 1689, Bodl. MS Smith 48, fo 41. Ironside claimed that the city corporation had not sent him a formal invitation to attend.

[3] A. Campion-Charlett, 8 Mar. 1689, MS Ballard 30, fo 31.

[4] Wood, *Life and Times* iii. 298. The visitors were the vice-chancellor and the resident doctors of divinity.

[5] Wood, *Life and Times* iii. 301; *CSPD 1689-1690*, 45 (28 Mar.). The warrant describes the deanery as vacant by the death of John Fell. In the light of later events it is strange that there should have been a contemporary rumour that Aldrich's appointment was on Gilbert Burnet's recommendation: A. M.[aynwaring]-J. Harrington, 28 Mar. 1689, BL Add. MS 36707, fo 63.

[6] Ironside-Ormonde, 26 May 1689, HMC *Ormonde MSS* viii. 23; Shrewsbury-Ironside, 11 June 1689, *CSPD 1689-1690*, 23.

with the tory past. They relied on an elaborate argument that, since James had withdrawn himself and could no longer afford them his protection, they were justified in giving a *de facto* obedience to William while continuing to acknowledge James as their *de jure* prince.[1] At the end of April that determined old-fashioned loyalist George Hickes was about to enquire of his Oxford correspondent 'what number of Confessors, you were likely to have with you' when he was astonished to be informed that in the whole university 'you are scarse like to have any more, than honest Mr Dodwell'. Further news that Thomas Turner, president of Corpus and brother of the Jacobite bishop of Ely, had conformed caused him to explode in wrath: to demand 'in what sense Mr President of CCC intends to take [the oath]'.[2] As the deadline drew near the rush to swear allegiance to William and Mary became positively undignified. It was reported that the quarter sessions 'are held twice every week for that purpose ... are constantly crowded with Heads and Fellows of Colleges'.[3] And in the end it was discovered that only eight obstinate traditionalists had held out. Of these only one proved troublesome: the minutely learned but eccentric Henry Dodwell, Camden professor of history. His unbridled denunciation of conformists, even to the point of waylaying them in coffee-houses to remind them of past sermons on loyalty, proved deeply embarrassing; and he was persuaded to quit Oxford before the vice-chancellor was forced to take action against him.[4] That matters should have come to such an anti-climax was a triumph for Gilbert Ironside and earned him powerful friends in the government. When he was nominated as bishop of Bristol few could deny that his services had been superb. He laid down the vice-chancellorship on 25 September after two years in which the university had been faced with a continuous crisis.[5]

The resident dons had taken the oaths almost to a man but during the course of the year 1689 they found themselves drawn into an increasingly vehement opposition to the policies of the new king. Indeed the university was to be primarily responsible for frustrating what was William's most cherished domestic project: that for the comprehension

[1] For a lengthy exposition of the theory see the paper composed by White Kennett at this time: BL Lansdowne MS 960, fos 20-150. Kennett was later to be an ardent supporter of the junto whigs: see G. V. Bennett, *White Kennett, 1660-1728, Bishop of Peterborough* (London 1957).

[2] G. Hickes-Charlett, 29 Apr. and 1 July 1689, MS Ballard 12, fos 45, 49. Thomas Turner (1645-1714), m. Hart Hall 1662; scholar CCC 1663, president 1687-1714. Francis Turner (1638-1700), sub. New College 1655; bp of Ely 1684-91.

[3] H. Fleming-D. Fleming, 22 July 1689, *The Flemings in Oxford* ii. 259.

[4] Wood, *Life and Times* iii. 309 (31 Aug. 1689). Henry Dodwell (1641-1711), incorporated at Hart Hall 1688; Camden prof. of history 1688-91.

[5] *CSPD 1689-1690*, 144. He was nominated on 10 June but permitted to delay his consecration until 12 October when he handed over to his successor, Jonathan Edwards (1629-1712, m. Ch.Ch. 1657; fellow Jesus 1662, principal 1686-1712; vice-chancellor 1689-92).

of the English presbyterians into an enlarged national church. From the time of his first arrival in England the prince had made no pretence about the fact that he wished to admit all protestants to a political equality with Anglicans. When planning his invasion he had promised the Dutch Calvinist ministers that he would 'take care of their brethren the presbyterians', and through his agents in England he had assured the leading dissenters 'that in due time regard should be had to them'.[1] Already, by the time of his arrival in London, Anglicans were gravely alarmed by reports of his discussions with nonconformists and by his gracious reception of an address from them which asked for a comprehension upon 'the Terms of Union, wherein all the Reformed Churches Agree'.[2] In these critical days he seems to have had an exaggerated idea of the strength of the old exclusionist party and scarcely to have realized the difficulties in the way of anything but the most carefully devised form of comprehension. He consulted with whigs like Devonshire, de la Warr, Lumley and Richard Hampden; and such advisers were only too ready to press on him an ecclesiastical settlement which would dismantle the whole system which restricted public office to the members of a narrowly defined Anglican church.[3] They were eager to encourage William in either or both of two policies: that of a 'comprehension' which would widen the membership of the church by changing its oaths, subscriptions, liturgy and ceremonies; and that of a 'toleration' which would admit to full civil rights those who stayed outside. It is clear that William did not realize how direct a threat he was offering to tory electoral prospects and to the entrenched position of the Anglican clergy. As one country divine wrote bitterly to an Oxford colleague: 'the fanaticks swear that they will cutt your Combes for you: The day is their own now, they are very uppish; they are amodelling of the State already. You Church of England men may hew wood and draw water under them.'[4]

That William did not find himself in open conflict with the clergy was in large measure due to a remarkable political initiative taken by Daniel Finch, second earl of Nottingham, aided by the distinguished body of London divines who looked to him as their patron. In these early weeks of 1689 Edward Stillingfleet, John Tillotson, John Sharp and Thomas Tenison worked to frame two moderate bills: one to grant a strictly limited comprehension to enable presbyterians to rejoin the establishment; the other to give dissenters who would not be so comprehended a bare liberty to worship separately without penalty. Their underlying aim was to preserve a monopoly of public office to members

[1] *A Supplement to Burnet's History of My Own Times*, ed. H. C. Foxcroft (Oxford 1902), 331-2.
[2] E. Calamy, *An Abridgement of Mr. Baxter's History* (London 1702), 634.
[3] [R. Sare]-Charlett, 17 Mar. 1689, MS Ballard 45, fo 31.
[4] A. Campion-Charlett, 19 Dec. 1688, MS Ballard 30, fo 22.

of the national church and thus maintain the electoral strength of the tory party.[1] It was their misfortune to be regarded with bitter suspicion by both sides, not least by the serried ranks of the Oxford clergy. Almost to a man Nottingham's clerical allies were, like the earl himself, Cambridge men. Stillingfleet, Tillotson and Simon Patrick were well known exponents of a rational divinity derived from the teaching of Ralph Cudworth and Henry More at their old university. During the exclusion crisis their attempts to conciliate the presbyterian leaders had earned them at Oxford the opprobrious label of 'latitudinarians'. Now their compromise was sabotaged from two directions. The king and his whig advisers revealed themselves as determined to press on with the repeal of the test and corporation acts; and on 16 March, just two days after Nottingham's two bills had received a second reading in the lords, William actually appeared in the house and made a speech from the throne advocating that 'all Protestants that are willing and able to serve' should be admitted to public office.[2] Tory anger was difficult to contain. 'The king', declared one Oxford man, 'is sett upon a Comprehension. It is his misfortune to fall in with a few men and to espouse their Interest whose credit, God knows, is not very Good.'[3] Indeed on 8 April Richard Hampden reported to the commons on a proposed whig comprehension bill of so radical a character that it would have erased every distinctive feature of Anglican churchmanship. One indignant tory MP called for the debate to be adjourned 'till Doomsday' while the news flew back to Oxford that the whigs intended to make 'the Church of England men Dissenters and not the Dissenters Church of England men'.[4] So great was the tory outrage that the next day William had to agree that parliament should drop the whole question of comprehension until it had been considered by a convocation of the clergy.[5] The tories were now willing to pass Nottingham's toleration bill since it provided only a bare liberty of separate worship. Nonconformists were still to be subject to the disabilities of the test and corporation acts; no permission was given for dissenting education; and it was stated in specific terms that the old laws about attendance at the parish church were still to apply to those who did not go to a licensed meeting-house.[6] Thomas Clarges, on behalf of his university constituents, was even ready

---

[1] D. R. Lacey, *Dissent and Parliamentary Politics in England 1661-1689* (New Brunswick 1969), chap. 10; R. Thomas, 'Comprehension and indulgence' in G. F. Nuttall and O. Chadwick (eds), *From Uniformity to Unity, 1662-1962* (London 1962), 243-53.

[2] Horwitz, *Parliament, Policy and Politics* 22.

[3] [R. Sare]-Charlett, 17 Mar. 1689, MS Ballard 45, fo 31; see also Campion-same, 2 Apr. 1689, MS Ballard 30, fo 26: 'A Convocation purely of Lay elders out does Geneva it self. I never knew these greycoated Ecclesiasticks reform to any good purpose. They fancy that Christ and his Apostles left the Government of the Church as Arbitrary as they conceiv [*sic*] that of the State to be, and that presbyterian Orders may become valid by an Almighty vote to Knights and Burgesses.'

[4] *Journals of the House of Commons* x. 84. [R. Sare]-Charlett, 9 Apr. 1689, MS Ballard 45, fo 31.

[5] Horwitz, 25.   [6] See Bennett, *Tory Crisis*, 10-12.

to limit these provisions further; and on 17 May he made a last-minute bid to have the intended toleration limited to a term of seven years.[1]

When King William gave the royal assent to the toleration act on 24 May it was thus a defeat and a crushing disappointment. The failure to achieve a comprehension in parliament meant that he now had to rely on Nottingham's 'moderate' friends if there was to be any chance of getting a scheme through the convocation of Canterbury. In the late summer, therefore, he abandoned his whig advisers and committed himself to the moderate Anglicans as to 'a party between the 2 extreames'.[2] On 4 September a royal warrant was issued out for an ecclesiastical commission, charged with the task of preparing such changes in the liturgy, canons and discipline of the church as might be laid before the convocation when it met in November.[3] The composition of this body is of the greatest significance for the ecclesiastical history of the reign and for the politics of the University of Oxford. It indicated not only the king's policy but where the future course of preferment was to lie. Apart from the ten bishops named there were twenty other divines. Of these fourteen had been educated at Cambridge, four at Oxford and two at both the universities. And within the next few weeks a series of promotions given to the Cambridge men on the commission emphasized the effect. Stillingfleet and Patrick were raised to the episcopate while John Tillotson, Sharp and Richard Kidder were given deaneries or promotion to better ones. Membership of the commission on the 'moderate' side was to be a sure road to a bishopric in William's reign.[4] Eleven were to become bishops, including eight who had been educated at Cambridge and one who had been at both universities. Of the Oxford men two only were to be thus promoted: John Hall, the austerely whiggish and Calvinist master of Pembroke, and John Williams, a London divine who was a client of Nottingham and an ardent advocate for comprehension.[5] The impression that the royal benison was bestowed on Cambridge and denied to the sister-university was reinforced when on 7 October the king paid a state-visit to Cambridge, walking from college to college, dining at Trinity and being present at an honorary degree-ceremony at which two prominent 'moderate' divines were given doctorates of divinity.[6]

[1] *Parliamentary History* v. 265.
[2] See H. C. Foxcroft, *Life and Letters of George Savile, First Marquis of Halifax* (2 vols London 1898) ii. 229–30 for William's conversation with Halifax on 8 August 1689.
[3] *CSPD 1689–1690*, 242. For the membership, meetings and the detailed revisions proposed see T. J. Fawcett, *The Liturgy of Comprehension 1689* (Alcuin Club collections liv Southend-on-Sea 1973).
[4] See G. V. Bennett, 'King William III and the episcopate' in G. V. Bennett and J. D. Walsh (eds), *Essays in Modern English Church History in Memory of Norman Sykes* (London 1966).
[5] John Hall (1633–1710), m. Pemb. 1650, master 1664–1710; Lady Margaret prof. of divinity 1676–91; bp of Bristol 1691–1710. John Williams (1636–1709), m. Magdalen Hall 1653; bp of Chichester 1696–1709.
[6] N. Luttrell, *A Brief Historical Relation of State Affairs* (6 vols London 1857) i. 590. See Tillotson-

When the commission met on 3 October the 'moderate' pressure-group appeared confident of success: they were a clear majority, and with their impressive weight of bishops, bishops-elect, and deans they quickly took charge of the business and pushed ahead with their proposals for comprehension.[1] But at once they encountered determined opposition from a minority led by the two Oxford figures, Aldrich and Jane. On the first day Jane demurred at the 'moderate' proposals, and at the second session he and Aldrich joined Bishop Sprat of Rochester in calling in question the legal basis of the commission.[2] At the third meeting, when discussion moved on to the subject of which ceremonies might be made optional or abolished, they ostentatiously stood up in the midst of the debate and walked out.[3] Their return to Oxford 'in discontent' was a symbolic act, and they were given an enthusiastic reception.[4] Of all the Oxford dons only one, John Hall, stayed behind among the Cambridge men to work on the revised liturgy of comprehension.

It was soon to be shown, however, that all these careful preparations were in vain. So far from preparing the minds of the clergy, the commission had set in motion a furious agitation. Bishop Burnet reported that

the universities, and particularly Oxford, took fire upon this; and began to declare against it, and against all that promoted it, as men that intended to undermine the church: severe reflections were cast on the king, as being in an interest contrary to the church.[5]

It was generally recognized that the agitation was primarily concerted in Christ Church, to which Lord Rochester had been paying frequent visits. Certainly it was William Jane who put out the most incendiary of all the pamphlets designed to influence the parish priests as they gathered to elect their proctors for the lower house of convocation. Entitled *Letter to a Friend containing some Quaeries about the New Commission*, it was a slashing attack not only on the whole idea of a comprehension but upon the 'Nine Men' who had undertaken to force it upon the church. What authority had been given to 'some few assuming men to alter the Established Worship, to make it comply with their own private conceits, or to serve their own private ends?' Such concessions would, in fact,

Shrewsbury, 30 Sept. 1689, *CSPD 1689-1690*, 280, in which he recommended that the king should nominate Kidder and Williams for the degree.

[1] Fawcett, 160-77; see also a transcript of the diary of John Williams in Lambeth Palace Lib. MS Secker 24/6; 'The autobiography of Symon Patrick' in *The Works of Symon Patrick, D.D., sometime Bishop of Ely*, ed. A. Taylor (9 vols Oxford 1858) ix. 522-5; T. Birch, *The Life of the Most Reverend Dr. John Tillotson, Lord Archbishop of Canterbury* (London 1752), 183.
[2] Thomas Sprat (1635-1713), m. Wadham 1651; bp of Rochester 1684-1713.
[3] Fawcett, 164.
[4] Kennett-S. Blackwell, 30 Oct. [1689], BL Lansdowne MS 1013, fo 260.
[5] *Bishop Burnet's History of His Own Time* [ed. M. J. Routh] (6 vols Oxford 1823) iv. 57, as corrected by the *Supplement*, ed. Foxcroft, p. 332.

bring in no more than a handful of dissenters. Even the presbyterians would not submit to a new episcopal ordination and yet, if they were not so ordained, churchmen would not 'own such Presbyters'. The Church of England was the best constituted church in Christendom but now it was to be 'transformed by Nine men, who may have tenderness and moderation enough to part with any thing but their Church-preferments'.[1]

Intense efforts were made on the 'moderate' side to get a majority in the lower house of convocation, and episcopal pressure was brought to bear on wavering deans and archdeacons. In fact, all their leading spokesmen were found a seat, but, as Bishop Burnet reported sadly, there was a groundswell of anger among the ordinary clergy which could not be contained: 'great canvassings were every where, in the elections of convocation men; a thing not known in former times.'[2] If the commission had had a majority of Cambridge men, the lower house of convocation which met for business on 21 November was composed overwhelmingly of Oxford graduates. Of the grand total of 132 members no fewer than 95 had been educated there. Of the 42 proctors of the diocesan clergy who can be identified 33 had a degree from the university. The contingent of Oxford dons who were returned to represent the clergy of many dioceses was formidable. It was headed by the vice-chancellor, Jonathan Edwards, who was accompanied by seven other heads of colleges and halls, two canons of Christ Church, and Bodley's Librarian, Thomas Hyde.[3] The Oxfordshire parish clergy elected John Mill, the principal of St Edmund Hall, and Henry Maurice, chaplain to the suspended Archbishop Sancroft and himself one of the foremost writers against comprehension.[4] The first business of the house, at which 85 members were present, was to elect a prolocutor. John Sharp proposed Tillotson, and he was warmly supported by the whole 'moderate' group as the man who had the confidence of the king and Nottingham. Aldrich then proposed William Jane, and after an embittered debate the vote was taken: to reveal that Jane had received 55 votes to Tillotson's 28. When the 'moderate' party made a special plea that Tillotson should nevertheless be placed in the chair, they were voted down a second time.[5] On 25 November the dean of Christ Church presented Jane to Bishop Compton of London in a speech which was long remembered as

[1] *Letter to a Friend containing some Quaeries about the New Commission* [London 1689], 2-4.
[2] *Bishop Burnet's History of His Own Time* iv. 57.
[3] Thomas Hyde (1636-1703), m. Queen's 1654; Bodley's Librarian 1665-1701; canon Ch.Ch. and regius prof. of hebrew 1697-1703.
[4] John Mill (1645-1707), m. Queen's 1661; principal SEH 1685-1707. Henry Maurice (1648-91), m. Jesus 1664; Lady Margaret prof. of divinity 1691. Maurice was author of *Remarks from the Country* (London 1690). For the official list of members see E. Cardwell, *A History of Conferences... connected with the Revision of the Book of Common Prayer* (Oxford 1840, 3rd edn Oxford 1849), 435-40.
[5] Luttrell, *State Affairs* i. 607; Cardwell, 440; L. W. Finch-Weymouth, 21 Nov. 1689, Longleat House, Thynne MS xvii, fo 206; Lindsay-Anderson, 21 Nov. 1689, *CSPD 1689-1690*, 325.

a classic statement of the university's resistance to comprehension, while Jane concluded his own oration with a rousing cry of 'Nolumus leges Angliae mutare [*sic*]'.[1] The 'moderate' party was now in despair. In the subsequent sessions Aldrich and Jane completely dominated the course of business, even leading their supporters in refusing to agree to a loyal address, proposed by the bishops, which associated the Church of England with the interest of 'the Protestant religion in general'.[2] Such an assembly was too dangerous for the delicate politics of the year 1689, and on 13 December it was adjourned by royal command, never to meet again.

This defeat of King William's scheme of comprehension at the hands of the men of Oxford was a significant moment in the history of the university. It now had to be faced that Oxford's political role had been fundamentally changed by the events of the Revolution. Until 1686 it had been the ally of a regime of personal monarchy, an institution which formed an essential part of a dominant political ascendancy. After 1689 it was to find itself deeply alienated from a king who regarded it with an intense suspicion and resentment. Like the tory party itself Oxford had to learn to live and act as an opposition interest, dedicated to defending the status and authority of church and clergy in a world of politics which had suddenly grown cold and hostile.

[1] [T. Long,] *Vox Cleri, or the Sense of the Clergy* (London 1690), 51; H. Prideaux, *A Letter to a Friend relating to the present Convocation at Westminster* (London 1690), 18. Henry Compton (1632-1713), m. Queen's 1654; MA Cambridge 1661; incorporated at Ch.Ch. 1666, canon 1669; bp of Oxford 1674-5, London 1675-1713.

[2] Cardwell, 440-51.

2

Against the Tide: Oxford under William III

G. V. BENNETT

DURING the course of King William's reign the university moved steadily into the position of a major centre of opposition to the government. To a casual observer life at Oxford would have seemed virtually unchanged by the Revolution. Academic ceremonies continued to be conducted with solemn decorum; heads of houses died, were briefly mourned and their successors elected; there was the usual strenuous competition for any vacancy, whether it was for a professor, an incumbent of a college living or a humble bedel. From time to time moral scandals came to light and provided endless gossip in common room and coffee-house; at regular intervals the young broke out into frolics which inconvenienced and irritated their elders. But, in spite of every such appearance of normality, it could not be disguised that the university was passing through a period of recession and reappraisal. During the decade from 1690 to 1699 the actual number of matriculations fell to a lower level than at any time since the civil wars, and it was apparent that many young men had begun to doubt whether an Oxford degree, which led to little save ordination, was worth the expense involved.[1] Such a loss of confidence stemmed from a wider crisis which was affecting the whole Church of England as it was forced to come to terms with the fact that its status and authority in the life of the nation had been gravely diminished.[2] The early years of William's reign were a time of grievous shock and trial for the ordinary parish priest. It was soon apparent that the toleration act had virtually destroyed ecclesiastical discipline over the morals and religious observance of the laity while heavy taxation for the great war with France brought about a sudden decline in the clergy's economic position. A new intellectual climate stressed 'Reason and Natural

---

[1] See L. Stone, 'The size and composition of the Oxford student body 1580-1909' in L. Stone (ed.), *The University in Society* (2 vols Princeton 1975) i. 91, table 1A, for an estimate of the number of matriculants. In the decade 1660-9 the average annual number was 458; in 1670-9, 400; in 1680-9, 321; and in 1690-9 it fell to 303, the lowest point until the great eighteenth-century recession began in 1720.

[2] For a fuller account see G. V. Bennett, *The Tory Crisis in Church and State, 1688-1730* (Oxford 1975), ch. 1.

Religion' and fostered a contempt for 'priestcraft' which extended even to some tory parliamentarians. For a generation the ministry of the established church appeared singularly unattractive, and many dons and their pupils, already committed to a clerical vocation, showed a sense of disappointment and betrayal. From this situation stemmed much of the anger and impatience which were to characterize university politics.

It was perhaps to be expected that whig politicians with long memories of the previous era would lose no opportunity to malign the universities on the floor of the house of commons. What was more serious was a new attitude of suspicion and cold indifference shown by the king's government. In the post-Revolution pattern of politics William worked with both whig and tory ministers but committed himself to neither side and strove constantly to preserve his administrations from domination by party zealots. Such a delicate balancing of forces required that, as far as possible, the civil service, the armed forces and the leadership of the established church should be composed of 'moderate' men, ready to support and work with any ministry of the king's choice. To prevent the church, in particular, from becoming a focus for extreme tory sentiment, care was taken that bishoprics and senior preferment should be given only to those who would work to prevent the clergy's involvement in political agitation. Thus those 'moderates' who had supported the scheme for a comprehension reaped rich rewards.[1] Oxford, with its deep attachment to old cavalier politicians and its body of assertive divines, could be seen as a standing threat to this policy of moderation, and ministers exhibited a strange nervousness about sermons preached by dons or pamphlets written by them. And yet the government's attempts to control the universities were always ill-informed and clumsy. It would have been sensible to build up connections with influential heads of houses who might try to moderate the politics of the ordinary dons, but those who offered themselves for this work were ill-supported and poorly rewarded. It might have been thought expedient to employ the crown's considerable resources of ecclesiastical patronage in a systematic way to encourage a 'moderate' toryism among the residents; but ministers, court peers and Williamite bishops too often directed their patronage away from Oxford or angered tories of all shades of opinion by bestowing it upon the tiny and unrepresentative group of whigs within the university. The result was to create not a useful body of ministerial support but a widespread belief among the ordinary dons that the government itself was an enemy to their aspirations and the author of many of their difficulties.

That Oxford was to face hostility in parliament and the law courts was quickly made apparent. In December 1689 Clarges and Finch introduced

---

[1] G. V. Bennett, 'King William III and the episcopate' in G. V. Bennett and J. D. Walsh (eds), *Essays in Modern English Church History in Memory of Norman Sykes* (London 1966).

a bill into the commons to give statutory force to the university's Caroline charter. In the light of James II's *quo warranto*, it seemed a reasonable precaution and a settlement of long accepted practice. To the general dismay, however, objections raised by the city of Oxford were quickly taken up by whig members, and the university, its lawyers and burgesses found themselves caught up in a bitter public controversy, with an exchange of pamphlets and a necessity 'to solicite parliament men and lawyers to stand on their side'. The outcome on the floor of the house was sufficiently uncertain for Clarges and Finch to decide to withdraw their bill.[1]   An even more disturbing indication of prejudice was to be found in the case of Henry Wildgoose, which came into the court of common pleas in January 1690. Wildgoose was an Oxford tradesman who had sought to avoid the expense and burden of city office by renouncing his citizenship and having himself matriculated in the university as one of the 'privileged men' or official servants of the academic community. When the ensuing case between the city and the university came into court, it turned out to be something of a *cause célèbre*. The duke of Ormonde, the earl of Clarendon, Viscount Weymouth, the bishop of Winchester and Sir Thomas Clarges attended, but even this impressive turnout of Oxford's great friends did not prevent the lord chief justice from giving an emphatic verdict in favour of the city. The effect was only that 'their appearance probably hindered the Bench from making reflexions, as formerly, on the Universitys Privileges'.[2]

Some hope for a greater sympathy in high places existed briefly in the spring of 1690 when the king decided to dissolve the convention parliament and throw the weight of the crown's influence behind the tories. On 19 February, at a special convocation held to elect burgesses for the new house of commons, there was no doubt of the mood of the ordinary MAs. The vice-chancellor, Jonathan Edwards, actually proposed the old members from the chair 'Whereupon they all cried up unanimously "Finch and Clarges", and named not at all a third person–which was a rare thing and not before knowne'.[3]   But this expectation of a new deal for churchmen proved groundless. The whig party in the commons remained deeply hostile and their anti-clerical attitudes affected even some tory members who seemed more intent on curtailing the political

---

[1] Wood, *Life and Times* iii. 322. See Bodl. Wood 423 for a collection of pamphlets concerning the bill. The principal one, *A Defence of the Rights and Privileges of the University of Oxford* (Oxford 1690) was written by James Harrington; see also T. Newey-Harrington, 26 Jan. 1690, BL Add. MS 36707, fo 78. For a powerful assertion of the city's case (among Lord Abingdon's papers) see Bodl. MS Top. Oxon. c. 325, fos 95 ff.

[2] Harrington-Charlett, 30 Jan. 1690, MS Ballard 22, fo 3; Wood, *Life and Times* iii. 323; Washington DC, Folger Shakespeare Library, Newdigate newsletter no. 206 (31 Jan. 1690).

[3] Wood, *Life and Times* iii. 325. From the moment of their election Clarges and Finch were working closely with Oxford personalities such as Charlett: Charlett-St John Brodrick, 13 Feb. 1689, Surrey Record Office, Guildford Muniment Room, Midleton MS 1248/1/232.

rights of dissenters than defending the position of their clerical allies. Clearly the heaviest stick which the whigs used to belabour the universities was the accusation, repeated in season and out of season, that the colleges were nests of secret Jacobitism; and the campaign had its effect. When in the summer of 1691 the time came formally to deprive the eight nonjurors at Oxford, the government made excessively heavy weather of the business. Threatening letters were dispatched from the secretary of state to the vice-chancellor, and his plea that the deprivation of fellows was essentially a college matter was dismissed as an attempt to evade his duty. In fact the seven nonjurors who held fellowships were all duly expelled by the beginning of 1692, but whig propaganda had already fixed on the university the reputation of having sheltered Jacobites until the last possible moment.[1] Indeed in January the whigs in the commons, led by the formidable Richard Hopkins, member for Coventry, launched themselves into a concerted attack on Oxford, and they actually managed to add a new clause to the land tax bill which imposed a double tax on any head, fellow or scholar of a college who did not offer voluntarily to swear the oath of allegiance. In 1692 the clause was removed before the bill became law but in 1694 it was revived and members of the university were subjected to the humiliation of queueing up before special commissioners to take an oath of loyalty which was imposed on no other of the king's subjects.[2]

All this might have been supportable if it had not been accompanied by a sharp recession in the professional prospects of ordinary clerical fellows. It was a recognized fact that the well-being of the colleges depended on there being a constant movement of senior fellows out into parishes or some comparable ecclesiastical preferment. The narrowness and enforced celibacy of college life was thought intolerable beyond a certain age, and places on the foundation were required for younger men. Most colleges, and especially the larger and richer ones such as New College, Magdalen and Christ Church, possessed the advowsons of livings of a value sufficient to make it worth a man's while to resign his fellowship and leave the university. There were, of course, never enough to satisfy all aspirants, and it was necessary for some fellows to seek chaplaincies or preferment from noble or gentry patrons, or to recommend themselves to the crown or to episcopal favour. But in the years of King William's reign there was a definite contraction in the opportunities available. It was not just that Oxford divines were being

---

[1] Nottingham-Edwards, 24 Sept. 1691, MS Ballard 10, fo 184; HMC *Finch MSS* iii. 283 [Nov. 1691]; Wood, *Life and Times* iii. 373 (14 Oct). In fact Edwards had designated those who had become liable to deprivation in the previous June; his difficulties stemmed from the reluctance of heads of houses to take any action which might be challenged at law: [E. Bernard]-Smith, 17 July and 14 Nov. 1691, Bodl. MS Smith 47, fos 89, 94; Wood, *Life and Times* iii. 374-7.

[2] W. Bromley-T. Bayley, 18 Jan. 1692, Wood, *Life and Times* iii. 380; see also iii. 445.

denied the preferment which had been open to them in the previous era; the fact was that a drop in benefice-income made far fewer livings worth the taking. The years from 1688 to 1691 saw exceptionally depressed prices for corn and thus low levels of income from tithe.[1] In the latter year William Sampson, rector of Clayworth, Nottinghamshire, and a diligent recorder of the annual value of his living, noted the lowest tithe for the whole of his incumbency.[2] Though corn prices recovered well from 1693 and only fell badly in 1700, the higher income obtained was eroded by a general dearness of food and commodities and unprecedented levels of taxation. From 1694 the land-tax was set at four shillings in the pound and, for a clergyman who derived most of his income from land in the form of tithes or the profits of his glebe, this could mean a loss of up to a fifth of his stipend. In addition tithes were assessed to the poor rate, and experiments during the 1690s at a poll-tax gave the clergy a rate akin to that of a gentleman. It is estimated that by 1695 rectors of parishes were paying out between a quarter and a third of their income in some kind of tax or levy. The result was a serious shortage of livings of the kind which a college fellow, accustomed to the comforts of university life, thought it proper to accept. The consequent immobility in academic life was noted on all sides. In 1691 Humphrey Prideaux's advice to the eminent brother of an aspiring young Oxford cleric was plain: 'I would by no means', he opined, 'advice you to putt your brother into such a living as would forfeit his fellowship, but rather to begin in some employment that might be consistent with it.' The reason was that 'as the world now goes, a curacy is better than a liveing, for, all country commoditys beeing soe low and taxes soe high, all liveings that depend on prediall tiths are fallen more than halfe in value'.[3] Soon complaints were heard of the length of time men were being forced to stay on at the university and the manner in which parishes were being filled by divines of lower status and less learning. As Prideaux himself put it: 'they that best deserve them, and whose labours would be most usefull to the publick, are condemned to their College chambers all day of their lifes, and the publick totally loose the benefit of their learning and piety.'[4]

The situation may be illustrated by a statistical survey of the fellows of an Oxford college which was to play a significant part in the political

---

[1] For the movement of corn prices and general prices see J. E. Thorold Rogers, *A History of Agriculture and Prices in England* (7 vols in 8 Oxford 1866-1902) vi. Average prices for wheat by the quarter were 28s 10d in 1690 but rose to 63s 5d in 1693; by 1701 they were down again to 27s 1d. On the other hand the price of flour rose from 48s in 1690 to 92s in 1693.

[2] See *The Rector's Book, Clayworth, Notts.* ed. H. Gill and E. L. Guildford (Nottingham 1910) for Sampson's figures. In 1691 the value of the benefice was £139 2s 11d. Apart from the poor years 1686 and 1688 it had not fallen below £150 since 1676. It was to exceed £230 in 1693, 1697 and 1698.

[3] *Letters of Humphrey Prideaux, sometime Dean of Norwich, to John Ellis, sometime Under-Secretary of State, 1674-1722,* ed. E. M. Thompson (Camden Soc. new ser. xv 1875), 148 (7 June 1691).

[4] HMC *5th Report,* 378.

struggle down to 1714.[1] Magdalen with its 40 fellows and 30 demies was one of the largest and richest societies, with a tradition of playing an active role in university affairs. The 40 fellows existing at the beginning of 1689 were a distinguished body, as befitted men who had just successfully defied James II and earned the plaudits of the whole Church of England. No less than 27 of them were, or subsequently became, ordained, and 13 of them were to take the degree of doctor of divinity. Yet their later careers in the church were singularly disappointing. Only 12 were to resign on preferment and no less than 14 were still in the college at the time of their death, though 3 of these had been elected as president. Those who did get a living had to wait on an average nearly 15 years from their election as a fellow, and their average age on resignation was just over 40. Life was even more difficult for the fellows elected during the period 1690 to 1701. Of these 24 men no fewer than 21 were ordained, and yet only 8 were able to resign on obtaining a benefice of sufficient value. Four appear to have given up the wait and resigned on marriage to take a curacy or a schoolmastership, while 5 continued in the college until their death. The picture would be a sombre one indeed were it not for 4 Magdalen fellows who escaped quickly from residence by allying themselves to the powerful network of patronage operated by whig peers and 'moderate' bishops. Three of these divines were to climb high up the ladder of preferment on their reputation as useful whig political supporters. Hugh Boulter became chaplain first to Archbishop Tenison and then to the third earl of Sunderland, and thereby began a career which led him to the deanery of Christ Church in 1719 and the archbishopric of Armagh five years later. Richard West became chaplain to Bishop Burnet, and was a leading spokesman for the 'moderate' cause in the convocation controversy and an effective political pamphleteer; it was only his early death in 1716 which deprived him of the bishopric for which his influential friends had been pressing since 1707. Richard Smalbrooke also began his career as one of Tenison's domestic chaplains, and his political services were amply rewarded. In 1709 he was presented by the archbishop to the rich rectory of Hadleigh in Suffolk, and in the following year received the 'golden prebend' of Hereford; in 1723 he was consecrated bishop of St David's and in 1731 translated to Lichfield and Coventry. Over against such dazzling careers the tory clergy of Magdalen of the same generation could show only Henry Sacheverell's rectory of St Andrew, Holborn, Thomas Yalden's preachership at the Bridewell, and a meagre clutch of country livings. The scene lightens somewhat for the group of fellows elected in the era from 1702 to 1714. Of these 31, 23 were in orders, and 15 able to resign on being presented to a benefice, all except 2 after

---

[1] This analysis is based on the information in Bloxham, *Reg. Magdalen* ii and Macray, *Reg. Magdalen* iv.

the death of Queen Anne. Perhaps because of the vehement tory politics of the college only one fellow of this generation, Joseph Wilcocks, found his way into the whig patronage system.[1] While his contemporaries remained parish priests he moved up rapidly, to be a prebendary of West-minster in 1715, bishop of Gloucester in 1721, and both bishop of Rochester and dean of Westminster in 1731. The conclusion must be that William's reign was a time of considerable strain for clerical fellows of colleges, with many able men denied senior preferment and even unable to find benefices of a sufficient income.[2] For a few who were prepared to break with the politics of the past and serve the new 'moderate' ascendancy there could be rapid advancement; for the great majority who remained wedded to their tory churchmanship the era was one of disappointment and mounting frustration.

The emergence of a vehement sense of grievance among the resident dons created serious problems for those who had to manage the politics of the university. Few could doubt that its position was dangerous and exposed, especially after 1694 when King William dismissed his tory ministers and turned to an administration which relied heavily on the services of the determined young court-whigs of the junto. The new ministry was easily alarmed by religious issues and particularly sensitive to attacks from the clergy; and, since Oxford was widely taken to speak for the established church, sermons, public addresses, votes and elections there were carefully scrutinized by ministers. Since the convocation of Canterbury was now effectively silenced, the universities provided the only medium through which a sizeable and formal body of the lower clergy could make its views known. The Oxford political managers thus exhibited a pardonable nervousness that wild or unguarded expressions of the ordinary dons' tory partisanship might bring grave difficulties on all their heads. The university needed tolerable relations with the

---

[1] Hugh Boulter (1672-1742), m. Ch. Ch. 1687; demy Magd. 1689-96; dean Ch. Ch. 1719-24; abp of Armagh 1724-42. Richard West (1671-1716), m. Merton 1689; demy Magd. 1689-97; archdeacon of Berkshire 1710-16. Richard Smalbrooke (1673-1749), m. Trin. 1688; demy Magd. 1689-98; bp of St David's 1723-31, Lichfield 1731-49. Henry Sacheverell (1674-1724), m. Magd. 1689, demy 1689-1701, fellow 1701-13. Thomas Yalden (1670-1736), m. Magd. 1686, demy 1690-8, fellow 1698-1713. Joseph Wilcocks (1673-1756), m. St John's 1692; demy Magd. 1692-1703, fellow 1703-22; bp of Gloucester 1721-31, Rochester 1731-56.

[2] In the New College Archives the register of fellows compiled by Warden J. E. Sewell provides comparative statistics for a college in which whigs formed a more significant group than at Magdalen. The lower value of New College fellowships and the high total of 27 college livings ensured a more rapid turnover. Of the 66 fellows of 1689, 36 are known to have been ordained but only 2 died as fellows. Twenty-five were provided for by the college itself: 17 in college livings, 6 as fellows of Winchester and 2 by being elected to the wardenship. The remainder obtained preferment elsewhere, often through the whig patronage network, which could ensure an early opportunity to leave college life. The relative security of fellows of New College seems directly related to its low level of political activity and its general mediocrity of achievement.

government for a whole variety of business and crown appointments; the heads of houses were not anxious to divert from themselves all possibility of royal patronage; and they were justifiably afraid of alienating ordinary public opinion, thus providing grist for the mill of whig accusations and inviting discriminatory measures against the university. For a generation Oxford politics were to be a study in the nice balance which the leading heads sought to hold between the angry politics of the college fellows and their own nervous self-interest.

At first view the constitution of the university seemed uniquely designed to encourage political assertion by the ordinary dons. All major business, parliamentary elections, the voting of addresses, appointments to university offices and the granting of graces for degrees took place in convocation, the formal assembly of doctors and regent masters. The precise qualification for membership of the house was not clearly defined and many elections were marked by accusations that 'bad' or 'doubtful' votes had been admitted by the proctors. It could be taken, however, that any MA 'on the foundation' of his college was entitled to attend, speak and exercise his suffrage, and that the small number of university officers and tutors in the halls could do the same. The total membership of convocation was thus about 440, though the prevalence of non-residence among fellows ordinarily reduced the number of those who answered the summons of the convocation bell to between 340 and 380.[1] For sufficiently important business or parliamentary elections candidates and their friends were ready to write to absentees urging them back to Oxford. It is evident, however, that few issues were decided on a free expression of the opinion of the ordinary MAs. Debates had to be conducted in Latin and many, perhaps most, of the younger dons were not prepared to risk ridicule by lapsing into bad grammar or false quantities before such an assembly. It is clear, too, that voting was affected by college loyalty, and that most matters were determined by the strength of certain large colleges, the members of which usually voted as a group behind the head of their house.[2] The most powerful of such interests was Christ Church which had no fewer than 60 members of convocation, drawn from its

[1] No official list of the members of convocation existed, and the earliest poll-book for an election of burgesses dates from 1722. This gives a useful view of the relative strengths of the colleges, though the total vote, at 432, was exaggerated by the inclusion of many bad or doubtful votes: see *A True Copy of the Poll for Members of Parliament for the University of Oxford, taken March the 21st 1721* (Oxford 1722), copy in Bodl. Oxon. 4° 6 (7). The register of convocation gives the votes cast during William III's reign, from which the approximate number of votes on each occasion can be calculated. At the general election of 1698 715 votes were cast in a four-cornered contest, indicating about 375 voters: OUA register of convocation 1693-1703, p. 186. At the general election in January 1701 612 votes were cast in a three-cornered contest, indicating about 337 voters, while at the by-election in March 1701 361 votes were cast in a straight contest: ibid. fos 225, 226ᵛ. On 11 March 1709 Hearne noted a contest for the bedelship of divinity in which a total of 372 votes was recorded: Hearne, *Collections* ii. 174-5.

[2] The clearest account of the voting strength in the various colleges is provided by Hearne in a list compiled in July 1709: *Collections* iv. 437-9 (appx A). Although the editor has failed to understand his

magnificent foundation of a dean, 8 canons, 101 Students and 10 chaplains. It was possible for 'the House' to muster as many as 55 votes in crucial contests, and the tradition was for them to follow their head's lead closely. Indeed the power of Christ Church and its ruthless use of its vote to press its own candidates for important university offices was deeply resented by smaller colleges. To some extent, however, this strength was countered by a traditional rivalry with the second most weighty college, Magdalen, behind which certain weaker societies gathered. Magdalen with its ample foundation of a president, 40 fellows, 30 demies and 4 chaplains could usually field as many as 47 votes, and its numbers were kept up by a firm refusal to allow its members prolonged non-residence. Three other colleges, All Souls, Queen's and St John's, had about 25 votes while Brasenose, Corpus, Exeter, Jesus, Trinity and Wadham had between 15 and 20 each. Five others, Balliol, Merton, New College, Oriel and Pembroke, usually had fewer than 15 MAs in the house, while University College and Lincoln could manage only single figures. Perhaps the greatest contrast between size of foundation and actual political effectiveness was provided by New College. Though it possessed a warden, 70 fellows and 10 chaplains, the existence of undergraduate and bachelor fellows meant that its actual number of regent masters was not above 24, and half of these would usually have been given permission to live away from Oxford. Indeed political divisions and a succession of weak wardens unable to enforce discipline ruined what otherwise might have been a major interest.

The fact that half the active members of convocation came from five large colleges obviously gave great influence to a small group of heads of houses, and in many respects the story of Oxford politics in William's reign can be told in terms of their rivalries and manoeuvres. The power of the heads was readily apparent. With the two annually elected proctors they formed the hebdomadal board and controlled the day-to-day administration of the university, under the presidency of the vice-chancellor who was always nominated from among their number. They had the sole right to initiate legislation in convocation and, as members of the various delegacies and boards of visitors or curators, directed important aspects of academic life. Most heads prided themselves on being able to answer for the votes of all members of their own societies, and some of the most virulent college disputes of the era had their origin in the obstinacy of a fellow or group of fellows who defied their head's whip. The affair of Jonas Proast of All Souls may stand as a case in point. For defying Warden Finch's request for his vote in the election of a Camden professor Proast was arbitrarily deprived and did not gain restitution until five years later.

annotations, it is clear that Hearne is giving not only the names under college headings but marking those who were usually non-resident.

Indeed, much of the intense ill-feeling in the college down to 1714 stemmed from attempts by Finch and his successor Bernard Gardiner to impose discipline on fellows who were determined neither to keep residence nor to abide by college statutes which required the taking of holy orders within a prescribed period. The defeat of the two wardens led in large measure to the slow eclipse of All Souls as a college important in university politics.[1] Other heads were more successful. Within their own societies they usually had the right to appoint to offices and tutorships and could be decisive in elections to college benefices. A fellow who attracted the enmity of the head of his college risked serious harassment. But, in spite of their power to influence and even tyrannize, the lot of those who presided over the smaller and less well endowed colleges was by no means easy. In 1699 the master of University College received only £110 annually, an income less than that of a substantial living.[2] For such a one the prospect of a deanery, a prebend or a valuable crown living, especially if this could be held with his headship, was intensely attractive and provided a clear inducement to ingratiate himself with the government of the day. It was equally tempting to form a connection with some prominent politician in opposition in the hope that his eventual attainment of power might lead to rich rewards. But the path of such a head was delicate. His own political convictions and the need to maintain leadership within the college might push him towards a clear tory stand, while self-interest and a fear of being held responsible for the extremes of the lower orders could lead him into temporizing over every issue.

For the whole of William's reign the dominant figure among the heads was Henry Aldrich, dean of Christ Church. For a generation, down to his death in 1710, he was to represent in the university the most uncompromising form of old-fashioned toryism. References abound to his vitality and personal charm, but contemporaries clearly stood in awe of a man of considerable force of personality who could be passionate and unpredictable. None could doubt his restless energy. As vice-chancellor from 1692 to 1695 he was an unremitting disciplinarian:[3] reimposing the dress

[1] For Proast see M. Burrows, *Worthies of All Souls* (London 1874), 308-11; Wood, *Life and Times* ii. 263, 382, 403, 467; W. Lancaster-Charlett, 11 Dec. 1694, MS Ballard 21, fo 56. Jonas Proast (d. 1710), m. Queen's 1659; MA Gloucester Hall 1666; chaplain Queen's and later All Souls. The Hon. Leopold William Finch (1662-1702), m. Ch.Ch. 1679; fellow All Souls 1682, warden 1687-1702. Bernard Gardiner (1668-1726), m. Magd. 1684; BA Magdalen Hall 1688; BCL All Souls 1693, warden 1702-26; vice-chancellor 1712-15; keeper of the archives 1703-26. In July 1709 Hearne noted eleven non-resident fellows of All Souls, a greater number than at any college except New College: *Collections* iv. 437-9.
[2] Hearne, *Collections* i. 300.
[3] See Wood, *Life and Times* iii. 427, 469; Folger Lib. Newdigate newsletter no. 219 (4 July 1693); Hickes-Charlett, 2 Apr. 1694, MS Ballard 12, fo 90. See also Wood, *Life and Times* iii. 404, (4 Oct. 1692). 'Dr Aldrich told the doctors and Masters that he will severely look after the discipline of the Universitie, disputations in Austins, wall-lectures, examinations, Lent exercises.'

regulations, requiring professors to give their lectures, and so curbing the 'insolences' of the undergraduate that in 1693 he was able once again to hold the Act, with its speeches, music and academic satire. Within Christ Church itself he was successful in attracting back the sons of the tory aristocracy. The new buildings of Peckwater quadrangle were designed to house them, and it even became a proof of tory loyalty among the squires of the midlands to have contributed to the cost. Following Fell's example, the dean offered prizes out of his own pocket to foster academic emulation among the aristocratic young, and each year his 'New-Year's gift' to the whole college was a finely printed and neatly bound volume, containing a literary essay by one of his youthful protégés. Aldrich stands as the very type of bachelor-don whose talent in letters and the arts acted as a honeypot to well-bred young men with intellectual pretensions. His skills were amazingly varied. He was a distinguished amateur architect whose work survives in the classical proportions of All Saints church, Trinity chapel, and Peckwater itself. He was the composer not only of church music which was popular into the twentieth century, but of cheerful songs and glees. His ability as a draughtsman meant that for many years he designed and supervised the execution of the intricate allegorical print which stood at the head of the annual university almanac.[1] The picture remains of him as generously hospitable, a witty and expressive talker, wreathed in clouds of tobacco smoke. Yet there was another side to him. His anger was easily aroused, and he was not above physically attacking one sprig of aristocracy who had irritated him.[2] As he grew older his charm began to wear somewhat thin. Suspicion began to gather at the length of time he spent in young men's rooms and references to his 'weakness' and 'faults' accumulated. In 1703 it was widely forecast that the tory administration would elevate him to the bishopric of Bath and Wells, but the appointment was mysteriously stopped. 'He had certainly been the man', reported Francis Atterbury, 'but for one objection, which his enemies urged warmly against him; and it hath succeeded. And the mischief of it is, that it is such an objection as, being entertained, will equally hinder him in his pretensions to any other Bishopric whatsoever.'[3]

Aldrich's political allegiance lay unmistakably with Lord Rochester, to whom he owed his original appointment as canon; and Christ Church

[1] H. M. Petter, *The Oxford Almanacks* (Oxford 1974), 4-9, 42, 46, 54-5, 121, 156.
[2] For this incident see *Letters of Prideaux to Ellis*, ed. Thompson, p. 72.
[3] Atterbury-Trelawny, 1 Dec. 1703, *The Epistolary Correspondence, Visitation Charges, Speeches, and Miscellanies, of the Right Reverend Francis Atterbury, D.D., Lord Bishop of Rochester, with historical notes, and brief memoirs of the author*, ed. J. Nichols (4 vols London 1783-7, 2nd edn 5 vols London 1799, i-iv printed and dated 1789-90, v 1798) i. 271. Francis Atterbury (1662-1732), m. Ch. Ch. 1680, dean 1711-13; bp of Rochester 1713-23; exiled 1723-32.

entered wholeheartedly into the earl's vehement opposition to William's regime. In these years the Hyde brothers were frequently in residence at the deanery where with Aldrich's aid they prepared the Oxford edition of the first earl of Clarendon's *History of the Great Rebellion.* At times Rochester appeared to treat the dean as a kind of domestic chaplain, using his house at will and ordering him to accompany him either to Oxford or to London.[1] But there is no doubt that Aldrich was a key figure in the important group of tory politicians and churchmen who met regularly at Rochester's house to discuss tactics. In particular its three episcopal members, Compton of London, Sprat of Rochester and Trelawny of Exeter, all former Students of Christ Church, provided the nucleus of a tory patronage network, centred on 'the House', which sought to offset the effects of the whig system. It was thus that a series of able young tory divines, including Atterbury, obtained their first preferment and a chance to enter on the wider political world.[2] After the part he had played in the defeat of comprehension Aldrich had nothing to expect from the government nor anything to fear from it, and he devoted himself wholly to opposition politics. In this he was supported by the other members of the chapter who had been appointed under the previous regime, and notably by William Jane and Robert South. If South was the most distinguished high-church preacher of the day, he was also a strident and acerbic exponent of Restoration churchmanship.[3] In 1690 the gentle William Wake, who had been appointed the previous year to Aldrich's vacant canonry, showed a distinct uneasiness at the thought of having to keep his periods of residence in Oxford amid such partisanship. 'Nor would I choose Christ Church for my retirement', he explained to an Oxford friend, 'had I espoused any party or interest opposite to that of those who must be my nearest companions in it.'[4]

---

[1] Hearne, *Collections* i. 43 (17 Sept. 1705). For an amusing incident see *Correspondence of Atterbury*, ed. Nichols i. 189 (18 Mar. 1703): 'My Lord R[ochester] being determined upon this journey, and desiring his company, he [Aldrich] was forced to comply sore against his will, and return for one month to the college.'

[2] For a series of letters from Compton and Sprat to Trelawny 1690-1703 see 'Collectanea trelawniana', pp. 263 ff. I am grateful to Mr F. T. Williams for permission to use these transcripts of manuscripts once at Trelawne, Cornwall. For Aldrich's pressing of tory candidates see Aldrich--Ormonde, 29 Dec. 1689, HMC *Ormonde MSS* viii. 26; same-Wake, 26 Jan. 1700, Wake MS 17, fo 41. Sir Jonathan Trelawny (1650-1721), 3rd bt; m. Ch.Ch. 1668; bp of Exeter 1689-1707, Winchester 1707-21.

[3] See R. South-Charlett, 11 May 1695, MS Ballard 34, fo 29, asking him to accept the vice-chancellorship after Aldrich: '. . . else our Old Noble Constitution and Religion be broken and borne down by Whigs and Latitudinarians.' Robert South (1634-1716), m. Ch.Ch. 1651; incorporated at Cambridge 1659. For an embittered sermon against comprehension, preached in Christ Church in 1710 by South, see Bodl. MS Carte 206, fos 75 ff. 'Toleration is the very pulling up of the Floodgates of Hell . . . for the pouring in a Deluge of Errour, Heresy and blasphemy upon the church': ibid. fo 87.

[4] Wake-Charlett, 2 Apr. 1690, MS Ballard 3, fo 57. William Wake (1657-1737), m. Ch.Ch. 1673; bp of Lincoln 1705, abp of Canterbury 1716-37.

Humphrey Prideaux, who had been involved in promoting the compre-hension scheme, was horrified to be offered a canonry at Christ Church and promptly refused it. 'I nauseate Christ Church', he wrote, 'I have an unconquerable aversion to the place, and will never live more among such people who now have the prevaileing power there.'[1] Since the dean and chapter were the sole governing body of Christ Church, making all appointments and disposing of all benefices, their control over the other members of the society was virtually complete. During Aldrich's time there was no division of the college's vote in convocation or at any public election[2].

Prominent among the other heads committed to high tory politics was Leopold William Finch, warden of All Souls. A son of the third earl of Winchilsea and a member of the powerful Finch clan, he worked closely with his cousin Heneage, the university burgess, and acted as his election agent. Warden Finch's career was bizarre and not a little pathetic. A Stu-dent of Christ Church of a notoriously riotous disposition, he had been elected a fellow of All Souls in 1682 in the teeth of Archbishop Sancroft's protest that he was unfit for holy orders.[3] During Monmouth's rebellion he had earned James II's gratitude by acting as captain of a company of volunteers and, to the archbishop's disgust, he had been appointed warden in 1687 by virtue of a royal mandate. Finch, who was still only twenty-four, was confirmed by the visitor only on the urgent plea of Wey-mouth and Clarges that otherwise a Roman Catholic would be forced on the college.[4] After the Revolution the youthful warden had some trouble in being accepted by the academic community and found it difficult to impose order in his own society. His convivial habits, brilliant but rash talk and lax observance of his religious duties contrasted sharply with his high tory stance and brought him into open conflict with a group of determined whig fellows.[5] While capable of astute manoeuvring in uni-versity politics, Warden Finch collapsed gradually under the strain into alcoholism and chronic debt before his death in 1702 at the early age of 39. At Jesus College Jonathan Edwards, vice-chancellor from 1689 to 1692, was a firm conservative in politics and theology, while at Corpus Thomas Turner created a college which earned the reputation of being the home of the most assertive high tories in the university.[6] President

---

[1] *Letters of Prideaux to Ellis* ed. Thompson, p. 150 (12 Oct. 1691).

[2] Stratford-Harley, 2 Dec. 1712, HMC *Portland MSS* vii. 118.

[3] Burrows, *Worthies of All Souls*, 292 ff; Sancroft-Nottingham, 2 Dec. 1681, Bodl. MS Tanner 36, fo 182; Nottingham-Sancroft, 2 Dec. 1681, ibid. fo 184.

[4] Clarges-Weymouth, 23 Apr. 1687, Longleat House, Thynne MS xii, fo 275.

[5] It was 1694 before he received the DD usually given to all heads on their election. Writing to Tanner on 28 May 1699 Thomas Rivers commented 'not one soul among us opens his mouth in the Warden's Justification, and almost every body avoids his Company': Bodl. MS Tanner 21, fo 74.

[6] In December 1703 Bishop Burnet in the lords attacked a sermon preached at Oxford by William Tilly (m. Wadham 1689; degrees CCC) and reflected seriously on Turner's influence as head of the

Turner took the oaths in 1689, and thereby preserved his headship and
his valuable prebends, but he remained deeply hostile to the new order.
His brother, the deprived bishop of Ely, spent much time at his lodgings;
and the president's correspondents consisted for the most part of non-
juring divines and of politicians like Clarendon and Weymouth who sympathized deeply with their position. Turner's influence in Oxford politics
was exercised almost wholly behind the scenes and he sought to avoid
public disputes, but the useful size of the Corpus vote and the fact that
many regarded him as a standard-bearer for old fashioned loyalism
meant that he was continually consulted by his colleagues.[1]

Most other heads, while affirming their tory principles, attempted to
follow more moderate courses and not alienate themselves wholly from
the government. This was not easy in the years from 1694 to 1699 when
whig ministers dominated business; and some found themselves accused
of having lost their 'honesty', gossiped about in the coffee-houses, and
sniped at in university sermons. John Hough, president of Magdalen, provides a case in point. In 1689 he stood at the height of his reputation as the
one man in Oxford who had withstood James II to his face, and as a former
chaplain to the duke of Ormonde his tory credentials were impeccable.
When in 1690 he was given the bishopric of Oxford to hold with his presidency it seemed that his leadership in university affairs must be unchallenged. Indeed for a while the heads deferred to him and employed
him as their spokesman in relations with the government and prominent
peers.[2] Hough was a kind and unauthoritarian man, much loved for his
open and generous style, but his succession to the bishopric weakened
rather than strengthened his standing in the university. Long absences
from Oxford about his parliamentary duties meant that from 1691 he took
little part in college business and the fellows of Magdalen were left to their
own devices under the leadership of successive vice-presidents.[3] His
increasing association with 'moderate' bishops and support for the
government led also to a growing alienation from a college of extreme
tory partisanship. At last on 5 August 1699 he gladly accepted translation
to the see of Lichfield and Coventry, though this can hardly have been
considered a promotion. When he resigned the presidency in early 1701 it
was to be succeeded by John Rogers, who can reasonably be considered a
crypto-Jacobite. As William Wake commented when the suggestion was

college: G. Hickes-T. Turner, 7 Dec. [1703], Bodl. MS Rawl. lett. 92, fo 181; J. Davis-T. Turner, 24 Feb.
1704, ibid. fo 196.

[1] 'The President of Corpus, who has the greatest authority amongst the Heads, is too wary a man
to enter into an open opposition of any one': Stratford-Harley, 12 Sept. 1711, HMC *Portland MSS* vii.
53.
[2] See Hough-e. of Abingdon, 30 July 1690, Bodl. MS Top. Oxon. c. 325, fo 77, in which he undertakes the delicate task of informing the earl that the heads have decided that Lord Nottingham and
not Abingdon is to be asked to present a loyal address.
[3] See Macray, *Reg. Magdalen* iv. 50.

made that he might himself succeed Hough in the Oxford bishopric: 'I have too much approved the Bishop's desire, and grounds of leaving it.'[1]

While other heads, like Roger Mander of Balliol, Fitzherbert Adams of Lincoln and Henry Beeston of New College, tried hard to walk the tight-rope, undoubtedly the greatest trimmer of all was Arthur Charlett, master of University College.[2] Fussy, garrulous and incorrigibly meddlesome, he might at first sight appear a political lightweight. He seems to have been elected by the fellows in 1692 as a clubbable man of ample private means who would live on a small stipend and not trouble them overmuch by enforcing discipline.[3] Indeed, Charlett quickly became the kind of university character about whom endless contrived jokes and mildly scurrilous stories were invented. His rambling chatter, his compulsive letter-writing and his eagerness to hear and report every piece of news or gossip made him a legend in his own lifetime. When in 1707 he published an almanac of assorted Oxford information and named it *Mercurius oxoniensis, or The Oxford Intelligencer* the university fell about with laughter.[4] In 1703 he was mercilessly lampooned in the 'Terrae Filius' speech at the Act, while in 1706 the whig periodicals the *Review* and the *Observator* reported a hilarious Oxford story about his getting drunk with the warden of New College and being led through the streets by a mischievous servant who held up before him a tankard instead of a lantern.[5] In 1711 even the *Spectator* ridiculed him under the pseudonym of 'Abraham Froth'.[6] Occasionally his ready familiarity with old and young led to stories which were positively unpleasant. In 1698 a junior fellow of University College was actually hauled before the vice-chancellor's court and deprived for circulating a wholly false story that the master had had an indecent relationship with a fellow of All Souls.[7] And yet Charlett was far from negligible in Oxford politics. His vast correspondence extended to virtually all the major politicians interested in Oxford; and many were glad to ask his advice on men and events. He had a fixer's outlook on the world and was

---

[1] Wake-Charlett, 31 Mar. [1699], MS Ballard 3, fo 34. John Rogers (1651-1703), m. Magd. 1668, president 1701-3.

[2] Roger Mander (1649-1704), m. Balliol 1666, master 1687-1704; vice-chancellor 1700-2. Fitz-Herbert Adams (1652-1719), m. Linc. 1669, rector 1685-1719; vice-chancellor 1695-7. Henry Beeston (d. 1701), fellow 1669, warden 1679-1701. Arthur Charlett (1655-1722), subs. Trin. 1669; DD Univ. 1692, master 1692-1722.

[3] G. Fleming-D. Fleming, 10 June 1692, *The Flemings in Oxford* iii. 61; Wood, *Life and Times* iii. 343.

[4] *Mercurius oxoniensis, or the Oxford Intelligencer for the Year of our Lord 1707* (London 1707). See Hearne, *Collections* i. 214: 'Dr Charlett commonly called the Gazzeteer or Oxford Intelligencer.'

[5] Hearne-T. Smith, 27 Apr. 1706, Bodl. MS Rawl. lett. 37, fo 81. Thomas Braithwaite (1661-1720), m. Queen's 1680; BCL New College 1687, DCL 1694, warden 1702-12; warden of Winchester College 1712-20; vice-chancellor 1710-12. For the 'Terrae Filius' speech see Bodl. MS Rawl. D. 697, fo 1: the mock question was asked 'whether a Doctor talks like an Apothecary?'

[6] *Spectator* No. 43 (19 Apr. 1711).

[7] C. Usher, *A Letter to a Member of the Convocation of the University of Oxford, containing the case of a late fellow elect of University College in that university* (London 1699). The evidence cited contained a series of words used in late-seventeenth-century Oxford to denote homosexual relations.

always ready to make roundings, propose candidates and work up parties. Behind the chatter there was an extremely ambitious man, desperately anxious for preferment and willing to work for any patron who might secure it for him. It was Charlett's tragedy that he should have been useful on many occasions to so many influential men but that none of them could bring himself to promote a divine whom Oxford itself refused to take seriously.

The number of heads who could properly be accounted whigs was small and in William's reign did not exceed four. They lived in a hostile environment and were subjected to scathing criticism. For the most part, therefore, they did not attempt to run a political interest in the university but kept their own company and attempted to provide in their colleges a refuge for those dons and undergraduates who wanted 'moderate' politics and liberal theology. The senior among them was John Hall, master of Pembroke since 1664 and to tory Oxford the very epitome of a latitudinarian divine. As Lady Margaret professor he had been the only Oxford theologian to take part in William's ill-fated comprehension scheme and remained in high favour with the king and leading whigs. In spite of being a pluralist, with long absences from Oxford, he contrived to play the part of an overbearing tyrant in his small college, eventually provoking the fellows to submit a list of complaints to the duke of Ormonde, their visitor.[1] It caused deep disgust throughout the university when in 1691 the king gave Hall the bishopric of Bristol to hold with his mastership and his professorship, and there was genuine alarm in 1694 when it was rumoured that he was the whigs' candidate to succeed Archbishop Tillotson.[2] Although as a bishop Hall played no part in university politics, he gradually remoulded his own college into the most thoroughly whig society in Oxford. In 1704 the author of a satirical account of a tour round the colleges could describe Pembroke in these terms: 'Here are whole Shoals of Low, Moderate, Groveling and Whiggish Churchmen, a Gang of Demiphanatical Blockheads that han't the Sense to sute their Religion with their Interest.'[3] In the popular estimate Wadham was likewise 'a nest of whigs'. Thomas Dunster, who became warden in 1689, was an unrepentant exponent of John Locke's politics, and his reputation has suffered from the spiteful comments of tory writers, but even the Christ Church wits' lapidary description of him as 'Dunstar ye Lowzy' cannot obscure the fact that under his rule the college had useful scholars and careful tutors.[4] In 1696 Humphrey Prideaux, who had no particular brief

---

[1] E. Bernard-Smith, 9 Apr. 1690, Bodl. MS Smith 47, fo 64; for the articles against Hall see MS Ballard 49, fo 135; and for Ormonde's reply of 2 June 1690, Bodl. MS Carte 131B, fo 232.

[2] Bennett, 'King William III and the episcopate', 117, 122.

[3] *A Step to Oxford: in which is Comprehended an Impartial Account of the University* (London 1704), 9.

[4] Hearne, *Collections* ii. 109 ('Dunstar ye Lowzy'); Thomas Dunster (1656–1719), m. Wadham 1673, warden 1689–1719.

for whiggery, thought it 'the best governed College in the University and stockd with the best Fellows'. Certainly Wadham's tradition of liberal learning was well exemplified in 'moderate' divines like Humphrey Hody and Richard Willis.[1] At Oriel the undistinguished and boozy George Royse[2] was elected provost in 1691. He had been chaplain to King William and had actually accompanied him on campaign to Ireland in 1690. Such a start carried him up the ladder of preferment and in 1694 he received what so many heads desired: the deanery of Bristol to hold with his provostship. To Hearne he was 'a rank whig' and, though he was conspicuous by his absence on virtually every public occasion, we learn of 'the club at Oriel' who in 1698 'stopt' Dean Aldrich's 'New-Years gift' of venison from the park at Woodstock.[3] At Merton it was virtually impossible for a known high tory to be elected to a fellowship, though the successive heads of the college appear to have exercised no influence in university affairs. The right of the archbishop of Canterbury to choose a warden from a shortlist put forward by the fellows ensured that only known 'moderates' would hold the office. In 1693 Tillotson appointed an elderly physician, Richard Lydall, who settled down in the lodgings with his large family and was not heard from again.[4]

If the whig heads refused to conduct any political campaign, there were not lacking certain irregular troops who made it their business to challenge and provoke the tory majority. From time to time a voice of dissent from high-church orthodoxy was heard in the pulpit of St Mary's as some college fellow sought to get himself noticed by whig patrons or 'moderate' bishops.[5] But the party cause was most persistently defended by a small group of Oxford residents who in the middle years of William's reign worked at the formulation of a new whig view of church and state. All were friends of Locke, though their views were far from being merely derived from his and were indeed often far more radical than anything he would have advocated. The most notorious was Matthew Tindal, fellow of All Souls, in which college he was a constant thorn in the flesh of Warden Finch.[6] Tindal had been briefly converted to Rome under

[1] Prideaux-R. Coffin, 7 Feb. 1696, HMC *5th Report*, 374. Humphrey Hody (1659-1707), m. Wadham 1676; regius prof. Greek 1698-1705; archdeacon of Oxford 1704-7. Richard Willis (1664-1734), m. Wadham 1684; fellow All Souls 1687; bp of Gloucester 1715-21, Salisbury 1721-3, Winchester 1723-34.

[2] George Royse (1655-1708), m. SEH 1671; fellow Oriel 1678, provost 1691-1708; dean Bristol 1694-1708.

[3] W. Bishop-Charlett, 22 Jan. 1698, MS Ballard 31, fo 16.

[4] Richard Lydall (1620-1704), m. Merton 1638, warden 1693-1704.

[5] For a particular example see Hearne, *Collections* i. 48.

[6] [E. Curll,] *Memoirs of the Life and Writings of Matthew Tindal* (London 1733). Tindal had a state pension conferred on him by William III: see ibid. 54 and S. Lalor, 'Matthew Tindal and the eighteenth-century assault on religion' (Trinity College Dublin M. Litt. thesis 1979), copy in All Souls, Codrington Library. Matthew Tindal (1657-1733), m. Linc. 1673; BA Exeter 1676; fellow All Souls 1678.

James II but after the Revolution he compensated for his lapse by emerging as one of the most trenchant and insulting of anti-clericals. Spending his time between Oxford and his civil-law practice in London, he was well aware of the bitter hostility with which he was surrounded in the university. Many would have loved to have public proof of his more outrageous opinions on morality or the clergy but he dextrously refused to provide any formal statement of his views which might be used in evidence against him. It was only the inexperienced young men who came to listen to his radical talk who found themselves in trouble for repeating his opinions. In 1706 Tindal published anonymously the book on which he had been working for years, *The Rights of the Christian Church Asserted,* an examination of early Christianity which merged into a bitter denunciation of the contemporary clergy and universities for 'priestcraft': for perverting the gospel, destroying liberty and seeking their own gain.[1] Close to Tindal in the middle years of William's reign was John Toland, the 'commonwealthman', who wrote in Oxford his *Christianity Not Mysterious,* which set the clergy in an absolute fury on its publication in 1696.[2] Perhaps, however, the most influential figure of them all was the massively learned James Tyrrell, who came to live in a country house at Shotover so that he could spend his days researching and writing in the Bodleian Library. A much neglected but important whig political theorist, he published in 1694 his *Bibliotheca politica,* a series of fourteen long dialogues setting out a view of the English constitution diametrically opposed to the usual tory affirmations.[3] With such formidable and articulate foes living among them, many an aspiring university preacher was spurred on to the attack. We learn that in 1695 both Tindal and Tyrrell were present in St Mary's on 31 January at the sermon commemorating the execution of King Charles I, when the pulpit thundered with a denunciation of Hobbes and Locke. The two whigs were

very attentive, and it's probable one or both of these may have given Mr Locke some account thereof this post. The Eyes of the congregation were as much fixed upon Mr Tyrrell this year, as they were upon the Scotsman the last; and if he had not finished Lib. Bibliotheca Politica I am apt to thinke this sermon would have cost him another Dialogue.[4]

In the autumn of 1695 the 'moderate' tory heads came close to a reconciliation with King William when they procured the election of Sir

[1] [M. Tindal,] *The Rights of the Christian Church Asserted* (London 1706).

[2] [J. Toland,] *Christianity Not Mysterious* (London 1696). See Bennett, *Tory Crisis,* 18–20. For the many replies to Toland (including those by Oxford residents) see G. Carabelli, *Tolandiana: materiali bibliografici per lo studio dell'opera e della fortuna di John Toland (1670–1722)* (Florence 1975).

[3] [J. Tyrrell,] *Bibliotheca politica* (London 1694). James Tyrell (1642–1718), m. Queen's 1657. For Tyrrell and his importance see J. P. Kenyon, *Revolution Principles: the politics of party 1689–1720* (Cambridge 1977), esp. 35 ff.

[4] T. Hinton-Charlett, 31 Jan. 1695, MS Ballard 38, fo 4.

William Trumbull, one of the secretaries of state, as university burgess. Indeed the death in early October of Thomas Clarges, their indefatigable opposition-tory member, presented them with a unique opportunity to take the initiative. There were only three weeks to go to a general election and at once a small group led by George Clarke of All Souls, the vice-chancellor Fitzherbert Adams and Arthur Charlett approached Trumbull even though he was already virtually committed to standing for Berkshire.[1] In many ways he was an ideal choice. A former fellow of All Souls, he had attained eminence at Oxford as a civil lawyer and had practised extensively in the ecclesiastical courts before embarking on a distinguished career in diplomacy. His marriage into the family of Cotterell of Rousham gave him something of the status of a local gentleman. His reputation as an ardent, even uncompromising churchman, could scarcely be faulted, though high office in an administration so dependent on whigs might well be looked upon with suspicion. But the fact is that Trumbull was not so much a party politician as a hardworking functionary put in by the king's manager, Lord Sunderland, to deny a critical office to the junto whigs. As such, anything which boosted his standing and thwarted whiggery was welcome to most tories, and there was a quite remarkable consensus of support for him. Archbishop Tenison of Canterbury and Bishop Burnet of Salisbury added their recommendation to that of their tory brethren of London and Rochester.[2] Some of the high tories in the university, however, had serious doubts. Trumbull's chief agent at Oxford was alarmed to hear 'a malicious story that you are Whiggish, that is an intimate crony of Wharton, who is now soliciting for you in Buckinghamshire. Nothing would do you greater injury here'.[3] Many of the younger MAs began actively to canvass for Sir Christopher Musgrave, a close ally of Robert Harley and a forthright member of the 'country' opposition which savaged King William's ministers in the commons so relentlessly.[4] It is clear that the real centre of support for Musgrave was in Christ Church where Aldrich was doggedly disinclined to have anything to do with Trumbull. But soon the dean found himself subjected to intense pressure. Not only did Bishop Hough seek to persuade him but

[1] S. Harcourt-Charlett, 3 Oct. 1695, MS Ballard 10, fo 92; G. Clarke-Trumbull, 3 Oct. 1695, HMC *Downshire MSS* i pt 2, p. 559; J. Holt-Trumbull, 9 Oct. [1695], ibid. 560. Sir William Trumbull (1639-1716), m. St John's 1655; fellow All Souls 1657; MP Oxford Univ. 1695-8. George Clarke (1661-1736), m. BNC 1675; fellow All Souls 1680-1736; MP Oxford Univ. 1685-7, 1717-36. Clarke was very influential as an MP and was a great benefactor both to All Souls and Worcester College.

[2] Tenison-Charlett, 9 Oct. 1695, MS Ballard 9, fo 26.

[3] W. Hayley-Trumbull, 10 Oct. 1695, HMC *Downshire MSS* i pt 2, p. 561.

[4] Sir Christopher Musgrave (1632-1704), 4th bt; m. Queen's 1651; MP Oxford Univ. 1698-1700. For a while there was a movement for Christopher Codrington (1668-1710, m. Ch.Ch. 1685; fellow All Souls 1690) the dashing young soldier-scholar from All Souls: see G. Fleming–D. Fleming, 10 Oct. 1695, *The Flemings in Oxford* iii. 246; W. Hayley-Trumbull, 13 Oct. 1695, HMC *Downshire MSS* i pt 2, p. 564.

even his own friends like Compton, Sprat and the earl of Clarendon.[1] It quickly became apparent that Musgrave had no chance in the face of such a consensus for moderation. When Hough secured all the votes of Magdalen and Warden Finch actually proposed Trumbull at a meeting of his own house, Aldrich knew that he had lost. One by one the trimming tory heads had written pledging the votes of their colleges to the secretary of state.[2] And so just before the poll on 21 October 1695 Musgrave prudently withdrew, allowing Trumbull and Heneage Finch to be elected unanimously. It was a triumph for those who sought a *rapprochement* with the government but distinctly unpopular with many of the ordinary members of convocation. Indeed so obviously had the election been 'fixed' by the heads that William Hayley besought Trumbull to cultivate some popularity by journeying down to Oxford and visiting the common rooms in person 'as what will please the younger Masters'.[3]

The immediate result of the secretary's election was that King William allowed himself to be persuaded to pay his first royal visit to the university. He came with obvious reluctance. Trumbull did his best to make the king's presence an occasion for reconciliation and a restoration of good relations with the government. He besought William to 'visit his own college, Christ Church, it would be a satisfaction to the University, and All Souls' College afterwards, but I must not press it'.[4] But to the new burgess's chagrin William made it clear that he would not enter the colleges of Aldrich and Finch, neither would he spend the night in Oxford; he would go only to the Sheldonian for a formal address and then leave at once for Windsor. On the actual day, 9 November, the king's attitude and demeanour made the visit something near to a disaster. The welcome from the crowd was tepid and he was uneasy. He spoke at length only to John Wallis, the Savilian professor of geometry and the government's code expert; he refused to eat anything from the magnificent banquet which had been prepared; and he left before proceedings moved on to the granting of honorary degrees.[5] It was an example of the poor face which William could present to the English world when he felt himself in hostile company. It was an equally bad piece of public relations when the next month Archbishop Tenison was commanded in the king's name to deliver

[1] C. Hedges-Trumbull, 11 Oct. 1695, HMC *Downshire MSS* i pt 2, p. 562; Clarendon-T. Turner, 27 Oct. 1695, Bodl. MS Rawl. lett, 91, fo 284.
[2] W. Levinz-Trumbull, 8 Oct. 1695, HMC *Downshire MSS* i pt 2, p. 560; R. Mander-[Trumbull], 12 Oct. 1695, ibid. 564; Trumbull-F. Adams, 8 Oct. 1695, Berkshire Record Office, Trumbull Add. MS 118.
[3] Hayley-Trumbull, 10 Oct. 1695, HMC *Downshire MSS* i pt 2, p. 561.
[4] See Trumbull-d. of Shrewsbury, 5 Nov. 1695 and Shrewsbury-Trumbull, 7 Nov. 1695, ibid. 580; Trumbull-Abingdon, 2 Nov. 1695, Bodl. MS Top. Oxon. c. 325, fo 79.
[5] Wood, *Life and Times* iii. 494-5; [E. Bernard]—T. Smith [10 Nov. 1695], Bodl. MS Smith 47, fo 183. John Wallis (1616-1703), incorporated at Exeter from Cambridge 1649; Savilian prof. of geometry 1649-1703; keeper of the archives 1654-1703.

a withering rebuke to the hebdomadal board for presuming to adjudge heretical certain propositions contained in a book by William Sherlock. Thus to menace the heads of houses so soon after their successful efforts to elect a secretary of state as their representative in parliament might be thought inopportune and a needless dissipation of painfully acquired goodwill.[1]

The years from 1695 up to the next general election in 1698 saw a new polarization of politics in the nation at large. King William and his whig ministers found themselves under bitter attack from an opposition which fed on a deep discontent with the growth of government power, patronage and corruption. Now the erosion in the position of the Church of England emerged as a major and emotive political issue. If Anglican toryism had once been a 'court' party, in these years it completed the transformation into being basically a 'country' movement of grievance and opposition. Much of this stemmed from country gentlemen and parish priests angered by what seemed a deliberate policy on the part of the ministers, judges and some bishops to reduce the church's influence in political life. In 1695 parliament did not renew the licensing act, and a flood of heterodox and anticlerical literature, much of it couched in the most insulting terms, poured forth upon the popular bookmarket. The church courts found it impossible to enforce the strict terms of the toleration act, while civil judges simply refused to assist those bishops who attempted to insist on the licensing of schoolmasters under the provisions of the act of uniformity.[2] But perhaps the greatest outrage to the feelings of tory gentlemen and clergy was the growing practice of occasional conformity, by which a dissenter paid a single visit to his parish church, received the sacrament and then obtained a certificate which qualified him for public office. That he henceforth was seen going openly to a conventicle was a standing cause of tory anger. Indeed William Bromley, that forthright defender of Anglican privilege in the commons, was later to describe the practice in emphatic terms: it was 'that abominable Hypocrisie, that inexcusable immorality of Occasional Conformity'.[3]

That Oxford was now the chief centre for the articulation of such grievance is shown by the fact that it was members of the university who launched the great agitation for a sitting and acting convocation of Canterbury, from which so much political division and controversy was to flow. In late 1696 Francis Atterbury, until the previous year a Student of

---

[1] Tenison-F. Adams, 24 Dec. 1695, MS Ballard 9, fo 28; W. Lancaster-Charlett, 28 Dec. 1695, MS Ballard 21, fo 62.

[2] For a discussion of the legal position see T. Tanner-Charlett, 14 May [1698], MS Ballard 4, fo 49; and for an account of a case at the Oxford assizes when the judges would not aid the bishop see ibid. fo 64 (14 Sept. 1702).

[3] Bromley-Charlett, 22 Oct. 1702, MS Ballard 38, fo 137. William Bromley (1664-1732), m. Ch. Ch. 1679; MP Oxford Univ. 1701-32; speaker of the house of commons 1710-15; secretary of state 1713-14.

Christ Church, published a brief, hard-hitting pamphlet which may well claim to be the most effective political tract of the decade. Entitled *A Letter to a Convocation-Man*, it attempted to prove by an examination of English law and constitutional practice that the clergy had a power to assemble and debate the pressing needs and grievances of their order and that the king had no just right to silence them as he had done since 1689.[1] It was not difficult for a writer of Atterbury's incendiary talent to set out a ringing statement of wrongs endured: 'a settled contempt of religion and the priesthood has prevailed everywhere.' When politicians conspired to diminish the church's legal rights and bishops were supine in her defence, when the clergy were insulted, over-taxed and discriminated against, an instant remedy was required and this could only be supplied by a convocation. At Oxford the tract caused an immediate sensation. George Smalridge reported the reaction in Christ Church. '*The Letter to a Convocation-Man*', he wrote, 'will be well worth your reading, it is much talked of, and much liked here. We are not able to guess at the Author: some will have it to be our Dean's, but I am certain they are in the wrong; some have done me the honour to father it on me, but they compliment me too highly who think I was able to write it.'[2] When William Wake, canon of Christ Church, undertook at Archbishop Tenison's request to write a reply, the controversy quickly began to assume the character of an Oxford internecine dispute. His book *The Authority of Christian Princes over their Ecclesiastical Synods Asserted* (1697) was received with immense anger in the common rooms and coffee-houses. 'I am heartily glad', he confided to a friend, 'that the subject of my book, which I hear has offended many here, and more at Oxford, has not much scandalized you.'[3] When the battle-line was drawn, the disputants on both sides were found to be Oxford men, with the formidable Atterbury opposed by Humphrey Hody of Wadham, White Kennett of St Edmund Hall and Edmund Gibson of Queen's.[4] When Atterbury returned to the charge in 1700 and wrote his *The Rights, Powers, and Privileges, of an English Convocation* dealing harshly with Wake, his contribution was at once hailed in the university as a complete victory.[5] During his residence at Christ Church the unhappy Wake had to endure much rudeness. 'I need not tell you', he wrote to Charlett on his return to London, 'the world here is as full of Mr Atterbury's book as I left it at Oxford . . . Some men, I am told, wonder at my impudence that I

---

[1] [F. Atterbury,] *A Letter to a Convocation-Man* (London 1697). See Bennett, *Tory Crisis*, 48–51.

[2] Smalridge–W. Gough, 10 Nov. 1696, *Illustrations of the Literary History of the Eighteenth Century*, ed. J. Nichols (8 vols London 1817–58) iii. 254. George Smalridge (1664–1719), m. Ch.Ch. 1682, dean 1713–19; bp of Bristol 1714–19; lord high almoner 1714–15.

[3] W. Wake–T. Tanner, 20 Apr. [1697], Bodl. MS Tanner 23, fo 23. W. Wake, *The Authority of Christian Princes over their Ecclesiastical Synods Asserted* (London 1697).

[4] Edmund Gibson (1669–1748), m. Queen's 1686; bp of Lincoln 1716, London 1723–48.

[5] [F. Atterbury,] *The Rights, Powers, and Privileges of an English Convocation* (London 1700).

have not yet hanged myself.'[1] So vehement was the feeling among ordinary fellows of colleges that Thomas Tanner was insulted in the streets for
having supplied Wake with items of historical information.[2]

It was unfortunate for the 'moderate' tory heads that the general election in the summer of 1698 should have to take place when feeling among
the ordinary MAs was so exacerbated. The university had gained nothing
from its election of Sir William Trumbull. Even Charlett had been scurvily
rewarded for all his activity in 1695. In the aftermath of the election he
had been handed out a royal chaplaincy but this small preferment
attracted the animosity of whig courtiers who began to circulate rumours
that he was a secret Jacobite.[3] In May 1698 he put in for his reward when
the valuable crown living of Marsh Gibbon in Buckinghamshire fell
vacant but, to his utter mortification, the benefice was given to Warden
Dunster of Wadham. Archbishop Tenison did nothing to defend him from
stories so malicious that they actually led the king himself to veto his
appointment; and it soon emerged that his rival's success had been due to
the earnest recommendation of Lord Chancellor Somers and Sir Thomas
Littleton, recorder of the city and a prominent Oxfordshire whig.[4] It was
no wonder that the arch-fixer of university politics decided to take no part
in the next election of burgesses. That he did so was all the more important in that the vice-chancellor, John Meare of Brasenose, had already
proved himself incapable of giving any kind of leadership to the 'moderate' heads. From the time of his assuming office in October 1697 he had
staggered from blunder to blunder. His servility to the government in procuring flattering addresses on the peace of Ryswick had utterly alienated
his more committed tory colleagues. Indeed Warden Finch was exasperated enough to pray aloud that the vice-chancellor might be transported to the colonies.[5] Charlett, whose disposition was more charitable
than that, saw him as merely pathetic and incompetent: 'in general he is a
very fair, Freindly candid Man, but these Infelicitys will on a sudden
destroy his credit, especially since some very considerable Men are res-
enting some things very loudly against Him.'[6]

In such hands the cause of Finch and Trumbull, the old members, was

[1] Wake-Charlett, 28 Mar. 1700, MS Ballard 3, fo 32.
[2] Tanner-Charlett, 10 May 1700, MS Ballard 4, fo 46. Thomas Tanner (1674-1735), m. Queen's
1689; fellow All Souls 1696; canon Ch.Ch. 1724; bp of St Asaph 1732-5.
[3] Charlett-Trumbull, 13 Dec. 1696, HMC *Downshire MSS* i pt 2, p. 716.
[4] For a series of letters from Charlett to Tanner, 21 May-14 June 1698, see Bodl. MS Tanner 22,
fos 21a, 22, 23, 55, 56, 57. Sir Thomas Littleton (1647-1710), 3rd bt; m. SEH 1665; speaker of the
house of commons 1698-1700.
[5] Finch-Weymouth, 14 Nov. 1697, Longleat House, Thynne MS xvii, fo 251. Meare reported to
Trumbull on the peace-celebrations at Oxford: 'There went a vein of loyalty and affection through
the whole performance.' Letter of 3 Dec. 1697, *Downshire MSS* i pt 2, p. 771. John Meare (1649-1710),
m. BNC 1665, principal 1681-1710; vice-chancellor 1697-8.
[6] Charlett-Tanner, 11 May 1698, Bodl. MS Tanner 22, fo 54.

already beginning to look dubious when canvassing began in June. Finch had been for some time too ill to attend debates in the commons while Trumbull had been forced out of office by the whigs in December 1697. Neither made any effort to visit the university.[1] Sensing disaster in the air, the chancellor, the duke of Ormonde, suggested tentatively that another 'moderate' candidate, John Ellis, an under-secretary of state, might be asked to stand.[2] Simon Harcourt, a rising young tory lawyer, whose own seat at Abingdon was in some danger, put out feelers for support.[3] But the disarray of the usual managers and the intense feeling among the ordinary MAs combined to give Dean Aldrich the opportunity for which he had been waiting since his rebuff in 1695. Now the Christ Church interest decided to appeal to the electorate at large, even in the face of the 'moderate' heads, and set up two 'country' opposition tories against the existing members. Immediately the split among the heads became open and unbridgeable. When Aldrich proposed Musgrave and Sir William Glynne, an otherwise unremarkable Oxfordshire backwoods squire,[4] Charlett was appalled at the personal acrimony which ensued, not least between the dean of Christ Church and Warden Finch of All Souls. The campaign, as carried on from Christ Church, was ruthless, with accusations flying thick and fast against the two former burgesses. In the midst of it, to avoid the noise of electioneering, and perhaps not to be seen neglecting Trumbull's interests too obviously, Charlett escaped out of town. When he returned it was apparent that the election was all but lost. He was concerned, he reported, 'both for the worth of the old Members, as also for the Peace and Quiet of the university, which is now like to be much disturbed'.[5] Though Magdalen held firm to its traditional antagonism to Christ Church, it was soon clear that the fellows of other colleges had given way 'to the zealous applications of Ch.Ch. who have caused all this disturbance in setting up a person only to show their resentment to the Court'.[6] No fewer than 375 doctors and MAs came to the convocation house for the actual poll and, after some heated speeches, the proctors took the votes as follows: Musgrave 207; Glynne 206; Finch 183; Trumbull 120.[7] It was a deeply divisive result. Not only had many ordinary MAs rejected the leadership of the head of their house but Finch had been defeated by Glynne whose sole

---

[1] For Trumbull's resignation see *Letters Illustrative of the Reign of William III*, ed. G. P. R. James (3 vols London 1841) i. 391, 404, 432.

[2] Ormonde-university, 14 July 1698, BL Egerton MS 2618, fo 182.

[3] W. Dobyns-Trumbull, 12 June 1698, HMC *Downshire MSS* i pt 2, p. 780; Vernon-Shrewsbury, 9 Aug. 1698, *Letters Illustrative of the Reign of William III*, ed. James ii. 148-9. Simon Harcourt (1661-1727), 1st visc. Harcourt; m. Pemb. 1677; hon DCL 1702; lord chancellor 1713-14.

[4] Sir William Glynne (1663-1721), 2nd bt; m. SEH 1679; MP Oxford Univ. 1698-1700.

[5] Charlett-Tanner, 21 July 1698, Bodl. MS Tanner 22, fo 202.

[6] T. Taylor-Trumbull, 23 July 1698, HMC Downshire MSS; pt 2, p 781.

[7] OUA register of convocation 1693-1703, fo 186.

recommendation was that he had been chosen to run with Musgrave. While high tories in Oxford received excited congratulations from their counterparts in Cambridge, the deep antagonisms which the conflict had aroused were still reverberating a month later, not least with the warden of All Souls whose kinsman 'took it amiss that he was left out'.[1] Indeed so great was the ill feeling that some began to regret what they had done. Charlett was of the opinion that 'many repent of laying aside Mr Finch, and not a few that any alteration was made at all, the heats being not yet over'.[2] It was not until the following November that the assiduous master was able to get Aldrich and Leopold William Finch back on speaking terms again.[3] Clearly the whole episode was one which the heads did not wish to see repeated.

With the ordinary college fellows increasingly assertive in their tory partisanship, it was fortunate for political management that the next general election in January 1701 could be made into an occasion for party unity. In these years when a headship fell vacant it became usual to choose some young man distinguished by the fierceness of his politics rather than by the gravity of his demeanour. Thus when in 1698 the easygoing president of St John's, William Levinz,[4] died, the contest lay between two youthful candidates, each of whom could well be accounted an extremist. The fellows' eventual election of William Delaune brought among the number of the heads a highly erratic personality who was not only financially profligate but ready for any measure of highflying tory-ism.[5] It is clear that the times were not conducive to moderation. During the course of 1699 the thunderous oratory of Robert Harley, Christopher Musgrave and Harley's one-time schoolfellow Simon Harcourt broke down the whig ministry's position in the commons. At last after a year's patching-up with a stopgap government, King William had to put him-self into the hands of ministers taken straight out of the ranks of the opposition, with Lord Rochester as the senior figure and Harley in charge of parliamentary management. It was natural that preparations for the ensuing general election should mark the high point of the

---

[1] Vernon-Shrewsbury, 9 Aug. 1698, *Letters Illustrative of the Reign of William III*, ed. James ii. 148; F. Roper-T. Turner, 9 Aug. 1698, Bodl. MS Rawl. lett. 91, fo 449.

[2] Charlett-Tanner, 4 Aug. 1698, Bodl. MS Tanner 22, fo 16.

[3] 'You have done a very good worke in bringing two honest Gentlemen together, who, I believe, had a mind to be friends, but wanted somebody to break the Ice. It is no new thing, for University Elections, to create little Animosities which last but too long': Clarke-Charlett, 19 Nov. 1698, MS Ballard 20, fo 59.

[4] W. Sherwin-T. Turner, 4 Mar. [1698], Bodl. MS Rawl. lett. 91, fo 432; G. Harbin-same, 13 Mar. 1698, ibid. fo 428; T. Crosthwaite-T. Smith, 4 Mar. 1698, Bodl. MS Smith 48, fo 345. President Levinz collapsed and died at a college meeting after becoming distressed over the destruction by the under-graduates of a plantation of young trees in the garden. William Levinz (1625-98), m. St John's 1641; regius prof. of Greek 1665-98; president St John's 1673-98.

[5] William Delaune (1659-1728), m. St John's 1675, president 1698-1728; vice-chancellor 1702-6; Lady Margaret prof. of divinity 1715-28.

influence of Dean Aldrich and the Hyde interest in the university. When the dean and the warden of All Souls sank their previous differences to propose that Christopher Musgrave and Heneage Finch should run together the combination was irresistible. To outward appearances it seemed like a resurrection of the predominance of the old cavalier families of the Hydes and Finches, but more percipient observers saw behind the scenes the growth of a new Oxford interest: that of Robert Harley, once a whig, alumnus of a dissenting academy but now a rising leader of the new tory party. Aldrich now bustled to set up Musgrave and consulted with Harley how best it could be done.[1] The election was not entirely uncontested. Some of the younger dons tried to run George Beaumont, a highflying tory baronet from Stoughton Grange in Leicestershire, who had the advantage of being a fellow of New College, but he prudently withdrew. Only William Glynne decided to battle it out, though now without the Christ Church support which had procured his election in 1698. On 3 January the voting in convocation was decisive. Musgrave received 275 votes and Finch 205 while Glynne trailed behind miserably with a mere 132.[2] It was a cause of quiet satisfaction for the vice-chancellor, Roger Mander of Balliol, who seems to have been much oppressed by the memory of the poor showing of his predecessor in 1698. That night one of the fellows of Balliol wrote in his diary: 'This evening I spent together with the fellow[s at] the Vice-Chanceler's Lodgings, who did not a little pride himself in the management of the Election.'[3]

It had been part of Lord Rochester's agreement with King William that the new ministry should allow the convocation of Canterbury once again to sit and debate.[4] To the Oxford divines such a prospect was even more exciting than that of a new house of commons with a 'country' majority and Harley in the speaker's chair. They knew that the lower house of convocation was sure to contain an overwhelming majority of clergy with a swelling sense of grievance and a determination to attack those whom they conceived of as having betrayed the church. Archbishop Tenison knew it too, and became increasingly alarmed. His chaplain, Humphrey Hody, was sent down on an exploratory visit to Oxford and returned with a quite frightening report of all the preparations for mischief being made by the university tories.[5] In real fear the bishops prepared themselves for total resistance and even for silencing the

---

[1] Harcourt-Harley, 21 Dec. 1700, HMC *Portland MSS* iv. 9. The major problem faced by Aldrich and Finch was the widespread belief that Musgrave would choose to sit for Westmorland: ibid. (14 Dec. 1700).

[2] OUA register of convocation 1693-1703, fo 225.

[3] Balliol MS 461, diary of Jeremiah Milles 1701-3, 3 Jan. 1701.

[4] Atterbury-Trelawny, 22 Feb. 1701, *Correspondence of Atterbury*, ed. Nichols i. 76.

[5] See Humphrey Hody's notes and his report of a conversation with Warden Dunster: Bodl. MS Add. A. 85a, fo 387.

assembly if their political masters would allow them to do so.[1] Indeed after visiting Oxford and dining with Aldrich, Lord Rochester himself began to be frightened by the spirit he had conjured up, and he exerted pressure to have George Hooper,[2] dean of Canterbury, elected as prolocutor instead of having the fierce and acidulated William Jane for a second time. But when the lower house first met for business on 21 February the proceedings turned out to be worse than either Rochester or the bishops could have imagined. Jane presented Hooper to the archbishop in a violent speech which introduced the theme of 'false brethren' which was to dominate the life of the assembly. To the deep mortification of the bishops present he described the rights of the church as *turpiter a suis prodita*.[3] Soon the house was engaged in drawing up an itemized list of *gravamina*: among them the 'open immorality' of the age, the propagation of heretical and anti-clerical books and the existence of dissenting seminaries in defiance of the law and the privileges of the universities.

The events in the lower house have in many ways the character of an eruption of Oxford politics on to the national scene. Of the total membership of 135, no fewer than 96 were Oxford graduates and of these 25 had been Students of Christ Church. Eight heads of houses and four canons of Christ Church were returned.[4] In the course of business the tory motions were proposed, and the debates dominated, by the contingent of Oxford dons. The reports show Aldrich, Finch, Jane and Jonathan Edwards as the principal speakers, closely supported by Francis Atterbury and Jonathan Kimberley.[5] The only Cambridge man to play an equal part was William Binckes, the vociferous representative of the clergy of the diocese of Lichfield and Coventry. By contrast the whig opposition numbered barely more than twenty in the whole house, and contained a significantly larger proportion of Cambridge men, among

---

[1] Bp Patrick-Wake, 17 Jan. 1701, Wake MS 17, fo 139; Atterbury-Trelawny, 15 Feb. 1701, reporting Hody's visit, *Correspondence of Atterbury*, ed. Nichols i. 73.

[2] Bp Sprat-Trelawny, 14 Jan. 1701, *Correspondence of Atterbury*, ed. Nichols i. 65; Atterbury-- Trelawny, 22 Feb. 1701, ibid. 76. George Hooper (1640-1727), m. Ch.Ch. 1657, classical, Hebrew and Arabic scholar; dean of Canterbury 1691; bp of St Asaph 1702-3, Bath and Wells 1704-27.

[3] Bodl. MS Add. A. 85a, fo 390. Hody's detailed notes on the sessions, the speakers and the votes are more valuable than the published accounts.

[4] This analysis of membership is based on information contained in *A True and Exact List of the Members of Both Houses of this present Convocation, summoned to meet on the sixth day of February, A.D. 1700* (London 1701). In only two cases has it not been possible to trace the university career of members of the lower house. The Oxford heads were Aldrich of Christ Church, Ralph Bathurst (1620-1704, m. Gloucester Hall 1634; scholar Trin. 1637, president 1664-1704; vice-chancellor 1673-6), Delaune of St John's, Edwards of Jesus, Finch of All Souls, Timothy Halton (1632-1704, m. Queen's 1649, provost 1677-1704), Mander of Balliol and Royse of Oriel. While three heads of Cambridge colleges were returned, none took any reported part in the business.

[5] See L. W. Finch-Charlett [25 Feb. 1701], MS Ballard 20, fo 8, where he reports 'the frightened Phiz of one [bishop], who particularly casts his eyes of Indignation on myselfe and my next Neighbour in the house the D. of C[hrist] C[hurch]'. Jonathan Kimberley (1651-1720), m. Pemb. 1667; dean of Lichfield 1713.

them Samuel Freeman, dean of Peterborough, their acknowledged leader. The character of the Oxford men in this small, embattled group is of interest. None of them, except William Lloyd, the impetuous young son of the bishop of Worcester, was actually resident in the university. Provost Royse of Oriel, a member of the lower house *ex officio* as dean of Bristol, was conspicuous by his absence from any session. Others, Charles Trimnell, John Tyler and John Evans, were men rising steadily in the church through their whig or 'moderate' episcopal connections and were all destined one day to be bishops themselves.[1] Their obstructive tactics, together with the prolocutor's nervous attempts to avoid open rebellion, meant that by the end of March relations between the two houses of convocation had become strained to breaking-point.[2] The crisis came suddenly on 8 April when Aldrich, Finch and Atterbury, leaving Hooper behind, marched to the upper house bearing a formal demand from the lower clergy that their lordships should delay no further in condemning John Toland's *Christianity not Mysterious* as a work of notorious heresy. On Tenison's refusing to receive them, the rage of the tory divines exploded. After much angry talk Professor Jane stood to propose a motion which marked a declaration of war: 'that, since the Upper House refused this correspondence with them, it was now time for that House to return their thanks to Mr Atterbury, for his learned pains in asserting and vindicating the Rights of Convocation.'[3] The majority present then revealed their Oxford connections by proceeding to vote overwhelmingly, and with only seventeen dissentients, that a letter should be sent to the vice-chancellor of the University of Oxford formally requesting that the degree of DD by diploma should be conferred on Atterbury as 'some public notice of so great a piece of service to the Church'. Such a doctorate 'by diploma' was an honour reserved for distinguished persons, and yet on 5 May the university duly obliged. It was the end of peace in convocation. In the following weeks the primate was insulted and his authority defied. The Easter recess found the lower house engaged in a full-scale attack on the previous ministry. When in June the king prorogued the assembly, the parties stood embattled against each other.

The degree of excitement engendered in Oxford by this conflict was shown in an extraordinary by-election contest which took placed in the university while the actual debates were in progress at Westminster. To the utter consternation of the heads it was learned that Christopher

---

[1] Bodl. MS Add. A. 85a contains lists of voters on the 'moderate' side in three separate divisions. In no case does the number exceed seventeen. William Lloyd (1627-1717), m. Oriel 1639; fellow Jesus 1642; bp of St Asaph 1680, Lichfield and Coventry 1692, Worcester 1699-1717. Charles Trimnell (1663-1723), m. New College 1681; bp of Norwich 1708-21, Winchester 1721-3. John Tyler (d. 1724), degrees (by decree of convocation) Magd.; bp of Llandaff 1706-24. John Evans (d. 1724), BA Jesus 1681; bp of Bangor 1702-15, Meath 1716-24.

[2] For a fuller account of events in convocation see Bennett, *Tory Crisis*, ch. 3.

[3] See *Correspondence of Atterbury*, ed. Nichols i. 90 for the entry in the *Journal of the House*.

Musgrave, after taking no less than two months to make up his mind, had opted to sit for his native county of Westmorland.[1] Such a slight to the university was sure to be bitterly resented and to reflect badly on those who had proposed him.[2] When the news broke, Aldrich, Jane, Finch, Delaune and the vice-chancellor, Roger Mander, were all up at the convocation. But it was the kind of situation for which Charlett was designed by nature, and he took the whole business of finding a candidate and managing his election into his own hands. Unerringly he hit upon the name of William Bromley, the very archetype of a midland tory squire, who had been MP for Warwickshire until turned out at the election of 1698. Bromley was humourless and moralizing, a writer of tedious narratives of his travels in Europe, but he had a vigour and consistency in asserting his high-church opinions which effectively obscured the almost total unoriginality of his mind. He was destined to exercise great influence over tory backbenchers. The heads in London were overcome with gratitude at this putting forward of a candidate who seemed likely to command a wide measure of support. 'The whole university', wrote Mander to Charlett, 'is indebted to you for your prudent care and management of affairs'.[3] Strangely enough, however, the whole university was not grateful. Bromley was a former Student of Christ Church and as its electoral machine went into operation on his behalf opposition was at once aroused in Magdalen and among fellows of the smaller colleges who objected to this fixing of things by their over-mighty neighbour. Rumours were even circulated that Bromley was not sufficiently fervent in the church's cause, and an alternative interest was made for Sir George Beaumont. Atterbury's attempt to compose matters by a personal appeal to his contacts in Magdalen met with no response: it was a Christ Church man who was asking and so their vote was 'pre-engaged'.[4] It was an unnerving experience for the vice-chancellor who hurried back to Oxford to find that in his absence even his own fellows at Balliol had begun to strain at the leash and were thinking of putting up Sir William Glynne again. His energetic efforts on behalf of Bromley were clearly resented by many younger MAs.[5] At the poll on 21 March the result was surprisingly close: 197 to Beaumont's 164.[6] It was not particularly consoling for Charlett, whose efforts had come perilously close to disaster, to find himself congratulated on the result by one of Tenison's

---

[1] Harcourt-Charlett, 3 Mar. 1701, MS Ballard 10, fo 113.

[2] C. Musgrave *junior*-[R. Harley], 25 Jan. 1701, HMC *Portland MSS* iv. 14; Sprat-Charlett [*c*5 Mar. 1701], MS Ballard 9, fo 140.

[3] Mander-Charlett, 6 Mar. 1701, MS Ballard 21, fo 166.

[4] Atterbury-Charlett, 3 Mar. 1701, MS Ballard 9, fo 91; Kimberley-same, 15 Mar. 1701, MS Ballard 30, fo 54.

[5] Mander-Charlett, 7 Mar. 1701, MS Ballard 21, fo 168. The vice-chancellor was unhappy to learn that Sir William Whitelocke had written to Charlett to sound out his chances and undertook 'to take him off, for we must not suffer any subdivision upon the account of more friends appearing'.

[6] OUA register of convocation 1693-1703, fo 226ᵛ.

closest allies on the grounds 'that you can keep the masters from breaking in upon the Vice-Chancellor and Heads of Houses'.[1]

The by-election of 1701, accompanying as it did the excitement in the convocation of Canterbury, marked a watershed in Oxford politics and the emergence of a movement of political extremism among the ordinary fellows of colleges which was to be a source of grave embarrassment to the usual political managers. Events at Oxford were always news, eagerly reported by the news-writers and improved upon by friend and foe. Whig periodicals like the *Review* and *Observator* were later to rejoice in anything which appeared to reflect on the loyalty or good sense of the university. Now in the early part of 1701 there came into existence a vociferous group of younger dons who were prepared to use the sermons in St Mary's and the business before convocation to propagate the most violent sentiments. In particular they were determined to harass and abuse any leading Oxford tory whom they suspected of 'trimming' or 'moderation'. Clearly this development owed much to the raw passions aroused by the party conflict of King William's last year, but it was not unconnected with the arrival on the Oxford scene of a new fellow of Magdalen, Henry Sacheverell, who had been elected a demy in 1689 and, after a period working in country curacies, had come back into residence at the beginning of 1701 on attaining sufficient seniority for election to a fellowship. On 13 April he signalled his return by preaching a university sermon which one fellow of Balliol noted as 'an ingenious discourse, the part of it as I imagine levelled against the Vice-Chancellor'.[2] Magdalen was now the recognized centre of Oxford political extremism. On 12 April the fellows had elected as president, in succession to Bishop Hough, one of their number, John Rogers, who was commonly believed never to have taken the oath of allegiance. And in July they elected Sacheverell himself to a fellowship. Immediately he and his allies were engaged in a running battle with university whigs such as Tindal and Tyrrell and conducting a campaign against the 'moderate' heads. Roger Mander, for his support of Bromley in the recent by-election, became a special object of their attentions. On 25 September, when he was about to enter on his second year as vice-chancellor, a concerted effort was made to prevent his re-election, which was secured only 'with some struggle'.[3] When King William died on 8 March 1702 Oxford had already become a chief centre for the articulation of Anglican grievance; it had also developed a propensity for political extremism which was to make its role dangerous in the troubled reign which lay ahead.

[1] W. Kennett-Charlett, 10 Apr. 1701, MS Ballard 7, fo 98.
[2] Diary of Milles, 13 Apr. 1701.
[3] Ibid. 25 Sept. 1701. On the following 7 December Milles noted: 'I heard Mr Willcox of Magd: [Joseph Wilcocks] at S. Maries a surprizingly imprudent discourse.' It would thus appear that even a whiggish demy of the college was ready to join in the fray.

3

The Era of Party Zeal 1702–1714

G. V. BENNETT

FOR a year after the new queen's accession the university waited with increasing impatience for a tory ascendancy to be inaugurated. Anne was a niece of Lord Rochester and, as befitted one who had been Bishop Compton's pupil, a devout churchwoman. That she had deeply disliked King William was well known, and she made no attempt to disguise her detestation of the whig junto. In the first hours of her reign she indicated to Archbishop Tenison that his presence at court was unwelcome; and in spiritual matters she leaned heavily on the advice of her confessor, Archbishop Sharp of York. At the dismissal of the old parliament she delighted all tories by declaring that her 'own principles must always keep me entirely firm to the interests and religion of the church of England and will incline me to countenance those who have the truest zeal to support it'.[1] The response at Oxford was fervent. Throughout the summer the literary stylists vied with each other in the composition of high-flown congratulatory verses and addresses, all upon the theme that the reign was to see a 'restoration' of church and university to their former places in the life of the nation.[2] In their talk in common rooms the dons were confident that now patronage and preferment would flow back to those who had been so long deprived of it, and that a new parliament would soon re-establish the Anglican monopoly of public office. There would be legislation to enforce the strict meaning of the toleration act: to confine office in central and local government to bona fide churchmen, and to restrict public education to the universities or to teachers who had been duly licensed by a bishop. This was the programme advocated by the earl of Rochester, who was expected by virtually everyone to be the new chief minister. And he, of course, was the politician whom the dons knew best of all. While working on the great Oxford edition of his father's *History* he spent long periods in the city, and usually stayed with either Aldrich at Christ Church or Thomas Turner at Corpus. He dined out regularly with other heads of houses and was known as a convivial guest and a vigorous

[1] Taken from *Parliamentary History* vi. 26.
[2] Delaune-Charlett, 3 Nov. 1702, MS Ballard 21, fo 189: he writes about the convocation address, composed by the Oxford divines, 'that Scurvy word *Restor'd* will not go down with the Bishops'.

conversationalist.[1] When in May 1702 the first volume of the *History* was published, its preface, written by Dean Aldrich, was taken as a forthright statement of the tory principles on which the new ministry was to be constructed. Indeed it was being eagerly read by the ordinary dons as they prepared for the first general election of the reign.[2] In many constituencies banners were carried high bearing the device 'No Moderation', and the clergy marched to the poll in a black-coated phalanx to vote for 'Church and Queen' candidates. But in Oxford there was no contest. Having been given Lord Rochester's approbation, Finch and Bromley, the old members, were impregnable. Bromley had already proved himself as a leading tory spokesman in the commons and an efficient defender of the university's interests,[3] and on 17 July he and Finch were re-elected without opposition. To complete this picture of the dawning of a new tory age, the queen herself came to visit the university at the end of August. There could have been no greater contrast between King William's unhappy visit in 1695 and this wildly enthusiastic occasion. On the day the vice-chancellor, Roger Mander, and the doctors, clothed in their scarlet, rode out to meet the queen and escort her into the city. In the High Street the excitement of the scholars and citizens was so great that the order of procession was broken and the university officials found themselves jostled from their place near the royal person by mere aldermen and townspeople.[4] Order was restored, however, in Tom quad and Anne listened to high-flown speeches delivered by the dean and his troop of aristocratic young men. At the deanery that evening relays of ordinary college fellows were admitted to kiss her majesty's hand. And the next day in the Sheldonian she listened to music and yet more oratory, and watched while a succession of rising tory politicians, Bromley, Harcourt and St John, were admitted to honorary doctorates.[5]

In such an excited atmosphere it was not easy to impose restraint on the younger dons, who seized every opportunity to express their tory partisanship not just in the university pulpit but by their votes in convocation.

[1] Rochester-T. Turner, 8 Sept. [1702], Bodl. MS Clarendon 125, fo 9: 'if I come, and you be at Oxford, if you will give me leave, I shall come to my old quarters'. Harcourt-Charlett, 12 Oct. 1704, MS Ballard 10, fo 118: 'I am glad to hear Lord Rochester is well and you were so merry, wee fail not to remember our Friends in our Cupps'.

[2] Balliol, MS 461, diary of Jeremiah Milles, July 1702.

[3] Bromley-Charlett, 27 May 1701, MS Ballard 38, fo 131. He writes in detail about his efforts to secure the university's privileges in two bills before the commons: one concerns its right to be represented on the commission of the peace, the other deals with the University Press. On 25 November 1701 Bromley and Finch had been elected to William's last parliament.

[4] The ensuing bitter dispute with the city lasted until the end of 1703: see Charlett-Weymouth, 7 Dec. 1703, Longleat House, Thynne MS xxv, fo 175. At the beginning of that year convocation voted to give the mayor one week to make his submission on pain of discommoning the whole corporation: W. Smith-Charlett, 20 Feb. 1703, MS Ballard 16, fo 46.

[5] Diary of Milles, 26 Aug. 1702; A. Boyer, *The History of the Reign of Queen Anne digested into Annals* (11 vols London 1703-13 i. 76-7.

It was all a sore trial to the vice-chancellor who, elderly and easily upset, found himself under constant attack. His own small college, Balliol, was noted for its passionate tory opinions and, to retain the support of his fellows, he attempted weakly to swim along with the popular tide. He soon had to face the fact that the ordinary MAs had acquired a leader of perverse genius. Surprisingly quickly after his return to Magdalen in 1701 Henry Sacheverell had emerged as a force in university politics.[1] Strikingly handsome, fastidiously dressed, he seemed always in evidence about college and university business. Contemporaries testified to his impressive appearance in the pulpit and his strong, clear voice. But virtually no one in Oxford appears actually to have liked him; indeed he was universally recognized as overbearing, ambitious and avid for personal publicity. What attracted the ordinary MAs to him was the constant zeal with which he propagated his violent tory opinions. He had the temerity to assert openly what others said in private company, and this same reckless boldness characterized his lieutenants, William Tilly and Edmund Perkes of Corpus, Joseph Trapp of Wadham and Thomas Hart of Magdalen.[2] On 31 May 1702 Sacheverell presented the vice-chancellor with his first serious challenge by preaching a remarkable sermon in St Mary's. Entitled 'The politicial union', it began with some routine tory assertions about the dependence of the civil power on the support of religion and the church.[3] It concluded, however, with some startling passages in an overheated prose which congregations would soon recognize as the preacher's inimitable style. He launched himself against 'Shuffling, Treacherous, *Latitudinarians*',

All those False and Perfidious Members, who under the Pretence and Hypocritical Disguise of *Charity* and *Moderation*, would have Taken down [the Church's] Fence, and Remov'd Its *Land-Mark*, to make Way, for All Men of a Free, and Unbounded Persuasion, to Enter, to Debauch its Doctrines, Overrun its Discipline, and to Subvert the very Being of That Constitution, which is at present the Onely Support of the Protestant Religion.

Against all such he exhorted his hearers 'to Hang out the *Bloody Flag*, and *Banner* of Defiance'; and he concluded with an attack on occasional

---

[1] For Sacheverell see G. Holmes, *The Trial of Doctor Sacheverell* (London 1973). His excitable character seems to have been apparent early in his career at Magdalen. The vice-president's register for 31 January 1693 records that he was admonished *propter contumaciam et contemptum* towards the dean of arts: Bloxham, *Reg. Magdalen* vi. 98. A fellow of Magdalen who knew him as an undergraduate later remarked 'I know just how far his warmth of temper may have transported him': T. Smith–Hearne, 23 Mar. 1704, Bodl. MS Smith 127, fo 35.

[2] Edmund Perkes (1676-1706), m. CCC 1691. Joseph Trapp (1679-1747), m. Wadham 1695; prof. of poetry 1708-18; chaplain to the lord chancellor of Ireland 1711. Thomas Hart (1669-1709), m. Wadham 1686; demy Magd. 1689, fellow 1696-1709.

[3] See F. F. Madan, *A Critical Bibliography of Dr. Sacheverell*, ed. W. A. Speck (Lawrence, Kansas 1978) for the first edition published at Oxford and dedicated to George Sacheverell.

conformists, 'These Crafty, Faithless and Insidious Persons, who can *Creep* to Our Altars, and Partake of Our Sacraments, that They may be *Qualify'd*, more Secretly and Powerfully to Undermine Us'.[1] That Mander two days later granted this diatribe the university's official imprimatur deeply scandalized 'moderate' churchmen and produced a crop of outraged answers. Yet within a fortnight the preacher was again in St Mary's pulpit to preach a passionate discourse on the occasion of the outbreak of war with France.[2] Not content with all this notoriety, in July Sacheverell joined in the election campaign by publishing a pamphlet, *The Character of a Low-Church-Man*, which was another assault on 'false brethren' and a plea for the return of 'true churchmen' to both parliament and convocation.[3] By the summer of 1702 Sacheverell was sufficiently well known for prominent tories who were not really acquainted with the Oxford situation to write to the speaker of the commons to suggest that the new Oxford celebrity should be his chaplain.[4]

The embarrassment which this kind of agitation could cause was soon to be shown in the case of William Nicolson, nominated bishop of Carlisle in May 1702. Nicolson was at this date generally accounted a tory; his promotion was due to the influence of his patron, Christopher Musgrave. But, as a distinguished medieval historian, he had ventured in print to dissent from Atterbury's theories about the nature and privileges of an English convocation. Moreover, he had actually referred to him, although so recently invested with an Oxford doctorate, as 'Mr' Atterbury. Unfortunately for the bishop-elect it had recently become the practice of the ordinary MAs in convocation to deny graces for the degrees of those whom they regarded as politically unacceptable; and, when Nicolson applied for the doctorate which the university invariably conferred on Oxford men who had been raised to the episcopate, plans were made to inflict on him an unprecedented humiliation. A group of MAs delivered to the vice-chancellor a paper announcing that they would vote against the degree, unless Nicolson made a public retraction of this insult to Atterbury and to the university which had just granted him a doctorate for his defence of the church. Mander was at once thrown into

[1] H. Sacheverell, *The Political Union: a discourse shewing the dependence of government on religion in general, and of the English monarchy on the Church of England in particular* (Oxford 1702), 48–9, 59, 61.
[2] H. Sacheverell, *A Sermon preach'd before the University of Oxford on the tenth day of June 1702*, with imprimatur dated 25 June 1702 and dedicated to Lord Weymouth.
[3] In answer to *The True Character of a Church-Man*, published in December 1701 by Richard West, also a fellow of Magdalen. Much of Sacheverell's pamphlet was devoted to a defence of Sir John Pakington (1671-1727, 4th bt; m. St John's 1688) the highflying MP for Worcestershire. Among the many replies was Daniel Defoe's *The Shortest Way with Dissenters* (London 1702).
[4] T. Foley-R. Harley, 1 Sept. 1702, HMC *Portland MSS* iv. 45. *The Character of a Low-Church-Man* was immediately recognized as Sacheverell's, and one leading 'moderate' wrote in mockery to enquire whether the vice-chancellor had given it an imprimatur as well: Kennett–Charlett, 1 Aug. 1702, MS Ballard 7, fo 107.

panic. Without consulting other heads he wrote to Nicolson saying that the degree would not pass and he sent off copies of the masters' paper to William Bromley and others.[1] It was a fatal error. Nicolson had to be consecrated as a mere MA, and at court and among senior tory politicians there was anger and sheer disbelief that the university should thus rebuff one whom the queen had chosen for the first episcopal appointment of her reign.[2] It was, of course, a fine opportunity for the Cambridge 'moderates' to deal a shrewd blow at Oxford and toryism, and Richard Bentley procured there the offer of a Cambridge doctorate not only for Nicolson but for White Kennett and Edmund Gibson, two prominent Oxford men who had also had difficulty in obtaining degrees at their mother-university.[3] Indeed the whole business tended so much to Oxford's prejudice that the leading heads felt bound to make it clear that the move against Nicolson had come not from them but from a cabal among the junior masters. Aldrich, Finch, Delaune and Jane at once proposed that the bishop should be given his degree by diploma without further application on his behalf, and they proceeded to whip in their troops to see that the vote passed in the house.[4] Mander's pitiful conduct showed that in an age of party faction a vice-chancellor needed to have strong nerves and steady political judgement.

The warm hopes which the tories entertained in the heady days of summer were, however, to wither in the cooler climate of the winter sessions of parliament and convocation. It gradually became apparent that the queen, for all her high-flown sentiments, had absolutely no intention of delivering herself into the hands of Lord Rochester or any other of the old tory party chieftains. In mid-October Archbishop Tenison's chaplain was able to give his correspondents the good news that the Oxford contingent in convocation 'have not that degree of encouragement from Court they expected; all their hopes being in the Earl of Rochester, and he forced to content himself with a less share of interest than was at first thought to belong to the Queen's Uncle'.[5] For all

[1] E. Gibson-Charlett, 14 May 1702, MS Ballard 6, fo 74; Nicolson-same, 15 and 18 June 1702, MS Ballard 4, fos 20, 18; 'Bishop Nicolson's diaries', 6 parts, parts 1-5 [ed. H. Ware], *Trans. Cumberland and Westmorland Antiquarian and Archaeological Soc.* new ser. i-v (1901-5), additions and corrections ibid. vi (1906), 337-40, pt 6, ed. R. G. Collingwood, ibid. xxxv (1935), pt 2, p. 161 (11 June 1702). William Nicolson (1655-1727), m. Queen's 1670; bp of Carlisle 1702-18, Derry 1718-27, Cashel 1727.
[2] Nicolson-Charlett, 9 July 1702, MS Ballard 4, fo 16. W. Bishop-same, 18 June, MS Ballard 31, fo 20: 'it's a direct affront to the Queen as they say, and it's plain, it was design'd to let Her know that the University would at least expect to be concern'd, if not to nominate Bishops, yet at least to approve of Them.'
[3] 'Nicolson's diaries' pt 2, pp. 162-3, 168; R. Brabant-Charlett, 27 June 1702, MS Ballard 35, fo 135. The Cambridge degrees were conferred on 25 June. For Kennett having his degree twice refused see Kennett-Charlett, 8 July 1701, MS Ballard 7, fo 101.
[4] Nicolson-Charlett, 9 July and 24 Sept. 1702, MS Ballard 4, fos 16, 14; 'Nicolson's diaries' pt 2, p. 171 (12 July 1702).
[5] Gibson-Nicolson, 17 Oct. 1702, Bodl. MS Add. A. 269, fo 4.

her fear and hatred of the junto, Anne was determined not to be governed by the party zealots of either side. Rather her confidence was to be given to two men who were her trusted personal friends, John Churchill, duke of Marlborough, and Sidney, earl of Godolphin; and it was their partnership which became the linchpin of the new administration. Soon they were caught up in the demands of the great war with France: the general engaged in his vast continental campaigns and the treasurer struggling to find money for the military machine. They came to dread any upsurge of party strife at home which would divide the house of commons on party lines and impede the voting of essential supply. And the issue which they feared above all was that of the church and religion, because they knew only too well how it could be used by the 'violent' party leaders to exercise power over the minds of the ordinary backbenchers. It was therefore with deep apprehension that Godolphin learned of the preparations being made by influential tories both in parliament and in convocation to introduce legislation to curb the political influence of dissenters. The prospect of such divisiveness was particularly distressing to the queen who, as a pious churchwoman, had an intense distaste for quarrels among the clergy and for preachers of inflammatory sermons. The ministry stood in dire need of an able ecclesiastical manager, and in the autumn Godolphin took an important decision: to entrust the affairs of church and university into the hands of Robert Harley, speaker of the house of commons, and perhaps the most brilliant and subtle politician of the day. In many respects Harley was an improbable figure to undertake the work. The son of a Herefordshire squire of puritan and whig background, he had not been to either university but had actually been educated at a dissenting academy. At his first entry into the commons in 1690 he had supported the most extreme measures of 'country' whiggism, and was even accounted by some 'an enemy of the church'.[1] But by 1702 a remarkable sea change had been effected in his politics. His hatred of the junto 'court' whigs had led him into association with Rochester and Sir Edward Seymour, and even to be accounted an advocate of the Anglican cause. Already he had established a mastery in the business of the house and built up a quite extraordinary range of political and religious contacts. In the last year of his reign King William had perceived that he had the makings of a political manager of real ability, and now Godolphin and the queen turned to him as the one man who could handle their most pressing problem. It was thus that the University of Oxford was brought into contact with the politician who was to be most influential in its affairs for the next twelve years.

[1] 'I am now going to meet with some grave divines and therefore must not converse too long with an enemy of the church': H. B[oyle]-R. Harley, 17 Oct. 1695, HMC *Portland MSS* iii. 572.

Harley's methods were quite different from those employed by William's ecclesiastical managers. They, by neglecting all tories and promoting only whigs, had alienated the great majority of the clergy and turned the universities into centres of political extremism. Harley's approach was at once more intelligent and more subtle, and designed to re-establish the dependence of the main body of the clergy on the government. He was concerned, primarily, to set up a new system of ecclesiastical patronage which would ensure that what the crown had to give was distributed in a consistent manner and used to forward a definite policy. Such a scheme would be useless unless the queen herself lent it her aid, and Harley went to great lengths to win her confidence and obtain access to her person. Eventually, by proposing himself as one who could quieten the disputes among the clergy, he obtained a working arrangement by which Anne, Archbishop Sharp and he himself chose the recipients of senior preferment.[1] By using the queen's authority, they even managed to secure control over the vast mass of lesser patronage which was usually administered by the lord chancellor.[2] Harley was anxious that it should rapidly become known that preferment was available to those tories who eschewed faction and extremism, and were ready to work closely with the queen's ministers. In this his aims did not coincide exactly with those of Anne and the elderly archbishop of York. They were devout Anglicans of an old-fashioned churchmanship who wished to promote men of mature years and ascetic disposition, scholarly divines who, in large measure, stood apart from the political conflict. He, politician that he was, was willing to recruit not just 'moderate' tories but even extreme partisans if only he could persuade them to forsake opposition and use their influence to support the government. It was not to be a matter of crude bribery. Harley was a master of both private persuasion and public propaganda, employing newsmen and journalists to give publicity to the ministry's arguments.[3] With the new patronage scheme, then, went an effort to win the minds of the tory clergy: to convince them that Anne herself was ready to provide a new deal when the time was ripe, that more would be gained by

[1] See G. V. Bennett, *The Tory Crisis in Church and State, 1688-1730* (Oxford 1975), 66-9. Godolphin-R. Harley [22 Oct. 1702], Longleat House, Portland misc. vol. fo 110: 'The Queen is full of hopes, from your encouragement and the pains you take in it, that the differences among the Clergy may be moderated.'

[2] R. Harley-Godolphin, 17 July 1704, BL Add. MS 28055, fo 94; Godolphin-G. Burnet, 7 Nov. 1705, Bodl. MS Add. A. 191, fos 29-30; Anne-duchess of Marlborough, 17 July 1706, *Private Correspondence of Sarah Duchess of Marlborough* (2 vols London 1838) i. 37.

[3] On 9 August 1702 Harley wrote to Godolphin: '[though] there are many Violent Whigs left out, yet those who come in their places wil [*sic*] be for moderate and safe counsels, unless deceiv'd by the artifice of some few hot men, whom I hope the Government will take care to prevent, by supplying proper antidotes . . . I cannot, but upon this occasion, again take the liberty to offer to your Lordship that it wil be of great service to have some discreet writer of the Government side.' BL Add. MS 28055, fo 3.

supporting the queen's ministers than by opposing them, and that the tories meanwhile had to be patient and show themselves responsible. In these first years of the administration Harley was indefatigable in seeking out ways to gain the goodwill of the clergy, not least by his scheme for the queen to devote the proceeds of the first fruits and tenths tax towards raising the value of the livings of the poorer vicars.[1]

The new management was to prove highly successful. In the days after the state opening on 21 October the speaker was active in a series of meetings with tory politicians and with many of the clergy who had been leaders of the opposition in the lower house of convocation. He was well aware just how much of the clerical attack had stemmed from Oxford, and he made a point of bringing particular pressure to bear on the Christ Church interest. Here, at least, royal influence could have an immediate effect. In May Harley had obtained the promise of a vacant canonry for Francis Gastrell, his chaplain as speaker,[2] and the queen and Godolphin agreed that he should have the filling of future vacancies in Christ Church. From this moment on, Harley became a figure of importance on the Oxford scene, attracting into his following a small troop of Christ Church clerics, including not only Gastrell but William Stratford, George Smalridge and, eventually, Francis Atterbury. If Dean Aldrich had any doubt about the situation, it was made clear to him on 28 October in a private audience with the queen.[3] He was informed that he was to be the new prolocutor and that he was expected to work to moderate the clergy in convocation. Similarly the speaker went out of his way to meet George Hooper, the prolocutor in the convocation of 1701, and to win him over to co-operation with the ministry. It was not long before the two deans were engaged in meetings with Godolphin and Nottingham to settle the business of the convocation.[4] All this clandestine activity was to provide a great surprise for the warmer Oxford partisans. On the day of the state opening William Bromley was in an excited mood as he prepared, on behalf of his constituents, to begin the new parliament with a bill to impose draconic penalties on occasional conformists. 'The Fanaticks', he wrote to Charlett,

could not be more dejected in Bucks than they seem at present every where else. Most of them are very quiet and silent, tho' some talk of Persecution, they forsee its Approaches, and their Liberty of Conscience they expect will be taken

---

[1] 'I find the Archbishop of York is highly transported with your notion about the first fruits': Godolphin-Harley [10 Jan. 1704], Longleat House, Portland misc. vol. fo 84.

[2] [Godolphin-Harley,] 21 May 1702, HMC *Portland MSS* iv. 39. Francis Gastrell (1662-1725), m. Ch.Ch. 1680; bp of Chester 1714-25.

[3] 'The Queen Commands me to tell you, she will bee ready to receive the D. of Christ Church tomorrow at 5, in the afternoon, and speak to him as you have proposed': Godolphin-Harley, 27 [Oct.] 1702, BL loan 29/64/8.

[4] See Bennett, *Tory Crisis*, 68-71; [Godolphin-Harley,] 4 Nov. 1702, HMC *Portland MSS* iv. 50.

from them. The Abuse of it I hope will, and a stop put to that abominable Hypocrisie, that inexcusable Immorality of Occasional Conformity.[1]

Yet strangely the great tory assault came to nothing. The Oxford contingent went up to Westminster, duly elected Aldrich as prolocutor and waited for him to lead the attack. They were astonished to find that he, Hooper and even Oxford tories like William Lancaster were holding back.[2] Even the pugnacious Atterbury had been subjected to the speaker's persuasive powers.[3] In the commons on 10 November Bromley and Arthur Annesley, as representatives of the two universities, introduced the occasional conformity bill; but when it reached the lords it ground slowly to a halt. Marlborough and Godolphin made a show of voting for it, while behind the scenes they exerted every effort to have it killed. It was only towards the end of the session that it became clear to the more aggressive tories that their aims had been frustrated by dextrous management and secret manœuvre.

This disappointment at Westminster in the winter of 1702 to 1703 did nothing to allay party feeling in Oxford. If anything it added fuel to a growing suspicion that there had been a betrayal by 'false brethren' in high places: and this was soon to be shown in an epic struggle at New College. In spite of the size of its foundation this society did not usually play a notable role in university affairs. Its fellowships were not valuable, and the majority of its MAs were non-resident, pursuing careers away from Oxford as physicians, lawyers or country parsons. While it had many college livings most were of so small a value that they did not require their incumbents to forfeit their fellowships. It is clear that the society was politically deeply divided. In most colleges a majority of the fellows could determine the party allegiance of their body but New College was recruited only from boys elected at the sister-college at Winchester, and those who could claim to be founder's kin had an absolute right to a fellowship. The result was a separation into two well-defined groups: on the one hand a body of clergymen, resident or dispersed in small livings and curacies, who were waiting for the falling in of a valuable benefice; on the other hand a more radical group of gentlemen, physicians, lawyers and well-connected clergymen who had attached themselves to whig patrons. The undergraduate and bachelor fellows appear to have gravitated towards the interest to which they were eventually to belong. When in June 1703 Warden Traffles died

---

[1] Bromley-Charlett, 22 Oct. 1702, MS Ballard 38, fo 137. On the same day Godolphin reported to Harley that Sir Edward Seymour was 'apprehensive of the heats of the Convocation, more than of the matter of Cadiz': Longleat House, Portland misc. vol. fo 128.

[2] Lancaster-Charlett, 14 Nov. 1702, J. Edwards-same, 19 Nov. 1702, MS Ballard 21, fos 65, 154. William Lancaster (1650-1717), m. Queen's 1670, provost 1704-17, vicar of St Martin's-in-the-Fields 1692: vice-chancellor 1706-10.

[3] Bennett, Tory Crisis, 66-70.

suddenly the 'moderate' party attempted to seize the initiative by proposing Charles Trimnell, archdeacon of Norwich, as his successor. It was
an astute move, for he was undoubtedly the most distinguished of the
former fellows, a well liked and very able man, clearly destined for the
episcopate and indeed one day to be a notable bishop, first of Norwich
and then of Winchester.[1] But of his whig connections there could be no
doubt. He had left New College to be tutor to Charles Spencer, third earl
of Sunderland, one of the most active members of the whig junto. In the
convocation of 1701 Trimnell had been leader of the tiny band of those
who had supported Archbishop Tenison and set themselves to thwart
the campaign of the Oxford tories. At once the whole whig and 'moderate' machine set to work on his behalf. Tenison 'and all his friends',
reported Atterbury, 'have moved every stone to secure this post for him,
and left no application untried, which it was possible for them to make
any where. If he is chosen, they have then five Heads in Oxford who are
sure and firm to them.'[2] Against Trimnell the New College tories could
put up only Thomas Braithwaite, a resident of no particular distinction;
but at once the whole tory world rallied to his support. Aldrich and
Charlett, aided by letters from Bishop Sprat, Trelawny, Rochester and
Heneage Finch, canvassed unashamedly.[3] It was hardly possible, wrote
Atterbury, to 'imagine how far this matter was driven into a party cause,
and how much concerned the great men of both sides were for the event
of it'.[4] On 25 June the fellows assembled in the college chapel, with the
eyes of the political world upon them, and proceeded to vote thirty for
Trimnell and thirty-one for Braithwaite, with the successful candidate
voting prudently for himself.[5] Even so, the whigs were not quite defeated
and, when some of Braithwaite's supporters departed back to their curacies, leaving the tories without a majority, they refused to certify the
election to the visitor, the bishop of Winchester. Soon all parties, with
their lawyers, were on the road to Farnham to appeal to the ancient
bishop, Peter Mews. But in spite of all kinds of pressure and lobbying,
Mews decided that Braithwaite had been statutorily elected and

[1] Writing to Trelawny on 4 February [1703] Atterbury commented 'it is now again strongly
reported, that Dr. Trimnell is the next man who is to sit on your Lordship's bench': *The Epistolary
Correspondence, Visitation Charges, Speeches, and Miscellanies of the Right Reverend Francis Atterbury, D.D.,
Lord Bishop of Rochester, with historical notes, and brief memoirs of the author*, ed. J. Nichols (4 vols London
1783-7, 2nd edn 5 vols London 1799, i-iv printed and dated 1789-90, v 1798) i. 157. For admiring
remarks on Trimnell from known tories see Hearne, *Collections* i. 218-19; *Letters of Humphrey
Prideaux, sometime Dean of Norwich, to John Ellis, sometime Under-Secretary of State, 1674-1722*, ed. E. M.
Thompson (Camden Soc. new ser. xv 1875), p. 200 (13 Sept. 1708). Richard Traffles (1648-1703), m.
New College 1665, warden 1701-3.
[2] Atterbury-Trelawny, 27 June 1703, *Correspondence of Atterbury*, ed. Nichols i. 222.
[3] Same-same, 3 July 1703, ibid. i 224; W. Bishop-Charlett, 15 July, MS Ballard 31, fo 26.
[4] Atterbury-Trelawny, 15 July 1703, *Correspondence of Atterbury*, ed. Nichols i. 228.
[5] NCA 5079, 'Case about Dr. Braithwait's Election'.

that it was entirely proper for a fellow of New College to vote for him-self.[1] The new warden's return to Oxford was a veritable triumphal progress, and he was rapturously welcomed into the city by a great throng of tory supporters. He was to prove a weak head and an even weaker vice-chancellor, while the college was to remain divided and embittered by internal conflict.[2]

The strong sentiments of Oxford toryism but its lack of direction or coherent leadership were soon to be shown in a strange by-election. In the parliamentary recess Heneage Finch was raised to the peerage as Baron Guernsey and the university had to find a new burgess to partner William Bromley. It is clear that the heads were deeply divided about the kind of representation they wanted. Time was lost in sounding out tory worthies like Lord Digby of Geashill and Sir Francis Dashwood, and it was well into the long vacation before it was discovered that neither was prepared to stand.[3] Now that indefatigable fixer, Arthur Charlett, inter-vened to work up an interest for Sir William Whitelocke of Phyllis Court, Henley. He was an odd choice. The son of Bulstrode Whitelocke, a notorious regicide, Sir William had worked his passage as a tory and had even become an object of whig ministerial spite in 1696. He was now sixty-eight years of age and had been out of the commons for eight years. A pompous and pedantic lawyer, who rapidly developed into a parlia-mentary figure of fun, Whitelocke was foisted on the university by a group of heads in concert with their tory aristocratic patrons.[4] On a visit to Longleat Charlett obtained the endorsement of Lord Weymouth; and that doyen of the old cavalier interest, President Turner of Corpus, was persuaded actually to propose him in the convocation house. This time,

---

[1] Bishop-Charlett, 15 July 1703, MS Ballard 31, fo 26.
[2] In 1709 a satirical poem commented:

> Next on *New-College* I bestow my Blessing,
> In Hopes that Animosities will lessen;
> That they in Time their Parties will give o'er.

Aesop at Oxford, or A Few Select Fables in Verse (London 1709), 74. John Ayliffe, *The Antient and Present State of the University of Oxford* (London 1714) i. 323 referred to the poor state of the college 'through the supine Negligence of a late Warden, and the Discouragements arising from domestick Quarrels'.
[3] Atterbury-Trelawny, 17 Mar. 1703, *Correspondence of Atterbury*, ed. Nichols i. 186; Bromley-[Harley], 25 Sept. 1703, HMC *Portland MSS* iv. 67. William Digby (1661-1752), 5th Bn Digby; m. Magd. 1679; MP Warwick 1689-98.
[4] See *Observator* vi no. 15 (19-23 Apr. 1707) for a hilarious description of Whitelocke, using his usual nickname of 'Old Shoe Strings'. See also *The University Ballad, or The Church's Advice to her two Daughters, Oxford and Cambridge* (np [1705]), reprinted in *The Bagford Ballads illustrating the Last Years of the Stuarts*, ed. J. W. Ebsworth (4 vols Ballad Soc. xiv-xvii 1876-8) iii. 829;

> The Wags so admire him, and love to make Sport
> With University Member, that they oft make effort
> To call him to Chair; do's this your Honour support?
> If *Ox[for]d* Jests be Re-printed, with Additions most rare,
> Her's a Jest for the House, and a Jest for the Bar,
> That you be not a Jest too, is worthy your care.

however, Charlett had not made an apt choice. Whitelocke received lukewarm support from Christ Church and was vehemently opposed in convocation when the election took place on 22 November. Indeed Bernard Gardiner, the new warden of All Souls, led a fierce campaign in favour of Francis Clarke, a high-tory squire from North Weston and the Magdalen candidate.[1] Given the powerful backing he had received, it is surprising to find that Whitelocke obtained only 174 votes against his opponent's 101. Tory though he was, the new member could not provide the kind of highflying oratory which the Oxford dons wanted, and his election was bitterly resented by many.[2]

The rejection of a second occasional conformity bill in December 1703 marked the end of the Oxford tories' patience with the Godolphin ministry.[3] Indeed the news of Bromley's defeat set off in the university an angry campaign of agitation which was to become a source of grave embarrassment to a government which still depended on tory support in the house of commons. The first salvo was fired by William Tilly of Corpus who on 30 January in St Mary's delivered an excited tirade against occasional conformity and attacked Bishop Burnet for defending the practice in the debate in the house of lords.[4] Tilly's example was at once copied, and week after week a succession of college fellows transformed the university sermon, preached before the vice-chancellor and senior and junior members, into a denunciation of dissenters, the bishops and secret 'false brethren' in high places.[5] On 9 March Sacheverell contributed his special rhetorical talent with a discourse before the assize judge on 'The nature and mischief of prejudice and partiality' which caused an immediate furore. He solemnly warned his hearers against those who were led by worldly interest to forsake their avowed principles and called for the closure of all dissenting academies, those *Illegal Seminaries . . .* for the Education of Youth in all the Poysnous Principles of *Fanaticism* and *Faction'.*[6] The vehemence of such preaching was matched by a wildness of talk and bitter denunciation in common rooms which many whigs and even some tories found insupportable. *The Oxford Dialogue between a Master of Arts, and a Stranger* attempted to

1 Francis Clarke (1655-1715), m. Magd. 1671; MP Oxon. 1710-15.
2 J. Davis-Weymouth, 22 Nov. 1703, Longleat House, Thynne MS xxv, fo 158; Charlett-same, ibid. fo 175; Whitelocke-T. Turner, 25 Nov. 1703, Bodl. MS Rawl. lett. 92, fo 188.
3 Godolphin himself had tried to dissuade Bromley from reintroducing the bill, but found him 'obstinate to the last degree': Godolphin-Harley, 9 Nov. [1703], Longleat House, Portland misc. vol. fos 209-10.
4 Davis-Turner, 24 Feb. 1704, Bodl. MS Rawl. lett. 92, fo 196.
5 Bodl. MS Eng. Th. f. 15 is a notebook for the years 1704-6 kept by an undergraduate and summarizing the content of university sermons. The texts indicate that the predominating topic was occasional conformity.
6 *The Nature and Mischief of Prejudice and Partiality stated in a Sermon Preach'd at St Mary's in Oxford at the Assizes held there, March 9th 1703/4* (Oxford 1704), 54. It was answered by Daniel Defoe in *More Short Ways with the Dissenters* (London 1704).

reproduce the authentic flavour of the language of 'those that are continually filling their Sermons, and their Tavern and Coffee-house Discourse with rude and vile Language, with ridiculous and false Stories of
their Civil and Ecclesiastical Superiors'.[1] If it was virtually impossible for
them publicly to challenge such conversation, the university whigs took
their revenge by publishing anonymous pamphlets and verses which
satirized Oxford life before a wider audience. One tract, *An Antidote
against Rebellion*, was of such bitterness as to start an inquiry as to its
author; it went so far as to attack Aldrich, Delaune and Gardiner as

Men whose very Faces are a sc[anda]l to their Gowns, these Men clap Honest
Sacheverel on the Back and pour College-Ale down his Throat; just as he would
stroke Touzer, and spit in his Mouth, to encourage him to take the Bull or Bear;
so they manage their Bulldog to set him upon the Back of some brawny
B[isho]p, *B[urne]t*, or *Ll[oy]d*, or *T[eniso]n*.[2]

In the autumn of 1704, as the new parliamentary session approached, the
tory preachers whipped themselves into a fury. On 7 September
Edmund Archer of St John's, one of the pro-proctors, turned the university sermon in thanksgiving for the victory at Blenheim into a denunciation of occasional conformity, and so infuriated Bishop Lloyd of
Worcester that he 'severely reprimanded him at the Vice-Chancellors
Lodgings'.[3] In such an atmosphere it was no surprise to learn that
Sacheverell was hard at work on a new tract against the dissenters and
that it would show 'more heat than in any thing he has done yet'.[4]

The Oxford tories had not, however, reckoned with the political skill
of Robert Harley. With the government facing a major parliamentary
test in the winter of 1704 Godolphin decided in May that the speaker
would have to come out into the open and take up the secretaryship of
state which Nottingham had resigned in disgust at the continued failure
of the occasional conformity bill. It was a difficult task, but in the following weeks Harley had extraordinary success in creating a new body of
support to fend off the coming tory assault. His tactic was to deprive the
opposition of some of its most effective leaders, and as the session began
he actually secured the defection of Simon Harcourt and Henry St John,

[1] *The Oxford Dialogue between a Master of Arts, and a Stranger* (London 1705), 33.
[2] *An Antidote against Rebellion* was published in Oxford on 25 May 1704; the extract is at p. 57.
Charlett suspected it to have been written by James Tyrrell 'but he absolutely denies it': Charlett--
Weymouth, 9 June 1704, Longleat House, Thynne MS xxv, fo 287.
[3] Hearne-T. Smith, 25 Sept. 1704, Bodl. MS Rawl. lett. 37, fo 31ʳ. Even Delaune, as vice-
chancellor, found the sermon offensive and refused to let it be printed: same-same, 29 Oct. 1704,
ibid. fo 35.
[4] Same-same, 13 Oct. 1704, ibid. fo 33. *The Rights of the Church of England Asserted and Prov'd* was
eventually published in 1705 in London. Sacheverell was assisted in it by his allies, William Adams
(1673-1714, m. Ch.Ch. 1691; fifteen of his university sermons were published by Sacheverell in 1716)
and Edmund Perkes of Corpus. See Madan, *Bibliography of Sacheverell*, 11; and Hearne-Smith,
20 July 1706, Bodl. MS Rawl. lett. 37, fo 87.

until then two of the hottest advocates for the bill. Harcourt, as MP for Abingdon and a rising Oxfordshire landowner, was a particularly useful agent within the university where he had many friends and clients.[1] The summer of 1704, indeed, had seen the consolidation of the new secretary's Oxford connection. In July Francis Gastrell obtained his promised canonry at Christ Church and quickly became the ministry's writer of 'faithful accounts' of the university scene. William Stratford, as speaker's chaplain, was assured of the next vacant canonry, while George Smalridge, who had been doing the duties of regius professor of divinity, was promised the succession after William Jane's death.[2] Francis Atterbury was given the deanery of Carlisle and actually promised that of Christ Church. In August the number of Harley's dependents in Oxford was increased when William Lancaster was, after much controversy, elected provost of Queen's. It is scarcely surprising that Dean Aldrich should send assurances of being the 'servant' of the new secretary and that the vice-chancellor, William Delaune, should seek, through Harcourt, to hitch his wagon to the rising star.[3] Within six months of taking office Harley was ready to bring all government patronage at Oxford under strict control. 'I wish now', he wrote to the treasurer, 'Her majesty would pledge to begin to recommend so many of each University to Lord Keeper (I have a Scheme for that purpose) . . . it would have immediately great effect in the universities.'[4] With so many preparations and with such defections among his supporters, Bromley's plans soon began to make heavy weather. The only way to get the bill through the lords was to 'tack' its clauses to the land tax bill for the ensuing year but this device was of doubtful constitutional propriety and directly threatened the war effort. Even some of the tory pundits began to sense defeat in the commons and it was reported that 'Lord Rochester and Lord Nottingham tried their credit with the University of Oxford to persuade them that in prudence the conformity bill shou'd not be brought in this session, but they would not be persuaded'.[5] Despite all warnings Bromley and Whitelocke pressed on until on the evening of 28 November the 'tackers' were heavily defeated by 251 votes to 134. Somewhat

---

[1] 'Perhaps thou mayest wonder at this unexpected change, but I am now convinced of my error . . . 'tis as ridiculous to hear an upstart Oxonian talk of Politicks as 'tis to see an unpowdered wig and dirty boots in a drawing room': Harcourt–A. Ottley of Christ Church, 9 Nov. 1704, National Library of Wales, Ottley MS 1983.

[2] Harley-Stratford, 8 July 1704, BL loan 29/191; F. Gastrell–[Harley], 27 Aug. 1704, HMC *Portland MSS* iv. 116; Smalridge–same, 12 Feb. [1707], ibid. 388; Atterbury-Trelawny [Nov. 1707], *Correspondence of Atterbury*, ed. Nichols i. 446. Stratford obtained his canonry by Harley's influence in July 1705: Bromley–[Harley], 7 July 1705, HMC *Portland MSS* iv. 203; Aldrich–same, 7 July 1705, ibid.

[3] [Harcourt-Harley], 29 July 1704, HMC *Portland MSS* iv. 105.

[4] Harley-Godolphin, 17 July 1704, BL, Add. MS 28055, fo 94.

[5] W. Simpson-J. Methuen, 17 Oct. 1704, Lawrence, Kansas, Kenneth E. Spencer Research Library, MS C. 163. xlv.

complacently, Bromley professed himself 'satisfyed, after the Disappoint-
ments we have met with, to find my endeavors to serve the Church and
Religion, are acceptable to those I have the Honour to represent'.[1] When
the news reached Oxford, however, it was received with grievous surprise and, among the ordinary dons, with something approaching outrage.[2]

In the excited era which followed the defeat of the 'tack', Harley and his
Oxford allies had to deploy all their reserves of subtle persuasion to restrain the wilder elements in the university. Rochester, Nottingham,
Seymour and Bromley were now in irreconcilable opposition, and their
campaign cry of 'the church in danger' progressively alienated the
queen, Marlborough and Godolphin from the tories. Hostile sermons
and insulting pamphlets, like James Drake's *The Memorial of the Church of
England* (London 1705), were fiercely resented by ministers, and it
became a standard tactic of whig politicians and writers to publicize
any overheated pronouncement by a high-church clergyman as proof
that the tories were incapable of responsible behaviour or political trust.
It was clear that the general election in the summer of 1705 would be a
testing time for the forces of moderation. In the previous year the
Christ Church interest, backed by Harley, had made plans to oust Sir
William Whitelocke by putting up George Clarke, a prominent pro-
administration tory and secretary to the queen's husband, Prince
George.[3] As a distinguished All Souls civilian and a popular personality
with royal connections he would have made a strong candidate. But the
failure of the 'tack' produced a new situation. Now the challenge to
Whitelocke came from a different quarter. It was known that he had sat
silent in the house of commons as Bromley had led the fight and, though
he had voted for the 'tacking' clause, it was impossible for him to pretend
that he had played a truly zealous part. He was thus horrified to learn
that Sacheverell and the Magdalen interest had decided to run Sir
Humphrey Mackworth, one of the hottest tories in the commons and a
leading speaker in the tacking debate.[4] Mackworth was just the kind of
histrionic highflyer likely to appeal to the ordinary MAs. Though his
shady mining speculations contrasted oddly with his piety as an original

---

[1] Bromley-Charlett, 23 Dec. 1704, MS Ballard 38, fo 142; see also Whitelocke-T. Turner,
16 December, Bodl. MS Rawl. lett. 92, fo 292.

[2] 'Most people in the university are mightily concerned at the Miscarriage of the Occasional
Conf. Bill': Hearne-T. Smith, 19 December 1704, Bodl. MS Rawl. lett. 37, fo 40.

[3] Atterbury-Trelawny, 23 May 1704, *Correspondence of Atterbury*, ed. Nichols i. 303; Charlett-
Weymouth, 9 June, Longleat House, Thynne MS xxv, fo 287; [Harcourt-Harley,] 29 July, HMC *Portland
MSS* iv. 105.

[4] All the world 'knows that he [Sacheverell] and the fellows of Maudlin, set up Sir H. Mackworth
some time since in the university, in order to throw out that worthless knight': R. Bridges-Trumbull,
12 Apr. 1709, Berkshire Record Office, Trumbull MS liii.

member of the Society for Promoting Christian Knowledge, he was a prolific writer of political pamphlets.[1] To Whitelocke's alarm the Magdalen interest now engaged in a thoroughly unprincipled campaign. Rumours were circulated that Mackworth was the real candidate of Rochester, Nottingham and Guernsey; bundles of his tracts were distributed free in the university; and crates of wine were delivered to college common rooms.[2] On 6 May, three days before the poll, Mackworth published a new pamphlet in the form of an open letter to his chief supporter, Henry Sacheverell.[3] Clearly his candidacy had a marvellous effect in concentrating the minds of all those who did not want to see the university represented by one who was at best a political maverick. Aldrich quickly withdrew Clarke's candidature: and tories as diverse as Delaune, Atterbury, Bromley and Hearne rallied to the support of Whitelocke.[4] Rochester and Nottingham even issued a public statement affirming their approval of the old member. Just before polling day Mackworth's friends came back with a hilarious ballad which indicated Whitelocke's whig background and his poor figure in the commons:

> If Br[om]ly and Mack[wor]th together are chose,
> You'l ne'er more be divided by any of those
> Who your peace and your Union do so much Oppose.[5]

But on 9 May when the members of convocation assembled it was clear that the heads had done their work well. Not a single MA voted against Bromley, who received 325 votes, while Whitelocke and Mackworth divided the second vote 214 to 110.[6] It was typical of Oxford politics that the contest should have been between candidates each of whom was a 'tacker'. At Cambridge, by contrast, the lord treasurer was confident enough to let his son, Francis Godolphin, stand against Arthur Annesley, a leading 'tacker', and Dixy Windsor, a virtually unknown tory zealot. There was even reason to believe that the government might achieve a moral victory by actually winning a university seat, and the vote of every head of house, save one, was secured. But on the day Cambridge erupted

[1] M. Ransome, 'The parliamentary career of Sir Humphrey Mackworth, 1701–1713', *Univ. Birmingham Hist. Jl* i. (1947–8); see also Atterbury-Trelawny, 27 Nov. 1703, *Correspondence of Atterbury*, ed. Nichols i. 270 for Mackworth's pamphlet *Peace at Home*, which was answered by Defoe's *Peace without Union* (London 1703). In March 1710 the commons were to vote him 'guilty of many notorious and scandalous Frauds': *Journals of the House of Commons* xvi. 391.

[2] Whitelocke-T. Turner, 10 Feb. 1705, Bodl. MS Rawl. lett. 92, fo 300; 'Nicolson's diaries' pt 3, p. 8 (7 May 1705).

[3] *A Letter from a Member of Parliament to his Friend in the Country* (London 1705).

[4] Writing to Trelawny on 21 April 1705 Atterbury reported: 'we shall certainly have the old members at Oxford. G. Clark hath desisted and Sir H. Mackworth it is supposed will desist, for it is certain he will not succeed', 'Collectanea trelawniana', p. 283. I am grateful to Mr F. T. Williams for permission to use these transcripts of manuscripts once at Trelawne, Cornwall.

[5] 'The university ballad 1705' in *The Bagford Ballads*, ed. Ebsworth iii. 834.

[6] Hearne-T. Smith, 14 May 1705, Bodl. MS Rawl. lett. 37, fo 50; OUA register of convocation 1704–30, fo 15.

with ugly scenes and an unpleasant demonstration by the undergraduates against Godolphin. When the poll was taken it appeared that 182 members of the senate had voted for Annesley, 170 for Windsor and 162 for the treasurer's son.[1] Even at the sister-university the tory partisanship of the ordinary dons had carried the day.

In the new house of commons the two parties stood almost equally balanced, and Marlborough and Godolphin, after all that they had suffered at the hands of the tory zealots, were clear in their minds that henceforth they would rely upon the whigs for a working majority. Now all Harley's skills were devoted to ensuring that the tories by factious opposition did not so alienate the queen and her ministers that a thoroughgoing whig regime was inaugurated. In season and out of season, whenever he could find a backbencher or a clergyman who would listen to him, the secretary preached the absolute necessity of responsible politics. But, seemingly oblivious of all danger, the highflyers pressed on with their former tactics. Indeed at Oxford Sacheverell and his cronies seemed almost to go out of their way to provide the whigs with ammunition. On 19 July William Tilly preached in St Mary's an assize sermon on 'the church in danger' which led to a formal complaint from the judges.[2] Indeed Harley, on reading it in print, so abandoned his usual judicial stance as to describe it 'as such a composition of incoherencys, nonsense in English, and impertinent with Greek, with the very spirit of Rage, that one would think it was written by some furious Presbyterian Scot'.[3] Week by week the university pulpit shook with denunciations of occasional conformity and assertions of the danger of the church, until on 23 December Sacheverell put all his allies into the shade by preaching in St Mary's an early version of the sermon 'In perils among false brethren' which in 1709 was to put the whole country into a crisis.[4] It was only natural that the whigs should seek to squeeze every advantage from the situation. When Bromley was proposed as a candidate for speaker in the new house he was mercilessly attacked in debate by Lord Hartington who went so far as to describe his Oxford constituents as 'Trumpeters of Rebellion'.[5] On 17 November the *Observator*, written by John Tutchin, demanded a full investigation of the colleges' use of their endowments while on 6 December the bishop of

---

[1] See MS Ballard 23, fo 114 for a detailed list of the voters on 17 May. Godolphin was defeated by his weakness in the large colleges, Trinity and St John's, each of which revolted against its head. Windsor did not obtain a single vote from the head of a college. See also A. Annesley-Charlett, 12 Apr. 1705, MS Ballard 10, fo 167; Boyer, *Annals* iv. 208-9.

[2] W. Tilly, *The Nature and Necessity of Religious Resolution, in the Defence and Support of a Good Cause, in Times of Danger and Trial* (Oxford and London 1705).

[3] R. Harley-Stratford, 10 Oct. 1705, BL loan 29/171. See also Hearne-T. Smith, 5 Aug. 1705, Bodl. MS Rawl. lett. 37, fo 57; Bodl. MS Eng. Th. f. 15, fo 30.

[4] Hearne, *Collections* i. 139; Bodl. MS Eng. Th. f. 15, fo 139.

[5] R. Bridges-Trumbull, 26 Oct. 1705, Berks. Rec. Off. Trumbull MS liii.

Ely in a speech in the lords called for a royal visitation of both universities.[1] It might now have been a prudent course for the Oxford divines to have held their peace, but any possibility of this was ruined by a deliberate piece of provocation from Matthew Tindal of All Souls. Early in the new year he published anonymously a small volume which was nicely calculated to set all tories, moderate as well as extremist, into a fury. Entitled, misleadingly, *The Rights of the Christian Church Asserted*, it was designed to show *'that they who raise the greatest Noise about the Danger of the Church, are the greatest Enemies to it'*. Religion was a matter of individual opinion and needed neither priests nor theology. Theology itself was 'artificial Cant and learned Gibberish, made up of obscure, and doubtful, and undefin'd Words'. He advocated a strict enforcement of clerical poverty to prevent the clergy having leisure enough to be a nuisance. He scarified Tilly's sermons as tending to the destruction of all liberty, and asked: 'Is there any Discourse S[acheverel]l has printed, which does not declare for it?'[2] The reaction was everything for which Tindal had hoped. Venerable heads of houses hurried to the pulpit to denounce him, and it was impossible to keep the lesser fry in check. Sitting in the cathedral on the morning of 21 April, Canon Stratford was miserably put out to hear a sermon from a Christ Church man who exhorted the congregation to 'arm themselves against the fiery trial that was now approaching'. Stratford went on to remark gloomily: 'it is said that Sacheverell has been outdone by one of Christ Church, and no doubt it is at Lambeth before you will receive this.'[3] But even this effort was eclipsed by a university sermon on 26 May by Thomas Hart of Magdalen, whose intemperate denunciation of Tindal produced nothing less than an official letter from the secretary of state demanding instant and condign punishment for the preacher.[4] It was becoming painfully obvious that the university's relationship with the queen and her government had deteriorated badly.

A reimposition of discipline was, however, quickly to be achieved by the strong-minded and energetic man who in October 1706 came to the vice-chancellorship. William Lancaster, provost of Queen's, was a complete contrast with his predecessor. Delaune had been a tory zealot, popular with the younger MAs, but devoid of real political sense and so confused in financial matters as to be perpetually tottering on the edge of fraudulent conversion.[5] Lancaster was a more subtle personality, persuasive and ruthless by turns, and his mastery of university business

---

[1] Boyer, *Annals* iv. 208-9, viii. appx, p. 166; 'Nicolson's diaries' pt 3, p. 36 (14 Dec. 1705).

[2] *The Rights of the Christian Church Asserted* (London 1706), pp. iii, 220-1, 301.

[3] S[tratford]-Gastrell, 22 Apr. 1706, HMC *Portland MSS* iv. 295; same-Harley, 27 Apr. 1706, ibid. 297; Bodl. MS Eng. Th. f. 15, fo 189. The text was Gal. 4. 29.

[4] Delaune-Ormonde, 1 Aug. 1706, HMC *Seventh Report* 781; Hearne-F. Cherry, 14 Aug. 1706, Bodl. MS Rawl. lett. 36, fo 290.

[5] For Delaune's inability to control business see R. Bridges-Trumbull, 3 July 1706, Berks. Rec. Off.

quickly established a dominance over the other heads of houses. 'The northern bear' was very much a self-made man. Of humble Westmorland origin, he had made his way, via a domestic chaplaincy to Bishop Compton, to the great living of St Martin-in-the-Fields. Even that fastidious diarist, John Evelyn, was impressed by the quality of his preaching and pastoral care. When in 1704 the fellows of Queen's elected him they quickly discovered that they had acquired a provost of formidable energy who pressed them on towards the completion of an ambitious programme for rebuilding the college in the Palladian style. Lancaster's tory credentials were impeccable, and his appointment as vice-chancellor was hailed by some whig publicists as the advent of yet another highflying zealot.[1] But in this they were wholly mistaken. The natural affinity of his mind was with men of business and government and not with faction and febrile opposition; and he was determined to restore the university to good relations with the queen and her ministers. Of course he kept up, as he had to do, a tory stance. In his inaugural oration he roundly attacked Tindal, and he was careful publicly to support tory candidates in parliamentary elections, even to the extent of caballing with Sir William Whitelocke.[2] He espoused Atterbury's cause in the lower house of convocation and professed to admire his pamphlets. But informed observers noted a new authority when it came to dealing with extremism and detected, behind the scenes, the subtle hand of Mr Secretary Harley. When, for example, the ministry wanted an address from the university on the occasion of the union with Scotland, in spite of vehement opposition among the ordinary MAs Lancaster at once prepared a way for it with the heads, and obtained what was required.[3] Similarly he enlisted their support to curb the increasing propensity of the members of convocation to deny degrees to those who had spoken or written against tory political orthodoxy. Gradually the worst kind of partisan preaching in the university was discouraged, and after a spectacular performance by Sacheverell in St Mary's on 18 May 1707 the vice-chancellor was able to take a decision not to have him or his closest supporters invited again.[4] Lancaster was a grave disappointment to the Oxford

Trumbull Add. MS 136/3. For his financial defalcations and Lancaster's pursuit of them see H. G. Carter, *A History of the Oxford University Press* i (Oxford 1975), 152–3; Hearne, *Collections* i. 315; Lancaster-Charlett, 10 May 1707, MS Ballard 21, fo 70.

[1] See *A Hymn to St Tack, sung at the election of the new vice-chancellour of Oxford* ([London] 1706): 'Now we may Hope for Glorious Days agen, And once more Ridicule both CHURCH and QUEEN.'

[2] Hearne, *Collections* i. 293–4; Lancaster-Charlett, 20 May 1708, MS Ballard 21, fo 77.

[3] Same-same, 8 Apr. 1707, MS Ballard 21, fo 67; Hearne–T. Smith, 14 Apr. 1707, Bodl. MS Rawl. lett. 27, fo 124.

[4] Bodl. MS Eng. th. f. 15, fo 352: 'I Tim.5.22: "Neither be partakers of other mens sins".' See Holmes *Trial of Sacheverell*, 89 ff. for this sermon which was later repeated at the assizes at Derby on 15 August 1709.

extremists, to Hearne, and even to the undergraduates whom he firmly disciplined; but he showed clearly that an able vice-chancellor, supported by his colleagues, was more than a match for the wild men.

It was well that some control had been reasserted, for the year 1707 was to see the university drawn into a struggle for power at the highest political level. In the spring Queen Anne decided to call a halt to the steady advance of whig influence in the Godolphin administration. Her resistance took the form of a stubborn refusal to accept the treasurer's proposal of two whigs for the vacant bishoprics of Exeter and Chester. With the clandestine support of Harley and Archbishop Sharp she offered the sees privately to two known tory divines. For the rest of the year the whole future of the government hung in the balance as Godolphin and the junto exerted intense pressure on the queen to get her to change her mind.[1] It was thus unfortunate that on 22 February William Jane at last died and added to the contest his canonry of Christ Church and the regius professorship of divinity. There can be no doubt that the preferments had been promised to George Smalridge, and that Anne and Archbishop Sharp regarded themselves as committed to him.[2] For some years he had been acting as Jane's deputy, and his firm tory opinions but peaceable disposition made him the candidate whom Christ Church itself wished to have. Indeed it was even rumoured that Dean Aldrich was ready to 'go over' to the government 'in hopes to secure Dr Sm[alridge] the Chair and that there are terms of accommodation offer'd'.[3] It can then only have been as a direct challenge to Harley's management of Oxford affairs that Marlborough and Godolphin now espoused the candidature of John Potter, one of Tenison's closest associates.[4] As the owner of the great palace of Blenheim, now rising at Woodstock, the duke seems to have chosen this moment to impose his influence on the university, though his notions were clearly derived from his duchess and her favoured whig informants in Oxford.[5] When the queen demurred at his recommendation the general exhibited irritation and personal pique. 'You know', he wrote to his wife, 'how often

---

[1] For a full account see G. V. Bennett, 'Robert Harley, the Godolphin ministry and the bishoprics crisis of 1707', *English Historical Rev.* lxxxii (1967).

[2] The queen 'was pleased graciously to remember the promises she had made to you and to his Lordship': Smalridge-[Harley], 12 Feb. [1707], HMC *Portland MSS* iv. 388. See also Godolphin-Marlborough [11 Apr. 1707], *The Marlborough-Godolphin Correspondence*, ed. H. L. Snyder (3 vols Oxford 1975) ii. 750.

[3] W. Bishop-Charlett, 17 Mar. 1707, MS Ballard 31, fo 61.

[4] Tenison-Harley, 28 Jan. 1707, HMC *Portland MSS* iv. 386. John Potter (1674-1747), m. Univ. 1688; fellow Linc. 1694-1706; regius prof. of divinity and canon Ch.Ch. 1707; abp of Canterbury 1737-47.

[5] 'I have been informed that the Dean of Carlisle [Atterbury], and Dr Smalridge, make compliments to Her Majesty, but at the same time are as violent as if they were governed by Lord Rochester': [Marlborough-Harley], 29 July 1706, HMC *Portland MSS* iv. 320; see also Hearne, *Collections* i. 104-5.

I spoke about Doctor Potter, and I do not hear that it is as yett done, though the consequence is, that if he has not the Professor's place, I will never more meadle with anything that may concern Oxford.'[1] As the struggle at court mounted in intensity the Oxford tories, moderate as well as zealot, looked to Harley to defend their cause.[2] By the autumn, when the queen's obstinacy still continued, the crisis had developed into a confrontation between Godolphin and the devious secretary. At one point, in November when Aldrich was desperately ill, it even began to look as though the contest was to extend to the deanery of Christ Church itself.[3] In the end, however, in January 1708, a compromise was reached. Anne obtained her two tory bishops but found herself forced to go back on her promise for the professorship. To the deep disgust of Christ Church and a widespread anger in Oxford, Smalridge was passed over in favour of the whiggish Dr Potter.[4] But for the whigs and Marlborough it was a dubious victory. Not only was the queen grievously offended by the way she had been treated but the duke had effectively ruined any future influence which he might have exercised in the university. When in 1709 the high stewardship was vacated by the death of Clarendon and Marlborough's name was suggested, the idea was treated with derision by the ordinary members of convocation.[5]

During the next two years the university passed through a time of great uncertainty. In February 1708 Harley was forced out of office and Godolphin had no recourse but to commit himself to the junto and their measures. When the whigs achieved a parliamentary majority at the general election in May, tories were deeply fearful that there would be a programme of legislation to strike down the privileges of the church and diminish its influence. In offering to forget all his past differences with Harley, William Bromley expressed the general view of his constituents 'that the gentlemen and clergy have everything to fear from some in power'.[6] Soon Henry St John and Simon Harcourt, both of whom had been turned out of their seats in parliament, were residing on their country estates near Oxford and building tory bridges by providing ample entertainment for university worthies.[7] The new party unity was cemented by a series of alarming rumours. In February 1709 there was

[1] Marlborough-duchess [12/23 June 1707], *Marlborough-Godolphin Correspondence* ii. 817.

[2] Smalridge-Harley, 23 May [1707], BL loan 29/194/82.

[3] Hearne-J. Barnes, 21 Nov. 1707, Bodl. MS Rawl. lett. 35, fo 223.

[4] Smalridge-[Harley], 8 Jan. 1708, HMC *Portland MSS* iv. 473; same-W. Gough, 17 Jan. 1708, *Illustrations of the Literary History of the Eighteenth Century*, ed. J. Nichols (8 vols London 1817-58) iii. 273; Tanner-Charlett, 23 Jan. 1708, MS Ballard 4, fo 87ʳ.

[5] Hearne-T. Smith, 19 Nov. 1709, Bodl. MS Rawl. lett. 38, fo 251.

[6] Bromley-[Harley], 18 Sept. 1708, HMC *Portland MSS* iv. 504.

[7] Ralph Bridges reported to Trumbull on 28 October 1708 that St John 'is like to grow honest agen, for he had the D. of C. Church and some of the Oxford Grandees at his country seat': Berks. Rec. Off. Trumbull MS liii.

much excitement when some whig MPs published a draft bill to take away the obligation imposed by some college statutes for fellows to enter into holy orders within a prescribed time. Even 'moderate' bishops and divines were convinced that their political allies had overreached themselves and were about to call forth a dangerous reaction from the clergy.[1] In the latter part of the year there were persistent reports of a project to repeal the test acts. Even Harley himself was not above initiating a rumour via the garrulous Canon Stratford that 'there has been a settled scheme laid of a visitation on both universitys also of all the Clergy to the old tune'.[2] And meanwhile the whig writers continued to lash and goad the university to a degree which was positively dangerous to their own cause. As one Christ Church man put it in writing to an old pupil who had become a 'moderate' bishop: 'nothing has exasperated the Clergy so much, as the insolent Liberties that have bin used against them from the Press. Tindal, Collins, De Foe, Tuchin, and that Gang have done the Whiggs more harm than good, infinitely.'[3] In such an atmosphere it was a considerable feat on the part of Vice-Chancellor Lancaster to maintain a firm control over university politics. With the assistance of the other heads, addresses acceptable to the government were voted, the extremists were rigorously excluded from the university pulpit and prominent whig undergraduates and dons were allowed to proceed to their degrees. But such repression of deeply felt opinion had its perils; and there were many signs that the eruption, when it came, would be sudden and fierce.

Few, however, seem to have predicted that the man to touch off the explosion would be Henry Sacheverell. By 1709 the Magdalen fellow was one of the failures of Oxford politics, and his incendiary activities within the university had virtually petered out. Many of his younger allies had left or been silenced by the heads of their houses. It seems clear that Sacheverell had accumulated far too many enemies both within his own college and in the university at large for continued residence at Oxford to be comfortable. His pushing ways and personal vanity, his violent talk in company and malicious stories about prominent university figures alienated even those who sympathized with his politics. His antagonism to Christ Church and to its candidates in elections was notorious. He was even reported to have said of one man *'that tho' an Angell should come from Heaven yet he would not be for him if Christ-Church appear'd in his*

---

[1] The move arose out of an obstinate attempt by the warden of All Souls to force Tindal and another whig to take orders or resign. See I. Doolittle, 'The organization of the colleges', p. 231 below; G. V. Bennett, 'University, society and church 1688-1714', p. 391 below; Whitelocke-Charlett, 24 Feb. 1709, MS Ballard 49, fo 166; W. Kennett-same, 26 Feb. MS Ballard 7, fo 124; Weymouth-same, 22 Mar., MS Ballard 10, fo 77.

[2] Harley-Stratford, 19 Dec. 1709, BL loan 29/171; see also Bridges-Trumbull, 7 Dec. 1709, Berks. Rec. Off. Trumbull MS liii.   [3] W. Wotton-Wake, 21 Mar. 1710, Wake MS 17, fo 243.

Behalf.[1] It was typical of the man that he should have put himself forward for his doctorate of divinity well out of his turn and thus have forced no fewer than nine other fellows of Magdalen to the expense of the degree rather than lose their seniority in the college.[2] But what seems to have given most offence to his contemporaries was the bloated language of his sermons, which contravened current conventions on literary style and all notions of decorum in the pulpit. If it is clear that his preaching was much to the taste of tory sheriffs, mayors and grand juries, it is equally apparent that it was anathema to his Oxford colleagues. After Provost Lancaster's accession to the vice-chancellorship the Magdalen orator had to remain silent or look outside the university for his pulpits and congregations. It was thus that in the spring of 1709 Sacheverell became a candidate for one of the two chaplaincies or preacherships at St Saviour's, Southwark, the great church at the southern end of London Bridge. He was strongly supported by Sir William Trumbull and Lord Weymouth, but his Oxford reputation preceded him: he was vexed to find himself faced with 'a terrible opposition by the Arch. Bp, the Fanaticks, and the Chrt Church men (Wondrous conjunction)'.[3] With wholly characteristic effrontery he called on Bromley at the house of commons to demand his support, but received what anyone else would have realized was a withering rebuke: 'Mr Bromley reply'd that there were sev'ral of our university which were candidates as well as he, and particularly one or two Xstchurchmen, and therefore he excused himself and they say referred him to Sir William Whitelocke.'[4] In fact, despite everything that Bromley, Whitelocke and Arthur Annesley could do to prevent it, Sacheverell was elected. And it was through his London connection that he was invited by Sir Samuel Garrard, the high-tory lord mayor, to preach in St Paul's cathedral on 5 November 1709.

The notorious sermon 'In perils among false brethren' was in many ways an irruption of Oxford politics on to the national scene. Its contents, involving wild denunciations of dissenters, 'moderate' clergy and secret enemies in high places, was hardly new.[5] As originally preached in St Mary's on 23 December 1705 it had attracted notice merely as an extreme example of the kind of harangue which the university had to endure week by week. But now, with the addition of some pointed references to Lord

---

[1] Hearne, *Collections* ii. 330.   [2] For this incident see Holmes, *Trial of Sacheverell*, 16.
[3] Bridges-Trumbull, 28 Mar. 1709, Berks. Rec. Off. Trumbull MS liii; Holmes 56-9.
[4] Bridges-Trumbull, 12 Apr. 1709, Berks. Rec. Off. Trumbull MS liii.
[5] For an eyewitness description of the sermon see J. Bennett-Hearne, 1 Dec. [1709], Bodl. MS Rawl. Lett. 2, fo 389: 'It lasted a full hour and a half, and was delivered with all the Assurance and Confidence, that violent Preacher is so remarkable for. I could not have imagined if I had not actually heard it my self, that so much Heat, Passion, Violence, and scurrilous Language, to say no worse of it, could have come from a Protestant Pulpit, much less from one that pretends to be a Member of the Church of England.'

Treasurer Godolphin, who was distinguished by use of his common nickname 'Volpone', it had power to set the world of politics into violent motion. The government's decision that Sacheverell should actually be impeached for 'high crimes and misdemeanours' put the official representatives of the university into grave difficulties. Vice-Chancellor Lancaster and the two burgesses, Bromley and Whitelocke, detested him and yet, as it became clear that the whigs intended to turn the trial into a grand debate on the meaning of the Revolution of 1688, it was essential for all tories to rally to the doctor's defence. It was important too that he should not be left to conduct his own case for fear that his unguarded statements might be exploited by the prosecution to fix a label of disloyalty, or even Jacobitism, on the whole tory party. And so, when on 13 December the whig spokesmen in the commons launched their attack, Bromley, Whitelocke and Annesley spoke strongly in defence of Anglican loyalist theory while pointedly avoiding any reference to Sacheverell or his personal character.[1] It was noted with wry amusement that the small group of lawyers and divines who now took the egregious doctor in charge was recruited mostly from the friends of Robert Harley and composed of Christ Church men. Simon Harcourt provided the legal expertise while Atterbury and Smalridge composed the speeches which Sacheverell spoke in his own defence. 'Those whom he has used brutally forget their past resentments on this occasion and visit him', reported Stratford in a letter full of amazement that there should be 'so solemn a prosecution for such a scribble'.[2] The situation was particularly trying for Vice-Chancellor Lancaster. His successful efforts to control extremism at Oxford had brought him into high favour with the Godolphin administration, and in May there was even talk of him for the bishopric of Chichester.[3] But now it was necessary for him to play his tory role, and on 14 December he took Sacheverell to the house of commons in his own coach and stood with him at the bar, accompanied by no fewer than a hundred black-gowned clergymen who had appeared to demonstrate their support. It was clearly gall and wormwood to Lancaster to have to pledge his personal fortune to the tune of three thousand pounds for Sacheverell's bail on 13 January.[4] He was not, however, to be pressed too far. When Sacheverell wrote in peremptory terms to demand a testimonial from the university as to his

[1] Lancaster-Charlett, 13 Dec. 1709, MS Ballard 21, fo 89; J. Perceval-W. Perceval, 10 Dec. 1709, HMC *Egmont MSS* ii. 244; Bridges-Trumbull, 20 Dec. 1709, Berks. Rec. Off. Trumbull MS liii.

[2] Stratford-[Harley], 21 Dec. 1709, HMC *Portland MSS* iv. 530.

[3] Bridges-Trumbull, 27 Apr. [1709], HMC *Downshire MSS* i pt 2, p. 874; Gibson-Wake, 17 May 1709, Wake MS 17, fo 211. See also Harley-Stratford, 19 Dec. 1709, BL loan 29/171 for Harley's malicious suggestion that Lancaster had conspired with Godolphin to bring a visitation on the university until the Sacheverell affair had ruined their plans, so that he found 'Lord Tr[easurer] will not own him, and [he] dare not let them know how far he countenanced that design'.

[4] Bridges-Trumbull, 13 Jan. 1710, Berks. Rec. Off. Trumbull MS liv.

life and good behaviour the vice-chancellor did not reply. 'I shall think my self most barbarously us'd', insisted the tory hero, 'to be Deny'd such a piece of Justice from a Body of People I now represent, and whose Interest so much depends on the Success of my Cause.'[1] But still there was silence. There were limits even to Lancaster's compliance with political necessity.

The great trial in Westminster hall could easily have been a disaster for the tories; in fact it effectively destroyed Godolphin's ministry. The managers of the impeachment had hoped to demonstrate that tory writing and preaching were inconsistent with the Revolution, the queen's title and the legal toleration granted to dissenters; instead defence counsel turned the trial into an emotional plea for the national church in the face of its enemies and detractors. As the news of each day's proceedings became known, popular excitement increased. Riots and demonstrations in the capital spread down into the cathedral cities and market towns, and before such a massive expression of public opinion the ministry crumbled and fell. The news that on 23 March Sacheverell had been found guilty but had escaped with a sentence so light as to be derisory was greeted in the country at large as a great deliverance. For the best part of a week the provinces gave themselves over to delirious rejoicing. In Oxford the tidings were received before the day was out. Soon bonfires were blazing in the High and the Broad and the mob burned whig books and an effigy of a dissenting preacher. Gown vied with town, and at one point 'the University resolved to defend Sacheverell with their blood'.[2] If it had not been for some firm action by the Recorder 'the advantages of a liberal education', as the vice-principal of St Edmund Hall put it dryly, 'would not have deterred the undergraduates from pulling down the meeting-house'.[3] In such an overheated atmosphere the vice-chancellor had to lie low. In fact he had recently made a bad miscalculation. Scarcely realizing that the Sacheverell affair would rebound on the government as it did, he and some other heads had decided to support the duke of Marlborough's candidate in a county by-election, and to do so against a known tory candidate. Now as the excitement mounted he came under vitriolic attack and, with Charlett and Delaune, was assailed as 'Turncoat', 'Weathercock' and 'Trimmer'.[4]

---

[1] Sacheverell-Lancaster, 5 Feb. 1710, MS Ballard 34, fo 78.

[2] [A. Harley]-E. Harley, 25 Mar. 1710, HMC *Portland MSS* iv. 539.

[3] R. Pearce-Kennett, 6 Apr. 1710, BL Lansdowne MS 1024, fo 210. Robert Pearce, m. Linc. 1698; MA SEH, vice-principal 1705. See also *High Church Display'd: being a compleat history of the affair of Dr. Sacheverell . . . in several letters to an English gentleman at the court of Hanover* (London 1711), 381; Hearne, *Collections* ii. 365.

[4] W. Bishop-Charlett, 14 Feb. 1710, MS Ballard 31, fo 78; Bridges-Trumbull, 27 Feb. 1710, Berks. Rec. Off. Trumbull MS liv; Hearne, *Collections* ii. 384. See also *The Oxfordshire Election* (London 1710), fo 78:

> We are told by the Town, that a Man of great Note,
> For the sake of Lawn-Sleeves is turning his Coat.

On 28 April Lancaster bowed to the wind and presided at a convocation which voted a loyal address promising the queen that if she would now dissolve parliament the University of Oxford would be ready to return members willing to secure the rights and safety of the church.[1] A fellow of an Oxford college had actually precipitated the collapse of an administration which had fought and virtually won the greatest war in the nation's history. It was an event long to be remembered by the politicians.

When in the summer of 1710 the great doctor set out on his triumphal progress across the midland shires he was eagerly awaited in Oxford. On 14 May William Tilly was once again permitted into the university pulpit to preach a sermon extravagant in his praise.[2] And the next day a vast throng of scholars and citizens made their way a mile out of the town to cheer the hero of the hour and escort him in. That evening he was magnificently entertained by the earl of Abingdon, with Thomas Rowney, MP for the city, the vice-chancellor and numerous heads of houses in attendance. Soon the doctor was reading daily prayers in Magdalen chapel before large congregations and graciously accepting the proceeds of collections towards his expenses.[3] Indeed the atmosphere of hero-worship was infectious and bore lesser men up upon the tide. On 2 June the fellows of Brasenose met and elected as their principal a young MA, Robert Shippen, who was distinguished by little other than the vehemence of his toryism and his vociferous support of Sacheverell.[4] When in late July the doctor at last ended his travels and settled down again on his fellowship at Magdalen there were many, including the great man himself, who thought that he would play a major part in university politics before being wafted away to some senior preferment. More percipient observers had a suspicion that the tory age, so eagerly looked for by the younger dons, would be slow in coming. Indeed, a first hint of where future political power was to lie came in early July when Robert Harley, not yet in any kind of office, recommended, through his agents Stratford and Gastrell, that an honorary doctorate should be conferred on an obscure divine named Samuel Palmer. According to the usual tests Palmer could hardly be

[1] OUA register of convocation 1704-30, fo 62ʳ⁻ᵛ. The address bewailed 'the danger of so many deluded souls as are misled into the damnable sin of schism'. It was attacked in the anonymous pamphlets *An Answer to the Address of the Oxford-University* (London 1710) and, more vehemently, *University Loyalty* (London 1710).

[2] W. Tilly, *A Return to our Former Good Old Principles and Practice the Only Way to Restore and Preserve our Peace* (Oxford 1710); Boyer, *Annals* ix. 202.

[3] Baynes-Charlett, 29 May 1710, MS Ballard 38, fo 207.

[4] Hearne, *Collections* iii. 8; R. W. Jeffery, 'History of the college 1690-1803' in *Brasenose Monographs* ii pt 1, no. XIII, pp 11-12; R. K[enyon]-Mrs Kenyon, 27 Oct. 1711, HMC *Kenyon MSS* 447. Robert Shippen (1675-1745), m. Merton 1693; fellow BNC 1699, principal 1710-45; vice-chancellor 1718-23.

considered a tory, and two of the heads were heard to complain in public that he was 'Mr Harley's convert, and that his converts were not to be trusted'. But the other members of the hebdomadal board were quick to back a Harleian candidate. When Charlett was approached for his support he at once replied that 'the kindness which he understood Mr Harley had for this gentleman was an obligation to him, without any other reason to serve him'. On the day when the degree came before convocation Sacheverell bustled up to Stratford on the floor of the house to announce 'that he, Dr Sacheverell, would engage the letter should pass' but Stratford was quietly contemptuous. He had already fixed the heads in Harley's name and this, he knew, was what counted. When the vote was taken 'the Heads and Doctors, who were above twenty, were unanimous for him. There was opposition, but to no purpose, amongst the Masters.'[1] The truth was that once again Oxford was to experience the devious management of Robert Harley.

The new ministry, as it emerged in the autumn of 1710, was the product not so much of the great Sacheverell excitement as of a quiet palace revolution. The queen had deeply resented the bullying to which she had been subjected by Godolphin and the whigs yet she had no intention, in escaping from them, of putting herself into the hands of the tories. Indeed Harley now became chief minister principally on the basis that he would work to preserve her freedom and a 'moderate scheme' in politics. It is clear that his position depended wholly upon her, and that he coerced her at his peril.[2] And so, in spite of a massive tory majority in the commons elected in November 1710, the minister had to refuse thoroughgoing tory measures when these were pressed upon him. In particular the queen was adamant in matters which concerned the church and ecclesiastical preferment. During the trial she had refused publicly to express any opinion about Sacheverell but privately in conversation with her trusted physician she revealed that she had actually wanted the doctor to be punished and that she thought him 'foolish' for his progresses round the country.[3] She was visibly offended by the high-flying expressions of some of the addresses presented to her. Her face was set like a flint against the promotion of any of the tory political divines, whether Sacheverell, Atterbury or Swift. And when it came to devising a policy for the universities she imposed severe restraints on her minister. Certainly no man was in a better position to establish a complete supremacy in Oxford. Even old Lord Rochester, now a surprising

[1] Stratford-E. Harley, 21-2 July 1710, HMC *Portland MSS* vii. 5-6. Virtually all the letters in this volume are from Stratford to Robert Harley's son Edward (1689-1741, from 1724 2nd e. of Oxford; m. Ch.Ch. 1707).

[2] For a convincing account of the queen's relationship with Harley see E. Gregg, *Queen Anne* (London 1980), ch. 12.

[3] *The Diary of Sir David Hamilton 1709-1714*, ed. P. Roberts (Oxford 1975), 6, 17.

convert to moderation and comfortably settled in as lord president of
the council, offered no challenge. When in May 1711 Harley became
lord treasurer and chose the title earl of Oxford his intentions seemed
clear. But, denied a free hand by the queen, he could work only by
hints, promises and excuses for delay rather than by a systematic
distribution of patronage. To the despair of William Bromley, who
pressed him continually on behalf of his constituents, he left bishoprics, deaneries and valuable crown livings vacant for months, and even
years, on end; and then at last filled them with pious but colourless
'moderate' tories out of the troop of Archbishop Sharp's protégés. This
curious paralysis in Oxford affairs became increasingly inexplicable to
the political world, and even led other ministers to attempt to fill the
vacuum. From the very formation of the administration there was
tension between the prime minister and two of his colleagues who
argued for a clear tory scheme: Simon Harcourt, the lord keeper, and
Henry St John, the secretary of state. Both had close Oxford connections, and the university was a tempting sphere in which to challenge
the treasurer's 'moderation'. Harcourt, indeed, was one of the great
parvenus of Oxfordshire society. His enormous earnings at the bar, put
into purchases of real estate at Cokethorpe, Nuneham and elsewhere,
had made him one of the largest local landowners. Down to 1704 he
had made repeated attempts to persuade various Oxford pundits to
put him up for a university seat in parliament.[1] Now, as lord keeper, he
was the master of a mass of minor patronage and determined to use it
to establish his influence.

It was unfortunate for Harley that, within a few weeks of the formation of his ministry, Henry Aldrich died and thereby vacated the magnificent deanery of Christ Church. As the key-position in university politics
its disposal could not be anything other than a crucial test of the government's ecclesiastical policy. It had been promised to Francis Atterbury as
long previously as 1704, and his assiduous service to Harley since that
time, and his more recent management of Sacheverell during the trial,
made it hard to deny his claim, even though his reputation for ecclesiastical assertiveness and the appalling quarrels in which he had been
involved as dean of Carlisle made him wholly unwelcome to the queen.[2]
On her behalf the archbishop of York pressed for the appointment of the
peaceable George Smalridge, who had been passed over for the professorship in 1708, while Christ Church signalled as clearly as possible
that this was the man the college would prefer.[3] Obviously Harley

[1] See [Harcourt-Harley] 29 July 1704, HMC *Portland MSS* iv. 105.
[2] 'God knows, I am far from being fond of that Deanry. But it hath been promised me ever since I
was Dean of Carlisle': Atterbury-Trelawny [Nov. 1707], *Correspondence of Atterbury* ed. Nichols i. 446.
[3] 'A.B. of York's endeavours failing for Dr Smalridge, His Grace acquainted me that Dr Att. was to

himself had every reason not to promote a man to whom he had given assurances of tory renewal which now could not be fulfilled. And so, when Harcourt, St John and Bromley took up Atterbury's cause, the minister was in a serious dilemma. There was nothing for it but pro-crastination, and a soothing message was circulated that 'the Queen will not dispose of the Deanery of Cht Chh as yet, till something falls, that she may at the same time please both the Candidates and Their friends'.[1] There were even hints that Atterbury was to be kept for some better pre-ferment—a bishopric or even the primacy itself if the ailing Tenison should die.[2] But by the summer the pretence had worn thin and a verit-able struggle was seen to be taking place at court. Neither Harcourt nor St John made any attempt to disguise the fact that their support for Atterbury was in protest against the obvious failure of Lord Oxford to promote any of the committed high-church divines. On visits down to Oxfordshire Harcourt whetted the appetites of his university guests with plans for a new distribution of preferment: not just the deanery for Atterbury but an Irish bishopric for Delaune, something for Sacheverell and a scheme to annex cathedral prebends in the crown's gift to some of the poorer headships.[3] Soon impatience in the university could not be contained, and on 9 July William Tilly preached in St Mary's an Act sermon which took the form of an elaborate eulogy of Sacheverell and a furious attack on those who had not yet given him preferment.[4] At last on 12 August at Windsor Mr Secretary St John brought matters to a head by presenting the queen and treasurer with an ultimatum, and with the peace negotiations at a crucial stage they were not prepared to risk his resignation. On 28 August, albeit with the greatest reluctance, Anne signed the warrant by which Atterbury became dean of Christ Church. As Harcourt's son Simon put it: 'the point was gained at last.'[5] As some palliative to the queen's feelings Smalridge was appointed to a vacant canonry of Christ Church and given the deanery of Carlisle. But the advent of a tory activist as formidable as Atterbury to the headship of the largest college in Oxford boded ill for moderation in university politics.

   During the next two years Dean Atterbury worked at an ambitious

be removed from the Deanery of Carlisle to that of Christ Church': 'Nicolson's diaries' pt 6, p. 141 (18 Dec. 1710). See also H. Bedford-Hearne, 27 Jan. 1711, Bodl. MS Rawl. lett. 2, fo 283; T. Rowney-Charlett, 8 Feb. 1711, MS Ballard 38, fo 192.

   [1] W. Bishop-Charlett, 6 Jan. 1711, MS Ballard 31, fo 86.
   [2] Kennett-S. Blackwell, 30 Dec. 1710, 13 Jan. 1711, BL Lansdowne MS 1013, fos 140, 142; HMC *Portland MSS* vii. 26.
   [3] HMC *Portland MSS* vii. 29, 33, 35, 45.
   [4] Ibid. 39; Hearne, *Collections* iii. 192.
   [5] Bennett, *Tory Crisis* 142-3; Atterbury-Weymouth, 30 Aug. 1711, Longleat House, Thynne MS xii, fo 297; Weymouth-Charlett, 7 Sept. 1711, MS Ballard 10, fo 79. Simon Harcourt (1685-1720), m. Ch.Ch. 1702; hon. MA 1712; MP Wallingford 1710-13, Abingdon 1713-14.

scheme to reshape and manage university politics. It was an uncertain time for Lord Oxford with serious difficulties in parliament in the winter of 1711 and an increasing challenge to his authority within the ministry itself. While he attempted to procrastinate over appointments, Harcourt and St John argued for a 'thorough' tory regime and a purging of whigs and 'moderates' from office. It was clear that their claim to speak for the 'Church of England interest' would have much greater credibility if they could mobilize powerful support for their policies from Oxford and its clergy; and this the dean now set out to secure. In the light of the bitter disputes which ensued it would be easy to consider his activities as mere clerical quarrelsomeness, and yet his schemes were not only plausible but had every likelihood of success. Atterbury was prolocutor of the lower house of convocation and his reputation as an earnest fighter for the rights of the clergy was important in attracting the ordinary MAs to his cause. At least in the beginning his campaign had the approval of his friend William Bromley, now as speaker of the house of commons at the height of his influence in the tory party. The voting strength of Christ Church was a useful base from which to work and the prospect that he and Harcourt would now become the distributors of valuable ecclesiastical preferment was sure to be tempting to many heads of houses. Indeed, to make the point that a formidable new interest had arrived upon the Oxford scene, the dean's installation at Christ Church was made an occasion of public splendour. The lord keeper came in state, bearing the great seal, tory peers and politicians were out in full force, and Mr Speaker Bromley's son was commissioned to bear his father's felicitations.[1] At the feast, as his university guests came up to greet him, Atterbury was free in offering them his interest with the ministers.[2] He was, of course, not unaware that his advent would be taken as a direct challenge to those heads who had become accustomed to managing the university's affairs. Since October 1710 the vice-chancellor had been the spineless and ineffective Warden Braithwaite of New College but behind him stood the formidable figure of his predecessor, Provost Lancaster. Lancaster was in many ways a disappointed man, often ill after a fall in the new building of Queen's, and anxious to re-establish himself with the government. Many of the heads still took their lead from him, and he remained a skilled operator in the business of the hebdomadal board. It was inevitable that he and Atterbury would soon clash, and in November the dean seemed almost to be relishing the prospect. As Canon Stratford expressed it in his usual pungent style: 'He owns he designs upon the first opportunity he can meet with to attack Lancaster. They are as well met as any two I know.'[3]

[1] Thomas Bromley (1693-1716), m. Ch.Ch. 1710; Hon. MA 1716.
[2] See Bennett, 144-7; HMC *Portland MSS* vii. 62; Hearne, *Collections* iii. 236-8.
[3] HMC *Portland MSS* vii. 68 (5 Nov. 1711).

Atterbury's principal need was to put together a group of heads of houses who would follow his lead on the hebdomadal board and who could bring their college votes into the convocation house for university elections. He knew quite well that the more cautious heads like Turner or Charlett would wish to stand neutral in a contest which seemed to reflect rivalry among the queen's ministers, but he had a strategy which was not without its ingenuity. He aimed to change the usual pattern of Oxford politics by uniting the voting strengths of Christ Church and Magdalen, hitherto thought to be implacable enemies; and to this end he made much of Sacheverell, now once again in residence on his fellowship. The great doctor was entertained to dinner, invited in to consultations and generally treated as though he was one of the select company of heads; he and the dean took to travelling up to London at the same times and were often seen in animated conversation.[1] But, even if Sacheverell could deliver the votes of the fellows of Magdalen, Atterbury had to have other heads in his party. He could be sure of the president of St John's: Delaune was now in desperate financial straits and in danger of having his income sequestered for bankruptcy; he lived in hope that Harcourt would be able to fulfil his promises about rich livings and Irish bishoprics. But to entice other heads the dean needed something more, and in November he revived talk of the lord keeper's plan to annex certain valuable cathedral prebends to some of the poorer headships. As Stratford put it succinctly:

The Lord Keeper is to ask the Queen's leave, and our Dean is to have the choosing of the Colleges. The end of this is too plain to need to be mentioned. It must draw applications to him, to be sure too before the places are determined, and is to make his Lordship absolute here, where our Governor is to be his Viceroy.[2]

But, in spite of all such temptations, only two other heads were drawn into the dean's schemes. Jonathan Edwards of Jesus had been closely associated with Atterbury in the early days of the convocation controversy; he was influential among the other members of the hebdomadal board and his college was strong in resident MAs, but he was now old and decayed in health. Robert Shippen of Brasenose was a tory zealot and closely linked to Sacheverell; he was certainly not immune to the lure of prebends and livings. As Stratford pointed out, it was not an entirely savoury alliance: 'By Sacheverell we hope to make Magdalen and Christ Church go together. Delaune is reckoned as dependent on us, and we court Shippen, because so corrupt a man will certainly fall in, if we can make him hope to find his own account in it. But these noble allies put me in mind of Hoppy and Toppy.'[3] In theory Atterbury could command a useful body of votes in convocation but, as he attempted to

---

[1] Ibid. 73, 76, 79.   [2] Ibid. 75 (17 Nov. 1711).   [3] Ibid. 72 (13 Nov. 1711).

intervene in university business, he found himself opposed and thwarted by men who were tough and experienced university politicians. His clashes with Lancaster became proverbial.[1] While the feeble Thomas Braithwaite was vice-chancellor the dean had some little success, but when Braithwaite left Oxford in 1712 for the lusher pastures of the wardenship of Winchester the vice-chancellorship came to a man of very different personality. Bernard Gardiner of All Souls had survived the bitter internal disputes of his own college remarkably unscathed, and he now joined with Lancaster in a formidable partnership to put down the dean of Christ Church, whose inexperience and frequent absences from Oxford made him no match for two such old campaigners. In May 1712 together they inflicted a resounding public defeat on him by exploiting a little-known provision in the statutes to prevent his being elected curator of the theatre.[2]

Atterbury's increasing weakness in university affairs was derived in large part from a collapse of his position within his own college. It is unfortunate that the story of the titanic quarrels at Christ Church in 1712 depends wholly on the bitterly partisan letters of William Stratford, who was himself a leading actor in the tragicomedy.[3] The impression conveyed is that the dean acted as a kind of madman, was at all times unreasonable, and himself received no provocation. Certainly Atterbury was of a volatile disposition and easily provoked to arbitrary measures by any appearance of opposition. His career at Carlisle and subsequently at Westminster is proof enough of that. It is apparent too that at Christ Church he was always uneasy in the presence of George Smalridge, for whom the college had expressed so decided a preference. But the aggression was not wholly on his side. Even before his installation Stratford, Gastrell and Smalridge were making ready for resistance, and in Stratford they had a spokesman who had conceived an intense personal antagonism to the dean. The three canons were unmistakably Lord Oxford's agents in the university and thought Atterbury ungrateful and treacherous to have transferred his allegiance to Harcourt and St John. Every detail of the quarrels was now reported back to the treasurer via his son Edward, Lord Harley. At first Atterbury made great efforts to secure his popularity in Christ Church: he was generous in entertaining the Students and donated prizes to revive a spirit of literary emulation.

[1] For an exchange after which Lancaster 'went off with a Flea in his Ear' see Hearne, *Collections* ii. 290.
[2] Ibid. 349. For Gardiner see M. Burrows, *Worthies of All Souls* (London 1874), 347 ff;for the alliance of Gardiner and Lancaster see the satire in the *Spectator* no. 43 (19 Apr. 1711) where they are referred to by their common nicknames, 'Dominic' and 'Slyboots'.
[3] See Bennett, *Tory Crisis*, ch. 8 for a fuller account. For a characterization of Stratford as 'a person of great intrigue and art' by another who had fallen foul of him see Lancaster-Charlett, 11 June 1709, MS Ballard 21, fo 87.

His mistake was at an early stage to seek to get into his own hands control over the college's massive ecclesiastical patronage and to do so on grounds which were legally dubious. Within months this dispute had escalated into a complex struggle which ranged over financial mismanagement, relations with tenants and the dismissal of the chapter clerk.[1] By December relations between the dean and his colleagues had reached deadlock; he refused to attend chapters, sign any document or even allow money to be paid out of the treasury. Whatever wrongs were suffered by the Harleian canons at the hands of their imperious head, the outcome was not entirely to Lord Oxford's disadvantage. Atterbury found himself 'blasted over all England', and even allies like Harcourt and Bromley were unnerved by some of the reports.[2] Soon the college was deeply divided, with many of the Students ranged behind Smalridge. When at the end of November Atterbury visited the common room to request their vote for his candidate in a university election he was shocked to discover that 'Half the students are resolved to vote with the Canons against the Dean'. To his utter chagrin he had to withdraw his man to prevent 'that which never happend before since our foundation, a division of the College upon a public election'.[3]

The Harcourt–Atterbury scheme was now in danger of collapse. In part this was a result of the dean's personal failures but it was due even more to their inability to deliver the government patronage which they had so confidently held out before the heads. Indeed it gradually became apparent that the queen and the treasurer had imposed a total ban on preferment for any Oxford divine. If Anne had been forced to appoint Atterbury rather than Smalridge, she had no intention of promoting anyone else whom she thought tainted with tory extremism. Even when Lord Oxford requested the deanery of Wells for Jonathan Swift she refused.[4] At first Harcourt and Bromley were merely disconcerted that their Oxford recommendations were set aside by the treasurer with his usual excuses and involved talk, but by the autumn of 1712 they had begun to exhibit anger and irritation. The lord keeper pleaded continually for Sacheverell and Delaune, while the speaker lost all patience when his modest plea for a prebend for Charlett was put off. He asked Lord Oxford to consider the discontent in the university 'that neither he nor any of the heads of Colleges . . . have been taken notice of,

<hr />

[1] Hearne, *Collections* iv. 36, 41; Gibson–Nicolson, 15 Nov. 1712, copy in Bodl. MS Add. A. 269, fo 18; Kennett–Wake, 7 Oct. 1712, Wake MS 17, fo 340; Smalridge–[Harley] [31 Oct. 1712], HMC *Portland MSS* vii. 103.

[2] [Bromley–Stratford] 29 Sept. 1712, HMC *Portland MSS* vii. 93; Harcourt–Oxford, 3 Dec. 1712, BL loan 29/138/(5).

[3] HMC *Portland MSS* vii. 117-18 (2 Dec. 1712).

[4] *Diary of Hamilton*, ed. Roberts, pp. 41, 43, 47, 54; J. Swift, *Journal to Stella*, ed. H. Williams (2 vols Oxford 1958) ii. 665.

which is discouraging to them and to the University, and exposes them to some contempt'.[1] By the end of the year Bromley was forced to the unhappy conclusion that this stop on preferment for the Oxford worthies was a deliberate act of policy.[2] The lord keeper was, however, desperately reluctant to abandon his plans. Since 1710 he had nurtured the hope that his own position in Oxford might be established by the election of his son Simon as university burgess. Bromley's position was, of course, massively secure, but at the time of the next general election in the summer of 1713 Sir William Whitelocke would be 78 years of age. Even in 1710 Warden Gardiner had expressed the hope that his 'Age and the Compliments already payd him by the Universitye' might induce him to retire in favour of George Clarke.[3] Now at the end of 1712 there was a small flurry of activity in the deanery in order to put up 'Young Sim' Harcourt. The lord keeper himself appeared and it was given out that the consultations had concerned Whitelocke: that he was 'old, that he will not desire to stand again, that if he should it would not be proper to choose on past service, and where can we choose better than Mr Harcourt?'[4] The young man was proposed for an MA degree, and presented in a speech by Atterbury which laid significant stress on his services as MP for Wallingford since 1710. Meanwhile the lord keeper pressed on with a new attempt to recruit some heads to his cause. There was again talk of annexing prebends to certain headships, and temptation was dangled before Colwell Brickenden, master of Pembroke, George Carter, provost of Oriel and John Baron, master of Balliol.[5] But the best hope of securing a compliant head was provided by the case of Worcester College. The settlement of Sir Thomas Cookes's benefaction had been delayed for over a decade by dispute as to which hall or college was to be the recipient. Lancaster as vice-chancellor had done something to expedite matters, and a committee had at last agreed that Magdalen Hall was the appropriate object of the baronet's confused bequest.[6] But in November 1712 by a decree in chancery Harcourt set aside the heads' award and fixed the endowment on Gloucester Hall. The immediate political implication of the judgement was seen a few weeks later when

[1] Bromley-[Oxford], 27 Oct. 1712, HMC *Portland MSS* v. 240. See also [Harcourt-Oxford] 22 Oct. and 24 Nov. 1712, ibid. 239, 247: 'Let me beg you to remember Dr Sacheverell.'

[2] Bromley-Charlett, 27 Oct. and 24 Nov. 1712, MS Ballard 38, fos 156, 158.

[3] Gardiner-Charlett, 27 June 1710, MS Ballard 20, fo 22.

[4] HMC *Portland MSS* vii. 121 (8 Dec. 1712).

[5] See HMC *Portland MSS* vii. 171 (16 Nov. 1713). Colwell Brickenden (1664-1714), m. Pemb. 1680, master 1710-14. George Carter (1673-1727), m. Univ. 1690; fellow Oriel 1694, provost 1708-27. Carter was a known whig but his desire for preferment led-St John (now Visc. Bolingbroke) to think he could be used: Bolingbroke-M. Prior, 3 Mar. 1713, *Letters and Correspondence of Bolingbroke*, ed. G. Parke (2 vols London 1798) ii. 285. John Baron (1670-1722), m. Balliol 1686, master 1705-22; vice-chancellor 1715-18.

[6] Lancaster-Charlett, 1 and 10 May 1707, MS Ballard 21, fos 69, 70; HMC *Seventh Report*, 782; L. S. Sutherland, 'The foundation of Worcester College, Oxford', *Oxoniensia* xliv (1979).

the lord keeper's chaplain, Richard Blechynden, was appointed principal of the hall and thus set to be the first provost of the new Worcester College. 'I own this to be very dexterous in Lord Keeper' was Canon Stratford's grudging acknowledgement.[1]

In the summer of 1713, however, as preparations for the general election got under way, Harcourt was forced to abandon all his Oxford ambitions. At Westminster the struggle for power within the ministry was mounting in intensity, and it was apparent that soon a decision would be taken at court rather than in parliament or in the remoter arena of the university. Atterbury now spent most of his time in London or at Windsor in close consultation with his friends; the deadlock at Christ Church was so notorious that he was desperate for a bishopric which would allow him to retreat in some semblance of order from a scene which he had so comprehensively mismanaged. Various other actors ceased to reside in Oxford, notably Sacheverell and Tilly. In April, after constant agitation, Harcourt obtained permission from the queen to present the great high-church doctor to the rich living of St Andrew's, Holborn, one of the benefices in the lord chancellor's gift. Immediately Sacheverell resigned his Magdalen fellowship and removed himself to London. And at last in June, at a time of great parliamentary crisis, Harcourt and St John forced the queen and the treasurer to end the misery at Christ Church by promoting Atterbury to the bishopric of Rochester and the deanery of Westminster. 'I never knew the queen do anything with so much reluctancy', recalled Lord Dartmouth, '... she said, Lord Harcourt had answered for his behaviour, and she had lately disobliged him, by refusing the like request for Dr Sacheverel, and found if she did not grant this, she must break with him quite.'[2] But if the lord chancellor had acquired a new ally in the lords, Atterbury's departure meant that there was no one to press 'Young Simkins's' candidature for the university seat. Smalridge succeeded to the deanery, and there was now little assistance to be expected from Christ Church; while the vice-chancellor and Lancaster were implacable in their hostility. Indeed in order totally to block Harcourt, Gardiner withdrew George Clarke's nomination and placed all his influence behind the re-election of White-locke. That ancient knight was not a little surprised to find himself invited to stand again by men who only recently had been plotting his involuntary retirement.[3] To Harcourt's anger he had difficulty in finding his son a seat at all. The Oxfordshire gentry, egged on by Clarke, refused to have him for the county and the seat at Wallingford which he had

[1] HMC *Portland MSS* vii. 115; see also ibid. 100, 126. Richard Blechynden (1668-1736), m. 1685 St John's; principal Gloucester Hall 1712-14; provost Worc. 1714-36.

[2] G. Burnet, *The History of My Own Time* [ed. M. J. Routh] (6 vols Oxford 1823) vi. 165.

[3] HMC *Portland MSS* vii. 139-53; Whitelocke-Turner, 1 Nov. 1713, Bodl. MS Rawl. lett. 92, fo 589.

held since 1710 appeared too unsafe to risk a contest. Eventually the young man was glad to be returned for his father's old seat at Abingdon. Such a fiasco marked the effective end of Harcourt's attempt to set himself up as the university's political patron.

In the last year of the queen's life Oxford fell back into a dull acceptance of the fact that it could do nothing to affect the course of politics. In the late summer the nation went to the polls to give the tories a victory even greater than that of 1710. Once again the clergy educated at Oxford exerted themselves in county and borough to return 'church' candidates; and their successes were reported back to their old colleges in glowing terms. Bromley who, with Whitelocke, was returned unopposed on 25 August was delighted to acknowledge that the results from the constituencies around Oxford were in large measure due to the vigorous electioneering of the clergy.[1] But, while enthusiasm remained strong among the ordinary squires and parsons, the leadership of the tory cause fell into disarray. As the queen's health decayed the question of the succession assumed alarming proportions, and was deeply divisive. In Oxford party zeal continued strongly among the MAs but there was no one among the heads to lead them. At Christ Church Smalridge succeeded in restoring order in the college but in August he received the bishopric of Bristol and the lord almonership to be held with his deanery. Thereafter he had little time to devote to university politics, and his interventions were rare and mostly unsuccessful. Power came to rest with a triumvirate of Gardiner, Lancaster and Charlett, who fixed elections, dealt firmly with dissidents, and waited patiently to see what would emerge when the queen at last died.[2]

It was not, of course, entirely possible to silence the lower orders, but the expression of their opinion, when it came, was anonymous and scurrilous. At the Act in the Sheldonian in July the vice-chancellor attempted to avoid any expression of politics by providing some excellent music and by banning the Terrae-Filius, the irreverent speechmaker who recited a drolling comment on the events and personalities of the past year. But, to Gardiner's intense discomfort, just as he was about to be readmitted to office in the following October, a pamphlet was sold in the streets which purported to be the suppressed Terrae-Filius speech.[3] He, Lancaster and Charlett were ridiculed as notorious tyrants within the walls of their own colleges but outside them political weathercocks, willing to turn with any change in the wind, and sell out

[1] Bromley-Charlett, 17 Sept. 1713, MS Ballard 38, fo 162. J. Johnson-Charlett, 5 Sept. 1713, MS Ballard 15, fo 96. In the government changes of the summer of 1713 Bromley became secretary of state but was still not successful in obtaining any preferment for Charlett.
[2] Hearne, *Collections* iv. 302, 329.
[3] *The Speech that was intended to have been spoken by the Terrae-Filius* (London 1713); Hearne, *Collections* iv. 243; HMC *Portland MSS* vii. 151.

church and university. Reference was made to a cabal of heads who met 'to settle the Church, disturb the University, and of late to abuse L — d Chance — r H — t'. Other Oxford trimmers were savaged, and not least John Cobb, warden of New College, a young man of minuscule scholarship whom the fellows had elected in 1712.

> In time ('tis much) But who can tell?
> The learned *Cobb* may learn to spell?[1]

The shafts found their mark. In solemn wrath, after his oration, Gardiner proposed that 'this Scandalous Libel' should be ceremonially burned in the schools quadrangle. But, to his chagrin and in spite of speeches from various heads, the motion was barely passed, and then only when the proctors arbitrarily assessed the strength of the shouts on both sides and refused a count when many called out for it.[2] Thereafter nothing stirred. At the end of October it was publicly announced that prebends of Rochester and Gloucester had been annexed to the headships of Oriel and Pembroke, but this seemed like an echo of a battle long ago fought and lost.[3] In the following July Lord Chancellor Harcourt hurried on the formal inauguration of the new Worcester College in fear that the impending revolution in politics might deprive him of any future connection with the university.[4] When Anne died on 1 August 1714 her death was the end of an era in Oxford. The toryism of the place was not dead but it slept. The queen's determined moderation and the effective management of her ministers had weakened it and so deprived it of leadership that now it stood virtually defenceless before the onset of the iron age of whig patronage.

---

[1] *Speech by the Terrae-Filius*, 22. John Cobb (1678-1725), m. New College 1697, warden 1712-20.

[2] Hearne, *Collections* iv. 243; Gardiner-Charlett, 4 Oct. 1713, MS Ballard 20, fo 23, *The University Miscellany, or More Burning Work for the Oxford Convocation* (Oxford 1713).

[3] Bridges-Trumbull, 29 Oct. [1713], Berks. Rec. Off. Trumbull Add. MS 134; HMC *Portland MSS* vii. 171.

[4] Harley-[Oxford], 15 July 1714, HMC *Portland MSS* v. 472.

4

Tories and Jacobites 1714-1751

P. LANGFORD

FOR many contemporaries Oxford's political position under the first two Hanoverians was a simple and straightforward one, that of committed and even traitorous opposition to the established regime. Historians have learned to distinguish between the opposition and the treason, but the essential outline of the traditional picture remains largely unchanged. That picture was perhaps most memorably presented in the elder Pitt's celebrated outburst in the house of commons in December 1754. In reply to a speech by one of the university's representatives, Sir Roger Newdigate, Pitt declared:

That he himself (Mr P—) had lately in Oxford been witness to what would have been high Treason anywhere else. He saw and heard, but this last summer, several persons of rank and standing in the University, walk publicly along the streets singing *God bless Great J — our King* &c. &c. ... He also saw the Pretender's Picture (or Print) in the printshops' windows, &c. This indeed he did not know at first, never having been at Rome to see the original as some others had, but he soon found it out by the civility of the Master of the shop and a latin line, and a half at the bottom, &c. The very streets were paved with Jacobitism, &c. He ran a very humorous and just comparison, betwixt our Alma Mater and an Old Hen—sitting upon and hatching two sorts of eggs, and her behaviour when the Ducklings, disregarding her care, admonitions, and example, took to an element so unnatural to her as water is.[1]

Exaggerated though such observations were, they were entirely compatible with the generally received view of the time. Even so the truth was less simple. Like most institutions, Oxford was very much more complex than the image which contemporaries entertained of it, and among the complexities were features which qualified, if they did not entirely vitiate, the customary generalizations.

As an integral part of the church the university was subject to all the currents and cross-currents of political opinion, intellectual fashion and

---

[1] R. Blacow-T. Bray, 3 Dec. 1754, Bray MSS. For other accounts see B. Williams, *The Life of William Pitt* (2 vols London 1913) i. 7, 257-8. William Pitt (1708-78), from 1766 1st e. of Chatham; m. Trin. 1727. Sir Roger Newdigate (1719-1806), from 1734 5th bt; m. Univ. 1736; MP Oxford Univ. 1750-80.

vested interest which characterized the eighteenth-century establishment. If anything, the conflicting tendencies implicit in such an institution were actually aggravated by the peculiar concentration in one
place of theological or at any rate polemical conflict, and of narrow but
often desperate placemanship and ambition. The political climate of this
hot-house might be described in terms of whig versus tory, low church
versus high church, court versus country, radical versus reactionary, or in
other ways which imply a relatively clear-cut division. But in practice
such terminology conceals more than it illuminates. In an age that was
deeply divided, deeply factious, deeply litigious, Oxford's politics were
considerably more complicated than that. Within the colleges there
were the incessant disputes which produced some of the classic battles
of the university's history; for instance the notorious struggles over the
statutes of All Souls, University College and Oriel, though these were
only the most spectacular of many such confrontations. Within the university at large there were the obvious tensions between colleges,
between political or patronage groups, above all between the heads of
houses on the one hand, and the younger MAs on the other, revealed
not only in such celebrated affairs as the parliamentary election of 1722,
but more frequently and with equal vituperation in purely internal contests such as that over the conferment of a degree on Archbishop Wake's
librarian David Wilkins in 1716, or that concerning the election of a curator of the Sheldonian Theatre, in 1723.[1] Nicholas Amhurst's complaint
about the universal nature of faction at Oxford was not entirely wide of
the mark: '. . . we see Whigs engag'd against Whigs, Tories against Tories,
masters against Doctors and Heads of Colleges, senior Fellows against
junior Fellows, one College against another College, and many Colleges
against themselves'.[2]

With the world outside Oxford's narrow affairs there were equally confusing amities and animosities. There was the city with its easily agitated
populace and its more predictable but often divided corporation, for
much of the eighteenth century strongly influenced by the university,
causing Swift to reflect that this was the great age of the dominance of
gown over town: 'For the Vicechancellor hath more power than the
Mayor, and indeed the University governs the City, although the latter in
my time was often disposed to be turbulent.'[3] Such testimony is
supported by the university's interference in municipal politics, often
with decisive results, for instance in 1721 in procuring the election of

[1] For Wilkins (1685-1745, a Prussian exile who was librarian at Lambeth 1715-18) see Smalridge–
Wake, 4 June 1716, Wake MS 20, fos 98-100; Hearne, *Collections* vi. 51, 98. For the Sheldonian
election see Hearne viii. 51.
[2] [N. Amhurst,] *Terrae-Filius* (52 nos. London Jan.-July 1721) no. viii (4-8 Feb. 1721). Nicholas
Amhurst (1697-1742), m. St John's 1716, expelled 1719.
[3] *The Correspondence of Jonathan Swift*, ed. H. Williams (5 vols Oxford 1963-5) iv. 274.

a former Student of Christ Church to the recordership against a strong
whig candidate from the city, 'an avow'd Enemy' of the university.[1] Outside the city Oxford naturally looked north to the old cavaliering shires
of Oxfordshire, Warwickshire and Northamptonshire, even Staffordshire, rather than south to Berkshire, east to the metropolis or west to
Gloucestershire. Oxfordshire itself boasted a far from negligible whiggish element based upon the Marlborough interest, but when the tory
gentry entered Oxford for their annual dinner, the High Borlace, or
when parliamentary candidates were needed for the tory interest in the
city and university there was little doubt where the natural allegiance of
the university lay. And finally there was the government itself, not subject in this period to quite the bitter party disputes of the early
eighteenth century, but by no means predictable even for its friends. The
interaction of local interest and national politics, and the varying concern of the major politicians with the church or with Oxford, not to say
the divisions of the court itself, all made a straightforward attitude of
either friendship or hostility to ministers a less simple matter than might
have been supposed. And thanks to the natural fascination of the newspapers with all this, 'the Nation having always an Eye to what passes in
the University',[2] and still more to the unwavering readiness of Oxford
men to put pen to paper, there was no shortage of incendiary material to
inflame or at least keep flickering this infinitely combustible mass.

The framework within which these patterns of conflict were to
operate in the early Hanoverian period was set in definitive and controversial fashion almost as soon as George I set foot in his new kingdom. In retrospect the importance of the years 1714 to 1717 is clear,
though contemporaries, used to the abrupt changes of political fortune
of the post-Revolution period, could hardly have been aware of that
importance. The university's conduct during these years permanently
discredited it with the monarchs and ministers who were to rule
England for nearly half a century, while the conduct of the latter
similarly alienated the most influential sectors of Oxford opinion. Yet it is
difficult to see that there was anything inevitable about this process, at
any rate as far as the university was concerned. In August 1714, on the
death of the queen, everything pointed or seemed to point to an adjust-
ment rather than a revolution in the political scene. With the exception
of the small, if vocal, squadron of those who had either resolved to trust
to hopes of a restoration or had become irrevocably committed to the
leadership of Bolingbroke, few tories foresaw the need to despair. As
White Kennett observed:

[1] Hearne, *Collections* vii. 246-7. The former Student was Mathew Skinner (1689-1749), m. Ch.Ch.
1709; recorder of Oxford May 1721; MP Oxford city 1734-9. The 'advow'd Enemy' was William
Wright, the deputy recorder.   [2] Hearne, *Collections* vii. 328.

None to all appearance more sanguine than they who would be still called Tories. They, forsooth, adhered to the Protestant Succession. They are most forward to go out and meet the King. They, by their principles, have been always for the Church and the Crown. They are the surest friends of the Prerogative, and they, if we believe them, are the majority of the Nation, and can command a new Parliament.[1]

Oxford, it must be admitted, was hardly the home of compromise in general or of moderate toryism in particular, but it clearly shared a good deal of this confidence and an acute sense of the necessity of forethought before declaring against the new regime. A Harleian like William Stratford of Christ Church placed great emphasis on the need to maintain a cautious position, whatever the temptations presented by the extremists, who had an obvious interest in engineering a confrontation with the new king:

I am afraid some will be for provoking him; it is certainly the interest of the late cabal to make an open breach betwixt him and the church party. I have some reason to think it is their design too. They may hope to escape in public troubles, or at least, if they are prosecuted, to say it is for the sake of their party and not their crimes. But I hope our friends will be on the defensive, and wait to see how they are used. I hope they will do nothing which may be a pretence for disgracing them.[2]

Later another moderate, though of different political complexion, George Smalridge, looking back on the last months of 1714, spoke of 'that Warmth and Zeal, which those of this place amongst the rest of his Majesties Subjects profess'd at his first Happy Accession to the Throne, in which Profession I am verily perswaded they were then Sincere'.[3]

That the outcome was quite unsatisfactory from the point of view of such as Stratford and Smalridge was in large measure a result of George I's apparent determination to become the exclusive property of the whigs, in a way which would never have occurred to William III in a comparable position. Apart from his brief flirtation with the Nottingham group he did nothing to suggest that tories who had grown used to the notion that they were as entitled to place, power and profit under a Revolution as under a Restoration monarch, would receive even passing consideration from the new regime. As it became clearer in the winter of 1714 to 1715 that 'there will be no mercy to any one', as Stratford put it,[4] the inevitable reaction set in, both in the tory party at large and more especially in Oxford, where young and hot heads were easily turned by the contrast between the growing attractions of a second Restoration

[1] *Original Letters Illustrative of English History*, ed. H. Ellis (2nd ser. 4 vols London 1827), iv. 288.
[2] Stratford-E. Harley, 5 Aug. 1714, HMC *Portland MSS* vii. 199.
[3] Smalridge-Wake, 9 Jan. 1715, Wake MS 15, fos 43–4.
[4] Stratford-E. Harley, 19 Nov. 1714, HMC *Portland MSS* vii. 207.

and the dwindling charms of Hanoverian rule. Hearne, not disposed to underestimate the natural strength of the Jacobite cause, had no doubt that George I's attitude had been responsible for a decisive change of opinion:

And what hath raised people's Wishes is this, that the Elector of Brunswick hath acted altogether according to the Direction of the Whiggs. He hath turned the Tories out, and filled all places with those of the Whiggish party. This hath justly caused Abundance of Discontent, and 'tis from hence that we have heard of so many Tumults and Riots. Those that were before against K. James are now zealous in his Behalf.[1]

The result in Oxford was indeed the occupation of entrenched positions which were to prove remarkably enduring. The university's ostentatious demonstration of its contempt for the new system of government was marked in the first instance by the bestowal on Sir Constantine Phipps, Sacheverell's counsel in 1710, of a DCL, conferred on coronation day. It culminated in the sensational election in September 1715 of Lord Arran as chancellor,[2] conduct which contrasted strikingly with the meek behaviour of Cambridge in selecting the new prince of Wales for its highest office. The scenes in convocation after the flight to the continent of the old chancellor, the duke of Ormonde, and the overwhelming support for his brother, Arran, make it plain that opinion in the university was seriously inflamed. Nor was the general atmosphere lacking in excitement. There was the inevitable spate of sermons devoted to the blessed memory of Queen Anne and her house, and even some more specific insults, like the sermon delivered before the assize judge in March 1716 by Thomas Haywood of St John's, who bluntly declared that 'King George had suspended his favours at present from the University by some misrepresentation, but that his heart was in God's hands'. 'This is the present behaviour of this place', commented one exasperated observer, 'Such is the perverseness of the Oxonians'.[3]

It is tempting to dismiss the excesses at Oxford as the inevitable result of provocation. Certainly there is much in the subsequent history of this crucial period to support such an interpretation. For the sequence of minor riots between 1715 and 1717 which deeply concerned a nervous government in London could easily be portrayed as trivial town and gown demonstrations stimulated by whig agents. In both 1715 and 1716 it was the juxtaposition of some emotive anniversaries which provided the occasion if not the cause of the disturbances. George I's birthday

---

[1] Hearne, *Collections* v. 97-8.

[2] Charles Butler (1671-1758), 2nd e. of Arran, from 1745 3rd d. of Ormonde; chancellor of the university 1715-68.

[3] D. Wilkins-Wake, 15 Mar. and 26 Jan. 1716, Wake MS 20, fos 58-9, 38-9. Thomas Haywood (1678-1746), m. St John's 1694; at this time vicar of Fyfield, Berks. (now Oxon.).

occurred on 28 May, and the anniversary of the restoration of 1660 on 29 May, a particularly unfortunate coincidence, and the birthday of 'James III' on 10 June. Later there was the anniversary of the new king's own accession, 1 August, and for that matter the prince of Wales's birthday, and coronation day, both in October. According to university apologists, the most accomplished incendiaries, despite their small number, were the younger whigs, organized in the notorious Constitution Club, 'a Sett of Men, whose Principles are opposite to Monarchy, and all good Orders and Government'.[1] It was claimed by the heads of houses that the notorious riot of 29 May 1715 in which a presbyterian meeting house was partly demolished was actually begun by these meddling spirits and Arthur Charlett's detailed report to the secretary of state, Lord Townshend, to the effect that the Constitution Club had opened the proceedings by erecting a bonfire on which were piled effigies of Sacheverell, Ormonde and even the late queen herself, was plausible enough and supported by other evidence.[2]

The Constitution Club was also involved in the most serious riots of all, which occurred on the prince of Wales's birthday in October 1716 and ended in a full-scale inquiry by the house of lords. On this occasion, however, it was the presence of troops, amounting to a full regiment of foot quartered in Oxford since late 1715, which seems to have been the chief provocation. Even the officer in charge admitted that the riots, which extended not merely to the breaking of windows but to armed conflict between some of the soldiery on one side and scholars and townsmen on the other, had begun when he and some other officers, together with 'honest gentlemen' of the Constitution Club, had built a large bonfire in front of the Star Inn and proceeded to toast King William and the duke of Marlborough, in addition to the royal family.[3] Naturally the university authorities made a good deal of his candour, alleging that neither this nor any other prince of Wales's birthday had ever been celebrated by the public and that the whole affair was deliberately provoked by the troops, a clear instance, as one of the city's MPs also put it, of 'the very peace and Quiet of the City broke and disturbed by those sent hither ... to see both preserved'.[4] Nor was corroborating evidence wanting. Typical of many minor incidents was the scuffle which broke out in Lyne's coffee-house on Carfax between an army officer and two students, ending in the arrest and detention of the latter for several hours. One of the students painted a picture of officers prejudiced against the university, particularly of one

[1] Representation of grand jury, 5 Aug. 1715, printed in B. Gardiner, *A Plain Relation of Some Late Passages at Oxford* (Oxford 1717), appx, p. 9.
[2] Ibid. 4-5.
[3] *Oxford Council Acts 1701-1752*, 326.
[4] Ibid. 328.

who 'came to him and said he knew his face and that he was a forward young fellow and we will humble your University of Oxford we will make you eat fire before we have done And as he was going from this Informant he said now let your Deanes release you . . .'.[1] Nor was the revelation that one of the officers involved was actually a local man, who nourished old resentments against the scholars, without its effect.[2] The protestations of the other side were naturally just as emphatic. The army was necessary, it was claimed, 'to prevent their rising in open Rebellion'.[3] There were 'severall thousands lying in and about Oxford ready to rise upon the first Signall or notice of the Pretenders Landing'. As for the university, it was rotten with Jacobites or crypto-Jacobites, from top to bottom.[4] The authorities encouraged or at any rate protected treachery, the colleges were, with a few honourable exceptions such as Merton and Wadham, themselves nests of rebels, and the students as a body were notoriously disaffected.

In retrospect it is easy enough to deny the force of such charges, to accept the well-meaning utterances of the moderates in politics who had the posts of responsibility in Oxford, and who were so anxious to gloss over the more alarming possibilities. We may not entertain, Bernard Gardiner observed, 'a general ill Opinion of a Body of Men, from the Behaviour of a few Strangers coming to reside some time amongst them; and those perhaps Irregular or Designing Men: Nor yet from the unguarded Sallies of Youth, namely the sudden Effects of Joy, Emulation or Humour, without any farther premediated Views'.[5] But perhaps this is too facile. Whatever the justification in terms of the actions of George I, whatever the qualifications in terms of the provocation of the friends and agents of government, whatever the mitigations in terms of the youth and naïvety of the undergraduate population, the fact remains that in 1715 and 1716 the atmosphere in Oxford was heated and hostile, at least sufficiently to concern a regime well aware of the underlying weakness of its position. Even if Oxford harboured few rebels for practical purposes—the presence in hiding of the notorious Colonel Owen seems to be the only fully attested instance—the temper and tone of life there were difficult to explain except in relation to a powerful swell of Jacobite sentiment. Whiggish testimony on this point is obviously suspect, and perhaps altogether inadmissible, but it certainly communicates something of the hot-house atmosphere of the period. A relatively unbiased visitor like Lady Anna Bertie found the state of affairs in Oxford at the time of Arran's election, for example, decidedly disturbing: '. . . all the

---

[1] Ibid. 336.
[2] Gardiner, *Plain Relation*, appx, p. 12.
[3] *Terrae-Filius* no. vi (28 Jan.-1 Feb. 1721).
[4] R. Smith-Lord Santry, 2 Oct. 1715, Bodl. MS Top. Oxon. c. 164.
[5] Gardiner, 1.

Cry I hear is Aron [Arran] and Ormond for ever and Down with the round heads, and treason hallied in the streat from morning to night so that you must think I am got into a very vile town'.[1] And the attempts of such as Stratford to explain away the evidence of student disaffection provided by the army officers were not always helpful: 'I believe the young scholars, who talked to the officers with the same freedom they talk to each other, might use expressions which men in town do not use to each other.'[2] When the house of lords concluded, admittedly on a partisan basis, against the university, it was not short of circumstantial and even material evidence to assist it.[3] Had Louis XIV lived, and had Ormonde and the pretender shown a little more initiative than they did, Oxford's conduct might perhaps have subsequently been construed by its defenders in a quite different light, as evidence of loyalty to the house of Stuart in the face of unremitting pressure from government.

The effect of Oxford's activities was to provide its enemies with large quantities of usable ammunition at a time when government was in the hands of men by no means disinclined to employ it. Especially after the decisive defeat of the Townshend–Walpole connection in 1717 had released the whig administration from its own factious preoccupations, ministers made it devastatingly clear that they intended to render the revival of toryism impossible. The earl of Sunderland's programme was designed not merely to establish permanent control of the house of commons with the septennial act, and of the house of lords with the peerage act, but to bring the church firmly to heel, with the repeal of the schism and occasional conformity acts, and above all with the definitive reform of the universities, the alleged breeding grounds of toryism. The conduct of the latter, and particularly of Oxford, since the accession of George I, provided obvious and potentially powerful supporting arguments. Indeed the draft university reform bill, prepared by the administration, incorporated a preamble which made this plain:

... it being notorious that many in those Nurseryes dedicated to Religion Learning Loyalty and Peace have been infected with principles of Sedition ... that Riots and tumults have disturbed the Peace of the Universityes and affronted your Government and the Offenders have been concealed or at least not detected and duly brought to Punishment.

That Party Principles are favour'd to the generall relaxation of Discipline and to the discouragement of Study and neglect of sound Learning, which ceases to be the way to preferment when Party is more regarded than Merit.

And whereas it is evident as well from the repeated endeavours to raise

---

[1] Lady Anna Bertie-Elizabeth Shirley, 22 [Feb. 1716], HMC *Townshend MSS*, iv. 232–3; see also HMC *Various MSS* viii. 91 ff.

[2] Stratford–E. Harley, 23 Nov. 1715, HMC *Portland MSS* vii. 214.

[3] *Journals of the House of Lords* xx. 436–7.

insurrections throughout the Kingdom as from the wild attempts of men of turbulent and fanaticall Spirits to make Schisms and Divisions in the Church and to overthrow the Supremacy of the Crown (which has allways been so carefully maintein'd by the Church of England) that there can be no reasonable expectation of enjoying Peace and Tranquility for any long time if the Youth of the Nobility and Gentry and especially such as are designed for holy Orders are infected with false Principles utterly inconsistent with our happy establishment in Church and State.[1]

The statute proposed to remedy this state of affairs was brief but draconian. It specifically vested the nomination and appointment to all university and college posts, including fellowships, scholarships and exhibitions, in the crown, and provided for the effective administration of this vast body of patronage by commissioners nominated by the king. Only appointments made by bodies not tainted by membership of the universities themselves (the governors of Charterhouse for instance) were permitted to retain their rights unfettered, and there were appropriate penalties for those attempting to evade the regulations. How real the danger of such legislation was, it is difficult to assess. Stratford, not unrepresentative of one prominent school of thought, rated it slight. Early in 1717 when talk of an attack on the universities diminished, he observed: 'I never was in much pain for the bill about the universities, it would have been so flagrant a breach of property, and so many private interests, besides that of those who are resident here, would have been concerned in it, that I can never think it would pass.' Even two years later when the government seemed more intent than ever on a bill, while admitting the apparent threat, he claimed: 'I believe they would have found it difficult to have formed any bill against us so as to have answered their end and not to have made all the property in England precarious. But we are safe for this session, Lord Harcourt assures us we are so.'[2] George Clarke, shortly to become once again one of the university's parliamentary representatives, made the same point to Lord Abingdon: 'when ever that sort of proceeding begins, it is hard to know where it will end, or who may not be affected by it.'[3]

Quite apart from the risk to chartered and propertied rights such a sweeping measure of reform would deeply have divided the church and caused a great deal of agonizing even among the whig bishops. Archbishop Wake and his colleagues were well disposed towards the cause of reform in general terms, but in practice there were considerable doubts. Thus Sir Jonathan Trelawny, who as bishop of Winchester was

[1] B. Williams, *Stanhope* (Oxford 1932) 456-7.
[2] Stratford-E. Harley, 20 Mar. [1717] and 24 Dec. 1719, HMC *Portland MSS* vii. 220, 266.
[3] *Oxford Council Acts 1701-1752*, 358.

accustoming himself to the new regime, declared his support for the proposition that 'both universitys ought to be scourg'd into perfect duty, and better manners to the King and His family'. Nevertheless he was horrified at the notion of remodelling electoral procedures at Christ Church, and announced his determination to vote against such measures, 'tho' I had a rope about my neck and was to be hangd the moment I gave it'.[1] Similarly the impeccably whiggish bishop of Ely, William Fleetwood, who had benefited by one of George I's earliest episcopal promotions and cheerfully agreed with his colleagues, early in the reign, in favour of some limited powers of removal for the crown in the universities, grew cautious when he discovered that such approval was being used at court to justify talk of more extensive control for a term of seven years. 'Your Grace sees what a wrong turn is allready putt upon what was agreed on by Us', he wrote to Wake, 'and I doubt not but Your Grace will take care to sett this matter right, Since whatever Odium may (as indeed much may) arise, on this Occasion, it must all be laid upon us, if we are represented as the movers and Advisers to this proceeding, originally.'[2] In the event at no time in these years did the threat materialize; even in 1717 no concrete move was made by government, and in 1719 the failure of the peerage bill understandably deterred the administration from further attempts at change. But had a universities bill appeared in either house, it is difficult to believe that it would not have produced a large measure of opposition, not only from tories, but from whig bishops in the lords, and perhaps from whig friends of Cambridge (they after all had done much to defeat the peerage bill) in the commons.

None the less the university was understandably concerned by the agitation of these years, and not least by the storm of hostile propaganda and anti-clericalism generated by Oxford's alleged disloyalty. The thunderings of John Toland, whose *State Anatomy of Great Britain* devoted considerable attention to the iniquities of the universities, and of Trenchard and Gordon in *Cato's Letters*, were merely the more effective examples of a general campaign launched by the whig press.[3] But more threatening in some respects than the attack on the political treachery of the universities were the more knowledgeable onslaughts on the internal structure of university life. Though Edmond Miller's *Account of the University of Cambridge* (London 1717) was devoted exclusively to Cambridge, it was naturally argued by the reformers that Cambridge, particularly after its election of the prince of Wales as chancellor and its address to the prince against the pretender in 1716,

---

[1] Trelawny-Wake, 17 Feb. 1717, Wake MS 15, fos 14-15.

[2] Undated letter ibid. fo 8.

[3] J. Toland, *The State Anatomy of Great Britain* and *The Second Part of the State Anatomy* (London 1717); J. Trenchard and T. Gordon, *Cato's Letters* (1st edn [anon.] 4 vols London 1724, 3rd edn 4 vols London 1733).

was less guilty than Oxford; in any case arguments deployed by Miller had some alarming implications for Oxford. His radical denunciation of the clerical basis of university education deeply perturbed church minds, and his advocacy of statutory changes to permit the election of large numbers of lay fellows was every bit as alarming to whigs and moderates as to tories, as indeed were his generalized hints about the sinister failure of the universities to abide by the terms of their statutes and charters. Moreover, his discussion of the oaths struck a particularly sensitive point, especially when taken up in a supporting pamphlet, *Reasons for a Royal Visitation, Occasion'd by the Present Great Defection of the Clergy from the Government* (London 1717).

The doctrine of 'customary oaths', by which the oaths required for matriculation, for the BA and for the MA, might be taken with un-expressed reservations or without moral commitment, was all too easily applied to the political oaths required by the government, according to the university's enemies. And the failure of the oaths introduced at the beginning of George I's reign to yield a flock of non-jurors, such as had appeared in 1689, seemed to many manifest proof of large-scale evasion and dishonesty. In short the university was a breeding ground of immorality as well as disloyalty.

There may be some particular Exceptions, but take the University together, 'tis certainly true, that the Men of the worst Morals, are generally the Government's worst Enemies; and 'tis for this Reason that I have said, that if the Politicks of the Universities were effectually reformed, they would the sooner reform their Morals.[1]

Perhaps few consciences were either sufficiently tender or guilty for indi-viduals to be deeply concerned at such charges, but they did touch a sensi-tive point corporately, and the pandora's box which they seemed to open, a world apparently involving not merely the imposition of whig dons, but the entire dismantling of the clerical structure of higher education, was naturally alarming. In the public mind Amhurst's biting witticisms about the university and its leaders doubtless constituted the most telling argu-ments;[2] but within the university they were merely the excrescence on a more dangerous and worrying substructure of reasoned argument against the traditional character of university life.

The effects of this difficult period of acute public criticism and poten-tial government intervention were, for Oxford itself, powerful if diverse. First and foremost there was a naturally defensive reaction, a tendency, particularly on the part of those in authority, to avoid any kind of

[1] *Reasons for a Royal Visitation* (London 1717), 63.
[2] *A Letter from a Student in Grub Street, to a Reverend High Priest and Head of a College in Oxford* (London 1720); see also *Diary of Mary, Countess Cowper, Lady of the Bedchamber to the Princess of Wales, 1714-1720* (London 1864, 2nd edn London 1865), 65.

extremism, an attitude which was in many ways to be the most marked feature of Oxford politics during the reigns of George I and George II. In positive terms there was little that could be done in the face of a court and ministry which were overtly hostile. Admittedly there were during the period of the whig split between 1717 and 1720 one or two serious attempts to cultivate the interest of the prince of Wales, already in opposition to his father. That period coincided with one of Arthur Charlett's spells as pro-vice-chancellor and involved him in elaborate schemes for attracting the prince's attention and support, extending to the translation and publication in English of an antiquarian work which particularly interested Princess Caroline. There seemed more than a little cause for optimism, and an obvious community of interest in this much-discussed alliance, for as one Student of Christ Church observed, 'the present Prince of Wales (as he is called) would certainly be for the Tories, when his Father (if K. George be his Father) should die, and that this would be the best way to establish him upon the Throne'.[1] But in the event such hopes were disappointed. Plausible schemes, like the proposed address to the prince in imitation of Cambridge, in 1716, had a way of blowing up in their authors' faces.[2] Moreover, the political turmoil which followed the South Sea Bubble was to reunite both the whigs and the royal family, at least to outward appearances. It may also be doubted whether the flirtation with the tories had ever been more than a temporary and half-hearted expedient on the part of the prince's household, at any rate as far as Oxford was concerned. After all, the embarrassment of Ormonde's flight and the university's studied concern to avoid electing the prince as chancellor in imitation of Cambridge was not easily erased. Thirteen years after that event, when the prince finally succeeded to the throne, this was advanced as the reason why he refused to talk of relaxing the proscription of Oxford tories. It was 'still remembered who was and was not chosen Chancellor here in the beginning of the late reign', Stratford then noted.[3]

The main concern of the university authorities, however, was less to curry favour with men in power than to prevent events in Oxford giving such men an opportunity to intervene. In this respect the most important conflict within the university was not that between whig and tory but that between the relatively moderate authorities in the centre and the extremes at either end of the political spectrum. To a great extent this was the ancient conflict between junior and senior, between the larger forces of the MAs and the controlling groups at the hub of university affairs. What was at issue, as one writer put it, was

[1] Hearne, *Collections* vi. 283, quoting Timothy Thomas (1694–1751), m. Ch.Ch. 1712).
[2] W. R. Ward, *Georgian Oxford* (Oxford 1958), 65.
[3] Stratford-E. Harley, 2 May 1728, HMC *Portland MSS* vii. 461.

the Power and Influence of the Heads of Houses and the Serious Part of the University. . . . If once the Young and Unthinking Part of the University meet with all Success against their Governours, they like a furious horse, will too soon feel their own strength, and throw off all Submission, and, consequently, Opposition and Rebellion will be their first Principles.[1]

In the delicate political situation encountered in George I's reign the essential requirement, as the authorities saw it, was to steer a careful course between outright hostility to the existing regime on the one hand, and betrayal of the sentiments of the great majority of the university on the other. And the activities of both extremes made such a course peculiarly hazardous. Men like Charlett did not see the threat in party political terms. On the contrary they even feared the overt junction of the extremists of each party, and the deadly consequences of 'Jacobites and Whiggs joyn'd together to do the University a Mischief'.[2]

The difficulties which followed the accession of George I, leading as they did to a massive campaign against the university in the press, and the serious possibility of government intervention, had given little room for confidence that it would be possible for Charlett and his like to avert the perils of their situation. By the early 1720s, however, their record had improved. At national level the disaster of the South Sea Bubble and its effects on ministerial politics proved a useful distraction from the affairs of the church, and the whigs were sufficiently occupied with their internal crisis. Moreover, in the university itself the hotheads were to some extent contained. Albeit with difficulty and a degree of danger, the threat presented by the Constitution Club was reduced, with a steady if unspectacular campaign against its members, and a running battle with the most irrepressible of the young whigs of the age, Richard Meadow-court, fellow of Merton.[3] Meadowcourt was a self-confessed incendiary, intent on obtaining the favour of government and attracting the maximum of attention both to Oxford and himself; he was a constant irritation, not least because his activities had the incidental effect of provoking the less sensible tories to acts of open rebellion against authority. He was also, not untypically of the university whigs, surprisingly unsuccessful in the long run. His obvious self-interestedness, and his flirtation with Bangorian doctrines, contrived to make him distasteful even to his hoped-for patrons, so that while he achieved preferment of sorts, notably a canonry at Worcester in 1734, the speedy and substantial promotion for which he laboured was not forthcoming. None the less he proved a menace in the university. His own sufferings, thanks to his part in the activities of the Constitution Club, were good for

[1] *Weekly Journal*, 24 Dec. 1721.
[2] Hearne, *Collections* v. 168.
[3] Richard Meadowcourt (1695-1760), m. Merton 1710.

considerable political intrigue and propaganda; prosecuted for his share
in the rioting of 1716 and allied misdemeanours he was successfully prevented from proceeding to his degrees for two years, but ultimately
forced the authorities, with the help of an act of grace from the king, to
admit defeat. More striking still was his use of the Warton episode, a
typical example of the kind of political flurry which so alarmed the
senior members of the university. Thomas Warton's sermon on Restoration Day 1719 was publicly denounced by Meadowcourt as treasonable.
Though the complaint was probably not without some justification,
there was little danger of serious consequences, despite the interest of
ministers in London. The sermon proved difficult to examine, since
Warton had unaccountably mislaid it; he said 'he had it not, nor knew
not where it was'.[1] Even so it was an embarrassing business, with the university made to appear ineffectual if not actually conspiratorial, and grist
to the mill of Meadowcourt and his superiors. As Amhurst observed, it
helped to convince ministers 'of the factious Spirit which reign'd at
Oxford, not amongst the *young Lads* only (as hath often been speciously
pretended) but even amongst the *Scarlet Gowns* and *veteran Doctors* of the
University'.[2]

None the less, the more dangerous threat to the policy adopted by the
rulers of the university under George I came not from such as Meadowcourt but rather from the opposite wing among the younger elements in
the university, and it was here that the heads of houses won a decisive
victory, which coming as it did at a time of considerable political sensi-
tivity, proved to be of the greatest consequence. For them the parliamentary election of 1722 had all the makings of a great disaster in an
area which had been relatively peaceful in the preceding years. The
sitting MPs at the death of Queen Anne, William Bromley and William
Whitelocke, had survived the general election of 1715 without contest.
On the death of Whitelocke in 1717 George Clarke, like Bromley a
moderate tory with Harleian rather than Jacobite connections, had been
permitted to take his seat after only a feeble protest on the part of the
angry young men, in the abortive candidature of Pierce Dod, also of All
Souls, who, according to Stratford, 'has been used to give drink to young
masters. In principles he is somewhat beyond a Tory.'[3] But in 1722 the
challenge of William King, the principal of St Mary Hall, presented a
stiffer test. King's notorious Jacobitism, together with his wide connections, made him a potentially powerful threat, and from the beginning he
was seen as the epitome of precisely those forces which the moderates

[1] Stratford-E. Harley, 28 June [1719], HMC *Portland MSS* vii. 256. Thomas Warton *senior* (1688-1745) m. Hart Hall 1706; demy Magd. 1706-17; prof. of poetry 1718-28.
[2] *Terrae-Filius* no. xvii (8-11 Mar. 1721).
[3] Stratford-E. Harley, 2 Dec. [1717], HMC *Portland MSS* vii. 232. Pierce Dod (1684-1754), m. BNC 1698; fellow All Souls 1705.

were so anxious to repress. 'He is lookt upon by some of the young and violent party here to be a much better Tory than George Clark; but I believe he will make nothing of it tho' he treats with French Wine, Burgundy and Champaign. Every Head as far as I can find is against him.'[1] It came as no surprise when the authorities bullied Arran into removing King from his office of secretary to the chancellor.[2] The atmosphere was heated, and the tension between 'masters' and 'heads' worse than perhaps at any time in the period. As a champion of the former pointed out, the issue was certainly not whig against tory, for 'as the W[hig]s were not to vote for Dr K[ing] because he was too great a T[ory]: so the T[orie]s were not to vote for him, for the *same Reason*'.[3] On their side indeed the heads left no one in doubt of their view that the election of King would be deeply discreditable to the university.

The manner of the election itself was predictably confused, with legal wrangles severely complicating matters. Bromley was accused of lacking the proper qualification for a university burgess, on the technical grounds that he was not a resident member of the university, and there was much controversy over the voting rights of MAs who appeared on buttery books but were not for practical purposes resident. At King's own college, Balliol, a large majority of the votes cast were of this questionable nature. Even with them, however, King failed to fulfil his promise. Bromley coasted home with 337 votes, and Clarke as the new-comer against whom King's campaign had been primarily directed followed with 278, leaving King to bring up the rear with 159. In one respect these figures were misleading. In a number of the smaller colleges King's toryism was plainly far more attractive than Clarke's moderation, and even many whigs seem to have seen in him a kindred spirit whose victory would at least cock a snook at authority. Corpus, Exeter, Jesus, St John's and Lincoln all preferred King to Clarke, and there was substantial support for him in a number of other societies—Magdalen, Merton, Pembroke, Trinity and Wadham. But he was over-whelmed by the big battalions with Harleian connections. At Christ Church, which cast 60 votes for Clarke against 2 for King, at Queen's where King received 2 votes against 22 for his rival, and at University College, the one college where (doubtless thanks to Charlett) King obtained no support whatever, he was utterly crushed.[4] Despite a nominal petition to the commons by King's supporters, it seemed an

[1] G. Carter-Wake, 26 Nov. [1721], Wake MS 16, fo 327. William King (1685-1763), m. Balliol 1701; principal St Mary Hall 1719-63.

[2] See Marquess of Carnarvon–T. Leigh, 17 Feb. 1722, Bodl. MS dep. c. 562, fos 59-61.

[3] [S. Harrison,] *An Account of the Late Election for the University of Oxford, By a Master of Arts* (London 1722), 20.

[4] *A True Copy of the Poll for Members of Parliament for the University of Oxford, taken March the 21st 1721* [OS] (Oxford 1722).

altogether decisive defeat for the forces which had threatened to drag Oxford further into official discredit, and reassuring evidence of the basic moderation of the university's toryism.

The pattern established at this time steadily hardened in the following years, with small prospect of real change either internally or externally. Indeed in retrospect the rigidity of university politics in the age of Walpole is particularly striking. There was, for instance, little progress on the part of university whigs, though it might have been expected that the relative stabilization of Hanoverian rule would have encouraged a powerful movement in favour of the existing regime. The influential whig bloc of Merton and Wadham and a group of supporters at Jesus were reinforced by the addition of Exeter, when the balance was finally tipped there in 1719, but otherwise was not augmented at all, if Christ Church is left out of consideration. The gradual transformation of Christ Church itself was inevitable, given its peculiar relationship with church and state. None the less it was slow and far from complete by the 1730s. Moreover, there were frights even in the reliable whig colleges. In 1725, for example, when Jesus was undergoing the double throes of electing a principal and instituting a new fellowship, the dean of Christ Church, William Bradshaw, dreaded for 'His majesty's interest in the College and the University' and prophesied that 'the College will be undone, and turn'd into a Nest of Jacobites'.[1] This disaster was averted, but successive leaders of the government's interest in Oxford had little on which to congratulate themselves during the 1720s and 1730s.

The impotence at Oxford of the whig interest during its national supremacy is only superficially surprising. In theory the deanery of Christ Church should have provided an ideal channel for the exchange of patronage from government for loyalty from Oxford; but in practice neither Smalridge, Boulter, Bradshaw nor even Conybeare[2] in the 1730s seems to have established the kind of connections and relationships which were needed. Typical of the frictions which arose was Townshend's denunciation of Smalridge,

calling him beast and wretched fellow, who being made Dean in order to strengthen the Whig interest there, did nothing but laze away his time, and suffered the Tories to increase their power and numbers in that University. He lamented that such a blockhead was ever made a Bishop.[3]

---

[1] Bradshaw-Wake, 5 and 26 Oct. 1725, Wake MS 16, fos 330, 331. William Bradshaw (1673-1732), m. Balliol 1692; dean Ch.Ch. 1724-32.

[2] John Conybeare (1692-1755), m. Exeter 1708, rector 1730-3; dean Ch. Ch. 1733-55; bp of Bristol 1750-5.

[3] HMC *Egmont Diary* i. 225 (22 Feb. 1732).

There were naturally grievances on both sides. If ministers found Oxford whigs ungrateful, Oxford whigs found ministers ungenerous and unco-operative. Admittedly government did make some attempt to organize new sources of patronage at Oxford, in combination with Cambridge. The Whitehall preacherships and the new regius chairs instituted under George I provided a degree of support for reliable whigs, such as David Gregory,[1] the first holder of the chair of modern history and languages. But useful though these innovations were, they were scarcely employed systematically, and at Oxford they lacked the far-flung and complex supporting network of aristocratic and propertied patronage with which they could be co-ordinated at Cambridge. Oxford's connection with the midland gentry offered a mass of unsystematized but none the less important patronage which ensured that a great majority of its products served interest as well as ideals in standing by tory principles. In college after college regional associations and ancient connections oiled the wheels of patronage, and whereas whigs often had to rely on external connection for preferment and expected too much of a direct line to London, the run of college fellows had a more secure and less speculative dependence on the loyal allegiance of the gentry. It would have needed a far bigger investment than Walpole and the Pelhams could be bothered to devote to Oxford, and an altogether higher calibre of personnel and organization among university whigs to shake this secure basis of Oxford's continuing toryism.

Intriguingly the main assault both on Oxford's patronage and its privileges in this period came not from the mainstream of whiggism at Westminster or in the university, but rather from the sudden and un-expected strength of 'Real Whig' agitation in the mid-1730s. The capacity of the universities to create their own patronage by purchasing advow-sons was a traditional grievance among dissenters and low-church radicals in the early eighteenth century, which clearly derived more from generalized anticlericalism than any coherent view that the practice reinforced the tory politics of the colleges. Lord Egmont, one of the lead-ing opponents of the universities in this matter, considered that the pur-chase of livings 'must prove of great detriment to themselves, as well as it is to learning', in particular because the preferment to such livings was determined by the seniority of individual fellows, 'to the great dis-couragement of study, for a learned man shall not have the preference over a blockhead, because it is not his turn'. Moreover, the pickings were far too fat: 'That numbers of livings in the University only made the Fellows lazy, whereas when pinched in their circumstances, and without prospect of College livings, they would study hard to go out in the world.'[2]

---

[1] David Gregory (1696-1767), m. Ch.Ch. 1714, dean 1756-67; regius prof. of modern history 1724-36.   [2] HMC *Egmont Diary* i. 109 (15 Oct. 1730), ii. 256 (5 Apr. 1736).

In retrospect it is doubtful whether colleges had pursued a systematic policy in recent years of accumulating this sort of patronage, and certain that the net effect was nothing like the feather-bedding alleged by the 'Real Whigs'. The statistical inquiry which was undertaken at Oxford at the instance of Stephen Niblett as vice-chancellor in response to the new challenge revealed that whereas the colleges boasted a total of 535 fellowships in 1736, they could lay claim to only 290 livings, of which virtually half (142) were worth less than £100 per annum.[1] At Queen's it was pointed out that 'Few or None of the Fellows go off till they are above 20 years standing and the rest stay much longer before they are promoted', and other colleges returned similar reports. The vice-chancellor himself felt the evidence was conclusive that 'there is no great danger of our becoming too powerfull with relation to advowsons, supposing no Restraint at all was laid upon us in this point', while the pamphlet which the university had printed to defend its case asserted:

as to the Number that the several Colleges are possess'd of, some have none, others but two or three of moderate Value; and none of them have so many, and of such Value, that it can possibly be any reasonable Invitation to the Fellows of those Colleges, to rest their Hopes of Preferment there; or, to make them indolent, or less careful to recommend themselves to the Patronage of others . . .[2]

In any case the anticlerical campaign clearly stemmed not from any novel or sinister access of patronage at Oxford and Cambridge, but from the sudden weakening of Walpole's political position in the mid-1730s. Ever since his elevation to the post of chief minister he had endeavoured to retain the general support of independent and often anti-clerically minded whigs without permitting them to unsettle the unchanging system which was the essence of his policy in church and state.[3] In particular he had stepped in when necessary to protect the church, not merely against attempts to repeal the test and corporation acts or to reduce the incidence of tithes, but against interference with the universities themselves. As a loyal son of Cambridge he had gone out of his way in 1722 to defend that university against the town of Cambridge in the matter of a land-tax dispute,[4] and still more significantly had intervened with decisive effect against a serious attempt to restrain the universities from purchasing advowsons three years later. But by 1735 he

---

[1] C. T. Martin, *Catalogue of the Archives in the Muniment Rooms of All Souls' College* (London 1877), p. 364, appeals and injunctions, nos. 509–24. Stephen Niblett (1697–1766), m. Queen's 1713; warden All Souls 1726–66; vice-chancellor 1735–8.

[2] *Reasons humbly offered to the Honourable House of Commons against the Bill now depending for Restraining the Disposition of Lands, whereby the same become Unalienable; so far as relates to the University of Oxford* [1736], see Martin, *Catalogue*, appeals and injunctions, p. 365, no. 530.

[3] See N. Hunt, *Two Early Political Associations* (Oxford 1961).

[4] *Parliamentary Diary of Sir Edward Knatchbull, 1722–30*, ed. A. N. Newman (Camden 3rd ser. xciv 1963), 117.

was no longer in a position to stop a frontal attack developing. His slowly weakening hold on the house of commons after the excise crisis, and his quarrel with his ecclesiastical manager Edmund Gibson, bishop of London, for example, made it considerably easier for the 'Real Whigs' to take the offensive against the church.[1]

The resulting onslaught, in the form of a mortmain bill, threatened to be doubly damaging to the universities, for it was designed to invalidate deathbed endowments to the colleges, as well as heavily restricting the number of advowsons which they could purchase. The response of the intended victims, however, was surprisingly effective. In both universities the counter-attack was carefully organized and skilfully mounted, with much lobbying of friends, much collecting of detailed information and much attention to detail. Naturally at Westminster the tories played an important part in debate and division. An intriguing feature, however, was the apparent readiness even of Oxford to woo whigs and ministers. Euseby Isham, the rector of Lincoln College, considered that Niblett had been 'a good Solicitor for us';[2] and indeed his readiness to lobby not merely independent whigs such as the speaker, Arthur Onslow,[3] but the prime minister himself, actually offended some tories. The spectacle of a vice-chancellor of Oxford attending Robert Walpole's levee particularly enraged Lord Cornbury.[4] Even so this campaign paid off handsomely. In the commons, despite an atmosphere which threatened to be unpleasantly hostile to the church, the universities were exempted from the prohibitions on deathbed legacies to charity. Moreover, when Cornbury moved a clause permitting colleges to purchase advowsons up to a number equivalent to half their fellowships it was carried overwhelmingly by 227 votes to 130 against Samuel Sandys's attempt to freeze them completely.[5] The net effect was that Oxford was permitted to acquire a further forty-eight livings, and Cambridge a further forty, a generous enough provision, considering that there had been little pressure to add to the existing numbers. In the lords the bishops attempted to make it more generous still with a clause which would have prevented the small livings worth less than £100 from being taken into account in calculating each college's complement; this, however, proved overoptimistic, being defeated by 57 votes to 42. None the less the end

[1] T. F. J. Kendrick, 'Sir Robert Walpole, the Old Whigs and the bishops, 1733-1736: a study in eighteenth-century parliamentary politics', *Historical Journal* xi (1968).

[2] Letter from Isham to his brother, 30 Mar. 1736, Northampton, Northamptonshire Record Office, Isham MS 1(c) 2491. Euseby Isham (1698-1755), m. Balliol 1716; rector Linc. 1731-55; vice-chancellor 1744-7.

[3] Arthur Onslow (1691-1768), m. Wadham 1708; speaker of the house of commons 1727-61.

[4] Cornbury-[Niblett], 23 Mar. 1736, Martin, *Catalogue*, p. 366, no. 539. Henry Hyde (1710-53), visc. Cornbury, from 1751 bn Hyde of Hindon; m. Ch.Ch. 1725; MP Oxford Univ. 1732-50.

[5] Cornbury-[Niblett], 23 Mar. 1736. Samuel Sandys (1695-1770); m. New College 1711.

result was an impressive tribute to the pressure brought to bear by the universities, if also to other forces. Though the bishops bitterly criticized Walpole for permitting the anticlerical campaign to develop in the first place, he had done sterling work behind the scenes in countering the activities of the radical whigs, and in the commons had again and again cast his influential support in favour of exceptions and exemptions designed to emasculate the mortmain bill. Otherwise much was owed to the relative tranquillity of the preceding years. Apart from a slightly heated atmosphere in Oxford, as elsewhere, at the time of the excise crisis, employed in vain by university whigs like Meadowcourt to draw the attention of the court once again in their direction, little had happened to bring the university into the public eye, and the low profile which the vice-chancellors of recent years, Mather, Butler and Holmes, had so assidously worked to cultivate had proved remarkably successful.[1] Had the mortmain bill been under serious discussion after the disturbances of 1716, or in the late 1740s in the midst of the troubles which were to plague Oxford in the wake of the Forty-Five, it is difficult to believe either that ministers would have been able to control the situation in the commons, or that the church would have been able to escape severe punishment.

Not even parliamentary elections seriously disturbed the underlying harmony of these years. The death in February 1732 of that old friend of Oxford, William Bromley, had opened the way for the advancement of a young and passionately committed Hyde, Lord Cornbury, who had proved eminently acceptable without the necessity of a poll. When George Clarke's death released the other seat in October 1736 there was more excitement, with Robert Trevor standing as a whig. But the result was scarcely a serious contest when the poll was taken the following February. A quarter of the electorate did not trouble to vote, and of those who did Trevor captured only 121 against the 329 secured by William Bromley's son. Only Wadham, Merton, Exeter and Christ Church, the latter by now well on its way to becoming a ministerial college once again, gave Trevor anything like a majority of their votes, while the remainder unhesitatingly closed ranks behind Bromley.[2] Even the strain of another election six weeks later caused by Bromley's premature death made little difference. Edward Butler, the popular and personable

[1] John Mather (1676-1748), m. Ch.Ch. 1693; president CCC 1715-48; vice-chancellor 1723-8. Edward Butler (1686-1745), m. Magd. 1702, president 1722-45; vice-chancellor 1728-32; MP Oxford Univ. 1737-45. William Holmes (1689-1748), m. St. John's 1707, president 1728-48; vice-chancellor 1732-5.
[2] *An Exact Account of the Poll, as it stood between the Honourable Mr. Trevor and William Bromley, Esq.* (London [1737]). Robert (Hampden) Trevor (1707-83), from 1776 1st Visc. Hampden; m. Queen's 1723; fellow All Souls 1725. William Bromley (1702-37), m. Ch.Ch. 1717; hon. DCL Oriel 1732; MP Oxford Univ. Feb.-Mar. 1737.

president of Magdalen, easily triumphed in a friendly contest with Peregrine Palmer, a fellow of All Souls newly turned country gentleman.[1]
There was talk of renewing Trevor's candidature to save some face for the
government, but in the event even this did not materialize. As Horatio
Walpole observed, explaining why he did not wish to see Trevor 'disgraced a second time', even with 'The tories at Oxford ... divided and in
the utmost confusion about a new member ... I do not see that the whigs
can make any advantage of it.'[2] It was a fitting tribute to the resilience of
Oxford toryism in the years of so-called proscription—years which saw
whiggism an almost impotent force in university politics, a generally
united and effective tory stance, and little by way of serious indiscipline or
indiscretion on the part of the great body of the university.

In retrospect, however, it can be seen that the 1737 election was one of
the last manifestations of this happy state of affairs. For the 1740s were
to witness much worsened relations with government, considerable ferment in the university and a general appreciation that the relative safety
of the twenties and thirties was past. By the forties many resident
members of the university had been largely educated in Hanoverian
England. Imbued with the same sentiments as their tory forebears and
connections, they were yet inclined to be less tolerant of a continuing
and apparently unrelenting victimization. The same disillusion which
swept the country gentlemen at the time of George II's accession and
again when Walpole's regime gave way to Pelham's was naturally
paralleled in the church. The fact that for practical purposes the issues
which had divided whig and tory a generation earlier were no longer so
lively merely added to the irritation and disillusion rather than diminishing them; a proscription based on name alone was even less tolerable
than suffering endured in a noble cause. Similarly the evident readiness
of a handful of tories to recognize realities and commit themselves
wholeheartedly to the regime augmented the anger of those who were
neither in a position nor of an inclination to follow their example. Oxford
had particular occasion to feel this resentment. Just as Lord Gower's
treachery in 1744 made him more odious than any whig to his old friends
and supporters among the tories in the north midlands, so the conduct
of Cornbury proved particularly galling to his constituents in the university. As early as 1741 there were grounds for suspecting his adherence
to the cause of his ancestors, but it was in January 1744 that, as Lord
Orrery put it, he 'has flung off the Mask, and has spoken and voted for
the Hanoverian Troops'.[3] Though he voted with the opposition on

---

[1] Peregrine Palmer (1703-62), m. Balliol 1719; fellow All Souls 1724; MP Oxford Univ. 1745-62.
[2] Walpole-Trevor, 15-26 Mar. and 22 Mar.—[2 Apr.] 1737, HMC *Buckinghamshire MSS* 5.
[3] *The Orrery Papers*, ed. the countess of Cork and Orrery (2 vols London 1903) ii. 174. John Boyle
(1707-62), 5th e. of Orrery; m. Ch.Ch. 1723; hon. MA Univ. 1743.

subsequent occasions, his conduct was scarcely that of an unwavering
tory. His price, it eventually emerged, was elevation to the upper house
as a peer in his own right, which he secured in January 1751.

In the face of such tendencies it became more and more difficult to
hold together that large body of ill-disciplined if basically moderate tory
sentiment which had kept Oxford out of trouble earlier. The old Harley-
ism was dying; and it was peculiarly appropriate for example that in
Christ Church itself, where the followers of Harley and Atterbury had
once fought so bitterly, by the middle of the century there remained only
moderate whiggism. Though the gradual transformation of Christ
Church did not decisively strengthen Oxford whiggism, it did help to
release the less-sophisticated tories of the smaller colleges into channels
at once more violent and dangerous. To a great extent the vice-
chancellors of the period, Isham of Lincoln, Purnell of New College and
Brown of University College, fought to maintain the old balance, but
their task was plainly growing difficult, and increasingly they bewailed
the fractiousness which, for instance, Theophilus Leigh, master of Balliol
and an active pro-vice-chancellor during Purnell's tenure, observed
around him: 'a Restless spirit', he called it, 'disrelishing Subordination
and Government'. 'There is a great Spirit, and it runs high, throughout
the University, against Government.'[1]

Events did not assist Leigh and his colleagues. The Forty-Five
received no aid from Oxford and hardly caused great excitement there.
But it did provide the occasion for a sullen demonstration of the resentment felt against the Pelham regime. The 'association' which Oxfordshire produced in imitation of most other counties was dutifully signed
by the vice-chancellor of the day, Euseby Isham, but otherwise by an
embarrassingly small complement of five heads and senior figures,
almost all whigs. Most of the university's tories plainly imitated the
example of the tory gentry of the county and refused to sign; some of
them who were to become prominent in Oxford's affairs later on, like
Joseph Browne,[1] a future vice-chancellor, were to be not a little embarrassed by their reticence on this occasion.[2]

This, however, was nothing to the storms which arose in the ensuing
years. The principal cause of outrage, the Richard Blacow affair of 1748,
had all the features of the troubles which had followed the accession of
George I, with the same mixture of Jacobite excesses and whig intrigues.[3]
Every year since the Forty-Five had seen high-spirited revels by drunken

[1] Leigh-J. Dolben, 6 Mar. and 6 Apr. 1752, Northants. Rec. Off. Dolben MSS D (F) 87, D (F) 82.
John Purnell (1707-64), m. New College 1727, warden 1740-64; vice-chancellor 1747-50. John Brown
(1687-1764), subs. Univ. 1704, master 1745-64; vice-chancellor 1750-3. Theophilus Leigh
(1693-1785), m. Trin. 1709; master Balliol 1726-85; vice-chancellor 1738-41.
[2] *An Authentick Copy of the Association entered into by Part of the Nobility, Gentlemen and Clergy of the
County of Oxford, at the Time of the Late Unnatural Rebellion in . . . 1745, together with the names of the persons
who subscribed thereto* (np 1745). Joseph Browne (1701-67), m. Queen's 1716, provost 1756-67; Sedleian prof. of nat. phil. 1741-67; vice-chancellor 1759-65.
[3] See L. S. Sutherland, 'Political respectability 1751-71', pp. 130 seq. below.

scholars, in which the appropriate form of conduct involved little more than ostentatious toasts to the king over the water, and on those occasions the university's authorities had done their best to prevent such excesses getting out of hand or into the papers.[1] As usual in such matters the official university view was that 'Mad Young Fellows get heated with Liquor and don't know what they do'.

Considering the multitude of young People that are here, many of them just let loose from the Restraint of a School, and all of them at a time of Life when their Passions are at the extravagent, it is wonderful there should be so few Instance of Disorder of any kind, as there really are.[2]

In all probability disaffection had relatively little to do with these difficulties, which owed much more to the activities of a particularly wild generation of aristocratic undergraduates, the most celebrated of whom was George Selwyn.[3] But not all offenders were as impeccably whiggish as Selwyn, and the misdeeds of 1748 did seem particularly disturbing, consisting as they did of open declarations for the pretender by two undergraduates, James Dawes and John Whitmore. No doubt these pranks could have been dealt with like their predecessors, but on this occasion the other element in university discord, that of whig provocation, was present. The affair was made the subject of official complaint by Blacow and subsequently taken up by London. The vice-chancellor, Purnell, declined to take Blacow seriously enough for the ministers. Dawes and Whitmore, who plausibly claimed to have been drunk at the time of their misdemeanours, were given 'a large work to translate' and prevented from taking their degrees for a year, in addition to being 'smartly punish'd in their Private Societyes'.[4] This was sufficient to threaten Purnell with serious consequences, but it was much aggravated by a repeat performance from the erring undergraduates, who on an October night toured the colleges with two musicians playing 'The king shall enjoy his own again'. On this occasion the full weight both of the university and the law descended, with Theophilus Leigh as pro-vice-chancellor nervously awaiting the reaction of the court.[5]

The ensuing furore involved a series of measures and counter-measures which raised whig hopes within Oxford, to some extent committed government at Whitehall and heightened the growing resentment and bitterness of Oxford tories. In this climate it was all too easy for new incidents to take place, much the most sensational being Dr King's provocative and publicized antics at the opening of the Radcliffe

[1] See University notices 1662-1821, Bodl. G.A. Oxon. b. 19.

[2] H. Sandford-e. of Shaftesbury, 18 and 27 Nov. 1748, PRO 30/24/28, fos 552, 558.

[3] George Selwyn (1719-91), m. Hart Hall 1739, rusticated 1745.

[4] Bodl. MS dep. 6. 48, nos. 34-5, 'The case of the late disturbance at Oxford, with the vice-chancellor's conduct therein'. See also Ward, *Georgian Oxford*. James Dawes, m. St Mary Hall 1744. John Whitmore, m. Balliol 1746.

[5] Leigh-duchess of Chandos, 31 Oct. 1748, Balliol MS 403, fos 76ʳ-7ᵛ.

Camera in April 1749. His speech on this occasion resembled countless sermons delivered in Oxford during the reigns of George I and II but the verve and timing gave it exceptional notoriety and led to a particularly brisk skirmish in the press, with King himself a characteristically vigorous participant.[1] But the really significant development had taken place earlier, and King's outburst, though spectacular, marked only the culmination of the crisis. For example the ministry had decided after the October outrage that it was high time for Oxford to be taught a sharp lesson. The anxiety of the cabinet to come down on what it called 'this treasonable and seditious Riot', despite the advice of the crown's lawyers that in point of law it would be difficult to proceed against either the offenders or the university, suggested a strong predisposition to make trouble regardless of the particular issue.[2] Subsequent events added to this suspicion. In the midst of the disturbances Cambridge embarrassingly hastened to congratulate the king on the making of peace at Aix-la-Chapelle, in plain contravention of the tradition that such addresses were presented only after parliament had met and pointed the way for lesser bodies. 'And yet', Leigh observed, 'I can't think Cambridge would have taken this new and extraordinary Step, without some Intimation from Great Persons (to whom They have easy access) that such measure would be agreeable.'[3] The sequel was still more alarming. When Oxford followed suit with an address which incidentally referred to the recent riots at the university, it was humiliatingly rejected, with a letter from the lord chamberlain to the chancellor explaining that 'His Majesty had seen a Copy of the University Address, and thinks it not a Proper one for Him to receive'.[4] Only an obsequious substitute would do; indeed Conybeare had originally proposed that the address should specifically apologize for the irregularities of the previous months. But as Leigh pointed out, such an apology would have admitted guilt in what was at worst an unwitting and insignificant offence, and would have paved the way for the legal proceedings which were in train against the vice-chancellor. Such reasoning did not appeal, however, to a ministry which was clearly contemplating interference with the universities on the lines of Stanhope's bill thirty years earlier.

Oxford was naturally inclined to put the blame for this state of affairs on its false brethren, from Conybeare at the top, with his direct line to

[1] See notably J. Burton, *An Answer to Dr. King's Speech* (Oxford 1750): *Remarks on Dr. K. . .'s Speech, before the University of O---d, at the Dedication of Dr. R . .'s Library, on the XIIIth of April MDCCXLIX* (London 1750); *The Wonder of Wonders, or Fresh Intelligence from Eton* (np 1750). King's part in the controversy may be followed in his own *Political and Literary Anecdotes* (London 1818, 2nd edn London 1819), 253 ff.
[2] Bedford–Leigh, 20 Oct. 1748, Bodl. MS dep. b. 48.
[3] Leigh–duchess of Chandos [12 Dec. 1748], Balliol MS 403, fos 82^r-3.
[4] Same–same, 9 Jan. 1749, ibid. fos 86^r-7^v.

the ministers, to Edward Bentham at the bottom, with his pamphleteering.[1] In fact, as under George I, it probably owed more to the disposition of the ministers themselves, who had recently emerged from a period of prolonged crisis involving the Forty-Five itself, a lengthy diplomatic battle over Flanders and Cap Breton, and finally a surprise general election. But by 1748 the difficulties both at home and abroad had largely evaporated, and ministers were inclined to consider meddling in areas which a Walpole would have avoided. In particular Newcastle, whose virtues did not include a sense of proportion, was particularly concerned with church affairs in 1749 and 1750. A pet scheme of Thomas Sherlock's, as bishop of London, for American bishoprics was under active consideration, and Newcastle, himself newly-made chancellor of Cambridge University, was involved in the internal reforms which were currently creating difficulties there. He was also busy with grandiose plans for the disposition of patronage. His list of 'Cambridge men, worthy of his Majesty's notice, and proper to be brought forward' drawn up at this time was merely one of many over the years. But his interest in Oxford is more intriguing, especially his intention of preferring such as 'Dr Bentham and Mr Blacow', a development which suggested that the ministry was preparing to take a more systematic interest than hitherto in the problem of strengthening Oxford whiggism.[2] At any rate by January 1749, with characteristic apprehension and hesitation, and with the prompting of the bishops, particularly Sherlock, who insisted that there were many 'who think it absolutely necessary that something should be done, and that soon', Newcastle had worked himself up to the contemplation of a commission of inquiry and redress in the universities.[3]

That nothing came of this, perhaps the most real threat to Oxford between 1714 and 1760, was the consequence of several factors. One was the attitude of Newcastle himself, who was much in favour of action against Oxford, but did not share the episcopal enthusiasm for reforming Cambridge. 'Any general academical Rules', he observed to Sherlock, 'may possibly comprehend both Universities; but I can never admit, That if the late and notorious, Conduct of the University of Oxford, should make a Visitation, or Enquiry there adviseable, That will be any Reason for the same at Cambridge whose Behaviour is as meritorious, as the other is justly to be censured.'[4] In this light his supplementary remarks in the same letter that 'in all Events, Something should be soon thought of, and determined, or others will have the Merit, and we perhaps be

---

[1] [E. Bentham,] *A Letter to a Young Gentleman, by a tutor and fellow of a college in Oxford* (Oxford 1748); *A Letter to a Fellow of a College, being the sequel of a letter to a young gentleman of Oxford* (Oxford 1749). Edward Bentham (1707-76), m. CCC 1724; tutor Oriel 1732-52; vice-principal Magd. Hall 1730; canon Ch.Ch. 1754 and regius prof. of divinity 1763-76.

[2] BL Add. MS 33061, fo 356.   [3] BL Add. MS 32718, fo 29.

[4] Ibid. fo 31 (21 Jan. 1747).

unavoidably drag'd into what may not have been well considered, and properly adapted' smacked rather of prevarication than resolution. The Cambridge consideration was a critical one, especially as that university was at this time seriously divided by disputes over its academic regulations and was hardly in a position to claim exemption from any general investigation.

Perhaps more important still, however, was the fact that on this occasion Oxford mustered a formidable political backing, with means somewhat akin to those of 1718 but altogether more effective. Then the attempt to woo and win the support of the prince of Wales had been a somewhat half-hearted and hesitant affair. Now the circumstances were quite different. Frederick, prince of Wales, and his advisers were heavily committed to opposition and in a mood to enlist the assistance of the tory country gentlemen in parliament. As early as June 1747 there had taken place a formal agreement between the two parties, on the basis of a patriotic programme which could attract widespread support. Though Oxford was not directly involved in these negotiations it was naturally represented by a number of those who were. The prince's secretary, Francis Ayscough, was a well-known Oxford figure, if hardly one likely to be loved by tories; the duke of Beaufort, Sir Francis Dashwood, the earl of Lichfield and Penyston Powney, all prominently involved in this business, were well known in Oxford.[1] Powney in particular had connections through his brother[2] with Theophilus Leigh, connections which were to provide a useful channel of communication for matters of special concern to the university. The most important manœuvre took place in the spring of 1749. A great number of tories, apparently amounting to 13 peers and 103 MPs, met in London. Arran himself was present, Beaufort presided and Dr Lee, the most important single influence in the prince's household, represented Leicester House. The pledges of support made for the university were an impressive signal of the political furore that was likely to greet any move by the government. In fact the ministers had already almost certainly decided to back down, thanks to the intervention of the prince. As Leigh put it: 'We are much beholden to a great Person, for sending in All under His influence, To our assistance; and, as we suppose, it may be now found, that some Fingers have been burnt; so we are in no pain lest our Adversarys should soon venture to Rally.'[3] Small wonder that the university's 'Gratitude is and will always be ready,

[1] Francis Ayscough (1700-63), m. CCC 1717. Francis Dashwood (1708-81), 2nd bt; hon. DCL 1749. George Henry Lee (1718-72), 3rd e. of Lichfield; hon. MA St John's; chancellor of the university 1762-72. Penyston Powney (1699-1757), m. Queen's 1716; MP Berkshire 1739-57.
[2] Richard Powney, m. Queen's 1719; fellow All Souls 1723.
[3] Leigh-duchess of Chandos, 5 May 1749, Balliol MS 403, fo 51. George Lee (1700-58), m. Ch.Ch. 1720.

when They shall be favour'd with an Opportunity of making a proper Exertion'.[1]

It was appropriate that this difficult period should be concluded with a parliamentary election which set Oxford by the ears. There had been no contest since 1737, and the worsted candidate in the second election of that year, Peregrine Palmer, had already been permitted in 1745 to take the seat vacated by Butler's death. But the stormy events of the late 1740s made it unlikely that the next election, due in 1754, would pass off peacefully. In fact it came prematurely when Cornbury finally acquired his peerage in his own right in 1751. The resulting election was a complicated affair, and marked by the emergence of novel forces which were to be of considerable consequence in later years. The most surprising candidate was one who had more in common with William King than with the common run of moderate MPs who had represented the university for most of the early Hanoverian period. Roger Newdigate was a thoroughgoing tory and a gentleman of impeccable 'country' background and principles. A substantial landowner in Warwickshire, and also in Middlesex, which he represented between 1741 and 1747, he was a fervent champion of the church and had some continuing associations with the University, notably through his friend, William Blackstone. He faced a weak candidate in Theophilus Leigh's brother-in-law Sir Edward Turner and a very strong one in Robert Harley. Harley had all the appeal of the house of Oxford, an ideal background as a moderate tory, excellent connections, particularly in Christ Church, and seemed an overwhelmingly attractive candidate. In party terms all three were tories. But Turner had whig friendships, through the Oxfordshire Keck family, and three years later was to stand on the 'New Interest' in the celebrated Oxfordshire election of 1754. Moreover, even the Harleys were scarcely aggressively tory at this time, and Lord Oxford, the cousin of the candidate, was not altogether averse to talk of a union with the Pelhams. It was presumably this and Newdigate's staunch high-church toryism which caused the upset. There was not a particularly heavy poll, nor so agitated an atmosphere as in 1722, but Newdigate's surprising victory reflected the strength of feeling in Oxford in the aftermath of the recent troubles. The victor secured almost as many votes as his two opponents combined, with 184 votes against 126 for Harley and 67 for Turner.[2] The polling figures demonstrated how utterly unsuccessful had been the

---

[1] Leigh-duchess of Chandos, 18 June 1749, Balliol MS 403, fo 54.

[2] *A True Copy of the Poll taken at Oxford January 31, 1750, with several papers sent to the common rooms of the respective colleges, relating to the election of a member of parliament for the university* (London nd). William Blackstone (1723-80), m. Pemb. 1738; fellow All Souls 1744; 1st prof. of English law 1758-62; principal New Inn Hall 1761-6. Edward Turner (1719-66), 2nd bt; m. Balliol 1735; hon. MA 1738, hon. DCL 1744; MP Oxon. 1754-61. Robert Harley (1727-74), m. Ch.Ch. 1744; hon. MA 1748. Edward Harley (1700-55), from 1741 3rd e. of Oxford; m. Ch.Ch. 1717; hon. DCL 1737.

efforts of successive whig groups to break down the hostility and coherence of university toryism. Quite the reverse had happened, for the
moderation of the twenties and thirties had been replaced by an
alarmingly aggressive, if despairing toryism. A Harley would have
romped home in the days of Bernard Gardiner and Arthur Charlett, but
in 1751 Newdigate's excellent organization, as managed by Blackstone,
and his unequivocal politics paid handsome dividends. College after
college which had studiously avoided supporting King in 1722 and had
settled for the safe candidates, Bromley and Clarke, had no hesitation in
plumping for Newdigate in 1751. All Souls, Balliol (depressingly for its
master who naturally strongly supported Turner), Brasenose, University
College, Magdalen Hall, Oriel and New College were all in this category,
and augmented the colleges which had supported King in 1722 and were
equally clear on this occasion. The combination overwhelmingly
defeated opponents who had the apparent advantage of a divided tory
cause, and strong support from university whigs.[1]

Newdigate's victory was deeply significant, though not perhaps for the
obvious reasons. Government men naturally saw it as new evidence of
the strength of Jacobitism in Oxford. Historians have fairly cast doubt on
the extent of this Jacobitism, though the question is of little real significance. The truth is that Oxford's toryism was much like the nation's, or
rather the gentry's toryism. It included some authentic Jacobites, and
some authentic Hanoverians. But it consisted largely of those in the
middle, who were occasionally brought, sentimentally, to contemplate
the possibility of a restored Stuart line prepared to respect the Church
of England, but who certainly did not think of acting themselves. For
most of the period the Hanoverian dynasty seemed sufficiently strong to
make the risks of rebellion unacceptably high. No doubt a major victory
by Stuart forces on English soil would have made a difference, and it is
difficult to envisage large-scale support at Oxford for the existing regime
if it had seriously faltered. As it is, Oxford's record was of a kind which
makes it possible to claim both that there was a basic acceptance of the
Hanoverian line while it prospered and at the same time substantial dis-
satisfaction with the personnel and policies of Hanoverian rule. The
important point, however, is that the problem of Jacobitism distorts
rather than illuminates the position of the university in the reigns of
George I and George II. To picture it either as treacherously unfaithful or
as loyal but misunderstood is scarcely helpful. Oxford's true role was as
the inspiration and symbol of tory resistance to the great proscription of
the period, a tory resistance whose durability and tenacity historians,
perhaps over-impressed with the solid grasp of the whig supremacy on
the machinery of power, have not always sufficiently recognized. Above

[1] *True Copy of the Poll.*

all Oxford's evolution strictly corresponded to that of the class to which, with the gradual dissolution of the court toryism which had been so influential under Queen Anne, it became naturally attached—the country gentlemen. It was they who sent their sons to the majority of colleges, they who provided the great mass of employment and patronage on which the clergy depended, they who elected Oxford's friends at West-minster, they, indeed, who were to accompany Oxford to court in 1760. It was peculiarly appropriate that one of their number should be elected a university burgess in 1751; it was also a powerful testimony to the endur-ing stamina of the Anglican squirearchy in church and state in a period when many thought both a lost cause.[1]

[1] Since this was written, L. Colley, *In Defiance of Oligarchy: the Tory Party, 1714-60* (Cambridge 1982), has redressed the balance.

5

Political Respectability 1751–1771

L. S. SUTHERLAND

IN THE twenty years following the election of Sir Roger Newdigate as university burgess in 1751 the foundations were laid of an Oxford politically very different from that of the first half of the century. The change was not complete until after Lord North,[1] as first lord of the treasury, was elected chancellor in 1772, nor, in the years immediately following 1751, was it apparent that such a change was on the way. Indeed the events of the Oxfordshire election of 1754-5 might have suggested that relations between ministers and the university had, if anything, deteriorated. But even at this early stage there were signs that these relations were beginning to be based more on old habits and the *partis pris* of individuals on the one side and frustration on the other than on any real conflicts of loyalty. It was not in the circumstances surprising that movements of national politics—the end of the 'Old Whig' political dominance, the excitement of war and victory and finally the accession of a new king—should erode the structure of past antagonisms within the university.

When, in 1750, ministers for political reasons abandoned one of the most formidable attacks they had ever planned to launch on the autonomy of the university,[2] it was tacitly assumed that it would have no successor. As 'all further Thoughts about the Universities seem to be laid aside', wrote Lord Chancellor Hardwicke, 'it seems to be the only thing left to give some Encouragement and Spirit to the well-affected there . . .'[3]

The most provocative speeches of William King, the well-known Jacobite principal of St Mary Hall, were delivered when his hopes for the Jacobite cause were fading, and, as a government spokesman in the university admitted, the number of genuine Jacobites there had become inconsiderable.[4] Yet cautious university politicians, who for years had

---

[1] Frederick, Lord North (1732-92), from 1790 2nd e. of Guilford; m. Trin. 1749; chancellor of the university 1772-92.

[2] See P. Langford, 'Tories and Jacobites 1714-1751', pp. 121-5 above.

[3] Hardwicke–Newcastle, 15 Apr. 1750, BL Add. MS 32720, fos 221-2.

[4] [H. Brooke,] *A Letter to the Oxford Tories* (London 1750).

made it their aim to repress the sallies of their extremist colleagues, found it if anything a harder task now than had their predecessors.

The policy of the whig Administrations had been apt to be feeble as well as hostile. Their attempts to offset the predominance of the tories in the university by offering preferment to members of its few whig colleges had been half-hearted, particularly after Newcastle became chancellor of Cambridge University in 1748, and they had on occasion alienated friends as well as foes by encouraging disreputable informers who, stimulated by hopes of clerical preferment, delated their colleagues as Jacobites. A singularly virulent specimen of this class, Richard Blacow, who had played a mischievous part in the troubles of the late forties, was still influential in ministerial circles in the fifties—indeed in 1754 he had been made a canon of Windsor—and was encouraging others, notably Thomas Bray, fellow of Exeter, and his younger colleague the Hebraist Benjamin Kennicott, to follow his example.[1] Though this group was the last to ply its unattractive trade, and was assailed by King and others with unexampled ferocity, it went further than anyone had gone before. In 1754 it went so far as to invent an entirely fictitious plot to promote its ends.

The general election of 1754 was not as a whole a difficult one for the Administration, but it saw, throughout the country, an unexpected flare-up of whig-tory animosity. The popular clamour against the Jewish naturalization act (so violent that the government ignominiously repealed it) was much less an outbreak of popular anti-semitism than a revival of the cry 'the Church in Danger'.[2] And when three Oxfordshire whig peers (the duke of Marlborough, Lord Macclesfield and Lord Harcourt) sponsored two whig candidates (Sir Edward Turner, a baronet rich from inherited commercial wealth, and Lord Parker,[3] son and heir of Macclesfield) to oppose the tories who controlled the county, the contest was bound to be bitter.[4] In this bitterness the university as the citadel of tory principles and closely linked with the county tories could hardly fail to share, however much its institutional leaders might hope to keep it out of a battle with which it had no formal connection.

[1] Thomas Bray (1706-85), m. Exeter 1726, rector 1771-85. Benjamin Kennicott (1718-83), m. Wadham 1744; fellow Exeter 1747-71; canon Ch.Ch. 1770; Radcliffe Librarian 1767-83. A close follower of Bray in politics, but also (what Bray had no claim to be) a dedicated scholar. Bray and Kennicott were already informing in 1749. Whether they were then in touch with Blacow is not clear. Blacow and Bray were on familiar terms by 1753.

[2] T. W. Perry, *Public Opinion and Politics in Eighteenth-Century England: a study of the Jew bill of 1753* (Cambridge Mass. 1962).

[3] Thomas Parker (1723-95), from 1764 3rd e. of Macclesfield; m. Hart Hall 1740; hon. MA 1743, DCL 1773; MP Oxon. 1754-61.

[4] The history of the election has been carefully studied, first by R. J. Robson, *The Oxfordshire Election of 1754* (Oxford 1949) and later by W. R. Ward, *Georgian Oxford* (Oxford 1958), more briefly but with the advantage of additional manuscript material. *The Oxfordshire Election of 1754*, ed. G. H. Dannatt (Oxfordshire County Council record publ. no. 6 1970) reproduces useful material.

The animosity on the tory side against their whig challengers was intensified by the advantages which their opponents enjoyed from the support of the Administration; and the university, always politically well informed, knew what these were as well as the county. They probably did not know that considerable sums had been promised to Marlborough and Macclesfield from the secret service funds, but they did know that the high sheriff, Thomas Blackall of Haseley, was pricked from among the stronger supporters of the local 'New Interest' (as the whigs now called themselves) and that the pro-government London press was lined up in their support.[1] This inevitably meant that the university writers also became involved. Indeed Blacow, who for some time had been active as a government writer, was by 1753 working for the whigs in the county and by the middle of 1754 had become editor of a new government paper the *Evening Advertizer* intended to do battle with the tory *London Evening Post*, whose writers were largely university supporters.[2] It also meant that the secretary of state's office was prepared to harass the publications of the Old Interest with all the means open to it before John Wilkes engaged in his campaign against general warrants.[3]

From the beginning a most active and organized press campaign was mounted by both sides. The challengers asserted that the tories were by definition Jacobites, fomenters of popery and fundamentally opposed to everything the Protestant Succession stood for. Those whom they challenged countered by accusing them of enmity to the church and of being self-interested supporters of an aristocratic faction disturbing the peace of the county for its personal ends. They also ridiculed their opponents' use of 'stale' anti-tory catchwords, the truth of which they stoutly denied. The course of the campaign was eventful enough to attract widespread interest: an unusually long run-up to the poll, a poll lasting seven days, followed by a demand for a scrutiny, which remained incomplete at the date for the return of the writ. This was followed by an irregular (and indeed illegal) return of all four candidates by the sheriff, so that when the new parliament assembled some five months later the house spent more than forty days of parliamentary time debating the

[1] On the promise of funding see L. B. Namier, *The Structure of Politics at the Accession of George III* (London 1929), 246-7. Blackall had been thought of as a possible New Interest candidate if, as was at first hoped, the city also had been contested: *VCH Oxon.* iv. 154; Harcourt–Bray, 22 Jan. 1754, Bray MSS.

[2] *The Evening Advertizer*, never very successful, came to an end in 1758. No full run appears to exist, though there are a number of issues in the Burney collection in the British Library. Blacow gives an account of its foundation in his *Letter to William King, LL.D.* (London 1755). Various references in the Bray MSS suggest that Macclesfield, in pursuance of New Interest publicity, had at one time a controlling interest over it. The *Evening Post* was a paper with a long and successful life, though for many years strongly anti-ministerial. Richard Nutt, its publisher and printer, was condemned for seditious libel in 1755—an end industriously sought by Blacow, who on one occasion tried to persuade Exeter College to prosecute him: Blacow–Bray, 17 and 23 Oct. 1754, Bray MSS.

[3] On this subject generally see L. W. Hanson, *Government and the Press 1695-1763* (Oxford 1936).

controverted election. In these debates, the case of the Old Interest was skilfully presented. The university's counsel, Charles Pratt, later Lord Chancellor Camden, was said to have founded his reputation on his management of it.[1] Several points of constitutional importance were raised by them,[2] though with the weight of the government majority relentlessly exerted against it, the Old Interest could not hope to avert defeat in the house, and the result of the poll was reversed. The issue was before the public for nearly three years, and these events, together with the legendary expenses incurred by both sides, gave the election a notoriety which was not forgotten for many years.

The university's concern in these events can be considered under various heads. In the first place, despite conscientious attempts by the vice-chancellor[3] and the hebdomadal board to keep the university out of the turmoil, their plans broke down as soon as polling began. The collapse was not due, as might have been expected, to indisciplined acts by colleges who favoured the Old Interest; it is easy to imagine the indignation of the Administration and its informers had such taken place. It was on the contrary the result of defiance of the ban imposed by the university authorities on political activities during the election by one of the whig colleges—Exeter—acting in collusion with the leaders of the New Interest in the county. The story is well known, how Exeter, on the morning of the day on which the poll began, threw open its gates to the New Interest voters indiscriminately and, having entertained them lavishly at the candidates' expense, let them go out through its north gate into the rear of the polling booths in Broad Street. They continued thus to outrage university opinion and assist the whig county voters during the seven days of the poll.

It is not clear how effective Exeter's aid to their allies was, though it won from them both praise and promise of reward.[4] It should be noted that there is no evidence that the ministry as a body encouraged or even

[1] John (Lord) Campbell, *Lives of the Lord Chancellors and Keepers of the Great Seal of England* (8 vols London 1845-69) v. 357.

[2] In particular the claims of a certain class of copyholder to vote in county elections and the conduct of the sheriff in returning all four candidates.

[3] At this time George Huddesford (1699-1776), m. Trin. 1715, president 1731-76; vice-chancellor 1753-6; keeper of the Ashmolean 1732-55.

[4] Writing to Bray on 30 April 1754 (Bray MSS) Harcourt thanked the rector, Francis Webber (1708-71, m. Exeter 1725, rector 1750-71) and fellows for their 'generous assistance'.

Such an instance of Zeal and Loyalty no other Society can pretend to. I am sure it is incumbent upon those who are invested with power, to take a particular notice of those who have dared to signalize themselves upon so trying an Occasion. All the Gentlemen that I have seen, declare that we could not have polled a hundred Votes, without the assistance of your College. But however we may be indebted to your Society, we are undoubtedly more to you, than to allmost any one person of the Party.

The praise is obviously exaggerated. The sheriff would not have closed the poll until all of his party had cast their votes; and, as Exeter's opponents pointed out, if the Old Interest supporters were able

approved such spectacular intervention in a county election by colleges from which it expected political support.[1] Certainly none of the other three whig colleges, Christ Church, Merton and Wadham, either followed Exeter's example or gave it support in the conflicts within the university which followed. Of the four whig colleges Christ Church was the only one which. could claim a solid bloc of county voters among its resident members and they cast their votes on the New Interest side as was expected of them but without great zest. On a vacancy in the office of under-treasurer it did, however, appoint a strong New Interest supporter to a position of importance for the college's relations with the city, but it was generally agreed that Christ Church's attitude as a whig supporter was lukewarm, and none of the other whig colleges was more active.[2]

Isolated though Exeter's gesture might be, it nevertheless was important, for it not only stimulated the university's concerns in the election contest, but also gave rise to a violent pamphlet war within the university itself which formed an interlude in the main controversy, having, when once it had begun, little direct concern with the election. On the contrary it soon developed into a continuation of the whig-tory conflicts of the forties. Even the contestants were the same, for Blacow threw himself whole-heartedly into the justification of Exeter, and (under cover of this) into an attack both on his old enemy Dr King and on the vice-chancellor; while King was delighted to renew hostilities against the government informers and delators whom he had earlier attacked. The only obvious difference between 1754 and 1747 was that the vice-chancellor now in office, unlike his predecessor, was of impeccable anti-Jacobite antecedents, though this made little difference to Blacow's line of attack.

There had been some sparring in the press between university partisans, and hostile comments were made by Dr King at Encaenia as early as July 1754 (on the occasion of the installation of Westmorland as high

and willing to block fourteen polling stations strung out along Broad Street there was clearly nothing to prevent their blocking Exeter's gate into the same street. Nevertheless, the college broke all attempts to keep the university neutral in the poll.

[1] Rewards to Exeter from the government were disappointing. Two years later, it is true, the rector was chosen dean of Hereford and Kennicott had already obtained the curacy of Culham from Thomas Secker, then bishop of Oxford, but he may well have earned it by his scholarship. Thomas Secker (1693-1768), m. Exeter 1721; bp of Bristol 1735-7, Oxford 1737-58, abp of Canterbury 1758-68.

[2] Macclesfield grudgingly admitted 'at least we may be certain, that the Weight of Christ Church upon their Tradesmen will not be turned against us; as I fear, it was in the time of the late Under-Treasurer': Macclesfield-Bray, 23 Oct. 1753, Bray MSS. Presumably he was speaking of city politics—there had been no opportunity of influencing county voters. Richard Hanwell was the new under-treasurer. Writing to Bray on 4 August 1754 (Bray MSS) Harcourt said of Christ Church: 'where between friends I may venture to say that nothing right will be done, as long as the Management of that place continues in the hands it is now in . . .'. John Conybeare was at that time dean.

steward of the university) but hostilities did not open formally until after the vice-chancellor's annual speech of 8 October, in which (reviewing the events of the year) he praised all societies other than Exeter for their behaviour during the poll, and attacked the conduct of the latter in no uncertain terms.[1] When the rector of Exeter and four of his fellows called on him with a request for a copy of his speech and it was refused them, they were able to use this as a *casus belli* and on 24 November a pamphlet was published entitled *A Defence of the Rector and Fellows of Exeter College* which not only sought to justify Exeter's actions, but attacked the vice-chancellor and his supporters on a wide front.[2]

If the Exeter pamphleteers were to be believed, the conflict which followed and which lasted without intermission for some five months was one in which the rest of the university were the attackers and Exeter the victimized defenders. It would be unwise to accept this interpretation without further examination. In the six months which had intervened between the end of the county poll and the vice-chancellor's speech there had been time for a good deal of action and, as the extensive correspondence of Thomas Bray in Exeter makes clear, much of the initiative came from that college and its friends in the county. The correspondence shows, for instance, that they had decided to launch an attack on the vice-chancellor in the public press before his speech had been delivered, and had planned the form of their pamphlet. It also makes clear that Lord Macclesfield, as leader of the New Interest in the county, was the authority in so doing.[3] It is obvious that he found the conflict within the university useful in keeping public interest alive during the lull made necessary before the new parliament met and could review the whig-tory party controversy.[4]

Equally significant was the fact that during these six months Exeter and its friends had put much work into engineering that curious con-

[1] The speech was not usually printed or recorded, but on this occasion the relevant parts of it were printed unofficially by the London and Oxford presses.

[2] It was dated 20 November 1754. On 26 Nov. Thomas Patten (1732-1806, m. CCC 1749) wrote to Newdigate: 'We cannot discover the Author of the Exeter Defence. No one cares to own it, tho' there are several who will take it kindly if the World will father it upon them.' Newdigate MS CR136/B2204. Francis Webber was later generally thought to be its author, though Blacow and Bray (and probably Kennicott) were obviously concerned in its production.

[3] You will see that I suppressed your Squib, and did not cause it to be inserted in the Evening [Advertizer]; for which I had these two reasons; in the first place I thought it might be right to conceal as much as might be from our Adversaries, that their and the Vice-Chancellor's conduct was likely to be brought before *the Tribunal of Fame*, or at least what parts of their conduct would be chiefly insisted upon in a pamphlet for that purpose; and secondly because nothing, which it might be proper to enlarge upon in the pamphlet, should in any degree be anticipated by a paragraph in a newspaper ... Macclesfield-Bray, 14 Oct. 1754, Bray MSS.

[4] He had already in July decided to call off the press campaign at least until the debate on the controverted election began, as its continuance was likely to 'create a nauseousness in the Generality of Readers': same-same, 15 July 1754, ibid.

spiracy known as the 'Rag Plot', the purpose of which was to smear the university with the imputation of active Jacobitism. The 'Plot' was based on the alleged discovery of some Jacobite verses among rags thrown down outside a shop on Carfax. The details of this ludicrous, even if somewhat sinister, conspiracy have long been known, since they were almost at once unravelled by a court consisting of the vice-chancellor, the mayor and William Blackstone, who exercised his formidable legal acumen on it.[1] What was not known until the Bray correspondence became available for examination was that Bray was the stage-manager of the 'plot' in Oxford—and one at least of its originators—and that not only was Blacow in London acting in collusion with him, but that almost to a man so were the leaders of the New Interest in the county.[2] Moreover, when Blacow brought his account of the alleged plot before Lord Holdernesse, the secretary of state (which owing to a foolish blunder it was at once known he had done), he acted with the support and under the recommendation of Macclesfield.[3] Nor was it then clear (as it is now) that when it was brought before the Administration the secretary of state entered into the affair without making any attempt to examine the evidence.

Thanks to the promptitude with which the university exposed the conspiracy it was soon discredited, and by the time the vice-chancellor made his speech on 8 October he must have felt some confidence that the danger of ill effects to the university was over, but the acerbity with which he spoke of Exeter must have been increased by the fact that he himself had received a threatening letter on the subject from Blacow.[4]

[1] A pamphlet describing the proceedings was published on 5 January 1755: *Information and other Papers relating to the Treasonable Verses found at Oxford, July 17 1754* (Oxford 1755) ran to two editions and was obviously written by Blackstone, who had interrogated the witnesses; there are several copies in Bodl. including one in Gough Oxford 39/16b. It would seem that Blackstone's pamphlet was ready for publication early in October 1754: Blacow-Bray, 5 Oct. 1754, Bray MSS. If it had come out as early as that Blacow believed he would have been able to get the secretary of state to stop its publication by king's warrant. Its contents had already been well ventilated in the London and Oxford tory presses. The mayor was Daniel Shilfox.

[2] Bray's responsibility is clear from Blacow's recriminations when the plan went awry: see for example his letter to Bray, 3 Aug. 1754, Bray MSS. Blacow was at once identified as the agent for spreading the story of the 'plot' through an identical error of dating which occurred in the stories printed in three separate London evening papers (and at once traced to him) and which was repeated when the secretary of state offered a reward for the discovery of the alleged plotters. The secretary of state and prominent New Interest JPs made attempts to discredit Blackstone's interrogation of New Interest supporters, but did so with total lack of success: see for example Blacow-Bray, 27 Aug. 1754, Bray MSS; Bodl. Gough Oxford 39/16b.

[3] See Blacow-Bray, 27 July 1754 (containing an extract of a letter from Holdernesse to Macclesfield), Bray MSS; and other correspondence ibid. No correspondence from Holdernesse is entered in the letterbooks of the secretary of state's office, though the text of the proclamation offering an award for discovery of the 'plot' is in the official papers: PRO SP 36, pt ii, fo. 242.

[4] Blacow-Huddesford, 3 October 1754 (copy in Bray MSS). The vice-chancellor replied civilly but firmly on 7 Oct. (copy ibid.). Blacow wrote a further letter to him of an even more threatening kind, to which he does not seem to have replied.

King's identification of the authors of the *Defence of Exeter* with the 'Society of Informers' is also explained by their present as well as their past activities.[1]

The most important concern, however, which the university had in the Oxfordshire election was its part in the phenomenal press campaign which accompanied it in all its phases: the election proper, the controversies in the university arising out of it, and finally the debates in the house of commons. The last two of these overlapped in time. It may be noted that the New Interest was actively concerned in the first and second of these phases only. As it was now dependent on the government's parliamentary majority and the government was anxious to avoid discussion of general principles, controversies 'without doors' were not only unnecessary but unwelcome. The press campaign during the struggle was by far the most voluminous and the highest in literary quality in the century. The presses in London and Oxford were kept in full activity; what became the flourishing local paper *Jackson's Oxford Journal* was founded in the first instance in order to publish election material from both sides. All existing newspapers and periodicals carried election news, and enterprising publishers reprinted collections of these ephemera for the use of distant readers. There is no doubt that most of this mass of printed material came from the pens of resident senior members of the university and was the result of careful organization and production.

The reader who has made his way through the bewildering variety of broadsheets, ballads, squibs, satires and pamphlets, short and long, some witty and clever, most of them scurrilous, and some simply coarse and unpleasant, is at first inclined to believe that they represent an entirely unorganized outburst of individual ingenuity in a society where, as one writer said, 'every young Fellow who has a Standish on his Table, and a thought in his Head, is too ready on the least Provocation, to vent it in a *Song*, a *Lampoon* or a *Satyr*'.[2] But further scrutiny shows that, though there were no doubt many such *francs-tireurs*, on both sides they depended on carefully planned campaigns. We are fortunate in having in the Bray correspondence the raw material of the activities of one of the parties, that of the New Interest, but it had far less talent to call on in the university than the Old Interest. Although most of the New Interest publications were produced in Oxford it was not to the university that they looked for the organization which lay behind them. Macclesfield took

---

[1] W. King, *Apology or Vindication of himself from the several Matters charged on him by the Society of Informers* ... (Oxford Feb. 1755) ran to three editions; in the second King added a note that by 'Society of Informers' he meant 'Authors of libels in the *Advertizer* and authors of a virulent Pamphlet called a *Defence of the Rector and Fellows of Exeter*'.

[2] *Jackson's Oxford Journal*, 2 Feb. 1754, signed 'L.M.', probably by Benjamin Buckler.

this over as part of the plan for his son's candidature, and he also was chief spokesman for the three whig aristocrats who were responsible for the campaign as a whole. In London it was he who employed Blacow, at first primarily for printing and publishing but later in a more responsible capacity. In Oxford he had the devoted assistance in all matters of party management including publications of Bray (neither a savoury nor a likeable man[1] but one who served him well), Harcourt and Marlborough. Harcourt played a smaller part in the organization, but was consulted on all major matters and could usually be relied upon to follow a lead given by Macclesfield. He made, moreover, one personal contribution of considerable value: he introduced to Marlborough an able young man who had recently taken his MA at University College to act as a factotum, Charles Jenkinson, younger son of a junior branch of a well-known Oxfordshire family, and later to attain high political office.[2] He carried out for Marlborough much the same duties as Bray did for Macclesfield, though he was able to move more freely in county society than could Bray. Many years later, after his death, his second son repeated a garbled family tradition that his father had run the literary campaign for the whigs and Blackstone that for the tories.[3] A tactful young man, Jenkinson worked well with both Macclesfield and Bray, and both he and Bray contributed vigorously to the press for their party. Macclesfield did not hesitate to turn down, however, any contribution from either which he thought unserviceable.[4]

There was another small group among the New Interest in the university whose lively literary campaign seems to have been largely

---

[1] Bray was at this time involved in proceedings at law against a young prostitute who accused him of fathering her child. The case against him was fanned by his political opponents, but her claim was defeated. Entries in his correspondence, however, do not give him an entirely clean sheet.

[2] Charles Jenkinson (1727-1808), from 1796 1st e. of Liverpool; m. Univ. 1746. For his introduction to Marlborough see N. S. Jucker, *The Jenkinson papers 1760-66* (London 1949); Harcourt-Bray, 17 Dec. 1752, Bray MSS, and other correspondence ibid.

[3] Charles Cecil Cope Jenkinson (1784-1851), from 1828 3rd e. of Liverpool; m. Ch.Ch. 1801; hon. DCL 1841. He thought the election to have been for Oxford city not county and said: 'It is curious that my father wrote the electioneering verses and squibs for the Whigs at this election, and Sir W. Blackstone for the Tories. There are two copies of verses, each celebrating their rival colours (blue and green). Blackstone's are far the best, but my father's not amiss.' Letter to J. W. Croker, 7 Dec. 1845, *The Croker Papers*, ed. L. T. Jennings (3 vols London 1884) iii. 178.

[4] Bray was greatly praised by both Macclesfield and Harcourt for a squib accusing the tories, the university, Lord Lichfield and the Radcliffe trustees of popery: *Jackson's Oxford Journal*, 19 Jan. 1754. As Harcourt said: 'It has allready done us infinite service, and will be a lasting advantage to us. In short there is a great deal of truth in it, and therefore is the more powerful.' Letter to Bray, 22 Jan. 1754, Bray MSS. On the other hand, he was smartly snubbed by Macclesfield for an incorrect rumour about Jacobite meetings: 'I find at last that there is no foundation for the report you had heard, relating to that Gentleman or his friends appearing in Plaids; for they only distinguished themselves by oak leaves in their hats, on that occasion. But had it been otherwise, the expression *Insensibility of Country Squires and clod pated Peasants* would have been too harsh, and improper to be used by the friends of two Gentlemen, who are carrying on a contest for a County Election.' Macclesfield-Bray, 19 Feb. 1754, ibid.

independent. This was composed of a few university men who owed their loyalty chiefly to Sir Edward Turner and whose moving spirit was his brother-in-law Theophilus Leigh, master of Balliol. Several of them were known for their wit, and Leigh was a famous punster. So much Old Interest fire was directed against them that their efforts must have been thought to be telling. Except where Jenkinson was the intermediary they appear to have had few contacts with Macclesfield or Bray, and with the Exeter supporters they seem at one time at any rate to have been on bad terms.[1]

With so much contribution to the pamphlet war from the whig party it would be surprising indeed were there not much more from that of the tories, predominant in the university; but as usual in tory politics little personal political material survives in the early years of the Hanoverian period, for obvious reasons. Indeed one historian has been so much struck by this in the years 1753 and 1754 that he has been led to believe that the university's tory party dissociated itself from the campaign which was in process.[2] It is true that no body of personal papers on the tory side has survived such as that fortuitously preserved at Exeter College for the whigs. It is also true that since most of the papers on both sides are anonymous their authorship can only be identified when internal evidence provides a guide. But a number of generalizations can be made about the participants.

In the first place, none of the tory peers played the directing part in the press campaign assumed by Macclesfield among the whigs. Indeed there are signs of disarray among tory leaders in the county. Nor did any London journalist exercise an influence comparable to that of Blacow. New Interest writers indeed often speculated without success as to who gave the *London Evening Post* its detailed Old Interest news from Oxford, but no one suggested that the fountain-head of this news was anywhere else but in the university itself; that some person or small group was controlling the main line of Old Interest publications was obvious. Relevant pamphlets, shorter prose pieces and even poems and ballads came out at the right time and made what were evidently agreed points. It was clearly the aim of those planning the tory campaign to concentrate on the present and not be forced back into what was for them an unprofitable past. Satires against Exeter College, against Blacow, the sheriff of Oxfordshire and ministers in general were a common line of defence or attack among them, and since they included the writings of

---

[1] In March 1755 Turner refused to let Blacow have franks for the postage of a violent attack he had printed on the vice-chancellor, '... a strange, strange, strange man' Blacow meditated (Blacow–Bray, 14 Mar. 1755, Bray MSS). The pamphlet was an *Address to the Rev. Dr Huddesford... occasion'd by what is called His Proper Reply to the Defence...* (London [early March] 1755).

[2] Robson, *Oxfordshire Election of 1754*, 71 suggests that the appointment in 1754 of Westmorland as high steward and not of Lichfield (as was tipped in *Jackson's Oxford Journal*, 5 Jan. 1754) was a sign of the divisions of opinion among tories which were later prominent.

some men who were both witty and acute they enjoyed considerable popular success.

The press campaign of the Old Interest was in fact obviously—like that of the New Interest—under some degree of central control; the control in this case rested within the university. It was generally agreed by their opponents that there were only two possible persons to give it such a lead: one was the old Jacobite William King, the other the young political leader William Blackstone. King had a great reputation among the tory friends of the university, wrote in excellent Latin and in English verse which was neat though his prose was heavy.[1] At the beginning of 1754 he had published a long satirical work somewhat after the nature of *Gulliver's Travels* called *The Dreamer*, to which the whigs attributed political significance but in which the tory writers did not show themselves much interested. He was in fact growing old, and his well-known Jacobite sympathies were not those favoured by the Old Interest writers of 1754, though the latter could be relied on to rally to his personal support when he was attacked by Blacow and his friends. Even Blacow did not believe that he wrote the election pamphlets for the Old Interest,[2] though it was conceived he might take the lead when purely university conflicts came to the fore.

The claims of Blackstone were very different. Though a tory he was at no stage of his life in the least a Jacobite. He was the most powerful university politician of his day, who had recently managed with skill the parliamentary election of Sir Roger Newdigate. He was able and ambitious, had legal contacts outside the university and parliamentary ones through Newdigate, who was by now influential in tory quarters in the house. Eight years later he told Lord Shelburne[3] that, tory though he was, he had 'laboured for ten Years together in this University, and I hope with some Success, in explaining, defending, and propagating the Principles of Loyalty and Liberty, and those of the Revolution in particular'.[4] He had obviously in mind the 1754 election. We know too that he steered the vice-chancellor through the shoals of the Rag Plot with discretion and that he was prominent behind the scenes in preparing the case for the Old Interest in the house of commons in

---

[1] D. Greenwood, *William King: Tory and Jacobite* (Oxford 1969).

[2] This was stated by Kennicott in his immensely long pamphlet *A Letter to Dr King Occasion'd by his Late Apology, and in particular by such Parts of it as are meant to defame Mr Kennicott*... (London 1755). The Bray MSS show that it was, as generally assumed, written by Kennicott himself, that it was written under Blacow's direct influence, and part of it in his house, though he was at the end disgusted by Kennicott's obstinacy in refusing to take advice about its presentation.

[3] William Petty (1737-1805), from 1784 1st marquess of Lansdowne; m. Ch.Ch. 1755.

[4] Letter of 22 Oct. 1762, Bowood MS S35. On 2 December 1754 in a letter to Newdigate he spoke of 'the noble Independence, which has ever been the Principle of the University' which 'however it may unjustly be branded with the Name of Disaffection, is thoroughly consistent with Loyalty, and inseparable from a Zeal for constitutional Liberty': Newdigate MS CR136/B1490.

1754-5.[1] Nevertheless the fact remains that, apart from an account of the Rag Plot published in January 1755 which bears all the signs of his authority and which was studiously factual, there is nothing written during the whole course of the election campaign which in the least resembles his known writings, and that none of his watchful enemies thought that there was.

This is not surprising. His personal position at that time made it obvious that he could not have taken an active part in party wrangles without loss of status.[2] He had just begun to deliver the lectures on law and the constitution which were later to be published as the *Commentaries on the Laws of England*.[3] He was at this very time lecturing on the delicate constitutional questions of parliamentary representation and the text of the *Commentaries* shows how cautiously he did so. He had no objection to government employment, and personal ambition and public principle combined to make a moderate line the only possible one for him. This does not mean, however, that we need conclude that he stood aside from his party's press campaign.

Blackstone's career as a university politician shows him to have been a past master in the art of presenting his own views through the mouths of others under his influence. We know the names of at least two such men in the university: Thomas Winchester of Magdalen and his lifelong *fidus Achates* Benjamin Buckler, fellow of All Souls, a man of much wit and miscellaneous learning and absolutely no personal ambition.[4] When the election started Buckler was chiefly known in the university as the author of *A Complete Vindication of the Mallard of All-Soul's College* (London 1750). His elegant style, light touch and ingenuity in the choice of subjects were eminently suited to the type of campaign the Old Interest was waging, and may indeed, to some extent, have determined its character. Though it is not possible to draw up a list of his writings during these years three major pamphlets were attributed to him by contemporaries with a considerable degree of probability. The earliest

[1] This is reflected in the entries in Newdigate's diary: Newdigate MS CR136/A [585] and [586]. It would seem that he had already produced at this time for the assistance of his party in the house the *Considerations on the Question, whether Tenants by Copy of Court Roll... are Freeholders qualified to vote in Elections for Knights of the Shire* (London 1758) which he published at the request of members.

[2] Both Robson and Ward believe that he was present at a meeting of Old Interest sympathizers in London on 1 March 1753, satirically described in *Jackson's Oxford Journal*, 12 May 1753. They assumed that Alderman Bl--k--st-n, described as at the head of the Independents at the meeting, to have been Blackstone. The context makes it clear, however, that the person in question was quite definitely Sir Matthew Blackiston, alderman and grocer of the city of London: see *Horace Walpole's Correspondence*, ed. W. S. Lewis *et al.* (48 vols New Haven, London and Oxford 1937-83) xx. 261 n. This error led them into a complete misunderstanding of other parts of Blackstone's activities in the press campaign.

[3] William Blackstone, *Commentaries on the Laws of England* (4 vols Oxford 1765-9).

[4] Thomas Winchester (1713-80), m. Magd. 1729, vice-president 1754. Benjamin Buckler (1716-80), m. Oriel 1733; fellow All Souls 1739; keeper of the archives 1777-80.

comes at the beginning of *Jackson's Oxford Journal* for 25 April 1753 and is entitled 'News Boys, News; More and More News', this counterblast to a New Interest publication in the same journal for 11 April 1753 headed 'News Boys, News' being attributed by some contemporaries to Jenkinson;[1] the second is *Serious Reflections on the Dangerous Tendency of the Common Practice of Card-Playing, especially of the Game of All Fours* (London 19 November 1754), a pamphlet attacking the sheriff's returns in the election, which Administration had serious thoughts of seizing as a seditious libel;[2] the last is *Proper Explanation of the Oxford Almanack for this Present Year MDCCLV* (London [March] 1755), attacking both the New Interest and Exeter College.[3] Blacow tried unsuccessfully to persuade Exeter to proceed at law against the publisher.

There is also good stylistic evidence to suggest that at least three other long pamphlets published between 1753 and 1755 came from his pen.[4] He would also appear to have been a frequent and effective contributor to *Jackson's Oxford Journal*.[5] It is significant too that he ended the election period in high favour with the tory leaders. In 1756 he was presented by Lord Abingdon[6] with two very favourably placed livings, the vicarage of Cumnor and the rectory of Frilsham which he could hold together with his All Souls fellowship. Moreover in 1759 when Westmorland was elected chancellor he was nominated to preach the official sermon at the inauguration ceremony and the chancellor ordered it to

[1] However, a contemporary manuscript note on the copy in Bodl. attributes it to Buckler, as does J. Nichols, *Literary Anecdotes of the Eighteenth Century* (9 vols London 1812-15) iii. 679 (note on William Jackson).

[2] In *Dissertations upon the Species of Writing called Humour* (London 1760) the author [T. Nowell] referred to 'those several Inimitable Pieces, generally allowed to be written by him [Buckler]', and gives among other illustrations of his work *The Game of All-Fours*. On the talk of a government prosecution of the printer of *All-Fours* see Blacow—Bray and Parker—Bray, 28 Nov. 1754, Bray MSS.

[3] The attribution to Buckler appears not only in *Dissertations upon the Species* but also in [G. Colman the elder] *Terrae-Filius* (4 nos London July 1763) no. 2, p. 27 and in a contemporary hand on the copy in Bodl. Gough Adds. Oxon 8° 53 (5).

[4] The first is *The Christian's New Warning Piece, or a Full and True Account of the Circumcision of Sir E[dwar]d T[urne]r Bart* (London 1753), a coarse and highly scurrilous piece, but the only amusing satire which appeared on the topic of the Jew bill, and not unlike some of Buckler's earlier works, for example *A Philosophical Dialogue concerning Decency* (London 1751). The second is *Mr Boots's Apology for the Conduct of the late High Sheriff in Answer to An Infamous Libel Intitled The Blackest of All Black Jokes* (London 17 Apr. 1755); there is no external clue to the authorship of this pamphlet, but in content and style it resembles the other pamphlets attributed to him. The third pamphlet is *The Last Blow, or an Unanswerable Vindication of the Society of Exeter College* (London [early March] 1753). Blacow had thought this was by King, and this opinion is accepted by Greenwood, but Kennicott classed it with the *Proper Explanation of the Oxford Almanack ...* as not accepted as his by Oxford opinion, and internal evidence seems to support this view: Blacow—Bray, 11 Feb. 1755, Bray MSS; Greenwood, *William King*, 277; [Kennicott,] *Letter to Dr King*.

[5] For instance it would seem likely from stylistic evidence that he was the 'L.M.' responsible for answering Bray's accusations of popery on 19 January 1754. His first letter appeared on 2 February 1754 and the interchange (in which 'L.M.' was much the more effective writer) continued until 2 March.

[6] Willoughby Bertie (1682-1760), 3rd e. of Abingdon; m. CCC 1707.

be published; if we exclude another humorous piece[1] this was the only sermon Buckler ever bothered to print.

The Old Interest put up a good fight in the university and the county but the election left the former in a disconsolate condition. The date coincided with that of its lowest undergraduate entry of the century and academics were uneasily aware of the effects on their numbers of their political reputation. And despite the care they had taken to rebut charges of Jacobitism, a speech by Pitt in the house of commons at the end of 1754 reiterated the accusation in memorable terms, a piece of oratorical irresponsibility for which the university never fully forgave him.[2]

The events of the political past were soon, however, swept aside by the beginning of radical changes at Westminster. The coming of war, the decline of the Old Whig dominance and the rise of Pitt with the aid of the disorganized tory party marked the beginning of the end of a long-established political system. In these changes the university was little concerned. Blackstone wrote to Newdigate on 27 February 1758 deploring the adherence of the country gentlemen to Pitt, the new minister:

... I cannot think all patriot Schemes and publicspirited Measures are to be dropped, merely to support a Minister, who has yet given You nothing but fine Words to depend upon. He has declaimed it is true against The Army, but saddled us with a larger than ever was granted before, in the time even of continental Wars; and all the Amends he has hitherto made for joining in the most pernicious Schemes of former Ministers, is by clapping his Hand on his Breast and crying 'Who is not sorry?' ... In the mean time the Spirit of the People is dejected; while They forget, or see others forget, all at once every one of those points, on which they have insisted for many years past, that the Salvation of the Nation depended. But these Attempts will destroy Mr P[itt]s Popularity:—It is fit they should, unless he studies to deserve that Popularity by Actions as well as Words. If he means well, let him join the Country Gentlemen in all proper Measures; Not in wild Schemes for annual, but in the Restoration of triennial, or at least quinquennial Parliaments; in a better Place Bill; in a Freeholder's Bill; in reducing not increasing, the Number and Influence of the Army; and in numberless other Measures, which are no Strangers to the Journals of your House.[3]

---

[1] *Elisha's Visit to Gilgal, and his healing the pot of pottage, symbolically explain'd: a sermon preached before the warden and college of All-Souls On Friday the second of November 1759* (published 29 Dec. 1759), copy in Bodl. Godwin Pamph. 111 (10). The publication of this was said to have been undertaken without Buckler's knowledge by some friends. It was criticized for its frivolity and is certainly very amusing.

[2] The wording of the speech varies in different accounts: see P. Palmer's report of it, 27 Nov. 1754, Bodl. MS Top. Oxon. c. 209,m fo 25; Blacow—Bray, 3 Dec. 1754, Bray MSS. The speech was made on 26 Nov. 1754 in a debate on the army estimates. Newdigate's notes on the debate, 26 Nov. 1754, are in Newdigate MS CR136/B2205. Blackstone also refers to it in a letter to Newdigate of 2 Dec. 1754, Newdigate MS CR136/B1490. [E. Bentham,] *The Honor of the University of Oxford defended, against the Illiberal Aspersions of E[dmun]d B[urk]e* ... (London n.d.) 7–8; listing well-known figures who had been at Oxford the author pointed out that Oxford might have added the 'British *Pericles*' (Pitt) had he not made an attack on Oxford as Jacobite long after Jacobitism was extinct there.

[3] Newdigate MS CR136/B1494.

When the great victories came to Pitt, both the university and the city rejoiced, and he enjoyed some personal popularity in Oxford as elsewhere, though its basis was always precarious.

During the last years of George II's reign the university's formal relations with the government remained unchanged. George II personally was unrelenting in his hostility. Archbishop Secker noted under the year 1758:

Sometime this summer, the University of Oxford presented an Address to the King. I took great personal pains with him to persuade him to receive it kindly. I could not prevail on him to speak to the Persons who presented it. But he read it afterwards: and then directed me to return the University thanks for it from him, which I did by a letter to the Vice-Chancellor.[1]

And when at the end of the same year the university had to elect a new chancellor the campaign was fought out bitterly on the traditional whig-tory lines, and Newcastle, despite his many more important preoccupations, found time both to work for the whig cause and to penalize those who had failed to support it.

Events within the university itself however were taking a happier turn. That they did so was due almost entirely to the enterprise of one man, William Blackstone. Between the years 1755 and 1760 he succeeded in carrying through almost single-handed one minor and three major administrative reforms.[2] The minor reform was the reorganization of the procedure of the vice-chancellor's court, of which vice-chancellor Huddesford had made him assessor in 1753.[3] The major were a complete reform of the University Press, carried through against intense opposition and sufficiently important to give Blackstone some justification to be known as the refounder of this important institution; the establishment of the Vinerian foundation for the study of common law; and finally, the most sweeping of all, the demonstration of the university's right to legislate in its own affairs without regard to the restrictions imposed on its freedom of action by the Laudian code.[4] This last was of such importance for the future development of the university that

[1] Lambeth Palace Library, MS 2598, fo 50ᵛ. The vice-chancellor in 1758 was Thomas Randolph (1701-83), m. CCC 1715, president 1748-83; vice-chancellor 1756-9; Lady Margaret prof. divinity 1768-83.

[2] He always had the assistance of a small band of close friends, mainly but not exclusively colleagues at All Souls.

[3] Some authorities give 1750 as the date he took up his office. No register of the vice-chancellor's court survives for his years of office, but a rough minute book (OUA Hyp/A/60) shows that there was a gap in the succession of assessors during the final illness and after the death in 1752 of Henry Brooke. During vacancies the vice-chancellor or a pro-vice-chancellor presided.

[4] For the reform of the Press see I. G. Philip, *William Blackstone and the Reform of the Oxford University Press in the Eighteenth Century* (OBS new ser. vii 1957) and H. G. Carter, *A History of the Oxford University Press* i (Oxford 1975), 325ff. For the Vinerian foundation see L. S. Sutherland, 'Evidence in literary scholarship' in R. Wellek and A. Ribeiro (eds), *Essays in memory of James Marshall Osborn* (Oxford 1979).

a separate chapter in this volume has been allotted to it.[1] It originated in the experiences of the campaign for the election of a chancellor to succeed the earl of Arran.

Arran died on 17 December 1758 in his eighty-ninth year. He had held office since 1715, had always been an inactive chancellor and in recent years had been entirely supine. The election of a successor, nevertheless, inevitably gave rise to intense party conflict in the university and in consequence to intervention by the Administration on behalf of the whig interest there. The Administration had of recent years relaxed a good many of its links with the whig colleges as a result of disappointment in university politics. How far they had lost touch is shown by the fact that just as Newcastle had decided to nominate Thomas Secker, archbishop of Canterbury, as a candidate, and had informed him of his intention, he accidentally discovered that approaches had already been made from whigs within the university to Richard Trevor, bishop of Durham, and that the latter had agreed to stand.[2] Newcastle was indignant and the bishop apologized 'with Tears in his Eyes',[3] but neither of the two proposed candidates can have viewed a campaign with much enthusiasm since it was generally accepted that the only hope of a whig success lay, as in the past, in the possibility of tory disunity.

No one living had seen an Oxford chancellor's election held under normal circumstances (though there were Cambridge analogies[4]) but there was ample evidence in parliamentary elections to show that, however much conflict there might be between tory colleges and the candidates they put up at the beginning of a campaign, the ranks could be counted on to close, through the withdrawal of the weaker candidates in time to prevent a whig victory. Though a parliamentary election was a more leisurely affair than that of a chancellor[5] the tactics were the same—personal pressure, the circulation of printed or manuscript flysheets and the posting of letters exhorting non-resident graduates to come up to Oxford to register their votes. The election of 1758-9 was only remarkable for the fact that from the beginning (and probably

---

[1] L. S. Sutherland, 'The Laudian statutes' below, pp. 191-203.

[2] Richard Trevor (1707-71), m. Queen's 1724; fellow All Souls 1727; canon Ch.Ch. 1735; bp Durham 1752-71. In *A Sketch of the Life and Character of... the Reverend Richard Trevor Lord Bishop of Durham* (Darlington 1776), Trevor said he was 'spurred on, more by the advice and importunity of his Friends, than by his own natural Temper and Inclination' (p. 2). Secker said it was 'by the advice I believe of Dr Dickens'. Samuel Dickens (1719-91, m. Ch.Ch. 1736; regius prof. Greek 1751-63) was at this time a prebendary of Durham.

[3] Lambeth Palace Libr. MS 2598, fo 52ᵛ.

[4] When the duke of Newcastle was elected chancellor at Cambridge in 1749 extensive investigations were pursued about university procedures: see D. A. Winstanley, *The University of Cambridge* (Cambridge 1922).

[5] The vice-chancellor, who set the date for the poll, was statutorily obliged to do so as soon as possible after the death or resignation of an outgoing chancellor, so that vacancies in the office should not be protracted. This rule was conscientiously observed.

even before the campaign officially opened[1]) there were really only two tory candidates, that they were both strong ones and that the animosity which sprang up between their supporters was so intense that it was not until the day before the poll that the leader of the less numerous party withdrew his name.

The tory candidates represented the dissensions within the county. They were Westmorland, uncle and political associate of Francis Dashwood and since 1754 high steward of the university; and Lichfield, leader of the tory interest in the northern part of the county. There had been evidence of rivalry between these factions in the university before when Westmorland had been nominated high steward by Arran in 1754.[2] By 1759 Westmorland had strong claims to be considered the officially favoured candidate. He had the support of the vice-chancellor, of most of the tory heads, of old Dr King (who was at this time devoted to him) and of Blackstone and his friends at All Souls. Lichfield, on the other hand, had a majority only at New College and among tory voters, themselves in a minority, at his own college of St John's. But he had substantial minorities at a number of other colleges, including even All Souls. Estimates of the numbers each party could count on varied considerably, but those which survive make it clear that Westmorland commanded a comfortable majority. The best estimate, drawn up on 1 January 1759, was 202 for the whig voters as a whole (extraordinarily close to the 200 they eventually polled), 196 for Westmorland and 119 for Lichfield.[3] When Lichfield showed an unwillingness to withdraw, whig hopes were raised and a strong whip was evidently sent round by the Administration. It also appears that the bishop of Durham's supporters, envisaging the possibility of a controverted return, sought procedural advice from Charles Yorke, a leading whig lawyer who had much experience of comparable problems at Cambridge.[4] The obduracy of the Lichfield

---

[1] On the day after Arran's death Lichfield at once resigned his freedom of the city: *Oxford Council Acts 1752-1801*, 30. His supporters must have been quick too in seeking legal advice from London, for two of the three lawyers consulted were able to report by 22 Dec. 1758: OUA/WPα/22/2, printed opinions endorsed by Blackstone 22 and 26 Dec. 1758.

[2] Robson, *Oxfordshire Election of 1754*, 71.

[3] Among the Blackstone MSS (OUA WP/α/22, fo 30) there is a paper, not in his hand but endorsed by him 'Rough Calculations of Numbers 1 January 1759'. It itemizes the expected votes of all colleges except University College (omitted presumably in error) for the two tory and one whig candidates. The estimate of the combined tory votes is appreciably higher than those ultimately polled. Westmorland is credited with 256 and Lichfield with 109. On the back Blackstone (in his own hand) added the votes of the two tory candidates together, but inserted as well a revised estimate giving Westmorland 196 and Lichfield 121 which seems much more reliable since contemporaries all state that the bishop of Durham (200) had more votes than either of the other candidates separately, and the estimated tory total here is close to the combined tory figure at the poll.

[4] OUA WP/α/3/4/1, 'Opinion of C. Yorke in reply to Queries about the qualification of voters 2 January 1759'. It seems unlikely that 'both parties', as suggested by Ward, *Georgian Oxford*, 209, invited the advice of this whig lawyer, who does not seem ever to have hitherto advised on Oxford affairs. The topics suggest that it was the whig supporters who raised the questions.

supporters seems to have been intensified by their anger at the tactics of opponents within their own party. The latter relied heavily on the legal argument first advanced by Blackstone that Lichfield had disqualified himself from acting as chancellor by a formal offence under the Laudian statutes, since he was a freeman of the city as well as a member of the university.[1]

It was not true, as Blackstone's enemies asserted, that he had concocted this argument for the occasion; he had advanced it in connection with the candidature of Turner for the university at a parliamentary election some eight years before in 1751.[2] Although on a strict interpretation of the statutes it was probably correct,[3] no one would have thought of raising the point if he had not suggested it. Nevertheless, it remained a central issue in the conflict and the campaign culminated in an authoritative paper on the subject by Blackstone published on 31 December after he had sent a copy of it to Lichfield himself.[4] How far this move precipitated Lichfield's final withdrawal it is hard to say, but feeling among the tory faction was very bitter and whether this tipped the balance or not he withdrew on 3 January. Charles Jenkinson, who had come down to vote for the whigs, reported from their point of view: 'I found the University in much better temper than I had expected; the friends of Lord Lichfield and Lord Westmoreland had so much exhausted their rancour upon one another, that they had very little left for any one else.'[5]

Westmorland's election was Oxford's last public event under the first two Hanoverians. His installation was celebrated with great pomp. On 7 July 1759 William King delivered one of his famous Latin orations at which Samuel Johnson clapped his hands till they were sore, and Benjamin Buckler preached a commemoration sermon on the association of religion and learning.[6] But all was far from peace and good cheer with either party. Among the whigs Newcastle refused to approve Humphrey Sibthorp's nomination to the regius chair of medicine, to which he thought he had every hope of preferment because he had voted against the bishop of Durham, and appointed a very mediocre

[1] He presented it in a paper headed 'Considerations on the Power of the University to make, alter, or repeal Statutes, without Royal Licence': see Sutherland 'Laudian statutes'.

[2] Langford, 'Tories and Jacobites', pp. 125-6.

[3] Two of the three legal authorities consulted supported Blackstone, one entirely and the other more hesitantly: OUA WP/α/22/2, endorsed by Blackstone 22 and 26 Dec. 1758.

[4] Blackstone-Lichfield, 31 Dec. 1758, OUA WP/α/22/1, fo 23. The flysheet is anonymous and has no title but the authorship is established by the catalogue of Blackstone's works in *The Biographical History of Sir William Blackstone* (London 1782), 22.

[5] Jenkinson-Grenville, 11 Jan. 1759, *The Grenville Papers*, ed. W. J. Smith (4 vols London 1852-3) i. 288.

[6] See Greenwood, *William King*, 287 ff; *Boswell's Life of Johnson*, ed. G. Birkbeck Hill, rev. L. F. Powell (6 vols London 1934-50) i. 123. Samuel Johnson (1709-84), m. Pemb. 1728; MA by dip. 1755; DCL 1775. [B. Buckler,] *The Alliance of Religion and Learning considered* (Oxford 1759).

candidate from Christ Church instead.[1] The dean of Christ Church acknowledged the favour but the tone of his letter was depressed.[2] Shortly afterwards the influence which Newcastle customarily exercised over the election of a warden of Merton, staunchest of all whig colleges, was defied by its fellows, who took up their stand—as they maintained— on the principle of college independence.[3]

Among the tories too the recent contention did not at once die down, though one of the first new statutes which was passed revoked the disqualification under which Lichfield was held to have suffered and in the same year, 1760, he was nominated by Westmorland to the office of high steward. Hostility against Blackstone remained particularly strong, and even in All Souls there was a flare-up against him, though it seems soon to have died down.[4] In March 1759 it was reported that he was bitterly disappointed at the 'perverse and evil spirit of opposition to all his well-meant designs' from those 'who should have applauded his independent actions', but who have 'show'd too good an inclination to misconstrue them'.[5] He began to disengage himself from university and college affairs (he seems to have resigned his position as assessor of the vice-chancellor's court in this year) and there is no doubt but that he was hurt and angry.

There may, however, have been other reasons for Blackstone's restlessness at this time. The introductory discourse with which he inaugurated his Vinerian lectures had been published in 1758 and was very well received by critics in the wider world;[6] and at the very time when he was alarming his Oxford friends by his discontent with events there he was

[1] Petition to Newcastle from Humphrey Sibthorp, 12 Feb. 1759, BL Add. MS 32888, fo 80. Humphrey Sibthorp (1712-97), m. SEH 1731; demy Magd. 1732-4, fellow 1734-41; Sherardian prof. botany 1747-84. John Kelly (1726-72), m. Ch.Ch. 1743; regius prof. medicine 1759-72.

[2] D. Gregory-Newcastle, 15 Feb. 1759, BL Add. MS 32888, fo 128.

[3] Newcastle had promised to bring pressure to bear on the archbishop of Canterbury to name as warden one of the three chosen candidates of the college, which under its statutes it had to submit to him as their visitor. Opposition in the college took the form of trying to prevent the name of the candidate in question being among the three submitted. Newcastle was adjured to get Lord Barrington to send down his brother (see p. 152 below) and his under-secretary Thomas Tyrwhitt (1730-86, m. Queen's 1747; MA Merton 1756), both fellows of Merton, to vote. When they came they supported the opposition side: Newcastle-J. Dodd, 1 Apr. 1759, BL Add. MS 32889, fo 330; J. E. Colleton-Newcastle, 9 Apr. 1759, ibid. fos 429 ff.

[4] On 20 March 1759 Blackstone was defeated at All Souls in an election for sub-warden, and one at least of the fellows challenged his right to continue in his fellowship since his election to the Vinerian chair. On 27 April Warden Stephen Niblett and other officers unanimously defended him against this challenge: All Souls, Warden's MS 59, Warden Niblett's notebook. Benjamin Buckler's sermon preached before the warden and fellows of All Souls on 2 November 1759—*Elisha's Visit to Gilgal*—published on 29 December 1759, indicates that there had been an outburst of feeling in the college against Blackstone but that the incident had ended.

[5] T. Winchester-Newdigate, 5 Mar. 1759, Newdigate MS CR136/B4099, Lo42.

[6] *A Discourse on the Study of the Law* (Oxford 1758); afterwards reprinted as an introduction to his *Commentaries on the Laws of England*. For its reception see for example *Annual Register* i (1758), 452; *Gentleman's Magazine* xxviii (1758), 541.

in correspondence with Lord Bute, tutor of the prince of Wales, who had consulted him on the education of the future king.[1] Within three years he had married, had been installed by Westmorland as principal of New Inn Hall and had become the first of the old Oxford academics to find preferment in the new reign.

The accession of George III in October 1760 changed the university's public position overnight, though it was some time before the full effects of the changes were to be felt in its internal affairs. The advent of a young king determined to reverse the policy of his predecessor and supported by new ministers who shared his views had a direct effect on the university. The attempts of the king to redress the nation's political balance in favour of the tories and Independents not only brought him and his ministers into touch with persons and issues with which the university had been closely associated, but also led to some signs of real and unaccustomed interest in the university as a place of learning and education.

One of the earliest moves in the political field was made by the king and Bute before the first general election of the new reign in order to solve the electoral problems left by the 1754 Oxfordshire election. Though no practical politician could envisage a repetition of the great struggle of that year, the rank and file of the tories in the county remained unreconciled to what they considered the injustices they had suffered, and they continued to pledge themselves in clubs formed for the purpose of redressing their wrongs. In this they had the support both of the county leaders and prominent members of the university.[2] Two of the very few personal interventions made by the Administration in the election campaign of 1761 were part of a complex electoral accommodation in the county. By this the two whig sitting members were provided with seats elsewhere: a brother of the new duke of Marlborough was put forward to associate the whig representation with that of the ducal family interest and Sir James Dashwood of Kirtlington Park came in to replace a traditional tory.[3] It was a pact achieved

[1] Lord Shelburne, who had attended Blackstone's earlier lectures when in residence at Christ Church, suggested to Bute that his pupil would benefit from them. This was taken up and eventually copies of his lecture-notes were sent to him: Blackstone-Bute, 15 March 1759, Isle of Bute, Rothesay, MSS of the marquess of Bute, MS 32. Blackstone referred with pride to the episode in his later correspondence with Shelburne: Bowood MS S35. His biographer asserts that he was first asked to deliver his lectures to the prince in person, but that he had to decline this honour owing to the obligations of his professorship: W. Blackstone, *Reports of Cases determined in the Several Courts of Westminster Hall from 1746 to 1779* (2 vols London 1781) i, p. xiii (the preface contains a memoir of Blackstone's life by his brother-in-law James Clitherow).

[2] For example, there were complaints that the vice-chancellor (at this time Joseph Browne) had attended in full regalia a meeting of the Old Interest supporters (Bray-unknown (n.d.), Bray MSS, folder 2; *Jackson's Oxford Journal*, 3 July 1760).

[3] L. B. Namier and J. Brooke, *The History of Parliament: The House of Commons 1754-1790* (3 vols London 1964) i. 64. Lord Charles Spencer (1740-1820, m. Ch.Ch. 1756; MP Oxon 1761-90,

with considerable difficulty and one which would have been impossible without the co-operation of the Administration. Memories of 1754 were as vivid in the university as in the county, and the operation was watched with interest there. Charles Godwyn, fellow of Balliol, writing on 28 November 1760 reported the

most remarkable occurrence which has lately happened here is the compromise, which is very much approved of. After a long debate it was agreed to join Lord Charles Spencer with Sir James Dashwood ... Lord Litchfield, Sir James Dashwood, and almost all the gentlemen on that side of the country were very strenuous for the compromise.[1]

Most of the peers and country gentlemen given places at court (because it was said the king liked to have such men about him[2]) had close university affiliations, and included their new high steward, Lichfield, who in 1760 was appointed a lord of the bedchamber and in 1762 captain of the band of pensioners.

The concern shown for the university in the early years of the new reign depended largely on Bute and the young Lord Shelburne, who was his keen supporter.[3] As an undergraduate at Oxford Shelburne had been in contact with two prominent academics with both of whom as a minister he now renewed his relations. It was he who presented William King to his royal master, having first checked with Blackstone that the doctor was no longer a Jacobite,[4] and it was through Shelburne that Blackstone himself was given a seat in parliament and offered political preferment. Moreover, though Shelburne in recommending him to Bute laid particular stress on his qualities as a 'man of business' and on his influence over certain major tory families, the surviving private correspondence between the two men shows a common interest which led Blackstone to hope not unreasonably for backing from the Administration in academic projects as well.[5] These hopes were to prove as illusory as the apparent strength of the new ministry. So too were the widespread expectations in Oxford in 1762 and 1763 that the king would revive a custom in abeyance since Queen Anne's reign and visit the

---

1796-1801) was the 2nd son of the 3rd d. of Marlborough, who had died on active service in 1758. The new duke was George Spencer (1739-1817), 4th d. of Marlborough; hon. DCL 1763. James Dashwood (1715-79), 2nd bt; hon. DCL 1743; high steward city of Oxford 1759-79; MP Oxon 1755, 1761-8.

[1] HMC *Buckinghamshire MSS* ix. 296.
[2] See C. Mordaunt-Newdigate, 4 Dec. 1760, Newdigate MS CR136/B1839a.
[3] E. Fitzmaurice, *The Life of William, Earl of Shelburne* (3 vols London 1875) i. The information is amplified in Shelburne's correspondence at Bowood (Wilts.), MSS of the marquess of Lansdowne, MS 535.
[4] Blackstone-Shelburne, 4 Aug. 1761, Bowood MS 535.
[5] Fitzmaurice [Shelburne]-Bute, Mar. 1761, quoted by Namier and Brooke under *Blackstone*; Blackstone-Shelburne, 27 Dec. 1761, 22 Oct. 1762, Bowood MS S35.

university during its Encaenia.[1] But although in fact he did not come, the new king's keenness in collecting his library won universal academic approval, and he contributed to learned projects in the university;[2] he also made considerable efforts to encourage professors (including the regius professors) to lecture,[3] and he bore Oxford in mind in the all-important matter of clerical preferment. 'Take care of Oxford', he told Archbishop Secker in 1765 when Newcastle was temporarily back in power, 'for the Duke will take care of Cambridge.'[4]

Senior members of the university were quick to express their satisfaction with these developments, though they did so with some significant reservations. Westmorland refused to accompany the vice-chancellor and others when they presented their loyal address in 1760, not because he disapproved of the terms in which they welcomed the new regime but because they paid formal tribute to the old.[5] Newdigate spoke for many of those whom he faithfully represented;

I can't answer your Qu. what my party is? I am only sure it is neither C[um]b[erlan]d nor Pelham, landed men must love peace, men proscribed and abus'd for 50 years together [should] be presented with fools caps if they make ladders for tyrant Whigs to mount by, I like the King and shall be with his Ministers as long as I think an honest man ought and believe it best not to lose the country gentleman in the courtier.[6]

Godwyn (usually a moderate man) wrote in 1762 words very similar to those of King (always an immoderate one) at the Encaenia of the following year: 'It is our happiness to be governed by a Prince who certainly means as well as any man in the kingdom; and, that his government may

[1] 'I take the Liberty of inclosing the subjects to be spoke next July in our Theatre, when, if we have a Peace, There will be a *Public Act*, and we flatter ourselves with the Hopes of being honoured with the Presence of the Royal Family here at that Time. I can assure you that the University were never better disposed to shew their Duty to his Majesty and his Family, and indeed they never had greater Reason. We have great Numbers of Youth of Genius and Learning and only want Encouragement to stir their Emulation. His Majesty's great Love of the fine Arts and Literature raise the highest Expectations in this Place, when they know also that *Augustus* has a *Maecenas*, the Patron of Ingenuity and Learning. . . .' T. Wilson–E. Weston, 1 Oct. 1762, HMC *Underwood MSS* 345; see also S. Barrington–C. Jenkinson, 31 Mar. 1763, BL Add. MS 38200, fo 282.
[2] For approval of his book-collecting see Godwyn–Hutchins, 22 Sept. 1762, Nichols, *Literary Anecdotes* viii. 230. There was some jealousy that £200 should be given to Kennicott for his Hebrew manuscripts: F. Wise–Guilford, 20 Oct. 1762, Bodl. North MSS, d. 9, vol. vi, fo 71.
[3] A beginning was made with the Savilian chair of astronomy in 1764. Writing to Hutchins on 3 Jan. 1763 Godwyn said: 'As an instance of reformation, he [the professor] is required to go through a course of Lectures in Astronomy every year. . . . In like manner all the professors who shall be nominated hereafter by the King and his ministers will be required to read, as we are informed, public lectures in a way that will be consistent with the present method of education in the university'. Nichols, viii. 232. In 1768 at the king's instance attempts were made to reform the activities of the regius professors of history at both Oxford and Cambridge: 'Papers on the Regius Professors of History [1768] Misplaced', BL Add. MS 38334, fos 149 ff.
[4] Lambeth Palace Lib. MS 2598, fo 62ᵛ.
[5] Westmorland–J. Browne, 9 Nov. 1760, copy in Bodl. MS DD Dashwood, Bucks. C.12, folder C.6.
[6] Newdigate MS CR136/B2311; quoted by L. B. Namier, *Crossroads of Power* (London 1962), 41.

be well carried on, I wish to see honest men placed about him.'[1] A few months later he applied his remarks to Oxford explicitly. 'It happens very fortunately for us in Oxford, that we are in some degree of favour, without being guilty of any mean compliance. I think it our duty as well as interest, to encourage this favourable disposition, so far as it can be done by persons who choose to be independent without disaffection.'[2]

The difficulty in translating these sentiments into practice only began to appear when political action was called for. Party divisions within the university and pride in its independence (both outcomes of past struggles) clashed uneasily with the new-found desire to gain the 'countenance of such a Prince' and to escape from 'those Distinctions at Oxford which [as they believe] have been so happily abolished Elsewhere'.[3] The political scene during the first ten years of the reign proved far from pacific in the university as in the nation. During this time the university had to deal with a contested election for a chancellor in 1762, two by-elections following the deaths of university burgesses in 1762 and 1768 respectively in which contests were narrowly averted, and a major contest in the general election of 1768. In 1762 and 1768 the Administration intervened in university affairs. In 1762 the intervention of Bute's administration was successful, in 1768 that of Grafton's was a striking failure. The outcome of neither was what those concerned had expected.

Westmorland died on 26 August 1762. His death had been expected for some weeks, during which the election campaign was mounted. It was generally known that Lichfield with his royal support would try to reverse his defeat of 1758-9. The group of Oxford tories which had brought success to Westmorland still opposed him.[4] They had difficulty, however, in finding a candidate to put in the field against him. Their first choice was well connected: the young earl of Suffolk, a member of Magdalen, the largest tory college, which supported him, and closely linked with Blackstone and the All Souls party which had been so successful in the last contest.[5] But not only was Suffolk very young but

---

[1] There is no full report of King's speech at this Encaenia. For short reports of it see Greenwood, *William King*, 318. Godwyn's words came from his letter to Hutchins of 11 Oct. 1762, Nichols, *Literary Anecdotes* viii. 230.   [2] Same-same, 3 Jan. 1763, ibid. 231-2.

[3] Lichfield-Newdigate, 24 Oct. [1762], Newdigate MS CR136/B1798, quoted by Ward, *Georgian Oxford*, 222.

[4] A suggestion was made by Harcourt and some of the whigs that Bute himself (following Newcastle's example at Camb.) should stand for chancellor. Fortunately he refused, and it seems unlikely the university would have gone so far as to choose him. If they had, given the intensely hostile publicity which pursued him all his life, the result would have been catastrophic for the university. Jucker, *Jenkinson Papers*, 52 ff.

[5] Henry Howard (1739-79), 12th e. of Suffolk; m. Magd. 1757; hon. MA 1759, hon. DCL 1761. Shelburne called Blackstone 'guardian or deeply connected with Lord Suffolk and Lord Abingdon': Namier and Brooke, *House of Commons 1754-1790*, under *Blackstone*, quoting Bute MSS. Blackstone was handling the embarrassed estate of the late 3rd earl of Abingdon on behalf of his executors.

the situation had by now greatly changed. In 1758-9 a whig candidate might conceivably have snatched victory from the disunited tories in a three-cornered contest, but could not possibly have formed an electoral alliance with any section of them. But this move was precisely what was now being engineered under the auspices of the new Administration. It was symptomatic both of the continuity of Oxford's political habits and the confusion of the party situation that those colleges which had faithfully supported the Old Whigs in the Pelhamite days now turned without question to their successors: Harcourt and Macclesfield were the local leaders from the county; Bray and Kennicott of Exeter and David Gregory, the dean of Christ Church,[1] the local leaders in the university, to whom was added an active young canon of Christ Church, the Hon. Shute Barrington.[2] And above all since that date, much grown in political experience, Charles Jenkinson was now attached to Bute.[3] The loyalty of those whig colleges to their new leaders was such that it was not till half-way through the campaign that they so much as asked for a *quid pro quo* in university politics for presenting their former opponents with the fruits of office. Stirred up at last by suspicions of some of Lichfield's tory followers, they got their leaders to extract from him a personal undertaking to nominate a prominent whig peer to act as his high steward, and in the future to give the heads of the whig colleges their turns in the vice-chancellorship which they had not hitherto enjoyed.[4]

Bute's aim was no doubt a step in the non-party politics he and his master favoured, but in view of the king's well-known statements about purity of elections his method of achieving his end was something of a shock to those of the university tories who opposed Lichfield. Blackstone, who though no longer a fellow of All Souls was still influential there, wrote a frank letter to Shelburne when he first discovered what was happening:

I have that Opinion of Lord Bute's Moderation as well as his Judgement, as to believe that he would not (at this time especially) disoblige two or three noble Families in order to direct the Weight of Government in favour of any one Candidate. And yet I have a Letter now before me, which says that 'Dr Barrington (the new Canon of Christchurch and a very intimate Friend of Lord Suffolk) has very genteely excused himself from following the Bent of his Inclinations in serving Lord Suffolk, by Acknowledging that he was personally applied to by his Patron Lord Bute in behalf of Lord Litchfield, even before the Death of our Chancellor. What (my correspondence adds) may we conclude from this Intelligence? Are we to have the whole Force of the Ministry drawn down, in

---

[1] Shelburne called him 'a gentleman, though not a scholar': Fitzmaurice, *Shelburne* i. 15.

[2] Shute Barrington (1734-1826), m. Merton 1752; bp of Llandaff 1769-82, of Salisbury 1782-91, and bp of Durham 1791-1826.

[3] See letters printed by Jucker, *passim*. Jenkinson was now private secretary to Bute and treasurer of the ordnance.

[4] Barrington and Bray raised these issues on 10 Sept. 1762: Jucker, 57-8, 59.

opposition to a Character so amiable and unquestionably loyal as that of the Earl of Suffolk?'—I have told him I could never believe it.[1]

But believe it he had to, as a carefully drafted reply four days later from Shelburne made clear. Bute was 'determin'd to support his Friend Lord Litchfield'. Shelbourne continued: 'I think it will not be difficult for me ... to convince you that in doing so, he not only acts agreable to your own Principles of Friendship, but becomingly as a Minister, in Regard to the public Light Lord Litchfield at this present stands in.'[2] Moreover, since Blackstone himself was now pledged as a member of parliament to the support of the Administration, and even sat for a seat provided by Bute, there was nothing for him to do but to swallow his indignation and accept for himself a compromise which left him free to vote for Suffolk, but not to take an open part in his campaign.[3] The reason could be seen among the large proportion of Oxford tories who still felt the euphoria of the new reign and who deprecated any opposition to the royally approved candidate. Lichfield as the candidate concerned might be expected to adopt this attitude,[4] but it was also the opinion of Godwyn, who wrote to a friend the day before the election:

We are to elect a Chancellor to-morrow, who, without doubt, will be Lord Litchfield, and, I hope without dispute too. An opposition at this time will be ill-judged. It is what our adversaries wish for, because it will be matter of triumph to them if the Chancellor owe his success to their concurrence. It so happens, that his election is, as I think, unavoidable. You will say, that Chancellor of the University of Oxford, and Captain of the band of pensioners, are titles which are not well connected together. If the Court had continued to frown upon us, we had been very secure from incurring any such reflection ... All that we have to say is, that we have at present such a Court that I hope no honest man need be ashamed of being connected with it.[5]

In view of the pessimism of one section of the party and the enthusiasm of the other, the cause of Suffolk or two other candidates later brought forward, Lord Aylesford and Lord Foley,[6] could not flourish. Suffolk withdrew[7] as did Aylesford. Only Foley persisted and he was beaten by 321 to 168.[8] The defeat was a rout.

---

[1] Blackstone–Shelburne, 7 Sept. 1762, Bowood MS S35.

[2] Shelburne–Blackstone, 11 Sept. 1762 (draft of reply on Blackstone's letter of 7 Sept.).

[3] This would appear to be the arrangement reached, and Oxford observers (no doubt unaware of it) found Blackstone's actions during the rest of the campaign baffling.

[4] See his letter to Newdigate of 24 Oct. [1762] in Newdigate MS CR136/B1798, quoted by Ward, *Georgian Oxford*, 222.

[5] Godwyn–Hutchins, 22 Sept. 1762, Nichols, *Literary Anecdotes* viii. 229.

[6] Heneage Finch (1715–77), 3rd e. of Aylesford; m. Univ. 1732. Thomas Foley (1742–93), 2nd bn Foley, m. Magd. 1759.

[7] Blackstone had advised him to entrust a formal letter of resignation to Benjamin Buckler: Suffolk–[T. Winchester], 18 Sept. 1762, MCA Bloxam MS collection ii. 175. Blackstone found himself pledged to vote for Foley and explained the circumstances to Shelburne in letter of 22 Oct. 1762, Bowood MS S35.   [8] OUA, Register of Convocation 1757–66, p. 396.

But this was a victory with little obvious gain to anyone. Lichfield was a feeble chancellor and exercised as little influence over the university as his predecessors had done, nor did he do more than the minimum to implement the personal undertaking he had given.[1] The high steward he nominated was neither Marlborough nor Harcourt, as the university whigs had hoped, but the earl of Corke,[2] a friend of Bute and Shelburne and a man of a very different background from that expected of the traditional whigs. So far as the pledge to elect whig vice-chancellors in their turn was concerned, Joseph Browne, the tory provost of Queen's who had been in office when Corke was elected, was both old and infirm. Lichfield kept him there for five years in all before replacing him, and then, under it was believed some pressure, he nominated as his successor the least influential of the whig heads, David Durell of Hertford who held office for three years, after which the experiment was dropped.[3] It was recognized throughout the university that there had been no change in the balance of forces there.

Nor did the enthusiasm for non-party unity as a means of peaceful government survive better in the university than in the country as a whole. The death in 1762 of Peregrine Palmer, who had been its representative in parliament for seventeen inconspicuous years, gave an opportunity to test the university's political attitude. With the greatest promptitude and without consulting either the chancellor or the supporters of the Administration a small group of heads sent an invitation, as they might have done at any time in the past fifty years, to an elderly country gentleman of impeccable tory background, Sir Walter Bagot.[4] When he accepted, both sides were thoroughly relieved to be spared a contest.[5] Sir Walter's only disadvantage as a candidate was his age. It was clear that a much more serious test of the university's political attitude was inevitable in the fairly near future. By 1766 at least one prospective candidate was laying his plans. On 25 May 1766 Charles Jenkinson wrote to Sir Robert Jenkinson, the head of his family in Oxfordshire:[6]

[1] He was at first somewhat unpopular, both with old and new supporters, but his benefactions, during his life and in his will, redeemed his reputation. His career was wrecked by drinking that was heavy even by eighteenth-century standards.

[2] Hamilton Boyle (1730-64), 6th e. of Corke; m. Ch.Ch. 1748; hon. DCL 1763 then high steward Oxford Univ.

[3] David Durell (1730-75), m. Pemb. 1747; BD Hertford 1760, DD 1764, principal 1757-75; vice-chancellor 1765-8. It might be argued that by that time the distinction between whig and tory was meaningless. It was nevertheless true that no head of a traditional whig college was nominated vice-chancellor until John Wills (1741-1806, m. Hertford 1758; degrees Wadham, warden 1783-1806), vice-chancellor 1792-6.

[4] Walter Wagstaffe Bagot, 5th bt. (1705-68), m. Magd. 1720; MP Oxford Univ. 1762-8.

[5] Writing to Jenkinson on 6 Dec. 1762 David Gregory remarked 'We have thus very luckily escaped a contest, which probably might have occasioned great heats and animosities among the younger part of the University, who are made of very combustible stuff'. Jucker, *Jenkinson Papers*, 101.

[6] Robert Jenkinson (1721-66), 5th bt. m. St John's 1738.

Permit me now ... to open to you a scheme, which I own I have very much at heart; the day after I saw Banks at Oxford it was suggested to me by some friends, who came over to me at Newnham, that if I thought fit to try it, I might have some chance of representing the University in case of a vacancy ... it was supposed I might very well stand upon the ground of having received the whole of my education there, and of some pretensions to publick merit, and that under this pretence my relations and friends of different denominations might unite the several parties in my favour.[1]

No longer attached to the fallen favourite Bute, he obtained in due course the full support of the king and of Grafton in his candidature.[2]

Bagot died suddenly on 20 January 1768, less than two months before the dissolution of parliament. Short though the tenure of a stopgap replacement must be, the university tories repeated their former tactics. On 25 January Blackstone moved the house for a writ and on 3 February Sir William Dolben, a candidate so eminently suitable that no rival could oppose him, was elected to the vacancy.[3] Admirable though he was, he had one serious disadvantage in that he was not free to stand for the university in the forthcoming general election. The only advantage his supporters gained by electing him was thus a delay of some six weeks in the opening of the formal election campaign.

The university election of 1768 is fully documented and has been described in detail by Ward.[4] It was the first campaign to be fought under the new statutes with regard to canvassing and voting and thus the first parliamentary election to be fought on a register of voters. But it was also the first Oxford election to take place since the virtual disappearance of the old tory party in the university. In consequence there was more than the usual uncertainty about the prospects of candidates.

Jenkinson, in putting himself forward as a government candidate, yet one hoping for the support of interests long hostile to such men, took a bold step, probably bolder than he initially realized. In the first place it was widely believed that the rapprochement between the university and the court was solid and permanent. Not only had there been no real

---

[1] Jucker, 411. 'Banks' was Bankes Jenkinson (1722-89), 6th bt; m. St John's 1739; fellow All Souls 1745. 'Newnham' was Lord Harcourt's house at Nuneham Courtenay.

[2] It should be noted, however, that the proposal that he should stand came from Jenkinson himself and his friends and not from the Administration, for as Namier and Brooke point out, 'it is probable that in 1768 the Treasury's activities were much less than at any other general election during this period' and when the time came Jenkinson was left very much to organize his own campaign. Chatham's reluctance to see the first lord of the treasury interfere in elections reinforced Grafton's disinclination to take the trouble upon himself; Namier and Brooke, *House of Commons 1754-1790* i. 68.

[3] Sir William Dolben (1727-1814), m. Ch.Ch. 1744; MP Northants. 1768-74, Oxford Univ. 1768, 1780-1806. Blackstone acted in the absence of Newdigate, and, as was said, '. . . in order to put a Stop to the Cabals and Intrigues, that were arising as soon as The News of ‹our› Dear Friend's Death arriv'd': C. Mordaunt-Newdigate, 26 Jan. 1768, Newdigate MS CR136/B1841.

[4] See in particular BL Add. MS 38457 (among the Liverpool MSS). Ward, *Georgian Oxford*, 226 ff.

opposition to the court candidate for chancellor in 1762, but the existence of this new friendship was the subject of good-humoured raillery at
the 1763 Encaenia, and at the beginning of 1768 the master of Balliol
could still write of 'the growing Reconciliation among Partys here' and of
'Prejudice' as 'in a Dying manner'.[1] In the second place he had failed to
realize the length of memories in a university constituency. So far from
gaining from the tory affiliation of many of his family, Jenkinson was
handicapped by the memory of his betrayal of his family's traditions in
1754. In fact it was believed that two of Blackstone's friends—the warden
of All Souls and the dean of Christ Church—had warned him that he
'must expect to see strong efforts of Tory resentment'.[2] He entered the
fray with no tory college supporting him, and the backing of the traditionally whig colleges, though it ensured him a fairly solid bloc of votes,
was for the same historic reasons something of a handicap in the course
of his campaign. Canon Tottie of Christ Church made a shrewd
comment when he told him that it was important that the whigs should
be united, but that this was not enough. 'For I am persuaded, that there
is not as yet such a change of Sentiment in this University, as to promise
Success to any Political Measure that is known to be set on foot and conducted by those that are called Whigs.'[3] Dean Markham pressed the
point home. Jenkinson must be presented by the head of a tory college
(the president of Corpus, who ultimately did not even vote for him, was
suggested, as Christ Church thought Nathan Wetherell, the master of
Jenkinson's own college, was not 'of sufficient consequence from the size
of his college'); and it was plain to the dean that Christ Church was too
remote from the rest of the university to provide effective campaigners.[4]
What were wanted were 'instruments to go among the young masters';
he added 'our people in general do not cultivate much acquaintance
abroad'. The dean also indicated that he thought he had taken almost
more than enough political action himself, and indeed he proved a
somewhat lackadaisical ally.[5]

   In the event it was Wetherell who became his chief agent, though he

---

[1] T. Leigh-Jenkinson, 24 Jan. 1768, BL Add. MS 38457, fo 34.

[2] Markham-Jenkinson, 21 Jan. 1768, ibid. fo 19. John Tracy (1723-93), 7th viscount; m. Univ. 1741, fellow All Souls 1746, warden 1766-93. William Markham (1719-1807), m. Ch.Ch. 1738, dean 1767-77; abp York 1777-1807.

[3] Tottie-Jenkinson, 1 Feb. 1768, BL Add. MS 38457, fo 99. John Tottie (1705-74), m. Worc. 1721; BA Queen's 1725; MA Worc. 1728; BD and DD and canon Ch.Ch. 1760.

[4] Markham-Jenkinson, 21 Jan. 1768, BL Add. MS 38457, fo 19. President Thomas Randolph of Corpus had been canvassed by the archbishop of Canterbury (who had supported his candidature for the Lady Margaret chair of divinity) but Randolph ultimately cast a single vote for Newdigate. Nathan Wetherell (1727-1807), m. Linc. 1748; higher degrees University College, master 1764-1807; vice-chancellor 1768-72. University College was not a particularly small undergraduate college but it had few members of convocation. Six fellows and six Independents voted in 1768. Only Worcester and Pembroke provided fewer voters.

[5] Markham-Jenkinson, 28 Jan. [1768], BL Add. MS 38457, fo 74ᵛ. He was absent from his college

was at this time still comparatively inexperienced in university politics, and his own college remained divided. It was a harsh introduction to the field in which he later became outstandingly proficient. He worked indefatigably, and even though his candidate failed it is difficult to think of any tactics which would have succeeded better. He worked within the university, interviewing voters and seeking out the names of all persons lay or clerical who might be able to exercise influence over any college or the humblest of its voting members. In this he was admitted to be remarkably effective; but he had not the contacts outside Oxford to enable him to follow the approaches through. This had to be done by Jenkinson himself, for there was no one else to do it for him. His official experience had made him adept in the role, but it was one foreign to the traditions of candidates at university elections, where even canvassing was proscribed, and it became increasingly damaging to Jenkinson's popularity as a candidate as the campaign proceeded.

Jenkinson was faced by four other candidates, and what would happen if any one of them withdrew was as important to him as the number of voters. Two of these represented the Old Tory traditions, and they were the two who proved successful. Newdigate, who enjoyed the advantage of a now long-standing university tradition to re-elect sitting members, behaved with admirable discretion. He retired to his country house in Warwickshire and left the campaign in the hands of faithful friends who occasionally wrote him reassuring letters[1] but made no attempt to keep him in close touch with what was going on. When polling day was drawing near the warden of All Souls sent him a civil letter, assuring him that all was well but suggesting that he send up for the occasion any non-resident voters of his acquaintance.[2] In fact he easily headed the poll and Wetherell, as master of his own college, where in the end every voter supported him, sent him his warm congratulations.[3]

The second candidate, Francis Page of Steeple Aston, a squire educated at New College, which put him up, was admitted on all sides to be amiable but almost painfully undistinguished.[4] Jenkinson's supporters were slow in recognizing that he could be a serious candidate.[5] One of Page's own supporters wrote to Newdigate after his election 'We wisht

for longer than expected and Shute Barrington obviously considered that he had let the younger members of Christ Church get out of hand: Barrington-Jenkinson, 20 Mar. 1768, ibid. fo 297.

[1] For example Thomas Winchester's letter of 6 Mar. 1768, Newdigate MS CR136/B2379.

[2] Tracy-Newdigate, 18 Mar. 1768, Newdigate MS CR136/B2303.

[3] Wetherell-same, 24 Mar. 1768, Newdigate MS CR136/B2338.

[4] Francis Page (1726-1803), m. New College 1743; hon. MA 1747, hon. DCL 1749; MP Oxford Univ. 1768-1801. For a short time William Drake (1723-96, m. BNC 1739), similar in interests to Page, was also a candidate, but their parties soon agreed to a vote whereby both sides were to accept the candidate with the greater support. When Page won Drake retired: Kennicott-Jenkinson, 10 Feb. 1768, BL Add. MS 38457, fo 144.

[5] See for example Theophilus Leigh's letter to Jenkinson, 25 Jan. 1768, ibid. fo 75.

to have return'd with you some person of more consequence, but he is truly a good natured, in many respects a worthy, and in every respect an independent man'.[1] Newdigate, accustomed to colleagues less able or energetic than himself, welcomed him with goodwill.

The other two candidates, George Hay and Thomas Fitzmaurice,[2] were more unusual and the support they relied on more puzzling to those concerned in the election. Hay, a civilian of some distinction, was notoriously a difficult person, but he had a high reputation at his college, St John's, and for some years had been thought of as a likely candidate for the university. Three weeks before the poll he persuaded his college to put him up and although they did so with tempered enthusiasm most of them voted for him.[3] Neither his contemporaries nor later historians have been able to explain his motives in standing but these may have resulted from a temporary difficulty in finding a seat elsewhere.[4] His chief victim was Jenkinson who had hopes of St John's—a college veering towards the government. Hay was certainly encouraged by a group hostile to Jenkinson with whom Blackstone was privately associated and some hoped to see in him a more effective anti-government candidate than had so far come forth.[5] But once nominated he won few outside supporters and ended the campaign with no more than sixty-two votes.

[1] Winchester-Newdigate, 30 Mar. 1768, Newdigate MS CR136/B2380. Dr Johnson was even more cutting: 'an Oxfordshire Gentleman of no name, no great interest, nor perhaps any other merit, than that of being on the right side.' *Letters of Samuel Johnson*, ed. R. W. Chapman (3 vols Oxford 1952) i. 201.

[2] George Hay (1715-78), m. St John's 1731; see Namier and Brooke, *House of Commons 1754-1790*, under *George Hay*. The Hon. Thomas Fitzmaurice (1742-93), m. St Mary Hall 1761.

[3] 'Diary of the Rev. Thomas Fry, DD. President of St John's College, Oxford, 1768-1772', 24, 26 Feb. and 6 Mar. 1768 (I am indebted to the late Dr Hargreaves-Maudsley for a typescript of this document which is in private possession). Thomas Fry (1718-72, m. St John's 1732, president 1757-72) put Hay forward, and tried to find out if there was any likelihood that he could get support from Queen's. The provost, Joseph Browne, was discouraging, and Fry's diary reports a good many criticisms of Hay and indicates no attempt to refute them. He was, however, obviously shocked when one of the fellows refused to give him any support.

[4] See Namier and Brooke, under *George Hay*.

[5] On 21 January 1768 Markham wrote to Jenkinson: 'What has been done towards gaining Dr Blackston without him you are not to expect much assistance from All Souls.' BL Add. MS 38457, fo 17. By 3 February Barrington wrote that the 'inveteracy' of Tracy and Buckler 'confirms the suspicion I formerly hinted with regard to B[lackstone]s sincerity': ibid. fo 116. He had already expressed these doubts on 27 January and insisted that the warden and Buckler 'who defer implicitly to his opinions' (ibid. fo 71) acted under Blackstone's influence and on 5 February Markham thought Blackstone's 'duplicity ... too clear to admit a doubt' (ibid. fo 121). Jenkinson's supporters (for example Peter Waldo, 1733-1803, m. Univ. 1748) pointed out that Hay was 'clearly not put up for nothing. There is some Artifice in it': letter to Jenkinson, Mar. 1768, ibid. fo 186. And Wetherell also wrote 'It is certain that Dr Hay can make no ground, and yet we may reasonably suppose that he is not set up without some view': letter to Jenkinson (n.d.), ibid. fos 188-9. The rumour was that Blackstone had advised Hay to stand. There is considerable support for this. First, when Hay's nomination came out Blackstone hastened to assure Newdigate that he need not be troubled for his own position: letter of 5 Mar. 1768, Newdigate MS CR136/B1498. Secondly, Suffolk, with his associations with this group, wrote [to Winchester] on 23 February 1768: 'But should some dignified character step forth to join Sir Roger Newdigate, I flatter myself such a person wou'd meet with your approba-

Thomas Fitzmaurice was a brother of Lord Shelburne, who had taken great pains with his education, having sent him to be a pupil of Adam Smith in Glasgow and then to Oxford to attend Blackstone's lectures and read classics with William King.[1] A vigorous, intelligent and somewhat radical young man he had at least for some time the support of the All Souls group associated with Blackstone, but depended mostly on the backing of the younger MAs over whom he exercised a great influence.[2] None of the experienced politicians expected him to be returned but he was seen as a force to be reckoned with, for he became the centre of what one of Jenkinson's supporters recognized as early as 3 February as 'The wild rant of independency'.[3] He was determined not to retire from the battle unless by so doing he could further his principle. In the last days of the struggle it became clear that he was merely splitting Page's vote and on 22 March, the day before the poll, he announced his withdrawal in favour of Page, asserting that 'if the *independance* of the University can but be secured, he is altogether heedless what becomes of him or his interest'.[4] Even before the formal announcement, Jenkinson's forces had begun to crumble. At Christ Church itself there was a revolt among some of the younger men.[5] The poll, in which Page defeated Jenkinson by the large margin of 296 to 198,[6] was held under conditions of the utmost excitement. As Wetherell told Jenkinson;

The day before the Election the cry of independance was so general, that all persons were to be proscribed who did not vote for Page. I read many parts of your *general* letter to some of your enemies, in which you very properly shew what independance really is. They could not help saying, that you were a Gentleman, had good sense, and that your conduct throughout was honourable; but still all persons were to be deemed the Proditors of the University.[7]

The elation of the victors was unbounded. Godwyn's confidence in the court had by now been exaggeratedly replaced by fear that the university

bation and best assistances—I look upon Dr Hay in this light—and have reason to apprehend that he will be thought of, and adopted by our particular friends.' MCA Bloxam MS collection ii. 189. Thirdly, Blackstone (though none of the rest of the group) cast his vote for Hay at the election

[1] W. R. Scott, *Adam Smith as Student and Professor* (Glasgow 1937), 239ff; Blackstone-Shelburne, 19 Oct. 1761, Bowood MS S35. Adam Smith (1723-90), m. Balliol 1740.

[2] When approached by Sir Bankes Jenkinson on Charles Jenkinson's account the All Souls men politely said they had 'so long a personal acquaintance with the other Candidate [Fitzmaurice], that I must excuse them for supporting his Interest': B. Jenkinson-Blackstone, 22 [Jan. 1768], BL Add. MS 38457, fo 25. By 3 March, however, they had begun to think he should give up before the poll: Blackstone-Newdigate, 3 Mar. 1768, Newdigate MS CR136/B1498. One of the younger MAs was Phipps Weston (1738-94, m. Magd. 1753); see Ward, *Georgian Oxford*, 232-3.

[3] G. Hoare-C. Jenkinson, [2 Feb. 1768.] BL Add. MS 38457, fo 111.

[4] Wetherell-C. Jenkinson, 22 Mar. 1768, ibid. fo 307.

[5] Led by Francis Atterbury (1736-1822, m. Ch.Ch. 1755; grandson of Bp Atterbury): Barrington-Jenkinson, 20 Mar. 1768, ibid. fo 297.

[6] *An Authentic copy of the Poll . . . for the University of Oxford* (Oxford 1768).

[7] Wetherell-Jenkinson, 1 Apr. 1768, BL Add. MS 38457, fo 324.

was 'in great danger of becoming a Court Borough'. He suggested on 14 March that 'some Nabob' might 'make a purchase of us before it be long' and thought that:

We never went through so great a trial, and have acquitted ourselves with honour beyond what we expected. All our connexions were inquired into, and every influence employed which could be thought of . . . we had a canvassing letter from our Visitor. But, in spite of all this management, we carried our election by a majority of near a hundred. Some Colleges had the credit of being unanimous, and others were nearly so.[1]

Samuel Johnson, who was in Oxford at the time, reported the result triumphantly to Mrs Thrale on 24 March 1768, the day after the poll:

Of this I am sure you must be glad, for without enquiring into the opinions or conduct of any party, it must be for ever pleasing to see men adhering to their principles against their interest, especially when you consider that these Voters are poor, and never can be much less poor but by the favour of those whom they are now opposing.[2]

But, as in the contest for the election of Lichfield as chancellor, the results of this sound and fury were short lived and left none of the bitterness of the county election of 1754, or even of the chancellor's election of 1758-9. It bore no resemblance to an expensive eighteenth-century borough election, nor could any pretence still be made that votes were swayed as in the past by party issues. In the same year Wetherell became vice-chancellor, and his close relations with Jenkinson were used for the benefit of the university. So too were those which he enjoyed with the latter's successful rival Newdigate. Four years later North was elected chancellor on an issue of major importance to the university. In consequence the reconciliation of university and court was well on its way to completion.

In the meantime there was only one flicker of old animosities. In 1769 when the petitions for Wilkes and against the government policy in the Middlesex election were at their height, the university was persuaded to send in one of the very few addresses to the crown supporting the government.[3] There was only one well-known Oxford figure who personally befriended Wilkes, this being the sole eccentricity of the normally unoriginal President Fry of St John's; but as he informed Wilkes, the petition only got through Convocation by a few votes after having been heavily amended.[4] Fry was apparently responsible for the expunging of

[1] Godwyn-Hutchins, 13 June 1768, Nichols, *Literary Anecdotes* viii. 252, 253. Brasenose and Worcester were unanimous in their votes for Newdigate and Page; New College, Oriel, Lincoln and Trinity virtually unanimous for the same candidates. Exeter and Hertford were virtually unanimous for Newdigate and Jenkinson. See *An Authentic copy of the Poll* . . .

[2] *Letters of Samuel Johnson*, ed. Chapman i. 201.

[3] Wetherell thought that 'Every individual in this place . . . is pleased with the Expulsion of Wilkes': letter to Jenkinson, 10 Feb. 1769, BL Add. MS 38206, fos 102-3.

[4] 'Diary of Thomas Fry', 14 Mar. 1769 and following days; Fry-Wilkes, 16 Mar. 1769, BL Add. MS 30870, fo 124.

some of the personal attacks on Wilkes himself. The other amendments represent rather the sympathy of a number of individual members of convocation for the national opposition to government policy.

The affair was nothing more than an interval in the slow but steady progress of Oxford into co-operation with the politics of George III.

6

Politics and Revolution 1772-1800

L. G. MITCHELL

IN ONE of Lockhart's novels a young man about to go up to Oxford is warned not to come back 'either a Whig or a Methodist'. 'By Jupiter, we'll make minced meat of the buck, if he ever dares but to be detected within smell of St Edmund's Hall, or insult CHURCH AND KING with a single hair's-breadth of day-light.'[1] In terms of standard Oxford opinion in the later eighteenth century, this advice was not unsound. It was clear what the phrase 'church and king' meant. The 'church' was the Anglican establishment, for which the university was the principal training ground. The 'king' represented an unalloyed devotion to the monarchical idea once it was freed from the hostility to, and of, the first two Hanoverians and their ministers. When the accusation of Jacobite disaffection lay far in the past it was even possible for a mild romantic sympathy with the old dynasty to be felt here and there. Whatever its context, however, both in the days of the university's 'proscription' and those when it no longer had anything to fear from government suspicion, its traditional stance in politics was pround 'Independence' of the activities of Westminster, which the mongrel phenomenon of the first whig kings had allowed to degenerate into a system of organized peculation.

As a result of these strongly held views, Oxford had a very clear idea of what kind of parliamentary representative it preferred: 'I am of Opinion that the University should always be represented by some Gentlemen of family and Fortune who have been bred at it—but never by any Body who is a present Member—and a mere Academical Man, that will open the Way to frequent Contests and produce endless Mischiefs.'[2]

Newdigate, who had represented the university for many years, exemplified the type of country gentleman in whom Oxford delighted. As recently as 1768 Charles Jenkinson had been defeated by Francis Page, and though his defeat was in part the outcome of his share in the controversies of an earlier reign it was joyfully received as indicating that 'the University is still superior to ministerial influence, and its

---

[1] J. G. Lockhart, *Reginald Dalton* (3 vols London 1823) i. 179. John Gibson Lockhart m. Balliol 1809. On St Edmund Hall see V. H. H. Green, 'Religion in the colleges 1715-1800', pp. 458-64 below.
[2] A. Biset-Newdigate, 1 June 1780, Newdigate MS CR136/B1481.

independency is sacred'.[1] The monumental integrity of a Newdigate was thought to be a more honourable and a more effective defence for the university's interests than any association with Hanoverian governments could possibly be.

Four years after Jenkinson's defeat, however, the attitude of the university towards the government underwent a revolution. For this, as will be shown, there were cogent reasons, but that the revolution was so easily achieved was partly due to conditions which were already in existence. It would be unwise to stress the significance of Jenkinson's defeat in 1768 as illustrative of university opinion without also noting the outburst of loyal enthusiasm which had accompanied the accession of George III and the ready acceptance by the university of Lichfield as a government nominee for the chancellorship two years later. Oxford's Independency in the new reign was a very different matter from its alienation from the rule of the early Hanoverians, or even the isolation into which it was forced by royal and government hostility when that alienation had for practical purposes disappeared. Both the university and its members had now much to hope for from government and little if anything to fear from it. The roots of the sentiment lay in the past, but a past sufficiently bitter for them to strike very deep. How long this sentiment would have prevailed is, however, impossible to guess had not a major practical issue forced a reconsideration of it.

All political activities in the university reflected the situation within the colleges. Christ Church as the largest college, with a voting power it carefully administered, was inevitably of importance in any election. Had Christ Church and the next biggest college, Magdalen, ever put together an alliance it would have been difficult to defeat them even by a coalition of the smaller ones. But Christ Church from at least 1730 onwards was a strong whig college and therefore it seldom took a lead in university politics, and indeed tended until the late years of the century to keep itself aloof from university business. Nor among the tory colleges did size by any means always tend to political initiative. This, in so limited a society as the university, depended greatly on personalities. And here, just as All Souls under Blackstone's leadership took the lead between 1751 and 1760, so now the lead fell to a still smaller body, University College, which achieved from 1768 to 1796 a remarkable dominance.

Among those who played the major part in winning this dominance was its master, Nathan Wetherell, vice-chancellor from 1768 to 1772. He was a friend of Dr Johnson and well known in the London literary

[1] L. B. Namier and J. Brooke, *The History of Parliament: The House of Commons 1754-1790* (3 vols London 1964), i. 359-60.

world. Quite clearly he cultivated his London contacts assiduously and tried to interest them in such local projects as the Oxford canal.[1] From these associations and the part he played in sponsoring Jenkinson's candidature in 1768 there is good reason to think he was ready to come to terms with the government. Between 1770 and 1771 his correspondence with Jenkinson is almost conspiratorial in tone.[2] As a channel of patronage it survived until at least 1796,[3] and as early as 1771 he had obtained, on the nomination of North, strongly pressed by Jenkinson, the deanery of Hereford.

As matters stood, a revision of opinion was most likely to occur either when the university had matters in hand which required parliamentary sanction, for example the passing of its improvement bill in 1771, or when the government began to interest itself in the forms and practices of Oxford. In both cases friends in London were needed, especially when the major issue of subscription to the thirty-nine articles by all undergraduates at their matriculation came up. The debate was to continue for some three years and would involve Oxford in a protracted and complicated round of national politics. There was no question of Oxford being independent if its own interests were under attack; the danger of parliamentary intervention could not be swept away by a lofty display of disinterestedness. The crisis about subscription brought Oxford rudely into the political market-place.

The problems started with the expulsion, in 1768, of six members of St Edmund Hall for attending unauthorized prayer-meetings in the house of a certain Mrs Durbridge in Bear Lane.[4] They were given a public trial amid 'a great number of gownsmen of all degrees'.[5] There was a certain artificiality about the case in that undergraduates had been attending such meetings for some time, and it would seem that the issue was only forced by violent tensions within the college itself.[6] Even so, the affair very quickly took on national importance. The six members were expelled from the university in a sentence pronounced by Durell of Hertford (the vice-chancellor), Randolph of Corpus,

---

[1] Wetherell-Newdigate, 10 Jan. and 10 Feb. 1772, Newdigate MS CR136/B2356.

[2] For example, Wetherell-Jenkinson, 17 June 1771, BL Add. MS 38206, fos 397-8.

[3] Same-same, 11 June 1796, BL Add. MS 38231, fo 48.

[4] See W. R. Ward, *Georgian Oxford* (Oxford 1958), 239 ff; Green, 'Religion', 458-64.

[5] J. S. Reynolds, *The Evangelicals at Oxford 1735-1871* (Oxford 1953, 2nd edn Oxford 1975), 34 ff. The trial was before the vice-chancellor, his bedels, assessors and the senior proctor, the vice-chancellor on this occasion acting *ex officio mero*: see S. L. Ollard, *The Six Students of St Edmund Hall* (Oxford 1911), 10 ff; All Souls, Warden's MS 59, Warden Niblett's notebook.

[6] St Edmund Hall was to remain a strong centre for evangelical or 'serious' studies, and for most of the 1770s the internal politics of the college turned on this question: see D. E. Jenkins, *The Life of the Rev. Thomas Charles B.A. of Bala* (3 vols Denbigh 1908, 2nd edn 3 vols Denbigh 1910) i; *The Life of the Rev. Richard Cecil*, ed. J. Pratt (London 1827); R. Cecil, *Memoirs of the Rev. John Newton* (London 1808).

Fothergill of Queen's and Nowell of St Mary Hall.[1] Significantly, the last three were, like Wetherell, to receive substantial preferment from the government within the next three years and were to be leading protagonists of a rapprochement with it in 1772. It is not perhaps too fanciful to suggest therefore that a group of 'government' men existed among the heads of houses well before the subscription debates came on in parliament. For these men the crisis of 1772 might well have been the excuse to consolidate and publicly avow a position which they had secretly favoured for some time.

Two conclusions could be drawn from the St Edmund Hall martyrdoms. Dr Johnson saw them as a vindication of Anglican orthodoxy as represented in the thirty-nine articles.[2] Alternatively, reformers in religion, increasingly centred on the Feathers Tavern group, were moved to greater efforts, on the simple observation that '*as these Six gentlemen were expelled for having too much religion, it would be very proper to inquire into the conduct of some who had too little*'.[3] By the beginning of 1772 it was clear that Oxford was facing a major challenge. It was known that a motion for the removal of the university tests would be brought in during the coming session of parliament as part of the movement aiming at the liberation of the Anglican clergy from the obligation to accept the thirty-nine articles. Ominously, a group of Cambridge academics was pushing for the same goal from within their own university. Wetherell, who succeeded Durell as vice-chancellor in 1768, lost no time in mobilizing Jenkinson: 'I see by the Papers that the young people at Cambridge are in motion in order to forward the Petition against Subscription—We have nothing of that sort here, and I will venture to say that Government could not do a more acceptable thing to this place than to quash it with a high hand.'[4] The invoking of government assistance in such a letter was an indication of future policy. The traditional independence of the university was distinctive, but as the events of earlier reigns had shown, it could also be frighteningly vulnerable.

The petition, including a section formally requesting the abolition of subscription to the thirty-nine articles as a pre-condition of entry into Oxford, was due to come before the commons in February 1772. Official Oxford opinion was stated a month earlier by Nowell, who had been

[1] Thomas Fothergill (1716-96), m. Queen's 1735, provost 1767-96; vice-chancellor 1772-6. Thomas Nowell (1730-1801), m. Pemb. 1746, principal St Mary Hall 1764-1801; regius prof. modern history 1771-1801.:

[2] *Boswell's Life of Johnson*, ed. G. B. Hill (6 vols Oxford 1887), rev. L. F. Powell (6 vols Oxford 1934-50) ii. 187; Green, 'Religion in the Colleges', 463.

[3] The Shaver [J. MacGowan], *A Sermon occasioned by the Expulsion of Six young Gentlemen from the University of Oxford* (London 1768), 8.

[4] Wetherell-Jenkinson, 6 Jan. 1772 (BL. Add. MS 38207, fo. 76). The situation at Camb. was somewhat different from that at Oxford, in that candidates for degrees had to take an oath to accept the thirty-nine articles, but no such oath was imposed at matriculation.

chosen to deliver the annual sermon before parliament on the anniversary of King Charles the martyr. The choice of one of the chief prosecutors of the St Edmund Hall evangelicals was itself provocative. Nowell left parliament in no doubt about the issues at stake in the coming debate, and what the government's response should be: 'So close is the connection between government and religion, so necessary the dependence of the one upon the other, that without this sacred band, all civil union would be dissolved; and mankind ... would by perpetually warring with one another reduce all things into a state of anarchy and confusion.'[1] Dr Johnson was so pleased with the highflying tory sentiments of the sermon, that he was anxious to see Nowell given immediate preferment.[2] Others were less happy. Coming before the debate in the commons on the reform petition, the sermon passed off without comment and was ordered to be published in the usual way. Once the debate had taken place it was resurrected as a point of controversy.

On 3 February 1772 Newdigate was warned by Page that the reform petition would be presented to the house by Sir William Meredith three days later.[3] This duly occurred, and Newdigate was at his post. Opposing even the mild proposition that the motion should lie on the table, he employed arguments and phraseology that were markedly similar to those of Nowell's sermon. There could be no doubt that he was speaking the official mind of Oxford; 'Civil and religious establishments are so linked and incorporated together, that, when the latter falls, the former cannot stand. They seem to me to be as inseparably connected as the soul and body.'[4] Much more significantly, North came out publicly with a defence of Oxford:

Certain I am that the consequence of the Petition would be the destruction of that right of private judgment for which it contends. All anarchy and confusion has a tendency to depotism. As civil dissensions terminate in the erection of a lord and master, so do ecclesiastical quarrels naturally lead to superstition, and an infallible guide.[5]

Although no formal bargain existed, the reform movement had forced Nowell, Newdigate and North to speak with one voice. The Oxford men won by 217 votes to 71.

Initially every one was pleased with the result. Theophilus Lindsey, one of the leading reformers, concluded a long account of the debate with the view that '... the 39 articles underwent such a scrutiny, and had

---

[1] T. Nowell, *A Sermon Preached before The Honourable House of Commons* (London 1772), 10.

[2] *Boswell's Life of Johnson* iv. 296.

[3] Newdigate's Diary, 3 Feb. 1772, Newdigate MS CR136/A [603]. Sir William Meredith (1725-90), 3rd bt; m. Ch.Ch. 1743; MP Wigan 1754-61, Liverpool 1761-80.

[4] *Parliamentary Debates* xvii. 255 (6 Feb. 1772).

[5] Ibid. xvii. 274 (6 Feb. 1772).

such a just exposition that the civil Power must soon be ashamed of imposing, what not one of our Adversaries defended except Sir Roger . . . Tho defeated we sing a victory, as truth and reason were all for us, and overpowered only by Power.'[1] In their view the debate was the beginning of a campaign with the honours of the first battle evenly divided. If Oxford was recalcitrant, Cambridge was still very much interested in reform.[2] Equally, an associated movement for a general relief of dissenters cleared the commons in May 1772; the tide running against the Anglican establishment would be difficult to stem.

After this first encounter, however, Newdigate was reasonably content. The majority had been comfortable, and what was particularly pleasing was the knowledge that he had forced the ministry into the open. He had held a meeting with North and the archbishop of Canterbury, who had been inclined initially to allow the petition to be read at least once. Only Newdigate's resolve had forced them to change their minds.[3] Oxford was duly appreciative. The heads of houses voted their thanks to the MPs for the 'noble defence of our ecclesiastical establishment'.[4] Wetherell hurriedly penned personal notes to Newdigate and Jenkinson.[5] A letter to Newdigate contained the pious hope that 'Debates in your House may in the future be confined to State-Politicks, leaving the Church to itself'.[6] No such respite would be allowed. The reformers had no intention of allowing the debate to die down.

In this new climate Nowell's sermon became a highly controversial target, at which the reformers now took aim.[7] On 21 February Thomas Townshend moved that Nowell be censured and that his sermon be burnt by the public hangman.[8] In a thin house, with no business of importance expected, the motion passed. Neither Newdigate nor Jenkinson was present, since no warning had been given by their opponents. In consequence the reformers scored a neat tactical victory and Oxford could only accept the censure with as good a grace as possible. Wetherell apologized to Jenkinson for the embarrassment caused, and indicated to Newdigate that Nowell would suffer this 'severe treatment patiently'.[9] The echoes of the Sacheverell case were strong,

[1] Lindsey-W. Turner [7 Feb. 1772], London, Dr Williams's Library, Lindsey MSS, Mod. fo. 144, folio 2.
[2] James Brown-Fothergill, 19 Feb. 1772, Newdigate MS CR136/B1524.
[3] Newdigate-Lady Newdigate, 8 Feb. 1772, Newdigate MS CR136/B4046 I.
[4] Ward, *Georgian Oxford*, 249.
[5] Wetherell-Jenkinson, 10 Feb. 1772, BL Add. MS 38207, fo 85; same-Newdigate, 10 Feb. 1772, Newdigate MS CR136/B2356.
[6] Wetherell-Newdigate, 19 Feb. 1772, Newdigate MS CR136/B2359.
[7] Wetherell-Jenkinson, 2 Mar. 1772, BL Add. MS 38207, fo 90.
[8] Newdigate-Lady Newdigate, 22 Feb. 1772, Newdigate MS CR136/B4046 B.
[9] Wetherell-Jenkinson, 6 Mar. 1772, BL Add. MS 38207, fo 100.

more particularly since Nowell had originally preached the offending sermon in 1766 without provoking any comment whatever. There could be no doubt that the reformers were determined to use the affair as a minor theme in the main campaign. On 16 March Townshend renewed the attack, but this time Newdigate was in his place and 'with extreme violence and heat justified both the preacher and Charles the 1st'.[1]

Oxford was clearly rattled by the Nowell persecution. There were signs that the leaders of the hebdomadal board were inclining to seek a compromise to meet the wishes of politicians such as North and Jenkinson, and 'a friendly correspondence' was entered into with Cambridge which had been advised to do the same.[2] A statement by Newdigate's normally silent colleague Francis Page, not apparently made in the house, that Oxford would undertake reform itself is probably a reflection of the views of the vice-chancellor, Wetherell, and other prominent members of the hebdomadal board and is significant for that reason, not as an indication of an initiative by Page.[3] Indeed Newdigate went out of his way to assure the new vice-chancellor (Fothergill of Queen's) on this point in his first official letter to him in the autumn. 'Mr Page and myself know too well the Deference due to your Superior Knowledge to obtrude our opinions upon our respectable Constituents as to the propriety of their Conduct.'[4]

Before the debate began Oxford hurried to strengthen its defences. The sudden death of its chancellor, Lichfield, in the late summer of 1772 was in this sense a piece of good fortune. Wetherell was off the mark even while Lichfield was still alive. In his mind there was no time to lose in securing the nomination of North as his successor, thereby cementing the new understanding between the government and the university.

I have just been acquainted that my Lord Litchfield is dangerously ill at Bristol. In case of Accidents I beg the favour of knowing from you, whether my Lord North has any Intentions of being our honoured Lord and Chancellor . . . for in truth his Lordship's general Character, and the peculiar Services he has lately done the Church and University ought to secure him the unrivalled honour of being at the Head of that Body.[5]

Wetherell was sent regular reports on Lichfield's health by Fothergill, who suggested that as soon as the chancellor's death was made official North should write to his old college, Trinity, to announce his

---

[1] *Parliamentary Debates* xvii. 311-17.

[2] D. A. Winstanley, *Unreformed Cambridge* (Cambridge 1935), 308.

[3] Some scholars (for example Ward, 249-50) have interpreted a phrase in a letter from Lindsey to Turner of 7 February 1772 as showing that Page had 'promised on his own authority that Oxford would bow before the storm'; but the evidence hardly bears the conclusion although Page certainly was among those who advised a compromise.

[4] Newdigate-Fothergill, 18 Nov. 1772, Newdigate MS C136/B2381.

[5] Wetherell-Jenkinson, 14 Aug. 1772, BL Add. MS 38470, fo 43.

candidature for the vacancy.[1] The Wetherell-Jenkinson link had never worked so smoothly.

Even so Wetherell was aware that in spite of the dangers raised by the recent parliamentary campaign there were still those in the university who thought a submission to the government too high a price to pay: 'I can conceive that the Independent Party (as it is called) will put some other person in Nomination, and if I guess right, they have their Eye chiefly fixed on Lord Radnor.'[2] The breaking of the Independent party was now the avowed aim of Wetherell's politics. It could only be an embarrassing business, in that Radnor was a member of his own college and his campaign was to be run by his son's tutor, William Scott.[3] University College votes would undoubtedly be split if the matter came to a poll. This provided an additional reason for Wetherell to want an undisputed election, and this could only be achieved by leaving the Independents no time in which to organize themselves.

At the beginning of September, with Lichfield now dead, Wetherell was already feeling confident: 'Things are in so favourable a Train, that I shou'd apprehend after the Independants have tried their strength for Lord Radnor, they will drop the contest, and Lord N. will be unanimously elected.'[4] By assiduous canvassing he had secured the support of the heads of All Souls, Brasenose, Corpus, Exeter, Jesus, Magdalen, St Mary Hall and Magdalen Hall, Merton, Queen's, St John's and Trinity, a formidable combination.[5] As a final security measure he was able, just before his term as vice-chancellor ran out, to set the date of the election as early as the statutes allowed. The Independents had very little time in which to manoeuvre.

In fact these precautions were rendered largely unnecessary by the simple point that the Independents could not agree on a common candidate. Radnor was challenged for this role by the duke of Beaufort and the earl of Abingdon, and predictably Wetherell was delighted: 'Lord Radnor's chief Interest is at New College—Seven or eight at University and a few Straglers in other Societies. D. of Beaufort will set out with Oriel, part of Jesus, and some individuals in other colleges.'[6] On 23 September only some sixteen individuals turned up to an Independent

[1] Same-same, 17 Aug. 1772, BL Add. MS 38470, fos 47-8.
[2] Same-same, 14 Aug. 1772, ibid. fo 43. William Bouverie (1725-76), 1st e. of Radnor; m. Univ. 1743.
[3] William Scott (1746-1836), from 1821 1st bn Stowell; m. CCC 1761; fellow Univ. 1767; Camden prof. history 1773-85; MP Oxford Univ. 1801-2.
[4] Wetherell-Jenkinson, 4 Sept. 1772, fo 55.
[5] Same-same, 5, 19 and 21 Sept. 1772, ibid. fos 57-9, 73-4, 77-8. The omission of Christ Church from the list does not mean that there was any danger of the college opposing the candidature.
[6] Wetherell-Jenkinson, 22 Sept. 1772, ibid. fos 79-80. Henry Somerset (1744-1803), 5th d. of Beaufort; m. Oriel 1760; hon. DCL 1763. Willoughby Bertie (1740-99), 4th e. of Abingdon; m. Magd. 1759; hon. MA 1761.

meeting, but even so it broke up without agreeing on a candidate, at which point Scott decided to bow to the inevitable.[1] Parson Woodforde, who as a loyal New College man had come up to vote in the college interest, described the collapse of the Independent campaign on 2 October. Beaufort's friends were installed in the Mitre and Radnor's further down the High Street. Each group refused any communication with the other. It was now obvious that North would be elected unanimously.[2]

Oxford had high hopes of its new chancellor, not least because at his installation he showed himself capable of a Latin oration without the aid of notes.[3] More importantly, his election represented political security. As the president of Magdalen put it:

To you, my Lord, your orthodox University looks up, as to him whose Eloquence, and Wisdom, and Authority are best qualified to preserve her Dignity and her Utility inviolate, to 'deliver her from unreasonable and wicked men, for all men have not faith', and by maintaining her laudable *Subscription*, to fix her as a lasting Bulwark of that genuine, apostolical Church, which Popery, Calvinism, and Infidelity have hitherto in vain united their efforts to overturn.[4]

The significance of the election was not lost on the reformers either. One of their leaders sadly reflected: 'I have however my doubts, whether we shall be able to get another hearing, since Lord North is made Chancellor of Oxford.'[5] The Radnor and Beaufort campaigns had demonstrated that in some colleges the Independent ideal lingered on as a force in Oxford politics, but it is fair to say that already in 1772 it was a diminishing theme. Oxford had once again come to put its trust in princes.

While North was eased into the chancellorship, the resident members of the university were confronted with a flood of pamphlets for and against subscription to the thirty-nine articles, in preparation for the debate in convocation which was promised in 1773 to buy off further parliamentary inquiry. In the month between 19 March and 18 April 1772 at least ten pamphlets were printed, together with an unknown number of individual flysheets. For the next twelve months or so there was to be no sign of this academic war flagging, with many of Oxford's leading personalities hurrying to the fray. The subscription issue was good campaigning ground, for there were excellent arguments on both sides.

The opposition's case was practical, undemonstrative and well supplied with common sense. They argued that, since any creed imposed

---

[1] Wetherell–Jenkinson, 23 Sept. 1772, BL Add. MS 38470, fo 81.

[2] *Woodforde at Oxford*, 191–2. James Woodforde (1741–1803), m. Oriel 1758; degrees New College.

[3] Wetherell–Newdigate, 16 Oct. 1772, Newdigate MS CR136/B2366.

[4] [G. Horne,] *A Letter to Lord North* (Oxford 1773), 42–3. George Horne (1730–92), m. Univ. 1746; president Magd. 1768–91; vice-chancellor 1776–80; bp Norwich 1790–2.

[5] Lindsey–Turner, 23 Oct. 1772, Dr Williams's Library, Lindsey MSS, Mod. fo 144, 12. 44, folio 8.

by man was necessarily fallible, to demand loyalty to such a creed was to institutionalize fallibility.[1] Further, since man's experience of God must be cumulative and progressive, to stand by forms generated in the sixteenth century was plainly ridiculous. It was not surprising therefore that many good men were lost to the Anglican ministry, for almost any intelligent man would find himself in difficulties with at least one of the articles. For a university to impose such a test was particularly odious in that 'it imposed the same Test on the Lay-Conformist, which had been originally devised as a Security against Diversity of Opinion in the Ministers and Teachers of Religion'.[2] Since there was now no necessary connection between an Oxford degree and a religious post, it was unjust to ask laymen to subscribe to a particular set of propositions drawn up in a special set of circumstances to give stability to the Elizabethan church.

The strongest opposition point, however, was the recognition that to ask boys of twelve to fifteen or sixteen years of age to subscribe to the articles was plainly ridiculous since no degree of comprehension could be guaranteed.[3] This was the most important argument both because it was the most attacked,[4] and because it suggested the compromise solution of simply asking entrants to affirm their membership of the Church of England without specifically mentioning the articles. This would remove the objection about the candidates' immaturity, in that the university test would then roughly be in line with regular Anglican confirmation. There was the further embarrassment of it being known that some colleges had become rather lax in going through the forms of subscription for their incoming members. These main points of the opposition case were presented with varying degrees of subtlety, but collectively they formed a not unimpressive body of argument.

In terms of the quantity of paper produced, if not always in terms of the quality of the arguments brought forward, the defenders of the tests won the debate. To the point that the articles were out of date came the answer that, if Elizabeth's reign had been 'troublous', so had 1772. Indeed, as Bagot of Christ Church pointed out, '*The two great*

[1] Anon, *A Defence of the Considerations on the Propriety of Requiring a Subscription to Articles of Faith* (London 1774), 4.
[2] [B. Buckler,] *Reflections on the Impropriety and Inexpediency of Lay Subscription to the 39 Articles ...* (Oxford 1772), 15. At the time this pamphlet was attributed to Buckler but Ward, *Georgian Oxford*, 262 n attributes it to President Fry of St John's. It can be shown, however, by the latter's diary that this is incorrect and it seems likely that the contemporary attribution was right.
[3] Anon. *Considerations on the Expediency of Making Some Alteration in ... the Present Mode of Subscribing to the 39 Articles in this University* ([Oxford] 1772); see also anon. *Observations on Two Anonymous Papers ...* ([Oxford] 1772).
[4] Anon. *A Vindication of the Test at Matriculation in its Present Mode ...* ([Oxford] 1772); see also anon. *Objections to the Received Test at Matriculation ...* ([Oxford] 1772); anon. *The Plain and Obvious Meaning of the Received Test at Matriculation, Examined and Vindicated* ([Oxford] 1772); anon. *Subscription at Matriculation Considered, with Respect to the Nature of the Act and the Extent of its Obligation* [Oxford 1772].

Factions of Papists and Puritans have been remarkably bold of late Years'.[1] In such circumstances, an established creed, far from institutionalizing error, was the only way of preventing the outbeak of all manner of sectarianism and heresy.[2] Indeed, as another canon of Christ Church observed, the articles were so liberally drawn that only men of malevolent intentions would find any difficulty with them. 'I am fully persuaded that different Persons may with a safe Conscience subscribe in different Senses, to those Articles.' On this reading the reformers were by definition fanatics, whose destructive tendencies would have the most terrible results. The conclusion was obvious therefore: 'An Establishment without a Test is an absurdity.'[3]

It followed from this premise that since the university was by foundation and practice a religious institution, it was entirely reasonable to ask laymen to take an oath of loyalty to the articles on becoming members, that is at matriculation. Subscription had been specifically extended to laymen between 1562 and 1581 in the realization that the security of the church demanded such an undertaking. From 'such persons our religious establishment might naturally expect the firmest support, or the deepest detriment; and no measure could be wiser than to attach them to its cause'.[4] In this context the Oxford pamphleteers in favour of the tests refused to take seriously the problem of asking for subscription from young boys. Rather contemptuously they pointed out that the degree of consciousness would be different for a child than for an ordinand making the same declaration before entering the priesthood. From the latter 'a full and entire Assent' would be expected, but a child would only be required to give 'an Acquiescence'.[5] With this caveat, lay subscription was eminently justifiable.

The most formidable argument in defence of the tests was to link them with the defence of the Anglican establishment as a whole. Two pamphlets by Bagot and Randolph made this point firmly. The main function of the university was still to provide ministers for the church: 'In any *Christian* University, a Proficiency in the Doctrines and Practice of the *Christian* Religion, is one Part of the Education intended, and that for *all* the Scholars in general, whatever their future Views or Intentions may be. . . . The University of *Oxford* is allowed to be a Seminary for the

[1] [L. Bagot,] *An Answer to a Pamphlet Entitled Reflections on the Impropriety and Inexpediency of Lay Subscription to the 39 Articles* (Oxford n.d.), 7. Lewis Bagot (1741-1802), m. Ch.Ch. 1757, dean 1777-83; bp of Bristol 1782, Norwich 1783, St Asaph 1790-1802.
[2] [T. Randolph,] *An Answer to a Pamphlet Entitled Considerations on the Propriety of Requiring a Subscription to Articles of Faith* (Oxford 1772).
[3] J. Tottie, *A Charge Relative to the Articles of the Church of England* (Oxford 1772), 6, 29.
[4] A Member of Convocation, *A Letter to the Rt Hon. Lord North Concerning Subscription to the 39 Articles* (Oxford [1773]), 25.
[5] Anon. *A Collection of Papers Designed to Explain and Vindicate the Present Mode of Subscription Required at Matriculation* (Oxford 1772), 16-17.

Church of *England*.'[1] Since the government of the university lay in a convocation of MAs, lay and clerical, tests had to be applied to prevent this Anglican institution running the risk of being governed by non-Anglicans. It was not enough to ask for a belief in the scriptures, because Jesuits would be admitted on that basis. The full articles were essential.

In firmly linking the subscription issue to the general question of the Anglican establishment both authors carefully pointed out that they did so in no spirit of persecution. Dissenters after all had alternatives open to them:

If they approve not the Doctrines of our *Articles*, they need not subscribe to them. If they dislike not the Terms of our communion, we compell them not to come in: they have a full Toleration to repair to any Conventicle they like best, or to set up one for themselves. . . . Nor do we think it would promote, either Peace, or Edification, if all Men of all Persuasions were allowed, and commissioned, to teach in our Churches whatever Doctrines they pleased. Would not rather every Parish have a System of Divinity peculiar to itself;[2]

The point was therefore a simple one for Bagot and Randolph. As long as the Anglican establishment was thought essential for the country's religious stability, and as long as Oxford produced its clergy, some specific subscription to the articles was unavoidable.

The war of pamphlets is also instructive as an insight into Oxford politics. Undoubtedly the majority of writers supported a hardline resistance to any change. Their official negotiators on the other hand, particularly Fothergill and Wetherell, were much more aware of Oxford's delicate position in national politics, and therefore much more inclined to compromise. In spite of securing the sevices of North,[3] they continued to believe that the reforming danger was real. They were accordingly anxious that, when Oxford took the matter into its own hands as promised, it should show itself to be moderate and accommodating.[4] In this sense, there developed a gulf between Oxford's official representatives and majority opinion. In late October 1772 Fothergill and Wetherell persuaded the hebdomadal board to compromise by eleven votes to five:

. . . at our late Board it was agreed that it shou'd be proposed To Convocation to rescind Subscription at Matriculation by substituting a Test of conformity in its place. The form of the Test is not yet determined; the more simple and open it is, surely the better. Some of the old people were very warm

---

[1] [L. Bagot,] *A Defence of the Subscription to the 39 Articles As it is required by the University of Oxford*... (Oxford [1774]), 11.
[2] T. Randolph, *On the Reasonableness of Subscription to the 39 Articles* (Oxford 1771), 17-18.
[3] Newdigate's diary, 23 Nov. 1772, Newdigate MS CR136/A [603].
[4] Wetherell-Jenkinson, 22 Oct. 1772, BL Add. MS 38207, fo 181.

against any Alteration; the President of Corpus for instance, the Provost of Worcester, the Rector of Lincoln, and above all the Warden of Wadham.[1]

When on 2 November a further meeting attempted to frame a new test, it was carried by only eleven to nine, with even Wetherell in the minority.[2]

Throughout these wrangles the dominating factor in Wetherell's mind was to discover exactly what could be defended in the commons, in other words what was the minimum price Oxford still had to pay for its peace. Allied to the wish not to embarrass North in the commons was the assumption that the new chancellor himself slightly favoured some relaxation of the tests. As described above, these considerations had led the heads of houses to fall back on the simple idea of asking each entrant to affirm that he was a member of the Church of England, that he held nothing contrary to its doctrines and would conform to its worship.[3] The strain of the situation was considerable and the peaceful installation of North as chancellor rather masked the reality. The battle of the pamphlets was real and unremitting, and the heads of houses were divided. As William Scott reported, the winter of 1772 found Oxford in a sad condition:

The University seems to be divided into Three Parties; one desirous of abolishing the present Subscription, without providing any Substitute; The Heads of this Party are Dr Tracy, and Dr Hoare Principal of Jesus; another willing to admit a moderate Test, amongst whom are our Master, Dr Huddesford, and I apprehend, a Majority of the University; a third Party headed by the President of Corpus Provosts of Worcester, and Oriel, and the Warden of New College declare against all Alteration.[4]

Clearly in this confused and bitter situation the opinion of Oxford's representatives in London would be crucial. Newdigate's views were characteristically straightforward and wholly unencumbered by nice points of theology or politics. He told Page that he could see no difference between the old tests and the proposed modifications.[5] In this same letter there is more than a hint of irritation with his colleague for promising a debate in Oxford at all. He wrote in the same vein to the vice-chancellor, expressing a willingness to advance any proposition put

---

[1] Same-same, 28 Oct. 1772, ibid. fos 184-5; Ward, *Georgian Oxford*, 264-5. William Gower (1702-77), m. Worc. 1715, provost 1736-77. Richard Hutchins (1698-1781), m. All Souls 1716; higher degrees Lincoln, rector 1755-81. George Wyndham (1704-77), m. Wadham 1722, warden 1744-77.

[2] Wetherell-Jenkinson, 2 Nov. 1772, ibid. fos 190-1.

[3] W. Scott-Newdigate, 17 Nov. 1772, Newdigate MS CR136/B2239.

[4] Ibid. Joseph Hoare (1709-1802), m. Jesus 1727, principal 1768-1802. John Clark (1732-81), m. Pemb. 1749; MA Oriel 1750, BD and DD 1768, provost 1768-81. John Oglander (1737-94), m. St John's 1756; degrees New College, warden 1768-94. It should be noted that the most conservative group bears some correlation with those supporting the Independent candidatures of Radnor and Beaufort earlier in the year.

[5] Newdigate-Page, 16 Nov. 1772, Newdigate MS CR136/B1674.

forward by his constituents, but strongly recommending a stern defence of the *status quo*. 'If we flatter ourselves that any concessions whatsoever can abate their [the reformers] Ill will, we shall find ourselves much mistaken ... it is now evident to all that they mean nothing but the Subversion of our Church from its foundations and that nothing less will content them.'[1] In the face of this letter Wetherell's party was only too happy to extricate itself from the muddle in Oxford by placing the matter entirely in the hands of 'a Conference, between the Chancellor and our Members'.[2] Accordingly, Newdigate set about stiffening his colleague's resistance.[3]

The proposal from the hebdomadal board suggesting the modified test came before convocation on 4 February 1773. Before the debate began Newdigate's letter insisting that the *status quo* was perfectly defensible in the commons was read out by Fothergill; and Thomas Patten, writing to Newdigate on 11 February 1773, said 'Lord North's Letter ... was encouraging enough' but Page still urged caution and moderation, which 'it is not unlikely ... will be remembered to his disadvantage'.[4] In the event all change was voted out by 111 to 64. An attempt by Fothergill to broach the matter again in March was negatived without a division.[5] For the first time in nearly a year, the voice of the university was heard in an unequivocal manner.

There could be no doubt that the honours of the day had gone to Newdigate. North had been lukewarm and Page had been simply timid. By contrast the baronet's firm sense of direction was much appreciated:

Had our Conduct on this important Trial betrayed such a Cowardice as had seized upon some of our Managers, it would have given the Cue to our adversaries to press upon us with redoubled Insolence; but the resolute Stand we made will I think give Pause to the boldest of them.[6]

Jenkinson was sent the same message by the rector of Exeter whose gout had prevented him from attending the actual debate.[7] William Scott divided the honours equally between Newdigate himself and Tottie and Bagot of Christ Church.[8] There can be no doubt that Newdigate's attitude was decisive in steering both the university as a whole and its new chancellor into open resistance to change. By the end of February 1773 therefore, the scheme for avoiding parliamentary interference by reform

[1] Newdigate-Fothergill, 18 Nov. 1772, copy in Newdigate MS CR136/B2381.
[2] Wetherell-Jenkinson, 23 Nov. 1772, BL Add. MS 38207, fo 197.
[3] Newdigate's diary, 5 Dec. 1772, Newdigate MS CR136/A[603].
[4] Patten-Newdigate, 11 Feb. 1773, Newdigate MS CR136/B2213).
[5] *Gentleman's Magazine* xliii (1773), 131, 148.
[6] Patten-Newdigate, 11 Feb. 1773, Bagot-same, 12 Feb. 1773, Newdigate MSS CR136/B2214, B1424.
[7] T. Bray-Jenkinson, 16 Feb. 1773, BL Add. MS 38207, fos 233-7; see also *Jackson's Oxford Journal*, 6 Feb. 1773.
[8] Scott-Newdigate (n.d.), Newdigate MS CR136/B2245.

from within had collapsed. The initiative once more lay with Sir William Meredith and the house of commons. Unlike the debates of the previous year, however, the university now knew its own mind and had the prime minister as its chancellor.

In preparation for this new onslaught Jenkinson in particular went in for considerable research as to the nature of subscription, how far it was formally applied, and how far Oxford colleges could still be called religious foundations.[1] In the event this homework proved unnecessary. Newdigate's view was vindicated. On 2 March he could report to his wife 'we have succeeded in preserving the Liturgy from being dismembered and thrown out Mr Montagu's Qu. for repeal by 125 to 97—no great majority but enough for the purpose—Lord North with us'.[2] Five days later he was able to notch up another triumph. A bill for the general relief of dissenters had passed the commons, but in such a way as to guarantee its death in the lords: 'I feel much lighter now the load of Presbytery is off my stomach and you may expect a very gallante Macaroni ready to take you out of your coach.'[3] These two victories were decisive. A motion for the repeal of the test act, presented by Meredith in 1774, was negatived without a division.[4] As Newdigate had all along believed, there was in fact no commons majority for changing the university's regulations. As the campaign in the house of commons for removing the disabilities of the dissenters continued on its course, the alliance between government and university to oppose it did not falter and after the outbreak of the French revolution became even closer.

Much space has been given to the politics of these years and this is unavoidable. In the confusion of warring pamphlets and political manipulation Oxford had taken its major decision. Its old, much vaunted Independence had been overturned, and after the ordeals of 1772 to 1773 there was good reason to make North's first Encaenia as chancellor a particularly splendid celebration of the university's deliverance from the ungodly:

... the splendor of the whole Celebrity is universally allowed to exceed every thing of the kind that has preceded it. The good order and discipline of the University was equally conspicuous. The vast appearance of Nobility upon this occasion was so great, that we have not yet been able to collect, with any degree of accuracy, a list proper to be laid before the publick.[5]

[1] Wetherell-Jenkinson, 20 Feb. 1773, BL Add. MS 38207, fos 239-42.
[2] Newdigate-Lady Newdigate, 2 Mar. [1773], Newdigate MS CR136/B40462.
[3] Same-same, 21 Mar. 1773, ibid. CR136/B4046 E.
[4] *Parliamentary Debates* xvii. 1327; see also Lindsey-Turner, 5 May 1774, *The Letters of Theophilus Lindsey*, ed. H. McLachlan (Manchester 1920), 49-51.
[5] *Jackson's Oxford Journal*, 10 July 1773.

In return for official protection Oxford willingly began to accustom itself once more to demonstrations of loyalty to kings, and even showed signs of enjoying the experience. The honorary DCL conferred on Dr Johnson in 1775 was pleasing both to the university and to the government. Indeed, as the American issue moved to the centre of the political stage it became much easier to correlate the responses of the North administration and Oxford. In 1775 Oxford sent a loyal address up to London deploring the Americans' 'artifices and seditious proceedings'. Parson Woodforde recorded the relevant division: 'I went to the Convocation House, and heard an Address to his Majesty on American Affairs read and unanimously approved of the second time of its being proposed. The first Time there were about 3. Non Placets — none the second Time.'[1] The claims of legitimacy had always carried a considerable appeal for Oxford. At the beginning of the century it had involved itself in a defiance of the Hanoverian usurpation. Now the same principle led it to defend the Hanoverians against their rebellious subjects. This consideration greatly eased the rapprochement with the government.

The university's view of American affairs produced a stinging attack by Edmund Burke in the commons debate of 26 October 1775, which in turn generated a full-blooded retort by Edward Bentham, the regius professor of divinity. In Oxford's defence Bentham pointed out that its teaching function was directly related to its politics: 'Here they imbibe the excellent precepts that no man is wiser than the laws, that none can wish for an opportunity of being emancipated from their authority, without deviating widely from the rules of virtue, and losing the valuable privilege of being entitled to the advantages of civil rights.' The American rebels, teaching by example the exact opposite of these principles, could only look forward to the 'tyranical administration of a military aristocracy'. The prayer of Oxford was therefore that 'the wild machinations of nefarious and factitious men might be rendered fruitless'.[2] The American difficulties now meant that the Oxford-government link was working on two levels, not one. A defence of a religious establishment had been widened to include a defence of political norms.

As far as any generalization can be drawn from the surviving evidence, Oxford's opinion about America held firm, even though the English war-effort staggered from disaster to disaster. When Newdigate informed the president of Magdalen about Saratoga, the latter philosophically observed that at least Burgoyne's troops were now released to

[1] *Woodforde at Oxford*, 301.
[2] [E. Bentham,] *The Honor of the University of Oxford defended, against the Illiberal Aspersions of E[dmun]d B[urk]e . . .* (London n.d.), 4-5, 17, 35.

deal with domestic sedition. He also, rather unfashionably, could find pity for the minister responsible for American affairs, Lord George Germain, 'who was to tell the sad tale in the face of *Messrs Fox & Co*. A less eligible situation cannot well be conceived'.[1] The more the situation in America deteriorated, the more stern Oxford became. In 1778, William Scott found 'our Alma Mater as warm in her Loyalty as ever', and positively looking forward 'to the Day of vigorous exertion'.[2] Even when American independence had to be conceded, Oxford's patriotism was bitterly disappointed, but not extinguished. 'Poor old England is pelted from all quarters, and has no friend to stand by her in her distress. May the good Providence of God shield her from destruction.'[3] The links between dissenting leaders and the American rebels were well known, and Oxford reacted accordingly.

Even while the war was at its height the problem of government support for the university in its religious difficulties was a pressing one. In 1779 the prospect of a further dissenters' initiative in the commons brought a sharp reaction from Lewis Bagot:

It was thought that the connection of a great man [Lord North] with this University would have proved a favorable circumstance to the establishment.— The crisis is come—and whatever his own fears or his own Policy may suggest— he ought to be apprized in a pretty firm tone of the sentiments of this Place ...[4]

The president of Magdalen was equally firm in thinking that '... an unbounded license for preaching and teaching ... is more than a Christian Government ought to grant'.[5] Oxford was an integral part of an ecclesiastical establishment which it was bound to defend.

In 1779 the campaign demonstrated how solidified the new system of politics had become. Once again Newdigate was for no change.[6] As in 1772 he sent an open letter to the university advising resistance. As before, he organized the official response. The vice-chancellor was summoned to London for a dinner with Bagot, Page and North. Convocation met on 27 March and the required petition arrived in London three days later in time to be presented to the commons by North himself. In it Oxford expressed its 'concern for the education of youth especially being, by the Bill depending, to be put into the hands of men, who did not so much as give assurance to the public that they believed the Scriptures'.[7] The smooth running of Oxford's successful

---

[1] Horne-Newdigate, 5 Dec. 1777, Newdigate MS CR136/B3859.
[2] Scott-Newdigate, 9 May 1778, Newdigate MS CR136/B2243.
[3] Wetherell-Newdigate, 31 Jan. 1782, Newdigate MS CR136/B2574.
[4] Bagot-Newdigate, 14 Mar. 1779, Newdigate MS CR136/B1425.
[5] Horne-Newdigate, 27 Feb. 1779, Newdigate MS CR136/1759.
[6] *Letters of Theophilus Lindsey*, ed. McLachlan, p. 58.
[7] Lindsey-Turner, 30 Mar. 1779, ibid. 60; see also *Gentleman's Magazine* xlix (1779), 209.

campaign in 1779, the mechanical interrelation between the university and the government, was remarked by contemporaries and demonstrated just how far a new pattern had been set since 1772.

Progress towards the complete alliance of university and government, however, could never be altogether smooth, and one of the most serious embarrassments to the university occurred when North, after his fall from power, joined Fox in the coalition of February 1783 for which he clearly expected Oxford's support.[1] Where should loyalty now be properly placed if Oxford's chancellor opposed the king in alliance with Foxite whigs? If the university hesitated at all, it was only momentarily. Forced to choose between the government alliance and its human symbol, Oxford opted for the substance.[2] When George III paid them a visit in August 1786 the displays of loyalty were once more deliberately ostentatious.[3] This rejection of North for the larger purpose was mitigated slightly by his gradual retirement from politics with the onset of blindness, but the difficulty remained until his death in 1792.

The general election of 1780 gave a superb illustration of how far the transformation in Oxford thinking had gone. It was the last election in which the Independent ideal was seriously mooted; it was the first election since Trevor's candidacy in 1736 in which a whig candidate dared to appear; and it was the first election since 1751 in which the university had to cope without Newdigate's guiding presence. The American background inevitably made it a rather gloomy affair. North was soon expected to give way 'to some of those factious demagogues who are at this moment defeating their own ends by rooting out all obedience from that people whom they are so ambitious to govern'.[4] In such circumstances the university would greatly have appreciated the quiet return of the two sitting members. Newdigate's sudden decision to resign his seat, in late April, came as an unwelcome shock and ruined any prospect of peace.

For some time the rumour about his retirement was simply not believed. The baronet was known to be something of a professional Jeremiah, and his groanings about the state of the nation were not initially taken seriously.[5] He therefore felt obliged to explain his views fully to the vice-chancellor, and his letter is worth quoting at length because it represents the last full expression of old Independent opinion:

[1] North–Dolben, 27 Oct. 1783, Northamptonshire Record Office, MS D (F) 115. Charles James Fox (1749–1806), m. Hertford 1764.
[2] Wetherell–Jenkinson, 26 May 1783, BL Add. MS 38471, fo 69.
[3] Diary of William Fletcher, Aug. 1786, Bodl. MS Top. Oxon d. 247, fo 165.
[4] J. Dolben–W. Dolben, 8 Apr. 1780, Northants. Record Office, MS D (F) 51. Sir John Dolben (1750–1837), 4th bt; m. Ch.Ch. 1768, BCL 1775; hon. DCL 1788.
[5] C. Parker–Newdigate, dated 'Sat: morn. 1780' and postmarked [Monday] 15 March, Newdigate MS CR136/B2141.

In five successive Parliaments in which I have receivd your Commands, my first and early opinions have been only confirmed. In all of them I have seen only a wretched abuse of talents and a dearth of public Virtue. In all of them, Majorities implicitly following the dictates of the Minister of the day, changing their opinions as the Minister was changed ... In all of them oppositions conducted by interested and factious Leaders, for private ends fomenting civil discord.... The people at large more corrupt than even the representative Body and that Body more corrupt than even the minister himself.... From this fatal source are derived, the too successful rebellion of one part of the Empire the sullen discontent and kind of armed truce in another and the ferment now raging under our feet and ready to burst out into flames.[1]

Independency had, for Newdigate, died in despair and disgust.

His sudden decision raised two disturbing possibilities. There was a real chance that what was called the 'tory' interest in Oxford would be split between those who accepted the 1772 pattern and those who continued to adhere to the old ways. Up to now Newdigate's presence had conveniently blurred this division. That it existed, however, was demonstrated by the fact that Jenkinson, remembering his defeat twelve years before, still thought himself too associated with the government to be an uncontroversial candidate, much to Wetherell's disappointment.[2] The longer Wetherell took to find a replacement, the greater the possibility of a tory schism. Should this happen, there might even be the nightmare possibility of a whig candidate. In the event all these things happened.

The hopes of the surviving Independents in Oxford centred on the formidable figure of William Scott, fellow and tutor in jurisprudence at University College. His followers were very similar to those who had supported the Radnor candidature for the chancellorship in 1772. Radnor had close connections with Scott, and there is evidence that the two men kept up a firm correspondence and patronage link.[3] The chances of success for Scott's candidature lay in the fact that he was first in the field, and in the hope that enough Oxford MAs would share Newdigate's revulsion against North's incompetence or corruption to repudiate the 1772 arrangement, which was still only eight years old.

The whig candidate, Sir William Jones, was also a fellow of University College. He claimed simply to 'stand upon the Whig interest, now much stronger than it was at Oxford 50 years ago; and as the Tories were divided, I should have a good chance of success ...'.[4] Certain aspects of

---

[1] Letter of 1 June 1780, copy in Newdigate MS CR136/B2012. The vice-chancellor was then Samuel Dennis (1738-95), m. St John's 1757, president 1772-95; vice-chancellor 1780-4.

[2] Jenkinson-Wetherell, 2 May 1780, copy in BL Add. MS 38307, fos 169ᵛ-70.

[3] L. G. Mitchell, 'The first Univ. dining club?', *University College Record* v no. 5 (1970).

[4] Jones-Lady Spencer, 13 May 1780, *The Letters of Sir William Jones*, ed. G. H. Cannon (2 vols Oxford 1970) i. 369. 'Oriental' Jones (1746-94), m. Univ. 1764; judge in supreme court of judicature, Bengal.

the whig campaign were new to Oxford's experience. That a whig should stand at all was astonishing, but that he should canvass for votes as 'a man, who loves learning as much as he does our genuine constitution'[1] was thought totally extraordinary. It challenged the cherished belief that honest Warwickshire baronets were the university's natural defenders, but clearly, if the idea of Independency was waning, the social type that represented that idea might also be under threat. Equally, Jones unashamedly based his campaign on London and the mobilization of the non-resident MAs by the whig aristocratic families.[2] Lady Spencer was sent a complete electoral register which, with the exception of Jesus College, contained 847 names of whom three-quarters were non-resident. A high proportion of the non-resident voters were either non-resident fellows or former fellows now ensconced in college livings. With these voters the colleges themselves normally kept in close touch, and outside intervention was likely to have, as was shown in the 1768 election, little effect. Jones's campaign was intended to exert influence on the independents among the non-resident voters. It was run from the Turk's Head tavern, and Fox, Dunning, Sir George Savile, the duchess of Devonshire and Richard Price were just a few of his sponsors.[3] This involvement of London and the non-residents was considered frankly underhand.[4] Oxford MAs with whig patrons would be placed in an impossible situation and, worse still, might in the special circumstances of 1780 turn out to be in the majority.

With Jones and Scott as declared candidates, Wetherell found himself in a very difficult position. They were both members of his college, and yet he would be forced to find and support a third candidate in defence of the 1772 understanding. In a senior common room of less than ten people this could hardly have made for an easy social life.[5] All attempts to smooth out differences within the college failed.[6] Mercifully he was once again able to call on the services of Sir William Dolben, as the university had done in the by-election of 1768, who was in many ways an

---

[1] Jones-Lord Althorp, 29 Apr. 1780, *Letters*, ed. Cannon i. 360. According to one source Jones was asked to stand by 'certain young lawyers' on a specifically reforming platform: see Parker–Newdigate, [13 March] 1780, Newdigate MS CR136/B2141.

[2] All foundationer MAs were qualified by the university's statute of 1760 to vote as members of convocation whether or not they were resident. Non-foundationers who were not in residence had to keep their names on the books of a college or hall for at least six months before the date of an election to be eligible to vote. To ensure the enforcement of this regulation lists were sent in by colleges and halls to the vice-chancellor at regular intervals. Thus the university was at this time the only parliamentary constituency for which there was an official voters' register: see L. S. Sutherland, 'The Laudian statutes in the eighteenth century'; pp. 196–7 below.

[3] Jones-Althorp, 8 May 1780, *Letters*, ed. Cannon i. 363–5.

[4] Jones-Lady Spencer, 3 June 1780, ibid. 400.

[5] L. G. Mitchell, 'Univ., Sir William Jones, and the 1780 election', *University College Record* vi no. 3 (1973).

[6] Jones-Althorp, 19 May 1780, *Letters*, ed. Cannon i. 381–2.

ideal candidate. As a Warwickshire baronet and friend of Newdigate Dolben stood in the apostolic succession of Oxford's MPs. Except on his hobby-horse of the slave trade he could be relied on as a supporter of the government throughout his parliamentary career.

Once the Dolben-Wetherell campaign started in earnest, Scott's chances were foiled completely and Jones had to revise his opinion. A reunited 'tory' interest meant that 'a Whig has as little chance *in* the University as a single bee would have in a wasp's nest'.[1] In fact his candidacy was killed by the outbreak of the Gordon riots. This was in itself thoroughly unfair, in that Jones himself shouldered a musket in defence of the Temple, but his potential constituents were not impressed:

From Oxford I have not heard very lately, but imagine that the late disturbances have contributed very unreasonably to make the resident Oxonians more adverse than ever to the advocates for Liberty, which they absurdly confound with Licentiousness, whereas the first is the basis of all human happiness; the second is incompatible with any idea of happiness.[2]

On 30 August he said he would 'certainly decline a poll',[3] but the Dolben candidature and the fear engendered by the Gordon riots had effectively destroyed his chances much earlier. He had now come to the sad conclusion that 'the University will descend to Whiggism by slow degrees, if ever'.[4]

After his uncontested election Dolben made the traditional progress around the common rooms of Oxford to make himself known to his new constituents.[5] In his victory Wetherell and the proponents of the 1772 arrangement were vindicated. The Independent idea was given its death blow. The whigs believed that they could 'transplant a little Whiggism into this rank soil', and indeed Jones was surprised to find himself 'very popular and my company ... much sought at Oxford ... and that not only by the young men but by the Dons, to use a word of the very young men'.[6] Undoubtedly the whigs in Oxford were in some ways more vigorous than before. George III, for example, believed that what he called the 'republican' principles of the young George Canning 'had done great harm at Christ Church'.[7] But it was all speculative. The whig candidature of 1780 was compelling by its novelty, but what it really showed was that a united 'tory' interest could never be in electoral danger in Oxford.

[1] Jones-Althorp, 3 June 1780, ibid. 398.
[2] Same-Lady Spencer, 16 June 1780, ibid. 417.
[3] Jones-Althorp, 30 Aug. 1780, ibid. 425.
[4] Same-same, 4 Sept. 1780, ibid. 432.
[5] W. Dolben-J. E. Dolben, 26 Oct. 1780, Christ Church library, MS 353/5.
[6] Jones-Lady Spencer, 21 Feb. 1781, *Letters*, ed. Cannon ii. 461; Jones-Althorp, 6 Apr. 1781, ibid. 465; see also letter of 28 Sept., 2 Oct. 1781, ibid. 499-500.
[7] D. Marshall, *The Rise of George Canning* (London 1938), 26. George Canning (1770-1827), m. Ch. Ch. 1787.

The period 1772 to 1789 therefore saw a major transformation in the university's political values. Forced into an association with the government in defence of its place in the religious establishment, it thereafter continued to need official backing. Any lingering feeling of guilt about 1772 was eased by the comforting thought that the university and North were at one on the American problem, the central issue of the 1770s. The retirement of Newdigate removed an important link with the old ways. Dolben's election in 1780 vindicated the new. Oxford had learnt to be loyal to the Hanoverians. George III was almost the university's favourite guest. Should there still be any doubts at the end of the 1780s about the 1772 arrangement, the outbreak of the French revolution eradicated them.

On the surviving evidence it is not easy to describe Oxford's attitudes in the early stages of the revolution, although, if the entries in the St John's book club are a true reflection of opinion, there was certainly no lack of interest in French affairs.[1] Individual Oxonians with some direct experience of France also spoke out early. Edward Nares, a fellow of Merton who had travelled in France in 1788, was quick to deplore 'those democratical principles, which have since done so much mischief'.[2] How far the university shared his views this early in the revolution can only be guesswork, but as it moved towards increasing violence attitudes predictably hardened, and on 9 June 1792 an address was sent from convocation praising Pitt's proclamation against seditious publications. With an unihibited tirade against 'wild theorists', Oxford seconded attempts 'to check and suppress those wicked and seditious Publications, which are disgraceful to every moral and civilized State; and which tend, not only to the destruction of Decency and Good Order, but totally to subvert that necessary Subordination, which alone can give Strength and Efficacy to Legal Authority.'[3]

Even before the fall of the French monarchy and the onset of the September massacres, which were the determining factors in many peoples' opinions, official and private Oxford had declared against the French experiment. In Brasenose 'old Langton croacks about the progress of democratic vulgarity, and the reapproach of night and barbarism—Stonard eats with unusual voracity'.[4] In Christ Church 'courage with vigilance' was thought essential, and although regretted, war was considered unavoidable by the beginning of 1793.[5] At a concert in

[1] St John's senior common room book club, Bodl. MS Top. Oxon. e. 361.

[2] The autobiography of Edward Nares, Merton MSS E.2.41 and 42. Edward Nares (1763-1841), m. Ch.Ch. 1779; fellow Merton 1788; regius prof. modern history 1813-41.

[3] Bodl. MS Top. Oxon. c. 296, fo 7.

[4] J. Richardson-R. Heber, 18 Nov. 1792, Bodl. Ms Eng. lett. d. 210, fos 16-17. John Richardson (1771-1841), m. Univ. 1789; judge of the court of common pleas 1818-24. Reginald Heber (1730-1804), m. BNC 1747. John Stonard (1769-1849), m. BNC 1789.

[5] T. Randolph-T. Lambard, 23 Jan. 1793, Bodl. MS Top. Oxon. d. 353/2, fo 56. Thomas Lambard (1759-1811), m. Ch. Ch. 1776.

the Sheldonian one enthusiast calling for the *Ça ira* 'was conducted by a body of Loyalists to the door of the Amphitheatre'.[1] Comparisons were being made with the American war, and the gloomiest conclusions drawn. On 6 January 1793 Tom Paine was burnt in effigy on Carfax, and 'the magistrates, in consideration of the *right feeling* thus roughly displayed, wisely connived at the tumultuous and somewhat riotous expression of it'.[2] There was official mourning for Louis XVI.[3] As a tangible expression of opinion there was, in 1793, a fashion for wearing waistcoats in 'loyal flannel'.[4]

With the outbreak of war Oxford's patriotism became even more frenzied. There were illuminations to celebrate Lord Howe's victory and a 'Roast beef and plumb pudding' dinner after the battle of the Nile.[5] The fall of Robespierre was received with delight, and a fellow of Brasenose gave voice to the joyful expectation that the whole of France would be plunged into chaos:

Glad the infamous Robespierre is gone at last. Gone to hell as sure as he's born, and Barrere and all the Tribe of them. I only wish that all the French Convention were gone with 'em—Aye, and the French nation too. It would be of signal Service to the human Race. Hope we shall drive the Ragamuffins back again now.... I was in hopes ... that both sides of the Convention would be plunging their Daggers in the Breasts of their Opponents. Charitable Wishes! you'll say I know—They are the best and most humane I can think of notwithstanding.[6]

An over-optimistic fellow of Magdalen lost a rump and dozen in 1794 by betting on the likelihood of a Bourbon restoration.[7] The acquittal of so many defendants in the state trials of 1794-5 was not received with pleasure in Oxford; rather it was simply viewed 'as a farther encouragement to the seditious'.[8]

This overdramatic show of loyalty was not simply unthinking and red-necked patriotism. Oxford shared the widespread feeling of malaise that dominated the 1790s. In many diaries and letters of the period the *fin de siècle* was thought to be apocalyptic, and Oxford agreed. The dearth of 1795-8 was particularly alarming:

I see now a good deal of the poor, and I know they can hardly live.... Much as I hate all popular Tumult and piously as I deprecate all popular Government,

[1] Richardson-Heber, 1 Dec. 1792, Bodl. MS Eng. lett. d. 210, fos 18-19.
[2] G. V. Cox, *Recollections of Oxford* (London 1868, 2nd edn London 1870), 12.
[3] Ibid. 13.
[4] Richardson-Heber, 16 Dec. 1793, Bodl. MS Eng. lett. d. 210, fos 32-3.
[5] Randolph-Lambard, 15 June 1794, Bodl. MSTop. Oxon. d. 354/1, fo 7ᵛ; diary of William Fletcher, Oct. 1798, Bodl. MS Top Oxon. d. 247, fo 208.
[6] Stonard-Heber, 19 Aug. 1794, Bodl. MS Eng. lett. d. 211, fos 11-12.
[7] W. Stevens-F. Burdett, 10 Oct. 1794, *The Journal of the Rev. William Bagshaw Stevens*, ed. G. Galbraith (Oxford 1965), 196. W. B. Stevens (1756-1800), m. Magd. 1772. A rump of beef and a dozen bottles of claret seem to have been the standard stake for Oxford wagers.
[8] Randolph-Lambard, 7 Nov. 1794, Bodl. MS Top. Oxon. d. 354/1, fo 16.

I should not wonder, and I declare I could hardly blame the lower Class of People, if they were to make, which God forbid, some desperate and dreadful effort to better their condition. It is not the romantic and absurd notion of French Liberty that will entice them to such an Attempt; the desire of Life and the hard struggle which men will make to preserve it, it is this alone will impel them to rise against their Governors.[1]

In Oxford this dismal economic situation put a new edge on the old rivalry between town and gown. In June 1799 the riots became so serious that the proctors were forced to read the riot act on Carfax and to order the closing of all college gates at eight o'clock.[2] Against the background of the Irish rebellion and the pendulum swings of the French wars the public peace of Oxford was often disturbed, and this fact gave substance to the idea of the times being always critical.[3]

In general therefore Oxford opinion ran in parallel with that in parliament, with an overwhelming majority against the French. As in the house of commons, however, there seems to have been a small but gifted group who persisted in supporting the new notions of liberty.[4] The great whig savant Dr Samuel Parr made it something of a personal responsibility to undertake semi-regular visits to Oxford in order to nourish the opposition point of view. Fox thought that if Parr could 'keep up a spark of Whiggism in Oxford' it would be 'a great point'.[5] For the orthodox in Oxford these visits were to be treated with a mixture of awe and distaste, as Lord Holland recorded:

At Christ Church, our superiors refrained from courting him [Parr] with any ostentation of civility, but they were wonderfully cautious not to offend by any remarks on his maxims in scholarship, politics and divinity, though printed in sermons and pamphlets and circulated very freely in conversation by his admirers in the University. A distant sneer or an arch inquiry was the utmost symptom of hostility ever hazarded against this active champion of every cause they disapproved.[6]

Predictably, the more radical undergraduates found themselves in conflict with the university authorities in the atmosphere generated by events in France. The poet Robert Southey was one of these: 'Is it not rather disgraceful, at the moment when Europe is on fire with freedom— when man and monarch are contending—to sit and study Euclid or Hugo Grotius? As Pindar says, a good button-maker is spoilt in making a king; what will be spoilt when I am made a fellow of Balliol?'[7]

[1] Stonard-Heber, 26 Feb. 1795, Bodl. MS Eng. lett. d. 211, fos 23-4.
[2] Randolph-Lambard, 9 June 1799, Bodl. MS Top. Oxon. d.354/4, fo 64.
[3] Same-same, 14 Apr. 1797, ibid. fo 8.
[4] The Diary of Joseph Farington, ed. K. Garlick and A. MacIntyre (New Haven and London 1978 onward) ii. 10ff. [5] W. Derry, Dr Parr (Oxford 1966), 198.
[6] Ibid. 14-15. Henry Richard Vassall Fox (1773-1840); m. Ch.Ch. 1790.
[7] Southey-Bedford, 20 Nov. 1792, The Life and Correspondence of Robert Southey, ed. C. C. Southey (6 vols London 1849-50) i. 169. Robert Southey (1774-1843), m. Balliol 1792; hon. DCL 1812.

As early as 1792 he had ceased to powder his hair as a material expression of his dissent.[1] He believed further that 'there is little good learnt at Oxford, and much evil'; and Coleridge, meeting Southey for the first time in Balliol, was forced to agree.[2] Differences about France, as was perhaps to be expected, put an almost impossible strain on the relationship between senior members and the more radical undergraduates.

In this respect the Oxford career of Walter Savage Landor was spectacular.[3] In later years he claimed to have been a martyr of the Oxford of the 1790s, and with some justification. Although pre-empted by Southey as the first man to wear unpowdered hair, Landor was warned by his tutor in Trinity that he ran the risk of being stoned for doing so.[4] He was then sent down, in 1794, for firing a gun into the rooms of a notorious tory whom he had nicknamed the 'duke of Leeds'. At a farewell dinner he gave the toast 'May there be only two classes of people, the republican and the paralytic', and then read out odes to George Washington, French liberty and the Polish patriots.[5] Together this created an Oxford career remarkable enough by any standards, and it is very expressive of the tensions of the 1790s. But as far as the evidence allows any general conclusion, the conservatism of Oxford's official face was welcomed by a clear majority of the university, with only a talented minority dissenting.

North's death removed the last outstanding embarrassment about the coalition of 1783. As soon as notice of it was received, certain of Oxford's leading figures, including the notable dean of Christ Church, Cyril Jackson, determined on 'a bold stroke'. Pitt was to be appeased as the leader of the anti-Jacobin campaign, and this entailed offering the chancellorship to the duke of Portland.[6] At this point in 1792 Pitt was engaged in an elaborate campaign to wean Portland, his money and influence away from Fox's whigs. It was rightly felt that to offer him Oxford's chancellorship would greatly facilitate this process. The university was only too happy to co-operate. Edmund Burke, who had already travelled the *via dolorosa* from Fox to Pitt, seconded the suggestion. According to him Portland's main virtue was that he had defended 'the Principles of this ancient tried Constitution, against all Innovation whatsoever'. As it was eloquently expressed, 'The Man, the Time, and the Object all speaks for it'.[7]

[1] *Life of Southey*, ed. Southey i. 171.

[2] Southey-Lamb, 3 Apr. 1793, J. W. Warter, *Selections from the Letters of Robert Southey* (4 vols London 1856) i. 19.   [3] Walter Savage Landor (1775-1864), m. Trin. 1792.

[4] J. Forster, *The Works and Life of Walter Savage Landor* (8 vols London 1876) i. 29. I am indebted to A. J. Petford of University College, Oxford, for this reference.   [5] Ibid. 41n, 44-6.

[6] Randolph-Lambard, 20 July 1792, Bodl. MS Top. Oxon. d. 353/2, fo 47ᵛ. Cyril Jackson (1746-1819), m. Ch.Ch. 1764, dean 1783-1809. William Henry Cavendish Bentinck (1738-1809), 3rd d. of Portland; m. Ch.Ch. 1755; chan. Oxford Univ. 1792-1809.

[7] 'A Letter from Mr Burke to a Member of this University', 7 Aug. 1792, copy in PCA 60/11/53.

188 L. G. MITCHELL

Portland's campaign was steered towards a unanimous election with barely any attempt at opposition.[1] Wetherell, still very much a political leader, was able to report in September 1792 that 'Oxford in general seems to be pleased with its future new Chancellor'.[2] It was thought that his acceptance definitely indicated a determination to 'leave the high priori road of Whiggism'.[3]

Portland took his responsibilities seriously. His main Oxford contact was Cyril Jackson, who was to become one of the greatest deans of Christ Church. Since the days of Dean Bagot the college had once again begun to play a more important part in university and government politics and Jackson made regular visits to Burlington House, Portland's London home, as the principal adviser on church preferment.[4] The bishop of Oxford, Edward Smallwell, was also a close friend and a major channel for the patronage of Oxford men.[5] In the tradition of North, Portland was also assiduously helpful in more mundane matters. When the university was anxious to present George III with an address congratulating him on his escape from an assassination attempt, Portland was asked to help with the drafting of it and to suggest the most acceptable manner of presentation.[6]

So far as the revolution was concerned there were pressing and tangible ways in which Oxford could express its views. The first French refugees arrived in 1791 and almost immediately there was talk of raising a relief fund in Oxford,[7] and by November it was in full swing:

You have heard no doubt of our exertions in behalf of the exiled Clergy. The University in convocation voted a donation of £100. The Chapter of Ch.Ch. contributed 50 to which the members added so much. . . . Magdalen gave from the public fund 100; the President added 20, and the members something more. Brazen Nose distinguished itself. The College voted 30, the Principal gave 20, and the contributions of individuals amounted to 50 more ... We collect at University nearly 50. Oriel makes a shabby figure. The Vice Chancellor has transmitted to town already £500—he will be able to send I should conceive half as much more.[8]

[1] Randolph-Lambard, 19 Aug. 1792, Bodl. MS Top. Oxon. d.353/2, fo 49.
[2] Wetherell-Jenkinson, 10 Sept. 1792, BL Add. MS 38228, fo 50.
[3] Hirst-Routh, 18 Feb. 1793, Magdalen MS 478, fo 31. George Hirst (1755-1802), m. Merton 1772; admitted Univ. Nov. 1772; demy Magd. 1774-6, fellow 1776-1802.
[4] Jackson-Portland, 29 Sept. 1794, 29 Nov. 1795, Portland MSS Pwf. 5764, 5767.
[5] Smallwell-Portland, 7 Aug. 1795, Portland MS Pwf. 8380. Edward Smallwell (1711-99), m. Ch.Ch. 1739, canon 1775-99; bp Oxford 1788-99.
[6] Wills-Portland, 8 Nov. 1795, Balliol College library, Jenkyns papers, VI. A (2), letterbook of John Wills; Jackson-Portland, 23 Oct. 1794, Portland MS Pwf. 5765.
[7] Randolph-Lambard, 9 Oct. 1792, Bodl. MS Top. Oxon. d. 353/2, fo 52.
[8] Richardson-Heber, 18 Nov. 1792, Bodl. MS Eng. lett. d. 210, fos 16-17. See also MCR 1.4, register 1731-1822, p. 410; PCA convention book 2/1/2; Wills-Wilmot, 5 Nov. 1792, letterbook of Wills. Martin Joseph Routh (1755-1854), m. Queen's 1770; demy Magd. 1771-5, president 1791-1854.

The giving of alms by the university was continued throughout the 1790s. The supporting of priests was maintained, and in 1797 there was a general subscription for the assistance of war-widows and orphans.[1] Most surprising of all, in 1796 Oxford decided to allow the University Press to print Copies of the Latin Vulgate for the use of the refugee French communities. Copies were to be distributed by the exiled bishop of St Pol.[2] For an avowedly Anglican university, whose politics over the previous twenty years had been narrowly concentrated on defending its monopoly, to assist in the propagation of Catholic literature was an astonishing feat. It clearly demonstrates the extent to which Oxford shared the fears of the 1790s. The French *émigré* clergy were the chief beneficiaries of this process.

With the elaboration of the war in 1793-4, Oxford's money began to be channelled directly towards defraying the cost of national defence. The county of Oxford as a whole was involved initially, but it is clear that the vice-chancellor and proctors took leading parts in promoting the idea. The former sought direction as to how the money could best be employed 'in this alarming and critical juncture of Affairs'.[3] In the first year £200 was given from the university chest and £2449 from other Oxford sources.[4] The donations were specifically intended to have symbolic value. It showed that Oxford was 'impressed with the most firm attachment to our happy Constitution', and was 'zealous to impress the same attachment on all those committed to our Charge'.[5] The understanding with the government now seemed to involve the direct subsidy of one by the other.

In the early months of 1798, when many people entertained a serious fear of invasion, Oxford's contribution to the anti-French campaign became even more direct. The university decided to raise a force of volunteers for the defence of Oxford, and presumably the country as a whole, in the event of a French landing. The money for this project began to come in during February.[6] The cost of maintaining the force was thought to be £350 per annum, of which the University guaranteed

William Cleaver (1742-1815), m. Magd. 1757; MA BNC 1764, BD and DD 1786, principal 1785-1809; bp Chester 1788, Bangor 1800, St Asaph 1806-15. The vice-chancellor at this time was John Wills.

[1] Heber-R. Heber, 30 Nov. 1797, Bodl. MS Eng. lett. c. 204, fos 129-30.
[2] Wills-Wilmot, 1 May 1796, letterbook of Wills. John Eardley Wilmot (1750-1815), m. Univ. 1766. The bishop of St-Pol-de-Léon played a leading part in securing and managing relief for the émigrés, clerical and lay; see *The Correspondence of Edmund Burke*, ed. T. W. Copeland (10 vols Cambridge 1958-78), vols vi, vii and viii.
[3] Wills-Portland, 7 Apr. 1794, letterbook of John Wills.
[4] Cox, *Recollections of Oxford* (1870 edn), 17; see also Pemb. Archives, convention book 2/1/2, 3 June 1794.
[5] Wills-Portland, 17 Apr. 1794, letterbook of John Wills.
[6] PCA convention book 2/1/2, 13 Feb. 1798. For details of individual contributions, see Randolph-Lambard, 6 Feb. 1798, Bodl. MS. Top. Oxon. d.354/2, fo 28; Richardson-Heber, 18 Nov. 1792, Bodl. MS Eng. lett. d. 210, fos 16-17.

£100. As a force they numbered 500 by June 1798 and were still in being in 1803, by which time the system of arming and provisioning had been placed on a regular basis by levying contributions from the several colleges.[1]

In spite of appearances, this was not an operetta army. Training was taken seriously and, as one resident reported: 'Everything ... [had] a most martial appearance. The haunts of the muses are molested by the din of arms, and nothing but words of command and volleys are to be heard from morning to night.'[2] The duke of Portland himself presented their colours to the volunteers at a grand parade in Christ Church meadow in June 1798, and the duke of York came down to review them a year later. For nearly ten years they kept up a regular military presence in the university.[3] The end of the century saw Oxford in arms to defend the Hanoverians.

It is clear then that in the last thirty years of the eighteenth century Oxford's political attitudes had undergone radical changes. The university was still sure of its basic values, still confident that the consequences of 'abridging their privileges' would be 'fatal' to the nation as a whole.[4] The dissenting challenge had been beaten off and the tests remained intact. In these basic assumptions Oxford opinion remained static for the whole of the century. What was new was the political manoeuvres required to defend them. The dissenting campaigns of the 1770s, linked with the rebellion in America, forced Oxford into an alliance with the government, which the outbreak of the French revolution made unshakeable. It guaranteed Oxford's unchanging standards and ethics. A member of St Alban Hall proudly boasted that eighteenth-century Oxford's greatest surviving achievement was to encourage 'Moderate abilities and learning, so well polished as to be fit for use upon all occasions.'[5]

---

[1] *Proposals Submitted to Convocation for Forming a Volunteer Corps to be raised for the Defence of the University and to go Beyond the Precincts Thereof* (April 1798), copy in OUA MR/3/4/1.
[2] Reginald Heber–Richard Heber 1798 (postmarked 5 June), Bodl. MS. Eng. lett. c.204, fo 137.
[3] Lockhart, *Reginald Dalton* iii. 46.
[4] J. Williamson, *Opinions Concerning The University of Oxford, and Subscription to the Thirty-Nine Articles* (Oxford 1774), 7. James Williamson (1743-1813), m. St Alban Hall 1769; fellow Hertford 1783.
[5] Williamson, 4.

7

The Laudian Statutes in the Eighteenth Century

L. S. SUTHERLAND

IN 1759-60 the University of Oxford made a bold bid for freedom to control its internal affairs. It challenged the authority of the code of statutes drawn up at the instance of its chancellor, Archbishop Laud, and imposed upon it by royal letters patent in 1636, to bind it in perpetuity except where dispensed or amended by royal licence.[1] The famous Laudian statutes, devised to cover in detail every aspect of university life, were certainly intended to provide a permanent framework within which the university was to operate. Not only was the university itself precluded from altering them, but it seems that neither did the crown intend under normal circumstances to intervene further. As Lord Clarendon told the university in 1662: 'Upon my Conscience, it was the Intention of those who made the Statutes, in that mannerly Reservation of the King's power to dispense, that he never should be moved to dispense but in case of extraordinary publick consequence for the visible and substantial benefit of the University.'[2] And the natural disinclination of a self-governing institution to call in outside intervention was strengthened, in the case of the university, by the deterioration of its relations with the crown after the 1688 Revolution and the hostility of governments to it under the first two Hanoverian monarchs. The vice-chancellor put the case in convocation in 1759. It might be said 'Ad Regem adire nos posse; plenum Opus Aleae. De Rege ipso praeclara omnia et dico et sentio, at Ministro Ministris Ejus . . .'.[3]

---

[1] The definitive edition of the statutes of 1636 is *Laudian Code*, ed. Griffiths; it has a valuable introduction by C. L. Shadwell. William Laud (1573-1645), m. St John's 1589, president 1611-21; incorporated at Cambridge 1626; chancellor of Oxford Univ. 1630-41; bp of St David's 1621, Bath and Wells 1626, London 1628, abp of Canterbury 1633; beheaded 1645.

[2] Quoted by the proctors in their *Representation of the Conduct of the Proctors, with respect to the Two Explanatory Statutes proposed by the Vice-Chancellor to them and the Heads of Houses* [Oxford 1759]; see p. 200 and n. 4 below. They quoted from the register of convocation.

[3] 'We can go to the king: the undertaking is full of risks [Horace, *Odes* 2.1]. Everything I say and think concerning the king himself is favourable. But his minister and his ministers. . . .' Quoted in *An Answer to the Objections made in Convocation to the Representation of the Conduct of the Proctors* (n.p. [1759]), for which see also p. 202 and n. 2 below.

There was indeed one loophole in the code, though a minor and ambiguous one. Title X, section ii, §2 of the statutes permitted the university to legislate without royal consent

If at any time it shall seem beneficial to the University, to make any new enactment or decree, or if at any time a doubt should arise concerning the decrees and statutes already made, or hereafter to be made, whereby a further explanation of them may become requisite (provided only that no sense is attached to any statute which, under the guise of explanation, eludes or emasculates its whole force, and that this power of explanation is not extended to statutes sanctioned or confirmed by the Queen's Authority, [*Statuta Regia Auctoritate sanctita vel confirmata*] without the special licence of the Queen herself . . .).[1]

Such statutes must be proposed by the hebdomadal board, declared in congregation and passed by convocation. This concession obviously permitted the university to pass statutes on matters arising after the promulgation of the code, for instance those regulating later benefactions, of which the statute drawn up in 1758 for the regulation of the Vinerian bequest provides an excellent example.[2] It might have been argued that any earlier statute which had survived supercession by the code—for no code would be entirely comprehensive—might be open to 'explanation', but university lawyers do not seem to have tried to exploit this possibility. A more ingenious interpretation was also sometimes advanced about the statutes open to 'explanation'. It was suggested that the 'Statutes sanctioned and confirmed by the Royal Authority' were not all the statutes embodied in the code, but only the so-called royal statutes imposed by Charles I shortly before the issue of the royal letters patent. These set up the proctorial cycle, laid down the powers and composition of the hebdomadal board, regulated appeals in the vicechancellor's court and (a matter no longer of significance) controlled the election of collectors at the Lenten disputations. Between 1636 and 1770 some eight statutes had been passed by convocation under this escapeclause, at least one of them (that of 1739 which extended to the sons of Irish and Scottish peers privileges which VI. i. 1 confined to the sons of peers sitting in the house of lords[3]) being legally valid only if the distinction between the royal statutes and the rest of the code was

---

[1] The translation is taken from the first English edition of the Laudian code: *Statutes*, trans. Ward i. 135-6.

[2] See J. L. Barton, 'Legal studies', pp. 601-4 below.

[3] Their privilege was to take their degree in a shorter time than others. The right of the sons of Irish peers had slipped in unnoticed, but that of sons of Scottish peers was raised in 1738 over the claim of George Hamilton (1718-85, son of the 6th e. of Abercorn; m. Exeter 1736; MA Merton 1742). A bundle of legal papers on Hamilton's claim is preserved in ECA box L.I.6 (studies). It includes no fewer than five legal opinions, all but one favourable to the claim, but none of them raises specifically its status in terms of the code.

accepted. The most important statute passed during this period was that setting up the standing delegacy for the University Press in 1757; it proved possible to pass this statute without infringement of the code, but its promoter William Blackstone, who was the central figure of the movement to free the university from this incubus, had anxieties lest it should be challenged.[1]

But in any case the loophole offered by this ambiguous statute was too narrow to let through substantial modification, and this was what those managing the university's affairs in 1759 wanted. Historians of the university have fully recognized the importance of this challenge to traditional assumptions and of the legislative freedom which the university believed it had gained therefrom. It was thanks to this challenge that it had by the end of the eighteenth century begun extensive and long-overdue reforms in its curriculum, and by the time the first royal commission was set up in 1850 it had 'abrogated large portions of the Laudian Code'.[2] But historians have paid little attention to the circumstances under which the challenge was made, or to the immediate purpose it was intended to serve. These were, in fact, nothing to do with the academic reforms which ultimately resulted from it.

The neglect of this episode in the university's history is not surprising, for the university made no attempt to preserve the relevant documents in its archives. Minutes of the hebdomadal board are lacking for this period, the relevant register of convocation contains no reference whatever to the matter, and the important statute which emerged from the challenge was disguised until 1888 by the fact that it appeared in the printed statutes as if it had been an integral part of the code to which it was in fact a substantial addition.[3] The major documents illuminating this incident are now in the Bodleian Library and the university archives. The most important of them are manuscripts and printed papers formerly in the possession of Blackstone, some of which were purchased at auction by the Bodleian Library in 1916, while others were procured for the university archives from the library of Blackstone's son some time between 1831 and 1852 through the enterprise of the archivist, Philip Bliss.[4] Blackstone, one of the most distinguished of the university's

[1] Bodl. MS Top. Oxon. c. 209 (Blackstone MSS), fo 28c. For Blackstone's concern in this question see I. G. Philip, *William Blackstone and the Reform of the Oxford University Press in the Eighteenth Century* (Oxford Bibliog. Soc. new ser. vii 1957); H. G. Carter, *A History of the Oxford University Press* i (Oxford 1975), 325 ff.

[2] *Report of Her Majesty's Commissioners appointed to inquire into the State, Discipline, Studies and Revenues of the University and Colleges of Oxford* (1852), 6.

[3] The first printed edition of the code appeared in 1768: *Corpus statutorum universitatis oxoniensis: sive pandectes constitutionum academicarum, e libris publicis et regestis universitatis consarcinatus* (Oxford 1768). It was this edition which Ward followed for his translation of 1845 (*Statutes*, trans. Ward i) which was the first English edition of the code.

[4] The papers purchased in 1916 came originally from the collections of John White (m. Oriel

lawyers, at that time a fellow of All Souls, recently elected the first Vinerian professor of law and already embarked on a course of lectures which were to win immortality as his *Commentaries on the Laws of England*,[1] was certainly the most powerful of the university politicians at this time and played a major part in this incident.

The issue in 1759 arose from the fact that the code, oddly enough, had failed to define the composition of the university's 'Great Convocation of Doctors and Masters Regent and Non-Regent'. Since the election, not only of many of the university's officers including its chancellor,[2] but of the two burgesses who since 1603 represented it in parliament rested with this body, this was obviously a matter of importance, particularly at a time when in the university, as in the nation, political controversies were acute, when the university set great store by its independence of the government, and when successive administrations exerted heavy pressure to gain control of the university's representation.[3]

The issue was a complex one. Even the authoritative modern *History of Parliament* gives a misleading description of the university electorate, for it is there described as composed of 'the doctors and masters of Arts'.[4] In fact, by long-standing custom before 1760 and by university statute after that date, it resided only in doctors and masters of arts who satisfied further qualifications, and was intended to exclude from voting in all types of election in convocation those not closely and regularly concerned with the university's business. Two points must be borne in mind if the events of 1759-60 are to be understood. In the first place, though the immediate result of the challenge was, and had to be, a university statute, those who made the challenge were primarily concerned with convocation not as a legislative but as an electoral body; and in the second place, even in the matter of elections they were aiming not at reform (which apart from all other considerations would have encroached on questions of parliamentary elections) but at providing a codification of existing custom. This was why Blackstone was so prominent in the incident.

Controversies within the university on the qualifications for voting in convocation, in which the state had frequently played an active part, had

1732; demy Magd. 1734-40; fellow All Souls 1753) colleague of Blackstone's at All Souls, and are in a volume bearing Philip Bliss's bookplate: Bodl. MS Top. Oxon. c. 209. Philip Bliss (1787-1857), m. St John's 1806, Bodley's Sub-librarian 1822-8; registrar of the university 1824-53; keeper of the archives 1826-57; principal St Mary Hall 1848-57. Blackstone's son was James Blackstone (1765-1831), m. Ch.Ch. 1781; principal New Inn Hall 1803-31; Vinerian prof. of common law 1793-1824; assessor in the vice-chancellor's court.

[1] W. Blackstone, *Commentaries on the Laws of England* (4 vols Oxford 1765-9).
[2] The vice-chancellor was nominated by the chancellor as was the high steward, but the registrar, a number of professors, the bedels and others were elected in convocation: see below.
[3] For a learned and comprehensive treatment of this subject see W. R. Ward, *Georgian Oxford* (Oxford 1958).
[4] L. B. Namier and J. Brooke, *The History of Parliament: The House of Commons 1754-1790* (3 vols London 1964) i. 35.

a long history. Most of them were concerned with the conflict over the elections of university proctors which caused recurrent turmoils in the university until the Caroline cycle of 1628 removed their election from convocation to the colleges, which were henceforth to provide proctors in specified rotation, as in a modified form they have done ever since. The Caroline cycle and the regulations governing it were included in an Appendix to the Laudian code. The definition of those within each college who were qualified to vote for proctors as there laid down transferred to the college electorate the qualifications at that time generally approved for voting in convocation. Voters must be MAs or doctors of the higher faculties *actualiter creati*, that is to say not holders of any kind of honorary degree, since this might favour (as at Cambridge) outside intervention. They must also be 'resident' and 'commorant'. In defining these terms a distinction was drawn between those who were permanent members of the foundation of colleges and halls, who were deemed to be resident without further proof, and those who were not on the foundation, described as *convictores* or *commensales* (in the eighteenth century they began to be called *extranei* or 'independents') who, since they had gone out of residence (*abire cum pannis* was the technical term, defined as early as 1594) were not eligible to vote again unless they returned to the university and had been personally resident for six months in their college or hall during the year in which an election took place.[1] Even in the seventeenth century such persons must have been very few; by the eighteenth century they were almost non-existent.

Disputes over claims by *extranei* to vote arose again before the eighteenth century. In 1691 sixteen university notables, including Bishop Fell, signed a protest before a notary public against the votes of two former canons of Christ Church, long out of residence, in an election for a Lady Margaret professor of divinity.[2] The regius professor of civil law, asked for an opinion, said that since there was no legal remedy the effects of their protest could 'only be such as those to free the Consciences from consenting to irregular Acts, to interrupt the Growth of Custom, etc.'.[3] The serious eighteenth-century disputes arose over some of the strongly contested political elections which began in the 1690s. Three of the eighteenth-century contests were for the university's parliamentary burgesses, one at the general election of 1722 and two at

[1] This early history has been sketched out by Shadwell in his introduction to the edition of 1888 (*Laudian Code* ed. Griffiths) and a valuable account was given in an anonymous counsel's opinion of 1772 preserved in the university archives (see p. 197 n. 1 below).

[2] The Lady Margaret professors were elected by members of convocation who belonged to the theology faculty.

[3] Bouchier–vice-chancellor (n.d.), MS Ballard 22, fo 91. Thomas Bouchier (1633–1723), m. Magdalen Hall 1650; fellow All Souls 1658; regius prof. civil law 1672–1712; principal St Alban Hall 1679–1723.

by-elections in 1737 and 1750. The first and third of these were fought with especial bitterness, as was the election for the chancellorship (the first in the history of the office since the election of Archbishop Laud) when in 1759 Richard Trevor, a candidate put up by the 'New' or whig 'Interest', seemed at one time likely to defeat the powerful 'Old' or tory 'Interest' by reason of a split in the latter between the supporters of the earl of Westmorland and those of the earl of Lichfield. In each of the contested elections the lack of a legal qualification for voters was recognized to be most unsatisfactory; in each the uncertainty of the qualifications of *extranei* was the trouble, and it caused the more anxiety as the number of such voters casting their votes was growing under the pressure on the university of national politics.[1] In both the 1750 and 1759 elections Blackstone, as a prominent university politician in the Old Interest, was actively concerned.

It was after the election of 1722 that the university first sought counsel's opinion on the qualification of voters. An anonymous opinion survives in its archives. Counsel began by making a strenuous attempt to argue that the qualifications for voting in convocation were in effect laid down by law, since they could be inferred from the provisions in the appendix to the Laudian code governing the elections of proctors by colleges; but he soon gave it up. Not only is there a statute (title X) dealing with convocation in which there is no reference whatever to proctorial elections, but (in addition to some other discrepancies) by the time he was writing and for many years before, the established custom at elections in convocation differed in an important particular from the practice laid down for the election of proctors in the appendix to the code. The code laid down that non-foundationers voting for proctors must have been resident in person for the requisite qualifying period. Established custom asked of such voters in convocation no more than that they should have kept their names on the buttery books of their respective college or hall. He therefore ended up not with a definition of a qualified elector to be deduced from the code but with what he judged to be one under the best custom he could find when he wrote. Though there had never been a determination at law, he held that all foundationers had a right to vote, even if absent; that the same applied to all those permanently resident in the university precincts, though not foundationers; that no honorary degree entitled its holder to vote (this he thought particularly important in parliamentary elections); and 'it may not be amiss to allow all *such as have had names in Buttery Books* for

[1] The number increased also for another reason. Honorary degrees began to be given not only, as in the past, to persons of distinction as a result of letters to convocation from the chancellor, but also in the form of MAs 'by creation', to undergraduate sons of noblemen, and soon also to gentlemen-commoners, who had been resident at least three years in the university: see L. S. Sutherland, *The University of Oxford in the Eighteenth Century: a reconsideration* (Oxford 1973), 6.

6-Months immediately preceding an Election of any sort, and have *paid Fees* and *submitted to the Moneos* for *Exercise* &c to have votes in such Election'.[1]

The trouble was, however, that these rules were apt to be flouted in the heat of elections. In the 1722 election not only did several holders of honorary degrees cast their votes, but their right to do so apparently won some authoritative support.[2] At all the contested elections the votes of *extranei* whose names had not been on the buttery books for the requisite period were challenged, and since no list of persons on these books in fact existed, doubtless others voted but escaped notice. An odd development was that at the 1750 by-election the master of Balliol had observed in his college (where he thought the malpractice originated and where for many years an entirely disproportionate number of *extranei* voted) that some men were putting their names on the books with the connivance of fellows without making any pretence of continued connection with the college.[3] Had the voting been close in any of the contested parliamentary elections, the defeated candidate would no doubt have petitioned the house of commons on the ground of undue return.[4] In the chancellor's case there would have had to be recourse (as on a later occasion at Cambridge[5]) to the courts.

On 2 January 1759, two days before the poll for the chancellor

---

[1] OUA SP/C/6, pp. 32-3. It was probably given by Nicholas Fazackerley (1685-1767, m. BNC 1702), a successful tory lawyer and later MP, who advised the university often at this time. 'Moneos' were orders from the vice-chancellor to undertake duties concerning graduation or other university functions. It is clear that in fact the university had ceased to issue such instructions to graduate *extranei*, and only spasmodically demanded fees of them, as in 1758 when the vice-chancellor 'has now ordered that all A.M-s who have not duly contributed to the Support of these Privileges as the Statute directs should be excluded the Right of Voting in the ensuing Election' (OUA/WP α/22/1, fo 15ᵛ.

[2] A curious copy of the poll of March 1722 (NS) printed at the University Press purported to show all votes queried, distinguishing between those finally considered valid and invalid, with votes of honorary MAs queried marked as 'good': *A True Copy of the Poll for Members of Parliament for the University of Oxford, taken March the 21st 1721* [OS] (Oxford 1722). A friend of the disappointed candidate William King in a savage pamphlet maintained that this list was got out by the hebdomadal board, and that they had agreed to accept the votes of honorary MAs when they found that most of them were on their side: [S. Harrison,] *An Account of the Late Election for the University of Oxford* (London 1722).

[3] There is a correspondence on the subject in the Dolben MSS: Northampton, Northants. Record Society, MSS D (F) 78-101. In general those keeping their names on the books of colleges did not withdraw their caution money and they were expected to pay the butler 1 *d* a week for writing them in. Leigh told Dolben, then visitor of the college, that he had counted on the buttery books of the college the names of 43 men who had kept no caution money, 'intending thereby to preserve to Themselves the Privylege of electing, in the University, Clerks to Benefices, Professors, Lecturers, and Burgesses; and which Privyleges, they have, in some respects, occasionally exercis'd': T. Leigh--Sir John Dolben, 5 Jan. 1752, ibid. MS D (F) 84. He maintained that they had done so in some cases against the New Interest candidate at the 1750 election, and manuscript annotations to a copy of the very imperfect *True Copy of the Poll taken at Oxford January 31. 1750* (copy in Bodl. Don. b.12) give the Balliol votes as 21, of which 9 were good and 12 bad, 10 of the bad votes being cast for the Old Interest candidate. Sir John Dolben (1684-1756), 2nd bt; m. Ch. Ch. 1702.

[4] In 1722 William King threatened to petition, but desisted.

[5] D. A. Winstanley, *The University of Cambridge in the Eighteenth Century* (Cambridge 1922), 145 ff.

was taken, a legal opinion was given by Charles Yorke, the most brilliant of the young whig lawyers.[1] It was asked for in the hope of preventing the vice-chancellor from burning the voting papers as soon as the result was declared, as was in fact obligatory by statute in the election of university officers,[2] but the occasion was taken in the case put before him to point out that:

There is no Test or Oath of the Qualifications, nor any publick Book of the University which ascertains the Voters, but it depends upon Collateral facts, besides the degrees, such as being bona fide members of some College or Hall, unless in a few cases excepted, and the Statutes or By-Laws of the University are silent as to the manner of examining the Validity of Votes in such Election.

All that Yorke could do was to stress (without success) the impropriety of burning the votes in the case of so important an officer, and to urge the returning officer to do his best to see that justice was done.

The hopes of the New Interest were dashed by the last-minute withdrawal of Lichfield. Westmorland won a resounding victory and his supporters saw their chance to remedy a long-standing abuse. They decided to do so by the introduction of a statute without seeking royal licence, and they based their decision on a revolutionary legal opinion drawn up by Blackstone. He presented it in a paper headed 'Considerations on the Power of the University to make, alter, or repeal Statutes, without Royal Licence'. The Bodleian Library's holograph copy of it, obtained much later, is the only one at present known to exist, though one or possibly two other copies can be shown to have been in existence in 1837, and it was quoted under the title of 'Mr Justice Blackstone's opinion' even by those who had not seen it.[3]

His line of argument was revolutionary, but it may be noted that he did not evolve it to meet the need of the moment. A document among his papers shows that he had already worked it out in detail nearly two years earlier in connection with the statute for the delagacy of the press which he was sponsoring.[4] Basically the argument was a simple one. All corporations had an inherent right 'to make By-Laws or Statutes for

[1] OUA/WPα/3/4/3.
[2] At the contested election for chancellor when Lord Grenville was elected in 1809 'there was a mixture of fun and annoyance, when the immense heap of voting-papers was (as the statute then required) "igne penitus *abolitus*" before the result of the election could be declared by the Proctors': G. V. Cox, *Recollections of Oxford* (London 1868, 2nd edn London 1870), 66. Cox adds in a footnote that the voting papers were burnt within the convocation house itself.
[3] Bodl. MS copy Top. Oxon. c.209, fos 27–8a. There is a rough draft in Blackstone's papers in OUA/WPα/22/1, fos 4, 5. In 1837 the duke of Wellington quoted from the paper as in his hands during a debate in the house of lords: *Parliamentary Debates* xxxix. 1395–6. Edward Hawkins, provost of Oriel, had a copy in 1836: see his evidence in *Report and Evidence upon the Recommendations of Her Majesty's Commissioners for inquiring into the State of the University of Oxford, presented to the Heads of Houses and Proctors* (Oxford 1853), evidence, p. 377 and note c.
[4] OUA/WPα/22/1, fos 4, 5.

their own domestic Government; provided such By-Laws or Statutes are not contrary to the Charter of Incorporation, or the general Law of the Land'. The university, being a corporation by prescription, time out of mind,

has no charter of Incorporation to restrain it, but its several Charters of Liberties . . . being confirmed by Act of Parliament 13 Eliz. are thereby become a part of the Law of the Land. A Statute therefore or By-Law made contrary to those Charters, or to the general Rules of Law, will not be valid or binding: But such as is consistent with both will be good.

Within these limits

It is certain that no Corporation has Power to make a Statute or By-Law abridging the Legislative power of their Successors, who have the same Right to *repeal* as the Predecessors had to *enact*; any more than one Parliament in being can make an effectual Act to abridge the Power of a future Parliament. Therefore any academical Statute or By-Law, which seems to assume such a Power, is either void in itself, or at least voidable and subject to Repeal by any subsequent academical Legislature.

He admitted that an attempt had been made to restrict the freedom of action of the university, though only, he maintained, with respect to the royal statutes issued and brought together in 1634, and not to the whole body of statutes included in the royal confirmation of 1636. But even in this limited sense 'it may be respectful indeed, though not indispensably necessary to sue for a royal licence', and was to be construed as a 'compliment' and not an obligation.

Since he had already worked out this line of argument, and it was accepted by the vice-chancellor and the majority of the hebdomadal board, progress was rapid. By March 1759 (if an endorsement in Blackstone's hand is accepted) the first draft of a statute defining voting qualifications was in print.[1] So too was the draft of a second statute of less permanent significance, but important to those who framed it. The clause in the Laudian code under which Lichfield's candidature was held to be invalid was II. 9, *De privilegiis universitatis et civitatis simul non fruendis*. Lichfield had accepted the honorary freedom of the city while still a member of the university and indeed with his name on the books of his college. It was opinions of counsel taken shortly before the election and, even later, a powerful anonymous paper by Blackstone himself, which forced his withdrawal.[2] But what had been a useful weapon in the

---

[1] OUA/WPα/22/2/4, endorsed by Blackstone 'First Draught of new Statutes Mar. 1759'.

[2] Opinions of C. Pratt, R. Wilbraham (1695–1770, m. BNC 1711; DCL by diploma (1761) and J. Morton (1705–80, m. Trin. 1720; created DCL 1749) concerning the qualifications of an unspecified candidate [Lord Lichfield] for the office of chancellor, 22 Dec. 1758, Bodl. Gough Oxf. 96 (61b). In Blackstone's papers in OUA/WP α/22/2/2 there is a copy with an addendum of 29 December endorsed by Blackstone 'Printed Opinions of 22 and 29 Dec. 1758 published 29 Dec.'. The

200   L. S. SUTHERLAND

conflict was now an embarrassment to those who had used it, for under
the terms of the code an offender was permanently excluded from the
university, and the Old Interest had no desire to alienate permanently a
prominent local tory peer, nor to perpetuate their own divisions.[1] A
short statute amending the rigour of this clause was therefore
introduced at the same time.

That there should be opposition to these proposals was inevitable,
and in the heated political atmosphere this soon took on a party colour.
Eight heads of houses, all supporters of the New Interest, were to go on
record against them, but the opposition does not appear to have been
organized until after the new proctors came into office: William Wright
of Merton and George Austen of St John's, both supporters of the New
Interest. The first drafts of both statutes needed considerable
amendment, and in the same month a further printed paper was
produced showing side by side the first drafts and extensive amendments, which were explained in voluminous notes. Both the form and
content of the amendments make it clear that Blackstone was their
author.[2] The amended document was followed by a third and final one,
embodying the most important of the amendments, which was ready for
discussion by the hebdomadal board at a meeting about 21 June, when it
passed after some heated debate.[3] The two statutes were then published
in congregation on 7 July and brought before convocation on 12 July.

In preparation for this meeting the proctors, leading the opposition,
printed and sent round to common rooms in the way then usual a paper
headed *A Representation of the Conduct of the Proctors.* . . .[4] The meeting of
convocation was a stormy one. Since all debates had to be in Latin
speeches were comparatively rare, but on this occasion the vice-
chancellor sought to refute the proctors' *Representation* in a long Latin

'Observations' on the above of 30 December 1758 in Bodl. Gough Oxf. 96 (61b) are certainly the
paper called 'Reflections on the opinions of Messrs. Pratt, Morton, and Wilbraham relating to Lord
Litchfield's disqualification' (1759) in the catalogue of Blackstone's works, apparently based on a list
of his own, in *The Biographical History of Sir William Blackstone* (London 1782), no. XIV. There is a copy
in OUA/WP α/22/2/3 endorsed by Blackstone 'Printed Observations 30 December 1758'. His
correspondence in OUA/WP α/22/1, fos 20-8 shows that it was printed on 30 December but held
up either until the evening of 31 December or the morning of 1 January 1759 in the hope that agreement would be reached without publication.

  [1] Westmorland appointed Lichfield high steward as soon as possible, and he later succeeded as
chancellor.
  [2] The second statute with which Blackstone was particularly concerned was entirely redrafted in
these amendments. The method of setting out documents in parallel lines on the same page for
convenience of comparison seems only to have been used hitherto in the course of the debates on
the Vinerian bequest, and the amendments and notes bear strong signs of his style.
  [3] The second draft was endorsed by Blackstone '2nd Draught of new Statutes June 1759': OUA/
WP α/22/2/6. The final draft was endorsed by Blackstone 'Last Draught of new Statutes, passed in
the hebdomadal Meeting circiter 21 Jun. 1759': OUA/WP α/22/2/7.
  [4] There are copies in Bodl. Gough Oxf. 69, no. 43 and OUA/WP α/22/2/8a, the latter endorsed
by Blackstone 'Proctors' Representation circ. 1 Jul. 1759'.

speech, and called on them to take a vote. This they refused to do (probably exceeding their rights[1]) and proceeded to impose their proctorial veto on both statutes. Though they complained that 'Reproaches and hissings were plentifully bestowed on them', they had for the time being blocked the proposals, and they promptly published in their own justification *An Answer to the Objections made in Convocation to the Representation of the Conduct of the Proctors.*[2]

Their success was, however, more apparent than real. They did not succeed in stirring up a campaign in the university against the measures,[3] nor did they gain the support of the ministry. Some years before ministers might well have been glad of a legal excuse for intervention in Oxford affairs, but times had changed. Though ministerial supporters had turned out to vote for the bishop of Durham as a candidate for the chancellorship in 1759,[4] ministers no longer wished to embroil themselves with the university. The supporters of the measures did not bother to answer the proctors' publications, and a year later, when new and more sympathetic proctors were in office, the statutes were reintroduced and passed, with no sign of opposition except a protest before a notary public signed by the eight New Interest heads of houses.[5]

It is noteworthy that the objections of the New Interest proctors were not directed at either of the statutes in themselves. The statute defining the membership of convocation and the right to vote in it was well drafted and sensible. It followed fairly closely the definition of the categories of voters laid down in 1722, and it made practical provisions for enforcing them. Thanks to Blackstone's amendments it evaded the imposition of oaths on voters but provided for annual lists to be drawn up by the university's bedels from the buttery books (counter-signed by

[1] Exercise by the proctors of their right of veto was rare, but on several occasions it was held that it was their duty to take the vote before applying their veto. A printed paper without heading dated 7 June 1770 on the business of convocation and congregation states that the proctors do not waive their negative by permitting a scrutiny to begin, 'Their negative right not to be declared till the Scrutiny is concluded': Bodl. G.A. Oxon, b.19, 17 (191).

[2] Copies in Bodl. Gough Oxf. 96, fo. 45, and OUA/WP α/22/2, unnumbered; the latter endorsed by Blackstone 'Proctors 2d paper circ. 12 Jul, 1759'.

[3] Only one important paper was later printed: *A Letter to a late Member of the University of Oxford with respect to the two Explanatory Statutes proposed to the C—n* (n.p. n.d.). This was written after 5 October 1759 when, it states, the vice-chancellor in his speech at the end of his year of office attacked the senior proctor and the proctor defended himself.

[4] C. Jenkinson–G. Grenville, 2 and 11 Jan. 1759, *The Grenville Papers*, ed. W. J. Smith (4 vols London 1852-3) i. 285, 288. The bishop of Durham had not been put up by the duke of Newcastle, whose candidate, Archbishop Secker, he forestalled, greatly to Newcastle's annoyance. I am indebted to the late Professor R. W. Greaves of Kansas University for this information from Secker's unpublished diary.

[5] Balliol MS 403. They were the master of Balliol (Theophilus Leigh), the principal of Jesus (Thomas Pardo, 1688-1763, m. Jesus 1705, principal 1727-63), the dean of Christ Church (David Gregory), the warden of Wadham (George Wyndham), the rector of Exeter (Francis Webber), the warden of Merton (Henry Barton, 1718-90, m. Merton 1733, warden 1759-90), the president of St John's (Thomas Fry) and the principal of Hertford (David Durell).

heads of houses and halls) and from the university's records. These lists
were to be deposited with the vice-chancellor. The only criticism made
of its terms was that it accepted the bona fides of those already on the
books before a stated date, a sensible provision though their opponents
hinted that the Old Interest might gain more from it than did the New.[1]

It was on the legal issue that the opposition had focused. Before the
battle was joined an attempt had been made to meet this criticism. As
the vice-chancellor informed convocation, 'to obviate this Difficulty, a
Case had been drawn by a *very skilful Person*, and laid before Two
eminent Counsil'.[2] The *Case*, though anonymous, was later included in
the catalogue of Blackstone's works and followed so closely the lines of
his *Considerations* that its authorship is self-evident.[3] The two 'eminent
Counsil' were Randle Wilbraham, the university's deputy steward, and a
younger man who later succeeded him in this office, John Morton. On
2 June 1759 they had produced a rather jejune joint opinion in which
they supported Blackstone's views without reservation. From that time
on Blackstone's *Case* and the opinions of Wilbraham and Morton were
always quoted as proof of the university's legislative independence,
occasionally supported by Blackstone's much fuller *Considerations*. The
independent value of counsel's opinion would be more convincing did we
not know from Blackstone's private correspondence that he was not only
in close personal and professional touch with Wilbraham at this time,
but that the latter admitted to depending heavily on him in all matters of
university law.[4] In any case the New Interest proctors remained quite
unconvinced by their views and argued that the case put before them,
though passed by the hebdomadal board without question, was faulty.
They were no match for Blackstone in the niceties of university legal
history, but they stuck firmly to the traditional view that the university
was precluded from changing or 'explaining' any of the statutes of the
Laudian code without royal licence, and they insisted that the code was
in effect a new charter which they were all sworn to obey.

And indeed the case the proctors put forward and the principles on
which they argued it were legally tenable. There was always an
undercurrent of uneasiness in the university about the basis of its new
and revolutionary claim for self-determination. It rose momentarily to

---

[1] This may have been true, as it certainly had been at Balliol when the master took steps to check
it, but it would be unjust to the New Interest to argue that they were primarily activated by this
consideration since this clause did not appear in the earlier drafts of the new statute, to which they
had been opposed.

[2] *An Answer to the Objections made in Convocation to the Representation of the Conduct of the Proctors* (n.p.
n.d.), copy in Bodl. Gough Oxf. 96 (45).

[3] *Biog. History of Blackstone*, catalogue of Blackstone's works, no. XV. Cf [W. Blackstone,]
*Considerations on the Question, whether Tenants by Copy of Court Roll . . . are Freeholders qualified to vote in
Elections for Knights of the Shire* (London 1758).

[4] OUA/WP α/22/1, fos 8-9, 16, 17.

the surface in 1770 and 1772-3[1] but it was not until the controversies surrounding the Hampden case in 1836 that it reached serious levels. Then legal opinion was once again taken on the question, and the attorney general and other prominent counsel were consulted; their views were hostile to those advanced by Blackstone and favourable to the position adopted by the proctors in 1759. There was nothing, they argued, in the statute of 1571 to prevent the university at a later date being given a new charter, and the Laudian code should be accepted as such.[2]

By this time, however, it was too late to put the clock back: too much legislative reform had been passed on the basis of the ruling of 1759, and the demands for still more radical reform which would sweep away the remains of the Laudian code altogether were so insistent that no attempt was made to tackle this legal problem. Nor was the conflict of opinion ever resolved. When the royal commission took the matter up in its *Report* of 1852 it gave little time to the consideration of old problems. After a summary investigation of the history of post-Laudian legislation its conclusion was that the university's legal position was 'to say the least so doubtful, that some step ought to be taken to set the matter at rest', and in the charter of 1856 the university was given full indemnity for any of its acts during this period which might have been illegal.[3]

Thus the university asserted its claim to self-determination against little serious opposition. Students of the history of eighteenth-century Oxford may regret that the issue was never brought to a conclusion, particularly when Blackstone was still there to defend his conclusions. They would not deny, however, that it would have been a bad day for the university if his attempt to liberate it had failed. Blackstone in this as in other cases during his short outburst of activity as a university politician deserved well of the institution which he served, not only because he cleared up the area of chaos he set out to deal with, but because he opened up much wider possibilities for change than he himself had envisaged.

---

[1] For 1770 see Bodl. G.A. Oxon. b.19, 17 (three pamphlets bound together opposing a new statute on university dress). In 1772-3 the question of subscription was raised. 'A few people in the University entertain a doubt of its Power to alter or explain a Statute confirmed by Royal Authority': W. Scott-R. Newdigate, 5 Mar. 1773, Newdigate MS CR136/B2241. Nathan Wetherell, just retired from the vice-chancellorship, had however assured Charles Jenkinson on 22 October 1772: 'It is a point universally acknowledged, that the University has inherent Powers of alteration of *any* of its *Statutes* without application to the Crown.' BL Add. MS 38207, fo 181. He had had difficulty in finding a copy of Wilbraham and Morton's opinion and apologized for its tattered condition.

[2] See Shadwell's introduction to *Laudian Code*, ed. Griffiths, pp. xxi-xxv.

[3] *Report*, 4; Shadwell, pp. xxv ff.

8

The Administration of the University

L. S. SUTHERLAND

IN THE eighteenth century the university's administration still fell, as it had long done, into two related but distinct parts. The first was the internal government needed for an institution devoted to religion learning and education, the stamp of which the university still bears. The second, which had disappeared almost without trace, was the organization which had been built up to preserve its liberties, particularly as against the city in which it was situated and with which its relations had always been uneasy and often actively hostile. Strengthened by the support of the crown in a series of royal charters (culminating in the Caroline charter of 1636) and by an act of parliament of 1571 which added statutory sanction,[1] the university had built up formidable legal powers and administrative claims *vis-à-vis* the city, which it sought to defend.

Both sides of the administration, like everything else in the eighteenth-century university, were steeped in the past, though the basic document on which they depended was the Laudian code of statutes, imposed by royal precept in 1636. The code defined the relations between the university and the city in the following terms:

Although the University and City of Oxford are distinguished from each other by their rights and magistrates, yet such is the prerogative of the Chancellor, that he not only has the peculiar custody of the whole University entrusted and committed to himself alone, under our Lady the Queen, but he also has common guardianship with the city mayor of the whole Borough or City of Oxford, and its suburbs, and he can with the consent of the University frame laws to have obligatory force on the burgesses also, or townsmen, and their commonality in subordinance to the University.[2]

The 'obligatory force' was imposed by the chancellor's (usually called the vice-chancellor's) court, which enjoyed a jurisdiction purporting to run throughout the realm and more certainly throughout the university's precincts, whenever a matriculated person was involved in a wide range

---

[1] 13 Eliz. I, c. 15.
[2] *Statutes* XVII.i.2, trans. Ward i. 176; for the Latin text see *Laudian Code*, ed. Griffiths, p. 164.

of causes both civil and criminal.[1] The term 'matriculated person' covered not only all academics, but certain privileged persons among the townsmen on the grounds that they provided a necessary background for academic studies.[2] The law administered in this court was based on the civil law, with which the university lawyers were familiar. Its sanctions over citizens were those of fines, imprisonment and the formidable power of 'discommoning'.[3] On the civil side it provided, among other things, a convenient and summary court for causes of debt, the usefulness of which long outlived its other activities.

How far the university had ever succeeded in subjecting the city to the full rigour of its claims and how far its privileged position had been justified in the past is not here the question. It is certain that by the eighteenth century any justification for such sweeping claims had disappeared and with it much of the will to enforce them, and that the period saw the beginning *de facto* if not *de jure* of the retreat which became virtually a rout in the following century. Nevertheless such matters remained a sufficiently serious concern of the university to demand consideration in any study of its administration.

In the internal administration of the university a clearly defined watershed can be discerned in the years between 1755 and 1760. Before the date, subject as they were to a Laudian code established in 1636 and intended to be perpetual but containing many detailed provisions which had not only become outdated but were virtually unenforceable, academics directed their attention to subtleties intended to maintain what they could of the form of the statutes even when the substance had been abandoned. Their anxiety in this respect was heightened by their disfavour in the eyes of the government between 1714 and 1760, and the fear that overt breaches of the code might be adduced by their enemies as a justification for attacking them by *Quo warranto*. After that date, on the other hand, they embarked on open though gradual change, at first tentatively then with growing confidence until, by the

[1] The university's precincts were variously defined but were generally accepted as covering the city and its suburbs and the four immediately adjoining hundreds. Its legal claims were to cover in civil causes all except those involving freeholds and in criminal causes all excepting treason, felony and 'mayhem'. These three last offences were by charter and statute triable under approval of the lord chancellor by a court sitting under the high steward of the university, but it was admitted that 'there has happily been no occasion to reduce them into practice for more than a century past': W. Blackstone, *Commentaries on the Laws of England* (4 vols Oxford 1765-9) bk IV, ch. 19, II.3 (pp. 274-6). The vice-chancellor's court also claimed privilege over all questions arising on testamentary causes among privileged persons with property within the precincts at the time of their death.
[2] There is no means of assessing the proportion of the citizens who enjoyed privileged status. In 1829, by which time its advantages were already much reduced, the university registrar guessed that there were some 250-300 enjoying it out of a total of some 15,000 citizens: OUA/WP α/56/3, fo 7.
[3] Discommoning was tantamount to civil excommunication and was capable of destroying the livelihood of tradesmen who depended largely on the university and the colleges for their prosperity.

end of the century, piecemeal changes had been made in many university institutions and had paved the way for the developments noted by the royal commissioners of 1850-2, who reported that they found that large portions of the Laudian code had already been abrogated.[1]

The causes of this development were complex and represented a deep-seated change in attitude. It was brought about by the work of one man, the university's greatest jurist of the time, William Blackstone. It was through his initiative that a radical reform in the administration of the University Press was forced through between 1756 and 1757,[2] and two years later it was his legal opinion which persuaded the university to attack directly the dead hand of the code and to assert its right to legislate for its own internal needs without any other restraint than that of the law of the land.[3]

The Laudian settlement had been essentially an attempt to rationalize a wide range of existing institutions (hence its conservative bias) while giving the system which emerged a slant towards whatever in these institutions best fitted the orderly and oligarchic tendencies of Laud's political thinking. It may be said that the organization of the university, taken in its widest sense, became for the next century the working out of the modifications in the balance of power imposed by the code, against the background of contemporary circumstances. The administration in the narrower sense of the officials responsible for its day-to-day affairs reflected the conservatism of the settlement. They were few in number and only two new offices were created.

The officials were listed in the code under the two headings of *officiarii* and *ministri sive servientes*. A few office-holders belonging to one or other of these categories were not included in the list but were entered under the institutions which they served: Bodley's Librarian, his deputy and the library's porter;[4] the assessor who sat as the vice-chancellor's deputy in his court and the registrar of the court and the proctors nominated to plead there; also the head printer of the University Press to whose office that of esquire bedel of law was to be attached.[5] The *officiarii* (apart from three honorific figures, the

[1] *Report of Her Majesty's Commission* (1852), p. 6.
[2] See I. G. Philip, *William Blackstone and the Reform of the Oxford University Press in the Eighteenth Century* (Oxford Bibliog. Soc. new ser. vii 1957); H. G. Carter, *A History of the Oxford University Press* i (Oxford 1975), pp. 325 ff. It was possible to reform the Press by statute without infringing the code, since it was there indicated that further reforms might be made to the Press: *Statutes* XVIII.v, trans. Ward i. 205. For a recent assessment of Blackstone see I. G. Doolittle, 'Sir William Blackstone and his Commentaries on the Laws of England (1765-9); a biographical approach', *Oxford J. Legal Studies* iii (1983).
[3] See L. S. Sutherland, 'The Laudian statutes' above.
[4] The statutes for the Bodleian Library were incorporated as an appendix to the code.
[5] For what actually happened see Carter, i. 144 ff.

chancellor, the high steward and the deputy high steward) were members of convocation, and heads or fellows of colleges, who also carried out university functions; the *ministri sive servientes* were rather officials in the full-time employment of the university. The list of officials included several whose duties were highly specialized, namely the public orator (first appointed in 1564) and the keeper of the archives (one of the two newly created offices).[1] There were also officers responsible for the university's interests in the city, the two clerks of the market, appointed annually, one by the chancellor and one by the vice-chancellor, and the masters of the streets, nominated annually by the proctors in congregation from among its regent masters who were to oversee lighting and sanitation and, if necessary, to assist in the keeping of the peace. Though not mentioned in the code the two university coroners were already in existence.[2]

Small in numbers though the university was, and though much of the life of the community was of course the responsibility not of the university but of the colleges, the business of central administration was in the hands of relatively few officers. First of these was the vice-chancellor, who as substitute for the chancellor assumed in his absence all his authority, though the chancellor was to be consulted on all 'business of weight and moment' were he present or absent. Second were those formidable 'maids of all work' the proctors, whose history stretched far into the past and who still, despite a considerable decline in their authority, exercised great power in the university's assemblies, where their presence was essential and where they carried out all scrutinies and exercised on occasion a joint veto. It was the proctors who were responsible for the administration of examinations and the conferring of degrees; and, subject to the vice-chancellor's general control, the maintenance of discipline both among members of the university and in the city. They employed a night-watch known as their *famuli*. Though not mentioned in the statutes the official known as the bedel or 'marshall of the beggars', who was to become the university marshal, was already in existence.

This small band of officers obtained support from the ranks of the *ministri*, though some of the latter occupied very humble positions.[3] The most important of them was the registrar, who might well have been included among the officers. He was required to be either an MA or BCL

[1] The keeper was intended to produce the material for the defence of the university's privileges, and his salary was raised by a levy 'for the defence of privileges'. This office was also in the first instance used as a reward for the services of the antiquary Brian Twyne for the work he had done in preparing the Laudian code. Brian Twyne (*c* 1579-1644), m. CCC 1594, was the first keeper of the archives (1634-44). See R. L. Poole, *A Lecture on the History of the University Archives* (Oxford 1912).

[2] *Reg. Univ.* ii pt 1, p. 262.

[3] For example the clerk and the *tintinabularius* (bellman).

and a notary public, and his duties included the affixing of the university seal, the compilation and preservation of the records of the main university bodies, the keeping of the major university accounts and the receipt of the university revenues. This was clearly a position in which an active man was bound to make his weight felt. It is not surprising that the *Oxford Almanack* of 1703, listing six university officers, gave them as the public orator, the librarian, the register [*sic*], the archivist, the assessor of the vice-chancellor's court, and the register of the vice-chancellor's court.[1]

The only other *ministri* of importance were the bailiff, the second new officer to be created by the code, who was responsible for collecting local rents and supervising university property in the city and acted as a kind of clerk of the works, and six functionaries whose office was as ancient as that of the proctors, the bedels (or beadles as they were still called).[2] There were three superior or esquire bedels, those of divinity, of law and of medicine and arts combined, and their subordinates the three inferior or yeoman bedels in the same faculties. The emissaries of the vice-chancellor in any business for which he called on them, essential in the performance of all ceremonies, on which they became the acknowledged experts, the organizers of the practical aspects of examinations and the conferring of degrees and the custodians of the matriculation registers, they were essential cogs in the administrative machine.[3] Almost all the officers and *ministri* obtained the greater part of their remuneration from fees,[4] and most of them, other than the vice-chancellor and proctors, held their offices for life. It should be noted that though no financial officer appears in the code, provision was made, following an earlier tradition, for the auditing of accounts. This was the responsibility of a standing delegacy of convocation whose members were appointed for life, the only standing delegacy of this kind recognized by the code.[5]

All these officials continued in existence throughout the eighteenth century, and some of them, in name at least, have survived until the

---

[1] Bodl. Gough Oxf. 31.

[2] On the antiquity of the offices of proctor and bedel see M. B. Hackett, 'The university as a corporate body' in J. I. Catto (ed), *The Early Oxford Schools* (*The History of the University of Oxford* i Oxford 1984), 82–7.

[3] This can be seen from the books of the yeoman bedels of divinity and law presented to the Bodleian Library by the two last holders of these positions in 1878 and 1879: Bodl. MS Add. B.63. The matriculation registers, until passed on to the keeper of the archives, were in the charge of the esquire bedel of divinity.

[4] Exceptions were the keeper of the archives (see p. 208 n. 1 above) and the assessor of the vice-chancellor's court, who drew a salary of £40 a year and took no fee. The yeomen bedels in particular frequently supplemented their earnings by engaging in outside activities.

[5] There was provision in the code for only two other standing delegacies, those for appeals to convocation and to congregation respectively, but their members held office for one year only. All other delegacies were supposed to be *ad hoc*.

present day. Given the incapacities due to old age among men appointed for life and the natural negligence of officials under little if any central control, it was hardly to be expected that they would in general bring much sense of urgency to their work, but in one way at least the university gained from the methods of administration it inherited: since its officials obtained so much of their remuneration in the form of fees exacted when their duties were performed, they had strong inducements to carry them out. The sinecure might be a major abuse among university lecturers and professors. The administrative officers might be inactive, but their positions were seldom complete sinecures.[1]

Thus, though the university might, well before the beginning of the century, have abdicated almost all its teaching responsibilities to the colleges and have become little but an examining body, and though its examinations might have become mere shadows of themselves,[2] the bedels maintained every detail of an elaborate examination system. They and the registrar preserved accurate records of all members of the university, which were of practical importance to themselves and are of great value to the historian. In the same way, though the control of the proctors over non-academics, over senior members and over what went on within the walls of colleges gradually disappeared, and a number of the regulations which the code expected them to enforce had fallen into complete desuetude, and though the standard of discipline they enforced varied greatly from year to year, both proctors and pro-proctors 'walked' assiduously at night, visited coffee-houses and alehouses and dealt with minor disorders.[3] Major disturbances such as those of a political nature in the

---

[1] An exception to this was the librarianship of the Radcliffe Library, the duties of which were in any case ill-defined until the last years of the century. Occasionally the work of officers was carried out by a deputy, for example the clerk of the market for some years before 1769, when the new delegates of privileges put an end to the arrangement: OUA/WP α/17/8/a, minutes of the delegates of privileges 1769-1819, 15 Feb. 1769. In the later years of the century it became increasingly common for one man to hold several offices. This was particularly so in the case of the registrar.

[2] See L S Sutherland. 'The curriculum', p. 470 f. below.

[3] For the proctors' powers over non-academics see p. 220 below. Their control over senior members was unsuccessfully challenged in 1683 when a pro-proctor, Arthur Charlett, won a case in the vice-chancellor's court against Matthew Morgan (1652-1703, m. St John's 1667; himself a former pro-proctor) who refused to pay his fine when taken up for being present in an alehouse after 9 p.m.: Wood, *Life and Times* iii. 40-3. There is an anonymous account of this case in *Oxford Magazine*, 15 June 1892, pp. 444-5; it was evidently already thought an excessive claim by the proctors. In 1762-3 when Richard Scrope (1729-87, m. Oriel 1747; demy Magd. 1748-57, fellow 1757-67) was junior proctor he pursued some malefactors into All Souls and was treated with insolence by William Craven (1738-91, from 1769 6th Bn Craven; m. Balliol 1756; fellow All Souls 1762) in whose rooms they took refuge. The proctors argued that it was customary for college officers to welcome and assist the proctors in removing riotous outsiders. Craven, later supported by All Souls, denied their right to exercise authority within the college. The case went to the vice-chancellor's court, and the advice of the chancellor and the deputy steward was asked. The court found that the proctors of the university were at all times 'sufficiently authorized by the statutes of the university to pursue any delinquent townsman into any college'. Craven appealed against this decree, and the appeal went, on a legal technicality, to chancery, where the case against him was confirmed: *A Letter to [Charles*

early years of the century, or the corn-riots at its end, might be beyond their powers. In addition the marshal and proctors' men kept the streets reasonably clear of prostitutes by high-handed methods which had not yet been challenged.

Finally, the keeping and auditing of the university accounts illustrate the strengths and weaknesses of this routine administration. The university was neither a big nor a rich organization, and its income from fees fell sharply with the decline in its numbers during the first half of the century, though this was offset by receipts from benefactions, increasing rents and other sources. Nor did its accounts cover the whole of its income or expenditure. The main account was divided, by an accident of history, into the general and the schools accounts;[1] there were also certain special accounts, of which those of the proctors, the Press, the Bodleian Library, and the Sheldonian Theatre were the most important. All of these, except the Bodleian account, were subject to the audit of the delegates of accounts, and all were kept in the traditional charge and discharge method inherited from the middle ages. Since the major purpose of this was to prevent the university from suffering loss due to the errors or dishonesty of accounting officials, they are not very informative, and were made the less so by a very clumsy method of dealing with balances. They were at their worst in commercial contexts, and for much of the period the University Press accounts were in a state of confusion.[2] But the delegates were honest and conscientious in the performance of their duties, and the only vice-chancellor who misappropriated the funds in his charge, William Delaune, vice-chancellor 1702-6, was forced to refund his defalcations.[3] The delegates were almost all heads of houses and inspired even powerful vice-chancellors with respect. For example in 1709 William Lancaster had £500 ready to purchase the great seventeenth-century collection of pamphlets later known as the Thomason tracts, but decided to hold back since he did not 'know but the Delegates of Accounts may expect that their consent should be had in laying out so great a Sum'.[4]

Penruddocke] Esq. Occasioned by a Late Misrepresentation of the circumstances of a Prosecution commenced A.D.1763 (Salisbury 1773). Nevertheless the claim does not seem to have been raised again. The university's critics sometimes claimed that the proctors' disciplinary duties were completely neglected at this time. The proctors' accounts 1564-1787 and 1788-1868 (OUA/WP β/23/2 and 3) as well as the diaries of individual pro-proctors show, however, that though there were inevitably variations in standards, much energy went into attempts to check brawls between undergraduates and citizens and in enforcing regulations. In making use of the proctors' accounts allowance must be made for the fact that at certain periods the normal penalty for minor undergraduate offences was an imposition rather than a fine.

[1] See I. G. Philip, 'Early accounts of the University of Oxford', The Accountant cxxix (1953).
[2] Carter, History of the Press i. 152 ff, 388 ff.
[3] See p. 215 below.
[4] Lancaster-Clarke, 17 Dec. 1709, MS Ballard 21, fo 91.

These routine activities provide, however, only the background to the political organization of the small and curious society which comprised the university, and in which a mixture of democracy and oligarchy, of inertia and restless activity, was a perennial feature. Clashes of persons, of colleges, of interests, were continuous, and all this against a setting provided by the conflicts of national party politics in which the university was deeply engaged.

This organization can best be illustrated by a brief examination of the constituent parts of university government and their relationships. The spectacular figure who stood at its head, with all the pomp of rank, ceremony and prerogative was the chancellor. His installation was something like a minor coronation, and a rumour of his death or mortal illness threw the whole society into turmoil; the one contested election in the century was a desperate political struggle. Yet before the century began his authority was already much in decline and was soon to fall even more sharply. It depended almost wholly on the influence he could exert at court or in the ministry and his own concern in exerting it on behalf of the university. Within the university itself he exercised little patronage. He held the nomination of the vice-chancellor, but this as will be seen gave him scant leverage. He also nominated to the headships of all but one of the declining number of university halls (which were of little financial value, though they carried with them membership of the hebdomadal board) and of a few minor offices, the most interesting and least known of which was that of his own academic secretary.[1] Such influence as he might hope to exert could arise in three ways: by bringing pressure to bear on elections to prominent positions in the university and colleges (though seventeenth-century experience had warned even crowned heads against this);[2] by seeking to influence the university's parliamentary elections (though this when attempted was apt to be counter-productive);[3] and by the use of the 'chancellor's letters' which under the provisions of the code empowered him to recommend to the hebdomadal board and through them to convocation the award of discretionary dispensations from the academic requirements for all types of degree.

These dispensations served two purposes, the relief of graduands from

[1] The first man known to have held this position was Dr William King, principal of St Mary Hall and academic secretary to Lord Arran. It finally fell a victim to nineteenth-century reform, to the annoyance of Lord Salisbury, then chancellor: OUA/WP γ/3/9.
[2] In the early years of the eighteenth century chancellors were known to have been more successful in influencing elections in certain colleges.
[3] 'I well remember that when the Duke of *Ormond* in the Height of his Glory recommended a Gentleman to be one of our Burgesses, the *Vice-Chancellor* and *Heads of Houses* refused so much as to open his *Letter*, the Purport of it being beforehand known [and later protested against it as an infringement of their privileges which] would in time destroy that Freedom and Liberty which he was principally obliged to maintain': [S. Harrison,] *An Account of the Late Election for the University of Oxford, by a Master of Arts* (London 1722).

some of the numerous obligations involved in the process of graduation,[1] in which the chancellor's part was purely that of an intermediary, and the award of degrees 'by creation'. Some of these, like the modern honorary degree, were purely honorific, others, particularly in divinity and medicine, were of value to candidates in their careers, and all chancellors found themselves pressed by influential friends to obtain degrees of both of these types for their protégés. The university viewed such attempts with deep suspicion, and the strength of a chancellor could be gauged by his success in handling such business. Clarendon, far and away the best chancellor the university was to have for many years, assured the vice-chancellor on 30 April 1662 that 'the University need have no Apprehension of any unreasonable Condescension in that kind from Me', but he admitted exceptions in the face of 'Importunity of very great Persons'.[2] The first duke of Ormonde was warned by the vice-chancellor in 1687 that inexplicit letters from his secretary 'gave occasion for dissent among those that had a mind to quarrel'.[3] The second duke of Ormonde, though his frequent absence on service overseas reduced his authority, was still, by comparison with his successors, a strong and certainly a popular chancellor. But it was his precipitate flight in 1715 attainted of high treason and the succession of mediocre and politically ineffective tory peers who followed him in the office which radically altered the nature of the chancellorship. Ormonde's successors were in no position to give political help to the university, but neither were they able to bring pressure to bear on it. By 1772 when Oxford made its peace with the government and elected Lord North, first lord of the treasury, as their chancellor, they stood to gain from his friendship, yet need not fear serious interference from him in their internal affairs. The eighteenth-century Oxford tradition of intransigent 'Independency' owed much to the history of its chancellorship.

As the chancellor's power declined, that of his deputy the vice-chancellor inevitably grew. He was nominated annually by the Chancellor in a letter the terms of which have survived into modern times. Clarendon took great pains to choose men whom he considered would make good vice-chancellors, but did not feel able to insist on the statutory obligation on the head of any college to accept the chancellor's nomination.[4] The elder Ormonde consulted Bishop Fell on the subject,[5] but there is no sign that later chancellors troubled themselves overmuch in the matter. In 1768 the earl of Lichfield, when reminded by the vice-chancellor of the need to nominate a successor, declined to mention

---

[1] See p. 219 below.
[2] Bodl. MS Tanner 338, fo 129.
[3] HMC *Ormonde MSS* vi. 494.
[4] Clarendon-R. Baylie, 19 July 1662, Bodl. MS Tanner 338, fo 144.
[5] HMC *Ormonde MSS* vi. 25 ff.

anyone. At no time in the eighteenth century did a convention about the succession such as later grew up come into existence. In 1796 the vice-chancellor told the duke of Portland that the office was usually accepted by one of the four pro-vice-chancellors who had been chosen by the existing vice-chancellor and who had not already served.[1] To arrangements of this kind was due, no doubt, the fact that between the beginning of the century and 1792 there had been no vice-chancellor who had been head of a traditionally whig college. As in the past, vice-chancellors were usually renominated, for two, three or four years and even on occasion five and once for six, but there were apt to be 'murmurings' if their term of office was unduly prolonged.

Though the office was one of prestige, it was not widely sought after, and a candidate was sometimes difficult to find, for it carried a heavy load of work and responsibility and was badly paid. The vice-chancellor's statutory income was ten pounds a year, and though he enjoyed some supplementary profits his colleagues in 1741 calculated that they rarely exceeded £70, which was far below the expenses of the office.[2] In that year Convocation added £100 a year to his stipend. When relations between the university and the government were good he might gain in another way. A successful term of office might help him towards ecclesiastical preferment, though seldom to the highest honours in the church. In the years when the university and the government were at loggerheads there was no hope of such a reward.[3]

On the whole those who agreed to act as vice-chancellor did so for reasons of personal obligation or of prestige or out of a desire for office (in most cases they had long sat on the hebdomadal board) and for the chance of some minor benefits to their college while they were in power. The vice-chancellor, supported traditionally by the proctors, presided over all university bodies and represented the university to the outer world. He also transacted in his own hand a surprising amount of written business and had to be as ready to draft a loyal address as to deal with trustees dilatory in handing over endowments to the university. The only personal power conferred on him by statute was that of exercising a veto

---

[1] Balliol College Library, Jenkyns papers, VI. A (2), letterbook of John Wills.

[2] OUA Register of Convocation 1730-41, fo 156ʳ (26 June 1741). The Royal Commission of 1850-2, which had no direct evidence, believed that the remuneration of the vice-chancellor came largely from the investment of university funds during his years of office: *Report of Her Majesty's Commissioners appointed to inquire into the State, Discipline, Studies, and Revenues of the University and Colleges of Oxford* (1852), 10. There is no evidence to support such a suggestion in the eighteenth century, and some evidence to the contrary. For example on 10 May 1707 Lancaster, as vice-chancellor, wrote to Charlett about claims for payment by men at work on the Bodleian building: 'I am sorry Dr Hudsons workmen should want money, but you know I have never received any but what the Bedles bring in at the end of Terms, which is most of it appropriated, tho if I were in Oxford I would find a little for that use.' MS Ballard 21, fo 70. John Hudson (1663-1719), m. Queen's 1677; fellow Univ. 1686-1711; Bodley's librarian 1701; principal St Mary Hall 1712-19.

[3] Of the thirty-five eighteenth-century vice-chancellors one only became a bishop after his term of office; a few became prebendaries or deans.

on the business of convocation and congregation if he so wished, but the vice-chancellor's veto, unlike that of the proctors, early disappeared as a political weapon.[1]

In the main those who undertook the task came through it reasonably well. In 1697, it is true, John Meare, principal of Brasenose, held office for one year only and left without the usual complimentary letter after a flaming quarrel in convocation about the dismissal of Roger Altham from the office of White's lecturer in moral philosophy.[2] The amiable reprobate William Delaune was the only vice-chancellor of the century whose living had to be sequestrated to refund the university money he had misappropriated. John Purnell, cited to appear before the king's courts in 1748 for disaffection in the wake of the student riots of the previous year, was a victim rather than an offender, and the government on legal advice dropped all charges against him.[3]

Judged by surviving evidence it would seem probable that the two ablest vice-chancellors of the period were William Lancaster (Thomas Hearne's *bête noire*) and Nathan Wetherell, the one before and the other after the university's years of eclipse, but as Langford has shown, even in the dark years vice-chancellors are found handling very difficult political situations with considerable adroitness,[4] and Stephen Niblett (considered in his college rather a nonentity when he was elected) was particularly successful in this area. At all periods the success of a vice-chancellor depended on his personality, the support he received from his college and his skill in handling the various bodies over which he presided.

The body on which he most closely depended was the hebdomadal board, Laud's oligarchic addition to the constitution, consisting of the heads of colleges and halls and the two proctors. According to statute they were required to meet at least every Monday in full term in the 'apodyterium'. In practice, though the meetings were numerous they were not as regular as the statute demanded, nor were they always held on Monday; and when the Clarendon building was built they met in the delegates' room instead of the gloomy apodyterium. At one time it was

---

[1] In 1756 during the struggle over reform of the Press George Huddesford vetoed a nomination made by the proctors to the delegacy, but the Press statute of the following year, a constitutional compromise, left no place in the arrangements for a veto. Later, if used at all, it was merely as a procedural convenience. In congregation in 1720, a pro-vice-chancellor tried to use his veto on the refusal of a degree, but it was parried by a subterfuge and it was not tried again: OUA Register of Congregation 1703-23, fo 127ᵛ (Mich. Term 1720).

[2] OUA Register of Convocation 1693-1703, fo 190 (1 Oct. 1698). There is a full account of the incident in Bodl. MS Rawl. D.912, fos 161ff. Roger Altham (1658-1730), m. Ch. Ch. 1677; White's lecturer in moral philosophy 1693.

[3] He was given no opportunity to clear himself and, as Blackstone pointed out, he was put to great expense, which however, the university met; the total paid out by the university seems to have been £298. W. Blackstone, *Reports of Cases determined in the Several Courts of Westminster Hall from 1746 to 1779* (2 vols London 1781) i. 45-6; OUA vice-chancellor's accounts 1735-69, WPß/22/1.

[4] See P. Langford, 'Tories and Jacobites 1714-51', pp. 99-127 above.

even suspected that much of their business was done in a rotating dining club known as the 'Ordinance' which met in the convenient absence of the proctors.[1]

The board was the centre of university administration. Through it business was passed on to the university's popular assemblies, and formal instructions from the chancellor to the vice-chancellor as his deputy always adjured him to consult his brethren on the board. Though these latter shared in the political and college controversies of the time, sometimes exacerbated by personal enmities, the board was on the whole a closely knit social unit whose individual members, being habitually cut off from the life of the fellows in their own colleges, often shared a sympathy which overrode college boundaries. Since their position was crucial in university politics it is the more unfortunate that the records of the hebdomadal board are very imperfect. Some early minutes were entered in the minute book of the University Press.[2] Then in 1738 Henry Fisher, when registrar, purchased a special book for their minutes and kept them, after a fashion, for almost a year, after which no further entry was made until 1759.[3] After that there is a gap until 1788 when brief records were entered in another book, until in 1803 John Gutch opened a full-sized folio register which was systematically maintained from then on.[4] Much of its routine business was never entered in any of these records, for the 'chancellor's letters' passing through it were entered in the register of convocation (if they were passed), and copies of the *programmae* or notices intended for circulation to the colleges and individual members of the university were printed and evidently kept separately, as was any statute that was passed. That some form of notes of proceedings was kept is clear from indirect evidence,[5] but the absence of an official record of transactions militated against the development of orderly administrative precedents.

In 1713-14 a savage campaign, creditable to neither side, was fought by Francis Atterbury, with the aid of Lord Chancellor Harcourt, against the leaders of the board; and in 1760 eight dissenting heads registered their protest before a notary public against the statute in which the

[1] For this body, at whose meetings outsiders were often present, see for example letters of G. Clarke-Charlett, MS Ballard 20, fos 74 ff.

[2] *The First Minute Book of the Delegates of the Oxford University Press, 1668-1756*, ed. S. Gibson and J. Johnson (Oxford Bibliog. Soc. extra publ. 1943).

[3] OUA registrar's accounts, WPα/56/4, p. 10 (back reversed): 'June [1738] Book for the Hebdomadal meeting 2/-.' OUA minutes of the Hebdomadal board 1738, 1759, WPγ/24/1. Henry Fisher (1691-1761), m. Jesus 1709; registrar 1737-61.

[4] OUA minutes of the hebdomadal board 1788-1803, 1803-23, WPγ/24/2, 3. A note in Bliss's hand inserted in the first of these books reads: 'This is the first Record of the acts of the Hebdomadal Board 1788.' John Gutch (1746-1831), m. All Souls 1765; registrar 1797-1824.

[5] For example BNCA B53/1-9, Principal Cawley's notebooks.

university asserted its independence of the Laudian code.[1] But on the political matters which most concerned the university the board usually presented a reasonably solid front of cautious moderation.

When we turn to the two popular assemblies on which the democratic traditions of the university rested we are faced with one of the anomalies of Oxford constitutional history which persisted for several centuries, namely the existence of two overlapping assemblies, one of which always waned in power as the other waxed. The Laudian settlement had ensured that convocation, or to give it its full name the great congregation of doctors and masters regent and non-regent, should wax and the congregation of regent masters should wane, just as the nineteenth-century reforms were to reverse the process. Congregation was the more restricted in its membership though the restriction was not quite as narrow as its title suggested. It consisted of all MAs who were necessary regents, that is in their first year after incepting,[2] who were theoretically obliged to attend, and certain *magistri ad placitum* who could attend if they so wished together with all professors, lecturers, resident doctors and the heads, deans and bursars of colleges who had gone through their regency. It was also more restricted than convocation in its activities, which were in the main confined to matters concerning the curriculum and the conferment of ordinary degrees. On these matters the statutes were so drawn as to leave it little discretion, and it was not surprising that the institution led a shadowy existence, impinging on the notice of the university only when it was necessary to find the nine persons necessary to 'make a house' to pass graces or confer degrees. The royal commission of 1852 found it completely dead.[3]

It is true that congregation did not accept its eclipse without a struggle. The one discretionary power of any importance left to it was that of granting or refusing graces to supplicate for degrees. Here its decision was final, and a complex procedure ensured that every individual member had the opportunity to express his views.[4] In the early years of the century this power was used not infrequently and aroused a great deal of interest. Graces were challenged on grounds of immorality, breach of statutory qualifications and, the issues which

[1] See L. S. Sutherland, 'The foundation of Worcester College, Oxford', *Oxoniensia* xliv (1979); Sutherland, 'Laudian statutes'.

[2] Theoretically regency lasted two years, but even at the time the code was drawn up a blanket dispensation for the second year was accepted.

[3] *Report*, 10.

[4] L. H. D. Buxton and S. Gibson, *Oxford University Ceremonies* (Oxford 1935), 67, do not give a full account of the procedure. If a grace was challenged, and the challenge renewed in two further congregations, the objector had to put his objection before the vice-chancellor who reported it to the house which then voted on it. There is evidence that it was customary for the vice-chancellor to seek legal advice on such occasions: see for example 'Opinion of Dr Bouchier Regius Professor of Civil Law', MS Ballard 22, fo 82.

raised the greatest interest, heresy and disaffection to church and state. But these activities died down with the fading of religious controversy and only in one short period thereafter did congregation seek to assert itself in university politics. When Blackstone and his friends successfully challenged the vice-chancellor and hebdomadal board over the administration of the University Press, the outcome was the promulgation of a statute. So rare was such an event that there was uncertainty about the interpretation of the Laudian procedure.[1] In the excitement of the moment the vice-chancellor permitted congregation both to debate the issue and to vote on it.[2] An attempt by some of its members to repeat this incursion into the preserves of convocation next year during a heated contest about the statute setting up the Vinerian professorship was firmly put down, and their brief outburst of activity in university politics came to an abrupt end.

Very different was the history of convocation, the general assembly of doctors and masters, regent and non-regent. Though the powers of the hebdomadal board left it little room to initiate measures, it had ample scope for important decisions. The affixing of the university seal, the election of a number of officers including the chancellor and the two university members of parliament, the passing of any statute and the granting of discretionary dispensations on the receipt of 'chancellor's letters', all rested with it. In consequence the university's active concerns in political issues found a focus there, particularly among what were generally called the 'young masters' whose political views were always more extreme than those of the cautious heads of houses. It was in convocation that the toryism which sometimes was justly described as Jacobitism found supporters in the years following the Hanoverian succession; and even in 1769 when anti-government feeling seemed almost extinct convocation passed an address to the crown against John Wilkes by no more than a few votes.[3] The characteristic feature of convocation, at its height in the first half of the century but still in existence later in a milder form, was its almost fanatical pride in its political independency which neither fear nor favour could demolish.

For this reason a constitutional weakness in its position was peculiarly worrying to it. The failure of the Laudian code to lay down any residence-qualification for its voters subjected it to the danger of pressure-groups from without. To a considerable extent, unlike its counterpart at Cambridge, it protected itself against the worst form of political infiltration by the convention that no graduate by creation should be a member, but it is significant that the first statute to be

---

[1] See Sutherland, 'Laudian statutes', pp. 198-9.
[2] Several flysheets on this matter are preserved in Bodl. Gough Oxf. 96, fos 51-8, 65.
[3] See L. S Sutherland, 'Political respectability 1751-1771', pp. 160-1 above.

passed in defiance of the limitations of the code was one which reduced (though it did not destroy) the danger of its measures being determined by what it called *extranei*.

Another danger to its effectiveness as a representative body might have seemed to be the strength of college feeling[1] and the possible predominance of one or two big colleges over the rest. But this danger can be overestimated: there were divisions within as well as between colleges, and the biggest of them, Christ Church, which in 1785 had 128 members of convocation,[2] always tended, for a variety of reasons, to be somewhat isolated in university politics.

Convocations were held frequently, if only to pass the 'chancellor's letters' necessary for the routine conferment of degrees. Many were no doubt purely formal, but excitement could quickly flare up and any controversial issue brought together a good house and quite a sizeable vote. The fact that the proceedings were in Latin, however, inhibited lively debate, though a good Latin speech was always appreciated, and most of the controversy took the form of flysheets or pamphlets circulated round the common rooms.

In the years when the university was at odds with the government, when a contested parliamentary election took place or a loyal address had to be sent in to the crown, and even when a proposed degree by creation had political overtones, a good deal of anxiety was expressed lest convocation should be captured by its extremist elements. But in fact the only Jacobite who ever stood for parliament was heavily defeated by a more moderate tory.[3] No proposed loyal address was ever rejected, though a few bold spirits voted against several; and though from time to time candidates for honorary degrees were turned down on political grounds against the advice of the vice-chancellor and the hebdomadal board, no major crisis arose out of this action. Convocation was much less irresponsible than its critics supposed, and fellows of colleges were at bottom no more anxious for a head-on collision with a hostile government than were the heads.

In the 1760s there began an unmistakable though unspectacular trend towards internal reform in the university. It was not a movement of convocation against the hebdomadal board, as Blackstone's short burst of reform had been in the 1750s. On the contrary, reforms were pushed by members both of the hebdomadal board and of convocation, and between 1768 and 1772 the lead was taken by a remarkably vigorous and

[1] This was shown in parliamentary elections, but even more so in elections to university offices: see G. V. Bennett, 'The era of party zeal 1702–1714', p. 91 above.
[2] Worc. College Archives, 'Members of Convocation 1760–87'. At this date Magdalen had 84 members, Queen's 74 and only two other colleges, St John's and Brasenose, more than 50.
[3] For William King's candidacy in 1722 see Langford, 'Tories and Jacobites', 112–4.

far-seeing vice-chancellor, Nathan Wetherell. The achievements of
Oxford reform in the later eighteenth century have been obscured by the
university's steadily increasing loyalty to the government in national
politics, and by its opposition to religious change in issues which took on
a new form and strength in the 1770s and after. Nevertheless they were
real enough, and the university used the new powers of legislation it
claimed for the purpose of removing existing abuses. In 1769 there was
the first reform of the Bodleian statutes (though major reform here did
not come until 1780), and in the previous year two standing delegacies of
convocation had been set up, both with provisions intended to prevent
their becoming oligarchic preserves: the delegacy of privileges and that
for the letting of university land. In 1770 university dress was reformed
(though this was unexpectedly forced on the authorities by a revolt of
the servitors of Christ Church[1]) and in the same year a group of
members of convocation began systematically to oppose all 'chancellor's
letters' which proposed reducing the residence required for a BA degree
below the three years to which it had been reduced in earlier years. In
the same year events took place which marked the beginning of the two
most sweeping reforms which were the main achievement of the period:
that in the internal academic organization of the university, which led to
radical changes in the curriculum and the examination system, and that
in the relations of the university and the city, a movement which affected
also the topography of the latter so that, as Salter put it, 'as regards the
geography of Oxford the year 1771 is the end of the Middle Ages'.[2]

The first reform is of such importance to the history of the university
that a separate chapter in this volume is devoted to it.[3] The latter, which
affected the city as much as the university, was in its way no less
important.

It was made possible only because during the century relations
between the city and the university had been markedly changing. The
century opened inauspiciously for university–city relations. In 1689 the
university had injudiciously tried to get through parliament a petition for
the confirmation of its last and most sweeping charter, that of 1636;[4] and
they had lost a case before the king's court in which they claimed a
citizen as a privileged person.[5] In 1702–3 the two institutions were locked
in violent conflict over the disorderly behaviour of citizens on the occasion of the visit of Queen Anne and the city's attempt to claim

[1] See L. S. Sutherland, 'The last of the servitors', *Christ Church Annual Report*, 1975.
[2] Salter, *Surveys and Tokens*, 6.
[3] Sutherland, 'Curriculum'.
[4] The city strongly opposed this but before the arguments were fully marshalled parliament was
dissolved, and the petition was never raised again.
[5] James Harrington gave an account of the hearing, adding that Ormonde, Clarendon,
Weymouth, the bishop of Winchester and Sir Thomas Clarges were at the trial and suggesting that
'Their appearance probably hindered the Bench from making reflexions as formerly on the
University Privileges': Harrington–Charlett, 30 Jan. 1690, MS Ballard 22, fo 1.

precedence over the university.[1] Isolated clashes occurred throughout the century and beyond.

Nevertheless relations between the two bodies were basically improving. Both university and city now held roughly the same views on national politics, and the university was never tempted into playing the active part in city which it did in county parliamentary elections.[2] The number of non-academics who thought it worthwhile to obtain privileged status was declining as the status became less valuable and the university grew increasingly slack in protecting its privileges. Of importance here was the effect of the systematic hostility evinced by the judges to the university's jurisdiction. In civil cases the vice-chancellor's court had to some extent held its own. An attempt in 1714 by Lord Chancellor Harcourt to deny its jurisdiction as between members of the university (on an issue full of political overtones) was a complete failure,[3] but in 1708-9 the university's authority to judge causes between members of the university and those outside its area of jurisdiction had been gravely questioned. Neither judgement, however, affected the city. This was more likely to be influenced by claims to criminal jurisdiction, and here the university was much less successful. At the end of the century it was left with some very uncertain precedents, several hostile *obiter dicta* by judges and a tendency to avoid the issue.[4] It is noteworthy that Blackstone, himself an assessor in the vice-chancellor's court and responsible for a reform in its civil procedure, was much less incisive in his *Commentaries on the Laws of England* on the university's criminal than on its civil jurisdiction.

If the relations of the university and the city were on the whole less hostile than before, the results of their joint efforts at civic administration made little if any progress. Lighting, scavenging and the upkeep of the roads were admitted to be deplorable, the university's masters of the streets were notoriously ineffective,[5] and the responsibility for the

[1] The minutes of a large delegacy set up by convocation to deal with the city's obduracy are included at length in the Register of Convocation 1693-1703 (minutes at the back of the book). For views within the university see W. Smith-Charlett, 20 [month obscured] 1702; same-same, 27 Sept. 1703, MS Ballard 16, fos 46, 50.

[2] There are occasional signs of activity by academics in support of county magnates concerned in elections to civic offices, but they were of negligible importance.

[3] OUA SP/A/13/6, Stratford *vs* Aldrich (1714); see also HMC *Portland MSS* vii and Sutherland, 'Foundation of Worcester College'. OUA WPα/34/3, 'Ch.Ch. Dr Woodroffe's Canonry 1709'.

[4] In the case of P. Welles *vs* E. Traherne, Willes CJ was reported by the university counsel (29 Nov. 1740) as saying 'he would always Support the Law of the land and tryalls by Jurys (on which all our libertys Depended) so farr as by Law he Could, against any particular Jurisdiction whatsoever': J. Wilmot-vice-chancellor, 29 Nov. 1740, OUA NW4/5.

[5] The author of a pamphlet published in Oxford in 1774 entitled *An Attempt to State the Accounts of Receipts and Expenses relative to the Oxford Paving Act, with Remarks* (copy in Bodl. Gough Oxf. m 138, fos 30 ff) pays tribute to the conception of such an office, adding however: 'But the office hath in a great Measure lost its efficacy by the Appointment of Masters inexperienced and often non-Resident.'

upkeep of the bridges and street-paving remained an obscure area. Though divided responsibilities between university and city no doubt added to the unsatisfactory situation, it was little better in most eighteenth-century towns or in local administration generally through-out the country. New methods of dealing with these problems under parliamentary sanction had, however, been developing: first there came the turnpike trusts undertaking the care of roads (largely a rural problem) and then a more complex equivalent for dealing with the manifold problems of urban improvement, the so-called improvement commissions.[1] Both of these techniques involved the setting up by act of parliament of *ad hoc* bodies with special powers; the numbers of such authorities had been growing, though improvement commissions did not become common until after about 1780. What was remarkable in Oxford was that the university on its own initiative planned and put through with the co-operation of the city a combined turnpike, toll-bridge and city improvement act of quite unusual complexity at the com-paratively early date of 1771.

It was once again the enterprising Blackstone who showed the way, though it was not he but Wetherell who could claim the credit for the measure which was passed. Blackstone, since 1762 no longer a fellow of All Souls and living at Wallingford, had become much engaged in local turnpike and bridge trusts. On the death of the third earl of Abingdon he found himself administering his seriously encumbered estates and in close touch with the town clerk of Oxford, Thomas Walker, who had acted as Abingdon's man of business and who was the brother of John Walker, partner with James Morrell in the leading firm of Oxford solicitors. Blackstone conceived the idea of improving the finances of the estate by turning the ferry over the Thames at Swinford near Eynsham into a toll-bridge and, supported by city and university friends, by repairing the derelict Botley causeway, Oxford's one direct link with the west, to take advantage of it.[2] A subscription opened among county magnates and members of the university and city having raised insufficient funds, he drafted and saw through parliament in February 1767 a turnpike act to provide tolls for this purpose, as well as the bridge act which set up a toll-bridge at Swinford.[3] The act proving to need

[1] F. H. Spencer, *Municipal Origins: An Account of English Private Bill Legislation relating to local Government, 1740-1785* (London 1911).

[2] There is an excellent account of this venture in E. de Villiers, *Swinford Bridge 1769-1969* (Eynsham History Group 1969), 9 ff. It is based largely on the Bertie Manuscripts in the Bodleian Library and the account-books of the Botley turnpike in the account-books of Morrell, Peel and Gamlen, Oxford, part of which are now in the Oxfordshire County Record Office.

[3] The subscriptions and the names of subscribers were printed in *Jackson's Oxford Journal*, Nov. and Dec. 1766. Those who lent money under the acts are listed in the accounts referred to in the preceding note. The largest lenders were Blackstone's All Souls friends, in particular Benjamin Buckler and John Tracy. The latter audited the accounts for many years.

amendment, he brought a further act before parliament in December of the same year, and thanks very largely to his personal efforts both bridge and causeway were opened on 4 August 1769.[1]

Though members of the university were active in the venture and the vice-chancellor gave it his support, it was not an official university venture. It might well have been so, for when Blackstone's amended bill was under consideration it was proposed that the opening of a toll-bridge at Magdalen should be added to it.[2]

Wetherell, even before he became vice-chancellor, had been concerned with the problems of the approaches to the city and the inadequacies of Magdalen bridge.[3] But he was also much exercised about the more complex questions within the city itself—with the un-satisfactory state of its cleansing and lighting, of its roads and paving—as well as with the need to provide a market-place instead of the stalls which encumbered the main streets. These aims could only be achieved by petitioning parliament for one of the new improvement acts and by combining it with some of the elements of a turnpike act. Such an act would not only make possible drastic remodelling of the streets and buildings of the city but would set up a completely new authority to administer the improvements.

Much careful preparation was put into the plan. On 6 February 1770 a document was submitted to convocation by the hebdomadal board, drawing attention to the inadequacies of the masters of the streets and asking for a delegacy to consider city administration.[4] A year earlier the new standing delegacy of privileges had already been anxious to hold discussions with the city on the question; and when convocation set up its delegacy the mayor appointed citizens to confer with it on 'removing nuisances and obstructions within the City and report'.[5] By 14 November 1770 the *Heads of a Bill*[6] were printed and disseminated throughout the university and city to form the basis of the petition the university was to put before parliament on behalf of both university and city.

In January 1771 the petition was submitted. The university and colleges anxiously canvassed their friends in both houses, the university burgesses adroitly steered the bill through its various stages, and James Morrell for the university and Thomas Walker for the city plied between

[1] *Jackson's Oxford Journal*, 5 Aug. 1769.

[2] According to *Jackson's Oxford Journal*, 27 Nov. 1767, and the correspondence between Wetherell and Newdigate (Newdigate MS CR136/B2332-4) convocation rejected his proposal. This is confirmed by the absence of any reference to it in the register of convocation.

[3] From 1768 he was a member of one of the mileway commissions which were supposed to manage the approach-roads to the city: Bodl. MSS Top. Oxon. c.175-7.

[4] OUA Register of Convocation 1766-76.

[5] OUA minutes of the delegates of privileges 1769-1819, WP α/17/8/a, 15 Feb. 1769. *Oxford Council Acts 1752-1801* 81 (19 Mar. 1770).

[6] Bodl. Gough Oxon. 138, no. 24.

Oxford and Westminster. There was some opposition both in committee and during the second reading from forces outside the city boundaries, but minor amendments including concessions to farmers coming to market subdued the resistance of county magnates and on 28 March 1771 the bill was passed and the commissioners appointed to operate the measure quickly set to work.[1] The act itself cost what was then thought to be the unprecedented sum of £1,027 2s.[2]

It was a proof of the skill with which the whole matter was handled that, though the powers of the commissioners were sweeping, no opposition was raised at the time within either the university or the city. The university's contribution to the provision of sites was that of the professor of botany's house and his library, both of which were in due course demolished, despite a rearguard action among a section of convocation. No college building was destroyed, though Balliol gave up an adjoining piece of land and Lincoln and Jesus some garden property to the new market. A number of houses on the north side of the High Street were demolished under the compulsory purchase powers of the act, and a vast number of shops, houses and other buildings (including those of colleges) were altered or had to give up their signs, overhanging guttering, bow windows, projecting steps and the like, to free the major streets from obstruction and to conform with their new alignment. The picturesque east and north gates, Bocardo, and the Carfax conduit were the main public victims of the widely acclaimed modernization.

If the passing of the act was a remarkable achievement, so was its successful administration by the joint university and city commissioners.[3] As always under such acts the number of commissioners was very large but those active among them small. The minute books both of the main and of the new market commissioners show that the active university members, who frequently included the vice-chancellor and always some heads of houses, played a prominent part among them.[4] They also show that the active citizens on the new organization were a small body of prominent men, not always members of the corporation, who were increasingly taking the lead in civic affairs.[5] With some of these the

[1] The episode is fully documented. A typescript entitled 'The Oxford Improvements, 1771-81' in the possession of the Victoria County History Committee gives a very sound account of it, though its author had not the advantage of using the Newdigate Manuscripts or the correspondence of the vice-chancellor with Charles Jenkinson in the Liverpool Manuscripts in the British Library. T. W. M. Jaine gives a full account of 'The building of Magdalen bridge, 1772-1790' in *Oxoniensia* xxxvi (1971).

[2] See *Attempt to State the Accounts*, p. [37].

[3] It was found necessary to amend the financial conditions laid down in the act when it was renewed in 1781 (21 Geo. III, c. 47).

[4] 'Acts of the Street Commissioners ... 1771-9', Bodl. MS Top. Oxon. c.278; M. Graham, 'The building of Oxford covered market', *Oxoniensia* xliv (1979).

[5] See the analysis of persons active among the commissioners in 'The Oxford improvements, 1771-81'.

university and colleges already had connections, and with many these were to become closer in the future, particularly in matters concerning the long-planned Oxford canal.[1] The setting up of the commissions and the co-operation of the university and the city on them did not put an end to old rivalries. In 1801 only the tact of the then vice-chancellor prevented a collision over the annual payment of St Scholastica's day money, that ancient source of bitterness, and as late as 1812 the delegacy of privileges was still hoping to assert the legal powers of the proctors over members of the city.[2] In the working of the commissioners there was inevitably some friction and incompetence, sectional interests from time to time delayed things seriously, but the achievements of the years between 1771 and the end of the century were remarkable, and gave Oxford a valid claim to be numbered among the pioneers of the coming age of local administration.

[1] Sir Roger Newdigate, a great encourager of canals, had early interested the university in this scheme, as his correspondence with Wetherell shows. In 1768 David Durell (the vice-chancellor who preceded Wetherell in office) had been deputed to attend a meeting of those encouraging the Coventry-Oxford canal: OUA vice-chancellor's computus 1735-69, WPß/22/1, account for 1767-8.

[2] OUA minutes of the delegates of privileges 1769-1819, WPα/17/8/a, 4 Feb. 1801, 26 Feb. 1812. The vice-chancellor in 1801 was Michael Marlow (1759-1828), m. St John's 1776, president 1795-1828, vice-chancellor 1798-1802.

9

College Administration

I. G. DOOLITTLE

IN 1688 the university could boast eighteen fully-fledged colleges: All Souls, Balliol, Brasenose, Christ Church, Corpus, Exeter, Jesus, Lincoln, Magdalen, Merton, New College, Oriel, Pembroke, Queen's, St John's, Trinity, University College and Wadham. There were also seven halls: Gloucester, Hart, Magdalen, New Inn, St Alban, St Edmund and St Mary, all living precarious existences but important as the potential nuclei of future colleges. Gloucester Hall formed the basis of the only new college to be founded in the eighteenth century, Worcester; Hart Hall was refounded as Hertford College and the moribund New Inn Hall was nearly resuscitated as a law college by means of the Vinerian benefaction.[1] The only other changes of note during the period were those substantial benefactions which added new 'foundations' to existing colleges, such as Eaton's in 1743 at the newly formed Worcester College and Michel's in 1764 at Queen's.

The government of the colleges depended, as it had always done, on their statutes. University College acquired a new set in 1736 after a full-scale wrangle over its mythical Alfredian foundation,[2] but other colleges, with less obscure origins, had to be satisfied with their original letters patent and charters. Needless to say, these precious documents were jealously guarded and inquiries, whether from disgruntled junior fellows or controversialists with an itch for transcription[3], were not encouraged, since, despite the passage of time, the statutes were always the first

---

[1] On Worcester College see L. S. Sutherland, 'The foundation of Worcester College', *Oxoniensia* xliv (1979). The foundation of Hertford College was due to the efforts of one man, Richard Newton, and in spite of every effort on Exeter's part to impede the passing of the charter: S. G. Hamilton, *Hertford College* (London 1903). On New Inn Hall see L. S. Sutherland, 'Evidence in literary scholarship' in R. Wellek and A. Ribeiro (eds), *Essays in Memory of James Marshall Osborn* (Oxford 1979).

[2] W. Carr, *University College* (London 1902), 172 ff; W. R. Ward, *Georgian Oxford* (Oxford 1958), 115-16; [R. Gough,] *Anecdotes of British Topography* (London 1768), enlarged, 2nd edn *British Topography* (2 vols London 1780) ii. 144 ff.

[3] 'Dr Baron, being a factious man, would allow only one Copy of the Statutes in the College which he kept himself. Mr Sanford being then a Fellow contrived to borrow Baron's copy, and shutting himself up in his room began to transcribe it. Dr Baron, thinking he kept it too long, and suspecting what he was doing, sent for the Book. But Mr Sanford, answering that he had not yet done with it, and that the Master should have it the next day, went on with the transcript, and did not go out of

resort in all disputes. 'Statutes', said President Cooke in 1786, 'are *stubborn* things'.[1] They might be considered, in certain colleges and at certain periods, as irrelevant and obsolete,[2] but they could not be ignored. At any time they might be used to overturn existing arrangements. The prospect of government-inspired inquiries *quo warranto* may have receded since the days of James II's attempt on Magdalen College,[3] but college charters remained vulnerable to domestic assaults.

Of course, the final arbiter in college disputes was the visitor, but he was scarcely the *deus ex machina* envisaged by founders. Even his identity could be the cause of furious debates. Until the 1720s the vice-chancellor, proctors and doctors of divinity (though not convocation[4]) were the collective visitors of University College; then in the wake of a protracted and bitter mastership election king's bench decided that the crown had that power, and it was a royal visitation which descended on the college in 1729.[5] This may be dismissed as atypical, but Oriel's contemporaneous experiences showed that more conventional arrangements could also lead to difficulty. In their dispute with Provost Carter the fellows dusted down the college's first and neglected set of statutes and claimed that the crown and not the bishop of Lincoln was the proper visitor. They won their case in the court of common pleas.[6]

The right of appeal was also much disputed. The principal of Brasenose brought the bishop of Lincoln swiftly to task when it appeared that the complaints of a single fellow, Thomas Beconsall, might elicit a visitation. The statutes required, he said, that the request be made either by the principal and six senior fellows or with the common consent of the college.[7] Some colleges put incoming fellows on oath not to appeal against internal decisions. This was certainly true of both Exeter and St John's in mid-century.[8] Such shackles probably had little effect. Victims

---

his room till he had finished the whole.' Quoted in H. W. C. Davis, *A History of Balliol College* (Oxford 1899), rev. edn by R. H. C. Davis and R. W. Hunt (Oxford 1963), 159-60. Joseph Sanford (1692-1774), m. Exeter 1709; fellow Balliol 1715-74.

[1] J. Cooke-G. Beaver, draft, 3 Jan. 1786, CCCA B/14/5/1. John Cooke (1735-1823), m. Hertford 1749; degrees CCC, president 1783-1823; vice-chancellor 1788-92. George Beaver, m. CCC 1744; BA Magd. 1747; MA CCC 1751, BD 1757.

[2] Provost Carter (1708-27) gave obsolescence as the reason why he could not impose the statutes on the Oriel fellows: OCA SII.94, Provost Carter's memorandum book, p. 31.

[3] For this celebrated episode see *Magdalen and James II* and G. V. Bennett, 'Loyalist Oxford and the Revolution', pp. 17-18 above.

[4] See T. Bouchier-A. Charlett, 17 June 1699, UCA misc. letters and papers.

[5] Carr, 175-6.

[6] F. J. Varley, 'The Oriel College lawsuit, 1724-6', *Oxoniensia* vi (1941); Ward, *Georgian Oxford*, 108-10, 281.

[7] Principal-bp of Lincoln [*c* April 1688], BNCA tower drawer 129, appeal of Thomas Beconsall. Thomas Beconsall (1664-1709), m. BNC 1680.

[8] W. K. Stride, *Exeter College* (London 1900), 73 ff; SJM LV.141, President Derham's notebook.

or troublemakers appealed anyway, while most of their colleagues were only too aware of the dangers of letting the reins slip out of their hands. For much of the century the episcopal bench, still less the alternatives of king's bench or parliament, were not the most comforting tribunals for tory Oxford colleges.

When obliged to refer to their visitors, colleges confined their consultations, so far as was possible, to informal correspondence on specific points. For their part the visitors generally were content to deal with cases one at a time; and though some of them (notably bishop Trelawny[1]) could be hard on individual aberrations, and partial too, they were reluctant to interfere systematically in college government. There were only two full-scale visitations in the period. The first at University College in 1729 was conducted by a set of unobjectionable dignitaries appointed by the crown, the second at Merton in 1738 by five Oxford commissioners.[2] On both occasions circumstances were such that some form of investigation was essential and in neither case was the college reconstructed.

The disputes with which visitors had to deal were many and various, but the most serious (as at University College and Merton) generally concerned the conduct or powers of the head of the college. At first sight this is surprising for in most colleges heads were elected by the fellows themselves out of their own ranks.[3] At Christ Church, it is true, the dean was appointed by the crown, and the two eighteenth-century incorporations of Worcester and Hertford provided for nominations not elections (the provost of the former being named by the chancellor and the principal of the latter by the dean of Christ Church from his Westminster Students). But otherwise, apart from the halls, the fellows had a free hand, even if their visitors might have the right to confirm the choice or make a selection from the two or three names presented to them.[4]

Headship elections therefore were usually determined with a view to the comfortable preservation of the status quo or a future benefaction.[5] This is not to say that there was unanimity on such occasions: the value

[1] Trelawny-Wake, 17 Feb. 1717, Wake MS 15, fos 14–15.

[2] For University College see Carr, *University College*, 176 ff. Visitors named in the commission were the bishops of Oxford, Bristol and Peterborough, the advocate general (George Paul), the serjeant-at-law (Sir William Chapple) and the admiralty advocate (Exton Sayer): see UCA register ii (1729–42), pp 1 ff. For Merton see B. W. Henderson, *Merton College* (London 1899), 158.

[3] For example, at Magdalen, from fellows of New College and Magdalen; at University College present or former fellows, scholars or alumni.

[4] Heads of halls were appointed by the chancellor, apart from St Edmund Hall whose headship was in the gift of Queen's. At Magdalen the senior fellows chose from two nominated by the junior fellows. All Souls presented two fellows, one artist and one jurist, and Merton presented three. In both cases the presentations were made to the archbishop of Canterbury.

[5] As when Charlett was elected 'in expectancy of his being a great benefactor': W. Smith, *Annals of University College* (Newcastle upon Tyne 1728), 260.

of the office, private intrigues and political manœuvring saw to that.[1] But the system seemed to preclude the election of the overbearing or the innovative. Why did it not do so in practice? The answer appears to be partly in the length of time heads stayed in their posts. Like fellows they were often comparatively young when appointed (with an average age of 43) and the majority stayed until death.[2] Unlike ordinary fellows they could accept preferment (even in some cases a bishopric[3]) without being obliged to resign, so they tended to outlast their own generation. The century saw some spectacular examples of such longevity, including Niblett (at All Souls), Leigh (Balliol), George Huddesford (Trinity), Wetherell (University College) and Gower (Worcester) who all lasted forty years or more. Heads, unlike fellows, were often able to marry without forfeiting their fellowships, and this too set them apart.[4] Their lodgings and attendant households were visible reminders of their privilege and influence.[5] They were also a good deal wealthier than fellows. Heads were generally entitled to a double, even treble, share of both the 'dividends' (or surplus revenue) and the fines on the renewal of leases which formed the major part of a fellow's stipend.[6] This, together with additional preferment (especially prebends) and various minor perquisites, gave most, though not all,[7] heads of colleges an enviable income.

If headships had been merely honorific, such marks of distinction would have been irritants and nothing more; but as they carried with them a wide range of administrative duties and constitutional powers jealousy could easily turn into anger. Not that the fellows quibbled much over their head's dealings with the undergraduates. His right of nomination to certain exhibitions and scholarships (either on his own or in conjunction with other trustees), admission of servitors and commoners, allocation of chambers, even the elevation of senior undergraduates to fellow-commoner status, and supervision of the residence-regulations were all powers either generally acknowledged or gladly disowned.[8] More controversial were those actions which

[1] For example the election as master of University College of Robert Shippen in 1710 or of Thomas Cockman in 1722: Hearne, *Collections* iii. 8 (Shippen); Carr 172ff and Ward, *Georgian Oxford*, 114-16 (Cockman). Thomas Cockman (1675-1745), m. Univ. 1691, master 1722-45. Or the election of Theophilus Leigh as master of Balliol in 1726: Davis, *Balliol*, 160-4.

[2] Of 151 heads whose age at appointment is known, 62 were appointed in their thirties. Out of 136 cases of which details are known, 106 heads remained in office until death.

[3] Especially the poor see of Bristol, often held by the dean of Christ Church.

[4] Principals of Jesus, however, were not allowed to marry until 1768: JCA box 4, folder 3, letters 1700-1800, no. 39. Wardens of Wadham were unable to marry until 1806: WCM 1/11.

[5] For their university powers on hebdomadal board and as vice-chancellor see L. S. Sutherland, 'The administration of the university', pp. 213-17 above.

[6] See pp. 236-7 below.

[7] For example the provost of Queen's: N. Bridges—Routh, 14 Dec. [no year], Magdalen MS 477, fo 30.

[8] For a head's right of sole nomination see F. Laurence-Cooke, 14 Oct. 1789 and A. A. Baker–same, 24 Apr. 1799, CCCA B/14/5/1. The trustees might for example be the fellows and outside dignitaries (QCA 21.123 exhibition book) or two senior fellows (All Souls, Warden's MS 36, Warden

impinged on the fellowship itself. Occasionally a head would make grand claims to a general veto on all college decisions. Usually such pretensions were summarily dismissed,[1] though in 1775 the visitor of Worcester, adjudicating in a dispute over the less than momentous question of table-cloths and napkins in hall, proclaimed that no order or decree concerning the government of the college had any force or authority without the approval of the provost.[2] More frequent and more durable were claims to a negative in elections, both of fellows and officers. Whenever a head became embroiled in a dispute with his fellows there was a chance that some form of veto would be claimed. Warden Gardiner of All Souls (1710-12), Provost Carter of Oriel in the 1720s and Warden Wyntle of Merton in the 1730s all made this claim. None of them won their point, though Gardiner gained a little more from his stand than Carter or Wyntle.[3]

The patronage at a head's disposal was another sensitive matter. In most, if not all, colleges it was the head who appointed the tutors and assigned pupils to them.[4] This, as a following section will show, was a most valuable perquisite and much coveted by the resident fellows.[5] Considerable diplomacy was required if charges of neglect, favouritism or interference were to be avoided.[6] Other appointments, or indeed

Niblett's notebook, exhibitioners, 17 Oct. 1760). For elevation to fellow commoner status see G. Fothergill-Smith, 29 Jan. 1742, 5 Apr. 1744, Queen's MS 473. George Fothergill (1705-60), m. Queen's 1722; principal SEH 1751-60. As to supervision of residence rules, President Cooke spoke of 'my official character to which the Charge of Our Members residence is more peculiarly committed': draft reply to Lord Kirkwall [14 Jan. 1800], CCCA B/14/5/1.

[1] The claims of the rector of Lincoln, the rumbustious Edward Tatham (1750-1834, m. Queen's 1769; fellow Linc. 1787, rector 1792-1834), to increase the stipend of the curacy of Combe were denied by the fellows, the visitor pointing out that it did not appear 'in a single instance the Rector has an exclusive Power over any part of the Revenues of the College'. However, he added that if the fellows refused the increase Tatham could appeal to him again: visitor-rector and fellows, 24 Dec. 1811, LCM Register 1739-1983.

[2] Letter of 11 Mar. 1775, WCA tin trunk, no. 10, quoted in J. C. Masterman, *Bits and Pieces* (London 1961), 17.

[3] The dispute at All Souls can be traced in Gardiner's letters 1710-11 at All Souls and in the Wake MSS at Christ Church; see also Ward, *Georgian Oxford*, 112. For Gardiner's right to veto elections of fellows see his letter to Wake of 11 Nov. 1719, Wake MS 16, fo 127. On Carter see Varley, 'Oriel College lawsuit'. For Wyntle see Ward, 100 ff; Henderson, *Merton College*, 158-9. The fellows of Merton once claimed that 'scarce any thing less than absolute Power' would satisfy their warden: fellows-visitor, 13 July 1738, MCR 1.4, register 1731-1822, pp. 65 ff.

[4] For the appointment of tutors see *Journal of the Rev. William Bagshaw Stevens*, ed. G. Galbraith (Oxford 1965), 470. The head assigned pupils at both Queen's and Trinity.

[5] It has to be noted, however, that President Fry of St John's was once chided for taking his duties in selecting tutors too seriously and was told that 'in other Colleges they often found it very difficult to meet with persons for that office': Costin, *St. John's*, 219. But the assertion stands alone and all the other evidence is against it.

[6] At Trinity one fellow complained to the visitor that the president had failed to give him any pupils: TCA visitor's letters 1576-1820, letter of 11 Aug. 1784. Hearne said that Lancaster 'was a great Favourite of Dr Halton's by which means he had most of the pupils in that College whom he shamefully neglected': *Collections* ii. 48. Joseph Smith (1670-1756, m. Queen's 1689, provost 1730-56) told George Fothergill that he could not assign him pupils in his own right 'considering the number

dismissals,[1] could occasionally arouse indignation, but not usually on the same scale.

Heads also possessed, either personally or in conjunction with the governing body, powers over another contentious issue, that of residence. A head could either permit fellows to be absent from college or make sure they performed their offices (in person or by deputy).[2] He might occasion further friction by exercising his privilege of first choice of all or some of the college livings. The master of Balliol had a general right of this kind, while the rector of Exeter could plump for the rectory of Bushey and was 'bought off' in the 1790s by an addition to his stipend.[3]

It is scarcely surprising, therefore, that the college records are peppered with accounts of disputes between heads and fellows which, when laced with politics or obstinacy, could lead to acrimonious and protracted feuds. To the cases of Carter and Wyntle may be added the controversial reigns of Matthew Hole at Exeter (1716-30) and Edward Tatham at Lincoln (1792-1834).[4] On the other hand, the power of a college's head could be a force for good as well as for evil, and some vigorous heads, notably Conybeare during his brief time at Exeter (1730-3)[5] and the celebrated Dean Jackson at Christ Church (1783-1809), were able to effect a virtual transformation in the government and reputation of their houses. 'Absolute Monarchy', as Cyril Jackson's reign at Christ Church was characterized, could work both ways: it could be autocratic or benevolent.

If a forceful head of house could sometimes escape from the shackles of statute or tradition, the fellows, naturally enough, had a good deal less freedom. Their lives were governed both by the wording of college constitutions and decrees and by the dictates of custom. To what extent did the resultant process of interpretation and reinterpretation change the character of college fellowships?

of the present Tutors, and how few Gentlemen there are in the College to be shar'd amongst them, they would be apt . . . to think it more improper now than ever to break in upon that privilege': letter of 5 Mar. 1731, Queen's MS 473.

[1] For example that of Jonas Proast, chaplain at All Souls, who on the face of it had been dismissed for not voting for the warden in a university election: W. Lloyd-abp of Canterbury, 17 Apr. 1688, All Souls, Warden's MS 50, pp. 320-2. Warden Finch agreed to restore Proast as chaplain in exchange for the archbishop's legally investing him with the wardenship: All Souls, Warden's MS 6; C. G. Robertson, *All Souls College* (London 1899), 159 ff.

[2] The Warden of All Souls had the power to license fellows to be absent: All Souls, Warden's MS 22(b), 161, Wenman's history of All Souls. For deputies see UCA new statutes of 1736.

[3] For Balliol see N. Docton-master and fellows, 5 Mar. 1725, BCA register 1682-1781, fo 56; and for Exeter ECA register 1737-1824, p. 245, 13 Mar. 1794, 10 Mar. 1798.

[4] ECA A.II.5, letter book 1720; Ward, *Georgian Oxford*, 106. Matthew Hole (1640-1730), m. Exeter 1658, rector 1716-30. V. H. H. Green, *The Commonwealth of Lincoln College, 1427-1977* (Oxford 1979).

[5] Conybeare went on to be dean of Christ Church and it is worth noting that the next person to hold a double headship was Lord Franks who was provost of Queen's 1946-8 and provost of Worcester 1962-76; see H. Button, 'Double headships and other notable heads', *Cambridge Review*, 22 Oct. 1982. I should like to thank Mr J. S. G. Simmons for drawing my attention to this article.

There was certainly little change in the way fellows were chosen. In Queen's, as in a number of other colleges, scholars on the foundation had a statutory general claim on a fellowship, though not by order of seniority. Queen's, however, maintained its established custom of electing its taberdars in strict succession.[1] Magdalen likewise saw no reason to reconsider its preference given by custom, not statute, to its own form of scholars called demies. Of the 422 Magdalen fellows elected between 1690 and 1800, 392 were demies. Jesus chose its scholars in the same way, though again it was under no statutory obligation to do so.[2] Only one exception to the general pattern has been found.[3] The preferences expressed by founders for candidates from certain counties, dioceses, schools and so on afforded perhaps less room for manœuvre, but again there were few signs of a desire for change. Preferred candidates invariably had to be 'habilis' and this might have been expected to arouse more controversy than it did. The principal and five fellows of Brasenose asked their visitor for an explanation of the term in 1788, but this seems to have been an isolated instance which is all the more surprising since the problem was clearly not an easy one to resolve.[4] It was one thing for the bishop of Lincoln to point out, as he had to Lincoln College in the previous year, that the candidate from the favoured area had only to be 'habilis' and not 'habilior' than a candidate from an inferior category, for that was plain enough.[5] It was quite another to state blandly that a candidate was 'habilis' if he was judged capable of performing most of the college offices to which he might be elected, 'correct' in his moral conduct and as having made considerable progress in learning. Elections, the visitor pronounced, should take into account both the preference of the Founder and the general (religious and educational) objects of the institution. Here indeed was scope for 'interpretation', but the opportunity was missed.

Many colleges were also obliged to give preference in one or two of their fellowships to founder's kin, but they did so with little apparent demur. It was only at All Souls, where unusually all the fellowships (save the faculty ones) were vulnerable to the claims of Chichele's descendants, that a sustained attempt to solve the problem was made.[6] It was a halting

[1] See QCA register K, 1 Mar. 1748 and other such entries. The rule of 'seniority is highly useful for the purpose of avoiding cabal and contention. It will be found also to have its inconveniences. From a love of quiet in the electors, and a desire to avoid dispute and litigation, and from the difficulty of ascertaining precisely the comparative degrees of merit in the several candidates, they will be frequently led to accept of the undeserving.' Queen's, MS 456, memoranda relating to Queen's College, p. 16.
[2] JCA box 5, misc. papers relating to appeals, 21 May 1750.
[3] TCA visitors letters 1576-1820, 17 June and 18 Aug. 1786.
[4] BNCA tower drawer 128, correspondence with visitor, letter of 28 June 1788.
[5] LCM register 1739-1983, letter of 9 Nov. 1787.
[6] The following is based on G. D. Squibb, *Founder's Kin* (Oxford 1972).

process, dependent upon the attitude of successive archbishops of Canterbury as visitor. The century began with a respite from the claims of kinsmen. Then in 1723 Archbishop Wake adjudged a test case and dictated that the founder's wishes must be literally obeyed. The college subsequently felt obliged to admit thirteen kin in the following twenty-five years, though it raised what objections it could to individual candidates. The arrival of the celebrated lawyer William Blackstone at All Souls inaugurated a fresh endeavour to stem the tide. Blackstone published his *Collateral Consanguinity* in 1750 to show the absurdity of such unlimited claims and fortified by such arguments the college admitted only one further kinsman. They were undone again by an archiepiscopal verdict in a case of 1762 and the kinsmen flooded in once more. Archbishop Cornwallis was pressed for his opinion but initially at least he was as unaccommodating as his predecessors. However, the continued influx of founder's kinsmen, who were filling by now three out of every four vacancies, convinced him of the need for action. In 1777 he pronounced that the fellows were not required to give preference to founder's kin while there were ten such kinsmen among the forty fellows in the college, though they could if they wished elect more than ten. This injunction, confirmed by Archbishop Moore[1] in 1792, kept numbers within reasonable bounds, at least until the second and third decades of the nineteenth century when they began to rise again.

Christ Church filled its 101 places for Students through the nomination of the dean (who had two selections) and the canons. One place was in the gift of the Vernon family and three were reserved for Westminster School, but otherwise the chapter had a free hand.[2] Occasionally, it is true, they showed a readiness to admit a boy on merit 'by the General consent' (the future Dean Jackson being one such case) and to postpone the entry of a candidate whose behaviour was not satisfactory;[3] but in the large majority of cases 'the roll' (filled up long in advance) was observed with scrupulous care. Patronage was not lightly relinquished.

In some colleges there was no restriction at all on the choice of fellows, but this tended to encourage not learning but faction.[4] Certainly Merton's fellowship elections were more notable for their political intrigue and bribery than their academic competitiveness.[5] There were examinations

---

[1] John Moore (1730–1805), m. Pemb. 1745; canon Ch.Ch. 1763; abp of Canterbury 1783–1805.

[2] E. G. W. Bill and J. F. A. Mason, *Christ Church and Reform 1850–1867* (Oxford 1970), 11–13.

[3] CA chapter book 1754–80, p. 100, 18 June 1763; chapter book 1776–99, p. 450, 16 Dec. 1782.

[4] 'Those Colleges in which men are elected into fellowships without having been previously of any inferior order in the house—as at Merton and Oriel—will have it in their power to choose the most deserving; so far . . . as their knowledge of them shall extend. And it may fairly be supposed, that, for the sake of their own credit, and independently of every other consideration, they will generally do this. No doubt however but that here also improper influence will sometimes find a place.' Queen's MS 456, memoranda relating to Queen's College, p. 17.

[5] See Ward, *Georgian Oxford*, 99–100.

of a kind too at All Souls[1] but they seem to have been regarded chiefly as a means of rejecting the claims of founder's kin. On at least one occasion the visitor was treated to examples of a candidate's sorry efforts.[2] It was not in fact until the very end of the century that even the unfettered colleges began actively to encourage open competition. Balliol deserves an honourable mention, but it was really Oriel which led the way when under Provost Eveleigh in 1795 it asked Edward Copleston to stand for election to a vacant fellowship for which he was not qualified.[3] The introduction of classified university examinations gave an impetus to similar moves in other colleges and in the early nineteenth century Brasenose is found struggling hard to reconcile the conflicting claims of founder's preferences and performance in the schools, but it is a story which belongs to another place and a later period.[4]

Given that for much of the period and in most colleges seniority (in various forms) and not merit was the decisive factor, it is important to consider how easy or difficult it was to succeed to a fellowship. Problems there undoubtedly were. Some were caused by the statutes, as at Merton, where there were attempts to keep up the number of 'bachelor fellows' for educational purposes by deferring their election into full fellowships until sufficient replacements had been gathered. This led to the multiple elections of 1711, 1717 and 1723 which aroused so much heat. After his visitation of 1738 the archbishop of Canterbury enjoined the college to fill up each vacancy without delay; and, though this was modified in 1752 to allow for three fellows to be elected together on a certain day, the earlier unsatisfactory arrangements were gone for good.[5] Other more serious problems were created by the failure of existing fellows to resign their fellowships at a rate commensurate with the influx of scholar-claimants. There is no discernible general pattern,[6] but in certain colleges at certain times the difficulties were acute. At Corpus in mid-century the *discipuli* (or scholars) were said to be waiting ten or twelve years from matriculation for a probationary fellowship, while the diary of that 'antiquated demy' William Bagshaw Stevens shows how long a man might have to wait at Magdalen if his 'county line' was blocked.[7] The customary age-limit

---

[1] Gardiner-Wake, 11 Nov. 1719, Wake MS 16, fo 127.

[2] Squibb, 43.

[3] Davis, *Balliol*, 274-84. John Eveleigh (1748-1814), m. Wadham 1766; higher degrees Oriel, provost 1781-1814. Edward Copleston (1776-1849), m. CCC 1791; fellow Oriel 1795-1814, provost 1814-28; prof. of Poetry 1802-12, bp of Llandaff and dean of St Paul's 1828-49.

[4] Principal and fellows—visitor (n.d.) and reply 3 June 1816, BNCA tower drawer 128, Notebook.

[5] Letters of 8 July 1738 and 20 July 1752, MCR register 1731-1822, p. 45; Henderson, *Merton*, 153.

[6] The sharp increase in the monetary value of fellowships at the end of the century might tempt one to apply more generally the remark of Bagshaw Stevens that 'from the increasing Value of Fellowships Senior Fellows will be less and less tempted every day to take college Livings': *Journal of Stevens*, ed. Galbraith, p. 106.

[7] CCCA A/5/5, correspondence with the visitor 1755; T. Fowler, *Corpus Christi College* (London

for demies of twenty-five had to be jettisoned for the sake of Stevens and others.[1] Of 191 demies who became fellows in the eighteenth century no fewer than 45, or approximately one in four, had to wait more than ten years.

There were various solutions to these difficulties, some legitimate and some not. At Lincoln it was decided to purchase advowsons to end the frustration of the eldérly senior fellows, and the scheme was in large measure successful. Eight of the fellows elected before or during 1750 lasted thirty years or more; none after that date did so.[2] Such a remedy was open only to the prosperous colleges (the advowson of a well-endowed benefice could well cost £1,000 or more) and after the mortmain act of 1736 was unavailable to colleges which had already purchased the permitted quota of one living to two fellows. Not surprisingly perhaps, private enterprise took over from corporate inactivity. Fellows were encouraged to resign by means of 'douceurs' from potential successors. Such at any rate was thought to be the practice at New College where candidates were anxious to be nominated to vacancies before the annual election at Winchester.[3] A number of wardens tried to put an end at least to corrupt resignations, if not to resignations themselves, but none had real success it seems until Thomas Hayward and John Oglander in the 1760s and 1770s.[4]

Concentration, however, on these particular problems should not obscure the fact that for long periods colleges could provide a smooth and relatively rapid promotion for their undergraduates. At Brasenose, for example, no one matriculating in the college who went on to become a fellow waited more than ten years, and most managed it in six (that is two years after achieving BA status). Even at Corpus, where the system broke down in the 1750s, scholars could generally expect to secure a fellowship after seven years or so.[5]

Once elected, most of a fellow's regular income came from a share in the college's surplus revenue each year. This 'dividend' took various forms: at All Souls it was called 'augmentation of commons'; at Corpus extra 'liveries' were granted; at New College 'increments' were announced. But the principle was basically the same: a double share perhaps to the

---

1898), 188. *Journal of Stevens*, ed. Galbraith, p. 106; Stevens was 39 when he secured his fellowship. 'County' and other preferences were common features of the fellowship system: see p. 233 above.

[1] Bloxham, *Reg. Magdalen* vii, p. vi.

[2] These calculations are taken from Green, *Lincoln College*, appx. See also J. P. D. Dunbabin, 'College estates and wealth 1660–1815', pp. 292–3 below.

[3] 'I hear four of the Fellows of New-College, amongst whom is Dr John Ayliffe, who is degraded and expelled the University (tho' not the College), have sold their Fellowships, which is a Custom here, under Pretence of Resignation, and so will go off.' Hearne, *Collections* v. 100.

[4] T. Hayward–Mr Speed, 25 Aug. 1765, NCA 3581 (copy). Thomas Hayward (d. 1768), m. Oriel 1749; BCL and DCL New College, warden 1764–8. NCA 1033 (appeal to the visitor by Mr Jeans 1773) and 9655, pp. 113 ff (copy).

[5] See CCCA balance books, where fellows' dates of election are shown, as in 1747 (C/22/1).

head of house; a single share to 'domus' or college funds; and single shares (sometimes varying according to status, both of degree and seniority) to the individual fellows, whether resident or not.[1] The dividend usually comprised all the revenues received from endowments, but some colleges made separate arrangements for the fines paid for fresh or renewed leases of their property. Allocations of these followed the same kind of system employed for dividends, though the college (domus) might receive a larger proportion by means of an immediate deduction of anything between a fifth and two-thirds.[2] Again fines usually went to all fellows on the foundation, but at Merton and Wadham only those present at the settling or sealing of a fine received a share.[3] There was also a tendency in certain colleges for senior fellows to regard fines as their personal perquisites (so Thomas Beconsall claimed at Brasenose) or at least as a fund to augment their stipends.[4]

Resident fellows were entitled not only to the 'commons' prescribed in the statutes but also to a series of extra allowances to offset their battels or living expenses. In theory the latter should have merely cancelled out the debts of frugal fellows, but since they had been commuted to money-payments they could produce in practice either a deficit or a surplus and might also be appropriated, in whole or in part, by absentees.[5]

It is no easy task to determine the value of fellowships during the period. There was considerable variation from college to college, from year to year and even from fellow to fellow. There may be some point, however, in giving a few figures from one college, All Souls, where arrangements were not untypical, and for which William Blackstone, bursar 1747-8 and 1751-2, provides a remarkable guide to the accounts.[6] The table below gives the income of the warden, a typical doctor (the highest-paid fellow) and a typical MA in certain years. The figures do not include the many additional, irregular sums a fellow might receive, such as fees for tuition, stipends as college officers (bursar, dean, lecturer and so on) and exhibitions attached to senior fellowships.

There are a number of points to be noticed: first, that the warden's income was three, if not four, times greater than that even of senior

[1] Pembroke was unusual in making the dividend proportionate to residence: 10 weeks entitled a fellow to a quarter-dividend, 36 to the whole. PCA convention book 2/1/1, p. 3, 10 Dec. 1725.

[2] CCCA C/22/1 balance book 1772 (one-fifth); W. Blackstone, *Dissertation on the Accounts of All Souls College, Oxford*, ed. W. Anson (Roxburghe Club cxxix 1898), 25 (two-thirds).

[3] MCR 1.6, Warden Wyntle's register, fo 22. WCM convention book III, p. 76, 13 July 1756: 'None should have any share but such as shall be present personally in the College before sun set the Day the Court is held or Fine agreed.'

[4] BNCA tower drawer 129, 1688. SJM LX.68-73.

[5] Green, *Lincoln* 388-9. MCR Wyntle's register, fo 159. It is not clear what happened when the archbishop of Canterbury tightened the rules on non-residence at Merton in 1738. There was some dispute about his injunction: MCR register 1731-1822, pp. 71 ff, 16 Aug. 1738.

[6] Blackstone, *Dissertation on the Accounts*.

TABLE 9.1

FELLOWS' INCOME AT ALL SOULS

Figures are for total income in pounds, with the portion derived from the augmentation of commons in brackets

	warden £	typical DCL £	typical MA £
1696-7	146 (77)*	60 (38)	33 (25)
1724-5	179 (80)	58 (40)	41 (26)
1749-50	161 (60)	45 (30)	30 (19)
1774-5	253 (135)	90 (67)	63 (43)
1793-4	357 (180)**	83 (57)	60 (37)
1799-1800	535 (310)	181 (155)	124 (100)

* Excluding £25 for servants.

** As there was a change of warden in this year the figures are for the following year

Source: C. T. Martin, *Catalogue of the Archives in the Muniment Rooms of All Souls College* (London 1877), p. 415 (song books e. 3, 5, 7, 52, 71, 77).

fellows; second, that a fellow's income depended heavily on the 'dividend' and hence on the college's property-revenue as well as on the number of fellows (a point of occasional controversy);[1] and third, that incomes seem to have remained static or declined in the first half of the century, rose somewhat in the third quarter and leapt dramatically in its final years.

There are a few hints which suggest that this pattern was repeated elsewhere. Certainly fellowships were reckoned to have been unremunerative in the first part of the century. In 1736 the master of Pembroke thought his fellows were receiving only about £20 yearly, and two years later senior fellowships at St John's were valued at £25 yearly, exclusive of college office and curacies.[2] John Wesley's income as a non-resident fellow of Lincoln in the 1730s and 1740s fluctuated a good deal but he too could count on only £20 or so yearly.[3] Later the totals rose markedly. When the fellows wanted to augment a fellowship at Balliol in 1775 they estimated its value at £70 yearly; in 1782 William 'Oriental' Jones, a non-resident fellow of University College, thought his fellowship

---

[1] Particularly at Merton where the fellowship, for reasons explained above, was often below strength. Eight bachelors had to wait 3½ years to be admitted after their election in 1705: MCR 1.3, register 1567-1731, pp. 694-5 (20 July 1710), p. 696 (1 March 1711). In 1716 John Bettesworth thought that the 16 fellows should make up their numbers to 24 and not pocket the extra revenues themselves: Wake MS 15, fos 57-8, 2 May 1716. At Lincoln in 1787 the visitor was chary of obliging the fellows to increase their numbers from 12 to the full 15 for fear of reducing their stipends and putting too much of a strain on the college's finances: LCM register 1734-1983, 22 December 1787.

[2] M. Panting-Niblett, 16 Mar. 1736, Martin, *Catalogue* p. 364, no. 510. Matthew Panting (1683-1739), m. Pemb. 1698, master 1714-39. SJM LX. 68-73.

[3] Green, *Lincoln*, 389n. John Wesley (1703-91), m. Ch.Ch. 1720; fellow Linc. 1725. When asking Archbishop Wake to increase the value of the 'uberius' benefice the Merton fellows claimed that their

worth £100 yearly; and from 1790 to 1804 the average annual value of a fellowship at Queen's was calculated at £120.[1]

The remuneration of heads of houses is even more difficult to establish, partly because their income often included substantial allowances for their household expenses and partly because they could hold lucrative preferments in conjunction with their college positions. William Derham of St John's, for example, enjoyed annual profits of approximately £120 from the rectory of Hanborough in addition to his income as president.[2] Nevertheless the assorted figures do tell some kind of story. If the warden of All Souls was receiving £179 in the mid-1720s, his counterpart at Merton was said to be enjoying, at roughly the same date, between £200 and £300 yearly.[3] Derham's income at St John's a few years later fluctuated wildly between £171 and £306. The increase in the later part of the century in property-revenues naturally had an even more noticeable impact on the emoluments of heads than on those of fellows. Again the All Souls figures find echoes elsewhere. The principal of Brasenose appears to have been receiving about £400 in 1770, £600 in 1778, and £800 in 1800 (rising to £1,100 in 1811).[4] New College's warden, though invariably translating to the better-paid wardenship at Winchester, was receiving £1,000 or so by the 1790s; while the rector of Exeter's receipts in 1811 amounted to about £700.[5] The dividend system gave heads a disproportionate advantage over their fellows and, in most cases at least, afforded them a substantial income.[6]

Stipends raise the related question of residence. Fellows plainly received a major part of their emoluments whether they were resident or not. By statute no fellow could be absent from his college without permission, and there is no doubt that in a formal sense the rules were upheld. The records abound with 'leaves of absence' granted to supplicant fellows. But equally there can be no doubt that the grants were made universally and almost automatically. There were of course some holders of 'faculty' fellowships (which were not restricted to those in holy orders and were assigned to studies like law and medicine which were often

fellowships were worth £100 p.a. exclusive of fees, perquisites and so on: Wake MS 16, fos 203ff; cf p. 245 below. This is hard to believe.

[1] Master and fellows-visitor, 23 Feb. 1775, BCA register 1682–1781, p. 148; *Letters of Sir William Jones*, ed. G. H. Cannon (2 vols Oxford 1970) ii. 599; QCA register K, 19 May 1804; J. R. Magrath, *The Queen's College* (2 vols Oxford 1921) ii. 147n.

[2] SJM President Derham's accounts 1748–57. William Derham (*c.*1703–57), m. St John's 1721, president 1748–57.

[3] Fellows-Wake, Wake MS 16, fos 203 ff. At Merton various perquisites were in dispute. Wyntle said that people thought the wardenship was worth £500 yearly; no one believed him when he said it was worth only £200: MCR Wyntle's register, fo 8[r-v].

[4] R. W. Jeffery, 'History of the college, 1690–1803' in *Brasenose Monographs* ii pt i, no. XIII, p. 60. Ralph Cawley (*c* 1721–77), m. BNC 1738, principal 1770–7.

[5] NCA increment books, 9857 (1793, £838), 9858 (1795, £1,227). ECA headship accounts, A.IV.(5).

[6] The president of Corpus, however, received a good deal less, for example £270 in 1772, £276 in 1779, £209 in 1783 (totals before battels were deducted): CCCA balance books, C/22/1.

pursued in conjunction with a career in London) and of 'travelling' fellowships (the terms of which envisaged extended periods away from the
university) who received special indulgence, but other fellows too could
expect to be allowed to go away to study, serve in the army or militia, discharge some royal or episcopal commission, act as a private tutor, preach,
recover from ill health, travel or even to prepare the ground for preferment.[1] Refusals appear to have been rare and easily explained. A mischief-
maker and suspected papist at Brasenose in 1688, Thomas Beconsall,
claimed that he had asked for leave on grounds of ill health but had been
denied; while the trustees of the newly established Michel foundation at
Queen's initially refused dispensation to a would-be curate and laid down
firm guidlelines on the subject (though later the rules were evidently
relaxed and all applications were approved).[2]

Such indulgence presumably explains why there were so few cases of
expulsion or even punishment for 'absence without leave'. A Christ
Church Student, it is true, was removed in 1787, but his offence was
aggravated by 'defiance' and undergraduate 'fellows' were anyway subjected to stricter regulations than masters and doctors.[3] Unauthorized
absence was usually punished, if punished at all, by a mild penalty known
as a 'sconce' from the head of house and even then the bark might be worse
than the bite.[4]

There was in fact very little excuse for such disobedience. The conditions attached to 'non-residence' were undemanding in the extreme. Only
if personal application for renewal was necessary could any inconvenience
arise and this was invariably required just once a year.[5] At election or
chapter day, usually in November or December, absent fellows would
return to their colleges to elect the officers for the ensuing year and have

[1] QCA Michel register 1765-1810, 30 Oct. 1765; CA chapter book 1776-99, p. 379, 2 Apr. 1778, chapter book 1754-80, p. 61, 22 Feb. 1760; All Souls, Warden's MS 35, orders of the warden and officers, 27
Oct. 1760; SJM register 1691-1712, p. 149, 9 Mar. 1694; QCA Michel register 1765-1810, 29 June 1767;
SJM Muniments, register 1691-1712, p. 135, 24 Dec. 1694; Cooke-G. Beaver, draft 3 Jan. 1786, same-W.
King, draft 15 May 1783, CCCA B/14/5/1.
[2] Principal-visitor, 2 June 1688, BNCA tower drawer 129, no. 6; QCA Michel register 1765-1810, letters of 30 Oct. 1765, 8 Sept. 1766.
[3] 'Having alledged no reason whatever for his Absence the Chapter considering this as a determined and obstinate Representation of the same Disobedience for which he received their former
solemn Censure on Nov: 21. 1785 have resolved to remove him from his Studentship': CA chapter
book 1776-99, pp. 521-2, 15 Feb. 1787. In 1734 New College ordered that fellows of under 5 years standing were to keep residence, especially in term time, on pain of being kept back from their degree: NCA
3581, p. 31, 28 Mar. 1734.
[4] At Wadham a Mr Allen who had been absent for 8 months was granted further leave for reasons of
health provided simply 'that he attended again whenever He should be sent for' to make up a majority
of fellows for purposes of sealing: WCM convention book III, p. 87, 11 Mar. 1761.
[5] At Worcester in 1780 it was agreed that the 'Rule of Indulgence of Absence to the Fellows, made
November the 30th 1768, be in part cancelled; and that in future they be obliged to appear in College
on or before the 30th November only in every ensuing Year': WCA tin trunk, no. 10, 19 Apr. 1780. See
also president-visitor [18 Dec. 1791] and visitor's reply, 6 Mar. 1792, TCA visitor's letters 1576-1820.

their leave of absence extended for another twelve months. Only if they themselves were elected into office would their calm be disturbed because most colleges insisted that their more important officers should reside, at least during term-time.[1] Sinecures in the *cursus honorum* there undoubtedly were (especially among the lecturing and catechetical posts) and deputies were sometimes permitted;[2] but most posts, and especially bursarships, were arduous and time-consuming. At the very least officers would be required to attend regular college meetings and absenteeism might be cause for a fine and even suspension of fellowship.[3]

College residents, therefore, tended to fall into two categories: senior fellows serving as officers and junior fellows waiting for preferment. Roughly half the fellows can be found present at any one time though the figures naturally vary a good deal. University College had usually half its complement; Balliol and Merton more than half.[4] And of course there was temporary absenteeism during the vacations.

From residence to seniority. It will already have become evident that the lives of fellows, whether resident or non-resident, depended heavily on seniority. For example, seniority determined a fellow's obligation to serve, by turn, in the various college offices.[5] In some colleges indeed the 'seniors' formed an autonomous quasi-oligarchy which kept a firm hand on office and emoluments. Such seems to have been the case throughout the period at Brasenose (though the evidence is decidedly one-sided) and for a brief time at Trinity.[6] Emoluments too, as seen above, varied somewhat according to seniority. That at least was true of both All Souls and Magdalen. The best rooms and the rents attached to them also went to the most senior fellows;[7] certain exhibitions or sinecures likewise; and even tutorships, though at the personal disposal of the head of house, tended to be granted

[1] At New College the warden declared 'that as the neglect of Officers is a matter directly under his Cognizance, he would not in future consent that any one should be elected into any Office, who did not propose to be resident ... during the Terms', NCA 960, p. 50, 20 Dec. 1776.

[2] As lecturer in moral philosophy at Magdalen in the 1790s William Bagshaw Stevens had only to deliver one lecture a term and did not trouble to go into residence, and he tried to get even these minimal duties performed by a deputy: *Journal of Stevens*, ed. Galbraith, pp. 359-60, 377-8, 455. The deanship of divinity at Magdalen made few demands on its incumbent and residence was evidently not obligatory: G. Hirst-president, 27 Oct. 1795, Magdalen MS 478, fo 41; W. Alcock-same, 26 Jan. 1796, MS 477, fo 49.

[3] At All Souls absenteeism was deemed to be harming college affairs and it was therefore agreed that any fellow 'absent without leave ... be sconc'd 6d.'; ASA acta in capitulis, MS 401 (a), fo 245^{r-v}, 5 Feb. 1704. At New College all officers were required to attend the meetings of the '13' under 'penalty of 5 Guineas': NCA 961, p. 1, 17 Apr. 1788. For suspension see WCA tin trunk, no. 10, 2 Apr. 1778.

[4] This estimate is taken from an analysis of the battel-books of the colleges in question.

[5] CA chapter book 1754-80. p. 293.

[6] BNCA tower drawer 129, case of Thomas Beconsall 1688; tower drawer 128, visitations and commissions. TCA junior bursar's order book A, 23 Dec. 1717; visitor's letters 1576-1820, 19 Dec. 1717.

[7] This was certainly true of Lincoln: Green, *Lincoln*, 393. See also the cases of Jesus and Wadham where only resident fellows were eligible for the best rooms: JCA box 4, folder 3, letters 1700-1800, no. 56; WCM convention book III, p. 106, 6 Dec. 1768.

in the same way. But of course most important of all was the senior fellows' right of first option on a vacant college living. The slightest acquaintance with the anxiety, sometimes even corruption, which attended the succession from fellowship to benefice will indicate how crucial seniority must have seemed.[1]

How natural then that there should have been such debate on the issue. Some colleges determined seniority simply by reference to the date of election and this caused no difficulty, save in exceptional circumstances.[2] But in colleges where preference was given to standing in the university considerable problems arose. Fellows were reluctant to take a doctor's degree (in most cases the DD) because of the expense involved but they were equally reluctant to concede status to juniors who might find the money and persevere. Aspiring DDs or BCLs might be obliged to renounce any claim to seniority over their MA colleagues.[3] Visitors were clearly uncertain about the practice, as the example of Trinity reveals. In 1713 the visitor agreed that the juniors taking DDs should have only honorific precedence (that is in hall, chapel and processions) and not in other matters; but his successor in 1760 thought otherwise and told the seniors that unless they could show statutable cause for not taking the degree they would have to forfeit their standing.[4] However, the signs are that the warning had little effect.[5] Only when it was clear that their privileges were immediately at risk would seniors take action. There was an amusing commotion at Magdalen in the 1790s when it was decided to distribute the dividend by magistral seniority and not by graduate precedence. A 'herd of doctors' hastily acquired their DDs by accumulation in 1798 to protect their position.[6]

So far the emphasis has been on privilege and remuneration. What were the obligations of a fellowship? The requirements of residence were largely nugatory and of office-holding short-lived. What were the others? In theory at least fellows were expected to read for a higher degree; and for aspiring clergy, as most fellows were, this meant the DD. Only a few faculty

[1] All Souls found William Wynne's offer of money to his immediate senior in orders to pass the living of Chesterfield 'shocking' but thought Wynne 'didn't fully realize what he was doing' and he was absolved: All Souls, Warden's MS 36, 22 Oct. 1781.

[2] The differences between the time fixed for elections to the various foundations at Worcester caused difficulty. In 1759 it was decided that standing in the university not date of election should be the criterion: WCA register, 8 May 1759.

[3] At St John's in 1714 a DD's claim to seniority over a DM was upheld by 8-2 and the DM acquiesced in the decision: SJM register 1712-30, p. 79, 26 and 31 Aug. 1714. In 1734 a fellow of St John's renounced the privileges and advantages which might accrue to him by his taking his BCL before another fellow took his MA: SJM register 1730-94, p. 41, 3 June 1734.

[4] TCA visitors letters 1576-1820, letters of 20 June 1713 and 3 June 1760.

[5] Following the intervention of a fellow in 1788 the rule had to be reinstated: ibid. 6 and 11 March, 23 June, 10 July 1788.

[6] *Journal of Stevens*, ed. Galbraith, p. 104 (17 Dec. 1796); G. Hirst-M. Routh, 20 Feb. 1797, Magdalen MS 478, fo 43; L. S. Sutherland, 'The curriculum', pp. 487-91 below.

fellows in law or medicine were formally exempt from the rule. But in practice, as the Trinity disputes have shown, many fellows evaded the rule on grounds of expense and almost certainly continued to find ways of doing so despite visitorial pronouncements.[1]

There was less reason, plainly enough, to escape from the obligation to take holy orders. But for those not intending to enter the church and not enjoying the exemption conferred by a faculty place, the incentive was less obvious; and on occasion they would cause a considerable rumpus. This was certainly true of All Souls where there was an unusually large number of lawyers and physicians. Warden Gardiner stood firm against the claims of certain of his fellows, including William Blencowe, an official 'decipherer of letters'. Despite pressure from the highest quarters, Gardiner refused to concede that such a post constituted a 'statutable lawful impediment' and won a notable, if melancholy, victory when Blencowe committed suicide in 1712.[2] But though the warden won considerable support from the university as a whole and though the government was deterred from implementing any plan for tampering with the rule concerning holy orders, his college remained obstinate. Against Gardiner's wishes (thus contravening their visitor's instructions of 1717 which enjoined unanimity), the fellows of All Souls continued to find reasons—royal or college service, for example—for granting dispensations.[3] Their circumstances, however, were exceptional and few colleges followed their lead.[4] Then, as now, All Souls was *sui generis*.

Of more general relevance was the need to conform to an elementary moral and social code. Naturally social misconduct might lead to expulsion or a year's probation; so too might serious misbehaviour, such as assaulting a fellow (and being taken by the proctor in a woman's company), calumny, drunkenness and profanity, or tampering with the bursarial accounts.[5] On at least one occasion heresy was cause for

[1] A list of fellows in 1768 showed 43 DDs, 50 BDs and 180 MAs: *An Authentic Copy of the Poll for Members to Serve in the Ensuing Parliament for the University of Oxford, taken March xxiii. MDCCC-LXVIII* (Oxford 1768).

[2] The episode can be followed in the Wake MSS and the college records. For a modern summary see Ward, *Georgian Oxford*, 34–5; also G. V. Bennett, 'The era of party zeal 1702–1714', p. 92 n. 2 above; G. V. Bennett, 'University, society and church 1688–1714', pp. 391–2 below. William Blencowe (1683–1712), m. Linc. 1697; demy Magd. 1697–1702; fellow All Souls 1702.

[3] There is a convenient history of the controversy in All Souls, Warden's MS 65, 'A Report on some of the Statutes ... Decr. 1837', fos 14–25. There are numerous other references scattered among the college records.

[4] Only two exceptions have been found, a student of medicine at Trinity and a librarian-fellow of Worcester: R. K. Pugh, 'Post-restoration bishops of Winchester as visitors of Oxford colleges', *Oxoniensia* xliii (1978), 182–3; WCA register, 30 Nov. 1797.

[5] For expulsion see ASA acta in capitulis, MS 401 (b), fo 20^{r-v} (22 Dec. 1752). See also the case of James Colmer at Exeter which sparked off a fierce struggle between the rector and the visitor: ECA register 1619–1737, 10 Oct. 1689, 27 Mar. 1690. For probation see WCM convention book III, pp. 65–6, 23 July 1752; for assault see SJM register 1730–94, p. 123, 13 July 1741, for calumny etc. see

removal, as seditious behaviour was too, at least when Bishop Trelawny, anxious to afford the government no pretext for intervention, came across it.[1]

Less problematical was the requirement that fellows should remain single. There could be no equivocation or 'interpretation' here, and if some men tried, as some did, to conceal wives and even children[2] they were expelled when discovered. Most fellows simply announced their marriage with a becoming display of pleasure mingled with sadness, and resigned.[3] Nor in most cases was there any uncertainty about the incompatibility of 'preferment' with a fellowship. Only lawyers and doctors had any claim to exemption. The Merton fellows allowed one of their number to practise medicine in Nottingham.[4] But such unqualified indulgence was most unusual. At All Souls only the jurist fellows had explicit permission to practise as well as to study law, and even they were unable to do so outside the precincts of the university.[5] It was not until 1757 that they were given leave to work in the court of the arches for seven years.[6] Artists had no such favour until Alexander Popham in 1760 won the right to keep his fellowship while pursuing a career at common law, and even then the visitor refused to make a general rule on the point, and Popham was elected steward to absolve him from the need to take holy orders (a subterfuge repeated in 1794).[7] Other colleges were not so insistent. A precedent of 1693 persuaded the future chief justice, Charles Abbott, to relinquish his probationary fellowship at Corpus exactly a century later on the grounds that he was a 'professional man'.[8] Such was the usual position. There was even a suggestion that a university professorship might not be compatible, though at length the claim was refuted.[9]

TCA register C, 1732, pp. 4 ff (Richard Hedges's case 1726); for tampering with the accounts see WCM convention book III, p. 26 (13 July 1738), p. 170 (30 June 1779).

[1] For a case of removal for heresy see Hearne-Wake, 11 April 1719, Wake MS 16, fo 115. On sedition see the correspondence in Wake MS 15 concerning Thomas Tooley; also SJM register 1712-30, pp. 306-10, 4 Feb. 1722 onward.

[2] QCA register K, 30 Dec. 1800. The same charge was made by Warden Wyntle of Merton against his enemy John Marten, the librarian, and others in the 1730s: MCR Wyntle's register, fo 90, 1737.

[3] 'Next to my own Father, I hold myself under the greatest Obligation in Nature to you. I have it not in my power to make you any return for all your Goodness.' 'I never thought of this Separation however partial it is between us, but with regret; Tho our Collegiate connexions are at an end, I have those of gratitude, friendship, and the highest esteem to attach me if possible more than ever to you.' J. W. Bourke's letters of resignation to the president, [2] Sept. [1799] and [5 Sept. 1799], CCCA B/14/5/1.

[4] MCR register 1567-1731, fo 797, 1 Aug. 1730.

[5] ASA acta in capitulis, MS 401 (c), 27 Nov. 1756.

[6] Ibid. Martin, *Catalogue* p. 323, no. 259, injunction of Archbishop Herring, 27 Jan. 1757.

[7] 'ASA acta in capitulis, MS 401 (c), 25 Feb. 1760; All Souls, Warden's MS 67, report on the statutes. Alexander Popham (*c*1729-1810), m. Balliol 1746; BA All Souls 1751, MA 1755.

[8] Abbot-president, 8 Aug. 1793, CCCA B/14/5/1. Charles Abbott (1762-1832), from 1827 1st Bn Tenterden; m. CCC 1781, fellow 1785, recorder of Oxford 1801; lord chief justice 1818-32.

[9] ASA acta in capitulis, MS 401 (b), fo 63, 26 Dec. 1720. For Blackstone's eligibility as sub-warden see All Souls, Warden's MS 36, Niblett's notebook, 27 Apr. 1759. This seems to have been an

Far more controversial, however, was the question of compatible livings and estates. Founders had designed their fellowships to provide a modest competence for future clergy during their period of study and training. A private income or succession to an endowed benefice made a college stipend unnecessary and thus forfeit; and figures were set defining such *uberiora beneficia*. The intention was simple enough but the passage of time, here as elsewhere, wreaked havoc with medieval arrangements. To take the more important question of livings first, founders had usually fixed ten marks or more (sometimes varying according to a fellow's status) as the highest permissible value. There was generally no problem if the benefice could be found in a contemporary *valor*, though the choice of *valor* (usually Pope Nicholas's of 1291 for earlier foundations and Henry VIII's 'King's Book' for later ones) sometimes caused difficulty and palpable evidence that the living had fallen on bad times might be taken into account.[1] If, however, there was no such contemporary valuation the difficulties began. In one or two cases the benefice was simply assumed to be compatible,[2] but most colleges properly felt obliged to establish whether it fell within some eighteenth-century equivalent of the statutable limit. Needless to say, fellows pestered their visitors, who decided questions of this kind, for higher and higher 'equivalents' as their stipends rose. Visitors, on the other hand, were keen to resist such pressures, fearing (as the bishop of Winchester told the New College fellows in 1711) that fellowships 'would become so desirable that there might be danger of your growing old upon them'.[3] The result was an uneven pattern which depended on the value of a college's fellowships and the attitude of its visitor. In the early part of the century, it is true, there was a little uniformity since the livings discharged by Queen Anne's commissioners from the payment of first-fruits and tenths as worth less than £50 yearly were deemed below the maximum. But though the figure was adopted at Merton (in 1711), All Souls (1719) and Oriel (1736), New College adhered to £80.[4] Later,

exceptional case; early in the century the fellows of Merton asked whether the professorship of physic was tenable with a fellowship merely in a rhetorical sense to urge a revaluation of their 'uberior' [*sic*] benefice: fellows-Wake, Wake MS 16, fos 203ff.

[1] Some fellows picked whichever *valor* suited them, but this was frowned upon: see All Souls, Warden's MS 35, orders of the warden and officers, 10 Feb. 1789, Scott's opinion. In 1758 Exeter's visitor decided that a living discharged from the payment of first-fruits and tenths by Queen Anne's commissioners as worth £50 p.a. or less was compatible with a fellowship even if it had been rated above the £8 statutory maximum in the King's Book: ECA register 1737-1824, pp. 100-1 (1 Nov. 1758).
[2] All Souls, Scott's opinion; BNCA tower drawer 128, visitor's injunction 1812.
[3] Letter of 29 Jan. 1771, NCA 9655, p. 111.
[4] Fellows of Merton-Wake, Wake MS 16, fos 203 ff; All Souls, Warden's MS 67, report on the statutes, fo 37; for fellows of Oriel see C. L. Shadwell, *Registrum orielense* (2 vols London 1893-1902) and G. C. Richards and C. L. Shadwell, *The Provosts and Fellows of Oriel College Oxford* (Oxford 1922). The visitor of New College fixed the figure at £80 in 1702 (NCA 9655, p. 109) and there it remained until the latter part of the century when it was raised to £120. Founder's kin were apparently allowed three times these figures: see Pugh, 'Bishops of Winchester as visitors', 174.

colleges went their separate ways, though Merton's figure of £80 in 1754 and Exeter's of £120 in 1804 may give a fair indication of the general trend.[1]

Establishing the 'equivalent' was one thing, valuing the benefice another. The findings of Queen Anne's commissioners were a useful, but by no means an infallible, guide. A discharged living was found in mid-century to be worth £180 yearly, that is above the £50 limit.[2] Individual assessment was essential. But what was to be included? Again there were rules. After the deduction of taxes and other burdens, said New College in 1728; 'tenths, synodals, and Procurations' excepted, declared Jesus College more specifically in 1743.[3] And if a fellow possessed two benefices? Then, remarkably enough, each benefice in turn was tested against the statutable limit.[4] If singly they were compatible, though collectively *uberiora*, they were not cause for resignation. Only benefices which were permanent or assured had to be compatible: those held in trust did not qualify.[5] And as for the definition of *beneficium*, there were still more rules. Chapels of ease were not so, nor were archdeaconries if worth no more than £80 yearly; but prebends, or at least some of them, were.[6] Brasenose made a distinction between vicarages and rectories: until 1812 the former were always considered incompatible, whatever their value.[7]

The question of private incomes or estates arose less often than livings, perhaps partly because they were easier to conceal. A man may hold anything provided he holds his tongue, was the contemporary saying.[8] When cases did occur they were treated in much the same way as benefices. The permissible limits were generally the same or slightly lower (at All Souls, for example, it was £40 not £50 in 1719) and were designed to be on a par with a fellow's stipend.[9] As with benefices, property was to be included only if it provided a permanent income—

---

[1] MCR register 1731-1822, pp. 177ff, 19 Dec. 1754; ECA register 1737-1824, p. 266, 22 Mar. 1804.

[2] JCA box 4, folder 3, letters 1700-1800, no. 42, 7 Aug. 1769, 'Opinion of Mr Blackstone re: holding of Fellowship and Living'.

[3] NCA 3527, 20 Dec. 1728, JCA box 4, folder 3, letters 1700-1800, no. 12, 16 June 1743.

[4] *The Conduct of the Right Reverend The Lord Bishop of Winchester, as Visitor of St Mary Magdalen College Oxford* (London 1770).

[5] Bray at Exeter took what appears to have been unscrupulous advantage of this rule: ECA register 1737-1824, pp. 54 ff, 1748. The injunction was repeated in 1802: ibid. p. 259, 30 June 1802. A similar decision was made at Merton in 1792 (MCR register 1731-1822, pp. 405-7, April 1792) but it was later rescinded.

[6] LCM register 1739-1983, 7 Oct. 1791 (chapels of ease); MCR register 1731-1822, pp. 349 ff, 24 June 1783 (archdeaconries); LC register 1739-1983, 18 Oct. 1746, Dr J. Andrews's opinion relating to avoidances, and MCR register 1731-1882, loc. cit. (prebends).

[7] Principal-visitor and visitor's reply, 1812, BNCA tower drawer 128, compatibility of holding fellowships with livings.

[8] *Journal of Stevens*, ed. Galbraith, p. 167 (19 July 1794). Gilbert White (1720-93, m. Oriel 1739, fellow 1746) was said to have followed the maxim: A. Clark, *The Colleges of Oxford* (London 1891), 121.

[9] All Souls, Warden's MS 67, report on the statutes, fo 37; QCA register K, 19 May 1804.

thus excluding estates in money and leases—and after deducting any *onera*.[1] Calculations were to be based on the real or improved value.[2]

Resignations of fellowships could be caused by any one of the reasons outlined earlier, but most were the result of marriage or preferment (the former, it need hardly be added, depending often on the latter). A large majority of Oxford fellows, it may confidently be stated, went into the church;[3] and, as they had hoped, many found preferment through their college, though the extent of this should not be overestimated. When the mortmain bill was under discussion in parliament the colleges produced information to show that there was no need to limit their patronage.[4] In the thirty years preceding 1735 Exeter had preferred only 3 of its 66 outgoing fellows; Jesus 13 out of 44; Magdalen 22 out of 86; Merton 9 out of 45; Oriel 4 out of 40; and so on. For a total university fellowship of 530 (including the Students of Christ Church) there were only 290 college livings, of which 92 were worth less than £50 and thus likely to be compatible with a fellowship. The act itself (1736), though taking account of these revelations, prevented colleges from acquiring advowsons equal to more than half the number of their fellowships. This remained the position from 1736 to 1805. Fellows were well advised not to wait for college preferment. Little wonder the Corpus fellow mentioned above asked for leave of absence to cultivate his prospects of promotion.[5]

There was no typical length of tenure for college fellows.[6] A comfortable and compatible living or curacy, together with an indisposition to get married, might persuade a fellow to stay for twenty years or more until as senior fellow he was able to pluck the right plum. Once he had decided on a living he was generally given a year of grace starting from the date of his institution, during which time he continued to hold and enjoy the emoluments of his fellowship and might opt for any other college living which came vacant (though without any extension of his period of grace).[7] If he declined, his juniors by turn were

---

[1] For the inclusion of permanent income only see LCM register 1739-1983, 18 Oct. 1746, opinions relating to avoidances etc. For the deduction of *onera* see All Souls, Warden's MS 24 (nd), pp. 233-7. According to a commentator at All Souls the exclusion of estates in money and leases was the view of the university and several other colleges, though he concluded in the case of his own college that all sorts of estates were to be valued: ibid.

[2] All Souls, Warden's MS 24, pp. 233-7.

[3] See Bennett, 'University, society and church'.

[4] Martin, *Catalogue*, p. 364, appeals and injunctions, nos. 509-24.

[5] Cooke-W. King, draft 15 May 1783, CCCA B/14/5/1; p. 240 above.

[6] Figures compiled for a number of colleges show no regular pattern. However it is worth recalling that Wadham's fellows were restricted by statute to 18 years after taking regency and this was certainly still being observed in the eighteenth century.

[7] He might alternatively be allowed 18 months from the death of the incumbent: JCA box 5, misc. papers relating to appeals, 21 May 1750. This rule was said to be followed in at least one other college. For the option of taking another living see UCA register 1729-1842, fo 91ᵛ, 28 June 1777.

given the chance to accept.[1] Resignation after acceptance entailed for-
feiture of the right of first option on subsequent vacancies.[2] This was
unusual, however, and most fellows made sure of their prize before
accepting.[3] Once safely ensconced in their rectory or stall, fellows
severed links with their college, except that those living within reasonable travelling distance kept themselves (or were persuaded to keep
themselves) 'on the books' for voting purposes.[4]

As the preceding section has shown, major college decisions, such as the
election of fellows and officers or the fixing and sealing of property fines,
were taken by the entire fellowship or at least a certain number of
'senior' fellows as defined by statute. Regular meetings of this kind would
be held once or twice a year on fixed dates, with the occasional addition
of extraordinary meetings to which non-residents would be specially
summoned.[5]

   Day-to-day decisions, however, were the concern of the officers—the
vice-principal, bursars and deans—chosen each year. The posts were
chores to be shared around not niches to be monopolized. In only a few
colleges (Brasenose and Trinity for example) were offices confined to the
seniors;[6] in most they were open to the fellowship as a whole. Usually
some kind of rota was observed, with fellows taking their turns in a fixed
succession of offices,[7] but there may well have been a certain amount of
picking and choosing in cases of inconvenience. It was certainly necessary to serve a full year before one could go on to the next offices as a
fellow of Magdalen discovered in 1773.[8] To what extent fellows did not
actually serve in person in the offices to which they were elected is hard
to tell. Substitution was certainly forbidden at New College from 1701
and makes no appearance at Trinity; yet at All Souls and (much more

---

[1] For example NCA 3527, 13 July 1786.

[2] For example LCM register 1739-1983, 6 May 1784.

[3] A BNC fellow of Brasenose in the 1690s refused to resign his fellowship on the grounds that the
living to which he had been presented was 'litigious': BNCA tower drawer 129, 'papers relating to
Mr Blackburn delaying to resign his fellowship 1697'.

[4] The president of Corpus wrote to J. W. Bourke that he would not remove his name from the
'bye books' (as Corpus called them) in case he wished to continue 'for the purpose of preserving
your Vote in Convocation'. Bourke replied that for so trifling a sum (20s p.a.) he would keep his
name on in the hope that he would 'have it in my power to offer you my vote on any occasion for any
friend of yours, as a small tribute of my gratitude': letters of 4 and 5 Sept. 1799, CCCA B/14/5/1.

[5] See A. Homer-Routh, 19 May 1800, concerning a special meeting, Magdalen MS 479, fo 44.

[6] This was so at Trinity, at least between 1717 and 1726: see p. 241 above.

[7] See the letters between C. Barton and President Cooke of Corpus in 1797: CCCA B/14/5/1.
The evidence from Magdalen conflicts. A fellow in 1796 understood that the office of dean of
divinity would devolve on him at the next election 'according to the order of seniority' but another
fellow had 'an indistinct idea' that the offices of vice-principal, dean of divinity and bursar came in
no set order: W. Alcock-Routh, 26 Jan. 1796, Magdalen MS 477, fo 49; G. Hirst-same, 27 Oct. 1795,
MS 478, fo 41.

[8] Bloxam, *Reg. Magdalen* vi. 300ff (case of Richard Chandler).

casually) at Magdalen even the bursarship might be served by deputies in the late 1790s.[1]

However, the All Souls arrangements notwithstanding, it is probable that for the most part bursars and deans had to serve in person, while it was possible, as the example of William Bagshaw Stevens indicates, to get one's lecturing duties performed by deputy. Similar conclusions can be made about residence. Attendance at least during term-time (which was how one visitor defined residence) was required of all officers in certain colleges[2] and of one dean and one bursar in all others. A fellow of Corpus, faced with a succession of offices and wondering whether to retain a distant living, was told by President Cooke in the 1790s that he would need to be present to discharge his duties as junior dean and senior bursar but would probably find the other offices compatible with his benefice.[3] Most of the senior officers of Balliol certainly seem to have been resident for much of the year.[4]

Service was theoretically for one year only, but a resident fellow, with no preferment to attract him away from Oxford, might well be persuaded to take on an office, and the emoluments that went with it, for a second time, either in his own right or as deputy for someone else.[5] He might also combine one of the onerous deanships or bursarships with one of the less demanding of offices (such as a lectureship). The Balliol evidence at least points to the existence of a small caucus of resident fellows swapping the offices from one to another.

Perquisites varied from office to office. There was generally a small statutable stipend with a set of fees directly or indirectly imposed on the undergaduates. During the century, however, colleges began to collect the fees for themselves (domus) and pay salaries instead. A wholesale change of this kind was effected at Wadham in 1767[6] and there were piecemeal changes elsewhere. There were also some less obvious advantages: Stevens at Magdalen in 1795 took the lectureship in moral philosophy because it enabled him to hold a living rated at twenty marks a year without a doctor's degree and excused him from the office of dean without excluding him from the evidently more lucrative bursarship.[7]

[1] At New College the 'warden and 13' ordered that in 'All elections of All Officers for the future, No substitution shall be Allowed': NCA 1092, 4 July 1701. On All Souls see G. Faber, *Notes on the History of the All Souls Bursarships and the College Agency* (np [1950]), 18-19; for Magdalen see the letters of Homer to Routh in Magdalen MS 479.
[2] See p. 241 above.
[3] Cooke-Barton, 9 Oct. 1797, CCCA B/14/5/1.
[4] During the Wyntle fracas at Merton it was claimed that a bursar had been absent for almost the entire year of his office, but the evidence is obviously suspect: H. Hall-J. Parsons, 1 Dec. 1744, MCR E.I. 30a, misc. papers 1738-90.
[5] OCA ETC/A/1.
[6] WCM convention book III, pp. 103-4, 17 July 1767.
[7] *Journal of Stevens*, ed. Galbraith, pp. 259-61.

The most senior of the college officers in formal terms was the deputy head of house, but the post was not quite as important as it sounded. The vice-principal or sub-warden, it is true, presided over college meetings when the head was away and supervised the election of a new head, but for most of the time his duties were much more humdrum. At St John's for instance he allocated the rooms, while at Brasenose he was in charge of divine service and of securing the attendance of under-graduates there.[1] The perquisites were correspondingly uninspiring: at both Brasenose and Magdalen the office is known to have been ill-remunerated.[2] The patronage accorded to the sub-dean of Christ Church—the right to nominate the canons' butler—was unusual.[3] The post was in no way a stepping-stone to the headship; it was simply part of the *cursus honorum* or *laborum*, to be avoided if at all possible. Magdalen, for example, experienced considerable difficulty in filling its vice-presidency.[4]

Each college possessed at least two bursars, senior and junior. There might also be an itinerant or 'riding' bursar. But usually the work was carried out by only one of the nominal bursars; the other posts appear to have been sinecures.[5] Then, as now, the bursar was responsible for the college's finances, both internal and external. Domestic housekeeping was more time-consuming than difficult, but estate-management required a certain degree of expertise and bursars were often given the assistance of a retained lawyer, sometimes a fellow and sometimes not.[6] There was, however, no separate 'estates' bursar concerned only with the college's property.

A bursar's duties can readily be ascertained from William Blackstone's long and open 'letter' of 1753 introducing his All Souls friend Benjamin Buckler to the mysteries of his new office.[7] The system was immensely intricate, bearing all the hallmarks of the medieval foundation, and much of the bursar's time must have been spent conforming to the obsolete rules. It was medieval too in the sense that bursars, like county sheriffs and borough chamberlains, were personally responsible for the monies they collected and disbursed. They gave substantial bonds for the honest performance of their duties and were only released when their accounts had been settled.[8] They were equally liable for the actions of their

[1] SJM Acc.V.H.I, vice-president's book of rooms 1772-1861; Jeffery, 'History', 41 (Brasenose).
[2] Jeffery, 61; Homer-president, 21 Jan. 1798, Magdalen MS 479, fo 41.
[3] CA chapter book 1776-99, p. 529, 16 Nov. 1787.
[4] See Homer's letters at Magdalen; also Hirst-president, 27 Oct. 1795, Magdalen MS 478, fo 41.
[5] For example the junior bursar at Balliol: BCA register 1794-1875, pp. 10 ff (21 Oct. 1799).
[6] For the retention of a fellow see NCA 3527, 14 Dec. 1775. For non-fellows see MCR register 1731-1832, p. 253, 14 Sept. 1767; SJM register 1730-94, p. 388, 27 Dec. 1766.
[7] Blackstone, *Dissertation on the Accounts*.
[8] PCA convention book 2/1/3, 20 Oct. 1772. The practice was started in Wadham in 1739: WCM convention book III, pp. 29-30, 6 Dec. 1739.

deputies. If an undergraduate ran up a bad debt which could not be recovered from his deposit or 'caution' money, then the bursar had to make good the deficiency;[1] and if a fellow was lent money by the bursar this was deemed a purely personal transaction for which too the bursar was responsible.[2] If the accounts were not settled in a reasonable time the college might be obliged to take the matter to law.[3] Sequestration of a fellowship was the ultimate sanction, but doubtless in practice compromises were generally possible.[4]

A bursar's perquisites were quite substantial: poundage (at varying rates in the pound) on the bills paid for various supplies, fees for the signing and renewal of leases, allowances for the administration of separate trust funds, and so on.[5] All these were in addition to the statutable stipend, which itself was usually larger than the others. Commutations of all or some of the bursar's fees were made at a number of colleges throughout the period: St John's in 1717, Queen's in 1755, 1769 and 1774 and at All Souls in about 1760.[6] When Wadham did likewise in 1767 it agreed that the taking of fees led to over-charging which the bursars were naturally disinclined to restrain.[7] Total pay is hard to assess: by 1777 Wadham's senior and junior bursars were receiving £22 and £25 over and above their statutable annual stipends of £20 and no more; while at Exeter in the 1790s the bursarship was worth about £35 yearly.[8] But the picture elsewhere is unclear.

Most bursars had assistance from the 'steward of the kitchen' who supervised the purchase and allocation of food by the manciple and cook and also kept an account of the residence and attendance of fellows and

---

[1] This was clearly an established principle at University College and started at Wadham in 1720: UCA bursar's general account c1706-39; WCM convention book III, p. 22, 6 Dec. 1720.

[2] Blackstone, *Dissertation*, 34-5; All Souls, Warden's MS 35, orders of the warden and officers, 22 Dec. 1770.

[3] 'Dr Jackson be call'd upon to Discharge the Money due upon Bond to the College, or to give such farther Security, as shall be satisfactory to the Society ... otherwise ... the Society shall proceed to take such Methods as the Law directs for the Recovery of the Same': QCA register K, 28 June 1750. The threat was realized at Wadham in the mid-forties: WCM convention book III, p. 44, 25 Mar. 1746.

[4] For sequestration see WCM convention book III, p. 28, 27 Mar. 1739. Speke compounded at Wadham in 1746 for part of the money due and all the legal costs: ibid. p. 44 (25 Mar. 1746), pp. 170-1 (30 June 1779). University College was willing to split the difference with William Denison (m. Univ. 1693; principal Magd. Hall 1745-55) for his bursar's debts: UCA early eighteenth-century accounts.

[5] For poundage of 15d in the pound from the brewers and 2s 8d from the bakers see BNCA tower drawer 129, Thomas Beconsall 1688; for leases see NCA 993, 30 Mar. 1678; for trust-funds see QCA register K, 13 Jan. 1797.

[6] It was 'order'd that the Bursars shall have Twenty pounds in Lieu of poundage from the Brewers, for the Time to come': SJM register 1712-30, p. 180, 26 Feb. 1717; QCA register K, 16 Aug. 1755, 3 Nov. 1769, 15 July 1774; Blackstone, *Dissertation*, 28n.

[7] WCM convention book III, pp. 103-4, 17 July 1767.

[8] Ibid., pp. 153-4, 17 July 1767, 6 Dec. 1777; ECA headship accounts, Mar. 1793 (£34 17s 8d), Mar. 1794 (£35 15s 0d).

undergraduates. The post rotated weekly among the fellows.[1] The activities of both bursars and stewards were scrutinized at least yearly by other fellows acting as auditors or 'accountants'.

Deans usually came in pairs or trios: a senior and junior dean, or deans of arts, law and divinity.·But again it is possible that, like bursars, only one was resident and operative. At New College, it is true, an undergraduate was told to submit his penal collection to the 'dean of his faculty', but the large number of resident junior fellows there may make this an exceptional instance.[2] At Magdalen, by contrast, the office of dean of divinity was virtually a sinecure.[3] Like their modern counterparts deans were in charge of discipline, and dealt with both the regular concerns of gate-hours and meal-attendance as well as the irregular cases of misbehaviour.[4] Serious problems, of course, would be taken to the head of the college[5] and perhaps also the senior fellows. Deans also acquired other duties either in the chapel or library.[6] Emoluments included the usual mixed bag of fees from undergraduates, particularly for presentation to degrees.[7] But the total may well not have been a considerable one. Certainly when the changes in library regulations increased the work of Balliol's dean it was thought necessary not only to introduce a composition salary of £16 per annum in lieu of fees but also to urge that future deans be automatically elected to the 'sinecure junior bursarship' and to the office of registrar.[8]

Every college appointed a number of lecturers each year in such subjects as Greek, logic, mathematics, philosophy and theology, as well as a moderator who presided over disputations (though the distinction between a lecturer and moderator was sometimes unclear).[9] These were the regular teaching posts laid down in the statutes or established by subsequent benefactions and to them only fellows could be elected; but it should be added that some colleges made a habit of hiring outsiders to teach foreign languages, while in others BAs helped with the instruction of undergraduates.[10]

[1] CCCA B/4/3/3, orders entered in loose papers, 4 May 1739; NCA 940, 20 Dec. 1766.

[2] NCA 961, 1 July 1773.

[3] Alcock-Routh, 26 Jan. 1796, Magdalen MS 477, fo 49; Hirst-same, MS 478, fo 41.

[4] Bloxam, *Reg. Magdalen* ii, p. clxxxvi (21 Feb. 1788); for hours and attendance see Queen's MS 475, fos 68-9; and for misbehaviour see president-Mr Bond, 14 Jan. (draft) and Mrs Bond-president, 17 Jan. 1798, CCCA B/14/5/1.

[5] CCCA B/4/1/1, acts and proceedings, p. 11, 29 Sept· and 9 Oct. 1749.

[6] For the chapel see Bloxam, *Reg. Magdalen* ii, pp. clxxx-ii; TCA liber decani I, 19 Nov. 1778; CCCA B/4/1/2, 29 Jan. 1806. For the library see BCA register 1794-1875, pp. 10 ff, 21 Oct. 1799; and see also the dean's books for the period.

[7] TCA liber decani I, 14 Feb. 1788; ECA headship accounts 1791, 1792.

[8] BCA register 1794-1875, pp. 10 ff, 21 Oct. 1799.

[9] University College's new statutes of 1736 provided for lecturers as well as moderators presiding over disputations: UCA statutes of 1736, title VIII, section v.

[10] At Merton 21*s* per quarter was to be paid to Fabre MA to teach French: MCR register

Lectureships were regarded quite differently from bursarships or deanships. Some fellows welcomed the chance to earn more money, especially if they were resident or could appoint a deputy in case of absence. Hence a tendency for senior resident fellows to retain the same office for a number of years.[1] How demanding were the duties is hard to say, though the practice of combining lectureships in different subjects is perhaps a tell-tale sign which lends significance to Warden Wyntle's allegation of neglect at Merton in the 1730s[2] and to William Bagshaw Stevens's distinctly casual performance of his lecturing duties at Magdalen in the 1790s. Moderators, by contrast, appear to have been junior fellows dragged into duties which the other fellows were keen to avoid.[3]

The bulk of lecturers' pay came from undergraduate fees, which heavily supplemented the basic stipends.[4] New College in 1765, through the efforts of Warden Hayward, introduced salaries in lieu of all fees. Calculations made on that occasion show just how much the lecturers were earning: mathematics (combined with the natural philosophy lectureship) £49 10s 0d; logic (combined with the catechetical lectureship) £55 3s 4d; Greek £9 0s 10d; moderator £8 7s 6d.[5]

Tutorships were not part of the statutory set of elective offices, but were unofficial posts personally granted to senior fellows by heads of colleges.[6] The college or public tutor—quite distinct from the private tutor-governors or student-companions some wealthy undergraduates had at college[7]—was a most important figure and could make or mar a college's reputation. Thomas Burgess won Corpus a great name in the 1780s.[8]

Tutors acquired their pupils either through personal contacts or the recommendation of the head of house. If there was more than one tutor in a college the work and the fees were sometimes, but not always,

1731-1822, p. 28, 1735. Isaac Abendana was paid £2 p.a. 1691-8 for teaching Hebrew at Magdalen: Macray, *Reg. Magdalen* iv. 48. For teaching by BAs see MCR 4.21, Warden Holland's register, 26 May 1714.

[1] The office of catechist at University College was usually taken by the senior resident fellow: UCA early eighteenth-century accounts.

[2] MCR Wyntle's register, fo 184.

[3] 'The Office of Moderator is declin'd by All': OCA ETC/A/1, provost's observations on neglect of the college chaplain, 2 Oct. 1750. WCM convention book III, p. 144, 6 Dec. 1776.

[4] MCR register 1567-1731, p. 735, 12 Nov. 1718; CCCA B/4/1/1, 23 Dec. 1748; WCM convention book III, p. 21 (6 Dec. 1735), p. 48 (6 Dec. 1746).

[5] NCA 940 (20 Dec. 1765), 237 (20 Dec. 1765).

[6] See also p. 231 above.

[7] For tutor-governors see Jeffery, 'History', 49 (Brasenose); CCCA B/4/1/1, 17 June 1703. For student-companions see Cooke-Mrs Wyndham, draft reply 28 Apr. 1789, CCCA B/14/5/1.

[8] J. Lewis-Cooke, 19 Oct. and draft reply 23 Oct. 1786, CCCA B/14/5/1; 'Mr Justice Buller'-'Dr Bathurst at Ch.Ch.', 6 June 1785, ibid. Thomas Burgess (1757-1837), m. CCC 1775; bp of St David's 1803, Salisbury 1825-37.

shared out in partnerships; or individual tutors might also choose to delegate some of their duties to sub-tutors or assistants.[1] One of Burgess's successors at Corpus was allowed to pay for another fellow to do the mathematical teaching, an arrangement that lasted some while.[2]

Tutors not only provided academic instruction for their pupils, they also acted as moral guardians. A tutor might take responsibility for an undergraduate's finances, both at the outset and during the course of his Oxford career; he would arrange for rooms to be available and help fit them out; and without his permission an undergraduate could not hope to obtain privileges and exemptions.[3]

At few colleges did tutors receive a fixed salary: the exceptions were New College, where two of the three tutors received £12 10s a term and the other £7 10s (with the customary increases in the 1790s) and Corpus where the mathematics tutor was virtually guaranteed £40 (later £50) per annum.[4] Elsewhere tutors depended on fees which were paid to them almost invariably at a fixed rate, either directly or increasingly via battels.[5] Totals depended on the number and status of the undergraduates, and estimating typical figures is impossible. All that can be said is that by the end of the century £100 yearly was a minimum, £200 quite common and over £300 not unknown.[6]

Librarian was probably the least important of the regular college posts. It often seems to have been regarded as an appendage to other more senior posts, such as senior dean at Balliol, bursar at Lincoln and

[1] Fellows were in tutorial partnership at Exeter 1770-84: ECA C.II.21. At University College and at Jesus the tutors worked both together and separately: UCA tutor's books 1736-98; Bodl. MS DD Jesus College, b.104-6. The provost of Queen's advised George Fothergill not to set up 'for a Head Tutor' but content himself with working under one: letter of 15 Mar. 1731, Queen's MS 473. See also G. L. Cooke–president, 26 Oct. 1815, CCCA B/6/1/1, resignations of fellowships 1783-1822.

[2] CCCA B/4/1/2, 10 Oct. 1799, 29 Jan. 1806.

[3] On finances see T. Patten-Cooke, 8 Oct. 1783 and draft reply [14 Oct.], CCCA B/14/5/1; letters of Erasmus Head, Bodl. MS Don. c. 152; *The Flemings in Oxford*. On rooms see Patten-Cooke, 8 Oct. 1783. If gentlemen-commoners and other undergraduates go out of town 'without Tutor's Privity and Consent . . . they shall be Sconc'd *Six Pence per Diem* 'till their return': Queen's MS 475, fos 68-9. At Trinity no undergraduate was allowed to give a dinner or supper unless permission was granted by the tutor: TCA liber decani I, 9 Apr. 1789.

[4] NCA battel books 1793. In 1793 the classical tutor was allowed £20 in addition to his salary and in 1797 £10: NCA 961. CCCA B/4/1/1, 10 Oct. 1799, 29 Jan. 1806.

[5] For fixed rates see BCA register 1782-1916, 29 Nov. 1800; CCCA B/4/3/3, 29 Jan. 1806; MCR register 1731-1822, p. 457, 27 Nov. 1800; LCM register 1739-1983, fo 12ᵛ, 26 Jan. 1748. But elsewhere, at Christ Church in particular, fees were a matter for private negotiation. Lady Gowran decided to determine the tutor's allowance herself—about 40 guineas per annum: T. Croft-Provost Smith, [8] May 1735, Queen's MS 482, fo 187. For direct payment see J. Borrett-Mr Marshall, 3 Nov. 1731, ibid. fo 174. For payment via battels see PCA convention book 2/1/1, p. 21, 2 July 1731: 'Agreed that the Tuition Money Due from every Under-Graduate should be Added to the Charge of his Battells at the End of every Quarter.' See also TCA register A.48, 9 Nov. 1780.

[6] These figures are taken from BCA payments to tutors 1772-3; Bodl. MS Top. Oxon. e. 124/14, pp. 34 ff; MCR D.2.19, tutor's book 1784-1800; JCA tutorage books 1682-1827, Bodl. MS DD Jesus College, b. 104-6.

vice-president at Trinity.[1] If it was attractive at all it was because of certain indirect privileges. At Worcester, for example, the librarian was dispensed from taking holy orders, while at Christ Church he could hold a benefice provided it was not in the gift of the college.[2]

It remains only to mention fellows' duties in chapel. Apart from such general supervisory powers over divine service as the vice-principal of Brasenose possessed, all fellows in holy orders—at least those in residence—were obliged to take weekly turns at reading in chapel.[3] Fees or 'priest money' were available for those who did so.[4] Securing the proper discharge of such duties was fairly difficult. In 1789 Lincoln's fellows had to be reminded that they would be fined for neglecting their turns, while at Corpus in 1806 it was decided that the junior dean should receive some money for undertaking the chapel-readings himself—perhaps no more than a regularization of what had become standard practice.[5]

College administration depended not only on the small nucleus of annually elected officers but also on the large contingent of permanent servants, ranging from butlers to bedmakers, cooks to platewashers. Some were chosen by the officers, others by the head of house.[6] There was an understandable tendency to appoint people already employed by the college, and men would either move from job to job or hold more than one post at a time.[7] As for pay, servants too had their multifarious perquisites commuted for fixed payments during the course of the century. There was a general change of the kind at Merton in 1791.[8]

The manciple was arguably the most senior servant. It was he who bought the food and charged for it, checked what each person ate, and either received the money himself or told the bursar what to put on

---

[1] BCA register 1794-1875, pp. 10 ff. Although the dean was officially librarian and kept the accounts, much of the actual work was done by others: J. Jones, 'Eighteenth-century Balliol', *Balliol College Annual Record* (1980), 61-3. LCM register 1739-1983, fo 1, 6 Nov. 1739; TCA liber decani I, 20 Dec. 1763.

[2] See p. 243 n. 4 above; CA chapter book 1754-80, p. 285 (3 July 1775), chapter book 1776-99, p. 390 (28 Oct. 1778). Laymen would be given a faculty place while they held the office.

[3] See p. 250 above; LCM register 1577-1739, fo 239, 12 June 1699; TCA liber decani I, 17 July 1758.

[4] NCA 3527, 22 Dec. 1735.

[5] LCM register 1739-1983, fo 83, 6 July 1789; CCCA B/14/1/1, 29 Jan. 1806.

[6] SJM LXII.65. At Queen's the provost had the right to appoint the butler and estate officers while at Christ Church the dean could appoint most *inferiores ministri*: Queen's MS 456, Provost Smith's farewell address to the society; CA chapter book 1776-99, p. 529, 16 Nov. 1787.

[7] At Corpus the underporter and chapelman was also the letter-carrier, while at Exeter the underporter was book-keeper and waiter on high table. Plural duties proved too much for the manciple of Wadham. CCCA B/4/1/2, 15 Feb. 1790; ECA register 1737-1824, p. 187, 26 Mar. 1790; WCM convention book III, p. 171, 30 June 1779.

[8] MCR register 1731-1822, p. 399, 20 July 1791.

battels.[1] In return he received the usual miscellaneous fees, later a salary, which totalled £60 or more by the end of the century.[2]

The butler's main task was to keep daily account of the college's domestic finances, entering battel charges in the buttery books against each resident's name and informing the bursar when battels exceeded cautions.[3] He might also have the duty, or profitable privilege, of supplying the college with certain basic provisions, such as beer and bread.[4] All this necessarily entailed some duplication with the manciple's work; and indeed at All Souls and for a time at St John's the two offices were merged.[5] Various other jobs were likely to devolve on the butler or his underbutler—for a price. The canon's butler at Christ Church, for example, looked after the noblemen's and gentlemen-commoners' tables in hall, the chapter house and lecture-rooms. This meant cleaning the cutlery, scouring the pewter, mending the linen and lighting the fires, as well as gathering the necessary supplies. He also had responsibility for room-rents.[6] Fees from the fellows and undergraduates, together with such perquisites as the surplus food, waste drink and profit on the allowances for provisions, amounted to nearly £60 at Merton in 1790 and over £100 at Christ Church in the 1780s.[7] Where salaries were paid Merton seems to have been closer to the norm than Christ Church.[8]

If the butler's duties overlapped with the manciple's, so too did the cook's. Provisions seem to have been generally the manciple's concern, but there are some indications that the cook too had a hand in buying and pricing the food. He certainly had the right to supply his kitchen with certain commodities: at Christ Church it was salt, at Wadham meat.[9] Merton's cook made around £70 in 1790 from the usual gamut of fees and profits.[10] The salaries introduced for the senior and

[1] NCA 1092, 1674, orders concerning the serving of commons out of the kitchen to the hall; LCM register 1577-1739, fo 292ᵛ, 28 Feb. 1725; WCM convention book III, p. 123, 16 Dec. 1773; CA chapter book 1776-99, p. 424 (8 July 1780), p. 583 (26 June 1790); NCA 961, 29 June 1769.

[2] TCA register A.48 17 Dec. 1781, 19 Nov. 1805.

[3] BCA register 1682-1781, fo 96 (nd); SJM register 1712-30, p. 560, 5 Oct. 1728.

[4] The two underbutlers at New College were granted the right to 'farm the Cellar' paying '30s for every Bar of Ale and 10 for Small': NCA 3527, 3 Apr. 1730.

[5] Blackstone, *Dissertation*, 4; SJM register 1730-94, p. 240 (28 Sept. 1751), p. 278 (16 Nov. 1756).

[6] CA liii.b.4, subdean's book, reverse of book; chapter book 1776-99, p. 333, 14 Dec. 1776.

[7] Surplus food was worth £40-50 p.a. for the canon's butler at Christ Church in the 1780s: subdean's book, reverse. For waste drink see NCA 993, 30 Mar. 1678. At All Souls the servants provided all save the beer and bread, and it is hard to believe that their takings or *allocationes super nomen* did not include a profit or 'cut' of some kind: Blackstone, 5. See also MCR misc. papers 1738-90, 1 Sept. 1790; CA subdean's book, reverse (the clear profit was calculated at £129 from which £20 was thereafter to be paid to the widow of the late canon's butler).

[8] QCA register K, 6 May 1756 (£40), about 15 July 1774 (£45); TCA register A.48, 19 Nov. 1805 (£60); All Souls Warden's MS 35, orders of the warden and officers, 23 Dec. 1797 (£30 plus £10 allowed 'for brewing').

[9] CA chapter book 1689-1713, fo 117, 24 Dec. 1708; WCM convention book III, pp. 118-19, 16 Dec. 1773.　　　　　　[10] MCR misc. papers, 1 Sept. 1790.

junior cooks at Trinity in 1775, after revision, were of much the same order.[1]

The porter had strict instructions to lock the gates of the college at a certain hour every evening. Before doing so he would make a tour of the chambers reminding people of the time.[2] Those who troubled him after that time, on their way out or in, would be reported to the dean or head of house.[3] Each morning the porter would wake the college and assist at chapel. He might also fetch and carry letters and messages, wait at high table, or even clean shoes.[4] He was usually paid by fees, but if by salary then the money was taken from latecomers' fines.[5]

Minor servants included gardeners, grooms, bedmakers (sometimes also called scouts), laundresses, hairdressers, shoecleaners and lamplighters. Two things only need be mentioned about them. The first is that their numbers increased towards the end of the century as the undergraduate-servitors who had formerly performed such menial tasks faded from the scene; secondly, many of the lesser servants were effectively employed not by the college but by its members, particularly the wealthy undergraduates. The college might fix certain minimum rates of pay and exercise a general supervision, but the money was paid directly from members to their servants and there was plainly scope for private and personal arrangements.[6]

Colleges' domestic administration revolved around three main concerns: finance, food and accommodation. Each deserves some attention here.

A college's finances, it will already have become apparent, centred on fees and dues. Fairly or otherwise, it was not the corporate estate but individual members who met the day-to-day expenses.[7] At the beginning of the period many payments were still made direct to the officers and servants concerned, but there was a growing tendency for the college to act as intermediary. At Corpus, for example, after 1787 tuition fees as well as room-rents were paid in the first instance to the bursar.[8]

[1] TCA register A.48, 18 Dec. 1775, 21 Dec. 1778, 9 and 19 Nov. 1779, 19 Nov. 1805.

[2] NCA 1092, 29 Oct. 1702.

[3] Queen's MS 475, fos 68-9; MCR Wyntle's register, fo 163; CA chapter book 1754-80, p. 226, 27 May 1772.

[4] NCA 993 (30 Mar. 1678), 3527 (22 Dec. 1735); TCA register A.48, 22 May 1780; TCA liber decani I, 19 Nov. 1778; NCA 3527, 22 Dec. 1735; CA chapter book 1776-99, p. 332, 19 Nov. 1776; BCA register 1682-1781, fo 96 (nd); Magrath, *Queen's* ii. 139; PCA convention book 2/1/1, p. 10, 6 Aug. 1776.

[5] CA chapter book 1754-80, p. 226, 27 May 1772.

[6] 'The Gardiner is to receive a Salary of £24 exclusive of the commons allow'd by the College ... to receive the profits of the Bowling Green but to defray the expences of Mowing the Green and keeping it in proper order, to receive 3d from each Gentleman for Greenage.' NCA 940, 21 Dec. 1764.

[7] Thomas Beconsall thought the practice unstatutable: BNCA tower drawer 129, 1688.

[8] 'Our College having Very lately established the Rule of Charging *Tuition* as well as Room-rent in

Battels therefore became more and more important and much bursarial time was spent trying to secure their speedy payment.

It was the undergraduates, of course, who presented the greatest risk. Bursars could always retrieve the debts of defaulting fellows by stopping all or a good part of their stipends,[1] but they had no such hold over junior members. Another form of security was required. Some colleges, such as Queen's and Wadham, retained for a time the old system of sponsors or signatories, persons who stood security for undergraduates' debts.[2] But by the end of the century most, if not all, exacted cautions or deposits instead.

Every undergraduate admitted to the college, as well as those who left their names on the books for voting purposes at their departure, were required to deposit a sum to cover bad debts. Bursars did their best to ensure that young men did not 'battel out their cautions'. As we have seen, their inattention could cost them dearly.

Not surprisingly strict rules governed battels. There were limits to the bills each undergraduate could run up against his name and limits to the time within which battels had to be paid.[3] The penalties for disobedience were severe: halting all further credit (known as 'stopping' or 'putting a cross' by the name in the books), refusing leave to go out of town, preventing a man from 'keeping' his terms, and denying testimonials or graces for degrees.[4] None the less, despite all these sanctions, bad debts were never eliminated entirely and colleges had occasionally to engage in heated correspondence with relatives or guardians in a desperate effort to gain satisfaction.[5]

As far as food and the provision of meals were concerned, attention was focused almost exclusively on dinner. Breakfast was not a public or regular meal, lunch did not take place, and supper was usually a private affair. Around the midday dinner, however, the college's day revolved. Regular efforts were made to ensure that everyone, at least the fellows,

the ordinary Battels; It has been thought proper to require an extension of Caution Money at the time of Entrance from 30 to 50 Guineas': draft reply of President Cooke—G. Glyn, 24 June [1787], CCCA B/14/5/1. See also p. 254 n. 5 above.

[1] ECA register 1737-1824, 28 Jan. 1758.
[2] QCA caution money books, 1720; WCM convention book III, p. 2, 6 Dec. 1720.
[3] For limits on the levels of bills see CCCA B/14/1/1, 10 Jan. 1786; NCA 961, 13 Nov. 1783, 3527, 24 Mar. 1784, 27 June 1793; SJM register 1730-94, p. 59, 12 Feb. 1736. For times of payment see BCA register 1682-1781, fo 96 (nd); CA chapter book 1754-80, p. 114, 24 Dec. 1764.
[4] For 'stopping' see NCA 3527, 24 Mar. 1784; TCA junior bursar's order book A, 2 Dec. 1692; UCA register 1729-1842, p. 81, 21 Mar. 1770. See also OCA SII G.5, Provost Hodges's memo book, p. 5, 15 Oct. 1734 and BCA register 1682-1781, fo 96 (leave to go out of town); QCA register K, 13 Jan. 1797 (terms); TCA liber decani I, scrutiny 1771 (graces for degrees).
[5] Writing to one guardian, President Cooke of CCC said he was 'unwilling to suffer so large an arrear to remain on our Books ... The Debt incurred bears date from his first entrance, The Bursars having *never* been able to bring him to any account, though regularly delivering up his Quarterly Charges.' Letter to J. Lynch, 11 May 1783, CCCA B/14/5/1.

scholars and commoners, dined in hall together. Both the university and the colleges recognized the importance of this for discipline and economy.[1] Private dinners in chambers were discouraged or forbidden.[2] Some colleges allowed members to choose their own food,[3] but others required them to eat in messes or combinations.[4] Seating in hall was strictly hierarchical: tables were allocated according to status and degree.[5] The qualifications for membership were in most cases obvious enough, but high table itself presented difficulties. In some colleges the privilege of eating with the fellows and using their common room had been extended automatically to noblemen and gentlemen-commoners.[6] It became more usual, as it had always been with other ranks, to wait for three or four years before admitting such men to what was sometimes called fellow-commoner status.[7] Waiting in hall was at first the duty of the servitors and bible-clerks, who carried the platters into hall and did the diners' bidding during the meal.[8] But, though some servitors continued to act in this way, their work increasingly devolved on other college servants—bedmakers, common-room men and simple 'waiters'.[9]

As for accommodation, it is clear that for much of the century many undergraduates lived out of college. Wadham in 1743 levied a small quarterly charge on those who did not take a room, but other colleges do not seem to have been concerned.[10] Then in the 1770s and 1780s came a series of attempts to tackle the problem.[11] Considerations of discipline and finance doubtless both contributed to the change of attitude. Whether it was as a result of such injunctions or because there was less 'chumming' or sharing of rooms is hard to say, but colleges were usually well-populated.[12]

[1] See for example Queen's MS 482, fos 123, 124; Magrath, *Queen's* ii. 111.
[2] CCCA B/4/1/2, 5 Apr. 1791; WCM convention book III, p. 257, 21 Nov. 1797.
[3] Jeffery, 'History', 54 ff (Brasenose); LCM register 1577-1739, fo 292ᵛ, 28 Feb. 1725.
[4] As at Magdalen and Christ Church: Macray, *Reg. Magdalen* iv. 54 (28 Jan. 1704); V. H. H. Green, 'The university and social life', p. 334 below.
[5] An exception was Trinity, where tables were arranged by 'orders'. H. E. D. Blakiston, *Trinity College* (London 1898), 62.
[6] Visitor–president and fellows, 17 Mar. 1727, TCA visitor's letters 1576-1820.
[7] For Queen's see Fothergill-Smith, 29 Jan. 1742 and 5 Apr. 1744, Queen's MS 473. At Brasenose no gentleman-commoner was to be 'admitted to the High Table or become a member of the Senior Common Room unless he has either taken his M.A. degree or been four years in residence and is a Bachelor of Arts or a Student of Civil law': Jeffery, 430. For delayed admission see UCA register 1729-1842, p. 92, 28 June 1777. St John's made an exception it seems for noblemen but Trinity did not: T. Dromore-president, 17 May 1797, SJM LXXXVI.S.3; TCA register A.48, 4 July 1777.
[8] LCM register 1577-1739, fo 292ᵛ, 28 Feb. 1725; Magrath, *Queen's* ii. 111.
[9] LCM register 1739-1983, fo 12ᵛ, 26 Jan. 1748; QCA register K, 13 Aug. 1796; WCM convention book III, pp. 260-1, 6 Dec. 1798.
[10] WCM convention book III, p. 36, 8 Oct. 1743.
[11] ECA A.I.10, order book, rules for payment of chamber-rent 1788; Queen's MS 456, 7 Dec. 1774; TCA register A.48, 14 Dec. 1787; BCA register 1794-1875, p. 9 (4 Dec. 1787), p. 13 (11 Nov. 1799); WCM convention book III, p. 165 (6 Dec. 1778), p. 174 (17 Feb. 1780).
[12] On room-sharing see WCM convention book III, pp. 120-1, 8 July 1773. Commoners of four years' standing at Trinity had to give up their rooms in college: TCA register A.48, 1 Feb. 1775,

Some rooms belonged, in effect, to the fellows who if non-resident, or content with a cheaper set, would sub-let to wealthy undergraduates. The rest were the concern of the college itself. One or two colleges had buildings or sets of rooms set aside for gentlemen-commoners, but otherwise members were accommodated in whatever rooms were vacant.[1] Once housed, however, undergraduates had a habit of lending and swapping rooms—a practice which colleges tried hard to suppress.[2] Rents paid to individual fellows were subject to private negotiation, but those to the college depended on the quality of the room and the status of the occupant.

Repairs and improvements, if undertaken by the college, were charged in part to those occupying the rooms. If they were undertaken by individuals, then the college might meet two-thirds of the cost itself; pay half of the cost and permit the occupier to levy the other half on his successor (who in turn could levy a third of the initial half on his successor, and so on by thirds down the chain); or pay nothing at all and allow the occupier to levy two-thirds (or more for certain work) of the cost on his successor (who again could begin the process of 'thirding').[3] If someone damaged his room he would either be obliged to pay for repairs himself or be forbidden to charge full 'thirds' to his successor.[4] Furnishings were provided by each occupant himself, but might be passed on to a successor and if ever 'thirded' became the property of the room.[5]

The student body of the university was a strictly hierarchical one and there were fine distinctions of both rank and dress from nobleman down to servitor. Considerable deference was paid to a young man's position in the world outside. But social status never entirely overrode university status and there was a sharp divide between foundationers and nonfoundationers. The latter were those 'independent members',[6] such as gentlemen-commoners and commoners, who in recent times had been permitted to enter the university for the sake of an education and perhaps also for the sake of a degree. They were temporary members,

30 May 1778. TCA registrum camerarum A shows few rooms empty. Contemporary comments confirm the picture, for example Queen's in 1762 and Christ Church in 1780: *The Correspondence of Jeremy Bentham*, ed. T. L. S. Sprigge *et al.* (London and Oxford 1968 onward) i. 58; *Reminiscences of Oxford*, 174; see also Green, 'The university and social life', 330-1.

[1] For gentlemen-commoners see for example C. Willoughby-president, 18 June 1786, CCCA B/14/5/1; H. L. Thompson, *Christ Church* (London 1900), 166.
[2] QCA register K, p. 40, 6 Aug. 1734; WCM convention book III, p. 174, 17 Feb. 1780; WCA tin trunk, no. 10, 29 Oct. 1785.
[3] LCM register 1577-1739, fo 239, 6 May 1699; CA chapter book 1689-1713, fo 125, 9 Dec. 1710; LCM register 1577-1739, fo 244, 22 Dec. 1703; SJM register 1730-94, p. 137, 23 July 1742.
[4] NCA 3527, 22 Dec. 1735; WCM convention book III, p. 174, 17 Feb. 1780.
[5] OCA SII.L2, thirding of rooms, 1775.
[6] QCA register K, 11 Sept. 1769.

still known as 'sojourners' in at least two colleges.[1] The former were the 'dependent members'[2] or scholars, significantly called 'portioners' or 'portionists' at Merton, who had been elected to a place on the foundation and who could expect to be elected to a fellowship in due course.

All undergraduates, save the well-born and wealthy, worked hard to obtain a foundationer's place or 'an establishment' either in their own college or in another. It was a regular practice for a student to obtain a commoner's place in a college such as Oriel where numbers were unrestricted and then move on to (say) a demyship at Magdalen, a junior fellowship at New College or a scholarship at Corpus, as and when he could. There is personal and statistical evidence for this phenomenon.[3] Colleges do not seem to have objected to the migrations, though they had formally to grant their permission. Only the grossly misbehaved were refused the *liceat migrare*.[4] But there was a tendency, sometimes a statutory obligation, to grant scholarships to internal candidates, so migration, heavy though it was, may well have been outweighed by changes of status within colleges.[5] The system may have appeared rigid, but it was in fact fluid and flexible.

The most elevated rank was that of 'nobleman' to which both peers and the sons of peers were entitled. But their numbers were small (save at Christ Church) and they were rarely distinguished from the general class of 'gentlemen-commoners', sometimes also called fellow-commoners, upper-commoners or *superioris ordinis commensales*.[6] Gentlemen-commoners were privileged and wealthy young men living a privileged and expensive life in the university. 'Better company' was usually the reason given for entering a man as gentleman-commoner.[7] A plain commoner's gown was sometimes regarded as below the dignity of certain families. The mother of a prospective member of Trinity was told in 1704 that 'none but sons of inferior clergymen, tradesmen and substantial countrymen are Commoners there'; only a gentleman-commoner's gown would do.[8]

[1] L. S. Sutherland, *The University of Oxford in the Eighteenth Century: a reconsideration* (Oxford 1973), 5 (Exeter); OCA Provost Carter's memo. book, p. 101.

[2] *Reminiscences of Oxford*, 135-6.

[3] For example C. Lawson-Cooke, 6 Nov. 1787, CCCA B/14/5/1; *Woodforde at Oxford*. The figures show Corpus, Magdalen and New College as heavy importers and poor colleges such as Oriel, Pembroke and Wadham as exporters. See Green, 'The university and social life', 316 and n. 5.

[4] See the exchange of letters between the visitor and principal of Brasenose concerning the case of Mr Dickinson: BNCA tower drawer 129, Apr.-Dec. 1778; Magrath, *Queen's* ii. 111.

[5] This was particularly true at Balliol.

[6] For 'fellow-commoners' see visitor-president and fellows, 17 Mar. 1727, TCA visitor's letters 1576-1820. Later in the century, however, the term was used only of those of 3 or 4 years standing who were deemed worthy of admission to high table or the senior common room (see p. 259 above). See also *The Flemings in Oxford*, i. 535 (upper-commoners); Sutherland, *University of Oxford*, 5n (*superioris ordinis commensales*).

[7] R. Dalton-Provost Smith, 10 May [*c*.1774], Queen's MS 476.

[8] Sutherland, 8.

Colleges made a number of exceptions for their gentlemen-commoners. Unlike other undergraduates, they might be allowed to use the library or be admitted to the buttery and cellar.[1] For much of the century they were permitted, in some colleges at least, to join the fellows at high table and in the senior common room. But such privileges were not gratuitously bestowed. The fees paid by gentlemen-commoners were exceptional too. The graded scale of charges imposed by colleges and the university was weighted heavily against the gentlemen-commoners. Bursars, servants and servitors were indebted to these wealthy undergraduates.[2] It was not an unreasonable arrangement.

The danger, of course, was that the gentlemen-commoners would exempt themselves from all academic responsibilities and bring the university into disrepute. In the first half of the century this seems to have occurred. One or two colleges showed a desire to oblige their gentlemen-commoners to submit themselves to exercises and discipline;[3] but without much success, it would appear, if the experiences of a University College man in the early 1720s are any guide. Alone of his contemporary gentlemen-commoners Nicholas Toke wanted to take a degree and he found preparation a hard task. Not only did the others refuse to 'dispute' with him, they ridiculed his diligence.[4]

In later years matters probably improved.[5] There is a certain amount of evidence to suggest that gentlemen-commoners began to play a proper part in the academic life of their colleges, and while formerly very few had taken BA degrees, towards the end of the century up to 20-30 per cent did so.[6] At the same time they tended to lose some of their privileges. No longer were they immediately admitted to high table and the senior common room, but were relegated to a table and a common room of their own.[7] All this helps to explain why numbers were falling.[8]

[1] BCA register 1794-1875, pp. 10 ff (library); TCA junior bursar's order book A, 1 Apr. 1686 (buttery and cellar).

[2] Sir William Dormer (1670-1726, 2nd bt; m. Trin. 1686) complained 'we gentlemen do maintain all the Colledge servants and serviters': Blakiston, *Trinity*, 171. Apart from their higher fees gentlemen-commoners were required to give 'plate-money': see for example LCM register 1577-1739, fo 287, 1 Feb. 1723.

[3] See for example NCA 3581, p. 31 (28 Mar. 1734), 3527 (21 Dec. 1731). In 1711 Warden Holland of Merton asked the college to agree to 'Subject the Gentlemen Commoners to the Exercise and Discipline of the College': MCR Holland's register, 1 Aug. 1711.

[4] See L. S. Sutherland, 'The curriculum', pp. 478-9 below.

[5] There was a complaint in 1763 that gentlemen-commoners at Corpus were 'left at liberty to do as they pleased', but this was from a guardian whose ward had been allowed to default on his bills: J. Lynch-Cooke, 21 May 1783, CCCA B/14/5/1.

[6] At Brasenose from 1768 gentlemen-commoners had to show up their themes with other undergraduates: Jeffery, 'History', 43. At Christ Church from 1774 the term's reading of noblemen and gentlemen-commoners is included in the collections books: see P. Quarrie, 'Christ Church collection books' below. The percentages relate to Christ Church, Corpus and Pembroke; numbers for Oriel were a little lower.   [7] TCA register A.48, 5 Mar. 1776, 4 July 1777.

[8] Especially in Balliol, Lincoln, New College and St John's; numbers in Oriel were falling proportionately though the total increased.

The class was never a large one and as soon as it no longer satisfied the snobbery on which it was based·it became smaller still.

Most non-foundationers were the simple commoners who formed by far the largest single class in the university. Perhaps two-thirds of those admitted to the colleges during the period 1690-1800 entered as commoners and, though a significant number subsequently found scholarships and fellowships, most of them remained commoners.[1] After three or four years in the university they left to find employment, more often than not in the church. Colleges accorded them few marks of distinction. A 'senior commoner' might be deputed to act on behalf of the rest of his rank and 'senior commoners', presumably of two or three years standing, might share a table with the bachelors, but otherwise there was no differentiation.[2] Privileges too were scarce. Libraries were closed to them, though a number of colleges had special collections of books which undergraduates could use; and until the very end of the period, when Pembroke seems to have led the way, there were no common rooms for the commoners.[3] Nor were there any exemptions from college exercises and church services, and commoners at least prepared for a degree. About 50-60 per cent obtained one.

Junior foundationers had various names. 'Scholar' was the generic term, but Magdalen called them demies and Merton postmasters. Queen's had two ranks: undergraduate scholars known as 'poor children' and BA scholars called taberdars. The 101 Students at Christ Church and the 70 junior fellows at New College, discussed earlier, might also be regarded as scholars. Some scholarships gave their holders a statutory or prescriptive claim to a fellowship. This was true of Corpus, Magdalen, Queen's, Wadham and (to a lesser extent) Trinity.[4] But at Brasenose, Merton and Oriel scholarships were 'merely exhibitionary' and terminated after a certain time without further rights.[5]

Colleges, such as Corpus, which had no simple commoner class

[1] At University College 859 out of 1,359 admissions were of commoners, excluding 26 outsiders who became fellows. At Balliol 1,098 of those admitted as commoners stayed commoners, 229 became scholars, 25 fellows, 45 scholars then fellows, 41 fellow-commoners.

[2] For a 'senior commoner' acting for the others see Magrath, *Queen's* ii. 208; *Correspondence of Bentham*, ed. Sprigge i. 75-6. Two men were assigned to wait on the bachelors and senior commoners in the Lincoln proposals of 1748: LCM register 1739-1983, fo 12ᵛ, 26 Jan. 1748.

[3] See I. G. Philip, 'Libraries and the University Press', pp. 749-52 below; *VCH Oxon.* iii. 295 (Pembroke).

[4] Of the 239 scholars of Corpus in the century 148 became fellows. At Magdalen 392 out of 422 fellows between 1690 and 1800 were demies (see p. 233 above). At Queen's taberdars had to vacate their places after a certain time, but retained their prior claim to a fellowship: see discussion of the question in Queen's MS 456, memoranda relating to Queen's College; and Bodl. MS Don. c. 152 for Erasmus Head's (m. Queen's 1727) personal experience of the system in the early part of the century. For Wadham see J. Wells, *History of Wadham College* (London 1898), 21-2. Scholars had a preference at Trinity but seniority did not count: visitor's letters 1576-1820, J. Dallaway's appeal to the visitor, 17 June 1786. James Dallaway (c1763-1834), m. Trin. 1778.

[5] See for example principal-visitor, 29 Apr. 1778, BNCA tower drawer 129.

recruited their scholars directly from schools, but most chose them from existing members, either commoners or servitors.[1] Seniority and the preference of the founder or benefactor played a part in the choice, and at Balliol fellows had the right to nominate scholars themselves; but by the end of the century at least examinations were held and carried weight.[2]

The perquisites attached to scholarships usually took the form of allowances rather than stipends. President Cooke said that the Corpus scholarships 'are to be considered as great *helps* to the young men who are so fortunate to obtain them in the course of education, and should be appreciated by what they *save* in the way of public Academical Expenses'.[3] Scholars enjoyed free or subsidized food and rooms, but rarely a direct share in the college's income. In 1771 Wadham's visitor pronounced that the surplus revenue was to be divided among the warden and fellows only. Four years later the scholars were given free rooms by way of compensation. Increased pay, it was thought, might have been misused.[4] The value of scholarships varied from benefaction to benefaction and from college to college, but £15 at the beginning of the century and £25 towards the end may have been typical figures and more or less covered the expenses of a frugal undergraduate.[5]

The most pressing obligation of a scholarship concerned residence. At the very least scholars had to 'keep' the terms laid down by the university and the requirements were often more demanding.[6] Absence without leave entailed loss of emoluments, suspension from a degree or rustication.[7] As far as undergraduates and bachelors were concerned, it seems

[1] Blakiston, *Trinity*, 189-90 (commoners); Queen's chose their 'poor children' from their servitors and batteles (see the sources cited in p. 263 n. 4 above). For a servitor being made a postmaster at Merton see MCR Holland's register, 19 Oct. 1730.

[2] Seniority seems to have played a part at Queen's, at least until the arrival of a new provost in 1796: Magrath, *Queen's* ii. 145 ff. For the preference of a benefactor see UCA statutes of 1736. On Balliol see J. Jones, 'Sound religion and useful learning: the rise of Balliol under John Parsons and Richard Jenkyns, 1798-1854' in J. Prest (ed.), *Balliol Studies* (London 1982), 92, 100 and n. 12. On examinations see J. M. Edmonds, 'Patronage and privilege in education: a Devon boy goes to school, 1798', *Trans. Devonshire Assoc. for the Advancement of Science* cx (1978), 106-8. See also two letters from the president of Corpus to parents of prospective candidates: Cooke-M. P. Wyndham, draft reply [19 June 1794] and same-R. Whittingham [28 Dec. 1798], CCCA B/14/5/1.

[3] Cooke-Whittingham [28 Dec. 1798], CCCA B/14/5/1.

[4] WCM convention book III, p. 113 (27 June 1771), pp. 132-3 (21 Apr. 1775).

[5] When Fothergill was made a taberdar in 1725 a taberdarship was thought to be worth about £16 a year, though only 9s 6d was received in money: *The Fothergills of Ravenstonedale*, ed. C. Thornton and F. McLaughlin (London 1903), 93. For a valuation of £25 in 1784 at Trinity see president and fellows-visitor, Nov. 1784, TCA visitors letters 1576-1820. The author of 'memoranda relating to Queen's College' said that 'a *poor child* who was an economist' would not have spent more than £20 at the beginning of the eighteenth century: Queen's MS 456. See also Green, 'The university and social life', 322.

[6] LCM register 1577-1739, fo 229ᵛ, 13 Apr. 1693; WCM convention book III, p. 30, 1 Mar. 1740; Cooke-Whittingham [28 Dec. 1798], CCCA B/14/5/1.

[7] WCA tin trunk, no. 10, 23 Feb. 1784.

likely that the rules were observed, but MA scholars, in two colleges at least, secured exemptions. In 1755 the Corpus MA scholars persuaded their visitor to grant a qualified dispensation; and their victory enabled their Trinity counterparts, already it appears non-resident, to secure a relaxation of the regulations governing the renewal of their leaves of absence.[1]

Since most scholars aimed at a fellowship or a career in the church, a high proportion are found taking degrees: perhaps 80 per cent of BAs and 60 per cent of MAs. Those who were forced to vacate their scholarships or found their path to a fellowship blocked took holy orders and left for marriage and an incumbency;[2] others who had a permanent place on the foundation stayed on to await their admission to a full fellowship.

Scholarships were the most desirable but not the only way of paying for an Oxford education. Most colleges, at least at the beginning of the period, offered a small number of servitors' places for the poor and deserving. Selection was often the right of the head of the college and an examination, or at least a rigorous examination, seems not usually to have been involved.[3] In return for free or cheap food and accommodation servitors were required to wait in hall and serve in chapel. They could earn some additional shillings by doing chores for fellows and gentlemen-commoners.[4] Brasenose servitors were even said to have composed essays for their wealthy contemporaries![5]

Two other classes need to be mentioned: batlers, who seem to have enjoyed a subsidized education little different from servitors; and bible-clerks who worked alongside the servitors in hall as well as in chapel.[6]

In the course of the century the number of servitors, batlers and bible-clerks fell dramatically, and in some colleges dwindled to nothing.[7] Other colleges abolished the menial duties of such students and employed servants instead. Servitor-choristers at Corpus were given the 'less degrading name of exhibitioners' and their Christ Church counterparts tried to have what they regarded as their exhibitioner

---

[1] Visitor-president, 19 July 1755, CCCA A/5/5; see also p. 240 above. Leave of absence was granted to bachelor scholars only in exceptional circumstances: Cooke-G. Beaver [3 Jan. 1786], CCCA B/14/5/1. TCA visitor's letters 1576-1820, 20 [Dec. 1768], [18 Dec. 1791], 1 July 1811.

[2] For an example see the plaintive letter of an ex-demy to the president of Magdalen in 1796: R. Houlton-president, 4 Jan. 1796, Magdalen, MS 476, no. 51.

[3] Provost Smith-W. Brownsword, 6 Jan. 1732, Queen's MS 482, fo 178. For the expenses of a batteler see Jeffery, 'History', 50-1.

[4] For the position at Queen's see Magrath, Queen's ii. 87-9, and provost Barlow-Sir J. Lowther, 5 Apr. 1670, HMC Lonsdale MSS 93-4.

[5] Jeffery, 45.

[6] Queen's certainly seem to have treated their batlers in much the same way as servitors. For bible-clerks see for example LCM register 1739-1983, fo 12ᵛ, 26 Jan. 1748; see also Green, 'Religion in the university', 426-8.

[7] Trinity declined a legacy in 1792 rather than revive their servitor class: TCA register A.48, 20 June 1792. See also L. S. Sutherland, 'The last of the servitors', Christ Church Record (1975), 37-9.

status recognized in their academical dress, though with only limited success.[1]

Exhibitions, properly speaking, were smallish sums, between £5 and £15 per annum, bequeathed for the partial maintenance of deserving undergraduates, either new or existing members of college.[2] The conditions varied enormously, but they often included geographical restrictions and injunctions about regular residence and the performance of academic exercises.[3] They were always terminable after a certain number of years or at a certain stage in a student's career, and rarely did they give the recipient any claim to a place on the foundation.[4]

An undergraduate's status was determined by his rank, but when he obtained a degree and stayed in college he enjoyed privileges which often overrode former distinctions. Bachelors might dine together, have their own common room or, in one or two colleges at least, have access to the main library.[5] A few might be admitted, usually on an *ad hoc* basis, to high table.[6] Masters were still more favoured. They invariably had the right to use the library and, though some had the privilege of a separate dining table and common room, others were admitted to high table and the senior common room.[7]

A Queen's taberdar in 1735 said that 'upon our foundation especially' taking an MA 'entitles a man to very extraordinary honours and priviledges, and is truly the greatest Change I have undergone since my Entrance'.[8]

[1] Cooke-A. A. Baker, 3 May 1799, 21 Feb. 1792, 20 June 1812, CCCA B/14/5/1, B/4/1/1, B/4/1/3; Sutherland, *University of Oxford in the Eighteenth Century,* 10, Green, 'The university and social life', 324-71.
[2] The Lady Hastings exhibitions at Queen's were for new members; but cf Cooke-Ironmongers Co, draft reply of 10 Feb. 1762 concerning the rules of Sir Charles Thorold's exhibition, CCCA B/12/5/1.
[3] For residence see Balliol's rules for the Bristol Grammar School exhibitions and the requirements imposed on the Crewe exhibitioners at Lincoln in 1723: BCA register 1682-1781, fos 20ᵛ ff, 1700; LCA register of Lord Crewe's exhibitioners to whom leave of absence is granted by the rector. For academic exercises see the Bridgeman exhibitions at Queen's and Hody's benefaction at Wadham: QCA register K, 3 June 1802; Wadham MS 10/2/4/6.
[4] However, at Balliol the scholars and fellows were said to have been chosen 'for the most part' from the exhibitioners: BCA register 1682-1781, fos 40 ff.
[5] For bachelors dining together see CA chapter book 1776-99, p. 676, 9 June 1798; for bachelors' common rooms see BCA register 1794-1875, fos 15ᵛ 16, 5 Mar. 1801, and Blakiston, *Trinity,* 200 (from at least 1688). At Trinity noblemen, gentlemen-commoners and BA commoners appear to have been permitted to use the library, but undergraduate commoners and scholars were not: TCA register A.51.
[6] As fellow-commoners at Queen's (see p. 259) above.
[7] For libraries see WCM convention book III, pp. 244-5, 6 Dec. 1794; BCA register 1794-1875, fos 10 ff, 21 Oct. 1799; Christ Church, library record 49, 22 June 1778. For a separate dining table see SJM register 1730-94, p. 233, Mrs Holmes's will 1750. For separate common rooms see CA chapter book 1776-99, p. 383, 20 June 1778; NCA 9655, p. 99, 27 May 1684; NCA 1033, 30 Aug. 1773. At Brasenose admission to high table appears to have been automatic, at Christ Church by invitation: Jeffery, 43; CA liii. b. 4, subdean's book, rules of the sub dean (loose folder). For admission to the senior common room see TCA register A.48, 13 Apr. 1775; BCA register 1794-1875, fos 15ᵛ 16, 5 Mar. 1801.
[8] Erasmus Head-parents, 5 May 1735, Bodl. MS Don.c.152.

The regulations governing the lives of undergraduates mainly concerned residence and degrees. Foundationers had to conform to college statutes and exhibitioners to the wishes of their benefactor, and failure to comply could entail the loss of all or a proportion of their emoluments. Commoners, of course, could be subjected to no such control. The university laid down certain requirements for the taking of degrees,[1] but much depended on how they were enforced by individual colleges. There are few signs of strictness until the end of the century. In 1783 Trinity laid down the dates by which undergraduates were to come up if they were to 'keep' that term; and Queen's in 1790 ordered its undergraduates to be in college within twelve days of the beginning of term and reside there till the end unless prevented by sickness, unavoidable accident 'or some necessary avocation'.[2] How often leave of absence was granted is hard to gauge; but even under the strict regime of President Cooke at Corpus in these same reforming times (1783-1823) dispensations were given for some less than necessary 'avocations' without damage to a person's 'residence'.[3] As for 'academic' rules, these will be treated elsewhere.[4]

Discipline varied from head to head and from dean to dean, but the punishments employed were much the same and ranged from additional exercises, public penance, loss of commons, fines and confinement to college, through to rustication and expulsion. The worst offenders could be subjected to an elaborate array of chastisements extending over many months, even years.[5] There were two main academic sanctions. Men could be 'put back' from their degree for a period or simply denied grace to supplicate altogether; others might be refused the testimonial needed to obtain holy orders. Again the problem is to determine how often such sanctions were enforced. There are instances where for the sake of peace or compassion colleges stayed their hand, but there is enough contrary evidence to suggest that these were not the rule.[6] Academic laxity might escape censure at times, but patent corporate indiscipline rarely went unchecked.

A large percentage of undergraduates left the university as BAs to

[1] See Sutherland, 'Curriculum'.

[2] TCA misc. iii, extracts from the standing rules and orders; QCA register K, 25 Nov. 1790.

[3] J. O. Parr-president and draft reply, 30 and 31 Oct. 1790, CCCA B/14/5/1.

[4] Sutherland, 'Curriculum'; and for the improvements effected at the end of the century Green, 'Reformers and reform', 621-8.

[5] CA chapter book 1754-80, p. 253 (7 May 1774), chapter book 1776-99, pp. 592 ff (1 Feb. 1791), p. 628 (6 Feb. 1794); NCA 9655, 14 June 1799.

[6] E. Jones-T. Pardo, 17 Mar. 1729, JCA box 3; WCM convention book III, p. 73, 8 July 1754 (the college's conditions were not accepted and the scholar, after giving further signs of political disaffection, was expelled without a degree). But for the contrary evidence, see NCA 961, 30 June 1774; CA chapter books, various entries (e.g. 1694, 1705-6, 1759); WCA tin trunk, no. 10, 1 June 1786; WCM convention book III, p. 30, 1 Mar. 1740; CCCA B/4/1/1, 13 Jan. 1748.

enter the church. Few of them kept their names on the books of their colleges. That was necessary only for those wishing to take a further degree or vote in university elections and it entailed the deposit of caution money and the payment of certain dues.[1] For the majority their three or four year 'sojourn' at Oxford was over.

[1] WCA tin trunk, no. 10, 2 Dec. 1784; CCCA B/4/1/1, 17 June 1783; Cooke-Lady Orkney, 27 July 1799, CCCA B/14/5/1.

10

College Estates and Wealth 1660–1815

J. P. D. DUNBABIN

AFTER the fall of Richard Cromwell, we are told,

The persons concerned in these mutations, having formerly got the revenues of the King, Church, loyal Nobility and Gentry, began a second time . . . to gape after the Lands of the Universities, and thereby to overthrow learning. At length it came to this result among most of them, that the Universities should be modelled after the Dutch fashion, as at Leiden, that is to say, that there should be but three Colleges left, and those for the three great Faculties, Divinity, Law, and Physic, each to have a Professor . . .[1]

How seriously this scheme was entertained is hard to assess. But the Restoration put it out of court, and such projects receded into abeyance for over two centuries. With the coming of the new order individuals were again replaced; but the colleges as corporations were left to work out their recovery on their own. In general they did so to good effect. And in the financial account of any period before the second world war their fortunes must overshadow those of the central university institutions.[2]

By no means all colleges had suffered financially under the Commonwealth. But a number emerged with debts; and some at least turned to benefactors for assistance. Thus after Balliol's civil-war problems had been compounded by the Fire of London, £518 was subscribed to set that poor college on its feet again;[3] while, at the other end of the financial

---

[1] Anthony Wood, *The History and Antiquities of the University of Oxford*, ed. John Gutch (2 vols in 3 Oxford 1792-6) ii pt 2, p. 695. The time-span covered by this chapter extends rather beyond that of the others in the volume. This is done partly to provide a greater continuity in the handling of this financial theme with other volumes in the series, but chiefly because of the nature of the sources and of economic developments generally. Thus for many colleges the Restoration permitted a new departure after two decades of financial difficulties and confusion, whereas the Glorious Revolution constituted no such turning point. Equally the university reforms of 1800 were of little importance in a financial context; rather the French revolutionary and Napoleonic wars represented for the colleges a long boom of prosperity qualified by inflation. Their termination inaugurated a very different period of falling prices and 'agricultural depression'.

[2] For a brief discussion of central university finances 1660-1815 see appendix II, p. 305 below.

[3] BCA Benefactions I (1636-76), pp. 33 ff; CA benefactions to Christ Church (temporary classification D.P.i.b.2), pp. 1 ff.

scale, Christ Church had already raised some £6,400 '*ad regale hoc Collegium restituendum*'. The colleges' fortunes had derived in the first instance from benefactions, and these always remained at least a potential source of wealth.

The sources of current income, or in this case of its deficiency, are well illustrated by the grumblings of the unfortunate bursar of Magdalen after James II's purge. He had 'received no rents or had any fines come in', with tenants declining to renew, 'for feare of a false title'. Furthermore, the commoners, 'who are to pay chamber rent at audit-time . . . are gone and pay nothing'. The college was accordingly 'behind hand'; and, for good measure, the extruded fellows had pawned much of its plate before leaving.[1]

Of these various items, charges levied on students are readily comprehensible to the modern mind, though they would probably have shocked the medieval colleges' founders. But the seventeenth-century system of rents and fines (the colleges' principal support) may well need explanation. It was governed by Elizabethan legislation that

(i) partially indexed incomes by insisting that at least a third of each ordinary college rent be linked to the market-price of corn. (Such rents came to be known as corn-rents, as distinct from the fixed sums receivable from copyholds, rent-charges and the like.)

(ii) prevented colleges, cathedral chapters and charities from selling real property or granting it on leases of more than twenty-one years, or three lives, in duration (or of more than forty years in the case of houses).

(iii) forbade the renewal of such leases until they were within three years of expiry.[2]

In our period the first two provisions by and large held. The third, though, was a dead letter. Technically leases were prematurely surrendered and then re-granted; but the process was in effect renewal and was always so called. It was expected to take place at fixed intervals, generally after the lapse of seven years (or one life) for lands, and of fourteen years for houses. Such renewals were conditional on the payment of premiums or 'fines'.

Colleges distinguished sharply between these fines and their 'old rents'. The latter formed the mainstay of general corporate income, and are always entered prominently in the annual accounts. But the bulk of the fines were divided directly between the head and fellows, and they were commonly recorded separately. Thus by the eighteenth century

[1] Wood, *Life and Times*, iii. 258 (Mar. 1688 NS), 530 (Dec. 1687).
[2] 13 Eliz. I, c. 10, 14 Eliz. I, c. 11, 18 Eliz. I, c. 6 and c. 11, printed in *Enactments in Parliament* i. 176, 188, 190.

college incomes can be viewed as a series of layers. This can be best illustrated from Balliol. Its oldest accounts are the *Computi*, concerned on the income side with rents and a few small traditional charges, and on the expenditure side only with the master, fellows and scholars. The *Computi* were later incorporated into the 'Final Accounts'. These survive only from 1672-3, and cover also the 'far larger number of students outside the college proper, the commoners and fellow-commoners, battelers and servitors, often significantly described as the *extranei*'.[1] They derived no direct benefit from the college endowments, but paid their way by battels, from which ('*ex altera parte Libri*') was covered the cost of providing food in hall and so on. Then in the eighteenth century a third category was added: *pro Domo*. Initially small, this was fed towards the end of the century with increases in the revenue of certain estates, with a share in the college 'dividends' and with savings on other accounts, and came to assume a considerable importance. 'Fines' entered into none of these headings; but there had been a separate record of them since at least the early seventeenth century.

All colleges kept accounts to prevent bursarial defalcation; and, in most, runs of accounts survive from at least the late seventeenth or early eighteenth century. But there was no common format; indeed no common language, with Latin surviving in Brasenose until the 1850s and roman numerals until the 1770s. Such tenacity had its absurd side: for over a century and a half Lincoln continued to enter as income the sum of 13s 4d once derived from premises destroyed by the fall of All Saints' tower, and then to adjust the expenditure side of the account accordingly. For the historian this conservatism has the advantage of permitting the comparison of some items over very long periods. But it risks obscuring new developments, especially if (like the New College Timber Fund[2]) they grew up outside the main accounts, and so excluded important components of college income—we have already noted the separate treatment of fines. In fact colleges differ markedly in respect of the comprehensiveness of their accounts, particularly with regard to internal fees and charges.[3] But in no college will every single receipt be listed.

[1] G. Beachcroft, 'Balliol College accounts in the eighteenth century' in J. Prest (ed.), *Balliol College Studies* (London 1982), p. 81.

[2] Faced in 1766 with the prospect of a temporary bulge in its receipts from timber, New College decided to feed the surplus into a special investment fund (outside the main accounts) to be drawn on when wood-sales again declined. In fact they boomed for the next half century, in some Napoleonic-war years even exceeding the yields of the 'old rents'. So the timber fund became for a time very large and was—predictably—raided: see NCA 1204, Warden Hayward's MS proposals, 1766; see also timber and underwood accounts and summary of college receipts and expenditure 1800-55, NCA 946, 3569, 973, 932, 51.

[3] Thus Lincoln kept its old form of accounts with only minor, and Wadham without any, alteration until the time of the Cleveland commission, the first to work out all college incomes on a consistent basis. Lincoln's 'calculus' for 1870-1 balanced on an appreciably lower figure than did the Cleveland form of accounts, but the Wadham bursars accounts on a distinctly higher one, since the

All this makes aggregation and inter-collegiate comparison difficult. But it does not render the accounts valueless as historical sources. They were audited by fellows with bursarial experience, a process that in 1801 took six Christ Church men from 9.30 a.m. to 2.15 p.m. on 21 December and from 9.15 to 12.15 the following day.[1] The results were not always impeccable; and it no doubt served the 1720 St John's bursars right for their faulty arithmetic that they should have been entered debtors to the college when they were in fact creditors. But though the imperfections would worry modern accountants, and sometimes did worry contemporaries, in my view the margin of error is not enough to obscure the general trends that chiefly concern historians.[2] One reservation, however, must be made. A number of colleges proceeded on a pay-as-you-go basis, treating as income payments of previous years' rent or arrears of battels, and carrying over to the future non-payments of current bills. Such a system could have gone disastrously wrong if arrears had been allowed to mount unchecked. But in practice this does not seem to have been the case. Payments may have lagged, but they were still made with tolerable regularity. Thus over the two centuries 1660 to 1868 St John's only wrote off from their main account some £4,600 in unpaid battels and rents, while in the eighteenth century no more than £434 of All Souls rents ever seem to have been overdue by more than two years.[3]

It is, then, possible to contend that accounts do offer historians a broadly acceptable guide to college incomes. But they were not, of course, published until 1883. And if seventeenth-century contemporaries had been asked about relative college wealth, they would probably have referred to an estimate of their 'old rents' made in the 1590s, on which (with minor adjustments) the colleges were still being assessed for poor rates in Charles II's reign.[4]

Cleveland format recorded not the true catering turnover but its net profit or loss: *Parliamentary Papers* (1873), xxxvii pt i, 79-80, 117-18; pt ii. 475-7.

[1] CA 'Annual Statements' of account, 1801.

[2] Two more technical points should be noted. The format of most accounts is one of simple income ('charge') and expenditure ('discharge'). But those of, at least, Balliol and Wadham offer the possibility of internal checks: thus Balliol generally records *recipienda/solvenda, recepta/soluta* and *non recepta/soluta*, while, in the case of Wadham, balance from previous account plus actual receipts should (though it does not always) equal actual expenditure plus carry-over to subsequent account. Secondly, in the eighteenth century as later, there was a tendency to include on both sides of the accounts constant non-income items (like the cash-float always maintained in the Balliol bursary). Sometimes, as with St John's, or the late-eighteenth- and early-nineteenth-century Balliol *domus* account, such items seriously exaggerate the actual turnover; and where I have edited them out to get a truer picture of college income, my figures will differ from the gross totals given by my sources.

[3] SJM computus annuus 1867 and 1868 (though admittedly subsidiary accounts were more disturbed). All Souls tres billae books, Bodl. MS DD All Souls, b.24-7; the peak of such arrears was reached in 1855 when £1,602 was more than two years overdue, £1,492 of which represented bad debts on a single property. It must, however, be conceded that the university's losses of rent had swollen by 1725-6 to £12,000 or many times its annual turnover: see appendix II, p. 305 below.

[4] The original assessment is printed in J. Gutch, *Collectanea Curiosa... Chiefly Collected... from the*

TABLE 10.1

THE 1592 ASSESSMENT OF 'OLD
RENTS' AS ADAPTED FOR USE
IN CHARLES II'S REIGN

	£
Christ Church*	2,000
Magdalen	1,200
New College*	1,000
All Souls*	500
Corpus Christi*	500
Merton	400
St John's*	400
Brasenose*	300
Queen's	c250[a]
Exeter	200
Oriel	200
Trinity	200
Lincoln*	130
University College	100
Balliol*	100
Wadham*[b]	100
Pembroke[b]	100
Jesus (1681)	100[c]

[a] £260 in the 1590s, £254 in 1662, £200 in 1681.

[b] Wadham and Pembroke were both founded after 1592.

[c] £70 in the 1590s, but considerable benefactions were received in Charles II's reign.

The gross figures were, as we shall see, far too low. But the relative position of the different colleges has, in the long run, altered less than one might have expected in view of their extensive financial independence. So it may not be unfair to study their collective fortunes on the basis of a sample; and what follows is chiefly based on the colleges starred in the table above.[1]

Most colleges came to possess some holdings of stocks or shares, perhaps starting with a minor investment in South Sea stock,

Manuscripts of Archbishop Sancroft (2 vols Oxford 1781) i. 190-1. For the early 1660s see Bodl. MS Rawl.D.317, fo 201 and for the early 1680s Wood, *Life and Times* ii. 565.

[1] The basic college accounts and the sample years (approximately 1 in 10) I have taken from them are:

All Souls: rent (and expense) rolls, 1660-1, 1669-70, 1679-80 etc.

Balliol: final accounts, 1672-3, 1679-80, 1691-2, 1699-1700 to 1719-20, 1730-1, 1739-40 etc.

Brasenose: engrossed books, 1663, 1670, 1680 etc.

Christ Church: register of treasurers' accounts, annual statements, receipt books, 1660, 1670 etc.

supplemented towards the end of the century with turnpike and canal bonds and then consols.[1] But this was essentially the investment of surplus balances, as at Corpus: 'taken out of the Tower all the cash, to be put to interest'.[2] The only proper vehicle for a college's basic endowment was freehold land. Worcester, which received most of its early endowment in stocks and leasehold estates, was directed by law to acquire freeholds, even though it was clear that: 'As punctual a payment of your rents, as you have had of the Dividends of your Stock is not to be expected.'[3] All colleges, therefore, possessed estates, and all accounts begin with entries for rents. These may be conveniently subdivided into 'money-rents', 'corn-rents' and an undifferentiated amalgam of the two (as in the All Souls heading *summa firmarum*). Table 10.2 gives an idea of their course over the period from 1660 to 1810, and also, as a control on the changing value of money, a rough translation of the gross receipts into constant 1740 pounds.[4]

The overwhelming impression is one of stability. Money-rents might occasionally be revised or added to. For example, the increase between 1719–20 and 1729–30 reflects Lord Crewe's[5] gift to Lincoln of an annual rent-charge of £474 on the manor of Bamborough. But one would not expect them to fluctuate greatly. Accordingly their total rose only slightly, and their real value was overtaken by the inflation of the French revolutionary and Napoleonic wars at the end of our period. Corn-rents too represented traditional sums; they were seldom adjusted, but a proportion of each rent was linked to grain or malt prices on the Oxford market. This

Corpus: libri magni, 1660, 1670 etc.
Lincoln: calculi, 1659–60, 1669–70, 1677–8 and 1682–3 (average), 1690–1 and 1692–3 (average), 1699–1700 to 1759–60, 1770–1, 1779–80, 1790–1, 1799–1800, 1809–10.
New College: computus bursariorum (and summary of college receipts and expenditure 1800–1855), 1659–60, 1669–70 etc.
St John's: computus annuus, 1660–1, 1679–80 to 1699–1700, 1710–11, 1719–20 etc.
Wadham: bursars accounts (generally made up twice yearly), 1661, 1670, 1680 etc.

Some colleges operated on the basis of calendar years, but most ended their financial year in or around October.

[1] South Sea holdings appear to have been retained for many decades, not dumped in the great panic. In 1809 New College held some £36,100 in the public funds (of which £3,692 was specifically for the purchase of advowsons), £1,500 in transferable bonds and £3,200 in loans repayable by instalments. NCA 2595, misc. papers. This total largely reflected the investment since 1766 of the surplus yield of the timber fund, and very few colleges could have matched it. Wadham held £3,720 in old South Sea annuities in 1731, £9,124 in 1790: WCM bursars accounts, 1731, 1790.

[2] CCCA C/7/2, tower book, under 1772.

[3] Lord Harcourt–provost, Dec. 1723, WCA box D, Thomas Cookes's papers. '[You] must not account them ill Tenants if they pay one half years rent before another is due': ibid. For the legal obligation to acquire freehold land see *Enactments in Parliament* ii. 41–4, 146–8.

[4] The translation is derived from the Schumpeter-Gilboy price indices (of contract consumer goods prices paid by institutions) printed in B. R. Mitchell (with P. Deane), *Abstract of British Historical Statistics* (Cambridge 1962), 468–9, the indices to 1690 are based on a more restricted series than those from 1700 and the index for 1661 has had to be applied to college rents received (mostly) in the previous year.

[5] Nathaniel Crewe (1633–1722), 3rd bn Crewe, m. Linc. 1653; bp of Oxford 1671–4, Durham 1674–1722.

TABLE 10.2

COLLEGE RENTS 1660-1810 EXPRESSED IN CURRENT AND
(IN ITALICS) IN CONSTANT 1740 POUNDS

	money-rents Brasenose Corpus, Lincoln, St John's	'rents' All Souls Balliol, Wadham	corn-rents Christ Church, Corpus, Lincoln, New College, St John's	total
1659-60	1,200[a]	3,500	7,600	12,400[a]
	900	*2,600*	*5,700*	*9,300*
1669-70	1,700[b]	3,000	9,300	14,100
	1,500	*2,700*	*8,200*	*12,500*
1679-80	1,700[b]	2,800	9,600	14,200
	1,500	*2,500*	*8,500*	*12,600*
1689-90	1,600	2,600	7,700	11,900
	1,600	*2,600*	*7,700*	*11,900*
1699-1700	1,800	3,400	10,400	15,600
	1,600	*3,000*	*9,000*	*13,600*
1709-10	1,800	4,300	11,600	17,700
	1,500	*3,500*	*9,500*	*14,500*
1719-20	1,800	3,400	8,900	14,000
	1,800	*3,300*	*8,700*	*13,700*
1729-30	2,300	3,100	10,700	16,100
	2,400	*3,300*	*11,300*	*16,900*
1739-40	2,300	3,900	9,700	15,900
	2,300	*3,900*	*9,700*	*15,900*
1749-50	3,000	3,500	8,400	14,900
	3,200	*3,700*	*8,800*	*15,700*
1759-60	2,700	3,700	10,300	16,700
	2,800	*3,800*	*10,500*	*17,000*
1769-70	2,700	4,900	11,300	18,900
	2,700	*4,900*	*11,300*	*18,900*
1779-80	2,800	5,000	9,500	17,300
	2,500	*4,500*	*8,600*	*15,700*
1789-90	2,800	6,000	13,500	22,300
	2,300	*4,800*	*10,900*	*18,000*
1799-1800	2,800	9,000	20,700	32,500
	1,300	*4,200*	*9,800*	*15,300*
1809-10	2,800	10,100	21,700	34,600
	1,400	*4,900*	*10,500*	*16,700*

[a] The figures for 1659-60 do not include the money-rents of Brasenose.

[b] If the Brasenose money-rents were excluded, the total of money-rents would be £1,300 (*1,200*) for 1669-70 and 1679-80.

was intended to achieve stability, and appears to have done so since fluctuations in their real value were much less than changes in gross receipts. These receipts were, of course, affected by the colleges' vigour in collecting, and by the tenants' ability to pay, arrears. But overall real income appears to have edged upwards over time, appreciably but not sensationally.

TABLE 10.3

I DECENNIAL AVERAGES OF FINES RECEIVED BY ALL SOULS, BRASENOSE, LINCOLN, NEW COLLEGE AND WADHAM EXPRESSED IN CURRENT AND (IN ITALICS) IN CONSTANT 1740 POUNDS

	1690s	1700s	1710s	1720s	1730s	1740s	1750s	1760s	1770s	1780s	1790s	1800s	1810s
fines	2,054[a]	2,214	2,344	2,297	3,121	2,636	3,165	3,738	4,978	5,047	6,913	10,523	14,075
	1,802	*2,259*	*2,232*	*2,344*	*3,507*	*2,804*	*3,297*	*3,665*	*4,445*	*4,241*	*4,973*	*6,118*	*6,900*

[a] The corresponding figures for All Souls, New College and Wadham are £1,168 (*927*) for the 1660s, £1,472 (*1,303*) for the 1670s, £1,484 (*1,387*) for the 1680s and £1,541 (*1,352*) for the 1690s. The figures for All Souls, Brasenose, New College and Wadham are £1,426 (*1,131*) for the 1660s.

II DECENNIAL AVERAGES OF FINES RECEIVED, AND RENTS RECEIVED IN GIVEN YEARS, BY ALL SOULS, LINCOLN, NEW COLLEGE AND WADHAM

	1690s	1700s	1710s	1720s	1730s	1740s	1750s	1760s	1770s	1780s	1790s	1800s	1810s
(a) fines	£1,702	1,736	1,953	1,911	2,589	2,202	2,578	3,020	3,996	3,985	5,783	8,641	11,295

	1690	1700	1710	1720	1730	1740	1750	1760	1770	1780	1790	1800	1810
(b) corn-rents, rents and	5,027	5,461	7,610	6,056	5,981	6,679	6,031	5,926	7,345	7,160	7,378	12,796	12,225
$\frac{b}{a}$	3.0	3.1	3.9	3.2	2.3	3.0	2.3	2.0	1.8	1.8	1.3	1.5	1.1

Sources: All Souls: rent rolls; Brasenose: principal's fine books (BNCA B.1.d.36, 37), calculation of fines 1789 onward (B.2.d.21); Lincoln: LCA register of fines; New College: register of fines for leases 1629–1788 (NCA 39), register of fines... 1634–1818 (NCA 9793, almost but not quite identical with NCA 39), record... of the college properties, their value and fees and fines... from c1770 to c1860 (NCA 9652); Wadham: bursars accounts.

The chief gains to the colleges from growing agricultural productivity (and, at the end of this period, changes in relative price levels) came rather from fines, since these were, as will be later demonstrated, directly related to the real value of the holding. We see from Table 10.3 that, at least for the colleges in question, fines never quite overtook rents as a source of income. But the gap between the two closed markedly in and after the second half of the eighteenth century, a development that had important repercussions on the internal life of many colleges.[1] Table 10.3.1 suggests that fines rose sharply between the 1660s and 1670s, more gently thereafter,[2] and then jumped in the 1730s. Receipts fell back in the 1740s, rose in the 1760s and still more in the 1770s, and then climbed rapidly from the 1790s to a peak in the first (war-time) half of the decade after 1810.

These increases had two sources, rising rents in the country at large and a determination on the part of colleges (and other ecclesiastical landlords) to secure better bargains. Fines were set as multiples of the 'clear value' of the land in question, that is of its gross rental value less the reserved rent payable to the college. So they would naturally be raised by any increase—of which the college was aware—in rent-levels. Equally, as time went on, colleges set fines at progressively greater multiples of the 'clear value'. In Charles II's reign one year's clear value was thought proper for the addition of seven years to a twenty-one-year lease with fourteen years unexpired (the commonest form of renewal): thus the Balliol fines book refers in 1674 to 'the usuall rate of paying one year in seven'.[3] But in practice settlements a little under this rate were not infrequent in the later seventeenth century. Thereafter they became rare. And in the 1750s it became usual to take fines of one-and-a-quarter year's value. 'This Practice', Principal Cawley of Brasenose tells us, 'commenced in the Year 1752 or 1753';[4] and it was followed by New College in 1759. In 1774 New College went to one-and-a-half-years, which soon became the going rate. Trinity followed in 1777, Brasenose in 1786 and Balliol in the same decade. A pamphlet of about 1802 still regarded one and a half years as normal, and noted that the chapters of Canterbury and Westminster had recently increased to this level (though that of Christ Church held out until 1811). But it added that Magdalen charged a fraction above.[5] So (quite often) did New College,

---

[1] Thus in Brasenose fines were divided only among the principal and six senior fellows; the resultant gap between the incomes of senior and junior fellows led many of the latter into non-residence, and occasioned sporadic outbreaks of discontent: *VCH Oxon*. iii. 211-13.

[2] Some further confirmation for this seventeenth-century pattern is provided by Balliol's receipts from fines: about £605 in 1660-9, £925 1670-9, £846 in 1680-9, £1,186 in 1690-9 and £1,156 in 1700-9 despite the college's resumption of some of the house-property adjacent to its own buildings: BCA lease log book 1588-1850, which is regrettably incomplete for much of the eighteenth century.

[3] Ibid. p. 126

[4] BNCA B53/11, Principal Cawley's observations on each Article of the Senior Bursar's Onus (1777); see also the sources for table 10.3.

[5] *A Brief Statement as to some Existing Calculations, and the Practice of Several Lords, and the Alterations*

which also now let its most profitable properties (tithes) on shorter leases with correspondingly higher fines. And in 1811 Brasenose increased again to just over one and three-quarter years.[1]

Of course a college could not derive much advantage from this system unless it knew the true value of its lands. And this brings us to perhaps the most important of our themes, the colleges' recovery of meaningful ownership over their estates. Even to say 'their estates' is to adopt the colleges' own perspective. Others might see things differently; and college fellows perambulating their lands were frequently struck by the fact that local opinion attributed ownership not to the college but to the lessee. Lessees, too, might share this view. One Oriel tenant, apparently unconsciously, used the term 'quit-rent' to describe his rent to the college.[2] Properties might 'have been for many Ages and Generations' in a given family 'as Tenants by Lease'. They could be settled, mortgaged, sold or subjected to charitable rent-charges by the lessees.[3] And, it was claimed in the 1730s, land-prices reflected lessees' rights: in Berkshire a twenty-one-year lease was worth fifteen years' purchase *de novo*, and as much as fourteen years' purchase after the expiry of seven years 'because it has been always taken that the Tenant may fill it up to twenty-one Years for one Year's Purchase. Yet if the College may and will refuse filling up such Lease, it is not worth more than seven Years Purchase . . .'[4]

The question of the true status of tenants under beneficial leases was not finally resolved until the extinction of the system. But it became especially heated on two occasions, in the mid-nineteenth century when this extinction was clearly imminent, and in the 1730s. At the beginning of our present period the house of commons showed itself clearly sympathetic to the renewal of leases 'upon reasonable Terms, according to antient

newly made and making by some of them, in the Mode of Fining [c 1802] pasted into BCA lease log book, p. 173. Besides Canterbury and Westminster the pamphlet cites the chapters of Chichester, Windsor, Gloucester, Lichfield and Bath and Wells, and Winchester College; it mentions that changes were in progress at Lincoln and that the chapter of Durham thought its fines were all too low.

[1] See the sources for table 10.3: also BNCA Cawley's Observations; TCA A.48 junior bursar's book, A48: Nov. 1777; CA xxiii.b.2, fine book 1799-1811. On top of these fines sealing fees were also payable, usually to the bursars and officials directly concerned in the transaction. These varied considerably from college to college—amounting in Brasenose to just over £6 15s and in New College to £10 12s for the renewal of a ten-year lease. One tenant told Balliol in 1804 that, with the necessary stamps, such charges raised the terms for renewing his brewhouse from one and a half to about two years. In addition Brasenose also collected periodic heriots from some of their leasehold as well as their copyhold property, but this was unusual.

[2] Richard Aston in a number of his letters to Oriel. Admittedly he was continually in dispute with the college, but his letters appear careful and moderate. Oriel College bursary, drawer LL.3, Wadley, Berks.

[3] College lease-books often record the prices paid for such sales—somewhat wistfully, since they were so much in excess of any college receipts from fines (these being in effect advance payments and thus greatly discounted). In 1722 Mrs Howell bequeathed her lease of Heckfield rectory (Hants) subject to the payment of £20 p.a. to charity, and at least until 1807 New College was still (*ex gratia*) allowing for this payment when calculating the fines. NCA 9652, record . . . of the college properties, their value and fees and fines . . . from c 1770 to c 1860', fo 35ᵛ.

[4] *To the . . . Commons of Great Britain, in Parliament assembled. The Humble Petition of Anne Lush* and *Observations on Mrs Lush's Case* [1734/5], Bodl. Gough Berks. 3 (22, 22a).

Use', and intervened on at least three occasions to promote it.[1] But disputes were probably rare, for ecclesiastical landlords appear at this time
to have been very cautious. Oxford colleges were often prepared to settle
for less than the conventional rate of one year's clear value by way of
fine; and to the end of the century Prebendary Grey of Durham recommended his colleagues

to keep to the old rule in Bishop *Morton's* time ... to be easy and moderate in
renewals of leases ... if they meant to avoid the evil of those unhappy civil wars
he had bitterly tasted of, and to which, he said, some rigid Clergy had not a little
contributed.[2]

Later, however, the clergy came to feel more confident, to see no reason
why they alone should forego rising rents, and to exhibit growing energy
and professionalism in establishing the true value of their lands.[3] There
is no reason to believe that the Oxford colleges were particularly
conspicuous in this process. But their receipts from fines certainly rose,
especially in the 1730s; and they got caught up in the general anticlerical
explosion of that decade.

In 1735 Queen's refusal to renew the lease of Sparsholt rectory was
appealed to the house of commons as something of a test case:

It may be objected, that this is a private Matter only, between the College and a
single Person; Yet it's observable, that it is a growing Evil; and tho only one
complains, yet many Families groan under the Burthen; and, if not speedily
prevented, will soon extend further.[4]

Actually the college's position was quite strong, since it was refusing to
renew not for its own benefit but to augment the income of the local
vicar, and the petition was rejected on a vote.

Next winter, according to Lord Hervey, 'All the considerable debates
... in Parliament were upon church matters'. One of the measures
involved was a bill to restrain legacies in mortmain. This was the
product, we are told, partly of lawyers' self-interest and of an antipathy to
the operation of Queen Anne's Bounty, but chiefly of 'the Difficulty that
Men of gainful possessions find, to turn their Money into Land'. Both
Universities and their alumni were among those who petitioned and

---

[1] *Journals of the House of Commons* viii. 304, 315, 382 (17, 29 July, 10 Mar. 1661 OS, the cases of
George Lowe, William Balaam and Thomas Culpepper, Sir Thomas Woodstock).

[2] J. Spearman and others, *An Enquiry into the Ancient and Present State of the County Palatine of
Durham* (Edinburgh 1729), 117–18. Thomas Morton was bishop of Durham 1632–59.

[3] For two views on this process see E. Fleetwood, *An Enquiry into the Customary-Estates and Tenant-
Rights of those who hold Lands of Church and other Foundations by the Tenure of Three Lives and Twenty-One
Years with some Considerations for Restraining Excessive Fines* (London 1731, 2nd edn London 1732);
W. Derham, *A Defence of the Churches Right in Leasehold Estates* (London 1731). Derham, a canon of
Windsor, stated (p. 20) that one and a quarter year's clear value was the highest fine he had ever
heard demanded for a seven-year renewal.

[4] *Observations on Mrs Lush's Case*; for the college's reply see *The Case of the Provost and Scholars of
Queen's College. . . in Answer to the Petition of Anne Lush* (nd), Bodl. G. A. Berks c.27(2). See also *Journals
of the House of Commons* xxii. 401, 3 Mar. 1734 OS.

lobbied against the bill—and to some effect, for they were exempted from the restrictions on legacies, though not from a ban on any college owning more advowsons than half the number of its fellows. Hervey says that the bill was a popular one:

The young men all ran riot on these topics and there were none to take the part of the poor Church but a few old Tories and the Jacobites. Sir Robert Walpole, however, who hated extremes and dreaded the consequences of all intemperance in Parliament whatever, though he voted for these bills, endeavoured to quell and soften the zeal of those who voted with him.[1]

This fear may have influenced not only Walpole's subsequent political reconciliation with the bishops but also his conduct next year when a petition was again presented against an Oxford college that had refused to renew a lease. Oriel's position on this occasion was the weaker since it was in no way altruistic. The college merely wished to allow the lease of the main property to run out to strengthen its hand in negotiations over the ownership of a subsidiary holding. Parliament was asked to 'interpose to prevent the Ruin of those Families, who (relying upon the Vertue and Honour of such Reverend and Learned Societies) have purchased upon the Faith of Colleges'. And clearly it was much inclined to do so; Walpole and other leading figures spoke for Oriel, but the petition was rejected only by 119 votes to 101.[2]

A pamphlet written shortly afterwards concluded with the hope that 'a general bill will speedily be brought in ... whereby all Complaints of this Sort may, for the future, be prevented'. And in 1739 one MP seems to have asked for a general briefing on the 'Case of Church and College Leases', which he expected soon to 'come under consideration' in the commons.[3] But in fact the question appears to have died down, albeit not without sporadic grumbles.[4] By the 1750s Balliol must have felt it safe to

---

[1] John, Lord Hervey *Memoirs*, ed. R. Sedgwick, ii (London, 1931), pp. 530-8. Petitions against the bill are to be found in *Journals of the House of Commons*, xxii (1732-7), 653-4 (Cambridge and Oxford Universities), 658, 666, 669, 676, 678; see also the collection of petitions against the bill in BL SPR 357 c.3 (esp. nos 59, 63) and 8133 b.9. The cost to Oxford was £48 19s 6d: OUA vice-chancellor's accounts, WPβ/22/1, fo 4, 1735. See also P. Langford, 'Tories and Jacobites 1714-51', pp. 115-18 above. The restriction on colleges holding advowsons was repealed in 1805: *Enactments in Parliament* ii. 25, 279.

[2] See the printed material (with manuscript annotations as to the parliamentary debate of 15 March 1737 NS) preserved in Oriel, dean's register ii, under 1737. The position was complicated since the manor of Wadley had, through an exceptional arrangement, been held without fine or normal renewal since 1539, and this provided plenty of scope for disputes as to precisely which properties it covered. But a compromise was reached in 1738 as to the renewal of the main lease (though it was still occasioning correspondence twenty years later) and over the disputed subsidiary 60 acres (after further litigation) in 1750: Oriel College bursary, drawer LL.3.

[3] *Reasons for a Law to oblige Spiritual Persons and Bodies Politick to renew their Leases for Customary and Reasonable Fines* (London nd, but from internal evidence 1737), esp. p. 24; *Reasons for altering the Method used at present in letting Church and College Leases, address'd to a Member of Parliament by the Senior Fellow of a College in Cambridge* [Dr Colebatch] (Cambridge 1739), esp. p. 3.

[4] In 1766 Lord Lichfield reacted to what he took (with some justice) to be a demand for an exces-

refuse to renew leases of the tithes of St Lawrence Jewry (London), the tithes and land of Longbenton (Northumberland), and land at Oddington and Woodstock (Oxfordshire), a very substantial fraction of its total holdings; these were accordingly run out and re-let on a purely rental basis.[1] Other colleges were less drastic. But they did show themselves, in the second half of the century, distinctly tougher bargainers than they had been earlier. For they were no longer necessarily prepared to renew a lease if the lessee had neglected to apply at the proper time,[2] and were quite ready to let it run out if he declined to pay the full renewal fine asked. New College resolved in 1761 that in such cases the fine due should be advanced to fellows from general college revenues;[3] other colleges followed the same practice. Usually the lessee soon accepted that he could do no better and paid up.

However, colleges did not go further and abandon the (to them extremely disadvantageous) system of beneficial leases; indeed on a number of occasions leases that had run out were re-auctioned, not converted into rack-rents. No doubt the chief reason for such conservatism was internal. As one tenant put it to the fellows of Balliol, if they refused to renew they might simply be impoverishing themselves and making a present of his fine to successors with fewer scruples.[4] But there were also external considerations. One New College radical (William Toovey)[5] pressed for a wholesale transition to rack-rents:

The Censure of the world and such arguments were urg'd against raising the fines, but all apprehensions of this kind were found to be groundless in that case, and there appears no better foundation for any fear in this, especially if the world was inform'd that we had recourse to this measure because we found all our endeavours to gain a certain knowledge of the real values of our Estates . . . every year frustrated and eluded.[5]

But his recommendations were not adopted. And others certainly differed as to the consequences of such a change. That eighteenth-century survivor President Routh of Magdalen is said to have 'deplored the coming in of the new system [of rack-rents], because the old system of leases interested so many persons of weight and position in the protection of College property'.[6] Nor was Routh altogether wrong about the

sive fine by observing, 'I find, that some of these exorbitant demands (which are much the subject of Conversation) will probably become an Object of *publick Notice*': NCA 39, fines and leases, p. 81, under Hardwick Farm (Seager's Close), Bucks.

[1] See BCA lease log book, under these places.

[2] In 1784 Christ Church resolved that 21-year leases were not to be renewed after 14 years had expired: CA xxiii. b. 3, fines and leases 1812-44, note on cover.

[3] NCA 940, reverse of liber licentiarum, orders of the 13.

[4] BCA lease log book, no. 25, under St Lawrence and Mickle-Benton (Longbenton). In fact the college held to its resolution in 1760, 1768 and 1788. In 1795 the property was re-let for a fine, but this practice was not repeated.

[5] NCA 1204, endorsed 'Mr Toovey's Observations on the renewal of our Rectories 1767'. William Toovey, m. BNC 1747; BCL New College 1758.

[6] Fowler, *Corpus*, 332n.

likely consequences of its abandonment in the nineteenth. For parliamentary intervention on behalf of the lessees was at one point a distinct possibility; and though college endowments were not appropriated (only taxed on behalf of the university), such an appropriation was at times by no means unthinkable.

One of Toovey's grounds for urging a change had been the impossibility of gaining 'a certain Knowledge of the real values of our Estates'. The reserved rent was no guide. So colleges had, once in seven years, to arrive at a figure for each holding on which to base a fine; and the lessee obviously had no incentive to help them if they pitched it too low. In the early part of our period colleges were reduced to expedients to check on their lessees' estimates. One was simply to observe their behaviour after a fine had been set. In 1666 the lessee of Great Horwood (Buckinghamshire) unwisely thanked New College 'as Benefactors acknowleding it to be worth much more and sent word to Sir Will Smith that fines went low at N.C.';[1] so the college doubled it next time, and then left it at the new level until the 1750s. Where leases were sold, their true value could be calculated from the sale-price if this could be ascertained. In the 1670s Balliol attempted to worm the details of its principal estate out of one of its undergraduates, Longbenton's joint lessee, by playing along with his wish to extrude his co-tenant, admittedly with only partial success.[2] Lastly one could always attempt to tap local knowledge, whether of the vicar or the subtenants. But they might have been discouraged from cooperating: in 1724 one vicar had to confess that, much as he would have liked to help Christ Church, 'for fear of a Discovery here in the Country I have destroyed every Note or Paper of any Significancy' about the value of East Garston rectory (Berkshire). He could not ask the subtenant of Maiden Court Farm, a nephew of the lessee, for a sight of a terrier for fear of arousing suspicion. And he believed that

ever since the Battens had their Lease of the Parsonage from the Dean and Chapter they have always been very careful to keep it in their own hands . . . or else in one of their Dependents and not let it to a Stranger, for fear of a discovery what the true value thereof might be.[3]

An armchair critic could feel that all this was making rather heavy weather. If fines were set too high, lessees soon provided evidence of their own receipts. So perhaps fines should have been raised until this point was reached. An alternative approach, at least for the eighteenth century, would have been to base them on rateable values, as was once suggested at New College.[4]

---

[1] NCA 39, fines and leases, p. 9.
[2] BCA lease log book, pp. 116-17.
[3] CA MS estates 3, fos 15 ff.
[4] NCA 1128, proposals for improving the fellowships and augmenting the small vicarages in the

Part of the difficulty was that it was often unclear just which pieces of land a college did own. For these mostly consisted not of estates within a ring-fence but of scattered small-scale holdings, a yardland here and a close there.[1] And their lessees might well occupy the adjoining land, either in their own right or by lease from other landlords, and cultivate (or more often sublet) the whole with no regard to legal boundaries. Thus the Wisdome family owned half of the hamlet of Wighthill in Tackley, Oxfordshire, and leased the remainder from Corpus; as a result the common fields became so consolidated 'by a long Unity of Possession (the same having been rented for many years by one Tenant, and he having ploughed up the Meer Balks and removed the ancient Land Marks' that in 1776–7 it became necessary to pass an act of parliament to re-apportion them.[2] Similarly when the last lease of the 'Red Lion at Wycombe' expired, the boundary-line between Brasenose's property and the neighbouring freehold tenement 'was found to run through two of the public rooms on the ground floor and down a corridor on an upper floor'.[3] Occasionally colleges gained by such confusion of possession, but more often (being at a distance) they lost. And it was their recurrent nightmare throughout and beyond our period that, in Thomas Tanner's words, in the 'process of time the Freehold will swallow up the Leasehold Lands'.[4] One place where this in fact occurred was East Walton in Norfolk, as is described below in appendix I.

To determine either the extent or the true value of their estates colleges needed to deal more systematically. In this direction they made much progress during our period. Perhaps the civil war served as a catalyst; certainly after the Restoration there was a multiplication of fine-books, books of evidences and similar material designed to serve as summaries of, and guides to, the information available about each holding. If properly used, they would at least save a college from being taken in by blatant untruths as to past practice,[5] while the accumulation of hearsay evidence as to the rents paid by subtenants and the like would provide ammunition for bargaining with the lessee. A second step was to secure that leases were renewed at regular intervals and at regular times

gift of New College (nd but from internal evidence c 1736). In a similar vein Lord Harcourt suggested to the provost of Worcester in December 1723 that he use land-tax demands to get a detailed knowledge of the college's newly purchased estate: WCA box D, Thomas Cookes's papers.

[1] This transpires very clearly from the detailed listing of all college holdings (as of Jan. 1872) in *Parliamentary Papers* xxxvii (1873) pt 2; and before enclosure they would have been even less consolidated.

[2] *Enactments in Parliament* iv. 313–14.

[3] A. J. Butler, 'The college estates and advowsons' in *Brasenose Monographs* i. no. VI, p. 19.

[4] CA MS estates 146, fos 389–90 (1728, with specific reference to Wood Norton, Norfolk).

[5] In January 1681 NS Brasenose was induced greatly to abate its proposed fine for the renewal of St Mary College by the plea that such fines had not been levied in the past; subsequent inquiries showed this to have been a lie.

of the year. Here again much had been done by the early eighteenth century to extinguish leases for more than the statutory term of years, and a fair amount to substitute twenty-one-year leases for leases by lives.[1] There was also a move to concentrate the business of renewals at fixed times of the year. Thus before 1712 Brasenose seems to have conducted it as and when lessees presented themselves: in 1707 (NS) there were sealings on 10 January, 20 and 28 February, 21 and 22 March, 1 and 30 May, 23 June, 8 July, 25 October and 22 December, but thereafter only at Lady day and Michaelmas. The new arrangements afforded scope for more systematic consideration; as Principal Cawley records (of the middle of the century): 'Fines are set or consider'd, at least, as soon as may be in Lent and Act Terms, that, in Case fresh surveys shou'd be wanted, there may be time to make them—They are never sent to the Lessees 'till the Corn-Roll is made up ... [but were payable by 15 May/19 November].'[2]

'Surveys' constituted the final step. Colleges had, of course, always been conscious of their value. The Balliol leasebook of the 1660s notes of Nethercote, Tackley (only a dozen miles from Oxford): 'This estate is one of those whereof we can get noe Terrier; and Consequence, noe Certain knowledge of it.' To remedy such deficiencies colleges begged a sight of old court rolls or, where possible, sought information of the lessees themselves. Thus Oriel intimated to Richard Aston, when he first sought to regularize the Wadley lease, that if he supplied a map and valuation 'it would induce the College to be more favourable to him; so he lent what material he had available, some of it by then over thirty years old.[3] An alternative course was for the college itself to commission a survey. Such surveys served as an invaluable check on the evaporation of college holdings, and they often led to substantial rises in the value set on particular estates. But it was not until the 1770s that they can be said to have become common, as a result (one presumes) of obviously rising land-values.[4] Nor were they entirely without pitfalls: assessments of potential value were

---

[1] In 1693 several of Merton's landed properties were still in fact leased for more than 21 years, but by 1700 all had been reduced to this term: MCR 1.3, register 1567-1731, pp. 612, 643.

[2] BNCA Cawley's Observations.

[3] *The Case of Richard Aston, Esq. in relation to a Dispute between him and Oriel College, Oxon* (printed pamphlet inserted into OCA dean's register ii, under 1737), p. 1.

[4] This generalization is based chiefly on fine-books. But one can be more specific about some colleges. Brasenose started systematic surveying earlier than most colleges: the first general valuation book of all its estates dates from 1754 (BNC B3.c.6) and it had long had in its accounts an item *Pro Scriptis et Munimentis*, described by Cawley as 'Monies paid for Mapping and Surveying the College Estates ... Letters etc.'. This overhauled *Expensa Equitantium* ('Monies expended in visiting the College Estates') in the 1730s, but still averaged less than £13 p.a. In the 1740s this became £15, in the 1750s £22, 1760s £25, 1770s £29, 1780s £41, £1790s £44, 1800s £133 and 1810-15 £350 p.a. The Corpus tower book records the expenditure of £10 or £13 on surveys in 1702-3. Some of the subsequent lawsuits may have involved surveys, but none is recorded *eo nomine* until 1767-9 when £35 was spent. 1770-2 saw a further £6, 1782 £133 and the 1790s £60. In the 1800s £228 went on surveys, and 1810-15 £300 (though this is put into perspective by the expenditure of £80 on illuminations for the visit of the allied sovereigns in 1814).

obviously subjective; so too, unless one actually went to the expense of measuring with a chain, were estimates of area, while much confusion could be caused by the difference between local and statute acres. Until the last quarter of the century, however, the function of a college survey was perhaps chiefly as a stimulus. New College invited aggrieved lessees to commission an alternative survey by any reputable person, and offered to accept whichever estimate was the lower. In the late eighteenth and early nineteenth centuries, however, colleges placed their trust increasingly in the work of professional land-agents who would survey whole sequences of estates. During the wartime boom such men may have been tempted to pitch their assessments on the high side,[1] and with the post-war depression further reductions had to be made.

In his description of the Christ Church estate papers Bill notes that the increase in valuations 'from about 1770' occasioned the exchange of more letters with lessees. But he adds that 'the method of estate management seldom led to correspondence directly about agricultural matters'.[2] For practical purposes the lessee stepped into the shoes of the landlord; and (subject to some exceptions to be noted shortly) colleges did not *manage* their estates, but merely drew the rents. Initially this was done through bailiffs or stewards. Christ Church had apparently discontinued these by the mid-seventeenth century,[3] but they survived a lot longer elsewhere. And in 1723 Lord Harcourt advised Worcester to acquire 'a proper Steward for making your Leases and Such an One as you may readily consult on all your occasions, and some Bayliffe or other proper person [he suggested the local vicar] to receive your rents [for a commission] and have an Eye over your tenants'.[4] But the colleges' establishment of London bank accounts by the third quarter of the eighteenth century rendered such intermediaries less necessary;[5] and a system grew up whereby, when the college had calculated the corn-rent

[1] Even in 1811 Mr Gale recommended the reduction by a sixth of the estimates of his assistant Mr Hiscock: NCA 9652, esp. Widdington (Essex) and Shearinghall (in Takeley, Essex).

[2] E. G. W. Bill, 'A catalogue of estate papers at Christ Church, Oxford' (typescript in CA).

[3] E. G. W. Bill, 'A catalogue of treasury books' (typescript in CA), p. 128. The run of bailiffs' accounts at Christ Church ends in 1633.

[4] See p. 274 n. 3 above.

[5] The process cannot be precisely dated since it might, as at All Souls, be 'originally only a private transaction between Banker and Bursar though now by long Use it seems to be publicly adopted . . . and is a great convenience to the whole Society': W. Blackstone, *Dissertation on the Accounts of All Souls College, Oxford*, ed. W. Anson (Roxburghe Club cxxix 1898), 21. The Merton bursars were already using bankers in 1737, but this departure from the traditional practice of paying all rents directly into the college treasury was ascribed by the warden to their set determination to exclude him from all share in, or knowledge of, college business: MCR 1.6, Warden Wyntle's register, under 1737, esp. pp. 119–22. For the gradual growth of college banking in London from 1718, and in Oxford from the close of the eighteenth century, see D. Adamson, 'Child's Bank and Oxford University in the eighteenth century', *The Three Banks Review* cxxxvi (1982); I should like to thank Mr J. S. G. Simmons for drawing my attention to this article.

due, it sent a receipt for that amount to the bank to be released to the tenant on his deposit of the rent.[1]

Under these circumstances the day-to-day involvement of the college was minimal. New College did pay for the rebuilding of sea walls at Writtle near Chelmsford at the cost of £1,350 (or more than two renewal fines). But all ordinary repairs were the responsibility of the lessee, though he could generally draw on his college-landlord for timber and might subsequently secure a reduction of his fine in respect of exceptional expenditures. Often, too, the defence of a college's rights was effected through its lessee. Thus in 1691 Balliol transferred the lease of the tithes of St Lawrence Jewry from the parishioners to a Mr Sayer on his undertaking to embark on a lawsuit to increase their amount.[2] In 1713 New College set a fine for land in St Giles's fields, almost literally on their doorstep, on condition that the lessee 'sue for the two acres which Mr Rowney enjoys to our prejudice';[3] and a century later they observed with pleasure that their lessee Mr Bearblock (partner in a firm of land-agents) 'proceeds with his usual activity in maintaining the rights of his Landlords, which indeed cannot be maintained by ordinary exertions, or without considerable expense, under the resistance which still continues to be made in Hornchurch [Essex] against the interest of the tithe-owners'.[4]

Even enclosures were principally for lessees to effect, the convention being that, by way of compensation for the costs involved, no notice should be taken of the resultant improvement in land-values when setting the fine for the next renewal. Admittedly colleges would formally join in petitions for enclosure, and might be drawn into a joint defence with the lessee of their rights.[5] Occasionally they might seek to monitor proceedings fairly closely or, more commonly, at least purchase a copy of the final award.[6] But it could as easily happen that they were kept in

[1] The system is described, as regards All Souls, in *Parliamentary Papers* (1873) xxxvii pt ii. 580. The run of such bank acquittances at Christ Church starts in 1770: CA lviii.c.8. New College resolved in 1775 to have a London banker into whose hands tenants could pay their rents without any demand for poundage; small tenants and quit-renters, however, might still continue to pay indirectly through bailiffs. NCA 961, orders of the 13, Dec. 1775. Trinity made a similar resolution in 1780: TCA register A.48.

[2] He succeeded, and the upshot was confirmed by act of parliament in 1695-6 (*Enactments in Parliament* iv. 303-4) supposedly at Balliol's and Sayer's joint expense. Sayer made difficulties about paying £90 of his £140 share of the costs, but ultimately did so to obtain his promised first renewal at the old rate.

[3] NCA 39, fines and leases, p. 60.

[4] NCA 9652, p. 111.

[5] See for example *The Case of . . . Queen's College, Oxford, and of the Reverend Philip Brown, Clerk, against the Bill for inclosing the Parish of Uffington* (nd *c* 1777), copy in Bodl. G.A. Oxon. c.247 (14).

[6] In 1806 Corpus paid £85 in expenses for attending meetings of the commissioners for Guiting Power, whose enclosure affected the college's woods, plus a further £117 for walling its new allotment; and in 1800-2 its claim to manorial rights at Northgrove had cost it £28. But four other enclosures monitored between 1800 and 1810 cost only a total of £55: CCCA tower book.

relative ignorance. Thus Brasenose was disturbed to discover in 1773 that its Faringdon lessee had (for a consideration of ten guineas to herself) 'consented that another proprietor ... should have a road thro the whole extent of the Land allotted to this Estate'.[1] And New College remained for forty-three years unaware of the existence of twelve acres allotted to it in the 1799 enclosure of Kirby Green, near Sleaford in Lincolnshire.[2]

But if the general rule is one of collegiate indifference to the actual management of estates, there are perhaps four main types of exception: special cases, manorial courts, timber, and ecclesiastical benefices. Fortunately for our purposes the legal framework governing college holdings was so strict that special cases tended to demand private acts of parliament. Some were of only minor importance. Enclosures apart, ten exchanges of property and one sale with a view to the repurchase of land elsewhere were so sanctioned between 1734 and 1814, mostly towards the end of the period.[3] A little land was also sold to canal companies; and in 1800 colleges acquired a right to dispose of land to finance the redemption of land-tax, which led to the sale of a limited number of peripheral holdings. More noteworthy was the involvement in urban development in three areas, London, Lancashire and Oxford. Thus in 1776-7 Magdalen was empowered to grant ninety-nine-year building leases in Tooley and Bermondsey Streets in Southwark.[4] Far more spectacular was the increase in the 1691 Hulme bequest (to trustees) of properties in and around Manchester to provide exhibitions at Brasenose: originally worth £40 yearly,[5] they were producing £360 per annum by 1770. An act of that year permitted the trustees to grant building leases and to spend money on developing and improving the estate. Their powers were further enhanced in 1795, by which time the estate yielded £1,180 annually. By 1814 this had risen to £2,500. And though they greatly increased the number and value of the exhibitions, the trustees could not manage to spend all their income: so by 1814 an interest-bearing capital of £23,700 had accumulated.[6] In this case

---

[1] Faringdon is under twenty miles from Oxford, but the estate was only visited because the lessee made difficulties about the fine: BNCA B.l.d.37, principal's fine-book 1705-1804.

[2] They were only discovered because a new lessee, in all innocence, showed them to a visiting fellow. Inquiry was then made and a copy of the award unearthed 'in the house of C. Chaplin, Esq.': NCA 9652 stewards' accounts, p. 43.

[3] These acts are listed in *Enactments in Parliament*, iv, appx 3.

[4] Ibid. iv. 314.

[5] R. W. Jeffery, 'History of the college 1690-1803', *Brasenose Monographs* ii pt 1, no. XIII, p. 8.

[6] By 1827 gross estate-income had risen to £3,300 plus £1,660 interest on an accumulated capital of £42,200, while expenditure was only £3,800 p.a. So the trustees were authorized to buy livings for the former exhibitioners, twenty-eight being eventually purchased. In 1839, by which time the estates produced £4,400 gross, the trustees secured powers to augment these livings and to build or rebuild churches. This represented a substantial diversion of the charity to Lancashire objects, a process taken further by Charity Commissioners' schemes in the 1880s that restricted to

Brasenose was only a recipient. But colleges were obviously more directly involved in the redevelopment of Oxford. The two chief schemes the university promoted were perhaps Radcliffe Square, which involved a considerable exchange and purchase of property under an act passed in 1720-1, and the provision of a new and commodious way between Worcester College and 'the adjacent Parts of the City and University of Oxford'—Beaumont Street, the assembly of land for which was authorized in 1774-5 though not completed until the 1820s. But in our period, as before and since, new college and university buildings encroached on neighbouring housing. More generally, university officers and professors and the head and one other representative of each college served with a city contingent as the commissioners under the Oxford mileways and improvement acts, the university and colleges paying (after 1800) two-fifths of the total costs involved. They also took advantage of the initial 1771 act to acquire general powers of selling houses in the city and suburbs. This was not, perhaps, a wise policy in the long run, but it was justified on the grounds that many 'are irregularly built, and by reason of their contingent Tenure are frequently suffered to fall in a ruinous state'.[1]

Two other areas in which colleges involved themselves directly were the holding of manorial courts and the growth and sale of timber. Conceptually they are quite different. But together they constituted the chief reason for the periodic 'progresses' in which college heads and others visited a selection of their estates. The right to hold manorial courts was often included in leases of other property, but most colleges probably kept some courts in hand.[2] Such courts could play an important role in local life; and some heads, for instance Warden Woodward of New College, clearly took their responsibilities in this connection very seriously.[3] But, economically speaking, their chief attractions were the

£2,000 p.a. the college's share of a total income that had reached some £6,900 p.a. by 1877. But in 1907 lobbying on B.N.C's behalf secured it a half-share in the capital and (after the deduction of £2,450 p.a. payable to local grammar schools) in the income of the fund. £2,400 of this half-share was to be devoted to scholarships, and of the remainder two-thirds to Brasenose and one-third to university purposes: *Enactments in Parliament* ii. 101-2, 229-30, 318-20, 402-3, iii. 84-5, iv. 230-9; E. Baines *et al. The History of the County Palatine and Duchy of Lancaster* (4 vols London 1836) ed. J. Crofton (5 vols Manchester etc. 1888-93) ii. 10-12; A. J. Butler, 'An account of the benefactions bestowed upon the college', *Brasenose Monographs* i, no. IV, p.30.

[1] *Enactments in Parliament* ii. 13-19, 102-36, 149, 168-83; C. H. Daniel and W. R. Barker, *Worcester College* (London 1900), 184; *VCH Oxon.* iv, sections on 'Early modern Oxford: development of the city' and 'Modern Oxford: development of the city'.
[2] In the course of the eighteenth century it became common to stipulate that lessees should at least forward to their college-landlords copies of the court-rolls and business transacted.
[3] See the 'Progress notes of Warden Woodward', transcribed and edited by G. Eland and D. Ogg, typescript (1936) in New College library. Portions of these notes have also been printed, for example *The Progress Notes of Warden Woodward round the Oxfordshire Estates of New College, Oxford, 1659-1675*, ed. R. L. Rickard (Oxfordshire Record Soc. xxvii [1949]). Michael Woodward (*c* 1602-75), m. New College 1621, warden 1658-75.

fines and heriots levied for the renewal of copyholds. These were never as important as the fines derived from leases, and were more tightly constrained by the custom of the manor. But they appear to have followed a broadly similar trend, provided of course that efforts were made to collect them; some figures are given in Table 10.4 below.

Progresses had their unpleasant side. The early eighteenth-century All Souls accounts include, under this heading, an item for the provision of pistols for the party. But the college visitors were always entertained by the principal tenants (lease-books contain a number of marginal notes about the quality of this hospitality) and they enjoyed convenient opportunities for viewing holdings and, more importantly, giving directions as to timber. In a much-quoted passage Warden Woodward records:

As wee were in the coppice there came unto us about 7 or 8 of the young maidens of Tyngeswyke [Buckinghamshire] and entreating pardon for being soe bold they desired a tree to make them a maypole. To encrease good neighbourhood and love among them ... and to weane them from conventicles, a tree was granted to them and marked out for them with a crosse.[1]

Less idyllically:

It was made to appear to the Gentlemen on the Spring-Progress, 1763, that Mr Duncan had obtain'd from the Warden in 1760 an unlimited Warrant for Timber on the Pretence of Building on the College Estate; And that he had put this warrant so strictly into execution, and committed such Waste thereby, that there will not be for many years a single stick of good Timber on the Demesnes.—Thus He built an Elegant House at a small expence, leaving at the same time the Old House, where the Progress is entertain'd, in a miserable ruinous Condition.[2]

As the last quotation makes clear, the system of management was not ideal. Tenants had plentiful opportunities to help themselves to college timber and no great incentive to protect young forest trees. Critics of the system said that as a result leasehold estates were noticeably bare of timber.[3] And from time to time lessees pushed for legislation to transfer to themselves the trees on (and mines under) their holdings, which were both as the law stood the exclusive property of the landlords. The university joined in resistance to such ideas.[4] Colleges derived little benefit from their mineral rights, but for at least some of them (and notably for New College) timber was an important resource, especially during the boom of the Napoleonic wars. Table 10.4 seeks to illustrate this.

[1] 'Progress notes', ed. Eland and Ogg, p. 96 (30 May 1670).
[2] NCA 9793, register of fines 1634–1818, Birchanger, Essex. Admittedly the progress was entertained in the new house in 1764, but it may be no coincidence that the renewal-fine was increased sharply in 1767.
[3] 'The deficiency of the growth of timber [on leasehold, as compared to ordinary, estates] is almost universally admitted': *Report of the Select Committee on Church Leases*, Parliamentary Papers (1839), viii, 249–50.
[4] See the vice-chancellor's summons of 1805 to a convocation to petition against a bill 'for encouraging Planting on Church, College, and Hospital Lands': Bodl. Don. b.12, p. 106b.

TABLE 10.4

DECENNIAL AVERAGES OF RECEIPTS FROM THE SALE OF WOOD AND THE PROCEEDS OF MANORIAL COURTS EXPRESSED IN CURRENT AND (IN ITALICS) IN CONSTANT 1740 POUNDS PER ANNUM

	sale of wood				proceeds of manorial courts		
	All Souls	New College	Wadham	total	All Souls (Edgware only)	New College (all courts)	total
1660s		247					
1670s		399					
1680s		584	63				
1690s		294	40				
1700s	107	316	47	470 *479*			
1710s	136	596	27	758 *722*			
1720s	102	752	90	944 *963*	*c* 53		
1730s	59	659	68	786 *883*	498		

1740s	184	719	137	1040	106	361	467
				1106			*497*
1750s	237	692	91	1020	90	498	588
				1063			*613*
1760s	210	985	118	1313	222	508	730
				1287			*716*
1770s	281	1436	193	1910	108	587*	695
				1705			*621*
1780s	165	1395	241	1801	218	732*	950
				1514			*708*
1790s	136	1882	234	2251	183	708*	891
				1620			*641*
1800s	486	3035	420	3941	275	1485	1760
				2291			*1023*
1810s	507	3190	636	4333	136	1159	1294
				2124			*634*

* The figure for the 1770s relates only to 1770-7; that for the 1780s to 1778-91 and that for the 1790s to 1792-9.

Sources: All Souls, rent rolls (the college held other courts besides that of Edgware, but their profits were smaller and less regular); New College, bursars' annual accounts under 'wood sales' (until 1766; allowance has been made for occasional years which are missing), timber and underwood accounts (after 1766), NCA 2595, misc. papers comprising analyses of college income and expenditure (for proceeds of courts until 1799) and NCA 51, summary of college receipts and expenditure 1800-55, receipts from progresses and *extra curiam* (for courts from 1800); Wadham, bursars' accounts, summaries (these record occasional small receipts from the sale of wood in the 1660s but none in the 1670s).

Ecclesiastical benefices constitute the final aspect of their external property in which colleges might take a direct interest. It must be admitted that, in our period, such interest was often at best spasmodic. Impropriated rectories were generally viewed as property to be leased out like any other; and the responsibility for finding and paying a vicar might well be included in the lease.[1] Even where the college retained the advowson, as was Christ Church's practice, its actual involvement might be very slight, since the man formally appointed might well be non-resident and it would then fall to him to procure a curate. A case in point is the poor living of Bledington in Gloucestershire, whose minister was twice deprived by the diocesan authorities for gross neglect, and which appears to have been left without any minister at all on three further occasions between 1689 and 1738.[2] Both here and elsewhere the contrast is very striking between the dean and chapter's eighteenth-century neglect of their functions as patron and their mid-nineteenth century contributions to promote the augmentation of livings, residence of ministers, repair of churches and establishment of schools.

None the less eighteenth-century colleges were not completely indifferent. Even the living of Bledington was on occasion slightly augmented.[3] As already noted, Queen's ran out the lease of Sparsholt in the 1730s to augment the living. And in 1766 New College bought out the lessee of Chesterton in Oxfordshire and re-let the rectory cheaply to the vicar. Colleges were assemblies of clerics, and were clearly not immune to general ecclesiastical concerns. But charity apart, there were also elements of enlightened self-interest in some of their dealings with their livings. For these constituted one possible vehicle for the investment of surplus funds. Thus in 1766 New College channelled what it expected to be a temporary bulge in timber-receipts into a special account to be 'put out to interest either in the publick funds, or in … trusts … for the Improvement of our Estates and Livings by Inclosure'; and by 1787 over £5,000 had been advanced in this way to various

---

[1] In 1708 New College conceded a small rebate in the fine for the renewal of Shutford in Oxfordshire 'in consideration of the Tenant's agreeing to pay £20 yearly to the Vicar, and to lett the College have the nomination of him after the next 6 years are expir'd': NCA 39, fines and leases, p. 48 (the second half of the transaction was rather unusual).

[2] CA MS estates 25, fos 19–20; M. K. Ashby, *The Changing English Village, A History of Bledington . . . 1066–1914* (Kineton 1974), esp. 171, 186–7. There also appears to be an appreciable difference between the list of early eighteenth-century ministers preserved locally and that given in the archives of Christ Church.

[3] Christ Church reduced the lessee's fine in 1706 on condition that he raised the annual stipend *from* £17 to £20, though this may have taken some time to become operative: CA MS i.c. 4, J. Gilpin's index to register of leases. At the 1769 enclosure it gave the vicar land worth £4 p.a. In 1806 it added further land worth £10 yearly, stimulating a gift of £3 16s 0d p.a. from Queen Anne's Bounty (which had already given a small Welsh farm *c* 1740): Ashby, *Bledington*, 189, 210. In the first half of the eighteenth century Christ Church property in the village yielded the college an annual corn-rent of £20 plus a fine of £80 every seven years.

rectories, Chesterton among them.[1] One reason for these advances was the 4 per cent interest charged. But another was that livings were then an extension of the college, since most fellows hoped in due course to leave Oxford for such ecclesiastical preferment as would enable them to marry.[2] The link is shown very clearly by New College's dealings with Steeple Morden in Cambridgeshire, 'value £47 *per annum*'. In 1782 the college resolved that since no fellow 'is willing to resign for it, the said Living shall be augmented by the addition [subject to an annual payment in lieu of fees] of the great Tythes and Demesne Lands upon the expiration of the leases'. 'Mr King was then nominated upon the usual terms of resignation' of his fellowship, a motion that he be permitted to refuse without forfeiting his option of subsequent preferment being defeated.[3] The college's dilemma was that it did not wish King 'to clog the succession' by hanging on until he could secure a living, and that the 1735 mortmain act had put a limit to the number of livings it could purchase. As soon as this bar was repealed in 1805, the college took steps to re-enter the market. Other colleges with fewer advowsons were not affected by the act, and they tended to buy livings as opportunities and ready cash presented themselves. The net effect was probably an appreciable addition to the numbers of college advowsons over the course of our period.[4]

This chapter has so far concerned itself with the colleges' external holdings. But with benefices we have come very close to their internal establishments. It is now time to look briefly at the latter in order to

[1] NCA 9743, register of fines 1634-1818; NCA 1204, Warden Hayward's proposals; NCA 946 accumulated timber fund accounts 1768-1820, pp. 41-2. A further £650 had been lent to two other rectors for purposes unspecified. Thereafter such loans continued to be made, but more rarely, the fund shifting towards investment in government stocks, turnpike and canal securities and the redemption of land-tax. Corpus made similar loans to incumbents from its tower money for enclosures and also for the rebuilding of their manses.

[2] Of the 20 fellows of Brasenose in 1770, 15 left in due course for college livings, 2 resigned for reasons unstated, and 3 died in office (one having so disgraced himself as to be debarred from all college preferment): W. T. Coxhill, 'Brasenose College in the time of Principal Ralph Cawley 1770-1777' (Oxford B.Litt. thesis 1946), 31.

[3] 'Mr King' was probably Richard King, m. Queen's 1767; degrees New College. Next year the college so far relented as to agree that if he or his friends bought another living it could be held in conjunction with Steeple Morden: NCA 9793, pp. 6-7 (reverse).

[4] Lincoln bought 2 livings in the decade before 1736, 2 more in the mid-century and one in 1808, at a total cost of £5,333: V. H. H. Green, *Lincoln College 1427-1977* (Oxford 1979), appx 10. The Corpus tower book records 2 small purchases in 1694-5, one in the 1720s, 2 (costing about £2,100) in 1725 and 1736, and then in 1819 the acquisition of Great Holland (Essex) for £2,850. Brasenose bought steadily until the passage of the mortmain act, spending £8,655 on 11 advowsons between 1676 and 1736 (and also acquiring 1¾ by gift); by 1811 it was again free to buy Tedstone Delamere (Herefordshire) for £3,500. In 1660 New College already had the presentation to 26 livings (plus most of the rights to Stratton, Norfolk), but it also had far more fellows to aspire to them. It was left one living in 1675, and then bought one in 1741 for £1,120, one in 1750 for £1,300, 2 in the 1760s for £3,850, plus the remainder of the rights to Stratton for £200. A final purchase (for £3,200) in 1784 seems to have brought it up against the legal limit. In 1824 2 more livings were bought for £6,550. See NCA, list of livings (compiled by Warden Sewell).

consider two final sources of collegiate wealth, internal charges and benefactions. Unfortunately internal college accounts are even less complete than external, since many fees passed directly to servants, tutors or college officers. Thus an eighteenth-century Lincoln commoner paid at admission 5*s* to the college (*domus*), 3*s* to the bursar, 4*s* to the manciple, 2*s* 6*d* to the cook and so on (total £2 2*s*). Only the *domus* sum figured in the accounts. He also paid 4*s* 3*d* a week (divided between the lecturer, the manciple and the cook), plus candle-money and room-rents, plus £4 per annum for tuition. Other colleges had innumerable permutations on this theme. The Brasenose bursars took poundage on beer and also on food in hall (3*s* in the pound on bread and raisins, but only 1*s*. on pepper and salt). One can perhaps make two general propositions: that overall charges tended to rise in the later eighteenth century, as reflected by a widespread increase in the sums demanded as caution money; and that collectively these charges could be quite important to the recipients. The Brasenose bursarial levy on beer was commuted for £40 yearly in 1770 at a time when 'a Fellow could live fairly comfortably on £100 per annum'. And in the 1680s one fellow of Lincoln

had for some years above twenty young Scholars (at a time) under his care; insomuch, that by his Fellowship, and advantage of Pupils, he had a yearly Income of £120 . . . It was the taking of Pupils that chiefly induc'd him to stay in that College so long (the Fellowship alone being hardly sufficient to maintain him there) and 'twas, perhaps, the taking of too many, that mov'd some of the Fellows [to accuse him of seditious opinions] . . .[1]

Few college accounts concern themselves greatly with such internal income, and even they probably understate it. They do, however, make clear that in the seventeenth century it was of very considerable significance, at least to poorer colleges. Individual college fortunes did not run exactly parallel; but there would seem to have been a general decline in both the amount and the salience of internal revenue in the first half of the eighteenth century (presumably as the result of falling admissions) and also a rise at the beginning of the nineteenth. It would be interesting to know what proportion of this revenue was derived from fellows and scholars (whose payments could be regarded as merely the recycling of money they had received from the colleges' external estates) and what from commoners (who constituted an entirely independent source of income). But we can only conjecture from the St John's figures that, while commoners initially contributed more (as they did also in Balliol in 1672-3), they soon fell behind the foundationers and in the second half of the eighteenth century contributed only a little over a quarter of the total battels.

[1] For Brasenose see Jeffery, 'History of the college 1690-1803', 60-1; for Lincoln see Green, 286, 405-7; see also I. G. Doolittle, 'College administration', pp. 251-4 above.

Internal fees sometimes faded into benefactions. Thus New College expected fellows to contribute £5 and fellow-commoners £20 apiece for building.[1] But many retained a continued feeling of identification with the college and made further, and entirely voluntary, contributions later in life. We have already noted the subscription made to pay off Balliol's debts after the Fire of London. Appeals to former members had many precedents. Indeed one of the complaints against Samuel Radcliffe, principal of Brasenose 1614-48, was that he had refused to allow fellows to collect subscriptions for the projected new chapel, thus losing many promised donations.[2] And they continued sporadically throughout the period. Thus in 1804 Corpus sought assistance when faced with a prospective repair bill of £2,000 for the front quadrangle. The president prepared the way with hints and the bursar then sent round a begging letter. Unwisely he asked the college butler to address the envelopes, which led some recipients to ignore them as circulars; more seriously, he gave no indication of the expected scale of contributions. But, after one or two prompting notes, the general response was good: some £1,400 was subscribed (though one banker's draft was accompanied by the remark that the work could have been done in stucco at a third of the cost), while at most a dozen people refused and fifteen omitted to answer.[3]

Such benefactions were commonly recorded in rather grandiose vellum books, but these were seldom kept up indefinitely, and in the words of a Brasenose historian, probably 'no list of benefactions that can at present be compiled can be regarded as exhaustive'.[4] But between 1681 and 1775 some £16,600 and a Caracci picture were contributed towards New College's buildings, plus £350 and four tenements to increase the warden's stipend.[5] Between 1660 and 1792 over £54,000 was given for buildings at Christ Church; the same source puts the eighteenth-century rental of the trust estates left to Christ Church to finance exhibitions at £2,760 per annum (and the value at £72,000).[6] Cash gifts to All Souls between 1676 and 1813 exceeded £32,800.[7] Balliol

[1] NCA 3693, benefaction book for the building of the garden quadrangle 1681-2 to 1684 (but continuing to 1775), loose note by p. 101 and *passim*.

[2] *VCH Oxon*. iii. 216, 210.

[3] Some fifty names appear as subscribers, but some of these were fellows: CCCA H1/4/4, notebook 'Cist: Aedific', H1/4/5, correspondence as to the building fund.

[4] Butler, 'Benefactions', 4. This is perhaps the most extensive list of benefactions we possess, but it is not easy to tabulate since gifts took so many different forms.

[5] The building contributions made before 1771 came from the following sources: Wardens and fellows £2,758; former fellows (besides the sums included above) £3,154; fellow-commoners £4,891; founder's kin £788; chaplains £96; Winchester College £1,789; holders of college benefices £933; outsiders £1,363: total £15,772. NCA 3693.

[6] CA D.P.i.b.2, benefactions to Christ Church, pp. 1, 90, 92-4.

[7] All Souls College library, L.R.5e.10 (ult.), benefactors register.

TABLE 10.5

INTERNAL REVENUE OF BALLIOL, CHRIST CHURCH, ST JOHN'S AND WADHAM

	1660	1670	1680	1690	1700	1710	1720	1730
Balliol								
battels and arrears, *proficua*, admissions etc.		£1,352[b]	1,304	1,286[c]	2,288	2,353	3,348	2,995
% of total ordinary receipts (net of gifts and legacies)		73%	76%	80%	73%	70%	77%	78%
Wadham								
battels, chamber-rents and decrements only	£1,780[a]	1,815	1,553	1,696	1,863	1,654	1,777	1,316
% of total receipts	62%	62%	62%	55%	60%	61%	60%	41%
Christ Church								
commons (and arrears of commons) and chambers	£100	443	562	356	356	400	374	449
% of total receipts	2%	6%	8%	7%	5%	6%	6%	6%
St John's								
battels:								
foundation	£465 (47%)	472 (46%)	764 (64%)	666 (72%)	808 (49%)	788 (51%)	842 (60%)	697 (43%)
commoners	530 (53%)	552 (54%)	436 (36%)	262 (28%)	854 (51%)	755 (49%)	568 (40%)	501 (38%)
total battels	£995	1,024	1,200	928	1,662	1,543	1,410	1,327
% of total real receipts	41%	44%	51%	43%	54%	45%	45%	47%

[a] 1661.   [b] 1672–3.   [c] 1691–2.

	1740	1750	1760	1770	1780	1790	1800	1810
Balliol								
battels and arrears, *proficua*, admissions etc.	£2,595	2,230	2,000	1,737	2,488	2,166	2,092	3,728
% of total ordinary receipts (net of gifts and legacies)	65%	61%	62%	44%	53%	42%	36%	44%
Wadham								
battels, chamber-rents and decrements only	£894	881	937	1,151	1,648	1,965	2,034	3,686
% of total receipts	29%	37%	40%	34%	47%	49%	34%	45%
Christ Church								
commons (and arrears of commons) and chambers	£225	136	232	475	367	642	812	752
% of total receipts	3%	2%	3%	5%	6%	6%	5%	5%
St John's								
battels:								
foundation	£697 (43%)	654 (75%)	626 (80%)	697 (71%)	939 (74%)	986 (65%)	1,628 (74%)	2,210 (63%)
commoners	939 (57%)	223 (25%)	154 (20%)	288 (24%)	334 (26%)	522 (35%)	576 (26%)	1,308 (37%)
total battels	£1,636	877	780	985	1,273	1,508	2,204	3,518
% of total real receipts	37%	34%	32%	32%	34%	34%	43%	44%

The items recorded above constitute the bulk of internal revenue, but other internal items appear discontinuously in the main or subsidiary accounts. The Wadham and St John's totals of receipts includes fines, those for Balliol and Christ Church do not; this will affect the ratio borne by internal revenue to total receipts.

seems to have accumulated benefices, receiving eleven (plus £200 towards the purchase of a twelfth) between 1692 and 1724.[1]

Some of these gifts could prove embarrassing, like that to Brasenose to endow an annual panegyric on James II. And they were not, as a whole, on a scale comparable with ordinary college revenues. But they were well worth having, and were looked out for. One of the reasons for Oriel's choice of George Carter as provost in 1708 was supposedly that he was rich and might become (as indeed he did) a significant benefactor.[2] And poor colleges could always aspire to encounter a 'second founder'. Lincoln had considerable hopes in this connection of Nathaniel, Lord Crewe, bishop of Durham; but in 1719 they partially undid them by first asking his advice as to the election of their new rector and then disregarding it.[3] Jesus was more fortunate. Its former principal, the diplomat and civil servant Sir Leoline Jenkins,[4] not only largely rebuilt its library during his lifetime, but roughly doubled its income on his death in 1685 by leaving it lands to the annual value of about £700 plus his old school in South Wales. The college had already been fairly successful in attracting gifts, and continued to be so into the next century, when Edmund Meyricke[5] left it further lands worth £150 per annum. As a result Jesus rose from being in the 1590s the poorest college to a position somewhere near the middle.[6]

But, if one disregards the shadowy eighteenth-century incarnation of Hertford (formally chartered in 1739 and dissolved in 1816), only one new college was actually founded in our period, Worcester. In the later seventeenth century Gloucester Hall was clearly anxious to upgrade itself. At first there was talk of doing so in connection with a scheme for educating the persecuted Greeks 'in the true doctrine of the Church of England'. And between 1692 and 1707 Principal Woodroffe[7] sought to realize this project, largely at Treasury expense: the result was a tragicomedy. Then in 1696 Sir Thomas Cookes, a Worcestershire baronet, let it be known that he wished to devote £10,000 to the foundation of an Oxford college. He was at once pursued by Woodroffe, and soon after by John Baron, master of Balliol (which had already in 1674-5 appealed to

---

[1] The college's visitor at this time was the bishop of London, and seven advowsons came from this source: BCA D.8. 1 and 3, lists of benefactors and benefactions 1263-1864 (compiled by H. Wall).

[2] D. W. Rannie, *Oriel College* (London 1900), 140-1 (citing Hearne).

[3] Green, *Lincoln*, esp. 294-301. Nevertheless Crewe still left the college the not inconsiderable sum of £494 p.a.

[4] Leoline Jenkins (1623-85), m. Jesus 1641, principal 1661-73; MP Hythe 1673-8, Oxford Univ. 1679-85.

[5] Edmund Meyricke (d. 1713), m. Jesus 1656; incorp. Camb. 1663; canon of St David's 1690.

[6] E. G. Hardy, *Jesus College* (London 1899), esp. chaps 5, 9. For its position in the 1590s see Table 10.1 above; in 1871 its external income was some 2.4 times that of Pembroke.

[7] Benjamin Woodroffe (1638-1711), m. Ch.Ch. 1656; principal Gloucester Hall 1692-1711.

the Worcestershire gentry and clergy to found fellowships at 'Balliol Colledge commonly known by the name of Worcester Colledge').[1] Between them Woodroffe and Baron so badgered Cookes that he thought of transferring his gift to the establishment of workhouses. But he died in 1701, leaving the disposition of his £10,000 to trustees (the heads of Oxford houses afforced by five bishops). Other halls now joined in the hunt, and for a time Magdalen Hall seemed likely to secure the legacy. But, after prolonged politicking, the high tory connection of Simon, Lord Harcourt ultimately carried the day for Gloucester Hall, which in 1714 formally became Worcester College and acquired the legacy (now swollen by interest to £15,000).[2] Other gifts followed: at least £18,800 plus land worth some £800 per annum by 1777, and in 1787 £15,200, which enabled the college to begin purchasing advowsons. But building had accounted for some £8,600.[3] And Worcester has always been among the poorer colleges, though in 1871 (the first date for which we have comparative figures) not quite as poor as Pembroke or Trinity.

That only one college, and that a poor one, was founded in our period is an important contrast with earlier centuries. And the chronology of the benefactions discussed in the previous paragraphs suggests something of a falling off as the eighteenth century proceeded. Fortunately they were the less needed since overall college income was on the increase. This tendency is illustrated by Table 10.6; but, given the growth of activities outside the main accounts which have been discussed at the beginning of this chapter the true rise is probably rather greater than that here shown.

The rise in college incomes naturally led to growing payments to their fellows. To explore these here would be to trespass on other chapters in this volume. But we may note, by way of conclusion, that some contemporaries eventually became aware of the new prosperity and wondered how long it could last. Thus in December 1809 Warden Gauntlett of New College formally recorded his

apprehension, that, notwithstanding the late increase of the Capital Stocks of the College by high prices of Corn, large receipts on the Progresses, and extraordinary profits on the sale of Timber, these sources of revenue may . . . eventually suffer a diminution, which may render it wholly inexpedient to divide so many Increments, as with the reluctant concurrence of the Warden it has been agreed to advance this present year.

[1] Wood, *Life and Times* ii. 308.
[2] L. S. Sutherland, 'The foundation of Worcester College, Oxford', *Oxoniensia* xliv (1979). One of the inducements at Harcourt's disposal was the annexation of cathedral prebends to the headships of Oriel and Pembroke and the conferment of similar patronage on Baron personally.
[3] Daniel and Barker, *Worcester*, chaps 7, 8, 10.

TABLE 10.6

TRENDS IN COLLEGE INCOMES

	All Souls	Balliol	Brasenose	Christ Church	Corpus	Lincoln	New College	St John's	Wadham	Total current £s	constant 1740s £s
c1660	2,900	—	1,000	4,000	2,900	500	3,600	2,500	2,900	—	—
1670	2,400	1,900	1,000	6,900	3,700	400	3,500	3,100	2,900	25,800	22,700
1680	2,500	1,700	1,300	6,900	3,700	500	4,500	3,200	2,500	26,800	23,600
1690	2,200	1,600	1,800	5,300	3,700	600	4,400	3,000	3,100	25,700	25,700
1700	2,600	3,100	1,900	7,400	3,700	800	3,800	3,800	3,100	30,200	26,300
1710	3,500	3,400	1,800	7,000	3,200	800	5,000	4,300	2,700	31,700	26,000
1720	2,300	4,300	1,800	5,700	4,000	700	4,800	4,000	2,900	30,500	29,900
1730	2,600	4,200	4,400	7,900	4,500	1,300	4,600	4,000	3,200	36,700	38,600
1740	3,300	4,000	2,100	6,600	4,400	1,300	4,900	4,700	3,100	34,400	34,400
1750	2,400	3,700	2,600	5,500	4,000	1,300	4,400	3,500	2,400	29,800	31,400
1760	2,900	3,200	2,700	7,700	4,500	1,300	4,500	3,300	2,400	32,500	33,200
1770	3,500	4,000	3,600	7,800	5,300	1,400	7,500	4,500	3,400	41,000	41,000
1780	4,200	4,700	3,400	6,300	4,700	1,300	6,700	5,300	3,500	40,100	36,500
1790	4,000	5,200	4,700	11,200	7,600	1,700	8,600	6,600	4,000	53,600	43,200
1800	7,000	5,800	6,100	17,000	7,900	2,800	13,900	8,400	6,000	74,900	35,300
1810	7,100	8,400	9,200	16,200	11,100	3,000	16,200	11,500	8,200	90,900	43,900

Since accounts differ greatly in their comprehensiveness, this table cannot be used to compare one college's income with another's.

Sources: principal land for St John's also subsidiary college accounts. For Balliol and, more importantly, Christ Church, these do not include any share of fines, wood money, etc.: for All Souls, St John's and Wadham they do contain such a share. The Corpus figures have been adjusted to include *all* the fines received in the sample years, those for Brasenose and Lincoln (from 1690) and for New College throughout to include the average of fines received in the appropriate decade. The New College figures also show the true proceeds of wood sales, rather than the sums transferred to the main accounts, but they exclude the copyhold fines etc. collected on progresses, which were first brought into the main account circa 1790.

The following March nine of his colleagues replied with a counter-state-
ment by way of

proof, that if any future vicissitudes should render a diminution of the present
eight Increments necessary, they were at the time justified in promoting such
an advance from the then actual state of the college Finances, viz its funded
property, corn rents, Progresses and sale of Timber . . . and that they are not
apprehensive of any future contingency that may create such a diminution.[1]

[1] NCA 960, letters inserted on the back of 'orders of the 13'. Samuel Gauntlett (*c* 1745–1822), m.
Trin. 1762; degrees New College, warden 1794–1822.

Appendix I

EAST WALTON, NORFOLK

WE have seen that beneficial leases often amounted to a system of dual ownership, with lessees as well as landlords feeling that they 'owned' the property in question and behaving accordingly. In such circumstances the establishment of title constituted a (perhaps the) major part of a college's estate-management. The problems this could occasion are dramatically illustrated by the Christ Church holdings at East Walton in Norfolk.[1]

The village contained three manors, whose history Christ Church traced in the early eighteenth century. Abbots Manor had been leased in the reign of Edward VI by the bishop of Norwich to the local landowning family, the Barkhams. Over the next three-quarters of a century the Barkhams also bought the freehold of Priors Manor and then the lease of Christ Church's own holdings, the united manors of Howards and Stranges. This last lease expired in 1649, and in 1653 and 1661 the college re-granted it to the chapter clerk; but by 1668 Sir Edward Barkham had again recovered it. Sir Edward's heiress later married Charles Yallop, to whom in due course the Christ Church lease descended. And in 1716 this, and most of the other Barkham estates in the village, passed to Yallop's creditor, Naish—in fact by way of mortgage, though it was represented locally as an outright purchase. Naish was himself in financial difficulties, and died abroad shortly after the expiry of his Christ Church lease in 1726 (NS).

This represented the college's apparent opportunity. The lease was re-granted to one of its lawyers, evidently as a holding operation, and Canon Tanner (who was also both a prominent Norfolk cleric and an antiquarian) started enthusiastic investigations into the extent of Christ Church's rights. Thus he cultivated Naish's former steward and gained access to the old court rolls; he 'opened some of the tenants' hearts with a little Beef and some thick Ale', and so ascertained the correct site of the manor court; and, armed with a transcript of a four-hundred-year-old survey, talked 'so that both Steward and Tenants thought I knew more of the Estate, than I fear we shall be able to make out'.

The chief problem was what Christ Church saw as the leakage of its property. In 1497 the owner of Howards and Stranges manors had held (or

[1] The following account is based on CA MSS estates 51, fos 1–282, 146, fos 380–7; Bill, 'Calendar of estate papers at Christ Church' vol. v, under East Walton; Gilpin's index to register of leases, under East Walton.

sublet) the manor sites, and demesnes amounting to 774 of the 2,150 acres in the common fields. But he had then leased them all out as copyholds by inheritance. In the course of the seventeenth century the Barkhams had bought these copyholds up as occasion arose, and had continued to hold them without the formality of any new grants until the advent of a family quarrel in about 1700. At that point Mrs Yallop was hastily admitted to some 193 acres of recent purchase; but as only a total of some 500 acres of copyhold could be traced, two to three hundred remained unaccounted for. Tanner hoped to regularize the position and collect the appropriate fines and arrears from Naish's heir, to whom he would then have renewed the lease of the manor, both for reasons of equity and since 'Naish can afford to give more than anybody else what ever, because it intermixes with his own lands, and it would be better the Chapter take a reasonable fine of him, than to go into Chancery, which we must for the discovery of our estate'.

Unfortunately Naish could not so afford. In 1733 he was imprisoned for debt in the Fleet and later he escaped abroad; his estate was settled by act of parliament on trustees empowered to compound with his creditors, and in 1741 Yallop's heir, Spelman, contracted to pay these creditors. The process involved very lengthy litigation, which spilled over into further lawsuits to distinguish the bishop of Norwich's land in Abbots Manor (leased to Mrs Barkham) from the Naish estates. Locally there was a great deal of confusion. In 1740 Christ Church's new agent was initially unaware of Mrs Barkham's precise identity and included Abbots Manor (as well as Howards and Stranges) in his account of 'Estates which are known to belong, and Estates which are supposed to belong to the Dean and Canons of Christ Church'. So it is not surprising that the college's inquiries into the true extent of the Naish copyholds proved unavailing. Since it could not locate them, it could not in any meaningful sense pronounce them forfeit for non-payment of fines and rent. Accordingly Christ Church was advised in 1746 that 'As the Boundaries by the Unity of Possession are so confounded', its only recourse was to file a bill in chancery for their determination. Rather than do this it compromised with Spelman, who had already come to terms with the bishop of Norwich for Abbots Manor. He was to pay £461 arrears of rent and be admitted in general terms to the copyholds; but their precise situation was to remain unspecified, a decision whose consequences did not work themselves out till the early twentieth century.

Further delay was occasioned by Spelman's indictment (in another connection) for forgery. But in 1753 the compromise came into effect and Howards and Stranges manor was again leased to him. Seven years later he sold his estate in the village, and by the end of the century this had passed by marriage to the wealthy Hamond family. By now it had become clear that the manor itself was of secondary importance, its income confined to quit rents and the occasional fines from the copyholds. These the Hamonds progressively engrossed; and in 1842 the family held, under a variety of tenures, the entire village. Among these holdings were 492 acres in copyhold from Howards and Stranges manor—that is virtually all that Christ Church had been able to trace as copyhold a century earlier. For good measure, at the enclosure of that year

Hamond claimed all the waste lands in respect of another manor—a fact of which Christ Church appears not to have heard till 1855.

Christ Church then determined not to renew the Howards and Stranges lease, rather to Hamond's annoyance. But just before his manorial lease ran out he put into his copyhold two new lives, the second of which lived until 1899. So Christ Church did nothing but collect quitrents until 1897, when the then Mr Hamond asked to buy the manor. The college received professional advice to sell, especially as the copyhold act of 1894 entitled Hamond to compel the enfranchisement of his copyholds. But instead Christ Church preferred to resurrect its claim to the missing manor-house and to 234 acres of demesne land which it had been unable to trace in the eighteenth century. (This claim might perhaps have been in order when the college recovered the manor in 1856, but it was now definitely debarred by the statute of limitations.) Christ Church further sought to reserve from enfranchisement the manorial wood, mineral and sporting rights; but, as Hamond repeatedly pointed out, these could not in fact be exercised since his copyholds, over which they obtained, could not be distinguished from his freehold property, over which they did not. Ultimately the possible costs of fighting the case induced a compromise, and full enfranchisement was effected in 1900 for £1,189. But since Christ Church had declined to sell the manor of Howards and Stranges, it found itself liable to a quitrent from that manor to another of 9s per annum; in 1902 it defaulted.

Appendix II

CENTRAL UNIVERSITY FINANCE, BENEFACTIONS AND BUILDINGS

The bulk of central university spending was carried on accounts with which each vice-chancellor was charged, his *computus*, the 'schools account' and later the 'theatre account'. Little or nothing was contributed—financially—to the university by the colleges. So its income was independently derived from a variety of sources: landed estates, investments, fees,[1] the takings of the University Press, licences to sell wine (thirty-nine at £2 10s 0d each in 1809-10), and the like. Expenditure went on general university purposes, on the Press and (especially in the earlier part of our period) on building. The accounts themselves left a good deal to be desired, and by 1725-6 were clearly felt to be distorted by purely paper transactions:

> whereas the foot of each Account is swelled to an extraordinary large Summ by charging one of them with most of the Expences of every year, and by several losses of Rents due to the same Account; it is ordered that £12,000 be left out of that Account where the V.C. is creditor, and the like summ of £12,000 be left out of the Schools Account where he is Debtor.[2]

And indeed such surgery could, with advantage, have been carried a good deal further. The following table represents an attempt to net out real income and expenditure.

The vice-chancellor, then, had a good deal less money at his disposal than had an affluent society like New College or Christ Church. (And the proctors had even less, since their receipts did not exceed £100 per annum until after the introduction in 1800 of examination fees.) In terms of benefactions and buildings, too, the university itself operated on a broadly collegiate scale. Table 10.8 attempts to list the chief academic benefactions of our period.

Lastly, buildings. The first part of our period witnessed the creation of the

---

[1] The Laudian statutes of 1636 had standardized degree and other fees and arranged for their collection by university bedels: *Statutes*, trans. Ward i. 208-9, 213-14. Towards the end of our period this system was developed, in a small way, to finance the expansion of university activities. In 1780 'A New Statute for Providing for the Maintenance of the Bodleian Library' imposed a *per capita* charge on all entitled to use it; in 1800 candidates for the new university examinations were charged £1 so that their examiners might each be paid £50; and in 1804 a 'preaching tax' of 3s a head per quarter was imposed to support university sermons: ibid. ii. 15 ff, 35, 50 ff. In the early nineteenth century such levies were collected through the colleges, together with a 'fire and water tax' and 'the annual charge for the public walks'. And from 1823 the university took to itself the fees previously collected by its bedels, in exchange placing the bedels on a regular salary: ibid. ii. 115.

[2] OUA vice-chancellor's accounts, 1725-6.

TABLE 10.7

COMPUTUS, SCHOOLS AND THEATRE ACCOUNTS—IN CURRENT
AND (IN ITALICS) IN CONSTANT 1740 POUNDS

	income	expenditure		income	expenditure
1659-60	869	782	1739-40	1,995	1,268
	(653)	(588)		(1,995)	(1,268)
1669-70	989	1,969	1749-50	2,038	1,931
	(871)	(1,735)		(2,145)	(2,033)
1679-80	1,167	2,142	1759-60	1,834	2,148
	(1,029)	(1,888)		(1,871)	(2,192)
1689-90	986	816	1769-70	3,130	2,839
	(986)	(816)		(3,130)	(2,839)
1699-1700	1,061	1,146	1779-80	3,328	4,447
	(923)	(997)		(3,025)	(4,043)
1709-10	1,619	1,436	1789-90	4,418	4,307
	(1,327)	(1,777)		(3,345)	(3,473)
1719-20	1,314	1,582	1799-1800	6,005	4,937
	(1,288)	(1,551)		(2,833)	(2,388)
1729-30	1,607	1,832	1809-10	10,608	7,379
	(1,692)	(1,928)		(5,125)	(3,565)

Sources: OUA vice-chancellor's accounts 1621-1803, WPβ/21/4-6, 22/1-2, OUA university accounts 1803-22, WPβ/22/3.

university complex to the north of the Bodleian Library. Here the Sheldonian Theatre was built between 1664 and 1669, at a cost to Bishop Sheldon of £12,200 (plus a further endowment of £2,000 for repairs). From 1678 to 1683 the university spent some £4,500 on the construction of the old Ashmolean Museum. And 1710-13 saw the erection of more spacious premises for the Clarendon Press, at a cost (to 1715) of some £6,200.[1] Then in 1714 the noted London doctor John Radcliffe died, leaving to trustees about £88,000 net.[2] They were to provide £40,000 for the erection of a library; and by 1748 the Radcliffe Camera had been built at a total cost of £43,200, though the university cannot be said to have derived much academic benefit from it until after 1810.[3] The trustees next proceeded to build the Radcliffe Infirmary, which, as a by-product, encouraged medical studies at Oxford (further assisted in 1780 by the Lichfield Trust for clinical instruction). And they were then persuaded by the professor of astronomy to embark on the construction of a proper observatory—between 1772 and 1800 its building and furnishing cost them some £31,700.[4]

[1] *VCH Oxon.* iii. 50, 54-5; Wood, *Life and Times* iv. 78.
[2] Bodl. MS DD Radcl. c.65, 'Abstract of the General Acct to 1718 St Mich to be pass'd 1720 in Augst' lists his effects as: personal estate £75,422, real estate £54,400, total £129,822; less debts owing from the estate £29,021, legacies, funeral charges and mourning £13,042. The legacies included £5,000 to University College, which was also to receive a further £600 p.a.
[3] *Building Accounts of the Radcliffe Camera*, esp. p. xlv and appx II. £20,000 is said to have been spent at the celebrations accompanying the opening of the Camera: W. R. Ward, *Georgian Oxford* (Oxford 1958), 178.
[4] C. Hussey, 'The Radcliffe Observatory, Oxford', *Country Life* lxvii (May 1930), 680.

TABLE 10.8

BENEFACTIONS FOR ACADEMIC PURPOSES

date[a]	benefactor	benefaction	beneficiary or purpose
1708	Henry Birkhead		professor of poetry
1717	Lord Almoner	£25 p.a.	professor of Arabic
1724	George I	£371 p.a. net	regius professor of modern history and languages
1734	William Sherard	£3,000	professor of botany and keeper of the physick garden
1749	Lord Crewe	£200 p.a.	
1758	Charles Viner	£12,000	law
1771	John Bampton	b	theological lectures
1780	earl of Lichfield	£7,000	clinical medical instruction
1793	George III	£182 p.a.	professor of botany and keeper of the physick garden
1795	Richard Rawlinson	c	professor of Anglo-Saxon
1796	John Sibthorpe	d	supplementation for the professor of botany
1798	Henry Aldrich	e	three professors
1807	John Wills	£4,765	the vice-chancellor, the Sheldonian Theatre, the Press, Bodley's librarian
1812	John Bird	f	an assistant to the astronomer
1812–20	prince regent	£400 p.a.	professors of mineralogy and geology; augmentation of other posts

[a] Derived from: *Historical Register of the University of Oxford* (Oxford, 1900), pp. 65, 117; *First Supplement to the Oxford Historical Register of 1900* (Oxford, 1921), pp. 33–40; Accounts of University Trusts and Benefactions (for the Rawlinson, Sibthorpe, Wills and Bird benefactions). The date shown in the table is that at which the benefaction took effect. The table does not include Sir Robert Taylor's bequest of £65,000 in 1788 to create an establishment for 'the teaching and improving the European languages', since the money did not come to the university until 1835.

[b] An estate that in 1900 produced £120 p.a.

[c] Bequeathed 1755 to come into effect in 1795. In 1768–70 the rents yielded £70 p.a.

[d] £275 p.a. gross rent in 1800.

[e] Dividends of about £350 p.a. 1804–10.

[f] Bequeathed 1794; proceeds initially ploughed back into the purchase of stock. 1812 saw the first recorded payment (£60 p.a.) for assistants to the astronomer.

I I

The University and Social Life

V. H. H. GREEN

THE most obvious feature of Oxford's history in the eighteenth century was the decline in the number of undergraduates. The number of fellows of colleges hardly changed; the number of colleges was marginally increased by the establishment of Worcester and the refounding of Hertford; but matriculations fell steeply. This decline had started in the later years of the seventeenth century; entries to the university, about 460 in the 1660s, had slumped to about 310 a year by the 1690s, fell as low as 200 a year in the 1750s, then began to recover slowly in the century's closing decades reaching approximately 250 in 1800.[1]

No college or class of the student community was exempt from this development. The total of entrants, for instance, in twelve representative colleges[2] amounted to 1,746 for 1700–9, 1,825 for 1710–19, 1,724 for 1720–9, 1,544 for 1730–9, 1,207 for 1740–9, 992 for 1750–9, 1,162 for 1760–9, 1,338 for 1770–9, 1,415 for 1780–9 and 1,350 for 1790–9. Though the figures for entry to individual colleges fluctuated considerably from decade to decade, the majority of colleges apparently had their lowest entry between 1740 and 1770, in general reaching a nadir in 1750–9. One significant exception to this general rule appears to have been Magdalen, which actually had its highest number of admissions in the decade 1750–9 (though since its entry was confined to gentlemen-commoners and those on the foundation, its numbers were always small and rarely fluctuated by more than 10 in the period; they were 68 in 1690–9 and 58 in 1790–9). The other was Lincoln, which was to reach its lowest ebb in the closing years of the century, a period when other colleges were seemingly on the edge of recovery. The decline at Lincoln was partly associated with the reputation of its unpopular rector, Edward Tatham. Although the intake in every college went down, it did not necessarily do so at the same time in all societies. Balliol, which had achieved a peak in 1710–19, underwent a progressive decline thereafter,

---

[1] L. Stone, 'The size and composition of the Oxford student body 1580–1909' in L. Stone (ed.), *The University in Society* (2 vols Princeton 1975) i. 6.

[2] Balliol, Brasenose, Christ Church, Corpus Christi, Lincoln, Magdalen, Oriel, Pembroke, St John's, Trinity, University College and Wadham.

reaching an all-time low in 1770–9, when 89 men were admitted by comparison with 318 in 1710–19. Lincoln and Wadham had their highest entry in 1690–9, but both thereafter declined, Wadham after 1730 (possibly reflecting in part the scandalous episode of Warden Thistlethwayte)[1] and Lincoln after 1740. Pembroke, which had its high-est intake in 1720–9, had a very poor entry in 1750–9, after which its numbers improved. University College too experienced an all-time low in 1750–9 (an entry of 57 by comparison with 170 in the decade 1730–9, 105 in 1760–9 and 165 in 1770–9). The principal exception to the prevailing trend, its history so often untypical of the university as a whole, was Christ Church. The college had a high entry of 378 in the decade 1710–19. Subsequently its numbers fell, as indeed was the case in most other colleges, more especially between 1740 and 1760 (341 admissions in 1740–9 and 227 in 1750–9); but then, unlike most other colleges, entries increased rapidly, admissions numbering 312 for 1760–9, 354 for 1770–9, 423 for 1780–9 and 478 for 1790–9. This astonishing reverse of fortune almost certainly reflected the high regard in which its deans, in particular the princely Cyril Jackson, were held by the established classes, as well as the competence of its tutors.

The rise and fall in numbers may then be associated with particular factors, such as the character of a college at any given time and the reputation of its head and tutors; but general features were at work, political and social in their nature, which must also be taken into account in seeking to explain the slump in admissions which the uni-versity experienced in the eighteenth century. Oxford's supposed ident-ification with Jacobitism, its associations with toryism and high-churchmanship (in the first half of the century) caused anxiety to whig politicians and were an obvious disincentive to parents who wished to ensure some measure of future patronage and preferment for their sons. Contrariwise the reconciliation between the crown and the university after 1760, demonstrated by royal visits to Oxford, was a significant factor in reassuring the established classes. Alarmed by the onset of subversion in church and state which it was the function of a university education to counter, they were encouraged to entrust their offspring to Oxford's care. As throughout its history, Oxford's current reputation in the public mind often reflected what it had actually been a decade or so earlier. In the early decades of the century the univer-sity had been continuously sniped at by whig publicists and pam-phleteers who stressed the incompetence and indolence of professors and tutors, the extravagance and dissipation of students. For some at

---

[1] Robert Thistlethwayte (1691–1744), m. Wadham 1707, warden 1724–39; canon of Windsor 1739. See *A Faithful Narrative of the Proceedings in a late affair between the Rev. John Swinton and Mr George Baker both of Wadham College, Oxford* (London 1739).

least the stream of criticism, if in some ways unjustified, ultimately had its effect, eroding the confidence of parents in the university's capacity to supervise the morals and to instruct the minds of their sons. For somewhat other reasons such criticisms were again gathering strength in the later years of the century.

The reasons for the decline may be clarified further by examining the classes of students who were most affected by it, on the one hand the children of the well-born and affluent, on the other hand those of plebeian birth. There was (by comparison with the seventeenth-century entry) a conspicuous fall in the admission of the children of the titled. 'From an estimated 45 a year in the late 1630s, the number of freshman sons of peers, baronets and knights fell to 16 in 1661, and dropped again to an all-time low of 7 in 1785–86.' It has thus been concluded that 'a smaller and smaller proportion of the children of the social élite' came to Oxford.[1] In practice those who entered with the status of noblemen (or even nobles who had the status of gentlemen-commoners) always formed a minute segment of the university and were largely confined to a single college, Christ Church. Although there was a pronounced decline in the number of nobles admitted between 1720 and 1760, by the final decade of the century the number was actually higher than it had hitherto been, though running even so at rarely more than 4 admissions a year.

The fall in the admission of gentlemen-commoners is more instructive. Not all the children of the titled wished to pay the much higher fees which noble status involved, and were content to opt for the status of gentleman- or fellow-commoner which gave them very similar privileges. The sons of the affluent and well-born supplied the bulk of the gentlemen-commoners. Their numbers certainly fell, though the fall appears proportionately not very much greater than that of the decline in the entry to the university as a whole. Christ Church had always had a lion's share of the gentlemen-commoners and by the end of the eighteenth century very nearly had a monopoly of them. Between 1700 and 1709 the college admitted 80 gentlemen-commoners: in the decades 1730–9 and 1740–9 this number was halved, but admissions rose again with comparative rapidity, with an entry of 91 gentlemen-commoners in 1760–9, 78 in 1770–9, 84 in 1780–9 and 105 in 1790–9. At some colleges, such as University College (where none was admitted after 1740, though there were compensatory increases between 1730 and 1750 in the number of candidates entering as *superioris ordinis commensales*) and Lincoln (where none was admitted after 1766), numbers had always been low. On the other hand, Brasenose, which became to some extent a rich and fashionable society in the later eighteenth century, saw an influx

[1] Stone, 'Size and composition', 47.

of gentlemen-commoners between 1750 and 1770, followed by a steep decline in their numbers thereafter. Pembroke, Wadham and Trinity, which witnessed a decline in the number of gentlemen-commoners admitted in the middle decades of the century, had in part retrieved the situation before its close. All told, given the drop in numbers in the university as a whole, the fall in the admission of the children of the social élite may have been less substantial and less significant than has sometimes been suggested.

None the less, the decline in this group of entrants was sufficiently significant to call for an explanation beyond the fluctuations of politics. 'The Universities, Oxford especially', Bishop Burnet commented as early as 1704, 'have been very unhappily successful in corrupting the principles of those, who were sent to be bred among them'.[1] 'The gentry and nobility', Dudley Ryder added in 1716, 'are afraid of sending their sons there, and begin to take them from thence and send them to foreign parts, particularly to Holland, for education.'[2] Yet there were reasons other than political which made the prospect of an Oxford education less attractive than it had once been for the sons of the well-born. To many the university was no longer providing what they expected of it for their children. A foreign tour under the guidance of a tutor could act as a more efficacious finishing school. Besides the rigidity of the curriculum and its fossilized character, widely publicized by Oxford's critics, there was the additional deterrent in the minds of some parents that an Oxford education might debauch the bodies as well as corrupt the minds of the would-be student, attracted by fast living and to over-indulgence, indolence and pleasure. 'The higher a young man's rank is', a writer commented in the *Gentleman's Magazine* for 1758,

the more he is suffered to be idle and vicious in our universities, an evil which arises partly from the fondness and vanity of parents, who must needs have their sons distinguished by their expences, even in a college; and partly from the conduct of tutors, who make their court to idle sons and weak mothers, in proportion as they suffer their wealthy pupils to live and return laden with ignorance and vice.[3]

The 'sending a son thither', Vicesimus Knox warned in 1781, was a 'most dangerous measure; a measure which may probably make shipwreck of his learning, his morals, his health, his character, and his fortune'.[4] Yet such arguments, to which must be added the notion that a young man of

[1] G. Burnet, *The History of My Own Times* [ed. G. Burnet and T. Burnet] (2 vols London 1724, 1734) ii. 380, quoted by Stone, 55.

[2] Quoted by Stone, 55.

[3] *Gentleman's Magazine* xxviii (1758), 175-6.

[4] V. Knox, *Liberal Education* (London 1781), 324. Vicesimus Knox (1753-1821), m. St John's 1771; headmaster Tonbridge School 1778-1812.

birth might be socially contaminated by mixing with men of lesser breeding, must not be overstressed. For, by the closing decades of the century, however much it might be criticized by the radicals, the university had become once more politically respectable. The impact of the French revolution and the subsequent spread of subversive ideas made many parents turn instinctively to what could be construed as the traditional home of social conservatism and religious orthodoxy.

In some respects more perplexing was the conspicuous drop in the admission of those described as of 'plebeian' origin. Men so described constituted 27 per cent of those matriculated in 1711, 17 per cent in 1760 and 1 per cent in 1810. In the years 1701-20 sons of plebeians represented some 36 per cent of those who graduated as BA; by 1781-1800 the figure had fallen to 11 per cent.[1] In the twelve colleges sampled the fall in the admission of plebeians seems to have been substantial and irreversible: 485 1700-9, 450 1710-19, 349 1720-9, 342 1730-9, 263 1740-9, 129 1750-9, 114 1760-9, 98 1770-9, 110 1780-9, 67 1790-9. Even in Christ Church only 32 men so described themselves in the decade 1780-9 and 17 in the final decade of the century. At other colleges sampled they practically disappeared altogether; Balliol, Corpus, Lincoln, Magdalen, Oriel, St John's, Trinity and University College had only single figures for their plebeian entry in the last decades of the century. Some caution is, however, required before any final judgement is made. For the term 'plebeian', as to some extent the term 'gent', had by the mid-century ceased to be a meaningful status category. For social reasons many children of plebeian origin preferred to describe their fathers as genteel, and since many of those who were plebeians were in fact comparatively affluent this was a reasonable enough thing to do. Thomas Charles recorded in 1814 how he came to Oxford:

about 40 years ago ... in the humblest form,—as '*pleb—fil:*'—whilst a number of my school-fellows, of the same class in life with myself were matriculated under a false designation, as 'gen:fil:' A batch of my class fellows had gone off to Oxford, above a year before I left school ... These gents had tassels to their gowns; and were not a little proud of them; my gown was plain, and my cap untasseled.[2]

It thus seems unlikely that the figures relating to the admission of those of plebeian status can be taken at their face value, or that they can be said to demonstrate conclusively the virtual disappearance of the undergraduates of humbler origins who had been relatively prominent at the university at an earlier period.

---

[1] N. Hans, *New Trends in Education in the 18th Century* (London, 1957), 45.
[2] D. E. Jenkins, *The Life of the Rev. Thomas Charles of Bala* (3 vols Denbigh 1908, 2nd edn 3 vols Denbigh 1910) i. 74. Thomas Charles (1755-1814), m. Jesus 1775.

Yet there was surely some closing of the ranks. The poor boy found it less easy to secure admission, less easy to pay the rising expenses of a university education and less easy to get preferment in the church once he had graduated. Furthermore there had been some decline in the facilities for acquiring that modicum of a classical education essential for entry, since many grammar schools, from which boys had come to the university in the past, were in a state of decay, and possibly fewer clergymen were taking pupils. Moreover, the decline in the number of servitorships and battelerships available at the colleges, precipitated by the wider employment of paid college servants, closed some of the openings which had hitherto made it possible for poor boys to come to Oxford. College scholarships and exhibitions, comparatively less valuable relative to the cost of living than they had once been, seemed to come less easily the way of the poorer boy. By the end of the century only Christ Church and Brasenose appeared to have had servitors in any numbers, and even in these two colleges there had been a significant decline in their numbers, at Christ Church from a high entry of 143 servitors for the decade 1720-9 to one of 73 in 1790-9; at Brasenose from 123 in 1710-19 to 15 in 1790-9. The rising cost of a university education and some change in social manners (it was no longer expected that the son of a poor man would be able, or even wish, to study at a university) both militated against the admission of men from the humbler social classes. Finally, even if the poor boy (and there were almost certainly more of them than the figures might suggest) stayed the course, emerged with a degree and was ordained, he found it difficult in an age when pluralism and patronage dominated the social structure of the established church to win any worthwhile preferment. The young graduate of Oxford or Cambridge might well spend the remainder of his life as a poorly paid curate.

Although it is difficult to provide precise figures, there was then some contraction in the social composition of the university. Neither the well-born nor the poor were any longer evident in their old numbers. The vast majority of the junior members simply described themselves as sons of gentlemen, though this word, like that of plebeian, was beginning to lose the definition it once had possessed. An analysis of the entrants to the university shows that for the most part undergraduates were the sons of country squires and parsons, with a smattering of merchants, lawyers, politicians and government officials.

The geographical complexion of the colleges was still very pronounced (which incidentally must also have influenced the accents of their members: there was no 'Oxford' English in the eighteenth century). Queen's, Brasenose and University College still possessed a predominantly northern character. These connections were rooted in the past, promoted for instance by a founder such as Robert of Eglesfield at Queen's or by benefactors who secured fellowships or scholarships for particular regions. The northern character of Queen's was further enhanced by the generous benefaction made by Lady Elizabeth Hastings, the daughter of Theophilus, seventh earl of Huntingdon, in 1737. She designed her benefaction for 'Youths of promising genius, but especially of sound Principles in matters of religion and well disposed', more especially from the West Riding of Yorkshire.[1] She expressed the wish that her exhibitions 'could be made Instrumental in Propagating the Xtian Religion in both or either of the Indies'. 'I have a strong bias to the East Indies, not only from the Notion I have of the Natives, but out of gratitude to them, as the Estate I enjoy was gain'd by Trading thither.'[2] Of the 1,846 men who came to Brasenose between 1690 and 1799 half came from the north (950), with a predominance of men from Cheshire (393) and Lancashire (491). University College had strong northern (especially Yorkshire) connections but also drew many men from the midlands. By contrast Wadham still drew the majority of its clientele, as it had done from its foundation, from the south-west of England, more especially from Dorset, Somerset and Devon, some 656 out of 1,477 men between 1690 and 1799. Balliol too had its roots in the west country, 983 out of 2,118 men. It also drew upon the midlands, but its connection with the north was minimal, though there was a regular small intake from Scotland (which included the economist Adam Smith). Christ Church, reflecting its solid aristocratic bias, drew largely from the London area (873 out of 3,754), but the midland region was also well represented (860, with 191 from Shropshire). Pembroke had a strong connection with the midlands as well as the south-west, together with a small but regular intake from the Channel Islands. Jesus drew most heavily on Wales, although there was a sprinkling of Welsh, Scots and Irish at other colleges. The sons of West Indian planters and East Indian merchantmen made their appearance in nearly all colleges in the closing decades of the century.

The geographical orientation of the college, the reputation and connections of its head and tutors, the personal recommendation of a local

[1] Eventually the bequest (originally intended for St Edmund Hall but diverted to Queen's on the appointment of Provost Smith in 1737) was to be used for the appointment of 5 exhibitioners to be selected from 12 schools, 2 in Cumberland, 2 in Westmorland and 8 in Yorkshire. Candidates, who had to have applied themselves to the study of Greek for at least 4 years, were to be examined at Aberford in Yorkshire by 7 clergymen who were to select the best 10, whose exercises were then to be sent to the college. The college selected 8 whose names were then put in an urn and the first 5 drawn out were to be elected. The drawing by lot went on until 1859. The schools originally named were Leeds, Wakefield, Bradford, Beverley (which lost its privileges in 1789 and was replaced by Richmond), Skipton (replaced by Pontefract in 1824), Sedbergh, Ripon (replaced by Hipperholme in 1784), Sherborne, Appleby, Heversham, St Bee's and Penrith.
[2] Magrath, *Queen's* ii. 98–102.

squire or clergyman, a father's or brother's or other relative's past membership, all go far to explain the choice of College and the means of entry. Humphrey Prideaux advised Richard Coffin that Wadham was the 'best governed college ... stockd with the best fellows', and 'Mr Doyly' the 'fittest person for a tutor' there. He rejected Exeter because of its reputation for 'drinking and duncery' but allowed that Christ Church had 'something of ingenuity and genteel carriage in the genius of the place'.[1] The Lincolnshire connections of John Morley[2] and John Wesley explain many of the admissions to Lincoln College during the rectorship of the one and the tutorship of the other; Morley's successors as rector, Euseby Isham and Richard Hutchins, both with connections among the Northamptonshire gentry, gave rise to a continuing inflow of men from Northampton and the neighbouring county of Leicester, a connection already established by the patronage of squirearchical families like the Crewes of Steane and the Knightleys of Fawley. Lord Crewe's foundation of exhibitions from his diocese of Durham may explain the intensification of the college's northern intake.[3] The choice of college was thus most likely to depend on personal or institutional connections. Some schools already had a significant association with a college, for example Westminster with Christ Church, Merchant Taylors' with St John's.

Once installed it was by no means unknown for a young man to migrate to another society, sometimes because it was cheaper, sometimes because of the promise of an exhibition or scholarship. James Woodforde, the diarist, had matriculated at Oriel on 8 May 1758 staying there until a vacancy for a closed scholarship for Wykehamists opened the way to his migration to New College. Joseph Somaster's move from Hart Hall where he had matriculated in April 1723 to Balliol, on the grounds that Balliol would be less expensive and that he had the promise of a scholarship there, led the then principal of Hart Hall, Richard Newton, to write a vigorous denunciation of his conduct.[4] Naturally elections to fellowships were a frequent cause of migration from one college to another. None the less, all in all, the number of migrants over a century remained small.[5]

The Oxford freshman entered a highly structured society, presided

---

[1] Letter of 7 Feb. 1696, HMC *Fifth Report*, 374. Robert Doyley (1661-1733), m. Wadham 1676, sub-warden 1692.

[2] John Morley (1670-1731), m. Trin. 1686; BA Pemb. 1689; further degrees Lincoln, rector 1719-31.

[3] V. H. H. Green, *The Commonwealth of Lincoln College 1427-1977* (Oxford 1979), 688-90.

[4] R. Newton, *University Education* (London 1726), 131-46. Richard Newton (1676-1753), m. Ch.Ch. 1694; DD Hart Hall 1710, principal 1710-40; founder and first principal of Hertford 1740-53; canon Ch.Ch. 1752.

[5] From a sample of colleges: 15 migrated from Balliol to New College, 57 from Christ Church to All Souls, 26 from Exeter to Christ Church (16 in the years 1730-9, presumably as a result of the

over by the head of the college and the fellows, and stratified by various grades of students, noblemen, gentlemen- or fellow-commoners, foundationers, scholars and exhibitioners, commoners, batteters, servitors and bible-clerks, down to the college servants. Every undergraduate's status was distinguished by the gown and cap he wore, by the fees he paid, the privileges he enjoyed, the table at which he sat in hall and by the place he occupied in chapel.

The sons of noblemen and of bishops could, if they wished, avail themselves of a privileged status, but nobles were few in number and tended to reside at Christ Church. 'The University', Arthur Charlett wrote to Lord Ormonde on 27 June 1705, 'is also very full at present of quality and all other ranks and orders of scholars. At Christ Church the table which has held the noblemen ever since the Restoration is now of necessity forced to be enlarged ... The last nobleman entered is the young Earl of Salisbury.'[1] When Charles Sharpe came to the college in 1798 the dean, knowing of his friendship with Lord Binning, warned him 'against vying in expence' with Binning, adding that 'very properly the fortune of a title was larger than that of none'.[2] Sharpe commented later somewhat ruefully that "tis scarcely in human nature to resist the foolish forms of respect to nobility which the college rules prescribe, or the crowd of flatterers which infests a gold tossel and a silk gown'.[3] The nobleman was a conspicuous figure in his gold-laced gown and cap with a golden tassel. He was under no obligation to take a degree, and if he decided to do so he was allowed a year's standing; on occasions he might be made an MA by creation. Nor was he obliged to submit to tutorial supervision and college exercises. At Christ Church, as at some other colleges, he dined at the high table and was allowed to use the senior common room. But in return for these privileges he was subject to higher fees and his expenses were high. When Lord Lewisham matriculated at Trinity his father reckoned that they would amount to at least £500 a year.[4]

appointment of Conybeare, rector of Exeter as dean), 21 to Christ Church from Jesus, 17 from Christ Church to Magdalen, 10 from Merton to Christ Church, 14 from Christ Church to Merton, 11 from Pembroke to Christ Church, 10 from Christ Church to St Mary Hall, 17 from St Mary Hall to Christ Church, 14 from Balliol to St Mary Hall, 21 from Jesus to Magdalen, 31 from Lincoln to Magdalen, 12 from Balliol to Magdalen and 19 from Brasenose to Magdalen.

[1] HMC *Ormonde MSS* viii. 161-2. James Cecil (1691-1728), 5th e. of Salisbury; m. Ch.Ch. 1705, hon. MA 1707.
[2] Charles Sharpe (1781-1851), m. Ch.Ch. 1798; Scottish antiquary. Thomas Hamilton (1780-1858), Lord Binning, from 1828 9th e. of Haddington; m. Ch.Ch. 1798.
[3] Letters to his mother, [Nov.] and May 1802, *Letters from and to Charles Kirkpatrick Sharpe, Esq.* ed. W. K. R. Bedford (2 vols London 1888) i. 79, 121.
[4] Bodl. MS North b.14, p. 224. William Legge (1731-1801), Lord Lewisham, from 1750 2nd e. of Dartmouth; m. Trin. 1749, hon. MA 1751, DCL 1756; high steward Oxford Univ. 1786-1801.

Young noblemen as well as some rich gentlemen-commoners sometimes brought their own servants, and even tutors, with them, and had them lodged in college.

The Scotch nobleman who is coming hither is my Lord Glenorchy's son; his mother was Lord Jersey's sister. His father ... has taken a house over against the Theatre, and designs to live here whilst his son is with us. His son's tutor is to live in the same chamber with him, and he designs to capitulate with him that he shall take no other pupils whilst he has his son ... I waited on his lordship to see some chambers; he has pitched I think on those which were Colonel Trelawney's ... He would have had Mr Periam's chambers if he could have had the whole floor, but poor Lord Strathallan's chambers had been taken before by Sir Charles Holt for his son, who is to [be] brought a student.[1]

Gentlemen- or fellow-commoners, the terms were virtually inter-changeable,[2] had similar privileges and often had fathers with titles or titled connections. Bishop Barlow, when provost of Queen's, defined their role in the college to Sir John Lowther:

we have two ranks of Gentlemen in the Colledge. 1. Those we call *Communars*, which are Gentlemen of inferior quality usually (though many times men of higher birth and fortune, will have their sonnes and heires in that ranke). 2. *Upper Communars*, which usually are Baronetts or knights sonnes, or Gentlemen of greater fortunes; these have some honorary priviledges above ordinary *Communars*, but are not (as in all other Houses generally) freed from any exercise the meanest gentlemen undergoe ... For a Tutor ... I shall commend him to such a one, as shall carefully endeavor to direct and instruct him in the grounds of Religion and Literature ... Lastly, to send a servant to attend him, will be some charge ... for he must have a boy (assigned by his Tutor) to be his servitor, who must be a gowne-man and a scholar, and will be able to doe all his little businesses for him ... Very few Gentlemen (though heires to very great fortunes) keepe any men to attend them here; and these few which sometimes doe, those servants haveing nothing to doe themselves commonly make their Maisters most idle.[3]

They mostly had the right to attend the senior common room and to dine at high table. They wore a distinctive gown. 'I hope', George

---

[1] W. Stratford-E. Harley, 8 Sept. 1711, HMC *Portland MSS* vii. 54-5. Lord Glenorchy's son was John Campbell (1696-1782), from 1752 3rd e. of Breadalbane; m. Ch.Ch. 1711; ambassador at Copenhagen 1720-30, St Petersburg 1731; MP Saltash 1727-41, Oxford 1741-6; vice-admiral Scotland 1776-82. Sir Harry Trelawny (1688-1762), 5th bt; m. Ch.Ch. 1703, aide-de-camp to the d. of Marlborough. William Periam (1679-1743), m. Ch.Ch. 1697. James Drummond, 3rd Visc. Strathallan (b. 1694 m. Ch.Ch. 1710) had died of consumption in May 1711. Charles Holt (1649-1722), 3rd bt; m. Magd. 1666, hon. DM 1695; MP Warwickshire 1685-7. His son John Holt, m. Ch.Ch. 1711.
[2] This was so in the majority of colleges, but not so in Queen's where fellow-commoners were commoners of at least three years' standing and were admitted to the high table and the fellows' stalls in chapel.
[3] Letter of 5 Apr. 1670, HMC *Lonsdale MSS* vii. 93-4. Thomas Barlow (1607-91), m. Queen's 1625, provost 1658-77; Bodley's Librarian 1652-60, Lady Margaret prof. of divinity 1660-76; bp of Lincoln 1675-91.

Selwyn told Lady Carlisle, 'that you approve of my choice of what the colour of his gown is to be. I think a light blue *celeste*, which Lord Stafford had, would be destestable, and scarlet is too glaring. No; it must be a good deep green.' 'I hope', he added, 'that he will have a very good collection of books in his own room, a sufficient allowance, and a hamper of claret, *en cas de besoin*.'[1]

Like noblemen, even though Queen's might have been an exception, gentlemen-commoners were not pressed to work and were comparatively free of normal college discipline. 'The gown a man wears', as George Kenyon told his cousin Lloyd Kenyon, 'excuses him from many exercises, as a lower gown obliges him to them.'[2] If 'he be a man of Fortune', Nicholas Amhurst commented satirically, he is 'soon told, that it is not expected from one of his Form to mind Exercises: If he is studious, he is morose, and a heavy bookish Fellow: If he keeps a Cellar of Wine, the good-natur'd Fellows will indulge him, tho' he shou'd be too heavy-headed to be at Chappel in a Morning'.[3] James Harris, later first earl of Malmesbury, who entered Merton as a gentleman-commoner in June 1763, recalled that men of his rank were 'under no restraint, and never called upon to attend either lectures, or chapel, or hall'.[4] When a gentleman-commoner of New College, living in a room above Woodforde's, made a 'great Noise all the Night', Woodforde appears to have taken no action to bring him to book.[5] Edward Gibbon, who entered Magdalen as a gentleman-commoner in 1752, later waxed sarcastic at the apparent indolence of his tutors, but in so indulging their clever if precocious pupil the tutors were themselves following the conventions of their own time.[6] Like noblemen, if they stayed for three years gentlemen-commoners could be given an honorary MA by creation.

For the most part gentlemen-commoners adopted a style of living that was both the envy and examplar of men of lesser birth. Lord Malmesbury recalled that his companions were pleasant but very idle, modelling their lifestyle on high life in London, spending their evenings playing cards and drinking claret (though not, he added, to excess).[7] In

---

[1] Letter [of Aug. 1790], HMC *Carlisle MSS* vi. 689. George Howard (1773-1848), from 1825 6th e. of Carlisle; m. Ch. Ch. 1790, hon. MA 1792, hon. DCL 1799. Lord Granville (Granville Leveson-Gower, 1773-1846, 1st earl Granville; m. Ch. Ch. 1789) is probably wrongly referred to here as Lord Stafford.

[2] Letter of 16 Nov. 1750, HMC *Kenyon MSS* iv. 492. George Kenyon (1735-70), m. BNC 1750.

[3] [N. Amhurst,] *Terrae-Filius* (52 nos. London Jan.-July 1721) no. x (11-15 Feb. 1721).

[4] *Reminiscences of Oxford*, 158.

[5] *Woodforde at Oxford*, 256 (6 Nov. 1774).

[6] E. Gibbon, *Memoirs of My Life*, ed. G. A. Bonnard (London 1966), pp. 54-5. On the other hand, Henry Fleming's tutor 'read to him once for the most part every day and sometimes twice': Magrath, ii. 74.

[7] *Reminiscences of Oxford*, 158.

their extravagance and dissipation they took the lead, as one commented, 'in every disgraceful frolic of juvenile debauchery', dishonouring, the university's critics averred, the name of Oxford. Such was the purport of a virulent attack in the *Gentleman's Magazine* for 1798.[1] The writer drew a pained reply from an Oxford graduate who recalled that when he had been at Oxford, some forty years earlier, young men 'in the *silken* and the gilded robe' had been regular in attendance at chapel and college exercise.[2] Since that time discipline had been further tightened, as he instanced by referring to the 'very strict discipline of the Dean of Christ church' and the 'still stricter of the Bishop of Chester, head of Brazen-nose college, who locks his gates *every* night at *eight* o'clock'.[3] Not all gentlemen-commoners, however, were improvident wastrels. Sir Erasmus Phillips, a fellow-commoner of Pembroke in 1720, spent much of his time hunting the fox, going to cock-fights and horse-races, fishing, riding or going up the river; on such expeditions he was sometimes accompanied by young fellows of the college and on one occasion, as he recalled, he actually prevented a fight breaking out between the vicegerent, Mr Wilder, and a Mr le Marchant at Nuneham. Yet he tried also to learn the violin, listened to declamations in hall and went to meetings of the Poetical Club at the Three Tuns.[4]

There can be little doubt however that, whether sober or not, gentlemen-commoners spent more money than the average under-graduate. Like noblemen they were liable for higher fees and they tended to rent more expensive rooms which they furnished more comfortably. John Robinson, who entered Lincoln in 1737, spent some £200 in a year; Arthur Annesley, a gentleman-commoner in the same college in 1751, expended some £180 in his first year which included £6 for his room, £12 12*s* for tuition, £41 15*s* 6*d* on battels, £12 on wine and ale, £2 14*s* for silk hose, £8 7*s* 4*d* on books, £13 5*s* for horse-hire, £4 14*s* 6*d* on a gun and £9 for prints for his room. Sir Michael d'Anvers and his brother, Sir Henry, were members of the Northamptonshire gentry who both came to Lincoln as gentlemen-commoners. Michael entered the college in 1757 and his accounts itemized the purchase of suits, buckskin breeches, stockings, buckles, boots and straps, hats, shirts, nightcaps, wigs and gloves, with payments

[1] *Gentleman's Magazine* lxviii (1798) 14-16, 95, 195, 282, 384.

[2] 'At the small excellent college of Trinity were Lord Lewisham (now Lord Dartmouth), Lord North.... all as regular as GREAT TOM. Of Lord Lewisham and Lord North it was said that, during their residence at Trinity, they never missed early prayers in their college chapel *one* morning, nor any evening when not actually out of Oxford.' Ibid. i. 283.

[3] Cyril Jackson, dean of Christ Church; William Cleaver, principal of Brasenose (1785-1809).

[4] *Notes and Queries* 2nd ser. x (1860), 365-6; C. Wordsworth, *Social Life at the English Universities in the Eighteenth Century* (Cambridge 1874), 172-3. Erasmus Phillips (1700-43), 5th bt; m. Pemb. 1720; MP Haverfordwest 1726-43. John Wilder (1681-1742), m. Pemb. 1696.

to the dancing master, tickets for the oratorio, sums for the hiring of horses and guns, visits to London and repairs to a gold watch which seemed frequently to be going wrong.[1]

Gentlemen-commoners doubtless provided the bulk of the 'smarts' or 'gallants' of whom Amhurst wrote with such disapproval:

He is a SMART of the first Rank, and is one of those who come in their *Academical Undress*, every Morning between *ten* and *eleven* to Lyne's Coffee-House; after which he takes a Turn or two upon the *Park*, or under *Merton-Wall*, whilst the dull *Regulars* are at Dinner in their Hall, *according to Statute*; about *one* he dines alone in his Chamber upon a *boil'd Chicken*, or some *Petti-toes*; after which he allows himself an Hour at least to dress in, to make his Afternoon-Appearance at *Lyne's*; from whence he adjourns to *Hamilton's* about *five*; from whence (after strutting about the Room for a while, and drinking a Dram of Citron) he goes to Chappel, to shew how genteely he *dresses*, and how well he can *chaunt*. After Prayers he drinks Tea with some celebrated *Toast*, and then waits upon her to *Maudlin* Grove, or *Paradise-Garden*, and back again. He seldom eats any supper, and never reads any thing but *Novels* and *Romances*.

When he walks the Street, he is easily distinguished by a stiff *Silk-Gown*, which rustles in the Wind, as he struts along; a *flaxen Tie-wig*, or sometimes a long *natural* one, which reaches down below his Rump; a broad *bully-cock'd Hat* or a *Square Cap* of above twice the usual size; *white Stockings*, thin *Spanish Leather Shoes*; his Cloaths lined with tawdry Silk, and his Shirt *ruffled* down the *Bosom* as well as at the *Wrists*: Besides all which Marks, he has a delicate Jaunt in his *Gait*, and smells very *Philosophically* of Essence.[2]

Richard Graves remembered such a set of 'smarts' at Pembroke who drank 'port-wine and arrack-punch' and sometimes claret and who kept late hours and 'drank their favourite toasts on their knees', although he did not find their company suitable to 'my fortune, or my constitution'.[3] Not indeed that all 'smarts' were necessarily men of good birth. As always there were men of less distinguished ancestry and less polished breeding who aimed simply to ape their example. 'I have scarce met with a conversible creature since I have been here', said a character in Miller's *The Humours of Oxford*, 'their fine Gentlemen are assuming Pedants, or aukward Fops; and their reigning Toasts—Taylors Daughters, and College Bed-makers.'[4]

The mass of the undergraduate population, except in colleges like Magdalen and New College which only took foundationers (and

---

[1] Green, *Lincoln*, 404-5. Woodforde had dancing lessons from a Mr Tole: *Woodforde at Oxford*, 22-3.

[2] *Terrae-Filius* no. lii (8-12 July 1721).

[3] *Reminiscences of Oxford*, 98. Richard Graves (1715-1804), m. Pemb. 1732, fellow All Souls 1736.

[4] [J. Miller,] *The Humours of Oxford* (London 1730), 2. James Miller (1706-44), m. Wadham 1726; rector of Up Cerne, Dorset, 1743.

gentlemen-commoners) were commoners. They were so diverse in type that it is virtually impossible to generalize about their social origins or lifestyle. Many, perhaps the majority, were the sons of country gentry, clergy and lawyers. At the lower end of the scale there were boys, like Samuel Johnson of Pembroke, who found it difficult to make both ends meet, and at the other end the children of rich landed families.

Some of the commoners would in due course be elected to scholarships and exhibitions and so come on the 'foundation'; others would be nominated for these awards before entry to the college. There were no scholars at the halls. Although scholarships were apparently much coveted, their real value, given the rising cost of a university education, had fallen, and it seems they were given less and less on grounds of genuine need. It was a common complaint that such awards, intended originally to enable poor boys to come to the university, were bestowed on the children of gentlefolk. As Richard Newton commented on Joseph Somaster's election to a scholarship valued at £32 0s 6d yearly at Balliol, 'He is eating the Bread of some poor Youth *duly Qualified* for this Scholarship, when He is not'.[1] Foundationers resented the gown which they had to wear as a symbol of a semi-servile status. At Lincoln the fellows ordered in 1748 that scholars were to read the lessons in chapel, except on Sundays and the greater feast-days, but were no longer obliged to help with the serving in hall.[2] Foundationers took to wearing unauthorized gowns, so distinguishing themselves from the servitors, and as a result gave rise to a constitutional crisis in the university in 1770.

The semi-menial class of servitors, batteters and bible-clerks[3] had very nearly disappeared before the close of the century, partly because the duties once performed by the servitors were now done by paid college servants and partly because the contemporary undergraduate, drawn in the main from the middle and upper social groups, resented the stigma that a servitor's status might seem to imply. He was, the *Gentleman's Magazine* noted in 1787, regarded in a humiliating light:

A servitor at present is almost always designed for the church; he is, therefore, to be considered hereafter as a gentleman, and qualified to keep company with the same man who now, perhaps, looks upon him in nearly the same light as a servant. This must naturally have a *tendency* to beget a contemptuous insolence in the one, and an abject servility or a gloomy reserve in the other . . . It may happen too, that the son of a poor clergyman of *good* family may be *servitor* to the son of a rich tradesman of *no* family. This is a very awkward relation.[4]

---

[1] Newton, *University Education*, 146.
[2] Lincoln, register 1739-1983, f 13, 26 Jan. 1748.
[3] See I. G. Doolittle, 'The organization of the colleges', pp. 265-6 above.
[4] *Gentleman's Magazine* lvii (1787), 1146-7.

There is, however, some evidence that in the early part of the century such posts were eagerly sought after. Rector Isham wrote to his brother Sir Edmund in 1739,

If it was only upon your Recommendation I should be glad to do everything I could for Nicholls; but I don't know anything more can be done for him at present than the admitting him a Servitor here which will be a Place of some Profit but small Expense ... We are frequently sollicited for these places and our number is limited, but I will contrive to let him in tho it should be a little irregular.[1]

It was possible for a servitor to rise in the hierarchy of his society;[2] the hebraist Benjamin Kennicott, who matriculated at Wadham as a servitor in 1744, later became a fellow. Other members of the college, however, tended to look down on them.

It was feelings of this kind that lay behind a long and sometimes acrimonious dispute about the wearing of academic dress.[3] Academic garb, originally prescribed by the Laudian statutes, was normal everyday costume, not merely for academic and collegiate occasions but for walking out in the town, not only differentiating dons and students from the townsmen but distinguishing, at least to the initiated, the different grades of the academic hierarchy, stretching from doctoral scarlet to the fustian of the servitor. Fashionable young men at earlier and later periods resented the drab sobriety of the uniforms prescribed by the university authorities. The latter sought constantly to stem flamboyance of costume and to insist on obedience to statute. The heads were distressed at the way in which many graduates and young scholars wore morning gowns without permission; gentlemen-commoners adorned themselves with square caps before they had performed the requisite exercises. Undergraduates seemed to be aspiring to be students of civil law, having taken to wearing the half-sleeve gown and square cap; some, more secularly minded, adopted the hat and cravat to the 'great scandal' of the university.[4]

The heads took a firm line on 28 April 1690 and laid down the requisite costume for the different classes of student with admirable precision.[5]

---

[1] Northampton, Northamptonshire Record Office, Isham MS 1(c) 2688, 10 Oct. 1739; see also G. V. Bennett, 'University, society and church 1688-1714' p. 374. Sir Edmund Isham (1691-1772), m. Wadham 1707; demy Magd. 1710-20, fellow 1720-36; admiralty advocate 1731-41; MP Northants in five parliaments 1737-61, 1768-72. John Nicholls of Northamptonshire, m. Linc. pleb. 1740 aged. 22.

[2] As late as 9 June 1786 *Jackson's Oxford Journal* advertised: 'Young Man, desires to enter a college as a servitor, but cannot afford to, appeals for support from ladies of Distinction, Nobility, Gent. Clergy etc. Refs given by 2 dignified clergymen. No objection to either Oxford or Cambridge.'

[3] See W. N. Hargreaves-Mawdsley, *A History of Academic Dress in Europe until the end of the Eighteenth Century* (Oxford 1963), 60-106; W. N. Hargreaves-Mawdsley, 'The commoner's gown', *Oxoniensia* xxii (1957), 111; D. R. Venables and R. E. Clifford, *Academic Dress of the University of Oxford* (Oxford 1957).

[4] Bodl. MS Don. b.12 (35, 50, 51, 71, 72).

[5] Bodl. G.A., Oxon. b. 19(17); MA Don. b. 12(35). Servitors were to wear round caps and gowns

Predictably, however, there were repeated breaches of the statute. In 1704, for instance, graduates were reprimanded for not wearing hoods at appropriate sermons, and others were told that they must not change the shape of their morning gowns.[1] Eight years later the hebdomadal board reminded juniors that all, excepting noblemen, must cap their seniors and wear black or subfusc.[2] In 1734 the heads once again stressed the need for uniformity and told the commoners that they must on no account wear a square cap or a square cap covered with velvet without special authorization.[3] When Erasmus Head of Queen's was made a fellow-taberdar in 1731 he wrote to his parents: 'I may be bold to say that, even tho' you had seen me but lately, you wou'd not know me in my present Habit . . . viz. A Full Gown, Square cap, and a Tuft, on Sundays and Holydays at Prayers a Surplice, with a Batchelor's Hood thereupon, a Band at all times as before.'[4]

The continued debate, often concerned with what might seem to be petty detail,[5] gave rise in 1770 to a serious constitutional crisis. Because of the difficulty in enforcing the regulations the heads decided that the statute *De vestitu et habitu scholastico* should be revised. In particular, servitors, though a fast disappearing group, resented the inferiority of their status being demonstrated sartorially to all the world. Equally scholars or foundationers had no wish to be mistaken for servitors. In March 1770 the dean of Christ Church (William Markham)

with sleeves hanging below the shoulder without buttons; battelers wore the same but could wear a square cap. Commoners' gowns were similar in cut but were made distinctive by having six buttons on each sleeve. Gentlemen-commoners were entitled to wear a half-sleeved gown, with four buttons on the sleeve. The buttons of baronets and knights might be made of gold or silver. Noblemen could wear coloured gowns with silver or gold buttons. BAs and foundationers who were undergraduates wore wide-sleeved gowns, sleeves not reaching below the finger ends; bachelors, sleeves hanging at full length; foundationers, turned up at the wrist. None was allowed to wear morning gowns without the explicit consent of the head of house and the vice-chancellor and proctors. Servitors, battelers, commoners, gentlemen-commoners, all being undergraduates, should wear only round caps. Gentlemen-commoners might have a hatband round their caps. Knights, baronets and noblemen who were undergraduates were allowed velvet caps with silver or gold hatbands. No one should wear a square cap contrary to statute, and they were not to be more than 12 fingers broad. Students of law and of four years standing and above were entitled to wear a half-sleeved gown without buttons and a square cap.

[1] Bodl. G.A. Oxon. b.19 (22).

[2] Ibid. (34).

[3] Bodl. MS Don. b.12 (50).

[4] Ibid. MS Don. 152, St Thomas's eve 1731. Edward Wood, who matriculated at Wadham in 1688, wrote to his father on 31 March 1689 that he was 'advised by the Vice Chancellour' that he was 'to speak a copy of Verses in order to [obtain] a square capp, in the Theater before all the Doctors and Masters' which verses were to cost him '3 Guineas': papers of the Wood family of Littleton: Wood-Harrison papers, Bodl. MS film 1691, p. 156.

[5] For example on 11 December 1738 undergraduates were ordered to abstain from foppish dress; all undergraduates upon the foundation, saving fellows and chaplains, were forbidden to wear tufts on their caps or to intrude into the bachelor's gallery. All BAs and undergraduates were to wear wide-sleeved gowns, not buttoned on the arms. Bodl. MS Don. b.12.51; G.A. Oxon. b.19 (54).

allowed the servitors to wear the scholar's gown and cap, a practice which appears already to have crept in at other colleges. 'The undergraduates of Corpus', Herbert Randolph told John Buckland, 'have been dignified with Tuffs some time.'[1] 'The Scholars of the First Year (Bray and Gill)', President Fry of St John's noted in his diary for 5 March 1770, 'had my permission to wear Tufts to their caps—the same privilege having been granted in some other Colleges—C.C.C.—B.N.C.—Trin: etc'; but the next day he refused an application to wear a tuft by the bible-clerk, since it would destroy the distinction between the servitors and scholars.[2]

The heads' attempt at revision did not meet with general approval and led to a scatter of pamphlets. 'Many People in the University', Randolph commented,

look upon this determination as unstatutable and unjust, confounding the distinction between Foundationers and non Foundationers, which is very precisely worked out by the Statutes. Davies of Merton the Pro-Proctors [*sic*] swears that he'll sconce every Servitor he sees in a Scholar's Gown. And there has been a meeting of the Masters at the Kings Head to consult of proper ways and means to remedy this breach of Statute.[3]

To stress their status some foundationers took to wearing the bachelor's gown, and were encouraged by some senior members to 'interpret away' the statute, a procedure which in the view of one critic encouraged the subversion of authority.[4] The heads' attempt at revision was held to be contrary to statute and the proctors were obliged to declare that the original statute still stood and issued a *moneo* or *programma* to the effect that it must be obeyed. On the last day of the Lent term 1770 an undergraduate foundationer who appeared in the proscholium as a candidate for a BA wearing an irregular habit was refused the grace for his degree.[5]

The controversy continued to simmer throughout the summer. On 9 May President Fry commented that 'after much altercation concerning wearing or not wearing Tufts', he and two of his fellows agreed with the view, of which Napleton of Brasenose was a strong advocate, that 'if the people of Ch.Ch. relinquished their claim to them we would

[1] Letter of 27 Mar. 1730, Bodl. MS Top. Oxon. c.126, fos 132-3, Herbert Randolph (1748-1819), m. CCC 1762; MA Magd. 1768, BD 1777. John Buckland, m. CCC 1762.
[2] SJM typed transcript of the diary of Thomas Fry, p. 54.
[3] Bodl. MS Top. Oxon. c.126, fos 132-3.
[4] Bodl. Gough Oxon. Adds. 8° 61 (23). The writer instanced that 'a servitor, the other day, during an examination in the natural philosophy school, had the assurance, after several other Indecorums, to place himself in the V.C.'s seat. The Regent Masters could not reduce him to order without interrupting the examination, and offering to go for a Proctor.'
[5] In their revision the heads recommended that servitors should wear the scholar's gown and a square cap, and that scholars, including demies, postmasters and Students of Christ Church should wear scholar's gowns and square caps with tufts. BAs were to wear their present gown with the addition of a tippet. Bodl. G.A. Oxon. b.19.

do the same, and they were accordingly to withdraw their opposition to the Degrees of Bowen, Ponton and Townley', these men in question having been refused their graces for having worn a tuft upon their caps.[1] Although the degrees were eventually conferred, and proposals for revising the statute still went ahead, the issue had widened. Since the statute was an original statute confirmed by the crown there were, it was alleged, strong constitutional objections to any reform promoted in convocation. The only pertinent objection to the present statute, it was said, was 'that there are young Gentlemen amongst us of some particular Ranks and Orders, who cannot, consistently with it, appear so much *like* Gentlemen, as they could wish to do'.[2] On the other hand, advocates of reform argued that 'in many instances' the statute had fallen into 'disuse [from] time immemorial' and its rigorous enforcement was a practical impossibility.[3] 'Were we now to habit ourselves according to the precise mode prescribed by the Statute, we should appear like so many fanatical Roundheads, and expose ourselves to the Ridicule of the World.' Who, in any case, comprised the foundationers? 'Why should not the lowest Scholar in the University be allowed to appear like a Gentn?' If the concession suggested was accepted 'it would improve the Decency of Academical Habits, and take off the mark of servility from the Sons of Clergymen and other reputable Persons on whom it is illiberal to continue it'. But not all agreed.[4] 'If the Exhibitioners of Ch.Ch. have any just Title to a Scholar's Gown', wrote one Christ Church critic, 'it is because the Scholar's Gown is their statuteable Habit; and then, what becomes of the Distinction, which has hitherto subsistd between COMMONER-Exhibitioners and Exhibitioner-SERVITORS?'[5] Another argued that while the wearing of tufts by foundationers might be justified by long practice, there was no justification for battelers and servitors ignoring the statute, nor was there anything in the proposition that the servitor's cap was a 'mark of Servility'.[6]

A further revision of the statute was promulgated and approved by convocation on 13 July 1770. 'The great Men', the *Daily Advertiser* had stated four days earlier,

[1] Fry's diary (transcript), 9 May 1770. John Napleton (1739-1817), m. BNC 1755. Thomas Bowen, m. St John's 1766, BA 1770, MA 1774. Thomas Ponton (1749-1821), m. St John's 1766, BA 1770, MA 1774. George Stepney Townley (1748-1835), m. St John's 1766, BA 1770, MA 1774.
[2] Bodl. Gough Oxf. 73, flysheet of 21 June 1770.
[3] Bodl. G.A. Oxon. b.19 (203a), 23 June 1770.
[4] *Observations upon the Statute Tit.XIV. De Vestitu et Habitu Scholastico, humbly offered to the Serious and Impartial Consideration of the Members of Congregation* [Oxford 1770], copy in Bodl. Don. b.12 (71b).
[5] B. Hallifax, *Remarks on Observations upon the Statute de Vestitu et Habitu Scholastico* (Oxford 1770), copy in Bodl. Gough Oxf. 80(24).
[6] *Remarks on Some Strictures lately published ... With a Brief State of the Controversy which gave occasion to them* (Oxford 1770), copy in Bodl. Gough Oxf. 80 (23).

had taken such Steps as they thought would secure Success. They expected to have finished the Business in Half an Hour, but it lasted for more than three Hours. The Friends of the present Statute debated upon every Article, and every Article was rejected that they wished to reject. They did not expect so great a Victory.[1]

Henceforth servitors and battelers were to be entitled to wear a gown similar to those worn by commoners without pleats, and with a square cap but void of a tassel. The scholar's gown was to be shorter than that of the bachelor but he was allowed a tassel on his cap as was the commoner. In order to prevent any unstatutable deviation in future, drawings and engravings were ordered to be made of all the different academical costumes as enacted by the new statutes, the plates to be deposited in the university chest.[2] The details of the controversy may now appear tedious and unimportant, but they reflect the social conservatism of the university and its aversion to change, and they point to its awareness of its function as an essentially distinctive institution.

One of the freshman's first purchases was obviously that of a gown. 'I had provided a gown', John James wrote of his arrival at Queen's on 8 October 1778, 'and cap in London, and thought I had made a cheap bargain, having heard of the extravagancy of college tradesmen. These I brought down, but upon putting them on, was told that I should be hooted at. The gown was of the mungrel kind, neither commoner's nor gentleman-commoner's, strangely made, and of bad stuff to boot.' He returned it and found that his Oxford gown was actually less expensive. 'And now *eccum!* see me strutting in my new robes, with my square cap and tossel, with as much dignity as Falstaff when he personated the King.'[3]

Once a young man had been admitted to the college, he came into residence, if a room was available for him, not necessarily at the beginning of term or on any special day. On his arrival he called on his tutor, who arranged for him to be taken to the vice-chancellor to be matriculated. He had entered a strange and unfamiliar society to whose customs and life he had soon to adapt himself. 'I remember your father', one of the college servants remarked to John James as he took his shoes to be cleaned, 'ah! he was a good kind man, and God grant you may be like him'.[4] James found that he had been allocated 'a very comfortable set of chambers', and the morning after his arrival was examined by Dr Nicholson on the 'ninth chapter of Acts and second

---

[1] Bodl. Gough Oxon. 73 (1).
[2] Bodl. MS Top. Oxon. c.16, fos 20–45.
[3] *Letters of Radcliffe and James*, 44. John James (1760–86), m. Queen's 1778.
[4] Ibid. John James (1729–85), m. Queen's 1745.

epistle of Horace'. 'He strongly admonishes to attend prayers regularly
... My box is arrived, safe and unhurt ... I beg to be informed by my
mother to what uses I must apply the napkins, and to what the towels;
how long a pair of sheets must be used before they are washed.' His
mother wrote back anxiously to inquire whether he had got 'china and
glasses'; 'have you got spoons? or a tea-chest; any green tea for your
genteeler company?'[1]

Throughout the eighteenth century the expense of an Oxford education rose steadily. By 1715 it was estimated that a commoner's annual
costs might amount to £60, that of a gentleman-commoner to twice as
much. William Pitt, it was remarked in 1726, 'must be maintained in
some degree like a gentleman at Oxford', at a cost of 'at least £150 or
£200 *per annum*'.[2] By 1750 a commoner might get through on £80 or
£100 yearly; by 1800 the sum might be between £200 and £300. In 1783
a mother commented that her son's expenses had 'a little exceeded the
£300 a year allowed him'. She did not think she had been strict with
him, and noted that his expenses had included some months abroad, a
tour of England and £50 for a piece of plate presented to his college, the
latter a ridiculously unnecessary expenditure but 'found it was expected'
of him.[3]

Such estimates can only be approximate, depending as they must do
on different costs in college and the more or less extravagant tastes of
the undergraduate and the allowance made to him by his parents. A
commoner, Charles Browne, who matriculated at Lincoln in, 1731 spent
£90 2s 0d in a year which included £26 3s 0d on his battels and room-
rent, £17 17s 0d on pocket-money, £1 1s 6d on boots and shoes,
£2 12s 6d on breeches and £13 6s 6d to his tailor. William Myers, who
matriculated at the same college in 1731 as a commoner, spent
£43 12s 6d in a half-year.[4] John Carnow Millett spent five years at Pembroke (1789-94) for £333 17s 6d inclusive of journeys to and from his
home in Cornwall (which he sometimes made by boat), but in 1790 he
seemed to reside in college for only a few weeks at a time.[5] In 1760 John
Higgon, speaking about the expenses of a servitor, thought 'a frugal
young man' could 'live pretty well on the yearly sum of 20 gns'.[6]

At his entrance each new member of the college was liable to pay
certain dues, the amount depending on his status. At Lincoln, by a ruling
of 1724, a gentleman-commoner paid £6 11s 4d, a commoner £2 2s 0d.
This sum was to be distributed among the officials and servants of the

[1] Ibid. 47. Thomas Nicholson (1728-1803), m. Queen's 1745, taberdar 1748, fellow 1762, DD 1773;
proctor 1764.
[2] R. Pitt-T. Pitt, 25 Nov. 1726, HMC *Fortescue MSS* i. 84.
[3] HMC *Various MSS* ii. 427-8, 13 Oct. 1783.
[4] Green, *Lincoln*, 407.   [5] Pembroke MS R10/1.
[6] J. Higgon-T. Pardo, 28 Jan. 1760, JCA box 3, misc. letters to Pardo.

college.[1] The freshman had also to deposit caution money, recoverable at the end of his residence; at Lincoln £4 for a scholar, £7 for a commoner and £12 for a gentleman-commoner.[2] When Jeremy Bentham went up to Queen's in 1760 he paid his tutor, James Jefferson, £8 as caution money. Like other freshmen he had to pay matriculation-fees, 17s 6d to the university, 10s 0d to the college, as well as table-fees of 10s 6d.[3]

In earlier times parents or guardians often sent the allowance for their son's expenditure direct to the tutor for him to take care of and to distribute, the tutor making himself responsible for the payment of the young man's bills. If the young man's allowance was exhausted or failed to arrive in time the tutor would normally lend him money. Some young men were irritated by a system so paternalistic in character. Erasmus Head of Queen's remonstrated with his parents for sending his allowance direct to his tutor, arguing that such a procedure was a

thing entirely unusual, since Parents have understood the unprofitableness of letting all the money remain in the Tutour's hands ... I know very well that most Parents have a prejudicial notion that 'tis the fittest, as the safest, and most frugal way, that Tutours shou'd be the keepers of their Son's money, as Persons of a more impartial and determined Judgement ... but I ... have found it ... much to the contrary; when I have been forc'd hitherto to have things at a dearer rate by half ... For you must know that Tutours employ and deal with ... certain Tradesmen of most callings ... The Book-seller we deal with is especially knavish, so that I am confident, if I'd had money in my own hands, and so dealt with another, that I cou'd have sav'd about 50 shillings in the few books I have bought already.[4]

Although Head's grievance may well have been justified, surviving accounts show that it was still a normal custom for the allowance to be sent to the tutor.[5]

In addition to entrance-dues, the undergraduate had to pay other fees while he was resident. These included tuition-fees, the cost of fuel and candles, room-rentals and terminal battels. The cost of tuition varied

[1] See Doolittle, 'College Administration'.

[2] Green, *Lincoln*, 406.

[3] *The Works of Jeremy Bentham*, ed. J. Bowring (11 vols Edinburgh 1838–43) x. 36. Jeremy Bentham (1748–1832), m. Queen's 1760. At Queen's table-dues were fixed at 14s for a fellow-commoner, 10s for a gentleman-commoner and 5s for a batteler. In 1761 the fee was raised from 10s to 12s 6d; by 1785 the batteler's table-fee had gone up from 5s to 7s 7d. Queen's MS 73.

[4] Bodl. MS Don. c.152, 25 Mar. 1728.

[5] In one instance in 1694 a tutor tried to arrange a marriage for his pupil: 'The Questions I am desir'd to propose to you are whether you are inclin'd to marry your son Mr Edward, if you are, whether the estate you intend to leave him will amount to £1600 p.anm. for that is the value required. I am ... to conceal the name, but in general am allowed to tell you, that whatsomever more your estate bee, the Fortune will be at least answerable, and that the young Lady for her quality, Education, and person is beyond all exceptions, in short 'tis suggested ... 'twill be an highly advantageous match.'; C. Whiting–T. Wood, 14 Apr. 1694, Wood-Harrison papers, fo 64.

from college to college, and according to status. At Queen's Bentham found that his own tutor, Jefferson, charged six guineas a year, the other tutor, Fothergill, eight guineas.[1] At Lincoln a commoner paid £4 4s 0d and servitors and the bible-clerk £2 2s 0d.[2] At Jesus a gentleman-commoner paid £2 a quarter, a commoner £1 and servitors 10s 0d.[3] To raise income many colleges increased tuition- and admission-fees in the closing decades of the century and a number of additional charges were also devised, for the fabric fund, for the library, for the upkeep of the garden and for the maintenance of the hall. The undergraduate might also pay small weekly sums towards the payment of the stipends of college lecturers and moderators, as well as to cover expenditure on candles and fires in hall. At Lincoln resident members paid 4s 3d a week out of which 1s 10d went towards the payments of the moderator and lecturer. If the amount contributed was insufficient to cover their stipends, then the deficit was added to what was expended on fuel and candles, the total of which was subsequently divided among the junior members.

All undergraduates had to reside in college. From time to time richer men would opt to take the better-situated rooms, occasionally occupying rooms allocated to non-resident fellows to whom they paid a rental. A college order at St John's, dated 22 May 1702, laid down that no gentleman-commoner or commoner should rent any of the fellows' or scholars' chambers till all the rooms in the commoners' quad were occupied.[4] To save money, more impecunious undergraduates might exchange their rooms for a garret in the vacation, a device which the fellows of Exeter sought to prevent by decreeing, on 30 June 1761, that once installed as a tenant a commoner should not move from his room without leave, and should continue to pay rent during the vacation (and 'shall not be permitted to throw up his Room under colour of renting a garret').[5] Garrets were, of course, very much cheaper than first- or second-floor chambers; at Lincoln garrets cost £3 per annum, first-floor rooms £6, increased to £10 in 1816.[6]

In 1693 George Fleming commented that at Queen's the college was so full that it will be 'very difficult to gett my brother Roger a Chamber'.[7] In 1800 Brasenose was said to be 'so superabundantly full that rooms are no where to be procured'.[8] At the end of the century Christ Church was

[1] Works of Bentham, ed. Bowring x. 37-8.
[2] Green, Lincoln, 406.
[3] Bodl. MS DD Jesus College, b.104-6.
[4] St John's Muniments, register 1691-1712, 22 May 1702.
[5] Exeter, B.IV. (23), register of chambers 1737-66. In Exeter in 1788 rents varied from 8 guineas p.a. to £2 for garrets.
[6] Green, Lincoln, 407.
[7] The Flemings in Oxford iii. 103. George Fleming (1667-1747), from 1736 2nd bt; m. SEH 1688, bp of Carlisle 1734-47. Roger Fleming, m. Queen's 1693.
[8] H. Heber, The Life of Reginald Heber (2 vols London 1830) i. 22-3.

bursting at the seams, so full, said George Colman, that he had to be put by his tutor in the rooms of an absent pupil.[1] Christ Church was 'never so full', Charles Sharpe told his father in 1799, 'as it is at present; we are as thick as three in a bed'. Three years later he averred that 'in spite of the absence of many of its members: two miserable servitors are obliged to huddle up in one stye, a thing scarcely ever known of before; and the Dean would melt an heart of stone by his lamentations for want of room'.[2]

Such demand for rooms represented a desire for both privacy and greater comfort. Gibbon was allocated three well furnished, elegant rooms in Magdalen's New Buildings.[3] On Richard Dodd Baker's arrival at Brasenose in 1801 he was given a comfortable suite of three rooms, a large sitting-room, a drawing-room and bedroom.[4] Many rooms were newly wainscotted at their tenants' expense. In most colleges, as a result of the system known as 'thirds', an outgoing tenant received compensation when he left the rooms. In 1742 St John's provided for a payment of four-fifths of the expenses laid out in fitting up and wainscotting a room by the incoming tenant.[5] 'My furniture is pretty good', John James commented on his arrival at Queen's in October 1778, 'and the thirds will run low, I believe, for I cannot be certain till Murthwaite returns to College.'[6] The amount of the 'thirds' was determined by adding the sum paid for the furniture on the man's entry to his chamber to the bills for any additional furniture acquired during his tenancy; of the total, two thirds was paid by the incoming tenant to the outgoing one.

Undergraduate accounts show substantial expenditure on furnishing. When Samuel Plomer, the son of the headmaster of Rugby School, left Lincoln in 1744, the inventory of his rooms showed that his furniture, valued at £12 4s 0d, included half-a-dozen chairs with seats of Spanish leather, a steel grate, a press and a chimney-glass, a mahogany table, mahogany stand, a tea-board and a music-desk, two other chairs, a sugar-box and a teapot. But the furniture of David Locock, though a gentleman-commoner, was valued only at four guineas and consisted of an oval table (broken), five matted-bottom chairs, two prints, two maps, a bed and bolster, blankets, sheets and a wig-block.[7] When Jeremy

[1] *Reminiscences of Oxford*, 173. George Colman (1762-1836), m. Ch.Ch. 1780.
[2] Letter to his father, 27 [Apr. 1799] and to his mother [Nov. 1802], *Letters from and to Sharpe*, ed. Bedford i. 91.
[3] E. Gibbon, *Memoirs of my Life*, ed. G. A. Bonnard (London 1966), 47.
[4] R. W. Jeffery, 'History of the college 1690-1803', *Brasenose Monographs* ii pt 1, chap. 13, p. 63.
[5] St John's Muniments, register 1730-94, 23 July 1742; see also Doolittle, 'College Administration', 259-60.
[6] *Letters of Radcliffe and James*, 45. George Murthwaite (1733-98, m. Queen's 1750) was the camerarius, the college officer who received and paid the 'thirds'.
[7] Green, *Lincoln*, 405, 407.

Bentham came up, he had his sitting-room newly papered and with his 'pictures' thought the room looked pretty enough.[1] In July 1735 Mr Astell of Lincoln laid out £4 9s 7½d on hangings for his bedchamber and study. A decade earlier a Mr Howson had paid the upholsterer £5 10s 6d; Robert Pindar, £6 7s 0d. When Francis Raynesford came into residence in the same college in October 1743 he had the casements, skirting and bookshelves of his room painted at a cost of £1 1s 9d.[2] The walls, in earlier times bare, whitewashed or crudely painted or covered by hangings, were often panelled and decorated by prints and pictures.[3] Parson Woodforde, though then a fellow of New College, purchased five pictures for his rooms in 1774, 'all fine Engravings of Bartolozzi', a Florentine engraver working in England.[4] Thomas Fry, when a fellow of St John's, attracted to Piranesi's prints, had engravings of 'Roman Ruins, fram'd', valued at £1 8s 0d, as well as others entitled 'Morning' and 'Storm'.[5]

But on coming into residence an undergraduate had more to do than pay college and university dues and furnish his rooms. He had a gown to buy, its cost often relating to his status, a cap and bands.[6] He would need one or more wigs and had to pay the barber. He needed a portmanteau for his luggage; and his journeys, even if he did not go home every vacation, could be expensive, whether by horse or coach. No wonder that poor boys like the brothers Wesley walked home. And all this was in addition to the linen, china, cutlery, tablecloths, napkins and snuffers that he needed for his room.[7]

Probably a student's principal expenses in college during his residence were his battels. These in the main comprised what he had to spend on his meals, as well as any purchases he might make at the buttery. They included also weekly payments for service and a number of small college dues. 'My expences', John James wrote on 17 May 1779,

for the last quarter had a good deal exceeded my expectations ... Under the account for eating (or battles, as it is called) are included several other little

---

[1] *The Correspondence of Jeremy Bentham*, ed. T. L. S. Sprigge *et al.* (London and Oxford 1968 onward) i. 21.

[2] Green, *Lincoln*, 407.

[3] 'Procure a flute whether you can play or not, and let it be always in sight, then who-ever sees it will give you credit for an elegant accomplishment ... Get the most expensive prints you possibly can, they will ornament your sitting room prodigiously, and in the end not cost you more than sixpence to the Porter who carries them back to the print-shop from whence you had them.' *A Few General Directions for the Conduct of Young Gentlemen in the University of Oxford* (Oxford 1795), 8.

[4] *Woodforde at Oxford*, 205.

[5] Transcript of Fry's diary, appx B.

[6] Lord Lewisham had two gowns. For the nobleman's gown he required 15½ yards of gold lace and 10 yards of damask costing £2 2s. His caps cost him £2 2s, his bands £1 8s. Bodl. MS North b.14, fos 232-5.

[7] Lord Lewisham spent no less than £39 16s 3d in this respect, including a close stool for 12s, globes costing £6, a bureau at 2 guineas, a writing-table and candle-screen at £1 8s. Ibid.

expences, such as for letters, College servants, charities at the Sacrament ...
My eating never almost exceeds one shilling [a] day, except upon very
particular occasions. We are indeed very much exposed to the frauds of
bedmakers, and a variety of tricks, which might easily be put a stop to if
proper inquiry was set on foot. But as the high amount of these expences is for
the interest of the College and its cooks, it is very improbable that any
regulation should soon take place.[1]

The day began with chapel and breakfast. Robert Larogue of Lincoln
wrote early in his undergraduate career: 'Well Chapel is no sooner over
than I run into my room and make an hearty breakfast upon Tea and
French Rolls.'[2] At Magdalen, *Terrae-Filius* commented in 1733, 'you may
see *little Brats* every Morning at the Buttery-Hatch calling for hot
Loaves and Butter in their *Papa's Name*'.[3] Woodforde often breakfasted
in his or his friends' rooms and sometimes at the local coffee-house on
chocolate, bread and butter or dry toast.[4] Rather to the alarm of his
mother, who suggested sending him some oatmeal, John James seemed
to breakfast at first only on milk.[5] Once breakfast was over, and with
guests it might take some time, the more conscientious man settled
down to study, 'at nine o'clock', so John James noted, 'at least half an
hour sooner than any body else'. 'The two first hours I have set aside
for composition or translation ... From eleven till one I read logic.'[6]

At the end of the morning dinner loomed ahead, becoming
increasingly late as the century advanced. Hearne commented morosely
in 1722 that several colleges had advanced their dinner hour from
11 a.m. to 12 noon, 'occasion'd from People's lying in Bed longer than
they us'd to do'.[7] Richard Newton laid down that dinner at Hertford
was to be at 1 p.m. but it was later moved to 3 p.m.; in 1791 it was at 4
p.m. At Trinity in 1775 'Hall dinner was at 3.0 p.m. and supper at 7.0'.
At Merton in 1795 dinner changed to 4 p.m. Joseph Pickford, who
entered Oriel in 1790, recalled that he dressed for dinner at 3 p.m.[8]
Dinner was indeed a ceremonial occasion. Hair had to be dressed and
powdered, and black or dark suits worn with silk stockings. 'Dinner',

---

[1] *Letters of Radcliffe and James*, p. 73.

[2] Yale University, Beinecke Library, Osborn Shelves, c.107. Robert Larogue (1753–72), m. Linc.
1771, elected to a scholarship *c* 1772 but died in an accident (Green, *Lincoln*, 413–15).

[3] *The Terrae-Filius's Speech, as it was intended to have been Spoken at the Publick Act in the Theatre in
Oxford* (London 1733), 25–6.

[4] *Woodforde at Oxford*, 2, 5, 20, 46 etc.

[5] Later (21 Dec. 1778) James came round to his mother's point of view. 'I am disgusted with the
water and milk of Oxford. Tea and coffee enervate and unhinge me ... This means no more than
that I want a barrel of oatmeal.' *Letters of Radcliffe and James*, 60.

[6] Ibid. 50, 51.

[7] Hearne, *Collections* vii. 327 (10 Feb. 1722).

[8] R. Newton, *Rules and Statutes for the Government of Hertford College* (London 1747), 70;
H. E. D. Blakiston, *Trinity College* (London 1898), 203; Merton, register 1731–1822, p. 425, 2 July
1795; 'Antiquities of Oriel common room', *Oriel Record* iv no. 10 (Dec. 1925).

Henry Ellacombe recalled of Oriel in 1809 'was at 4, where none could appear without silks, breeches with knee-buckles, silver or gilt. The gentlemen commoners wore the *dress* gown at dinner and in chapel. Gaiters were not allowed with gown. Cloth boots came in. We called them *buskins* ... Men were sconced if accidentally they appeared in Hall undressed.'[1] At Balliol the young men wore swallow-tail coats, knee-breeches, silk stockings and pumps; the college barber prepared their hair, starting with the junior freshman and ending with the senior fellow.[2] The senior don presiding would normally say grace. Everyone sat at tables according to their status and year, the dons and others privileged at the high table, masters, bachelors, scholars and commoners; the servitors dined afterwards. 'We all dined at our proper Tables', Woodforde noted on Christmas day 1762.[3]

By and large the food provided seems to have been inferior in quality, unless the diner had, as he was able to do, ordered at his own expense something additional from the kitchen. In the winter of 1798 Charles Sharpe of Christ Church told his mother that

dinner is hardly worth the grudging, being served up on pewter or silver the Lord knoweth which, at the first course; and a joint of meat is set down at the head of each table, which descends gradually to the bottom, the students cutting huge slices from it all the way down. Then comes potatoes; and your beer is put down to you in a stone mug. Then if you choose pudden or a tart you must vociferate for it with the voice of a fisherwoman, and often not get it neither.[4]

Reginald Heber reached a similar verdict about the dinners at Brasenose in 1801: 'the dinners we get here, at least the commoners, (for the gentlemen commoners have a table to themselves and fare very well,) are the most beastily things that ever graced the table of a poor-house or house of correction.'[5] But conditions obviously varied from college to college, and even from day to day.

Once dinner was over, most senior and junior members retired to recreation. Joseph Pickford went off to the senior common room and had pipes and ale before walking up and down the High Street till five, returning to his rooms to read and write until seven or eight. Presumably after supper he went back to the common room to play cards and to drink brandy and water, 'to a very late hour'; occasionally some of those present were the worse for drink.[6] 'After dinner', so Larogue told his

[1] J. W. Burgon, *Lives of Twelve Good Men* (London 1888), 386n. Henry Ellacombe (1790-1885), m. Oriel 1808.
[2] H. W. C. Davis, *A History of Balliol College* (Oxford 1899), rev. edn by R. H. C. Davis and R. W. Hunt (Oxford 1963), 167-8.
[3] *Woodforde at Oxford*, 101.
[4] *Letters from and to Sharpe*, ed. Bedford i. 80-1.
[5] Heber, *Life of Reginald Heber* i. 26-7.
[6] 'Antiquities of Oriel common room'.

friend Simpson, 'I again retire into my little Apartments and resume the book, which generally throws me into a fine knap till four, at which time we again attend Chapel. Immediately after this I take a walk, call upon my friends.'[1] In his recollections of William Shenstone, who entered Pembroke in 1732, Richard Graves recalled

I was invited ... to a very sober little party, who amused themselves in the evening with reading Greek and drinking water ... But I was at length seduced ... to a very different party; a set of jolly, sprightly young fellows, most of them west-country lads; who drank ale, smoked tobacco, punned, and sung bachanalian catches the whole evening.[2]

'Now and then, after supper', wrote John James, 'I sit with my friends, and seldom walk out without company, and, as our conversation is either literary or at least innocent and entertaining, I hope to receive benefit from it.'[3]

The young men would have supper, either in the college hall or buttery (or if there was one, as for instance the bachelors' common room at New College, in the common room) or at an eating-house or tavern. Woodforde's diary shows him supping with his friends sometimes in their rooms, sometimes at the King's Head or in other colleges, as at Brasenose on 17 November 1774 (when he was a fellow and subwarden of New College) where he supped on roast hare, veal-collops and woodcock, with port wine and punch to drink afterwards.[4] At Trinity in 1792 supper was at 9.30 'followed by negus or "hot egg-flip" '.[5]

College gates were closed at certain hours and latecomers had to pay a fine for entry. At Trinity the gate was shut every night at 10 p.m. The names of those who returned to college after that hour were inserted in a special book, a copy of which was delivered at 10 every morning to the vice-president and dean.[6] At Queen's all BAs and undergraduates who knocked at the college gate after 11 p.m. were fined 1s, and after 12 a.m. 2s.[7]

While there was probably a greater abundance of serious-minded reading men than is normally allowed by historians of the eighteenth-century university, contemporary undergraduates then and later were charged with extravagance and dissipation. Oxford, as the editor of *The Student* (1750) put it in his first editorial, 'we know has for some time been used as a term of reproach, and become a bye-word amongst many.

[1] Yale Univ., Beinecke Library, Osborn Shelves, c.107.
[2] *Reminiscences of Oxford*, 97–8.
[3] *Letters of Radcliffe and James*, p. 51.
[4] *Woodforde at Oxford*, 259.
[5] Blakiston, *Trinity*, 212.
[6] Trinity, liber decani I, 19 Nov. 1778.
[7] Queen's, MS 475, fos 68–9.

Pamphlets have been designedly written, and measures industriously persued, to lessen her credit.'[1] The high cost of a university education, in Vicesimus Knox's view, was the result of the 'luxuries and extravagances which the fashion of the age introduces', an accumulation of unnecessary expenditure on fashionable clothes, private dinners, the keeping of horses, the expense of hunting, gambling and trips to London, all of which led young men to borrow money at a high rate of interest.[2]

In every college there is a set of idle people called *Lowngers*, whose whole business is to fly from the painful task of thinking. These are ready to catch at every young fellow at his first admission, and imperceptibly teach him to saunter away his time in the same idle spiritless manner with themselves ... There is another set still more dangerous, who assume to themselves the name of *jolly fellows*, and ridicule every body who has the folly to be sober.[3]

The university authorities, earlier and later, tried to curb such excesses, but probably without much effect. In 1723 the hebdomadal board reminded innkeepers and keepers of coffee- and eating-houses that they were not to entertain scholars in their houses for whom commons were provided in their colleges.[4] In 1748 the vice-chancellor (John Purnell) and heads, disturbed by breaches of the peace in the streets caused by undergraduate parties attended with 'great intemperance and excess', together with 'expences that are both needless and hurtful', ordered all junior members to attend their college halls and threatened that the perpetrators of the 'irregularities' practised 'at coffee-houses, cook-shops and victualling-houses' would be punished.[5] Eighteen years later Thomas Falconer of Brasenose commented that 'the growing expenses of eating have at last obliged the seniors to enforce some new ordinances with vigour against Cook-shops'.[6] In 1772 convocation passed a statute to check luxury and the unacademical expenses of servants, horses, dogs, racing and cock-fighting, drawing a reply in the *Gentleman's Magazine* in defence of horse-riding on good medical grounds.[7] Similarly the university promoted sumptuary regulations to prevent flamboyant costume, in 1793 for instance forbidding the wearing of red waistcoats.[8]

The coffee-house and the tavern were the favourite resorts of both

---

[1] *The Student or the Oxford (and Cambridge) Monthly Miscellany* (2 vols Oxford 1750-1) i, p. v (no. 1, 31 Jan. 1750).

[2] Knox, *Liberal Education* (9th edn 2 vols London 1788), ii. 208 ff.

[3] 'A letter to a young gentleman on his entrance at the university', *The Student* i. 21 (no. 1).

[4] Bodl. G.A. Oxon. b.19.17 (43), 30 Sept. 1723.

[5] *Gentleman's Magazine* xviii (1748), 11 Apr. 1748.

[6] T. Falconer-C. Gray, 30 Aug. 1766 HMC *14th Report* ix. 300. Thomas Falconer (1737-92), m. BNC 1754.

[7] OUA register of convocation 1766-76, NEP/*supra*/register, pp. 239-42, 11 July 1766; *Gentleman's Magazine* xlii (1772), 401.

[8] OUA minutes of the hebdomadal board 1788-1803, WPγ/24/2, fo 79.

senior and junior members. The first coffee-house had been apparently opened by Jacob, a Jew, 'at the Angel in the parish of S. Peter in the East Oxon', in the 1650s.[1] In the next century many more were spawned, catering for different groups, social and collegiate. They did not confine their catering to the provision of coffee or chocolate but served alcoholic liquors. Tom's in the High was socially exclusive and expensive;[2] Horseman's, also in the High opposite to Brasenose, catered principally for members of Merton,[3] All Souls, Corpus and Oriel; Harper's at the corner house of the lane leading to St Edmund Hall, for Queen's and Magdalen; Bagg's, at the corner of Holywell, facing the King's Arms, for New College, Hertford and Wadham, and Malbon's at the north-east corner of the Turl for Trinity and other colleges in the neighbourhood.

No doubt drinking to excess was often the bane of junior as well as of senior members (and indeed of eighteenth-century society as a whole). 'We went to the Coffee house in the evening, where almost all the Gownsmen we saw were tipsy', an Irish visitor, Dr Thomas Campbell, commented in 1775, 'and the streets re-echoed with bacchanalian crys ... The next night also, we went to another Coffee house, and there the scene was only shifted, all muzzy. This, happily abated my enthusiasm conceived for an Oxford education.'[4]

In theory undergraduates were forbidden to frequent taverns and alehouses. When young Henry Fleming of Queen's was actually apprehended at an alehouse by the head of his college, Timothy Halton, he was given the choice of whether he and his companions 'would be whipt or turn'd out of their places'. They chose the latter penalty but were pardoned.[5] Although the colleges complained and the proctors continued to visit alehouses to turn away and sometimes to fine junior members, it was naturally extremely difficult to combat an accepted social habit:

> Nor Proctors thrice with vocal heel alarms
> Our joys secure, nor deigns the lowly roof
> Of Pot-house snug to visit: wiser he
> The splendid tavern haunts, or coffee-house.[6]

---

[1] Wood, *Life and Times* i. 168 and note.

[2] But it was a proposed sale of apparently pornographic literature at Tom's (and at the Black Horse in St Clement's) which led the proctors to consult the vice-chancellor on 15 Apr. 1774.

[3] In 1723 the fellows of Merton complained of the sale of wine and punch there: Merton, 4.22, Warden Holland's register, 22 July 1723.

[4] *Diary of a Visit to England in 1775, by an Irishman (the Reverend Doctor Thomas Campbell)*, ed. S. Raymond (Sydney 1854), 19-20.

[5] *The Flemings in Oxford* i. 313. Henry Fleming (1659-1728), m. Queen's 1678.

[6] 'A panegyric on Oxford ale' in *The Poetical Works of the late Thomas Warton, B.D.* ed. R. Mant (2 vols Oxford 1802) ii. 185. In 1723 the fellows of Merton complained that tavern-keepers kept their houses open on Sunday, and an order was made that no tavern-keeper should receive any person in their tavern to drink wine there on Sundays on penalty of a fine of 10s: Merton, 4.22, Warden

There is too much evidence of drunken revelling to push the point further, as Woodforde's diary demonstrates. When William Crowcher of Merton spent an evening in the bachelors' common room at New College he became 'develish drunk indeed, and made a great Noise there, but we carried him away to Peckhams Bed in Triumph'. Afterwards, Woodforde recalled, at 3 a.m. in the morning, 'Peckham broke my doors, being very drunk' and the next morning 'Several of our Fellows went at four o'clock in the Morning for Stow, and all drunk'. Although Woodforde had himself 'made a resolution never to get drunk again, when at Geree's Rooms in April last, when I fell down dead, and cut my Occiput very bad indeed', there can be no doubt that many undergraduates as well as fellows drank to excess.[1] Yet, as with other generalizations, a note of caution has to be injected. As a young fellow John Wesley was to become increasingly abstemious. In April 1799 Charles Sharpe of Christ Church told his mother that 'so dull and disagreeable are such entertainments [viz. the holding of 'wines'] to me, that I am resolved ... to give them up entirely and go to none'.[2]

Gambling was another social vice of the age in which the more affluent and well-born undergraduates may sometimes have indulged beyond their means. Woodforde certainly liked to gamble but the sums involved, which he spent on wagers at cards, bowls, horse-racing and billiards, were all of trivial dimensions. On 4 November 1761 Dyer of New College bet Mr Williams 2s 6d that he would drink three pints of wine in three hours and write out six verses from the Bible correctly, but he was so 'immensely drunk' that he 'could not write for his life'. On 4 June 1761 Peckham wagered Woodforde himself that 'his first Hands at Crickett [the first stroke of an innings] was better than Bennett Senrs', but 'he was beat' and Woodforde won 5s.[3]

Nominally Oxford was a society of celibates; but young women, either friends from home or more notoriously from the town, naturally enough

Holland's register, 22 July 1723. 'I walk'd to Ale-houses, and took near 30 schollars'; 'visited the Ale-houses, and turned out 16 or 17 schollars': Balliol, MS 461, diary of Jeremiah Milles. 'I found two Gentlemen at the Goats drinking whom I sent home and desired their Company in the morning': *Woodforde at Oxford*, 230, 12 June 1774.

[1] *Woodforde at Oxford*, 32 (11 Mar. 1761), 132 (1, 2 June) 151-2 (7 Sept. 1763). 'Occiput' refers to part of the skull. Henry Peckham (1740-87), m. New College 1759. At Trinity the dean was empowered to inflict the following penalties on any undergraduate or BA guilty of intoxication: for the first offence translation of a paper in the *Spectator*; for the second and third, translation of sermons; for the fourth, confinement to college for a week, strict attendance in hall and translation of two sermons or repetition-sermons of 200 lines; for the fifth, notification of the offence to the father or guardian, and for the sixth, rustication for four terms. Trinity, liber decani I, 20 Mar. 1788. Apparently Trinity had the reputation for having the fewest drunkards since good beer was available in the college and therefore men were less tempted to go to alehouses in the town.

[2] *Letters from and to Sharpe*, ed. Bedford i. 83.

[3] *Woodforde at Oxford*, 41, 57; the editor suggests that 'Bennett senr.' may have been Woolley Leigh Bennett (1733-90), m. Hertford 1752.

occupied the attention of the young men. Even Woodforde found some innocent enjoyment in the company of Nancy Bignell and her sister. Larogue of Lincoln called on his friends in the evening 'when we toast our inamoratas! and towards midnight stagger home'.[1] Others wanted and procured more distinctively physical satisfaction, feeling doubtless like the Cambridge undergraduate who observed in chapel to his companion in 1700 that *'tho' I have the Word of God in my Mouth, to tell the Truth on't I have a* Lyn *Devil in my Breeches'* (King's Lynn had at that time 'so fair a Reputation for the foul practise of Venery').[2] Proctorial authority extended to a surveillance of women of the town, with powers to expel them from the city's precincts and to incarcerate them in Bridewell. At night, Jeremiah Milles noted on 14 March 1702, 'I was in pursuit of an ill woman to put her into Bridewell, but failed'. He was more successful on 15 May when he 'walk'd till 1 a clock', and put 'two whores in Bridewell'.[3] Offenders brought to the notice of the college for such indiscretions were punished summarily. Charles Wake, a BA of Corpus, had had the temerity to bring in a 'lewd woman' disguised in a scholar's gown and 'kept her in College for 2 nights'; but the fortunate intervention of his father, a prebendary of Westminster, led to proceedings against him being dropped.[4]

Even before the development of organized games which have in more recent times absorbed the attention of the undergraduate, sometimes to an obsessive extent, there were opportunities for exercise: walking, riding, hunting for the rich, and boating. Some undergraduates had their own horses but the majority hired them from the many stables. Erasmus Head, in 1733, hired a horse 'once a Day at the rate of 5s per Week, which, how expensive soever it may seem, is the cheapest I can possibly hire one in all this term'.[5] Woodforde hired a horse from Jonathan Jackson who had a stable in Holywell, 'very good Hack indeed', for 2s a day and rode with his friend Geree after disputation to drink 'half a Pint of Cherry at the White Hart in Dorchester'. On other occasions he rode out to Foxcombe Hill and towards Burford. In May 1763 he had his own grey horse brought from Ansford so that he could ride home, bedding him and feeding him at 5s a day at Jackson's stable.[6] A gentleman-commoner of Lincoln, David Locock, paid 14s for a velvet hunting-cap and £15 for the hire of a horse for ten days from Mr Dry at the Eastgate in 1743. In 1737 a Mr Charlton expended £7 8s for horse hire in addition to paying 1s 6d for shoeing and £1 11s for saddlery.[7] Woodforde went

[1] Yale Univ. Beinecke Lib. Osborn Shelves, c.107.
[2] E. Ward, *A Step to Stir-Bitch-Remarks upon the University of Cambridge* (London 1700), 15.
[3] Milles's diary, 14 and 16 March, 15 May 1702.   [4] CCC B14/1/1, 16 Jan. 1769.
[5] Letter of 13 July 1733, Bodl. MS Don. c.152.
[6] *Woodforde at Oxford*, 122, 123, 126, 128-9, 130.
[7] Green, *Lincoln*, 405, 409.

shooting in New College woods at Stanton St John: 'I had out my Dog being the first time, and he did pretty well.'[1] Although college and university regulations forbade the keeping of dogs, undergraduates often contravened the rule. Trinity gentlemen whose dogs were seen in any part of the college were to be fined 1s by the porter 'for his own use'; at Worcester a college order of 1785 imposed a fine of 2s 6d for keeping a dog.[2]

In summer excursions were often made up the river, though there was as yet no organized rowing. 'Sometimes', Robert Larogue commented, 'after [evening] chapel we take Boats and go up the water. This is to me a delightful recreation'.[3] Such expeditions usually ended at a local tavern, either at Binsey or Godstow, where the company played skittles and refreshed themselves with bread, cheese and beer.[4] Occasionally undergraduates walked or rode to Blenheim or other great houses; Woodforde's visit to Blenheim cost him 2s 6d for admission, 6d each to the porters at the house and the park gate and 11s 6d for dinner for himself and his two friends at the Bear at Woodstock.[5] Earlier, a member of the university had vowed never to spend the summer in Oxford again because of the time that he had to spend in showing the sights to visitors and taking them out to Blenheim, then being built. 'That Blenheim is a curse upon this poor place, I would at any time make one in a rising of the University, town and county, to raze it to the ground.'[6]

Cricket had made its appearance. Woodforde mentioned that he was a member of a cricket club, and referred to matches between Winchester and Eton, and some Milton men and some gownsmen 'eleven on a side', but the game could apparently be played between two opponents (like modern 'French cricket').[7] More universal was the appeal of the annual horse-races on Port Meadow.[8] Although Erasmus Head of Queen's admitted that he could 'never in my Life . . . take any Delight' in such a 'Kind of Diversion', he described what went on to his parents:

On the first Day was a Plate of 50 Guineas value run (for he did *run* too) by one Horse; when . . . a great many Gentlemen and Ladies, some Dukes, Earls &c. were present to see the Gelding run by himself; and to win with Ease, without

---

[1] *Woodforde at Oxford*, 19 (4 Nov. 1760), 67 (28 Dec. 1761).

[2] Trinity, liber decani I, 15 Apr. 1778; Worcester, book no. 10, 29 Oct. 1785.

[3] Yale Univ. Beinecke Lib. Osborn Shelves, c.107.

[4] See for example *Woodforde at Oxford*, 13, 15, 47, 137. See too Milles's diary, 3 June 1703: 'This morning Mr Baron and all the Gent. Commrs &c were up the water with the University Mus: we dined at Godstow, and got home about 10 a clock.'

[5] *Woodforde at Oxford*, 32 (12 Mar. 1761); on 13 July of the same year he paid 2s to see the house and gave 1s each to the porters (ibid. 46).

[6] Stratford-Harley, 11 Sept. 1711, HMC *Portland MSS* vii. 55.

[7] *Woodforde at Oxford*, 12, 13, 14, 41, 134.

[8] E. H. Cordeaux and D. H. Merry, 'Port Meadow Races', *Oxoniensia* xiii (1948).

Touch of Breast, as the saying is. The Gentleman, whose he was, was so generous as to give the Plate to be run for again the next year ... The next day was a Plate of £30 value run for likewise by one Horse.[1]

When Woodforde attended the competition was keener, even though on one day there was 'but one Horse enter'd ... Molly Long Legs'. Nine horses entered for the £50 stake on 20 August 1761 and in 1763 'Three horses started for the Plate, viz. Mr Stamford's Horse, Bosphorus; Mr Snell's mare, Crimp; and Mr Stroud's Horse, Prospect ... If Bosphorus wins, I win of Reynel's, Bedford, Waring and Gauntlett, of each o.1.o.' In 1774, though he did not himself go, there was 'A great deal of Company in Town as our Races begin to Morrow—and great Sport expected'.[2]

There were other diversions to attract the undergraduate, provided by the play-actors, musicians and conjurors attracted by the possibility of a gullible audience: a little boy playing upon glasses with his fingers at the King's Arms, a waxwork display in the town, Monsieur Rosignol imitating birds at the Mitre, Hyman Palatine doing sleight of hand in Ship Street, Thomas Heyne displaying a mandrake, 'a very curious Root, found in water, representing a Human Body'.[3] Jeremiah Milles in 1702 noted, among other entertainments, a 'magick Lanthorn', 'the rope-dancers', a 'ladder dancer' and 'the Elephant'.[4]

Some such entertainments were gruesome, even unpleasant. Milles was fascinated by the dissection of a dog, but when a dissection took place on a live dog he was repelled by the cruelty.[5] Woodforde went to the Old Ashmolean to watch the dissection of a woman 'for which I paid o.o.6'.[6] The holding of the assizes provided an enormous attraction for the young men, so much so that the authorities tried to deter them, more especially from attending the public executions. When the highwayman Dumas was tried in March 1761 junior members were forbidden to attend the trial and in retaliation hissed at the vice-chancellor. When Dumas was sentenced to be hanged (at the castle on 23 March at 7.40 a.m.) all college gates were ordered to be shut from 10 the previous evening to 9 a.m. But, in 1762, Woodforde was present at the execution of a gipsy sentenced to death for robbing a girl with violence. Thirteen years later as pro-proctor he was present with some thousands of others at the execution of George Strap. 'A Methodist prayed by him in the Cart for some Time under the Gallows ... I think I never saw such Sullenness and Villainy in one Face. Jack Ketch kissed him twice before he went of[f].' Woodforde took the opportunity to

[1] Letter of 1 Sept. 1730, Bodl. MS Don. c.152.
[2] *Woodforde at Oxford*, 51-2, 149-50, 243-4. Carew Reynell (1730-81), m. New College 1748.
[3] Ibid. 43 (18 June 1761), 61 (2 Dec. 1761), 160 (5 Mar. 1764), 283 (7 Apr. 1775).
[4] Milles's diary, 8 Apr. and 25 July 1701, 11 and 13 July 1702.
[5] Ibid. 4 and 11 Oct. 1701.   [6] *Woodforde at Oxford*, 80 (10 Apr. 1762).

exercise his proctorial powers by apprehending two gentlemen 'for wearing different Capes to their Coats, than the Coats were of'.[1]

There were more decorous pastimes, dancing, bowls, chess,[2] billiards, cards and, in hard winters, skating on the river. Cards played for smaller or greater sums of money were perhaps the most normal occupation for both don and undergraduate after dinner: piquet, quadrille, brag, beat the knave out of doors, putt, whist, loo and lansquenet among others.[3]

At first sight there would appear to have been an absence of the clubs and societies which festoon the modern university; but there were societies of like-minded young men, often apparently brief in duration. By and large they were social in purpose; though the notorious Constitution Club was, as its name implied, political.[4] It had its venue at the King's Head tavern in the High; its members included five fellows and a number of gentlemen-commoners (from New College, Oriel, Christ Church, Hart Hall, Worcester, All Souls, Merton, St John's and Trinity). It was whiggish in complexion and designed to overcome disaffection. Another Oxford society, the Freecynics, was apparently a kind of philosophical club, 'who ... have a set of symbolical words and grimaces, unintelligible to any but those of their own society'.[5] Jeremy Bentham was introduced to Oldfield Bowles, a gentleman-commoner, who belonged to an Oxford club of more radical inclinations, 'Unbelievers, Atheists and Deists',[6] a strong contrast to the Wesley brothers' Holy Club. There was a Poetical Club in existence in 1721 to which Erasmus Phillips belonged. Its members 'motto'd and epi-gramatized' at the Tuns tavern where, at their meeting on 17 August, they subscribed 5s towards Evans's *Hymen and Juno*, drank Galician wine and were entertained 'with two Fables of the Doctor's Composition, which were indeed masterly in their kind', though the club aroused the sneers of Nicholas Amhurst in *Terrae-Filius*.[7] Others were of a narrowly social character.[8]

Towards the end of the century a number of young men, Thomas Dibdin of St John's, a future founder of the Roxburghe Club, John Stoddard of Christ Church, George Forster of Lincoln and others, formed a Society for Scientific and Literary Disquisition which met in

[1] *Woodforde at Oxford*, 31 (6 Mar. 1761), 33 (23 Mar. 1761), 277-8 (13 March 1775).

[2] Jeremiah Milles was a member of a chess club: see entries in his diary for 9 October, 2 and 6 December 1701, 10 and 17 February, 21 and 22 December 1702.

[3] See *Woodforde at Oxford, passim.*

[4] J. C. Jeaffreson, *Annals of Oxford* (2 vols London 1871) ii. 233.

[5] A. H. Gibbs, *Rowlandson's Oxford* (London 1911), 82.

[6] *Works of Bentham*, ed. Bowring x. 38-9.

[7] 'Diary of Erasmus Phillips', *Notes and Queries* 2nd ser. x. 365-6, 443-5; Wordsworth, *Social Life at the English Universities*, 149-50. *Terrae-Filius* nos. xix (15-18 Mar. 1721), xx (18-22 Mar. 1721).

[8] See D. Fairer, 'Oxford and the literary world', pp. 795 ff below.

each other's rooms where essays were read.[1] The topics were mainly literary or philosophical, and studiously avoided all controversial, political and religious issues. The founders tried to get the approval of the vice-chancellor, John Wills, and the proctors for the rules they had drawn up, but while the vice-chancellor saw nothing 'subversive of academic discipline' in the scheme, he felt unable to give the society his official approval, 'as innovations of this sort, and in these times, may have a tendency which may be as little anticipated as it may be distressing to the framers of such laws'. Subsequently they adopted the nickname LUNATICS; 'Mad', indeed, Dibdin commented, 'we were, and desired to be so called—if an occasional deviation from dull and hard drinking, frivolous gossip and Boeotian uproar, could justify that appellation'.[2]

The best-known Oxford club was probably the High Borlace, high tory in sympathy, which used to meet on 18 August, unless this was a Sunday, to eat and drink at the King's Head tavern; but though Theophilus Leigh, the master of Balliol, was at its annual dinner in 1734, it was not essentially a university society. Its members were taken from the county as well as the university and it had a lady patroness.[3]

College clubs may have existed but their life was very ephemeral, and their object convivial. Woodforde was a member of a breakfast club which had three members, himself and his friends Geree and Dyer; they called themselves the Sasafras Club and used to breakfast in each other's rooms.[4] The most important exception was the Phoenix Club, founded at Brasenose by Joseph Alderson and three others at the close of 1781 or early in 1782, though its continuous existence appears to date from 1786. In that year a set of rules was drawn up, restricting the membership to twelve. The members dined together each evening (every member had to dine at least once a fortnight), and an anniversary dinner was held at the King's Arms. There was an annual subscription of 5s (and, after 1801, 2s 6d for the common-room man).[5] It had its own wine-cellar and bought its own papers. It had many of the aspects of a junior common room (and was indeed called the Phoenix Common Room), of which so far few definite traces, except possibly at Corpus and New College, can be found.

It is hardly surprising that undergraduates' high spirits, sometimes stimulated by drink and spurred on by boredom, occasionally erupted

---

[1] Thomas Dibdin (1777-1847), m. St John's 1793. Sir John Stoddard (1773-1856), m. Ch.Ch. 1790; judge of vice-admiralty court, Malta 1826-9.

[2] *Reminiscences of Oxford*, 218-21.

[3] C. E. Mallet, *History of the University* (3 vols London 1927) iii. 32; Wordsworth, *Social Life at the English Universities*, 153-5.

[4] *Woodforde at Oxford*, 112 (26 Feb. 1763).

[5] F. Madan, *A Century of the Phoenix Common Room (Brasenose College, Oxford), 1786-1886* (Oxford 1888); F. Madan, 'A short account of the Phoenix Common Room 1782-1900', *Brasenose Monographs* ii pt 2, pp. 93-135.

into violence with each other or with the townsfolk. Edmond Bolton of Brasenose was spending an evening in December 1725 at the room of one Wyndham Napier to drink punch. 'Everyone at first design'd to get drunk soberly, and took their Glasses together very friendly: each drinking his right-hand man's good health over the right thumb.' One of the party, Mr Trogee, ill-content with drinking over the glass, swigged from the bowl, so arousing the anger of his comrades. 'Now glasses clash'd with glasses, and pipes with pipes in terrible Confusion, and the punch ran in rapid streams down their throats.' A brawl ensued. Trogee was 'kick'd from the top of the stairs, and wou'd inevitably have broken his skull' had not 'Alford catch'd him at the bottom ... some hurt and some unhurt in the scuffle they went to bed themselves, and so very prettily concluded the Sunday night. Trogee is gone down into the Country and has carry'd with him a terrible black Eye and Bruis'd face.'[1] Even Woodforde engaged in fisticuffs with his friend Macock of Lincoln in the High on 2 November 1760. Two years later 'Webber and myself had a Quarrell in the BCR and fought in the Garden, where he ... beat me unmercifully'. When Woodforde was sub-warden in 1775 'there was a great Riot in College by the Junior People—who broke down Dawbenys Doors, and broke Jeffries's Windows'.[2] In 1729 Thomas Hylton and four others from Lincoln were charged with breaking into the college buttery and 'by rioting and drunkenness first on the water and after in Colledge, where your company could scarce be dispersed by the Tutors and Officers of the Colledge'.[3]

From time to time relationships between town and gown flared into violence. Charles Sharpe described one such occasion which occurred in June 1800:

For these four nights past there hath been regularly a battle between the gownsmen and town-people, which last night came to such a pitch that swords were produced, and the devil and all to do, in spite of the Vice-Chancellor and Proctors, who were called the most villainous epithets to their very beards. Had our two Censors not come out to quell the Ch.Ch. *men*, the consequences would have been serious ... I am sorry to say that some of my friends, whom I should never have thought capable of such childish absurdity, were in the last battle ... The evil originated in Mr K---- (a brother of Lord K----'s), who, though very good-natured when sober, is a very fiend drunk; and the quarrelling with some men, by whom he was much abused, brought all the students into the scrape.

---

[1] 'An undergraduate of 1723', *Oxford Magazine* lxvi (1947-8), 90. 'Trogee' cannot be identified in the registers of Brasenose or University College.
[2] *Woodforde at Oxford*, 19, 71, 293. Henry Macock (1743-1816), m. Linc. 1758. John Webber (1740-89), m. Univ. 1758; BA New College 1763, MA 1767; proctor 1774. Charles Daubeny (1745-1827), m. Oriel 1762; BCL New College 1773.
[3] Quoted in Green, *Lincoln*, 411. Thomas Hylton (1711-39), m. Linc. 1728.

A night or so later Sharpe feared a repetition of the troubles when, returning from a concert which Madame Mara had been giving in the Holywell music room, he found a 'great crowd of fellows assembled at eight o'clock, armed with cudgels and stones'. Sharpe told his mother that he would not venture outside the college walls in darkness, being insufficiently proficient at 'cudgel-playing or boxing'.[1] The city's humiliation at the hands of the university was still recalled by the annual service held at St Mary's on St Scholastica's day (10 February), which was only to be abolished in 1825.

The university and colleges had machinery, sometimes in practice a little rusty, for dealing with several forms of misbehaviour. The proctors and pro-proctors were the university's agents for policing the streets, imposing fines and apprehending offenders; but they seem by and large to have been concerned with minor offences, such as irregularities in wearing academic dress (even John Wesley was once 'progged' for failing to wear his cap), turning undergraduates away from alehouses and places of ill-repute and dealing with riotous behaviour. But the penalties they imposed were relatively lenient. When Woodforde was a pro-proctor he was often content with an apology. Mr Woodhouse, a gentleman-commoner of Christ Church, who had vomited in the Sheldonian during Encaenia, had to translate one of Pope's *Pastorals* into Latin hexameters. His companion, a Mr Peddle, a gentleman-commoner of St Mary Hall, and already in holy orders, had his name put in the black book.[2]

College discipline seems to have been administered in a similar way. The anger of the authorities could be provoked by 'rude and unmannerly' behaviour, by disturbances of the peace, by insolence to the head or tutors.[3] Breach of college rules could lead to fines or impositions, the normal punishment. Colleges were reluctant to proceed to the final penalty of expulsion. At Trinity in 1707 a Mr Knollys, a fellow-commoner, was expelled because, as the president, William Dobson, put it to Knollys's cousin John Foyle, a barrister and former member of the college who had remonstrated with the president, 'in disturbing the Peace of the Society he lives in, and when no admonitions will prevail with him to return to a more sober behaviour . . . I think the removal of such a one (be his Quality what it will) absolutely necessary'. Knollys's work, as his tutors testified, had been satisfactory nor was he guilty of 'drinking, whoring, or swearing'; but he had missed prayers and insulted the dean, and 'at length to crown the rest, he made a publick disturbance

[1] *Letters from and to Sharpe*, ed. Bedford i. 96, 98.
[2] John Chappell Woodhouse (1750–1833), m. Ch.Ch. 1767; dean of Lichfield 1807–33. John Peddle (1752–1840), m. St Mary Hall 1771.
[3] Green, *Lincoln*, 411–12.

in the Chappel, while Divinity disputations were perform'd he with some others setting up a loud Laugh (an unheard of Insolence) to affront the Vice-President in the Execution of his Office'. Besides he had, though the president did not mention it, 'kick'd at the Cat of Thomas Hasker Clark and Bursar of the said College, which Cat (as it was said) ran afterwards into the Chappell'. The President sought to mollify Knollys's cousin: 'no doubt', he wrote, 'you design'd a benefit to the College', but 'it may be better for us to loose £500 than have the company of one so prejudic'd and sour'd against us'; unusual sentiments in college governing bodies where benefactions are concerned.[1]

Fines or sconces or impositions were the more normal punishment for breach of college rules. In a clerical society the withholding of a testimonial for orders or the grace for a degree were effective sanctions sometimes used to ensure good behaviour. Tom Hylton and his friends, who had disturbed the peace of Lincoln by their drunken revels, were threatened with such a penalty.[2] The threat to withhold the certificate of good conduct which the bishop required before ordination was not uncommon, as the case of the Methodists expelled from St Edmund Hall in 1768 was to demonstrate.[3] Occasionally offenders were still obliged to confess their faults in chapel or at dinner in hall.[4] In the case of men rusticated it was normal to demand a certificate of good conduct from a local clergyman before they were allowed back into residence.[5]

The senior members of the university often adopted a style of social life that was not dissimilar to their juniors. The centre of this world was the senior common room, which had, in most colleges, made its appearance after the Restoration, reflecting the general advance in amenities typifying the lifestyle of the period. Every don had his set of rooms in college, often panelled and sometimes elegantly furnished; if he was absent from college he could let the rooms and use the rent to supplement a stipend that became steadily more lucrative as the century advanced. But it was in the common rooms that he foregathered with

---

[1] Bodl. MS Ashmole 1820, b. fos 45-6. William Dobson (1650-1731), m. Trin. 1666, president 1706-31.

[2] Lincoln, register 1577-1739, fo 296b, 13 Mar. 1729.

[3] See L. G. Mitchell, 'Politics and Revolution 1772-1800', pp. 165-6 above; V. H. H. Green, 'Religion in the colleges 1715-1800', pp. 458-64 below.

[4] At Christ Church in 1726 two young men who had been involved in a duel over a love affair were not expelled 'but were required to ask pardon publickly in the Hall': H. L. Thompson, *Christ Church* (London 1900), 149.

[5] Regulations for the conduct of undergraduates at Queen's, more especially for the Lady Elizabeth Hastings's exhibitioners, stressed the need for juniors to show respect to their seniors, to attend regularly in hall, in chapel and at lectures, and to show sobriety and discretion in their public conduct. All who missed prayers twice a week were liable to be fined 1s or set an imposition. A similar penalty was imposed on all who missed a disputation or exercise in the hall. A sconce of 6d could be imposed on all who went out of town without the permission of their tutors: Queen's, MS 475, fos 68-9.

the other fellows and, where they enjoyed the privileges, with the fellow-commoners, and here the seniors played cards after dinner, drank wine and brandy, smoked their pipes, read the journals and made their wagers. The accounts of Oriel's senior common room itemize the annual purchase of cards, dice, clay pipes and, until 1762, a mistletoe (presumably for the Christmas festivities); a chess-board was bought in 1789, a tea-chest in 1789; maps of Toulon and the Mediterranean procured in 1744 were presumably intended to help the fellows follow the fortunes of war.[1] At Lincoln the college paid for the maintenance and repair of the fabric of the senior common room and, in 1815, for its new furnishings.[2] On All Saints day, a festal day when fruit and tobacco were free, members had to pay for tea, coffee or wine taken from the common-room stock. Every common room had its own wine-cellar, and a few colleges continued also to brew their own beer. The consumption of liquor was often considerable. At Queen's in 1811 no less than 1,470 bottles of port, 171 of sherry and 48 of madeira, in addition to quantities of gin, rum and punch, were consumed.[3]

John James wrote somewhat censoriously in 1779:

The fellows of a college that spend half their lives in poring over newspapers and smoking tobacco, seem to live to no end, to be cut off from all the dearer interests of society, to possess, or at least to exert, no benevolence. What in the name of wonder can these men think of themselves when they look back upon a life that has been spent without either receiving or communicating pleasure.[4]

Senior common room bets were usually laid in port, sometimes a single bottle, occasionally a half-dozen or dozen of claret or burgundy. The wagers themselves helped to provide some entertainment, satisfy some curiosity, passed the time and assisted in supplying the common room with wine to drink. Bets were made on the weather, politics, national as well as local, marriage possibilities, the war (if there was one), the turf, the boxing ring, the results of university and national elections, preferment to high office, literary allusions, even the weights of the fellows present. Corpus's common room was plainly interested in sporting matters. One of the earliest entries in a book which dates back to 1745 referred to a bet as to whether Firetail and Pompkin would complete the mile heat (probably in the summer races on Port Meadow) in one minute four seconds. The doings of Shirley's horse in the sweepstakes, the fight between Big Ben and Perrins, the success of the Pig and of Dutch Sam in his pitched battle, the fight between Humphries and Mendoza, or the several encounters of Oard in the ring do not

---

[1] 'Antiquities of Oriel common room'.
[2] Lincoln, register 1739-1983, fo 136, 24 Feb. 1815.
[3] R. H. Hodgkin, *Six Centuries of an Oxford College* (Oxford 1949), 165n.
[4] *Letters of Radcliffe and James*, 85.

suggest a highly elevated intellectual conversation in the common room.[1] Mr Coates waged Mr Beaver that he would not get into Merton grove from the Corpus common room with coat, breeches and boots on, a challenge which Mr Beaver manfully accepted. The convivial Mr Modd bet Mr Weller, a fellow of apparently similar tastes, that he could hold out a heavier weight at arms length than Mr Weller. Mr Beaver wagered Mr Wake that he weighed no more than 17 stone. Dr Williams won two bottles of port by betting that he was not less than 18 stone 6 pounds.[2] A similar series of wagers appears in the Lincoln betting book in the 1820s; though the fellows' average weight would appear to have been somewhat less than their colleagues at Corpus in the closing years of the century. In 1787 Mr Jacob of Corpus bet Mr Skelton two bottles that he could with the same leg on which he was to hop touch with any part of his foot a mark 6 feet from the ground. Mr Skelton was clearly of a more athletic physique than the portly Mr Wake, wagering Mr Stockwell[3] three bottles that he could beat him at tennis, the best of three sets.

But not all wagers were on trivial matters. The advent of the French wars provided ample opportunity for speculation as to the possibility of peace or the outcome of some particular campaign. Will Mr Pitt contrive to have an armament in a month before 15 October 1792? Will the combined armies be in possession of Paris before 1 September 1793? At Lincoln, where the surviving betting book dates back to 1809, the subject-matter was often local in content, though in 1812 Mr Wilson wagered Mr Yeadon that their colleague William Harby had fitted up his rooms before the taking of Seringapatam 'when Tippoo was killed', and in 1813 another fellow, Clarke Jenkins, opined that Lord Spencer would not contribute towards the erection of a memorial to the murdered prime minister, Spencer Perceval, in All Saints church, Northampton.[4]

Excessive indulgence in strong drink was, as Gibbon's well known statement on the fellows of Magdalen testifies, a supposed feature of senior common room life and nor can its wide prevalence be denied. 'Yesterday Morning, at two Clock', Hearne recounted, 'the Duke of

[1] CCC wager book 1745-1808, contents summarized in *The Pelican Record* xiii no. 2 (Mar. 1916), 56-8.

[2] John Modd (1745-91), m. CCC 1762. Samuel Weller (1736-95), m. CCC 1751. Sam Weller, so much to the fore in the Corpus wager book, had as an undergraduate been disciplined for drunkenness: 'ebrius in Festo C C in sacello tumultuatus fuerim'. He had given an entertainment in the BAs' common room and as a result he had been deprived of his commons for a week and other scholars had to do written impositions: CCC wager book 1745-1808. George Williams (1762-1834), m. CCC 1777; Sherardian professor of botany 1796-1834; physician Radcliffe Infirmary 1789-1834; Radcliffe Librarian 1810-34; FRCP 1799.

[3] Thomas Stockwell (1744-1825), m. CCC 1759; sub-dean of Salisbury 1801.

[4] Lincoln senior common room betting book. 'Mr Wilson' was probably Harry Bristow Wilson (1775-1854), m. Linc. 1793. William Yeadon (1775-1848), m. Linc. 1790, fellow 1797-1823; clerk Magd. 1791-3. William Harby (1769-1823), m. Linc. 1787. Clarke Jenkins (1778-1865), m. Linc. 1796.

Beaufort (who is of Univ. Coll.) rid out of Town with that vicious, loose Fellow, Mr Ward (commonly call'd Jolly Ward) of Univ. Coll. It is said they had sate up 'till that time drinking. Ward was so drunk that he vomited four times between Queen's Coll. Lane and East Gate.'[1] Woodforde's diary and other contemporary records afford ample evidence of intemperance in senior common rooms. It was apparently the fellows of Oriel who in the next century, according to Burgon, 'were the first in Oxford to break through the tyranny of fashion by abandoning the immoderate use of wine which prevailed in the upper ranks of English society . . . This was the first Common-room where *tea* was drunk . . . The Oriel tea-pot became a standing joke in the University.'[2]

Every college had, as it still does, its statutory feasts when the food tended to be more sumptuous than on normal evenings: as, for instance, the new year feast and the commemoration of Archbishop Laud at St John's; the Christmas day boar's head at Queen's; the chapter days at Lincoln; St Katherine's day at Balliol,[3] and many another. All Souls kept, though not annually, the strange feast of the mallard, a glimpse of which Reginald Heber caught as he leaned out of his window at Brasenose in the early hours of the morning (and caught a chill in consequence).

I had a full view of the *Lord Mallard* and about forty fellows, in a kind of procession on the library roof, with immense lighted torches, which had a singular effect . . . I am sure that all who had the gift of hearing, within half a mile, must have been awakened by the manner in which they thundered their chorus, 'O by the blood of King Edward'.[4]

There was too a regular round of private dinner parties at which the host was sometimes the head of the college, for the heads and their wives (where the college statutes allowed) formed the epicentre of Oxford's social life, as well as 'treats' and other entertainments for departing or newly elected fellows.[5]

In a society statutorily celibate there were inevitably some occasions of scandal. Some young dons, like their junior members, doubtless availed themselves of the services of the ladies of the town, professional and otherwise. William Cradocke, fellow of Magdalen and chaplain to

---

[1] Hearne, *Collections* viii. 24 (15 Dec. 1722). Henry Somerset (1707-45), 3rd d. of Beaufort; m. Univ. 1720; hon. DCL 1725. George Ward (1686-1733), m. Univ. 1702, fellow 1708.

[2] Burgon, *Lives of Twelve Good Men*, 386-7.

[3] See the entry in Jeremiah Milles's diary for 25 Nov. 1702: 'This being S. Katharine's day, and our chiefe festival, I was busy in preparing necessaries, and sending to invite Strangers. After dinner we were in the Com. Room, and had the Univers. musick. At night we play'd at Cards till past 12.'

[4] Letter to J. Thornton, 15 Jan. 1801, Heber, *Life of Reginald Heber* i. 25. Heber was himself elected a fellow of All Souls in 1804.

[5] For 'treats' see for example the entries in John Wesley's diary when he was a fellow of Lincoln (1726-51).

the bishop of Oxford, George Fleming noted on 10 June 1692, 'hath got by stealth or as of others will have it run a way with a daughter of one Esq Nurse a great fortune'.[1] In a predominantly youthful male society some degree of homosexual affection and activity was inevitable. The most widely publicized scandal concerned the warden of Wadham, Robert Thistlethwayte, accused of sodomy with a college servant and one of his undergraduates, Mr French, the latter unwillingly, in 1739. Another fellow, a Mr Swinton, seems to have escaped prosecution for the same offence.[2] In November 1732 Thomas Wilson, then a Student of Christ Church, deplored the leniency with which Merton treated its chaplain, John Pointer, 'long suspected of Sodomitical Practices', who had done 'some very indecent things' to one of the commoners.[3] Pointer escaped to his living in Nottinghamshire but subsequently returned to Oxford where he lived in St Giles.[4]

The social apex of the university's year had been for many years the Act, an occasion which was designed, as the Laudian statutes make plain, to commemorate the conclusion of the act or exercises required for graduation, so marking the commencement of the young man's career as a BA. The academic exercises, which took place in early July, lasted several days, though the Act day itself was celebrated on the first Tuesday in July; when in 1669 it was transferred for the first time from St Mary's church to the newly built Sheldonian Theatre it lasted from 11 a.m. to 7 p.m. More and more, however, the academic procedure was overshadowed by the entertainments and general junketing which accompanied it. 'This publick Act', as Bloom, a character in Thomas Baker's comedy *An Act at Oxford*, declared,

has drawn hither half the Nation, Men o'Fashion come to shew some new French Cutt, laugh at learning and prove their want of it ... The Company, the Diversions have rais'd us a pitch above our selves; the Doctors

[1] *The Flemings in Oxford* iii. 63. William Cradocke (1659-92), m. Magd. Hall 1675; demy Magd. 1676-9.

[2] *A Faithful Narrative of the Proceedings in a late affair between the Rev. Mr. John Swinton and Mr. George Baker...* (London 1739). John Swinton (1697-1777) m. Wadham 1713; BD Ch.Ch. 1759; keeper of the archives 1767-77.

[3] *The Diaries of Thomas Wilson, 1731-7 and 1750*, ed. C. L. S. Linnell (London 1964), 81-2. Thomas Wilson (1704-84), m. Ch.Ch. 1721. John Pointer (1668-1754), m. Merton 1687; author of *Oxoniensis Academia* (London 1749).

[4] Hearne's account is as follows, 'On Wednesday night Nov. 29 Last Mr John Pointer, Chaplain of Merton College, was examined before the Warden of that College, Dr John Holland [1666-1734; m. Magd. Hall 1682; BA St Alban Hall 1685; fellow Merton 1691, warden 1709-34], on the point of sodomy, he having been accused of sodomitical practises. Two persons of the College, Post-masters, I hear, of a good reputation, were ready to make their oath, but their oaths were foreborn, and for quietness Pointer was advised to go off from the College, and forbid reading prayers as Chaplain there any more ... He hath been guilty of this abominable vice many years ... But this and other Vices are become so common in England ... that they are not by many looked upon as sins.' *Collections* xi. 133.

have smugg'd up their old Faces, powder'd their diminutive Bobs, put on their starch'd Bands, and their best Prunello Cassocks, with shining Shoes that you might see your Face in.—The young Commoners have sold their Books to run to Plays.—The Servitors have pawn'd their Beds to treat their shabby Acquaintance, and every College has brew'd such a store of strong stupifying Belch, in hopes to level sheer Wits to their own Mediocrity.[1]

Dr Coode of All Souls, writing to Charlett on 12 July 1713, spoke of the 'ball of the best quality at the Council Chamber and a supper at 12 at night in the town hall, in short there has been nothing but social doings tho no Terrae filius'.[2]

The recreational side was represented by the musical concerts and, less seriously, by the sometimes scabrous figure of the Terrae-Filius. The Terrae-Filius of seventeenth-century Oxford had been the licensed jester of the university, originally intended to poke fun at Romanists and unbelievers, but he had become a witty, sometimes libellous critic of the *quaestiones disputatae* of the Act itself and of leading figures in the university, so outspoken and abusive that he was sometimes expelled and his oration suppressed. The diarist John Evelyn, who had been present at the Act in July 1669, commented:

The *Terrae filius* or Universitie bouffoone entertaind the Aditorie with a tedious, abusive, sarcastical rhapsodie, much unbecoming the gravity of the Universitie, & that so grossly, as that unlesse it be suppress'd, it will be of ill consequence, as I plainly expressed my sense, both to the Vice Chancellor and severall heads of houses afterwards[3]

In the late seventeenth and early eighteenth centuries the Terrae-Filius still appeared occasionally; by 1703 he was giving his oration in English. After 1713, however, the name of no Terrae-Filius is recorded, and after the solitary Act in 1733, when a speech attributed to him but probably never given was published, he disappeared altogether.[4] The content of his animadversions can, however, be gleaned from the printed

[1] [T. Baker,] *An Act at Oxford* (London 1704), 2.
[2] Ballard MS 20, fo 175^r-v. Philip Coode (1674-1718), m. Queen's 1691; fellow All Souls, MA 1698, BM 1703, DM 1707.
[3] *The Diary of John Evelyn*, ed. E. S. de Beer (6 vols Oxford 1955) iii. 532, 10 July 1669.
[4] There are extant orations of Joseph Brooke (m. Ch.Ch. 1657) in 1663: Bodl. MSS Rawl. D. 191, 1110, Top. Oxon. e.202, Don. f.29, Add. A.368, Locke, e.17. Henry Gerard (m. Wadham 1662) in 1669: Bodl. MSS Rawl. D.191, Top. Oxon. e.202; Don. f.29, Add. A.368; Queen's MS 478; *Opera posthuma latina...Roberti South* (London 1717), 139 ff. John Rotherham (m. Ch.Ch. 1664) in 1671: Bodl. MSS Top. Oxon. e.202, Don. f.29; *Opera Roberti South*, 123 ff. John Shirley (m. Trin. 1665) in 1673: Bodl. MSS Rawl B.403, Don. f.29; Wood, *Life and Times* ii. 266-7 (fragment only). John Aylworth (m. Magd. 1669) in 1693: Bodl. MS Rawl. D.912; Hearne, *Collections* i. 188-90. Robert Roberts (m. Ch.Ch. 1697) in 1703: Bodl. MSS Tanner 338, Rawl. D.697, printed in *The University Miscellany* (London 1713). Although the vice-chancellor had the intended speech of 1713 year burned, it was later printed as *The Speech that was intended to have been spoken by the Terrae-Filius* (London 1713). It sold well: Hearne, *Collections* iv. 243. The authorship of the pamphlet was attributed to John Willes of Christ Church. For 1733 see *The Terrae-Filius's Speech, as it was intended to have been spoken at the Publick Act* (London 1733).

pamphlets. The speech of 1713, composed in a mixture of Latin and English, alluded to Lancaster, the provost of Queen's, as a trimmer, old 'Slyboots', mentioned a corrupt election at Merton, stressed the whiggish character of Jesus, and the sale by the university of books at a quarter of their true value in order to build a printing house.

In 1733, the writer described the bishop of Oxford as a 'mitred Hog' who in his seventieth year had married a girl of eighteen; ascribed the dean of Christ Church's recent preferment to his support for the excise scheme, spoke of the 'egregious' warden of Wadham as a sycophant and of the fellows of St John's as Jacobites. Exeter was governed by 'old women', Jesus was enveloped in a smell of toast and old cheese. The fellows of All Souls were drunkards and 'smarts'. The warden of New College, a 'blessed Seminary of Learning governed by a *Boy*, who was elected by *Boys*', had secured his election by bribing the fellows with French wine and arrack punch. At Worcester 'there could not be found a *Priest* ... that could read the Service in *Latin*'. Lincoln, 'always was, and always will be, under the D---l's Inspection'.[1] Brasenose buys up advowsons and brews ale. Oriel men are always in debt. At Magdalen the dons live scandalous lives.

Although the Terrae-Filius speech of 1733 was never spoken or probably never intended to be, the Act of that year was a memorable occasion, one of the 'Grandest Doings', Erasmus Head anticipated, 'that have ever been known in Oxford since it was a University, by reason of a Publick Act, which has not been celebrated here for these 19 years last past. All the Lodgings in Town have been long ago bespoke for the Accommodation of Gentlemen and Ladies, who then intend to visit us.'[2]

But the revival of the Act in 1733 was, as it were, a flash in the pan. In its fullness it was never to be repeated, and was replaced by one of its component parts, the commemoration of founders and benefactors, which came to be known as Encaenia; on occasions the celebrations were grander than usual, such as the Encaenia held in July 1756 in honour of the countess of Pomfret at which many honorary degrees were bestowed in the three days of the proceedings, and again in 1763 to mark the conclusion of the treaty of Paris.[3] Encaenia had been given added substance by the benefaction bestowed upon the university by Nathaniel, Lord Crewe, bishop of Durham, formerly rector of Lincoln. By

---

[1] The reference was to the carved gargoyle over the gable at the northern end of the west wing of the front quad, 'the Lincoln Imp', which was removed in 1731 after the head had been damaged in a storm two years before.

[2] Letter of 20 May 1733, Bodl. MS Don. c.152.

[3] A periodical entitled *Terrae-Filius*, four issues of which were printed in London in July 1763, described Encaenia, but was not an oration: copies in Bodl. G.A. Oxon. 4°(6). Woodforde bought four copies on the successive days of the commemoration at 6*d* each, commenting that the supposed authors were Bonnell Thornton (1724-68, m. Ch.Ch. 1743), Charles Churchill and George Colman, all of whom were present at the proceedings: *Woodforde at Oxford*, 138-40.

his will, dated 24 June 1720, Crewe designed £200 for the university.[1] Eleven years later, on 2 July 1731, his former chaplain Richard Grey[2] reaffirmed to convocation the bishop's intention (Crewe died in 1722) as to how the money was to be spent. In addition to supplementing the stipends of certain officials £20 was to be paid to the university orator and £20 to the poetry lecturer, each of whom should be obliged in alternate years to make a speech in the Sheldonian in commemoration of the university's benefactors; £10 a year was allocated to the heads of houses, doctors and professors for an entertainment at Encaenia.[3]

So Encaenia came to replace the Act as the distinctive social occasion of the academic year. An account of the 1750 Encaenia shows the heads and others being entertained in New College Hall, then proceeding at 4 o'clock to the Sheldonian where there was music, an honorary degree was conferred on the earl of Plymouth and the university orator spoke for an hour. 'The theatre was quite full, a very handsome appearance of ladies; and the whole was conducted with great decorum.'[3] Woodforde, who was present at the Encaenia in 1763, described the events in detail. The chancellor, Lord Lichfield, 'dressed in Gold Brocade all over' presided. On the first day, 5 July, 'Doctor Wilson's speeches for his Prizes, spoke by Sandys of All-Souls, and Cooper of Braze-nose-Coll: and likewise Mr Thomas Warton's Speech in Commemoration of Bene-factors'. The next day the chancellor conferred honorary degrees on Lord Corke, the duke of Manchester and Sir John Trevor. A performance of Handel's *Acis and Galatea* was given in the Sheldonian Theatre. More degrees were conferred on 7 July, the oratorio *Judas Maccabaeus* being performed in the afternoon. On the final day, in the presence of the chancellor, garbed in a silver-brocade suit, there were further speeches, among them a trenchant oration from the high tory Dr King, the principal of St Mary Hall; Handel's *Messiah* was the final musical offering.[4]

Commemoration had then taken the form that it was long to have, the gathering of the doctors and heads in their scarlet for Lord Crewe's benefaction, the conferring of honorary degrees by the chancellor, speeches by the public orator or the professor of poetry, the recital of prize-exercises. 'Friday next is the grand day', John James wrote of the

[1] C. E. Whiting, *Nathaniel Lord Crewe* (London 1940).

[2] Green, *Lincoln*, 688. Richard Grey (1696-1771), m. Linc. 1712; incorporated at Cambridge 1732; archdeacon of Bedford 1757-71.

[3] *Gentleman's Magazine* xx (1750), 328 (2 July). Other Lewis Windsor (1731-71), 4th e. of Plymouth and Lord Windsor; m. Queen's 1749; hon. MA 1750.

[4] *Woodforde at Oxford*, 140; *Gentleman's Magazine* xxxiii (1763), 348-9. On the third day Lord Lichfield wore 'a light Silk Suit, very handsomely trimmed with flowered Silver-Lace': *Woodforde at Oxford*, 139. William Sandys (1740-1816), m. Queen's 1756; fellow All Souls 1759. Thomas Warton junior (1728-90), m. Trin. 1744, fellow 1752; professor of poetry 1756-66; Camden professor of history 1785-90.

ceremony in 1779, 'The Creweian Oration is to be spoken before a strange, miscellaneous assembly of ladies, doctors, fiddlers, and breeches-makers . . . To-morrow we are to have the Dettingen Te Deum performed in the University Church.' Three years later James, as the successful candidate for the prize poem, was himself a participant:

On Friday and Monday I rehearsed in the Theatre before a pretty considerable number of spectators . . . At half-past ten I repaired to the Theatre, which had at that time a tolerable show of company; and was perpetually filling. At eleven o'clock one gallery was crowded with ladies, the area was lined with Masters of Arts, &c, &c. Close by the Vice-Chancellor sat the Bishop of Oxford, and near him the Doctors, many of them medical, assembled to confer a degree in physick. This done, and the Creweian Oration, by Dr Bandinel this year, having been delivered, the assembly fastned their eyes on me, stuck up in my rostrum . . . My colleague spoke next, a modest and fearful man, and almost broad Scotch. About one the company broke up. I waited on the Vice-Chancellor with my composition before dinner.[1]

In 1785 *Acis and Galatea* together with the *Messiah* were again performed, the orchestra reinforced by 'double drums and double bassoon from Westminster Abbey' to an audience estimated at a thousand.[2]

Yet for the most part dons' lives, if they resided in college, were likely to be, as they have doubtless always been, somewhat humdrum, not even punctuated, unless they held office as tutor, by tutorial contacts. Many more were probably reading men than the surviving evidence would suggest; witness the lists of books bought for and taken out of college libraries. Jeremiah Milles would sometimes miss dinner to prevent an interruption of his studies.[3] But for others the time must sometimes have hung heavily. The coffee-house and tavern,[4] the common room, the daily saunter, were all welcome breaks in the day's monotony, punctuated by chapel and hall. For exercise, like their students, they walked or rode horses, went up the river, enjoyed the occasional 'treat' or even went shooting over college property in Oxford's vicinity.[5] Progresses to college property and visits to London, together with the clerical duties that they were likely to perform in parishes near Oxford, provided a welcome change of scene and company. In summer they went like the undergraduates to the horse-races in Port Meadow. If the winter was a severe

[1] *Letters of Radcliffe and James*, 79, 221-2. James Bandinel (1734-84), m. Jesus 1752; public orator 1776-84.
[2] Diary of Richard Paget (c 1766-1794, m. Magd. 1780, demy 1780-94), Bristol Univ. Library, Paget Collection, DM 106/419, 21 June 1785.
[3] Milles's diary, for example 9 Jan. 1701.
[4] See the entries in Milles's diary for 14, 15 and 22 Feb. and 27 Mar. 1701. There are also ample illustrations in Woodforde's diary.
[5] For 'treats' see the entries in Milles's diary for 21 Oct. and 27 Nov. 1701. In 1825 Lincoln reserved sporting rights over its property to the fellows: Green, *Lincoln*, 399n.

one, as was that of 1763 when a sheep was roasted whole on the ice near Hythe Bridge, they went skating. They were dutiful in their attendance at university sermons, less so at university exercises.

College life could be, and often was, made rancorous by dissensions among the fellowship itself, usually arising from differences over the interpretation of statute or divisions of the fellows' income or the elections to fellowships, leading to appeals to the college's visitor to intervene and arbitrate. There were even occasional acts of violence as when in 1741 Richard Mainwaring, a young fellow of St John's, committed a violent assault on one of his colleagues, John Harbin, 'at an unseasonable time of night'. Mainwaring had earlier been apprehended by one of the Proctors for being 'in company with a woman of bad fame'.[1] Not surprisingly he was subsequently deprived of his fellowship. Many younger fellows found college life frustrating. Nothing exercised the minds of the clerical fellows more than preferment to a college living, opening the way to probably a larger income as well as connubial bliss. Since preferment to college livings depended on seniority, intense interest was generated among the more senior fellows as to their chance of promotion. 'Little Eli Harrison', so Richard Radcliffe told John James on 27 January 1759,

was just then dead, who had a college living in Hampshire, and as it happened to be one of an inferior value [£279 yearly c 1830], it came down to Bolton Simpson[3], and was accepted by him with all thankfulness. It seems he has had a housekeeper ready this dozen or fourteen years, and wanted nothing in all that time but a house to put her in, and an income to maintain her upon.

'Our very best living', he wrote to his mother on 27 December 1765, 'was vacant in summer by the death of the immortal Holmes, and has fallen to the share of the very oddest Fellow belonging to us. You will know that I mean Dr Sewell.'[2]

Indeed, as with the junior members, the majority of the senior members hoped and expected that college life would form only a comparatively brief interlude in their lives; for preferment to a living was the obvious sequel to a fellowship. However much they might look back nostalgically to college rooms and comforts, a parish provided the opportunity for marriage, a parsonage house and, with luck, the promise of canonries, archdeaconries and even possibly a deanery or a bishopric. Twelve heads of houses became bishops in this period; though as the

[1] St John's Muniments, register 1730-94, p. 173, 14 July 1741. Richard Mainwaring, m. St John's 1738; expelled 1741. John Harbin (1722-62), m. St John's 1738.
[2] *Letters of Radcliffe and James* 14, 23-4. Richard Radcliffe (1727-93), m. Queen's 1743, fellow 1762-93. Heley Harrison (1701-59), m. Queen's 1717, fellow 1733. Bolton Simpson (1718-86), m. Queen's 1734, taberdar 1739, fellow 1752. George Holme (1676-1765), m. Queen's 1694, fellow 1704. William Sewell (1722-1800), m. Queen's 1738, fellow 1753; rector of Headley, Hants 1765-1800. Sewell does not seem to have taken a doctor's degree.

bishopric of Bristol, an impoverished see, was virtually appropriated to the deanery of Christ Church the figures may be deceptive. Seven became deans; and the majority of the others could at least look forward to a prebendal stall. For former fellows a country living was a more likely prospect and one which may have made them look back to their Oxford rooms with an occasional sigh: as Tom Warton summed up the situation in 1750:

> These fellowships are pretty things,
> We live indeed like petty kings:
> But who can bear to waste his whole age
> Amid the dulness of a college,
> Debarr'd the common joys of life,
> And that prime bliss—a loving wife!
> O! what's a table richly spread,
> Without a woman at its head!
> Would some snug benefice but fall,
> Ye feasts, ye dinners, farewell all!
> To offices I'd beg adieu,
> Of Dean, Vice-praef,—of Bursar too;
> Come joys, that rural quiet yields,
> Come, tythes, and house, and fruitful fields![1]

What was true of most dons was equally true of the majority of undergraduates, a very high proportion of whom proceeded to holy orders. If they had sufficient family ties, or rich patrons, they could hope for livings in town and country. Oxford men had their fair share, perhaps more than that, of high offices in the established church, in some cases rewarded by the government of the time for loyal services rendered to it. Of 158 bishops in the province of Canterbury in this period 85 were Oxford graduates while 67 came from Cambridge. Out of 7 archbishops of Canterbury, 4 were graduates of Oxford: Wake, who had been a canon of Christ Church, Potter, a fellow of Lincoln who had been regius professor of divinity, Secker and Moore, the last also a canon of Christ Church. In the province of York 14 out of 22 bishops came from Oxford; Archbishop Markham of York had been dean of Christ Church.[2] Of 133 Irish bishops 34 were Oxford men, 27 came from Cambridge and 22 from Trinity College, Dublin. No doubt many Oxford graduates who lacked connections remained impoverished curates all their lives; the prospect for a poor boy was such that it was a disincentive to entry to the university. Yet, all in all, the Church of England seemed in many respects an extension of the ethos of Oxbridge. Its university-trained clergy, influenced by loyalty to the alma mater as well as by their early upbringing, were, unless they had been seduced by whiggism, concerned

---

[1] 'The progress of discontent', *Poetical Works of Warton*, ed. Mant. ii. 194.
[2] Of the English and Welsh bishops mentioned some 31 had connections with Christ Church.

to support the university against the insidious forces of infidelity and dissent, radicalism and secularism. The university's inert conservatism, then and later, owed much to the intimate connection which existed between the university and the established church.

Even in the eighteenth century, however, it was not merely through diocesan administration and parochial supervision that Oxford's graduates exerted a profound influence on the nation's life. Many graduates, a high proportion in holy orders, became schoolmasters, feeding into the school curriculum the academic pabulum, in some respects increasingly stereotyped, which they had absorbed at Oxford and which for years to come was to shape grammar-school education.

Apart from the church and education, it was probably in the legal profession that Oxford graduates were most likely to be found making a career for themselves.[1] In spite of the prestigious careers of Blackstone and Chambers[2] Oxford made little impact on legal studies as such, although many of those who did not go forward to ordination went to study at the Inns of Court and became practising lawyers. Of some 218 judges 67 were Oxford graduates (and 42 were from Cambridge). Three of the nine chief justices of England were Oxford men; Lord Mansfield,[3] for instance, was a Christ Church man. Perhaps even more pervasive, though difficult to calculate in absolute terms, was the influence by the Oxford-educated gentry who served as justices of the peace.

The impact which Oxford made in the sphere of policies and of government is equally difficult to assess since many other factors, apart from university training, must have gone towards the moulding of political attitudes. Moreover, as has been fully demonstrated elsewhere, the relationship between Oxford and the government fluctuated from one of hostility and suspicion in the early part of the century to an alliance founded on mutual trust in later years. Many Oxford graduates found their way to positions of high political influence. Carteret[4] had been at Christ Church as was Shelburne later. Henry Pelham and Charles James Fox were at Hertford, Chatham and Lord North at Trinity, Henry Addington at Brasenose.[5] Arthur Onslow, speaker of the house of commons from 1727 to 1761, was a graduate of Wadham. In the political sphere the preponderance of Christ Church men, as it was long to continue to be, was a very striking feature. Of some 590 MPs between 1715 and 1754, 176 were Oxford men (by comparison with 70 from

---

[1] At least 1,100 out of 13,200 graduates in the period 1689-1800 attended the Inns of Court and/or became practising lawyers: figures taken from unpublished tables compiled by Mrs Valerie Jobling.

[2] Robert Chambers (1737-1803), m. Linc. 1754; fellow Univ. 1761.

[3] William Murray (1705-93), 1st e. of Mansfield; m. Ch.Ch. 1723.

[4] John Carteret (1690-1763), 2nd Earl Granville; m. Ch.Ch. 1706; DCL by diploma 1756.

[5] Henry Pelham (1695-1754), m. Hart Hall 1710. Henry Addington (1757-1844), m. BNC 1774.

Cambridge) and of another sample of 660 between 1754 and 1790, 157 were Oxford educated (by comparison with 123 from Cambridge).[1] There is comparatively little to indicate that their political affinities were in any way significantly determined by their college loyalties. Of some 170 Oxford men who served in parliament between 31 May 1754 and 30 March 1761 approximately 84 were government supporters (of whom 30 had been at Christ Church), 63 were tories (of whom 14 had been at Christ Church and 9 at Balliol) and 12 were opposition whigs. Yet it is fair to say that especially in the debates relating to subscription in 1772 many Oxford men sprang to the defence of Oxford's traditional religious position.

Outside the professions, and in this respect there was a steep decline in the number of those taking medical degrees, Oxford graduates were few and far between, a few army and naval officers, some merchants. In general the developing commercial and industrial world remained a *terra incognita* for the mass of Oxford students. Indeed, the limitation of Oxford's sphere of influence in this respect, its partial alienation from the predominant trends in the emergent social and political economy of early nineteenth-century England, may go some way to explain the crisis of credibility with which the university was to be faced in the first half of the coming century, a crisis which was to envelop but happily not to suffocate.

---

[1] The samples are taken from entries A-D in R. Sedgwick, *The History of Parliament: The House of Commons 1715-1754* (2 vols London 1970) and entries F-H and R-T in L. B. Namier and J. Brooke, *The History of Parliament: The House of Commons 1754-1790* (3 vols London 1965).

12

University, Society and Church
1688-1714

G. V. BENNETT

AT THE end of the seventeenth century the universities were regarded
by most literate Englishmen as performing a function essential to the
public good. They were the guardians of a body of traditional learning
on which religious orthodoxy, political obedience and social order were
thought to depend. It is true that the era saw a veritable crisis among
European intellectuals when much of this knowledge, with the
academic methods which it employed, was called in question. The rise
of a new interest in science and mathematics led to a vigorous attack
on the value of ancient texts and revered authorities. A reliance on the
guidance of the past was decried and the new cult of 'Nature and
Reason' demanded careful observation of natural phenomena, inductive
reasoning and the making of general theories based strictly on the
evidence. Some scientists went so far as to reject traditional religious
doctrine and to appeal to pure reason as the basis of religion; they
insisted that the scriptures alone, interpreted in that light, were a
sufficient basis for faith without the pedantry of patristic scholarship or
a minute linguistic exegesis. But in England the fiercer advocates of this
new approach were few in number, and many of the most distinguished
scientists and mathematicians protested movingly that their discoveries
supported rather than diminished the value of the older world of
learning. Certainly a majority of informed Englishmen feared that the
new natural philosophy would be socially disruptive and felt the need
for a learned activity which espoused a theologically and historically
oriented approach to the intellectual life; and they looked to the
universities, and to Oxford in particular, to articulate a defence of the
traditional order. Few imagined that a university ought to be concerned
with pure research or disinterested scholarship. Doubtless there were
some academics who devoted themselves to the pursuit of learning for
its own sake,but they were usually regarded as mildly eccentric. For the
most part the historical, linguistic and textual studies of the dons were

part of a sustained endeavour to defend the existing ecclesiastical and social order, even when occasionally that defence took the form of a cautious attempt to update old patterns of thought. Where the worth of such literary scholarship was generally acknowledged was when it was used to provide a detailed apologia for the English version of protestant Christianity in the face of what was conceived of as the ever-present threat of the Church of Rome.

It was this body of learning, and the educational activity which went with it, which justified the university's existence as an 'institution' in the sense of being a definite group of persons, working by strict rules and procedures, and dedicated to serving the public interest in some particular way. An institution, thus understood, formed a social grouping: its members had to be recruited, taught distinctive attitudes and modes of operation, and invested with the tokens of authority which distinguished their function in the community. In one sense, such an institution was itself a product of the dominant social order: in its corporate life it affirmed existing ranks and inequalities and exhibited contemporary patterns of deference; and its functionaries disseminated the assumptions and prejudices of the society within which they worked. Indeed it was as bulwarks of stability that the universities and their colleges received royal and aristocratic patronage, were granted legal immunities and privileges, and were permitted to accumulate property and substantial endowments. But, in another sense, such institutions could easily acquire the character of a vested interest, concerned above all with the prestige of their function and the status of their members; and it was never easy for them to adjust rapidly to changes in the social balance or to new directions in state policy. Without careful handling they could be a dangerous source of opposition to the government and an irritant to some newly established social predominance.

It is, then, with the University of Oxford as such an 'institution' that this chapter is concerned. It will attempt to show the university's relationship to the existing social order, the manner in which its members were recruited and how, with their various origins and in their ranks, they were identified with the institution and its purposes. Inevitably there will be much about the formation of the clergy of the Church of England, for it was those of the university's graduates who entered the priesthood who did most to propagate its learning and its values. Oxford and Cambridge were the key-institutions in the national religious establishment. At a time when it was virtually impossible to be ordained without a degree, and the great majority of graduates joined the ranks of the parochial clergy, the profession was in large measure an extension of the universities' function into innumerable parishes spread throughout the country. Such a close association of university and church had, of course, its weakness. A partly secularized aristocracy and gentry regarded with suspicion an education so directed to the making of clergymen, and their participation in it was always less than wholehearted. In the early eighteenth century few members of the true social élite were actually to graduate and be ordained, and they played only a small part in furthering the universities' basic purposes. For such young men a more attractive alternative education was available. Unlike their continental counterparts, Oxford and Cambridge did not monopolize legal education. They provided training for the 'civil' or ecclesiastical lawyers, whose professional qualification was a university degree in law; but the education of those who wished to practise in the main branch of English law, the common law, could be acquired only in London. There the four Inns of Court, with their ancient buildings and venerable customs, had much of the character of a 'third university', with able barristers ready to take pupils to read in chambers. The distinctly secular and practical approach to learning which characterized the common law led many men of wealth and position, who had no intention of being ordained, to ignore Oxford and Cambridge, or to spend a minimum period of residence in either before removing themselves to an Inn of Court. And there could be no doubt of the social superiority of common-lawyers to clergymen. The profession of barrister was confined strictly to 'gentlemen' and denied to any involved in 'trade'; the expenses of those who wished to be called to the bar were large, and there was no way by which a man from a humble background could find help in paying them. Thus, although there was some overlap between those who had been at a university and those who entered the legal profession, this connection was not to be compared with that which existed between the universities and that host of men of modest origins who graduated and went on to join the ranks of the eighteenth-century clergy.

An Oxford freshman entered into an academic community which was intensely conscious of the disparities of wealth and status which existed in contemporary English society. Indeed, every undergraduate had his position in life impressed upon him each day and at every stage of his university career. At matriculation each young man was required to state his parent's social rank and have this formally certified by his tutor. Henceforward he paid dues and fees according to a tariff of ranks. Freshmen were entered in the register as *pauperes pueri* or as the sons of plebeians, clerks in holy orders, gentlemen, doctors, esquires, knights, baronets or peers.[1] Such formal categories must, of course, be used with

---

[1] The description 'doctor' may indicate a clergyman, a civil lawyer or a medical practitioner, though an analysis would suggest that the vast majority in this category were physicians. In the

TABLE 12.1

PARENTAL STATUS OF MATRICULANTS 1690, 1700 AND 1710

	1690		1700		1710	
	no.	%	no.	%	no.	%
pauperes pueri	47	18	31	11	13	5
plebeians	30	12	68	23	76	27
clerks in holy orders	38	15	48	16	46	17
gentlemen	101	39	104	35	97	35
esquires	24	9	33	11	33	12
knights and baronets	13	5	9	3	6	2
peers	4	2	1	—	6	2
total of matriculants	257		294		277	

caution; and it is by no means clear that they indicated the precise economic status of a freshman's father. A 'plebeian' might be one who had prospered substantially in trade and was well able to give his son a handsome allowance at Oxford. Similarly a 'clerk in holy orders' could be an impoverished country curate, a wealthy rector, or even a major cathedral dignitary. The most comprehensive category was that of a 'gentleman'. In England such a description had no precise legal connotation, and there is evidence that during the course of the eighteenth century it was increasingly adopted by those who earlier would have been quite content to be included among the plebeians.[1]
How the categories remain valuable, however, is as indications of a man's own estimate of his social standing. In a community which was intensely conscious of rank he would wish to place himself in the highest group to which he might aspire without incurring ridicule, yet he might well hesitate before choosing the higher fees and grander lifestyle which the superior category involved. The son of a 'gentleman', for example, would be thought socially disgraced if he performed menial services in a college, and it was certain to cause him great embarrassment if he were entered on the college books as less than a commoner. Similarly no man would be described as *pauper puer* unless he were to be a servitor and work his way through college by acting as a domestic servant. The higher ranks from 'esquire' upwards present fewer difficulties. An

statistics used in this study it has been thought most useful to include all 'doctors' under the category of 'gentlemen'.

[1] L. Stone, 'The size and composition of the Oxford student body 1580–1909' in L. Stone (ed.), *The University in Society* (2 vols Princeton 1975) i. 48.

'esquire' or 'armiger' was simply one from a family whose armorial bearings were recorded at the College of Heralds, while knights, baronets and peers had a recognized place and privilege on every national occasion. That there was some stability about the social categories in which freshmen placed themselves is shown by the fact that during the years covered by this study there was from year to year no significant variation in the proportion of those in the various ranks.[1]

Corresponding to parental status were the ranks by which freshmen were entered in the books of a college. The various societies differed in their precise terminology but it could usually be taken that those who were not admitted directly on to the 'foundation' would be given the description of servitor, batteler, commoner, gentleman-commoner, or nobleman. A detailed analysis of all the entrants to Christ Church and Brasenose, two colleges of very different social composition, from 1690 to 1700 (table 12.2) illustrates the way in which college rank went with parental status. At the bottom of the social scale *pauperes pueri* to a man were entered as servitors or battelers. The great majority of plebeians were in the same classes with the exception of a few fortunates whose financial circumstances lifted them out of the usual disadvantages of their status. It is perhaps of interest that more well-to-do plebeians went to Christ Church than to any other college, and their fathers may well have been purchasing for their sons the standing and circle of personal acquaintance of a gentleman. At the other end of the social hierarchy noblemen were recruited exclusively from the sons of peers, while gentlemen-commoners were drawn mainly from the children of baronets, knights and esquires. The category appropriate to a mere gentleman was clearly that of a commoner, though it was always more comprehensive than that. What is apparent from the statistics is that the convention that no gentleman should be entered as less than a commoner was a strong one, and the notion of one who claimed 'gentle' birth actually wearing a servitor's gown was abhorrent to dons and undergraduates alike. There are indeed instances of men matriculated as the sons of gentlemen demoting themselves to plebeian status on later occasions to avoid the accusation that they had demeaned the rank they claimed by accepting servile duties. Occasionally men whose fathers ranked above mere gentlemen were matriculated as commoners, but they seem to have been younger sons seeking a career in the church or men for whom their parents were seeking a more modest mode of life

---

[1] See table 12.1. During the three decades from 1690 to 1719 a total of 8,932 freshmen were matriculated, an average of 298 p.a. It has not been thought necessary to trace the career of each one. This study derives its statistics from the freshmen of three sample years, 1690, 1700 and 1710. Detailed information has also been compiled on all those admitted to ten colleges during the thirty-year period: Balliol, Brasenose, Christ Church, Lincoln, Magdalen, New College, Pembroke, Trinity, University College and Wadham.

TABLE 12.2

CORRELATION BETWEEN COLLEGE RANK AND PARENTAL STATUS 1690–1700

Christ Church

college rank		parental status	
nobleman	8	peer	8
gentleman-commoner	58	knight/baronet	21
		esquire	15
		gentleman	22
Student	58	peer	3
		knight/baronet	5
		gentleman	28
		clerk	20
		plebeian	2
commoner	130	knight/baronet	3
		esquire	3
		gentleman	75
		clerk	33
		plebeian	11
		unknown	4
servitor	55	gentleman	2
		clerk	8
		plebeian	27
		pauper puer	17
		unknown	1
total	309		309

Brasenose

college rank		parental status	
gentleman-commoner	19	knight/baronet	3
		esquire	7
		gentleman	8
		clerk	1
commoner	64	knight/baronet	5
		esquire	16
		gentleman	24
		clerk	15
		plebeian	3
entrance scholar	2	gentleman	1
		clerk	1
battelers	122	gentleman	6
		clerk	29
		plebeian	65
		pauper puer	19
		unknown	3
unknown	3	clerk	1
		plebeian	2
total	210		210

than that usually associated with gentlemen-commoners. The sons of the clergy, as a professional category rather than a social grouping, exhibited the greatest diversity. It was possible for the son of a dean to be entered as a gentleman-commoner while country parsons were often glad to get their boys in as servitors and batelers. Out of 576 clerical offspring entered at five colleges between 1690 and 1719 no fewer than 148 were entered in these lowly categories.[1] But what is perhaps surprising, in view of the frequent assertions of the poverty of the parochial clergy, is the high proportion of their children who were entered as commoners. This may well reflect the sacrifices which Oxford-educated priests were prepared to make to give their children a good start or the grim realization that servitors and batelers virtually never found themselves elected to college scholarships or fellowships.

By the end of the seventeenth century a scholarship or some equivalent junior place on the foundation of a college was no longer a sign of poverty nor necessarily an indication of exceptional academic merit. In most colleges its monetary value was quite small, and its real advantage lay in the free rooms and the dinners in hall which it provided. At Wadham, for example, the stipend of a scholar remained fixed at the £10 a year which had been laid down by the founders in 1613.[2] Essentially a scholarship committed its holder to remain in residence long enough to take a degree, and usually continued after graduation to allow him to proceed to the MA. In all colleges the scholars were the category which had the highest proportion of those taking degrees. In the period 1690 to 1719 the percentage of those in each category admitted as BAs was: at Balliol, scholars 88, commoners 46, servitors/batelers 63; at Christ Church, Students 86, commoners 43, servitors 64; at Pembroke, scholars/exhibitioners 86, commoners 47, servitors/batelers 65; at Wadham, scholars 97, commoners 42, servitors 60. It is clear that the electors thought primarily in terms of young men with the declared intention of taking holy orders, and it was understood that the scholars would have a preference in any election to a vacant fellowship within the college. While some societies, such as Merton and Lincoln, seem to have made a point of choosing fellows from outside, most simply filled up a vacancy from their own members. Thus in a sample group of five colleges (Balliol, Brasenose, Pembroke, University College and Wadham) 156 elections to fellowships were made between 1690 and 1719, 110 from among the scholars, 42 from the commoners, 3 from the servitors and only 1 from another college. Junior places on the

[1] The five colleges are Balliol, Brasenose, Lincoln, Trinity and University College, none of which gave more than a few scholarships on admission and therefore admitted all freshmen to one of the usual categories.
[2] Stone, 'Size and composition', 42.

foundation, scholarships, exhibitionerships, demyships, postmasterships and studentships, were awarded in various ways, some colleges giving them before admission and others having elections in which those already in residence could compete. What emerges most clearly from an analysis of the elections made after admission is that the very poor were rarely successful. At Balliol, for example, 71 scholars were elected from the commoners as against only 5 from the servitors and battelers; at Wadham 172 were elected from the commoners and not a single servitor. Only at Brasenose, a college of an exceptionally depressed social composition, was there any consistent policy of promoting poor boys, and 195 battelers were elected as against 23 commoners. Even here, however, some attempt was made to protect the character of the body of fellows, and of 36 elections to fellowships between 1690 and 1719, 16 were from those who had begun as commoners, 16 as battelers and 4 as admission-scholars. Before any election to a junior place on a foundation immense pressure was brought to bear by bishops, former fellows and incumbents of college livings; and the result was what might have been expected. The majority of scholars came from a moderately prosperous background, many were the children of the better-off clergy and virtually all were committed to ordination. In most colleges there was, then, little social distinction between the scholars and the ordinary commoners: both sets of undergraduates dined in hall, lived in much the same kind of chamber, and were taught by the same tutors. The difference lay only in the much greater commitment of the scholars to graduation, ordination and academic careers. Yet the rivalry between the two groups was proverbial and took the form of endless disputes over precedence and the privileges to be accorded to 'members of the foundation'. In 1693 William Smith of University College, who was vicegerent in the absence of the master, wrote plaintively about a fierce dispute which had broken out over where the respective parties should sit in hall, 'the Scholars and Commoners standing on so ill terms as they do in most of the Colleges of the Town'.[1]

At three prestigious colleges the junior foundationers had real pretensions to social eminence. At Christ Church the 'Students' were either Westminsters or 'Canoneers'. The former were chosen at West-minster School on a grand election day attended by the dean of Christ Church and the master of Trinity College, Cambridge, each concerned to acquire the most promising youths for his own college. Westminster under the famous Dr Busby[2] was the pre-eminent school of the later seventeenth century and its education was sought out by parents,

[1] W. Smith–Charlett, 16 Nov. 1693, MS Ballard 16, fo 21. William Smith (1652-1735), m. Univ. 1668, fellow 1675-1705; incorporated at Cambridge 1678.
[2] Richard Busby (1606-95), m. Ch.Ch. 1626; headmaster of Westminster School 1638-95.

ambitious for their able sons and not unaware of the school's connection with the two most magnificent foundations in the English university world. Westminsters had a reputation for poise, elegance and stylish classical learning, and at Christ Church they formed a self-consciously superior set of young intellectuals. The canonical Students were appointed by the canons of Christ Church, acting in turn; and, though their choice was usually made from among the commoners, the influence exerted by great men in such elections was only too obvious. The junior Students of Christ Church included the sons of peers, baronets and knights while the overwhelming majority were drawn from the children of gentlemen and the prosperous clergy. In the years from 1690 to 1700 only two plebeians were elected to a Studentship, and these were the sons of wealthy merchants.[1] Indeed in the whole thirty years 1690-1719 only 172 undergraduates of plebeian origin were admitted in a society through which there passed 54 noblemen, 206 gentlemen-commoners, 211 Students and 361 commoners. For a would-be divine a Christ Church Studentship was a magnificent base on which to build a career. Once elected he had a freehold for life or until such a time as he resigned, married, failed to proceed to his degrees or neglected to take holy orders within the prescribed time. In like manner the scholars of New College entered into their world of security and privilege. Elected exclusively from the other Wykehamist foundation at Winchester, they served a two year 'probation' and then, without further test and while still undergraduates, were admitted as full or 'actual' fellows of the college with freehold tenure. Since admission to Winchester had come to be narrowed to gentry families, New College by 1690 had managed virtually to eliminate the children of the poor from its membership. In the period 1690 to 1719 149 men were admitted as fellows: 12 sons of baronets or knights, 10 of esquires, 86 of gentlemen, 24 of medical practitioners and 13 of clergymen, with only 4 acknowledging plebeian origins.[2] Only marginally less socially exclusive were the 'demies' of Magdalen. These junior foundationers were chosen on admission, or shortly afterwards, by the president, vice-president and one other fellow; an electing body which seems to have shown a strong preference for the sons of former fellows.[3] A demyship was also a most valuable position for an intending divine: it could be retained even after a man had taken

---

[1] See table 12.2, p. 364 above.

[2] Founder's kin were admitted directly as freshmen into full fellowship with voting rights and financial dividend, at New College called an 'increment'. For the increasingly aristocratic style of the college after the Restoration see P. Williams, 'From the reformation to the era of reform 1530-1850' in J. Buxton and P. Williams (eds), *New College Oxford 1379-1979* (Oxford 1979), 58-9. In 1677 the visitor permitted the introduction into the college of 16 noblemen and gentlemen-commoners on the grounds that they would be afterwards 'useful in acquiring honour and dignities' for the fellows: see H. Rashdall and R. S. Rait, *New College* (London 1901), 186.

[3] Out of 67 demies elected between 1700 and 1719 45 were elected on matriculation, 12 after less

his MA, and if he were prepared to wait for a period which varied between seven and twelve years he was virtually certain to be elected to a fellowship. In fact in this period no fewer than 70 per cent of all demies became fellows of Magdalen with the usual freehold for life. Demyships were of course withheld from the very poor; and in the thirty years, out of 102 demies, 6 were the sons of baronets and knights, 7 of esquires, 43 of gentlemen, 37 of clerks and only 8 of plebeians (1 was of origin now unknown). Even so, the plebeians were a disappearing class. Only 3 were elected in the decade 1710 to 1719, and during the rest of the century this number dwindled to nothing. These richly endowed colleges exercised great care in the selection of their junior foundationers and protected their fellowships and the social prestige of the society by excluding rigorously the low-born or unsophisticated. A very small group of poor boys, by showing exceptional talent, mounted the ladder of academic promotion but the great majority of their kind found that their lot was an undergraduate existence as a servitor or batteler, followed by departure from Oxford for some ill-paid curacy. Scholarships, demyships, studentships and fellowships were not for them.

An academic body containing within itself such diversity in social class and manner of life was given a sense of common identity by participation in an elaborate protocol and ceremony. An Oxford freshman had quickly to initiate himself into the special terminology and intricate procedure of both college and university. By the time he graduated he would have become an adept in a world of communal ritual. Central to it was the peculiar mystery of academic costume, on the subject of which vice-chancellors orated regularly and with passion and issued numerous directives. Becoming a member of the university was often referred to as 'wearing a gown' or 'putting on a gown', while a man's college rank was described as 'his gown'. The dress regulations of the Laudian statutes, reissued (with additions) by convocation in 1689, decreed in solemn detail the gown appropriate to each degree and undergraduate status and ordered that patterns should be deposited in the registry so that the Oxford robemakers should be in no doubt.[1] In 1675, in a beautifully executed engraving, David Loggan had shown the academic community both in its diversity and unity by drawing a procession with members of the university walking in their order of precedence, each wearing the costume appropriate to his rank or degree.[2] At the front is a humble

than 1 year, 3 less than 2 years and 7 less than 3 years. It was not unusual for undergraduates with Magdalen connections to matriculate at another college while waiting for a vacant demyship.

[1] L. H. D. Buxton and S. Gibson, *Oxford University Ceremonies* (Oxford 1935), 20-2; OUA register of convocation 1693-1703, (at end); Wood, *Life and Times* iii. 469 for Aldrich's fulminations in his vice-chancellor's oration, 11 October 1694; V. H. H. Green, 'The University and social life' above, for example p. 324.

[2] D. Loggan, *Oxonia illustrata* (Oxford 1675), plate X, 'Habitus academici'. David Loggan was the university's engraver.

servitor and towards the end is a youthful nobleman, taking his place above a doctor of divinity and immediately before the vice-chancellor and bedels. The servitor is illustrated wearing an unadorned gown with a round flap-collar and a 'streamer', or strip of cloth, instead of a sleeve; a batteler has a similar gown with a square collar, while a commoner sports a pattern of 'tufts' on his streamers to indicate his superior status. A gentleman-commoner is shown wearing the 'half-sleeved' gown of the civilian or legal pattern with tufts on sleeves and hem. Such of the gentlemen-commoners as were the sons of baronets or knights were allowed the additional privilege of having tufts in silver or gold braid. Noblemen were permitted not only to have an even more extensive area of braid but to have their gowns tailored in a colour of their choice. Loggan's careful engravings of Oxford street-scenes show that a man's degree or status was instantly recognizable at a time when all wore their gowns about the city, in the parks and walks, and even out in the countryside. It is, in fact, difficult to view the public life of the university as other than a series of elaborate ceremonies, punctiliously performed by men who were well aware of their symbolic character. The examination system, for example, bore little relationship to the actual educational work of the university and had already become by 1689 a succession of rituals derived from the forms of the medieval academic disputations. The undergraduate who wished for a degree 'kept his terms' and, at the appropriate times, walked in procession, attended religious services, listened to formal orations and repeated well-worn formulas.[1]

Those who continued in residence after they had obtained a bachelor's degree were drawn from a much narrower social range than those originally matriculated (as may be seen in table 12.3). It is these men, nearly all intending to be ordained, who were to form the essential personnel of the university as an institution. Already the members of the social élite had departed. Noblemen and gentlemen-commoners rarely stayed in Oxford longer than two years; and, apart from a very small number who were destined for the church, they did not take a degree. It was considered proper for them to read privately with a tutor but it was thought socially demeaning for them to dispute or declaim in the college hall or in the schools in company with their inferiors. In the period from 1690 to 1719 there were 734 men who entered as noblemen or gentlemen-commoners at eight Oxford colleges: Balliol, Brasenose, Christ Church, Lincoln, Pembroke, Trinity, University College and

---

[1] For a serious account of the requirements see J. Ayliffe, *The Antient and Present State of the University of Oxford* (2 vols Oxford 1714) ii. 117-52; and for a livelier and satirical description [N. Amhurst,] *Terrae-Filius* (52 nos. London Jan.-July 1721) no. xlv (14-17 June 1721). See also L. S. Sutherland, 'The curriculum' below, for example p. 470.

TABLE 12.3

DEGREES TAKEN BY THE MATRICULANTS OF 1690, 1700 AND 1710

year of matriculation	1690				1700				1710			
number of matriculants	257				294				277			
	BA		MA		BA		MA		BA		MA	
degree	no.	%	no.	%	no.	%	no.	%	no.	%	no.	%
pauperes pueri	37	79	9	19	16	52	4	13	11	85	3	23
plebeians	21	70	8	27	57	84	22	32	64	84	24	32
clerks in holy orders	30	79	21	55	38	79	21	44	37	88	16	35
gentlemen	50	50	31	31	52	50	33	32	59	61	40	42
esquires	3	12.5	2	8	5	15	3	9	3	9	1	3
baronets/knights	2	15	0		1	11	1	11	1	17	1	17
peers	1	25	0		0		0		1	17	1	17

The percentages represent those taking degrees as a proportion of the total of matriculants in each category.
The figures under BA include those who proceeded to the degree of MA.

Wadham. In all, only 20 of them (or 3 per cent) took a degree and no more than 8 remained in residence for an MA, though certain of the grandees after departure were complimented with an honorary degree. In spite of all the attention and deference which they were accorded, the noblemen and gentlemen-commoners were of all Oxford under-graduates the least identified with the institution and its purposes. Their stay was too short, their reading too secular, and their social status and future careers were to be in no way dependent on the university.

Of far greater importance to Oxford were the foundationers and others who remained to study theology and prepare themselves for ordination. Most stayed not so much to obtain the MA as to pass the time until they attained the canonical age of twenty-three when they could be ordained deacon, and meanwhile to acquire sufficient biblical and doctrinal knowledge to satisfy a bishop's examining chaplains. Of course, as resident BAs they took part in the elaborate sequence of cere-monies which qualified them for an MA: they 'determined', did 'Austins' and 'quodlibets' and delivered their 'wall lectures' and Latin declama-tions. Some parts of these exercises actually retained a certain vitality and an elegantly composed and felicitously delivered oration could earn much applause and even be published. But for most purposes the degree involved no more than payment of fees and continued residence in a college or hall. The usual time required was seven terms, though it was possible to have this reduced by a term if a 'chancellor's letter' were obtained recommending a dispensation. It was primarily the expense which made the whole business so difficult for the poorest classes of undergraduate. In the face of all their financial difficulties they hung on grimly long enough to get a BA degree because this was the minimum requirement for ordination. In the eight colleges between 1690 and 1719 1,276 men were entered as servitors or batteless and no fewer than 941 (or 74 per cent) took the degree. But at that point funds ran out and benefactors withdrew their support, and only 295 (or 23 per cent) managed to stay on to take an MA. The great majority of those who did so were the sons of gentlemen or the better-off clergy; and more than half had been originally entered as commoners. Indeed, out of 2,270 commoners in the eight colleges only 1,162 (or 51 per cent) graduated but no fewer than 639 (or 31 per cent) went on to the higher degree. The group which thus provided the highest proportion of resident bachelors was that of the foundationers. A survey of five colleges shows them to have had between them 495 scholars or the like entered between 1690 and 1719; and of these 422 (or 85 per cent) took a degree, and 336 (or 79 per cent) became MAs.[1]

[1] Not all of the eight colleges previously cited had junior foundationers. In this calculation the five colleges were Balliol, Christ Church, Pembroke, University College and Wadham.

Those who remained on in Oxford after receiving the degree of MA were socially an even more select group. In theory all newly created regent masters were obliged to attend the meetings of convocation and congregation for two years; in fact the only non-foundationers who continued in residence were those who thought that the university might provide a useful base for what was often a desperate search for a curacy or a living. It was the fortunate few with fellowships who formed the élite corps of defenders of the university's system of beliefs and its role in English society. Apart from the heads of houses and a few professors they were for the most part young, unmarried clergymen, overwhelmingly of a gentry or professional background. The number of college fellows not in orders or intending to be ordained was, at this period, quite small and confined to the places reserved for physicians and civil lawyers. Few had any intention of remaining permanently in the university and their hopes for a future career and an eventual settlement lay in obtaining some substantial preferment in the church. Despite the leisure and the opportunities which they had for study, their academic work was almost wholly apologetic and controversial rather than original study and research. They acted in all respects as the learned spokesmen of a professional interest, and they waited anxiously for the time when some preferment came their way of sufficient value to allow them to resign their fellowships, marry and move on to become a gentleman, pastor and keeper of order in some local community. What imported some difficulty into their position was that in the reigns of William and Anne there was a real shortage of such livings. Most fellowships provided their holders with benefits and income equivalent to more than £100 a year outside the college.[1] Gentlemen, used to ample rooms, 'domus' (college) meals and wine and the attention of servants, were wholly reluctant to leave until they were sure that their position would be bettered. It was inevitable that the controversial and political activity of the university should thus be directly related to their aspirations and discontents.

The lifestyle and career-prospects of an Oxford undergraduate depended largely on his social origins. It was, for example, expected that a man's expenses and expenditure would vary greatly according to the rank by which he had been entered in the college books.[2] In this

---

[1] At All Souls in the year 1697-8 the total income of a fellowship for an MA was £33. Rooms, meals and payments for tuition and college offices were extra. Many clerical fellows could earn more by supplying curacies in the Oxford district or obtaining periods of leave of absence to act as stipendiary curates.

[2] See Atterbury–St John Brodrick, 21 Oct. 1690, Surrey Record Office, Guildford Muniment Room, Midleton MS 1248/1/237 for Charles Boyle's expenditure from June to September. The initial fees came to £32 14s 2d and expenses for a quarter to £63 3s 2d. Boyle (1674-1731, from 1703 4th e. of Orrery, m. Ch.Ch. 1690) was a studious man, not given to the lifestyle of many noblemen.

period a gentleman-commoner required £120 a year if he was to preserve his dignity and reputation, a commoner would need between £60 and £80, while even a batteler found himself in difficulties if he had less than £40.[1] Thomas Brockbank, the son of a Westmorland parson of modest means, was at Oxford between 1687 and 1695. He was entered as a batteler at Queen's and was glad to take on the menial duties of 'poor child' and 'larderman' to help pay his way. His letters show him to have been a frugal young man, who read hard, wore clothing sent from home, and wasted little time on idle pleasures.[2] His ambition was to gain a place on the foundation, perhaps eventually a fellowship, and his father was ready to stretch his own resources to the very limit to give him his chance. Thomas stayed for eight years and took his MA before admitting failure, though the result was hardship for his parents and penury and debts for himself. In all his father paid out £273 for fees and living expenses, an average of £34 a year, rising to a peak of £46 in 1692 when he took his bachelor's degree. Such an outlay has to be seen in the light of the levels of clerical stipends at this time when £40 was typical for a country living and an income of £80 was well above average.[3] Some very poor men, however, scraped by on even less than Brockbank. In 1732 George Whitefield was a servitor at Pembroke, and he later claimed that in three years he had spent only £24 of his own money, but he was a popular youngster, handy in his work and able to earn by exercising the skill at drawing beer which he had learned at his home, the Bell Inn at Gloucester.[4] That life could be financially impossible for *pauperes pueri* without any kind of parental support is shown by the high proportion of them who did not graduate, even though a degree and the church could have been their only aim in coming to Oxford. It was generally agreed that a commoner should not attempt to get by on less than £60, but there were bitter complaints from others that charges had risen steeply since the 1670s, for the better-off by as much as 50 per cent. It is interesting to find that Bishop Nicolson of Carlisle expended no less than £446 in the five years that his son Joseph was in residence at Queen's as a commoner.[5] There was now strong pressure on a substantial landowner to enter his son as a gentleman-commoner with all the

[1] *The Life of the Reverend Humphrey Prideaux* (London 1748), 196; Stone, 'Size and composition', 43.

[2] *The Diary and Letter Book of the Rev. Thomas Brockbank 1671–1709*, ed. R. Trappes-Lomax (Chetham Soc. new ser. lxxxix 1930).

[3] Ibid. 84. For a table of the values of benefices in one midland county see J. H. Pruett, *The Parish Clergy under the Later Stuarts: the Leicestershire Experience* (Urbana, Illinois 1978), 34. Also J. L. Salter, 'Warwickshire clergy, 1660–1714' (Birmingham Ph.D. thesis 1975), 24, for a table of values of Warwickshire benefices which shows the average for rectories at £80 and for vicarages at £40. In 1705 no fewer than 70 per cent of all livings had a value of £60 or below.

[4] C. Wordsworth, *Social Life at the English Universities in the Eighteenth Century* (Cambridge 1874), 413. George Whitefield (1714–70), m. Pemb. 1732.

[5] N. Sykes, *Church and State in England in the Eighteenth Century* (Cambridge 1934), 194. Joseph Nicolson (1689–1728), m. Queen's 1707.

additional expense which this involved. In 1704 Theophilus Leigh of Adlestrop, Gloucestershire, explained the situation in a letter to his sister:

My nephew being your eldest son, and Heir to a good estate, which will quickly be known there, without possibility of concealment I think indeed you ought to allow him £100 by the Year. Our Cosin Chamberlayne allowed his Son as much, and he spent much more. You must of necessity enter him a Gentleman Commoner. It will be otherwise very reflective upon You, and discouraging to him. Such as were Commoners in my time, are . . . Gentlemen Commoners now.[1]

Not only were the disparities of expenditure great but the evidence is that all costs were increasing. After 1720 the numbers of those at Oxford who described themselves as plebeian or who were admitted as servitors or battelers dropped away rapidly as men from a poorer background found the expenses and hardship intolerable.[2] And many of the social élite considered that the 'grand tour' itself was not much less expensive and of more educational value for a young aristocrat than two years at Oxford.

In the era from 1689 to 1714 there was, however, still a recognized place in the university for men from a humble background. Indeed this was inevitable when there were so many small livings which did not provide an income fit for a gentleman and while there was a continuing demand for stipendiary curates who would minister in place of a non-resident incumbent at a fraction of the benefice's real value. Contemporaries viewed the problem of the impoverished undergraduate strictly in terms of supply and demand at the lower end of the clerical market. There were some, like John Eachard in his *The Grounds and Occasions of the Contempt of the Clergy and Religion*, who appeared to be campaigning vigorously against schoolmasters and local benefactors who encouraged the children of labourers and artisans to embark on a university career which could lead only to a life of penury as a poor curate without hope of a living. 'We are', he complained, 'perfectly overstocked with professors of divinity.'[3] But the excess supply of young men seeking ordination and lowly clerical employment was, in fact, quite modest. In William's and Anne's reigns, when benefice-income was depressed, the need for clergymen without high economic expectations was real enough, and the numbers of such Oxford men known to have been ordained rose perceptibly. The servitors and battelers were an accepted part of the Oxford scene, though contemporaries did not deny that their condition was unenviable and humiliating. Perhaps the sons of manual workers accepted their lot as part

[1] T. Leigh-Mrs Sarah Wight, 22 Apr. 1704, Northants Record Office, MS D (CA) 354, fo 51. Theophilus Leigh (1648-1725), m. Queen's 1663. His nephew was William Wight, m. Ch.Ch. 1704. Chamberlayne's son was Edmund Chamberlayne (1670-1755), m. Trin. 1687.

[2] During the decade 1710-19 a total of 438 servitors and battelers were admitted to Balliol, Brasenose, Christ Church, Lincoln, Pembroke, Trinity, University College and Wadham; in the decade 1760-9 the same colleges admitted no more than 112.

[3] J. Eachard, *The Grounds and Occasions of the Contempt of the Clergy and Religion* (London 1670), 115.

of their position in the hierarchy of deference; but there were others, usually the children of penurious clergymen, who felt keenly the demeaning nature of the services they had to perform, the shame of the debts they contracted and the shabby mode of life which was forced on them.

The worst humiliations were reserved for the servitors who did domestic labour on staircases and in hall and kitchen in return for food and small fees. In 1670 Eachard had written of the 'Bed-making, Chamber-sweeping and water-fetching' which they performed, and even in the reign of George I a 'poor child' at Queen's, George Fothergill, could describe his labours in similar terms. He wrote to his parents:

> I cannot tell well how to give you a notion of what we Servitors do. We are seven of us, and we wait upon the Batchelors, Gentlemen Commoners, and Commoners at meals. We carry in their Commons out of the kitchen into the Hall, and their bread and beer out of the Buttery. I call up one Gentleman Commoner, which is ten shillings a quarter when he's in town, and three Commoners, which are five shillings each, on the same conditions. My Servitor's place saves me, I believe, about thirty shillings a quarter in battels, one quarter with another.

He congratulated himself at least on having escaped the position of a junior servitor, 'a slavery which I always dreaded, and which I could not well have undergone'.[1] The word 'slavery' recurs in these letters of undergraduates who were forced to do servants' work. Thomas Brockbank, as the son of a priest who had been at Cambridge, had some pretensions to gentility, and his letters show concern about the state of his clothes, his wig and his linen. In an attempt to procure a little extra money he accepted a place as larderman where his duties were 'to set down each mans commons for which I was equal with the Poor Children at Table'. This he endured for three years, hoping to be elected as one of the bachelor-foundationers or taberdars, but in 1692 his hopes were dashed and he found himself left as 'Senior pore child'. Not being 'willing to stay any longer under that Slavery', he took his degree, thereby abandoning any hope of a place on the foundation.[2] As late as 1728 Erasmus Head, another north-country batteler at Queen's, described his situation similarly. Finding it impossible to make ends meet he put in for a poor child's place, 'tho' I shall enter upon a long slavery, and be at much more trouble and uneasiness than what I am now at, which makes me not a little abhor the change'.[3] Much worse, however, than the actual duties was the stigma of social inferiority which attached to them. Until well into the eighteenth century it was not thought fitting for one who did menial

---

[1] G. Fothergill-parents, 11 July 1724, *The Fothergills of Ravenstonedale*, ed. C. Thornton and F. McLaughlin (London 1905), 88, 79.

[2] *Diary of Brockbank*, ed. Trappes-Lomax, pp. 16, 42.

[3] Head-parents at Foxlakenning, Rose-Castle, Cumberland, 25 Mar. 1728, Bodl. MS Don. c.152.

services to mix socially with undergraduates of a superior rank. It is even recorded that at Pembroke one son of an impoverished Warwickshire clergyman found that he could not keep up a friendship with a school-fellow except by stealth: 'Mr Shenstone had one ingenious and much-valued friend in Oxford, Mr Jago, his Schoolfellow, whom he could only visit in private, as he wore a servitor's gown; it being deemed a great disparagement for a commoner to appear in public with one in that situation.'[1]

To the mind of the early eighteenth century it seemed only fitting that those who had existed in such demeaning circumstances should be confined to the most lowly and poorly paid positions in the church. There were, of course, a few servitors who rose to high office. Edmund Gibson, later bishop of London, was a batteler and poor child at Queen's, while John Potter, who was a servitor at University College in 1689, went on to become regius professor of divinity, bishop of Oxford, and eventually archbishop of Canterbury. But these were very able men whose exceptional qualities were apparent even in their college days.[2] They set themselves on the ladder of promotion by putting their talent as writers at the disposal of Archbishop Tenison and his whig allies, and thereby reaped a rich reward. But such success-stories were rare, and most poor graduates were more faithful to the conservative politics and divinity in which they had been raised. Over two-thirds of servitors and battelers left on obtaining the degree of BA, and all but a few became country priests. They had been given little formal training in theology and virtually none in pastoral care, but apart from the church there was no profession open to them. It was necessary to eke out an existence until they were of age for deacon's orders, and meanwhile find some clerical employment which a bishop would accept as sufficient for ordination. A detailed study of the clergy of Leicestershire in the later Stuart era has shown how disadvantaged were men of plebeian origins who possessed only a bachelor's degree. Such poor divines provided a clear majority of the stipendiary curates who had no security of tenure and worked for stipends which averaged between £20 and £30.[3] Even for those who became incumbents there was a strong probability that they would find themselves in the poorer livings. Of those who had been 'plebeians' at the university 68 per cent held a benefice of less than £100 in value while only 34 per cent of those who had been 'gentlemen' or above did so.[4] And yet this clerical proletariat was far from being radical. They might be the section of the clergy most vulnerable to

[1] Macleane, *Pembroke*, 371.

[2] For Gibson's early career see N. Sykes, *Edmund Gibson, Bishop of London, 1669-1748* (Oxford 1926), ch. 1.

[3] As late as the period 1715-18 stipendiary curates in the diocese of Rochester with only a BA degree had an average stipend under £30 a year, while those with MAs had an average of £36: bishop's act book 1713-1821, legal secretary to bishop of Rochester, 1 The Sanctuary, Westminster, SW1.

[4] Pruett, *Parish Clergy*, 54-7, 70-2.

recession in the economic position of the church, but their anger was directed not so much at their better-off brethren but against those whigs and anticlericals who sought to diminish the status and prestige of the profession. The poor country parsons in their worn black clothes and gowns, and their BA hoods, were strident in their advocacy of the traditional learning and politics of the university. Their college careers might have been marked by penury and domestic drudgery but they went on to propagate to their flocks the conservative teaching which they had imbibed at Oxford.

Among the better-off undergraduates the real divide lay between those who intended to stay at the university long enough to take a degree and those who wished to acquire just enough literary polish to pass in the world as men of quality. For the most part the foundationers, drawn as they were from the sons of gentlemen and the more prosperous clergy, remained until they had an MA, and then proceeded to ordination, either as fellows of colleges or as incumbents. Just over half the commoners likewise committed themselves to ordination by taking a degree, and of these about half stayed on to read theology before taking an MA. It was from these foundationers and commoners that the well-to-do rectors, cathedral dignitaries and bishops of the next generation were to be drawn. Often living in the university for five years or more, they set much of its social tone. But beside them were other commoners, perhaps eldest sons of members of the landed gentry, who had no intention of being ordained. These came up, on average, a year earlier and resided for two years or less. For them Oxford was a kind of finishing school; they read the classics with a tutor and looked to acquire independence and the social graces in the other Oxford world of country sports, clubs, coffee-houses and fashionable tailors. It is clear that the dons were acutely sensitive to the accusation that they were providing an education unfitted to a cultured man of leisure and that colleges were bringing the aristocracy into contact with persons of a low social class. One trenchant critic was John Aubrey, who wrote that there was ample provision in the universities for the education of divines but no care had been taken for the right breeding of gentlemen of quality: 'instead of giving to young Gentlemen the Accomplishment according to Juvenal, they returne home with the learning (if any at all) of a Benedictine Monke; with some Scholarly Canting. Thus in lieu of giving him the Breeding of a Gentleman, he is sent home with that of a Deacon.'[1] A fear that the sons of the landed gentry might go to special academies to learn 'manners' or be sent abroad to foreign universities recurs in academic correspondence and explains the vehement campaign which Oxford and its political friends launched in 1700 against Lewis Maidwell's

---

[1] Bodl. MS Aubrey 10, fo 143 (nd), quoted by Stone, 'Size and composition', 50. John Aubrey (1626-97), m. Trin. 1641.

parliamentary bill to establish in Westminster an academy to teach gentlemen the classics, modern languages, dancing, singing and 'riding the Great Horse'.[1] The result was that, after the Revolution, Oxford increasingly brought its lifestyle into conformity with that of the cultivated gentry and acquired a reputation for comfortable living and 'gentlemanly' manners among the dons, and expenditure and adherence to fashion among the young. In 1700 no fewer than two fencing masters and four dancing masters were active in the city.[2]

There was certainly no lack of diversion for young men who did not find themselves unduly pressed to severe academic study. In his diary from 1701 to 1703 Jeremiah Milles, fellow of Balliol, recorded his efforts as a pro-proctor to impose some restraint on the extra-curricular activities of the undergraduate body: he dispersed great numbers from alehouses, attempted to drive scholars away from the bull-baiting at Gloucester Green, and kept up a relentless campaign against strolling prostitutes by having them 'carted' out of town by the proctors' men. He and others recorded the other amusements of the academic year: a journey with the gentlemen-commoners up to Godstow on the water with the 'University Music', the horse-races at Port Meadow and the arrival of the London players at the time of the Act.[3] Clearly a period of residence at Oxford could present serious temptations to a young man of social standing. Tailors, in particular, were ready to extend unlimited 'tick', though the penalty for not meeting their bills could be a persistent and humiliating 'dunning'.[4] It is apparent that clothes and fashions were an intense preoccupation. Even the correspondence of the poorer undergraduates is taken up with the necessity of money for coats, breeches and wigs, while the better-off made a point of walking in the meadows and parks to show off the latest finery. As Nicholas Amhurst put it, 'all the SMARTS in OXFORD are not *Noblemen* and *Gentlemen-Commoners*, but chiefly of a meaner Rank, who cannot afford to be thus *fine* any longer than their *Mercers, Taylors, Shoe-makers*, and *Perriwig-makers* will *tick* with them'.[5] The *Guardian* of 18 March 1713, in a mock-letter signed 'Simon Slack', ridiculed under-graduate fashion-consciousness by suggesting that the architects of style

---

[1] For 'Maidwell's Project' see 'Dr. Wallis's letter against Mr. Maidwell, 1700', ed. T. W. Jackson, *Collectanea*, ed. Fletcher, pp. 309-31; L. W. Finch-Charlett, 28 Feb. 1700, MS Ballard 20, fo 10; J. Hough-same, 27 Feb. 1700, MS Ballard 9, fo 122. Hough argued that if only tutors would instil into young gentlemen 'good learning, good manners, a reasonable insight into the grounds of their religion, and a habit of Obedience to their Superiors, I am perswaded that neither they nor their Parents would thinke they had lost their time amongst us, or complain that we did not make 'em what the Town calls fine Gentlemen': quoted by Jackson, 291.   [2] *Collectanea*, ed. Fletcher, p. 304.

[3] Balliol, MS 461, diary of Jeremiah Milles; Bodl. MS Rawl. lett. 36, fo 277; *Diary of Brockbank*, ed. Trappes-Lomax, p. 62.

[4] See A. D'Anvers, *Academica, or the Humours of the University of Oxford* (London 1691).

[5] *Terrae-Filius* no. lii (8-12 July 1721).

were seeking 'to introduce several pretty Oddnesses in the taking and tucking up of Gowns, to regulate the dimensions of Wigs, to vary the Tufts upon Caps, and to enlarge or narrow the hems of Bands'. So widespread was the obsession that some individualists, like Edmund Neale (alias Smith) of Christ Church, made a point of flouting convention and appearing in public in tattered clothes. But he was a poet and a young man of exceptional good looks, known to the ladies of Oxford as 'the Handsome Sloven'.[1]

What seems to have caused the most concern to parents was the heavy drinking which was prevalent among both dons and undergraduates. As early as 1677 Anthony Wood had drawn attention to the time spent in taverns and alehouses, and by William's reign the situation was in danger of becoming a public scandal and providing ammunition for the university's enemies. In 1696 Humphrey Prideaux warned a relative of the 'drinking and duncery' which went on in many colleges, while one commoner advised that a brother who had failed to get a place on the foundation should be removed from Oxford on the grounds that 'it cannot be very elegable to buy a little, a very little learning . . . at the expence of money's, and corruption of morrals'.[2] In 1700 the vice-chancellor's court forbade all coffee-houses to sell spirits and strong wines but still in 1708 the author of *Advice to a Son in the University* thought that drink was the most dangerous vice. As one worried father of a potential gentleman-commoner wrote in 1704: 'There is indeed so generall a complaint, now of the expence, increase of conversation, and other alterations . . . that for my own part, I do not think of sending my eldest Son to either of them nor any of my Younger but such whom I design for the Church.'[3]

The commoners who were not aiming for a degree had much in common with the undergraduates who were the social élite of Augustan England: the noblemen and the gentlemen-commoners. Although these gilded young men stayed only for a year or eighteen months and their residence in Oxford was usually intermittent, the whole academic community regarded it as of immense importance that those who were one day to direct the national and local life of the nation should be associated with the university and the established church. The rank of 'nobleman' was reserved for peers with suffrage in the house of lords, for their eldest sons and the younger sons of dukes and marquesses. Nearly all went to Christ Church, and the fifty-four of them who resided there

---

[1] See *Johnson's Lives of the English Poets*, ed. G. Birkbeck Hill (3 vols Oxford 1905) ii. 1-22. Smith carried on a personal feud with Dean Aldrich whom he satirized unmercifully in his poem *The Town Dis-play'd* (1701); he was expelled from his Studentship in 1705 and died in 1710. For the proceedings of the chapter of Christ Church against him see Bodl. MS Tanner 314, fo 205.

[2] Wood, *Life and Times* ii. 396; Prideaux-R. Coffin, 19 Feb. 1696, HMC *5th Report*, 374; G. Fleming-D. Fleming, 20 Sept. 1696, *The Flemings in Oxford* iii. 310.

[3] T. Leigh-Mrs Sarah Wight, 22 Apr. 1704, Northants Rec. Off. MS D (CA) 354, fo 51.

between 1690 and 1719 were taken as a sign of that college's pre-eminence in the university. In the summer of 1703 it proved necessary to enlarge the size of the noblemen's table in hall, and the glad news was at once circulated to the chancellor and Oxford's other highly-placed friends. Henry Worseley, MP for Newton, Isle of Wight, replied enthusiastically: 'I wish the Noblemen's table in every Colledge was proportionately lengthened with that of Christ Church, for the happiness of our Nation depends very much upon the education of our Noblemen, and the Principles they suck in in their Minority.'[1] Under Aldrich Christ Church made great efforts to encourage its aristocrats to some literary endeavour and to keep them away from the temptations which the city had to offer to immature men with money and social prestige. The dean himself donated prizes, and chose his noble protégés to deliver high-flown orations to important visitors. It was well understood by the dons that to be tutor and friend to a nobleman with important connections could lay the foundation of a successful career in the church, and young academics were eager to be chosen for the work. Francis Atterbury's relationship with the Honourable Charles Boyle, later earl of Orrery, in 1690-1 illustrates the subtle blend of authority and deference which a tutor exhibited.[2] In three decades no Christ Church nobleman except Boyle proceeded to the degree of BA though eleven of them were presented to honorary MAs. Their role in life had been marked out for them from birth, and no one in contemporary Oxford saw fit to question it.

The sons of leading county families and the younger sons of peers were usually entered in the rank of gentleman-commoner. A few parents sought to protect their offspring from a pretentious style of living by deliberately choosing an ordinary commonership, but the convention that a man should abide by his known place in society was a strong one. It was clearly expected that the tory politicians of the west midlands and south-west should send their sons to Oxford, even if it were only for a term or two. Simon Harcourt, though himself at Pembroke, entered his son as a gentleman-commoner at Christ Church in 1702, while Edward Harley and Thomas Bromley enjoyed the same rank there in 1707 and 1710. Though these young men remained in residence no more than a few months, in honour of their famous fathers each was presented to an honorary MA by the public orator in a full convocation. Few gentlemen-commoners graduated and were ordained. Out of 674 entered in eight colleges between 1690 and 1719 only 20 took a degree, and all these appear to have

---

[1] Worseley-Charlett, 28 July 1705, MS Ballard 39, fo 32; Charlett-Ormonde, 27 June 1705, HMC *Ormonde MSS* viii. 161. Henry Worseley (1675-1740), m. SEH 1690.

[2] See the letters in *The Epistolary Correspondence, Visitation Charges, Speeches, and Miscellanies, of the Right Reverend Francis Atterbury, D.D., Lord Bishop of Rochester, with historical notes, and brief memoirs of the author*, ed. J. Nichols (4 vols London 1783-7, 2nd edn 5 vols London 1799, i-iv printed and dated 1789-90, v 1798) i. 29-42. All quotations are taken from the second edition.

been younger sons who wished to be ordained. On the other hand, no fewer than 232 went on to the Inns of Court. A few went into the army, some remained at the law as barristers, but the majority simply took up their obligations as country gentlemen, landowners and magistrates. As many as 158 became members of the house of commons. It was this body of young men who provided the university's real connection with the nation's social élite. While the noblemen were congregated at Christ Church, gentlemen-commoners existed in every college. Clearly some colleges were smarter and could promise grander rooms and better food. There was vigorous competition to build new staircases with spacious sets of rooms in which a gentleman could live in style. In 1708 New College added six new sets overlooking the garden, and assured the Honourable James Brydges, a wealthy old member who had made a generous donation, that the money would be faithfully 'apply'd to a Pile of building lately raised for Noblemen and Gentlemen Commoners'.[1] During Anne's reign the grand staircases of Peckwater quadrangle were being constructed at Christ Church to provide accommodation without parallel elsewhere, and much of the expense was borne by contributions from the tory gentry of the midlands. But if Christ Church took 206 of the 674 gentlemen-commoners, other colleges were not lacking in their efforts to attract young men likely to prove useful to both dons and undergraduates. Balliol had 120 and Trinity 104. Wadham and Pembroke had, for their size, large numbers of gentlemen-commoners with 86 and 30 respectively, and this seems due to political sympathies which appeared reassuring to whig families who refused to entrust their sons to the extreme toryism of Christ Church, Balliol or Trinity. Other colleges managed to attract their gentlemen-commoners because of strong regional connections. Brasenose in this period, with 340 battelers admitted as against 204 commoners, might well have been regarded as of such low social character that gentlemen-commoners would prefer to avoid it in favour of some more prestigious society. In fact its 34 members in that rank were drawn almost entirely from the gentry families of Lancashire and Cheshire, counties which supplied over half of the college's entrants.[2] And similarly a Welsh magnate like Sir Watkin Williams-Wynne chose to join his humbler fellow-countrymen at Jesus rather than betake himself to Christ Church.

The careful attention lavished on the sons of the ruling class did not necessarily mean that in their future careers they espoused the ideas in politics or divinity which Oxford propagated. Their stay was too short and their lifestyle too much out of accord with that of the clergy who managed

[1] Sub-warden-Brydges, 15 June 1711, San Marino, California, Huntington Library, MS ST 58.6, fo 140. Hon. James Brydges (1674–1744), from 1719 1st D. of Chandos; m. New College 1690; MP Hereford 1698–1701.

[2] In the period from 1690 to 1719, out of the college's total entry from England of 599, no fewer than 315 came from Lancashire and Cheshire.

the affairs of the university. It is likely, too, that their study at the Inns of Court was more influential in forming their constitutional notions than the reading prescribed by their Oxford tutors. In fact, the voting pattern of Oxford men who became members of the house of commons disposes of the belief that their political allegiance was overwhelmingly to the tory party. The most reliable division-list for the reign of Anne is that for the election of a speaker at the beginning of a new parliament on 25 October 1705.[1] It is significant that this was understood to be a 'party' contest between a court whig candidate, John Smith, and a tory, William Bromley, who was burgess for the university. Of the 513 members elected in 1705 no fewer than 186, or 36 per cent, had spent some time at Oxford and most had been gentlemen-commoners; as many as 44 were former alumni of Christ Church. Only 20 had actually acquired a degree but 108 had been students at an Inn of Court. In the actual division the votes cast by the Oxford men were 84 for the court whig candidate and 79 for Bromley with 20 absent and 3 involved in disputed election returns.[2] An analysis of the same Oxford members' voting in a series of 'party' divisions in Anne's reign shows that 54 voted consistently with the whigs and 66 with the tories, while 12 appear to have switched their votes across party lines.[3] It is clear then that the nobility and landed gentry who had been at the university were in themselves somewhat unreliable defenders of its political and religious beliefs. It was fortunate that their real importance for Oxford and Oxford men lay elsewhere. Both tutors and undergraduates looked to them for the ecclesiastical patronage upon which the whole life of the university depended. In 1699 the colleges between them possessed the right of appointment to 179 benefices, and in the 147 cases where the annual value can be calculated no more than 67 benefices were worth £100 or more.[4] The number was wholly insufficient for the preferment of the fellows of the colleges, much less to provide for the settlement across the country of the 125 or so Oxford men who were ordained each year. This work had to be done by the nobility and gentry, whose extensive powers of appointment in this era scarcely need to be emphasized. In Warwickshire, for example, noblemen and major landowners in the county had the presentation to 48 per cent of all livings and 60 per cent of all those worth more than £80 a year; those who resided outside the county had an additional 9 per cent and 4 per cent respectively. In an area which sent so many

[1] For the list, with a careful analysis, see W. A. Speck, 'The Choice of a Speaker in 1705', *Bull. Inst. Hist. Research* xxxvii (1964).

[2] The actual vote was 248-205 in favour of Smith. A small number of tories attached to Harley and St John voted with the court, though a placeman like George Clarke, fellow of All Souls, earned dismissal by voting for Bromley. John Smith (1656-1723), m. St John's 1672; speaker of the house of commons 1705-8; chancellor of the exchequer 1708-10.

[3] This analysis is based on the seven division-lists cited by Speck, 37.

[4] I am grateful to Mr Garry Lynch for this detailed research into the value of college livings.

gentleman-commoners to Oxford it is not surprising to find that in the years from 1700 to 1714 no fewer than 66 per cent of incumbents were graduates of the university.[1] By contrast neighbouring Leicestershire was a county which was predominantly orientated to Cambridge with very few of its landowners finding their way as gentlemen-commoners to Oxford. Here 58 per cent of all advowsons were owned by the local peers, baronets, knights and esquires. It is significant that in 1714 63 per cent of all incumbents had been to Cambridge as against 30 per cent who had graduated at Oxford.[2] Compared with the mass of patronage in the hands of local landowners, that possessed by the crown, bishops or corporate bodies was relatively insignificant. It was essential to the maintenance of the university's influence that it should cultivate a close relationship with those who had the power to place its members in local communities across the country.

Important to the functioning of a national institution was that it should bring disparate elements in the nation's life together into a common purpose without destroying their sense of separate identity. It has been seen that the university could include in its membership men from widely differing social groups while continuing to affirm the importance of rank and privilege. And similarly Oxford could draw its students from the various regions of England and Wales while letting them retain a strong feeling of local affinity. In the early eighteenth century an individual's home 'country', with its network of loyalties and patronage, determined not just his accent but the course of his future employment. At a time when travel was notoriously difficult and expensive, a university was one of the few institutions which could draw young men for a while from the place in which they had been born and where eventually they would live and die. The correspondence of the time illustrates in painful detail the laborious journeys by carrier and horse and on foot which Oxford men undertook. For the very well-to-do the 'flying coach' from London took a whole day in summer; in winter, when the ways were wet and muddy, the same journey took two days, with an overnight stop at High Wycombe. In 1693 the passengers were held up and brutally robbed by six highwaymen.[3] From Westmorland it was a ten-day ride on an ordinary saddle-horse, and more than a week from Cornwall.[4] On Gloucester Green there was a regular market in horses with the price fluctuating as members of the university arrived and departed. Poor students or those who lived at a great distance rarely went home during the whole period of their university course. It was, then, only to be expected that each of the two universities should have

[1] Salter, 'Warwickshire clergy', 33-4, 52.

[2] Pruett, *Parish Clergy*, 45, 60.

[3] Washington DC, Folger Shakespeare Library, Newdigate newsletter no. 2232 (10 Oct. 1693).

[4] See *Diary of Brockbank*, ed. Trappes-Lomax, pp. 48 ff for an account of his journey from Cartmel to Oxford in 1693.

a region from which it drew its members; and in fact a line drawn from the Mersey to London roughly delineated the two areas. The figures in table 12.4 show that over half of all Oxford freshmen came from the south-west, the west midlands and Wales while only a small proportion came from the east midlands or East Anglia. But of the two, Oxford covered by far the most prosperous and populous parts of the country, and actually penetrated into its rival's territory with a number of important outposts.

Within the university, colleges had strong connections with particular areas or counties and provided havens where men of a similar local background might congregate. The most obvious example was of course Jesus College, which was and remained virtually a Welsh enclave. Among the freshman of 1700 every one of the 27 had been born in the princi-

TABLE 12.4

MATRICULANTS BY REGION OF ORIGIN

year of entry	1690		1700		1710	
	no.	%	no.	%	no.	%
local	24	9	33	11	18	6
south-west	47	18	59	20	54	19
west midlands	40	16	59	20	58	21
Wales	32	12	35	12	38	14
north	22	9	29	10	27	10
east midlands	18	7	9	3	12	4
east	4	2	11	4	5	2
London	28	11	22	7	34	12
south-east	20	8	26	9	16	6
Scotland, Ireland, overseas	3	1	7	2	12	4
not known	19	7	4	1	3	1
	257		294		277	

local: Oxon., Berks., Bucks.
south-west: Cornwall, Devon, Dorset, Somerset, Wilts.
west midlands: Bristol, Glos., Hereford, Shropshire, Staffs., Warwicks., Worcs.
Wales: all counties, including Mon.
north: Cheshire, Cumberland, Durham, Lancs., Northumberland, Westmorland, Yorks.
east midlands: Beds., Derbys., Hunts., Leics., Northants., Notts., Rutland
east: Cambs., Essex, Herts., Lincs., Norfolk, Suffolk
London: Middlesex, including cities of London and Westminster
south-east: Hants., Kent, Surrey, Sussex

pality, and in 1710 all 32 were Welsh, though 2 had actually been born in the border-counties of Shropshire and Worcestershire. The wretched poverty of their homeland meant that most Jesus men were of humble origin, and in each year from 1690 to 1719 the college contributed the largest number of freshmen who matriculated as 'plebeians' or *pauperes pueri*. Many of these did not stay to take a degree and it is known that Welsh bishops had despaired of finding graduates to staff their poorer livings. Even those who struggled through to become BAs could look forward only to a meagre existence in some meanly endowed Welsh vicarage.[1] Equally striking was the connection of Exeter College with the south-west of the country and, in particular, with the area of the diocese of Exeter. In 1700, out of 22 freshmen, 17 had been born in the counties of Devon and Cornwall; and in 1710, out of 23, 18 came from the south-west. It is clear, too, that they returned there. Between 1689 and 1707 Bishop Trelawny of Exeter ordained 229 men known to be Oxford graduates, of whom no fewer than 128 had been at Exeter College; in the same period he laid hands on only 29 Cambridge men.[2] Among the other colleges only Brasenose exhibited quite so firm an affiliation with a particular region. Between 1690 and 1719 out of 626 freshmen as many as 315 had come from the two counties of Cheshire and Lancashire. Two colleges made significant inroads into areas which were otherwise regarded as Cambridge territory. Lincoln College took 26 per cent of its overall entry of 303 from the east midlands, while University College recruited 21 per cent of its freshmen from the single county of Yorkshire. The statistics show, however, that Oxford men came predominantly from the south-west and the west midlands. Five colleges, Balliol, Christ Church, Magdalen, Trinity and Wadham, admitted between them 3,061 freshmen during this period, of whom 788 (or 25.7 per cent) came from the south-west and 803 (or 26.2 per cent) from the west midlands. Studies of the Anglican clergy at county and diocesan level confirm a remarkable correlation between a man's geographic origin, the university and college he attended and the area in which he was later to exercise his ministry. A simple illustration of this may be found in the 117 Oxford freshmen of the year 1700 who are known subsequently to have been ordained. No fewer than 49 of them found a living in the county of

---

[1] For a sad account of the condition of the Welsh clergy, written by a Jesus man who matriculated in 1690, see E. Saunders, *A View of the State of Religion in the Diocese of St. Davids about the beginning of the 18th Century* (London 1721). William Lloyd, when bishop of St Asaph from 1680 to 1692, had had to abandon his efforts to secure an all-graduate ministry: A. T. Hart, *William Lloyd* (London 1952), 63-71. Between 1689 and 1713 136 men were ordained deacon in the diocese of Bangor, 78 from Oxford, 17 from Cambridge, 3 from other universities and 38 who do not appear to have attended any university; in fact only 64 of the 136 had actually graduated: A. I. Pryce, *The Diocese of Bangor during Three Centuries* (Cardiff 1929) (figures corrected).

[2] M. G. Smith, 'The administration of the diocese of Exeter during the episcopate of Sir Jonathan Trelawny, 1689-1707' (Oxford BD thesis 1964), 287.

their birth while 20 more were preferred in adjacent counties. It was a sign of the effectiveness of the university that it could thus combine a local and a national function: that it could confirm regional loyalties while providing a unifying set of beliefs and a profession trained to propagate them.

In the early eighteenth century the prime function of the university was conceived to be the recruitment and formation of a learned profession, the clergy of the national religious establishment which set forth the Anglican version of the Christian faith in the cathedrals, parishes and schools of the country. It was generally understood, however, that the clergy were far from being a homogeneous body and that standards of education and theological competence varied widely. Oxford had to prepare men for the ministry whose way of life ranged between that of a stipendiary curate on a miserable £30 a year to that of a substantial rector with many hundreds from tithe-income and perhaps a valuable cathedral prebend. Such differences were, of course, to grow even greater in the course of the century as agricultural improvement and enclosure acts increased the value of tithes for certain fortunate incumbents. An example of such sudden wealth may be found in the story of Joshua Reynolds, fellow of Corpus, who in 1707 was presented by the college to the rectory of Stoke Charity in Hampshire. This advowson had been purchased in 1693 when the annual value of the benefice was well under £100. But between 1718 and 1728 the rector's position was transformed. An enclosure award in 1724 raised his net profit from £117 to £380. Reynolds stayed on until 1740, living the life of a substantial country gentleman on this income from a parish of only sixty-eight people.[1] Although the actual value of a living rarely corresponded to the weight of pastoral responsibility attached to it, it was clearly understood that only a parish with a sufficient competence could expect to have a gentleman and a scholar as its parish priest and that a poor living would be filled by a man of modest origins whose university career had been brief and whose knowledge of theology might well be vestigial.

Merely to spend three years at Oxford and proceed BA was admitted to be a poor preparation for ordination. The undergraduate course of study was entirely secular in character, and the lists of reading which have survived show that it consisted of philosophy, with a heavy

[1] CCCA F11/19/2 (copy at 3), the rector's book of Joshua Reynolds of Stoke Charity. Reynolds's vigorous exaction of what was due to him and the gradual diminution of his pastoral concern make sad reading. In 1692 Corpus also purchased the advowson of the rectory of Pembridge, Herefordshire, worth over £300 per annum.

emphasis on formal logic, and a working through of well known Greek and Latin texts. A plan of work drawn up for a man at St John's in 1696 suggests that a 'Preparatory Insight into Divinity' might be included but the works prescribed were devotional in character rather than exegetical or doctrinal.[1] Clearly much depended on how seriously an individual tutor took his duty of religious instruction but even more on the disposition of the undergraduate. Tutors obviously differed greatly. The diary of Jeremiah Milles shows that at least some were men of deep spirituality. Milles went daily to early morning chapel and received the sacrament at least once a week; he was at the university sermon every Sunday, kept Lent with fasting and private prayer and read extensively in scholarly theological topics. Each morning he 'read lectures' to his pupils, and the death of one of them from smallpox in October 1701 threw him into an agony of sorrow. He was a young clergyman of transparent sincerity and Christian faith, willing to spend time with his young charges. That many ordinands had something of the same religious character is shown by the careful notes taken by Matthew Hawes, a commoner of Christ Church and later a Buckinghamshire incumbent. Between 1704 and 1707, when he graduated, he recorded and analysed the argument of 364 university sermons.[2] Milles and Hawes were perhaps unusual examples of religious zeal, and some colleges made a point of excluding from their fellowship men such as these whose enthusiasm might prove embarrassing to their colleagues. In 1693 Anthony Wood recorded the case of a candidate not elected at Merton 'because he was too precise and religious and therefore not fit to make a societie man'.[3] All colleges insisted on attendance by undergraduates at a chapel service at an hour between 6 and 7 o'clock, and levied fines and impositions on absentees, but the non-appearance of fellows or gentlemen-commoners was often winked at. Most colleges appear to have had a single celebration of the holy communion in the course of a term, and dons and undergraduates who wished for more were obliged to go to Christ Church cathedral where, according to some accounts, there was a weekly service. Regular attendance at this was, however, enough to earn a man the mildly approbrious 'character of a Sanctify'd Person'.[4] The general impression is of a regime in most colleges where a decent religious observance was required of all members and regular

---

[1] Bodl. MS Rawl. D.1178. For a similar list with introductory religious works see MS Rawl. D.188.
[2] Bodl. MS Eng. Th. f.15, 'methods of sermonizing'.
[3] Wood, *Life and Times* iii. 424 (15 June 1693). The candidate was Peter Wood (1673-1703), m. Merton 1689; MA New College 1696.
[4] Hearne, *Collections* i. 34. Arthur Bury (1624-1713, m. Exeter 1639, rector 1666-90) was to claim it as a sign of unusual piety that he had instituted a monthly sacrament at Exeter: *The Account Examined, or A Vindication of Dr Arthur Bury* (London 1690), 20.

absenteeism was unacceptable, but where services were often per-functorily performed by stipendiary chaplains.[1]

A young man who was forced to give up his university course on completing the degree of BA was hardly ready for ordination. It was thus important that for most of them there was a period of compulsory waiting before they could be admitted to deacon's orders at the canonical age of 23.[2] Some had to return home, hoping to read a little theology before presenting themselves to a bishop's chaplain for examination. It was this class of candidate which earned the vehement criticism of reforming bishops, and many of them were rejected. Bishop Burnet of Salisbury was particularly troubled at the theological ignorance of poor ordinands 'especially the servitors, who if they had not a good capacity and were well disposed of themselves were generally neglected by their Tutors'. With the boldness of a Scottish graduate he defied the English universities by setting up at Salisbury a 'nursery' of 'students in divinity who should follow their studies and devotions till I could provide for them'. But the bitter attacks which this produced from Oxford led him eventually to choose the better part of valour and end his experiment.[3] In the middle years of King William's reign most bishops made the ordination of the poorest class of candidate as difficult as possible, and on 10 July 1695 Archbishop Tenison actually issued a circular letter to all his suffragans urging that they should require a university degree, definite testimonials and a proper title to a curacy or a living before they ordained anybody. Suddenly candidates found themselves in great difficulties. Thomas Brockbank was reduced to despair. 'How to get a title', he wrote, 'I am allmost at a loss, for now none but real ones will be taken.'[4] Of course, a candidate who had stayed in Oxford for an MA and studied theology for two or three years rarely had any difficulty, though most bishops made it a matter of conscience that they and their examining chaplains should give each ordinand a searching test. It was certainly the only serious examination which Oxford men faced in their lives. In December 1694 Thomas Tanner's performance in the chapter house of St Paul's was something of a triumph. 'I was examined', he reported, 'above two hours by the Bishop himself, and Dr Beveridge, Dr Stanley, Dr Isham, Dr Alston, and Dr Lancaster; I had a note writ by the Bishop himself on the back of my Testimonials signifying that I had passed their examinations.' His friend Edmund Gibson added the information that 'The Gentlemen examin'd for Orders were, according to their several Performances, rang'd under

---

[1] For the attention attracted by the absences of Warden Finch of All Souls from the college chapel see J. Rivers-Tanner, 28 May 1699, Bodl. MS Tanner 21, fo 74.

[2] See Sykes, *Church and State*, 113-14.

[3] *A Supplement to Burnet's History of My Own Times*, ed. H. C. Foxcroft (Oxford 1902), 500-1.

[4] *Diary of Brockbank*, ed. Trappes-Lomax, p. 81.

the heads of *Very well, Indifferent*, and *Tolerable*, by the Examiners. Only two had the honour to come under the first, and Mr Tanner was one of them.'[1]

Not every bishop was as strict as Compton of London, yet there is evidence that many candidates were refused. In November 1692 George Fleming of St Edmund Hall, son of a baronet, returned to Oxford after taking his degree and presented himself to the bishop's chaplain. He was utterly mortified to find himself rejected, and he was not in fact to be ordained until 1694 after a period of residence studying theology.[2] Probably more was expected from a gentleman like him than from the plebeians and poor vicars' sons who were hurried into orders as soon as possible after graduation. Many bishops made an exception for such candidates because of their 'poor and discouraging circumstances' and the wretchedness of the cures to which they were going.[3] A really conscientious bishop like William Wake of Lincoln found that virtually all the Oxford graduates whom he had to reject or defer were simple BAs who were almost wholly ignorant of theology. In 1716, when archbishop of Canterbury, he sent Charlett an urgent plea that the university should take its responsibilities more seriously. Every tutor must see that his undergraduates had a grounding in systematic theology and, instead of limiting their studies to the classics, he should expect from his pupils a constant reading of the Greek Testament, so as to make them well acquainted with the text. He deplored the way in which colleges issued testimonials for candidates who were manifestly unprepared for ordination. 'For, indeed', he concluded, 'you cannot beleive how great the defects of our Clergy in all respects are, especially when they first apply to Us for Holy Orders.'[4]

A strongly developed sense of personal vocation was not required of Oxford men proceeding to ordination. Indeed, the notion of being members of a learned profession which performed recognized public duties was much more characteristic of the clergy than any high concept of the priesthood. Many ordinands were simply following in their father's footsteps and each year the sons of clerks provided the highest proportion of ordinands of any group.[5] Sons of poor vicars like Thomas

[1] Tanner-Charlett, 22 Dec. 1694, MS Ballard 4, fo 26. Gibson-Charlett, 22 Dec. 1694, MS Ballard 5, fo 81. William Beveridge (1637-1708), incorporated from Camb. 1669; prebendary of St Paul's 1674. Zaccheus Isham (1651-1705), m. Ch.Ch. 1667; prebendary of St Paul's 1686. Charles Alston, incorp. from Camb. 1676; prebendary of St Paul's 1681.
[2] G. Fleming-D. Fleming, 9 Nov. 1692, *The Flemings in Oxford* iii. 91.
[3] Sykes, *Church and State*, 113. For Bishop Wake's searching examination of ordination candidates see N. Sykes *William Wake, Archbishop of Canterbury 1657-1737* (2 vols Cambridge 1957) i. 160-7.
[4] Wake-Charlett, 27 June 1716, MS Ballard 3, fo 64. For another example of the bitter complaints made by bishops about college testimonials see J. Williams of Chichester-Charlett, 3 July 1707, MS Ballard 9, fo 83.
[5] Thus 58 per cent of the sons of the clergy among the freshmen of 1690 are known to have been

390   G. V. BENNETT

Brockbank listened to pious advice from their parents about their future ministry, but their own correspondence is full of discussion about curacies, stipends and the value of possible livings. If they had a lively sense of priestly vocation it is rarely, if at all, mentioned. For the poor graduate there was simply no other profession except that of teaching and most schoolmasters' places were reserved for clergymen. The only real doubts about being ordained were expressed by the better-off, perhaps because it was they who were most often pressed towards the church against their own inclination by their parents and families. George Fleming strove in vain to dissuade his father from forcing him to embrace a way of life for which he felt an 'innate aversion', but the baronet was determined that his expenditure on a younger son should be limited to the bare minimum needed to put him through Oxford and make him eligible for ordination and a decent benefice. A pathetic appeal that he be allowed to become a barrister or that his father would 'grant me that liberty, which I would employ no otherwise than either in serving his Majesty this Spring in his Fleets or Armies, or in some place about court' was peremptorily rejected.[1] Even an intervention by the principal of St Edmund Hall was to no avail. George Fleming was ordained, duly preferred and eventually in 1734 (when he had succeeded as the second baronet) became a civilized but wholly unenthusiastic bishop of Carlisle.

Some of the heartsearching over ordination stemmed from the fact that the statutes of most colleges required fellows after a certain lapse of time to take orders or resign. A fellow who had adopted a secular mode of existence as a common lawyer, a journalist or in government service, perhaps as a non-resident in London, could find himself faced with a grievous decision. Some heads used the statute as a way of ridding themselves of those who were politically or personally unwelcome to them, and Arthur Charlett of University College was a great stickler for the strict letter of the law. In 1701 he formally deprived the Honourable Albemarle Bertie, a son of the earl of Lindsey, for allowing two ordinations to pass after being publicly admonished in the chapel.[2] Most accepted their lot, even in cases where they could summon up no great enthusiasm for the duties, the dress and the new, graver deportment expected of them. In 1699 William Adams, Student of Christ Church, explained his situation in plain terms to a close friend:

I've bin preparing my self for Orders: now all is over, & I've bin with the Bp and his chaplain; and have nothing to do but to pay my Riches, and receive

ordained, 66 per cent of those of 1700, and 52 per cent of those of 1710. The actual percentages will certainly be higher.

[1] G. Fleming–D. Fleming, 9 Nov. 1692, *The Flemings in Oxford* iii. 91; ibid. 92 for the reply of 29 Nov.
[2] For the details see MS Ballard 49, fo 16. Hon. Albemarle Bertie (1669–1742), m. Univ. 1686.

Imposition of hands. I've no particular call to that holy profession, besides a good resolution, which I took very lately to enter into it, and have had the Grace to Keep it.[1]

The most serious struggle over the obligation to take orders was fought out in All Souls where Bernard Gardiner used the statutes against a group of whig secularist lawyers who grouped themselves around the person of Matthew Tindal. The warden's pressure on the fellows to attend chapel and the sacrament and to be ordained within the prescribed time produced fierce resentment and something approaching a state of open warfare.[2] Indeed, at the beginning of 1709 an ultimatum to one fellow, William Blencowe, actually produced a minor political crisis. Blencowe, who was a staunch whig, was currently employed in the government's deciphering service, and it thus proved relatively easy for him, Roger Meredith, Thomas Dalton, Fisher Littleton and other lawyer-fellows to get a bill introduced into the commons to repeal any obligation for college fellows to take holy orders. For a moment it seemed as though the whig majority might pass into law a measure which would have affected radically the whole relationship of the university and the clerical profession.[3] Even a 'moderate' churchman like White Kennett joined in the general alarm: the bill would 'take away the Encouragements allotted to the Studies of Divinity; nor will such an Exemption from Holy Orders lead to any thing so much as to the breeding of Sparks and Beaux instead of grave Divines'.[4] Archbishop Tenison had been influential in Blencowe's election, but even he knew that something essential to the university's character was at stake, and he threw all the weight of the bishops against such 'dangerous experiments'.[5] The result was that the bill failed, though the archbishop and the earl of Sunderland exercised all their influence to see that the full rigour of the statutes was not applied to Blencowe while he continued in government service. But with the fall of Godolphin's ministry and the removal of the whigs from any position of power, the reluctant fellow found himself left to the warden's mercy. On 25 August 1712 with all time expired and dismissed from his deciphering post, Blencowe was discovered with his

[1] [W. Adams]-Tanner, [1] June 1699, Bodl. MS Tanner 21, fo 90; J. A. W. Bennett, 'Oxford in 1699', *Oxoniensia* iv (1939).

[2] [B. Gardiner]-E. Gibson, 12 Jan. 1708, C. T. Martin, *Catalogue of the Archives in the Muniment Rooms of All Souls College* (London 1877), p. 402, no. xiii.

[3] [W. Bromley]-Gardiner [2 Mar. 1709], Martin, *Catalogue*, p. 343, no. 213. Roger Meredith (1677-1739), 5th bt; m. Linc. 1693; fellow All Souls 1701; barrister Middle Temple 1703; MP Kent 1727-34. Thomas Dalton m. Queen's 1699; fellow All Souls 1706; barrister Middle Temple 1711; accused by Hearne (*Collections* i. 52) of having taken part in the notorious dinner on 30 Jan. 1707 which parodied the execution of Charles I. Fisher Littleton (1679-1740), m. Pemb. 1696; of Wadham 1702; fellow All Souls 1703; barrister Middle Temple 1708.

[4] W. Kennett-Charlett, 26 Feb. 1709, MS Ballard 7, fo 124.

[5] Tenison-Gardiner, 5 Mar. 1709, Martin, *Catalogue*, p. 344, no. 219.

brains blown out.[1] He did not perhaps die entirely in vain. After 1714 the readiness of college visitors to countenance dispensations from orders allowed serious inroads to be made on the clerical monopoly of fellowships.

It is not possible to determine exactly how many men who were at Oxford during this period were subsequently ordained. The university did not itself keep information on the ecclesiastical careers of its members and college records are inadequate. The task of correlating the names of Oxford graduates with those admitted to orders in the various English dioceses is a formidable and ultimately impossible undertaking since some bishops' registers have not survived. Even when statistics have been laboriously compiled from a variety of manuscript and printed records they will necessarily always understate the true numbers. It must, therefore, be the patterns which are accounted significant rather than the totals arrived at. For the purposes of this study an attempt has been made to trace the career of all those matriculated in the years 1690, 1700 and 1710, and this information is set out in table 12.5. On this basis 314 men are known to have been ordained out of 828 who matriculated and 489 who proceeded

TABLE 12.5

MATRICULANTS OF 1690, 1700 AND 1710 KNOWN TO HAVE BEEN SUBSEQUENTLY ORDAINED

	1690		1700		1710	
number of matriculants	257		294		277	
subsequently BA or BCL	144		169		176	
subsequently ordained	no.	%	no.	%	no.	%
pauperes pueri	23	49	16	52	7	54
plebeians	13	43	34	50	39	51
clerks in holy orders	22	58	32	67	24	52
gentlemen	24	24	31	30	41	43
esquires	1	4	3	9	1	3
baronets/knights	0		1	11	1	17
peers	0		0		1	17
total ordained	83		117		114	
percentage of graduates ordained	58%		69%		65%	

[1] Hearne, *Collections* iii. 439; I. Doolittle, 'The organization of the colleges', p. 243 above.

to a bachelor's degree. It may thus be reasonably estimated, allowing for the incompleteness of the records, that an average of 125 went into orders in any one year, and that about 70 per cent of graduates made the church their career. It is, however, the pattern of the social status of those taking orders which seems to account for the profession's conservative character and its fierce defence of its rights and privileges. The Oxford-educated clergy were drawn predominantly from the children of the poor and of the clergy themselves. Half of those matriculated as plebeians or *pauperes pueri* (132 out of 265) are known to have been ordained. The priesthood was the only profession to which they could aspire, and their status depended on its reputation and authority. The largest proportion of any group of undergraduates going into the church was provided by the sons of the clergy, and 78 out of 132 such matriculants (or 59 per cent) followed into their father's profession. For them, perhaps, the priesthood had been an expectation since childhood and the object of such influence and connection as their families could muster. Of those matriculated as 'gentlemen' only 96 out of 301 (or 32 per cent) went into orders. And when it came to the sons of esquires and above, 8 out of a total of 129 constituted an insignificant contribution to the clerical profession. It is difficult to avoid the conclusion that, while the dons and prosperous incumbents were drawn from the sons of gentlemen and the richer clergy, the influence of Oxford as an institution was mediated to the country as a whole by a clerical profession drawn overwhelmingly from the children of plebeians and the poorer parish priests. In this single fact may lie an explanation for the strong resistance which the church offered after 1714 to the whig attempt to subordinate its life to the political system of a semi-secularized aristocracy.

The effectiveness of the university as a national institution depended in large measure on the public respect accorded to the body of learning which it and the clerical profession set forth. In the anglican version of protestantism great store was laid by an appeal to the authority of the past: to the fathers of the early church, the definitions of the councils of the first four centuries of the Christian era and the formulations of traditional western academic theology. It was taken for granted that the defence of orthodoxy was entrusted to those who had been trained up to possess the necessary philosophical, exegetical and historical expertise. The basis of the parish priests' authority among their flocks was that they shared, albeit in a humble way, in this traditional knowledge and skill. But it was not hard to see that the new ideas of 'reason and natural religion', if taken to their logical conclusion, left no place for historic orthodoxy or the authoritative status of churches and university faculties. There were, of course, many learned churchmen who strove valiantly to find some accommodation between the traditional formulas and the new doctrines.[1] John Tillotson, in particular, revolutionized preaching by setting forth a Christianity which was eminently reasonable and which consisted above all in living in charity with one's neighbours. Such prominent anglican exponents of 'natural religion' usually left much unsaid and they attempted to avoid pronouncements on the nature of the church's authority or on the person of Christ. But there were others, often devout and intelligent men, who felt a compelling need to free Christianity from what they thought of as the complexities and accretions of the past, to cast aside academic theology and all intricate learning and to set forth the simple, direct message of the gospels in terms which accorded with the age of Newton and Locke. It was inevitable that the clash between the old and the new approaches should come to centre in a struggle over the doctrine of the trinity, as this had been worked out in the fourth and fifth centuries, and particularly in the Chalcedonian definition of the person of Christ. The trinitarian controversy of William's reign may seem like febrile academic bickering; contemporaries recognized that it concerned the very place and authority of the universities in society.

The dispute had its origin in the great attempt at comprehension of 1689. While Aldrich and Jane were up at Westminster, leading the resistance to King William's scheme, another Oxford divine, Arthur Bury, rector of Exeter, prepared a short book designed to persuade the members of the convocation of Canterbury to a 'charitable' view of changes in the doctrinal formulations of the church. His work, which he called *The Naked Gospel*, was printed anonymously and privately without an imprimatur from the vice-chancellor, and at first copies were restricted to a few of his Oxford friends. When, however, the convocation was prematurely dissolved, he produced a second issue with a new 'conclusion', addressed to a wider public.[2] Nobody was in any doubt as to the author or failed to see that his book, brief as it was, constituted a pungent attack not just on traditional formulations but on the whole character of Oxford theology. Bury adopted the disingenuous argument that the contemporary decay of the Christian religion was due to 'those who have perverted the Gospel'. Its original, plain meaning had been 'clouded with human learning'; 'Logick, Metaphysicks or any other Scholastick Arts' were not only unnecessary but tended to 'make the Gospel an enemy to its own great design, which we have found to be the advancement of Natural Religion'. 'The Law of Nature', he continued, 'is written in the heart by the hand of God, as a tran-

---

[1] On this see M. C. Jacob, *The Newtonians and the English Revolution 1689-1720* (Hassocks 1976), together with the perceptive review by G. Holmes in *The British Journal for the History of Science* ii no. 38 (1978).

[2] A copy of the original version of *The Naked Gospel* (np 1690) in Bodl. Antiq. e. E. 22 (5) is inscribed *Ex dono Rever: et Clariss: Autor*. There is a copy of the second issue (np 1690) with the conclusion which refers specifically to the commission ibid. (6).

script of his own nature, and must be, like its original, immortal: The Gospel came not to deface it, but to make it more legible; to new write it upon our Understandings, with clearer glosses; upon our Reason, with brighter arguments.' From such a position he could move on to dismiss the traditional orthodox formulations on the grounds that they were unintelligible to the simple souls to whom the gospel was primarily addressed. The Chalcedonian definition of the person of Christ he set aside as 'not required as Necessary for Salvation; and consequently [it] was no member of that Faith which our Lord required as necessary thereto'. The teachings of Arius were asserted to 'answer all the designs of Faith, Love, Thankfulness, Obedience, &c. Can none be Believers but Metaphysicians only?' It was priests who had, in their own selfish interests, obscured the real gospel: 'By this art have we gotten a vast army of new Doctrines of faith, and the Gospel, of whose Simplicity the greatest of the Apostles gloried, is become a Science of all others most perplexed. Our modern Theology hath so much more of Metaphysicks than of the Gospel.'[1]

No regius professor of divinity could countenance such opinions, expressed in Oxford by a DD who was charged with the spiritual formation of the young, and William Jane took immediate action. Even when the book was still in only a few hands the rumour went round that this was a formally heretical work, and the second issue at the end of March caused a minor sensation among those fortunate enough to secure a copy. As one learned observer put it, such views 'if more openly known would rid him of all his places in Church or College'.[2] It was ill luck for Bury that the moment of publication found him already involved in a dispute over the manner in which he had recently expelled one of the fellows of Exeter, James Colmer, on a charge of fornication. Soon the latter's counter-accusation of bribery, immorality and heresy brought the visitor of the college, Sir Jonathan Trelawny, bishop of Exeter, onto the scene. He, a former Student of Christ Church, now spurred on by Aldrich and Jane, determined to rid the university of a notorious heretic.[3] On 16 June he arrived at the college to hold a formal visitation. To his anger, the front gate was slammed in his face and Bury shouted that he was denied entrance. When the bishop and his servants forced their way in by a side-door, the rector and other fellows made a formal protest in the middle of the quadrangle in terms which provoked Trelawny into snatching the paper and treading it underfoot.[4] On 24 July he came again to complete his

[1]   *The Naked Gospel*, preface and pp. 4, 7, 8, 43 (2nd issue only) 49 (2nd issue only), 79.
[2]   E. Bernard-T. Smith, 22 Mar. and 1 Feb. 1690, Bodl. MS Smith 47, fos 60, 62.
[3]   Bernard-Smith, 9 Apr. 1690, ibid. fo 64: 'that Prelate threatens that he will expell the Rector'.
[4]   For the story see *Reg. Exeter Coll* pp. cxxix-xxxi. The two sides gave their versions in: J. Harrington, *An Account of the Proceedings of Jonathan, Lord Bishop of Exeter, in his late Visitation* (Oxford 1690); [A. Bury,] *The Account Examined* (London 1690); and A. Bury, *The Case of Exeter-Colledge Related and Vindicated* (London 1691).

visitation. He marched in solemn procession from Christ Church to find that this time Bury's enemies within the college had forced the gates from the inside. Upon 'the breaking of them open', reported one delighted observer, 'the opposite party went to fisty cuffs for about 3 or 4 minutes, which ended in the utter ruin and destruction of a great many caps and periwiggs'.[1] But in the following three days the bishop proceeded to execution: Bury's supporters were suspended, and the rector himself deposed and actually excommunicated for 'heresy, taking of bribes, and grievous incontinency'.[2] Soon the excitement spread to the university at large. When a body of sixty MAs petitioned the vice-chancellor for formal action against *The Naked Gospel* he had no alternative but to refer the work to a commission of theologians.[3] Professor Jane pretended to stand aside, but it was in fact he who drew up the text of a formal decree of condemnation which the hebdomadal board submitted to convocation.[4] There can be no doubt of the strength of feeling among the ordinary MAs. On 19 August even William Wake joined the troop of Christ Church men who went to condemn 'the impious and heretical propositions' of the book and who ordered it to be burned to ashes in the schools quadrangle.[5] It was not until 1696 that the destruction of Bury was completed by a decision of the house of lords in Trelawny's favour, but the case had already shown the university's fierce reaction in the face of any questioning of its learned expertise.

Of course, the burning of Bury's book did nothing to silence the theological conflict. Indeed, it provoked a spate of acrimonious literature from real radicals and anticlericals like the Socinians Stephen Nye and Thomas Firmin. Oxford found itself continually held up to execration as an enemy to free and 'reasonable' inquiry. One pamphlet worked itself into a fury over 'Academick Inquisitors (like supream infallible Tribunals) burning Articles and Books, afterwards embracing and practising the very same; expelling and recalling, canting and recanting . . . very angry that the laity would not believe things against their Sense and Reason'.[6] Soon answers and counter-answers were being composed on all sides, giving Oxford a superb opportunity to demonstrate the kind of patristic learning at which it excelled, and its opponents a chance to denounce it all as outmoded pedantry. In the midst of all this, early in 1691, Bury issued out a revised and completely rewritten version of his book. Disingenuously he attempted to claim that this, with two wholly new chapters on the trinity

[1] T. Crosthwaite-Smith [27 July 1690], Bodl. MS Smith 48, fo 339.
[2] Bernard-Smith, 27 July 1690, Bodl. MS Smith 47, fo 66.
[3] Same-same, 17 Aug. 1690, ibid. fo 70.
[4] Wood, *Life and Times* iii. 338.
[5] Wake-Charlett, 2 Apr. 1691 MS Ballard 3, fo 58; T. Crosthwaite-Smith, 29 Aug. 1690 Bodl. MS Smith 48, fo 337.
[6] *An Historical Vindication of the Naked Gospel* (np 1690), preface.

and the resurrection, represented his real opinion in doctrinal matters. But, as one learned critic put it bluntly, it was 'quite another Book', and the only effect was to inaugurate a new round in the pamphlet warfare.[1] In such a state of theological agitation it was as easy for an incautious friend to run into trouble as an actual enemy, and this was the fate which befell William Sherlock, dean of St Paul's and master of the Temple. Sherlock was a controversialist of formidable learning and literary power. In 1690 he undertook to confute Nye and Firmin in a work which he imagined would establish him as the foremost champion of orthodoxy. But his *Vindication of the Doctrine of the Holy and Ever-Blessed Trinity* at once ran into terrible trouble with the Oxford pundits. The cause of his offending lay in his abandonment of patristic language in favour of a more modern terminology with a Cartesian flavour. Instead of 'terms of art, such as Nature, Essence, Substance, Subsistence, Hypostasis, Person, and the like' he preferred to write of 'self-consciousness' for the basis of personality and 'mutual consciousness' for the co-inherence of the divine persons in the trinity.[2] But to the Oxford theologians this was nothing more than an attack on the theology of the schools and, worse, it smacked of tritheism. So in 1693 Robert South, canon of Christ Church, launched himself into thunderous *Animadversions upon Dr. Sherlock's Book*.[3] To a modern reader his attack seems exaggerated and misdirected. For all the novelty of his expressions, Sherlock was dealing with real doctrinal problems while South was demanding a strict adherence to patristic language under pain of anathema. Certainly this was how the matter appeared to a young but exceptionally learned fellow of University College named Joseph Bingham. Preaching in the university pulpit on 28 October 1693 he set about South with some boldness, arguing that it was absurd to maintain that the terminology even of the fathers was final in setting forth the mystery of the trinity. Such impertinence from a young man at once set the Christ Church machine in motion. Bingham was delated before the hebdomadal board, and on 25 November the heads issued out a formal censure of two propositions (identical with those of Sherlock) which the sermon was alleged to have maintained.[4] On 23 November, to avoid the loss of his degrees, Bingham thought it prudent to resign his fellowship and retreat to a small country living. The university thus lost the presence in Oxford of the man who between 1708 and 1711 published *Origines ecclesiasticae*, perhaps the most learned work of early ecclesiastical history published before the nineteenth century. But this time the Oxford theologians had overreached themselves. Sherlock, a Cambridge man,

---

[1] T. Long, *An Answer to a Socinian Treatise, call'd The Naked Gospel* (London 1691), preface.

[2] W. Sherlock, *Vindication of the Doctrine of the Holy and Ever-Blessed Trinity* (London 1690), 48, 81.

[3] R. South, *Animadversions upon Dr. Sherlock's Book* (London 1693).

[4] Wood, *Life and Times* iii. 492. For the text of the sermon see *The Works of the Rev. Joseph Bingham*, ed. R. Bingham (9 vols London 1840, new edn 10 vols London 1855) x.

published an insolent reply;[1] and just before Christmas 1695 the vice-chancellor was horrified to receive a message from the king, conveyed by the archbishop of Canterbury. He was informed that the decree of the hebdomadal board had been referred to the judges who had unanimously pronounced it 'a High Usurpation upon his Majesty's Prerogative and a manifest violation of the Laws of this Realm'.[2] The following 23 February King William issued out a set of directions commanding an end to all preaching, writing and disputing over the doctrine of the trinity.

The year 1696 was thus a low point for the morale of the university's theologians and roused them and their country clerical followers to frustrated anger at what they conceived to be an imminent danger to orthodoxy and traditional learning. In 1695 the licensing act had been allowed to expire and at once a flood of heterodox and insultingly anticlerical literature poured forth onto the popular book-market. Among the most notorious of the new writers was John Toland, whose *Christianity Not Mysterious*, published in 1696, set the clerical world in an uproar. Actually written while the author was living in Oxford, it was a brutal, frontal assault on the value of academic theology. Christianity, it was asserted, was simple, reasonable and agreeable to the common notions of unlearned men, who had no need of professors or priests:

> How many voluminous Systems, infinitely more difficult than the Scripture, must be read with great Attention by him that would be Master of the present Theology? What prodigious Number of barbaric Words, (mysterious no doubt) what tedious and immethodical Directions, what ridiculous and discrepant Interpretations must you patiently learn and observe, before you can begin to understand a Professor of that Faculty?[3]

It was a sense of an expertise and a profession derided which now gave the impulse to the famous convocation controversy. In its essential features Francis Atterbury's *Letter to a Convocation-Man* (1697) was a Christ Church tract which finds its place among the other Oxford contributions to the trinitarian dispute, and was a response to the king's peremptory command to silence. It was an appeal for a sitting and acting convocation to deal authoritatively with a situation which the universities could no longer control. It was directed against Sherlock and Bingham as much as against Locke and Toland. There was 'an universal Conspiracy amongst a sort of Men under the Style of Deists, Socinians, Latitudinarians, Deniers of Mysteries, and pretending Explainers of them, to undermine and

---

[1] [W. Sherlock,] *A Modest Examination of the Oxford Decree* (np [1695]), 46: 'these heads; Decreeing, Heresy-making Heads'; J. Edwards, *Remarks upon the Examination of the Oxford Decree* (Oxford 1695), 3: 'he hath treated the Governors of the University with great insolence and contempt'. See also Lancaster-Charlett, 28 Dec. 1695, MS Ballard 21, fo 62: 'it will be very hard if he escape after he has treated the Learning and even the Latin of the place with so much Ignorance and disdain'.

[2] Tenison-F. Adams, 24 Dec. 1695, BL Add. MS 799, fo 149.

[3] [J. Toland,] *Christianity Not Mysterious* (London 1696), p. xxiv.

overthrow the Catholick, Faith'. The authority of the universities had been rendered ineffective or Toland 'had not else in publick Conversations dispersed his pernicious Notions in one of 'em so long as he did unpunished'. Such power as they had had been used 'not without some difficulty and Check, and have, when exercis'd, been pursu'd always with the Calumnies and Outcries of the whole Party'.[1]

With the meeting of convocation in 1701 the attempt of university and clergy to enforce traditional orthodoxy was in large measure transferred to the assembly at Westminster, and there the struggle was brought to nothing by the deadlock between the two houses. After 1701 Archbishop Tenison and his episcopal brethren were in great difficulty. Many of them shared to the full a detestation of writers like Toland, Anthony Collins and William Whiston, but they were well aware that no government was prepared to allow the kind of heresy-hunt which could so easily inflame the politics of the day. It was obvious, too, that the Oxford pundits were as concerned to pay off old scores as to defend a traditional learning. Indeed, their attempt to initiate synodical censures against Sherlock, Bingham and Burnet led many, including conservative theologians like George Bull,[2] to throw their weight against any kind of action. Gradually, with the failure of convocation, a new situation came into being; and it became apparent that the universities, like the church, could no longer claim to represent the 'official' ideology of English government and society. If their learning was still widely accepted as a conservative and stabilizing element in the national life, it had ceased to command universal acceptance. Thus in the course of Anne's reign something of the old assertiveness went out of Oxford theology. After 1703 William Jane was slowly dying, and in 1708 he was succeeded as regius professor by John Potter, a scholar whose politics made him wholly averse to any campaign against theological deviation. With the passing of champions like Jane, South and Jonathan Edwards, the heroic age of Oxford patristic learning drew to a close. The young continued to be instructed in traditional theology but the scholarly emphasis moved towards a philosophical divinity, intended to defend the Christian faith against the arguments of contemporary deists. Of this, Joseph Butler's *Analogy of Religion* was the most famous example.[3] By the mid-eighteenth century it was possible for writers like Conyers Middleton, Benjamin Hoadly and Richard Watson to ignore the argument from historical tradition and to treat the fathers with a lofty condescension as representing the opinion

[1] [F. Atterbury,] *Letter to a Convocation-Man* (London 1697), 6, 12; cf G. V. Bennett, 'Against the Tide: Oxford under William III', pp. 51-2 above.

[2] George Bull (1634-1710), m. Exeter 1648; bp of St David's 1705-10.

[3] J. Butler, *Analogy of Religion* (London 1736). Joseph Butler (1692-1752), m. Oriel 1715; bp of Bristol 1738-50, Durham 1750-2.

of a remote and crabbed age.[1] The contempt in which educated men of the Enlightenment held both academic theology and the clerical profession worked a severe loss of confidence in both universities, and is itself sufficient to account for their decline in numbers and their retreat from playing a major role in national affairs.

---

[1] N. Sykes, *From Sheldon to Secker* (Cambridge 1939), ch. 5; G. V. Bennett, 'Patristic tradition in Anglican thought, 1660-1900' in G. Gassmann and V. Vajta (eds), *Tradition in Luthertum und Anglikanismus; Oecumenica* 1971/2 (Gütersloh 1972).

13

Religion in the University 1715-1800

R. GREAVES

WHILE eighteenth-century Oxford was not wholly uninfluenced by developments which had led to questioning of the established order in the Church of England and criticism of the rescripts of orthodox theology, for the most part it remained firmly entrenched behind its ramparts of conventional religious observance and traditional divinity. With its sister-university, Cambridge, oxford continued to be a main supplier of ministers for the established church, and a majority of its graduates were destined for holy orders. The greatest number of the fellows of its colleges were in priest's orders or under obligation to proceed to them and many were to find their future career in preferment to a college living. Almost all the heads of houses were also in orders.[1]

Thomas Secker, first as bishop of Oxford (1737-58) and then as archbishop of Canterbury (1758-68) was, like his predecessors, clearly not satisfied with the preparation commonly afforded to ordinands in the two universities which were the seminaries of the national church. He told the clergy of his diocese in 1766: 'You will earnestly labour to complete yourselves in all proper knowledge; not merely the introductory kinds, which unhappily are often almost the only ones, taught the candidates for holy orders; but those chiefly, which have a closer connection with your work.'[2]

Besides the furnishing of the clerical mind, he was concerned also with the formation of the clerical character. 'Form yourselves therefore thoroughly by devout meditations and fervent prayer, to seriousness of heart, and zeal for the eternal welfare of souls'.[3] In Secker's view, clerical

---

[1] In 1760 all the heads of houses were DD and two of them, the provost of Oriel (Chardin Musgrave, 1723-68, m. Oriel 1740, provost 1757-68) and the master of Pembroke (John Ratcliff, 1700-75, m. Pemb. 1718, master 1739-75) had canonries annexed to their offices, the provost at Rochester and the master at Gloucester (the latter union lasted until 1938). William Cleaver, the principal of Brasenose (1785-1809) was from 1788 to 1809 bishop successively of Chester, Bangor and St Asaph; and John Parsons, the master of Balliol (1798-1819) was from 1813 to 19 also bishop of Peterborough. Both these men wee efficient hads and promoted university reform, particularly of examinations: see V. H. H. Green, 'Reformers and reform in the university' below.

[2] *The Works of Thomas Secker, LL.D.* ed. T. Hardy (4 vols London 1805) iv. 191.

[3] Ibid.

persons should live clerically, and not like laymen. 'Fellows of Colleges should be men of collegiate Dispositions', which for him meant clerical dispositions.[1] His was the old doctrine, with many years of life before it, that the universities were not only academies of learning but also schools of Christian *askesis*, of Christian mortification.[2]

To all appearances the two universities were magnificently equipped for the training of the clergy. Each was replete with chapels, churches and clerics. The gentlemen were bound to statutory religious observances by the Laudian code of 1636, and besides the chaplains, catechists and tutors in the colleges in both universities there were the professors of divinity and at each of them a regius professor appointed by the crown who was also head of the theological school. At Oxford in addition there was the Lady Margaret professor, elected by the doctors and bachelors of divinity on the books, as well as professors of Hebrew and Greek and Archbishop Laud's and the lord almoner's professors of Arabic. In the libraries stood serried rows of works by the fathers (the finest continental editions richly represented), these last, in the words of a regius professor, 'remarkable for Invention, for Argumentation, for Oratory, for their Depth and Penetration in Judgement',[3] as well as a fair sprinkling of less orthodox writers. There were also substantial manuscript collections in the old oriental tongues, which were regarded as necessary for the serious study of the Christian scriptures.

In his celebrated Act sermon of 1733, well before he became bishop of Oxford, Secker had enlarged upon the advantages enjoyed by the English universities over those of Europe, such as Paris and Leiden; academies which, as a medical student, he had known at first hand, and where he had spent almost as many years as he had months at Oxford. He laid great stress on English college-residence and tutorial supervision; he had himself been fortunate in having as his tutor at Exeter college the redoubtable and orthodox John Conybeare. In Oxford, he pointed out, there were means helpful 'to preserve ... that Temperance of living, Simplicity of Appearance, and Frugality of Expence, which are usually brought hither ... which keep the Mind in fit Temper for the Exercise of its Faculties, and defend it from the Corruptions of Luxury and Vanity' as well as from youthful indiscretion and unguarded conduct, such as 'will be treasured up in many a malicious Memory to their future Disadvantage'.[4]

Like the dissenting academies, the two universities were at once places for the training of religious teachers and of education for laymen. Two

[1] T. Secker-G. Onslow, 24 Feb. 1762, Lambeth Palace Library, VV 1/4/5/22.
[2] See for example G. Herbert, *A Priest to the Temple* (London 1671), ch. 2; *The Works of George Herbert*, ed. F. E. Hutchinson (Oxford 1941), 226.
[3] Manuscript notes on lectures in divinity read by Edward Bentham, Bodl. MS Top. Oxon. e.225.
[4] T. Secker, *Fourteen Sermons preached on Several Occasions* (London 1766), 'Sermon preached before the University of Oxford on Act Sunday, July 8, 1733', pp. 23, 25.

conflicting types of criticism were directed at them in contemporary literature. According to the one, university men were represented as monkish, narrow, devoid of social grace and lacking in civility, a convention fortified by Hogarth's savage cartoon of 1737 which pilloried the coarse, bucolic and cunningly stupid faces at the lecture of Henry Fisher, the university registrar.[1] According to the other they were wealthy, luxurious and worldly, and though the worldly were largely the lay element, some of those intending to enter the church were also among them, particularly as the social status of the clergy rose during the eighteenth century.

The provision made by the university for formal instruction in divinity had behind it centuries of academic tradition. Divinity, as the queen of the sciences, was to be approached by the uninstructed only after sufficient groundwork had been laid in humane studies. It was accepted that previous qualifications for embarking on a study of the Christian faith were 'a due knowledge of the rules of right reasoning, and of the moral and religious truths which nature teaches; of the state of the world in its earlier ages, and in that when Christianity first appeared'. Then and then only, should come the professional and 'diligent search into Holy Scripture'.[2] For that reason there were no university exercises in theology for the degrees of BA or MA. Formal theological training was the business of the higher faculty. When once the MA was achieved, first the BD and then the DD could follow, though only a small minority of those entering the church proceeded to the higher faculty, and if they did they no longer obtained from the university the traditional instruction for it. This did not, however, mean that religious education was intended to be neglected while the students' formal university studies took their course. On the contrary, whether they wished to take holy orders or enter worldly pursuits their religious education rested, according to the Laudian code, with the tutors in the colleges.[3] The latter consequently provided a religious framework for the daily life of all their undergraduate members, and such religious instruction as they, the tutors, *in loco parentis*, thought suitable for them; prospective ordinands being taught not in clerical separateness but together with men who had in view secular pursuits.

Edward Bentham, who first as fellow and tutor of Oriel, then as canon of Christ Church and ultimately regius professor of divinity, dedicated himself for forty-five years to achieving Secker's ideals of clerical education and drew up schemes of self-examination both for teachers and taught. He asked himself:

---

[1] See for example W. Darrell, *The Gentleman Instructed in the Conduct of a Virtuous and Happy Life* (London 1720), 2-3. R. Paulson, *Hogarth's Graphic Works* (2 vols New Haven and London 1965), no. 154 (cat. no. 143). In 1766 Secker commented on the curious way in which some, getting into country parishes, 'acquire uncouth accents one knows not how': *Works of Secker*, ed. Hardy iv. 200.

[2] Ibid. iv. 67, charges to the clergy 1738.

[3] *Laudian Code* III.2, ed. Griffiths, p. 31 (Latin text); *Statutes*, trans. Ward i. 15 (English).

What are the Amusements and diversions in which I delight? Are they proper for a Clergyman?

Are the times of my lecturing fixed and stated?

Do I give them any stated Lectures on the Subject of Religious Knowledge?

Do I give them a good Example by my constant Attendance upon the University Sermon?

Do I leave them to shift for themselves?

Upon what Principle is my remissness founded? . . . because I would maintain the character of being gentleman-like and good-natured?[1]

He had always striven at Oriel to give his pupils a fair impression of the Bible as a whole, and of the New Testament in Greek, with due attention to the period between the Testaments. Even an elementary study of the Greek Testament could not be taken for granted. All too often men came up from their grammar schools poorly trained in the classical languages.[2] Westminster scholars in their first year at Christ Church were encouraged to take Hebrew not only because they had studied it at school but also on the grounds that they were likely to be more advanced in their Greek than pupils from other schools.[3] But all undergraduates (one suspects even Edward Gibbon under his first tutor at Magdalen[4]) received some sort of informal instruction in divinity and, in the last years of the century, Edward Tatham, a highly critical observer, thought the colleges generally had provided reasonably for their men. Contrasting the uselessness of the university with the activity in the colleges, he went so far as to commend the tutors for their 'more modern and useful learning'.[5]

Basic religious training of the undergraduates therefore depended primarily on the conscientiousness of their tutors, and on the whole, as much family correspondence shows, a lofty tutorial ideal survived. John Conybeare supervised his gentlemen-commoners and 'sojourners' at Exeter more vigorously than Gibbon's amiable and devout Mr Walde-

---

[1] *A Sketch of Academical Institution, to which is subjoined a Self-Examination* (London 1761), identified by Secker as Bentham's in the manuscript table of contents of a volume of pamphlets bound together in Lambeth Palace Library.

[2] See the savage comments of Edward Tatham, *The Chart and Scale of Truth* (2 vols Oxford 1790) ii. 115; and for the decay of grammar schools, L. Stone, 'The size and composition of the Oxford student body 1580–1909' in L. Stone (ed.), *The University in Society* (2 vols Princeton 1975) i. 11, 51.

[3] P. Quarrie, 'Christ Church collection books', pp. 502–3 below.

[4] Thomas Waldegrave (1711–84), m. Linc. 1728; degrees Magd. Gibbon refers to him as 'one of the best of the tribe': E. Gibbon, *Memoirs of My Life*, ed. G. A. Bonnard (London 1966), 54–5. Waldegrave had been a pupil of Wesley, who held the strongest views on tutorial responsibility: see Green, 'Reformers and reform', 611. Waldegrave, a very pious man, spent much time walking round Shotover talking to his difficult pupil. Such conversations, given his interests, must almost certainly have been largely on religious topics, and it may be noted that Gibbon was well informed about Oxford views on recent theological controversies: Gibbon, *Memoirs*, ed. Bonnard, p. 55.

[5] E. Tatham, *A Letter to the . . . Dean of Christ-Church respecting the new Statute upon Public Examination* (Oxford 1807), 5–6, citing his *Chart and Scale of Truth* i. 363–70.

grave. Some colleges, although not all, maintained a continuous tradition of care for students which extended throughout the century, as for example Corpus, where it was notably exemplified for twelve years (1721–33) by John Burton and was continued by his successors.[1] Edward Bentham looked back, years later, on his old tutor with admiration.[2] But if they had a certain success with the teaching of their undergraduates in religious knowledge as well as in subjects in the curriculum, they were less successful when it came to their graduates. Despite the fact that the university did not even purport to provide formal theological training for young graduates until after they had taken their MA degree, it was expected that at the age of 23 those who were to enter the church would be able to appear prepared for a professional examination in theology for deacon's orders. This meant that many, if not most, young men did whatever systematic reading they undertook in theology before they completed their MA. It was at this point that one of the most serious weaknesses of the educational system appeared. While colleges, in accordance with the precepts of the Laudian code, placed all their undergraduates under tutors and these drew tutorial fees from them, no such arrangement was made for the bachelors, though their former tutors might continue to take a friendly interest in them. The colleges, it is true, tried to arrange for disputations in divinity between BAs and resident MAs, particularly in the earlier years of the century, and sometimes laid down a condition that reading in theology should be undertaken before their candidates were presented for the degree of MA. But these efforts were for the most part feeble and they proved ineffective, if only because their efficacy depended on the bachelors being in residence, and though some colleges were successful in imposing a good deal of residence on their foundationers, the steady decline in the length of residence imposed on bachelors reading for an MA meant that arrangements made in Oxford for their instruction were frequently circumvented.

The maintenance of the professional standards of ordination depended, of course, not on the university or colleges, but on the individual bishops or those they appointed to conduct the examinations. The ordinal, the canons, the laws gave only general directions: that the candidates must have reached 23 years of age, be of certified virtuous life and good reputation, competent in Latin and sufficiently versed in scripture. Besides the basic scriptural knowledge the young man was supposed to have had some instruction in the liturgy, the thirty-nine articles and even ecclesiastical history, particularly of the reformation, sufficient to defend the tenets of the Church of England against papists, sectaries and enthusiasts. While some bishops' examinations were no

[1] John Burton (1696–1771), m. CCC 1713, fellow 1721.
[2] E. Bentham, *De vitâ et moribus Johannis Burtoni, S.T.P.* (Oxford 1771), 12.

doubt perfunctory, others were more demanding. James Woodforde of New College found his examination for deacon's orders in 1763 at the hands of the chaplain of the bishop of Oxford no trifling affair. He was called on to construe a difficult passage in the middle of Romans 5 and was asked a good many hard and deep 'Quaestions'. 'I had not one Quaestion that yes, or no, would answer ... Mr Hewish is a very fair Examiner, and will see whether a Man be read or not soon.'[1]

Every university man offering himself for ordination had to bring a *testimonium* from his college or hall certifying his fitness. Archbishop Wake had given instructions as to the nature of these 'letters testimonial' and John Potter when bishop of Oxford had taken considerable pains to ensure that they were observed.[2] Up to a point the colleges tended to take the responsibility seriously;[3] they usually issued testimonials exclusively to graduates, refused them to men of bad character or with whom the college had lost touch, and tried to ensure that they were given under the college seal and not by individuals,[4] but they tended to take a detached view as to the candidates' professional qualifications. How far this was true at different colleges at different times during the century will be examined more fully in the next chapter which concentrates on developments within the colleges as distinct from those in the university. Here it is necessary to make two points: first that though no place was found for theological education in the university's arts curriculum as laid down by statute, the university played a striking and all-pervasive part in the provision of a religious atmosphere for all its members, lay and clerical; and secondly that in the second half of the century Edward Bentham, sponsored by Secker, introduced a striking innovation in the provision of theological instruction for intending ordinands.

The statutory duties of the regius and the Lady Margaret professors of divinity had by the nature of their positions nothing to do with the instruction of undergraduates or bachelors. Their concern had been solely with the higher faculty of theology. So long as the annual 'Acts'

---

[1] *Woodforde at Oxford* 129-30 (23 May 1763). As to Romans 5, Woodforde would have been well prepared by a careful reading of Gilbert Burnet's *Exposition of the Thirty-Nine Articles of the Church of England* (London 1720), 136-48.

[2] Potter-Wake, 8 Oct. 1723, Wake MS 22, fo 248.

[3] There were of course exceptions. For instance E. Jones of Jesus wrote to the principal on 17 March 1729: 'I knew Williams was an arrant block-head before I signed his testimonium, and I told him so and cautioned him not to appear before the Bishop of St Asaph till he was better provided, but I was obliged to sign his Testimonium for Peace sake because if I had refused it would have been interpreted as a piece of spite and malice against his Tutor and some of his other Friends in College, and they would be sure to be upsides with me whenever a pupil of mine should appear.' JCA box 3. At St John's, on the other hand, it was resolved on 23 July 1742 that every candidate under the standing of MA or BCL should 'submit himself to an examination by such persons as the Convention should appoint, before his Testimonium is granted': SJM register 1730-94, p. 137.

[4] There was a dispute on this issue at Exeter in 1720 between the rector and the fellows: ECA box L.I.5, visitor's decrees 1673-1810.

continued the professors had to take the leading part in the disputations of the graduating doctors of divinity who were the major participants. During the long illness of William Jane (regius professor 1680-1707) one of the chief reasons given why an Act could not be held was his incapacity to oppose in the annual disputations.[1] The regius professor had also to play his part in the other disputations in which every inceptor in theology had to prove his quality. He had to lecture to those proceeding to this highest of university honours, and in addition by his sermons, his publications and his opinions on theological matters he was the recognized head of the faculty for which the university was peculiarly famous.

But by the early years of the century the situation had changed; the Act had given way to the Encaenia where theology had no pride of place. The lectures and the disputations for those qualifying had ceased to be of significance or even for the most part to exist at all. From the point of view of the instruction going on in the university the duties imposed on the professors had now become negligible. Some of the incumbents of the chair, such as Robert Sanderson, had done more than was required of them, but not until Secker as archbishop concerned himself with the question was any systematic instruction in divinity provided by the university (as distinct from the colleges) for resident BAs intended for the church.[2] It was when John Fanshawe[3] died in 1763 and the office of regius professor of divinity became vacant that Secker, who saw in Edward Bentham a man more likely than any other to carry out such a scheme of instruction, immediately promoted his claims, representing him to ministers as 'a very good Scholar and Divine: hath always been a hearty Friend to the Government'.[4] 'I have got Dr Bentham', he wrote in May 1763,

against his will, the professorship of Divinity: for who might have got it else, I could not tell: and the Dean of Christ Church wished for Him: and as the Duke of Marlborough wanted a Canonry for Mr Moore, the procuring of it was easy. But they have, I think very unkindly forced Dr Bentham to quit his good House for an extremely bad one, and to become Junior Canon, though the only parallel Case was that of Dr Allestree 100 years ago: and he kept both his former Canonry and his House. I am sorry for poor Bentham: but I am glad for the University.[5]

[1] For example OUA register of convocation 1703-30, p. 36, 19 June 1707.

[2] Bentham had a fondness for lists of great names, but mentioned only two of his predecessors in the *praelectio* whose examples he wished to emulate: Robert Sanderson (1588-1663, m. Linc. 1603, regius prof. of divinity 1642-8, 1660-1; bp of Linc. 1660-3) and John Potter; E. Bentham, *De studiis theologicis* (Oxford 1767), 9.

[3] John Fanshawe (1698-1763), m. Ch.Ch. 1716; regius prof. divinity 1741-63.

[4] Secker-G. Grenville, 10 May 1763, BL Stowe MS 119, fo 152. He probably did not remember, or perhaps chose to forget, that in the university election of 1737 Bentham had voted as a tory; *Exact Account of the Poll . . . between . . . Trevor . . . and Wm Bromley esq.* (London [1737]); see also P. Langford, 'Tories and Jacobites', pp. 118-19 above.

[5] Secker-R. H. Drummond, 31 May 1763, York, Borthwick Inst. of Hist. Research, MS Bp. C. & P. VII (20C/68). Richard Allestree (1621-80), m. Ch.Ch. 1637; regius prof. divinity 1663-80. The dean

Bentham, as might be expected from his record as a college tutor, entered on his new duties as regius professor with a deep sense of the importance of his office, applying to himself, with a moving eloquence, II Corinthians 2.16: 'Who is sufficient for these things?'[1]

In 1764 at Secker's suggestion he offered a series of lectures covering the whole body of divinity to be given three times a week without charge to all 'Students from Three to Seven Years Standing, as came recommended by their Tutors or Governors'.[2] In all, he gave in his course between sixty and seventy lectures occupying the larger part of the academic year. Just how revolutionary this proposal was, his first announcement, issued from Christ Church on 3 July 1764, shows: 'But it is hoped that no Person will make his Attedance on the Lectures a pretence for neglecting any Duty or Exercise to which he may be called by the Rules of his College.'[3] Secker gave him money for books to distribute to the poorer part of his audience.[4]

To judge by one surviving, incomplete set of notes on Bentham's lectures they repeat, not unnaturally, sentiments—even continuous passages—found in his printed works.[5] On basic doctrine he was ortho-dox. Speaking as a professor nominally to BAs, he emphasized the importance of an accurate understanding of the biblical languages, important even for the expositions of the ordinary parochial clergyman. There was an old and strong Oxford tradition of close study in the biblical and other oriental languages, represented at this time in the monumental labours of Kennicott on the Hebrew text of the Old Testament, probably the most considerable exercise in the collation of biblical manuscripts of the century.[6]

Close textual study was the more important because, as he told his pupils, 'the Transcribers were not certainly inspired by the Holy Ghost . . . often they might be nodding . . . many of them adapted their Copies to

was David Gregory and the duke's friend was John Moore. The unkind treatment of Bentham suggests that a majority in the chapter had their own candidate, but had been defeated by Secker's promptitude. Bentham's reduction to the status of junior canon must have seemed particularly invidious, as in 1760 he had been pressed to serve a sixth year in the burdensome office of subdean: Bentham-Newcastle, 5 Jan. 1760, BL Add. MS 32901, fo 100. 'Mrs Bentham . . . seems very sorry she is oblig'd to part with her house and Garden as there is so little or no Garden to their new house, and her whole delight seems to be in one': J. Bentham-his father, 19 June 1763, *The Correspondence of Jeremy Bentham*, ed. T. L. S. Sprigge *et al*. (London and Oxford 1968 onward) i. 76-7.

[1] E. Bentham, *De studiis theologicis* (Oxford 1764), 4.

[2] E. Bentham, *Reflexions upon the Study of Divinity* (Oxford 1771), advertisement.

[3] For the announcement see Bodl. G.A. Oxon. b.19, no. 152. See also Bentham, *Reflexions*, advertisement: '. . . at Seven o'clock on Sunday, Wednesday, and Friday-Evenings; so that the number of Lectures in the whole are between Sixty and Seventy. In this course I have now proceeded for more than Eight Years, and it is my purpose to continue it so long as God shall give me health.'

[4] Lambeth Palace Lib. MS 2598, fos 62-3 (£20 in 1765, £21 in 1766).

[5] Notes by Henry Hall (1749-1839, m. Queen's 1768) in Bodl. MS Top. Oxon. e.226.

[6] See D. Patterson, 'Hebrew studies', p. 540 below; I. G. Philip, 'Libraries and the University Press', p. 735 below.

their particular Tenets and Systems of Religion, as had been the Case in the Romish Church in regard to the Fathers'.[1] Towards the fathers of the church, who in Oxford had been generally regarded as of great authority on the interpretation of scripture, his attitude was much like Secker's: to treat them with respect but not excessive veneration, and as having the more weight the nearer they were to the apostles' time. He, like Robert Sanderson, thought better of the great medieval doctors than did many of his contemporaries, particularly on moral questions. He strongly urged the study of the *Secunda secundae* of Aquinas.[2] Nor did he neglect more recent thought. He seems to have been not at all afraid of scientists, such as Newton, Boyle, Ray, Wallis, Hales and James Bradley, men in whom, he said in his inaugural lecture, theology rejoices.[3] It was practical and useful that his course provided for some instruction in the laws of the land, so far as these affected, under the legal establishment, the clergy as ministers and as possessed of ecclesiastical property.[4] There were also, as was only to be expected, the characteristic objections to papists, schismatics and enthusiasts.[5] Bentham did not apparently feel himself capable of providing for gentlemen seeking holy orders an exposition of Anglican divinity comparable in learning and urbanity with Blackstone's account of English law, though it is significant that the parallel occurred to him. He could but hope that 'some man of Genius and Learning ... may apply his powers to build up a system of Divinity for the use of younger Students, with the same comprehensiveness of matter and accuracy of disposition ... which remarkably distinguish the pages of our Law-Commentator'.[6]

We do not know how influential Bentham's lectures were in the university, how many took advantage of them nor from which colleges his students came. We do know, however, that by the beginning of the nineteenth century attendance at the lectures he had founded was demanded as a prerequisite for the acceptance of all Oxford men for ordination not only by the bishop of Oxford but by others. Bentham was essentially a middle-of-the-road man but one who gave good service to his university. As a pro-government pamphleteer he was evidently well

---

[1] Henry Hall's notes, fo 135.

[2] Hall's notes, fos 29-30. He also thought well of Peter Lombard's Sentences, as 'a very useful and celebrated Book, grounded upon the Scriptures and collected from the Fathers', though even here metaphysics was creeping in.

[3] Bentham, *Praelectio*, 18-17: 'Sed ea propero, quorum subsidiis, arctiori quodam necessitudinis vinculo, gaudet Theologia.' James Bradley (1693-1762), m. Balliol 1711, Savilian prof. astronomy 1721-63, prof. experimental phil. 1749-60.

[4] Bentham, *Reflexions*, p. xv.

[5] In 1757 Bentham refused to sign the evangelical Thomas Haweis's testimonial for orders. Secker's objection to ordaining Haweis was tempered by George Berkeley (m. Ch.Ch. 1752), one of Secker's protégés, and he was finally privately ordained deacon at Cuddeson by Secker along with George Berkeley, Samuel Glasse (1735-1812, m. Ch.Ch. 1752) and Charles Poyntz (1735-1808, m. Ch.Ch. 1752). See A. S. Wood, *Thomas Haweis 1734-1820* (London 1957), 54-6.

[6] Bentham, *Reflexions*, p. xxi.

thought of, though his mild and civil approach contrasted with the more
flamboyant style of his tory opponents. As a logician he was, as Professor
Yolton shows, by no means negligible.[1] In his later years he refused to join
the vice-chancellor in sitting in judgement on the St Edmund Hall
Methodists, and in the crucial debate in convocation on subscription to
the thirty-nine articles in 1772 he spoke so quietly that he was not heard.

His successor, Benjamin Wheeler, continued the lectures and,
according to John James of Queen's, the restriction against students of less
than three years' standing was relaxed. Writing to his father on 5 November 1779 young James said:

We have a divinity lecture every Sunday and Wednesday evening, by Dr Wheeler,
at Christ Church. In his advertisements last spring he requested the attendance
of graduates, or those of three years' standing, alone. This prevented me from
going, save once or twice, at that time. But finding of late that his restriction, if
observed, would almost demolish his audience, I have, out of respect to him and
to myself, paid regular attendance.[2]

Wheeler's lectures were printed posthumously in 1819. In the introductory lecture he outlined his proposed course under three heads:
applicable to the divines of 'whatever local denomination' and 'proceeding upon the broad basis of scriptural truth'; applicable 'to the divine considered as a scholar, and as such desirous of becoming acquainted not only
with the grounds of his faith, but also with the precise meaning and
authenticity of those writings which profess to deliver it'; applicable 'to
the divine, as a member of the Church of England'.[3]

In the later years of the century when Wheeler's successor John
Randolph continued to deliver them, the lectures were attended by
George Valentine Cox, recently appointed esquire bedel of law. His judge-
ment, given later, was scathing:

Those lectures were then given late in the evening, by candle-light; one effect of
this (and not a very surprising one, considering the hour, the subject, and the
audience) was, that many of the class slept through the lecture, waking up now
and then at the sound of a Greek quotation ... Attendance, not attention (and
that very irregular attendance), was all that was required to obtain a certificate to
be presented to some bishop for ordination ... In short, the only things really
carried away by the majority of the class, were the Syllabus given to each one at
the commencement of the course, and a formidable printed list of authors recommended for future reading, presented at the close of the lectures.[4]

---

[1] J. Yolton, 'Scholars, logic and philosophy', below, for example pp. 572-3.

[2] *Letters of Radcliffe and James*, 93. Benjamin Wheeler (1733-83), m. Trin. 1751; fellow Magd. 1769;
prof. poetry 1766-76, Sedleian prof. nat. phil. 1767-82; canon Ch.Ch. and regius prof. divinity 1776-83.

[3] T. Horne, *The Theological Lectures of the late Rev. Benjamin Wheeler* (Oxford 1819), 14-15. Horne
refers in his preface to 'several courses in which the Lectures were delivered' (p. viii). He prints only
fifteen in the first volume, 'a promised second not being issued for want, it may be presumed, of
encouragement': Macray, *Reg. Magdalen* v. 105.

[4] G. V. Cox, *Recollections of Oxford* (London 1868, 2nd edn London 1870), 140. G. V. Cox

In May 1792 John Randolph printed a five-volume *Manual for the Use of Divinity Students*. In the preface he said that the intention was to 'lay before the Student in Divinity some short and comprehensive Tracts' which 'deserve to be frequently read and studied' and to 'shew the genuine sense of the Church of England in her earliest days, both as to the grounds of separation from the Church of Rome, and the Doctrines, which after a long struggle having entirely emancipated herself from that Yoke, she at length finally adopted and ratified'.[1]

The innovation of a university lecture intended for ordinands may have contributed less than was hoped to the religious life of the university. Of much greater significance to this life, however, were the statutory university sermons. Few topics were more carefully regulated by the Laudian code, and the eighteenth-century university tried hard to keep these regulations intact. The arrangements which the code incorporated, intended to provide the preaching of official sermons by senior members in holy orders for the edification of the rest of the university, were the culmination of a succession of sixteenth-century regulations (little changed in the code itself) designed to implement the puritan ideal of the teaching of the word.[2] The result was an elaborate framework of religious observances in which sermons played the predominant part and in which all members of the university were expected to be actively or passively involved.[3] Its foundation rested on two official university sermons preached every Sunday of the year, except on Easter Sunday when the morning sermon was replaced by one preached in the chapel of every college at its communion service.[4] There were also university sermons on the morning of every feast-day recognized by the Church of England; on each of a variety of public occasions (sometimes accompanied by music[5]) notably on the anniversaries of the accession of the reigning monarch, of the discovery of the gunpowder plot, the martyrdom of Charles I, the restoration of the monarchy and on special occasions such as national thanksgivings or fasts. There were also two sermons each year on Act

(1786-1875), m. New College 1802; esquire bedel of law 1806-66. John Randolph (1750-1813), son of Thomas Randolph; m. Ch.Ch. 1767, canon Ch.Ch. and regius prof. divinity 1783-1807.

[1] J. Randolph, *Manual for the Use of Divinity Students* (5 vols Oxford 1792) i, pp. iii, iv.

[2] In 1847 Dean Gaisford (1779-1855, m. Ch.Ch. 1797, dean 1831-55) gave the hebdomadal board a short but useful *Summary* of the origin of the system. A printed copy is to be found in G.A. Oxon. c.63 (81).

[3] Everyone was expected to attend these sermons, but no means of enforcement was provided, and indeed there was not enough church accommodation for such numbers.

[4] Though some college sermons were allowed to die out, these statutory ones were delivered in all colleges. As Parson Woodforde noted in 1763, 'all Colleges and halls have Sermons in their Chapels this day': *Woodforde at Oxford*, 118.

[5] Provision was made in the vice-chancellor's computus for 'special payment for the organist' (the professor of music) on 29 May (Restoration day) and on 5 November (Guy Fawkes day). On Restoration day 1691 'a new anthem and new service was sung in the organ loft by singing men and choristers': Wood, *Life and Times* iii. 362.

Sunday,[1] and two on the occasion of the visits of the judges of assize. After
the foundation of the Radcliffe Infirmary in 1770 an annual service of a
kind hitherto unknown in the university was set up, a charitable service
with a sermon (preferably preached by a distinguished visiting cleric) at
which alms for the new institution were regularly solicited from the
fashionable congregation which attended.[2] All these sermons were in
English, but there were also six sermons a year in Latin: one at the
beginning of each of the four terms, one on Ash Wednesday as part of the
ceremonies of the determination of BAs and one on the Tuesday after Act
Sunday which was supposed to mark the end of the academic year.[3]

These sermons were to be preached as a duty by senior members of the
university who were in holy orders, and for the most part the preachers'
names were taken by rota from two preaching cycles, in one of which each
man had his 'preaching turn'.[4] Unless there were special reasons to the
contrary they were to be preached in the university church of St Mary the
Virgin. Exceptions to this rule were made for all sermons by the dean and
canons of Christ Church as also for those on Christmas day, Good Friday,
Ascension day (traditionally preached by the dean), and a variety of other
feast-days which were allotted to certain specified colleges, and all
sermons in Lent and that on the afternoon of Easter Sunday, which as a
gesture to past university custom were preached in St Peter's in the East.[5]

The most prestigious of the routine sermons were those preached on
Sunday mornings during term. The preachers allotted for them were
taken from a small and highly select group of scholars consisting of the
heads of houses, the two professors of divinity and the professor of
Hebrew. All preachers nominated were permitted to 'sink their turn'[6] if
they wished, and arrange for a deputy or representative to preach in their
place. The preachers on Sunday afternoons in term-time and on both
Sunday mornings and afternoons out of term, as well as on all but the
most important feasts of the church, were chosen from a much wider
cycle, which included all doctors and bachelors of divinity, all doctors and
bachelors of civil law, provided they were in orders and (if BCLs) were of
over six years' standing in that degree, and all MAs in holy orders
provided they were of four years' standing. Those liable for service were

[1] Even after the disappearance of the Act 'Act Sunday' was still celebrated: *Jackson's Oxford Journal*,
8 July 1759.
[2] The Infirmary depended almost wholly on subscriptions and the sums taken at the sermon and
the concert which followed it were important. In 1790, for instance, the collection after the sermon by
the bishop of St David's brought in £148 15s 6d: ibid. 15 June 1790.
[3] These six sermons survived well into the nineteenth century: see *Oxford University Calendar*
(1849).
[4] Those with 'turns' in the smaller cycle by virtue of their office were also included in the bigger one
with all others of their academic standing. The names of some men appear in both cycles.
[5] *Laudian Code* XVI. 3, ed. Griffiths, pp. 157–8; *Statutes*, trans. Ward i. 169.
[6] For this term see OUA MR/10/1/1 and Bodl. Top. Oxon. e.66.

not confined to men in residence, but included all who had kept their names on their college books. These preachers too were permitted to arrange for deputies to carry out their duties. The esquire bedel of divinity was responsible for seeing that the vice-chancellor's *moneo* or warning was delivered to them in good time; in person if they were in Oxford or to their colleges if they were not.[1] He had also to ensure that a preacher was always available.

The preachers of all other English sermons, known as special or extraordinary sermons, and of all the Latin sermons were nominated *ad hoc* by the vice-chancellor,[2] though for convenience their names were often included in the bedel's lists. These occasions varied considerably in character. Two sermons which were preached on Shrove Sunday and the last Sunday in June were the only endowed university sermons until the Bampton lectures began in 1780. The chosen candidate had to preach on pride or humility taking a text from a preselected list.[3] For each he received 50s from the university. An odd arrangement in connection with the Easter sermons also came under the vice-chancellor's direct care. On Low Sunday a preacher was nominated to preach a 'repetition sermon' in which he collated from memory the sermons preached over the Easter feast-days, a feat of endurance greatly admired by his audience.[4] More important for the university's reputation were the two sermons on Act Sunday, where there was often a big congregation of visitors. Until the ceremony of the Act gave way to that of Encaenia, vice-chancellors tried to find preachers among those incepting for the doctorate on the occasion. On 8 July 1733, for instance, the last year in which a traditional Act took place, Hearne noted 'This being Act Sunday, the sermon was preached at St Marie's in the morning by Dr Cockman, Master of Univ. Coll., and in the afternoon by Dr Secker of Exeter Coll. both Inceptors, the Ladies both morning and afternoon sitting, as usual in Act time, in the Gentlemen's Galleries'.[5]

But at times when relations between church and state and university and government were tense, the choice of preachers for many of these special sermons taxed the political acumen and judgement of vice-chancellors to the utmost, and even when the preachers had been carefully chosen their words when they entered the pulpit might be unexpected and sometimes acutely embarrassing. The Laudian statutes had made provision for such indiscipline and placed special powers

---

[1] Though for convenience Christ Church preachers were included in the bedel's list, the *moneo* did not go out to them, and deputies for canons were sanctioned by the dean: Dean Gaisford's *Summary*.

[2] *Laudian Code* XVI. 4, ed. Griffiths, p. 158; *Statutes*, trans. Ward i. 170. Ward and Heywood, *Statutes* i. 170.

[3] It was endowed in 1684 by William Master (1627-84), m. Ch.Ch. 1647; fellow Merton 1651.

[4] Hearne frequently spoke with approbation of these sermons, as did Woodforde of one he attended in 1779: *Woodforde at Oxford*, 125.   [5] Hearne, *Collections* xi. 227.

(without appeal) in the hands of the vice-chancellor, and in the earlier years of the century vice-chancellors had to exercise them on several occasions. An acute case of difficulty in finding a preacher was experienced in June 1716 when a sermon was required for the thanksgiving for the crushing of the 1715 rebellion. Hearne reported:

It was very, very hard to get any one to preach. Many Guineas were offered. All refused, except one Dingley, Fellow of Corpus Christi College, a Man who some Years agoe (namely about sixteen or seventeen Years since) was pretty famous for Preaching, but since not, unless it be for his Dullness. This Dingley (commonly called Paul Dingley) undertook the Task at first, but having slept upon it one Night, he grew discontented, and got himself rid of the Burthen. Upon which the Vice-Chancellor, Dr John Barron, Master of Balliol College, and a very silly man, was put to his shifts to procure a Preacher. But being not able to succeed, he fixes upon Dr John Hudson, one that will do any thing for Money. The Dr undertakes to procure one, or else to do it himself, there being a Reward of nine Guineas, besides the Excuse of a common Turn. The Dr, therefore (who is principal of St Mary Hall), gets Mr Bromwich (who is his Vice-Principal) to do it for three, himself putting the other six Guineas into his own Pocket, and at the same time being excused a Turn, which excuse is equal to three Guineas more. Accordingly therefore Bromwich preached, like a Fool as he is, and the Dr ran away with nine Guineas, which he will look upon (as he does all Roguery) as a Piece of Cunning. The name of the Preacher was not stickt up as usual, the person that preached being ashamed of what he was to do, and not willing to have it known.[1]

When preachers used their opportunity to launch attacks on government policy, the vice-chancellor found himself in a difficult position. Hearne remarks that William Tilly's assize sermon before the judges in 1705, in which he attacked occasional conformity, was very much approved, but it was attacked both in the lords and in the commons and provided the university's foes with a pretext for a royal visitation of the two universities.[2] Sacheverell's famous sermon against 'perils among false brethren' escaped disciplinary action in the university when it was preached there on 23 December 1705, only to touch off a nation-wide movement when repeated before the lord mayor of London in 1709.[3] Complaints from ministers to the vice-chancellor about the content of university sermons were not uncommon and had to be taken up. Often little came of the inquiries but not all preachers so challenged were fortunate.[4] On 1 February 1727 vice-chancellor Mather summoned six

---

[1] Hearne, *Collections* v. 235. William Dingley (1673-1735), m. CCC 1691. Thomas Bromwich (1683-1724), m. Univ. 1698; vice-principal St Mary Hall 1713-24.
[2] Ibid. i. 10; W. R. Ward, *Georgian Oxford* (Oxford 1958) 27-8.
[3] See G. V. Bennett, 'The era of party zeal 1702-14', pp. 82-6 above.
[4] See Hearne, *Collections* vii. 24: 'Complaint being made above of the Sermon preached at St Marie's on the 29th May by Mr Warton of Magd. Coll., a Messenger came down last Night to urge the V.Chanc. to proceed against him. Accordingly, this Day, in the Afternoon, was a Meeting, in the

doctors of divinity to consider complaints against George Coningsby of St Mary Hall for his sermon on 30 January, on the grounds that it had given 'great offence not only to himself but to the audience, by reason of scandalous reflexions on the present Government and particularly on the bishops'. Coningsby like some others similarly challenged said he could produce neither a copy of the sermon nor notes on it. Less lucky than some of them, he was suspended from preaching within the university precincts. The vice-chancellor was promptly thanked by the secretary of state, Lord Townshend, for zeal so acceptable to his Majesty.[1]

A good deal of the lively interest which the sermons aroused throughout the university in the early years of the century was undoubtedly political, but politics and religion were still hard to distinguish. Even Hearne, though his heart warmed to a good anti-Hanoverian discourse, often praised sermons on purely theological grounds and most of the numerous sermons which their preachers had printed were understandably of this nature. Moreover, there were many devout men like young Jeremiah Milles of Balliol who regularly went to St Mary's twice of a Sunday and on saints' days and who carefully noted in his diary what he thought of preachers. A confirmed and critical sermon-taster, he took the greatest pains with his own script for a sermon on 3 March 1701, beginning to prepare nearly two months earlier, and on one occasion 'studied all of this day without eating about my sermon for the University'.[2]

It is easier to account in general terms for the decline of the influence exerted by university sermons than to trace it in detail. No doubt it was largely due to the secularization of the age to which all drew attention and the reduction in religious controversy which accompanied it. Long before the university's political hostility to the Hanoverian regime came to an end, the fires of theological controversy which had done much to inspire it began to die down. They were to flare up again in the seventies when subscription to the thirty-nine articles was assailed, and the pulpits were active again in this war of words; but until the nineteenth century brought a new ecclesiastical atmosphere the sermon tended to decline in importance as a weapon in favour of the pamphlet.

Complaints also began to be made of the poor congregations, though

Delegates' Room at the Printing House, of the V.Chanc. and six Doctors about the Matter. Warton's Sermon was demanded, but he denyed that he had it, and took an oath that it was purloyn'd or stole from him. Who gave him such Advice I know not, But 'tis certain I little expected that he would thus prevaricate. He ought by statute to have delivered a true copy, eisdem terminis, of his Sermon, and to have stood to what he preached.'

[1] OUA register of convocation 1704-30 (back of volume). A note appended in the register indicated that the ban was lifted twelve years later. George Coningsby (1683-1766), m. Wadham 1710; MA St Mary Hall 1717; BD and DD Balliol 1739.

[2] Diary of Jeremiah Milles, Balliol Coll. MS 461, 8 Jan. 1701.

more in the vacations than in term-time, and changes in academic custom led to a sharper distinction between term and vacation as the century wore on. A special occasion was necessary to attract Woodforde to church when he was resident between 1759 and 1774, unless in pursuit of his duties as a pro-proctor. On 5 May 1763 he noted: 'Went to St Mary's this morning and heard Jeffrison of Queens-Coll. preach; and after it heard the Coronation Anthem sung there. This is the Thanksgiving day for the late Peace between France, Spain and England.' 'There were', he added, 'vast Numbers of People to hear the Coronation Anthem.'[1] He also attended assize sermons, and the assizes after them, but he would perhaps in any age have been a reluctant sermon-goer. Even in the years when the enthusiasm for university sermons was at its lowest, a congregation would collect whenever 'a "great gun" . . . was expected to fire away (as was then the wont) at a methodistical or a dissenting target'; and Edward Tatham preached to a crowded audience a sermon lasting two and a half hours in defence of a disputed verse in St John's Epistle (5.7) in the course of which he wished 'all the German critics' (which he pronounced 'Jarman') at the bottom of the 'Jarman Ocean', and which he brought to a close by declaring that he would leave the question to the bench of bishops 'who have little to do, and do not always do that little'. He held the attention of his hearers so well that few left before the close, though one old head of a college was said never to have recovered fully from the ordeal.[2]

A good deal of the decline into which the university sermons fell was, however, due to weaknesses in their administration. These were inherent in the system and became increasingly obvious with the falling away of theological zeal. In the first place there were far too many of them. More than 120 were preached every year with the full panoply of official support. There were also sermons preached on public occasions in city churches on behalf of the corporation,[3] and lecturers were appointed. All the preachers had to be provided from the university's resources. In the second place the arrangements for the provision of the university preachers were in themselves unsatisfactory. The statutes had always made provision for preachers to hand over their 'turns' to deputies. So far as one can determine, the intention was that this would be primarily a question of exchange of dates. In fact, from as early as records enable us to judge, a number of those with turns, particularly in the larger cycle, but even in the smaller and more select one, failed to take them up and far too

[1] *Woodforde at Oxford*, 125. James Jefferson was Jeremy Bentham's tutor.

[2] Cox, *Recollections*, 233-4.

[3] Cf Hearne, *Collections* x. 47 (12 Sept. 1728): 'Tho' the Mayor, Recorder, Aldermen, &c., of the City of Oxford go to Cairfax Church, as the City Church, yet the City hath properly no church. . . . That church . . . no more belongs to them than St Marie's doth to the University. The University pays so much a year to St Marie's Parish for the use of that Church, which Church they have used time out of mind.'

many substitutes or representatives had to be found for their supply to be easily handled. Though the use of substitutes increased as the century wore on, already at its beginning a system based on cash-payments, largely organized by the bedel of divinity, was obviously in operation.[1] Those anxious to 'sink their turns' were prepared to pay for a substitute and already there was a fixed rate—in the case of a 'common turn' three guineas by 1716—and the bedel served as an intermediary in the payment.[2] At first there seems little if any complaint that the quality of preaching was affected, though in 1716 Hearne lamented the fact that the vice-chancellor no longer preached in person the sermon on the afternoon of Easter Sunday traditionally allocated to him.[3] From the surviving bedels' lists it would seem that some pains were taken to see that reputable deputies were provided for the Sunday morning sermons in term, and at Christ Church for instance all substitutes for canons' preaching had to be approved by the dean.[4] But only among the preachers of special sermons who were approached directly by the vice-chancellor were substitutes comparatively rare.[5] In 1681 the hebdomadal board had met to discuss special arrangements for providing suitable preachers during the king's residence in Oxford, changing the turns so that 'able and grave men should preach, especially such that should not give offence by flashy notions and expressions or make reflections as the yong [sic] masters do'.[6]

It was in the last years of the century that the employment of paid substitutes became so general as to constitute a scandal and that the quality of preaching became gravely affected by it. This was particularly marked in the ill attended vacation services. George Valentine Cox claimed to have listened to more sermons than anyone alive. He stated that by the end of the century it had become customary for a few residents

[1] Official records kept by the bedel of divinity covering the years 1744-52 and 1797-1804 survive: OUA MR/10/1, 2 and 3. They are roughly kept and not strictly comparable in form, those covering the later period being more informative (for example about deputies preaching) than the earlier ones.

[2] Anthony Wood thought that the use of substitutes markedly increased after the Restoration, when the restored fellows returned. He quoted 40s a sermon as the cost of a substitute and knew a Christ Church man who boasted that he gained more than £10 a year by such substitute preaching: *Life and Times* i. 361. That the bedel acted as intermediary would seem to be indicated by the entries in Bodl. MS Top. Oxon. e.66, where 'Pd.' is written against the names of many preachers who were employing substitutes.

[3] Hearne, *Collections* v. 256.

[4] See Gaisford's *Summary*. The bedel's list shows that in the last years of the century the universal Christ Church substitute, from the dean's turn downwards, was Simon Stanton (1764-1817, m. Ch.Ch. 1781), the precentor.

[5] It is not clear where the money came from for the special sermons arranged by the vice-chancellor. A fee of 9 guineas was quoted on two very different occasions and at widely different times, for a sermon of thanksgiving in 1715 and for the repetition sermon in 1774: see *Woodforde at Oxford*, 213. In the reforms of 1803 they were valued at 6 guineas. They do not appear in the vice-chancellor's computus; presumably he found the money from some confidential petty cash.

[6] Wood, *Life and Times* ii. 522.

who became known as the 'Oxford hacks' to add substantially to their incomes by taking up unwanted turns and to monopolize university preaching, particularly in the vacation, but also increasingly during term.[1] Though lists surviving among the papers of his colleague, the bedel of divinity, suggest that he may have exaggerated both the extent of their monopoly and the poverty of their preaching, they show that the problem was real enough, and it was the increasing use of such substitutes in term-time preaching which led at last to reform.[2]

When it came it was one of the quiet and practical internal reforms which became possible after the hold of the Laudian statutes was relaxed. In 1803 an amending statute was passed which concentrated on four main changes.[3] In the first place the Sunday afternoon sermons and those on feast-days during the long vacation were suspended. In the second place convocation was henceforth to choose ten select preachers to hold office for two years from a list drawn up by the vice-chancellor, proctors and the regius professors of divinity and Hebrew. These were to undertake to act as substitutes for all preachers unwilling or unable to take their turns as term-time Sunday preachers. In the third place, remuneration was made general for all preachers and at fixed rates. All Sunday preachers were to be paid five guineas, all special preachers six guineas, and all others four guineas. In the fourth place an ingenious scheme was drawn up whereby fees were to be collected by the bedel from all colleges and halls on behalf of their preaching members and, together with certain other funds the university collected, were to be used to pay every preacher according to the new statutory scale.[4] Thus the man who preached in his own turn was to get back what was supposed to be equivalent to his contribution, and the substitute for a man who failed to carry out his preaching duty drew his fee from the university direct. That the arithmetic involved soon proved faulty and that in fact individual contributions to the central pool soon ceased to be required mattered little. The improvement in preaching standards was said to have been immediate,[5] and the suspension of the long vacation Sunday afternoon sermons was followed in 1819 by those of Sunday morning in the long vacation as well. The cutting down of

---

[1] Cox, *Recollections*, 233, 237.

[2] The lists show that a high proportion of the vacation preaching, and quite a considerable share of that during term-time, was done by three persons: Samuel Forster (1728–97, m. Wadham 1746, registrar of the university 1761–97), John Gutch (registrar 1797–1824) and Isaac Crouch (m. SEH 1774, vice-principal 1783). Of the quality of their preaching Cox himself admits that Crouch was 'always listened to with great respect'; Forster he remembered only as 'a dismal-looking preacher with a solemn black wig': Cox, 29, 31.

[3] *Statutes* title XVI, trans. Ward ii. 43–56.

[4] A series of lists of payments from colleges for their members after 1803 giving the fees of preachers is in OUA WPγ/2/9. The bedel collected them as 'culets', adding them to minor contributions already in existence.

[5] Cox, 237.

unwanted sermons, the stimulus given to good preaching by the establishment of the select preachers, soon to be followed by the coming of the high-church movement, revolutionized preaching. The high-church preachers 'relieved the University pulpit, in general', Cox thought, 'from a succession of dry, cold discourses and occasional elegant essays' which were, in his experience, 'attended by a thin and listless congregation'.[1] The criticism may be somewhat unfair, since many of the sermons which survive, though tedious to the modern reader and void of critical content, are nevertheless replete with scriptural and patristic learning. In 1748 Edward Bentham wrote:

I am for having you attend our University Sermons not only as a Christian but as a scholar. Exert all your faculties of criticism; but do it with seriousness. Preaching here, whatever it may be in other places, is intended by way of exercise for the divine, as well for the instruction of his hearers.[2]

One of the most interesting innovations affecting the university sermons which came to fruition during the latter half of the century was the founding of the Bampton lectures. John Bampton, who died in 1751, bequeathed lands to the university for the endowment of eight lectures in defence of the Christian religion, as found within the Church of England. The lecturer was to be in holy orders and an MA of either university. He was to defend particularly the orthodox doctrines of the trinity and the incarnation and, in strongly Oxford tradition, the authority of the scriptures and the early fathers of the church. He was to 'confute all schismatics and heretics', to treat of the articles of the Christian faith, as comprehended in the apostles' and Nicene creeds—not it will be noted as comprehended in the thirty-nine articles nor as in the *Quicunque vult*. He was to be chosen by the heads of houses only 'and by no others, in the room adjoining to the Printing-House'.[3] The lectures were designed by their founder to fortify undergraduates and bachelors in a sensible and conservative Anglican orthodoxy. They were delivered in lieu of Sunday morning sermons in term-time.

The first eight of these sermons or lectures were given in 1780 by James Bandinel. He presented a general defence of the Christian revelation, with what for 1780 were optimistic undertones. 'The capacities of man as an individual are progressive; so are those of human nature taken collectively; and God has always been pleased to accommodate his dispensations to this law of progression: he brings mankind from nature to grace, from grace to glory.' He expressed strongly Arminian opinions (as against the church's evangelicals) on Christ dying for all, and, perhaps

---

[1] Ibid.

[2] E. Bentham, *Advices to a Young Man of Fortune and Rank on coming to the University* (Oxford 1748), 13.

[3] OUA Bampton papers, WPα/2/3 and 1. John Bampton (1689-1751), m. Trin. 1706.

temerariously, dissented somewhat from St Augustine on this point.[1] From these lectures alone it would be possible to construct a list of those dangers to the minds and souls of the junior members which the heads collectively most feared, chiefly enthusiasm and scepticism. Enthusiasm, which could be taken to include Methodism and evangelicalism, led to schism, schism to sedition and sedition to the sort of things which were happening in France. As to scepticism, the young were especially warned against Hume, Gibbon and Priestley.

In 1791 Henry Kett, 'Horse Kett' of Trinity, a character well known about the university, taking a line which he flattered himself was peculiarly conformable to the directions of Bampton, lectured on the primitive fathers, whose antiquity gave them an advantage 'which cannot be counterbalanced'. To them the first attention of the ecclesiastical student should be turned, to Clemens Romanus, Ignatius, Polycarp, Justin Martyr, Irenaeus, Athenagoras. Kett was particularly concerned to display the misrepresentations of these divines by Gibbon and Priestley, to which gentlemen he said there clung an unpleasant air of novelty. Kett referred particularly to Gibbon's cleverly suggestive 'language of diffident hesitation'.[2]

Provost Eveleigh of Oriel, in lectures which were prefaced by an affectionate address to the undergraduates, for whose benefit primarily they existed, was pleased to cite Josiah Tucker for the opinion that 'the idea of being a consistent Protestant never entered into the head of any man for upwards of seventy years after the Reformation'.[3] Eveleigh was a staunch upholder of the reformation, who believed that from Luther's time, 'Christianity began to assume its genuine appearance'.[4] Great as was his devotion to the thirty-nine articles, he directed that the beliefs of the church were to be looked for also in the liturgy, catechism and homilies. The articles were controversial and had a limited purpose: 'to regulate the belief and doctrines of those among us, who are intrusted with the public instruction'.[5] In 1804 Richard Laurence devoted his lectures to showing that the Articles were not, as Evangelicals asserted, 'Calvinist', but largely Lutheran.[6]

[1] J. Bandinel, *Eight Sermons . . . at the Lecture founded by . . . John Bampton, M.A . . . . to which is added a Vindication of St Paul from the Charge of wishing himself Accursed* (Oxford 1780), 112–13.

[2] H. Kett, *A Representation of the Conduct and Opinions of the Primitive Christians, with Remarks on certain Assertions of Mr Gibbon and Dr Priestley* (Oxford 1791), 20–2, 23–6, 158. Henry Kett (1761–1825), m. Trin. 1777; Bampton lecturer 1790. In 1793 Kett unsuccessfully stood for election to the chair of poetry but was defeated by James Hurdis (1764–1801, m. Magd. Hall 1780; demy Magd. 1781; prof. poetry 1793–1801).

[3] J. Eveleigh, *A View of our Religion* (Oxford 1792), 135n, citing J. Tucker's *Letters to Kippis* (London 1773), 32. Eveleigh was Bampton lecturer in 1792. Josiah Tucker (1713–99), m. St John's 1733.

[4] Eveleigh, 134.

[5] Ibid. 160–1.

[6] R. Laurence, *An Attempt to illustrate those Articles of the Church of England which the Calvinists improperly consider as Calvinistical* (Oxford 1820). Richard Laurence (1760–1838), m. CCC 1778; BCL

The lectures varied somewhat, but at no time became so specialist or technical in character as to render them wholly unsuitable for the captive audience to which they were addressed. In 1794 Thomas Wintle, who had been a protégé of Secker's, concentrated his attention on the correct understanding of some difficult passages in the Psalms. He defended, not for the first time, the Hebrew learning of his great patron, which had been belittled by Bishop Hurd and others. He seems to have had a 'high' doctrine of the eucharistic sacrifice and a live doctrine of faith as more than merely speculative assent.[1] He dedicated his work to the evangelically disposed Shute Barrington, bishop of Durham, who had honoured his general plan with his approbation.

Perhaps the most remarkable of all the early Bampton lectures were those of Edward Tatham delivered in 1789 and published in a considerably expanded form in two large volumes in 1790. Like almost everything else this forceful man did, they were out of line with normal practice and in some ways were out of line with the founder's intentions. For one thing, they were not addressed primarily to the junior members of the university. They were addressed, as their dedication to the heads of houses indicated, to its governors. They did not set out merely to provide a defence of a threatened orthodoxy, but instead to bring about the breaking of some old and venerated forms; he provided a salvo for reformation. He did not, for example, share Bampton's veneration for the fathers, as providing aids to the understanding of scripture. The fathers knew nothing about collation. They had no textual skills. They embarked on fantasies of their own which produced misunderstanding rather than light.[2]

Within the framework of a very impressive discussion of the degrees and kinds of certainty appropriate to the various forms of logic, philosophical, mathematical, physical, historical, ethical, poetical and musical, Tatham both defended the university against some of the charges made against it and advanced his own plans of reformation. He declared against those who represented Oxford as a school of vice: the ancient discipline of the place made for a 'Modesty of manners and demeanour' which 'has always characterized and distinguished the sons of Oxford'.[3] Like Bentham he defended the authority of Aristotle on

and DCL University College; Bampton lecturer 1804; canon Ch.Ch. and regius prof. Hebrew 1814–22; abp of Cashel 1822–38.

[1] T. Wintle, *The Expediency, Prediction and Accomplishment of Christian Redemption Illustrated* ... (Oxford 1794), 99, 108, 193 ff, 211. Sermon VII, ibid. 225 ff, included discussion of grace with an approving reference (p. 237n) to Hooker's *Ecclesiastical Polity*. Wintle was announced as having lately published *Daniel, an Improved Version Attempted, with a Preliminary Dissertation and Notes, Critical, Historical, and Explanatory* (Oxford 1792). Thomas Wintle (1738–1814), m. Pemb. 1753; Bampton lecturer 1794.

[2] Tatham, *Chart and Scale of Truth* ii. 105–6.

[3] Ibid. i. 368.

moral questions, but unlike Bentham he was anxious to see Aristotelian logic and the old disputations driven out as altogether unsuitable for the modern world, and the methods of Bacon and Locke given pride of place.[1] Above all, he urged a thorough and scientific study of the scriptures, for which the first requirement was competence in the learned languages, to be pursued 'radically and grammatically'. The Greek tongue was 'of infinitely more importance to Theology than all other languages'. Yet too often boys come up from school inadequately prepared in it, 'an evil, which, perhaps more than any other, disgraces the literary discipline of the present age'. It even outweighed the attention so admirably being given to the old oriental languages.[2] Indeed, one of the great reforms to which he looked forward was a new translation of the Bible, 'philosophically grounded ... An *unprejudiced*, a *literal*, a *faithful*, and an *uniform* translation of the whole Bible, both Old and New Testaments, is that learned work, which is more earnestly to be desired than any other.' Christians of all denominations could take part in its production and he was able to point to much useful preliminary work already done, much of it at Oxford.[3]

Finally, another agency which could be made to play its part in the improvement of instruction not only of students in general but of ordinands in particular was the University Press. This is not the place to examine its activities in general, but it is necessary to point out that the delegates had always regarded themselves, and in no light-minded spirit, as publishers to the Church of England. Hence when in 1768 a 'Reverend Mr Scott' had offered them a new translation of the New Testament in two quarto volumes they replied that they did not print

at the Expence of the University the Works of any private Person containing either a Translation or an Exposition of any Part of the Sacred Scriptures, lest they should seem by so doing to give the Sanction of their Approbation, and thro' them that of the University to Works which comprise Matter of Controversy or of dubious Interpretation.[4]

On the other hand, when the Church of England was threatened, for example by a move to repeal the test and corporation acts, the Press was there as always and ready to reprint a pamphlet entitled *When is the proper time to apply for a repeal of the Test Act* which was sent to all members of both houses of parliament along with Bishop Sherlock's arguments.[5]

[1] Tatham, *Chart and Scale of Truth* i, esp. ch. 14.
[2] Ibid. ii. 111–15.   [3] Ibid. 179, 230; but cf. ibid. 163–232.
[4] Oxford University Press Archives, orders and accounts of the delegates of the Clarendon Press 1758–94, p. 73, 10 May 1768.
[5] OUA minutes of the hebdomadal board 1788–1803, WPγ/24/2, pp. 29, 264: '1500 copies of Bishop Sherlock's Argument against the Abolition of the Corporation and Test Acts ... viz., so much of the Pamphlet as was printed and published in 1787.'

The widespread and increasing fear of infidelity which was engendered by the French revolution, moreover, had important results in the policy, energetically pursued in the 1790s, of issuing cheap editions of useful books for the common use of schools, universities and the clergy, as 'stock-work' for the Press in slack periods. This was not a new policy: Daniel Prince had suggested the printing of the early Christian apologists Lactantius and Minucius Felix in 1766.[1] William Cleaver, when bishop of Chester, also played a leading part in encouraging the production of cheap editions, and in so doing may have had in mind the needs of another class of men, of whom in his widespread diocese of Chester he had much experience: candidates for orders who had no university education. For the benefit of such men, among others, he published an elaborate reading list, though he would have agreed with Bishop Pretyman Tomline that reading lists were not enough.[2]

The Press's cheap editions were well bound and attractively printed, though in somewhat small type. A start was made in 1790 on the catechism with notes by Thomas Marshall, first published by the Press in 1679, which soon became commonly referred to as the 'Oxford Catechism'.[3] Thereafter almost every year there followed an inexpensive edition of an Anglican classic: in 1792 a thousand copies of Hooker's *Ecclesiastical Polity* and five hundred of his other works; Burnet on the articles to be 'on the same paper with the Hooker'; Pearson on the creed, as soon as a 'corrector' could be found for it;[4] a volume of Barrow's sermons; Wells's *Geography*;[5] Synge's *Gentleman's Religion*;[6] to name only a few. Here was a body of religious knowledge for the young cleric or theological student that was orthodox, learned and widely acceptable.

[1] H. G. Carter, *A History of the Oxford University Press* i (Oxford 1975), 376.

[2] [W. Cleaver,] *A List of Books intended for the use of the Younger Clergy and other Students in Divinity within the Diocese of Chester* (Oxford 1791), 2nd edn, enlarged, *A List . . . to which is added the learned Dr Dodwell's catalogue of the Christian writers and genuine works that are extant of the first three centuries, together with an extract from his second letter of advice &c.* (Oxford 1792). He recommended Bishop Lavington's *Enthusiasm of Methodists and Papists Compared* (London 1749-51); Chrysostom, *De sacerdotio*, ed. J. Hughes (Cambridge 1710); S. Clarke, *Being and Attributes of God* (London 1705); Butler's *Analogy*; and a good deal of Waterland, whose eucharistic theology of 'a feast upon a Sacrifice' was much like his own. Pretyman Tomline, *Elements of Christian Theology designed principally for the Use of Young Students in Divinity* (2 vols London, Cambridge and Oxford 1799) i, p. vii; the second volume was largely occupied by an exposition of the articles.

[3] Orders of the delegates of the press 1758-94, p. 266, 12 Mar. 1790. Cleaver's book-list included this under the title 'The Oxford Catechism'. Thomas Marshall (1621-85), m. Linc. 1640, rector 1672-85.

[4] Orders of the delegates of the press 1758-94, p. 291, 3 Feb. 1793. Ibid., p. 293, 24 June 1793: '1500 copies of Pearson as soon as Hooker is finished.'

[5] Probably E. Wells, *History and Geography of the Old and New Testament* (Oxford 1801). Oxford University Press Archives, orders of the delegates of the press 1795-1810, p. 46, 30 Mar. 1798. Arrangements were made for the re-engraving of the maps under the supervision of Dr Randolph 'together with a reduced Map of Palestine according to D'Anville': ibid., p. 50, 11 July 1798.

[6] Ibid., p. 64, 2 July 1799. Edward Synge (1659-1741), m. Ch.Ch. 1674; DD Trinity College, Dublin; bp of Raphoe 1714; abp of Tuam 1716-41.

At the end of the century, in spite of all that Bentham and Tatham and others had tried to do, Oxford theology remained defensive and there was still no systematic provision, nor indeed was there at Cambridge, for the training of ordinands in 'those studies belonging peculiarly to their profession'.[1] It was in the early nineteenth century therefore that the reformers of the university's curriculum and statutes began in a more serious atmosphere (the terrors of the French revolution frightened many into piety[2]) to assess afresh the requirements of these men. Behind the reformers were the ordinary clerics of the country who had been taught by men such as Bentham and Conybeare and had taken their moral stance from bishops such as Secker and the more influential eighteenth-century heads of houses, and there can be little doubt that, in spite of weaknesses in the system, these clerics helped to lay the foundation for the great religious revival which was to come.

[1] *Report of Her Majesty's Commission* (1852), p. 71.
[2] See C. Smyth, *Simeon and Church Order* (Cambridge 1940); *Annual Register* (1798), 221.

14

Religion in the Colleges 1715–1800

V. H. H. GREEN

ALTHOUGH the university made demands on seniors and juniors alike in respect of their religious exercises, the colleges remained, as indeed they had always been since their foundation, the conscious setting within which their individual members were to find, or fail to find, an outward expression of their faith. Undergraduates and graduates received some instruction in scriptural and theological learning through the university sermons and the lectures delivered by the professors of divinity, but in practice performance fell short of what the statutes laid down. It was in the colleges rather than in the university that the real instruction in divinity took place, teaching was done and religious observances were upheld. Every college had its own place of worship. Three college chapels were consecrated in the eighteenth century: that of Hertford on 25 November 1716, the new chapel of Queen's on 1 November 1719 and the chapel of Pembroke on 10 July 1732.

The statutes of every college made provision for a measure of compulsory attendance at chapel by the junior members as well as for lectures on the Greek Testament and instruction in divinity which under-graduates were required to attend. Besides, as the majority of college fellows were in holy orders, all teaching took place within what may be described superficially as a religious setting. Most fellows retained their fellowships for a comparatively limited period, spending the greater part of their careers in livings, many of them advowsons in the gift of the colleges. Many of these had been bought in the first half of the eighteenth century to enable senior fellows to marry and so find a satisfactory niche in the established church as well as a better remunerated position than that of the average fellow. On paper the colleges might then seem to represent the Church of England at prayer, acting as seminaries for young men a majority of whom were themselves eventually to seek holy orders.

Evidence is scattered and scanty about liturgical observances both in the colleges and elsewhere. Some information can be found in college registers and accounts and in personal letters and reminiscences. For example, as the purchase of wine and the laundering of linen mentioned in the accounts make plain, the holy communion was usually celebrated in college chapels on the great festivals and generally on the first Sunday in every term.[1] 'Went to Chaple', Parson Woodforde noted on Easter Sunday (3 April) 1763, 'this Morning at half an Hour after nine o'clock, and received the Holy Sacrament ... Mr Hayward our Sub-Warden preached in our Chapel before the Sacrament this morning.' On Christmas day 1773 he attended New College chapel at 9 a.m., read the epistle and assisted the warden 'going round with the wine'.[2] As a fellow of Lincoln John Wesley preached in the college chapel on Easter day (2 April) 1738. In the majority of colleges—Christ Church was in this respect an exception—undergraduates were actually required to attend communion once a term. The statutes for Hertford (1747) for instance laid down that the sacrament should be administered on Christmas day, Easter day, Whit Sunday and on the first Sunday in every term 'and every Member of the Society then resident shall receive it'.[3]

The responsibility for the practical preparation of the chapel for the communion rested with the bible-clerk, junior in status, socially midway between commoner and servitor, who received emoluments in return for his duties. These varied from college to college, but what he was generally required to do can be deduced from the careful notes on the bible-clerkship prepared by Ralph Cawley, principal of Brasenose (1770-7).[4] The bible-clerk had to tell the butler on Friday night or Saturday morning to procure the bread for the communion, to inform the cleaner, to see that the chapel was fit and ready, to spread the altar with the appropriate cloth before prayers on Saturday evening, obtaining the linen from the hallman and the wine from the manciple. He was to lay out the cushions on the steps leading to the altar, to put a marker in the principal's prayer book at the appropriate place and to find out from the celebrant when he was ready to ring the chapel bell. At the communion itself he was to make his own celebration last, so that after communion had been given he could pour the wine into the flagon or chalice and close the rails. During the service itself he was warned to be careful not to read louder than the rest of the communicants. When the service was at an end he was to hand their caps to the principal and the vice-principal, and then remove the altar-linen before evening prayers. On other Sundays and holy days he was to mark the appointed lessons in the Bible, the first lesson being read by a bachelor on the foundation, and the second by the vice-principal or a senior fellow. On weekdays it was his duty to call on the

[1] At the cathedral in Christ Church, there had been monthly sacraments since 1660, although John Wesley and the early Methodists talked of attending weekly: see for example L. Tyerman, *The Life of the Rev. George Whitefield* (2 vols London 1876-7) i. 17; see also the diaries of John Wesley and Benjamin Ingham cited in p. 438 n. 8 and *passim* below.

[2] *Woodforde at Oxford*, 118, 119.

[3] R. Newton, *Rules and Statutes for Hertford College* (London 1747), 14.

[4] BNCA Principal Cawley's notebooks, B53.

fellow in orders whose week it was to read prayers a quarter of an hour before the bell was rung. He was required to make the responses 'with an audible voice', to take his turn with the rest of the scholars in reading the lesson, and to make a note of absentees and late-comers, the latter defined as those who came into chapel after the general confession. Absentees were to be reported to the vice-principal or fellow on duty after each service, and to the principal himself every Thursday. In the winter the bible-clerk ensured that the chapel was properly illuminated; he obtained the candles from the butler. The large wax tapers on the altar were to be lighted only on surplice-days: that is on Sundays and festivals. He had also to ensure that the chapel, or rather the antechapel, was prepared for the academic disputations which also took place there. On the eves of commemorative services, which in Brasenose amounted to some nineteen days a year, he had to remind all the fellows of their incidence, taking to the bursar the names of those who were to attend the service.

Nor did the bible-clerk's duties stop at the chapel. In hall he had to take note of the fellows who were to dine. He stayed behind till the end of the meal in order to give the senior fellow who was presiding at high table the 'knocker' with which he could call for grace. The bible-clerk had himself to say the initial grace and, after the first course, he might have to read (in Latin) a portion of the Psalms, Bible or other book appointed by the principal or vice-principal; we may reasonably doubt the extent to which this obligation was put into practice in the eighteenth century. He had also to take an account of the bread consumed at high table and to produce weekly bills for it for the butler. If the account was inaccurate the bible-clerk might have to make up the deficiency, 'it being plac'd to his Name in the Books'. When an incumbent of a college living died he was required to ring the bell for half an hour and to toll it for another half. When a new fellow was to be elected he had to attend the candidates in the cloisters, ring the large bell for the general fellowship examination, carry two books of the statutes and a Greek Testament into the chapel and ensure that a table and chair were placed behind the eagle (the lectern or reading desk) with pen, ink, paper and a burning candle for use at the outcome of the election. In like manner he had to be present when a fellow at the end of his period of probation was made a permanent fellow. He had some responsibility for drawing up testimonials for graduates of the college who were seeking ordination.

The perquisites of the bible-clerk at Brasenose included 10s 6d on the death of a college incumbent, 2s 6d for writing a testimonial, £1 10s for the remains of the candles in chapel, 2s for the entrance of a gentleman-commoner, 1s for a commoner, 6d for a batteler, 2s 6d on the election of a scholar; and for the changing of a gown 2s for a gentleman-commoner, 1s for a commoner or a scholar and 6d for a batteler. He was permitted free commons when there were a greater number of absentees than servitors present, and was entitled to the wine left over at the high table, to take his dinner from high table on gaudy days and to what remained of any dish with which any one fellow may have treated his fellow diners.

In most colleges morning prayer took place daily between 7 a.m. and 8 a.m., though the time was sometimes adjusted according to the time of year. At the cathedral in Christ Church Latin prayers had been moved from five in the morning to six, and 'at present' (in 1777) they were at seven both summer and winter. Evening prayers in 1660 took place at 8.30 p.m. but had been 'for many Years by Customary usage at $\frac{1}{4}$/9'.[1] 'We have prayers daily', George Fothergill of Queen's wrote, 'twice in our new chapel, for the most part at 6 a.m. and always at 5 in the afternoon.'[2] In the draft statutes for Hertford College Richard Newton laid down that morning prayer (between 1 October and 1 February) should be at 7.30 a.m. and from 1 February to 1 October at 6.30 a.m.; evening prayers throughout the year were to be at 6.30 p.m. On Sundays and holidays the first service was as on weekdays, but a second service with the litany took place at 9 a.m.[3] Traditional or college usage gave some chapel services unusual features. At Merton in 1796 the fellows recommended that the 'Warden be requested to direct the Chaplains to omit the First and Second Lessons at Morning and Evening Prayer, except on State Days, Sundays, and Holy days, and their Eves'.[4] At Brasenose on Easter day the sermon was always placed after morning prayer, instead of being in the normal rubrical place, and was followed by the communion service. On Good Friday, by notice given in 1773, prayers were to be at 3 o'clock, and dinner took place immediately afterwards. 'The old Custom was to have no Dinner on this Day; and about 3 years ago, Prayers began at 4 o'Clock, and Dinner was serv'd immediately after: But many inconveniences ensu'd from both these Practices.' Principal Cawley apparently suffered much, liturgically and extra-liturgically, on 3 July 1771 when, on behalf of the newly-founded Oxford Infirmary, there were 'almost 3 Hours in the Church' of prayers, singing and sermon. Dinner was at about three o'clock in the town hall for 120, but as only half that number turned up the rest had to pay 6d for eating and 1s 6d for wine which was 'generally thought an Imposition', and after that, to cap it all, four hours of Handel's *Jephthah*.[5]

---

[1] CA iv. a. 3, treasurer's notebook.

[2] G. Fothergill-his parents, 18 June 1722, *The Fothergills of Ravenstonedale*, ed. C. Thornton and F. McLaughlin (London 1905), 168. From 1 October until Easter they were at 7 a.m. and 5.30 p.m. according to the diary of Benjamin Ingham (1712-72, m. Queen's 1730). Ingham's diary has been transcribed and edited by Richard P. Heitzenrater of Southern Methodist University, Dallas; I am most grateful to Professor Heitzenrater for allowing me to use the typescript of his transcript, on which all quotations from the diary in this chapter are based, in advance of its publication.

[3] Newton, *Rules and Statutes*, 12-13.

[4] MCR 1.4 register 1731-1822, p. 433, 21 Nov. 1796. Perhaps no more was meant than that one or other of the lessons might be omitted.

[5] BNCA B53/1, pp. 18, 50. Did this represent a decline in Good Friday observances? Cf

In the larger chapels—Christ Church, New College and Magdalen—there was a choir whose singing sometimes attracted a considerable congregation. 'Norris, singing Boy sung (in our chapel this Evening) a very fine Anthem', Woodforde (who himself occasionally played the chapel organ) recalled on 21 March 1762. Later, in 1771, he noted that 'our Chapel this Evening . . . was so crouded with Ladies &c. that many of the Senior Fellows were obliged to sit out of their Seats'.[1] In Provost Smith's day (1730-56) a college jubilee at Queen's inspired the composition of a special Latin eucharistic hymn of five verses, strong on the incarnation and the virgin birth. 'The quire belonging to Magdalen College and Mr Powel the Oxford singer performed on that occasion.'[2]

Plainly there were some fellows and undergraduates, a Jeremiah Milles or a John Wesley, who attended chapel services with genuine devotion, and found the daily liturgy satisfying. 'I spent the morning', Milles wrote in his diary on 8 March 1702, 'in prayer and meditation'; on 4 April following he prepared himself 'as much as I cou'd, having company most of the day, for the H. Eucharist at night I went to bed at 10, and Hunt read to me a sermon'.[3] Benjamin Ingham and like-minded undergraduates at Queen's never missed morning and evening prayers in the chapel. Half a century or more later, in 1760, the young Jeremy Bentham, then a freshman at Queen's, although only twelve years old, was put through a rigorous preparation for the first of his college communions as an undergraduate. He wrote to his father:

On Saturday we received the Sacrament upon which account we were lectured in the New Testament three days before, and as many after that day: to prepare for which awful duty I read Nelson on the Sacrament . . . I intended to fast that morning, but it would not do, for I began to grow sick for want of victuals: and was forced to eat a bit of breakfast with Mr Cooper, with whom I lived this ten days. We did St Paul's Epistle to the Hebrews for lecture in the Greek Testament, which I found very difficult and indeed it is allowed here to be the hardest Greek there is.[4]

On the other hand, Gibbon's experience at Magdalen might have been more representative some years earlier, 'left', as he recalled it, 'by the dim light of my Catechism, to grope my way to the Chappel and communion-table'.[5]

E. Vernon-J. Smith, 12 Feb. 1752, Queen's MS 473: 'As you are good Observers of Lent at Oxford—I have this day sent you a small Keg of Sturgeon to diversifye your Fish entertainments.'

[1] *Woodforde at Oxford*, 78, 189.

[2] Queen's MS 475, fo 212; the couplet *Qui corpus cibo reficis, Cælesti Mentem Gratiâ* is reminiscent of the *Quod ore sumpsimus* in the Roman Missal.

[3] Balliol MS 461, diary of Jeremiah Milles. Joseph Hunt (1681-1726), m. Balliol 1697, Master 1722-6.

[4] *Correspondence of Jeremy Bentham*, ed. T. L. S. Sprigge *et al.* (London and Oxford 1968 onward) i. 21.

[5] E. Gibbon, *Memoirs of my Life*, ed. G. A. Bonnard (London 1966), 58.

For the majority of the juniors, as in all probability of the seniors, attendance at chapel services may well have entailed a perfunctory duty. The services themselves may often have been conducted in a slovenly manner and were not infrequently marked by misbehaviour and connivance on the part of the conscripted congregation. Edward Bentham commented:

It is not less lamentable than ridiculous to see GENTLEMEN during the time of Divine Service, sometimes affecting many airs of negligence and Irreverence— such as in persons of meaner condition would be universally condemned as arising from want of sense and want of manners.[1]

It is doubtful whether the fellows themselves attended the services with any degree of regularity. In some colleges which did not, as at New College, always employ a chaplain, the growing practice of non-residence reduced the number available for conducting the services. Some of the resident fellows were irregular in their attendance. Woodforde, apparently a fairly regular attender at evening prayers, noted on 14 November 1762 that he had not been to Sunday evening service for three weeks.[2] In 1716 there were three fellows at All Souls in priest's orders resident, and the reading of 'surplice prayers' was apparently sometimes in default.[3] Eighty years later, either because of negligence or non-residence, the fellows of Lincoln agreed to appoint a chaplain from among their number, paying him a stipend for his duty.[4] At Oriel in 1750 towards the end of the long vacation the bible-clerk had been ordered to ring the bell for prayers, although the chaplain who had 'undertaken the cure of so many Churches' was not there, so that 'our Neighbours might not know that we had no Prayers'. The provost complained 'that other Fellows ought to reside and Share in the Duties of the College—that We should be deservedly Censurd and Reproachd for Such a Neglect as We had 18 fellows founded for Divinity'.[5] On 3 September 1769 Woodforde had himself to take the service at New College, 'or else there would be none', and he sconced (fined) the chaplain in course, Mr Tawney, five shillings

[1] *Right Behaviour in Church*, identified in the copy in Lambeth Palace Library (YC 911.13, no. 8) by a manuscript note in Secker's hand as 'By Edw. Bentham D.D.'.

[2] *Woodforde at Oxford,* 94.

[3] B. Gardiner—Wake, 22 Dec. 1716, Wake MS 15, fo 185.

[4] LCM register 1739-1983, fo 98, 8 Dec. 1796: 'a chaplain shall be appointed, to do the ordinary duty of the chapel, with a stipend of £40 per annum.' Seven years earlier the college, that is the rector (John Horner, 1747-92, m. Merton 1764; BD and DD Linc. 1778 and 1785, rector 1784-92) and the major part of the fellows had agreed that 'if any resident Fellow shall neglect to enter upon his turn of Reading in Chapel or leave any part of the Duty unprovided for during the week, his next Senior resident shall, if he Chuses, take the turn and be allowed fourteen shillings, to be paid immediately by the Manciple, and be charged to the account of the Person so neglecting—or if the Duty be discharged by more than one of the Fellows; the Mulct to be proportionately divided'. Ibid. fo 83.

[5] OCA ETC/A/1, observations on neglect of the college chaplain, 2 Oct. 1750, by the provost (Walter Hodges, 1695-1757, m. Oriel 1711, provost 1727-57; vice-chancellor 1741-4).

for neglect of duty. Although New College had usually more than one chaplain, and even a chaplain's common room, Woodforde commented six years earlier (30 July 1763) that he began 'the Prayers this morning at 8 o'clock in our Chapel, there being no Chaplain there for some time'.[1] The German Pastor Moritz could hardly disguise his surprise, and distaste, at hearing Mr Modd, a chaplain at Corpus, suddenly exclaim after an all-night sitting at the Mitre Inn in 1782, 'd—mn me, I must read prayers this morning at All-Souls'.[2] Not surprisingly, three years earlier Thomas Randolph, the president of Corpus, had had occasion to reprimand Modd for his 'drunkenness, extravagance, and other irregularities'.[3]

With their seniors apparently often lax, it was hardly to be expected that the undergraduates would show much enthusiasm for attendance at church services. Governing bodies of colleges found it necessary to apply a lesser or greater degree of compulsion. To ensure attendance at chapel undergraduates at Queen's were mulcted if they missed morning prayers twice a week.[4] At Trinity, by a ruling of 1788, they were to be punished by the imposition of some literary exercise if they missed more than four times in a week without the dean's permission. In March 1798 the fellows of Trinity laid down that every undergraduate was required to be at chapel at morning prayers either on the second or third Sunday in the Michaelmas term or Lent term according to the date of the term's commencement; failure to fulfil this comparatively modest requirement meant that an undergraduate might be debarred from keeping terms.[5] Trinity seems to have been an easy-going college in this respect; it was noted, however, of one of its noblemen, Lord North, that he seldom missed evening prayers.[6] There is, however, some evidence that gentlemen-commoners were generally treated more sympathetically; at Corpus they were not obliged to attend early chapel on any day but Sunday and Thursday.[7] At New College Woodforde, noticing that there was no gentleman-commoner present in chapel on 23 April 1774, 'sent the Clark to each of them to desire they should attend oftener'. Fourteen years earlier he had himself been the object of disciplinary attention for failure to attend.[8]

---

[1] *Woodforde at Oxford*, 143.

[2] C. P. Moritz, *Travels, chiefly on foot through Several Parts of England in 1782* (London 1795), 169.

[3] Fowler, *Corpus*, 190.

[4] They were sconced 6*d*: Queen's, MS 475, fo 68.

[5] Trinity, liber decani I, 20 Mar. 1788, 22 Mar. 1798.

[6] *Gentleman's Magazine* lxviii (1798), 283, quoted in L. S. Sutherland, *The University of Oxford in the Eighteenth Century: a reconsideration* (Oxford 1973), 20.

[7] *Memoirs of Richard Lovell Edgeworth* (2 vols London 1820) i. 94. Edgeworth (1744–1817), entered Corpus as a gentleman-commoner on 10 October 1761, having been previously at Trinity College, Dublin.

[8] *Woodforde at Oxford*, 218–19 (1774), 8, 9 (1760).

For the run-of-the-mill candidates college chapel became just another, and in some respects a disagreeable or at best a tedious chore:

> Now shuffling to the Chapel door
> Behind two sloven Students more
> I follow up the aisle,
> Displeas'd, good natur'd Chapman stares,
> for nearly half-done are the Prayers,
> And lessons read meanwhile
>
> At five, the Chapel bell again
> Rings a loud peal but rings in vain
> To move a single guest.[1]

Richard Newton laid down that all members of his society, Hertford, who did not appear in chapel at the tolling of the second bell—the first warning bell had been rung a quarter of an hour earlier—should be fined 2*d*, and he also tried to insist on decent appearance and behaviour. The less serious, he commented, were tempted to rise only when the second bell was being rung, and as a consequence appeared 'in a Slovenly Dress in every part Unfinish'd, to drop into the Chapel, one after another, during the whole Service, most Offensively to God and Man'. Among other offences, he noted '*Laughing, Talking, Sleeping, Lolling* as if asleep, *Sitting* when they should *Kneel*'.[2] Since college chapels were used for disputations and academic exercises, as well as for the elections of heads and fellows, in some respects they must have acquired secular associations in the mind of undergraduates which may have helped to make religious worship even more of a formality. Formal it had certainly become for the majority of its congregations, and long continued to be. 'We are in Chapel at Seven every morning', David Ker of Christ Church wrote, 'which it is impossible to escape attending without having an imposition and if such a thing was at all made practice of, your company would be no longer required.' 'These prayers', he added, 'are nothing more than a muster, and do not last more than ten minutes.'[3] Robert Larogue wrote to a friend in 1772: 'At about 7 o'clock in the Morning I rise and go half a-sleep to Chapel, where instead of praying I am too apt to spend my time in gaping and yawning.'[4]

In addition to the requirements for chapel attendance undergraduates had also to receive a variable amount of public instruction in divinity through the medium of lectures and tutorial advice. By the statutes of

[1] 'Letters from Oxford, from 1790 to 1794', *Reminiscences of Oxford*, 187, 194. Joseph Chapman (1743-1808), m. Trin. 1759, president 1776-1808; vice-chancellor 1784-8.

[2] Newton, *Rules and Statutes*, 11-12.

[3] Letter to his father, 19 Apr. 1796, Belfast, Public Record Office of Northern Ireland, MS D2651/2/132B.

[4] R. Larogue—S. Simpson, 8, 15 Apr. 1772, Yale University, Beinecke Library, Osborn Shelves, c.107.

Hertford on Sundays and holy days immediately after the first service, in term-time, the catechist was to give instruction in some part of the catechism or in some '*Moral Duty*, in a manner Useful to the *Servants*', and on Sunday evening at eight o'clock in winter and nine in summer, 'a *Catechetical* or *Theological* Lecture, for the Improvement of the Undergraduates of the Society'. Besides this, lessons in chapel and chapters in hall were to be read by the undergraduates in turn, that 'Persons trained up here for holy Orders may become well acquainted with the Scriptures early, and also learn to read them distinctly, and audibly'.[1] At Corpus in the earlier days of President Cooke (president 1783-1823) all undergraduates and bachelors on the foundation were required to prepare an 'Abridgement of Dr Randolph's Divinity Lectures'. When in 1791 a BA, seeking the grace of his college for his MA, had been prevented from attending these lectures, he was called upon to present to the president instead an abridgement of the fourth and fifth books of St John Chrysostom, *De sacerdotio*, a work which had from the seventeenth century a remarkable vogue in the Church of England.[2] What particularly exacerbated the evangelically minded young men of St Edmund Hall in 1768 was the vice-principal's decision, at the principal's suggestion, to lecture on the thirty-nine articles at nine in the evening 'that He might satisfy Himself whether they held any erroneous Doctrines'.[3] At Lincoln lectures on the New Testament were given by the Greek lecturer, who earned a stipend of three shillings a time, on Tuesdays and Thursdays during November, and from Ash Wednesday to early July; at other times of the Year he was to perform on Tuesdays.[4] Such instruction was intended in the main, it would seem, for young graduates. While the careful scheme of studies drawn up for disputation by the undergraduates of Queen's included a little theology, more extensive instruction had to wait on graduation. On 13 August 1731 the college decided that the taberdars 'shall from Michaelmas Day next be obliged to render upon Divinity Questions not only on the Sundays, but on all the Holydays in the year, excepting those following the Festival of the Incarnation of our Blessed Lord', and that they

be obliged to go on regularly in the said rendring according to the List of Questions given them by the Provost for that Purpose, and be call'd upon by the Dean once in three Months to exhibit each of them their Books in their own Handwriting, to be laid before the Provost when required. In which their

---

[1] Newton, *Rules and Statutes*, 13-14, 51-2.

[2] CCC acts and proceedings 1783-1810, fo 46, 26 Jan. 1791.

[3] T. Nowell, 'Materials for an answer to a pamphlet entitled *Pietas Oxoniensis*', Bodl. Higson MSS, fo 4. John Higson (1721-87), m. Wadham 1740; vice-principal SEH 1751-68. George Dixon (1709-87), m. Queen's 1729; principal SEH 1760-87.

[4] Lincoln, register 1739-1983, fo 40ᵛ, 6 Nov. 1770.

Questions are to be Clearly stated, and proper Arguments urg'd from Scripture and Reason and the Authorities of the Church for the Proofs of the several Points they undertake to maintain.[1]

Several of these books survive and indicate that the writers had a sound knowledge of the Bible, as of some modern and patristic theologians, and were independent in their conclusions.[2] At Christ Church, in 1773, the dean and chapter gave encouragement to James Chelsum, the catechist and *praelector theologiae*, to go on with the 'very useful Plan of Lectures in Divinity for the Instruction of Youth in this College', which he had been giving once a week in full term, apparently devised on his own initiative.[3]

It is of course impossible to estimate the extent of the influence, or the nature of advice, as to theological reading which individual junior members received from college tutors. John Wesley was probably exceptional in the care he took to advise on books and the instruction he gave to his pupils;[4] but there must have been many other clerical dons who were in this respect conscious of their responsibility and tried to be helpful. 'My tutor', George Fothergill commented in 1723, 'ordered me the other day to go to the Hebrew Lecture.'[5] Such full and careful provision for worship and instruction may lend some, if tendentious, support to the claims often made by the university's advocates, more especially at the time of the debate about subscription, that the university was a true school of Christian orthodoxy.

Nevertheless, university and college religion, if all-pervasive, had become in many respects conventional, and was indeed long to remain so. On such soil scepticism inevitably reaped a crop, albeit a very thin one, while religious enthusiasm, reacting against current formalism, attracted a vigorous yet again a small minority, perhaps more influential through the percolation of its views into the outside world than in the university itself. In the early decades of the eighteenth century fashionable thinking outside the university had fostered not merely latitudinarianism but deism and infidelity, and its spread naturally aroused uneasiness among

[1] Queen's, MS 475, fo 93.

[2] (1) Two anonymous volumes: MS 489 (beginning at Question 43), MS 496 (beginning at Question 42); (2) Books 3 and 4 by Cuthbert Barwis (m. Queen's 1736), MS 491-2; (3) Book 2 by Thomas Denton (m. Queen's 1740) covering Questions 19-41, MS 487: (4) Three books by Thomas Bland (m. Queen's 1742), covering Questions 16-60, MSS 493, 494, 495; (5) Book 3 (dated 1743) beginning from Question 23 by Richard Graham (m. Queen's 1737), MS 488, and (6) Book 3 by Cuthbert Wilson (m. Queen's 1738), MS 490.

[3] Christ Church, chapter book 1754-80, p. 238, 6 Jan. 1773.

[4] But such books, in the main theological (though including Aldrich's textbook on logic), appear also in the reading lists of like-minded members of the so-called Holy Club: see Ingham's diary, *passim*.

[5] Letter to his parents, 18 Oct. 1723, *Fothergills of Ravenstonedale*, ed. Thornton and McLaughlin, p. 82. His tutor was Joseph Steadman (1686-1773), m. Queen's 1702, fellow 1711; prebendary of St Paul's 1731.

the clerical dons. The Bangorian controversy had won more attention at Cambridge since Hoadly as well as some of his principal critics had been graduates of that university, but he had some followers among the more whiggish fellows at Oxford. Yet there was never more than a sparse sprinkling of deists and even fewer, like the precocious Edward Gibbon, who flirted with Roman Catholicism. Nevertheless, deistic thinking was evidently considered a serious menace. Its prophet, Matthew Tindal, an undergraduate at Lincoln (where he had studied under the learned and nonjuror high churchman George Hickes) and later at Exeter, had become a fellow of All Souls in 1678. His *The Rights of the Christian Church asserted against the Romish and all other Priests who claim an Independent Power over it* (London 1706) was to provoke such a furore that it was burned on the orders of the house of commons, together with Sacheverell's sermon, on 25 March 1710. In 1730 he published his best-known work, the deistic *Christianity as Old as the Creation, or the Gospel a Republication of the Religion of Nature*. Although years earlier denounced as an unbeliever by an All Souls' chaplain, Jonas Proast, in a letter printed by George Hickes in his preface to William Carroll's anonymous *Spinoza Revived* of 1709, Tindal remained a fellow of his college until his death in 1733.[1] Because of his radical thought his reputation in Oxford was naturally low. Hearne spoke of him as a 'notorious ill-liver' and a 'noted debauchee'.[2] Though in fact an abstemious man, Tindal's supposed lack of moral principles was considered a natural sequel to his unbelief, as a pamphlet printed after his death makes plain.[3] Although Tindal only made a few converts to his ideas, he had injected a critical note into the religious scene at Oxford; to conservative-minded clerics and their pupils deistic ideas were anathema.

Traces of direct influence of deistic ideas on junior members are few. In May 1728 an Oxford graduate, Robert Jennens, a relative by marriage of the high churchman, Lord Aylesford, had cut his throat and thrown himself out of a window in the Middle Temple. He was formerly of Trinity College, and letters were discovered in his desk from a college friend, Nicholas Stevens, 'now a regent master, in deacon's orders and designing for priest's orders, curate of a village near Oxford, and probationer fellow of Trinity'.[4] The letters criticized orthodox Christianity and were deistic in tone; Stevens boasted of the converts he had made to deism and urged Jennens to follow his example, recommending the advocacy of Bangorian views. 'My brother', he wrote, 'I take to be a sceptical Christian, and therefore while he hopes Christianity may be true, does not care to give so much countenance to *Deism*, as to say he doubts of the truth of

[1] [M. Tindal,] *Christianity as Old as the Creation, or the Gospel a Republication of the Religion of Nature* (London 1730); [W. Carroll,] *Spinoza Revived* (London 1709).

[2] Hearne, *Collections* i. 93, 237.

[3] *The Religious, Rational and Moral Conduct of Matthew Tindal, by a Member of All Souls* (London 1735).

[4] Stratford-Harley, 23 Oct. 1728, HMC *Portland MSS* vii. 468.

Christianity.'[1] Jennens's suicide was attributed to the tensions set in train by reading such 'horrible stuff'.[2]

The incriminating literature was passed to the bishop of Oxford and as a consequence a prosecution against Stevens was initiated in the vice-chancellor's court. Stevens, who had collapsed on hearing of the discovery of his letters to Jennens, fled abroad, as did another Trinity man, John Cater, whom the bishop of Oxford had already refused to make a priest because of his alleged Arianism. Stevens's father, a lawyer, took his son's name off the books, and the vice-chancellor's court subsequently, in October 1728, expelled him from the university. The case caused something of a furore; among Stevens's critics was John Wesley's brother Samuel.[3] Trinity was apparently not the only college affected. In 1730 *Fog's Weekly Journal* alleged that Magdalen was infested with deists on the strength of the expulsion of two members of the college. 'On Friday, June 12', Hearne wrote,

Mr Pescod, a young M.A. and Demy of Magdalen College, Mr Lisle, Mr Wells (formerly a commoner of Lincoln) and Mr Barnes, three Bach. Demys of the same College, were convened before the President &c. of that College and on Thursday morning, June 18, Pescod and Wells were expelled the College for Blasphemy and other Vile Practices.[4]

The seniors were so uneasy at the signs, however slight, of deistic thinking by the undergraduates that the vice-chancellor (Edward Butler) called a meeting in late November 1728 to publish a *Programma* condemning the 'ill Designing Persons' who sought to implant such views into the 'Unguarded Inexperience of less inform'd Minds'.[5] His fellow heads were wary of appearing intolerant; only four members came to the first meeting and eight to the second. 'Four for the programma', Stratford noted, 'The Vice-Chancellor, Corpus, Trinity and our Proctor. Four

[1] *Two Letters from a Deist to his Friend, with Remarks*, ed. S. Wesley (London 1730), 5.
[2] HMC *Portland MSS* vii. 468; see also J. Spence, *Anecdotes, Observations, and Characters of Books and Men*, ed. S. W. Singer (London 1820), 387-8; 24 Jan. 1729, letter from R. Downes, Hearne, *Collections* x. 69, 71, 86, 305. In his first letter Jennens had written: '*Bayle's* Dictionary is in the *Bodleian* library, where I now and then carry some body or other with me to read in't, and find I shall make more heretics by this means than I design'd ... I have consider'd your letter, yet cannot find that Christianity has done so much mischief in the world as you apprehend it to have done ... the evils of Christianity are not so great as to require an open denial of it, especially considering the ill consequences that may attend such a denial ... I must own it proper that *Deism* should be propagated among friends, where there are no particular reasons to the contrary.' *Two Letters from a Deist*, 1, 2.
[3] In his preface to *Two Letters from a Deist*, pp. iv-v, Samuel Wesley wrote: 'The following Letters indeed pull off the mask, and present a very unusual spectacle, a *Deist* speaking his real sentiments, which are as contrary to his pretensions, as light to darkness.' Samuel Wesley (1691-1739), m. Ch.Ch. 1711.
[4] Hearne, *Collections* x. 297. Robert Pescod, m. St Mary Hall 1721; Balliol 1723; degrees Magdalen, expelled 1730. Thomas Lisle (1709-67), m. Magd. Hall 1725; demy Magd. 1726-32, fellow 1732-47; public orator 1746-9.
[5] *Programma* (2 Dec. 1728), copy in Bodl. G.A. Oxon. b.111, fo 39.

against it, our governor, Jesus, your acquaintance Felton of Edmond Hall ... and the Proctor of New College.'[1] When the meeting was renewed on 2 December, sixteen being present, the whig Dean Bradshaw suggested that the *Programma* might infringe the rights of college visitors, but in the upshot only he and the principal of Jesus voted against it.[2] The *Programma* thus went out, reminding tutors of the need to instruct their pupils in the 'Articles of the Religion which They Profess, and are often call'd upon to subscribe to' by 'recommending to Them, the frequent and careful Reading the Scriptures and such other Books, as may serve more effectually to promote Christianity, Sound Principles and Orthodox Faith'. Although the object seemed harmless enough—'to guard', as the vice-chancellor put it, 'the Youth of this Place against these Wicked Advocates for Pretended Humane Reason against Divine Revelation'— Dean Bradshaw persisted in his opposition and refused to post the notice, an action which confirmed Charles Wesley,[3] then a Student at Christ Church, in his poor view of whiggish religion, and of the invidious threat to the true faith which cool-minded clerics like Dean Bradshaw seemed to represent.

The need to rebuff deistic thinking was a frequent theme with preachers at St Mary's in the first half of the eighteenth century. So Thomas Hind, chaplain to the earl of Halifax and rector of Lillingstone Lovell, preaching on Act Sunday, 7 July 1717, attacked the profane teaching of Samuel Clarke and William Whiston in order to demonstrate the divinity of Christ from scriptural sources. 'For this', he told his congregation,

is the only true *Primitive Christianity*, the only *Scripture Doctrine of the Trinity*. Is it not amazing then, that Men, nevertheless, by little Quibbles and Distinctions ... should dare attempt to pull our Saviour out of his *Royal Throne*, and, as much as in them lies, strip him of his Majesty and eternal Godhead, and thrust him down into the rank of creatures, the works of his own hands ... For did ever mortal, before *Arius* and *Socinus*, and their Forefathers started these Absurdities in Divinity, which their Successors and Disciples are now endeavouring to revive amongst us ... hear of an *Independent* and *Dependent* God.[4]

'Must They' (the clergy), Joseph Betty declared in a university sermon on 21 September 1729, 'be Exposed to the Capricious Humours, the Witty

---

[1] Stratford-Harley, 26 Nov. 1728, HMC *Portland MSS* vii. 469. Those counted, besides the vice-chancellor, were John Mather (Corpus), William Dobson (Trinity), Robert Manaton (m. Ch.Ch. 1715; proctor 1728), William Bradshaw (dean of Christ Church, 'our governor') Thomas Pardo (Jesus), Henry Felton (1680–1740, m. SEH 1696; BD Queen's 1709; principal SEH 1722–40) and Carew Reynell (1694–1745, m. New College 1712; proctor 1728).

[2] Stratford-Harley, 2 Dec. 1728, HMC *Portland MSS* vii. 470.

[3] Charles Wesley (1707–88), Student Ch.Ch. 1726.

[4] T. Hind, *The Divinity of our Saviour prov'd from the Scriptures of the Old and New Testament, in a Sermon Preached before the University of Oxford at St Mary's on Act-Sunday, July 7. 1717* (Oxford [1717]), 29. Thomas Hind (1683–1748), m. Linc. 1697.

Malice, and the Raging Insolence of *Arians* and *Atheists*, of *Libertines* and *Latitudinarians*, of *Socinians* and *Deists*?'[1] Betty's sermon led to a battle of pamphlets, which may have contributed to the author's suicide on 8 January 1731 from an overdose of laudanum.[2] Thomas Hutchinson, a prebendary of Chichester, made a not dissimilar point in his university sermon of 1 July 1739. 'The surprising effects of zeal, without knowledg [*sic*] ... of free-thinking, without the just exercise of reason, have no where appear'd more remarkably, than in the writings of modern enemies to reveal'd religion.'[3] Preachers constantly reaffirmed the dangers of infidelity. There is here, said William Cleaver on 24 January 1762, inquiring into the character of King David and referring to his polygamy, 'no Room for the Triumphs of Deism, the licentious Principles of which on this Subject are so notorious under the Light of a better and more perfect Dispensation'.[4]

It is against this background that the work of John and Charles Wesley and the rise of the so-called Holy Club must be set, since what they and their friends in other colleges were to try to do was to provide both an effective antidote to deism and to the lukewarm Christianity so characteristic of university religion. John Wesley had entered Christ Church in 1720 after schooling at Charterhouse, graduated in 1724, was ordained the next year and on 25 March 1726 was elected into the Lincolnshire fellowship at Lincoln College recently vacated by Sir John Thorold.[5] His election resulted from his father Samuel's[6] friendship with Lincoln's head, John Morley, who held the living of Scotton, near Gainsborough, with his rectorship. John was plainly a comely and conscientious young man, who appears in his diaries and letters as studious, sociable and devout. He had esteemed his first tutor at Christ Church, George Wigan, and remained a personal friend of his second, Henry Sherman.[7] His early diaries show the exceptionally wide range of his reading, not simply in theology and church history but in English literature, poetry, geography, history and popular science.[8] He entered fully into college life. An entry in his diary for 9 March 1725 lists some

---

[1] J. Betty, *The Divine Institution of the Ministry and the Absolute Necessity of Church Government: a sermon preach'd before the University of Oxford on Sunday the 21st of September, 1729* (Oxford 1729). Joseph Betty (1687-1731), m. Hart Hall 1714; fellow Exeter 1719.

[2] Hearne, *Collections* x. 374, 378.

[3] T. Hutchinson, *The Use and Scope of the Ceremonial Law briefly represented ... in a sermon preach'd before the University of Oxford, at St Mary's, on Sunday, July 1st 1739*, 3. Thomas Hutchinson (1698-1769), m. Linc. 1715; B and DD Hart Hall 1738.

[4] W. Cleaver, *An Inquiry into the True Character of David King of Israel. A sermon preached before the University of Oxford, at St Marys, on Sunday, Jan. 24 1762. In which the exceptions of a late writer to the conduct of David on some occasions are obviated*, 21.

[5] John Thorold (1703-75), 8th bt; m. Linc. 1721.

[6] Samuel Wesley (1662-1735), m. Exeter 1683; rector of Epworth 1695-1735.

[7] George Wigan (1683-1776), m. Ch.Ch. 1711. Henry Sherman (1681-1739), m. Ch.Ch. 1710.

[8] John Wesley's Oxford diaries (1725-35) are in the Methodist Archives in the John Rylands

seventeen Oxford friends, some from Christ Church but including three
from his future college, Lincoln. With them he breakfasted and dined,
went to the tavern and the coffee-house, played billiards and tennis,
sometimes rode, hunted and shot; he went to the summer races on Port
Meadow, made the occasional wager and was a voracious reader of plays
and, if opportunity offered, a playgoer as well. He noted in cipher the
steps of a new dance and took lessons on the lute. He had already, as his
close relations with Kitty Hargrave at Epworth and with his lady friends
in the choice Cotswold villages of Stanton, Buckland and Broadway,
where he was a welcome visitor, were to demonstrate, a discerning eye for
feminine company.

John Wesley's religious faith, so powerfully moulded by his parents,
more especially by his mother Susanna, was fundamental to his existence.
His early diaries and letters reflect not simply a strong sense of vocation
but an underlying feeling of religious inadequacy. Although the faults so
carefully pinpointed, if often screened in cipher, indolence, untruth-
fulness, intemperate sleep (by which he meant too much sleep, a fault to
which already he ascribed many of the evils of mankind) and detraction
(backbiting), appear both venial and common-place, they reveal already
his obsession with perfectibility, a concept promoted further by his
reading of Thomas à Kempis's *Imitation of Christ*. A religious intensity
bordering on scrupulosity appears beneath the social surface. His affairs
of the heart, soft and genteel as they were, left him with qualms; he must,
he wrote after dallying with Kitty Hargrave, never touch a woman's breast
again.[1] His resolution to do better found fruit in an iron self-discipline, a
careful regulation of time spent and a routine of reading the Bible and
religious devotion. 'Removing soon after to another College', that is
Lincoln, he was to comment in 1738:

I executed a resolution, which I was before convinced was of the utmost
importance, shaking off at once all my trifling acquaintance. I began to see more
and more the value of time. I applied myself closer to study. I watched more
carefully against actual sins. I advised others to be religious, according to that
scheme of religion by which I modelled my own life.[2]

Shortly after his election at Lincoln he had returned to Epworth to help
his father in his parish, only returning into residence in 1729 in response
to an insistent summons from Rector Morley to act as tutor at the college.

University Library of Manchester; they have never been published but are now being edited by
Richard P. Heitzenrater of Southern Methodist University, Dallas. For billiards, tennis etc. see the
entries for 27 Feb. 1730, 10 Sept. and 18-19 Aug. 1725. Between 18 June 1725 and 26 May 1726 he had
read *The Ambitious Stepmother, Jane Shore, Lansdown, The Fair Penitent, Theodosius, The Silent Woman, Half-
Pay Officers, The Royal Consort, The Orphan*, and *The Rehearsal* among other plays.

[1] Wesley's diary, 17 Oct. 1726.
[2] *The Journal of the Rev. John Wesley, A.M.* (4 vols London 1827) i. 94.

His younger brother Charles, who had followed him to Christ Church in 1726, was less of an intellectual, but equally sociable. The envious eye which he momentarily cast over the fortunes and dress of more gilded youths, even a passing infatuation for an actress herself apparently well experienced in the wiles of life and sex, evidently did not linger long. The influence of Epworth and the advice of his elder brother John formed an effective rampart against indiscretion. He began to attend the weekly sacrament, to read the Bible, to say his prayers regularly and to study harder. He 'persuaded', so he wrote later, 'two or three young scholars to accompany me, and to observe the method of study prescribed by the Statutes of the University'.[1] One of these friends was Bob Kirkham of Merton, the son of his brother's friend, the rector of Stanton in the Cotswolds, to whom he wrote somewhat censoriously, '... you can't imagine how wretchedly lazy he is, and how small a share of either learning or piety will content him. Four hours a day he *will* spare for study out of his diversions ...'.[2] If Bob Kirkham, invited to stay at Epworth where brother John could give him tuition, eventually decided to toe the line, some were critical of Charles's admonitions, calling him 'hick-homily' and his friends 'Methodists', 'Bible-Moths', 'Sacramentarians'.[3]

In his enthusiasm, Charles had begun to proselytize. 'I have', he told John in May 1729,

a modest, humble, well-disposed youth lives next me, and have been (I thank God!) somewhat instrumental in keeping him so. He was got into vile hands, and is now broke loose. I assisted in setting him free, and will do my utmost to hinder his getting in with 'em again ... He was of opinion that passive goodness was sufficient, and would fain have kept in with his acquaintance and God at the same time.[4]

Charles persuaded his friend William Morgan to take the sacrament regularly and recommended him to read Robert Nelson's *A Companion of the Festivals and Feasts of the Church of England*, with such good effect that William became 'resolved to spare no pains in working out his salvation'.[5] If the Holy Club was then in the making at Charles's initiative, it was John Wesley's return to a tutorship at Lincoln which gave its work an added dimension.[6]

The Holy Club, like many other religious societies of late seventeenth-

[1] F. Baker, *Charles Wesley* (London 1948), 14.

[2] Ibid. 15. Robert Kirkham (1708–67), m. Merton 1727.

[3] The name Methodist was first used in the summer of 1732: J. Clayton–J. Wesley, 5 Sept. 1732, *The Journal of the Rev. John Wesley, A.M.*, ed. N. Curnock (8 vols London 1909) viii. 281; *Fog's Weekly Journal*, 9 Dec. 1732 and a tract in reply entitled *The Oxford Methodists* (London Dec. 1733).

[4] *Letters*, ed. F. Baker (2 vols in Works of John Wesley xxv–vi Oxford 1980, 1982) i (1721–39), p. 237.

[5] Ibid.

[6] The name 'Holy Club' was not used until November 1730 and was apparently dropped six months later: see Ingham's diary.

and early eighteenth-century England, was designed in the first instance to promote and deepen individual piety, and so to limit the appeal of deism and to overcome the formalism of Oxford religion. Such a response might be expected to have evoked sympathy rather than hostility among the more religiously minded dons. For the prevailing ethos of the Anglican establishment in the university was traditionalistic in character, and rooted in patristic theology, of which for instance John Potter, the future primate, for long bishop of Oxford and regius professor of divinity, was himself a learned exponent. Nor was pietism unknown in Oxford life. Anthony Horneck of Queen's, who was made chaplain of All Saints, had earlier as preacher at the Savoy attracted attention by founding a religious society for the reformation of manners and by writing devotional tracts, more especially for the preparation of the sacrament.[1] Into the pattern of piety not unfamiliar to Oxford men and of the religious societies of which Josiah Woodward wrote,[2] Wesley and his friends at first fitted without difficulty. What they were doing may have seemed at first no more than a somewhat firmer expression of pietistic activities familiar to churchmen of the early eighteenth century. Wesley's philanthropic ventures were thus to win the high regard of the pious layman Sir John Philipps, and the pastoral work which he and his friends undertook in the Oxford prisons had the approval of Bishop Potter as well as that of the tory head of Lincoln, who in 1731 was Euseby Isham. It was only later that Wesley's apparent enthusiasm seemed to outrun orthodox discretion and consequently aroused criticism. At first John believed it to be his prime duty to further the academic studies of Charles and his Irish friend, William Morgan, by instructing them in theology.[3] But such tutorials were to be also vehicles for deepening spirituality, in particular for the rediscovery of the supposed practices of the early church, for making frequent early communions, for the reading of the scriptures, for stressing the practice of fasting, on both Wednesdays and Fridays. It was to the apostolic and patristic writings that John turned for enlightenment, earning appropriately enough the nickname of 'Primitive Christianity' from his friends in the Cotswolds.

The infant society, if such it could be called, had only a small membership, John, Charles, William Morgan and possibly Francis Gore and a few others. 'A gentleman of Merton College [Bob Kirkham] who was one of our little company, which now consisted of five persons',

[1] Anthony Horneck (1641–97), MA Heidelberg; incorporated at Queen's 1664.

[2] J. Woodward, *An Account of the Rise and Progress of the Religious Societies in the City of London &c. and of their Endeavours for Reformation of Manners* (2nd edn London 1698). Josiah Woodward (1656–1712), m. SEH 1673.

[3] William Morgan (1712–32), m. Ch.Ch. 1728, one of the original members of the Holy Club, he later suffered a nervous breakdown ending in madness and death. Many attributed his end to the austerities of the Holy Club society, a charge which Wesley repudiated vigorously.

Wesley was to recall later, 'acquainted us that he had been rallied the day before for being a member of the Holy Club'.[1] The membership was plainly a shifting one, with a small hard core and an ampler periphery, probably never more than twenty at the most. The Holy Club was hardly an organized society in the modern sense of the word. While its members took direction in some sense from John, in practice they met in small groups in college rooms, clustered usually around young dons, meeting independently of each other to share in prayer, the reading of devotional books and religious talk. 'I hope in God', John Clayton, high tory and high churchman, the son of a Manchester bookseller, wrote to Wesley on 6 September 1732, 'we shall get at least an advocate for us, if not a brother and a fellow labourer, in every College in town.'[2]

This formed indeed the general pattern of the early organization. Small groups appeared in a number of colleges, Christ Church, Lincoln, Queen's, Brasenose, Merton, Corpus, Magdalen, Exeter and Pembroke. At Brasenose Clayton, who was to return in 1734 to Manchester to become chaplain to the collegiate church there, had at least two other sympathizers in his college, William Nowell who later moved to Oriel and Matthew Salmon. At Corpus the lead was taken by another Manchester man, Thomas Patten, a young fellow and friend of Clayton's who impressed his contemporaries by his regular attendance at communion and his diligence in fasting;[3] John Burton, who was closely associated with the Society for the Propagation of Christian Knowledge, was Patten's senior colleague, and a third sympathizer was another young don, Charles Kinchin, who held the Hampshire living of Dummer.[4] There was also a small group of young dons at Magdalen, among them William Haward and Matthew Horbery, who were joined by another of Wesley's Lincoln pupils, William Clements, the nephew of an Oxford bookseller.[5] None of these was to long persist in their complete commitment to the society. At Queen's the lead was taken by the sturdy Yorkshireman Benjamin Ingham; a group of undergraduates, Henry Washington, Robert Watson, Thomas Smyth, Christopher Atkinson and John Ford, were regularly in

[1] J. Wesley-R. Morgan senior, 19-21 Oct. 1732, *Letters*, ed. Baker, i. 338.
[2] Journal of John Wesley, ed. Curnock viii. 281. John Clayton (1709-73), m. BNC 1725.
[3] Thomas Patten (1713-90), m. BNC 1730; degrees CCC 1733. Patten eventually became rector of Childrey in Berkshire and was esteemed as a conscientious parish priest: *Boswell's Life of Johnson*, ed. G. B. Hill (6 vols Oxford 1887), rev. L. F. Powell (6 vols London 1934-50) iv. 162.
[4] Charles Kinchin (1711-42), m. CCC 1725.
[5] William Haward (1703-56), m. Merton 1720; degrees Magd. Matthew Horbery (1707-73), m. Linc. 1726; degrees Magd. Horbery (later dean of divinity and vice-president) refused the suggestion that he should stand for the presidency being 'of such uncommon modesty and invincible diffidence'. He was successively vicar of Eccleshall and of Standlake; his sermons were much esteemed both by Dr Johnson and David Garrick: J. Nichols, *Literary Anecdotes of the Eighteenth Century* (9 vols London 1812-15) ix. 558-63. William Clements m. Linc. 1726; BA Wadham 1730; MA Magd. 1733. Clements's commitment to the Holy Club fluctuated: see for example Wesley's diary under 25 Oct. and 7 Nov. 1732, 6 Nov. 1733; see also Clayton's letters to Wesley of 1 Aug. and 4 Sept. 1732, *Letters*, ed. Baker i. 331.

his company; 'we appointed', Ingham wrote in his diary on 9 November 1733, 'to meet every Friday night for the future, to read and encourage one another in virtues and religion'. There were also sympathizers in Merton (under Bob Kirkham), at Jesus and Wadham (under another young don, Richard Watkins), at Exeter (under Thomas Broughton, a young fellow) and in Pembroke—all colleges, whig in complexion, where the Holy Club may have formed some means of relief from the establishment in church and state.[1]

Naturally the two colleges where the club was strongest were Christ Church and Lincoln. It had been started in Christ Church but enthusiasm eventually ebbed there, possibly because of the scorn which the group's activities evoked, the less surprising if it is remembered that, apart from Charles Wesley, its leaders there included the impulsive and ultimately unbalanced Irishman, William Morgan, and the melancholic Welshman, John Gambold who, like Ingham, eventually became a Moravian.[2]

The development of the fortunes of the Holy Club in Lincoln can be charted with some precision. 'There is a society of gentlemen, consisting of seven members', Richard Morgan was to inform his father in 1734, 'whom the world calls Methodists, of which my tutor [John Wesley] is president'.[3] Wesley denied indignantly the charge that he used his tutorial position to proselytize, but circumstances created both by his personality and function made it unusually difficult for the young men under his supervision to evade his influence. He advised his pupils on extra-curricular reading and went with them on expeditions outside Oxford to Blenheim, Rousham and elsewhere. Initially he was allotted ten pupils: John Westley, Jonathan Black, Thomas Hylton, Robert Davison, John Bartholomew, John Sympson, Edward Browne, Richard Bainbridge, George Podmore and Thomas Waldegrave (the latter eventually became Gibbon's tutor at Magdalen). None of them appears to have been influenced decisively by his religious views, but later the intensity and rigidity of these views made Rector Isham unwilling to entrust more men to his care. In 1733 Wesley told his mother that he had as many pupils as he wanted, adding however: 'If I have no more pupils after these are gone from me, I shall then be glad of a curacy near you.'[4] The next year Richard Morgan, who had come to resent Wesley's paternalistic control, asked his father to transfer him to the care of the other tutor in college, presumably

---

[1] Richard Watkins (1702-76), m. Wadham 1720. Thomas Broughton (1712-77). m. Univ. 1731; fellow Exeter 1734-41.

[2] John Gambold (1711-71), m. Ch.Ch. 1726.

[3] R. Morgan junior-R. Morgan senior [14 Jan. 1734], *Letters*, ed. Baker i. 365. Richard Morgan junior, m. Linc. 1733; brother of William. Their father was Richard Morgan (1679-1742), m. Hart Hall 1696; 2nd remembrancer in the court of exchequer in Dublin (a post later occupied by Richard Morgan junior).

[4] *Letters*, ed. Baker i. 355.

Richard Hutchins. 'He has what few are in college (except one gentleman-commoner and two servitors who are Mr Wesley's pupils) under his tuition.'[1] By 1734 Wesley had apparently only three pupils, Westley Hall, a gentleman-commoner, Matthew Robinson and either Joseph Green or Joseph Leech, both servitors.[2] Yet, by contrast with the men first placed under his supervision, Hall, Robinson, Green and Leech, as well as Richard Morgan, were all very much under Wesley's influence and closely linked to the Holy Club.

The pressure which Wesley brought to bear was for some difficult to resist. 'Poor starving Johnny' Whitelamb from Wroot near Epworth, where he had been employed originally by John's father as an amanuensis, entered Lincoln as a servitor at the late age of 22.[3] With very limited means he depended much on Wesley's charity and goodwill. 'John Whitelamb', John told his brother Samuel on 17 November 1731, 'wants a gown much, and I am not rich enough to buy him one at present. If you are willing my twenty shillings should go toward that, I will add ten to them.'[4] Wesley held high hopes of Whitelamb. 'He reads one English, one Latin, and one Greek book alternatively', he informed his father,

and never meddles with a new one in any of the languages till he has ended the old one. If he goes on as he has begun, I dare take upon me to say that by the time he has been here four or five years there will not be such an one of his standing in Lincoln College, perhaps not in the University of Oxford.[5]

Almost inevitably Whitelamb was drawn into the activities of the Holy Club, supervising the children from the school and workhouse. But Wesley soon became uneasy about him, charged him with 'vanity' and made him promise to give up the unsuitable acquaintances that in Wesley's opinion he had evidently made. Nor were the unsuitable acquaintances exclusively male, which was somewhat disturbing, since Whitelamb was already contracted to Wesley's sister Mary, 'patient, grizzle Moll', whom he was shortly to marry.[6] Through the elder Wesley's influence, the lord chancellor offered Whitelamb the dreary parish of Wroot, which Samuel himself had held in plurality with Epworth since 1725. Mary died in childbirth on 1 November 1734, and Whitelamb, in spite of some attempt to persuade him to work in America, remained at Wroot a further thirty-five years, steadily growing

---

[1] Letter [14 Jan. 1734], ibid. 366.
[2] Westley Hall (1710-76), m. Linc. 1731. Matthew Robinson (1713-45), m. Linc. 1730; MA BNC 1737.
[3] John Whitelamb (1707-69), m. Linc. 1731.
[4] *Letters*, ed. Baker i. 322.
[5] J. Wesley-S. Wesley senior [11 June 1731], ibid. 282.
[6] See Wesley's diary under 18 June, 3, 11, 14 Aug. and 14, 15, 17, 18, 19, 24 Sept. 1733.

more embittered. 'Oh, why did he not die forty years ago, while he knew in whome he had believed!' was John Wesley's somewhat harsh comment on hearing of his death.[1] But perhaps Johnny had the last word: 'God grant you and your followers', he wrote after hearing Wesley preach at Epworth in 1742, 'may always have entire liberty of conscience! Will you not allow others the same?'[2]

Wesley's experience with Whitelamb had its parallels in similar relationships with other Lincoln men who became associated with the activities of the Holy Club. Matthew Robinson was another Lincolnshire boy, the son of the vicar of Blyborough, who had entered the college as a servitor in 1730. Wesley talked with him about the sacraments, with the result that he asked the rector's permission to take communion at Christ Church in December 1732. But within a year he was having some doubts about the Holy Club. Wesley called him for long talks in his rooms and in the college garden. Robinson avowed that he no longer wished to take communion at Christ Church, but he was no match for his tutor's fervent arguments. Entries in Wesley's diary suggest how disappointed he was at Robinson's defection, more especially as the young man had actually used his 'theme' (corresponding to the modern weekly essay) to criticize the Methodists.[3] When some years after Charles Wesley met Robinson, by now a fellow of Brasenose, and his friend Oliver Battely in the Long Walk, they were distant, if not hostile, urging Charles to export more of the 'Cowley saints' to Georgia and charging the Methodists with 'intrusion, schism, and bringing neglect upon the ministry'. Charles warned them, 'Remember, you will be of my mind when you come to die'.[4]

John Robson, yet another Lincoln undergraduate, showed similar signs of faltering.[5] Wesley recorded his attendance at, or failure to attend, communion as a sort of spiritual temperature gauge. When he failed to rise in the early morning, Wesley invariably talked with him at some length and 'prevailed', once with the young man 'in tears'. But, in the long run, Robson too ceased to persevere.[6] 'I charge Mr Robson', Wesley wrote on 30 September 1735, 'in the name of the Lord Jesus that he no longer halt between two opinions'; he urged him to keep the fasts on Fridays and Wednesdays, and advised him to read Tilly's sermons on free will; but, alas, in vain. 'I met', Charles noted in his journal in June 1743, 'poor, languid, dead Mr Robson.'[7]

[1] *The Letters of John Wesley, A.M.* ed. J. Telford (8 vols London 1931) v. 151, 4 Oct. 1769.
[2] L. Tyerman, *The Oxford Methodists* (London 1873), 382.
[3] Wesley's diary, 30 Dec. 1732, 25 June, 22, 31 July and 10, 12 Aug. 1733.
[4] C. Wesley, *The Journal of the Rev. Charles Wesley* (2 vols London 1849) i. 73.
[5] John Robson (1715–1802), m. Linc. 1732; MA New Inn Hall 1742.
[6] Wesley's diary, 30 July 1730, 16, 23 Apr., 4, 11, 22 Nov. and 8 Dec. 1733, 18 Jan., 1 Mar., 25, 30 May and 5 June 1734; Ingham's diary, 8 Apr. 1734.
[7] J. Wesley–R. Morgan junior [30 Sept. 1735], *Letters*, ed. Baker i. 438. *Journal of Charles Wesley* i. 319.

Not all encounters had such lame endings. The most dramatic of all was a sequel to the admission to Lincoln of Richard Morgan. Convinced of Wesley's rectitude and high endeavour, Richard's father decided, somewhat unwisely, to entrust his younger son to his care. Richard had, however, no intention of following the example of his brother William. As an affluent gentleman-commoner he tried to be something of a 'smart', buying a dog (in spite of an order banning dogs in college) which Wesley persuaded him to return. To his growing resentment he soon found that his life seemed to be controlled at every turn by his tutor, who told him not merely what to read but when to rise, what friends to choose, what expeditions to take. Wesley at least once extracted him from the congenial company of the senior common room, of which, as a gentleman-commoner, he was a member. No wonder Wesley's colleague Richard Hutchins told Wesley that Morgan felt confined.[1] When Morgan refused to leave the common room to attend a meeting of the Holy Club one Saturday evening he felt obliged to apologize. In a subsequent talk Wesley 'opened religion' to him, persuading him to read the gloomy moral tract the *Second Spira* and later fortunately found him 'affected', 'Warm'd'.[2] Wesley was sufficiently confident of his success with his pupil to write, in spite of a cautionary letter from Richard's father that he should not press his son too far, that

Mr Morgan usually rises about six, and has not yet been wanting in diligence. He seldom goes out of college, unless upon business or to walk for his health . . . He loses no time at taverns or coffee-houses, and avoids as much as possible idle company . . . Some evenings every week he spends in the common room, and others with my brother and me.[3]

Yet the young man undoubtedly chafed at a surfeit of religious books and what to him appeared to be too pious a company. During Christmas he caused Wesley some concern by staying up too late.[4] Angry and overwrought, Morgan complained to his father:

He has lectured me scarce in anything but books of devotion . . . By being his pupil I am stigmatized with the name of a Methodist, the misfortune of which I cannot describe . . . I am as much laughed at and despised by the whole town as any of them, and always shall be so while I am his pupil. The whole college makes a jest of me, and the fellows themselves do not show me common civility, so great is their aversion to my tutor . . . I think it incumbent upon me to inform you that it is my opinion that if I am continued under Mr Wesley I shall be ruined.[5]

---

[1] Wesley's diary, 10 and 14 Nov. 1733.
[2] Ibid. 18 Nov. 1733.
[3] Letter of 17 Dec. 1733, *Letters* ed. Baker 359-60.
[4] Wesley's diary, 27 Dec. 1733, 1, 2 Jan. 1734.
[5] Letter [14 Jan. 1734], *Letters*, ed. Baker 367.

Unfortunately Morgan left the letter open on his desk where it was seen and read by Wesley when he called at his room while Morgan was out. Wesley noted in his diary grimly that evening that there was no sincerity in him and at once prepared a letter to Morgan's father in extenuation of his own conduct and in condemnation of his pupil.[1]

The outcome was curious but not unpredictable. The elder Morgan, sensible and placatory as ever, admonished his son, urging him to work rather than to play: 'Squander not away the morning in tea and chat.' But he advised Wesley not to bring too much pressure to bear on Richard to make him become a fully committed member of 'that strict religious society'.[2] It was advice that Wesley did not find easy to accept. The long heart-to-heart talks continued, and Morgan was among the small group of friends who said farewell to the brothers when they embarked at Gravesend for Georgia. 'Mr Morgan', Charles told his brother Samuel on 31 July 1734, 'is in a fairer way of becoming a Christian than we ever yet knew him.'[3] After leaving Oxford Morgan's religious enthusiasm was to evaporate, but he had sufficient esteem for his old tutor to entertain him when he visited Dublin in July 1769 where Morgan was second remembrancer.[4] In Queen's Ingham was occasionally faced with similar problems. 'At night', he observed on 1 November 1733, 'I had a dispute with Knail, whom I had obliged to observe the fast; he held that the Church did not [have] power to institute such things, neither are we obliged to keep them.' Momentarily his friend John Ford, Ingham noted, also proved recalcitrant. At 7.30 a.m. on Friday morning 26 April 'Ford came, he told us the story of his fall, his father and mother the chief causes; religious talk of his great sin, he seemed insensible of it, objected against many things; we exhorted him to go to the Sacrament at Christ Church, he did not consent'. Yet by the same evening he had come round and, in addition to taking the sacrament, agreed 'to meet with us on Wednesdays, Saturdays, and Sundays; and Fridays'.[5] The moral pressures were substantial; yet, as in other religious societies, the membership was often fleeting and fluctuating.

Others, such as James Hervey and George Whitefield, found in the activities of the Holy Club the roots of a lifelong commitment to evangelical religion, even if they did not hold precisely to the views which the Wesleys were later to fashion. While, for instance, Ingham took his lead from John Wesley (though he did not meet him until 18 April 1733), he was in the main associated with the group which met at

---

[1] Wesley's diary, 14, 15 Jan. 1734; *Letters*, ed. Baker i. 367–71.
[2] R. Morgan senior-his son, 31 Jan. 1734 and same-Wesley [31 Jan. 1734], ibid. 325 n, 374–6.
[3] Quoted in *Letters of John Wesley*, ed. Telford i. 160n.
[4] *Journal of John Wesley*, ed. Curnock vi. 329.
[5] Ingham's diary, 1 Nov. 1733, 26, 27, 28 Apr. 1734.

Charles Wesley's rooms at Christ Church.[1] On the other hand, Lincoln men, James Hervey, John Robson, Thomas Greive, went to Ingham's own group in Queen's or met in each other's rooms in Lincoln.[2] These 'gathered' groups, in number ranging from two to six persons, usually headed by a young graduate or don, were concerned above all to stress the need for Christian commitment. They met regularly, sometimes at 1 p.m. more often between 7 and 9 p.m. On fast-days they sometimes met for breakfast at 3 p.m. They sought to deepen their spiritual lives by rigorous self-examination of their thoughts and actions many times a day, interspersing their meditations by prayer and the reading of devotional books and the Greek Testament, and by 'religious talk' with their friends.[3] After the example of John Wesley, they described their day in diaries, modelled as exactly as possible after Wesley's own, the keywords of which were sometimes screened by abbreviations, symbols and cipher.[4] But they were not intended as secret documents, for they discussed their diaries with each other, accepting reproof and surer progress in their spiritual pilgrimage. 'We agreed', as Ingham put it on 9 May 1734, 'to tell one another our faults and to pray for one another.' Ingham himself was apt to make a spiritual balance sheet at the end of each day under the headings 'Blessings' and 'Sins'.[5] They made resolutions, especially during Lent, regulating their devotions, rationing the amount of food and drink and redeeming the time.[6] Wesley's strong belief in the virtue of early rising led his followers to copy his example. Ingham, for instance, who tried to rise at 4 a.m. found difficulty in complying with this rule. 'From sufficient and sad experience I do consider that it is sinful to lie waking in bed, or to sleep longer than the health and strength of our bodies require.'[7] In consequence he purchased a 'larum' to wake himself, tried sleeping on his bed without sheets, sconced himself a penny for going back to bed after rising, did without

[1] Ingham's diary, 17 Mar. and 11 Apr. 1734.

[2] Ibid. 8 Apr. 1734.

[3] The books which they read in their private groups were very similar, for example *The Country Parson's Advice*, John Goodman's *Winter-Evening Conference*, P. Browne's *Human Understanding*, Jeremy Taylor's *Holy Living and Holy Dying, The Life of M. de Renty* and *The Spiritual Conflict*, attributed to Juan de Castiniza.

[4] Heitzenrater observes in his introduction to Ingham's diary (typescript, pp. 1-4): 'We know that at least fifteen of the Oxford Methodists learned the coded system of diary-keeping that Wesley was developing.' Cf Ingham's diary, 1 Nov. 1733, 'this day I taught Ford, Atkinson, and Washington to write a diary'; 1 Mar. 1734, 'at Charles Wesley's, he taught us to keep an exacter diary'.

[5] Ibid. 22 Apr. 1734.

[6] Ingham's ten resolutions for Lent included setting apart 4 to 5 a.m. for devotion (and 8 to 9 p.m. also on Monday, Tuesday, Wednesday and Friday). If he failed to rise 'before the larum ceases', he was 'to miss one meal that day or at least to sconce myself one pence to be given to the poor'. He was to meditate on his knees for set hours, to eat no butter 'unless with strangers', to have only one meal on Wednesdays and Fridays 'if possible', to eat no baked pudding on Sunday. Ibid. 4 Mar. 1734.

[7] Heitzenrater, p. 20.

dinner or supper and even persuaded a friend to sleep on chairs in his room to act as a 'sentry' to wake him.[1]

Aiming at a life of salvation and perfectibility, they took their models from the teachings of the early church, more especially from its observance of the 'stationary' fasts on Wednesdays and Fridays. In addition to regular attendance at their college chapels they took the sacrament on Sundays and other days at St Mary's or Christ Church. Occasionally communion was celebrated for the sick in a private room.[2]

What brought the members together was above all their participation in common works of charity. Colleges had long sent donations to the prisoners in the Oxford prisons, the castle and the Bocardo; John Wesley's father, Samuel, had visited the prisons while he was an undergraduate at Exeter. But it was novel to undertake this task in so regular a fashion. The young men conducted services, preached, celebrated holy communion once a month. They distributed Bibles and tracts among the prisoners. 'Pray, don't forget', Clayton reminded Wesley, who was in London winning the support of the blind philanthropist Sir John Philipps, 'a few Common Prayer Books for the Castle.'[3] Wesley and his friends provided medicines, fuel and other necessities. They taught the prisoners and their children how to read. 'There are only two in the jail', Clayton reported to Wesley, 'who want this accomplishment,—John Clanville, who reads but moderately, and the horse-stealer, who cannot yet read at all.'[4] They took a deep interest in the prisoners' cases and tried to ensure that they received appropriate legal aid. While it is not always plain what the charges were, the reiteration of certain names—Topping, Salmon, Blair—and the constant visits made testify to the amount of time spent in these charitable operations. Clayton remarked:

You must know then that last week I writ out a state of her [Mrs Topping's] case and sent it up to London to one Mr Waddilove, an eminent attorney, who sent me down his opinion . . . informing me that the whole of Mr Sheldon's proceedings were null and invalid, and that if we had but a small sum of money we might sue him for a trespasser, and recover very considerable damages.[5]

The case of Blair engrossed Wesley's attention for several months and brought the Methodists unfavourable publicity. Blair was accused of alleged sodomitical practices.[6] Throughout the autumn and winter of

[1] Ingham's diary, 21 Nov. 1733: '*This day* I hired a larum for two shillings *a year*; Atkinson *was to pay* one half *and I to call him*.' Ibid. 1 June 1734: 'N.B. Atkinson stood sentry all night by my bedside in two chairs.'
[2] Ibid. 14 May 1734: '11.15 Hughs came, I Hervey, and Atkinson with three women and the clerk received the Holy Sacrament with the sick person.'
[3] Letter of 1 Aug. 1732, *Letters*, ed. Baker i. 334.
[4] *Journal of John Wesley*, ed. Curnock viii. 276.
[5] Letter of 4 Sept. 1732, ibid. 278.
[6] Oxford, County Record Office, sessions minutes 1726–32, pp. 144, 147.

1732 and the first six months of 1733 Wesley was constantly visiting him, instructing his lawyer and, after the unfortunate man had been found guilty, helping him, for Blair could not pay his fine and was persecuted by his fellow prisoners. Wesley's intervention in this case, coinciding with the first open criticisms of the Holy Club, was critically received. Thomas Wilson noted in his diary on 22 November 1732:

Mr Horn and I had rather a warm dispute about the Methodists taking the part of Blair who was found guilty of Sodomitical Practices and fined 20 marks by the Recorder. Whether the man is innocent or no they were not proper judges, it was better he should suffer than such a scandal given an countenacing [*sic*] a man whom the whole town think guilty of such an enormous crime. Whatever good design they pretend it was highly imprudent and has given the occasion of terrible reflections.[1]

Nor was their work confined to the prisons. They visited St Thomas's workhouse by the south-west corner of Little Hythe Bridge Street to read prayers and the Bible with the inmates, to talk with the old people and to catechize and teach the children.[2] Ingham and his friends also visited the local almshouse, St Bartholomew's Hospital (Bartlemas) in the Cowley Road, but found no almsmen there,[3] as well as the workhouse at Whitefriars on Gloucester Green. Wesley was especially concerned to further the education of poor children, giving money to the local charity school, the Grey-Coat School, and with William Morgan setting up a special charity school. John Gambold wrote:

The school was, I think, of Mr Wesley's own setting up; however he paid the mistress, and clothed some, if not all of the children. When they went thither, they inquired how each child behaved, saw their work (for some could knit or spin), heard them read, heard them their prayers or their catechism, and explained part of it.[4]

Such practical activity was, in the Methodists' view, a manifestation of virtue and interior holiness rather than a means of attaining it.

Although the numbers involved were small, the diffusion of the Holy Club through the colleges, its members' unusual tenacity in religious observance and their charitable activities attracted attention throughout the city and university. In London they had acquired sympathetic well-wishers, among them Sir John Philipps and the publisher Charles Rivington, and in Oxford itself they received some encouragement. Bishop Potter was at first friendly, confirming one of the prisoners

[1] *The Diaries of Thomas Wilson*, ed. C. L. S. Linnell (London 1964), 81.
[2] See for example Ingham's diary, 23 Jan. and 5 Apr. 1734.
[3] Ibid. Easter Tuesday, 16 Apr. 1734, 'did not meet with the poor people'; 21 Apr. 1734, 'could not find the poor people, resolved to go no more'.
[4] *Journal of John Wesley*, ed. Curnock viii. 267.

(Irwin) at Cuddesdon at John Wesley's request.[1] When Wesley visited the bishop there on 2 October 1732 they had a long and friendly talk on the administration of the communion at Christ Church and St Mary's, on fasting and the penal laws. Such sympathy underlay the point that Wesley's piety in his early days was an exaggeration of a religious tradition which Oxford found congenial.

But before the end of 1732 the mood was changing, so that even the well-wishers became apprehensive and critical. The death of young William Morgan, Blair's case and a hostile letter on 9 December in *Fog's Weekly Journal* brought the criticism to a head. The letter in the *Journal* evoked a strongly worded reply, possibly from the pen of William Law, and Wesley did what he could to rebut the charges made against his society, calling on the vice-chancellor to allay the fears of those in authority.[2] The crisis passed, but it is doubtful whether the Holy Club was ever to be quite as strong again. Of William Smith, the only other fellow of Lincoln closely identified with the Methodists, Clayton had reported as early as August 1732 that he was a target for the venom of his colleagues. Clayton visited Lincoln every day, 'big with expectation to hear of some mighty attack made upon Mr Smith; but, I thank God, I have always been disappointed; for not one of the Fellows has once so much as tried to shake him, or to convert him from the right way'.[3] Undergraduates sometimes jeered at the Methodists as they went to church. 'Public Prayers, Sermon and Sacrament at St Mary's', Ingham wrote on Tuesday 23 April 1734; 'I was very bold and not at all concerned at the crowds of gazers'.[4] As is often the way with minority groups, the situation had been over-dramatized; but there could be no doubt that the activities of the Holy Club were causing concern. If, outside Lincoln, Wesley's university sermons won some warm applause, others were critical of his 'enthusiasm'. Although there were new recruits, and growing interest among a small group of townspeople, the Holy Club was making less impact than Wesley hoped it would, so adding to a growing feeling of disillusion.

John and Charles Wesley were to leave for missionary work in Georgia towards the end of 1735. John's religious discontent, his lack of success in affairs of the heart, the death of his father and his own unreadiness to succeed him at Epworth, his long interest in the Society for the Propagation of Christian Knowledge, his desire to be free from the sophisticated society of Oxford without resigning his fellowship, may all have helped to explain his decision to take the American chaplaincy. While the Holy Club continued its activities—a boast of the Wesleys—it

[1] Wesley's diary, 15 June 1732.
[2] Wesley's diary, 14 Dec. 1732. The vice-chancellor at this time was William Holmes.
[3] *Journal of John Wesley*, ed. Curnock viii. 276, 1 Aug. 1732. William Smith (1707–65), m. Linc. 1726.
[4] Ingham's diary, 23 Apr. 1734.

seemed to lack the impetus of earlier days. A list which gives the names of twenty or so members at this time included Whitefield, Gambold, Horne, Smith, Evans (of Christ Church) Hervey, Robson, Gridsley (no one of this name is known, possibly Greive is meant) Westley Hall, Salmon, Broughton, Chapman, Kitchen (probably a mistake for Kinchin of Corpus) Ingham, Atkinson, Watson, Washington, Bell, Wilson and Smith (of Queen's); many of these were graduates who were soon to leave Oxford. The lead seems momentarily to have been taken by Richard Morgan who continued to visit the Bocardo and to encourage the religious society in which townspeople, notably Mr and Mrs Fox, appeared to be taking a prominent part. Rector Isham censured Morgan for undue recourse to fasting, drawing a somewhat bitter response from the young man:

You cannot sufficiently arm me against the Rector. I suspect him of insincerity to you [i.e. Wesley]. I want to know whether you ever did. I believe, and Mr Horn is of the same opinion, that my going into Ireland depends on my going into the hall on fast days. The Rector said as much as if you frightened others from religion by your example; and that you might have done a great deal of good, if you had been less strict . . .[1]

But Morgan left Oxford in 1736. The most dynamic man among the others was undoubtedly George Whitefield who soon grew to admire the Wesleys: 'For above a twelve-month my soul longed to be acquainted with some of them, and I was strongly pressed to follow their good example, when I saw them go through a ridiculing crowd to receive the Holy Eucharist *at St Mary's*.'[2] Charles Wesley invited Whitefield to breakfast and advised him to read Francke's *Against the Fear of Man* and the well known *The Country Parson's Advice to his Parishioners*, almost a textbook for members of the Holy Club.[3] But Whitefield was only to be in Oxford for a relatively short time after the Wesleys' departure; he acted as a curate for Kinchin at his Hampshire vicarage at Dummer before he too made his way to America.

Kinchin, Broughton and Gambold all had country cures, at Dummer, Cowley and Stanton Harcourt. Ingham, the leading Methodist in the relatively strong group at Queen's, was with the Wesleys in Georgia. The only deeply committed Methodist remaining in Oxford was the delicate, introspective and pious James Hervey who had neither the capacity nor the inclination to take the lead in a group, some of whose teaching he regarded with growing suspicion. Charles Wesley's return to Oxford on 8 February 1737 momentarily breathed new life into the Holy Club. He

[1] Tyerman, *Oxford Methodists*, 22.
[2] *Reminiscences of Oxford* 105.
[3] A. H. Francke, *Nicodemus: or a treatise on the Fear of Man*; the third edition of the English translation (Newcastle upon Tyne 1744) has a preface by John Wesley. [William Holmes,] *The Country Parson's Advice to his Parishioners of the Younger Sort* (Oxford 1742).

stayed with his old friend, the Oxford mercer John Sarney, ostensibly to cast his vote in the parliamentary election in favour of the independent tory William Bromley. But he took the opportunity to revisit the castle. Although his stay was short, Ingham, who had also returned from America, wrote to Wesley in October 1737 in a reassuring way: 'All friends at Oxford go on well. Mr Kinchin, Mr Hutchins, Mr Washington, Bell, Sarney, Hervey, Watson, are all zealous.'[1] Charles Wesley managed to persuade a young fellow of Jesus, Christopher Wells, at first hesitant, to commit himself to the cause. He noted on 29 September 1737:

In the afternoon I met Mr Wells alone and had some close talk with him upon the new birth, self-renunciation, &c. He confessed reputation was his idol; rejected his own righteousness: convinced, but fearful: longing to break loose. I went with him to the chapel; and afterwards resumed the subject. He seemed on the brink of the new birth.[2]

It appeared, however, that support was shifting from the university, where the numbers involved had always been small, to the townsfolk, among them John Sarney (although Charles was to note that by 28 September 1738 he was 'my friend that *was* ... now entirely estranged by the offence of the cross'[3]) and Fox, whom John had befriended in the debtors' prison. Such was the situation in Oxford when John himself returned to England, uneasy in spirit and intensely concerned about his soul's salvation. In Oxford he preached to a 'numerous and serious congregation' at the castle on Sunday, 19 February 1738, but the experience in Georgia had led him to outgrow the formal devotion and practical charity of the Holy Club.[4] He was accompanied to Oxford by the Moravian Peter Böhler, who had so profound an influence over him at this critical juncture of his life. At Oxford over Easter his heart being 'so full', he engaged for the first time at Mr Fox's house in extempore prayer. After rising at half past four, he preached at Wytham on Easter Saturday and attended two religious meetings, one at Fox's house and the other in Washington's rooms in Queen's. On Easter Sunday he preached at 9 a.m. in Lincoln College chapel on the text 'The hour cometh, and now is, when the dead shall hear the voice of the son of God, and they that hear shall live'. At the subsequent celebration of the holy communion, 'all serious, all stayed'. Some days earlier he had gone with Kinchin to visit a condemned man in the castle. After they had prayed, the man confessed: 'I am now ready to die. I know Christ has taken away my sins; and there is no more condemnation for me.'[5] The episode confirmed Wesley in his own need

---

[1] *Letters*, ed. Baker i. 521.
[2] *Journal of Charles Wesley*, i. 76.
[3] Ibid. 131.
[4] *Journal of John Wesley*, ed. Curnock i. 440.
[5] Ibid. 449 and n, 448.

for reassurance, forming a fitting prelude for the 'conversion' experience of the Aldersgate Street meeting of 24 May 1738.

This experience was not simply a turning-point in Wesley's own life, but a landmark in the history of Methodism in Oxford. In the sermon which he preached before the university on 11 June 1738 he stressed strongly the necessity of justification by faith and the impossibility of good works before justification.[1] By implication it was a criticism of the Holy Club's past activities, an attitude which puzzled some of his Oxford friends. Although he remained a fellow of Lincoln, drawing his stipend annually, until his unfortunate marriage obliged him to resign in 1751, Oxford had ceased to be the focal point of his interest. To his former pupil James Hervey, who had remonstrated with him for not undertaking parochial work, Wesley wrote strongly on 25 October 1739:

... you would have me preach ... in a Parish? What Parish, my Brother? I have none at all. Nor I believe ever shall ... Indeed, I cou'd not serve (as they term it) a Cure now. I have tried, and know it is impracticable, to observe the Laws of the English Church, in any Parish in England ... See the matter in another Light, and it comes to a short Issue. I everywhere see GOD's people perishing for lack of knowledge. I have power (thro' GOD) to save their Souls from Death. Shall I use it, or shall I let them perish—because they are not of my Parish?[2]

Yet he was still in 1739 toying with the idea of fulfilling the exercises for the BD, which the statutes of the college required him to take. 'In a few days', he wrote to his brother Samuel on 27 October 1739, 'my brother and I are to go to Oxford to do exercise for our degree. Then, if God enables me, I will prove my charge against Bishop Bull, either in my Latin sermon, or Supposition Speech.'[3] But Samuel died suddenly on 6 November following, and the idea seems to have been put into cold storage. In June 1741, however, he 'inquired concerning the exercises previous to the degree of Bachelor in Divinity' and wrote a plan of a Latin sermon incorporating, as his earlier letter to his brother suggested, passages from Bishop Bull's *Harmonia apostolica* which denied justification by faith.[4] But his interest in taking the step waned as he began to compose his university sermon on 'The Almost Christian' which he preached at St Mary's on 25 July 1741.

This sermon suggested the widening of the gap between conventional university religion and Wesley's position. It demonstrated that he was increasingly critical of the university for what he considered to be a disregard of its own statutes, and of the diluted Christian faith it seemed to espouse. In 1741 he had originally prepared a passionate denunciation

---

[1] *Wesley's Standard Sermons*, ed. E. H. Sugden (2 vols London 1921) i. 35-52.
[2] Lincoln College, Wesley MSS; *Letters*, ed. Baker i. 692.
[3] *Letters*, ed. Baker i. 693-4.
[4] *Journal of John Wesley*, ed. Curnock ii. 468-71.

of Oxford's indolence and moral indifference. But he was persuaded, apparently by the countess of Huntingdon, to change his mind and to substitute a discourse less offensive to his listeners.[1] But the notion did not die and the sermon which he delivered before the university on 24 August 1744 was to be a vigorously worded broadside, denouncing juniors and seniors alike. We are lucky in having an account of it from a very different type of Oxonian, the young William Blackstone, who wrote:

We were last-Friday entertained at St Mary's by a curious Sermon from Wesley the Methodist. Among other equally modest Particulars, he informed us, 1st That there was not one Christian among all the Heads of Houses, 2ndly that Pride, Gluttony, Avarice, Luxury, Sensuality, and Drunkenness were the general Characteristicks of all Fellows of Colleges, who were useless to a proverbial Uselessness. Lastly, that the younger Part of the University were a Generation of Triflers, all of them perjured, and not one of them of any Religion at all.[2]

'O my brethren!', Wesley concluded, 'what a Christian city is this!! It is time for Thee, Lord, to lay to Thine Hand!'[3]

The Hebraist Benjamin Kennicott, representing a very different party in the university, commented that the words were 'full of such presumption' that a 'universal shock' went through the congregation;[4] and after the service the bedel told Wesley that the vice-chancellor (Walter Hodges) wished to have his sermon-notes. He sent them without delay, not without admiring the wise providence of God: 'Perhaps few men of note would have given a sermon of mine the reading if I had put it into their hands; but by this means it came to be read, probably more than once, by every man of eminence in the University.'[5] John Mather, the pro-vice-chancellor, told Rawlinson on 24 September 1744:

The Affair of Wesley, I have had but little concern in, besides the mortification of hearing him preach for about an hour or more. For when I sent the Beadle for his Notes, which he deliver'd to me sealed up, he told me it was well he went soon for 'em, for he found him preparing to go out of town ... Being thus disappointed of summoning Mr Wesly before proper persons, I thought it adviseable to keep his Notes in my own Custody till the Vice-Chancellor came home, who was expected in a little time ... I suppose it will not be long 'ere the Vice-Chancellor does something in that Affair, tho' it is now a busy time with him, just at the removal of the Office from himself to the Rector of Lincoln, where Wesly is still Fellow.[6]

---

[1] Ibid. 478–81.

[2] W. Blackstone–S. Richmond, 28 Aug. 1744, Godalming, Charterhouse Archives, Blackstone colla. MS 1.

[3] *Wesley's Standard Sermons*, ed. Sugden i. 53.

[4] Tyerman, *John Wesley* i. 449.

[5] *Journal of John Wesley*, ed. Curnock iii. 147–8.

[6] Bodl. MS Rawl. lett. 29, fo 102. Richard Rawlinson (1690–1755), m. St John's 1708.

Euseby Isham, who was about to become vice-chancellor, would have been embarrassed had he had to undertake the prosecution of a man whom he still greatly esteemed. It was decided to do nothing but, as Wesley rightly predicted: 'I preached, I suppose the last time, at St Mary's. Be it so. I am now clear of the blood of these men. I have fully delivered my own soul.'[1] He came once more to Oxford as a fellow, at the rector's request to cast his vote in the parliamentary election in favour of Isham's friend Edward Turner. He was surprised at the civility shown to him: 'There was no pointing, no calling of names, as once; no nor even laughter.'[2] In June 1751, on his marriage, he resigned his fellowship.

Once the Wesleys had ceased to reside in Oxford, the religious societies in the colleges tended to evaporate, even though Methodism had a small but growing following among the townsfolk. 'There are very few of them [Methodists] now left among the scholars at Oxford', Wesley told Steinmetz in 1741.[3] 'The Society', Charles Wesley noted on the other hand on 27 June 1743, 'is in a flourishing condition, chiefly by means of a discreet sister from London.'[4] Moreover, it was to blend with Oxford evangelicalism, which had roots somewhat different from those of Methodism proper. Pious undergraduates, finding college and university religion indifferent if not hostile, attended the services of evangelicals in the town parishes, notably Joseph Jane, a tutor of Christ Church since 1738, who had been appointed to the college living of St Mary Magdalen, his curate Thomas Haweis and James Stillingfleet, elected to a fellowship at Merton in 1752.[5] Jane's views appear somewhat unclear but he leaned, as James Stillingfleet was later to do, towards the Hutchinsonians.

Hutchinsonianism, a somewhat freakish movement, had only a small following at Oxford, but it had there at least one influential spokesman in the kindly and estimable George Horne. John Hutchinson, who had died in 1737, was a self-educated man whose imagination had been inflamed by learning that the geologist John Woodward was collecting evidence (in the form of fossils) to testify to the Mosaic account of the flood in the biblical story of the creation, subsequently writing *Moses's Principia* in 1724 to confound the recent scientific views of Newton.[6] Horne had a close friend in William Jones, who had studied with him at University College and with whom he collaborated in writing *A Full*

---

[1] *Journal of John Wesley*, ed. Curnock iii. 147.

[2] Ibid. 511.

[3] *Letters*, ed. Baker ii (1740-55), p. 49.

[4] *Journal of Charles Wesley* i. 319.

[5] James Stillingfleet (1729-1817), m. Wadham 1748; MA Merton 1754; grandson of Bp Stillingfleet.

[6] [John Hutchinson,] *Moses's Principia* (London 1724).

Answer to the Essay on Spirit in 1753.[1] When Horne became Bishop of Norwich, he appointed Jones, then perpetual curate of Nayland in Suffolk, as his chaplain. Horne and Jones, better scholars than Hutchinson, modified Hutchinson's aberrant theology, but they, and their sympathizers, embraced his 'scriptural philosophy', with its intrinsic symbolism, simultaneously holding to high-church views and hostile to all forms of rationalism. In his tract *A Fair, Candid, and Impartial State of the Case between Sir I. Newton and Mr Hutchinson* (Oxford 1753) Horne, for instance, had argued trenchantly against the Newtonian concept of a vacuum, implicit in his theory of gravitation, as conducive to atheism. Horne and Jones, like other Hutchinsonians, maintained that if Hebrew was read without points, this would confirm their scriptural philosophy.[2] Newton was not the only target of the Hutchinsonians' criticism; Horne disapproved of William Law's mysticism, attacked the philosophy of David Hume and engaged in debate with Kennicott. In their emphasis on spirituality and Biblicism the Hutchinsonians were sometimes suspected of sympathizing with Methodism (and Horne at least expressed disapproval of the expulsion of the six students from St Edmund Hall), though as far as Oxford was concerned, Hutchinsonianism appeared mainly as an expression of contemporary high churchmanship. It was, however, too intellectual and too eccentric to attract the attention of more than a few dons.

By contrast evangelicalism eventually had a vigorous if limited following among undergraduates and townsfolk. One of its leading exponents, Thomas Haweis, had been at Christ Church but had migrated to Magdalen Hall for fear of the dons' disapproval of his religious views. There he attracted a following among undergraduates which Charles Wesley commended. Other junior members reacted differently. When some threw stones and jeered, the proctor, Thomas Nowell, refused to interfere. Matthew Powley was told by his tutor to disconnect himself from Haweis, but he refused to do so and as a consequence forfeited the prospect of a fellowship.[3] Woodforde, who heard Haweis lecture in St Giles's church on 19 November 1761, thought his address 'very stupid, low, and bad stuff'. On 3 December following he noted that there was 'a great dust at Haweis's lecture this evening', and this time Nowell acted, for four days later Goring of Magdalen and Skipp

---

[1] W. Jones, *A Full Answer to the Essay on Spirit* (London 1753). William Jones (1727-1800), m. Univ. 1745. The *Full Answer* was in reply to R. Clayton, *An Essay on Spirit, wherein the Doctrine of the Trinity is Considered* (London 1751).

[2] See L. S. Sutherland, 'The curriculum'.

[3] J. W. Middleton, *An Ecclesiastical Memoir* (London 1822), 78; A. S. Wood, *Thomas Haweis* (London 1957), 72; J. S. Reynolds, *The Evangelicals at Oxford 1735-1871* (Oxford 1953, 2nd edn Oxford 1975), 22-42. Matthew Powley (1741-1806), m. Queen's 1760. His tutor was Thomas Fothergill, provost of Queen's.

of Merton 'were had up . . . for making a disturbance at his Church last Thursday Evening'.[1] The vice-chancellor (Joseph Browne) complained to the bishop about Haweis, and the bishop warned him that if he had had a licence (the bishop's predecessor Secker had waived this formality) he would have had it withdrawn. Faced with the displeasure of the bishop and the university, Haweis left Oxford in 1764 for the Northamptonshire rectory of Aldwinckle All Saints which he was to hold until 1820. The same year Jane accepted the living of Iron Acton in Shropshire. Three years later, in 1767, Stillingfleet also retired from Oxford to a country living, that of Coychurch in Glamorgan.

Stillingfleet, a friend of the countess of Huntingdon, had regularly led the Bible-reading on Sunday evening at the house of a Mrs Durbridge, the widow of a townsman who had been converted by George Whitefield, and it was at her house that some undergraduates from St Edmund Hall were accustomed to foregather. The hall, still a dependency of Queen's, had evidently attracted a small group of evangelicals, some of whom enjoyed the patronage of the countess. The principal, George Dixon, valued her friendship and was in some respects sympathetic towards her views, for as an undergraduate at Queen's he had been associated with Ingham and other members of the Holy Club.[2] Not so the vice-principal and tutor, John Higson, a choleric and opinionated man who, his critics alleged, had 'laboured at times under an insanity of mind' which made him consider taking his own life: 'Mr Higson expressed himself in such a manner, and gave such intimations of making away with himself, that, except he got better, he must necessarily be confined.'[3] Higson repudiated the charge indignantly but admitted that he had suffered from a 'Lowness of spirits', and as a result he had in April 1766 gone into the country to recover his health. He had, he added, never been under discipline 'except the comfort and conversation of his Friends and very nourishing Diet'.[4] Higson's relations with the principal became so strained that when he learned that Lady Huntingdon had written to get a ward of hers admitted to the hall, he remonstrated with Dixon, urging that the hall's reputation in the university had already been tarnished by its Methodist associations. 'This put the Principal into a violent Passion.'[5] In reply Higson argued that he knew that at least two of the hall's young men had preached at Methodist meetings, and he surmised that a third was a follower of Wesley. If they were Methodists

[1] *Woodforde at Oxford*, 59, 62, 63. Henry Goring (1739-1824), 6th bt; m. Magd. 1757; MP Shoreham 1790-6.

[2] Ingham's diary, 28 May 1734.

[3] S. L. Ollard, *The Six Students of St Edmund Hall* (Oxford 1911), 4, 5; see also Bodl. MS St Edmund Hall 56 (the Higson MSS), *passim*.

[4] Bodl. MS St Edmund Hall, 56, fo 44ᵛ.

[5] Ibid. fo 42ᵛ.

or had preached at Methodist meetings, Dixon snapped back, he thought none the worse of them, and challenged Higson to prove what he had said.

Put on his mettle, Higson determined to vindicate himself and to humiliate the principal. On 29 February 1768 he formally laid before the vice-chancellor, as the hall's visitor, charges against the seven young men involved—Benjamin Blatch, James Matthews, Thomas Jones, Joseph Shipman, Erasmus Middleton, Benjamin Kay and Thomas Grove—with a view to investigating their so-called Methodist affiliations, a procedure which so shook the young men that they complained to the principal. In March 1768 Dixon in his turn summoned Higson in the late evening, 'tho' it rained very fast and Mr H[igso]n had a severe Cold', and rebuked him for his 'ill behaviour', threatening him with dismissal from his tutor-ship.[1] Next day Higson had a talk with the provost of Queen's who re-assured him that the principal could not dismiss him without the express permission of the vice-chancellor.

But the principal's order to Higson to lecture his pupils on the thirty-nine articles played into the vice-principal's hands. Close interrogation revealed that the undergraduates' views were Calvinistic in character, for they accepted election, reprobation and irresistible grace. One of them, Middleton, absented himself from the lecture without leave, and when rebuked by Higson said that it 'was like being sent to the Gallies, and refused to come'.[2] Higson declared that he could not honestly sign the students' testimonials. His attempts to get any real satisfaction from the principal were, however, still of no avail. He decided to invoke higher authority. Although the vice-chancellor, not a very powerful character, was at first lukewarm, his fellow heads, probably encouraged by Bishop Hume,[3] thought that the time had come to make an example of these religious enthusiasts. They were charged with illiteracy, hostility to the doctrine and discipline of the Church of England, either by preaching or frequenting illicit conventicles, and misbehaviour towards their tutor. Blatch was dismissed from the case on the ground that, although he was incorrigibly idle, he was a man of fortune and not a candidate for holy orders. Three of the accused, like Higson himself, were mature students of humble origin. Matthews had been apprenticed to a weaver at Alton 'and afterwards lived with his elder brother, who kept a reputable inn', or, in the more slanted language of the charge-sheet, 'followed the low occupation' and 'vented the Tap at an Inn in Alton'.[4] Shipman had

---

[1] Ibid. fo 43.   [2] Ibid. fo 16.

[3] John Hume (1706–82), m. Merton 1721; degrees CCC; bp of Bristol 1756–8, Oxford 1758–66, Salisbury 1766–82.

[4] Ollard, 12; Bodl. MS St Edmund Hall 56, fo 15. The whole issue bears the marks of the sharpening of social distinctions within the church and the divisions of church and chapel characteristic of the nineteenth century.

been a draper. Thomas Jones, son of a labourer, had trained as a barber and worked at his brother's shop where Mr Blackham, the curate of Newport, Salop, and a hostile witness, averred that he 'made me a very good Periwig, which I now wear'.[1]

Their Methodist, or rather Calvinistic affiliations were beyond doubt. Matthews had been befriended by John Fletcher of Madeley, a close friend of John Wesley, who had at one stage designed that he might follow him as leader of the movement. Matthews himself told Higson that 'the said Fletcher used to preach, to the Colliers, standing upon an Oven Bank'.[2] Shipman—'at first he was very wild'— fell in with the Methodists, and 'nothing would serve him but he would be a Clergernam [sic], so he gott acquainted with one Davies a Parson at Benjworth near Evesham in Worcestershire who is a very strenuous Methodist and have putt strange notions in Mr Shipman's head'.[3] Jones was infected with Methodist views by staying with a Methodist family in London, 'Thinking himself I suppose wiser than his Neighbours, he took upon him to censure some whose Sentiments or Practice did not correspond with his', notably Mr Blackham whom he had rebuked for his addiction to cards and dancing.[4] It was with some gusto that this cleric reported to Higson that he had taken

a Ride to Wheaton-Aston on Monday last, when by means of a Friend, I had some Conversation with five or six methodists of the lower Rank. Not suspecting my Design, these men freely told me they had often ... heard Mr Jones's Performances. Their description was this: He had a Table before him and a Bible plac'd upon it, which he took up, and out of it read a Chapter, and then proceeded to *expound* it to, and to *exhort* them. But previous to this I should have observ'd they generally sung an Hymn in which Mr Jones join'd, and *that*, they remark'd with an extraordinary good voice. They also told me that Mr Jones had explain'd several of the 39 articles of Religion to them at different times.[5]

Mr Jones was not only in friendly contact with Mr Davies but also with John Newton of Olney, the evangelical friend of William Cowper, with whom he sometimes stayed during the vacations. Middleton agreed that he went to meetings in Mrs Durbridge's rooms, where they sang hymns, from the collections of Mr Madan, and where Stillingfleet and Foster expounded the gospel. He denied that he had ever been one of Wesley's preachers, though he admitted that he had been a scholar of Wesley's school at Kingswood, near Bristol. One of the witnesses, a Mr Browne,

[1] C. Blackham–Higson, 26 Dec. 1767, Bodl. MS St Edmund Hall 56, fo 5. Charles Blackham of Newport, m. All Souls 1757.
[2] Bodl. MS St Edmund Hall 56, fo 15ᵛ.
[3] S. Wintle–Higson, 23 Feb. 1768, ibid. fo 7.
[4] Blackham–Higson, 26 Dec. 1767, ibid. fo 5ʳ⁻ᵛ.
[5] Blackham–Higson, 31 Jan. 1768, ibid. fo 1.

I. Henry Aldrich, dean of Christ Church

II. James Bradley, Savilian professor of astronomy

III. William Blackstone

IV. Benjamin Buckler

V. Edward Lhuyd, keeper of the Ashmolean Museum, taken from the Museum's Benefactors Book

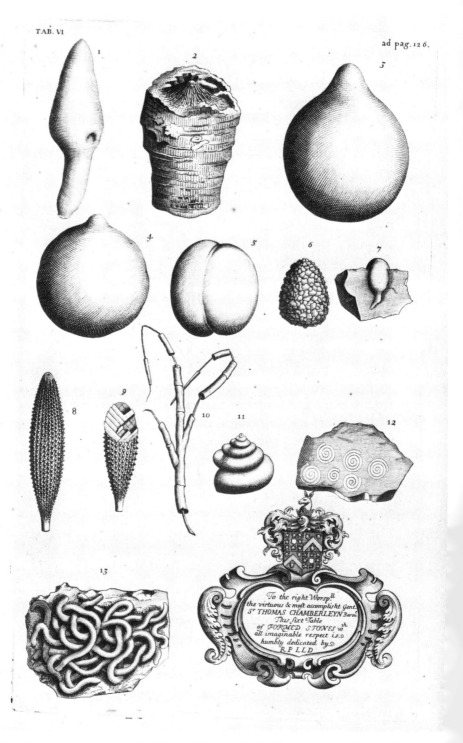

VI. 'Formed Stones', from *The Natural History of Oxfordshire* by Robert Plot, (Oxford 1677 p. 126

VII. Tories and the High Church party triumphing over Toleration and the Whigs: the Oxford Almanack for 1712

VIII. The Opening of the Radcliffe Camera: the Oxford Almanack for 1751

IX. Chapel of New College, taken from [W. Combe], *A History of the University of Oxford*, (2 vols. London 1814), p. 159

X. Hall of University College, taken from [W. Combe], *A History of the University of Oxford* (2 vols. London
1814) 2, 39.

XI. The Radcliffe Observatory

XII. A View down St. Aldates from Carfax, 1755. Bod. Lib. Gough Maps 27 (no 31)

XIII. 'A Varsity Trick—Smuggling In', taken from A. H. Gibbs, *Rowlandson's Oxford*, (London 1911), p. 45

XIV. Frontispiece to 'The Humours of Oxford', a comedy by James Miller, April 1730,
British Library: Paulson 217

XV. Minerva and Hercules raising the Student from the Seductions of Pleasure: the Oxford Almanack for 1718

XVI. Christ Church: the Oxford Almanack for 1776

affirmed that he knew that Middleton despised the prayers of the Church of England, for, sitting next to him in the college chapel, he noticed that he never said the responses. Grove, who confessed to attending Methodist meetings, had told a Mr Bromhead that the prayers of the Church of England were but 'Cold and Dead Letters, nothing comparable to extempore Prayers'.[1]

It was thus easy for Higson to demonstrate his pupils' ignorance and illiteracy. He said of Matthews that he 'found Him so destitute of Classical Knowledge, that he frequently cou'd not tell the Case, or Time and Person, of a common *Latin* Noun or Verb'. Jones, though ignorant of Latin or Greek, sought permission to devote his time to Hebrew.

I took great Pains in explaining to him the Nature of Sylogism; and when he came to attend Disputations, he had forgot his Instructions, and said moreover, That he thought such Kind of Learning useless ... Mr Middleton told me he could not declame and indeed he could not. Nor dispute and in his English Themes frequently misspelt a common English Word ... When he attempted to read a Latin Sentence, He hummed and hawed ... in such a Manner as his Tutor had never heard before.[2]

Blatch, the tutor added, 'did not know the Difference between an Entry in a Hall-Buttry-Book and a Matriculation in the University', while Shipman was unable to read the statute *De reverentia juniorum erga seniores*.[3] Blatch had shown himself to be insolent as well as idle.

But what did this catena of trivialities amount to? If the young men were demonstrably not very clever, their illiteracy was more a matter of degree than substance among the undergraduates of that time. Their affiliation to Calvinistic and Methodist societies seemed proved. On the other hand, the good faith of the witnesses against them was in doubt. The two young men from St Edmund Hall, Browne and Bromhead, had obviously been pressed into service by their tutor. The curate from Newport, Blackham, wanted to have his own back on Jones. Even less reliable was the evidence of a Mr Welling who was soon to be himself in difficulties as a result of indiscreet remarks he had made on religion when under the influence of drink at the St John's gaudy. The verdict on the case was delivered in the college chapel by the vice-chancellor, acting in a twofold capacity. As visitor of the university halls he expelled the offending students from St Edmund Hall. Then, under the special powers of his *imperium merum*, he also expelled them from the university.

A war of pamphlets followed the case. In his *Pietas Oxoniensis* Richard Hill argued that the Calvinistic doctrines for which the six students had

[1] Ibid. fos 20, 21, 23 (Middleton), 29 (Grove). Martin Madan (1726–90), m. Ch.Ch. 1742. Edward Bromhead, m. SEH 1763; BA CCC 1768.

[2] Bodl. MS St Edmund Hall 56, fos 48^{r-v}, 18, 20.

[3] Ibid. fos 24, 26.

been expelled were 'the ancient, undoubted, received tenets of the Church of *England*'. It was, moreover, objected against the young men

that they were connected with Mr FLETCHER, Mr NEWTON, Mr DAVIES, Mr VENN, &c. who were reputed Methodists.—And wherefore so reputed? Why because they believe the Articles they have subscribed to; and instead of spending their time in idleness and sensual indulgence, or in talking of raising their Tythes, and how much such and such a Minister's Living brings in, whether such and such benefices are tenable together, where the cheapest Curates are to be had, and whether there is easy duty or not, preach several times in the week, go to their Parishioners houses, inquire into the state of their souls.[1]

In *Goliath Slain* the same writer asked whether, had the young men all been present at Mrs Durbridge's, 'perhaps there would have been no more harm in this than in going to lownge for hours together at Billiard-tables and Tennis-Courts, or at the fruit-stalls of KIT, PAT, or NAN GILL'.[2] George Whitefield wrote to the vice-chancellor to inquire:

As it now stands one of the Questions proposed to every candidate for Holy Orders runs thus: 'Do you trust that you are inwardly moved by the Holy Ghost?' But if all Students are to be expelled that sing Hymns, pray extempore, attend upon, or expand a verse now and then in a religious Church of England Society, should it not rather, Reverend SIR, be worded thus, namely, 'Do you trust you are *NOT* inwardly moved by the Holy Ghost to take upon you the office and administration of the church?'[3]

Other critics included Augustus Toplady, author of the hymn *Rock of Ages*, and John Fell, a dissenting minister, who published *Grace Triumphant, a Sacred Poem submitted to the Serious and Candid Perusal of Dr Nowell.* The Reverend John MacGowan, under the pen-name of *The Shaver*, published a widely read attack on the Anglican establishment at Oxford. He dressed his theme in indifferent verse:

> My thanks, and the nation's to the doctors be given,
> Those Guardians of Virtue, those Porters of Heaven
> For their timely wise care in suppressing the growth
> Of praying, expounding and hymn-singing youth.

> Should praying be suffer'd by our learned Sages
> (What has not been known in Ox. . .d for ages)
> Instead of gay parsons, with cassock and band,
> There would be none but Puritans all o'er the land.

[1] R. Hill, *Pietas Oxoniensis or a Full and Impartial Account of the Expulsion of the Six Students from St Edmund Hall, Oxford* (London 1768), 53, 67. Richard Hill (1733–1808), 2nd bt; m. Magd. 1750; MP Shropshire 1780–1806; see also L. B. Namier and J. Brooke, *The History of Parliament: The House of Commons 1754–1790* (3 vols London 1964) ii. 623–5.

[2] R. Hill, *Goliath Slain: Being a Reply to the Reverend Dr Nowell's Answer to Pietas Oxoniensis* (London 1768), 29.

[3] G. Whitefield, *A Letter to the Reverend Dr Durrell. . . occasioned by a late expulsion of Six Students from Edmund Hall* (London 1768), 26–7.

Expounding the Scriptures! this still is more wicked,
Therefore from college be they instant kicked;
For scripture and priestcraft as distant do well
As some PARSONS from Virtue, or HEAVEN from HELL.[1]

Thomas Fry, the president of St John's, a moderate man, deplored the verdict;[2] Edward Bentham, then regius professor of divinity, refused to join in sitting in judgement on the students. The defenders of the university's action had a less easy task, though Thomas Nowell insisted that the undergraduates' teaching manifestly tended to the 'impeaching or depraving the doctrine of the church of *England*, the book of common prayer ... and discipline established in the church'. 'And surely', he urged,

in this place there can be no occasion or pretence for such religious meetings: there are prayers here in every chapel twice a day; there are sermons at the University church twice every Sunday, and once every holiday ... If this were not sufficient, those pious gentlemen might have joined together in prayer within their own halls, or colleges. But to hold such meetings in private houses in the town was directly contrary to the discipline and rules of the University to the canons of the church, and the statutes of the realm.[3]

No doubt Nowell, whom Lord North was to make regius professor of modern history and who in 1772 was to raise the ire of the house of commons by preaching a sermon in which he compared Charles I with George III, pointing out that the grievances against both monarchs were equally illusory, reflected the feeling of the majority.[4] 'I talked', Boswell wrote on 15 April 1772,

of the recent expulsion of six students from the University of Oxford, who were methodists, and would not desist from publickly praying and exhorting, JOHNSON. 'Sir, that expulsion was extremely just and proper. What have they to do at an University who are not willing to be taught, but will presume to teach? ... Sir, they were examined, and found to be mighty ignorant fellows'. BOSWELL. 'But, was it not hard, Sir, to expel them, for I am told they were good beings?' JOHNSON. 'Sir, I believe they might be good beings; but they were not fit to be in the University of Oxford. A cow is a very good animal in the field; but we turn her out of a garden'.[5]

This was, as Lord Elibank told Boswell, 'an illustration uncommonly happy', and one surely with which even Horace Walpole would have

---

[1] The Shaver [J. MacGowan], *Priestcraft Defended, a sermon occasioned by the expulsion of six young gentlemen from the University of Oxford* (London 1768); The Shaver, *A Further Defence of Priestcraft* (London 1768), 39–40.
[2] Costin, *St John's*, 220.
[3] T. Nowell, *An Answer to a Pamphlet, entitled Pietas Oxoniensis* (London 1768), 40–2.
[4] See L. Mitchell, 'Politics and revolution 1772–1800', p. 167 above.
[5] *Boswell's Life of Johnson*, ed. Hill, rev. Powell ii. 187.

agreed, for, as he wrote to William Cole, 'Oxford has begun with these rascals, and I hope Cambridge will wake'.[1]

John Wesley was himself strangely silent. He certainly had little sympathy with the Calvinistic doctrines to which the young men adhered, and may have regretted the assertion that this was what Methodists believed. His occasional visits to Oxford aroused memories of a happy past but were tinged with melancholy; when in 1778 he went to Christ Church he wrote that he could not but still retain a peculiar affection for Oxford. 'What lovely mansions are there! What is wanting to make the inhabitants of them happy? That without which no rational creature can be happy—the experimental knowledge of God.'[2] At St Edmund Hall Higson, whose position as vice-principal had become untenable, retired to his vicarage of Batheaston. Dixon remained as principal for another nineteen years, continuing to admit students of evangelical leanings, among them the well-known future Methodist, Joseph Benson. In 1769 a St Edmund Hall man Stephen Seager, was summoned before the vice-chancellor (Nathan Wetherell) on information provided by Dixon, to explain his religious views. Consequently he was refused leave to matriculate. No doubt, however, the foundations which were to make evangelicalism in early nineteenth-century Oxford the 'religion of Teddy Hall' had been laid.

In 1778 Brasenose refused testimonials for orders to one of its members, a Mr Roe. He had attended 'meetings of the Methodists at Macclesfield and other places as well as in the university', professed to be a follower of Wesley and 'repeatedly denied the necessity of episcopal ordination'. Roe appealed to the college visitor, who, irritated by the amount of college business which came before him 'at my age and infirm state of health . . . a great load upon me', interviewed both Roe and his father (who was said to have built a church for worship which the bishop of Chester, William Markham, had refused to license) and was reassured as to the young man's orthodoxy.[3] The principal was less sanguine. 'I wish', he wrote on 18 December 1778, 'Mr Roe does not endeavour to mislead your Lordship . . . It does not appear to me possible, that the College should sign any testimonial of Mr Roe's.'[4]

So throughout the eighteenth century, the university remained a bulwark of the established order in the church as in the state. Its theo-

---

[1] *Horace Walpole's Correspondence*, ed. W. S. Lewis *et al.* (48 vols New Haven, London and Oxford 1937–83) i. 135.   [2] *Journal of John Wesley*, ed. Curnock vi. 213.

[3] J. Green–T. Barker, 1 Dec. 1778, BNCA tower drawer 129, visitorial documents. The visitor was John Green (1706–79), incorporated BA from Cambridge 1731; bishop of Lincoln 1761–79. The principal was Thomas Barker (1727–85), m. BNC 1745, principal 1777–85.

[4] Barker–Green, 18 Dec. 1778, BNCA tower drawer 129, visitorial documents.

logical teaching, its liturgy, its sermons, its social views continued to be founded on the *antiqua via* of the Tudor apologists and Caroline divines, threaded by patristic learning and dosed by some degree of latitudinarianism, but rarely tinged by textual criticism or original thought. Only a few scholars deviated from the solid phalanx of traditionalism, some were attracted to the obfuscated notions of Hutchinsonianism. The Methodists and evangelicals had made only a minor dent in what seemed to many an unwarranted religious complacency. Yet, behind this, there were signs of unease. Even within Oxford there were some who were beginning to query the demands made on students at matriculation, and were indeed becoming unsure of the validity of the thirty-nine articles themselves. But these constituted only a tiny minority of the whole.

In 1772, when Sir William Meredith's petition to parliament to relieve members of the university from subscription to these articles was rejected, severe remarks were made. William Scott wrote to Newdigate:

The truth is, and I confess it to be a disgraceful one, that we put our Names down in a common Register (at the front of which is the text of the Articles) Our Master always acquaints the young Men with what they are about to do, and what the Act implies in the Understanding of the University. But it is not I believe the common Practice.[1]

Even if they had been told, uninstructed lads were hardly capable of judging the theological nuances of what they were subscribing. Thus the uninstructed subscription of the freshman was regarded quite differently from the instructed subscription of the graduate. It was, for the former, perhaps not unreasonably, explained to mean no more than a promise of general conformity to the Church of England while *in statu pupillari*. Even friends of the university were reported as pressing for change. The heads were divided. Some were for abrogation of the subscription at matriculation; others for explanation or modification: others for standing fast.[2] At Cambridge, where the liberalizing movement was stronger, the subscription at BA was changed for a general declaration of conformity, which led John Tottie to liken that university to a monkey that had lost its tail.[3] Edward Bentham, following the example of his great predecessor Robert Sanderson, favoured an *eponimis* or 'explanation'. To the rank and file of the university the campaign was part of a wider one to change the Church of England itself. 'The Attack upon our Subscription took its rise from that which was made upon the whole Body of the Articles, the Church of England was not to be taken by Storm: our

---

[1] Scott–Newdigate (nd), Newdigate MS CR136/B2444. See also Mitchell, 'Politics and revolution', 177.
[2] Scott–Newdigate, 17 Nov. 1772, Newdigate MS CR136/B2239.
[3] Same–same (nd), Newdigate MS CR136/B2444.

Adversaries have a Mind to see what they can do by *Sap*.'[1] What was feared was a radical change in the university, from being a seminary of the Church of England, where its faith and religion were taught and practised, into an ecclesiastically miscellaneous seed-bed of schism.[2] Certainly, the promoters of change outside the university held principles repugnant to many in it. A strong taint of Erastianism hung about some of them, who held that the church as a public institution was merely a creature of the secular power.[3]

Yet it is difficult to believe that if Bentham and the middle party had got their 'explanation', any great difference would have come about in the educational processes in the university. BAs still having to subscribe would have had to be taught about the articles, and know their Burnet, Welchman or Veneer.[4] Later generations were to reach the opinion that too much weight was put upon the articles and that *lex orandi* as also *lex credendi* might have been more in mind than it was. It might even have happened that there would have been less need to fit the conclusion of every disputation to what the articles were at that time believed to convey. Perhaps also, 'it is our Fault', said an Oxford man, 'in this Place to see everything in too *Clerical* a Light'.[5]

Bentham died in 1776, puzzled and alarmed by much that he saw in the world around him. The disturbances in America had increased in virulence during the past ten years, and he was fearful that a situation similar to that of the 1640s would develop once again. As so many 30 January sermons explained, the dissolving of the fabric of church and state was brought about by destructive demagogues, parsons and politicians, playing upon the passions and ignorance of the multitude. He had every reason to be disturbed. The late 1780s saw the deepening of the troubles in France. The attack on the French church and subsequent de-Christianization strengthened, indeed romanticized, the identification of altar and throne. More were made anxious by the spread of dissent. In some places the dislike was made vocal. A close-at-hand, if not quite immediate, knowledge of excesses in France, and a shrewd anticipation

[1] Bodl. G.A. Oxon. b.7 (nd), Principal Cawley's papers, noted by Cawley as 'by Dr T—' (that is by Dr Tottie).

[2] Anon., *A Collection of Papers, Designed to Explain and Vindicate the Present Mode of Subscription Required at Matriculation* (Oxford 1772), 11.

[3] *Letters on the Subscription to the Liturgy and XXXIX Articles* (London 1772); the copy in Bodl. Gough Camb. 45 (8) has the manuscript note, 'Mr Jebb'.

[4] G. Burnet, *An Exposition of the Thirty-Nine Articles of the Church of England* (London 1720). E. Welchman, *XXXIX articuli . . . in usum juventutis academiae* (Oxford 1713), English edn, 'new translated into English according to the 6th edition', which had come out in 1738. J. Veneer, *An Exposition on the Thirty Nine Articles of the Church of England* (London 1734).

[5] [B. Buckler,] *Reflections on the Impropriety and Inexpediency of Lay Subscription to the 39 Articles* (Oxford) (1772).

of revolutionary imperialism, enabled Edward Gibbon almost to forgive Edmund Burke his devotion to Church establishments.[1]

In the face of these national and international dangers, the social turmoil of which the French revolution seemed to be the herald, the sniping at the university by radicals, dissenters and intellectuals alike, it is not surprising that the vice-chancellor should assure the duke of Portland in the first year of his chancellorship that 'the sole purposes of our academical Institutions' are 'maintenance of Order, the Advancement of Learning, and the furtherance of Religion and morality'.[2]

[1] E. Gibbon, *Memoirs of My Life*, G. A. Bonnard, p. 195.
[2] J. Wills–d. of Portland, 25 Sept. 1793, Balliol College Library, Jenkyns papers, VI.A (2), letter-book of John Wills.

15

The Curriculum

L. S. SUTHERLAND

THE university exercises[1] qualifying candidates for the degrees of BA and MA and for those of bachelor and doctor of the higher faculties—divinity, law and medicine—as also for the anomalous degrees of bachelor and doctor of music, were governed by the Laudian code of 1636, modified statutably only by the addition of two declamations to be delivered by candidates for the MA, introduced in 1662 to strengthen the non-dialectical part of the curriculum. Well before the eighteenth century began, however, the system of university instruction which these exercises were intended to test had broken down, and the tests were recognized to be unsatisfactory in themselves and laxly administered.

The code, following antiquarian traditions, had laid down the methods and content of the curriculum in great detail, particularly for the degrees of BA and MA as the bases of the academic system. It was composed of two types of university exercise, the one traditional, the other an innovation. The first was the pride of the medieval university, the system of scholastic disputations which the code incorporated with loving and antiquarian care, though these exercises, except as a training in logical thought and exposition, no longer attracted the support which even in the sixteenth century they had still enjoyed. The second, the innovation, was what the code conceived of as a searching oral examination both for BA and MA candidates to be based on a series of compulsory lectures. These were intended to counteract the preponderance of the dialectical training of 'the last age' and to encourage 'learning and polite letters among all persons taking degrees in Arts'. Following the humanist tradition great stress was laid on the importance of expressing 'thoughts in Latin' and on translation from colloquial English into Latin.[2]

---

[1] In 1767 Jeremy Bentham referred to what 'in their barbarous jargon they call "exercises" ': *The Correspondence of Jeremy Bentham*, ed. T. L. S. Sprigge *et al.* (London and Oxford 1968 onward) i. 116. The term was sometimes restricted to the disputations as distinct from the work for the examination.

[2] *Laudian Code* IX.ii, *De examinandis gradum candidatis per magistros necessario regentes*, ed. Griffiths, pp. 88–92; *Statutes*, trans. Ward i. 85 ff. For reasons which remain obscure members of New College were exempt from this obligation, the college providing its own examination: see H. Rashdall, *The Universities of Europe in the Middle Ages* (2 vols Oxford 1895), new edn by F. M. Powicke and A. B. Emden (3 vols Oxford 1936) iii. 221–3. They had no exemption from the public disputations.

A candidate for the degree of bachelor of arts was expected to reside for four years or sixteen terms (the four-term year was maintained throughout the period) within his college walls, but even the code itself contained provisions which could be used to reduce the residence required to three years or twelve terms.[1] Throughout the century it was by no means uncommon for undergraduates to reside for four years for their BA and the statutes of many colleges imposed this residence on their foundationers. Three years had, however, become the basic university requirement, and strength of purpose on the part of convocation was necessary to prevent discretionary dispensations becoming common which would have further reduced the necessary residence.[2]

During these years candidates had to present themselves for three exercises in the traditional disputations, and one oral examination in the new style. It was also intended that they should regularly attend the public disputations and the public lectures on which their examination was based. Though these requirements had fallen into desuetude well before the period began (if indeed the public lectures had ever come into full operation) the exercises in which candidates had personally to take part continued to be strictly required. After a man had been in residence for at least two years he was expected (if he wished to take a BA) to dispute on grammar and logic *in parviso* both as opponent and respondent under the moderatorship of a BA or senior sophister. These disputations were held three days a week during full term and regent masters, proctors, pro-proctors and, up to the earlier years of the century, the vice-chancellor himself were expected to intervene to ensure that they were well conducted.[3] When a candidate took part in them in

[1] The obligation to reside within the college walls was frequently avoided by subterfuges during this period; see I. G. Doolittle, 'College administration', pp. 239–41 above. Candidates could count towards residence the terms in which they matriculated and graduated, whether or not they had been in residence during them. Congregation was also empowered to grant them up to 2 terms' dispensation (and did so on demand). The residence required was 28 days in the Easter term and 14 days in the Act term. Sons of peers and the eldest sons of baronets and knights were allowed to take their BA at three years standing; the concession was at first confined to sons of English peers but later extended to sons of Scottish and Irish peers: L. S. Sutherland, 'The Laudian Statutes', p. 192 above.

[2] Discretionary dispensations could be given (for a considerably higher fee) by convocation on receipt of a 'chancellor's letter' (in which he asked convocation to grant degrees and dispensations in individual cases) explaining the circumstances. These were primarily given in connection with the degree of MA but at certain periods were also obtainable fairly easily by undergraduates. In the 1770s convocation clamped down on the grants to such applications, as is apparent from its register. An anonymous pamphlet, attributed to John Napleton, *Considerations on the Residence Usually Required for Degrees in the University of Oxford* (printed but not published 1773), explained why this step was taken. On 17 May 1773 the hebdomadal board resolved that no 'candidate for the BA should on any pretence petition Convocation for dispensation, even for one term': BNCA Principal Cawley's notebooks, MS B53/2.

[3] Regent masters were MAs within one year of incepting; by statute the period of regency was two years but in the code itself a dispensation of a year was permitted, and congregation gave a blanket dispensation reducing the period. Among the sins of omission and commission which Hearne attributed to the egregious William Delaune, vice-chancellor 1702–6, was that he 'has hardly been once at any Publick Exercise': *Collections* i. 100 (26 Nov. 1705).

the course of qualifying himself, he was said to do so *pro forma*, and when he had successfully completed the exercise, he was created a 'general Sophister'. In the eighteenth century the process was usually described as 'doing Generals'. Thereafter he was supposed to take part in the same disputations at least once a term until he graduated—though even in the earlier years of the century he was held to have fulfilled this obligation when he had taken part in three of them; it was called 'doing Juraments' and by 1773 attendance at such disputations had died out.[1] Finally he had to 'answer under Bachelor' in the elaborate Lenten disputations in which those who had recently graduated were said to 'determine', an exercise necessary to make the BA degree more than a courtesy title, and which was essential for those who wished to proceed to the MA. The undergraduate 'answering under Bachelor' had to respond twice to a BA (known as his 'father') in logic and rhetoric.

Though the taking of these tests was strictly enforced, the administration of them was slipshod. They aroused little if any interest, and the subjects disputed (chosen by the candidates themselves, though countersigned by their college and a master of the schools) were banal and stereotyped. It was easy to cheat in them by learning by heart the stages in the disputations offered through the use of cribs called 'strings'.[2] Nor were the disputations by any means always adequately supervised. Jeremy Bentham, himself an able and enthusiastic disputant, thought in 1765 that 'Austins' (part of the MA syllabus) which 'consists in disputing for 2 hours in the presence of the Proctor for the whole time ... is ... the least of a farce of any of the disputations in the Schools, at the rest of which the Proctors are only present occasionally, and sometimes not at all'.[3] When James Woodforde of New College did the first part of his 'generals' in 1761 he noted in his diary:

I went into the Metaphysical Schools where was Mr Baldwin and Berkeley Secundus the Moderator and opponent. A quarter after two, Scrope of Magdalen Coll. Pro-Proctor came in and kept us on and put us out 'till almost three. We came of [*sic*] very well. We were up in the Schools from one 'till three—being the usual time.[4]

---

[1] Applications for dispensations in Convocation by 'chancellor's letters' (recorded in the registers of convocation) show that attendance at three disputations as an undergraduate was expected throughout the first half of the century. But Napleton said 'the article of attendance is by Universal consent, totally neglected and forgot': [J. Napleton,] *Considerations on the Public Exercises for the First and Second Degrees in the University of Oxford* ([Oxford] 1773), p. iii.

[2] These are frequently referred to by contemporary satirists, and were said to have passed from hand to hand freely among undergraduates, apparently in manuscript form. No copy has so far been found.

[3] *Correspondence of Bentham*, ed. Sprigge i. 87. For his success as a disputant in college see also ibid. 50.

[4] *Woodforde at Oxford*, 57. Charles Baldwyn (m. Univ. 1756, BA New College 1760) was the college chaplain. 'Berkeley Secundus' was probably George Berkeley (m. Ch.Ch. 1752), son of the bishop of Cloyne.

But when three weeks later he did the second part, he noted that after being up all the night before at a farewell party for a friend he 'went up again in the Schools, with Berkeley Secundus and was set over by Stubbs of Queen's Coll. being Master of the Schools, only one medium', suggesting that there was only one subject of disputation instead of the regulation three. Apparently no proctor or pro-proctor was present.[1]

So much for the traditional side of the university curriculum. The examination for the BA was taken separately and usually late in the undergraduate's career. The senior proctor was responsible for nominating and swearing in three regent masters as examiners.[2] Since the examination was intended to be a searching one, no more than six candidates were to be examined in a day (though at least by the eighteenth century it was usual to take them in pairs). Oddly enough the subjects of the examination, apart from the provisions for spoken Latin, were only indirectly defined. These were to be determined by the content of the compulsory lectures. Most of them were to be given by regent masters, and the subjects and authors on which they were to lecture were laid down in detail and on conservative lines. The subjects were grammar and 'selected heads out of Greek and Roman Antiquities'; rhetoric (based on Aristotle, Cicero, Quintilian and Hermogenes); and, after the end of their first year, logic and moral philosophy, both on strictly Aristotelian lines. After the end of their second year they were to attend the first part of the lectures, primarily intended for BAs, of the Savilian professor of geometry and of the regius professor of Greek. This last was to lecture on Homer, Demosthenes, Isocrates, Euripides and others of the 'more ancient and classical authors'; these too were intended primarily for the BAs. No provision was made for teaching in divinity, which was explicitly left to college tutors and lecturers.[3]

In fact the system of public lectures broke down completely so far as those to be delivered by regent masters were concerned, and with few, if notable, exceptions the professorial lectures fared no better. Lectures, or rather classes, still seem to have been made available for the few who cared to attend them in Hebrew and Arabic, and 'the sciences' seem to have been better provided for than the arts, partly because of the enterprise of two Savilian professors of astronomy, David Gregory and John Keill, the latter of whom was also lecturing in 1703 as deputy for the Sedleian professor in natural philosophy, and partly too because of

---

[1] *Woodforde at Oxford*, 60. Baldwyn again acted as moderator.

[2] Nicholas Amhurst said it was notorious that most candidates paid the proctor's man a crown to choose their own examiners: *Reminiscences of Oxford*, 94. His evidence must be accepted with caution but Napleton makes it clear that the college or the candidate in fact had to find the examiners.

[3] *Statutes* III. ii, trans. Ward i. 15 ff.

special arrangements for instruction in anatomy.[1] But with few exceptions the lectures given during the century were thought of as extraneous to the curriculum, and indeed often owed their popularity among under-graduates precisely to this fact.[2] Some were given by professors or their deputies, others by individuals with no university obligations. They delivered them on their own initiative and generally charged fees, occasionally heavy ones, to those attending them.[3] Undergraduates had to get permission to attend them from their tutors who were not always anxious to give it, and were loath to rearrange a man's college work to make attendance at them possible.[4] For financial reasons men also usually asked their parents leave to enrol for them. In the second half of the century in particular scientific lectures laying stress, as the older type of instruction did not, on experimental work became increasingly popular with undergraduates as they did with the world outside the universities.[5] On the arts side, Blackstone's lectures on English law which began in 1753 and formed the basis of his famous *Commentaries on the Laws of England* (a most successful innovation) were specifically intended to supplement the existing legal curriculum.[6] The purpose of the lectures

[1] For lectures in Arabic see P. J. Marshall, 'Oriental studies', pp. 551-2 below. David Gregory (1661-1708), incorporated from Edinburgh at Balliol 1692; Savilian prof. of astronomy 1692-1708. John Keill (1671-1721), incorporated from Edinburgh at Balliol 1695; Savilian prof. of astronomy 1712-21; for his lectures in natural philosophy see *Oxford Almanack* (1703), copy in Bodl. Gough Oxf. 31, and G. l'E. Turner, 'The physical sciences', pp. 670-1 below. For instruction in anatomy see H. M. Sinclair and A. H. T. Robb-Smith, *A Short History of Anatomical Teaching in Oxford* (Oxford 1950); C. Webster, 'The medical faculty and the physic garden' below.

[2] This is well illustrated by the numbers attending the lectures of James Bradley; see Turner, 'Physical sciences', pp. 673-4.

[3] Three guineas was the usual charge for a first course. It might be reduced or remitted for later courses. Blackstone's charge was six guineas. An undergraduate's accounts for 1754 show also a charge of 5s to his servant, no doubt for enrolling: Bodl. MS Top. Oxon. e. 256 (the undergraduate was William Deedes, a gentleman-commoner at Corpus 1752-5). Richard Browne (1712-80, m. Hart Hall 1727; fellow Trin. 1731; regius prof. Hebrew 1774-80), however, stated that when lord almoner's professor of Arabic (1748-80) he delivered lectures for fifteen years 'All which time he had taken no money or Present of any of his Scholars (except a trifle once to shew his right to do so) that he might the more effectually encourage the cultivation of Eastern Learning': L. S. Sutherland, 'The origin and early history of the lord almoner's professorship in Arabic at Oxford', *Bodleian Library Record* x (1978-82), 175.

[4] John James's tutor at Queen's in 1782 (Thomas Nicholson) was reluctant to give him his certificate to attend the Hebrew lecture of the regius professor because of 'the disrepute into which ... the study of the language had been brought by the extravagancies of some Hutchinsonian divines *of this University*': *Letters of Radcliffe and James*, 190-1: On 10 March 1762 Jeremy Bentham reported to his father: 'Mr Jefferson [his tutor] began Natural Philosophy with us yesterday, but whether we shall improve much or no I can't tell, as he has no apparatus; but today Dr Bliss's Lectures will begin, which I hope I may attend his next Course, which will be next Year.' *Correspondence*, ed. Sprigge i. 60.

[5] When Jeremy Bentham succeeded in attending the lectures of Nathaniel Bliss (1700-64, m. Pemb. 1716; Savilian prof. of geometry 1742-64; astronomer royal 1762-4) in 1763 on 'The Science of Mechanics' he was disappointed in them. He commented: 'Mr Bliss seems to be a very good sort of a Man, but I doubt is not very well qualified for his Office, in the practical Way I mean, for he is oblig'd to make excuses for almost every experiment they not succeeding according to expectation; in the speculative part, I believe he is by no means deficient.' Ibid. 67.

[6] W. Blackstone, *Commentaries on the Laws of England* (4 vols Oxford 1765-9).

in divinity, begun by Edward Bentham as regius professor in 1764 with
the encouragement of Secker, then bishop of Oxford, and continued by
his successors, was to prepare young men for the church.[1] Thomas
Bever's lectures on jurisprudence and the civil law were on the other
hand intended to deal with the legal curriculum as well as catering for
more general interests, but they were not successful.[2] The first successful
lectures on a subject cognate to the curriculum on the arts side were
those of William Scott as Camden professor of history, who began
lecturing in 1779.[3] The lectures of the professor of poetry founded in
1708, a unique institution in any university, were conceived by the
founder, Henry Birkhead, to be a valuable supplement to the curriculum:
'the reading of the ancient poets gave keenness and polish to the minds
of young men as well as to the advancement of more serious literature
both sacred and human . . .'.[4] It was customary to hold the chair for two
periods of five years, and its holders were often distinguished. One of
them, Thomas Warton the younger, in the forty lectures he delivered
between 1757 and 1766, may well have played a prominent part in the
rise of interest in Greek literature, which was so marked a feature of the
later eighteenth century.[5]

An interesting but on the whole not very satisfactory contribution to
public lectures on the arts side were those of the regius professor of
modern history and his supporting lectures in modern languages,
founded in 1724 under the auspices of George I. The enterprise, whose
sponsors were Edmund Gibson and Robert Walpole, was intended to
encourage loyalty to the Hanoverian regime as well as interest in
modern historical scholarship. The scheme covered the needs of Oxford
and Cambridge. The first two Oxford occupants of the chair, David
Gregory (1724-36) and William Holmes (1736-42) carried out their
duties with some energy, but their successors were frequently less successful. On the accession of George III the crown and some of its ministers (particularly Lord Bute) inaugurated a more vigorous educational
policy at both universities, first in 1763 and later as a result of direct
intervention in 1768 and 1769, apparently as the result of the influence of
Blackstone's   lectures   on   the   king   as   a   young   man.   Obstacles

---

[1] See R. Greaves, 'Religion in the university 1715-1800', pp. 403-6 above.
[2] See W. S. Holdsworth, *A History of English Law* (17 vols London 1903-72) xii. 644. Thomas Bever
(1726-91, m. Oriel 1744, fellow All Souls 1749) lectured as deputy to the regius professor of civil law.
[3] John James reported in 1779: 'The lectures on ancient history that were read here last spring by
Scot the Professor . . . are perhaps superiour to anything of the kind in point of elegance and erudition.' He would have attended more of them 'had not the Doctor's [his tutor's] lecture interfered'.
Letters of Radcliffe and James, 92. It was expected that they would be printed but Scot always refused
to publish them.
[4] OUA register of convocation 1703-30, fo 47ᵛ. Henry Birkhead (1617-96), m. Trin. 1634; fellow
All Souls 1638-57.
[5] See M. L. Clarke, 'Classical studies', pp. 513-33 below.

on the side of the universities rendered the reforms less far reaching than had been hoped.[1]

By the eighteenth century the examination for the BA, towards which the lectures were supposed to be leading, was held to consist of three parts: spoken Latin; questions on what were called 'the Sciences' as envisaged in the code, namely logic, rhetoric, Euclid, morals and politics; and—the part taken most seriously by colleges but not based on the code—the works of three classical authors of the undergraduate's own choice, either one Greek and two Latin or two Greek and one Latin. This convention reflects at least one good result of the breakdown of the Laudian plan: the much greater attention given to classical reading than it had provided for. Jeremy Bentham in 1763 chose to be examined in Demosthenes, Anacreon and Cicero's *Tusculan Disputations*. A friend from Queen's examined with him chose the Greek Testament, Horace and Sallust.[2] A reasonably prepared candidate was expected to construe passages from his texts accurately. The 'sciences', however, with the exception at some colleges at least of logic where Yolton has unveiled interesting post-Lockean developments,[3] were prepared largely from compendia, and often enough from manuscript *schemae* which passed from hand to hand and consisted of questions and answers on the most obvious topics extracted from them.

The examinations themselves were summary and failure in them almost unknown. Unlike the disputations, however, on occasion they aroused a certain amount of public interest. Jeremy Bentham boasted to his father in 1763:

I had a very numerous audience, the seats were cover'd with people, besides a good many that stood in the body of the place. I was up for near an hour together, which was nearly as long again as the usual time. I hope I have acquitted myself tolerably well; and am pretty certain, if I have not gain'd credit, that at least I have not lost any.[4]

In 1781 another Queen's man, John James, a hard-working and extremely scholarly man whose reading would have been creditable in any age, gave a gloomier account:

[1] For the contributions to reform of Oxford and Cambridge see BL Add. MS 38334, fos 132 (1763), 138 (1768). Some of the official papers have been misplaced but can be put in order again. See also for Cambridge *The Times Literary Supplement* (1926), p. 168; and for Oxford, J. Vivian-C. Jenkinson [2 Nov. 1769], BL Add. MS 38206, fo 143. The king had originally expressed his hope that all public lectures with which he was concerned should be read in a way 'consistent with the present method of education at the University': C. Godwyn-J. Hutchins, 3 Jan. 1763, J. Nichols, *Literary Anecdotes of the Eighteenth Century* (9 vols London 1812-15) viii. 232. See also K. Sharpe, 'The foundation of the chairs of history at Oxford and Cambridge: an episode in Jacobean politics', *History of Universities* ii (1982).
[2] *Correspondence of Bentham*, ed. Sprigge i. 72.
[3] J. Yolton, 'Schoolmen, logic and philosophy'.
[4] *Correspondence of Bentham*, ed. Sprigge i. 71.

You wish perhaps to know the issue of the examination which I think I told you I was to pass on Monday sennight, but which was deferred till the Friday following for want of Masters. Besides the gentleman I mentioned as my associate I had another, a person of Merton, who, being to take Orders on Sunday last, was under absolute necessity of having his degree. Trifling [and] farcical as these things are known to be, I never saw a man under more apprehension, or with greater reason; for he protested to us with vehemence that he had not looked in any Latin or Greek book since his matriculation; and as for the sciences, he was hardly acquainted with their names . . . yet he escaped . . . After this I hope I need not take much pains to assure you I was successful. It was my luck to answer all their questions but one which I did not exactly hear, and to perform the other exercises, which consisted of only a few lines in my classics to construe, without any blunder. The very small share of regard paid to literary qualifications in the candidates for a degree is a real disgrace as well as disadvantage to *the Universities of this land*.[1]

One is bound to conclude that there was little if any organized stimulus for undergraduates in the eighteenth century and such as there was depended entirely on the colleges. The idea, popularized by Gibbon in his *Memoirs*, that this was virtually non-existent stands up neither to the evidence left by individual undergraduates of their studies nor to the surviving records in college archives.[2] There was wide variation in the value of what was provided not only between different colleges but also within any one college at different dates. Nevertheless it is possible to arrive at some conclusions about the system at which colleges were aiming. In reaching these conclusions we are greatly assisted by one remarkable record which survives, the three-volume series of 'collections books' at Christ Church, so called because they record the regular oral submissions of written work or 'collections' for each term by which the reading of undergraduates at Christ Church was tested. From 1699 to 1717 they record individually the termly or annual reading of undergraduate foundationers (Students), commoners and servitors reading for a degree; from 1717 to 1772 they contain basic schemes of required reading and lists of the persons collected, and from 1768 until well into the nineteenth century they provide once again individual reading lists. From 1773 onwards they were intended to include all undergraduates, including noblemen and gentlemen-commoners, and do so reasonably well.[3] Their value in showing changes and developments in the biggest and most distinguished college of the university is obvious, though it must be borne in mind that it was in many ways atypical. There also

[1] *Letters of Radcliffe and James*, 160-1. William Baron Cattell, m. Queen's 1777; BA Merton 1781.
[2] E. Gibbon, *Memoirs of my Life*, ed. G. A. Bonnard (London 1966), pp. 46 ff. Care must be taken, however, not to assume that resolutions passed by governing bodies were always implemented, or if they were at the time, were persisted in.
[3] See P. Quarrie, 'The Christ Church Collections Books' below.

survives an account of the books on which Magdalen undergraduates were said to have been 'collected' between about 1770 and 1800 and a list of books for examinations appointed at Trinity about the year 1800. In Brasenose in 1809 termly collections provided for reports to the principal, vice-principal, senior fellows, tutors and the dean. At Queen's an interesting reading list is attached to a scheme for undergraduate disputations dating from the time of Provost Joseph Smith, probably in the 1730s, though there is no evidence that it was actually in use there.[1] But the most valuable personal records to survive are the numerous commonplace books which, usually at the instance of tutors and friends and relations, undergraduates were in the habit of keeping, thereby laying the foundation for the books which it was customary for educated men to keep throughout their lives.[2]

With the aid of these documents and more scattered references from other sources[3] we can reach certain conclusions. It is clear that all colleges, however varied the quality of the education they provided might be, saw undergraduate education as fitting into a common framework, and that this framework had evolved out of the curriculum which the Laudian plan had either recognized or created. Three general points can be made: all colleges subscribed to the obligation to provide some sort of religious education for their undergraduates; they based their curriculum primarily on the requirements of their own foundationers, battelers and servitors; and, since these were almost without exception aiming at the degree of BA, the curriculum which the colleges provided was based on the requirements for it. They added to it however three further subjects treated by the Laudian code as part not of the BA but of the MA examination: natural philosophy, metaphysics and history, which last was held to include geography and chronology.[4] In theory studies were based on the

---

[1] [J. Hurdis,] *A Word or Two in Vindication of the University of Oxford, and of Magdalen College in particular from the Posthumous Aspersions of Mr. Gibbon* (np nd), repr. in *Reminiscences of Oxford*, 130–48. TCA misc. iii. In 1789 it was resolved at Trinity that there would be two examinations of all undergraduates in hall each year, and that the books for the next examination should be given out immediately after the preceding one: TCA liber decani I, 12 Feb. 1789. W. T. Coxhill, 'Brasenose College in the time of Principal Ralph Cawley 1770–1777', BNCA no. 101. Queen's MS 482, no. 23. These were confused with Smith's better-known *quaestiones* for the theological training of taberdars (bachelor foundationers): see J. R. Magrath, *The Queen's College* (2 vols Oxford 1921) ii. 135.

[2] See for example James Blackstone's notebook (Balliol MS 430); the diary of Jeremiah Milles (Balliol MS 461); Dr Grandorge's commonplace book 1690 (Bodl. MS St Edmund Hall 72).

[3] For example 'Hints at the method of studying in the university, Nov. 1704' and 'Some short hints at a method of studying in the university, Sept. 1696', Bodl. MSS Rawl. D. 40, D. 1178: W. Cleaver, *List of Books recommended to the Younger Clergy and other Students within the Diocese of Chester* (Oxford 1791, 2nd edn, enlarged, Oxford 1792); Oriel College library, case D.C.V.4, 6, 7, registers of books taken out of the library.

[4] This was probably due to the assumption which had grown up that all basic arts teaching, as distinct from disputations, declamations and lectures to be delivered by the candidates, was to be completed in the BA course. A summary of the requirements for the university courses written about 1757 by Charles Coxwell (1741–1829, m. Pemb. 1757) mentions among

BA curriculum even when undergraduates were not aiming at a degree, though in practice this theory was seldom adhered to in full in the case of noblemen and gentlemen-commoners, who until the last years of the century rarely took the BA, receiving instead, if they so wished and remained long enough in residence, an honorary MA by decree.[1] While by no means all men in these classes neglected, as was generally believed and as Gibbon certainly did, their college duties, and a few read up to the highest contemporary standards, colleges had little success in submitting them to the full range of the college exercises, and their reading was apt to be tailor-made for them.[2] Some commoners also evaded the BA by entering after two years or more 'the Law Line', becoming thereby nominally candidates for the BCL, though in fact they seldom took that degree and by 1773 it was 'usually and with good reason discouraged'.[3]

In order to meet these academic requirements colleges acted as follows. Every college kept in operation undergraduate disputations in their halls or antechapels part of what had once been a more comprehensive system—under the supervision of a dean or moderator. Undergraduates seem to have been expected to take part in them as soon as they had completed some preliminary reading in logic with their tutors (as was certainly the rule at both Queen's and Brasenose). Evidence from a number of colleges suggests that this exercise was reasonably well attended, except by noblemen and gentlemen-commoners. Indeed, for those intending to enter the schools some practice in disputing *secundum artem* was almost essential. Nicholas Toke, a gentleman-commoner at University College in 1721 and alone among his 'gown' in taking a BA, found his greatest difficulty to lie in the fact that gentlemen-commoners considered it beneath their dignity to dispute in the hall. If he did so he would be 'guilty of great singularity and be accounted a Person proud of

the advantages of becoming a BA that one 'is exempted from attending lectures either public or private, as being supposed no longer to need a Tutor, but to have a competent Knowledge of the rudiments of academic learning': Gloucester, Gloucestershire Record Office, MS D269B/F108.

[1] This right was an extension from the provision in the code permitting sons of peers and the eldest sons of baronets to take their degrees at three years' standing: *Statutes* i. I, trans Ward i. 31. It was not there suggested that the degrees should be by decree, nor is any reference made to gentlemen-commoners. In fact in 1723 the hebdomadal board, giving permission to one such candidate to get an MA by decree, resolved that henceforth no degree of MA by decree should be given to a gentleman-commoner unless he had already taken his BA 'regularly'. This was a dead letter.

[2] The high standards achieved by some are amply demonstrated by the Christ Church collections books after 1773 when the reading of noblemen and gentlemen-commoners was for the first time incorporated with that of others. The registers of many colleges contain resolutions at one time or another submitting noblemen and gentlemen-commoners to the full rigour of college exercises, but until late in the century it seems unlikely that these resolutions were put into operation, or at any rate were maintained. Certainly most undergraduates believed they were not.

[3] Napleton, *Public Exercises*, 54. The BCL was the only degree which was not necessarily approached *via* the BA.

his own performances', yet unless he could 'practice disputations' he thought he would be 'very much at a loss' when he came 'to the exercise for a Degree'.[1] Since these disputations usually took place twice a week during most of the full terms, the subjects to be disputed on had to be arranged according to some plan. At Christ Church the subdean posted up a programme once a week based on a plan drawn up for the term.[2] However, only one college scheme covering the whole BA course has so far been discovered, the one at Queen's to which reference has already been made.

Every college also expected from each undergraduate, with the exception in some cases of noblemen and gentlemen-commoners, a number of declamations of themes, both oral and written, which were presented in the hall, nominally at least to the head of the house, and which were often corrected and resubmitted.[3] They were usually in Latin verse or prose and were no doubt intended to improve the undergraduates' Latinity, but were occasionally in Greek and in the later years of the century were sometimes in English. They excited a good deal of interest, banal though most of them now appear, and were frequently sent home for the admiration of the declaimer's family.[4] The composition of poems on public occasions and for the Encaenia was also frequently urged on undergraduates and was the object of emulation among them.[5]

The main part of the undergraduates' curriculum, however, consisted of lectures on and reading for the subjects deemed to be covered by the BA examination. Every undergraduate was placed under the direction of a tutor on entering the college, and (*pace* Gibbon) the general evidence from undergraduates is that their tutor played, for good or ill, a

[1] 'A gentleman commoner at Univ.', *University College Record* iii (1956–60), 264–5. It was suggested that he might get out of his difficulty by employing a skilled disputant in the college to dispute with him in his rooms, but ultimately he got the necessary practice by working through some 'strings' with his tutor.

[2] They are in a loose folder of manuscripts (nd but probably late eighteenth century) in CA liii.b.4, subdean's book.

[3] At Christ Church a compromise was evidently reached regarding noblemen and gentlemen-commoners. David Ker, a gentleman-commoner there in 1796, reported that they had to show up a theme in English once a week but that 'our Themes are never read over, but the best of the Commoners are': letter to his father, 24 June 1796, Belfast, Public Record Office of Northern Ireland, MS D2651/2/132B. There is a collection of 'themes' in the rare book room of Pembroke College and in CCCA B/10/1/2; the latter in verse and prose and in Greek, Latin and English.

[4] Jeremy Bentham sent a number home, one of which (in Latin) is entitled 'Despise Pleasures, every pleasure is injurious that is purchased by Regret'. He boasted that it had 'the approbation of all my Acquaintance, who liked the thing itself very well, but still better my Manner of speaking it. Even a Batchelor [of arts] of my Acquaintance went so far as to say, that he never heard but one speak a Declamation better all the time he has been in College': *Correspondence of Bentham*, ed. Sprigge i. 49–50.

[5] At Brasenose in 1773 'all members under the Degree of MA' were expected to send in to the principal work intended for the prizes at Encaenia. He sent on the best to the vice-chancellor. BNCA Cawley's notebooks, B53/1, p. 26 under *commemoration exercises*.

considerable part in their college life, teaching them individually or in small classes, organizing their reading and the work they did for other teachers, besides, right up to the end of the century, maintaining a considerable and rather surprising control over their finances.[1] All colleges also had lecturers in special subjects, though the part they played in undergraduate education varied greatly according to the good order of the individual college. At Queen's and Brasenose for instance it was taken for granted that they lectured once or twice a week in full term.[2] On the other hand, we know that in the bad years at Merton, between 1735 and 1740, when Warden Wyntle was at loggerheads with his fellows, and at Exeter when Conybeare and his successors began their reforms, their duties had been totally neglected; and at Magdalen, even in the 1790s when things were generally reforming, William Bagshaw Stevens, a non-resident fellow, considered he had done his duty as lecturer in moral philosophy when he had arranged for one lecture a term to be delivered by a deputy.[3]

The greater part of the reading of undergraduates consisted of classical literature, and its range was wide. In the later part of the century at Christ Church the collections books show a great and growing interest in Greek literature, including the tragedians and orators as well as the historians and the traditional study of Homer. Scholarly undergraduates at other colleges shared this enthusiasm, though by no means always with the same official assistance from their colleges.[4]

Outside the classics, in the study of the 'sciences', less work was done, and indeed there is, as one would expect, less sign of interest than in the later years of the seventeenth century. The books read were largely seventeenth-century compilations, though Locke's *Human Understanding*

[1] See Doolittle, 'College administration', 254.

[2] At Brasenose, for instance, John Kenrick, a first-year undergraduate, wrote to Lloyd Kenyon on 14 November 1750: 'That you may the better understand the method we go upon, I shall divide our lectures into public and private. First, then with our private tutor, we are lectured in Plato's Dialogues and logic, whenever he pleases to call upon us; for our public lectures in the hall, we have particular days in the week, which consists of Zenophon's *Memorabilia*, and Horace, by two different lecturers, one of them is Mr Mather, a very ingenious man, whom, I dare say, you have heard of. As for our exercises, they are disputations, three times a week, besides a declamation every term.' He added 'I must not omit telling you that I came on to dispute last week, a work which I do not like much as yet, though I chop logic pretty fast'. HMC *Kenyon MSS* iv. 492. Roger Mather (1719-68), m. BNC 1735; public orator 1749-60.

[3] For the conflict at Merton see MCR 1.6, Warden Wyntle's register. Robert Wyntle (1683-1750), m. Pemb. 1699, fellow Merton 1705, warden 1734-50. For Exeter see Exeter register 1737-1824, p. 7; regulations laid down in 1733 were by 1737 again neglected, and further stringent rules were again laid down. For Magdalen see *The Journal of the Rev. William Bagshaw Stevens*, ed. G. Galbraith (Oxford 1965), 370, 377. Stevens achieved this arrangement after a tussle with President Routh: see Doolittle, 232.

[4] This was certainly so with John James at Queen's: see *Letters of Radcliffe and James, passim*. It is unfortunate that we have no good information on the curriculum at either Oriel or Brasenose in this later period, when their reputation stood very high.

was read at Christ Church within a year of its publication and Newton's *Principia* appears in the last two decades of the century. Aristotle's *Nicomachean Ethics*, often thought of as a nineteenth-century educational revival, began to be read at Christ Church again in the seventeen-seventies. Throughout the century the only works of Aristotle widely read were the *Poetics* and the *Rhetoric*. At Christ Church, from about 1768, a great deal of attention was paid to mathematics; to Euclid and Maclaurin's algebra were added plane and spherical trigonometry and conic sections, though there are signs that the subject was not very popular with undergraduates, and more men were referred back at collections on a term's work in mathematics than in any other subject.[1]

It is easy to see how the nineteenth-century honour school of literae humaniores evolved from the best side of this eighteenth-century curriculum. At its worst, undergraduates and more experienced critics could justly complain that it gave them nothing but practice in construing classical texts (many of which they might well have read already if they had been at a good school) a grounding in formal logic and a smattering of non-literary knowledge based on outdated texts.

If the course for the degree of bachelor of arts as conceived in the Laudian code survived (if barely) in a recognizable form throughout the century, that for the degree of master of arts to which it led changed even more radically, not indeed in its nominal contents but in its real character. Like the BA course it was composed of two parts, one traditional, the other an innovation. It was intended to be a course of three years (twelve terms) of study, though, as with the BA, the code itself contained provisions which reduced the residence required for it. The traditional side of the course consisted of scholastic disputations and the delivery of six solemn lectures, the proof that when a candidate

---

[1] Abraham Robertson (1751-1826, m. Ch.Ch. 1775; Savilian prof. of geometry 1797-1810, astronomy 1810; Radcliffe's Observer 1810-26) was a Scotsman who came to Oxford on his own initiative believing he would be able to keep himself by private teaching. He tried unsuccessfully to open an evening school for young mechanics but failing became servant to an Oxford apothecary. Here his mathematical ability came to the attention of a well-known student in medicine at Christ Church and he obtained a servitorship in the college: see G. V. Cox, *Recollections of Oxford* (London 1868, 2nd edn London 1870), 144-7. David Ker said of his mathematics lecture, 'at ten I proceed to a Mathematics Lecture, which by the bye is very thinly attended, but that is so much the better for those that are there': letter to his father, 19 Apr. 1796, PRO Northern Ireland, MS D2651/2/135B. It seems likely that this lecture was in fact a university lecture given by Robertson as public reader in mathematics, for this year he advertised two sets of lectures one in conic sections, and the other 'the Elements and Application of Fluxions, in which the most important parts of Sir I. Newton's Principia will be explained': *Oxford University Notice*, 16 Feb. 1796. In the early years of the century, however, things were different—as George Carter shows. Writing to Archbishop Wake on 7 September 1721 he pointed out, 'Mathematics are studyed, Your Grace knows very well, but little amongst us, especially by such as I should be glad to recommend to this Place [the Savilian chair of astronomy]': Wake MS 16, fo 88.

'incepted' he was qualified to teach in the schools.[1] The innovations were an oral examination intended, as with the BA, to test his achievements in 'polite letters', and, after 1662, the delivery of two Latin declamations intended for the same purpose.

The beginning and end of this course were signalized by public ceremonies; those at the beginning were the Lenten disputations in which the recently incepted BA 'determined', thereby summing up his career as a bachelor; the end was the culmination of the academic year, the annual vespers and Act, the great disputations in which all those graduating in the higher faculties and a selected number of graduating MAs disputed, and in which they all 'incepted'. As late as 1669 the Sheldonian Theatre had been inaugurated for these 'solemnities' with all possible pomp. The ceremony had its lighter side, and entertainment was provided as well as learning, but its centre was seen as the clash between skilled and learned disputants before an expert and enthusiastic audience.

In the years separating the candidate's part in these ceremonies he was expected to qualify in two further philosophical disputations, that *apud Augustinenses* (known as Austins) and the *quodlibeticae* (quodlibets). He had also to deliver his solemn lectures, three in natural and three in moral philosophy, to be read from texts of his own composition. He was also supposed to attend the lectures of the Savilian professors of geometry and astronomy, the Sedleian professor of natural philosophy, the White professor of moral philosophy, the Camden professor of history, and the regius professors of Greek and Hebrew. He was to be orally examined on the contents of these lectures, and his two Latin declamations were chosen by the junior proctor from three themes presented by himself.

By the beginning of the period the situation with regard to these exercises was at least as unsatisfactory as that in the BA course. The disputations were as banal, and as easy to cheat in, though 'Austins' were, as has been said,[2] held to be better conducted than other public disputations. The solemn lectures were delivered—or not delivered—to empty rooms and were known as 'Wall Lectures'. A confession by a Magdalen MA to President Routh in 1798 draws attention to a more serious irregularity with regard to them;

knowing that no such thing [was] ever thought of in our College as composing the Lectures in Natural and Moral Philosophy, I read those which had been for many years almost invariably taken into the Schools by our Men. Indeed I well remember that I should have grudged the time it would have taken from my

---

[1] The 'solemn' lectures were distinct from the 'cursory' lectures (those explaining a text) which had been previously demanded but were now thought to be unsatisfactory. To 'incept' was to obtain recognition at the Act for the degree for which the candidate had done the 'exercises'.

[2] See p. 471 above.

favourite pursuits, to gain such a knowledge of those Sciences, as would have enabled me [to] make those Lectures.[1]

Though some of the professors were men of distinction and some of them lectured from time to time, there was no compulsory attendance and dispensations were regularly given in congregation for abstention from them.[2] The examination nominally dependent on them was admitted to be even more summary than that for the BA since no convention had grown up for the presentation of texts, and it would seem that such an examination of comparatively senior men, some of them already in holy orders, was generally held to be something of an indignity.[3] The declamations were the only part of the whole which retained any vitality, partly no doubt because of candidates' experience in declaiming in their colleges.[4]

But the MA course underwent two fundamental changes which did not affect that for the BA. The first was the disappearance of the Act to which its exercises were supposed to lead. From the early 1690s it became increasingly common for the chancellor formally to recommend the 'intermission' of the Act for the year and for convocation to vote a blanket dispensation for all due to incept at it. Though the Act of 1713 was said to have called forth a record attendance,[5] it proved the last of the old tradition. There was only one attempt, in 1733, to revive it, and though as late as 1772 some members of Convocation were still pressing for its resumption, the cause had long been a lost one.[6] The Encaenia which gradually took its place, arising out of what was at first called an 'Act Philologica', fulfilled none of the same academic functions.[7] The reasons given each year for its 'intermission' were varied; when they were academic they related to developments in the higher faculties.

The second fundamental change in the MA course was the erosion,

[1] Magdalen, MS 473, fo 1. Unfortunately the name of the writer has not survived, nor do we know what Routh replied. The young man was much upset at the knowledge that he had foresworn himself and asked for guidance. He had thought at the time of confessing that he could not take the oath prescribed for graduands but 'through want of resolution at the moment, I fell'.

[2] OUA registers of congregation, *passim*.

[3] Speaking of the MA examination even after the reforms in the curriculum had begun, Archbishop Whately said: 'when I first went to Oxford and for some years after, there was a regular public examination for the degree of MA. But, in fact, it was *not* public, all the undergraduates and Bachelors making it a point of delicacy never to attend because several of those examined were men of middle age, and many clergymen.' Moreover, examiners could not be persuaded to reject anyone. *Report of Her Majesty's Commissioners appointed to inquire into the State, Discipline, Studies and Revenues of the University and Colleges of Oxford* (1852), evidence, p. 25. Richard Whately (1787-1863), m. Oriel 1805; principal St Alban Hall 1825-31; abp of Dublin 1831-63.

[4] OUA junior proctors declamation books, SP/107-9, give a list of the subjects approved and the dates on which the declamations were given 1723-97, the names of the candidates and the very varied topics on which they declaimed.

[5] W. Dolben-A. Charlett, 15 July 1713, Ballard MS 21, fo 192.

[6] OUA register of convocation 1766-76, p. 222, 22 Apr. 1772.

[7] See V. H. H. Green, 'The university and social life', pp. 352-3 above.

and finally the almost complete disappearance, of the residence qualification. Under the rules of the Laudian code the twelve terms of residence were reduced to ten by excluding the requirement for the first and
last terms (as for the BA), and congregation had power to dispense up to
three further terms (as against the two terms for the BA) and exercised it
without question. These provisions in themselves reduced the qualification to seven terms of residence, less than two years. But it was through
the discretionary dispensations made in convocation in response to individual 'chancellor's letters' that the great change took place. The number
of applications accepted increased steadily throughout the century. In
1715-16 the total number of 'chancellor's letters' passed was seventeen
out of a total of some eighty men taking their MAs. By 1793-4 it was
fifty-three out of much the same total but the length of time dispensed
for each candidate also increased.[1] In 1715-16 no application was passed
for more than three discretionary terms, a concession which, when
added to the five terms already dispensed or counted in, brought the
residence required down to one year. About 60 per cent of the applicants
asked for less and thus resided longer. By 1772 Napleton admitted that
discretionary grants of four terms had become so regular that 'the
Candidate, unless indeed there be something very particular in his case,
has a moral certainty of obtaining it'.[2] He spoke for the group in convocation supported in 1773 by the hebdomadal board, which was concerning itself with the subject. Their success in maintaining residence
requirements for the BA was not reflected in the case of the MA. They
reluctantly came to the conclusion that they could not stand out against
demands for five-term dispensations by convocation which reduced the
requirement to two term's residence, the 'Master's Term' of the nineteenth century. By 1793-4, however, more than 50 per cent of the
recorded dispensations by convocation were for six terms, and dispensations for five and six terms between them made up nearly 80 per cent of
the dispensations granted.

This did not mean that at any time in the century there were no BAs
in residence. Even in 1793-4 nearly 40 per cent of the candidates resided
for seven terms or more. Men staying on for their MAs were, as statistics
collected by the university showed, mostly those intending to take holy
orders, and a very high proportion of these were foundationers of
colleges.[3] Colleges varied greatly in the strictness with which, despite the
universal relaxations in the rules for the residence of fellows, they sought

[1] The numbers of dispensations by convocation are taken from the appropriate registers of
convocation, those of the total number of graduates from the registers of congregation.
[2] *Considerations on the Residence*, 4.
[3] Of the 491 men proceeding to the MA between 1765 and 1772, the university statistics show
that all but 12 were 'either foundationers or in Orders or both'.

to enforce their founders' statutes on their BA foundationers. As late as 1799 Corpus, a particularly strict college, having considered the application of a BA fellow to go out of residence as a tutor in a private house, noted that consent was given only after much deliberation:

... so much do our Statutes dwell upon the obligation to *Residence*, and particularly (for obvious *Reasons*) with respect to the *Junior* part of the Society; whose literary *Proficiencies*, and *Moral Conduct* can be best ascertained during such Residence by those who are to determine their fitness or usefulness for the master's degree, and afterwards for their admission into Holy Orders.[1]

Other colleges were less successful in their efforts.[2] Another reason, which also influenced bachelors who were not on the foundation to spend at least some time at the university before taking their MA, was the need to put in time before they were of age to take deacon's orders, and to obtain a testimonial of fitness for those orders from their college.

These factors were, however, largely offset by two others which were in the main more telling: the pressure of economic need among foundationers, the value of whose endowments were eroded by the decline in the value of money; and the absence of any systematic instruction for the graduate. The decay of university instruction for the BAs was not, as in the case of the undergraduate curriculum, counteracted by any development in college teaching. The bachelor had no college tutor; no college lectures were for the most part provided for him. Most colleges, unless they were in great disarray, continued to provide bachelor disputations in hall, and sometimes to exact fines for non-attendance at them.[3] The deans also presented bachelors for degrees, and it was common for colleges to insist on some form of declamation, lecture, or formal disputation from candidates before they granted them the grace to proceed to their degree; but these requirements necessitated little exertion from them.

In so far as even the most conscientious colleges concerned themselves with the training of their bachelors, this was rather in connection with their preparation for ordination than with the MA itself. In general

---

[1] CCCA acta B/4/1/1. The strictness of Corpus was widely admitted. On 13 April 1789 Mrs Wyndham, whose son was going to Corpus, wrote to the president that she had warned him 'I thought it but fair, to tell him, that in *many* others, he would have more liberty;—nay, perhaps in *any* other . . .': CCCA B/14/5/1.

[2] One of the issues over which Warden Wyntle of Merton was embroiled with his fellows in 1735 was the extremely inconvenient statutory arrangement hitherto in force in the college to keep up a body of bachelor fellows, so that they might receive instruction in the college before being elected fellows proper. This was done by deferring elections of fellows, and withholding graces from bachelor fellows qualified to proceed to their MA until an adequate quorum of bachelors was in residence to replace them. See Merton, Warden Wyntle's register. The system broke down completely, as did at this time the provision for enforcing residence on the bachelors.

[3] CA subdean's book, rules of the subdean (loose folder); BNCA Cawley's notebooks, B53/1, p. 26 under *College exercise*; LCM box of correspondence, mainly seventeenth- and eighteenth-century, 1770.

the colleges took the responsibility seriously.[1] They even made some, for the most part feeble, efforts to meet the demands of episcopal Visitors and other bishops to ensure that their candidates had some systematic training in divinity other than that provided while they were still under-graduates. In the early years of the century Balliol was especially praised for the training it provided through the work of catechistical lecturers and others, and at Corpus by 1791 an abridgement of the divinity lectures of the late Thomas Randolph was demanded of each candidate for the MA before he was given his grace.[2]

Only one college however, Queen's, appears to have made a syste-matic and sustained attempt to provide its bachelors with training in theology. Some time before 1731 Provost Joseph Smith drew up, and the college accepted, a comprehensive system of theological *quaestiones* and written work arising out of them for the use of the taberdars which can be shown to have been in active use for some twenty years, and remnants of which can indeed be found in use in the college as late as 1823.[3]

Of the small number of 'independent' BAs not aiming at the church but who felt it worthwhile to complete their Oxford course and proceed to the MA, Jeremy Bentham provides in the sixties an illustration, though not in all ways a representative one. He took out a 'chancellor's letter' for three terms, which he evidently thought the normal time, leaving himself liable to four terms of residence. He did not keep these terms consecutively, but worked them in with reading for the Bar. When in Oxford he attended part of Blackstone's famous lectures, and the less successful ones in civil law of Thomas Bever, and he also fitted in a short course on 'air' by the popular professor of astronomy Thomas Hornsby. He looked up some musical manuscripts in the Bodleian Library, fre-quented the physic garden and some concerts, bought books and became exasperated by the formalities of presenting himself for his degree.[4] Others no doubt spent their time less profitably.

The Laudian code laid down the details of the courses leading up to the university's highest awards, the DD, the DM and the DCL, the last still then commonly called the 'doctorate in laws'. In all of them the candi-date had to be an MA and of a certain number of years' standing. In due course after incepting MA he was eligible for the appropriate doctorate. There was considerable variation in the number of years' standing

[1] See Greaves, 'Religion in the university 1715-1800'.
[2] CCCA acta B/4/1/2.
[3] Queen's, MS 475, fos 93 ff and MS 442 (1).
[4] *Correspondence of Bentham*, ed. Sprigge i. 84 ff. Thomas Hornsby (1733-1810), m. CCC 1749; Savilian prof. of astronomy 1763-1810, prof. of experimental phil. 1763-1810, Sedleian prof. of nat. phil. 1782-1810; Radcliffe's Observer 1772-1810; Radcliffe Librarian 1783-1810.

required in the different faculties. In divinity the BD had to be of seven years' standing from his MA. In medicine the BM had to be of three years' standing from his MA. In law the BCL who had taken his MA had to be of three years' standing from it, while the BCL who had not done so had to be of five years' standing since he had entered the 'Law Line', which he was entitled to do after two years of work for the BA. In the few cases in which colleges admitted scholars or undergraduate fellows to read law at entrance, the preliminary two years of reading for the BA were statutably waived. There was less variation in the standing required for bachelors proceeding to the doctorates. It was four years in every case except that of the BCL who had not taken his MA; for him it was five years.

The exercises required for these degrees were intended to be strictly professional. Candidates were supposed to have followed during the years leading up to each degree the lectures of the appropriate professor, and to obtain each degree they had to take part in professional disputations in the schools. The BD was also required to preach a Latin sermon in St Mary's. The BCL who had not taken his MA had also to take the oral examination imposed on arts candidates to ensure their achievements in 'polite letters' and to dispute three times on civil law; his examination was the same as that for the BA, but with the addition of two more 'sciences', jurisprudence and history. For the doctorate each candidate had to deliver either six solemn lectures or at least three cursory lectures on specified parts of his subject. These were laid down and were conceived on strictly traditional lines.

There is no direct statement in the code which would suggest that residence was not required for the higher degrees as it was for the MA (only for the undergraduates reading for the BA or BCL was residence defined as residing within a college or hall). Indeed, it would seem by implication that it was; but it was clearly impracticable for most candidates to reside for such long courses unless they were fellows of colleges. In fact residence was not demanded, and there was no occasion for the stream of dispensations by convocation through 'chancellor's letters' which brought about the change of the MA during the century from a resident to a virtually non—resident degree. A provision in the code suggests that even when it was drawn up there was some recognition of this problem, for provision was made, though obviously as an exception, for what was called 'accumulation', the omission of the higher bachelor's degree and the taking of it and the doctorate at the same time (fees were paid for both degrees, but exercises done only for the doctorate). When dealing with the doctorate in divinity the code goes into some detail about the conditions under which dispensation could be given by convocation to permit 'accumulation'.[1] The applicant had to be four to five

[1] *Statutes* IX. iii. 4, trans. Ward i. 54.

years' longer standing than if he had taken his degree in the normal way, and he had to be normally resident more than thirty miles away from the university. This method of taking the doctorate was already widely used at the beginning of the period and became increasingly common as time went on.[1] The condition about residence was not insisted on and convocation made its own rules about the necessary years of standing for degrees other than those in divinity, rules considerably less strict than those laid down in the code for the latter.

In the eighteenth century the degree of bachelor in the higher faculties was not widely taken by those aiming at a doctorate, nor indeed by those taking the bachelorships without further ambition, except by fellows of colleges who could fit them in without difficulty. Even here they were much neglected despite university and college statutes. In theory throughout the century all MAs who kept their names on the college books were expected to enter on the 'lines' of one of the three higher faculties.[2] Since the great majority of fellows of colleges were obliged to proceed to holy orders and only a small number of 'faculty' fellowships existed for those intending to proceed to law or medicine, this should have meant that the great majority of fellows would proceed by regular process through the degree of BD to that of DD. In fact this obligation was widely neglected, except when internal disputes within colleges brought the question to the fore.[3] The cause given for the neglect was largely that of expense.[4] It could hardly have been the burden of work which the obligation imposed. The compulsory lectures which candidates were supposed to attend were not given, college disputations for MAs in divinity died out, despite some efforts in the earlier years of the century by college Visitors to insist on them, and both in divinity and law those who did proceed to the higher bachelor's degrees had frequently to obtain dispensations to postpone their statutory disputations on account of the difficulty in 'finding a class'.[5]

The doctorates were essentially high professional qualifications, and since most Oxford graduates entered the church, and this was a field where higher qualifications were widely sought—by the higher clergy,

[1] OUA registers of convocation, *passim*.

[2] In the OUA/WPα/2/5, official returns of members of colleges and halls on the books for 1804, the MAs are returned under these headings. MAs on the divinity line were returned as 638, on the physic line as 5 and on the law line as either 8 or 15 (there was some confusion about the entry from Queen's). The figures include men who had gone down but kept their names on the books.

[3] See Doolittle, 'College administration', pp.241-2.

[4] This excuse was accepted by one Visitor of Trinity but doubted by another. On 17 March 1727 the bishop of Winchester wrote to the president and fellows as to the complaint about divinity disputations: 'I am sorry to find there is so much truth in it because I take that exercise not only to be plainly injoined you by your Statutes but also to be of great use for the improvement of the College in the knowledge of Divinity, and in a readiness and ability to defend it, as there shall be occasion . . .' TCA Visitors' letter 1576-1820. See also MCR Wyntle's register.

[5] See for example OUA register of convocation 1703-30, fo 291, 26 Jan. 1727.

the heads of houses, the more prominent headmasters of schools and so on—the numbers who qualified as doctors of divinity were much greater than those in medicine or law. The numbers graduating in medicine at Oxford were always small, but their influence in the university was considerable.[1] The professional qualification was carefully guarded by the profession itself through the activities of the Royal College of Physicians of London, which, though it was losing its control over the profession as a whole at this time, had a special interest in preserving the professional status of the Oxford and Cambridge doctorates. In 1722 the college warned both universities against incorporating as doctors of medicine the doctors of other universities, or awarding honorary degrees in this field, and the universities accepted the warning.[2] There was always in Oxford, moreover, a nucleus of DMs holding university positions and faculty fellowships, which they combined with private practice. Their cohesion was increased by the foundation of the Radcliffe Infirmary and its opening in 1770 and then by the foundation of the clinical chair associated with it, and they saw that convocation watched jealously for any infringement of professional standards. It is characteristic of their vigour and solidarity as a group that they were the first of the higher faculties to persuade convocation to make use of the powers it claimed after 1760 to depart from the provisions of the Laudian code and to modify their examination requirements. In 1781 the length of the medical course was reduced by two years by making candidates eligible for the BM one year after taking their MA, instead of the three years hitherto required.[3]

The position of the faculty of law was much weaker. The decline in the importance of civil law meant that the degree of DCL was of little professional value except in the restricted field of Doctors' Commons. Oxford's distinguished lawyers looked to the Inns of Court and, with notable exceptions such as Blackstone and William Scott, played little part in university affairs. It was not until 1789 that Scott took up and steered through the hebdomadal board and convocation a statute intended to assist the professional interests of the civilians by reducing the length of the course to match that of their Cambridge contemporaries and even then the proposal ran into difficulties. The result of the lack of professional interest in the status of the DCL was the dilution of its professional character. This happened in two ways. The first was by the award of honorary degrees in the modern sense of this term, the award of doctorates to distinguished public men as an honour conferred on them by the university both at Encaenia and on other occasions; the DCL was,

[1] See Webster, 'Medical faculty', 685.
[2] G. N. Clark, *The Royal College of Physicians of London* (2 vols Oxford 1964-6) ii. 509-10.
[3] On the importance of the resident physicians and the length of the medical course see Webster, esp. 688-9.

except for churchmen, the only suitable doctorate to offer them. Though this custom reduced the professional character of the degree, it in no way impaired its distinction. The conferment of honorary DCLs might reflect the university's political views and the respect in which the higher aristocracy was held at the time, but convocation never awarded them lightly. The second way in which the professional aspect of the DCL was diluted was less to its credit and seems to be largely an eighteenth-century phenomenon. This was the taking of the doctorate by 'mutation', a method not authorized by anything in the code, though not in itself illegal. It arose from the wide discrepancy in the years of standing necessary to qualify for the DD and the DCL. The practice grew up for MAs who would naturally have looked to the DD to obtain dispensations from convocation to 'commute' their MAs into BCLs, and then to obtain a DCL by accumulation. In this way a number of clergy sought and obtained the DCL. The method is described in a letter from an MA, the headmaster of an academy in Soho, in 1786:

The wild report you heard of my Dr's gown was not more wild than true. I am *bona fide* LL.D. at your service. The transition or transportation from arts to Law or Divinity is easy and frequent; and as I was not of standing for the latter, and all I wanted, the inania nomina rerum, the same in both, I preferred the former now to the other at a time when my character must have been fixed one [way] or other without it. MA is entitled to be dubbed LL.D. at about eleven years standing. And the Convocation, for economy's sake, and to encourage the going out in arts first, grant the degree of LL.D. without any other exercise than three wall lectures, MA having been previously commuted by a Chancellor's Letter to LL.B.[1]

Charles Coxwell in his 'Abstract' of 1757 gave practical information on the question: 'A person of sufficient standing may take a Doctors degree, tho he never took a batchelors in Divinity; the expense in that case will be greatly increased; or by commuting, he may take a doctor of Laws, which will be something less.'[2]

There was always an undercurrent of dislike for the procedure of 'mutation'. In 1708 Provost Lancaster of Queen's, one of the best of the university's vice-chancellors in the earlier years of the century, wrote '. . . the University knows no difference between what a man studys in the College and in the University, but the Statutes expect everyone should study in his College what he professes out of it', and towards the end of the century, in 1789, a group of members of convocation, anxious to prevent abuses in the award of degrees, challenged a number of 'chancellor's letters' proposing mutations, though they only succeeded in defeating

---

[1] W. Barrow-J. James junior, 26 Jan. 1786, *Letters of Radcliffe and James*, 264. William Barrow (1755-1836), m. Queen's 1774; archdeacon of Nottingham 1830-6.
[2] Glos. Rec. Office, MS D269B/F108.

one.[1] But so common had the practice become that when in the same year the hebdomadal board, under Scott's influence, tried to reduce the length of the course by permitting the DCL to be taken a year after the BCL if a candidate had already taken the MA and four years after if the MA had not been taken, the statute had to be withdrawn and amended by confining the concession to those who were prepared to take an oath before the proctors that they intended to enter 'the Maritime and Ecclesiastical Courts'.[2]

The number of men proceeding to the doctorates remained at a fairly steady level throughout the period,[3] though references to the 'paucity of proceeders' often made in convocation would lead one to think otherwise. When the Act was 'intermitted' as became common form, a reason often adduced was the absence or paucity of proceeders in the 'superior faculties'. It is evident, however, that the university officers excluded from their calculations all doctors proceeding by accumulation and mutation, no doubt on the reasonable grounds that they would not have been able to take their part in the disputations of the traditional Act. In 1783, for instance, when some members of convocation made a special drive to restore the Act, the chancellor informed the house that 'on account of the small number of Proceeders in the Superior Faculties' the Act would be intermitted. In fact the registers show that seven DDs and two DCLs incepted, but four of the DDs were by accumulation, and both the DCLs by mutation and accumulation.[4]

As the century wore on clearly the advantages of staying on at the university for the purpose of taking a higher degree became less and less attractive. Other careers beside the church and university were opening up and this, together with the increasing expense, weighed heavily against the higher faculties. By the end of the century the possibility of reforming the curriculum had become real, and the need urgent.

[1] Lancaster-Charlett, 20 May 1708, MS Ballard 21, fo 77. OUA register of convocation 1776-93, pp. 375-7, 4 Apr.-10 July 1789.

[2] OUA WPα/12/2.

[3] L. Stone, 'The size and composition of the Oxford student body 1580-1909' in L. Stone (ed.), *The University in Society* (2 vols Princeton 1975) i. 94.

[4] OUA register of convocation 1776-93, p. 175, 10 Apr. 1783; register of congregation 1769-84, pp. 514-15, 521.

16

The Christ Church Collections Books

P. QUARRIE

THE importance of the Christ Church collections books for the history of the curriculum in the eighteenth century can hardly be overestimated, as they give a detailed circumstantial account of undergraduate reading in the largest college of the university. Such information can otherwise be gathered in part only from scattered sources, for example the odd list of books read by an individual, chance mentions in letters and so on. Indeed, although these are records of readings in only one college they form a kind of control against which the readings of someone such as John James at Queen's in the 1770s or Henry Fynes Clinton at Christ Church itself at the end of the century can be judged.[1] Moreover, they do this over such a long period that it is possible to gain a detailed impression of the major shifts in reading, and indeed in general education both within and outside the university. For in the eighteenth century both the schools and the universities saw a great change in the type and numbers of books read: authors, many of whom had been widely read since the middle of the previous century, disappear and others previously neglected, or in some instances new books, take their place. Handbooks of ethics and natural philosophy disappear and modern original works take their place, as for example the *Institutionum metaphysicarum libri duo* of Frank Burgersdijk, professor at Leiden 1620-35, a work published posthumously in 1640 and many times reprinted both on the continent and in England. This was a book specified from 1717 for the fourth 'class' (a 'class' being a set of books prescribed for reading) and much read before, the use of which climbed steadily, reaching a peak in the years 1730-50; in the 1760s it is no longer mentioned.[2]

---

[1] Henry Fynes Clinton (1781-1852), m. Ch.Ch. 1799; MP Aldborough 1806-26; see M. L. Clarke, 'Classical studies', pp. 513-33 below.

[2] A list of editions of Burgersdijk is given in P. Dibon, *La Philosophie néerlandaise au siècle d'or i L'Enseignement philosophique dans les universités a l'époque précartésienne 1575-1650* (Paris 1954), 124. This work never attained the same popularity in Cambridge (where it was frequently printed) of his *Institutiones logicae*: see J. E. B. Mayor, *Cambridge under Queen Anne* (Cambridge 1911), 251-2. In 1687 the Oxford bookseller Anthony Stevens held most of his books in stock, including thirty-three copies in quires of his *Collegium physicum* (perhaps the Oxford edn of 1664) and twenty-one of the logic: see D. G. Vaisey, 'Anthony Stevens: the rise and fall of an Oxford bookseller', *Studies in the Book*

The collections books fall into three divisions. The first (1699–1717) gives details of authors read by individuals, the second (1717–74) gives schemes of required reading for the four (or three) 'classes' with the lists of persons 'collected' (that is to say examined as to their reading) and the third (1768 into the nineteenth century) again gives lists of individual readings. They are in various hands, written by the censors, and include very brief details of authors and titles: in one case only is a particular edition of a text specified, Rollin's edition of Quintilian.

The development during the eighteenth century which strikes one above all else is the enormous increase in the study of Greek writers. From being a small part of the reading at the beginning of the century, in the last two decades (even allowing for the large increase in the numbers of undergraduates) it became a very important study; and in the decade 1780–9 the Greek readings even exceeded the Latin.

In the early years there is no very commonly read book: Aristotle's *Rhetoric* was read by a small number; some few read Homer; others a little Theocritus (generally in conjunction with Virgil, one supposes the *Eclogues*); occasionally an obscure work makes an appearance. In 1706 Charles Fairfax read the paraphrase of Aristotle's *Nicomachean Ethics* by Andronicus of Rhodes, as did two others.[1] One finds Xenophon's *Memorabilia* and *Cyropaedia* (both of which had recently appeared in new editions by Edward Wells, printed at Oxford in 1690 and 1703) in a total of thirty-one and forty-eight readings in the first two decades. The latter of these texts was edited by Wells *in usum scholarum*, and the book had been for generations used as a schoolbook.[2] In the years 1720–50 there is an increase in the reading of Homer: the four class-lists for the period, which give the names of those collected, required in classes 1–3 the reading of the whole of the *Iliad* divided up into three divisions of eight books. Apart from the New Testament in Greek, this is the only Greek book read. The general level of attainment in Greek is manifestly not high.

This situation changed in the middle of the century, and from then onward the number of authors read and the frequency of the readings increases dramatically. Part of the reason for this must lie in the greater availability of texts and part in a change of attitude towards Greek studies. In the early years of the century Cambridge rather than Oxford was the place whence came new editions. In 1703, for example, appeared

Trade in Honour of Graham Pollard, ed. R. W. Hunt, I. G. Philip and R. J. Roberts (Oxford Bibliog. Soc. new ser. xviii 1975), 108, 110, 113.

[1] Charles Fairfax (1685–1723), m. Ch.Ch. 1702; dean of Down and Connor 1722.

[2] Edward Wells (1667–1727), m. Ch.Ch. 1686. John Gilman (1675–1741, m. St John's 1693; undermaster of Merchant Taylors' School 1707–19) published an edition of the *Memorabilia* (London 1720) for the use of his school, in the preface to which (pp. ix–x) he refers to the paucity of separate editions of Xenophon's various works, except for the *Cyropaedia*.

an edition of two plays of Euripides, *Medea* and *Phoenissae*, by a fellow of Emmanuel, William Piers, who is said by Hearne to have cribbed Barnes's edition of 1694.[1] This was clearly meant for undergraduate reading, and 850 copies were printed (Cambridge produced at this time a number of editions of the philosophical compendia used at both universities). There were also editions of Latin authors from the Cambridge Press. Obviously the Oxford Press produced editions of Greek texts, but these were grand works, not meant for the undergraduate market, which everywhere had been largely supplied in the seventeenth century, and indeed into the eighteenth century, by imports from Holland. Gradually this situation changed and Oxford began to produce books meant for its undergraduates, some of which went through several editions. In the fifty years from 1730 to 1780 some fifty editions of classical texts appeared (including reprints) and in 1760 Blackstone suggested printing an edition of Cicero as 'part of a great plan for publishing an intire edition of all the classics in an elegant Manner and at a very cheap Rate for the benefit of Students'.[2] This series did not come to pass. Cambridge produced some much used works, notably Mounteney's edition of some of the speeches of Demosthenes (*Philippic* I and *Olynthiacs* I–III) which, appearing first in 1731, was reprinted in London and at Eton eight times before the end of the century.[3] In the schools the amount of Greek read was increasing, and the frequency of editions of *Poetae graeci* (first published 1755) an anthology of Greek verse and *Scriptores graeci* (1767) which contains small selections from Xenophon, Herodotus, Thucydides and (largely) Lucian (from Kent's Cambridge edition of 1730) are testimony to this at Eton.

In many ways one of the most influential books of this second half of the century was the *Pentalogia* of John Burton. This was a collection of five plays—*Oedipus Tyrannus*, *Oedipus Coloneus* and *Antigone* of Sophocles, Euripides's *Phoenissae* and the *Septem contra Thebas* of Aeschylus—first published in 1758 at the Clarendon Press, and again in 1779, revised by Thomas Burgess of Corpus. Burton had considerable influence at Oxford, and shortly after 1754 he addressed a letter to his nephew Edward Bentham, who had just vacated his fellowship at Oriel and become a canon of Christ Church, entitled *De litterarum graecarum institutionibus dissertatio critica*. In this Burton stresses the importance of a proper command of Greek idiom, which he said could be gained only from a detailed study of certain prose writers: Plato, Aristotle, Lysias, Isocrates, Demosthenes, Herodotus, Thucydides and Xenophon, who

[1] Hearne, *Collections* ii. 212. *Euripidis quae extant omnia*, ed. J. Barnes (London 1694).
[2] See I. G. Philip, *William Blackstone and the Reform of the Oxford University Press in the Eighteenth Century* (OBS new ser. vii 1957), 15, 115.
[3] Mounteney's *Demosthenes* is several times mentioned in the collections books and was read twenty-one times 1760–9.

must not only be read but imitated in composition also. He strongly condemned the use of editions with Latin cribs, which he said allowed the reader not to understand fully the nuances of the Greek: making this too easy was an impediment to learning (*scientiae incremento obest ipsa discendi nimia facilitas*) and a deeper understanding was to be gained from the use of dictionaries and notes which reduced grammatical and stylistic peculiarities (for the purpose of explanation) to a norm. The application of some of these ideas can be seen in Burton's *Pentalogia*, in a selection (*Tetralogia*) from Euripides (*Medea, Hippolytus, Iphigenia in Aulis* and *Iphigenia in Tauris*) published by the University Press in 1771, and in the large quarto edition of Theocritus published in 1770 (edited by Warton) but originally mooted in 1758, when it was agreed by the delegates of the Press 'that there be no Latin translation, but that all difficult words be explained in the verbal index at the end of the work'.[1] It was also agreed that the edition be printed without accents; this was another of Burton's ideas set out in some detail in his *Dissertatio* and observed in some of his own Greek prose writings.

It is in the *Pentalogia* and the *Tetralogia* that the most-read plays of the later part of the century are to be found. For Aeschylus it is the *Septem*, read thirty-two times in the 1780s and thirty-one in the 1790s. From 1790, however, it is the *Prometheus Vinctus* which becomes the most-read play. A separate edition of the play (reprinted at least four times by 1807) had been available from the year 1767, edited by Thomas Morell, chiefly famous as the compiler of the text *Judas Maccabaeus*. This edition seems from the preface to have been undertaken at the instance of John Foster, headmaster of Eton 1765–73, for use as a school textbook. For Sophocles, who begins to be read in the 1760s,[2] the most-read plays in the last two decades and the early nineteenth century are the two Oedipus plays, although all the plays are frequently read (except *Trachiniae*). For Euripides the most-read play is *Medea*, the two Iphigenia plays and the *Phoenissae*, with *Medea* far outstripping the rest in the last decade. In the final years (1790–1800) *Hecuba* had seventy-two and *Hippolytus* forty-four readings. Both *Medea* and *Hippolytus* were available singly, the former in a straight reprint from Barnes's edition of 1694 published in 1734 by the Eton bookseller Joseph Pote (reprinted 1785, 1792 and 1795 and available without the Latin version) and the latter in Samuel Musgrave's edition (Oxford 1756, reprinted Eton 1792 and 1799). *Phoenissae* was available in an edition with two other plays (*Hecuba* and *Orestes*) edited by John King and published in Cambridge in 1726 and

---

[1] Philip, 97.

[2] *Electra* was among those plays edited early in the century by Thomas Johnson of King's whose collected edition of Sophocles appeared first in 1746 in London and Eton: a complete Sophocles in Greek with an *index verborum* by Thomas Morell appeared in Eton in 1786.

reprinted *in usum scholae etonensis* in 1748. That it was these editions, and particularly the two, so to speak, 'anthologies', which were used is clear from the number of annotated copies of them that survive.[1]

Among the prose writers it is, for the second half of the eighteenth century, the historians, Herodotus, Thucydides and Xenophon, who are read the most.

In the final period books I and II of Polybius were also read.[2] An example of how these texts were read towards the end of this period is given below.[3] It is interesting to note that John Burton stressed the importance of elucidating texts *ex historiae monumentis* and praised for this very reason Edward Bentham's collection of the three funeral speeches (λόγοι ἐπιτάφιοι that is Thucydides, Lysias and the *Menexenus*

TABLE 16.1

READINGS OF GREEK PLAYWRIGHTS

	1770–9	1780–9	1790–1800
Aeschylus			
Septem		32	31
Persae		9	27
Prometheus Vinctus		8	53
Agamemnon			10
Euripides			
Medea		49	90
Hecuba		15	72
Iphigenia in Aulis		47	53
Iphigenia in Tauris		45	34
Phoenissae		38	48
Orestes		22	48
Hippolytus		15	44
Alcestis			37
Sophocles			
Ajax	1	52	63
Antigone	6	64	43
Electra	60	60	40
Oedipus Coloneus	9	83	49
Oedipus Tyrannus	38	92	63
Philoctetes		43	61
Trachiniae		7	10

[1] The *Phoenissae* was read at Cambridge in the 1770s: see C. Wordsworth, *Scholae academicae* (Cambridge 1877), 356.

[2] Fynes Clinton says that Polybius was not read in the original: *The Literary Remains of Henry Fynes Clinton, Esq., M.A.* ed. C. J. Fynes Clinton (London 1854). Several translations were available.

[3] See p. 498 below.

TABLE 16.2

READINGS OF GREEK HISTORIANS

	1760-9	1770-9	1780-9	1790-1800	total
Herodotus	47	192	273	327	839
Thucydides	13	119	208	263	603
Xenophon					
Anabasis	22	119	112	103	347
Cyropaedia	48	101	114	82	345
Hellenica	21	43	113	215	392
Memorabilia	13	119	208	263	388

of pseudo-Plato) for the inclusion of historical tables. Bentham's book came out first in Oxford in 1746, and in 1759 he published an English translation in London. The Greek text was reprinted at Oxford in 1768, and there were other editions printed at Eton with a Latin translation added. Bentham's notes are in English and in the preface he stresses the importance of these texts as illustrating Greek history. He then gives an account of the writers, both ancient and modern, on Greek history, and it is particularly interesting to note in the light of the large number of readings of Raleigh's *History* (81) recorded at the end of the century, that Bentham enumerates those chapters which deal with Greek history.[1]

The most-read texts of Aristotle (hardly any Plato seems to have been read throughout the period) are the *Rhetoric* and the *Poetics*. The former was read a little in the early years of the century, but in the last thirty years or so it became by far the most-read text (1770-1800: 169, 194, 151 readings) with the *Poetics* (108, 125, 38) well behind and very few readings of the *Nicomachean Ethics* and *Organon* (for logic one relied on Aldrich).[2] There was an Oxford edition of the *Rhetoric* (1759) and the *Poetics* went through three editions in twenty years, the last of which (1780) was reported by the editor, Thomas Winstanley, to be much wanted in the university (over half of the 1,500 copies of this edition printed had been sold by 1804).[3] The *Rhetoric* and *Nicomachean Ethics* were both reprinted several times in the early nineteenth century in Oxford.

---

[1] Bentham (1746), introduction, p. 86. For Bentham's involvement with the Press see Philip, *Blackstone and the Press*, 7.

[2] See below, p. 504.

[3] H. G. Carter, *A History of the Oxford University Press* i (Oxford 1975), 404. Thomas Winstanley (1749-1823), m. BNC 1768; BD and DD St Alban Hall; fellow Hertford; Camden prof. of history 1790-1823; principal St Alban Hall 1796-1823; Laudian prof. of Arabic 1814-23.

The amount of Latin writers read remained remarkably constant from 1720 to 1780 (apart from a drop in the 1750s when total numbers in the college sank), far exceeding readings of any other type. In the first decades of the century Latin, Greek, divinity and ethics readings are grouped very closely together, but after 1730 the study of Latin authors pulls ahead. Cicero is beyond any doubt the most-read author and his most popular work was *De officiis*, of which there were many editions available: that by Thomas Cockman being constantly reprinted.[1] The *De oratore, Orator, Brutus* and *Tusculanae disputationes* were also much read up to about 1750. At no time were the *Orationes* much read; the four speeches against Catiline (which were included in the *Orationum* XII *selectarum liber*[2]) had a total of eighty-five readings in the closing twenty years or so of the period.

The Latin historians make a considerable impact towards the end of the century, Caesar, Livy and Sallust in particular. Of Caesar the reading in both school and university increased dramatically in the final thirty years of the eighteenth century. An edition (Oudendorp's text) was printed in Oxford in 1780 in an edition of two thousand copies (it sold badly) and there were several London and Eton editions. The most-read book was *De bello gallico*, but *De bello civili* and the lesser works were also read. From 1767 onwards Caesar was specified as reading for the first class. *De bello gallico* was read in some cases over three terms, followed by *De bello civili* over two, and the remainder all together. Livy was read by very large numbers, and again the reading was spread over a number of terms. It was at school that a boy gained knowledge of this writer: the volume *Conciones et orationes ex historicis latinis excerptae*, originally published in 1649 in Leiden *in usum scholarum Hollandiae* (it is in fact the Latin part of Henri Estienne's *Conciones . . . ex graecis latinisque historicis excerptae* of 1570) and printed thus in Oxford in 1667, was taken over by Westminster School in the early eighteenth century (there are editions of 1713, 1727 and 1770 in the British Library) and later by Eton (it was used at Eton and in 1819 an edition *in usum scholae regiae etonensis* came out there). By far the greatest part of this volume is devoted to Livy, with

---

[1] John James wrote to his son suggesting the purchase of Ernesti's *Cicero* (it should be noted that it was the intention to print Ernesti's *index verborum* in the abortive Oxford Cicero) and recommending the Oxford 1717 edition of *De officiis* (and other works) edited by Thomas Tooley (1688-1758, m. St John's 1705) or by Zachary Pearce (London 1745); he also mentions Pearce's *De oratore* (Cambridge 1716, 1732 and London 1746); *Letters of Radcliffe and James*, 48, 6 Nov. 1778.

[2] This volume, *Orationes quaedam selectae*, was originally a Delphin Classic; it includes, in addition to the speeches against Catiline, all the other orations of Cicero (*Pro Archia, Pro Caelio, Pro Milone* etc.) which from the 1760s onwards were read at Christ Church. The book was used in schools also. The 11th edition (1789) was published by a number of London booksellers among whom were Pote of Eton and Ginger, whose name appears in many Westminster schoolbooks. In addition to the speeches the volume also included *De senectute* and *De amicitia*. It first appeared in England in 1692 without *De senectute* etc. which were added in the 1699 edition.

TABLE 16.3

READINGS OF INDIVIDUAL SPEECHES BY CICERO

	1720–9	1730–9	1740–9	1750–9	1760–9	1770–9	1780–9	1790–1800
De natura deorum	197	118	152	7	25	62	37	44
De officiis	238	192	161	98	96	57	50	152
De oratore	188	155	143	98	62	74	64	86
Orator	93	160	151	62	21	29	1	6
Brutus				64	23	29	6	
Tusculanae disputationes	160	148	139	66	48	48	20	87
Orationes					194		97	108
total	876	773	746	395	469	299	275	483

some speeches from Sallust and Quintus Curtius. By the end of the eighteenth century there were many editions of Livy available, the most successful being Drakenborch's, and in Oxford there were two editions from the Press (1800 and 1813) and two published by Parker in the first twenty years of the nineteenth century, which is proof of the tremendous growth in reading. Sallust again, although read in the first two decades of the century, increases in popularity from 1763 onward. Initially it is the full *Opera* that are specified, but from the 1770s it is his account of the Catilinarian conspiracy which is most read.[1]

TABLE 16.4

READINGS OF LATIN HISTORIANS

	1760–9	1770–9	1780–9	1790–1800
Caesar				
De bello gallico	9	105	154	24
De bello civili	22	54	95	19
Others		56	177	6
Livy	41	198	245	195
Sallust				
Opera	72	29	8	2
Bellum catilinarium	8	54	44	50
Bellum iugurthinum	6	47	30	30

Of the poets only Virgil, Horace and Lucretius (surprisingly) make constant appearance. In the first fifty years of the century it is the *Aeneid* (read in two stages of six books in the first and second class) which dominates; from 1760 the *Georgics* are read more (the edition of John Martyn, the botanist, appeared first in 1741 and was often reprinted). From 1717 until 1756 no Horace was required but after that, while the *Ars poetica*, which in the first two decades had been read together with the *Epistles* and *Satires*, is still being read, it is the two latter titles which are widely read.[2] Lucretius, listed in the reading of the third class for the years 1717–71, was read most from 1720 to 1750: indeed the number of readings for the next decade is less than half that for 1740–9. Lucretius had attained some considerable popularity in the second half of the previous century, and in the 1690s Bentley was working on the text. A

[1] Cf the figures for readings of Cicero's four speeches against Catiline in table 16.3.
[2] John James expressed his predilection 'at the hazard of my taste perhaps' for the *Epistles* and *Satires*. He used the Horace of André Dacier and Noël Etienne Sanadon. Letter to his father, 10 Mar. 1780, *Letters of Radcliffe and James* 111.

standard edition with succinct if not distinguished notes was published
in Oxford in 1695 by Thomas Creech of All Souls, and reprinted many
times in London.[1] The absence of authors such as Ovid is to be
explained by their being read at school, where much Latin poetry was
read, and where the cultivation of Latin verse writing was becoming the
gentlemanly pastime. Juvenal and Persius are read in the closing years
(particularly the former) and Lucan not at all.

TABLE 16.5

READINGS OF LATIN POETS

	1710-	1720-	1730-	1740-	1750-	1760-	1770-	1780-	1790-1800
Virgil									
Aeneid	120	237	202	174	136	88	12	23	39
Georgics	27				40	101	55	70	69
Lucretius	39	162	146	142	67	22	22	4	30
Horace									
Epistles					40	34	56	58	146
Satires	10							35	142
Odes	13				23	38	50	26	31

Turning to the remaining fields of reading, divinity included readings
of the scriptures and what we may generally term philosophy. In the
first instance this is limited to the Greek New Testament, or for those
from Westminster School certain small portions of the Old Testament in
Hebrew. At Westminster the foundation scholars were obliged by statute to be taught Hebrew. This was done with the aid of a small grammar specially written by the great Dr Busby and said to have been
circulated in manuscript form before its publication in 1708 (there were
several reprints) and the Psalter again specially printed. Basically this
was repeated at Christ Church, with the addition of two books of the
Pentateuch, Genesis and Deuteronomy (rarely Exodus). In the first class
the Psalter was read, in the second Genesis and in the third Deuteronomy. Occasionally some other part of the Old Testament makes an
appearance, as in the case of Benjamin Marshall who, matriculating in
1700, was elected Student in 1701 and in 1703 read the seven minor prophets and the Qur'an.[2]

[1] Thomas Creech (1659-1700), m. Wadham 1677; fellow All Souls 1683.
[2] He was one of the scholars whose name is appended to a Hebrew address on the accession of
Queen Anne in 1702: see D. Patterson, 'Hebrew studies', p. 546 below.

For those who were not from Westminster the reading was the New Testament in Greek. From 1717 this seems to have been divided thus: first class, Gospels; second, Acts, Romans and Corinthians; third, Galatians to the end of the New Testament. At the end of the century the numbers drop, having been at their highest for 1730-49.

TABLE 16.6

READINGS OF THE NEW TESTAMENT

	1720-9	1730-9	1740-9	1750-9	1760-9	1770-9
Gospels	194	149	114	115	109	111
remainder of New Testament	178	148	137	119	111	55

Allied to the reading of the scriptures was the reading of Bishop John Pearson's *Exposition of the Creed*, published at London in 1659, which was read divided up into three portions, each dealing with four articles (by far the longest is that dealing with articles 1-4, which was read in the first class). For most of the century this was read over three successive years, and again the greatest number of readings is to be found in the period 1720-50. Having completed Pearson the candidate's Anglican faith was further strengthened by the reading of John Ellis's *Articulorum* XXXIX *ecclesiae anglicanae defensio*, originally published at London in 1660 with the title *Defensio fidei*, and several times reprinted, intended for *tyrones praesertim sacris ordinibus initiandi* (signature π, folio 2, recto, of the 1694 Cambridge edition). Again for this little book the greatest number of readings lies in the years 1720-49 after which it virtually disappears.

But the favourite defence of Christianity, used almost from the date of its original publication (1627) was the *De veritate religionis christianae* of Grotius. This was several times printed in Oxford from 1650 onwards, and in 1709 an edition appeared at Amsterdam with the notes of Jean le Clerc (Joannes Clericus) and his tract *De eligenda inter Christianos dissentientes sententia*. This was the edition used (it was reprinted at Oxford well into the nineteenth century) at Christ Church. Among the English translations those by Simon Patrick and John Clarke were frequently reprinted, and from the late eighteenth century selections from the work were made for school use.[1] In the early eighteenth century the book was read at Christ Church, and more frequently from 1758 when it was

---

[1] For example *De fide & officio christianorum: excerpta ex T. Burneti & Grotii libellis* (Eton 17??).

prescribed for second-year reading. After that the number of readings rises to over a hundred (1760–1800: 142, 119, 121, 124). Indeed, it seems unlikely that it was not read at all times, even if the collections books do not mention it.

The pattern of what we may call philosophical reading, under which heading is included logic, ethics and natural science, shows a marked change in the period. In the early years most of the reading is done out of compendia. Henry Aldrich's *Artis logicae compendium* appeared first in 1691 and was often reprinted, being used throughout the eighteenth and into the nineteenth century.[1] Its major use begins from 1717 (it was read in the first class) but it was still being read by over two hundred in the closing years of the century. The handbook of ethics used right up to the middle of the century is termed *Eustachii ethica*. This is *Ethica: sive summa moralis disciplinae, in tres partes divisa* of Eustachius a S. Paulo, a Cistercian. This little book was much read from the mid-seventeenth century, and printed frequently in London and Cambridge (a Cambridge edition of 1707 was printed in an edition of five hundred copies). This was read right up to the 1750s by the second class, its greatest use being in the twenty years 1720–40. The textbook of physics by Caspar Bartholinus, professor of medicine at Copenhagen, entitled *Specimen philosophiae naturalis, praecipue physices capita exponens* was printed at Copenhagen, then at Amsterdam (1697), and at Oxford first in 1698 (this edition and the later Oxford editions were not printed at the University Press but were published by the firm of Clements). In the years 1710–19 it was read 82 times, in the next decade 162 and in the next 138, having been prescribed as reading for the third class from 1717. Its use gradually died away and it is last mentioned in 1756. In the 1740s Burgersdijk's immensely long-lived book entitled *Institutiones metaphysica* yielded in the fourth class to Locke's *Essay*, which we know from other sources was much studied. John James records the making of an abridgement of Locke, and there were several printed abridgements available.[2]

---

[1] William Hamilton wrote: 'The Compend of Aldrich ... has furnished, for above a century, the little of all Logic doled out ... by the University of Bradwardin and Scotus.' W. Hamilton, *Discussions on Philosophy and Literature, Education and University Reform* (London and Edinburgh 1852), 123, quoted in *OED* under *compend*. Robert Sanderson's *Logicae artis compendium*, called in slang the 'compend', was used a little at Christ Church according to the collections books at the beginning of the eighteenth century but not afterwards. It was still being used in the 1770s: *Letters of Radcliffe and James*, 50, 55. James also read Gerard Langbaine's *Ethices compendium* (Oxford 1714).

[2] James to his father, 31 Oct. 1781: *Letters of Radcliffe and James*, 165–6. J. Locke, *An Essay concerning Human Understanding* (London 1690). Locke's *Essay* flourished at Cambridge from shortly after its publication until well into the nineteenth century, but did not meet with approval at Oxford, although some tutors abridged it and lectured on it: see Wordsworth, *Scholae academicae*, 126–7. Hearne mentions the abridgement by John Wynne (1667–1743, m. Jesus 1682, principal 1712–20; Lady Margaret prof. of divinity 1705–15; bp of St Asaph 1715–27, Bath and Wells 1727–43) published first in 1696: *Collections* ii. 282. In 1796 a *Syllabus of Locke's Essay* appeared in Cambridge which by 1830 had gone through eight editions.

The level of readings in logic and ethics is very much the same for the whole period, even allowing for the addition of further books which, as already mentioned, generally took the place of something which had had already a long life. Samuel von Pufendorf's *De officio hominis et civis*, originally published at Lunt in 1673, appeared first in England (Cambridge) in 1682 and thereafter was often reprinted. The Cambridge 1701 edition, printed for sale by the London bookseller Timothy Childe, consisted of one thousand copies, which suggests that a fairly large sale was anticipated, and in 1735 another edition with the notes of Thomas Johnson of Magdalene appeared. According to the collections books it was read most in the 1760s, but it is clear that it was lectured on at Christ Church earlier: Richard West, the friend of Thomas Gray, mentioned in a letter of December 1737 attending his tutor's lecture on Pufendorf, 'a very jurisprudent author'.[1] The other work of political philosophy read in the middle years of the century is Burlamaqui's *The Principles of Politic Law* which appeared in English in a translation by the Irishman Thomas Nugent in 1752.[2]

The situation with mathematics is, however, very different. From 1760 onward readings of mathematical books climb very sharply, and by the end constitute the sole 'scientific' reading. The most-read book is Euclid, which is first mentioned in the class-lists in 1763, when books I–VI are set down as required for the second class together with John Keill's *Introductio ad veram physicam* (printed in Oxford for Thomas Bennett; the reprints of 1705 and 1715 were again for a London bookseller), or Worster's 'Phys.', that is *A Compendious and Methodical Account of the Principles of Natural Philosophy* by Benjamin Worster, first published at London in 1722 (second edition London 1730). The Euclid used was the edition of books I–VI and XI and XII (in the sixteenth-century translation of Commandino) produced by Keill in 1701 *in usum juventutis academicae*. The enlarged edition of 1715 (*quibus accedunt trigonometriae planae & sphaericae elementa. Item tractatus de natura & arithmetica logarith. morum*) was published again in Oxford by Clements, and the 1747 edition is described as the fifth. Keill's edition was also translated into English. From 1763 readings of Euclid increase enormously and by the final decade there are over 350 readings. From 1768 books I–IV were read in the first class and the remainder in the following year with the first part of Maclaurin's *Algebra*, a popular work at the end of the century (the fifth edition was published in 1788).[3]

[1] Letter to Gray dated 2 Dec. [1737] from Christ Church: *The Correspondence of Gray, Walpole, West and Ashton (1734-1771)*, ed. P. Toynbee and L. Whibley (3 vols Oxford 1935), rev. H. W. Starr (3 vols Oxford 1971) i. 71. West's reading in the first term (Michaelmas 1737) comprised: *Iliad* I–VI; *Aeneid* I–VI; Cicero, *De oratore* I–III; Aldrich; Pearson, articles I–IV; four gospels.

[2] J.-J. Burlamaqui, *Principes du droit politique* (Amsterdam 1751), trans. T. Nugent as *The Principles of Politic Law* (London 1752).

[3] C. Maclaurin, *A Treatise of Algebra* (London 1748).

Keill's own *Trigonometriae elementa* (printed with his 1715 edition of Euclid) is cited as being read at the end of the century and on into the nineteenth (an edition appeared in Oxford in 1806). All the mathematical reading was concentrated in the last stages of the undergraduate's career.[1]

[1] For examples of the reading of undergraduates over the period see figures 1–5.

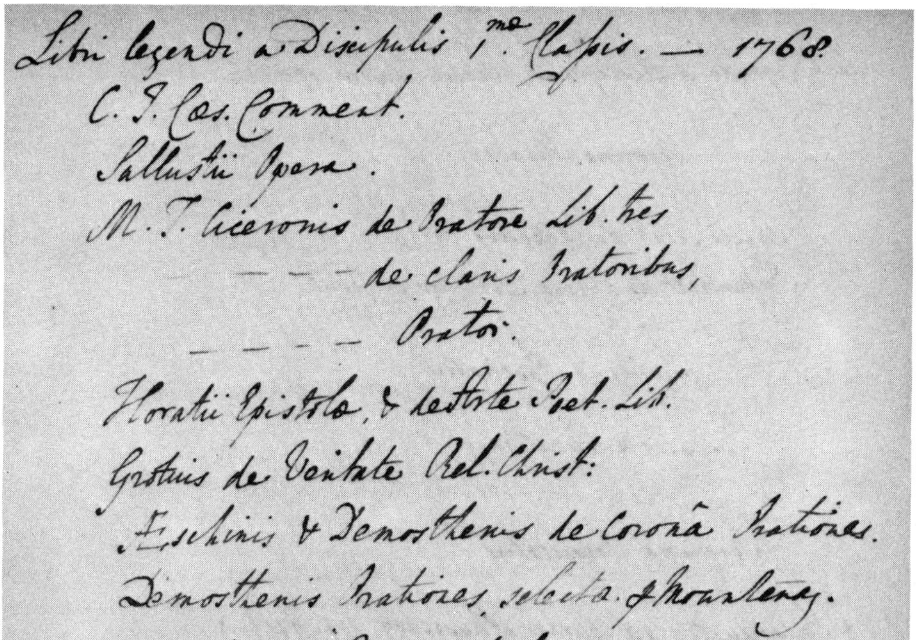

Libri legendi a Discipulis 1.mæ Classis. — 1768.

C. J. Cæs. Comment.

Sallustii Opera.

M. T. Ciceronis de Oratore Lib. tres
— — — de claris Oratoribus,
Orator.

Horatii Epistolæ, & de Arte Poet. Lib.

Grotius de Veritate Rel. Christ:

Æschinis & Demosthenis de Coronâ Orationes.

Demosthenis Orationes, selectæ. & Mounteney.

Xenophontis Memorabilia
— — — Anabasis

Aldrichii Artis Logicæ Compendium.

Quatuor priores Libri Euclidis.

Quatuor Evangelia, & Acta Apost.

A Westmonasteriensibus 50 priores Psalmi. Hebr:

Figure 1

Prescribed reading for the first class, 1768

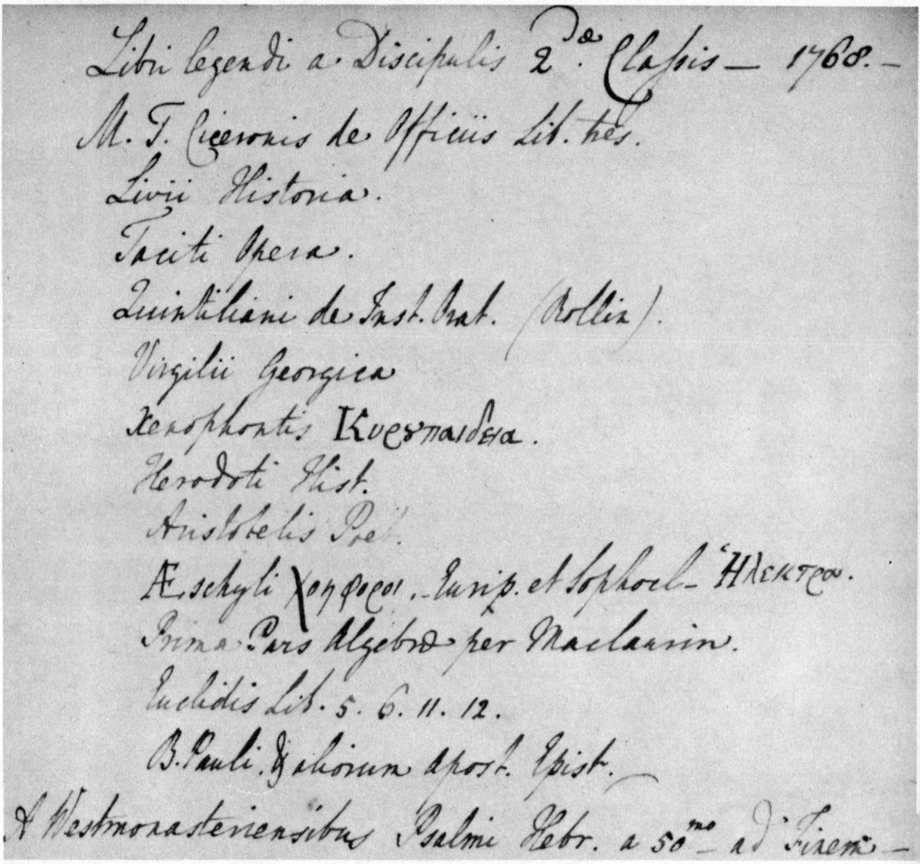

Libri legendi a Discipulis 2da Classis — 1768. —
M. T. Ciceronis de Officiis Lib. tres.
Livii Historia.
Taciti Opera.
Quintiliani de Inst. Orat. (Rollin).
Virgilii Georgica
Xenophontis Κυρουπαιδεια.
Herodoti Hist.
Aristotelis Poet.
Æschyli Χοηφοροι. Eurip. et Sophocl. Ηλεκτρα.
Prima Pars Algebrae per Maclaurin.
Euclidis Lib. 5. 6. 11. 12.
B. Pauli & aliorum apost. Epist.
A Westmonasteriensibus Psalmi Hebr. a 50mo ad finem —

Figure 2
Prescribed reading for the second class, 1768

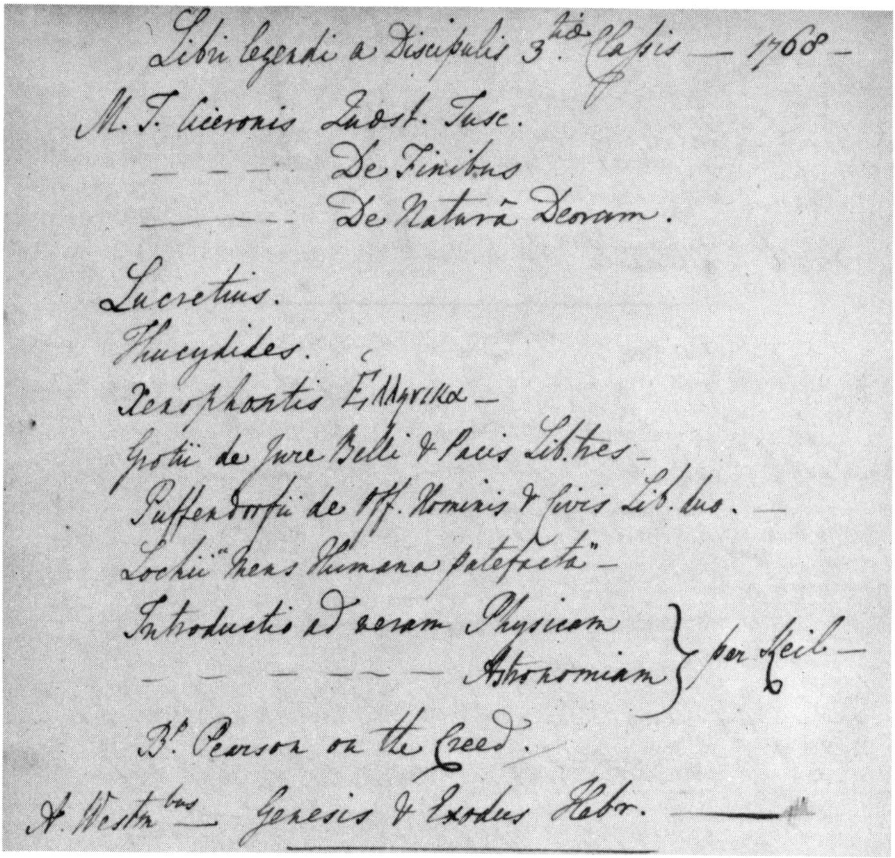

Libri legendi a Discipulis 3.^{tiæ} Classis — 1768 —

M. T. Ciceronis Quæst. Tusc.
— — — De Finibus
— — — De Naturâ Deorum.

Lucretius.
Thucydides.
Xenophontis Ἑλληνικα —
Grotii de Jure Belli & Pacis Lib. tres —
Puffendorfii de Off. Hominis & Civis Lib. duo. —
Lockii "Mens Humana patefacta" —
Introductio ad veram Physicam
— — — — — Astronomiam } per Keil —
Dr Pearson on the Creed.
A. Westm.^{bus} Genesis & Exodus Hebr. ——

Figure 3
Prescribed reading for the third class, 1768

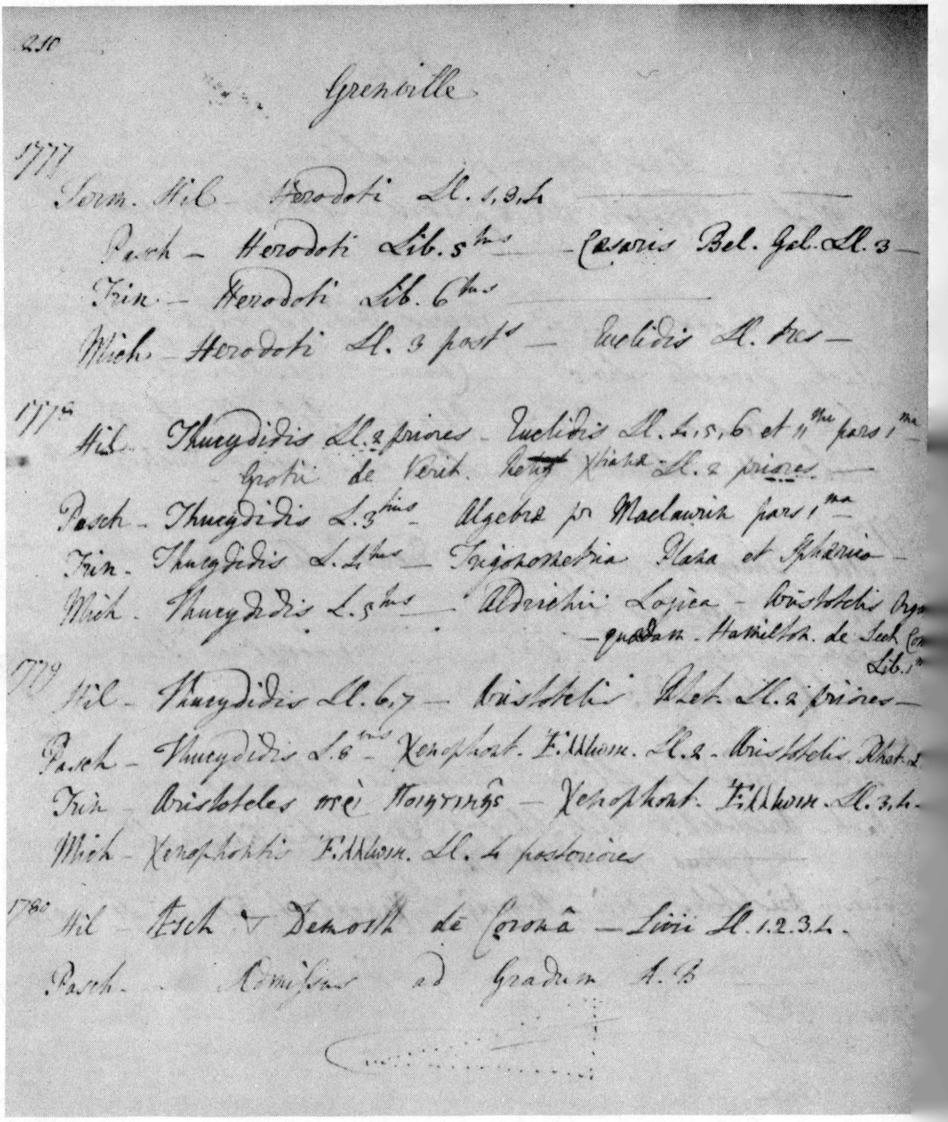

Grenville

1777

Term. Hil. Herodoti Ll. 1,2,3,4

Pasch — Herodoti Lib. 5tus — Caesaris Bel. Gal. Ll. 3

Trin — Herodoti Lib. 6tus

Mich. Herodoti Ll. 3 post — Euclidis Ll. 1us

1778

Hil. Thucydidis Ll. 2 priores. Euclidis Ll. 4,5,6 et 11tus pars 1ma
Grotii de Verit. Relig. Ll. 2 priores

Pasch. Thucydidis L. 3tius. Algebra pro Maclaurin pars 1ma

Trin. Thucydidis L. 4tus — Trigonometria Plana et Spherica

Mich. Thucydidis L. 5tus. Aldrichii Logica — Aristotelis Org...
— quaedam. Hamilton. de Sect. Con. Lib. 1us

1779

Hil. Thucydidis Ll. 6,7 — Aristotelis Rhet. Ll. 2 priores

Pasch — Thucydidis L. 6tus. Xenophont. F. Hellen. Ll. 2. Aristotelis Rhet.

Trin — Aristoteles περὶ Ποιητικῆς — Xenophont. F. Hellen. Ll. 3,4.

Mich — Xenophontis F. Hellen. Ll. 4 posteriores

1780

Hil — Aesch & Demosth de Coronâ — Livii Ll. 1.2.3.4.

Pasch — Admissus ad Gradum A.B

Figure 4
The reading of William Wyndham Grenville, 1777–80

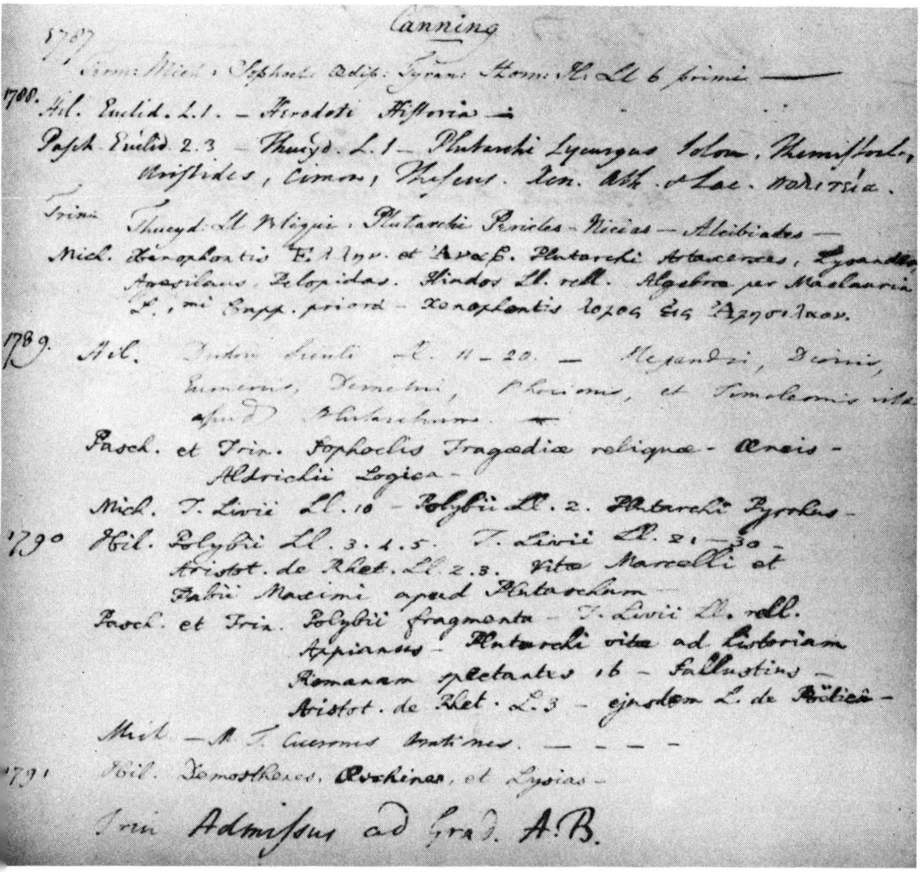

Canning

1787 Term: Mich: Sophocl: Oedip: Tyrann: Hom: Il. Ll 6 primi —

1788. Hil. Euclid. L. 1. — Herodoti Historia —

Pasch. Euclid 2.3 — Thucyd. L. 1 — Plutarchi Lycurgus Solon, Themistocles, Aristides, Cimon, Theseus. Xen. Ath. et Lac. πολιτεία.

Trin. Thucyd. Ll reliqui. Plutarchi Pericles — Nicias — Alcibiades —

Mich. Xenophontis Ἑλλην. et Ἀναβ. Plutarchi Artaxerxes, Lysander, Agesilaus, Pelopidas. Herodot. Ll. rell. Algebra per Maclaurin L. 1mi Capp. priora — Xenophontis λογος εις Ἀγησιλαον.

1789. Hil. Diodori Siculi L. 11–20. — Alexandri, Dionis, Eumenis, Demetrii, Phocionis, et Timoleontis vitae apud Plutarchum. —

Pasch. et Trin. Sophoclis Tragoediae reliquae — Aeneis — Aldrichii Logica —

Mich. T. Livii Ll. 10 — Polybii Ll. 2. Plutarchi Pyrrhus —

1790 Hil. Polybii Ll. 3. 4. 5. T. Livii Ll. 21—30 — Aristot. de Rhet. Ll. 2. 3. Vitae Marcelli et Fabii Maximi apud Plutarchum —

Pasch. et Trin. Polybii fragmenta — T. Livii Ll. rell. Appianus — Plutarchi vitae ad historiam Romanam spectantes 16 — Sallustius — Aristot. de Rhet. L. 3 — ejusdem L. de Poetica —

Mich. — M. T. Ciceronis Orationes. — — —

1791 Hil. Demosthenes, Aeschines, et Lysias —

Trin. Admissus ad Grad. A.B.

Figure 5
The reading of George Canning, 1787–90

17

Classical Studies

M. L. CLARKE

WHEN the examination statute of 1800 required that all candidates for a degree should be examined *in literis humanioribus* it was no innovation. The Laudian code had included the same requirement, and it had been re-emphasized in 1662 in an addendum to the statutes. The Laudian code used the words *bonae literae*, the addendum preferred *humaniores literae*; in either case the meaning was the same, the study of the best Greek and Latin authors. Throughout the period 1688-1800 the classics were an essential part of university studies.[1]

Little was done to promote such studies by university as opposed to college teaching. Of the eleven professors of Greek in this period the only one of note was Humphrey Hody, professor from 1698 to his death in 1707. He was a good scholar and he lectured regularly.[2] But the only lecture course of his which is known, one which he prepared for publication before his death but which did not appear in print until 1742, was not related to undergraduate studies. Contrary to the statutes, which directed that the professor should expound a Greek text, he took as his subject the revival of Greek studies in western Europe at the renaissance and the learned Greeks who contributed to this revival.[3] He was followed by Thomas Milles, vice-principal of St Edmund Hall, 'a Person', according to Hearne, who had a grudge against him and was otherwise not unprejudiced, 'void of Integrity, Parts or Learning, especially that part of Learning he is to profess, he not understanding the Rudiments of the *Greek* Tongue'.[4] His tenure of the chair was brief. He was appointed to an Irish bishopric before he had even given an inaugural lecture and was succeeded by Edward Thwaites of Queen's, who was, to quote Hearne again, 'well vers'd in Greek, and in several Parts of Learning; but his chief

---

[1] *Statutes* IX.ii.1, trans. Ward i. 85-7, addendum to IX.ii.2, trans. Ward ii. 33.

[2] Hearne, *Collections* ii. 108.

[3] H. Hody, *De Graecis illustribus linguae graecae literarumque humaniorum instauratoribus* (London 1742). That the work was originally delivered as lectures, which one would not guess from the text, is stated in the life of Hody prefixed to the work (pp. xxxiii-xxxiv). It is probably to be identified with the 'History of the Greek Tongue' which according to Hearne, writing shortly before Hody's death, was almost ready for the Press: *Collections* i. 317.

[4] Ibid. i. 326. Hearne has numerous other derogatory remarks about Milles.

Excellency lay in the Saxon Learning'.[1] He delivered an inaugural of which Hearne thought little—'nothing but an History of the Greek Tongue in the old beaten road'—but after that was as silent in his capacity as Greek professor as he was in the role of professor of moral philosophy, a post which he held at the same time.[2] His successor, Thomas Terry, appointed in 1712, gave an inaugural which Hearne thought very good, in which he dwelt on 'the Excellency of the Greek Tongue' and exhorted his young hearers to study the language, but that was all.[3] For the rest of the century the Greek professors were equally silent and equally undistinguished as scholars. The professorship was regarded as a sinecure, and it normally went to Christ Church. In 1783 when John Randolph, who held it along with two other professorships, gave it up on his appointment to yet another, that of divinity, Thomas Burgess of Corpus, who was probably the resident best qualified for the post, hoped to succeed and intended to give lectures, but the Christ Church interest was too strong and the chair went to William Jackson, a member of that society and brother of its dean.[4]

Two other professorships, that of history founded by Camden[5] and that of poetry, are relevant to classical studies. The statutes of Camden's professorship required its holder to lecture on one of the ancient historians, mentioning in particular an elementary work of no value as an authority, Florus's epitome of Roman history.[6] The preamble to the statute regarding the poetry professorship referred to 'the reading of the old poets',[7] and though Robert Lowth,[8] in the best-known series of eighteenth-century lectures on this foundation, took Hebrew poetry as his subject, the lecturers generally concerned themselves with that of Greece and Rome, though not to the exclusion of English literature, and it is reasonable to assume that they did something to encourage a literary as opposed to a purely linguistic interest in ancient poetry.

In 1688 Henry Dodwell was appointed to the Camden professorship, which he held until 1691 when he was ejected as a result of his refusal to take the oath of allegiance to William and Mary. After an inaugural

[1] Hearne, *Collections*, ii. 115 (Milles), iii. 278 (Thwaites). Edward Thwaites (1667-1711), m. Queen's 1689; regius prof. of Greek 1707-11; Whyte's prof. of moral philosophy 1708-11. See also D. C. Douglas, *English Scholars 1660-1730* (London 1939, 2nd edn London 1951) and D. Fairer, 'Anglo-Saxon studies', p. 812 below.
[2] Hearne, *Collections* ii. 108, 127.
[3] Ibid. iii. 391-2. Thomas Terry (1678-1735), m. Ch.Ch. 1696; regius prof. of Greek 1712-35.
[4] J. S. Harford, *The Life of Thomas Burgess* (London 1840), 72. Thomas Jackson (1751-1815), m. Ch.Ch, 1768; regius prof. of Greek 1783-1811; bp of Oxford 1812-15. Cyril Jackson was dean 1783-1809.
[5] John Camden (1551-1623), m. Magd. 1566; migrated to Broadgates Hall; graduate of Ch.Ch.
[6] *Stat. Tit. IV.* Sec. 1, chapt. 2; Ward and Heywood, *Statutes*, i. 23.
[7] Ibid. 298.
[8] Robert Lowth (1710-87), m. St John's 1729; fellow New College 1733; prof. of poetry 1741-51; bp of Oxford 1766-77, London 1777-87.

lecture on the difficulties and uncertainties of early Greek history he began a course on the collection of lives of Roman emperors known as the *Historia Augusta*. After six introductory lectures on the authorship of the different lives he proceeded to the text of the first, that of Hadrian, and in the sixteen lectures delivered before he was deprived of his post, and the three prepared but not delivered which he published with them, he reached no further than the fourth chapter.[1] He followed the traditional, and statutory, method of prelecting on a text, but for him the text was merely the occasion for disquisitions on Roman institutions and chrono-logical problems in the period in question. Dodwell was the author of an 'Invitation to gentlemen to acquaint themselves with ancient history' in which he claimed that the practical value of the subject made it more suitable for gentlemen than for scholars;[2] but his Oxford lectures, full as they are of solid matter, were essentially for scholars. After his deprivation he continued to make valuable contributions to ancient chronology. He was a true scholar, and it is to the credit of the electors that they appointed a Dublin man who had no previous connection with Oxford simply because he was the best man for the job. This was not a principle followed in subsequent appointments.

Of Dodwell's successor Charles Aldworth Hearne wrote: 'He has never yet shew'd himself in print, and whether he be well qualify'd for the Place or no 'tis hard to judge from anything which he does, seldom or never reading [lecturing].' By the time he died Hearne was more sure about his qualifications: he was 'a Person of no Learning, and very unfit for this Post'.[3] The next professor, Sedgwick Harrison, a lawyer of All Souls, was not a good choice. 'He was a man', to quote Hearne again, 'that might have done good Things, had he minded his Studies. But being of an invi-dious, malicious, furious temper, he seldom spoke well of any one, but was for doing what mischief he could.' Perhaps it was mischievousness that made him, on the rare occasions on which he lectured, follow the statutes literally and require his listeners to bring paper, pens and ink to take down his elementary explanations of Florus.[4]

After a lawyer the electors appointed a physician, Richard Frewin. It was said that soon after his appointment he bought £100 worth of books on history in order to qualify himself for the post, but what if anything resulted from this purchase is not recorded.[5] Frewin's successor John Warneford occupied the chair for twelve years and remained silent

[1] H. Dodwell, *Praelectiones academicae in schola historices camdeniana* (Oxford 1692).

[2] The 'Invitation' was prefixed to the second edition of D. Wheare's *Method and Order of reading both Civil and Ecclesiastical Histories* (London 1685, 2nd edn London 1694).

[3] Hearne, *Collections* i. 228, vii. 117. Charles Aldworth (1649-1720), m. St John's 1666; demy Magd. 1668-72; Camden prof. of history 1691-1720.

[4] Ibid. ix. 336, viii. 213, ix. 89. Sedgwick Harrison (1683-1727), m. Gloucester Hall 1697; fellow All Souls 1706; Camden prof. of history 1720-7.

[5] Ibid. xi. 436. Richard Frewin (1681-1761), m. Ch.Ch. 1698; incorporated at Cambridge 1707; Camden prof. of history 1727-61.

throughout.[1] The prestige of the chair was restored later in the century by William Scott, professor from 1773 to 1785. He broke with tradition not only in lecturing but also in lecturing in English. His lectures, which were never published, were highly thought of: 'perhaps superiour to anything of the kind in point of elegance and erudition' was how John James described them, and Samuel Parr was struck by the 'variety of learning, acuteness of observation, and elegance of style' of a part of one of them, read to him by Scott, 'which contained some curious matter on the revenues of the Grecian States'.[2] Scott was followed by Thomas Warton the younger, less suited, one might think, to this chair than to that of poetry which he had previously occupied. He delivered an inaugural oration in elegant Latin, in which he declined to be bound by obsolete statutes and give schoolboy lessons on Florus. He proposed rather in future lectures to choose one of the ancient historians and discuss his virtues, and by way of foretaste he gave a brief survey of these writers. His intention was to give only occasional lectures, *ut haec non omnino frigescant rostra*. Even this he failed to do; as his biographer put it, he 'suffered the rostrum to go cold'.[3] It remained so under his successor Thomas Winstanley.

The first poetry professor, Joseph Trapp, took as his subject poetry in general, its nature and its different kinds. He was mainly concerned with the classical poets, particularly those of Rome, from whom he took most of his examples. He had an unbounded admiration for Virgil (he was the author of a verse translation of the *Aeneid*) and had little to say on the Greeks.[4] The next professor, apart from Lowth, to publish his lectures was William Hawkins, professor from 1751 to 1756, and comparing him with Trapp we are conscious of a change of taste, a movement away from traditional classicism. He champions the bold genius unfettered by rules, and in drama, which he chose as his subject, he prefers the moderns, Shakespeare in particular, to the ancients.[5] So far as the ancients are concerned he shows himself well acquainted with Greek tragedy, and his admiration for Aeschylus went beyond what was usual at that time, when the tendency was to depreciate him as rude and unpolished compared to Sophocles and Euripides. Greek poetry was the subject of the lectures of

[1] See H. S. Jones, 'The foundation and history of the Camden chair', *Oxoniensia* viii–ix (1943–4). John Warneford (1721–73), m. CCC 1735; Camden prof. of history 1761–73.

[2] *Letters of Radcliffe and James*, 92; *The Works of Samuel Parr, LL.D.* ed. J. Johnstone (8 vols London 1828) ii. 562. W. E. Surtees knew little of the lectures, but 'a character of Alexander the Great has been mentioned to me, as uniting the splendour of the poet and the integrity of the historian': W. E. Surtees, *A Sketch of the Lives of Lords Stowell and Eldon* (London 1846), p. 24.

[3] *The Poetical Works of the late Thomas Warton B.D.* ed. R. Mant (2 vols Oxford 1802) i, pp. lxxxiv, cxi; the inaugural lecture is printed in ii. 361–73.

[4] J. Trapp, *Praelectiones poeticae* (3 vols Oxford 1719, 3rd edn 1736).

[5] *Praelectiones poeticae* in vol. iii of Hawkins's *Works* (3 vols Oxford 1758). He quotes long passages of Shakespeare by way of illustration, passages which are not improved by being translated into Latin iambic verse in order to harmonize with the language in which he was required to lecture. William Hawkins (1722–1801), m. Pemb. 1737; prof. of poetry 1751–6.

Hawkins's successor the younger Warton, in which 'he exerted himself to fulfil the duties of the office, by a constant recommendation of the elegance and simplicity of the classic poets'.[1] The only lecture that was published, that on Theocritus, included in revised form in his edition of the *Idylls*, ends with a comparison between him and Virgil which shows a clear preference for the Greek poet over his more polished but artificial imitator. Warton was a professed admirer of Greece, and we can think of him as a leader of taste and not merely a follower.

One more set of eighteenth-century poetry lectures remains to be discussed, that of John Randolph, the professorial pluralist who has been mentioned as a silent occupant of the Greek chair. His lectures on Homer (1776-83) were exhumed by his son and published in 1870, to remain equally unread in print.[2] Unlike Trapp, Hawkins and Warton, Randolph was not a poet, and his lectures, which are rather dry and academic and which deal at length with the society of the Homeric age before coming to the poet's treatment of his material, would have little interest for the aspiring poet or critic. For a studious undergraduate they would at least provide something he would not get from any other source, but how many would be able or willing to stay the course when it was still not completed after seven years, with one lecture a term and that in Latin?[3]

With so little help or stimulus from the professors, undergraduates had to rely on the resources of their colleges. In the colleges there would be lectures and prescribed exercises, supplemented by private reading. Lectures would be either private, conducted by the tutor in his room, or public, by a college lecturer in the hall. At Queen's in 1760 Jeremy Bentham had to attend his tutor's lectures on the *Characters* of Theophrastus and, on days when these did not take place, public lectures by the college lecturer in Greek.[4] In either case the lectures would be in effect construing lessons like those at school. Dr Johnson recalled that when he was at Pembroke he was so mortified by the superior abilities of one of his contemporaries that 'at the classical lecture in the Hall' he sat as far from him as he could so as not to hear him construe.[5] John Burton of Corpus, lecturing twice a week on Xenophon or Demosthenes in his capacity as college lecturer in Greek, 'used to hear his pupils construing and by his own observations led them to the study of criticism'.[6]

---

[1] *Poetical Works of Warton*, ed. Mant i, p. xli.

[2] J. Randolph, *Praelectiones academicae in Homerum*, ed. T. Randolph (Oxford and London 1870). In 1980 I found the pages of the Bodleian copy uncut.

[3] Randolph resigned the poetry professorship before his ten years were up on his appointment to that of divinity.

[4] *The Correspondence of Jeremy Bentham*, ed. T. L. S. Sprigge *et al.* (London and Oxford 1968 onward) i. 19, 21.

[5] *Boswell's Life of Johnson*, ed. G. B. Hill (6 vols Oxford 1887), rev. L. F. Powell (6 vols Oxford 1934-50) i. 272.

[6] E. Bentham, *De vitâ et moribus Johannis Burtoni* (Oxford 1771) 11.

Burton was described by Peter Elmsley as *ab omni critica disciplina alien-issimus*, but though he may have been ill qualified for textual criticism he was a good tutor and he had ideas of his own about the teaching of Greek.[1] He would have something of his own to contribute. Not all tutors however were like Burton. Gibbon found that a Terence lecture with his tutor Dr Waldegrave was no more than 'a dry and literal interpretation of the Author's text', and according to Vicesimus Knox undergraduates were usually left to construe with little or no interruption on the part of the tutor.[2]

For exercises, apart from disputations, which although conducted in Latin do not concern us here, there were themes, declamations, trans-lations and verses, and in a well disciplined college one such exercise would probably be required each week.[3] A theme was a Latin essay on some moral commonplace. Richard Newton in his statutes for Hertford College was exceptional in requiring that themes should be in English.[4] A declamation was a Latin speech delivered orally in hall or chapel on a dis-puted question which could be argued either way. The theme was an exer-cise regularly practised at school; the declamation was in the main confined to the university and in some colleges to the final year of the undergraduate course.[5] Woodforde's diaries record some of the subjects set at New College. He writes a theme on *Summum jus summa injuria*; he declaims, to give two examples, on the relative value of courage displayed in war and justice exercised in peace, and on whether a wise man changes his mind, supporting in the first case the claims of courage and in the second the right to change one's mind.[6] The distinction between the two types of exercise was not however clearly drawn; Woodforde's theme on *Summum jus summa injuria* had to be read in chapel, and a declamation which Bentham delivered was on the non-controversial subject *Sperne*

---

[1] Sophocles, *Œdipus tyrannus*, ed. P. Elmsley (Oxford 1811), p. iv. Peter Elmsley (1773-1825), m. Ch.Ch. 1791; BD and DD St Alban Hall; Camden prof. of history and principal St Alban Hall 1823-5.See Burton's *De linguae graecae institutionibus quibusdam epistola critica* prefixed to his account (in Greek) of a journey in Surrey and Sussex (London 1752) also published separately under the title *De literarum graecarum institutione dissertatio* (Oxford 1758), and his *Pentalogia* (Oxford 1758, Oxford 1779 edn) i. 12-15. See also p. 521 below.

[2] E. Gibbon, *Memoirs of my Life*, ed. G. A. Bonnard (London 1966), p. 54; V. Knox, *Liberal Education* (London 1781, 9th edn 2 vols London 1788) ii. 177, 202-3, 250.

[3] But the 'Ode on the Death of the King' in 1760 which Jeremy Bentham sent home on 22 Novem-ber was the only exercise he had so far done that term: *Correspondence of Bentham*, ed. Sprigge i. 22.

[4] R. Newton, *Rules and Statutes for the Government of Hertford College* (London 1747), 23. An earlier version had been published in 1720 as *A Scheme of Discipline with Statutes intended to be established by a Royal Charter for the education of Youth in Hart-Hall in the University of Oxford*.

[5] [J. Hurdis,] *A Word or Two in Vindication of the University of Oxford, and of Magdalen College in particular from the Posthumous Aspersions of Mr. Gibbon* (np nd), repr. in *Reminiscences of Oxford*, 135-6. Newton, *Rules and Statutes*, 23.

[6] *Woodforde at Oxford*, 3, 8, 15. In a declamation at Queen's John James argued paradoxically that Anacreon was wiser than Aristotle: *Letters of Radcliffe and James*, 52.

voluptates, nocet empta dolore voluptas and might more properly have been called a theme.[1]

Translations were less often required than original compositions. Newton however directed that there should be regular exercises in turning English into Latin and Latin into English, and some students practised the method of retranslation; John James translated Cicero's *De officiis* and later put his English version into Latin and compared it with the original.[2] Newton laid down that 'When any Undergraduate shall write *Latin* correctly and with Purity, he may be directed to translate a Portion of *English* or *Latin* into *Greek*, or any *Other* useful Language', and Bentham was made to translate Caesar into Greek prose, an exercise which he found more difficult than writing original Greek verse.[3]

In the Hertford statutes Newton directed that if any undergraduate chose to make verses instead of theme or translation he might do so if the principal thought fit and if 'it shall not be found to draw off his Mind from serious Studies'.[4] This cool attitude was by no means generally shared. Indeed, verse-making was a part of university life. It was the practice to greet royal births, deaths and marriages and other appropriate occasions with outpourings of loyal verse, mainly though not exclusively Latin.[5] Undergraduates as well as senior members had to contribute, and the best of their compositions were published. Thus in 1760, on the death of George II, Bentham was asked by his tutor to write some appropriate verses, and two or three days later 'it came out as a publick exercise for every body to do'.[6] His comment made later in life says all that need be said about these productions:

Meantime, according to custom, at that source and choice seat of learning, loyalty, and piety, a fasciculus of poetry—appropriate poetry—was called for, at the hands of the ingenious youths, or such of them whose pens were rich enough to be guided by private tutors. My quill, with the others, went to work; though, alas! without learned or reverend hand to guide it. In process of time, by dint of hard labour, out of Ainsworth's Dictionary and the Gradus ad Parnassum, were manufactured stanzas of Latin Alcaics, beginning *Eheu Georgi!* certifying and proclaiming the experienced attributes of the dead god and the surely-expected ditto of the living one, with grief in proper form at the beginning, and consolation, in no less proper form, at the end.[7]

---

[1] *Correspondence of Bentham*, ed. Sprigge i. 47-9. Another prose exercise of Bentham, on the non-controversial subject *Numquam minus solus quam cum solus*, was delivered in hall. It is printed in *The Works of Jeremy Bentham*, ed. J. Bowring (11 vols Edinburgh 1838-43) x. 43n.

[2] Newton, *Rules and Statutes*, 24; *Letters of Radcliffe and James*, 50.

[3] Newton, 26; *Correspondence of Bentham*, ed. Sprigge i. 37.   [4] Newton, 26.

[5] There were always a few Greek verses. English, completely absent from the collections of the late seventeenth century, had crept in by the mid-eighteenth. In the 1750s and 1760s from 30 to 40 per cent of the contributions were in English.

[6] *Correspondence of Bentham*, ed. Sprigge i. 22.

[7] *Works of Bentham*, ed. Bowring x. 42.

What Bentham says about the help given by tutors is confirmed from other sources. It was an open secret that the Latin hendecasyllabics on the death of the prince of Wales in 1751 allegedly by George Brome of Christ Church were really the work of William Markham, then a tutor of the House.[1] If therefore anyone looking through the published collections notes the rather high proportion of sons of peers and baronets whose names, with particulars of parentage, appear beneath these Latin odes and elegies, he should not be too hasty in drawing conclusions about the high classical culture of the English aristocracy.[2]

Latin verses were also demanded at the Lent disputations for determining bachelors. It was the custom for each disputant to recite on Ash Wednesday a short Latin poem, usually five or six elegiac couplets, on his subject for disputation. The subjects were philosophical or scientific; the verses were not, and it was enough if they illustrated the theme somehow. They were in the nature of epigrams, designed to entertain. Thus to give one example, on the subject *An idem semper agat idem*, one versifier produced a pleasant sketch of the monotonous daily life of a college fellow.[3] Christ Church specialized in this form of composition. Two volumes of Lent verses by members of the House were published, in 1723 and 1748, and after they were given up in the schools their composition was continued as a college exercise.[4] This was the sort of thing which those with any gift for versifying did rather well, and the Lent verses are more attractive than the routine congratulations and condolences demanded by royal occasions. But not everyone had the gift. Those who had not would have to find someone to provide the requisite verses for them, as Jeremy Bentham did for a friend of his.[5]

After celebrating in quick succession the death of George II, the marriage of his successor and the birth of a prince of Wales the university gave up the practice of issuing collections of loyal verse, and at about the same time the Lent verses came to an end. Hence perhaps the institution in 1768 of the chancellor's prize for Latin verse. Competition for this aroused a good deal of interest. In 1779, when the subject set was Electricity, wagers were laid that it would go to Christ Church. 'I confess', wrote John James, 'they bid fairer than any other single college, from their

[1] *Poetical Works of Warton*, ed. Mant i. 24.

[2] There were, however, some men of noble birth who were expert composers of Latin verse, notably Lord Wellesley (Richard Colley Wellesley, 1760-1842, from 1781 2nd e. of Mornington; m. Ch.Ch. 1778) who won the chancellor's prize for Latin verse in 1780.

[3] The first poem in the first of the Christ Church collections (1723) cited in next note.

[4] Collections entitled *Carmina quadragesimalia ab aedis Christi alumnis composita* were edited by Charles Este (Oxford 1723) and by Anthony Parsons (Oxford 1748). Charles Este (1696-1745), m. Ch.Ch. 1715, bp of Ossory 1736-40, of Waterford and Lismore 1740-5; Anthony Parsons (1706-78), m. Ch.Ch. 1725. See also H. L. Thompson, *Christ Church* (London 1900), 142-3. Several Lent verses by Christ Church men are included in *Anthologia oxoniensis*, ed. W. Linwood (London 1846).

[5] *Works of Bentham*, ed. Bowring x. 44.

superiour number of verse writers. I have heard some so arrogant in it that I felt a very strong wish to be able to disappoint them.'[1] The prize did in fact go to Christ Church in that year and the two following, but in 1782 James had the satisfaction of disappointing them by being the winner.

In the colleges verses were among the regular exercises, or were set on special occasions. Samuel Johnson was required to write on the gunpowder plot (though he failed to do so and got away with an apology in Latin verse) and at Christmas to translate Pope's *Messiah* into Latin.[2] At Christ Church there were prizes for Latin verse in addition to the usual obligatory exercises. In 1712 the subject set was *Atrium peckwateriense*, on which the contestants were required to write about eighty lines of hexameters; the prizes were suitably classical, the works of Plato and Demosthenes for the winner, with those of Dionysius of Halicarnassus and Livy for the next best and of Homer for the third.[3] Latin verse could also be set as an imposition for breaches of discipline. Woodforde once missed a service in chapel and was set the task of translating David's lament for Saul and Jonathan into Latin sapphics. Evidently he found this too much for him; a later entry in his diary reads: 'Gave my imposition to Mr Pye [the sub-warden] . . . made by Nicholls in Sapphic metre.'[4]

Such easy ways out were common, for verses and other exercises. The subjects were likely to have been set before. Old copies were kept, handed down and reused. According to Vicesimus Knox university exercises were 'usually such as a school-boy could equal; often stolen from books, most frequently handed down by tradition; and when they are original, which is indeed very seldom, they may, often do, abound with grammatical and other errors, uncorrected and unpunished by the officers who hear and receive them'.[5] Not all tutors of course left exercises uncorrected; Burton was extremely conscientious in this respect, and himself wrote numerous themes, declamations and verses to serve as models.[6] But it may well be that by the 1770s, when Knox was at Oxford, interest in these exercises was declining. The old humanist tradition had grown weak.

In addition to lectures and exercises there was private reading. Samuel Johnson recalled that while at Pembroke he read in Greek Homer and Euripides and 'now and then a little Epigram', and in the same college a few years later there was 'a very sober little party, who amused themselves in the evening with reading Greek and drinking water' and who chose authors seldom read at school such as Theophrastus, Epictetus and Phalaris.[7] Clever undergraduates who found college lectures too

---

[1] *Letters of Radcliffe and James*, 65-6.
[2] *Boswell's Life of Johnson*, ed. Hill, rev. Powell i. 60-1.
[3] J. Pointer, *Oxoniensis academia* (London 1747), 84.   [4] *Woodforde at Oxford*, 8-9.
[5] Knox, *Liberal Education* ii. 202.   [6] Bentham, *De vitâ et moribus Johannis Burtoni*, 12.
[7] *Boswell's Life of Johnson*, ed. Hill, rev. Powell i. 70; R. Graves, *Recollections of . . . William Shenstone Esq.* (London 1788), 13-14; *Reminiscences of Oxford*, 97-105.

elementary were sometimes excused attendance and left to read on their own. One such was William Jones at University College in the 1760s, who 'perused with great assiduity all the Greek poets and historians of note, and the entire works of Plato and Lucian, with a vast apparatus of commentaries on them'.[1] John James used to devote the mornings to compositions and logic and the rest of the day to reading the classics, which he considered to be in the nature of amusement compared to logic. He read in Latin Terence, Livy and Horace, and in Greek Lucian, a play of Aristophanes, the Odyssey, Plato, Xenophon's *Anabasis* and the whole of Herodotus.[2] It seems from his letters that this reading was done on his own initiative rather than as a result of tutorial direction; on the other hand, Jeremy Bentham mentions in one of his letters that his tutor, James Jefferson, who appears to have been fussily conscientious, was 'plaguing me about doing Homer', as a result of which he read more than three books and a half of the Odyssey in two days; and later in life he recalled that Jefferson forced him to read Cicero's speeches, all of which, so he claimed (surely with some exaggeration) he knew by heart.[3]

In some colleges there was a prescribed programme of reading, notably at Christ Church, where we have particulars of the prescriptions for the whole of the eighteenth century in the collections books. Collections were defined by Richard Newton, who had been a tutor at Christ Church, in his statutes for Hertford College. The tutors were to allot each class of undergraduates four classical authors for the year, from which each student was to make

Collections consisting of such beautiful Expressions or Reflections as the Reader *Admires*; or of such difficult and obscure Passages as he *Explains*; or of such Characters of Persons, or Descriptions of Actions as he thinks worthy of *Imitation*; or of such Geographical or Chronological Remarks as appear to him *Material*; or of whatever else he conceives either useful for himself to *Remember*, or to *Impart* to others.

These were to be shown each week to his tutor and at the end of the year to the principal, 'that thereby his Industry, and Accuracy, and Penetration, and Learning may be seen'.[4] Newton was an educational reformer and he may be going beyond current practice at his old college, but something like this was presumably the original meaning of a word which came to be applied to termly college examinations. Whether the student merely showed up his extracts or was further tested on his

---

[1] *Memoirs of the Life, Writings and Correspondence of Sir William Jones*, ed. Lord Teignmouth (London 1804), 31. Others similarly excused were Thomas Burgess at Corpus and Robert Southey at Balliol: Harford, *Burgess*, 9; *The Life and Correspondence of Robert Southey*, ed. C. C. Southey (6 vols London 1849-50) i. 215.

[2] *Letters of Radcliffe and James*, 49-52, 55, 67-8, 80-1.

[3] *Correspondence of Bentham*, ed. Sprigge i. 52; *Works of Bentham*, ed. Bowring x. 37.

[4] Newton, *Rules and Statutes*, 27-8.

knowledge of the books, the system would ensure that he had read what was prescribed.

Some account has been given in an earlier chapter of the classical reading at Christ Church as recorded in the collections books. Two points may be added here. First, in the period 1717 to 1755, when the prescribed books remained unchanged and were common to all undergraduates, the range of reading was very narrow and two of the books in the list, the *Aeneid* and the *Iliad*, are likely to have been already familiar, in part at any rate, from school reading. The total amount required was very much less than what was read at Trinity College, Dublin, in the same period, and Dublin was a university where subjects other than classics were studied more seriously than at Oxford.[1] On the other hand, reading would not necessarily be confined to what was prescribed for collections. Lord Shelburne, who entered Christ Church in 1753, read with his tutor some Livy and some speeches of Demosthenes, though neither author was included in the list for collections.[2]

The second point concerns the increased emphasis on historical texts from 1768 onwards. It looks as if this was the result of a deliberate policy, due perhaps to William Markham, who became dean in 1767. Markham is not known to have had any special interest in ancient history, but he had been headmaster of Westminster and he knew that there, and indeed at other schools, reading was almost exclusively poetical. Homer and Virgil could be taken as read; if the university was not to involve a repetition of schoolwork it should concentrate on prose writers. But there was probably another consideration. Christ Church was pre-eminently the college for those destined to play a part in public life, and for them ancient history was considered to be particularly suited. When Gilbert Elliot, the future Lord Minto, went up to Christ Church in 1768 Markham informed him that 'only classical and historical knowledge could make able statesmen'.[3] For those unlikely ever to become statesmen the reading list was less biased towards historical writers. Thomas Gaisford, who is said to have been told by Dean Jackson that he would never be a gentleman but would certainly succeed as a scholar,[4] had a varied programme which included in addition to a considerable amount of historical reading the whole of Euripides, all Pindar, six plays of Aristophanes and four books of Lucretius.

---

[1] J. M. Stubbs, *History of the University of Dublin from 1591 to 1800* (Dublin 1889), 199–200; R. B. McDowell and D. A. Webb, *Trinity College Dublin 1592–1952: an academic history* (Cambridge 1982), 45–6.

[2] E. Fitzmaurice, *The Life of William, Earl of Shelburne* (3 vols London 1875, 2nd edn 3 vols London 1912) i. 14; *Reminiscences of Oxford*, 150.

[3] *Life and Letters of Sir Gilbert Elliot, First Earl of Minto, from 1751 to 1806*, ed. countess of Minto (3 vols London 1874) i. 38.

[4] W. Tuckwell, *Reminiscences of Oxford* (London 1900), 130.

By contrast with Christ Church the list of books prescribed at Magdalen in the latter part of the eighteenth century does not appear to be based on any particular principle. It includes the whole of the *Aeneid* and the first half of the *Iliad*, much of which should have been familiar from school reading. Apart from that Latin verse is represented by the *Georgics*, the *Epistles* and *Ars poetica* of Horace and six satires of Juvenal, and Greek verse only by one play of Sophocles. There is a fairly representative selection of Latin prose writers. Among the Greek prose texts are selected dialogues of Plato and speeches of Demosthenes; there is a large amount of Xenophon, but no Herodotus or Thucydides.[1] Many of the undergraduates, who would include, to use the nineteenth-century terms, pass men as well as class men, would no doubt find this quite as much as they could manage, but, to compare Oxford once again with the only comparable university in the kingdom, Dublin at the end of the eighteenth century required a good deal more.[2]

College teaching of course varied from time to time and from college to college, but generally speaking it was not on a high level. According to Vicesimus Knox undergraduates derived little benefit from tutorial lectures, which were seldom superior to those of the higher classes in a good school.[3] It could be said in extenuation that a college tutor was expected to teach logic, ethics and metaphysics as well as classics, and that his pupils might be of very different attainments; but the tutor himself could well be a man of mediocre ability who owed his fellowship to his place of birth. Moreover, there was then little of that competitive spirit which was bred by the examination system of the nineteenth century and which served as a spur to endeavour on the part of both teachers and taught.

Even at Christ Church, the largest and richest college and the one which drew on the best classical schools,[4] the teaching was not of much help to a man of scholarly tastes like Henry Fynes Clinton, author of books on Greek and Roman chronology, who entered in 1799. In his case we have not only his programme of reading recorded in the collections books but also his own comments on his university course. In his four years as an undergraduate he read in Greek the whole of the *Odyssey*, all the plays of Aeschylus, all Herodotus and Thucydides, Xenophon's

[1] Hurdis, *Vindication* in *Reminiscences of Oxford*, 136-7.
[2] Stubbs, *University of Dublin*, 257-8; McDowell and Webb. *Trinity College Dublin*, 69. Cambridge, with its primarily mathematical curriculum, is not comparable; nor are the Scottish universities, where the students were a good deal younger and the classics were regarded as belonging to the earlier stages of the course.
[3] Knox, *Liberal Education* ii. 177, 202-3.
[4] According to George Colman the younger, who entered Christ Church in 1779, boys from Eton and Westminster were never examined on entry in classics, as their competency was assumed as a matter of course: *Reminiscences of Oxford*, 169. This assumption, however, must often have proved unjustified.

Hellenica, five books of Diodorus, a considerable amount of oratory, but of Plato (or pseudo-Plato) only the two Alcibiades dialogues. His Latin reading was confined to Livy, and this he says was the only addition to the stock of Latin he had brought with him from Southwell, the grammar school which he had left at the age of fifteen and a half to go to Westminster. As he was already interested in Greek history he was glad that Herodotus and Thucydides were among the first authors he was set to read. But when he left Oxford after seven years in all he had never heard of Dio Cassius and had read no Plutarch in the original; he knew nothing of Callimachus, Apollonius Rhodius, Theocritus or Hesiod, and fourteen tragedies of Euripides were still unread. He 'never received a single syllable of instruction concerning Greek accents, or Greek metres, or the idiom of Greek sentences; in short, no information upon *any one point* of Grammar, or Syntax, or Metre. These subjects were never named to me.' He learnt more from his contemporaries, one of whom was Gaisford, than from his official tutors; he considered that when he entered Oxford 'Greek learning was perhaps at the lowest point of degradation'.[1]

This verdict would no doubt have surprised Dean Jackson and might in any case be hard to substantiate;[2] and the deficiences which Clinton found in his education when he looked back later in life were hardly glaring. They do, however, point to the weaknesses of the traditional eighteenth-century scholarship represented by Christ Church, a scholarship which was content with an empirical knowledge of the ancient languages based on the reading and imitation of the best authors, and did not encourage a more profound and critical study.

Universities are judged not only by the efficiency of their teaching but also by their contributions to the advancement of learning. In classics an assessment of Oxford's contribution in our period can conveniently begin with Richard Bentley's incorporation at Wadham in 1689. He had come to Oxford as tutor to James Stillingfleet,[3] the younger son of Bishop Stillingfleet, and he spent about a year there, making good use of the resources of the Bodleian Library and getting to know the leading scholars of the university, such as Hody, then tutor at Wadham, Dodwell and John Mill, the future editor of the New Testament. While he was in Oxford the curators of the Press decided to publish the chronicle of John Malelas (or Malalas) the only manuscript of which was in the Bodleian Library, with prolegomena by Hody on the identity and date of the chronicler. Mill, who exercised a general supervision over the publication,

[1] *Literary Remains of Henry Fynes Clinton, Esq., M.A.* ed. C. J. Fynes Clinton (London 1854), 8-13, 22, 230.
[2] In 1758 Burton wrote gloomily of *Literarum graecarum studia quae quidem languere indies et exolescere sentio*: Burton, *Pentalogia* (1779 edn) i. 2.
[3] James Stillingfleet (1675-1746), m. Wadham 1689; dean of Worcester 1726-46.

invited Bentley to contribute some notes, and this he did in a substantial
Epistola ad Millium which was published in 1691 as an appendix to the
edition. Thus Oxford can claim some credit for the work which established Bentley's reputation as a scholar; and though Hody's contribution
was put in the shade by Bentley's, it was a thoroughly competent piece of
work.

Oxford also occasioned Bentley's next and more famous work, the dissertation on the letters of Phalaris, and here the scholarship of the
university does not show up so well. It was the practice at Christ Church,
started by Fell and continued by Aldrich, for the dean to give one of the
most promising scholars of the House the task of editing a classical text,
which was then printed, distributed in the college as a new year's gift and
put on sale to the general public. In 1693 Aldrich chose Charles Boyle, a
young man of only seventeen, as one of these editors, and assigned to
him the epistles of Phalaris. The edition, which was completed by the
beginning of 1695, was an unpretentious piece of work, and Boyle did
not commit himself on the authenticity of the epistles, which had
already been questioned; but in his preface he made a slighting reference
to Bentley which provoked him to publish a dissertation showing them
to be spurious. This was taken as an attack on Christ Church, and in the
next year there appeared what claimed to be Boyle's examination of
Bentley's *Dissertation*, but was in fact not his work at all but a joint
production of a group of Christ Church men led by Atterbury. This in
turn gave rise to a greatly enlarged *Dissertation* in which Bentley showed
to the full his learning and critical powers.[1]

Boyle's examination was a clever production, plausible enough to convince many at the time, but it was superficial and more concerned to
score points off Bentley than to arrive at the truth. Moreover, Bentley
was right and Christ Church was wrong. The men who joined together
to answer Bentley were all products of Busby's Westminster, and Busby,
as Samuel Johnson put it, 'advanced his scholars to a height of knowledge very rarely attained in grammar-schools'.[2] Hence a certain over-
confidence on the part of the Christ Church Westminsters. Among them
was John Freind, who was responsible for the edition of Ovid's *Metamorphoses* which appeared from the Oxford Press in 1696. Of Freind and
Anthony Alsop (another Christ Church author) Bentley wrote: 'If they
can but make a tolerable copy of verses with two or three small faults in

[1] *Phalaridis epistolae*, ed. C. Boyle (Oxford 1695); R. Bentley, *A Dissertation upon the Epistles of Phalaris, Themistocles, Socrates, Euripides, and others; and the Fables of Aesop* (London 1797); 'C. Boyle', *Dr. Bentley's Dissertations on the Epistles of Phalaris and the Fables of Aesop Examined* (London 1698); R. Bentley, *A Dissertation upon the Epistles of Phalaris with an Answer to the Objections of the Honourable Charles Boyle, Esquire* (London 1699).
[2] *Johnson's Lives of the Poets*, ed. G. B. Hill (3 vols Oxford 1905) i. 416.

it, they must presently set up to be Authors; to bring the nation into contempt abroad, and themselves into it at home.'[1]

The Oxford Press had no monopoly of classical publications, but it regularly produced editions of Greek and Latin texts and its lists give a good indication of the interests of the university in this field. The omissions are significant no less than the inclusions. In Greek, Homer's works were several times reissued, anonymously and without editorial matter. Hesiod was edited in 1737 by Thomas Robinson of Merton, who had more of his own to contribute than many editors of the period.[2] Less satisfactory was the Oxford Pindar of 1697 by two young fellows of Magdalen, Richard West and Robert Welsted, of which Hearne wrote that the editors 'being careless and not much versed in old MSS ... and being not withall diligent enough in collecting materials and consulting Authors there are a great many Blunders in it'.[3] Nothing of any note was produced in the field of Greek drama until the second half of the century, when we find a new interest in Greek tragedy developing. When Burton published his edition of five plays with the title *Pentalogia* in 1758 he included in the preface a plea for the reading of the dramatists in schools and universities in addition to the hexameter and elegiac verse beyond which few then progressed.[4] His edition was designed to be useful to students. More important from the scholarly point of view were the works of Heath and Musgrave, both of whom are still remembered for their contribution to the textual criticism of the tragedians. Benjamin Heath, town clerk of Exeter and an Oxford man only by virtue of the honorary degree which the university conferred on him, was the author of a substantial volume of notes on the three tragedians published by the Press in 1762. Musgrave, whose complete Euripides appeared in 1778, was a physician who had travelled on the continent as Radcliffe fellow of University College, and having collated important manuscripts of Euripides in Paris was better equipped in this respect than many editors of the period who used only those manuscripts that were easily accessible, which were often of slight value.[5]

Aristophanes, then generally regarded as little more than a scurrilous

[1] Bentley, *Dissertation upon the Epistles of Phalaris* (London 1727 edn), p. xxxv. On Freind see G. l'E. Turner, 'The physical sciences', p. 663 below.

[2] Thomas Robinson (1699-1761), m. Oriel 1716; BA Linc. 1720; higher degrees Merton 1722; archdeacon of Northumberland 1758-61.

[3] Hearne, *Collections* i. 153. Robert Welsted (1671-1735), m. SEH 1687; demy Magd. 1689; practised medicine in Bristol and London. Richard Dawes criticized the Oxford Pindar in his *Miscellanea critica* (Cambridge 1745), section ii.

[4] Burton, *Pentalogia* (1779 edn) i. 4. Some Greek tragedy was read in a few schools. In 1729 the *Choephori* and the *Electra* of Sophocles and of Euripides were published (by the Oxford Press) for the use of Westminster School.

[5] The Oxford Press had previously (1756) published Musgrave's *Hippolytus*, with notes by Jeremiah Markland, whose name alone appeared on the title-page. Samuel Musgrave (1732-80), m. Queen's 1749; BA and MA CCC; BM and DM Univ.

buffoon, was ignored by Oxford scholars. Not so the Hellenistic poets. In 1697 appeared a sumptuous folio Lycophron edited by John Potter, then a young fellow of Lincoln. Equally sumptuous was Warton's two-volume Theocritus of 1770. This was described by Housman as 'large and empty', and certainly it is open to criticism.[1] Warton printed in an appendix some of the collations made by or for the antiquary James St Amand of manuscripts in foreign libraries, but made no use of them in his text; he included a hitherto unpublished life of Theocritus by the long-dead Joshua Barnes to save himself the trouble, as he admitted, of producing one of his own; and he acknowledged that the contributions of Jonathan Toup[2] which were included in the edition were superior in point of scholarship to his own work. But empty though Warton's Theocritus may have been there was more substance in it than in the Apollonius Rhodius of John Shaw in which the Dutch scholar Wytten-bach could find little to praise apart from the paper and type.[3]

There was an Oxford edition of Thucydides, but none of two other major Greek historians, Herodotus and Polybius.[4] The Thucydides (1696) was the work of John Hudson, fellow of University College, later to become Bodley's Librarian, a conscientious scholar who edited a large number of classical texts. The complete works of Xenophon appeared between 1690 and 1703, edited by Edward Wells, whose own contribu-tions were very slight; the most valuable feature of the edition was the *Chronologia xenophontea* contributed by Dodwell.[5] In 1727 Thomas Hutchinson edited the *Cyropaedia* followed in 1735 by the *Anabasis*. Hearne described him as 'a much worse Scholar than he takes himself to be', and probably with justice; a better scholar than Hearne, Richard Porson, had a low opinion of Hutchinson's work.[6] There was a negligible edition of the *Memorabilia* by Bolton Simpson of Queen's published in 1741 and often reprinted, and one of rather more substance by Edward Edwards of Jesus, published posthumously in 1785.[7]

While the popularity of the *Memorabilia* is evidence of an interest in the Socratic moral teaching, Plato was little regarded in Oxford—or

[1] *The Classical Papers of A. E. Housman*, ed. J. Diggle and F. R. D. Goodyear (3 vols Cambridge 1972) iii. 1005.

[2] Jonathan Toup (1713–85), m. Exeter 1733; MA Pembroke Coll. Cambridge 1756.

[3] Apollonius Rhodius, *Argonautica*, ed. J. Shaw (2 vols Oxford 1777, 2nd edn 1 vol. Oxford 1779). John Shaw (1750–1824), m. Univ. 1764; demy Magd. 1767–71. Cf *Bibliotheca critica* (Amsterdam 1777 onward); i pt 3 (1778), 113–17.

[4] In 1706 Hugh Hutchin (m. Linc. 1695; degrees Ch.Ch.) began an edition of Polybius: Hearne, *Collections* i. 195. It came to nothing, as did other later projects for an edition: H. G. Carter, *A History of the Oxford University Press* (Oxford 1975), 335.

[5] As Wells himself said in the preface to the complete edition of 1703. J. G. Schneider agreed: see his edition of Xenophon, *Historia graeca* (Leipzig 1821), p. xviii.

[6] Hearne, *Collections* viii. 413. See Porson's *notae breves* appended to the 1785 edition of Hutchin-son's *Anabasis*.

[7] Edward Edwards (1726–83), m. Jesus 1743.

indeed elsewhere—in this period. No complete edition of his works was produced, though some individual dialogues, or groups of dialogues, were edited by Oxford scholars in the course of the eighteenth century.[1] The only editor who showed a serious interest in Plato's thought was John William Thomson, whose *Parmenides*, published in 1728, included prolegomena in which he attempted to expound the Platonic theory of ideas; but he thought it necessary to apologize for devoting himself to such an obscure and uninviting subject, and at the beginning of the nineteenth century half of the five hundred copies printed of the work were still unsold.[2]

More surprising than the neglect of Plato was the neglect of Aristotle in a university supposedly devoted to Aristotelianism. An edition of the *Ethics* appeared in 1716, and one of the spurious *De virtutibus et vitiis* in 1752. Otherwise the only works in the Oxford lists are the *Rhetoric* and the *Poetics*. The edition of the *Rhetoric* by William Holwell of Christ Church which appeared anonymously in 1759 was designed to be useful to students; Holwell considered a Latin version to be more of a hindrance than a help and consequently dispensed with one, but he provided extensive notes aimed at explaining and illustrating difficult passages.[3] An edition of the *Poetics* appeared in 1760 and another in 1780. The latter, by Thomas Winstanley of Brasenose, had its merits as well as its defects, but it was outclassed by that of Thomas Tyrwhitt, published posthumously in 1794.[4] The other famous Greek work of literary criticism, Longinus, *On the Sublime*, was edited by John Hudson in 1710 and again by Toup in 1778. Toup, a country clergyman in Cornwall, was rather a difficult man. One of the notes which he contributed to Warton's Theocritus was considered blasphemous and obscene and was suppressed, whereupon he repeated the substance of it in another publication, with an offensive attack on his critics. The delegates of the Press however valued his work; they published not only his Longinus but also, after his death, four volumes of his *Emendationes in Suidam* (1790) and they paid for the memorial tablet to him put up in his parish church.[5]

[1] In addition to John William Thomson's *Parmenides* (published 1728) there was an edition of *Erastae, Euthyphro, Apology, Crito* and *Phaedo* by Nathaniel Forster (1718-57, m. Pemb. 1732, fellow CCC 1735) in 1745; of *Alcibiades* I and II and *Hipparchus* by William Etwall (1747-78, m. Magd. 1764, demy 1764-71) in 1771, and of *Euthydemus* and *Gorgias* by M. J. Routh in 1784.

[2] Carter, *History of the Press* i. 294. Thomson was encouraged to produce his edition by John Burton, who contributed a prefatory letter in Greek.

[3] Holwell also published, not at Oxford, an edition of selected literary treatises of Dionysius of Halicarnassus (London 1766) on which see *Dionysius of Halicarnassus: Three Literary Letters* ed. W. R. Roberts (Cambridge 1901), 211. Hudson edited the complete works of Dionysius (Oxford 1704).

[4] On Winstanley's edition see *Bibliotheca critica* ii pt 3 (1782), 114-16. In his preface Winstanley attributed to poor eyesight and ill health his failure to add more explanatory notes. Aristotle, *Poetica*, ed. T. Tyrwhitt (London 1794).

[5] J. Nichols, *Literary Anecdotes of the Eighteenth Century* (9 vols London 1812-15) ii. 345-6.

Thomas Tyrwhitt like Toup was not an Oxford resident, but he had held a fellowship at Merton and he kept in touch with the university. He was always ready to help other scholars, and gave financial assistance to Thomas Burgess at the beginning of his career. Burgess was, in the words of his biographer, 'the most zealous, able, and successful promoter of Greek learning at Oxford, towards the close of the eighteenth century'.[1] While still an undergraduate he published his notes on the five plays in Burton's *Pentalogia*,[2] and a few years later, in 1781, he produced a new edition of Richard Dawes's *Miscellanea critica* with extensive additional notes. He travelled on the continent and met the leading foreign scholars of the day, and it was he who made the arrangements for Wyttenbach to edit Plutarch's *Moralia* for the Oxford Press. His plan to start a quarterly classical journal came to nothing, but he was responsible for something very like a learned journal, with contributions by various hands, the *Museum oxoniense literarium* of which one volume appeared in 1792 and a second in 1797.

While the university and its Press had a creditable record in Greek scholarship it was noticeably weak in Latin. Two editions of some value appeared in 1693, a Velleius Paterculus by Hudson[3] and a Quintilian by Edmund Gibson, then a BA of Queen's, who made use of some new manuscript material. Hearne edited Livy in 1708 with variant readings from six Oxford manuscripts collated by himself. He ended his preface with the promise of an edition of Cicero; this never materialized, but his collations of numerous Ciceronian manuscripts, none of them unfortunately of much value, were included in the handsome ten-volume Oxford Cicero of 1783, which otherwise contained nothing new.[4] Editions of individual works of Cicero which appeared in the late seventeenth and early eighteenth century were of little value; for the rhetorical works the Press was content to reprint the inferior Delphin edition of Jacob Proust.[5] No edition was produced of Tacitus, and with the exception of Ovid's *Metamorphoses* (the edition of 1696 condemned by Bentley), Lucretius and Virgil (an edition of 1795), Latin verse writers were neglected, partly no doubt because they, or some of them, were so familiar that no need was felt for any further work on them. The only Oxford Latinist of the period whose scholarly work is remembered today is Thomas Creech whose edition of Lucretius was published in 1695.

---

[1] Harford, *Burgess*, 20.

[2] *Observations*, etc. 1778, reprinted in a new edition of Burton's *Pentalogia* (1779).

[3] In the preface of his edition of Velleius (Leiden 1719) Peter Burman spoke highly of Hudson's edition and praised his industry and other services to scholarship. Hudson's Velleius was soon sold out and a second edition appeared in 1711.

[4] The text was that of Olivet, and the final volume consisted of Ernesti's *Clavis ciceroniana*.

[5] *M. T. Ciceronis omnes qui ad artem oratoriam pertinent libri*, ed. J. Proust (2 vols Paris 1687, 3 vols Oxford 1718).

Creech was described by Munro as 'a man of sound sense and good taste, but to judge from his book of somewhat arrogant and supercilious temper'.[1] Unlike most editions of the period, which tended to consist of an uncoordinated accumulation of *variorum* notes and manuscript readings, his bears the mark of a definite personality. His notes are brief and to the point and sometimes forcibly expressed; his edition proved eminently useful and was often reprinted.[2]

In ancient history, apart from Dodwell's chronological studies, Oxford had little or nothing to show. Gibbon acknowledged no obligation to the university where he spent those 'idle and unprofitable' months,[3] and it can claim no credit for the *Decline and Fall*. The same can probably be said of William Mitford's *History of Greece*.[4] Jeremy Bentham, who was a contemporary of Mitford's at Queen's, saw no sign in him of the future historian.[5] Historical study, as has already been mentioned, was encouraged at Christ Church toward the end of the eighteenth century, but it was confined to the reading of the ancient texts; it remained so during the first half of the nineteenth century and it was only after the separation of 'Mods' and 'Greats' that a more specialized study of ancient history developed.

Two useful works ancillary to classical studies were printed by the University Press in the years around 1700. John Potter's *Archaeologiae graecae, or The Antiquities of Greece*, published in 1697, was followed in 1704 by the third edition of *Romae antiquae notitia, or The Antiquities of Rome* (first published in London in 1696) by Basil Kennett of Corpus.[6] Both works proved popular and were many times reprinted. They were companions to Greek and Latin studies, dealing with the constitutional, religious, military and social institutions of the two peoples. They were not concerned with classical archaeology as it is now understood. This had then no place in Oxford studies and little in the interests of members of the university. The university had, however, in its custody the inscriptions from Lord Arundel's collections which had been presented by his grandson, and in 1755, after various vicissitudes, a substantial part of Arundel's sculpture collections also came into its hands. A catalogue by Richard Chandler of Magdalen was published in 1764.[7] In the next year Chandler

---

[1] Lucretius, *De rerum natura*, ed. H. A. J. Munro (London 1860, 3rd edn 2 vols Cambridge 1873) i. 17.

[2] Though the second Oxford edition did not appear till 1818 the book had been reprinted elsewhere in the meantime.

[3] Gibbon, *Memoirs of my Life*, ed. Bonnard, p. 48.

[4] W. Mitford, *History of Greece* (5 vols London 1808-20). William Mitford (1744-1827), m. Queen's 1761.

[5] *Works of Bentham*, ed. Bowring x. 40.

[6] Basil Kennett (1674-1715), m. SEH 1689; scholar CCC 1689, president 1714-15.

[7] Chandler's *Marmora oxoniensia* superseded the catalogue of the same name by Humphrey Prideaux printed at Oxford in 1676; the imprint is Oxford 1763 but it was not put on sale until 1764.

set out for Asia Minor on a mission sponsored by the Dilettanti Society which resulted in a number of publications, *Ionian Antiquities, Inscriptiones antiquae* and two volumes of travels.[1] Oxford thus had a share in the eighteenth-century discovery of Greek art and architecture, but though Chandler was elected to a fellowship at Magdalen after his return from his travels, it cannot be said that his work and that of other travellers in Greek lands impinged much on the studies of the university. These were primarily literary, and were indeed narrower than they had been in the late seventeenth century when Kennett and Potter compiled their books and Dodwell was engaged in his chronological studies.

The late seventeenth century was also a period of considerable activity in the field of Greek and Latin literature. Indeed if one judges solely by the number of classical editions published, Oxford scholarship was most flourishing in the last decade of that century and the first of the eighteenth. After that there was a falling off in quantity of output, and perhaps in quality too until the 1750s; then, in the latter half of the century, we find some work of high quality being produced in Greek, though nothing of any note in Latin. For an objective view of Oxford scholarship in the last three decades of the eighteenth century we can turn to the reviews in the *Bibliotheca critica*, edited and largely written by Wyttenbach. Here we find Shaw's Apollonius Rhodius severely handled and Winstanley's *Poetics* lukewarmly reviewed. There is high praise, however, for Musgrave, Toup and Tyrwhitt, and Burgess is looked on as a promising young man likely to develop into a distinguished scholar.[2]

It will be observed that the three best Oxford scholars in the opinion of a foreign contemporary, an opinion which would not be disputed today, were none of them resident in the university. Musgrave and Tyrwhitt were laymen, and there was little scope for laymen in Oxford; and scholars in holy orders were always likely to leave for other work in the church. Toup pursued his Greek studies in his Cornish parsonage; others would give up classics for studies more directly related to their profession, as Burgess did, and as Potter had done about a century earlier.[3] When we add the requirement of celibacy and the closed character of the majority of college fellowships it is easy to see why the university so often failed to keep the services of its best men and why even in a subject

See Carter, *History of the Press* i. 392-5. Richard Chandler (1737-1810), m. Queen's 1755; demy Magd. 1757.

[1] R. Chandler, *Ionian Antiquities* (London 1769); R. Chandler, *Inscriptiones antiquae* (Oxford 1774); R. Chandler, *Travels in Asia Minor* (Oxford 1775); R. Chandler, *Travels in Greece* (Oxford 1776).

[2] *Bibliotheca critica* i pt 2 (1777), 120-8, i pt 3 (1778), 32-52, 113-17, i pt. 4 (1779), 1-44, ii pt 3 (1782), 111-16, ii pt 4 (1783), 85-94, iii pt 2 (1790), 133-5.

[3] In the preface to his *Lycophron* (1697) Potter announced his intention of devoting himself in future to theological study and to the service of the church. He refused the offer of the professorship of Greek in 1707 on the ground that he had 'turned his study wholly to divinity': W. R. Ward, *Georgian Oxford* (Oxford 1958), 32.

like classics which had a monopoly of school education the general level of its teaching was not high. Yet classical scholarship flourished none the less; indeed it is a curious paradox that what Housman called our great age of scholarship which began in 1691 with the publication of Bentley's *Epistola ad Millium* and ended in 1825 with 'the successive strokes of doom which consigned Dobree and Elmsley to the grave and Blomfield to the bishopric of Chester' was the age in which the universities were least mindful of their responsibilities as teaching institutions.[1]

[1] *M. Manilii astronomicon liber primus*, ed. A. E. Housman (London 1903, 2nd edn Cambridge 1937), p. xlii. It is another paradox that Cambridge, which gave much less encouragement to classical studies than Oxford, was yet the university of Bentley and Porson, Markland and Dawes.

18

Hebrew Studies

D. PATTERSON

THE serious study of Hebrew at Oxford may be attributed to the founding of the regius chair of Hebrew in 1546 by Henry VIII, who made it chargeable on the dean and chapter of Christ Church.[1] The Edwardian Visitors in 1549 ordered Hebrew lectures to be delivered from 8 a.m. to 9 a.m. immediately before those on theology, while the Laudian statutes of 1636 laid down that the regius professor should lecture twice a week on Tuesdays and Thursdays between one and two 'from the fountains of holy writ'. The lectures were to be attended by undergraduates and by BAs for a year unless they were entered on the law or medicine line. But although the names of the Elizabethan and other early Hebrew professors are all known, they seem to have left little mark, being otherwise engaged. John Harding, for example, had two periods of office, but for much of the time he was also president of Magdalen.[2] Yet there were sufficient Hebrew scholars available under James I for the production of the Authorized Version of the Old Testament.

In addition, the university permitted 'shagglyng'—extraordinary or temporary—lecturers who often taught *gratis*, but were otherwise paid by individual colleges or students or even by the king or bishops. They also permitted extraneous teachers of Hebrew, mostly converts, who from the seventeenth century onward found their way to Oxford to teach Hebrew and were encouraged to do so by churchmen and academics alike.

Hebrew was largely regarded as a branch of theology. As the statute implies, the concern with the language was primarily for a better understanding of the scriptures.[3] 'The natural method is to begin first with the Hebrew Bible', wrote a correspondent to Charlett in 1711, who was also pleading for the teaching of Chaldee.[4] Bodley debated with his first Librarian, Thomas James, whether a Hebrew grammar and dictionary

---

[1] I am indebted to Mr R. Judd of the Oxford Centre for Postgraduate Hebrew Studies for his help in many ways with this chapter.
[2] John Harding (d. 1610), fellow Magd. 1577-8; incorporated at Cambridge 1584; regius prof. of Hebrew Oxford 1591-8 and 1604-10; president Magd. 1608-10.
[3] See P. J. Marshall, 'Oriental studies' below.
[4] A. Bedford-Charlett, 11 Dec. 1711, MS Ballard 34, fo 111.

should be classed under theology or arts.[1] Nevertheless, the Hebraic factor in English literature during the seventeenth century has been clearly demonstrated.[2]

Of the few professors of note in the seventeenth century was John Morris, for whom Charles I added a cathedral canonry by letters patent in 1630.[3] Many others were proficient in both Hebrew and Arabic. Indeed, the early tendency for the same scholar to hold the regius chair of Hebrew and the Laudian chair of Arabic gave a biblical slant to Oxford Arabic studies. Together with the new growth of trade and curiosity about the middle and far east, it deflected the interests of the orientalists at the university in the late seventeenth and early eighteenth centuries away from Hebrew to Arabic and other oriental languages. But it also encouraged an approach to Hebrew as a language in its own right. An *Essay on the Usefulness of Oriental Learning*, dedicated to the governing body of Lincoln College, quoted the preface to a Hebrew grammar in such vein:

If we enquire into the excellencies which usually recommend the learned languages we shall find the *Hebrew* to be an original and essential language, that borrows of none, but lends to all. Some of the sharpest Pagan writers, inveterate enemies to the religion and learning of both Jews and Christians, have allowed the *Hebrew* tongue to have a noble Emphasis and a close and beautiful Brevity. Then *Hebrew* is a language, for uniformity and simplicity, of all others the most easy, and yet, at the same time, so full of excellent wisdom and skill in the contrivance of it, as, considering it merely as a language, will afford exercise for the acutest parts and give pleasure to the most curious.[4]

The second half of the seventeenth century produced a more distinguished line of professors of Hebrew of whom the first was Edward Pococke, also Laudian professor of Arabic.[5] He had been chaplain to the Levant Company in Aleppo and was both Hebraist and Arabist. An outstanding Hebraist, his share of the London polyglot Bible (1657) was unmatched by any other editor, while his commentaries on some of the prophets display familiarity with rabbinic exegesis as well as a wide knowledge of the Christian commentators. His *Porta Mosis*, an annotated edition of six sections of Maimonides's *Mishnah* commentary with the Arabic text in Hebrew characters and a Latin translation, was the first

---

[1] Thomas James (*c*1573-1629), m. New College 1592, fellow 1593-1602; Bodley's Librarian 1602-20.

[2] A. H. Fisch, *Jerusalem and Albion* (London 1964).

[3] John Morris (1594-1648), m. Ch.Ch. 1609; chaplain All Souls and MA 1632; incorporated at Cambridge 1623; BD 1626; DD and canon Ch.Ch. 1632; regius prof. of Hebrew 1626-48. See also p. 544 below.

[4] Philoglottus [Gregory Sharpe], *An Essay on the Usefulness of Oriental Learning* (London 1739), 15-16.

[5] Edward Pococke (1604-91), m. Magd. Hall 1619; degrees CCC; incorporated at Cambridge 1628; canon Ch.Ch. 1648-50; regius prof. of Hebrew 1648-51, 1660-91.

Hebrew book printed in Oxford (1655). He also published a Latin version of Maimonides's preface to the *Mishnah* at Oxford in 1690. Pococke won deserved acclaim for his scholarship, but Anthony Wood said of his successor Roger Altham that he 'became Hebrew professor as canon, but doth not read because he is no Hebritian'. 'Yet being a Ch.Ch. man he was admitted canon. Partialty! Others of other houses were fit for it; but the place is reserved for a Ch.Ch. man.'[1] On the other hand, Hearne, although stating that Altham was put in by the influence of Radcliffe with the earl of Portland, commented that he 'is a good Scholar, and a most Excellent Preacher, but as yet has done nothing remarkable in the way of his Profession' and that either for 'not taking some Oath, or not making some subscription in due time lost the Place and was succeeded by Dr Thomas Hyde the Library-Keeper'. 'After the death of Dr Hyde, as 'tis suppos'd by the Interest of the Archbp of York and other Friends, he obtained the Place the 2d time.'[2]

Like Pococke, Thomas Hyde succeeded to both chairs, the Arabic from 1691 and the Hebrew from 1697. Hearne referred to him as the greatest master in Europe of the oriental languages.[3] Hyde had been a reader in Hebrew at Queen's in 1658, and as librarian of the Bodleian Library from 1665 had compiled its catalogue. His publications included Latin translations of Abraham Farissol's cosmography, *Iggeret Orhot Olam*, published as *Itinera mundi* in 1691, and of Hebrew material concerning the history of chess.[4]

Robert Clavering, professor from 1715 until 1747, was clearly conscious of his duties as a teacher:

> I am glad to find some people sensible of the great decay of that sort of learning which our Ancestors priz'd so much and we value so little; It is to be hopd that some time or other a Genius may arise that will revive the Repute of Eastern Literature: But when that will be I cannot tell.[5]

A correspondent of Charlett's referred to 'the learned Mr Claverings authorities out of the ancient Rabbinical Authors in Vindication of our old English Psalter'.[6] In 1705 he published in Oxford an annotated Latin

[1] Wood, *Life and Times* iii. 375 (14 Nov. 1691). Roger Altham (1649-1714), m. Ch.Ch. 1668; canon Ch.Ch. and regius prof. of Hebrew 1691-7, 1703-14.

[2] Hearne, *Collections* i. 228 (18 Apr. 1706). William Bentinck (1649-1709), 1st e. of Portland; hon. DCL 1670.

[3] Ibid. 235 (26 Apr. 1706).

[4] *Catalogus impressorum librorum bibliotechae bodleianae, in academia oxoniensi* (2 vols Oxford 1674); *Itinera mundi*, ed. T. Hyde (Oxford 1691); T. Hyde, *De ludis orientalibus* (Oxford 1694). The history of chess in the latter work had first been published in Oxford in 1689: H. G. Carter, *A History of the Oxford University Press* i (Oxford 1975), 228-9.

[5] Clavering-Charlett, 25 Sept. 1705, MS Ballard 9, fo 139. Robert Clavering (1671-1747), MA of Edinburgh, admitted Linc. 1693; hon. BA 1693, hon. MA 1696; fellow and tutor Univ. 1701; canon Ch.Ch. and regius prof. of Hebrew 1715-47; bp of Llandaff 1725, Peterborough 1729-47.

[6] J. Johnson-Charlett, 31 Dec. 1708, MS Ballard 15, fo 79.

translation of the third and fifth chapters of Maimonides's *Mishneh Torah*.[1]

Clavering's successor Thomas Hunt was also professor of Arabic and was encouraged to begin with 'reading in Hebrew, (as that would be useful to many Young Students)'.[2] Hunt was a sound oriental scholar who exerted considerable influence, although his published work may seem a little lightweight. His *Dissertation on Proverbs VII. 22 and 23* (Oxford 1743) was addressed to students of Arabic and other oriental languages,[3] while the prefatory discourse to his lectures as regius professor of Hebrew, *De usu dialectorum orientalium* (Oxford 1748) repeated the old theme of the importance of Arabic for Hebrew studies.

Richard Browne echoed Hunt's views that Arabic was necessary for the understanding of Hebrew. He was neither a distinguished scholar nor an impressive person, and was put in by Lord North and Lord Dartmouth.[4] He did, however, assemble a large collection of oriental coins which were presented by his executors to Christ Church and deposited in the library.

George Jubb gave his inaugural lecture on 16 December 1780.[5] As he was also principal registrar of the prerogative court of Canterbury, archdeacon of Middlesex, prebendary of St Paul's and chancellor of York from 1781, he may have been too occupied outside Oxford to have engaged in much teaching or research.

The last professor to hold the chair in the eighteenth century was Benjamin Blayney, a distinguished scriptural commentator whose Jeremiah was being read at Oriel from 1785 onwards.[6] He took great pains in correcting the text of the edition of the English Bible printed by the Clarendon Press in 1769, for which he was paid £350 by the university[7] but unfortunately a large part of the edition was lost in a fire at the Bible warehouse in Paternoster Row. His revision included a large number of additional references in the margin, and for all its faults, it became for many years the standard by which Oxford Bibles were corrected. In a letter to the *Gentleman's Magazine* he described the methods used for his revision:

Frequent recourse had been has [*sic*] to the Hebrew and Greek Originals; and as on other occasions, so with a special regard to the words not expressed in the

[1] Carter, *History of the Press* i. 447.

[2] Hunt-Rawlinson, 18 Nov. 1740, Bodl. MS Rawl. lett. 96, fo 38. Thomas Hunt (1696-1774), m. Ch.Ch. 1715; fellow Hart Hall 1721; Laudian prof. of Arabic 1738-74; regius prof. of Hebrew 1747-74.

[3] See Carter, i. 524.

[4] Bodl. MS North, d. 15, fo 218; see also L. S. Sutherland, 'The origin and early history of the lord almoner's professorship in Arabic at Oxford', *Bodleian Library Record* x (1978-82), 175.

[5] George Jubb (1718-87), m. Ch.Ch. 1735, canon and regius prof. of Hebrew 1780-7.

[6] Benjamin Blayney (1728-1801), m. Worc. 1746; fellow Hertford 1786, vice-president; canon Ch.Ch. and regius prof. of Hebrew 1787-1801.

[7] OUA vice-chancellor's computus 1769-70, p. 7, schools account.

Original Language, but which our Translators have thought fit to insert in Italics, in order to make out the sense after the English idiom, or to preserve the connexion. And though Dr Paris made large corrections in this particular in an edition published at Cambridge, there still remained many necessary alterations, which escaped the Doctor's notice in making which the Editor chose not to rely on his own judgment singly, but submitted them all to the previous examination of the Select Committee, and particularly of the Principal of Hertford College, and Mr Professor Wheeler.[1]

In spite of the contributions to learning made by some of the regius professors in the period, it was not they but other scholars such as Humphrey Hody, Robert Lowth, Benjamin Kennicott and Joseph White[2] who were justly regarded as the major Hebraists of the century.

Humphrey Hody, whose memory is perpetuated at Wadham by the scholarships he founded for the encouragement of Greek and Hebrew, was a brilliant scholar whose biblical studies were widely acclaimed. At the age of 22 he published a dissertation on the *Letter of Aristeas* in which he argued that the story embodied a Jewish legend intended to enhance the credit of the Septuagint.[3] The severe criticism which it aroused led Hody to devote almost twenty years to the composition of his great work *De bibliorum textibus originalibus*, which examined the history of the Septuagint and the original Hebrew texts as well as the Latin Vulgate and the later Greek versions.

Very different in character but of no less importance was Robert Lowth's seminal course of lectures on Hebrew poetry. Appointed professor of poetry in 1741, Lowth delivered a series of thirty-four Latin lectures on the literary qualities of biblical poetry, published as *Praelectiones de sacra poesi Hebraeorum* (Oxford 1753) and translated into English as *Lectures on the Sacred Poetry of the Hebrews* (London 1787).[4] Lowth was the first modern scholar to formulate the theory of parallelism as the foundation of biblical Hebrew poetry, although Azariah de Rossi, whom Lowth quoted, had anticipated him in part in the sixteenth century. Whereas Renaissance scholars had made unsuccessful attempts to scan poetic passages in the Bible as though they were classical hexameters, Lowth demonstrated the antiphonal nature of Hebrew poetry, with the latter part of each verse echoing the idea of the first by corroboration or contrast. 'Dr Lowth's lectures do great honour to the Nation, and to the University in part', wrote Charles Godwyn to Richard Hutchins.[5]

[4] See p. 540 below.

[1] *Gentleman's Magazine* xxxix (1769), 517-18.
[2] Joseph White (1745-1814), m. Wadham 1765; Laudian prof. of Arabic 1774-1814; canon Ch.Ch. and regius prof. of Hebrew 1802-14.
[3] See G. H. Box in *The Legacy of Israel*, ed. E. R. Bevan and C. Singer (Oxford 1927), 369.
[5] Letter of 31 Dec. 1763, J. Nichols, *Literary Anecdotes of the Eighteenth Century* (9 vols London 1812-15) viii. 239.

Lowth's keen appreciation of the importance of Hebrew is clearly discernible in his concluding address to the university:

The Hebrew language, which was for a series of years in a manner obsolete and neglected, has been lately cultivated by you with such attention and application, and has obtained so respectable a place among the other branches of erudition, that it seems, through your means to have recovered, after a tedious exile, all its former dignity and importance. Proceed, therefore, in the same career with the same ardour and success, and consider it as a work worthy of your utmost exertions to illustrate and cultivate this department of literature. You will find it no less elegant and agreeable, than useful and instructive; abounding in information no less curious for its extent and variety, than for its great importance and venerable sanctity; deserving the attention of every liberal mind; essential to all who would be proficients in Theology; a branch of literature, in a word, which will confer credit upon yourselves, will be an honour to the University, and an advantage to the Church.[1]

Lowth's translation of Isaiah (1778) also represented a new approach in so far as he distinguished between the prose and poetry of the original Hebrew. It is notable for the emphasis he placed on the sublimity of biblical literature in an age of prudery and circumlocution.

Perhaps the most familiar name in Hebrew scholarship in the period is that of Benjamin Kennicott, who learned Hebrew from Thomas Hunt, then regius professor, and whose interest in textual criticism was aroused by Robert Lowth. In 1753 Kennicott published a dissertation on the printed text of the Hebrew Bible attributing obscurities and conflicting passages to scribal errors and the ambiguities inherent in the script; to a second dissertation, published in 1759, he appended a survey of existing manuscripts of the Hebrew Bible attributable to the age before printing and a catalogue of those in Oxford libraries.[2] When the delegates of the Press asked Hunt in 1750 to suggest books that should be undertaken, he proposed the collation of the Old Testament manuscripts in Oxford; and in 1760 the delegates agreed to support an enlarged project, suggested by Kennicott, of a comparison of the Hebrew manuscripts prior to the invention of printing without restriction as to place.[3] For the next twenty years Kennicott devoted his time and energies to the project, with the assistance of many home and foreign libraries. 'Dr Kennicott meets with great encouragement, and goes on very briskly', wrote Godwyn to Hutchins in 1763.

There are hands at work for him in most parts of Europe. Probably the House of Commons may grant him a supply. He gives to his encouragers a translation of

[1] This passage from Gregory's translation was printed in the *Gentleman's Magazine* lxxiv (1804), 919.
[2] B. Kennicott, *The State of the Printed Hebrew Text of the Old Testament Considered* (Oxford 1753); B. Kennicott, *The State of the Printed Text of the Old Testament Considered* (Oxford 1759).
[3] Carter, *History of the Press* i. 410.

the 42d and 43d Psalms, as a specimen of the use which may be made of various readings.[1]

At home, however, relations between the editor and the delegates became very strained. His application to borrow manuscripts from the Bodleian Library was twice considered in convocation and rejected, although the University of Cambridge and the British Museum were more accommodating.[2] Sixteen years after the work was commissioned, volume one (Genesis to II Kings) appeared in 1776 in 650 copies. The 649 manuscripts consulted were identified by numbers, and omissions and evasions are indicated by signs. Vowels and accents were omitted altogether, because to notice variations in them would have added too much to the editor's labour. The second, thicker, volume followed in 1780. It contained at the end Kennicott's *dissertatio generalis* on what he had done and his methods of work. He went so far as to say that none of the variants was a threat to essential doctrine or increased historical knowledge. Though 'the text should not be much mended thereby', Samuel Johnson concluded, 'yet it was no small advantage to know, that we had as good a text as the most consummate industry and diligence could procure'.[3] But as the historian of the University Press has pointed out, 'What was a comfort to Johnson and to his fellow Christians is a disappointment to a more inquisitive generation'.[4]

Although Joseph White did not succeed to the regius chair of Hebrew until 1802, his early concern with Hebrew is shown by the award of a Hody exhibition for Hebrew in 1766-73. Well versed in Syriac, Arabic and Persian, he is still remembered for the first printed edition of the Gospels used by the Jacobite sect in eastern Syria (1778) on the basis of four manuscripts sent in 1730 from Mesopotamia to Glocester Ridley, fellow of New College.[5] Much of his time was devoted to the textual study of the Old Testament as well as the New. Although of a somewhat indolent disposition, his linguistic attainments were great, and compare favourably with those of the most eminent orientalists of his time.

There were other teachers of Hebrew at Oxford than the professors. Jean Gagnier was active as deputy for the regius professor of Hebrew in 1715, and was supported by William Lloyd to teach ten scholars Hebrew, being paid £20 yearly to do so.[6] In 1706 Gagnier had published *Josephus*

[1] Godwyn-Hutchins, 21 Dec. 1763, Nichols, *Anecdotes* viii. 239.

[2] See for example OUA register of convocation 1766-76, p. 81, 4 Dec. 1768. Earlier the curators of the Bodleian Library had been more accommodating: see I. G. Philip, 'Libraries and the University Press', p. 735 below.

[3] *Boswell's Life of Johnson*, ed. G. B. Hill (6 vols Oxford 1887), rev. L. F. Powell (6 vols Oxford 1934-50) ii. 128. [4] Carter, i. 413.

[5] Ibid. 402-3. Glocester Ridley (1703-74), m. Trin. 1721; BCL New College 1729; DD by diploma 1767.

[6] See Sutherland, 'Lord almoner's professorship in Arabic', 172; and for Lloyd's support, Lloyd-Charlett, 10 Nov. 1710, MS Ballard 9, fo 50.

Ben-Gorion. Hearne said that Gagnier 'is now a Teacher of the Hebrew Language in Oxford, and is esteem'd by able Judges to be a compleat Master of it'.[1]

During the eighteenth century there were few practising Jews in Oxford.[2] Luzena the Jew, 'a very learned man', was consulted about an inscription on a ritual cup, and William Henry Vorstius, 'very considerable for his skill in the Hebrew Tongue', translated Rabbi David Gans's *Chronology*.[3] But the Jews who taught officially in the university were converts. Isaac Abendana transferred from Cambridge to Oxford in 1676. At Trinity 'some of the scholars were taught Hebrew by a learned Jew, Dr Abendana, whose fees are charged in Computus from 1689'.[4] He seems to have been an accomplished Hebraist, and John Willes called him 'my old master Abendana'.[5] 'I perceive you have got another Rabbi in the University whom I should be glad to hear has given you sufficient Tokens of Real Conversion', Humfrey Wanley wrote to Charlett in 1705 about Philip Levi who taught at Magdalen and Lincoln, the latter college paying him £6 yearly.[6] Like many other extraneous teachers Levi was poorly paid and suffered from severe financial difficulties during his years at Oxford. William Lloyd told Charlett in 1708 that he had not been paid 'punctually', and went on to add:

it cannot be that you Heads of Houses should suffer so needfull a part of Learning to be lost. I doubt not you will look out for a Teacher of Hebrew, and employ the best man you can finde. If you chuse on one between this and Michmas, and make him certain of £40 a year which is a bare Subsistence I will add my Allowance of £8 a year to make it a little more comfortable for him. If you cannot finde one to your mindes within that time . . . I will endeavor to persuade Monsr Gagnier . . . the ablest man that I know in all parts of Hebrew Learning, to accept of the employment on those terms . . . and if at any time you dislike him, I will willingly receive him again.[7]

Levi must have died in 1708 because in that year the university paid £2 10s for his funeral, and in 1709 Magdalen gave £2 to his widow.[8] Levi had support from both Charlett and Robert Clavering. In thanking Charlett 'for all he had done for Levi' Lloyd, however, added;

[1] Hearne, *Collections* ii. 308 (14 Nov. 1709).
[2] See C. Roth, 'Jews in Oxford after 1290', *Oxoniensia* xv (1950).
[3] 'It is a pity Mr Luzena had not transcribed the Inscription in the Beautiful square Characters which he found on the pot. Instead of which, he has given the Rabbinical Character, which few people can read, and which was very difficult for the engraver to copy.' T. Hunt-R. Rawlinson, 1 Dec. 1743, Bodl. MS Rawl. C.369, fo 3. For Vorstius see N. Marsh-Charlett, 14 Apr. 1698, MS Ballard 8, fo 3ᵛ.
[4] H. E. D. Blakiston, *Trinity College* (London 1898), 173n.
[5] J. Willes-Charlett, 15 Mar. 1695, MS Ballard 25, fo 21. John Willes (c1647-1700), m. Trin. 1663; canon of Lichfield 1688-1700.
[6] Wanley-Charlett, 1 Aug. 1705, MS Ballard 13, fo 116. Humphrey Wanley (1672-1726), m. SEH 1695; for the payment by Lincoln see A. Clark, *The Colleges of Oxford* (London 1891), 191.
[7] Lloyd-Charlett, 9 Aug. 1708, MS Ballard 9, fo 48.
[8] OUA vice-chancellor's computus 1707-8; Macray, *Reg. Magdalen* iv. 54-5.

How the Bp [Clavering] came to choose him to teach young men and paid him. Now finds he's leading young men out of translating the Pirke Avoth in Mishna. Will you please charge him never to teach anything but the Text Hebrew of the Holy Scriptures.[1]

Clavering allowed Levi to publish under his own name a compendium of Hebrew grammar which the bishop had written. Levi dedicated it to the vice-chancellor, heads of houses and 'their respective Societys as a gratefull acknowledgement of their great and extraordinary favours'.[2]

Perhaps the most famous of the Jewish teachers in Oxford at the beginning of the eighteenth century was Isaac Bernard, who was a native of Prague. Writing to Charlett in January 1711 Wanley called him

a Scribe or Notary, as also a Pedling or little Merchant. He is extremely well skill'd in the Hebrew Literature, in the Jews Laws, Rites, Customs and Ceremonies; and write's a most Incomparable Hand, having Ingross'd 34 copies of the Law for the Synagogues ... If Mr Clavering ha's any Queres for him, I'le endeavour to find him out, and gett them answer'd.[3]

'Aaron' was employed by the university from 1726 until 1734 at a fee of £4 per annum. He taught Hebrew and Rabbinic to anyone who would pay and was regarded as an authority in all things Hebraic. He was in high favour with the principal of Magdalen Hall, Digby Cotes.[4]

Mark Moses Vowel, 'Reader of the Hebrew Language at Oxford', sent a letter to the *Gentleman's Magazine* in 1751 concerning the authority of the Massorah, at that time the object of much discussion in learned circles.[5] Joseph Smith appointed him Hebrew lecturer at Queen's about 1745 and assigned him £5 yearly—half the real stipend of the lecturership. When Vowel protested he promised him £1 10s out of his own pocket. Twelve years later Joseph Smith junior wanted to stop his father's contribution.[6] Payments to Vowel as Hebrew lecturer at Magdalen ceased in 1751,[7] and like Levi he seems to have suffered from financial problems. The date of his death is not known, but in 1772 *Jackson's Oxford Journal* proposed to print by subscription 'critical remarks upon certain passages of the Hebrew Bible ... by the late Moses Vowel, teacher of Hebrew in the University, for the benefit of his destitute widow and family'. Vowel had lived in Oxford for twenty-nine years.[8]

There was also a 'Mr Wratislava', teacher of German, French and Hebrew, who lodged at Tubb's in High Street.[9] 'Lates' (Lattes) of Turin

[1] Lloyd-Charlett, 6 Aug. 1707, MS Ballard 9, fo 47.
[2] Macray, *Reg. Magdalen* iv. 54-5; Carter, *History of the Press* i. 245n.
[3] Wanley-Charlett, 15 Jan. 1711, MS Ballard 13, fo 121.
[4] Digby Cotes (1684-1745), m. Magd. 1698; fellow All Souls 1707; principal Magd. Hall 1716-45.
[5] Roth, 'Jews in Oxford', 69; *Gentleman's Magazine* xxi (1751), 317-18.
[6] Vowel-Smith junior, 11 Jan. 1757, Queen's, MS 482, fo 346.
[7] Macray, *Reg. Magdalen* v. 15.
[8] *Jackson's Oxford Journal*, 7 May 1772.
[9] Ibid. 9 Feb. 1771.

taught Hebrew, music and modern languages in Oxford. He wrote an extremely rare brochure which includes rules for reading without points and a glossary of Hebrew abbreviations of considerable originality but little utility.[1]

Certain free grammar schools were supposed by their statutes to teach Hebrew as well as Latin and Greek, but the high master of St Paul's writing to Charlett in 1697 pointed out that

Generally speaking such persons as have attain'd to any excellency in it have been very little owing to any body but themselves, and to their Books for it; It being taught but in very few schools, and there only a little before Boys were sent to the University.[2]

Westminster scholars coming to Christ Church were better prepared than most.[3] Richard Busby, headmaster 1638–95, produced not only a Latin and Greek grammar but also a Hebrew Grammar,

which after it had been handed about in MSSt and continually transcrib'd for the use of the Boys of Westminster Schoole was printed at ye Theater ... I have been inform'd by one that was lately Student of Christ-Church and once a Scholar to Dr Busby that he also writ an Arabick Grammar, which Language was likewise taught in that schoole, the Dr having some skill in it.[4]

Hebrew was also taught at Winchester.

Several colleges had special benefactions for Hebrew studies. John Morris, in addition to a bequest of rare oriental books, left a small annual sum for the purchase of books and a perpetual annual rent-charge of £5 to be paid to a Student of Christ Church who was to be an MA and to be chosen by the dean for a speech in Hebrew in praise of Thomas Bodley, and thus as an encouragement of Hebrew studies. These speeches were made in November of each year and are still given today.[5] The Symes scholarship at Exeter could be held for eight years unless a fellowship was meanwhile obtained; if at the end of five years the scholar could not render any chapter of the Greek Testament into Latin, and also any chapter in the Hebrew Bible in any of the five books of Moses at an examination by order of the bishop of Bath and Wells, he lost his scholarship.[6] John Maynard also gave money to found a catechistical and

[1] D. F. Lates, *Regulae generales legendi linguam sanctam sine punctis masoreticis, breviter & methodice in usum tyronum propositae, & in ordine alphabetico expressae* (Oxford 1758); see Roth, 70.

[2] J. Postlethwayt-Charlett, 1697, MS Ballard 34, fo 86.

[3] For example the numbers reading the Psalms in Hebrew at Christ Church were as follows: 13 1700–9; 47 1710–19; 50 1720–9; 46 1730–9; 41 1740–9; 39 1750–9; 39 1760–9; 14 1770–9; 1 1780–9; 1 1790–1800.

[4] Hearne, *Collections* ii. 307–8.

[5] W. D. Macray, *Annals of the Bodleian Library* (Oxford 1890), 150 ff.

[6] W. K. Stride, *Exeter College* (London 1900), 249.

a Hebrew lecturership at Exeter.[1] Provision was made for the study of Hebrew as well as Greek and Latin in the founding statutes of Jesus in 1571.[2] At Lincoln a fellow was appointed to teach Hebrew in 1624 and in 1708. President Horne at Magdalen ordered that the 'divines and chaplains' were to attend the Hebrew lecture; the BA members were to attend the Hebrew and Greek lectures. The Hebrew lectures were begun in 1565 by Thomas Kingsmill.[3] At Pembroke Benjamin Slocock gave £200 for the support of a Hebrew lecturer.[4] 'What do you say to my request for Hebrew books?', wrote young John James of Queen's in 1782.

To day we had our first lecture, upon the alphabet and vowels! The Professor is a young man, preferred to this post I believe, by Lowth. He lectures at home in a snug private room, which will no doubt assist in *familiarizing* the language.

James goes on to say he is

learning Hebrew by the Points. This is certainly the most difficult method, and, perhaps for that reason, appears now the more agreeable. I confess I cannot see why the other party declaim so vehemently against punctuation as a rabbinical corruption, for their own method is doubtless as great a deviation from the ancient mode of pronouncing as that of the Masorites.[5]

Wadham was certainly one of the leading colleges in the encouragement of Hebrew studies. From 1738 until 1800 there were ninety-two Greek exhibitions, two Greek and Hebrew and fifty-four Hebrew exhibitions. The first meeting of the warden and the two professors to appoint the exhibitioners took place on 9 June 1738.[6]

Evidence is scanty regarding the amount of formal teaching and lecturing that was actually done. In his *Vindication* (printed about 1800) of Magdalen College against Gibbon's attack James Hurdis declared that the regius professor of Hebrew was reading on certain days of every week during term.[7] 'I began my Hebrew Lecture', wrote Thomas Hunt, 'in the beginning of Act Term, at which were present upwards of 50 Scholars.'[8] Richard Browne read lectures 'on the Hebrew and Arabic Languages both, constantly to considerable numbers in the University, two of which are now Heads of Colleges and others gentlemen of Standing in the Place'.[9] Both Robert Clavering and George Jubb,

---

[1] Stride, *Exeter College*, 57. Sir John Maynard (1602–90), m. Exeter 1621; the Protector's serjeant 1654 and for the Commonwealth 1658, dismissed on the Restoration but re-created king's serjeant 1660.   [2] J. N. L. Baker, *Jesus College, Oxford 1571–1971* (Oxford 1971), 1.

[3] Macray, *Reg. Magdalen* ii. 148, 192.   [4] Macleane, *Pembroke*, 300.

[5] *Letters of Radcliffe and James*, 191–2, 199. The professor was Henry Ford (1753–1813), m. Pemb. 1776; BA and MA Christ Church; DCL and principal Magd. Hall 1788; lord almoner's prof. of Arabic 1780–1813.   [6] WCM 10/2/4/6, Hody's benefaction.

[7] [J. Hurdis,] *A Word or Two in Vindication of the University of Oxford, and of Magdalen College in particular from the Posthumous Aspersions of Mr. Gibbon* (np nd), repr. in *Reminiscences of Oxford*, 146.

[8] Sutherland, 'Lord almoner's professorship in Arabic', 174.

[9] Ibid. 175.

however, had appointments outside Oxford and in the case of Jubb there is little evidence that he did any teaching. 'How the bishopric of Llandaff and deanery of Hereford will be consistent with a Regius professorship in Oxford, I cannot see', wrote Stratford of Robert Clavering; and Thomas Hyde commented, 'seeing that lectures though we must attend upon them will do but little good, Hearers being Scarce and Practicers more Scarce'.[1]

Lord Eldon's famous account of his examination for his MA may have been true:

An examination for a degree at Oxford was a farce in my time. I was examined in Hebrew and in History. 'What is the Hebrew for the place of a skull?'—I replied—'Golgotha'—'Who founded University College?'—I stated, (tho' by the way, the point is sometimes doubted), that K. Alfred founded it—'Very well, Sir' said the Examiner, 'you are competent for your degree'.[2]

Certainly the churchmen and academics felt uneasy about the weaknesses in Hebrew teaching and tried to keep the lecturerships going.

As to the quality of the teaching, apart from its quantity and the proficiency in Hebrew of undergraduates, graduates and teachers alike, it is instructive to examine a representative sample of the addresses in Hebrew which the universities of Oxford and Cambridge offered to the sovereign and other dignitaries on state occasions.[3] For the period under review fourteen honorific addresses containing Hebrew and printed at Oxford have been examined. The Hebrew parts consist of a total of thirty-seven Hebrew poems, and although one is unsigned and another only initialled, the rest are followed by the names of twenty-two contributors.[4] The honorific addresses containing Hebrew delivered at Cambridge during the same period, with a total of thirty-two poems, have also been examined. Five are unsigned while the rest are contributed by a total of twenty-two scholars.

The quality of the poetry varies greatly, with the Oxford collections having a decided edge over Cambridge. Among the former five poems

[1] Stratford-Harley, 29 Aug. 1724, HMC *Portland MSS* vii. 382; Wake MS xvi, fo 50 (Hyde, 10 Mar. 1701).

[2] Quoted by C. E. Mallet, *A History of the University of Oxford* (3 vols London 1924-7) iii. 163. John Scott (1751-1838), from 1799 1st e. of Eldon; m. Univ. 1766; high chancellor of England 1801-6 and high steward of the university 1801-38.

[3] I am grateful to Professor A. Karp of Rochester University, USA and to Mr J. Sparrow, formerly warden of All Souls, who kindly supplied me with copies of the texts of these addresses from their private collections.

[4] The Oxford contributors, in alphabetical order, were: Roger Altham, John Bagwell, Joseph Betts, Richard Brown, Robert Clavering, John [Jean] Gagnier, James Hemming, Thomas Hunt, Benjamin Kennicott, Robert Lowth, Benjamin Marshall, John Moore, John Pettingal, Carew Reynell, Henry Rigby, James Stephens, James Stillingfleet, 'J.T.' of Queen's, Thomas Troughear, John Wallis, Benjamin Wheeler, William Wilkinson. One poem was unsigned, another was by a non-Oxford contributor.

are—in this writer's opinion—outstanding, while a further eight may be classed as good. Fourteen constitute reasonable academic exercises, while seven are poor and three are very weak. None of the Cambridge poems is outstanding, although seven are good. A further eighteen may be categorized as respectable exercises, while six are poor and one extremely weak. The great majority of the poems suffer from lapses in grammar and syntax, while some contain passages which are scarcely comprehensible. As might have been expected, the overall impression is contrived and artificial. Frequent resort is made to the introduction of biblical phraseology and reference, often dragged in clumsily and without ceremony. Many of the poems are in rhymed couplets, triplets or quatrains, reflecting contemporary patterns in English literature. There are examples of poems in monorhyme, in partial rhyme and without rhyme of any kind. The most common metrical patterns approximate to tetrameters and pentameters, although some of the poems display no recognizable metrical system. Such attempts as there are to reproduce the rhythmic qualities of biblical Hebrew poetry remain largely unconvincing. With few exceptions the poems are unpointed—that is printed without the vowels.

Of the five poems which deserve high praise, the earliest is by John Bagwell, fellow of Exeter, in a *vota* published in 1689 on the accession of William and Mary.[1] The poem is printed with vowel points and composed in the metrical tradition of Hebrew poetry deriving from the medieval Spanish-Arabic schools. The metre is constructed from three units each comprising two *tenuʿot* and a *yated* followed by three *tenuʿot* (- - - -ᴜ - - -ᴜ - - -ᴜ - -). The metre is skilfully maintained throughout the poem, which consists of four quatrains each with its own monorhyme.[2] In praising king and queen, the poem urges Britain to rejoice in its good fortune. The author demonstrates a pleasing command of Hebrew.

The death of Prince George of Denmark prompted the publication of a poem by Robert Clavering in 1708.[3] This poem, which bears the superscripture *carmen hebraicum incisum & resonum* is cleverly constructed and may be regarded as the most sophisticated technically of all the poetry in these collections. It consists of twelve lines, each with a strong caesura, arranged in couplets, with the half-lines rhyming with the last end of each first line, while the latter halves of the several lines have a common rhyme throughout. Hence the pattern is aaab, cccb, dddb and so on.

---

[1] John Bagwell (1664-1725), m. Exeter 1681, fellow 1687-97; canon of Exeter cathedral 1700.
[2] For a concise and helpful survey of the development of Hebrew poetry see *The Penguin Book of Hebrew Verse*, ed. T. Carmi (Harmondsworth 1981), 57-72. A *tenuʿah* (plural *tenuʿot*) consists of a single syllable. A *yated* consists of a syllable preceded by a sounded *sheva*. These are the two basic metrical units from which Hebrew poetry in the Spanish-Arabic tradition is constructed. The metres are read from right to left.
[3] A copy of this poem is in Bodl. Pamphlets 277 (14).

Moreover, the last word in each couplet echoes the preceding word, as for example *be-nimharim harim, ha-amarim marim, ve-nisharim sarim* and so on. This echoing feature was used as a dramatic device by the great Hebrew poet Moses Hayyim Luzzatto in his play *La-Yesharim Tehillah* (Praise to the Righteous), published in Amsterdam in 1743, which in itself borrowed the technique from *Il Pastor Fido* by Giovanni Battista Guarini. Each half-line of Clavering's poem comprises a *yated* and four *tenu'ot* (- - - - - ∪ - - - - - ∪). But, apart from the beginning of each line and half-line, the sounded *sheva* is treated as a silent *sheva* so far as the metre is concerned. The poem is fully pointed, with very few omissions, and the occasional poetic licence with respect to grammar and syntax is explicable in the light of the exigencies of the metre and the echo device.

In 1715 Jean Gagnier published an elegy on the death of John Radcliffe in ten quatrains of which the second and fourth lines rhyme.[1] The poem is written in the metrical pattern of the well-known Jewish hymn *Adon Olam*, and consists of a *yated* and two *tenu'ot* in repeated sequence (- - - ∪). Moreover, the poem contains a number of phrases reminiscent of *Adon Olam*. Where the latter, for example, runs 'Into His hand I will entrust my spirit', Gagnier's poem contains the line 'Into the hands of God he has entrusted his spirit'. The poem praises Radcliffe's medical skills in extravagant terms, applauds his generosity and laments his passing. Again, a number of infelicities may be regarded as poetic licence because of the metrical pattern. In this poem, as elsewhere, there are occasional misprints and the Hebrew is unpointed. On the whole it is an effective poem.

On the death of the prince of Wales in 1751 James Hemming composed an *epicedium* lamenting Frederick's passing and praising his virtues.[2] The most interesting feature of the poem is its alphabetic structure, with the first line beginning with an *alef*, the second with a *bet* and so on throughout the alphabet. The poem consists of eleven rhymed couplets, the twenty-two verses thereby utilizing the twenty-two letters of the Hebrew alphabet. Although this form is a common device in Hebrew poetry which started with the Bible and proliferated in the liturgy, this is the only example of its kind in the collections under review. The structure naturally places certain constraints on the poem, but apart from the occasional lapse and a certain air of contrivance, the author demonstrates a considerable cleverness and a real feeling for the language. It is an interesting exercise and indicative of Hemming's skill.

The birth of a son, George Frederick, prince of Wales, to King George III and Queen Charlotte in 1762 occasioned a Hebrew poem by

---

[1] *Exequiae clarissimo viro Johanni Radcliffe M.D.* (Oxford 1715), copy in Bodl. M. 6. 6. Art.
[2] James Hemming m. SEH 1748, BA 1752.

John Moore, fellow of St John's College.[1] The thirty lines of print comprise fifteen lines of poetry reminiscent of the Psalms. It displays the two main features of biblical poetry, namely parallelism and a system of rhythmic stresses. Each line is divided by a strong caesura, with the second half echoing in whole or in part the thought expressed in the first. The feel of the poem is authentic, and it reads more naturally than any other poem in the collections under review. The poet had clearly mastered the principles of biblical Hebrew poetry outlined by Robert Lowth, and the composition demonstrates his mastery of biblical idiom. In comparison the poem by Benjamin Kennicott in the same collection is disappointingly mediocre, although an accompanying contribution by Henry Rigby, scholar of Wadham, represents another brave attempt to catch the spirit of the Psalms.[2] As a yardstick for measuring the level of Hebrew studies at Oxford and Cambridge in the late seventeenth and eighteenth centuries these collections of Hebrew poems deserve serious consideration.[3]

It is interesting to conclude by comparing the standards at Oxford with those elsewhere in the country, and more importantly in continental Europe. As at Oxford, there was a chair in Hebrew at Trinity College, Dublin, although the teaching of the subject was not pursued vigorously. Indeed, little can be said of the professors, since they published nothing related to Hebrew studies. It was not until after 1790 that any works on the subject issued from the college.[4] However, it is a very different story, and one which has not received the attention it deserves, with the dissenting academies formed after the ejection of 1662. Although it is true that the lasting achievements of the academies lie in fields other than Hebrew, and that in Hebrew itself their energies were dissipated in the controversy about vocalization—'points'— which raged in the eighteenth century, their standards were high. Solomon Harris of Carmarthen Academy was said to have been deeply read in rabbinical learning and to have owed much to personal acquaintance with Jewish scholars. At Tewkesbury Academy from 1708 to 1734 Samuel Jones taught Hebrew without points; two verses of the Old Testament were translated at sight into Greek every day by each student. Lectures on Jewish antiquities included the history of the text, the Talmud, Massorah, Versions, Targums and Cabbalah. The study of Hebrew was followed by Arabic and Syriac.[5]

[1] John Moore (c1743-1821), m. St John's 1759.
[2] Henry Rigby (c1742-1819), m. Wadham 1759.
[3] Copies of the addresses examined in this chapter have been deposited in the library of the Oxford Centre for Postgraduate Hebrew Studies at Yarnton Manor, Yarnton, Oxford.
[4] R. B. McDowell and D. A. Webb, *Trinity College Dublin 1592-1952: an academic history* (Cambridge 1982), 59.
[5] For more details see H. McLachlan, 'Semitics in the nonconformist academies' in his *Essays and Addresses* (Manchester 1950). I am indebted to Mr John Stephens for drawing my attention to this essay.

In continental Europe the study of Hebrew was widespread. The high frequency with which Hebrew grammars were published (and reprinted) at places such as Wittenberg, Jena, Leipzig or Basle implies a large student market. The Leiden and Amsterdam presses, as also to a lesser degree those of Lund and Uppsala, printed the doctoral dissertations of students of Jewish texts. The typical set task was to translate into Latin a tractate of the Mishnah, or a section of Maimonides' Code, or a rabbinical commentary to part or all of one of the biblical books.[1] In this world the Oxford scholarship mentioned earlier had exerted a great influence, in particular because Lowth's *Praelectiones* came to the notice of the most eminent orientalist in Germany. J.D. Michaelis (1719-91) brought out an expanded German translation in 1780 but Lowth's gratitude for his pains was ambiguous:

I was favoured with a sight of the Gottingen edition, published under the inspection of the learned and ingenious Professor of Philosophy in that University, John David Michaelis, and greatly improved and illustrated by him. To this were added his Notes and additions, in which he has with great candour supplied my defects, and corrected my errors.[2]

The effect of the translation in Germany was electrifying. It deeply impressed Herder and led to the inception of his great work on the spirit of Hebrew poetry (1782-3) and its influence is discernible in the pioneering work of Johann Gottfried Eichhorn, the founder of modern Old Testament criticism.

[1] See the article 'Hebraists, Christian' (by R. Loewe) in *Encyclopaedia Judaica* (16 vols Jerusalem 1971-2) viii, cols 9-71.

[2] R. Lowth, *De sacra poesi Hebraeorum* (Oxford 1753, 1763, 1775), trans. G. Gregory as *Lectures on the Sacred Poetry of the Hebrews* (2 vols London 1787, 3rd edn London 1835), p. xii.

19

Oriental Studies

P. J. MARSHALL

BEFORE the nineteenth century the concern of European universities with Asia and its civilizations was largely a theological one.[1] The Jewish people, their scriptures, their language and their history were the principal objects of study; interest in other eastern peoples tended to depend on the degree to which knowledge pressure of Islam on Europe presented for at least some learned military means. From early in the fourteenth century the study of Arabic and the Arabs was recognized as a proper subject for a university.[2] This tradition later went into decline, but there was a marked revival in Arabic learning in the seventeenth century, especially in the Netherlands and in England. Seventeenth-century scholars, like their medieval predecessors, valued a knowledge of Arabic as a useful adjunct to Hebrew in biblical studies, but with varying degrees of enthusiasm they also pointed out that through Arabic, Persian and Turkish Europeans could gain access to a civilization with considerable literary, philosophical and scientific achievements to its credit. By the eighteenth century the role of the universities as educators of Europe about Asia became a minor one, as merchants, missionaries and travellers produced their accounts, not only of the middle east but of India and China, and as philosophers incorporated such accounts into their speculations. Nevertheless, the European universities continued to produce scholars who were learned in Asian languages apart from Hebrew and whose studies showed some concern for Asian civilizations as worthy of attention for their own sake.

Eighteenth-century Oxford had two endowments for oriental studies in this sense, both of them for Arabic: Archbishop Laud's professorship and that which came to be known as the lord almoner's. The duties of the holder of the Laudian chair were laid down by the archbishop himself in a statute of 2 July 1640. He was to lecture for one hour each week on Wednesdays during vacations. In these lectures he was to expound

---

[1] This chapter has benefited greatly from the suggestions and criticism of Professor P. M. Holt of the School of Oriental and African Studies of London University.

[2] R. W. Southern, *Western Views of Islam in the Middle Ages* (Cambridge Mass. 1962), 72.

the work of an ancient and approved author, explaining points of grammar and showing the similarities of Arabic, Syriac and Hebrew. BAs were to attend until they were eligible to graduate as MAs and those studying medicine until they became BAs. The lecturer or professor was also to offer instruction to those who wished for it on the afternoon of the lecture day, and to act as curator of Laud's Arabic manuscripts. The great Arabist Edward Pococke already held the chair when Laud defined its duties and he continued to do so until his death in 1691. He was then succeeded by Thomas Hyde, who held it until 1703. John Wallis followed Hyde as Laudian professor from 1703 until 1738.[1] Wallis was succeeded by Thomas Hunt, who held the chair until 1774. In that year Joseph White, the last of the eighteenth-century professors, was appointed. White's tenure lasted until 1814.

The origins of the lord almoner's chair are much more obscure.[2] It seems to have grown out of a grant of £100 a year instituted by William III in 1699 for 'some young students in our University of Oxford to be instructed' for 'the service of the Publique in . . . the modern Arabick and Turkish Languages'. Forty pounds were to go to two young men named in the grant and twenty to Thomas Hyde, the then Laudian professor, who was to teach them.[3] The 'public service' was the translation of diplomatic and commercial correspondence with the Levant. Hyde himself had frequently been employed by the government in such work since the reign of Charles II, and ministers clearly hoped that he would train his eventual successors.[4] The endowment was put on a new footing at Anne's accession in 1702. The hundred pounds were now to come from the money allocated for the queen's 'private charities', which was administered by the lord almoner. The declared accounts of the queen's charities indicate that the hundred pounds were disbursed every year until 1707. There was then a break until 1712, when payments were resumed and continued until the accession of George I in 1714, when the hundred pounds began to be distributed in an entirely different way. Payments of fifty pounds were now made directly to what the treasury warrants and declared accounts variously called 'professors' or 'students' of Arabic, one at Oxford and one at Cambridge.[5] There is no further mention of the recipient of the grant at Oxford being under the instruc-

[1] John Wallis (1674-1738), m. Wadham 1691; demy Magd. 1693; Laudian prof. of Arabic 1703-38.
[2] See L. S. Sutherland, 'The origin and early history of the lord almoner's professorship in Arabic at Oxford', *Bodleian Library Record* x (1978-82).
[3] H. Hall, 'The origin of the lord almoner's professorship of Arabic', *The Athenaeum* no. 3238 (16 Nov. 1889), 673.
[4] *Syntagma dissertationum quas olim auctor doctissimus Thomas Hyde...* ed. G. Sharpe (2 vols Oxford 1767), prolegomena, i, p. xxii: J. Vernon-T. Hyde, 20 and 27 Sept. 1698, *Calendar of State Papers, Domestic Series, of the Reign of William and Mary, preserved in the Public Record Office*, ed. J. W. Hardy and E. Bateson (11 vols London 1895-1937) ix. 389, 392.
[5] PRO E/351/2720; AO/1/1922; T/61/21, p. 243; T/52/26, p. 408; AO/1/1924/12; Hall, 674.

tion of the Laudian professor, and in time he came to be known as the lord almoner's professor, although the endowment, still worth fifty pounds, was still being called 'King William's pension' in 1740.[1]

It seems likely that when the hundred pounds were divided between Oxford and Cambridge in 1714 Oxford's share was awarded to Jean Gagnier. Gagnier was a French catholic priest who had spent some years in England and been converted to protestantism. In 1716 he was said to be enjoying a pension worth fifty pounds and a year later he was actually called 'Arabic Professor or Lecturer' by one of his competitors.[2] The earliest surviving almonry records, dating from 1724, leave no doubt that Gagnier was in possession of the endowment by then. He kept it until 1740, when it was obtained by Thomas Hunt, who held it jointly with the Laudian chair until he resigned it in 1748 on becoming a canon of Christ Church. His successor was Richard Browne, who called his office 'in some sort a King's Professor',[3] and held it until 1780. Browne's successor, Henry Ford, saw the century out.

Only fragmentary evidence survives about the teaching offered by the holders of either of the two Arabic chairs in the eighteenth century. What does survive does not seem to suggest that any of the professors was an enthusiastic lecturer or that there was much demand in the university for instruction in oriental languages other than Hebrew. Laud's injunctions about attendance at the Arabic lectures were not observed in the century; proficiency in Arabic was not in fact a requirement for any part of the curriculum. Even so, although there were long periods in which lectures were not given at all, persistent attempts were made to revive them. John Wallis was one of those who did not lecture, but in 1718 John Baron, the vice-chancellor, who had himself sat at the feet of Pococke and Hyde, persuaded him to appoint Gagnier, by this time holder of the almoner's endowment, to deputize for him.[4] The lectures were given on Wednesdays in vacations, as prescribed by Laud.[5] Hunt appears to have done some Arabic lecturing, but by 1763 he had ceased to do so, although 'considerable numbers in the University' were said to attend lectures given by Browne, the lord almoner's professor.[6]

[1] T. Hunt-R. Rawlinson, 16 Nov. 1740, Bodl. MS Rawl. lett. 96, fo 38. In 1748 he again described the endowment as 'a Pension paid by the Lord Almoner call'd King William's pension': same-same (nd but endorsed 24 Oct. 1748), ibid. fo 291.
[2] *Letters on Various Subjects ... to and from William Nicolson*, ed. J. Nichols (2 vols London 1809) ii. 447-8,470.
[3] Browne-Guilford, 12 Mar. 1763, Bodl. MS North d.9, fo 104.
[4] *Ismael abu'l-Feda, De vita, et rebus gestis Muhammedis*, ed. J. Gagnier (Oxford 1723), praefatio, p. 1. Gagnier evidently ceased to be Wallis's deputy in 1723. He was replaced by another deputy who was said to be entirely ignorant of Arabic: W. Stratford-E. Harley, 2 Apr. 1723, HMC *Portland MSS* vii. 354.
[5] A. Bedford-Charlett, 11 Dec. 1719, MS Ballard 34, fo 111.
[6] Hunt-Rawlinson, 16 Nov. 1740, Bodl. MS Rawl. lett. 96, fo 38; Browne-Guilford, 12 Mar. 1763, Bodl. MS North d. 9, fo 103.

Eight years later his Arabic lectures were being heard by a solitary student.[1] White, the Laudian professor, announced a course in 1776, and planned but never delivered an ambitious series on the history of Egypt.[2]

Irregularly given and ill-attended lectures may not be a reliable indicator of the amount of instruction actually imparted. But assessment of Oxford's contribution to oriental studies in the eighteenth century seems to depend much more on the quality of the scholarship of the Arabic professors and of a few others with similar interests than on the vitality of their teaching. Some of the professors clearly failed both as scholars and as teachers. Not only did John Wallis give no lectures for most of his long tenure, but he did nothing to advance knowledge either. Thomas Hearne dismissed him as a man who 'if ever he understood' Arabic 'may be suppos'd now to have forgott it, he having the Character of one that keeps much Company and few Books, intirely neglecting his Studies'.[3] Richard Browne published nothing and was said to have 'little or no taste' and to seem 'in all respects, to be a low, lick-spittle fellow'.[4] But four of those who held Arabic chairs—Hyde, Hunt, White and Gagnier— were active scholars, respected by their contemporaries, as was John Swinton. Finally, the most accomplished English orientalist since Pococke was educated at Oxford and became a fellow of University College. For the first phase of his scholarly career, the period of his translations from and commentaries upon Persian and Arabic literature, William Jones was closely connected with the university and was scrupulous in acknowledging his debts to it.

For much of the century Oxford orientalists worked in the shadow of the great Arabic revival which had begun in the 1630s. In the following decades Pococke became professor, the Press started to publish books using oriental types, and, beginning with that of Laud himself, very large collections of manuscripts were acquired. The continuity between the eighteenth century and the past is very strongly suggested by the inaugural lectures of three of the most creative holders of the Arabic chairs, Hyde, Hunt and White.[5] In these lectures the new professors tried to define the scope of their subject and to defend its continued study at Oxford. Although the lectures were delivered over a period of some eighty years between 1691 and 1776 they are remarkably similar to one another and indeed to a lecture with the same purpose given by Pococke.[6]

---

[1] St John's Muniments, typed transcript of diary of Thomas Fry, 22 Mar. 1771.

[2] J. Wells, *History of Wadham College* (London 1898), 138; p. 560 below.

[3] Hearne, *Collections* ii. 63.

[4] Fry's diary, 22 Mar. 1771.

[5] T. Hyde, 'Oratio de linguae arabicae antiquitate, praestantia et utilitate' (1691) in *Syntagma dissertationum*, ed. Sharpe ii. 451-9; T. Hunt, *De antiquitate, elegantia, utilitate, linguae arabicae, oratio* (Oxford 1739); J. White, *De utilitate linguae arabicae, in studiis theologicis, oratio* (Oxford 1776).

[6] Subsequently printed as the preface to Pococke's edition of *Carmen Tograi, poeta arabis doctissimi* (Oxford 1661).

By training and inclination Hyde, Hunt and White were first and fore-most biblical scholars. All three of them were to combine their Arabic chairs with tenure of the regius professorship of Hebrew. It is therefore hardly surprising that all three laid great stress on the value of Arabic in biblical studies, partly because of the affinity between Arabic and Hebrew, and partly because much important work had been written in Arabic on the Bible by Jewish and eastern Christian commentators.

As Pococke had done, Hyde, Hunt and White also defended the study of Arabic for secular reasons, and the terms they used were very much the same as his. The Arabs had been the custodians of Greek learning at a time when Europe had lain in the deep sleep of barbarism.[1] Hyde and Hunt insisted that the Arabs had also brought much from their own tra-ditions and from other sources to what they had learnt from the Greeks, especially in mathematics, geography, astronomy and medicine.[2] Whether Arab learning was now of more than historical interest and whether it had anything that was still of value to teach the west were matters for debate. Pococke had been prepared to argue that the Arabs had more to teach than to learn, but a much more sceptical view had been expressed by Thomas Smith of Magdalen, when he reported that he had found 'little of ingenious or solid learning' on his travels in the Levant in the 1660s.[3] The kind of scepticism which Edward Gibbon showed when he commented that 'since the sun of science had arisen in the west ... Oriental studies have languished and declined' was domi-nant in the eighteenth century.[4] Astronomy and medicine seem to have been the only branches of Arab learning that continued to arouse any interest. Hyde took Arab astronomy seriously. He believed that the Arabs had been the first to calculate the position of the fixed stars and the tracks of the planets.[5] In 1665 he had published at Oxford the tables of Ulugh Beg with a commentary, which was reprinted in 1767.[6] Hunt believed that medical treatises written in Arabic contained much that was still important.[7] It was on his recommendation that the University Press brought out a Latin text in 1778 of the *De chirurgia* of 'Abulcasis' (al-Zahrawi).[8]

---

[1] White, *De utilitate*, 5.

[2] *Syntagma dissertationum*, ed. Sharpe ii. 456; Hunt, *De antiquitate*, 25-8, 33-8.

[3] *Carmen Tograi*, ed. Pococke; L. Twells, *The Theological Works of the Learned Dr. Pococke* (2 vols London 1740) i. 35, 59. T. Smith, 'Historical observations relating to Constantinople', *Miscellanea curiosa* (3 vols London 1708) iii. 58.

[4] E. Gibbon, *The History of the Decline and Fall of the Roman Empire*, ed. J. B. Bury (7 vols London 1896-1900) vi. 28-9.

[5] *Syntagma dissertationum*, ed. Sharpe ii. 457.

[6] Ibid. i.

[7] Hunt, *De antiquitate*, 38-9.

[8] H. G. Carter, *A History of the Oxford University Press* i (Oxford 1975), 401-2. 'Abulcasis' was an Arab physician who died in 1098.

In advocating the claims of historical material written in Arabic the Oxford professors were on much less contentious ground. Pococke had already made a number of texts available in translation,[1] and the curiosity of so many eighteenth-century intellectuals about the variety of human experience ensured that further histories of the Arabs from their own sources would be eagerly received. The major English contribution of the century to Arabic historiography, Simon Ockley's *History of the Saracens* (1708), was the work of a man who eventually held a chair at Cambridge. But Ockley had gathered most of his material from the Bodleian Library's collection of manuscripts, had been made an MA at Oxford and wrote in his dedication that 'his little Book . . . took its Rise and Original' from Oxford.[2] Hyde, Hunt and White all worked on new editions and translations of Arabic historians, while John Swinton was responsible for some of the essays on the history of Asian peoples in what came to be known as the 'ancient' sections of the *Universal History*.[3] Finally, Hyde and Hunt followed Pococke's example yet again in commending Arabic and Persian poetry to the west. Hyde left in manuscript Latin translations of Saʾadi and Hafiz, while Hunt's inaugural lecture suggests that he had an extensive knowledge of Arabic poetry, including the *Muʿallaqat* and other pre-Islamic survivals.[4] But Asian poetry was not to be presented in a form that made it acceptable to a wider public in England until the appearance in 1772 of William Jones's famous *Poems, consisting chiefly of translations from the Asiatick languages*.[5]

The eighteenth-century professors of Arabic may have been conservative in their perception of their subject and may, as later generations were often to complain, have presented their findings in unappetizing Latin treatises; but for much of the century there were men at Oxford whose learning was certainly not superficial and whose interests, within traditional limits, were not narrow. Hyde was perhaps the most wide-ranging of all. He was a richly eccentric personality about whom many anecdotes have survived, varying from Humphrey Prideaux's tale of his having been beaten by his wife to Hearne's account of his having preached for an hour and a half without his audience hearing a word, he being so 'wonderfull slow of speech and his delivery so very low'.[6]

---

[1] See P. M. Holt, 'The study of Arabic historians in seventeenth-century England: the background and the work of Edward Pococke', *Bull. School of Oriental and African Studies* xix (1957).

[2] S. Ockley, *The History of the Saracens* (2 vols London 1708, 1718, vol. i entitled *The Conquest of Syria, Persia, and Aegypt, by the Saracens*) ii, p. iii.

[3] For the *Universal History* see pp. 560-1 below.

[4] On Hyde's translations see R. W. Ferrier, 'Anglo-Persian relations in the seventeenth century' (Cambridge Ph.D. thesis 1970), 435; for Hunt see his *De antiquitate*, 15.

[5] See pp. 562-3 below.

[6] *Letters of Humphrey Prideaux, sometime Dean of Norwich, to John Ellis, sometime Under-Secretary of State, 1674-1722*, ed. E. M. Thompson (Camden Soc. new ser. xv 1875), 46; Hearne, *Collections* xi. 368-9.

Hyde was something of an oriental polymath. He had a fine knowledge of Persian, having worked when young on the Persian sections of the polyglot Bible, but he was also an insatiable collector of at least a smattering of other languages. He bombarded the Levant Company, the East India Company and individual merchants with requests for books and manuscripts. He helped to publish a Malay dictionary. He possessed vocabularies of 'two of the languages of Tartary . . . that of the Ouzbek Tartars about the great city Samarcand and that of the Tartars above the China wall who now govern China', as well as a 'Singala vocabulary' from Ceylon. He had been given 'the numbers and a parcell of other words in the Numidian language of Africa' and an 'alphabet of the Chaldaens about Bassora and thereabouts towards the Persian Gulph'. He was interested in India and Hinduism, trying to distinguish the various fragments in Indian languages which came his way. Unusually for a British orientalist, Hyde showed some awareness of the great discoveries about China that were beginning to be debated on the continent, and he tried to make some contribution to them. He brought to Oxford a Chinese Christian, whom he called Michael Shin Fo Sung, closely interrogated him in Latin and compiled a book of *varia chinesia* from what he learnt.[1] He was interested in astronomy, botany, eastern games,[2] sea monsters and mermaids.

This multifarious activity did not prevent Hyde from producing one long and very important book, his *Historia religionis veterum Persarum*, now recognized to have been a major contribution to western understanding of Zoroastrianism.[3] A number of seventeenth-century travellers had reported that the Parsis of western India claimed descent from the ancient Persians. Hyde applied himself with great tenacity to the task of obtaining Parsi scriptures and translating them. Even after his book had been published he was still trying to get more texts from Surat 'by a little bribing one of their Priests with a little money, and telling him its for me who is a great lover of their Religion'.[4] To modern scholars Hyde seems greatly to have overestimated the age and authority of his two most important Parsi sources, the *Zaratusht Nameh* and the *Sa'dar*, but his version of Zoroastrianism was a very great advance on previous European accounts which had relied almost exclusively on Greek tradition.[5] It was

[1] Hyde's curiosity about language is very vividly brought out in his letters to the East Indian merchant Thomas Bowrey in the period 1700-2 and to Humfrey Wanley in 1699: London, India Office Library and Records, MS Eur. E. 192; BL MS Harley 3781.

[2] 'In the same manner as another Gentleman went to Dr Thomas Hyde, the famous Orientalist, to be directed in the Game of Chess. The Dr told him he knew nothing of it, notwithstanding he had writ a Book about this Game, as he had about other Oriental Games.' Hearne, *Collections* vi. 197. See also D. Patterson, 'Hebrew Studies', p. 537 n. 4 above.

[3] T. Hyde, *Historia religionis veterum Persarum* (Oxford 1700).

[4] Hyde-Bowrey, 13 Apr. 1701, India Office Lib. MS Eur. E. 192, no. 15.

[5] J. Duchesne-Guillemin, *The Western Response to Zoroaster* (Oxford 1958).

only to be superseded in the 1760s when the French traveller Anquetil Duperron began his deciphering of Avestan.

Hyde's *Historia* is a long sprawling book, written in what was regarded as indifferent Latin. Hyde was warned to prepare himself for the 'obloquy the men of phantasy and the young fry of wits and poets may ever endeavour to cast upon your Book', which attracted few subscriptions. Members of the Royal Society when canvassed were said to show little interest in a work 'not so agreeable to the studies of experimental philosophy, mathematicks and natural history which they are pursuing'.[1] Hyde was so discouraged by the reception of his book that he abandoned his projected translation of what he called 'the works of Zoroaster'. After his death, however, his work gained greatly in esteem. Copies of his book were 'mightily bought up in Holland and other parts of Germany', and it was a Dutch professor who referred to Hyde as *stupor mundi*.[2] Various attempts were made to reissue his book and to publish his essays and manuscript papers in a collected edition. The *Historia religionis veterum Persarum* finally reappeared in 1760, selling much more briskly than the original edition had done, and the collected papers were published in 1767 in two volumes.[3]

Zoroastrian studies made little progress at Oxford after Hyde's death. A copy of the *Vendidad* was acquired from India, but it remained undeciphered.[4] In 1762 Oxford's ignorance of ancient Persia was exposed by the arrival of the precocious Anquetil Duperron fresh from his remarkable linguistic triumphs in the east. Thomas Hunt, who regarded visits by foreigners 'that travel hither out of curiosity, or for their improvement' as 'a compliment to us',[5] must quickly have discovered that he was receiving a young foreigner who intended to improve Oxford rather than be improved by it. In his *Zend-Avesta, ouvrage de Zoroastre* Duperron gloated over the confusion in which he had found the oriental manuscripts kept in the Bodleian Library, over the misapprehensions about the age of Hyde's sources and over the lack of knowledge of any ancient Persian script.[6] Duperron's discourtesy provoked the young William Jones to publish what contemporaries regarded as a crushing retort, but what has now come to be seen as a thoroughly ill-judged attempt to ridicule and deny the importance of Duperron's discoveries.[7]

Hyde's successor in the Laudian chair, John Wallis, was a man of no

[1] Correspondence of Hyde and T. Smith, *Syntagma dissertationum*, ed. Sharpe ii. 488–93.
[2] Hearne, *Collections* i. 295.
[3] Carter, *History of the Press* i. 390; *Syntagma dissertationum*, ed. Sharpe.
[4] See *The Zend-Avesta*, ed. J. Darmesteter (3 vols Oxford 1800–7), i, p. xiv.
[5] Letter to G. Sharpe, 11 Aug. 1755, Bodl. MS Eng. lett. d. 146, fo 124.
[6] A. H. A. Duperron, *Zend-Avesta, ouvrage de Zoroastre* (3 vols Paris 1771) i. pp. cccclx–i.
[7] 'Lettre à Monsieur A*** du P***', *The Works of Sir William Jones*, ed. A. M. Jones (6 vols London 1799) iv. 583.

account, but he was followed in 1738 by Thomas Hunt, universally recognized to be a deeply learned, if largely unproductive, scholar. In a long tenure of both the Arabic and the Hebrew chairs Hunt's only publications were his inaugural lecture and another lecture entitled *De usu dialectorum orientalium ac praecipue arabicae, in hebraico codice interpretando* (Oxford 1748). His *Observations on Several Passages in the Book of Proverbs* appeared after his death, edited by Benjamin Kennicott and published at Oxford in 1775. Kennicott commented in his preface that Hunt was 'remarkably timorous, and distrustful of his own judgement', growing 'more and more fearful of the severity of Public Criticism'. It was Hunt's views on the relative antiquity of eastern languages which exposed him to criticism. Hunt regarded Arabic and Hebrew as 'sister' languages, both descended from a common 'oriental' original.[1] There was, however, a vociferous school of thought that believed that such claims merely served 'to exalt the *Arabic* Tongue, and no less to depress and degrade the *Hebrew*', and that attempts 'to explain the *Divine Volume* by the Language of the *Alcoran*' should be given short shrift.[2] Had Hunt possessed the necessary resolution, energy or soundness of health to see his projects to completion, he would have produced an Arabic grammar and an edition of the description of Egypt written at the end of the twelfth or the beginning of the thirteenth century by Abd al-Latif of Baghdad, for which he had collected a great quantity of material and issued an elaborate prospectus.[3] In spite of his lack of published work, the range of sources quoted in the inaugural lecture suggest very great learning and there are many acknowledgements of his generosity in making this available to other scholars.

An edition of Abd al-Latif, which had attracted many scholars since Pococke, was finally completed by Joseph White, Hunt's successor in the Laudian chair, and eventually published in 1800.[4] Son of a journeyman weaver, White 'united a degree of roughness with great simplicity of manners' and little of 'what is called knowledge of the world'.[5] He gained some notoriety through a scandal connected with his Bampton lectures, in the composition of which, it was later disclosed, he had received help for which he had made no public acknowledgement. But he was an accomplished and versatile scholar. Although his most notable work

[1] Hunt, *De antiquitate*, 3–4; Hunt, *De usu dialectorum*, 2.

[2] B. Holloway, *The Primaevity and Preeminence of the Sacred Hebrew … vindicated from the repeated attempts of the Reverend Dr Hunt to level it with the Arabic, and other oriental dialects* (Oxford 1754), 3.

[3] For the Arabic grammar see J. Williams–G. Sharpe [Aug. 1750], Bodl. MS Eng. lett. d. 145, fo 16. Thirty copies were printed 'for private use': Hunt–Rawlinson, 19 Mar. 1750, Bodl. MS Rawl. lett. 96, fo 310. Hunt's prospectus was entitled *Proposals for Printing by Subscription, Abdollatiphi historiae Ægypti compendium* (Oxford 1746).

[4] *Abdollatiphi historiae Ægypti compendium*, ed. J. White (Oxford 1800).

[5] *Illustrations of the Literary History of the Eighteenth Century*, ed. J. Nichols (8 vols London 1817–58) iv. 858–65.

was on the Bible, especially an edition of a Syriac New Testament,[1] he had wide interests in the languages and civilizations of the near east. His edition of Abd al-Latif was intended to be the precursor of an ambitious 'General History of Egypt' in two volumes, which would make its first appearance in the form of lectures for which a fee of one guinea would be charged, making the project 'uncommonly lucrative'.[2] He also collaborated with Major William Davy of the East India Company's army in an edition, published at Oxford in 1783, of *The Institutes Political and Military ... by the Great Timour* from a Persian text.

Of those who held the lord almoner's endowment on its own, the first, Jean Gagnier, was the most distinguished. He too moved to other oriental languages from Hebrew and the Bible. Contemporary opinions on him as an Arabist varied. After calling him 'a man of a steddy Head and great Industry', Hearne came to believe that he was 'a very mean piddling Author' and it was said of him that he 'does not understand Arabick, notwithstanding his great pretenses to it'.[3] But Humphrey Prideaux, by no means a mild critic, thought him 'well skilled in this sort of learning'.[4] Gagnier devoted much of his career to the works of Abu'l-Fida, the Syrian prince who wrote in the early fourteenth century. He made a significant contribution to western attempts to portray Muhammad in a relatively objective way as a historical figure in his *De vita et rebus gestis Muhammedis*, a part of Abu'l-Fida's universal history, which was the basis for his more accessible two-volume life of Muhammad.[5] At the very end of his life Gagnier brought out a Latin translation of Abu'l-Fida's geography, on which he had worked for many years.[6]

The 'erudition' of John Swinton was said to be 'so well known' as to need no comment by those who were proposing to publish a new Persian dictionary.[7] In a note in his hand which passed to Dr Johnson, Swinton claimed authorship of a string of articles which appeared in the last of the seven volumes of the 'ancient' part of *An Universal History from the Earliest Account of Time to the Present* (London 1736-44) and in a volume of *Additions to the Universal History* (London 1750).[8] Some of the articles, on 'The Turks, Tartars and Moguls', 'The Indians', 'The Chinese', together with a 'Dissertation on the independency of the Arabs', are on Asian subjects. They are not, however, remarkable either for their range

[1] *Sacrorum evangeliorum versio syriaca philoxeniana*, ed. J. White (2 vols Oxford 1778).
[2] *A Statement of Dr. White's Literary Obligations to the late Rev. Mr. Samuel Badcock and the Rev. Samuel Parr* (Oxford 1790), 64-5.
[3] Hearne, *Collections* i. 206.
[4] Prideaux-F. Gwynne, 5 Feb. 1722, HMC *Leyborne-Popham MSS* 256.
[5] J. Gagnier, *La Vie de Mahomet* (2 vols Amsterdam 1731).
[6] Abu'l-Fida, *Descriptio peninsulae Arabum*, ed. J. Gagnier (Oxford 1740); cf Carter, *History of the Press* i. 519.
[7] India Office Lib. MS Eur. G. 37, box 17, no. 66, proposals for printing a Persian dictionary.
[8] *Gentleman's Magazine* liv (1784), 892.

of sources, depth of knowledge, or sophistication of approach. The 'Dissertation on the Arabs' seems to have been intended as a tilt at 'free thinkers and infidels of all descriptions' by showing that the statement in Genesis that Ishmael, progenitor of the Arabs, was 'a wild man' had been proved true by subsequent history and therefore that Moses was 'an inspired writer'.[1]

With the obvious exception of Hyde's work on the ancient Persians, oriental scholarship at Oxford throughout the eighteenth century had been largely concerned with elaborating themes and material explored by Pococke and his contemporaries. But from the 1750s changes were beginning that were in time to bring about the most striking development in British oriental studies since Laud took up the patronage of Arabic. The main focus of British interest in Asia was shifting from Aleppo, Smyrna and the Levant Company to Calcutta, Bombay and the East India Company. For two or three decades, largely because of intractable linguistic problems, this shift of emphasis in Asia stimulated a new slant on Islamic studies rather than bringing British scholars into contact with Hindu India. In particular it produced a heightened interest in Persian, the diplomatic and administrative language of Mughal India and the language of cultured Indian Muslims. A number of East India Company servants came home with some knowledge of Persian, and sometimes with manuscript collections.

The university's response to the new interest in Persian was less than whole-hearted. In the late 1760s Warren Hastings tried to raise endowments to found a chair of Persian. Although an attractively worded prospectus was printed, the project failed to win support and was dropped.[2] A proposal to publish a Persian dictionary, based on the famous *Thesaurus* of oriental languages of Meninski (published at Vienna in 1680) and specifically intended for use in India, also received little support. The proposers reflected that 'Perhaps there never was at Oxford at any one time so many gentlemen capable of giving assistance in such a work'.[3] In the event, however, the dictionary was finally completed and published in two volumes in 1776 and 1780, virtually singlehanded by John Richardson, one of the proposers, a feat for which the university awarded him an MA by diploma.[4]

[1] *Additions to the Universal History*, 261-2, 289. 'The history of the Arabs' in vol. i and part of vol. ii of the *Modern Part of the Universal History from the Earliest Account of Time* (44 vols London 1759-66), which appeared in 1759, is much more impressive. Its author had mastered a great many Arabic manuscripts. He shows himself to have been a rigidly orthodox Christian, criticizing George Sale and Gagnier for excessive tolerance towards Islam. It is possible that this too was the work of Swinton.

[2] *A Proposal for Establishing a Professorship of the Persian language in the University of Oxford* (np nd). For further details of the project see P. J. Marshall, 'Warren Hastings as scholar and patron' in A. Whiteman, J. S. Bromley and P. G. M. Dickson (eds), *Statesmen, Scholars and Merchants* (Oxford 1973), 245-6.

[3] India Office Lib., MS Eur. G. 37, box 17, no. 66, proposals for printing a Persian dictionary.

[4] For the dictionary see J. Richardson, *A Dissertation on the Languages, Literature, and Manners of*

Richardson, a Scot, was one of a younger generation of scholars who believed that oriental learning must be directed to a wider public by relating it to contemporary interest in India and Persia and by presenting it in a form that would appeal to men of taste. He condemned 'editors and commentators' who marred 'instruction or entertainment' by 'an unnecessary display of learning', presenting their 'Latin versions without elegance'.[1] These were precisely the views of William Jones. The study of Persian, he wrote, had been 'checked in its progress by the learned themselves' with their 'minute researches of verbal criticism'.[2] He was even prepared to commit the sacrilege of including Pococke in a list of worthies, in whom one would find 'beaucoup d'érudition, mais, peut-être, un peu trop d'étalage'.[3] But he himself would be different. 'All my thought and feelings are concentrated on anything sensitive and delicate in the fine arts ... any thing that is sublime or charming in painting or poetry'.[4] He would write as a critic, not as a philologer, as a poet in his own right, not as a mere translator.[5] In his treatment of Arabic and Persian poetry, he would follow the example of Robert Lowth, who had directed his Lectures on the Sacred Poetry of the Hebrews not to 'the student of theology' but to 'the youth who is addicted to the politer sciences, and studious of the elegancies of composition'.[6] In short, he would incorporate Asian literature into the stock of polite learning.

Jones's career as an orientalist falls into two more or less separate halves. For some eight years, between 1766 and 1774, while he was actually at Oxford or closely connected with the university, he worked on a series of literary studies and translations of Arabic and Persian. From 1774 to 1783 he had little time for scholarship in a legal career interrupted by occasional forays into politics. But from 1784, when he arrived in Calcutta as a judge of the supreme court, he became an orientalist once again and produced his famous essays on Hindu India and Sanskrit.

When Jones had entered University College in 1764 he was already regarded as something of a prodigy of learning and taste. He took up Arabic and Persian and mastered both in a relatively short space of time. His first translation appeared in 1770, a version of a Persian history of

Eastern Nations (Oxford 1777, 2nd edn Oxford 1778), 490. The dissertation had first appeared prefixed to the first volume of Richardson's Dictionary, Persian, Arabic and English (2 vols Oxford 1777, 1780). John Richardson (1741-c1811), m. Wadham 1775; MA by diploma 1780.

[1] J. Richardson, A Grammar of the Arabick Language (London 1776), p. viii.
[2] 'A grammar of the Persian language', Works of William Jones, ed. Jones ii. 122.
[3] 'Dissertation sur la littérature orientale', ibid. v. 512n.
[4] Jones-C. Reviczky, 29 Jan. 1770, The Letters of Sir William Jones, ed. G. H. Cannon (2 vols Oxford 1970) i. 45.
[5] 'Poeseos asiaticae commentariorum libri sex', Works of William Jones, ed. Jones ii. 336.
[6] R. Lowth, De sacra poesi Hebraeorum (Oxford 1753), trans. G. Gregory as Lectures on the Sacred Poetry of the Hebrews (2 vols London 1787) i. 51.

the usurper Nadir Shah, done to fulfil a commission given to him by the king of Denmark.[1] An essay on poetry was appended to the translation. In 1771 he published a Persian grammar with various literary dissertations and some specimens of translated verse. His most famous early publication, *Poems, consisting chiefly of translations from the Asiatick languages*, appeared at Oxford in the following year. It included the much anthologized 'Persian song of Hafiz' with its invocation of 'all Bocara's vaunted gold' and 'all the gems of Samarcand'. In 1774 Jones brought out his Latin commentaries on the poetry of Asia, which at the time he believed would be his last work of oriental scholarship.

Jones considered that persons of taste and discrimination could enjoy oriental poetry because they would find in it much that was familiar and recognizable, as well as much that was strange. He presented his translations in strictly metred rhyming verse and stressed the parallels and similarities between Asian and European poetry. He described the *Shāh-nāmeh*, for instance, as written in 'the spirit of our Dryden and the sweetness of Pope'.[2] But within a familiar frame the reader would encounter new and exotic images. 'It has always been remarked, that the *Asiaticks* excel the inhabitants of our colder regions in the liveliness of their fancy, and the richness of their invention.'[3] Jones was sure that his contemporaries would respond to such liveliness and richness if it were presented to them in a palatable form, and the reception of his translations by critics was in general favourable. They were praised for their 'elegance and vivacity' as well as their 'correctness and simplicity'.[4]

University opinion seems to have taken pride in the reputation which Jones won for himself, but there is little to suggest that his example had a potent effect on oriental studies at Oxford. The orthodoxies continued to be practised until well into the nineteenth century. But in a longer perspective Jones's career did help to bring about profound changes. His work on Sanskrit in Calcutta, as later refined in France and Germany, was one of the elements in the great transformation of European oriental scholarship which was eventually to transform Oxford as well.

---

[1] The translation originally appeared in French in 1770. An English version was published as *The History of the Life of Nader Shah* (London 1773).
[2] 'Grammar of the Persian language', *Works of William Jones*, ed. Jones ii. 313.
[3] 'An essay on the poetry of the eastern nations', ibid. iv. 533.
[4] *Critical Review* xxxii (1772), 247; *Monthly Review* xlvi (1772), 511.

20

Schoolmen, Logic and Philosophy

J. YOLTON

IN THE Oxford curriculum there was not a subject called 'philosophy'.[1] Students read ethics or metaphysics, not philosophy. They also studied divinity or theology and such sciences as physics, physiology and anatomy. The term 'science' covered any body of knowledge. Locke spoke, for example, of 'natural philosophy and all the other sciences', or of 'divinity, ethics, law, politics and other sciences'. He also contrasted experimental science with a perfect science of natural bodies. The latter was the notion of a demonstrative or deductive knowledge of nature, based on some few first principles. The former was Locke's reference to natural philosophy, that is science in our sense: physics, physiology, anatomy and so on. The term 'philosophy' referred to the ancients—Aristotle, Plato, the Stoics, Epicureans—and also to the scholastics and to modern writers. Questions Locke identified with 'philosophy' included: are body and extension the same?; can matter be made to think?; how are qualities related to substances?; what role in knowledge can identical propositions play? Other issues discussed by Locke and Descartes fall under this use of 'philosophy': is matter passive or inert?; what are the essential properties of matter?; how do bodies act on mind? (and vice versa); must the soul be immaterial?; is the will free?

In looking for philosophy in the Oxford curriculum, we should keep in mind that these and other issues which we recognize as philosophical topics are found, in the seventeenth and eighteenth centuries, just as easily in lectures and books on theology, physics or medicine as they are in the writings of Locke, Berkeley or Hume. Philosophical issues cut across all the 'sciences'; books which we categorize as 'philosophy' usually attended to issues in other areas of knowledge as well. Even when problems about the nature and extent of knowledge were in question, the contemporary debates in religion or in science are clearly discernible in, and often integral to, the writings of Locke, Berkeley and Hume.

[1] I am indebted to the late Gilbert Ryle for his extensive and detailed comments on an earlier version of this chapter. His interest and advice in this project have been most helpful. The help and guidance of the late Dame Lucy Sutherland have also been instrumental in bringing the chapter to its final form.

In the eighteenth century logic became the focus for many of the philosophical issues, especially those concerned with knowledge and understanding. The traditional logics, the standard manuals of logic, were still very much in use at Oxford; but there were certain changes, both in the attitudes towards the subject and in the nature of logics written in the century, which made its study something more than just a methodological tool, even though that was its stated purpose. The role of Locke's *Essay concerning Human Understanding* in these changes, as well as in eighteenth-century British philosophy in general, was fundamental.[1]

The role of logic in the university's curriculum was mainly as a method to be used in the disputations, the form of examination which was still prescribed but which came under increasing criticism. The student who could find value in the disputations was rare. We are told that Shelley took very kindly to logic and felt a keen interest in it.[2]

Jeremy Bentham also seems to have enjoyed his role in the disputations:

I have disputed too in the Hall once and am going in again tomorrow, there also I came off with Honour, having fairly beat off not my proper Antagonist but the Moderator himself: for he was forced to supply my Antagonist with Arguments, the Invalidity of which I clearly demonstrated ... I am sorry that it does not come to my turn to dispute every disputation day, for, for my part, I desire no better sport.[3]

It was not until the following year that he moved from disputing in the college hall to disputing in the schools. On Friday:

I went up for the first time as Respondent, since which I have been up twice as Opponent, this day for the 3d. time, and on the 24th shall go up again as Respondent. It is very uncomfortable work, as we stay an hour and a half or more in the Cold.[4]

He added at the end of this same letter, 'I find the answering under Batchelor to be very easy, as 2 out of 3 times no Proctor came into the School'. George Fleming wrote somewhat earlier (1689) about his studies in logic without complaints. In fact he seems to have read rather more than his tutor suggested, which is unlikely if he found the logics (they were the standard school logics of the seventeenth century) distasteful.[5]

In 1729 a tutor at Queen's writing to the father of one of his pupils

[1] J. Locke, *An Essay concerning Human Understanding* (London 1690).
[2] *Reminiscences of Oxford*, 278-9.
[3] Letter to his father, 30 June 1761, *The Correspondence of Jeremy Bentham*, ed. T. L. S. Sprigge *et al.* (London and Oxford 1968 onward) i. 49-50; see also L. S. Sutherland, 'The curriculum', p. 475 above.
[4] Bentham to his father, *Correspondence of Bentham*, ed. Sprigge i. 59, 60.
[5] 'At my first arrival my chief studies was Logick, for the obtaining of which my Tutor read unto

reported that his son was to begin his studies in logic, 'in company of some few others of about the same standing', and later that he was 'busy about the rules for Syllogism which he allready finds are not so mysterious as He apprehended them to be'.[1] Late in the century John James wrote to his father: 'I have conquered the logic Compend, and got over the threshold of the Temple of Aristotle. Logic seems a kind of free masonry. It is mysterious, dark, and apparently impenetrable: but the mystery consists in its being unknown.'[2]

Of course, studying logic was not the same as disputing, but the usual complaints were directed against both. It became very popular to ridicule and satirize them, but especially the disputations. Sidney Graves Hamilton remarked on the farcical nature of these public exercises, citing a letter from one student who could not even remember doing his 'quodlibets'.[3] Vicesimus Knox talked of the disputations not being taken seriously. Arguments were in fact handed down from generation to generation 'on long slips of paper, and consist of foolish syllogisms on foolish subjects'.[4] Knox took his BA in 1775, so this attitude was still current later in the century.[5]

John James queried the value of the logics also: 'What the definitions I have learnt may do for me I am not able to judge. They will assist me in a verbal engagement in the hall I doubt not, but such knowledge is at best superficial.'[6] Nicholas Amhurst (briefly at St John's in 1716, then expelled) talked of the 'art of Chopping logic', saying it was 'the easiest art in the world; for it requires neither natural parts, nor acquired learning, to make any one a compleat master of it; a good memory is the only one thing necessary'.[7] He confirmed the existence of 'strings',

me Sanderson's and Du Treus Logicks, over and aboue [*sic*] which I myself read Aristotles Organon, and Chrackanthorps Logick with others of the same subject.' G. Fleming–D. Fleming, 4 May 1689, *The Flemings in Oxford* ii. 251-2. Jeremy Bentham did not begin logic until his second term. Writing to his father on 15 February 1761 he says 'I expect to begin Logic tomorrow with 4 more of us'. In November 1760 he had reported that 'Mr Jefferson [his tutor] does not intend beginning with me in Logic yet awhile': *Correspondence of Bentham*, ed. Sprigge i. 35, 21.

[1] J. Steadman–J. Smith, 22 May 1729, and nd (endorsed 1730), Queens, MS 482, fos 150, 151.
[2] *Letters of Radcliffe and James*, 55, letter xxii (nd).
[3] *Collectanea* iii. 313.   [4] *Reminiscences of Oxford*, 161-2.
[5] Cox said that in 1799 such was still the practice. The examination for the BA 'had dwindled into a formal repetition of threadbare "Questions and Answers" (in Divinity, Logic, Grammar, "et in omni scibili") which had been transmitted in manuscript from man to man, and were unblushingly admitted, if not adopted, even by "The Masters of the Schools" '. Cox also reported being asked by a divinity student to 'supply him with a Latin *Epigram* ... to fit on to his old "*strings*" '. G. V. Cox, *Recollections of Oxford* (London 1868, 2nd edn London 1870), 38-9 and note.
[6] *Letters of Radcliffe and James*, 55.
[7] *Reminiscences of Oxford*, 72. There is some ambiguity surrounding Amhurst's expulsion from St John's. He said it was for his whig views; others suggested it was, as the *DNB* biographer wrote, for 'his libertinism and misconduct'. Amhurst went on to an active literary career, the Oxford expulsion never far from criticism and lampoon in his poems and journals. The series of periodical papers *Terrae-Filius* (52 nos. London Jan.-July 1721) gives his version of life at Oxford.

answer-books for arguments. Amhurst also remarked that the 'opponent' in these exercises usually lost because he was on the wrong side of the question, although 'oftentimes that side is palpably the right side, according to our modern philosophy and discoveries'. It is worth noting that Amhurst did at least know what the modern philosophy taught, although he later complained about the 'unedifying questions in logic, metaphysics, and school divinity'.[1] Even as late as 1764 William Jones complained 'that he was required to attend dull comments on artificial ethics, and logic detailed in such barbarous Latin, that he professed to know as little of it as he then knew of Arabic'.[2]

The school logic and the way it was used in disputations was also the subject of satire and ridicule outside the university. The *Spectator* of 16 August 1711 carried a letter in which coffee-house debaters were said to use the method of the schools to 'prove Matters which no Body living denies', or to wager bets and then debate on any claim, whether true or false. A later number, for 4 December 1711, detailed various methods of arguing or convincing. The writer remarked that 'The Universities of Europe, for many Years, carried on their Debates by Syllogism', and they 'cut and minced into almost an Infinitude of Distinctions'. This writer then said:

When our Universities found that there was no End of wrangling this way, they invented a kind of Argument, which is not reducible to any Mood or Figure in *Aristotle*. It was called the *Argumentum Basilinum* (others write it *Bacilinum* or *Baculinum*) which is pretty well expressed in our *English* Word Club-Law. When they were not able to confute their Antagonist, they knock'd him down. It was their Method in these Polemical Debates first to discharge their Syllogisms, and afterwards to betake themselves to their Clubs, till such time as they had one way or other confounded their Gainsayers. There is in *Oxford* a narrow Defile, (to make use of a Military Term) where the Partisans used to Encounter, for which Reason it still retains the Name of *Logic Lane*. I have heard an old Gentleman, a Physician, make his Boasts, that when he was a young Fellow he marched several times at the Head of a Troop of *Scotists*, and Cudgell'd a Body of *Smiglesians* half the length of *High-Street*.[3]

A war of differing logics, a different sort of battle of the books!

A sober and trustworthy critic of the method of disputation was John Napleton. In 1773 he prepared a critical report of this method of examina-

[1] *Reminiscences of Oxford*, 73, 91.
[2] *Memoirs of the Life, Writings and Correspondence of Sir William Jones*, ed. Lord Teignmouth (London, 1804), 31.
[3] *The Spectator*, ed. D. F. Bond (5 vols Oxford 1965) ii. 71, 429. Duns Scotus influenced a number of the logics in use at Oxford in the seventeenth century. The references to 'Smiglesians' is to those who followed Marcin Smiglecki's *Logica selectis disputationibus et quaestionibus illustrata* (Ingolstadt 1618, Oxford 1634). The *Spectator*'s account may be more accurate than satire for the seventeenth century, for there were team debates which did end in physical fights. Logic Lane of course still exists.

tion, making suggestions for changes. Napleton, who also wrote a logic, confirms that even as late as 1773 the subject-matter of the disputations *in parviso*, and frequently the general discussions themselves, 'are trite and uninteresting'. Even the questions used in the 'determination', the formal process for BAs to conclude their course and begin that of the MA, were lightweight and unimportant, 'the arguments arising out of them are consequently still more so'; they are long and tedious and 'become languid, uninstructive, and uninteresting'. The 'quodlibets' were a mere lifeless form, given to an empty room. The schools were 'solitary and unfrequented'. Nevertheless, with certain changes, Napleton thought that the logical disputations could teach the student to think clearly and with order and precision.[1]

Isaac Watts, whose logic of 1741 began to be used around mid-century in the Oxford curriculum, also had criticisms of the disputations, as well as recommendations for improvements. He put some of the blame on to the logics then in use: 'the greatest Part of Writers on that Subject have turned it into a Composition of hard Words, Trifles and Subtilities for the meer Use of the Schools, and that only to amuse the Minds and the Ears of men with empty Sounds.'[2] The author of several other eighteenth-century logics, Edward Bentham, did not reject everything in the older scholastic logics, but he did remark that those logics were 'generally suited to the taste of the time' and hence

when Scholastick Learning was most in vogue, all the treatises on this subject borrowed from thence a very disagreeable cast: And though the method of writing was strict and close, yet the matter of the observations was generally jejune and insipid; the language was harsh and overcharged with abstruse subtleties, many of them useless as well as unpleasing.[3]

In his *Introduction to Logick* Bentham was more critical and dismissive: the 'old Scholastick form of Logick was disgusting, and the matter of it unsatisfactory'.[4] Sanderson's logic, Bentham suggested, 'remains a monument

[1] [J. Napleton,] *Considerations on the Public Exercises for the First and Second Degrees in the University of Oxford* [Oxford] 1773). Napleton's *Elementa logicae* (Oxford 1770) is not a logic that one hears about or finds cited. It is essentially Aristotelian, but it shows a number of influences of the more modern, eighteenth-century logics, Locke's among them. See also V. H. H. Green, 'Reformers and reform in the university', pp. 615-18 below.
[2] I. Watts, *The Improvement of the Mind: or a supplement to the art of logick* (London 1741), 4.
[3] E. Bentham, *Reflexions upon Logick* (2nd edn Oxford 1755), 5. A similar but slightly different remark is found in the 1st edition of this logic: *Reflections upon the Nature and Usefulness of Logick* (Oxford 1740), 6. In an English translation of *Monitor monitori* Bentham is described as:
Half a Casuist, half Lawyer, half Courtier,
Half Cit,
Half a Tory, half Whig (may I add, half a Wit?).
D. Greenwood, *William King, Tory and Jacobite* (Oxford 1969), 189.
[4] E. Bentham, *An Introduction to Logick* (Oxford 1773), preface, p. i.

of his Industry and Judgment', suited 'to the Age in which it was compiled'. Aldrich's logic was also antiquated.[1]

While changes to the curriculum were being suggested, Bentham tells us that he was using his logic, citing very recent authors in a variety of subjects, in his tutorials at Oriel. To what extent the new eighteenth-century British logics were used at Oxford is a question on which we will have to hazard a guess later in this chapter. But before doing so, it is useful to remind ourselves of Locke's extended attack upon the old school logic and philosophy.

Locke's influence on eighteenth-century thought was enormous. Even some of his doctrines which were most strongly opposed by many writers found their way into an extensive range of literature over the century. Lockean ideas, terminology, and examples were everywhere. A number of the topics in disputation questions used at Oxford were taken from Locke or from issues which he raised and which were debated in the eighteenth century. His influence on the new logics was direct and extensive. It is probable that his thorough criticism and rejection of syllogistic logic was instrumental in the logics of Watts, Bentham and Duncan,[2] gradually replacing those of Sanderson, Aldrich and Wallis (to cite just a few of the older logics, themselves modelled on somewhat earlier seventeenth- and later sixteenth-century works). Locke's *Essay* and his *Conduct of the Understanding*, published after his death,[3] also appeared on some reading lists. Both works were considered to be contributions to logic by the eighteenth-century philosophers.

His criticism of the old logics centred on three points: they insisted that all knowledge must be derived from basic principles; the formal nature of the syllogism presupposed, and rested upon, a natural logic or ability all men had to reason; and disputations were only good for stopping the mouths of wranglers. These three objections amounted to saying artificial logic was not useful for the discovery of truth, was not a logic of discovery. Whenever he talked about the abuse of language 'the learned gibberish of the Schools' came in for its share of blame: their talk of genera and species, their invention of terms which designated nothing were examples of 'that eminent trifling in the Schools', or of 'the useless Imagination of the Schools', or of the 'empty unintelligible noise and jargon'.[4]

[1] Bentham, *An Introduction to Logick*, preface, p. ii. The second edition of Robert Sanderson's *Logicae artis compendium* (Oxford 1615) was printed at Oxford in 1618. Henry Aldrich's *Artis logicae compendium* (Oxford 1691) was extensively used at Christ Church.

[2] W. Duncan, *The Elements of Logick* (London 1748); see also pp. 576-7 below.

[3] In *Posthumous Works of Mr. John Locke* (London 1706); it was published separately in 1741.

[4] Locke, *Essay*, 3.4.8; 3.10.4. These numbers refer respectively to the book, chapter and sections, as given in P. H. Nidditch's edition (Oxford 1975).

Besides the misuse of language, the schoolmen and their logic made a false start by insisting that 'all Reasonings are *ex praecognitis, et praeconcessis*'.[1] The principles from which they reasoned were trifling and tautologous: 'it is impossible for the same thing to be and not to be', 'the whole is equal to all its parts', 'what is, is' and so on. Genuine knowledge for Locke started from truths established by experience and observation, the method of the scientists of the Royal Society, of which Locke was a member from 1668:

the beaten Road of the Schools has been, to lay down in the beginning one or more general Propositions, as Foundations whereon to build the Knowledge that was to be had of that Subject. These Doctrines thus laid down for Foundations of any Science, were called *Principles*, as the beginnings from which we must set out and look no farther backwards in our Enquiries.[2]

It was these principles to which the disputants appealed. Such appeals only served 'to silence Wranglers, and put an end to dispute'. Truth is not served.[3] The combination of empty words and useless principles wrongly used enabled the disputants to make the true appear false, white appear black. The proceedings of the school debates passed, Locke observed, 'commonly for Wit and Learning', but it was really a cheat.[4] Such a method of arguing had been carried outside the university too:

this artificial Ignorance, and *Learned Gibberish*, prevailed mightily in these last Ages, by the Interest and Artifice of those, who found no easier way to that pitch of Authority and Dominion they have attained, than by amusing the Men of Business, and Ignorant, with hard Words, or imploying the Ingenious and Idle in intricate Disputes, about unintelligible Terms, and holding them perpetually entangled in that endless Labyrinth.[5]

Even the 'material Truths of Law and Divinity' had been obscured and perplexed.[6] If at university, students were taught that it was a virtue 'obstinately to maintain that side of the Question they have chosen, whether true or false, to the last extremity; even after Conviction'; small wonder that 'they should not in civil Conversation be ashamed of that, which in the Schools is counted a Vertue and a Glory'.[7] That letter in the *Spectator* may have contained more truth than satire.

Locke had another, more substantive objection to the standard logics of the day: their formalism was not needed. He even tells us that at one time he thought the syllogism was a good device for revealing fallacies and incoherence of arguments, but he has since found that 'laying the intermediate *Ideas* naked in their due order, shews the incoherence of the Argumentation better, than Syllogism'.[8] He defined knowledge as

---

[1] Ibid., 4.7.8; cf 4.2.8.   [2] Ibid. 4.12.1.   [3] Ibid. 4.7.11.
[4] Ibid. 3.10.5.   [5] Ibid. 3.10.9.   [6] Ibid. 3.10.12.
[7] Ibid. 4.7.11.   [8] Ibid. 4.17.4.

the perception of the agreement or disagreement of ideas, a definition cited frequently in the eighteenth century, even in several lists of questions for the school disputations. But he thought natural, unaided reason was better equipped to see the connection of ideas than mode and figure of syllogism:

a due and orderly placing of the *Ideas*, upon which the Inference is made, makes every one both Logician or not Logician, who understand the Terms, and hath the Faculty to perceive the Agreement, or Disagreement of such *Ideas* (without which, in or out of Syllogism, he cannot perceive the strength or weakness, coherence or incoherence of the Discourse) see the want of Connection in the Argumentation, and the absurdity of the Inference.[1]

Syllogism will not furnish us with the intermediate ideas which show the connections of more remote ones: our natural sagacity does that. In short, truth is to be found not by the use of the artificial method of the syllogism but by our own careful attention to ideas and their connections, using experience and observation for the acquisition of ideas.

Some of Locke's criticisms of the syllogism were found in Descartes and in the Port-Royal logic of Antoine Arnauld and Pierre Nicole.[2] The Port-Royal logic was translated into English as early as 1685, with several other translations in the next century. It was well known in Britain. But its main influence in this country was due more to Locke than to its original publication: he was in effect the transmitter of the Cartesian concept of logic as the art of thinking. It was his criticism of the syllogism and his call for 'another sort of Logick and Critick, than what we have been hitherto acquainted with'[3] which Watts, Bentham and Duncan tried to fulfil. Locke did not think he himself had supplied 'those right helps of Art' which Richard Hooker had earlier sought, but he did think it plain 'that *Syllogism*, and the Logick now in Use, which were as well known in his days, can be none of those he means'.[4]

Edward Bentham confirmed Locke's censure of school logic. Locke in his *Essay*

[1] Locke, *Essay*, 4. 17.4.
[2] *La Logique, ou l'art de penser* (Paris 1662). Two other continental logics, influenced by the Port-Royal logic but also carrying considerable influence from Locke, are Jean Le Clerc's *Logica: sive ars ratiocinandi* (London 1692) and Jean Pierre de Crousaz's *La Logique, ou système de réflexions, qui peuvent contribuer à la netteté et à l'étendue de nos connoissances . . .* (Amsterdam 1720). Both of these logics were later translated into English and were well known in Britain.
[3] Locke, *Essay*, 4.21.4.
[4] Ibid. 4.17.7. It is of course always easy to show that logic exercises are not very exciting, that philosophical jargon lacks meaning. But the significance of Locke's attack against the logic and language of the schools is twofold: it enabled him to call for a logic of use more natural and more relevant to actual problems, and it was part of a general change from logic as formal and artificial to an epistemic logic more concerned with the nature of knowledge and belief, with human understanding and its processes.

hath dropp'd many disparaging reflexions upon Scholastick distinctions and disputations: But this might be accounted for from the circumstances of the Times in which he wrote; particularly from the absurd chicaneries of some Logical disputants, who having nothing solid in their genius or valuable in their stock of acquired knowledge, studied to shelter these defects under the appearance of great subtlety to surprize and confound their Readers.[1]

Bentham wanted to salvage some of the good features of the scholastic logics. He suggested that the excesses were due more to the 'warmth and inexperience of youth' than to the schools and their logic.[2] Nevertheless, he acknowledged most of Locke's points: the need to have distinct ideas and words determinate in their signification; to pay close attention to the use of words; that judgement was defined as the apprehension of the agreement and disagreement of ideas; and he conceded that natural sagacity should not be over-formalized.[3] He held that unaided reason needed some guidance, that thinking and speaking were related in such a way that 'Logick and philosophical Grammar must often coincide', that there were close analogies between the use of the rules of grammar in writing and speaking and the use of some basic rules of reason in thinking and that the usefulness of both grammar and logic 'entirely depends upon their application'.[4] These were points Bentham feared might be lost if logic and disputations were entirely ignored.[5] Moreover, he thought the modern logics, and here he included Locke's *Essay*, had not been of sufficient assistance to young learners because they had given greater prominence to 'enquiries into the nature of our Souls, our Sensations, our Passions and Prejudices, with other springs of wrong judgment', than they had to the rules for the ordering of thoughts and arguments. These inquiries 'make a part of the natural History of Man, rather than a part of Logick'.[6]

This last remark of Bentham's is important, for it calls attention to a feature of Locke's *Essay*, and of his *Conduct*, as well as the eighteenth-

---

[1] This passage (p. 46) and others on Locke were added in the second edition of Bentham's *Reflexions upon Logick*.

[2] Bentham remarked that science had made great progress, but he thought the 'common run of reasoners as bad as ever;—not more knowing, but much more conceited;—not so ambitious to improve their knowledge, as to conceal their ignorance;—determining magisterially upon points, even those of the greatest moment, without knowing or considering the first principles of what they are discoursing of;—taking themselves to be masters of every subject, upon which they can raise an objection.' Ibid. 47-8.

[3] Ibid. 16, 17, 27.

[4] Ibid. 24, 14.

[5] Cf his *Introduction to Logick*, preface, p. ii, where he characterizes logic as 'the GRAMMAR of REASON'.

[6] Bentham, *Reflexions*, 6-7. In the preface to his *Introduction to Logick* (p. ii) Bentham added: 'Although the Art of thinking hath received great improvements from the labour and ingenuity of many excellent Writers, Mr Locke, Bishop Butler, &c. yet the philosophical matter serving to illustrate their observations, as it lyes in their books, is commonly too copious, the reflexions too abstruse to fall within the grasp of such as are Novices in Thinking.'

century British logics which followed Locke, that needs to be noticed. Locke's *Essay* was a contribution to that natural history of man—what Hume called the science of man—that Bentham wanted to see treated on its own, not in books of logic. Yet Locke's *Essay* was recognized by Bentham as a contribution to logic.[1] In fact, the logics of Watts and Duncan had the same combination of logic with analysis of the nature and function of the human understanding. Even Bentham's *Introduction to Logick* opened with a chapter on the 'Soul, its powers and operations'. Later sections in this book dealt with 'Sensation, external and internal', with the role of reason in mathematics and metaphysics, with different kinds of certainty and belief, with faith, doubt and opinion. The fact is that the new logics incorporated most of the philosophical and psychological issues then being discussed in many of the eighteenth-century tracts in science, theology and ethics.[2]

Both old and new logics, and also Locke's *Essay*, took their divisions and arranged their material around the faculties or acts of the mind, but the analysis of those acts became in most of the new logics a major part of their account. The old logic used the divisions mainly as an organizing principle, but the expansion into a more epistemic logic is implicit in these divisions. Usually the division is into three, as it is in Richard Burthogge's *Organum vetus et novum: or, a discourse of reason and truth* (London 1678): first, apprehension of simple terms; secondly, the composition of those terms, as in affirmation and negation; and thirdly, discourse or illation. This threefold division of acts of the mind appears not only in works on logic and theory of knowledge. Typical of many works on religion in the latter part of the seventeenth century is John Wilkins's *Of the Principles and Duties of Natural Religion* (London 1675). Wilkins said it was generally agreed that the acts of the mind were reducible to three:

---

[1] 'The Logical Theory contained in *Mr Locke's Essay*, so far as it goes, generally coincides with that of the Schools; though it confessedly receives a different aspect from those episodical dissertations upon several philosophical subjects which he hath interspersed throughout that work in a very delightful manner.' Bentham, *Reflexions* 7. In his *Letters concerning the English Nation* (London 1733), 94, Voltaire said of Locke: 'Perhaps no Man ever had a more judicious or more methodical Genius, or was a more acute Logician than Mr *Locke*.'

[2] The editor of Jeremy Bentham's *Correspondence* characterizes Edward Bentham as a 'virtuous, industrious, and plodding man' who 'published books on moral philosophy and logic': *Correspondence of Bentham*, ed. Sprigge i. 20. (Incidentally, he mistitles Bentham's *Reflexions upon Logick* as *Reflexions on Logic with a Vindication*: ibid. (i.28) Edward Bentham's *Introduction to Logick* may be a bit routine. but the two editions of his *Reflexions* are quite good essays in what we would call today 'philosophical logic'. Well written and succinct, they constitute a thoughtful examination of old and new. His *Introduction to Moral Philosophy* (Oxford 1745) is also a good, clear account of contemporary discussions in this area. It does not contribute an original discussion but it is a valuable account and, I would think, a helpful guide to students. It has an extensive list of topics with recommended reading for each topic, as well as a long list of authors in moral philosophy. It is up to date. The only other eighteenth-century work that has a comparable survey of contemporary moral philosophy is Philip Doddridge's *Course of Lectures on Pneumatology, Ethics and Divinity* which appeared posthumously (London 1763).

'Perception of such single objects as are proposed to them, which is called *simple Apprehension*'; 'Putting together such single objects, in order to our comparing of the agreement or disagreement betwixt them, by which we make Propositions, which is called *Judging*'; and 'The discerning of that connexion or dependance which there is betwixt several Propositions, whereby we are enabled to infer one Proposition from another, which is called Ratiocination, or Discourse'.[1] The use of this same threefold distinction in an older logic can be found in one written by Zachary Coke as early as 1654, *The Art of Logick*. Coke spoke of 'degrees' rather than of 'acts' of the understanding: 'The first degree of the understanding is simple, *viz.* the apprehension of a single Term or Theme, as *Peter, Paul*, a living Creature'; secondly, the 'conception of two Terms by way of composition, as when we think, *A man is a living Creature*'; and thirdly, 'when in order we think of more than two Terms passing the thought from one to the other, till you come to a third. This is discourse.'[2] Sanderson's much better known logic, *Logicae artis compendium*, which was steadily in use in the Oxford curriculum in both the seventeenth and eighteenth centuries, identified the three operations of the mind as simple perceiving, which dealt with terms; unifying and dividing, which dealt with propositions; and discoursing, which dealt with argumentation and method. The very popular logic of Dean Aldrich of Christ Church—his *Artis logicae compendium* of 1691—listed the three operations as simple apprehension, judgement and discourse. Sometimes there are four divisions, as in the Port-Royal logic, the logic of Peter Ramus (Pierre de la Ramée)[3] and in some of the eighteenth-century British logics: conceiving, judging, reasoning and ordering or method.[4]

As the titles of Aldrich's and Sanderson's books indicate, and in this they were typical of the pre-eighteenth-century logics in use at Oxford, they were compendia, essentially of Aristotle's and later scholastic logical principles and rules. They were in effect manuals designed as aids to reasoning and argumentation. Bentham tried, in his *Introduction to Logick*, to write a manual in more modern terms and with more attention given to the operations of the mind. Watts and Duncan made them the centre

[1] Wilkins's book anticipates some of Locke's language. It was also used by Edward Bentham in writing his *Introduction to Logick*.

[2] Z. Coke, *The Art of Logick; or, the entire body of logick* (London 1654), 6.

[3] *The Logike of P. Ramus Martyr newly translated... per M. R. Makylmenaeum Scotum* (London 1574).

[4] For a discussion of the seventeenth-century logics see W. S. Howell, *Logic and Rhetoric in England, 1500-1700* (Princeton 1956). An even better discussion, which relates these logics to the Oxford curriculum of Locke's time, is John Kenney, 'John Locke and the Oxford training in logic and metaphysics' (St Louis Ph.D. thesis 1959). Commenting upon the divisions in logic according to the faculties of the mind, Kenney points out that the early logics prepared the way for and did anticipate some of the developments in theory of knowledge in the eighteenth-century British logics (p. 207). I am indebted to Dr M. A. Stewart of Lancaster University for calling Kenney's work to my attention.

piece of their discussions. Isaac Watts's *Logick: or, the right use of reason in the enquiry after truth* (London 1725)—a subtitle taken from that of Descartes' *Discourse*—opens by saying that true logic 'is not that noisy Thing that deals all in Dispute and Wrangling, to which former Ages had debased and confin'd it'. The design of logic is, he says, to teach the right use of reason in the sciences and in the actions of life.[1] There were sections late in his book which gave some hints on the right use of reason, and others that talk about the syllogism and methods of reasoning, but a large bulk of his logic dealt with the theory of ideas, borrowing both from Locke and Malebranche, with representative perception, the debate over innate ideas, the relations or lack of relations between ideas and things. In short, Watts continued in the tradition started by Locke, although he was not nearly as systematic.

Duncan's *Elements of Logick* of 1748 is even more significant than Watt's *Logick* in that it was much more a work of general philosophy than of pure logic. First published in Dodsley's *The Preceptor*, a publication designed for schools as a compendium of learning, it was also separately published in the same year.[2] Large portions of it were later used as the article on logic in the first edition of the *Encyclopaedia Britannica* (1768-71).[3] The significance of Duncan's logic lies in its being a very close paraphrase—frequently even a copy—of Locke's *Essay*. In this feature of his book, Duncan reflected most of the debates in eighteenth-century philosophy. He defined logic itself as 'the History of the human Mind, inasmuch as it traces the Progress of our Knowledge, from our first and simple Perceptions' (p.4.). With this conception of logic (which was Watts's conception also, but the one Bentham sought to modify) Duncan naturally had discussions of the operations of the mind (for example perception, judgement, reasoning, abstracting) of the nature of ideas and their origin, of simple and compound ideas, the idea of substance, of relations: in short, discussions of all the concepts and doctrines Locke had examined in book II of his *Essay*. Words as signs of ideas were also given a similar detailed analysis. The first half of Duncan's book covered the same ground, with the same language and examples, as books II and III of the *Essay*. The second half followed book IV of Locke's *Essay*. Duncan adapted Locke's definition of knowledge, as the perception of the agreement or disagreement of ideas, to the syllogism, the

---

[1] Watts, *Logick*, pp. vi, 2.

[2] Logic was defined by Dr Johnson in the preface to Robert Dodsley's *The Preceptor* (2 vols London 1748) as 'the Art of arranging and connecting Ideas'. The preface goes on to say (p. xxiv): 'The *Logic* which for so many Ages kept Possession of the Schools, has at last been condemned as a meer Art of Wrangling, of very little Use in the Pursuit of Truth; and later Writers have contented themselves with giving an Account of the Operations of the Mind.' Watts's *Logick* and Locke's *Essay* were cited in the preface as other logics that could be consulted with profit.

[3] Readers of the *Encyclopaedia* were doubly exposed to Locke, for the article on metaphysics consisted of large extracts from the *Essay*.

syllogism being one way in which the relations of ideas could be exemplified. He also used some of the older terminology here and there, but such material was well integrated into the general account of the human understanding, especially into his account of the method of trial and experiment in the natural sciences. The result was a reinforcement of Lockean philosophy in mid-century, with most of the topics in philosophy and theology then exercising people being either discussed or cited.[1]

In drawing inferences about students' assignments and reading from disputation-questions, we must keep in mind the testimony of several students that 'strings' were used in their preparation and that summaries or compendia rather than original authors constituted much of their reading.[2] Nor do we have many lists of disputation-questions from which to infer possible contents of the curriculum. Nevertheless, there are four such lists extant, two of which were used in the schools in 1774. Another long list is to be found in Edward Bentham's *Introduction to Logick* of 1773. It is reasonable to think that Bentham's list was constructed with typical questions in mind, since he says that this logic

was compiled, and the much greater part of it printed, long ago, by an Academical tutor [Bentham himself], for private use: it being his practice to initiate his Pupils in all parts of Philosophy, by the help of an English Introduction, adding thereto, in course, the Latin Definitions and principal Questions, with their explication.[3]

[1] Howell exaggerates only a little when he says (*Logic and Rhetoric*, 360): 'On balance, Duncan's *Elements of Logick* must be regarded as the most challenging and most up-to-date book of its time, place, and class. Its analysis of the foundations, the instruments, and the reliability of natural philosophy and history meets the challenges that had to be met in releasing scholarship from the awkward limitations still being imposed upon it in the name of Aristotle.' Howell also tells us that the *Elements* went into eight editions in *The Preceptor* up to 1793, and nine as a separate title by 1800. He gives a good account of the contents of this work, but he fails to note the heavy reliance upon Locke's *Essay*. Duncan's *Elements* was not, as Howell claims (p. 349), original. However, its importance is hardly reduced by recognizing its derivative nature.

[2] A typical second-hand summary in ethics is the one Jeremy Bentham used at Queen's: *Ethices compendium in usum juventutis academicae*. According to the editor Bentham refers to this as the Oxford compendium in his *Deontology*. John James, somewhat later at Queen's, used Langbain's compendium, very likely the same one used by Bentham: see P. Quarrie, 'The Christ Church collections books', p. 504 n. 1 above.

[3] Bentham, *Introduction to Logick*, preface, p. i. Cf. the verse quoted by Greenwood, *William King*, 191–2:

> What all concerns I advertise,
> Whether they foolish are or wise;
> All Fathers, Mothers, Guardians that
> Have Sons or Wards to educate:
> I. *E.B.*, long since known
> A *mighty Tutor* in the Town
> Hight [Oxford] and in [Oriel College],

There are also several lists of questions written by Provost Smith of Queen's, some with reading lists attached.[1] It is not clear whether these lists were ever used at the college but again it seems reasonable to think they were composed with the actual curriculum in mind. In addition there is an extended collections book (three volumes in fact) from Christ Church with names of students and their reading assignments throughout the eighteenth century. From these, certain conclusions can be drawn about what Christ Church men were expected to read. How typical these assignments were of all colleges is unclear. It may perhaps be suggested, though, that this heterogeneous group, consisting of explicit assignments at Christ Church, proposed questions and readings at Queen's, Edward Bentham's carefully constructed list of topics which he used at Oriel and the two university lists, gives some basis for at least a partial reconstruction of the logic and philosophy curriculum in eighteenth-century Oxford.

Out of a list of sixty questions (*Quaestiones logicae in parvisiis discutiendae* (1744))[2] there is a number of straight logic topics, typical of the older logics: topics on genera, species, definitions, the nature of propositions, on the syllogism. But there is also a number of more general philosophical questions. Some of these latter hint at some influence of Locke and of the newer logicians. For example:

1 Whether logic is an art?
2 Whether the rules of artificial logic are useful for perceiving truth?
4 Whether a simple apprehension is capable of being false?
5 Whether simple ideas may be given?
6 Whether the mind is purely passive when receiving simple ideas?
7 Whether all human cognition be derived from simple ideas and be capable of being resolved into them?

Questions 5, 6 and 7 are typical Lockean topics, although of course Locke came from a tradition where these were accepted or debated. Other questions later in this list are of more interest:

43 Whether all discourse be derived from prior concepts and presuppositions?
44 Whether science (knowledge) consists in the perception of relations among ideas?

> Expose to Sale a Stock of Knowledge
> Of ev'ry Kind and ev'ry Price,
> Each Chap to please, however nice:
> And all is good, I will be bold
> To say, and new as e'er was sold.

[1] Queen's, MS 475, fos 93 ff.
[2] Bodl. G.A. Oxon. b.19, fo 231. I have retained the numbers of the questions as they appear on the printed sheet. The questions were always given in Latin; I give the English translation of those I cite.

46 Whether representations of external senses ought to be considered veridical?
50 Whether human reasoning be an adequate measure of truth?
52 Whether moral certainty in some matters be equivalent to demonstrative science?

Question 43 was a standard scholastic maxim but, as has been pointed out, Locke launched a sustained attack against it. Question 44 contains Locke's definition of knowledge, a definition used by Watts and Duncan. Question 52 was a claim that Locke made about moral philosophy; it attracted much attention and was referred to frequently in the eighteenth-century literature. Question 46 was not restricted to Locke, but he again gave greater prominence to the issue of knowledge of the external world; it was repeatedly discussed by eighteenth-century philosophers and in the new logics.

The *Quaestiones in augustinensibus discutiendae* were the subject of disputations for bachelors.[1] They were held once in every week during full term. Each bachelor performed once after his determination. Thus these questions were for more advanced students. This particular list is a combination of ethics and natural philosophy. Some of the questions on the previous list reappear here, but these questions more obviously reflect the eighteenth-century philosophical scene, again with Locke's influence very much in evidence:

1 Whether an innate moral sense is given?
2 Whether moral philosophy is a science?
3 Whether moral philosophy is capable of demonstration?
4 Whether a division of moral philosophy into ethics, economics and politics may be justified?
9 Whether the will necessarily follows the last judgement of the intellect?

The claims for a moral sense were being made by a number of writers in the first half of the century. This was an eighteenth-century development, so the first question was certainly reflecting the contemporary debates. Questions 2 and 3 again are Lockean topics, 3 more than 2 perhaps. Question 9 was the focus of much of the controversy in the eighteenth century over free will and determinism. It originated with Hobbes and some of those who attacked him but it was a question discussed by Samuel Clarke in his Boyle lectures, in various tracts written against Clarke by Anthony Collins, and by many other writers on ethics in the century.[2]

One other question in this list also reflects a controversy raised by

[1] Bodl. G.A. Oxon. b.19. fo 232, Quaestiones in augustinensibus discutiendae (1774).
[2] Clarke's Boyle lectures were published as *The Being and Attributes of God* (London 1705).

a suggestion which Locke made, that God might be able to add to matter the power of thinking. This suggestion produced a storm of protests, led by Stillingfleet and some defences in an extensive literature. It was a controversy closely linked with the debate over freedom and necessity. If the mind or soul was not immaterial, immortality would be threatened and man would be only a thinking machine. Thus the question, to be defended in the affirmative, that the immateriality of the soul could be demonstrated. Two other questions must reflect Lockean issues:

20 Whether the mind always thinks?
21 Whether the idea of God is innate?

The first of these was a topic on which Locke wrote against Descartes; the second was one of the main claims of the defenders of innate ideas, against whom Locke's attack in book 1 of the *Essay* was directed.

There are also on this list a number of questions in physics: whether electrical and magnetical phenomena can be explained mechanically, without reference to immaterial forces?; whether light is a body?; whether gravity is an essential property of matter? (a question of some concern to Newtonians). These questions were all issues debated by Newtonians and anti-Newtonians in the eighteenth century. They also appeared in some philosophical and theological books. It was not always easy to separate the theological from the strictly scientific concepts when dealing with the basic properties and principles of matter. One question in this list indicates another overlap between science and philosophy:

32 Whether the sensible qualities of bodies arise from the various forms and figures of particulars?

This principle in fact represents both old and new attitudes. Taken in the scholastic way, where *form* meant *substantial form*, this principle came under attack by the modern writers in philosophy and science. But given its scientific interpretation by the corpuscular theory (for example as formulated by Boyle or as used by Locke) this principle became generally accepted by most writers in the century: it was often cited in such popular publications as the *Spectator* or the *Annual Register*. In the scientific sense, this principle, or something very close to it, said that observed qualities of body are not at all like the real properties of body but they are causally dependent upon the extension, figure and motion of the insensible corpuscles of body.

An interesting list of questions was drawn up by Joseph Smith, provost of Queen's. Whether it was used at Queen's or whether it was just a proposal it is significant for our purposes because some of the questions are the same as those on the two lists already discussed, which certainly were used in the schools. Moreover, Smith's list for third-year students contains books to read against each question. These questions and their reading lists thus tell us at least what the head of one college thought important. The list contains questions on science, ethics, logic and theology, and underlines the close interlocking of the topics and issues then being studied and discussed.

The questions drawn up by Provost Smith for first-year students include most of the traditional topics in logic: are relations real?; do universals exist outside the mind?; questions on the predicaments of Aristotle, on abstraction, on the syllogism. That stock Aristotelian question which was also closely associated with Locke—whether anything may be in the mind which was not first in the senses?—appears here. Smith's questions for second-year students include a number of issues on ethics, standard issues in Aristotle and in scholastic discussions, but some of which were also topics in eighteenth-century moral philosophy. Questions were set on free will, on happiness as an end and on conscience as an adequate guide for human action (a question of great importance in the seventeenth-century debates in moral philosophy). The issue Locke raised is here also: 'whether moral philosophy is able to become a demonstrative science?' Another Lockean question to be defended was 'whether innate speculative principles are given?'

The third-year list combines questions in ethics and logic with some of the current issues in physics. The logics cited are Sanderson's *Logicae artis compendium* and Smiglecki's *Logica*, but a number of eighteenth-century works in ethics and philosophy appear in this list, together with Locke. Typical of the ethical questions are: whether virtue lies in the mean?; whether all actions aim towards some end?; whether happiness is the aim of virtue?; whether the will is free?; whether the will follows the last judgement of the intellect?' All but the last two of these are standard Aristotelian topics, while the last two refer to recent debates. Included in the authors to be read on these topics are Pufendorf on the law of nature; Henry More's *Enchiridion ethicum* (London 1668, 2nd edn London 1669); Francis Hutcheson, probably his *Inquiry into the Idea of Beauty and Virtue* (London 1727) or his *An Essay on the Nature and Conduct of the Passions and Affections* (Dublin 1728); Cheyne's *Philosophical Principles of Religion* (London 1705); and Clarke's Boyle lectures. Among the topics in physics are these: whether matter and form are natural principles of body?; whether all matter is homogeneous?; whether all the effects of body can be explained mechanically?; whether there is a vacuum?; whether light is a body?; whether quality is infinitely divisible? The reading suggested for these issues in science is Cartesian and

Newtonian, for example Jacques Rohault, whose system of natural philosophy was translated by John Clarke in 1723 and given, in his notes, a Newtonian commentary; George Cheyne's *Philosophical Principles of Religion*; Jean Le Clerc; s'Gravesande, a friend and follower of Newton; Benjamin Worster, another Newtonian and John Keill, a Newtonian who was lecturing at Oxford on natural philosophy in 1700 and whose *Introductio ad veram physicam* was published in 1702.[1] Provost Smith was obviously up to date in his knowledge of Newtonian publications in the century.[2]

For the principle that nothing is in the intellect but what is first in the senses, Locke and Burgersdijk are recommended, probably the latter's *Institutiones logicae* (The Hague 1640) along with P. Browne's *The Procedure, Extent and Limits of the Human Understanding* (London 1728) a work antagonistic to but influenced by Locke. Henry Lee's *Anti-Scepticism* (London 1702) a full-scale critique of Locke, and Robert South's sermons are suggested for the topic 'whether there are innate ideas?' Locke and Lee are again the sources for defending the affirmative 'whether sensations are proper representations of things?' The same two authors, along with Peter Brown, are cited for that issue inflamed by Locke, 'whether matter is capable of thinking?' It is again Locke, Lee and Brown who are cited for the topic, 'whether we have as clear ideas of incorporeal as of corporeal substance?' Locke is the only author cited for the topic 'whether the mind always thinks?'

At the end of his *Introduction to Logick*, which Bentham said he used when he was a tutor at Oriel (1732–52) there are four pages of sample questions for disputations. Again, we need to keep in mind that stock answers to any of these questions were probably available in answer-book form or in second-hand summaries. The fact that the topics on this list echo those on the previous three lists may even reinforce the suspicion of pat answers to stock questions rather than thoughtful reading in primary sources. Still, the fact that most of those topics associated with the new way of ideas (the Lockean philosophy) are on Bentham's list

---

[1] See *Rohault's System of Natural Philosophy*, trans. J. Clarke (2 vols London 1723); G. Cheyne, *Philosophical Principles of Religion* (London 1715); W. J. S. van s'Gravesande, *Physices elementa mathematica* (2 vols Leiden 1720), trans. J. Keill as *Mathematical Elements of Physics* (London 1720); B. Worster, *A Compendious and Methodical Account of the Principles of Natural Philosophy* (London 1730); J. Keill, *Introductio ad veram physicam* (Oxford 1702).

[2] The usual claim is that Cambridge was much stronger in science and mathematics than was Oxford. For the formal part of the curriculum this claim may be more or less true, although Frank has recently shown that the opportunities to study science at Oxford were much more extensive than has been recognized. He shows also that many students debated scientific questions; see R. G. Frank jr, 'Science, medicine and the universities of early modern England', *History of Science* i pts 3–4 (Sept.–Dec. 1973).

does show that, however it occurred, those Lockean issues did find their way into the Oxford curriculum.[1]

Bentham's list is, like his own approach to logic and philosophy, evenly balanced between old and new topics. There are all the standard logical ones on species, universals, division, forms of syllogism and so on, on which the older logics centred. But there are also a number of questions which clearly presuppose a knowledge of Locke—whether acquired directly or second-hand—and of some of the discussions of his philosophy in the late seventeenth and early eighteenth centuries. For example:

Whether there are innate principles?
Whether anything may be in the mind which was not first in the senses?
Whether all ideas arise from the senses?
Whether simple ideas are given?
Whether the mind can create or destroy ideas at will?
Whether it is especially proper to divide corporeal qualities into primary and secondary?
Whether the Lockean distinction of substance, mode and relation is to be preferred?
Whether universal ideas are made by abstraction?
Whether the representations of the external senses ought to be considered veridical?
Whether knowledge consists in the perception of a relation among ideas?
Whether all reasoning is made from prior concepts and presuppositions?
Whether moral certainty in some matters is equivalent to demonstrative science?

An interesting question from Aristotelian and Thomistic philosophy, but a question which had relevance to Cartesian and Lockean theory of knowledge, is 'whether ideas of spiritual being and their affects are formed through the assimilation of them to material beings and their affects?'[2]

The account already built up of the doctrines and issues in the Oxford curriculum from these diverse but admittedly restricted sources is fairly consistent. In logic and ethics students were exposed to some old and some new concepts. In more general philosophy and in the natural

[1] Christopher Wordsworth's remark is worth keeping in mind: 'in gauging the philosophical reading of the University we must distinguish between works read by individual scholars more or less widely, and books which were actually or virtually acknowledged text-books received by the tutors, examiners, &c., representing a college or university'. C. Wordsworth, *Scholae academicae* (Cambridge 1877), 121. Frank, 'Science, medicine and the universities', 200, has also pointed out that 'the statutory requirements of the arts course' (especially under the Laudian code) were 'overly specific concerning procedures, and overly vague on the substantive content of the curriculum', thus allowing for recommendations as to content by individual tutors.

[2] In the long list of topics in moral philosophy in his *Introduction to Moral Philosophy*, Bentham cites some of these same questions. He also cites most of the eighteenth-century writers on moral philosophy in whose works many of these same issues were debated, for example Samuel Clarke, William Wollaston, Thomas Rutherforth, Edmund Law's translation of William King on evil, Francis Hutcheson the elder.

sciences the issues and doctrines were more contemporary to the eighteenth century. The twin influences of Locke and Newton are confirmed. Some informed guesses can be made about probable books which lay behind the disputation-questions in the first two lists. The third list, that of Provost Smith, provides us with many explicit authors and titles, some of which confirm our guesses based on the first two lists. The validity of taking the third and fourth lists as representative lies in the considerable overlap of questions between the last two and the first two lists. We still do not know whether any or many students read these titles; or whether, like some students in all times, they pursued the easier course of using compendia and 'strings'.

Another source of information, the Christ Church collections books, does, however, reinforce the general impression which has been gleaned from the disputation lists. A brief account of the books cited in logic, philosophy, theology and natural science will give some idea of what was thought relevant to undergraduate education at that college. By noting what the general reading programme was for these students, some impression may be formed of the role of logic and philosophy in the curriculum. Starting in 1699 with lists for individual students (four or five titles per student) we find Le Clerc's 'Physica', probably his *Ontologia et pneumatologica* (London 1692), Sennert's *Epitome naturalis scientiae* (Amsterdam 1671) and Burgersdijk's *Institutiones metaphysicae*.[1] Locke's *Essay* appears on a few lists in 1702, also Wilkins's *Principles and Duties of Natural Religion*, a work used by Edward Bentham.

Throughout these lists in the first part of the century, the logics are invariably those of Sanderson and Aldrich, with John Wallis's *Institutio logicae* (Oxford 1687, 5th edn Oxford 1729) being used on several occasions. It is not surprising that Aldrich's logic should be so heavily used, since he was the dean of Christ Church. Logic does not appear on every student's list, though. In 1705, for example, a logic was assigned to only one student. In that same year Malebranche (probably his *Recherche de la vérité*, in the Oxford translation of 1694) is listed along with some of the more traditional works of Burgersdijk, Pufendorf and Le Clerc. Malebranche is an interesting figure, for his influence in eighteenth-century Britain was strong. He represents the more modern views in philosophy and theology, although they were in conflict with those of Locke.

Locke continues to appear, not on many lists but regularly, usually along with Pearson, Grotius and Cicero or Wilkins. In 1711 there is one entry for John Keill's *Introductio ad veram physicam*. Rohault's *Physica* in Samuel Clarke's Latin edition with his notes (London 1710) also appears in 1711, together with Locke's *Essay* and Wilkins's work on *Natural*

---

[1] Sennert was only recommended in the early years of the century, not beyond 1719. Burgersdijk was heavily recommended up to 1759; in the 1760s his *Collegium physicum* (Leiden 1632) took over.

Religion. Wallis's logic appears in 1713 on several lists. In 1714 there is a rather curious assignment of the third book of Locke's *Essay*, the book on language. This was given to several students in that year. Du Hamel's *Metaphysics* (2 volumes Nuremberg 1681) is cited (another Cartesian, of sorts). In 1714 also, logic is much more often assigned, the logics of Wallis and Aldrich mainly, though Sanderson gets an entry or two. Another logic, hardly ever mentioned, appears here too, that of Samuel Smith, *Aditus ad logicam* (Oxford 1665).

The lists starting in 1717 and running on for some years are given by year of student in groups. In 1717 fourteen students are all assigned the same books, including Aldrich's logic; similarly in 1718. Most groups, however, do not have logic on their list of recommended books, the tendency is for it to be given to the first-year students only. Up to 1721 at least, most first-year lists include Aldrich's logic. Students for other years are assigned mainly ethics and theology. Burgersdijk's *Institutiones metaphysicae* is regularly assigned to fourth-year students up to 1744. For the rest the recommended books are mainly classical authors (Cicero, Virgil, Homer) together with standard works of divinity. Eustachius's *Ethica* (London 1677), one of the outlines of ethics, is heavily recommended up to 1756.

In 1744 the fourth-year lists drop Burgersdijk and add Locke's 'Metaphysics', that is his *Essay* or possibly some lectures on Locke. But in 1755 Locke is taken off that list. The list for the second year in 1757 has an interesting entry for physics, a contemporary work influenced by Newton: John Rowning's *A Compendious System of Natural Philosophy* (published in London in parts between 1735 and 1744).[1] In 1757 also, Locke reappears on third-year lists, and then to the end of the 1770s is on many lists. Aldrich's logic seems to be replaced in the 1760s by that of Wallis. Keill's *Physics*, now published in English, is assigned in 1765.[2] Aldrich's logic appears regularly in the earlier period.

The pattern of reading assignments to the end of the century is pretty much the same as these last few entries: Locke occasionally, Aldrich, once in a while Keill; but for the most part they become more classically oriented from 1772. What is perhaps surprising is that there is no work of eighteenth-century philosophy or theology assigned, only a few contemporary works of natural science. Only three students in the entire period are given Newton's *Principia* (in the 1780s and 1790s). Le Clerc's logic may possibly have been read, since all his other works appeared a few times on these lists. Since Le Clerc followed Locke and the Port-Royal logic, it is possible that Christ Church students may have been exposed to some of the newer concepts in logic *via* this route, as well as

---

[1] Rowning's book appears 59 times in the 1750s; it does not appear again.
[2] Keill, *Introductio ad veram physicam*, trans. as *An Introduction to Natural Philosophy* (London 1720).

through Locke. But there is not in these collections books the sort of orientation towards the eighteenth century which Provost Smith's recommendations show, or which Edward Bentham's writings recommend and embody. The differences may be due to the attitude of a tutor drawing up the ideal list of books and a college working within the official structure. Or it may be that Christ Church was more conservative than Oriel or Queen's. Nevertheless, with Locke steadily appearing on many of the lists at Christ Church, something of the new philosophy must have been imparted to these students.

His presence on these lists from 1702 is interesting, since an effort was made in 1703 by the heads of houses in Oxford to suppress the *Essay*, along with Le Clerc's *Physics* and *Logica*. James Tyrrell told Locke that the reason for such an attempt was that the students were reading too much of the new philosophy. Tyrrell did not indicate whether they were reading Locke and Le Clerc as part of the curriculum or just out of interest. He did go on to tell Locke that it was believed by the heads of houses that reading his new philosophy was subverting scholastic logic and disputations.[1] Perhaps Locke's extended critique of the old logics did have some effect. The editor of Jeremy Bentham's *Correspondence* says that John Burton 'introduced the study of Locke into the schools'.[2] Sprigge does not cite any evidence for this claim but it is consistent with the reconstruction that has been suggested from the lists of disputation questions and the Christ Church collections books.

John James indicated that he was reading Locke, although this seems to have been on his father's advice rather than that of his tutor. James's tutor did recommend Watts and Duncan, however:

From eleven till one I read logic. As the Doctor recommended it, I am running over Watts. On Duncan, which I take up next, I will bestow no little care, and will imprint him on my mind by abridging and digesting him. After him you recommended Locke, and with these I shall have my hands pretty full for a good while.[3]

But James went on to say:

[1] Tyrrell-Locke, Apr. 1704, Bodl. MS Locke, c.22, fo 167. For the details on the reactions to Locke's *Essay* by the heads of houses see J. Yolton, *John Locke and the Way of Ideas* (Oxford 1956), 3-4, 11-12.
[2] *Correspondence of Bentham*, ed. Sprigge i. 27. Wordsworth, in commenting on the regular occurrence of Locke in the Cambridge reading lists, says that the *Essay* was 'cast out from Oxford' and took root at Cambridge: *Scholae academicae*, 127. I think we now have evidence suggesting that this view of Locke's rejection at Oxford is not true. Locke and Lockean logics were making steady inroads, even at Christ Church. That his critique of the older logic was resented, even as late as 1764, is suggested by a note Lord Teignmouth reports from William Jones at University College. Jones said that 'one of the fellows, who was reading Locke with his own pupils ... carefully passed over every passage in which that great metaphysician derides the old system': *Memoirs of the Life of Sir William Jones*, 31.
[3] Letter to his father, 21 Nov. 1778, *Letters of Radcliffe and James*, 51.

Sanderson is the great oracle next to Aristotle, to whose bust the wranglers in the hall seem to pay a more profound reverence than to common sense. In the Compend we have entered the third book, and I have had the honour of proving to the Doctor's great satisfaction than it must be either night or day. The Doctor construes a few chapters, which the next lecture we repeat to him.[1]

James complained that his tutor 'does not explain a single term, and were I to rely only on the instructions I receive from him, I should find myself very deficient'. He wondered about the value of Sanderson's 'Compend': 'Is it worth the labour to retain all the terms, definitions, &c., it abounds with?' He suggests an alternative, namely the use of a *scheme* where all the definitions and terms are put down in a concise and easy method. It is interesting to learn that James looked to the new logics for help: 'From a careful perusal of Watts and Duncan I hope e'er long to acquire a competent knowledge, and to be able at least not to be silent in the Hall'.[2] He was to be disappointed in Watts, but held out hope for Duncan:

Watts descends into so many minutiae; he calls off the attention from the main object by such a quantity of dry observations, definitions, &c., &c., that I neither read him with pleasure or improvement. From a careful persual [*sic*] of Duncan I expect a great deal. I am now engaged with, and will soon finish him.[3]

James's final comment, not on Duncan but on disputation, was that he preferred 'morality to wrangling and verbal disputes'.[4]

Jeremy Bentham confirms that Sanderson's *Compendium* was used at Queen's and that he had to learn some of it by heart.[5] Bowring confirms that Watts was the English logic in use at Queen's while Bentham was there. He says that Bentham always called it 'Old woman's logic'.[6] Bentham makes no mention of Duncan. His namesake, Edward Bentham at Oriel, invited Jeremy to dinner on several occasions, and even helped him with his translation of Cicero. After one such dinner Edward sent Jeremy back to Queen's with a copy of his *Reflexions*.[7] There

---

[1] Ibid. 50. The third book of Sanderson's *Artis logicae compendium* was on the syllogism. The first two parts on simple terms and propositions provided all the definitions and distinctions.

[2] *Letters of Radcliffe and James*, 51, 50.

[3] Ibid. 55. Duncan's *Elements* was also read at Cambridge. Richard Watson told of attending lectures in the college hall, where the 'lecturers explained to their respective classes certain books, such as Pufendorf's *De Officio Hominis et Civis*, Clarke on the Attributes, Locke's Essay, Duncan's Logic, &c': quoted in P. Beasley, *A Search of Truth* (Philadelphia 1822), 69. The editor of James's *Letters* cites (p. 50n) George Dyer's *The History of the University and Colleges of Cambridge* (2 vols London 1814) i. 197-8, where it is said that Duncan's *Elements* is 'the best system of logic, or, at least, that most favourably now [1814] received at Cambridge'. Dyer also noted that Duncan's book was 'little more than an Abridgement of Locke's Essay'. See also Wordworth, *Scholae academicae*, 13.

[4] *Letters of Radcliffe and James*, 55.

[5] Letter of 12 June 1761, *Correspondence of Bentham*, ed. Sprigge i. 47; letter of 4 Mar. 1761, ibid. 36.

[6] *The Works of Jeremy Bentham*, ed. J. Bowring (11 vols Edinburgh 1838-43) x. 37.

[7] *Correspondence*, i. 28: Letter of 26 Nov. 1760, *Correspondence of Bentham*, ed. Sprigge i. 28.

are a number of other letters in Bentham's published *Correspondence* which mention Edward, but he never gives any indication of whether he read the *Reflexions* or, if he did, what he thought of it.

Jeremy Bentham was hardly the typical student. Before coming to Oxford he had read, at the age of 10, Dodsley's *The Preceptor* and hence, perhaps Duncan's *Elements*, Locke's *Essay* and Mandeville's *Fable of the Bees*, an important new work on moral philosophy.[1] When he went to Oxford he took with him more than sixty books.[2] Jeremy's father kept a close watch on his son's education, even when he went to Oxford. He served as an additional tutor, receiving frequent letters, pressing him for his translations of Cicero, which he was doing for his father not for the college tutor, and in general supervising his progress. John James's father seems to have played a similar role with his son. Jeremy complained about his tutor's lack of enthusiasm and guidance. John James's father levelled a more general charge: the college did not really help the student. Beyond 'a logic or ethic compend', no book was recommended by the tutor. 'From the genius of the place, the emotions it inspires, the connections that may be formed, the opportunities of libraries, &c., much may be expected from a lad of spirit—but from tutors, I verily believe, *nothing*.'[3]

The close supervision of son by father was undoubtedly a typical custom as was also the buying of books when at Oxford, presumably often at the father's recommendation, and the bringing to college of a small working library.[4] The account of the Fleming brothers at Oxford in the last years of the seventeenth century confirms these practices. For example Henry Fleming asked to borrow from his father a copy of Kenelm Digby's *Two Treatises* (Paris 1644), an interesting early work of (*inter alia*) psychology.[5] Other books bought in 1682 by Henry Fleming were by Gassendi and Aristotle, and Wilkins's work on *Natural Religion* as well as on language, *An Essay Towards a Real Character and Philosophical Language* (London 1668). He also bought a number of volumes of the *Transactions* of the Royal Society and several volumes of Boyle. He was right up to date, buying the most recent books. George Fleming told his father in 1689 that he was studying moral philosophy, receiving lectures

---

[1] B. de Mandeville, *The Fable of the Bees* (London 1714).

[2] C. W. Everett, *The Education of Jeremy Bentham* (New York 1931), 23-4. Samuel Johnson brought with him to Oxford over one hundred volumes. Among his books was Locke's work on education and Mandeville's *Fable of the Bees*: J. L. Clifford, *Young Samuel Johnson* (London 1955), 120.

[3] *Letters of Radcliffe and James*, 53.

[4] Frank points out the importance of the Oxford booksellers (he has the late seventeenth century in mind more than the eighteenth) for the more advanced and curious scholar. 'When the stock of the largest of the Oxford booksellers Richard Davis, was put up for auction in the late 1680s after his death, it numbered over 30,000 volumes. Over 6,500 of these were works in philosophy, natural philosophy, mathematics, and the medical sciences.' Frank, 'Science, medicine and the universities', loc. cit.   [5] *The Flemings in Oxford* ii. 49.

from his tutor 'along with which I read myself Aristotles Ethicks'.[1] George had with him at Oxford in 1689 the following books: Seneca's philosophy, Philippe du Trieu's *Manuductio ad logicam* (Liège 1620), Bacon's *Essays*, Richard Crakanthorp's *Logicae libri quinque* (London 1641), Smiglecki's *Logica*, Sennert's 'Physics' and Sanderson's *Physicae scientiae compendium* (Oxford 1671) and some works of Boyle.[2] He also told his father in 1690 that his tutor, Dr Mill, recommended to him Sanderson's work on conscience, *De obligatione conscientiae* (London 1647) and 'the new Philosophy, saying he wonder'd I should be without them so long, being such books, as without them one could never be a good Philosopher'. He asks his father to let him have these two books 'though they be of a high price'.[3]

It would be interesting to know what Mill meant by 'the new Philosophy'. Since George told his father that Mill wondered how George had been so long without these two books, he would hardly seem to have had Locke's *Essay* in mind, although the phrase was quickly identified with Locke after 1689. Equally it would be too early for him to have referred to Newton, although that label was applied to Newton's *Principia* (London 1687) but not as early as that. Perhaps it was Bacon's *Novum organum*[4] or Bacon as expressed in some of the writings of the Royal Society scientists. The editor of the Flemings' correspondence suggests, perhaps implausibly, that it might have been Ralph Cudworth's *True Intellectual System of the Universe* (London 1678).[5]

One other source tends to support the general account, so far reconstructed, of a move away from the standard logics to the modern epistemic logics; of the appearance of more recent books on ethics and theology in the Oxford curriculum; and of a slow addition of Newtonian works. In 1755 Daniel Waterland published at Oxford a second edition of his *Advice to a Young Student, with a method of study of the first four years*. The first edition of 1730 (published in London) was written for students at Cambridge, while the second was designed to fit Oxford as well. Waterland praised Locke in both editions, his *Conduct of the Understanding* being cited as a work which usefully exemplified reasoning, rather than merely (as Wallis's logic was said to do) defining terms of art. Waterland added in the second edition such recent works as William Wollaston's *Religion of Nature Delineated* (np 1722), Joseph Butler's *Analogy of Religion* (London 1736) and Robert Jenkin's *Reasonableness of the Christian Religion* (London 1700). All three of these books carried forward the discussions

---

[1] Ibid. 252, 273-4.

[2] Ibid. 273, 274, 278, 279. The Seneca was perhaps *Annaei Senecae tum rhetoris tum philosophi* (Savoy 1604, 2nd edn Geneva 1646) and the Sennert probably *De scientia naturali* (Amsterdam 1671).

[3] *The Flemings in Oxford* ii. 296-7.

[4] F. Bacon, *Novum organum* (London 1620).

[5] *The Flemings in Oxford* ii. 296.

of many of the disputation-topics cited above. Jenkin's book in particular (though now an obscure and overlooked work) echoed most of the debates over thinking matter and the nature of ideas and knowledge which Locke's philosophy passed on to the eighteenth century. Both editions of Waterland's *Advice* cited contemporary Newtonian books by Keill, Rowning, James Gregory, Cheyne and Newton himself. Francis Hutcheson was recommended for ethics in the second edition only, a significant new entry. Hutcheson wrote several very influential books on ethics. The notion of a moral sense was given a systematic exposition in his *Essay on the Nature and Conduct of the Passions and Affections* (London 1730). He also wrote a compendium in Latin, probably designed for use in the universities.[1]

The examples of the Flemings, John James and Jeremy Bentham may all be of serious students seeking to learn. How typical they were of the general run of Oxford students in the eighteenth century would be difficult to say. Nevertheless, their example probably shows us what were the reading habits of the serious student. One such, William Mills, may have been over-zealous about his reading (or perhaps he was only looking for additional income): he stole in 1785 a number of books from an undergraduate library at Trinity College.[2] Undergraduates as a rule did not have access to college libraries. Thus their holdings are not sources from which conclusions can be drawn about student reading. They are, however, of some relevance for the general intellectual climate among tutors and graduates.

Apart from purchases of books by the colleges themselves, bought with money from legacies and library subscriptions, benefactions were considerable, both from former members and outside well-wishers. On looking over a variety of eighteenth-century library collections one is immediately struck by the fact that they were very up to date. Many colleges had the new logics of Watts and Duncan, some had the Port-

[1] F. Hutcheson, *Philosophiae moralis institutio compendiaria, ethices et jurisprudentiae naturalis elementa continens* (Glasgow 1742). Waterland recommended with Hutcheson another work on ethics, David Fordyce's *Elements of Moral Philosophy* (London 1754). Waterland said the works of Hutcheson and Fordyce were 'the latest and best Systems you will meet with'. Waterland also recommended another work by Hutcheson, which he referred to as 'Hutcheson's Metaphysics': *Metaphysica synopsi ontologiam et pneumatologiam* (Glasgow 1742). For an interesting discussion of moral philosophy in the seventeenth and eighteenth centuries in Britain see W. Whewell, *Lectures on the History of Moral Philosophy in England* (London 1852); Whewell was master of Trinity College, Cambridge.

[2] TCA misc. iii, pp. 42 ff. The books taken from this library by Mills included works by Hooke, Richard Willis, Boyle, Newton, Molyneux, Thomas Sprat, Pufendorf and Rohault and copies of the *Transactions of the Royal Society*. The library had apparently fallen into disuse and the books were unguarded in a separate room. Mills kept the books he stole in his rooms for years. He said he found little advantage in them, but his intuition as to what books were important was sound. William Mills (1769-1848), m. Trinity 1785.

Royal logic. Locke's *Essay* and other works of his were in almost every college. While Berkeley occurred in a few collections, Hume does not seem to have reached the Oxford libraries in the eighteenth century. It was routine for colleges to acquire contemporary tracts and books on theology, science, ethics and philosophy, and the eighteenth-century holdings in these areas were extensive.[1]

It is tempting to think that books in the college libraries reflected the content of tutorials, readings and examinations, but it must be borne in mind that much instruction was perfunctory. The constraints of the Laudian statutes and of tradition worked against change, and the frequent use of summaries, compendia and the like did not encourage tutors or students to read or think critically about examination-questions. But even taking a cautious view, the evidence left to us— limited though its range may be—suggests that changes were taking place in eighteenth-century Oxford. The old disputation-system was being criticized and overhauled internally. The old logics, even as they were still being used, were viewed more critically. New British logics were appearing and being used, not perhaps extensively and not always with complete satisfaction, as an aid to disputation.[2]

This last point—that Watts and Duncan may not have been as good aids to disputations as Sanderson or Aldrich—indicates another and more important change taking place in the Oxford curriculum, the move away from disputation as a hollow exercise. What was happening was the replacement of the old by the new logics, a change of emphasis from scoring points to understanding and discovering truth. The very thing that Edward Bentham complained about in Locke and the new logics, that they contained too much material on science and psychology, was the main instrument of this change, in the move from formal wrangling over trite issues to the serious pursuit of truth in science, religion and ethics. It is possible to suggest that the new logics became the instruments by which the important issues in these areas came into the Oxford curriculum. In this, Locke's *Essay* played a major role, both directly, in that it was read at Oxford, and indirectly through the new logics and through the variety of books in science and theology which took up some of the issues raised by him.

---

[1] I have checked lists of collections in Brasenose, Corpus, Christ Church, New College, Oriel and Trinity. In some colleges there were two or three extensive collections.

[2] One other feature of these changes which may be important, and which needs examination and consideration, is the fact that the newer books in logic and philosophy were written in English, replacing the Latin compendia.

21

Legal Studies

J. L. BARTON

ONE eighteenth-century lord chancellor and one chief justice had studied law at Leiden before reading for the English bar.[1] When Lord Mansfield presided over the king's bench, Junius accused him of attempting to engineer an English reception.[2] Junius was making use of the rhetorical commonplace that the civil law was the law of despotism, so that in a sense a partiality for the civil law was a necessary characteristic of any judge who was proposing to reduce Englishmen to slavery. None the less, it is significant that he should have thought this charge plausible enough to be worth making. The prestige of the civil law was not confined to legal circles. The authors of the later seventeenth century had developed, or rather had inherited, a theory of the law of nature which depended heavily on civilian texts and doctrine, and to the modern eye at least the moral and political philosophy of the time was quite startlingly legalistic in its approach. Archdeacon William Paley was led to publish his own little book on this subject in the hope that it might replace the works of Grotius and Pufendorff in the hands of undergraduates.[3] These authors were not only excessively 'juridicial' in their general attitude, they made so liberal a use of classical illustrations that they might give the unwary young the impression that upon questions of morals the authority of pagan antiquity was comparable to that of revelation. Paley himself can certainly not be accused of undervaluing revelation, but whatever he may say in his preface, it is precisely in its 'juridicial' approach that his book differs from a modern work on the same subject, and his sources are obvious enough. Indeed Thomas Wood, who published a *New Institute of the Imperial or Civil Law* in 1704, ventured to hope that it might prove of use to divines in resolving cases of conscience.[4]

---

[1] Peter King (1669-1734), 1st Bn King of Ockham in Surrey; chief justice of common pleas 1714-25, lord chancellor 1725-33. Dudley Ryder (1691-1756), chief justice of king's bench 1754-6.

[2] *The Letters of Junius*, ed. C. W. Everett (London 1927), letter xli (pp. 177-85).

[3] W. Paley, *Principles of Moral and Political Philosophy* (London 1785).

[4] Thomas Wood, *A New Institute of the Imperial or Civil Law* (London 1704), pp. xiv-xv. Thomas Wood (1661-1722), m. St Alban Hall 1678; fellow New College 1679.

The intellectual prestige of the civil law in this period may have owed something to the decay of the civil-law courts. One consequence of the Revolution of 1688 was to render it politically impossible for the king to attempt to interfere with the activities of the courts of common law. The king's bench improved this opportunity by completing, in a singularly ruthless fashion, that process of crippling the ecclesiastical courts and the admiralty which Sir Edward Coke had begun. They were thus left exercising a jurisdiction 'confined within a very narrow compass; limited to a few objects; and so much blended with the canon, common, and statute, law, that it is hardly possible to invent a name, that will suit it precisely'.[1]

In the result, even the most violently prejudiced of common lawyers could hardly imagine that his profession was in any danger from the rivalry of the civilians, and though the occasional pamphleteer might repeat the old warning that the liberties of England were in danger of being trampled underfoot by a despotic monarch surrounded by cringing legists, this was a possibility which no one took very seriously any more. If, however, the old political hostility to the civil law had largely disappeared, this was of very little advantage to the Oxford faculty.

The courts before which the civilians practised could support only a small Bar, and the number of students who were proposing to become advocates of Doctors' Commons was correspondingly small. For the intending advocate who was concerned merely with his prospects of success in his profession, the obligation to obtain the degree of DCL was more a burdensome formality than an essential stage in his professional training. The abolition of university lectures in canon law in the sixteenth century had already rendered the university course much less useful to the lawyer whose future practice would be largely in the ecclesiastical courts. The rigorous supervision which the common-law courts now exercised over the ecclesiastical courts and the admiralty alike ensured that the law which they administered bore even less resemblance to that taught at the universities. The future advocate, like the future barrister, now learned his profession largely by attending upon the courts and making his own notes of decisions. For the student who did not have Doctors' Commons in view, the faculty of civil law possessed three attractions which, if not in themselves fatal, were somewhat unfortunate. In the later middle ages priests had not been permitted to study civil law. Hence the holders of legist fellowships were not bound to take holy orders. The practical consequences of this disability (or privilege) convinced Lord Macclesfield that to abolish the requirement that fellows of colleges should take orders would not be a desirable reform. He observed:

[1] T. Bever, *A Discourse on the Study of Jurisprudence and the Civil Law* (Oxford 1766), 37.

That generally speaking, those who have the Faculty places get them purely to avoid going into Orders, and that they may lead a more gay life without designing to follow any profession.

That on this account they are too often filled by the younger sons of families of good estate; and were this incumbrance of going into Orders taken off, I fear, most of the Fellowships would gradually come into their hands, to the great detriment of learning, by excluding those from Fellowships, who really want such an help in their education.[1]

In the second place, Henry VIII's statute against pluralities had permitted bachelors of canon law, among other persons, to purchase dispensations to hold two benefices with cure of souls.[2] It was widely held that the civilians had acquired this privilege by succession when the faculty of canon law was suppressed.[3] John Ayliffe might object that a bachelor of laws was not and never had been a bachelor of canon law,[4] but there is no evidence that those who relied upon this vulgar error suffered for it, and it increased the attractions of the BCL for those 'younger sons of families of good estates' who did intend to take orders, and whose fathers' means would stretch to the acquisition of more than one benefice.[5] Finally, and perhaps worst, the degree of BCL was the least exacting alternative open to the undergraduate who desired to complete his statutory exercises with as little trouble as possible. One of Humphrey Prideaux's suggested reforms had been that

whereas the Lawyer's Gown ... is often made an *Asylum* for the idle and the ignorant such as have not, by their proficiency in their studies, qualified themselves for the Degree of B.A., it be ordained, that no person for the future, shall be allowed in either of the said Universities, to put on the Lawyer's Gown, till he hath first taken the Degree of B.A., or till three years after that, be admitted to take the Degree of Batchelor of Law.[6]

Nothing was done, and in the last years of the century it was still possible for an undergraduate to enter the law faculty without first studying arts. John Napleton wrote in an anonymously published pamphlet:

This degree, I apprehend, is contrary to the general tenour of our present system; and, though it be allowed by Statute in other cases, seems originally to

[1] 'A memorial relating to the universities' in *Collectanea curiosa* ed. J. Gutch (2 vols Oxford 1781) ii. 61-2.
[2] 21 Hen. VIII, c. 13, s. 12.
[3] J. Godolphin, *Repertorium canonicum* (London 1680), ch. 26, sect. 3, p. 294.
[4] See *The Case of Dr Ayliffe at Oxford* (London 1716) which is thought to have been written by Ayliffe himself. John Ayliffe (1676-1732), m. New College 1696, expelled 1715. The idea that a degree in laws was to be deemed a degree in both laws apparently retained sufficient vitality in the nineteenth century to make it usual for a DCL of Oxford appointed to judicial office in the ecclesiastical courts to adopt the style of doctor of laws in official documents: C. Wordsworth, *Scholae academicae* (Cambridge 1877), 265.
[5] J. Ayliffe, *Parergon juris canonici anglicani* (London 1726), 417-18.
[6] C. Wordsworth, *Social Life at the English Universities* (Cambridge 1874), 556.

have been granted to such Students only, as were obliged by the rules of their College to turn aside early into the Law Line.[1]

In truth undergraduates had been entitled to enter the law faculty on their first arrival at the university for as long as there had been a law faculty, and the compilers of the Laudian code, though they did not feel able to forbid the practice, had done what they could to discourage it. The candidate for the BCL who was neither an MA nor a foundation fellow was obliged to spend two years in dialectic, moral and political philosophy and other humane letters, as well as five years in civil law, so that he saved no time by choosing the BCL rather than the MA. Two oppositions and one responsion were substituted for the single disputation of the Elizabethan statutes.[2] However, a legal disputation attended only by the professor was no very serious ordeal, and the faculty still provided a comfortable refuge for the idle man.[3] We may therefore suspect that it was not wholly through the fault of the professors that lectures in civil law ceased to be delivered during the period. Once it had become the regular practice to grant the candidates for degrees in the higher faculties a general dispensation for non-attendance at statutory lectures, the idle would have no incentive at all to attend, and the prospective advocate might be excused for feeling that a course upon a portion of the *Pandects* was too academic to be worth the time which it would take up. The last but one occupant of the civil law chair during the period, Thomas Francis Wenman, was an amiable and aristocratic botanist who was destined to end his life a martyr to science by drowning in the Cherwell while in search of waterplants.[4] James Hurdis named him among the professors of his day who had attempted to lecture but had been obliged to abandon their courses for want of auditors.[5] We have no means of judging his attainments as a civilian, for he wrote nothing on this subject, but this in itself, taken in conjunction with his distinction in quite a different field, suggests that the choice of professor was no longer governed primarily by his knowledge of the texts upon which the statutes required him to read. Indeed Thomas Bouchier, a civilian and canonist of the old school who occupied the chair when the period opened, enjoyed before his death the melancholy distinction of being

---

[1] *Considerations on the Public Exercises for the First and Second Degrees in the University of Oxford* ([Oxford] 1773), 54.

[2] *Laudian Code* VI. iv. 1-2, ed. Griffiths, pp. 60-1; *Statutes*, trans. Ward i. 50-1.

[3] According to G. V. Cox, *Recollections of Oxford* (London 1868, 2nd edn London 1870), 377-8 civil-law disputants in the early nineteenth century were provided with their 'strings' by the clerk of the schools.

[4] Thomas Francis Wenman (1745-96), m. Univ. 1762, fellow All Souls 1765; prof. of civil law and keeper of the university archives 1789-96.

[5] [J. Hurdis,] *A Word or Two in Vindication of the University of Oxford, and of Magdalen College in particular from the Posthumous Aspersions of Mr. Gibbon* (np nd), repr. in *Reminiscences of Oxford*.

considered by his contemporaries to be the only knowledgeable member of his faculty.[1] In the memorable controversy over Thomas Cockman's election as master of University College it was Bouchier who suggested that the 'canonical election' mentioned in the statutes should be taken to mean an election conducted according to the forms of the canon law. In the result, Cockman's party took their case to the king's bench, the university lost its right of visiting the college to the king, as the lawful successor of King Alfred, and upon a second visitation the king's delegates confirmed Cockman's election.[2] Old Thomas Bouchier did not live to suffer this final humiliation, but upon his deathbed he observed more than once that Cockman had killed him. Since he was past ninety at his death, it is unlikely that his life was very drastically shortened by disappointment, but this detracts only slightly from the merit of the story. His death, as recounted by Hearne, might serve as a fable to illustrate the destruction of the old learning at the hands of the encroaching common lawyers.[3] He was succeeded in the chair by his son James but it was said of him that he had 'no capacity himself, but does all by his father's direction'.[4] Wenman's successor, French Laurence, was a contributor to the *Rolliad*, and helped Burke to prepare the preliminary case against Warren Hastings. He was chancellor of the diocese of Oxford, and according to Napleton was intending to lecture. Whether he ever did so does not appear.[5]

Attempts were certainly made during the period to encourage the study of the civil law, but they seem to have been intended primarily for the benefit of students in the faculty of arts. For the artist a grounding in the principles of the civil law and the law of nature—the latter was largely based upon the former—might be considered a necessary part of his grounding in moral and political philosophy. Locke had expressed this view with great emphasis, and in 1708 Thomas Wood tells us that 'young Men think themselves obliged to read an *Institute* of the Imperial Law, and a Comment upon the Title *De Regulis Juris*, and then to study *Grotius* and *Pufendorff*.[6]

He may have been exaggerating their sense of obligation to some extent, but in 1689 young George Fleming began the study of moral

[1] HMC *Portland MSS* vii. 92.
[2] See W. R. Ward, *Georgian Oxford* (Oxford 1958), 114-15; W. Carr, *University College* (London 1902), 172-6; UCA disputed election of the master 1722-9.
[3] Hearne, *Collections* viii. 102, 74.
[4] Stratford-Harley, 24 Sept. 1712, HMC *Portland MSS* vii. 92. James Bouchier (1683-1736), subs. St Alban Hall 1698, principal 1723-36; regius prof. of civil law 1712-36.
[5] [Hurdis,] *Vindication*, 147. French Laurence (1757-1809), m. CCC 1774; regius prof. of civil law 1796-1809.
[6] T. Wood, *Some Thoughts Concerning the Study of the Laws of England in the Two Universities* (London 1708), 4. Cf J. Locke, *Some Thoughts on Education* (London 1693), §175.

philosophy with the *Ethics* of Cursellaeus and Justinian's *Institutes*.[1] So also when William Blackstone's friend Thomas Bever was induced by the success of the former's lectures to attempt to revive lectures in civil law, he was not concerned to provide instruction for the prospective advocate, or indeed for the members of his own faculty, of whom he seems to have had no very good opinion, but to offer his hearers an opportunity of acquiring that knowledge of the nature and characteristics of law in general which an educated gentleman ought to possess.[2] Jeremy Bentham in his later years said, incorrectly, that Bever succeeded Blackstone as Vinerian professor, and 'read lectures on Roman law, which were laughed at'.[3] Bever's course would have been more correctly described in the language of the time as a course on the law of nature. It would today be called a course on jurisprudence. Since at that date it was taken to be self-evident that the civil law approached more nearly to the rational ideal than any other positive system, a lecturer on this subject would naturally make extensive use of civilian materials. Whether or not the course was laughed at, it was not a complete failure. The amount of rewriting in the lecturer's manuscript suggests that it was repeated a number of times, and the 'directions to the reader' which the rewriting rendered necessary show that it was upon occasion delivered by deputy in Bever's absence. It may be questioned, however, whether the lectures would be likely to dissuade any auditor from going to study the civil law abroad, a practice which Bever lamented, as did Blackstone.[4]

So also the greater part of the literature on the subject which was produced during this period by Oxford men was not designed for the professional student. Thomas Wood's *New Institute* was compiled, according to its title-page, 'for the use of some persons of quality', whom we may assume to have been pupils of the author. It was his modest aim to 'encourage young Scholars to spend some few Hours in the Study of the

---

[1] *The Flemings in Oxford* ii. 256, 257. George's account of his studies suggests that the *Institutes* were read second.

[2] The introductory lecture was revised for the Press, and published as his *Discourse on the Study of Jurisprudence and the Civil Law*. The manuscript of the complete course was deposited in All Souls (it is now MS 109) upon condition that it would not be printed. It is sometimes said that Bever was acting as deputy for Professor Jenner (Robert Jenner, 1714-67, m. Trin. 1730; regius prof. of civil law 1754-67) but this seems to be a mistake. He obtained Jenner's permission to lecture, but if the contents of his course was any guide it was a private rather than a statutory one. For Bever's opinion of the members of his own faculty see his *Discourse*, 28: 'those nominal students, whom private convenience, or college statutes, oblige to wear the gown, are generally contented with a slender, mechanical smattering, barely enough to entitle them to the honor and benefit of a degree; after which they soon lose the little remembrance they ever had of it'.

[3] *The Works of Jeremy Bentham*, ed. J. Bowring (11 vols Edinburgh 1838-43) x. 45.

[4] 'A fashion has prevailed, especially of late, to transport the growing hopes of this island to foreign universities, in Switzerland, Germany, and Holland; which, though infinitely inferior to our own in every other consideration, have been looked upon as better nurseries of the civil, or (which is nearly the same) of their own municipal law': W. Blackstone, *Commentaries on the Laws of England* (4 vols Oxford 1765-9) bk I, p. 5.

Civil Law'. With this end in view he had concentrated upon the leading principles of the subject, omitting 'matters of practice and useless knowledge'—a very significant juxtaposition.[1] To the second and subsequent editions (there were four in all) the author added his own translation of the preliminary part of Domat's *Lex Loix civiles dans leur ordre naturel*, under the title of *A Treatise of the First Principles of Laws in General* and without the name of the original author. The approach of Robert Eden, whose *Jurisprudentia philologica* appeared in 1744, was somewhat different. He stated in his preface that when he was a tutor at University College with Francis Walwyn, there were not a few who thought that a knowledge of the civil law would be of use to the young men committed to their care. The author had, however, been unable to find any book on the subject that was not over-technical, and likely by its want of elegance to disgust the reader who had been brought up on the best classical authors. He had therefore attempted to produce a work more classical in style than the *Institutes* and enriched with select references to good authors, which, he ventured to hope, would serve not only to render an otherwise dry and jejune study pleasanter to the young but also to shed new light upon many passages of the classical authors which could not be well understood without some knowledge of the civil law. No second edition was called for. Eden's text is the *Elementa juris civilis secundum ordinem institutionum* of Heineccius, with minimal adaptations.[2] The notes are his own, or largely so, but it may have been felt that it was simpler for those who wished to read Heineccius to go to him direct, and for those in search of an explanation of legal passages in classical authors to go to John Taylor's *Elements of Civil Law*, which first appeared in 1754 (at Cambridge) and had the advantage that it was written in English. The only attempt at a comprehensive scholarly treatment of the civil law from the Oxford of the period was that of the unfortunate John Ayliffe. His *New Pandect of the Roman Civil Law*, which had cost him twenty years of labour, did not find a publisher until 1734 and appeared posthumously.[3] It failed so completely that the second volume never appeared. It was a singular, and indeed for the age in which it was published, a unique work. The author relied primarily upon the Italian jurists of the later middle ages, who were now very much out of fashion. He used them, however, as authorities for the interpretation of the texts, and did not attempt anything in the nature of a comprehensive account of medieval doctrine, and he indicated what portions of the Roman law were no longer applied in the continental practice of his day. It has been said that he never

---

[1] Wood, *New Institute* (4th edn London 1730), pp. xiii, 87.

[2] On this see H. Coing, 'Das Schrifttum der englischen Civilians und die kontinentale Rechtsliteratur', *Ius commune* v (1975).

[3] J. Ayliffe, *A New Pandect of the Roman Civil Law* (London 1734).

seems to have asked himself the question, whether he was proposing to expound the law of Justinian, the law of the medieval commentators or the *usus hodiernus* of the contemporary continental jurists.[1] In other circumstances this fact alone might not have caused the book to fail so disastrously, but the market for scholarly works on the civil law in English was at best a very small one. The same author's *Parergon juris canonici*, which was based upon the abridgement of the canon-law commentators which he had compiled for his own use when he was engaged in practice, went through two editions (1726 and 1734) and is still sometimes cited at this day. Ecclesiastical practitioners could find a use for a concise abridgement of the old canon law, which would enable them to see at a glance which portions of it were still applicable in England and would save them in most cases the labour of going to the original source.[2]

At the beginning of the period covered by this volume the introduction of what may very broadly be termed 'modern subjects' into the universities was already a topic of discussion. In 1708 Thomas Wood argued that instruction in the elements of English law was a necessary part of the education of a gentleman, and that the universities ought to provide it. In the pamphlet which he wrote upon this subject he pointed out that one of the difficulties of his proposal was that there existed no elementary textbook of English law that was not seriously out of date.[3] This want he subsequently attempted to supply. His *Institute of the Laws of England* is clearly intended as the modernized version of Finch's *Law, or a Discourse Thereof* which he had thought would be the kind of work which would best serve as an introductory textbook for students.[4] It went through ten editions. Its success was certainly due in part to the fact that it was the only book of its kind in print until Blackstone's *Commentaries* was published, but it is only fair to say that the tenth edition appeared as late as 1772, when the *Commentaries* had been in circulation for some years.

It is possible that Wood himself provided some instruction in English law for his pupils at New College, but no major step was taken until the

[1] Coing, 28-9.
[2] Thomas Bever's *History of the Legal Polity of the Roman State and of the Rise, Progress, and Extent of the Roman Laws* (London 1781) is hardly a legal work, but more an attempt at constitutional history. For completeness, we should also mention the two little pamphlets by Alexander Schomberg (1757-92, m. Queen's 1775; demy Magd. 1776): *An Historical and Chronological View of the Roman Law* (Oxford 1785) and *A Treatise of the Maritime Laws of Rhodes* (Oxford 1786). Both are very slight and contain nothing original. Whether they were designed to satisfy the temperate curiosity of undergraduates or to benefit the reputation of the author (the first is dedicated to Lord Camden, then lord chancellor) it would be difficult to say.
[3] Wood, *Study of the Laws of England in the Two Universities*, 19.
[4] H. Finch, *Law, or a Discourse Thereof* (London 1627 etc.). T. Wood, *An Institute of the Laws of England* (2 vols London 1720).

middle of the century. Blackstone had failed to meet with the success for which he had hoped at the Bar, and was coming to the conclusion that his talents were not suited to legal practice. He had resolved to return to Oxford, and had been encouraged to think that he might hope to be appointed to the chair of civil law on the next vacancy. Indeed it would seem that the assurances which he had received were specific enough to induce him to begin to prepare his lectures.[1] His hopes, however, were disappointed. He resolved nevertheless to lecture on the law. It would seem that his friends had encouraged him to offer a general course of the same type as was later to be given by Bever, which would necessarily take in a great deal of civil law. He felt, however, that this might look like a deliberate attempt to steal the thunder of the new professor and thought it better to confine himself to the common law.[2]

In this he may have been unnecessarily delicate. In 1754, after a vacancy of two years, the chair was finally given to Robert Jenner. Lord Campbell may or may not be exaggerating when he states that Jenner had not only never read the texts upon which he was appointed to lecture but would have been unable to construe them had he attempted to do so.[3] He certainly refrained from lecturing himself—from ill health, or so it was said—and saw no reason to discourage others from doing so. He made no difficulties about giving Bever permission to deliver his course on legal theory.[4] It is very possible, however, that Blackstone had another motive which he did not think it prudent to relate to his correspondent. Charles Viner had already resolved to leave his estate to the university to provide an endowment for the teaching of English law.[5] The first detailed scheme for his benefaction was drawn up in 1752. It was prepared in consultation with William King, the Jacobite principal of St Mary Hall. We may suspect that in the summer of 1753, when Blackstone advertised his first course of lectures in English law to commence in the Michaelmas term following, he fully appreciated that upon Viner's death a member of the university who was already lecturing regularly on this subject would be the obvious candidate for the new chair. The success of his lectures was such that he proved in the event not merely the obvious but the only candidate, but the controversies which arose over the settlement of the benefaction earned him a fund of ill will which was to render his life at Oxford somewhat uncomfortable thereafter.

[1] For this, and for what follows, see L. S. Sutherland, 'Evidence in literary scholarship' in R. Wellek and A. Ribeiro (eds), *Essays in Memory of James Marshall Osborn* (Oxford 1979). The account in J. Holliday, *The Life of William late Earl of Mansfield* (London 1797), 88–9 is apocryphal.

[2] See his letter quoted by Sutherland, 'Evidence', 235.

[3] J. Campbell, *The Lives of the Chief Justices of England* (2 vols London 1849, 3rd volume London 1857) ii. 378–9.

[4] Bever, *Discourse on the Study of Jurisprudence*, advertisement.

[5] Charles Viner (1678–1756), m. Hart Hall 1695.

Under the terms of the final will, which was dated 29 December 1755, Viner's estate was to provide for a professor, a fellow or fellows, and a scholar or scholars in English law. The professor was to be an MA or a BCL at the least, and a member of the Bar. He was to receive a 'handsome salary', and was to deliver four 'solemn lectures' at such times as convocation should appoint, outside the law terms at Westminster. The fellows were also to be MAs or BCLs, and one of them was to be appointed to act as tutor to those students who were studying the common law. The scholars were to be of two years' standing at least at the date of their election. The details of the benefaction were to be settled by convocation.[1] This enabled Blackstone and his supporters to contend successfully that the report of the delegacy which had been appointed to consider these details should be brought directly to convocation and not placed before the hebdomadal board, though the anonymous author of *A Serious Address to the Members of Convocation* argued that this was a fatal irregularity which would prevent convocation from considering the proposals for new statutes.[2] Viner's unfortunate specification of 'solemn lectures' presented a graver difficulty. The only lectures which the university statutes described as 'solemn' were ceremonial lectures. The epithet was applied to those lectures which the praelectors in arts were to deliver in their formalities upon the morning of the *vesperiae* before the general inception. The BA was required to deliver six 'solemn lectures' upon natural and moral philosophy as part of his form for the MA. In the superior faculties, the candidate for the doctorate might deliver either six cursory lectures upon prescribed texts, or six 'solemn lectures' upon subjects of his own choosing.[3] The delegacy recommended that the professor should be required to deliver one solemn lecture in every term, and that he should in addition be required to deliver in every year a complete course of lectures on English law, to consist of sixty lectures at the least, which the Vinerian scholars should be entitled to attend gratis, and for which his other auditors should pay such fee as convocation should appoint. He should receive a stipend of two hundred pounds annually, out of which he was requested to allow fifty pounds a year to Viner's widow during her lifetime. Since the professor's stipend would absorb the greater part of the income of the fund, it was proposed that the establishment of fellowships should be deferred until there was more money available. It could be, and was, argued that this scheme had clearly been prepared with an eye to Blackstone's convenience rather than to the founder's intentions. An anonymous author inquired:

[1] There is a collection of the various documents which were circulated during the controversy in Bodl. Gough Oxf. 96, and there are further references in Sutherland, 'Evidence', which I have plagiarized freely in the ensuing account.

[2] A copy of the *Address* (np nd) is in Bodl. Gough Oxf. 96 (18).

[3] *Laudian Code* VII.i.2, VI.ii.13, VI.iv.4 (cf VI.v–vi), ed. Griffiths, pp. 67, 58, 61–2, 62–5; *Statutes*, trans. Ward i. 58, 47, 52, 52 ff.

Whether the great Character and Merits of any one particular Person can justify the University in paying him a Compliment at the Expence of violating any Part of the Will of so great a Benefactor?[1]

The argument that Viner had contemplated that his professor should be a distinguished absentee rather than a resident teacher derived some additional force from his proposal that one of his fellows should be required to serve as tutor to the students of the common law. The duties which the delegacy suggested should be imposed upon the professor would leave a tutor with very little occupation. Again, it could be argued that the proposed salary was at once excessively handsome for a professor who was to be bound merely to deliver a certain number of solemn lectures, and inadequate for the occupant of a teaching chair such as the delegacy had in view, who would be obliged to abandon his practice at the Bar. There was no doubt a suitable candidate available at the moment, but there was no guarantee that it would be possible to find a successor to him.[2] The delegacy's proposals were finally carried by a majority so narrow as to set off a controversy upon the question whether the vice-chancellor and proctors had votes in convocation.[3] The proposed statutes were also carried. Blackstone, however, had exhausted his influence in the process. His success had been so complete as not merely to enrage his opponents, but to cause the friends whom he had mobilized ruthlessly in support of his proposals to feel that they had done as much as could be expected of them. Under the terms of the will the fellows and scholars on his foundation were to be attached to some college or hall in the university. Blackstone, according to his brother-in-law and biographer James Clitherow, had entertained hopes that the principalship of one of the halls might be annexed to his chair, that the Vinerian fellowships and scholarships might be attached to the hall, and that the hall itself might become a house of common lawyers, as Trinity Hall at Cambridge was a house of civilians.[4] When Blackstone became principal of New Inn Hall in 1761 he may have intended this as a first step towards the realization of his project, but he cannot have long continued to think that it would be possible in the conditions then existing. Convocation now took a positive pleasure in thwarting him, and rejected his most trivial and reasonable requests. Under the new statutes the Vinerian scholars were required to attend two courses of the professor's lectures before they proceeded to the degree of BCL. Blackstone asked for a dispensation for those scholars who had attended his lectures before he

---

[1] *Queries Humbly Proposed to the Members of Convocation* (np nd), copy in Bodl. Gough Oxf. 96 (32).
[2] Bodl. Gough Oxf. 96 (20, 22, 23, 25).
[3] Ibid. (26).
[4] The short life by Clitherow which is prefixed to W. Blackstone, *Reports on Cases determined in the Several Courts of Westminster Hall from 1746 to 1779* (2 vols London 1781) is the only contemporary biography.

was elected to the chair. It was denied.[1] The statutes allowed the professor to deliver his solemn lectures by deputy if he should be prevented from doing so in person, but the deputy had to be approved by convocation, and such approval could not be obtained at very short notice. Blackstone proposed that convocation should approve a list of persons, any of whom might act for him if the need should arise. The vicechancellor (George Huddesford) refused to propose that they be approved for more than one year, a restriction which Blackstone thought so insulting to his nominees that he withdrew the proposal altogether.[2] It had been resolved that the Vinerian scholars should remain for the present in their former colleges, and it could safely be assumed that a proposal to move them to New Inn Hall would be sure of rejection merely because Blackstone was known to desire that it should be carried. In 1759 he had again taken chambers in the Temple, and thanks to the reputation which he had acquired at Oxford he had met with better success in his profession than formerly. In 1766, the year after the publication of the first volume of the *Commentaries*, he resigned his chair and his principalship and left the university. In 1770 he was raised to the bench. Whatever irritation may have been caused in the university by the manner in which he had succeeded in forcing his own statutes for the chair through convocation, these statutes were drawn strictly enough to render it difficult for the chair to degenerate into a sinecure appointment.

His successor, Robert Chambers, the friend of Dr Johnson and eventually chief justice of Bengal, has left nothing in print save a *Treatise on Estates and Tenures* which—characteristically—was published posthumously in 1824 by his nephew, as the only portion of his uncle's lectures which a health broken by the climate of India had allowed him to prepare for the press. He had had equal, if not greater difficulty, in preparing them for his auditors, for it was not until 1770 that he was able to deliver a full course. Even this was the result of unrelenting pressure from Johnson, who did not easily tolerate procrastination in his friends, and whose intervention proved more effective than the fines inflicted by the university. Johnson provided practical help as well as exhortation, and which passages of the manuscript of Chambers's course (preserved in the British Library) are from Johnson's pen and which from Chambers's is something of a controversy among the learned.[3] It is, however, because of Johnson's intervention that his protégé's lectures are now being prepared for publication by Professor Thomas Curley, of Bridge-

---

[1] Bodl. Gough Oxf. 96 (37).
[2] Ibid. (42).
[3] See R. L. McAdam, *Dr. Johnson and the English Law* (New York 1951). For the legal, as distinct from the literary content of the lectures see Rupert Cross, 'The first two Vinerian professors: Blackstone and Chambers', *William and Mary Law Rev.* xx (1978-9).

water, Massachusetts.[1] During the last three years of his tenure he was permitted to lecture by deputy, to give him the opportunity to decide whether he would remain permanently in India or return to the university. His deputy was his fellow Newcastle man John Scott.[2] Richard Wooddeson, who succeeded to the chair in 1777, published his lectures in 1792 under the title *A Systematical View of the Laws of England*.[3] For beauty of style they cannot bear comparison with the *Commentaries*, but in the opinion of informed contemporary critics they were a more useful work for the student, since the author was more cautious in his views than Blackstone, and less likely to lead the reader astray on controversial points.

The reform of the examination system appears to have had a bad effect on the teaching of English law at Oxford. One consequence of the very unexacting character of the old degree examinations was that the syllabus did not have any great influence on the course of study actually pursued by an industrious undergraduate, nor was it expected that it should have. The university could require the Vinerian scholars to proceed with all convenient speed to the degree of BCL, without any apparent fear that the obligation to take a degree in civil law might distract them from the study of the common law. With the introduction of examinations which were a genuine test of attainment the ambitious undergraduate was less able to afford the time to embark upon a serious study of a subject which was not examined, and the unambitious undergraduate was no more inclined than before to embark on a serious study of anything. None the less, even in the middle of the following century the Vinerian professor was still lecturing to an audience of somewhat more than thirty, though the number of lectures required of him had been reduced from sixty to twenty-four.[4]

---

[1] The preceding observations I owe to an unpublished paper of Professor Curley's, which has been communicated to me by the kindness of Dr Fleeman, of Pembroke College, Oxford.

[2] John Scott (1751-1838), from 1799 first e. of Eldon; m. Univ. 1766; lord chancellor of Great Britain 1801-6 and high steward of the university 1801-38.

[3] R. Wooddeson, *A Systematical View of the Laws of England* (3 vols London 1792-3). Richard Wooddeson (1745-1822), m. Pemb. 1759; demy Magd. 1759.

[4] H. G. Hanbury, *The Vinerian Chair and Legal Education* (Oxford 1958), 92-3.

22

Reformers and Reform in the University

V. H. H. GREEN

IN THE first half of the eighteenth century Oxford was constantly under criticism. Its critics were for the most part whig publicists and intellectual deists. They held that the univesity was first and foremost a seminary for the established church and thus committed to a rigid doctrinal stance, and that its senior and junior members were largely sympathetic to the tory, even the Jacobite, interest and consequently must be suspect of treason. Furthermore the critics considered that Oxford was so deeply imbued with political and spiritual reaction that it could only be restored to its rightful function by root-and-branch reform.

These criticisms were often biased as well as extremely ill informed, nor when it came down to brass tacks were many positive or constructive proposals for reform made to soften the invective. One of the few who made some attempt to do this was Humphrey Prideaux, who had been earlier a Student of Christ Church and who was from 1702 to 1724 dean of Norwich. In 1715, at Lord Townshend's request, Prideaux submitted a scheme for the reformation of the universities. He criticized life fellowships, and dismissed the majority of the tutors as men 'such as I could scarce committ a dog to their charge'. He argued that no fellow should be permitted to hold his fellowship for more than twenty years and, with an unusual shaft of humour, suggested that an institution called Drone Hall should be set up to house superannuated dons. If the university was to be made genuinely efficient the government would have to intervene to reform the statutes. He recommended that a board of arbitration should be set up to deal with disputes that might arise among the colleges. Moreover, aware of the threat from contemporary deistic writing, he argued for the better teaching of divinity, suggesting, as a Hebraist himself, greater study of the scriptures in their original tongues.[1] Even though the possibility of government interference remained for some years to come, Prideaux's scheme never got further than the secretary of state's desk.

A limited tenure of twenty years for fellows was also the recommenda-

---

[1] R. W. Ketton-Cremer, *Humphrey Prideaux* (np 1955), 28-9.

tion made by the author of 'A memorial relating to the universities', published in 1759: 'many persons, spending their whole life in a College, without doing any the least service to their country, but to their own hurt, being generally, as they advance in years, over-run with spleen, or taking to sottishness.' This writer's main concern was to reduce or eliminate the disaffection to the government, 'the disloyal behaviour of the Universities, since his Majesty's happy accession to the Crown', which 'blind zeal for a party' had seemingly injected into so many members of the university. Parliament would have to intervene to remedy these abuses since the university was clearly incapable of putting its own house in order.[1]

There must therefore be some limitation on the university's autonomy. The appointment of heads of houses should be vested, not indeed in the crown, but in the 'great Officers of State, and such of the Archbishops and Bishops as shall be thought proper'. Since many fellows continued to reside in their colleges 'waiting for their turn of a College Living, without endeavouring to improve in learning', fellowships should not only be limited in length of tenure but colleges should in future be forbidden to purchase advowsons, any future advowson bought by a college becoming automatically forfeit to the crown. The only exceptions to the rule relating to tenure should be college tutors of fifteen years' standing or more who because of the nature of their academic duties would have lacked the opportunity to 'make those pushes in the world that others have time to make'. Moreover, college statutes would have to be revised to ensure that no fellow could be given leave of absence 'to make a push in the world' within five years of his election to a fellowship.[2]

While the writer in some sense sympathized with the current demand for the laicization of fellowships, he disagreed with the assumption that the too great increase of the clergy and 'their unhappy behaviour of late years' was connected with the bestowal of ecclesiastical benefices on former fellows of colleges. The unhappy state of the church was more a sequel to the university's graduates who had become 'most noisy and zealous tools of faction in the hands of cunning men'. Yet in those colleges which made provision for the election of laymen to fellowships in such subjects as medicine and law, laymen should be appointed, even though 'generally speaking, those who have the Faculty places get them purely to avoid going into Orders, and that they may live a more gay life without designing to follow any profession'. New statutes should be made to allow for 'an equal number of Fellows not in Orders, to the number of Faculty places allowed by the Founders', with a tenure limited

---

[1] 'A memorial relating to the universities' in *Collectanea Curiosa*, ed. J. Gutch (2 vols Oxford 1781) ii.
[2] Ibid. 56, 53, 54, 55, 57.

to ten years which should suffice to 'qualify them for their profession, if they really designed to follow one'.

If the university was to be won over to the new regime, then its members must be assured that there were likely to be rewards for their loyalty. The king should establish a professorship for the 'study of the law of nature and nations' in the universities at an annual stipend of £50 with the obligation of giving twenty lectures a year, both to prevent the professorship from 'turning into a sinecure, as most of them are' and to provide political instruction. 'I am of opinion', the writer declared, 'that if youth were thus instructed in the solid foundations of right and wrong, and the true original and design of all government, they would not entirely be perverted to notions in politicks, so injurious to mankind, and ruinous to their country.' All preferments, such as scholarships, exhibitions and fellowships, together with the exercise of discipline, should be henceforth placed in the hands of a 'well chosen set of Commissioners, constantly residing in each University, and inspecting the behaviour, and knowing the characters of all their members', at least for the next seven years.[1] The government should establish a fund which would enable it to provide annual pensions of £20-30 for fellows sympathetic to the regime, while others could be rewarded with reasonable preferments in the church. Deserving young men might be given awards and exhibitions of £10 or £20.

And I doubt not but by the encouragements just mentioned, on which the Government needs not lay out more than from 1500 to 2000£ per annum in each University, with the concurrence of the other methods before considered, there would in a few years be wrought a very sensible change in the affections of the Universities, towards the present Establishment, besides a great increase of learning.[2]

In 1714 another whig publicist, John Ayliffe of New College, published two volumes on *The Ancient and Present State of the University of Oxford*. He was similarly critical, condemning the behaviour of contemporary heads of houses, the source of 'many foul and scandalous Corruptions', and illustrating his case by mentioning the misappropriation of the funds of the Clarendon Press (attributed to the mismanagement, if not the corruption, of Delaune, the president of St John's).[3] Ayliffe's book created something of a furore, so much so that the university decided on his expulsion; but before this could happen he resigned his fellowship.[4]

[1] Ibid. 60, 61, 62, 63, 67, 66.
[2] Ibid. 68.
[3] J. Ayliffe, *The Ancient and Present State of the University* (2 vols Oxford 1714) i. 216. See also L. S. Sutherland, 'The administration of the university', p. 215 above.
[4] *The Case of Dr. Ayliffe, at Oxford* (London 1716).

Perhaps the most bitter and widely publicized series of attacks on the early eighteenth-century university came from the pen of Nicholas Amhurst, a fellow of St John's until the college expelled him from his fellowship in 1719, allegedly for debauchery, more likely for his stout adherence to whig opinions. In his *Terrae-Filius* he flayed the university for its adherence to tory politics, for its slothfulness and indifference to learning, all of which made a mockery of its claim to be a centre of piety and scholarship. He had a low opinion of the academic body. A fellow who is elected for life

wastes the rest of his Days in Luxury and Idleness; he enjoys himself, and is dead to the World; for a *senior Fellow* of a College lives and moulders away in a supine and regular Course of eating, drinking, sleeping, and cheating the *Juniors*.[1]

Amhurst compared the hebdomadal board to the South Sea Company, so recently discredited, since the heads of colleges, like the directors of the company, had

as perfidiously broken as great a Trust reposed in them ... under pretence of advancing national Religion and Learning ... they have debauch'd the Principles of Youth instead of reforming them ... they have embezzled or squandered away great Sums of publick Money.[2]

There was, he thought, very little to be said for contemporary scholarship at Oxford.

I have known a profligate *Debauchee* chosen Professor of *Moral* Philosophy; and a Fellow, who never look'd upon the *Stars, sober* in his Life, Professor of *Astronomy*; we have had *History* Professors, who never read any thing to qualify them for it, but *Tom Thumb, Jack* the *Gyant-killer, Don Belliamis* of *Greece*, and such-like valuable Records.[3]

Amhurst dismissed the examination system set up by the Laudian code with contemptuous scorn: 'It is a notorious Truth, that most Candidates get Leave of the *Proctor*, by paying his Man a Crown ... to choose their own *Examiners*, who never fail to be their old *Cronies* and *toping* Companions.'[4] He readily admitted that there had been some minor improvements in the public exercises of the university, 'that *Locke, Clarke* and Sir *Isaac Newton* begin to find countenance in the schools, and that *Aristotle* seems to totter on his antient throne';[5] but the changes had not been radical enough to make him modify his verdict that the colleges were principally 'Nurseries of Pedantry instead of sound Learning', the

---

[1] [N. Amhurst,] *Terrae-Filius* (52 nos. London Jan.-July 1721) no. xliii (7-10 June 1721).
[2] Ibid. no. xiii (22-5 Feb. 1721).   [3] Ibid. no. xi (15-18 Feb. 1721).
[4] Ibid. no. xlv (14-17 June 1721).
[5] *Terrae-Filius, or The Secret History of the University of Oxford in Several Essays* (2 vols London 1726), pp. xviii-xix.

'publick Discipline ... wretchedly neglected, and the publick Exercises confin'd to nonsensical Jargon and the meer Burlesque of true Knowledge'.[1]

Amhurst was a whig polemicist, preaching in the main to the converted; his criticisms served to confirm their prejudicies but may well have made his victims more complacent in their defence, as they saw it, of true religion and honest learning. James Miller, a Wadham man, clergyman and dramatist, shared Amhurst's views on the university, and in a play entitled *The Humours of Oxford*, published anonymously in 1730, he too gave rein to his contempt for dons and undergraduates, 'a parcel of Sad, Muzzy, Humdrum, Lazy, Ignorant old Caterpillars'. Why, says one of the characters, 'he is a Fellow of College; that's to say, a Rude, Hoggish, Proud, Pedantick, Gormandizing Drone—a dreaming, dull Sot, that lives and rots, like a Frog in a Ditch, and goes to the Devil at last'. Nor are Miller's undergraduates in much better shape: 'What between Dressing, Dancing, Intriguing, the Tennis-Court, and Tavern, I am so perpetually taken up'.

I had a good-for nothing, musty Fellow for a Tutor, who made me read *Latin* and *Greek*, and would certainly have ruin'd me, if two or three honest Fellows had not got me out of his Clutches, carried me to Town, and show'd me the World.

'When I came to his Chamber', says the servant of the don Mr Conundrum,

I found him entrench'd amongst a Parcel of musty old Books, like a Bug in a Bedstead—with half a Dozen Woollen Night-caps on his Head; a short black Pipe in his Mouth; a great pair of Spectacles on his Nose; and a Book in his Hand, as big as himself.

And this character, described by the author as a 'great pretender to learning', was also shown to be involved in a seamy affair with a local flirt.[2]

Although many dons undoubtedly read Amhurst's *Terrae-Filius* with wry amusement, and may have been agreeably entertained by Miller's somewhat ponderous satire, there was as yet very little evidence of any widespread desire for reform within the colleges themselves. Such uneasiness as was expressed came from single individuals, in some way or another disillusioned with the lifestyle of the university, manifest in the trenchant condemnation of Oxford in John Wesley's final sermon at St Mary's in 1744,[3] or in the pertinacious criticisms flowing from the pen of the founder of Hertford College, Richard Newton, keenly critical of the older foundations.

[1] *Terrae-Filius* no. i (11 Jan. 1721).
[2] *The Humours of Oxford* (London 1730), esp. pp. 7, 23, 25, 47.
[3] See V. H. H. Green, 'Religion in the university 1715-1800', pp. 455-6 above.

Newton gave voice to his criticisms in a series of articles which he contributed to the *General Evening Post* between January 1750 and July 1751.[1] Writing under the pseudonym of 'Well-Wishers' Newton urged the government to intervene to correct abuses since it was 'a thing absolutely impossible for it [Oxford] to amend itself'. Is it not reasonable, he argued, that

the parliament should once more interpose their authority, to alter such ... statutes of their founders, as shall seem to them to be a hurt to *discipline* in the place of education, and consequently to learning and virtue.

Characteristically, it was not the syllabus that he found so much at fault but rather the university's moral attitudes, the luxury which tempted don and graduate alike, reflecting contemporary decadence in society at large, the 'emulation in persons of great affluence, and high stations, to excel in dress, and equipage, and entertainments'. 'Luxury had over-run the country, and had subdued it', with the natural consequences that the rising generation, the young men of Oxford, were themselves drawn to '*excesses* in eating and drinking, in apparel and diversions'. Colleges had ceased to abide by their statutes; heads were elected by intrigue; discipline had been undermined. Fellowships were awarded to 'Men of *family* and *fortune*' who lived not

in a simple frugal manner, so necessary to health, and study, and virtue, which their founders *designed* they should. A *plain* diet, in a *moderate* proportion ... at *stated* hours, *twice* a day, so acceptable to the scholar going to bed in sobriety, and rising early, no longer pleases.

'Misrepresentation, and Obloquy, gratuities and entertainments, and late hours, and perfunctory exercises, and silent statutes' all helped to promote a relaxation of discipline. Because of the opportunity for preferment made available by the purchases of advowsons by colleges, the present-day colleges 'consist ... wholly of *young men*, with a power *still* of choosing their own governor, the *true cause* of the want of discipline in this place'.

The ancient discipline is lost. And the publick are deprived of the good intended them, to which they have still a right, and loudly and justly complain that it is with-held from them, and which, yet, they cannot recover without a reformation of the university.

Without such reform 'the University will not be a proper place for the education of youth'.

Newton's animadversions fell on stony ground, at least within the portals of the university. Outside it, the Jacobite rebellion of 1745 had released again some suspicion of the university's loyalty and encouraged

---

[1] *General Evening Post*, 9-11 January, 11-13 January, 29-31 March, 14-16 June 1750, 9-11 July 1751.

its critics to call once more for its reform. In 1749 a pamphleteer, probably George Coade, demanded a reform of the university so as to rid it of its tarnished politicians and to bring it into line with the progressive spirit of the times.[1] Like Newton, he held that government intervention alone could overcome the 'Sink of Debauchery and School of Sedition' into which Oxford had for so long slumped.[2] Newton's criticisms had been answered, somewhat ineffectively, in a series of letters in the *General Evening Post* and the *Whitehall Evening Post*. The writer, who signed himself 'Oxoniensis', stressed the sacred character of the statutes and oaths, rooted in immemorial tradition, which could not be tampered with lightly. The comparative youthfulness of fellowships was no bad thing. When, 'some thirty or forty years ago', there were several elderly men in the colleges, there was a general complaint that fellows, 'by staying too long here, contracted a sourness and moroseness, or a stupid indolence, regardless of their own and the college's reputation'.[3] He reminded Newton that the colleges' power to purchase advowsons had been already restricted by legislation.

Let him seek for a remedy of abuses in an academical and statutable method, attending on his duty in the University, and giving his assistance, when called upon, as he is, by statute and oath, obliged to do ... let him keep within the bounds of truth, and inform himself better of facts, and of the statutes and constitutions of colleges, before he pronounces so hastily and confidently upon them.[4]

So, after a brief recurrence in the summer of 1751, the minor controversy petered out in a desultory and inconclusive fashion. The Laudian code was amended, but it was still unlikely that the hebdomadal board would take the initiative in reform.[5]

Among Oxford's alumni one rather surprising voice stressed the need for reform, that of the conservative-minded jurist William Blackstone. Writing to Lord Shelburne on 27 December 1761 (to secure Shelburne's good offices for his appointment to the post of chief justice of Chester), Blackstone argued that should he be successful in his application, it would give him an opportunity to

open another Plan which I have long meditated, and which my present Situation in the University (as Principal of a Hall) would give me Opportunity to put in Practice. I mean some Improvements in the Methods of academical Education; by retaining the useful Parts of it, stripped of monastic Pedantry; by

---

[1] *A Blow at the Root: or, an attempt to prove that no time ever was, or very probably ever will be, so proper and convenient as the present, for introducing a further reformation into our national church, universities, and schools* (London 1749). [2] Ibid. 43.

[3] *General Evening Post*, 15 Feb. 1750.

[4] *Whitehall Evening Post*, 19 May 1750.

[5] See L. S. Sutherland, 'The Laudian statutes'.

supplying its Defects, and adapting it more peculiarly to Gentlemen of Rank and Fortune: Whereas the Basis of the present Forms is principally calculated for the Priesthood; while the Instruction of Laymen (whatever be their Quality or Profession) is only a collateral Object. The Universities were founded when the little Learning of the Times was monopolized by the Clergy.[1]

How concerned Blackstone was with this objective is unclear. Perhaps he realized that it was a subject likely to appeal to his correspondent. By the following autumn he confessed to Lord Shelburne that the appointment of the new chancellor (Lord Lichfield) closed any prospect 'of regulating those Errors in our Theory and Practice of Education, which Your Lordship and I have often lamented together'.[2]

Yet Blackstone cannot have been alone in thinking that reforms were necessary. 'I am glad', Sir Edward Turner informed the master of Balliol, Theophilus Leigh, 'to hear that you and others think of Reformation at Oxford. The Town talk freely of the want of Discipline (which by the by some of the Town are answerable for) that one is almost afraid to trust a Child there.'[3]

The movement for eliminating the thirty-nine articles had stronger backing in Cambridge than in Oxford, for its leaders, Francis Blackburne, rector of Richmond in Yorkshire, and his son-in-law, Theophilus Lindsey, were Cambridge graduates. In his *Confessional*, published anonymously in London in 1766, Blackburne claimed that the thirty-nine articles were theologically unacceptable, that the current latitude allowed to those who subscribed was fundamentally dishonest and that the rule of scripture was a sufficient guarantee of faith. The movement to scrap the obligation to subscribe to the articles led to the so-called Feathers' Tavern petition, and a motion to be proposed in the house of commons to annul the requirement to subscribe to the articles at the universities.[4]

For the majority of Oxford's clerical dons the thirty-nine articles constituted an essential bulwark against the insidious onslaught of dissent and infidelity which they associated with the growth of political radicalism which threatened to bring about the overthrow both of church and society. The expulsion of six undergraduates from St Edmund Hall in 1768 had demonstrated the high feeling running in Oxford at the time, more especially as some evangelicals claimed that the expulsion itself was a contravention of the doctrines contained in the articles. There was clearly a number of dons who would readily have agreed with the substitution of a more general form of subscription, as the subsequent war of

[1] Blackstone-Shelburne, 27 Dec. 1761, Shelburne MS S.35.
[2] Same-Same, 22 Oct. 1762, ibid.
[3] Turner-Leigh, 24 May 1766, Bodl. Dep. c. 568, fos 67-8.
[4] See L. G. Mitchell, 'Politics and revolution 1772-1800', pp. 166 ff above.

pamphlets demonstrated. Even so, it is significant that the initiative to modify or abolish the subscription to the thirty-nine articles at matriculation owed more to Cambridge (where no subscription at matriculation was required) than to Oxford, and that it was defended by established authorities at Oxford.

Yet the question gave rise in some respects to uneasiness. Even in Oxford itself the possibility of reform began to be discussed in some quarters, if only to forestall possible government intervention and to counter the threat of dissent. Idleness, it was argued, was a vacuum which could be filled not merely by immoral practices but by subversive political ideas. Some tightening of tutorial as well as of moral discipline could be regarded as an indispensable corollary to the proper object of a university education. That there was currently talk of reforming the traditional examination system is clear from a letter which his father addressed, on 9 June 1773, to young Martin Routh, the future president of Magdalen, in the course of which he commented that 'the alterations talked of in the examinations for degrees I suppose you will hear no more of for two or three terms—unless you have made a greater progress in those articles than your friends here imagine'.[1]

It was in this year, 1773, that John Napleton circulated anonymously his *Considerations on the Public Exercises*.[2] Napleton, who by no manner of speaking could be called a radical, had been a fellow of Brasenose since 1760 and he was later to occupy various profitable preferments in the church, among them the so-called 'golden' prebend of Hereford. He had the reputation as a college tutor of being, as Edward Collins commented, 'uncommonly strict'.[3] His short book was the first to highlight the problem posed by the outmoded examination system, and to suggest that there was a measure of serious concern in Oxford for reforms. He referred to a meeting of 'several respectable members of the University' which had condemned the 'low condition' into which the academic exercises had fallen, and which had expressed strongly the need to restore them 'to their ancient dignity and importance', conceivably the occasion to which Routh's father had been alluding.

Napleton considered the exercises for the BA at length and found them all to some extent deficient. The disputations *in parviso* were negligently performed, the questions put there 'trite and uninteresting' and the obligation of further attendance 'totally neglected and forgot'. Much the same could be said of the second exercise, *answering under bachelor*, 'except that, as it is held in Lent, the Schools are more frequently visited

---

[1] MCA iii. 21.

[2] *Considerations on the Public Exercises for the First and Second Degrees in the University of Oxford.* ([Oxford] 1773).

[3] R. Polwhele, *Reminiscences in Prose and Verse* (3 vols London 1836) i. 107.

by the Proctors and Masters'. The final examination was completely perfunctory. 'In the present Method, the Candidate sollicits Three Masters to
be his Examiners, and then obtains the Proctor's appointment or *Liceat*.
The Masters usually permit him to chuse his own Classics.' Nor were the
six exercises for the mastership more impressive. Determination was
intended to be performed with great dignity and solemnity. It still started
with prayers and a sermon at the university church to which the dean of
each college went with his determining bachelors, and it was followed by a
disputation in the schools, but the disputation was more often than not
'languid, uninstructive and uninteresting'. *Disputationes apud augustinenses*
and *disputationes quodlibeticae* had become lifeless forms; at the latter 'the
Regent Master proposes an argument on some trite question, and the
quodlibetical disputation is at an end'. The *sex solennes lectiones*, three in
natural and three in moral philosophy, which had to be given in the
schools between one and two in the afternoon, had become equally moribund. 'No private person ever hears these lectures; the Proctors attend
them occasionally: they are generally read *pro forma* in an empty school';
hence the phrase by which they were generally described, 'wall lectures'.
The two final exercises had also ceased to have any real meaning. 'They
are', Napleton commented, 'in truth for the most part performed in so negligent a manner, that it is equally impossible they should contribute to the
advancement of learning, to the improvement or reputation of the Candidate, or to the honour of the University.'[1]

After his attack on these 'lifeless unedifying formalities', Napleton's
positive recommendations seem unduly mild. 'This', he wrote, 'is an age
of improvements as well as of extravagancies: if it sometimes proposes
alterations unnecessary and excessive, it sometimes presents us too with
schemes that are rational and laudable.' His suggestions at least could
not be charged with being 'absurd refinements' or 'dangerous innovations'. He made much of the need to inspire the candidate with emulation by expanding the number of exercises in which he had to dispute to
an annual function in the Sheldonian Theatre in the presence of congregation. No man, he argued, will give of his best if there is no real inducement for him to do so.

Can it be supposed that a Young Man of ingenuity and learning will be accurate
in preparing matter for a Philosophical Disquisition, and take pains to clothe it
in reputable language, in order to read a Solemn Lecture, to which he is morally
certain he will have but One Auditor? . . . The necessity of appearing before so
numerous and respectable an audience, where he may lay the foundation of his
reputation and future fortunes, must be a wonderful incitement to the Student
to pursue his preparatory studies.

[1] *Public Exercises*, esp. pp. iii, v, vii, ix, x, i.

Napleton recommended the appointment of special examiners who would rank the candidates in three classes according to their achievement at the end of the examination. Surprisingly he thought that the actual 'Matter' of the examination was in general 'so well conceived, as to be capable of little, if any, improvement', but he thought that new material ought to be incorporated to test the candidate's proficiency in mathematics for both the BA and MA degrees. For the BA he should be

examined in the first six books of Euclid, in the nature and use of Numbers, particularly vulgar and decimal Fractions, and in the elements of Algebra; and for the Master's, in the eleventh and twelfth books of Euclid, in some convenient System of Conic Sections and Trigonometry, in the nature and use of Logarithms, and in the principles applying Algebra to Geometrical Subjects.

He stressed how important it was for the candidates to express themselves fluently in Latin, not simply the more effectually to assist in carrying out the business of convocation and the discipline of the schools, but to stimulate correspondence between learned men in all parts of Europe which had been imperilled by the way in which the 'ready use of Latin' had 'gone down in the world within these last hundred years'.[1]

To the criticism sometimes made that the degree course was 'not sufficiently directed to that Profession, for which the greater part of our Graduates are intended', Napleton replied that the course was sufficiently general in its scope to 'introduce' the candidate 'with advantage, either to the study of his particular profession, or to the ordinary duties of public or private life'. In fact college and professorial lectures should or ought to provide a training in professional skills in divinity, anatomy and chemistry, in civil and English law. But for students in divinity the New Testament should be studied in Greek as a 'test of the Candidate's acquaintance with the learned languages'. Aware of the controversy in which the university had so recently been involved, Napleton recommended that better provision ought to be made for instruction in the thirty-nine articles.

I need not enlarge on the extensive utility of such a measure, taken in every point of view; in an age which renders it peculiarly necessary, to send out our Youth well instructed in the principles of Christianity, engaged early on the side of Truth and Virtue, and steadily attached upon mature convictions to the purest Church in the world.

This was an opinion which reflected Napleton's basic conservatism. All in all he seemed to put too much faith in a modest and simplistic reform of the examination system by the provision of a 'numerous and respectable audience' at the academic exercises, by the incorporation of a 'few additional specimens of Mathematical Knowledge' and by placing 'the

[1] Ibid. esp. 60, 13, 24, 19, 33-4, 35.

Logical Disputations upon a useful and respectable footing'. These seemed somewhat paltry remedies for a deep-seated disease.[1]

For the most part Napleton's recommendations fell on stony ground. Did they produce any effect? Vicesimus Knox, writing a few years later, noted that in spite of its 'author's delicacy and moderation . . . the public knew it not, and, with all its merit, it soon sunk into total oblivion. The drowsy genius of dulness laughed, as he lolled on his sofa, at its utter failure.'[2] Knox was a more vehement critic than Napleton, though hardly a more constructive thinker. He was so prolific a writer that a modern scholar has commented somewhat harshly that he simply made a 'hodge-podge of the journalistic common-places of the day'.[3] Knox found both universities (though it was from Oxford that he took most of the illustrations for his theme) equally defective in their moral discipline and academic standards. If Richard Newton had held that the university's shortcomings were rooted in the low standards of contemporary society, and in the cultivation of self-indulgence at Eton, Westminster and Winchester even before the young men entered Oxford, Knox thought that contemporary immorality and infidelity were encouraged by the lack of tutorial supervision.

In no places of education are young men more extravagant; in none do they catch the contagion of admiring hounds and horses to so violent a degree; in none do they learn to drink sooner; in none do they more effectually shake off the fine sensibilities of shame, and learn to glory in debauchery; in none do they learn more extravagantly to dissipate their fortunes; in none do they earlier acquire a contempt for their parents; in none do they learn so much to ridicule all that is serious and sacred.[4]

In such respects he found the authorities wanting in responsibility. 'I never could discover', he wrote of the vice-chancellor, 'that he is much engaged in any superintendence immediately conducive to moral and literary improvement.'[5] The proctors were only concerned with trivial breaches of university regulations.

A man might be a drunkard, a debauchee, and a very ignorant person, and yet long continue to escape the Proctor's animadversion and penality; but no virtue or regularity could protect you from his severe censure, if you walked on Christchurch-meadow, or the High-Street with a band tied too low, or with no band at all; with a pigtail, or with a green or scarlet coat.[6]

The attitude taken by college deans was similar; they confined themselves to making sure that the undergraduates attended chapel, and

[1] *Public Exercises*, esp. 36, 37, 39, 46.
[2] V. Knox, *Liberal Education* in *The Works of Vicesimus Knox, D.D.* (7 vols London 1824) iv. 255. The first edition of *Liberal Education* was published in London in 1781.
[3] W. R. Ward, *Victorian Oxford* (London 1965), 6.   [4] Knox, 163.
[5] Ibid. 158.   [6] Ibid. 159.

otherwise turned a blind eye to all except flagrant offences, only too aware that some of the undergraduates would shortly become fellows and their own colleagues.

Knox's main complaint was that the standard of scholarship was low; but he did not in any detail recommend major changes in the curriculum, simply a more effective operation of the existing system. He held that fellows and tutors should perform their duties with greater efficiency, that professors should lecture regularly, that college exercises should be performed in a less perfunctory fashion, and that the period during which undergraduates should be required to reside in Oxford should be lengthened. 'With respect to the present state of learning in the universities, I am certain I should be destitute of candour, if I asserted that the most conspicuous characters in them are deficient in this prime requisite of an academical life.' 'The common rooms of Oxford abound with wits, from the punster and acrostic manufacturer, to the scoffer at all reformation.'[1]

Knox had no high hopes that the university would set its house in order. He recognized that there had been recent improvements in tuition and discipline at some colleges, notably at Christ Church; but he knew all too well that his opinions were unlikely to carry favour with most of Oxford's residents, but were far more likely to evoke implacable hostility, contending, as he believed he was, against power, riches, pride and prejudice. In an odd aside he wondered whether it might be for the good of the nation if the 'colleges were dispersed; if their revenues were employed in building and supporting separate colleges in various parts of the kingdom'.[2]

Knox's book on *Liberal Education* was published in 1781; eight years later, in 1789, he addressed an open letter to Lord North as the university's chancellor (which was annexed to the tenth edition of his book), in which he set out his recommendations for reform under twenty headings.[3] Once more he concentrated his attention on the need for a more rigid discipline and moral reformation. Undergraduates should be required to reside for eight months of the year. Tradesmen should be prevented from giving credit to importunate students. Their tutors should superintend tradesmen's bills and transmit quarterly accounts to parents and guardians. The keeping of horses and dogs and the frequenting of stables should be forbidden. He advised also that the oaths taken at matriculation and on other occasions should be simplified. Noblemen and gentlemen-commoners should no longer be entitled to exemption from public exercises and university discipline. The number of tutors in each college should be increased, and their stipends doubled. College

---

[1] Ibid. 162, 153.   [2] Ibid. 148.
[3] V. Knox, *A Letter to the Rt. Hon. Lord North* (London 1789).

examinations should be instituted, but should be 'conducted with such delicacy as not to hurt the feelings of the diffident and modest'. The university exercises, which should for the greater part be conducted in English, should be 'better accommodated to the present state of learning and the views of students of the present age'. Professors should be obliged to read three lectures a week in every term or provide a substitute; the 'professor of modern languages' should employ at least one foreign assistant to teach his pupils the elements of a foreign language. He recommended the establishment of a school of elocution, and the opening of the Bodleian and Radcliffe Libraries to all members of the university. He also suggested 'that all useless and antiquated forms whatever, which savour of monkery, popery, slavery, and Gothicism, should be utterly abolished'. He appealed to the chancellor in the hope, vain as he must have known it to be, that he would countenance such proposals for reform in parliament. 'Posterity', he said somewhat tactfully, 'will forget the misfortunes of the minister, while it profits by your wisdom as an academical chancellor.'

Knox's criticisms, coming from a former fellow of a college, naturally raised an angry response. One Oxonian wrote:

Your veracity as a Writer, and your feelings as a Man have been materially injured by your imprudent digressions into subjects, which, from their connection with the Moral Characters of Individuals, demanded the utmost delicacy of treatment, and the most faithful correctness of information.[1]

The writer went on to insist that he could vouch that the most 'rigorous' discipline was in fact imposed upon all members of the university, including noblemen and gentlemen-commoners; he asserted that the professors discharged their duties by giving courses of lectures and surmised that the expenses of a university education were not unduly great. To the suggestion that oaths at entry should be modified he, like so many traditionalists, reacted violently: whatever the status of the university decrees 'the Statutes of private Colleges, which we bind ourselves to observe at our Admission upon a Foundation, cannot with propriety be changed or diminished by any Power on Earth'. Oxford maintained, in this critic's view,

an acknowledged pre-eminence over every Seminary in the World. It is confirmed and consecrated in its Establishments by the approbation and practice

[1] *A Letter to the Rev. Vicesimus Knox on the subject of his Animadversions on the University of Oxford by a resident member of that University* [signed 'Philalethes'] (Oxford 1790), p. i. See also E. Tatham, *The Chart and Scale of Truth* (2 vols Oxford 1790) i. 34: 'He has drawn the *Discipline* of our Universities, both literary and moral, in features the most distorted, and painted the whole academical scene [*sic*] in the blackest and most offensive colours.' In *A Letter to the Dean of Christ Church respecting the New Statute upon Public Examination to which is added a Third Address to the Members of Convocation* (Oxford 1807), p. 5, Tatham claimed that Knox had 'left unnoticed every thing of more modern invention and more useful learning which had been substituted by Colleges in a liberal and beneficial manner to supply the place of an antiquated Discipline'.

of Ages: And it is endeared to every classical and patriot mind by the long train of celebrated Progenitors, who, descending in a glorious and uninterrupted succession, have illustrated the Annals of their Country by matchless Examples of Excellence, and reflected by the splendor of their Names an unfading Lustre on their common Parent.[1]

Although most Oxford dons might dismiss Knox as a windbag, the demand for reform of the examination system was slowly growing. 'I mean not to defend the utility of those Exercises', even Knox's critic recognized, 'in the present state of Learning: But I am unwilling to infringe upon antient Establishments, when a compliance with their original Forms and Customs does not materially affect the Welfare of the Institution.'[2] In the Bampton lectures on *The Chart and Scale of Truth* which he delivered in 1789 Edward Tatham, then a fellow of Lincoln, voiced his apprehensions about some aspects of the syllabus, more especially what as a Cambridge man he regarded a little unfairly as Oxford's uncritical acceptance of Aristotelian thought, accounting in part for the obsolescence of the public exercises. He held that college exercises had recently improved (there was some evidence for this in Christ Church and Balliol, though not much in his own college) even though the university exercises remained notably defective.

Since the Schools were neglected, the Colleges have improved: and, however the main spring of the great literary machine may be worn out by time, and never as yet replaced, there are other wheels in action of better mechanism, improving and to be improved, which move to the honour and emolument of great learning.[3]

Seven years later, in 1796, the publication of Edward Gibbon's widely read autobiography gave additional publicity among the non-Oxford public of the university's shortcomings, even though Gibbon's experience was four decades old.[4] The book evoked a spirited response and a strong defence of the university. Samuel Parr, though a Cambridge man and a whig friend of Charles James Fox, recited a list of Oxford's more illustrious sons to underline the 'excellency of our strength and the joy of our glory'.[5] James Hurdis, himself a fellow of Gibbon's college, Magdalen, made a somewhat peevish and not wholly convincing defence of the Oxford professoriate and of Magdalen's tutorial practices.[6]

The university's ship of state, represented by the hebdomadal board,

---

[1] *Letter to Knox*, 4-5, 16, 28-9. [2] Ibid. 22.

[3] Tatham, *Chart and Scale* i. 363.

[4] Gibbon's autobiography is in the first volume of *Miscellaneous Works of Edward Gibbon, Esquire*, ed. [John Holroyd,] Lord Sheffield (2 vols London 1796, 3rd volume London 1815); there is a modern edition by G. A. Bonnard under the title *Memoirs of My Life* (London 1966).

[5] S. Parr, *A Spital Sermon* (London 1801), 120-38.

[6] [J. Hurdis,] *A Word or Two in Vindication of the University of Oxford, and of Magdalen College in particular from the Posthumous Aspersions of Mr. Gibbon* (np nd), repr. in *Reminiscences of Oxford*.

was indeed by now beginning to move, creaking and cumbrous, towards modest reform of the examination system. That this should have co-incided with the immediate aftermath to the outbreak of the French revolution was no accident. The explosion in French society represented for many dons the sequel to the subversion of true religion, to what Ralph Churton in a university sermon termed 'the want of subordina-tion, the impatience of discipline, in the seminaries of learning' in France. If, he added, 'there is the remotest Tendency to similar passions in our own country and among ourselves, we should crush the growing evil in the bud'.[1] Like so many other Englishmen, most Oxford dons believed that sound religion, encompassed in the teaching of the estab-lished church, was the best safeguard against the anarchical ideas of social and political revolution, which 'tramples on religion and speaks blasphemy against God'.[2] Samuel Parr was to declare in 1800:

After the recent downfall, and amidst the rapid decay of similar institutions in foreign countries, our Universities are the main pillars, not only of the learning, and perhaps the science, but of the virtue and piety, *whether seen or unseen*, which yet remain among us, and therefore, woe be to every frantic visionary, and every ruffian vandal, who would raze them from their old and sacred foundations.[3]

But how well fitted were the universities to fulfil this important task? There was a growing suspicion that the English seminaries might be no better equipped than their French counterparts to cope with the spread of dissent and subversion. Their spiritual and academic fibre seemed defective. Too many dons took their duties with insufficient seriousness. Too many undergraduates whiled their time away in idleness and dissi-pation. Both religious dissent and political radicalism could fill the vacuums thus created. In the minds of many the connection between revolution and unorthodoxy, let alone outright atheism, was uncom-fortably close. 'By a most impertinent and obtrusive Conduct', Tatham said of the dissenters, 'they opened a correspondence with that country [France], and formed clubs . . . to celebrate it.' The dissenters 'labour to deprive us of the political learning of antiquity, and of the collected wisdom and experience of them'. 'When our safety or honour of the country is concerned, we know it is not to the Dissenters that we are to look to Right our battles.'[4]

---

[1] R. Churton, *A Sermon preached before the University of Oxford at St Mary's on Friday, April 19, 1793* (Oxford 1793), 17. Ralph Churton (1756-1831), m. BNC 1772; Bampton lecturer 1785; rector of Mid-dleton Cheney, Northants 1792.
[2] Ibid. 18.
[3] Parr, *Spital Sermon*, 112.
[4] E. Tatham, *A Sermon preached before the University of Oxford, on the 5th of November 1791* (London 1791, 2nd edn London 1792), 32, 38.

Although the direct evidence is lacking the deliberations of the heads of houses who constituted the hebdomadal board must be seen against this backcloth. There was indeed no doubt, as a writer in the *British Magazine* for 1800 made plain, that the new examination statute was intended to help stem the tide of political and religious subversion.[1] The article showed that the French revolution was in the writer's view an international conspiracy designed to overthrow religion and society. Intellectuals had been its principal advocates. 'Human depravity has engendered a moral pestilence, which has spread its deleterious effects over the whole of the civilized world.'

We have witnessed a *gradual progress* in the learned upon the continent towards those principles, which by being secretly and extensively disseminated, and at length by being openly avowed and acted upon, have filled the world with its present miseries ... in the foreign seminaries was fostered the moral plague which has so long desolated the fairest portions of the globe.

Although there were other sound reasons for reform, 'the nation in such an exigency calls with a far more earnest and authoritative voice upon her public seminaries of learning', and it was the 'conviction of this danger' which had led the university to consider proposals for reforming the examination system. Fountains now contaminated must be purified, 'and no method can be more effectual for the accomplishment of this end, than that which the university of Oxford now proposes to adopt ... It is high time ... to think of laying some restraint upon the profligacy which will always be found among young men who are too much their own masters.' Improved religious instruction will help to that end, providing the means for 'repelling and detecting the sophisms of that reptile philosophy, which would materialise and brutify the whole intellectual system'.

If such was the background to the passing of the new examination statute, rooted perhaps as much in fear of what might happen if there was no reform than in any deep-felt conviction of the need for change, it was likely that the reform would be of a conservative character. Yet the statute undoubtedly formed the thin wedge which was eventually to open the door to far-reaching changes. Unfortunately the absence of minutes of the hebdomadal board for the priod 1793-1800, apart from one meeting in 1796, two in 1798 and one in 1800, makes it impossible to trace the history of the statute in detail. John Eveleigh, provost of Oriel since 1781, has been described as the 'chief promoter' of the new examination system.[2] Of all who were present, Edward Copleston asserted in the course of a sermon which he preached at Eveleigh's funeral in 1814,

---

[1] 'J.M.' on 'The proposed regulations in the University of Oxford', *British Magazine* i (1800).
[2] M. Pattison, *Memoirs* (London 1885), 73.

'I believe I am best able to say how anxious he was for its adoption, and what pains he took to overcome the inertness and prejudices of many who were adverse to its introduction'. When it seemed that the plan was likely to be frustrated, he intimated that he would himself offer a substantial benefaction 'for the purpose of providing rewards and honours for the more distinguished candidates, if the university would consent to a reform of the whole system of examinations'. This helped to promote the acceptance of the scheme, 'if any individual can with propriety be named as its author, to him, I firmly believe, is that praise justly due'.[1] A mild-mannered man he was much esteemed by his contemporaries for his lack of personal ambition and 'singular uprightness'.

Eveleigh appointed tutors who raised the academic tone of the college. In this respect the election of Copleston of Corpus (who was to succeed Eveleigh as provost of Oriel in 1814) in 1795 was significant in that a Devonshire man was elected to a fellowship reserved for candidates from Wiltshire.[2] Copleston had not applied but was elected on his reputation alone. He became one of the best tutors in the university, teaching by means of small tutorial classes, deeply, even vituperously, concerned with maintaining high intellectual standards, and attracting others who shared his interests—John Keble, Richard Whately and Edward Hawkins.[3] By temperament Eveleigh himself was a conservative churchman; in the Bampton lectures which he preached in 1792 he had tried to counter the dangers of 'an adventurous and sceptical philosophy' by stressing the necessity of an orthodox theology.[4]

John Parsons, the master of Balliol from 1785 to 1809, was as orthodox and rigid a tory as Eveleigh, so suspicious of the newly formed junior common room that he burned its rules and banned its meetings; he was later rewarded with a bishopric. Yet, though some time elapsed before Balliol's academic record improved, Parsons had been keen to appoint good tutors and to encourage industry and ability, introducing an entrance examination and termly collections.[5]

If Eveleigh was the begetter, Cyril Jackson, the dean of Christ Church, would seem to have been the principal architect of the new examination. Personally he was as outstanding among his fellow heads as his college was without equal for social distinction in the university. Jackson, a pupil

[1] W. J. Copleston, *Memoir of Edward Copleston* (London 1851), 63.
[2] Ibid. 5; *Remains of the late Edward Copleston*, ed. R. Whately (London 1854), 3–6.
[3] John Keble (1792–1866), m. CCC 1806; fellow Oriel 1812–35; prof. of poetry 1831–42. Edward Hawkins (1789–1882), m. St John's 1807; fellow Oriel 1813–28, provost 1828–82; Bampton lecturer 1840, Dean Ireland's prof. of the exegesis of holy scripture 1847–61. Whately, elected a fellow of Oriel in 1811, was Bampton lecturer in 1822.
[4] J. Eveleigh, *Sermons preached before the University of Oxford* (Oxford 1794), 2–3.
[5] H. W. C. Davis, *A History of Balliol College* (Oxford 1899), rev. edn by R. H. C. Davis and R. Hunt (Oxford 1963); J. Jones, 'Sound religion and useful learning: the rise of Balliol under John Parsons and Richard Jenkyns, 1798–1854' in J. Prest (ed.), *Balliol Studies* (London 1982).

of William Markham at Westminster, had been appointed sub-preceptor to the prince of Wales through Markham's influence and so gained an entry into court circles which, though his appointment as preceptor terminated in 1776, he never relinquished; in 1783 Portland secured his nomination as dean of Christ Church. His earlier whig associations were no disservice to him and, a strong critic of catholic emancipation, his basic assumptions always remained conservative. A princely figure, not without a touch of self-importance and pomposity, he exercised, as Heber recalled, 'an absolute monarchy of the most ultra-oriental character'.[1] He obviously enjoyed his contacts with eminent politicians and the glittering world of the metropolis, and delighted in the young men of illustrious birth who came to the college. But he had a genuine appreciation of scholarship. He was, in spite of Tatham's sneers, a cultured man with a wide range of interests and he was concerned to improve both the discipline and academic standing of his college, which indeed already stood high.[2] He expected Christ Church to encompass an academic as well as a social élite. He took a keen interest in his more gifted pupils, in Canning who gained the chancellor's prize in 1789 for a Latin poem on the pilgrimage to Mecca, and in Peel with whom he carried on a long and intimate correspondence.[3] He certainly raised the tone of the place: 'all undergraduates at Christ Church', it was reported with some exaggeration, 'read the *Principia*'.[4] He appointed notable tutors, among them the Greek scholar Thomas Gaisford, who was Peel's first tutor, and the able if eccentric scholar Charles Lloyd.[5] It is a loss to university history that Jackson, who retired in 1809, should have given instructions for all his private papers to be destroyed.

It was then hardly surprising that under the lead of such conservative figures the new statute should have been sufficiently modest in its character to win the support of the other heads as well as of the majority of the masters in spite of the charges of chicanery which, possibly with some justification, Tatham was to bring against Jackson.[6] When it was

[1] R. Heber, *The Life of Reginald Heber* (2 vols London 1830) i. 499. Reginald Heber (1783-1826), m. BNC 1800; fellow All Souls 1804; bp of Calcutta 1822-6.

[2] 'Does he intend to sink the education of the whole University down to the humble standard of his own College?' Tatham, *Letter to the Dean*, 9. Gibbon wrote, referring to Cyril Jackson's two predecessors: 'Under the auspices of the late deans a more regular discipline has been introduced ... a course of classical and philosophical studies is proposed, and even pursued, in that numerous seminary; learning has been made a duty, a pleasure, and even a fashion; and several young gentlemen do honour to the college in which they have been educated.' Quoted in H. L. Thompson, *Christ Church* (London 1900), 167.

[3] N. Gash, *Mr Secretary Peel* (London 1961), 71, 210, 212. Robert Peel (1788-1850), 2nd bt; m. Ch.Ch. 1805, MP Oxford Univ. 1817-29; first lord of the treasury 1834-5 and 1841-6.

[4] *The Diary of the Right Hon. William Windham 1784 to 1810*, ed. C. A. Baring (London 1866), 244. In actual fact, according to the collections books at Christ Church, the *Principia* was read only once in the decade 1780-90 and twice in the decade 1790-1800.

[5] Charles Lloyd (1784-1829), m. Ch.Ch. 1803; bp of Oxford 1827-9.

[6] '[You may] bring all your Canons, and all your students, and all Others whom you command,

presented to convocation some fifteen out of the eighteen sections of the scheme were passed unanimously.[1] There were, however, some college tutors, among them Copleston of Oriel and 'Horse' Kett of Trinity, who opposed two sections of the new statute on the grounds that they were not radical enough.[2]

The statute certainly was the reverse of revolutionary.[3] The subjects in which men were to be examined were the traditional ones: for the BA, 'Grammar, Rhetoric, Logic, Moral Philosophy, and the Elements of Mathematics and Physics'; for the MA, 'Mathematics, Physics, Metaphysics and History. And to these is to be added . . . the Hebrew tongue.' The only novelty was the compulsory examination on 'every occasion' in the 'Elements of Religion, and the Doctrinal Articles', an attempt obviously to reinforce instruction in the orthodox faith, regarded as vital to the preservation of public order and social stability. The examination in Grammar, 'in Humane Literature . . . especially one in the Greek and Roman writers, three of whom at the fewest, of the best age and stamp, are to be used', was also compulsory. To stir the spirit of emulation the examination was to take place in public: 'it is a most desirable and momentous object, that as many members of the University as possible . . . should be present.' There were to be six examiners, three of whom constituted a quorum, who were to examine six candidates viva voce (for the examination was at first oral, not written) each day. Candidates who aspired to honours were to be examined by the whole board of examiners upon a somewhat wider range of books; the first twelve were to be listed in order of merit, though in fact fewer than twelve men were to present themselves in the first few years of the examination's existence, and for many years to come only a minority of undergraduates sought honours.

Hardly surprisingly the new examination statute was criticized, partly because of the apparent limitation on the numbers deemed worthy of honours; nor did there appear to be an effective way of amending the statute in convocation without a lead being given by the hebdomadal board. The heads listened sympathetically to the complaints but they were cautious, conservative-minded men, and the changes that they at first suggested were not strong enough to satisfy the complainants. An

---

and range them in just order in Convocation'; 'what *beckonings*! and *crossings*! and *whisperings*! and *consultations*! . . . Never was the Corporate Body in the solemn act of discharging its legislative functions, upon an occasion the most momentous, insulted in so public and barefaced a way'. Tatham, *Letter to the Dean*, 3, 7.

[1] OUA register of convocation 1793–1802, fos 376–96; Balliol College Library, Jenkyns papers, VI. A (12), 21 May 1800; *The Times*, 25 Apr. 1800.

[2] Broadsheet of 20 May 1800 ('The undersigned Tutors . . .'), copy in Bodl. G.A. Oxon b.19, fo 296.

[3] *Statutes* IX. ii, trans. Ward ii. 29–41.

'expected opposition, powerful both in numbers and eloquence, which they could neither satisfy nor resist, confined their deliberations for six years within the walls of that mysterious conclave, known to the younger members of the University by the profane appellation of Golgotha'.[1] At last, in 1804, after the proctors had themselves raised the expediency of amending the statute, the heads agreed to refer proposals for change to a small committee for 'very mature Deliberation'.[2] As is the wont with committees, it took its time, eventually reporting two years later, 13 June 1806, that the members had 'Proceeded in their Deliberations with all the Expedition which was consistent with the Nature and Importance of the Subject'.[3] The committee recommended that the Easter and Act terms should be consolidated to form the Trinity term, and that for the future the academic year should consist of three terms of eight weeks. They proposed some comparatively minor amendments in the conduct of the examination itself. Attendance on the bachelor's determining exercises should be substituted for 'answering under bachelor' and for 'juraments' an attendance on 'generals' should be required; that at the conclusion of each examination the examiners should arrange 'the Undergraduates ... according to their proficiency in Literis Humanioribus'. The committee also suggested that an exercise for bachelors during Lent described as determination should replace the old exercises for the MA. They further recommended that the office of master of the schools should be made separate from that of pro-proctor.

The hebdomadal board discussed the report at some length at a number of meetings throughout 1806, and in December issued a draft statute. The complainants were dissatisfied, objecting to various individual clauses. The first statute was rejected, as was a second amended statute in February 1807. It was then proposed that the statute should be divided into sections and that a vote should be taken on each of them. In the event only one section was thrown out, that which contained a provision for publishing the names of the lowest class of candidates. The new statute, once more amended, received the approval of convocation on 17 June 1807.[4] It did not in any fundamental sense change the content of the examination as it had been laid down in 1800. But it provided that in future all candidates were to be classified according to merit; the names in the first two classes, both in literae humaniores and in mathematics, were to be published after the end of each half-yearly examination. In effect a school of mathematics and physics was made available for those who had already taken or were taking the examination 'Greats' in

[1] H. H. Drummond, *Observations suggested by the Strictures of the Edinburgh Review upon Oxford* (Edinburgh 1810), 29-30.
[2] OUA minutes of the hebdomadal board 1803-23, 25 June 1804, WPγ/24/3, fos 63-6.
[3] Ibid. 13 June 1806, fos 109-11.
[4] *Statutes* IX. ii, trans. Ward ii. 56-8.

classical studies. The number of examiners was reduced from six to four, two annually going out of office, and declared incapable of re-election without the interval of a year. The examiners' emoluments were increased from £50 to £80 per annum. The examination for the MA was abolished. A second statute, passed on 2 June 1808, substituted, in place of the old forms, a minor examination in the classics, the study of a Greek and Latin book, together with logic and the elements of Euclid and translation from English into Latin; the new examination received the old appellation of *responsiones in parviso* or 'responsions'. When, in 1809, the examination statute of 1807 was reissued, a clause was added forbidding the admission of a candidate to the final examination without a certificate of his having passed 'responsions'. A line subdividing the second class effectually created three classes.[1]

The new examination system had its teething troubles and did not lack its critics. It attracted few candidates and was disliked by many college tutors. The statutes had been produced by the heads meeting in the hebdomadal board without any effective consultation with the masters who made up convocation; inevitably there was talk of 'skull-duggery' and evasion.[2] Edward Tatham argued forcefully that the heads were whittling away the rights of the masters. Moreover, since the heads were unready to risk a defeat in convocation, their proceedings had often been dilatory and unnecessarily protracted. Others, like Tatham, criticized the narrowness of the curriculum, more especially its neglect of natural philosophy.

Tatham constituted himself the leading critic of the examination as well as of the tactics which the heads had employed to have the first and following statutes accepted. 'A bad Reform', he concluded in 1807, 'is worse than none. Better, much better, had we been under the Public Discipline which obtained before the Statute of 1800, however faulty.'[3] The new examination had been 'patched and tinkered up out of the rubbish of the Old Discipline of the Schools, without any regard whatever to the Advancement of the Learning and Knowledge of *these present times*'.[4] He objected to the fact that although he was the head of a house and therefore a member of the hebdomadal board, he was sometimes purposely (and perhaps understandably) excluded from their meetings. In his view sessions of the board became merely a forum for the views of the wicked dean of Christ Church, Cyril Jackson. The dean

---

[1] *Statutes*, trans. Ward ii. 78-81, 101-2.
[2] After the 'Public Commemoration was over the last year, when most of the Academical business was at an end, and most of the Masters ... gone for the long Vacation' the statute was revived: E. Tatham, *A Fifth Address to the Free and Independent Members of Convocation* (Oxford 1808) 4.
[3] E. Tatham, *An Address to the Members of Convocation at Large on the Proposed Statute on Examination* (Oxford 1807), 17.
[4] Ibid. 6.

is the Father of that anomalous production, called the New Statute, born in the nineteenth century to blast the fame of this famous University in the estimation of Europe ... For your Person I have a high regard, and of your *Learning*, though you have given no public testimony of it, from *Reputation*, I entertained a high opinion ... for there is nothing I find so fallacious as *Literary Fame* in the University of Oxford.[1]

'There has long been an endeavour, I know and lament, to draw all power into a *Certain Place*, which place I have told, and told it truly, That it either mistook or abused its rights, or rather both.'[2] With the dean Tatham seemed to associate the whole college which he regarded with grave suspicion:

However great his affection of the Peripatetic learning, and however strenuous his exertions may be to make it fashionable, the great Framer of the New Statute, with all the power he possesses, may be disappointed in his hope of making the young members even of his own College, men of quick sensibility, vivid imagination, and elastic genius, philosophers or logicians of the Peripatetic school. Should it, however, be a part of his ambition, that his young-men may figure in the world as accomplished Foxhunters, which appears, from the pursuits of his College, to have less of affectation; he may entertain more sanguine hopes.[3]

Tatham accused the dean of overruling the rights of the free and independent members of convocation. He had so arranged for the passing of the statute of 1807 that no proper notice had been given, and the determination meeting had been held in the vacation.[4] Tatham, as was his manner, was blunt to the point of rudeness. In order 'to retrieve, as far as I am able, the injured Honour of my Alma Mater, I will cause your half-formed and mis-shapen offspring to stink in the nose of every scholar in Europe'.[5]

He had, however, deeper grounds of criticism than his dislike of Jackson. 'An University', he declared justly,

is the seat of *Universal Learning* increasing and to be increased, from the nature of men and things, with the lapse of time ... its *Discipline* should accordingly be *adapted to the Increase or Advancement of Learning improving and to be improved according to the times*, otherwise it may occupy young-men in studies that are obsolete and in errors that are exploded.[6]

---

[1] Tatham, *Letter to the Dean*, 3.

[2] E. Tatham, *A Second Address to the Members of Convocation at Large on the Proposed New Statute respecting Public Examinations* (Oxford 1807), 4.

[3] Tatham, *Letter to the Dean* 11.

[4] E. Tatham, *A Fifth Address ... respecting Public Examination, and the Alterations to be Proposed in Convocation* (Oxford 1808), 4-5.

[5] Tatham, *Letter to the Dean*, 4.

[6] Tatham, *Address to the Members of Convocation at Large*, 1.

He was an astringent critic of the dominance of Aristotelian philosophy at Oxford, comparing it unfavourably with Cambridge where he had been an undergraduate and which, unlike his adopted university, had admitted both Bacon and Newton into its curriculum. 'From being the *Instrument* of all truth and learning . . . the Organon of Aristotle has upon the whole been the *Instrument* of ignorance and error; by which that great philosopher has proved in the event the greatest tyrant in the universe.' Aristotle, in Tatham's opinion, had kept 'learning and science in a dark and gloomy prison . . . drawing a cloud over the disk of the literary sun, by which it was for centuries eclipsed, and of which more than a single limb is now obscured'.[1] He had to lament, he wrote in 1811, recalling his admission to the university, that university learning

was radically and generally defective, that it was founded upon false and contracted principles, applied without philosophical discrimination to the different branches of knowledge, which were cultivated by one method of reasoning only, the Aristotelian Logic; and that the truths of all these branches were confounded together, and considered in the mass as of equal force, commanding the same assent of the understanding. This root of prejudice and error was an insurmountable barrier against the progress of truth and sound learning in every part of science in this University.[2]

Tatham contended that the new examination statute should have provided an opportunity to bring into being a course of study more suitable to the present age. But instead of modifying Aristotle's influence the new statute had actually perpetuated and even strengthened this

absurd and antiquated Discipline, which have holden Oxford in inglorious slavery . . . [the] framers of this New Form of a Statute . . . are doughty Schoolmen, disciples and slaves of Aristotle and the Ancients, blind to all improvement, and bigotted to antiquity . . . the Old Moral Philosophy of Aristotle, Cicero, or Epictetus, however admirable in their days, is at this day not worth a louse . . . how preposterously absurd . . . is it, to send the Youth of a Christian University, in the nineteenth century, to learn their Moral Philosophy from Aristotle, that uncircumcized and unbaptized Philistine of the Schools?[3]

The stress laid on logical and dialectical studies could only have the effect of cramping the mind and stunting the development of the rational faculties.

And when, after your four-years' labour in studying Dialectica is crowned with the desired success in ranking your names, though only alphabetically, in the

---

[1] Tatham, *Chart and Scale* i. 331-2, 333.

[2] E. Tatham, *An Address to the Rt Hon. Lord Grenville, Chancellor of the University of Oxford upon Great and Fundamental Abuses in that University* (Oxford 1811), 29.

[3] Tatham, *Address to the Members of Convocation at Large*, 2, 6. Cf ibid. 15: 'That the old University-Motto, DOMINUS ILLUMINATIO MEA, may be changed for one which will be more appropriate to its character, and more worthy of its renown, ARISTOTELES TENEBRAE MEAE.'

First Class, well may you deserve to be pronounced *Egregie*, for, doubtless you will prove *Egregious Blockheads*, unqualified to cope with Art or Science, and unprepared for the study of the Learned Faculties.[1]

Positively, he asked why the reforms had neglected to embody modern philosophy as well as mathematical and scientific studies more thoroughly in the syllabus. 'Why . . . is NATURAL PHILOSOPHY the Queen of all Theoretic Science, one of the fittest subjects of academical Education, *totally omitted?*' Was it because the makers of the statute refused to take any guidance from Cambridge which in recent years had produced abler mathematicians, better philosophers, greater poets and better classical scholars than Oxford?[2]

Tatham's blunt speaking outraged his fellow heads as well as many others in the university. He was an unpopular figure, often at logger-heads with his own fellows as well as with the other heads, with only a very limited influence in the university. His criticisms were the more likely to be counter-productive. 'I know not', said one such critic writing under the pseudonym Philalethes, 'which forms the greatest cause of astonishment, the effrontery or the falshood . . . with which you have so illiberally attacked the Dean of Christ Church.' He critically accused Tatham of undermining the authority of the heads in such a way as to promote subversion and indiscipline among the undergraduates, a charge which must have infuriated the obstreperous Yorkshireman. Such an address was 'actually inciting them to discontent, and complaints little short of rebellion against their tutors and guardians'. His 'invidious comparison between this and a Sister University' could only be un-popular.[3]

Tatham's condemnation of his fellow heads' behaviour appeared so intemperate that the hebdomadal board decided to take legal advice.[4] Meeting on Thursday 28 June 1810 the heads considered the 'false and scandalous Charges' which Tatham had made 'against Individuals, and against this Board', stating that its meetings 'have been holden in an *artful, collusive*, and *smuggling* Manner for the purpose of effecting the objects of interested Individuals, and particularly for the purpose of passing the Statutes respecting the Public Examinations, and other Exercises for Degrees'. 'This Board, considering that such Conduct . . . deserves the severest Reprobation, as tending to create Divisions in the University,

---

[1] Ibid. 11. [2] Ibid. 8.

[3] 'Philalethes', *A Letter to the Rector of Lincoln College* (Oxford 1807), 6, 5, 7.

[4] For example, Tatham referred to 'These new and capricious Meetings . . . set up in the place of the old Hebdomadal Meetings, which, in the abundance of their liberty, they hold in contempt as slaves chained down to time and place' and asked how the vice-chancellor could 'expect that the junior members of the University, consisting of generous youths full of high blood and spirits, will strictly obey the Statutes which relate to them': E. Tatham, *A New Address to the Free and Independent Members of Convocation* (Oxford 1810), 8, 12.

to injure its Discipline and to degrade its Character, Resolves That a Case be prepared', and instructed Mr Wooddeson, the counsel for the University, to advise whether proceedings should be instituted under the statutes *De famosis libellis cohibendis* and *De contumeliis compescendis* against the author. On 2 July following the vice-chancellor, John Parsons, and twenty heads of houses together with the two proctors signed a document for circulation repudiating the charges which Tatham had made.[1]

Tatham was unrepentant. In a lengthy open address to the chancellor, Lord Grenville, he justified his actions, 'I stand forward as the Public Corrector of these Abuses ... I consider myself directly the Advocate and Assertor of the Rights of Convocation.' 'I do not shrink for a moment from my resolution to maintain inviolate the Hebdomadal Statute. I do not shrink for a moment from my duty to vindicate the rights of Convocation. I do not shrink for a moment from my endeavour to reform the Abuses of the University of Oxford.' 'Am I,' he declared stoutly, 'in the act of reforming great Abuses, to be frightened with threats and Lawyers?—Alas! However you may think of the head; you know little of the heart, of *Edward Tatham*.'[2] But he was too unpopular and lonely a figure to win much support. The heads wisely decided to take no further action in the matter. The new examination statute had come to stay.

Such reforms had made a minimal impact on the outside world. Oxford was still, as Copleston expressed it, 'assailed on every side, and by every poisoned weapon the press can discharge'.[3] In this the *Edinburgh Review* was to be to the fore. Towards the close of a learned review of la Place's *Traité de méchanique céleste* in 1808 the writer (John Playfair) took occasion to remark that the inferiority of mathematical scholarship in Britain resulted from the deficiency of the universities, notably Oxford, 'where the dictates of Aristotle are still listened to as infallible decrees, and where the infancy of science is mistaken for its maturity, the mathematical sciences have never flourished; and the scholar has no means of advancing beyond the mere elements of geometry'.[4] Then, in July 1809, after a somewhat caustic sidelong glance at Oxford's affluence and standing, another critic (Payne Knight) struck at the edition of Strabo by the Oxford Press as a 'ponderous monument of operose ignorance and vain expense'. The editor, Thomas Falconer, was charged with inaccuracy, ungrammatical Latin and lack of genuine scholarship; his book, was a 'pile of rubbish heaped up with so much labour'; and the reviewer went on to say that though

---

[1] OUA minutes of the hebdomadal board 1803-23, 28 June 1810, WPγ/24/3, fos 195-6, ibid. 2 July 1810, fos 202-3.

[2] Tatham, *Address to Grenville*, 3, 15, 28.

[3] *The Examiner Examined or Logic Vindicated, addressed to the junior students of the University of Oxford by a graduate* (Oxford 1809), 1.

[4] *Edinburgh Review* xi (Jan. 1808), 283.

this learned Body have occasionally availed themselves of the sagacity and erudition of Rhunken [*sic*], Wyttenbach, Heyne, and other *foreign* professors, they
have of late, added nothing of their own, except what they derived from the
superior skill of British manufacturers, and the superior wealth of their establishment; namely, whiter paper, blacker ink, and neater types.[1]

Finally a reviewer of Richard Edgeworth's book *Essays on Professional
Education* (London 1809) criticized the undue emphasis placed on
classical education in England, for which the universities were largely to
blame. 'An infinite quantity of talent is annually destroyed in the Universities of England, by the miserable jealousy and littleness of ecclesiastical
instructors.' They 'fancy that mental exertion must end in religious scepticism; and, to preserve the principles of their pupils, they confine them
to the safe and elegant imbecility of classical learning'. 'Classical literature', the reviewer noted meaningly, 'is the great object at Oxford.' He
added: 'Sad, indeed, is the fate of this University, if its object has been
classical literature alone; and it has failed even in that.'[2]

The university found a champion in Copleston, fresh from a victorious
sortie against a fellow tutor, Henry Kett, with whom he had once been
associated in pressing for further reforms in the original examination
statute. Copleston felt that Kett's scholarship, or rather lack of it,
degraded the university: in his earlier works 'the conceptions were indistinct and confused; the information scanty and unconnected; the
remarks superficial; the errors, beyond all bearing, abundant and disgraceful; the language turgid, frothy and impotent'.[3] He concluded his
article, which showed that he had nothing to learn in point of method
from the *Edinburgh Review*, with the words:

my labours are not yet over . . . If the vile imposture of *quackery* deserves to be
scourged and pilloried, the foul lurking fiend of *defamation*, of deliberate and

---

[1] Ibid. xiv (July 1809), esp. 441, 431. He had commented (p. 430): '[We have] often contemplated,
with sentiments of patriotic pride and exultation, the spacious and comfortable abodes, and ample
revenues provided for the instructors; which exempt them from all worldly cares, but those of learning and teaching; and, at the same time, protect them from those dangerous lures of pleasure and dissipation, which so often distract and unnerve the mind of the scholar amidst the busy bustling throng
of a great and luxurious metropolis. To the Fellow of a College, the public library is the theatre of
recreation and the private study the office of business; from the fatigues of which, the morning's ride,
and the evening's lounge, present constant, regular, and tranquil means of relaxation.'

[2] Ibid. xv (Oct. 1809), 50-1. The reviewer was Sydney Smith (1771-1845, m. New College 1789)
one of the originators of the *Edinburgh Review*.

[3] Copleston, *Examiner Examined*, 2. Copleston reserved a stinging and resolutely destructive pen
for Kett's most recent book, *Logic made Easy, or a short view of the Aristotelic system of reasoning* (Oxford
1809). Kett's *Elements of General Knowledge* (2 vols Oxford 1802) was the substance of a course of lectures given to his pupils; though it went into a number of editions, it had been shown to be full of
errors, for example by 'Philalethes' [John Davison] in *A Short Account of . . . Discoveries contained in a
Recent Work* (2 parts Oxford 1803-4). Kett had been a classical examiner in 1803-4 and was familiarly
known as 'Horse' Kett because of his equine countenance. Copleston was thought culpable of bad
taste in printing on the title-page of his *Examiner Examined* lines from Virgil ending with *Equo ne
credite, Teucri*. Kett committed suicide by drowning on 30 June 1825.

systematic defamation, must not be allowed to spit his venom with impunity . . . I have begun, indeed, with chasing a flea; I shall end, perhaps, with rousing a lion.[1]

In his *Reply to the Calumnies of the Edinburgh Review* Copleston endeavoured to show that its picture of an Oxford education was both outdated and ill informed. It was 'time to raise the voice of injured freedom and insulted honour' when 'the public are taught with unwearied and malicious industry to look upon us either as gloomy bigots, or lazy monks, or ignorant pretenders to learning and science', charges which had been born of the 'vile serpent-brood which have been hatched in our own bosom'. Oxford's attitude to Aristotelian studies had for instance not been uncritical, but its critics had ignored the sound qualities of Aristotelian philosophy and of classical learning. In any case Oxford education was not confined to classical literature; there was ample opportunity to study strict logic, divinity and mathematics; lectures were available in experimental philosophy, astronomy, chemistry, mineralogy and botany. If the reviewer had been once correct in suggesting that an Oxford student had 'no means of advancing beyond the mere elements of geometry', the establishment in the previous year of the honour school of mathematics and physics went some way to remedy the position. All in all the Edinburgh reviewer had produced a frivolous and narrow interpretation of classical literature which Copleston refuted by a detailed analysis of the Oxford curriculum which he hoped to show was sufficiently liberal and penetrating to enrich the mind of all who studied there. 'The writer confounds the *cultivation* of *literature* with the *acquisition of science*.'[2] Copleston's vigorous defence was indeed much appreciated. Grenville wrote him a personal letter of thanks and the university conferred on him the degree of DD by diploma.

Some who were well acquainted with Oxford may have felt that Copleston's verdict was too complacent. Whatever its merits, the new examination as yet attracted few candidates; the majority remained passmen (whom Copleston would personally have wished to be named in lists). In 1802 there had been only two candidates, one of whom, Hendy of Oriel, as Copleston much later described the occasion, 'tried for two days successively, and during four hours each day, before a most crowded audience in Divinity, Ethics, Rhetoric, Logic, Mathematics, Natural Philosophy, and the chief Latin and Greek classics'.[3] In 1803 there were

---

[1] Copleston, *Examiner Examined*, 57.

[2] *A Reply to the Calumnies of the Edinburgh Review against Oxford, containing an account of studies pursued in that university* (Oxford 1810), esp. 4, 10, 12, 16-17, 132, 136-55. On pp. 16-17 Copleston stated that '*for more than a century*, the Physics of Aristotle have been set aside, and, except for the sake of satisfying liberal curiosity . . . they are never even consulted'. See also Copleston's *A Second Reply to the Edinburgh Review* (Oxford 1810) and his brief *A Third Reply to the Edinburgh Review* (Oxford 1811).

[3] *Oxford Magazine*, 2 Nov. 1887. Abel Dottin Hendy (1783-1808), m. Oriel 1799.

four candidates, in 1804 three and in 1805 two, one of whom was W. H. Tinney of Magdalen, who earned the distinction of being entitled *maxime*, and the other Benjamin Symons, the future warden of Wadham.[1] From 1807 the candidates were classified, both in 'Greats' and mathematics, ten in the former in 1807 and thirty-two in Easter term 1808. One of the candidates in 1808 was Robert Peel, who was placed in the first class in both subjects (he was the first to win this distinction in mathematics); the double distinction was also achieved by John Keble in 1810 and by the future Provost Hawkins in 1811.

In content the examination remained conservative. None of its supporters would have wished an opportunity for debate about revealed theology or have given occasion for speculative thought. 'The more I think on it, the more am I convinced', Copleston wrote to John Penrose, 'that, to *exercise* the mind of the student is the business of education, rather than to pour in knowledge'; but he also believed that revealed knowledge was the basis of a good education and that it was better to produce 'an annual supply of men, whose minds are . . . impressed with what we hold to be the soundest principles of policy and religion' than to turn out a few great minds 'exploring untrodden regions'.[2] H. H. Drummond, who had also sought to refute the arguments of the *Edinburgh Review*, held similar views. Drummond agreed with Tatham, albeit the rector of Lincoln wrote with 'some bad taste and extravagance', that the curriculum remained defective through its failure to recognize modern philosophy, more especially Bacon's *Novum organum*. He surmised that the 'narrow policy of attempting to conceal from the eyes of undergraduates the arguments for any system of opinions, is now, I trust, utterly extinct'. None the less he still believed that it was most important 'to teach, in the first place, those old and established principles that are beyond the reach of controversy'.

Young men who are really desirous to be wiser and better for what they read, and to learn to think rightly and sensibly upon the most important subjects, must subdue every unreasonable desire of novelty, and, relinquishing the vain applause of all that is witty and superficial, assiduously labour to trace the steps by which their predecessors advanced on the road of useful discovery.[3]

---

[1] William Henry Tinney (1784-1871), m. Magd. 1801; fellow Oriel 1806-28. Benjamin Parsons Symons (1785-1878), m. Wadham 1802, warden 1831-71.

[2] Copleston, *Memoir of Edward Copleston*, 38, 150. Cf *Reply to the Calumnies*, 150-1: 'Let not this be construed into an admission that speculation is discouraged . . . But it is not, and it ought not to be the business of a body. It is for us to execute an established system; to teach and to recommend what is thoroughly approved . . . The scheme of Revelation we think is closed, and we expect no new light on earth to break in upon us.' John Penrose (1779-1859), m. Exeter 1795; degrees CCC; Bampton lecturer 1808; vicar of Bracebridge and Langton, Leics. 1802, and perhaps curate of N. Hykeham 1838-59.

[3] H. H. Drummond, *Observations, suggested by the Strictures of the Edinburgh Review upon Oxford* (Edinburgh 1810), 30, 34, 17, 79. Henry Home Drummond (1783-1867), m. CCC 1802; MP Stirlingshire 1821-31, Perthshire 1840-52.

Drummond's views in this respect were surely representative of the majority of Oxford dons.

Such reforms then as had taken place were conservative in content and inspiration. They were designed primarily to protect and promote received standards and not to stimulate original or speculative thought. They might almost be said to be a part of the establishment's attempt to sustain the orthodoxy and privileged position of the Church of England and to ensure social stability in the state. Even the erosion of the viva voce system and of public debate was itself a self-imposed limitation on the possible circulation of critical views. Yet, in spite of these and other defects, the new examination system constituted a watershed in university history. A good performance in the honour school was to count as something prestigious in itself. It not merely gave an accolade to the search for academic honours, but stimulated the colleges into competitiveness. Soon colleges would select the majority of their fellows from those who had acquitted themselves well in the schools. Many colleges had already tried to raise their own standards by introducing their own examinations and 'collections'. At St John's from 1802 it was decided that the 'undergraduates shall at the end of every Michaelmas, Lent and Act Term attend in the College Hall ... and be examined before the President and Senior Fellows as to the Progress they have made in their Studies'; book-prizes for academic achievement were introduced in 1811.[1] At Trinity the system of collections, originating in 1789 but only sporadically applied, was revised in 1809; henceforth it was laid down that future examinations would be conducted on lines similar to those of responsions, no more than six men being examined at once. Every undergraduate was to be examined in science and divinity as well as in classical books. A 'literary prize fund' was resurrected to provide prizes for those who distinguished themselves in collections.[2] As a result there was a slow, but steady improvement in the teaching both at college and university levels. John Coleridge recalled to Arthur Stanley in 1843 the excellence of the tuition he and Thomas Arnold, who had gone up to Corpus in 1811, received at that small college:

not by private lectures, but in classes of such a size as excited emulation, and made us careful in the exact and neat rendering of the original, yet not so numerous as to prevent individual attention on the tutor's part, and familiar knowledge of each pupil's turn and talents. In addition to the books read in

---

[1] Costin, St John's, 244-5.

[2] H. E. D. Blakiston, *Trinity College* (London 1898), 207. At Lincoln, a backward college, termly examinations 'for the improvement of the College discipline as well as to ascertain the progress of the undergraduate members in Literature' were not introduced until 1828: Lincoln, register 1739-1983, fo 174. Writing to his mother on 2 April 1808, W. S. Hamilton said he had been 'busy with Collections, which are public examinations, at the end of each term, on all the books we have read during the continuance of the term, before the master and public lecturers': Jones, 'Sound religion and useful learning', 97.

lecture, the tutor at the beginning of the term settled with each student upon some book to be read by himself in private, and prepared for the public examination at the end of term in Hall.[1]

However slow reform might appear to be to the outside observer, by the early nineteenth century it was beginning to make an impact on the university, even though it was not to reach its apogee for half a century and more.

---

[1] Fowler, *Corpus*, 205. Sir John Coleridge (1791-1876), m. CCC 1809; fellow Exeter 1812-18; hon. Student Ch.Ch. 1867-86. Arthur Stanley (1816-81), m. Balliol 1833; fellow Univ. 1838-51; regius prof. of eccles. history and canon Ch.Ch. 1856-64. Thomas Arnold (1786-1842), m. CCC 1811; fellow Oriel 1815; headmaster of Rugby School 1826-42; regius prof. of modern history 1841-2.

23

The Ashmolean Museum

A. G. MACGREGOR and A. J. TURNER

THE *Musaeum*, a large and stately Pile of squared Stone, was built at the Charge of the University, who found such a Building necessary in order to the promoting, and carrying on with greater ease and success, several parts of usefull and curious learning, for which it is so well contrived and designed.[1]

Edward Chamberlayne's emphasis in this remark on the usefulness of the Ashmolean Museum to the university was entirely justified, for despite its name the original building was not constructed merely to house Ashmole's bequest. That Elias Ashmole, antiquary, collector, astrologer and herald, might give his collection of specimens (the vast bulk of which had originated in Tradescant's 'Ark' at Lambeth) to the university was intimated to the vice-chancellor by Thomas Barlow during Trinity term 1675, although Ashmole seems to have been considering their ultimate destination some years earlier.[2] Discussion continued, and in July 1675 Ashmole reported that he had asked Barlow to suggest 'the building of some large Roome, which may have Chimnies, to keepe those things aired that will stand in neede of it'.[3] Clearly

---

[1] E. Chamberlayne, *Angliae notitia, or the present state of England* (London 1669, London 1684 edn), pt 2, pp. 325-8. Edward Chamberlayne (1616-1703), m. SEH 1634; LL.D. Cambridge 1671; DCL Oxford 1672; FRS.

[2] See Ashmole-T. Hyde, 3 July 1675, bound in a copy of Hyde's edition of the astronomical tables of Ulugh Beg (Oxford 1665) in the Bodleian, printed in C. H. Josten, *Elias Ashmole* (5 vols Oxford 1966) iv. 1433. As early as 1670 John Evelyn referred in a letter to John Beale to rumours in Oxford: 'our *Alma Mater* men will be forc'd to play the Apes; You heare they talke already of founding a Laboratorie, have beg'd the Reliques of old Tradescant, to furnish a Repository'. Evelyn MS Lb no. 329. M. Hunter, *Science and Society in Restoration England* (Cambridge 1981), 146-7, quoting an unpublished Evelyn manuscript; see also Ashmole-Griffinfield, 18 Sept. 1674, Josten, *Ashmole* iv. 1395. In his letter of presentation to the vice-chancellor in May 1683 Ashmole remarked that not only had he been tempted to sell his collection for a large sum, but 'was also prest by honourable persons to consign them to another Society': OUA register of convocation 1671-83. Presumably he was referring to the Royal Society. The most recent account of Ashmole's acquisition of the Tradescant collection is in M. Welch, 'The foundation of the Ashmolean Museum' in A. MacGregor (ed.), *Tradescant's Rarities: essays on the foundation of the Ashmolean Museum 1683, with a catalogue of the surviving early collections* (Oxford 1983). See also Josten, *Ashmole* and M. Allen, *The Tradescants, their plants, gardens and museum 1570-1662* (London 1964). P. Liath-Ross, *The John Tradescants, Gardeners to the Rose and Lily Queen* (London 1984). Elias Ashmole (1617-92), BNC 1644.

[3] Ashmole-Hyde, 3 July 1675.

this was an opportunity the university did not wish to lose. The collection was extremely valuable (it contained large numbers of natural and artificial rarities, coins and medals, scarce books and manuscripts) and when Ashmole made his formal proposal there was no demur in accepting.[1]

The offer came at a propitious moment, for the University Press was printing a work of exactly the kind of empirical study that had seemed to be promised by the Royal Society in its early years and which some influential members of the university wished to see encouraged: that was Robert Plot's *The Natural History of Oxford-shire*, which seems from its first appearance to have been enthusiastically received and 'approv'd of generally very well'.[2] This is confirmed by the fact that the university immediately began to plan the establishment of a lectureship in the subject of 'philosophicall history' for Plot to fill, a move which suggests that there was considerable support within the university for the institutional recognition of this subject.[3] There was also encouragement for such a project (perhaps stimulated by Plot himself) from outside the university, in particular from the naturalist and physician Martin Lister.[4] Probably also of significance was the fact that at this time the vice-chancellor, Ralph Bathurst, was himself a fellow of the Royal Society and a close friend of the anatomist Thomas Willis, with whom he worked on medical problems.[5] He was also one of Plot's chief encouragers in the writing of natural history, and was well disposed towards the new 'scientific' studies. It may well have been through Bathurst's agency that the scheme for a lectureship in 'philosophicall history' was combined with the need to build a home for Ashmole's gift, and a further element, a laboratory for chemistry, incorporated. Certainly by July 1677 all this seems to have been decided, for Prideaux reported:

[1] A. Wood, *Athenae oxonienses, an exact history of all the writers and bishops who have had their education in the University of Oxford from 1500 to 1690* (2 vols London 1691), 3rd edn with additions and a continuation by P. Bliss (4 vols in 5 London 1813-20) iv, col. 357; Josten, *Ashmole* iv. 1494.

[2] T. Dixon-D. Fleming, Aug. 1677, *The Flemings in Oxford* i. 227. The publication date of *Oxfordshire* is not entirely clear. According to Wood it was published about 17 May 1677: Wood, *Life and Times* ii. 376. The imprimatur, however, is dated 13 April 1676, and it was noted as 'in the press' by Humphrey Prideaux in the following August: *Letters of Humphrey Prideaux, sometime Dean of Norwich, to John Ellis, sometime Under-Secretary of State, 1674-1722* ed. E. M. Thompson (Camden Soc. new ser. xv 1875), 50, 60-1; Josten, *Ashmole* iv. 1482-3. Robert Plot (1640-96), m. Magd. Hall 1658; fellow and secretary of the Royal Society 1682; keeper of the Ashmolean Museum 1683-90.

[3] Bodl. MS Ashmole 1136, fos 114-15; Josten, *Ashmole* iv. 1500-1; Prideaux-Ellis [June/July 1677], *Letters of Prideaux*, ed. Thompson, pp. 60-1.

[4] For Lister (c1638-1712; St John's College, Cambridge; DM of Oxford by diploma 1684) see G. L. Keynes, 'Dr Martin Lister, F.R.S.', *Book Collector* xxviii (1979) and xxix (1980). Twenty years later Charlett writing to Lister commented: 'I think I can charge my memory so far back, that being at that time very familiarly intimate with Dr Plot, it was your Letters, Gifts and offers that encouraged the then VCr and Bp Fell to undertake the erecting of that Noble Building, so that to you is due our Thanks for every thing belonging both to the Fabric, Contentes and Uses thereof.' Letter of 22 June 1705, Bodl. MS Lister 37, fo 88.

[5] Thomas Willis (1621-75), m. Ch.Ch. 1637; FRS, FRCP, Sedleian prof. of natural philosophy 1660-75.

we have set forth the philosophicall History of Oxfordshire and are now on a designe of erecting a Lecture on that booke; to which end, as soon as we are agreed on the ground, we shall build a school on purpose for it with a laboratory next and severall other roomes for other uses, whereof one is to hold John Trades-kins raritys, which Elias Ashmole in whose hands they are, hath promised to give to the University as soon as we have built a place to receive them.[1]

The university was committed. Ashmole's formal offer was duly accepted at the end of October 1677, and in December of that year Plot, with an introductory letter from John Evelyn, went to London to meet Ashmole and gain his approbation of the university's choice. At some time between 8 October 1677 and 26 August 1678, the university acquired land from the city and from Exeter College, and in the follow-ing spring work started on the foundations.[2] The master mason and building contractor who designed and erected the building was the local stonemason, Thomas Wood, although its design has in the past been attributed to Wren.[3] On 15 May 1679 the foundation-stone was laid and thereafter progress was steady, until in May 1683 the almost completed building was visited by the duke and duchess of York and the Lady Anne. On 23 May 'yeoman bedells went to several colleges and halls to give notice to all Doctors and Masters that the Musaeum Ashmoleanum would be open the next day'.[4]

If the University of Oxford had been antagonistic towards empirical studies of the natural world, as is often suggested, then the museum could never have been erected. The fact of its existence indeed forces recognition of the need to distinguish more clearly between the philo-sophical ideas which were found disturbing and the empirical or tech-nical studies which were found valuable. In the Ashmolean chemistry,

[1] Prideaux-Ellis [June/July 1677].

[2] *Oxford City Properties* 283 ff. The cost was £326 9s 6d: OUA vice-chancellor's computus 1666-97, fo 50ʳ. For the general building costs of the museum see R. T. Gunther, 'The building accounts of the Ashmolean Museum', *Notes and Queries* xii (1923), 183-4. The accounts were analysed by Josten using the vice-chancellor's computus 1666-97, 12 Oct. 1682-30 Oct. 1683: *Ashmole* i. 254, iv. 1720 n.4. The collapse into the foundations in May of the general privy of Exeter College caused much discomfiture to the workmen and much merriment to local wits: Wood, *Life and Times* ii. 452 (May 1679): Josten, *Ashmole* iv. 1642; Dixon-Fleming, 11 May 1679, *The Flemings in Oxford* i. 284-8.

[3] For Wren's association with the building there is no documentary evidence although the sug-gestion dates back as far as 1756: *A Pocket Companion for Oxford* (Oxford 1756), 17-18. The case was extensively argued by R. T. Gunther and Sir Reginald Blomfield in a correspondence in *The Times*, 19, 22, 26 Feb. 1923, in which Blomfield seems to have the better argument. Evidence for Thomas Wood was adduced by H. E. D. Blakiston (ibid. 8 Feb. 1923) when he drew attention to a print of the museum by Michael Burghers, the university engraver, ascribable to 1685/6. This is inscribed in the lower left-hand corner *T. Wood, Archit.* It is reproduced in R. T. Gunther, *Early Science in Oxford* (14 vols Oxford 1923-45) as the frontispiece to volume iv, and by Welch, 'Foundation of the Ashmolean Museum', where an account of the progress of the building is given along with extracts from the accounts. For a general survey of the building see *VCH Oxon.* iii. 47. The building in question is now the 'Old Ashmolean' and houses the Museum of the History of Science.

[4] Wood, *Life and Times* iii. 54-6; Josten, *Ashmole* iv. 1721.

the various branches of natural history, and antiquarian studies were provided with an institutional home. In the process an important development took place, in which antiquarian study and natural history were equally linked. Fossil remains and the remains of man were studied not in parallel but as two parts of a single subject. Man was studied in his environment, as a part of the natural world and of the general history of nature. Necessary distinctions were of course made, but in the works of the museum's first two keepers, Robert Plot and Edward Lhuyd,[1] as in the museum's collections themselves, man and nature were considered together as two elements in a single system controlled by a providential deity.

While the Ashmolean building was being erected, Ashmole drafted statutes and made the first arrangements for his donation.[2] The collection itself was sent from London by river and arrived in Oxford on 20 March 1683 in twelve cartloads.[3] Ashmole's formal letter of gift followed on 26 May 1683.[4] Plot, who had packed and dispatched the collection from London, had also been arranging contributions from other sources. The most important of these was the presentation by Lister of two Roman altars, a gift which he followed with many others in succeeding years.[5]

Gradually the administrative structure of the museum was established. Plot, who had been named keeper of the museum by Ashmole and professor of chemistry by the university, resided in the museum and received a salary not greater than £50 per annum, to be paid from the income derived from admission fees.[6] An underkeeper was also appointed by Ashmole's statutes of 1686 who was to be paid not more than £15 per annum. An annual visitation of the museum was set up in 1684 at Ashmole's request, and in June 1686 formal 'statutes, orders and rules' were drawn up.[7] The museum's opening hours were to be the same

[1] Edward Lhuyd (c1660-1709), hon. MA 1701; keeper 1690-1709.

[2] For the statutes see Bodl. MS Rawl. D.912, fos 666 ff, printed by Josten, *Ashmole* iv. 1707-9.

[3] Bodl. MS Wood's diaries 27, fo 12; Josten, *Ashmole* iv. 1714-15, 1717.

[4] OUA register of convocation 1671-83, pp. 362-3. A slightly variant version is printed by Josten (iv. 1721-2) from the Ashmolean Library, MS 1.

[5] Plot-Lister, 2 Sept. 1682, Bodl. MS Lister 25, fo 19; Same-same, 10 Feb. 1683, Gunther, *Early Science* xii. 365-6; J. Lloyd-Lister, 10 Apr. 1683, MS Lister 35, fo 94. The altars arrived on 10 Mar. 1683: *Philosophical Transactions of the Royal Society* no. 14 (1684), 457.

[6] Statutes, orders and rules for the Ashmolean Museum in the University of Oxon. 24 June 1686, no. 13, Bodl. MS Ashmole 1820a, fo 296. The annual figures given by Plot were: June 1683-4 £81 17s 1d; 1684-5 £77 10s 8d; 1685-6 £60 8s 8d. Ashmolean Lib. MS 1, no. 11. In the following year receipts fell to £51 0s 3d and expenses amounted to £3 19s. There was left therefore £47 1s 3d which had now to be divided between Plot and his two assistants.

[7] For the visitation see Ashmole-vice-chancellor, 1 Sept. 1684, Ashmolean Lib. MS 1, no. 4. Item 2 in the same manuscript is a copy of the letter which is printed in Josten, *Ashmole* iv. 1743-4. The letter was read in convocation on 19 September: Wood, *Life and Times* iii. 109 19 Sept. 1684. A much mutilated draft of the statutes in Ashmole's handwriting dated 21 June 1686 survives as Ashmolean Lib. MS 1, no 3 and is considered by Josten to be the final version. A copy of it is to be found in Bodl.

as those of the Bodleian Library and visitors were to be conducted round the museum personally by the keeper or underkeeper. Catalogues of the objects and books were to be compiled and a donor's book was to be kept. No object or book might be lent and the right of consultation was strictly regulated. Later revisions in 1696-7 and 1714 established scales of admission fees for visitors to the museum, although junior members of the university were excluded from using the libraries.[1] These statutes provided the basis for administration throughout the eighteenth century.

For the university, however, the museum was not simply a collection of objects to enable the curious to pass an idle hour. It was intended as a centre for study and teaching; an 'institute' in modern parlance. The way in which it was envisaged by contemporaries is clearly shown by the vice-chancellor in a graceful letter of thanks to Lister:

Our University having design'd a new Library which may containe the most conspicuous parts of the great Book of Nature, and rival the Bodleian's Collection of Mss. and printed volumes, in whose neighbourhood it is placed.[2]

When the doors of the new building were opened Ashmole's collection was displayed, arranged in a logical manner we may suppose by Plot. At the same time other aspects of its work began. The chemical laboratory in the basement had been equipped at a cost of over £60 and an operator, Christopher White, had been appointed to assist with chemical

MS Rawl. D.864, fos 187-9. This copy was printed by Gunther *Early Science* ii 312-16 and by Josten *Ashmole* iv. 1821-5; Josten incorporated a number of additional phrases from MS 1, no. 3. Further manuscript copies may be found in Bodl. MS Ashmole, 120a, fo 396; Bodl. MS Rawl. D.912, fos 666-7, in an unidentified hand, but certified by Christopher Harrison, Rawlinson's amanuensis; and in Bodl. MS Hearne's diaries 121.4.43-51.

[1] The revisions were proposed by Edward Lhuyd. Bodl. MS Ashmole 1820a, fos 217-18, is a 'Summary of the statutes and [rules] of the Ashmolean Musaeum, with additions proposed to the visitors [MS torn] at their visitation October 29 1696' in Lhuyd's handwriting; there is a fair copy ibid. fos 1-2. The statutes were printed in English and Latin and were hung up in the main rooms of the museum; a Latin copy of the 1714 rules is still displayed in the present Ashmolean Museum. Copies of both the English and Latin versions of 1714 are preserved in Bodl. MS Ashmole 1820b, fo 37 (English) and fo 38 (Latin). Cf *Oxford in 1710 from the Travels of Zacharias Conrad von Uffenbach*, ed. W. H. and W. J. C. Quarrell (Oxford 1928), 24: 'On 23 August [1710] we wished to go to the Ashmolean Museum; but it was market day and all sorts of country-folk, men and women, were up there (for the *leges* that hang up on the door *parum honeste & liberaliter* allow everyone to go in). So, as we could have seen nothing well for the crowd, we went down stairs again and saved it for another day.'

[2] Quoted in Lloyd-Lister, 10 Apr. 1683, Bodl. MS Lister 35, fo 94. A similar sentiment had been expressed by Ashmole in the preamble to the 1686 statute of the museum. His gift was bestowed on the university: 'Because the Knowledge of Nature is very necessarie to humaine life, health, and the conveniences thereof, and because that knowledge cannot be soe well and usefully attain'd, except the history of Nature be knowne and considered; and to this [end], is requisite the inspection of Particulars, especially those as are extraordinary in their Fabrick, or useful in Medicine, or applyed to Manufacture or Trade.' That the new centre for natural philosophy was the university's major preoccupation in the last decades of the seventeenth century is underlined by a remark of Thomas Hyde to the effect that the building of the laboratory had exhausted all the university's money: see I. G. Philip, 'Libraries and the University Press', p. 725 below.

demonstrations and with preparations for Plot's lectures and to make up medicines which could be purchased.[1] Soon afterwards Plot began his lectures.[2] Interchanges of specimens and ideas were begun with, for example, the keeper of the physic garden, Jacob Bobart.[3] Although the museum undoubtedly benefited in some ways from such intercourse, the practice of giving away duplicates from the collections, sanctioned by the statute of 1686, set a pernicious precedent which posed a real threat to the integrity of the entire collections which individual benefactors deposited in the museum. Cataloguing was started and a steady flow of donations and gifts began.[4] Interest within the university was also considerable, and in October 1683 a formal Philosophical Society was established, meeting regularly each week in the Ashmolean. The Society carried out experiments, heard and discussed discourses from its members and entered into an extensive correspondence with the Royal Society in London, with the Philosophical Society in Dublin and with a wide circle of individuals who reported observations and sent donations to the museum.[5] Although the society survived for only seven years it was during that period active and important, revitalizing a somewhat moribund Royal Society and providing an important focus for the vast amount of interest in empirical natural philosophy to be found among local men scattered throughout the English provinces.[6] From 1684 to 1686 Plot also edited the *Philosophical Transactions of the Royal Society* from Oxford, thus bringing the discussions and activities there before a wider international audience.

[1] For the laboratory see G. l'E. Turner, 'The physical sciences' below; Chamberlayne, *Angliae notitia*, pt 2, pp. 326-7; Gunther, *Early Science* i. 43-5. That the laboratory was almost totally independent of the museum is underlined by the fact that in the original arrangement of the building there was no internal connection between the basement and the other floors. Access to the basement was only by the exterior double flight of steps below the Broad Street entrance. This may of course have been planned so as to avoid the risk of fire. For the cost of the laboratory see OUA vice-chancellor's computus 1666-97, fos 69ʳ-70ᵛ, 12 and 30 Oct. 1683. The exact figures were £17 9s disbursed by Plot and £44 17s disbursed by White. Christopher White (1651-96), privileged person 1676.

[2] Chamberlayne, loc. cit. For Plot as chemist see F. S. Taylor, 'The alchemical papers of Dr. Robert Plot', *Ambix* iv (1949-51).

[3] For instance the undated notes probably in Bobart's hand taken from Plot with a list of metals and ores in the museum: Bodl. MS Lat. misc. e.29, printed by Gunther, *Early Science* iii, appx C, pp. 440-7.

[4] For early catalogues see Ashmolean Lib. MS 1, nos. 7-10, 12-14. The primary catalogues (MSS 8 and 18) together with the 'Book of Benefactors' of 1683-1766 (MS 2) are reproduced as microfiches 1-4 in MacGregor (ed.), *Tradescant's Rarities*. Gifts of manuscripts and books were encouraged by the belief reported by John Aubrey in 1688 that 'now there is such care and good method taken, that the Bookes in the Musaeum, are more safe than those in the Librarie, or Archives': Aubrey-Wood, 22 Dec. 1688, Bodl. MS Aubrey 12, fo 2, printed by Josten, *Ashmole* iv. 1861-2.

[5] For the Philosophical Society in general see Gunther, *Early Science* iv and xii, *passim*. For the Dublin Philosophical Society see K. T. Hoppen, *The Common Scientist in the Seventeenth Century: a study of the Dublin Philosophical Society, 1603-1708* (London 1970).

[6] See Hunter, *Science and Society*, 55-6, 81, 82.

In 1689 Plot resigned the chair of chemistry in which he was succeeded by Edward Hannes of Christ Church.[1] The following year he also resigned from the museum, being succeeded by Edward Lhuyd.[2] Lhuyd's first association with the institution had been as 'Register to the Chymicall courses of the Laboratory', but 'being a person who was naturally addicted to the study of Plants, Stones, &c. as also Antiquities, he was made by Dr Plot underkeeper'.[3] In time Lhuyd became one of the most significant scholars of his day: he was an important contributor to the augmented English edition of Camden's *Britannia*, published in 1695, and his own works, the *Lithophylacii britannici ichnographia* (London 1699) and *Archaeologia britannica* (Oxford 1707) earned him the support of his contemporaries and still serve as monuments to the diversity of his talents.[4] The intensive field-work which took him on extended visits between 1695 and 1701 to Wales, Ireland, Scotland and Brittany earned only qualified approval from the university administration: he was awarded an honorary MA in 1701, but the annual lectures he was obliged to deliver over the following six years may have been intended partly to ensure at least his periodic presence in Oxford.[5] Like Plot, many of

[1] Edward Hannes (*c*1664-1710), m. Ch.Ch. 1682; prof. of chemistry 1690-1704. See Josten, *Ashmole* i. 249, 255, 293, iv. 1867n. for this professorship.

[2] For a glimpse of Lhuyd preparing the ground see Bodl. MS Ashmole 1816, fos 74, 69.

[3] Hearne, *Collections* i. 244. Both these posts were regarded as menial and were sought after only by the most impoverished of scholars: Gunther, *Early Science* xiv. 7. For the keepers and their assistants, see F. R. Maddison, 'The staff of the Ashmolean Museum, 1683-1894' (typescript in the Museum of the History of Science, Oxford).

[4] For some recent appraisals of Lhuyd see J. L. Campbell and D. Thomson, *Edward Lhuyd, F.R.S. 1660-1709* (Cardiff 1971); J. L. Campbell and D. Thomson, *Edward Lhuyd in the Scottish Highlands 1699-1700* (Oxford 1963); F. V. Emery, *Edward Lhuyd F.R.S. 1660-1709* (Cardiff 1971); F. V. Emery, ' "The best naturalist now in Europe": Edward Lhuyd F.R.S. (1660-1709)', *Trans. Hon. Soc. Cymmrodorion* (1970); P. W. Carter, 'Edward Lhuyd the scientist', ibid. (1962); A. and W. O'Sullivan, 'Edward Lhuyd's collection of Irish manuscripts', ibid.; J. L. Campbell, 'The contribution of Edward Lhuyd to the study of Scottish Gaelic', ibid. Lhuyd's original commitment to William Camden's *Britannia* (London 1586, London 1695 edn) had been to survey three counties only, but after the withdrawal of other contributors he 'offer'd to doe all Wales; and to take a journey speedily quite through it, for ten pounds in hand; and twenty copies of the Book, when it shall be publish'd': Bodl. MS Lister 36, fo 51. The *Lithophylacii* was conceived as a methodological catalogue of 'formed stones' from the Oxford region but, with the encouragement of John Ray, it was expanded to encompass the whole of England: Gunther, *Early Science* xiv. 21. The volume of the *Archaeologia* published in 1707, subtitled *Glossography*, was intended as only the first instalment of a four-part *Archaeologia*. It was an introductory study of the language which laid the foundation of comparative Celtic philology and was the standard work until the mid-nineteenth century. The second volume was to have been a survey of customs and traditions; the third 'an Account of all such monuments now remaining in Wales as are presumed to be British; and either older or not much later than the Roman conquest'; and the fourth 'An Account of the Roman Antiquities there, and some others of later date, dureing the Government of the British Princes'. A fifth part on natural history was also planned. See Bodl. MS Ashmole 1820, fo 228; F. V. Emery, 'Edward Lhuyd: *A Natural History of Wales*', *Studia celtica* xii-xiii (1977-8). The cost of publishing the *Lithophylacii* was borne by Hans Sloane, Isaac Newton and others. Lhuyd also corresponded frequently with Ray, Lister, Aubrey and other scholars: Gunther, *Early Science* xiv, *passim*; see also M. E. Jahn, 'A note on the editions of Edward Lhwyd's *Lithophylacii britannici ichnographia*', *Jl Soc. for the Bibliography of Natural History* vi (1971-4).

[5] Lhuyd's tract *De stellis marinis*, published at Leipzig in 1733, was based on his public lectures delivered at Oxford between 1701 and 1707.

whose methods he developed, Lhuyd viewed man and his remains, whether artefactual or linguistic, as a part of the total complex of studies which made up natural philosophy, and his range of interests reflected the unified approach embodied by the Ashmolean.[1]

Hardly had Lhuyd taken charge of the museum when, in 1691, it suffered its first robbery. The losses were mainly of coins and medals but some small pictures, including a miniature of Aubrey by Cooper, were also taken. Lhuyd was much agitated by the loss and by the prospect of incurring Ashmole's displeasure by it: pleas were circulated through Walter Charleton in London for news of the stolen items and of the 'outlandish gentleman' on whom Lhuyd's suspicions fell.[2] The incident seems not to have deterred further benefactions however, and within two years Aubrey himself wrote to Lhuyd that he had 'a great mind' to dedicate his 'collection of letters (now 50 years compleat) to the museum', notwithstanding that the 'R[oyal] S[ociety] are utterly against sending any thing to Oxon'.[3]

Brief accounts of the principal rarities in the museum during Lhuyd's keepership have been left by two visitors. In 1694 H. L. Benthem noted that

Among other things shown are the picture of a man who lived to be 152 years old; Henry VI's iron cradle; Anne Bullen's straw hat, the episcopal mace of

---

[1] In particular he developed Plot's use of the printed query to elicit precise information from local residents about the flora, fauna, language, customs, land forms, fossils, agriculture and so on in a given region. Lhuyd's printed *Parochial Queries* appeared in 1696 with thirty-one questions, as a preparative towards his projected *Natural History and Antiquities of Wales*. Plot had used printed queries in the preparation of his books on Oxfordshire and Staffordshire. The earliest set he issued dates from 1674. Queries had similarly been used by John Ogilby in 1673, as they were later by Aubrey: M. Hunter, *John Aubrey and the World of Learning* (London 1975), 71. They were also used by Christopher Wase in his survey of the free schools of England. Of the ultimate origin of the query as a method of scholarly investigation we know little. The first published example is apparently that appended to Arnold and Gerard Boate's *Ireland's Naturall History* (London 1652) but the method was known and used by Francis Bacon. On the Boates' *History* see C. Webster, *The Great Instauration: science, medicine, and Reform 1626-1660* (London 1975), 431. An example concerning metals was appended by William Rawley to his *Resuscitatio* (2 pts London 1657-70). That it originated with Bacon is possible but as yet unproven.
[2] Several names were put forward by Lhuyd, some of them suggested by 'Mr Beverland'. In a fictitious letter written to himself and dated 1700 Hadrian Beverland mentioned that Lhuyd, whom he described as 'an insidious, malitious, quickly displeased, soon angry Welshman', claimed that the locks had been picked: Bodl. MS Rawl. C.344, no. 1, fo 6. See also letters from Lhuyd to Charleton, Gunther, *Early Science* iii. 322-3 and from Aubrey to Ray, *Philosophical Letters between . . . John Ray and Several Correspondents* ed W. Derham (London 1718), 251. For a list of the missing items dated 25 September 1691 see BL MS Sloane 118, fo 111. Walter Charleton (1619-1707), m. Magd. Hall 1635; hon. DM 1643; physician to Charles I and II; FRCP, president 1690, 1691.
[3] Bodl. MS Ashmole 1814, fo 91. Hunter, *Aubrey*, 90 and 243 notes that Aubrey's determination to leave his books, manuscripts and antiquities to a 'publick repository' benefited the Ashmolean greatly; see also R. T. Gunther, 'The library of John Aubrey, F.R.S.', *Bodleian Quarterly Record* vi (1929-31). For other benefactions see the letters of thanks in Bodl. MS Lister 36, fos 231, 237, 239, 240 and MS Lister 37, fos 37, 72, 88.

Augustine the Monk; many *Hieroglyphica* and other Egyptian antiquities presented by Dr Robert Huntington; a whole mummy; and all kind of rarities such
as Roman altars, Money, Lamps, etc. found in England, and collected by Martin
Lister.[1]

In 1706 C. H. Erndtel saw several of the same items but considered the
pre-eminent exhibit to be 'an entire *Egyptian Mummy* which Mr *Goodyear* lately gave to this treasury of nature'.[2]

In 1701 Lhuyd had been only narrowly unsuccessful in his efforts to
persuade the university to purchase the enormous natural history collections of William Cole of Bristol. These were valuable in Lhuyd's view
because, unlike most collectors of his time, Cole had carefully noted the
provenance of each piece as he obtained it.[3] In 1708 Lhuyd presented his
own collection of fossils to the museum, and during his extensive travels
he collected large numbers of new items for it which he later arranged
there.[4]

Lhuyd died at the height of his powers in 1709, aged 49 and heavily in
debt. The asthma which had dogged his latter years was aggravated by a
chill, allegedly caught through sleeping in a damp room at the museum
and ultimately by pleurisy.

A successor was found within the museum in the person of David
Parry, although his election as keeper did not go uncontested. Parry had
been an able assistant to Lhuyd in the field as in the museum, but he had
an addiction to drink which led to his death in 1714 while he was still in
his early thirties.[5] Parry's talents as well as his fatal flaw are referred to in
the latest and fullest description of the museum which survives from the
eighteenth century, contained in an account of a visit to Oxford in 1710
from the diary of Zacharias Conrad von Uffenbach.[6] While conceding
that Parry was 'little inferior to his predecessor Lloyd in natural history
or in the knowledge of Cambrian, Anglo-Saxon and other languages',
Uffenbach complained that Parry was 'too idle' to continue the cataloguing of the collection which had been begun by Lhuyd and that he was
always 'lounging about in the inns, so that one scarcely ever meets him

---

[1] H. L. Benthem, *Engeländischer Kirch- und Schulen-Staat* (Lüneburg 1694), 329-30. For the portrait of 'Old Parr' and the iron cradle erroneously associated with Henry VI, see MacGregor (ed.),
Tradescant's Rarities, nos. 210, 275. The Gothic ivory crozier head given by Lady Dorothea Long in
1683 as Augustine's episcopal staff also survives in the Ashmolean.

[2] C. H. Erndtel, *The Relation of a Journey into England and Holland, in the Years 1706 and 1707*
(London 1711), 52.

[3] See A. J. Turner, 'A forgotten naturalist of the seventeenth century: William Cole of Bristol and
his collections', *Archives of Natural History* ii (1982).

[4] On Lhuyd's collections see Ashmolean Lib. MS 2, Ashmolean Museum Book of Benefactors; see
also Gunther, *Early Science* iii. 238-9; M. E. Jahn, 'The Old Ashmolean Museum and the Lhywd
collections', *Jl Soc. Bibliog. Nat. Hist.* iv (1962-8). Lhuyd's manuscripts, however, were seized by the
university and sold to defray his debts: Gunther xiv. 45-8.

[5] Hearne, *Collections* v. 4-5. David Parry (c1682-1714), m. Jesus 1705; keeper 1709-14.

[6] Uffenbach, *Oxford in 1710*, ed. Quarrell, pp. 26-31.

in the museum'. The administration of the museum suffered correspondingly, to judge by Uffenbach's account:

The specimens in the museum might also be much better arranged and preserved, although they are better kept than those in Gresham College, London,
which are far too bad considering their splendid description. But it is surprising
that things can be preserved even as well as they are, since the people impetu-
ously handle every thing in the usual English fashion and . . . even the women
are allowed up here for sixpence; they run here and there, grabbing at everything and taking no rebuff from the *Sub-Custos*.[1]

Under Parry's successor John Whiteside, 'a Gentleman of a bashfull,
Sheepish, cloudy, Mathematical, unpromising Aspect', the museum once
more prospered and visitors came in larger numbers than at any other
time in the eighteenth century. Whiteside, who gave 'a Collegiate-
Course on Mathematics', re-ordered and expanded the exhibits and
repaired the display rooms.[2] At the same time, unlike some of his predecessors, he seems to have been able to establish good relations with the
university authorities so that somewhat larger funds were made available
for refurnishing the museum, and the publication of a full-scale printed
catalogue was considered.[3]   On this topic Arthur Charlett, a former

---

[1] Uffenbach, *Oxford in 1710*, 31.

[2] John Whiteside (1680–1729), m. BNC 1696; chaplain Ch.Ch.; keeper 1714–29. See Charlett-
Sloane, 26 Aug. 1715, BL MS Sloane 4044, fo 88 ('. . . unpromising Aspect'); same-same [July 1715],
MS Sloane 4058, fo 113 ('Collegiate-Course in Mathematics'). A year later Charlett wrote 'I am very
glad to find our Tutors, and young Brs of Arts, are so pleased with his [Whiteside's] Experiments, as
well as the Young Gentlemen, the Number being Double, and Treble, to what they used': same-
same, St Catherine [25 Nov.] 1715, MS Sloane 4044, fo 112. It has been suggested that during Whiteside's keepership the Ashmolean Museum came to be established as the recognized repository for
local finds of coins: J. G. Milne, 'Oxford coin-collectors of the seventeenth and eighteenth centuries',
Oxoniensia xiv (1949). Outgoings from the museum during his tenure included £1 5s 9d to the
'joyner for setting up drawers for coins' and other sums for cloth to line the drawers and glass to
cover them: Ashmolean Lib. MS 5, under 1721. Other payments towards planting and maintaining
yew trees in the museum's precinct, polishing the exhibits and 'refreshing and guilding pictures' (a
process which included painting titles—many of them erroneous or inaccurate—on the canvasses)
give an impression that some industry and order was being applied to the collections. The arrival of
some items can be traced in the accounts, as when five guineas were paid for 'Q. Anne's medals', 6s
for 'a tub and carriage of a tortoise', 6s 6d for 'a box and carriage of Bradshaw's hat' and other sums
for transporting a fragment of roman hypocaust, two urns and Dr Plott's pictures: MS 5, *passim*. The
loss of certain items prior to Whiteside's appointment was also recorded in an 'Account of the coins
missing before the year 1715, in Mr Whiteside's hand', Ashmolean Lib. MS 21.

[3] Writing to Sloane on [25 Nov.] 1715 Charlett said he wanted him to know 'in what good
condition, our Musaeum is in, and what charges the University has been at this last yeare, in
cleansing and adorning the Particular Room of the Repository; which was scarce ever in so decent
an Order as now under the care of Mr Whiteside, and his assistant Mr Hansted a modest diligent
Young man of this College, of addresse proper for his Office, and here with pleasure I can tell you
that our general Audit of Accounts this Yeare the Expences were passed by most of the Delegates,
we being nine in number with great Chearfull noise, which I cannot say has always happened, and
the Accounts ran very high by reason of a new library filled up to receive our excellent Friend Dr
Listers Books . . . so that now in the Musaeum besides Sir William Dugdales MSS, are three Librarys
in distinct Rooms for Anthony Woods Dr Lister and Mr Ashmole.' BL MS Sloane 4044, fo 112. Cf
same-same [July 1715], BL MS Sloane 4058, fo 113: 'It has been our misfortune to have

member of the Philosophical Society and from time to time one of the statutory Visitors of the museum, took advice from Sir Hans Sloane who was then making occasional donations to the museum from his own rich collections. Whiteside visited Sloane in London. In June 1717 Charlett reported to Sloane the great success of Whiteside's course of philosophical experiments, and these continued for some years. The initiative for these lectures, although given in the Ashmolean where the apparatus was kept, came, as Hearne makes clear, from Whiteside himself who personally purchased the apparatus. This was extensive, for in November 1723 Whiteside told Hearne that he valued it at over £400.[1] Certainly if it was at all comparable with the clock bought in 1720 from George Graham it must have been a remarkable collection, for Graham's clock embodied the first example of his new deadbeat escapement and was the most accurate and advanced piece of horological machinery in Europe.[2] At about the same time the idea originally proposed by Obadiah Walker in 1682 of centralizing all the university's collections of rarities in the museum was once more being considered.[3] Nothing came of it, however, nor of the project to print a full catalogue of the museum.

While Whiteside lectured on experimental philosophy and displayed 'Knick Knack or Gim-Cracks' to visitors,[4] the courses of chemistry had continued in the basement. In 1704 John Freind gave a course of lectures.[5] These were later published with a dedication to Newton. In the researches for these lectures Freind was assisted not only by the operator (one of Christopher White's sons) but also by Richard Frewen, who had succeeded Freind as lecturer by 1708 and was still holding the post in 1715.[6] Meanwhile gifts continued to arrive in the museum, notably in 1716 a collection of fossils and relics of the great flood from John Woodward and in 1718 the Alfred jewel, which remains one of the principal treasures of the museum.[7] Hearne, who was a friend of Whiteside,

our Former Keepers, that had some vanityes adheare so closely to thyr virtues, that they rather [MS torn] te the officers of the university an aversion rather to the Place, from the [dis]like of thyr Persons.'

[1] Hearne, *Collections* x. 209, 231, 242.

[2] See A. J. Turner, 'The introduction of the dead-beat escapement: a new document', *Antiquarian Horology* viii (1972), 71.

[3] Charlett–Sloane [1717], BL MS Sloane 4045, fo 81. Cf Bodl. MS Rawl. D. 912, fos 670–1, 'Propositions sent to my Lord Bishop of Oxford (by Mr Walker Master of University College) from Mr Ashmole', 30 Sept. 1682; see also Walker's notes on them, ibid. fos. 672–3.

[4] Hearne, *Collections* x. 209.

[5] John Freind (1675-1728), m. Ch.Ch. 1694; MP Launceston 1722-4; physician to George II when prince of Wales and to Queen Caroline 1727. Whiteside also gave some lectures on chemistry since notes taken at a course given by him in 1720 survive in Bodl. MS Ashmole 1820a, fo 302.

[6] Charlett–Sloane [25 Nov.] 1715, BL MS Sloane 4044, fo 112.

[7] For Woodward's collection see Ashmolean Lib. MS AMS 2, p. 20ᵛ; Bodl. MS Ballard 24, fos 81, 83, 85. Woodward also sent Whiteside a copy of his recently printed catalogue and a print of his infamous 'antient votive shield . . . a monument that has much erudition in it . . . If you find some place for it in your Museum I believe the sight of it will not be unacceptable to the Lovers of Antiquity,

tried in vain to persuade Ralph Thoresby to give his extensive collection to the museum.[1]

Whiteside's energies and time were applied not only to administering the museum and to lecturing but also to ecclesiastical duties, for he was chaplain of Christ Church from 1713 to 1729. In Hearne's opinion the fact that Whiteside was a clergyman—'the only objection I ever thought should be made against him'—was not only 'contrary to the Founder's intentions but was likely to form a Precedent afterwards for other Clergyman to be chosen', and in time his fears proved well founded.[2]

The successor to Whiteside, George Shepheard, was elected keeper on 3 December 1729. Hearne thought he would certainly have failed in his bid for the post, 'had the Vice-Chancellour been guided by Principles of Honesty and not of Party'. Considered by some as a talented mathematician, Shepheard was thought by others 'a muddy-headed man' with 'a very dark notion of things'.[3] He had in any case little time to make much impact on the museum for within fifteen months of his appointment he died of smallpox.

The tenure of Joseph Andrews, who followed Shepheard, was equally contentious and short-lived.[4] Hearne records that in London as in Oxford the post was widely expected to go to James Bradley, the Savilian professor of astronomy, who had actually applied for it: 'he being a Person every way qualified with respect to his skill in Mathematicks (tho' he be no Antiquary), and being a man that performs Courses of Experiments at the Museum in the great Lower Room, he having purchased Mr Whiteside's Instruments.'[5] In the event the appointment was made by a committee of only three Visitors, one of whom was Andrews himself, present in his capacity as senior proctor. Considerable controversy was aroused both by the choice of candidate and the manner of his selection: Hearne judged him unsuitable by virtue of being a clergyman and a Visitor, and further because he was 'no scholar and understands nothing in the least of Natural History, Mathematicks and Antiquities'. Although Andrews enjoyed a certain popularity within the university he was clearly nervous about his new position as keeper of the

especially Forreigners.' The print, formerly Bodl. MS Ashmole 1821, is now Ashmolean Lib. MS 4, fo 2. For Woodward and the shield see J. M. Levine, *Dr Woodward's Shield: history, science and satire in Augustan England* (London 1977). For the Alfred jewel see Ashmolean Lib. AMS 2, under 1718. It was given by Thomas Palmer on the death of his father, Colonel Nathaniel Palmer. It seems, however, that the latter had intended it for the Bodleian Library: see D. Hinton, *A Catalogue of the Anglo-Saxon Ornamental Metalwork, 700–1100, in the Department of Antiquities, Ashmolean Museum* (Oxford 1974), 29–48; see also S. Piggott, 'Antiquarian studies', p. 771 below.

[1] *The Diary of Ralph Thoresby, F.R.S.* ed. J. Hunter (2 vols London 1830) i. 174, ii. 428–9.
[2] Hearne, *Collections* x. 407.
[3] Ibid. x. 208, 391–2. George Shepheard (1689–1731), m. Trin. 1705; keeper 1729–31.
[4] Joseph Andrews (c1696–1754), m. Magd. 1713, vice-president 1737; keeper 1731–2.
[5] Hearne, *Collections* x. 406.

museum, for when Hearne called there on 21 May 1731, a month after the appointment, he found 'Mr Andrews was out of Town, and had locked up the door and carried the key with him, being apprehensive his Election would be contested, because of his having but three votes'. Andrews's apprehension proved well justified for on 22 February of the following year, after a protracted campaign of agitation, George Huddesford, the president of Trinity College, secured the keys and the keepership for himself. The entire episode was shrouded in intrigue and the ensuing scandal rocked the whole university.[1]

Quite apart from the personal dimension of the antagonism surrounding Huddesford's appointment, a new irritant had attached itself to the keeper's post. Since the death of Whiteside an annual salary of £50 had been settled on the keeper, which ought to have provided welcome release for an industrious keeper from the necessity of personally showing off the museum's exhibits. The incumbent, however, was to receive this sum 'be he where he will', so that the post was reduced to 'a perfect Sine-Cure, and nothing is to be done by the Keeper for the honour of Learning, unless he have a strange inclination to Learning, and will follow it himself at his own natural Genius'.[2] A significant outcome of this development was that Sir Hans Sloane, who had intended to supplement his modest donations to the museum with a large benefaction, now resolved to bestow his gifts elsewhere. The conduct of the museum under George Huddesford seems to have acted as a further deterrent to Sloane's munificence, for (according to Richard Rawlinson) he was said to have turned against the museum after being informed 'how ill' the 'natural curiosities had been preserved in the Museum, and that the famous Tradescants Collection was much the worse for wear, and even worse if possible by the conduct of some Keepers and their understrappers'.[3]

Richard Rawlinson's reservations about the Ashmolean Museum and his antipathy to George Huddesford in particular weighed heavily when the time came to bequeath his own collection to it, a transaction characteristically hedged about with conditions.[4] The museum had benefited

---

[1] Ibid. 407, 418, xi. 31.

[2] Ibid. xi. 31.

[3] Bodl. MS Rawl. C.989, fo 188. Confirmation of George Huddesford's ineffectual leadership as Keeper comes from Richard Gough: 'Nothing can equal the negligence with which the Ashmolean museum was kept. The librarian being one of the heads put in a scholar for 5£. who made a perquisite of shewing the curiosities, which lay in the utmost confusion. Lhwyd's fossils were tumbled out of their papers, and nobody regarded or understood them till his catalogue of them was republished by Mr Huddesford the late librarian, son of Dr Huddesford.' [R. Gough,] *Anecdotes of British Topography* (London 1768), 2nd edn, enlarged, *British Topography* (2 vols London 1780) ii. 134n.

[4] *The Deed of Trust and Will of Richard Rawlinson, of St. John Baptist College, Oxford, Doctor of Laws, containing his endowment of an Anglo-Saxon lecture, and other benefactions to the college and university* (London 1755).

along with the Bodleian Library and institutions elsewhere from periodic donations made by him over several years. From the late 1740s, however, Rawlinson became increasingly anxious about the fate of his collection, both in the immediate future when he faced the possibility of moving house to premises which lacked adequate storage space, and in the longer term after his death when he foresaw the need (as urged by him upon Ballard) to 'Dispose of [his] Treasure so as to be faithfully preserved for the advantage of a better age than the present'.[1] Oxford was by no means an automatic choice, however, since Rawlinson was apprehensive of the possibility that universities might become 'a morsel for some future Henry'.[2] He had in any case no very good opinion of the Ashmolean Museum and its staff, and the fact that his previous benefactions secured him no exemption from the 'dishonour' of the charges and formalities imposed for consulting manuscripts in the Ashmolean library proved particularly irksome, especially as they were of direct benefit to the keeper. For a period his flow of gifts to the museum was suspended until such time as the whole question of charges was reviewed, and parcels of books sent to the Bodleian Library arrived with the stipulation that they were not to be opened until his differences with the museum had been resolved. Rawlinson's one-man blockade finally succeeded in 1751: the fees were withdrawn and the statutes amended by the Visitors.[3] New benefits accrued to the museum immediately and in drawing up his will in 1755, the year of George Huddesford's retirement, Rawlinson sought to improve the lot of future keepers by establishing a foundation to supplement their salary. Again there were conditions: clerics were to be expressly excluded from holding the post, as were 'Scotchmen' and graduates of Scottish universities; later codicils banned natives of Ireland or the plantations abroad and any of their offspring, members of the Royal Society or the Society of Antiquaries, married men, widowers, graduates of any university but Oxford and Visitors elected 'out of their own body or number of electors'.[4]

While the museum benefited materially from Rawlinson's generosity,[5] his attempts to exclude the clergy from holding office there failed immediately. On his resignation from the keepership in 1755 George Huddesford was succeeded by his son William, then an inexperienced 23-year-old, who was also to hold the living of Bishop's Tachbrook from

[1] B. J. Enright, 'Richard Rawlinson, collector, antiquary, and topographer' (Oxford D.Phil. thesis 1956), 326.
[2] Ibid.
[3] Bodl. Gough Oxf. 101, no. 4.
[4] *Will of Richard Rawlinson*, 10-29.
[5] Most of Rawlinson's collection, including his cabinet of seal matrices, was inherited by the Bodleian Library. His benefactions to the Ashmolean Museum included a model of a Venetian gondola, an Indian palanquin, and a white fox from Muscovy: Ashmolean Lib. MS 2.

1761.[1] His youth and a religious frame of mind did nothing to prevent William Huddesford from becoming one of the most successful keepers of the eighteenth century, and the energy he brought to the task of re-arranging the natural history collections was happily combined with a desire to seek the advice and guidance of more senior scholars. Among William's correspondence are several letters responding to his declared intention immediately to reform the exhibits.[2] The enthusiasm with which his proposals were met is typified by a letter from Smart Lethieullier of 29 December 1755:

I cannot help expressing the Pleasure I have in hearing that you earnestly apply yourself to the Digesting into some order the confus'd heap of natural Bodies which are under your Care in the Musaeum. You are no stranger to my having long wish'd to see that Repository in order. Tis the only means by which it can increase and become an honour to the University, instead of being the contempt of Strangers.[3]

In a later communication Lethieullier advised the separation of natural from artificial rarities, while acknowledging that some collections such as that of Lhuyd should be kept intact.[4] More detailed advice came from William Borlase, with whom Huddesford developed a relationship which was both closely personal and also fruitful for the museum. On 17 December 1766 Borlase wrote to Huddesford that he was 'entirely of the opinion that you should classify all the Fossil, Vegetable and Animal curiosities in the Manner of Linnaeus', although he went on to

[1] William Huddesford (1732-77), m. Trin. 1749; keeper 1755-72.

[2] In a letter to William Borlase of 17 February 1759 Huddesford betrayed early misgivings about his self-appointed task. He had lately made an excursion to London: 'Where I met with great civilities from learned in Nat. Hist. and have by viewing so many noble Collections in all its Branches much increased my own Knowledge in that Science. Neither am I in the least (as I expected I should) put out of Humour with our Oxford Repository—I am now more sensible than ever of its value, and am certain that we have many Good and Valuable Specimens. I hope to be able to convince the World of this also by bringing them to Light in proper and decent Ornaments and fear not but that we shall meet with friends who like you will contribute to increase its value.' Penzance, Morrab Library, Borlase papers, OL.IV. 296-7.

[3] Bodl. MS Ashmole 1822, fos 3-4. Smart Lethieullier (1701-60), m. Trin. 1720; hon. MA 1723. The Book of Benefactors (Ashmolean Lib. MS 2) records Lethieullier's gift in 1756 of zoological specimens contained in sixteen glass jars, some of them having been acquired by him from Woodward.

[4] Letter of 12 Mar. 1756, Bodl. MS Ashmole 1822, fos 13-14. In the same letter Lethieullier goes on to say of Lhuyd's collection that: 'if compar'd with the printed catalogue [i.e. the *Lithophylacii*], many articles would be found wanting. May they not be suppli'd with specimens of the things he describs taken from other cabinets? The more full it appears the less neglect will seem to have been in the former Keepers of it.' Opposing advice came from Mendes da Costa who wrote on 10 October 1758 of Lhuyd's cabinet: 'such as it is, retreived by you with great assiduity and indefatigable Labour, I would never Augment; that is, I would never replace anything lost in it ... I would take some few drawers of the Cabinet, and noting that they were of my replacing, I would ... replace therein the specimens lost which I could Acquire, and those I could not Acquire I would place a Label in them informing future Students I could not replace them, and have therefore left them in that Manner. This proceeding would claim you the Approbation of the Learned as being a just proceeding.' Ibid. fo 92.

recommend also the system adopted by the compiler of the Royal Society's catalogue, Nehemiah Grew, 'who tho his names are become obsolete yet in things and sublime speculation was I think a better philosopher than any of them'.[1]

Huddesford's attention to the arrangement of the collections was clearly maintained over a number of years and his initiative was no doubt a factor in encouraging many new and important donations which arrived at the museum during his term of office. Borlase (who gave an entire mineralogical collection and a volume of original drawings of the same, all presented in a cabinet inscribed with his name) and Thomas Pennant were among the most important of these, and mention is made in various letters of material sent from Switzerland, Denmark, Sweden and South America.[2] Huddesford also took pains to acquire archival material relating to the museum and its benefactors, prepared a new edition of Lhuyd's *Lithophylacii* and republished the *Historia sive synopsis methodica conchyliorum* of Martin Lister.[3] Other projects which Huddesford had in mind or actively worked on included a life of Edward Lhuyd, and a 'History of the Foundation of the Museum, its progress, and Lives of its Keepers and a catalogue of its cheif treasures digested according to the Linnaean System', towards which 'I have try'd part of the Animal Kingdom and found it possible'.[4] Elsewhere he mentioned an *Index*

---

[1] Bodl. MS Ashmole 1822, fo 126. William Borlase (1695–1772), m. Exeter 1713; FRS 1750. Borlase was described as 'my First and greatest Patron' by Huddesford: Morrab Lib. OL.IV. 305b. On Borlase see P. A. S. Poole, 'William Borlase, the scholar and the man', *Jl Royal Institution of Cornwall* new ser. v (1965–8).

[2] Borlase's cabinet still survives in the present Ashmolean Museum, though the minerals are lost. The gifts of Thomas Pennant (1726–98, m. Queen's 1743) were again minerals, metals and rock specimens: Ashmolean Lib. MS 2. Huddesford mentions also 'a great addition to our Collection from our Friend Platt': Huddesford–Borlase, 10 Nov. 1759, Morrab Lib. OL.IV.305b. A nineteen-page manuscript catalogue in the Ashmolean Library (MS AMS 1) is inscribed on the cover: '1765 November the 22d. I presented the following Collection of Fossils to the Ashmolean Museum, Oxon. Joshua Platt, Aged 67.'

[3] In a letter to John Loveday (1711–89, m. Magd. 1728) of 12 April 1769 Huddesford told of nearly a hundredweight of papers given to him by Dr Fothergill, the Quaker physician, including three volumes of letters to Lhuyd, several bundles of letters to Lister and a number of Lister's notebooks: there is a copy of the letter in Oxford, Museum of the History of Science, MS Gunther 45. Similar information is given in a letter to Borlase, Morrab Lib. OL.VII.59. Huddesford explained that he undertook the republication of the *Lithophylacii* (Oxford 1760) 'in order to give some small Testimony of my Gratitude to those Members of the University who gave me the Keepership of the Museum, and to convince those, who might and did think such a favour very undeservedly bestowed, that I would endeavour to fill with decency, though I could not adorn, that Station'. Letter to Borlase, 6 Feb. 1760, Morrab Lib. OL.VII.308-9. He also explained to Borlase that in undertaking his new edition (Oxford 1770) of Lister's *Historia conchyliorum* (first published at London in 1685–92) he had 'endeavoured to lay a nest egg towards the improvement of Nat: Hist: in Oxford, by accepting a mean gratification for my Labour, upon Condition "That the Profits arising from the Sale of the Work should be applied to the Use of Ashmoles Museum" ', letter of 31 July 1770, ibid. 62. At least some of the copper plates for the *Historia* were in the Museum of the History of Science and were identified by Mr F. R. Maddison; they have now been transferred to the Bodleian Library. The fact that these plates were still extant may have been one of the reasons why the Press agreed to a republication; see also the committee of the Museum of the History of Science's 11th *Annual Report* (1944–5), 31.

[4] Morrab Lib. OL.VII.311-12.

materialis of Wood's manuscripts, which he published 'by way of Tryal, if it meet with encouragement I intend to proceed with Ashmoles and Dugdales'.[1]

In the field of antiquarian studies Huddesford's interests were less developed and indeed he 'claimed no merit in that Branch of Literature'.[2] Only in the matter of biography did he feel qualified to contribute, as when moved to rescue the proposed 'Lives of Hearne, Leland, and Wood' from being 'put into the Hands of, perhaps, some Cantab: who could know no more of them than I do of a Cardinal of Rome'.[3] Various antiquities were contributed to the Ashmolean during his keepership, however, notably by Borlase. The latter also sent numerous coins, including Greek, Roman and oriental issues, some of them in response to Huddesford's plan for 'ranging the coins of the Museum'.[4]

At Huddesford's premature death in 1772 the writer of his obituary wrote of 'his eminent Learning, his amiable and social virtues, distinguished piety, undissembled sincerity, and universal love and benevolence to all mankind'.[5] To the scholarly world he was undoubtedly the most effective keeper of the Ashmolean Museum of the eighteenth century, although to judge from the progressive decline in admissions which accompanied his period of office, the public at large was little affected by the changes he wrought.[6]

Even under such exemplary care the collections were at risk from pilfering and from the more insidious dangers of decay. The techniques of preparing natural history specimens for display were still primitive more than a century after some of them had found their way into the Tradescant collection, and the displays were housed in an environment which was far from ideal. Fluctuations in temperature and humidity, along with the injurious effects of the coal-fires which provided winter heating, all took their toll of the exhibits, particularly the organic items.[7] The

[1] Morrab Lib. OL.VII. 47.

[2] Ibid. 58. Huddesford declined election to the Society of Antiquaries on the grounds of insufficient qualification.

[3] Ibid. 62.

[4] Morrab Lib. LB.III.215.

[5] *Jackson's Oxford Journal*, 6 Oct. 1772. Personal modesty appears to have been one of Huddesford's principal characteristics. He wrote to Borlase that 'Fidelity and care in preserving what is committed to my Trust can be my only merit': Morrab Lib. OL.VII.53.

[6] In a letter to Huddesford dated 25 January 1766 J. West assured him that 'No one can be so proper as yourself, who have done more for the honour of that Museum under your care than all your predecessors since Mr Ashmoles time': Bodl. MS Ashmole 1822, fo 187. For admissions see table 23.1.

[7] Even the inorganic specimens presented problems. For instance in a letter to Borlase Huddesford declared himself 'sorry to find the Mundics so perishable a treasure—some of the best specimens being crumbled to peices'. Borlase replied that their self-destruction was inevitable, owing to the natural presence of plentiful 'Salts Vitriolic Arsenical &c', and in due course Huddesford had to report that the former mundics were 'gone to decay in spite of varnish and every other care'. Morrab Lib. OL.IV.311-12, OL.VII.53 and LB.III.364.

TABLE 23.1

RECEIPTS FROM ENTRANCE FEES TO THE ASHMOLEAN MUSEUM
1683-1810*

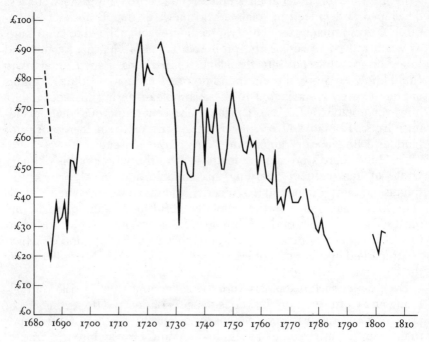

* The figures are taken from a discontinuous series of day-books in the Ashmolean Library (MS AMS 5/1-29) in which the numbers (and in some instances the status) of visitors, the time of their arrival and the fee paid (normally 6*d*) are recorded daily by the underkeepers and the takings confirmed quarterly by the keeper. Although the general decline in the museum's fortunes during the latter half of the eighteenth century is reflected in the figures, there is some evidence that they do not tell the whole story; in particular the sums specifically mentioned by Plot for the years 1683-7 (see p. 642 and n. 6 above) and shown here by a broken line are at variance with the totals recorded in the day-books.

processes of decay advanced to such a degree that some items fell into utter ruin and had to be destroyed. The most dramatic instance of this occurred in 1755 when, with the sanction of the vice-chancellor and proctors, one of the museum's most renowned exhibits, a stuffed dodo, was discarded.[1] Indeed the entire climate of academic opinion was by this time inimical to the well-being of the collections, as can be gauged

[1] See also K. C. Davies and J. Hull, *The Zoological Collections of the Oxford University Museum* (Oxford 1976), 9. Ashmole had stipulated in the statutes of 1686 (para. 6) that 'whatsoever natural Body that is very rare, whether Birds, Insects, Fishes or the like, apt to putrifie and decay with tyme, shall be painted in a fair Velome Folio Booke, either with water colors, or at least design'd in black and white, by some good Master with reference to the description of the Body itselfe, and the mention of the

from Huddesford's letters. On 4 December 1760, for example, he had written to Borlase: 'You will perhaps laugh to see me tri[f]ling about a Place now despised and undervalued—and when soe little encouragement is given *here* to labours of this kind.' Elsewhere he continued the same theme: 'Every Science is dead at present especially Nat[ural] H[istory].'[1] It was a situation which was not to improve until well into the following century.

The tenure of Huddesford's successor William Sheffield, keeper 1772-95, is best remembered for a sensational loss of a different kind which occurred in 1776.[2] Thompson has gathered together all the contemporary accounts of the manner in which one Peter le Maitre, who lodged close by and was a frequent caller at the museum, first of all secreted two medals about him during one such visit and subsequently managed to hide beneath the staircase until after the museum had shut in order to make off with further valuables.[3] His haul on this occasion was more impressive, including fifteen gold medals, two gold chains and several gold coins, the whole variously valued at between £174 13s 9d and £400. The following morning le Maitre fled the city, travelling *via* London, Norwich and Birmingham to Dublin where he was finally arrested. All the stolen items were recovered with the exception of one of the chains, which had been melted down. The incident is given added piquancy by the possibility that le Maitre, who was sentenced to five years hard labour on the hulks off Woolwich, was in reality Jean Paul Marat.

Less sensational but more significant events which took place during Sheffield's twenty-three-year keepership include the acquisition of important South Pacific material from Johann Rheinhold Forster.[4]

The keepers who followed Sheffield were all equally ineffectual in their direction of the museum. William Lloyd, who saw out the

Donor, in the Catalogue'. No such book is known to exist, although some specimens are recorded as having been drawn: see Morrab Lib. LB.III.364.

[1] Ibid. OL.IV.311-12, 314-15. See also OL.IV.316-17. Two years later, in 1763, Huddesford noticed that 'a Spirit of Botanical Enquiries reigns here' in which 'Numbers of all ages employ themselves in Simpling': ibid. OL.VII.52-3. More enthusiasm than learning seems to have been expended, however, for elsewhere he exclaimed: 'It is astonishing to see what Numbers are collecting natural Rarities. Men of all ranks, without the least Science, have ample Museums; and when they die their reliques are bought up at Immense price. All this while we want *Scholars* that would make proper use of these materials.' Ibid. OL.VII.60.

[2] William Sheffield (1732-95), m. Worc. 1750, provost 1777-95; keeper 1772-95.

[3] J. M. Thompson, 'The robbery from the Ashmolean Museum, 1776', *English Historical Review* xlvi (1931); J. M. Thompson, 'Le Maitre alias Marat', ibid. xlix (1934).

[4] OUA acts of convocation 1766-76, p. 371, 8 Mar. 1776, records Forster's gift of clothing, arms and furniture. All these items are now in the Pitt Rivers Museum, Oxford, catalogued by P. B. Duncan, *A Catalogue of the Ashmolean Museum* (Oxford 1836), 184-5 (35 entries). For Forster see *The Resolution Journal of Johann Rheinhold Forster, 1742-1775*, ed. M. Hoare (4 vols Hakluyt Soc. 2nd ser. clii-clv 1982).

eighteenth century, is dismissed by Gunther as 'a retired, quiet (not to say idle) gentleman having no pretensions to science or scholarship; seldom, indeed, coming out of his lodgings in Holywell, where he amused himself in what his neighbours called "strumming" on his harp.'[1] Thomas Dunbar made no recorded impact, while his successor William Thomas Philipps had not 'the heart to cleanse the Augean Institution, nor face enough to keep so unsatisfactory an office' and resigned after a year.[2] Only under the successive leadership of the brothers John Shute Duncan and Philip Bury Duncan were radical reforms introduced and the first printed catalogue of the collections produced.[3] The most significant developments of the nineteenth century, however, were to be the progressive separation of major parts of the collections.[4]

Before the great reforms of the nineteenth century there had been changes in the role and character of the Ashmolean Museum since its auspicious opening in 1683 which were almost equally far-reaching in significance, for all that they were more insidious in character. During the eighteenth century, according to Gunther, 'the Keepers of the museum slept, and their charge fell into the condition of a dusty and neglected curiosity shop'.[5] While this blanket condemnation fails to acknowledge some of the positive contributions noted above, it must be admitted that the efforts of those such as William Huddesford resulted in only temporary checks in the museum's protracted slide into decline. The collections gradually lost all relevance as teaching aids and it was only with the advent of new and practical approaches to the study of natural science and material culture in the nineteenth century that they began to regain their rightful importance.[6]

---

[1] Gunther, *Early Science* iii. 330. William Lloyd (1760–1815), m. Wadham 1776; keeper 1796–1815.

[2] Gunther iii. 330–1. Thomas Dunbar (1783–1831), m. BNC 1801; keeper 1815–22. William Thomas Philipps (1787–1854), m. Pemb. 1806; demy Magd. 1808–20, fellow 1820–42; keeper 1822–3.

[3] John Shute Duncan (c1769–1844), m. New College 1787, fellow until 1829; keeper 1823–6. Philip Bury Duncan (1772–1863), m. New College 1790; keeper 1826–54.

[4] See D. M. Metcalf, *Sylloge of Coins of the British Isles* (London 1958 onward) xii *Ashmolean Museum Oxford* (2 pts 1967, 1969) pt 2, p. vii; R. W. Hunt, 'The cataloguing of Ashmolean collections of books and manuscripts', *Bodleian Library Record* iv (1952–3).

[5] Gunther, iii. 327.

[6] Many useful insights into the early history of the Ashmolean are to be found in A. V. Simcock, *The Ashmolean Museum and Oxford Science* (Oxford 1984), published after this chapter was written.

24

The Physical Sciences

G. L'E. TURNER

THE eighteenth century is not generally regarded as a period of great scientific significance, yet it was characterized by the expansion of interest in science among all kinds of people. James Keir wrote in 1789:

Nevertheless, the age in which we live, seems to me, of all the periods in history, the most distinguished for the sudden and extensive impulse which the human mind has received, and which has extended its active influence to every object of human pursuits, political, commercial, and philosophical. The diffusion of a general knowledge, and of a taste for science, over all classes of men, in every nation of Europe, or of European origin, seems to be the characteristic feature of the present age. The study of the sciences principally has expanded the mind, and laid it open for the reception of every kind of truth. Some individuals of rare genius in former times may perhaps seem to excel those of the present day; although in justice to these, it should be remembered that luminous bodies shine brightest in obscurity. But in no former age, was ever the light of knowledge so extended, and so generally diffused. Knowledge is not now confined to public schools, or to particular classes of men.[1]

The growing interest in science, and particularly in its practical aspects of observation and experimentation, as proposed by Francis Bacon, did not leave the University of Oxford untouched. Throughout the century, however, the teaching and study of the physical sciences remained largely outside the university's formal teaching and examining structure. The various acts of uniformity, enshrined at Oxford in the Laudian statutes of 1636, had given the established church a monopoly over matriculation in both Oxford and Cambridge and also over the granting of degrees and emoluments, all of which were denied to nonconformists. Since the Anglican church had no affiliation with religious groups outside the British dominions, the English universities were peculiarly insulated against foreign influence. But dissenters had international affiliations, and many English nonconformists, as well as Scottish presbyterians, studied at Dutch universities, where the new experimental philosophy was quickly absorbed into the curriculum.[2] The

---

[1] J. K. [James Keir], *The First Part of a Dictionary of Chemistry, &c* (Birmingham 1789), p. iii.
[2] De Volder introduced experimental physics to Leiden University in 1675: see E. G. Ruestow,

Scottish universities were transformed on the continental pattern, Edinburgh in particular looking towards Leiden as a model.[1] At Oxford and Cambridge the colleges had long since secured predominance over the university.[2]

In Oxford the colleges were obliged by their statutes to elect fellows on criteria not exclusively based on intellectual distinction. Most of the undergraduates were destined to become clergymen, to care for their country estates, or to enter politics. For those wishing to follow an academic career and be elected to fellowships, qualifications in classics not in science were required, and the system was therefore self-perpetuating. This is not to say that Oxford men were without intellectual curiosity about science. William Markham, dean of Christ Church, for example, told an undergraduate in 1768 that while 'only classical and historical knowledge could make able statesmen ... mathematics and other things were very necessary for a gentleman'.[3] The eighteenth-century young gentlemen being educated at Oxford University eagerly attended lectures and courses in experimental philosophy, their lecturers being more often than not either professors of astronomy or independent teachers.

Experimental philosophy was taught in the Ashmolean Museum from about 1714 but the subject did not become formally incorporated into the university until the establishment of the readership in experimental philosophy in 1810, paid for by a grant from the crown.[4] The creation of university posts in scientific subjects came about for a variety of reasons, making it difficult to consider the different branches of science separately. Medicine and chemistry were closely associated, as were mathematics with astronomy, and astronomy with natural or experimental philosophy, and several posts were often held by a single man.

It is said that the first public teacher of chemistry in Oxford was Peter Stahl, a native of Strasbourg.[5] With some assistance from Samuel Hartlib he came to England in 1658. He went to Oxford and joined up with Robert Boyle the following year, giving his first course of lectures in

Physics at Seventeenth and Eighteenth-Century Leiden: philosophy and the new science in the university (The Hague 1973), 96.

[1] Edinburgh was reformed after the act of union of 1707: see N. T. Phillipson, 'Culture and society in the 18th century province: the case of Edinburgh and the Scottish Enlightenment' in L. Stone (ed.), *The University in Society* (2 vols Princeton 1975) ii. 427-9.

[2] C. E. Mallet, *A History of the University of Oxford* (3 vols London 1924-7).

[3] *Life and Letters of Sir Gilbert Elliot, First Earl of Minto, from 1751 to 1806*, ed. [E. E. E. Elliot-Murray-Kynynmound,] countess of Minto (3 vols London 1874) i. 38, quoted by L. S. Sutherland, *The University of Oxford in the Eighteenth Century, a reconsideration* (Oxford 1973), 27.

[4] *Oxford University Calendar* (1817), 65.

[5] Wood, *Life and Times* i. 290, 472-5. Wood is one of the sources used by G. H. Turnbull, 'Peter Stahl, the first public teacher of chemistry at Oxford', *Annals of Science* ix (1953), from which the following information concerning Stahl has been taken; see also R. T. Gunther, *Early Science in Oxford* (14 vols Oxford 1923-45) i. 22-4.

1660. He moved to an apothecary's house and, according to Anthony Wood, lectured there to, among others, John Wallis, Christopher Wren, Thomas Millington, John Locke, Nathaniel Crewe, Thomas Brancker, Ralph Bathurst, Henry Yerbury, Thomas Janes, Richard Lower and Richard Griffith.[1] Stahl moved again and built an 'elaboratory' behind the Ram Inn, where Wood himself joined the chemistry course on 23 April 1663. He paid thirty shillings when the course began and thirty shillings more when it ended on 30 May. The class consisted of at least ten people, and Wood said he 'got some knowledge and experience' from the course. Stahl was, then, operating outside the university, and was making at least thirty pounds in five weeks. His 'elaboratory' was a concept that was incorporated by the university in the basement of the Ashmolean Museum. This barrel-vaulted room bears a strong resemblance to the laboratory built at the University of Altdorf, completed in 1682.

The *officina chimica*, as it was called, was Oxford's first university chemistry laboratory, and it functioned as such until a move in 1848 to a new building next to the physic garden. The first chemical 'operator' (that is demonstrator) was Christopher White, described by Wood as 'the Universitie chymist'.[2] The German scholar Zacharias Conrad von Uffenbach visited the laboratory and wrote in his journal:

But to return to the *laboratorium*, I must admit that it is very well built. It is as long or deep as the Ashmolean though not so wide. It is vaulted throughout and fitted with many really curious furnaces with architectural and other embellishments of the most costly description, most of them planned by Boyle ... the furnaces look entirely uncared for, though, as mentioned above, they are still fairly intact and not only are the finest instruments, crucibles and other things belonging to the place almost all of them lying in pieces, but everything is covered in filth.[3]

It must be noted, however, that Uffenbach was highly critical, and said much the same about the rooms of the Royal Society at Gresham College in London. He saw the museum's laboratory when he went to hear the opening of an anatomy course which was held 'under the Ashmolean' in a 'small vaulted room behind the *laboratorium*, very well suited for anatomy on account of the low temperature'.[4] There was

[1] Thomas Millington (1628-1704), BA Trinity Coll. Cambridge; intruded fellow All Souls 1649, MA 1651, incorporated at Cambridge 1657; BM and DM 1659; Sedleian prof. of natural philosophy 1675-1704. Thomas Brancker (1633-76), m. Exeter 1652, expelled 1666. Henry Yerbury (c1628-86), m. Magd. Hall 1642; demy Magd. 1642-8; incorporated at Cambridge 1668. Thomas Janes, incorporated from Cambridge 1650 and again 1652; fellow Magd. 1652, DM 1659. Richard Lower (1631-91), m. Ch.Ch. 1651; FRCP 1675. Richard Griffith (c1635-91), m. Univ. 1655.
[2] C. H. Josten, *Elias Ashmole* (5 vols Oxford 1966) i. 254 ff; Wood, *Life and Times* iii. 55, 227.
[3] *Oxford in 1710 being the Travels of Zacharias Conrad von Uffenbach*, ed. W. H. and W. T. C. Quarrell (Oxford 1928), 37-8.
[4] Ibid. 37.

a *schola anatomica* in the Schools Quadrangle, but this, as again described by Uffenbach, was really a museum rather than an anatomy theatre, and anatomy lectures, particularly if they involved dissection, took place elsewhere, for example in the Ashmolean Museum. The *schola anatomica* was taken over for library use in 1789 because it, and probably also the anatomy room in the museum, were made unnecessary by the new anatomy school at Christ Church.[1]

Another foreign visitor to the museum was the Dutchman Pieter Camper, who noted in his diary for 1749:

The collection is a poor one and not worth seeing. Underneath the Museum is a magnificent chemical laboratory provided with all the furnaces that Terchmeyer describes. There are also a large number of engines according to Becker. There is also a good dissecting room. Mr Alcock gives lectures here on Chemistry and Anatomy.[2]

The association, referred to by both these travellers, between chemistry and anatomy runs through the whole of the eighteenth century, and it was by no means an accident that both subjects were catered for in the museum's basement. The chemistry lecturers were all medical men, and chemistry formed a part of the medical course at the university.

It was at the university's expense that the chemical laboratory had been equipped with all the latest apparatus. A description of what it contained is to be found in a letter written by Plot in 1695:

As for the Goods or Utensils in the Laboratory: the great Alembic, Barrel and Worm, were bought by the University: and so were the great Pewter and small Copper Heads of the Balneum Mariae, and the Iron pots at the bottom of the Chappel Furnaces. All the ironwork of the Alkanor, and Great Reverberatory was also bought by the University, and all the Furnaces buylt at their charge. The great iron digester at the West end of the Laboratory is also theirs.[3]

No sooner was the Ashmolean building finished in 1683 than it was put to use by a group of scholars led by Plot who met each week to follow a course of chemistry. Meetings took place on Friday afternoons in the *schola naturalis historiae*, and the following year the informal gatherings evolved into the meetings of the Philosophical Society of Oxford.[4] Plot held the office of 'director of experiments',[5] echoing the

[1] H. M. Sinclair and A. H. T. Robb-Smith, *A Short History of Anatomical Teaching in Oxford* (Oxford 1950), 36-8.
[2] P. Camper, *Petri Camperi itinera in Angliam, 1748-1785* (Opuscula selecta neerlandicorum de arte medica xv Amsterdam 1939), 83. Nathan Alcock (1707-79) studied at Edinburgh and Leiden; incorporated at Jesus 1741; FRS, FRCP.
[3] Bodl. MS Ashmole 1819, fo 39, quoted by Gunther, *Early Science* i. 50-1, xii. 405.
[4] Josten, *Ashmole* i. 255; Gunther i. 47-50. For the Philosophical Society of Oxford see Gunther iv and A. G. MacGregor and A. J. Turner, 'The Ashmolean Museum', p. 644 above.
[5] Gunther iv. 45.

curator of experiments of the Royal Society of London. A similar philosophical society was formed in 1683 in Dublin, and the three societies
communicated regularly with one another, their proceedings being
very similar in character.[1] Plot served as secretary to the Royal Society
of London from 1682 to 1684 and was elected secretary again in 1692.

Plot's reputation as an antiquarian and natural philosopher, which led
to his becoming a fellow of the Royal Society in 1677 and to his appointment by the University of Oxford as first keeper of the Ashmolean
Museum and first professor of chemistry rested on his book *The Natural
History of Oxford-shire*.[2] While exploring to gather material for his book
he also amassed a large collection of minerals, fossils and other natural
curiosities. As a chemist he subjected the medicinal springs of Oxfordshire to analysis based on the methods of Boyle and Willis. On 12
November 1689 Plot resigned his Oxford chair, married and settled on
his family estate.[3] He was succeeded as professor by Edward Hannes,
who became physician to Queen Anne in 1702 and was knighted in 1705.
Hannes was the last holder of this chair, since it never became an established university post, but chemistry continued to be taught in the
museum by the laboratory operators and by lecturers in anatomy, some
but not all of whom held university posts.[4]

The association of John Freind with the Ashmolean Museum began in
1704, when he gave, by invitation, nine lectures on chemistry.[5] He
adopted the principles of Newtonian attraction, which he derived from
lectures at Oxford by John Keill, and used them in an attempt to explain
chemical processes, such as calcination, distillation and fermentation.
The publication of a second edition of his lecture course involved him in
the Leibniz-Newton controversy. But Freind had left Oxford shortly after
delivering his lectures and had become a physician with the army. He
was elected a fellow of the Royal Society in 1712, and of the Royal College of Physicians in 1716. He published a number of books on medical
topics. The teaching of chemistry in the university was revitalized in
1739 by the arrival in Oxford of Nathan Alcock. The career of Alcock
provides some pointers to the attitude towards science shown by members of the university in the mid-eighteenth century. He was born of landowning parents in Runcorn, Cheshire. He lost interest in the classics at
school, and decided to study medicine. For this purpose he set

[1] K. T. Hoppen, *The Common Scientist in the Seventeenth Century: a study of the Dublin Philosophical
Society 1683-1708* (London 1970).
[2] MacGregor and Turner, 640.
[3] On Plot's resignation see Josten, *Ashmole* i. 293.
[4] Ibid. 249, 255, 293, iv. 1867n.
[5] The lectures were published as *Praelectiones chymicae* (London 1709) and in an English edition by
'J.M.' as *Chymical Lectures in which almost all the operations of chymistry are reduced to their true principles
and the laws of nature, read in the museum at Oxford, 1704* (London 1712).

out for Edinburgh University because it was 'the nearest, and reckoned the cheapest university, as well as a very good one for the cultivation of the several branches of physic'.[1]

The medical school that attracted Alcock had been founded in 1726; nevertheless, it could not satisfy his ambitions. The biographical account written by his brother Thomas continues:

But this university, which was then rather growing into fame, than become famous, did not satisfy our ambitious and knowledge-thirsty pupil. Boerhaave's name at this time was sounded all over Europe; and the aspiring Alcock could not rest until he had feasted his eyes and senses with a sight and hearing of that great man.

Alcock first matriculated at Leiden as a medical student in 1732. His teachers there included Boerhaave on the praxis, Gaubius on chemistry, Albinus on anatomy and 'sGravesande on experimental philosophy and astronomy. He seems to have arrived in Oxford in 1739.[2] His brother described how this came about:

Oxford was, at this time, reported to him to have little or nothing done in it for the benefit of students in physic. It was said, that old Professor Woodward made a sinecure of his place—that Doctor Nicholls had left the anatomy, and was set-tled in London—that the readers in this, and in chemistry, either were not quali-fied, or not disposed to prosecute those sciences with any effect, and that a fair opening now appeared there for an ingenious industrious man to introduce himself . . . He therefore very gladly embraced the advantage of this fair open-ing at Oxford, and very soon presented himself to this celebrated university, as a Praelector in Chemistry and Anatomy.[3]

Alcock's brother knew of the situation at Oxford because he himself had been an undergraduate at Brasenose. The regius professor of medicine, William Woodforde, was old and ailing, spending much of his time at Bath. He had not made the necessary official arrangements for the replacement of Francis Nicholls, a very successful lecturer in anatomy both in Oxford and London. In about 1736 Nicholls decided to confine his teaching to London, and it was planned that his place would be taken by Thomas Lawrence, a bachelor of medicine of Oxford.[4] It was this appointment that Professor Woodforde failed to confirm, thus providing Alcock's opportunity.

But Richard Frewin, Camden professor of history, and his friends

[1] [Thomas Alcock,] *Some Memoirs of the Life of Dr Nathan Alcock, lately Deceased* (London 1780), 6. The present account of Alcock's career is based on these *Memoirs* together with Sinclair and Robb-Smith, *Anatomical Teaching*, 31-4 and E. A. Underwood, *Boerhaave's Men at Leyden and After* (Edin-burgh 1977), 73-5.
[2] Underwood, *Boerhaave's Men*, 73.
[3] *Memoirs of Alcock*, 8-9. 'Professor Woodward' (*sic*) was William Woodforde (d. 1758), subs. New College 1699; regius prof. of medicine 1730-58. 'Doctor Nicholls' was Francis Nicholls (1699-1778), m. Exeter 1715; Tomlins reader in anatomy and FRS 1728; physician to George II 1753-60.
[4] Thomas Lawrence (1711-83), m. Trin. 1727; FRCP, president 1767-74.

objected to Alcock's successful lecturing, and soon a strong opposition to him was formed. The high-church party controlled Oxford, and Alcock was most likely suspected of being a heretic, having been a pupil of Boerhaave, a liberal Calvinist. Thomas Hughes of Trinity was persuaded to read chemistry, Thomas Lawrence was brought from London to read anatomy, and both of these doctors lectured publicly in the Ashmolean Museum in the spring of 1740. Alcock could only give his lectures privately in a room provided for him by the principal and fellows of Jesus. The contrast was, apparently, marked by the numbers of pupils, and Hughes and Lawrence withdrew, leaving the field to Alcock, who became the undisputed public praelector in the museum. The opposition, however, had still not finished with him. When, in 1741, friends proposed the degree of MA for him, it was rejected by the heads of houses, who suggested that a BA would be more appropriate. The quarrel then resolved itself into a fight between convocation and the heads of houses, and the MAs imposed their will by voting *non placet* on all university business until Alcock was granted an MA. Oddly, it was after he received his Oxford degree that he returned to Leiden, matriculated for the third time on 21 February 1742, and received his doctorate in medicine on 24 February.[1] He then returned to Oxford, where he practised as a physician and lectured both in anatomy and chemistry. He took a BM at Oxford in 1744, became a DM in 1749 and was elected FRS in 1750. He left Oxford in 1757 to live in Bath, and was offered the regius professorship of medicine the following year, on the death of Woodforde. He refused the offer, however, and retired to his estate at Runcorn, where he practised medicine until his death in 1779.

Alcock was succeeded as lecturer in anatomy by John Smith who also included some chemistry in his curriculum. From the lecture-notes of a Merton undergraduate, George Wingfield, made in 1759, we know that Smith lectured in 'the laboratory' and included descriptions of mineral waters and 'a chymical production called Phosphorus' in his lectures.[2] These lectures on anatomy are also remarkable for the analogies which Smith drew between the structure of the human body and machines: 'a Congerie of organs or Mechanical Engines ... consisting of Different Machines such as Pullies, Serringes, Tubes, Columns, Strainers, presses, receptacles, &c.'[3] *Jackson's Oxford Journal* recorded that on 25 May 1761 Smith began a series of lectures at the museum on philosophical and mechanical chemistry. Following the university's common practice in

<hr>

[1] Underwood, *Boerhaave's Men*, 74.

[2] George Wingfield, 'Anatomical Lectures just as they were taken, at a Course read by Doctor Smith of St Mary Hall Oxford, in the Laboratory there 1759', Bodl. MS Add. A.302, quoted by Gunther, *Early Science* i. 59 ff. See also the notes compiled by William Blackstone: Oxford, Oxfordshire County Record Office, MSS Blackstone, XXVII/a/1-4.

[3] Bodl. MS Add. A.302, fo 3.

the eighteenth century of regarding its chairs simply as general appointments, not tied to scholarship in a particular subject, Smith was elected
Savilian professor of geometry in 1766. He may, however, have continued
his association with the Ashmolean Museum, for it was not until 1781 that
a new chemistry lecturer appeared.[1]

This was Martin Wall, a fellow of New College, who in 1781 delivered
An Inaugural Dissertation on the Study of Chemistry which he published in
1783 in his *Dissertations on Select Subjects in Chemistry and Medicine*; in 1782
he published his lectures in chemistry.[2] Again, we have the comments of a
student who attended the lectures. John James of Queen's wrote to his
father on 12 December 1781:

Our course of chemistry, which was to consist of twenty-seven lectures, is now
approaching to a conclusion. The class has hitherto held out pretty well: our
numbers are however beginning to fall off daily. From his success in this first
attempt the professor has conceived greater expectations from a second. He certainly merits encouragement from his diligence, modesty, and the real excellence
of his instructions . . . The present arrangement consists of six heads. One, saline
bodies; two, earthy; three, inflammable; four, metallic; five, aerial; six, aqueous . . .
Thus, if metals compose an order themselves, it may be asked why animal and
vegetable substances have not the same honour. The apology offered for this
omission is perhaps plausible enough; for both animal and vegetable matters
may be reduced by chemical decomposition to the four substances, called elementary.[3]

Wall may have been a conscientious lecturer, but his successor, Thomas
Beddoes, was considerably more than that. Beddoes studied medicine at
London and at Edinburgh, where he attended the lectures of Joseph
Black, which he described as the source of 'any just views I may entertain
of chemistry'.[4] He graduated DM at Pembroke College but he had more
friends at Christ Church, where the dean, Cyril Jackson, had an interest in
science and attended meetings of the Lunar Society. When Joseph Black
visited Oxford he stayed with Jackson, who became a close friend of

[1] In his inaugural lecture Charles Daubeny (1795-1867, m. Magd. 1810; Aldrichian prof. of
chemistry 1822-54; Sherardian prof. of botany 1834-67) implied a gap: 'Dr Wall, who ought also to be
mentioned as having revived the study of Chemistry in this University, (having delivered a course of
lectures in this school after they had been long discontinued,) . . .' C. Daubeny, *Inaugural Lecture on the
Study of Chemistry, read at the Ashmolean Museum November 2, 1822* (Oxford 1823), p. 28. This gap was
also implied in Walls's own inaugural lecture (cited in next note).
[2] M. Wall, *An Inaugural Dissertation on the Study of Chemistry, read in the Natural Philosophy School,
Oxford, May 7, 1781* in his *Dissertations on Select Subjects in Chemistry and Medicine* (Oxford 1783); M.
Wall, *A Syllabus of a Course of Lectures in Chemistry, read at the Museum in Oxford* (Oxford 1782). Martin
Wall (1747-1824), m. New College 1763; clinical professor 1785-1824; FRCP 1787.
[3] *Letters of Radcliffe and James*, 171 ff.
[4] T. Beddoes-J. Black, 23 Feb. 1788, Edinburgh Univ. Library, Black MSS, quoted by T. H. Levere,
'Dr Thomas Beddoes and the establishment of his Pneumatic Institution: a tale of three presidents',
Notes and Records of the Royal Society xxxii (1977). Thomas Beddoes (1760-1808), m. St John's 1775; BA
Pemb. 1779, MA 1783, BM and DM 1786; father of the writer Thomas Lovell Beddoes.

Beddoes.[1] In May 1787 Beddoes produced a document entitled *A Memorial concerning the State of the Bodleian Library*.[2] This well-deserved attack stressed how lacking the library was in scientific books and journals, and how poorly it compared in that respect with European libraries. During the few years he remained in Oxford Beddoes was a most conscientious lecturer, teaching in the museum every day except Saturday and Monday, when he worked in the library. In 1790 he published at the Clarendon Press an account of the writings of John Mayow,[3] and in 1791 he read to the Royal Society a paper entitled 'Observations on the affinity between basaltes and granites'. He also corresponded with Lavoisier and Guyton de Morveau.

Moves were being made during Beddoes's residence in Oxford to establish a chair of chemistry in the university. He would have been the obvious candidate for such a post, and all might have been well had he not made himself the focus of political controversy by his outspoken approval of the French revolution.[4] Oxford University was not going to appoint a self-confessed Jacobin to a professorship, and Beddoes left for Bristol in 1793, leaving Oxford still without an established teaching post in chemistry.

It was ten years later, in 1803, that the Aldrichian professorship of chemistry was filled, and much of the credit for this event must go to Beddoes, who vigorously advocated an established teaching post in chemistry. For the hundred years from Hannes to John Kidd, who was the first Aldrichian professor, the lecturers in chemistry appear to have been unestablished.[5] There has been debate as to whether Beddoes himself held an official position in the university. Gibbs and Smeaton have tried to establish the facts:

References to the time when Thomas Beddoes began actively working and teaching chemistry in the University of Oxford are so conflicting that we have compared notes to see if a consistent account of the order of events in 1786-7 can be given. The records of the two Colleges with which he was associated (St John's and Pembroke) and the University archives reveal nothing, and this suggests that he had an independent status throughout his stay. He certainly had no remuneration from the University, and he was entirely dependent on fees received from the students who attended his lectures. Whether he is called lecturer,

[1] E. Robinson, 'Thomas Beddoes, M.D., and the reform of science teaching in Oxford', *Annals of Science* xi (1955).
[2] A copy of the *Memorial* [Oxford 1787] is bound with other related material in Bodl. Bodleian Library Records; see also I. G. Philip, 'Libraries and the University Press', pp. 742-4 below.
[3] [T. Beddoes,] *Chemical Experiments and Opinions Extracted from a Work Published in the Last Century* (Oxford 1790). John Mayow (1641-79), m. Wadham 1658; fellow All Souls 1660.
[4] T. H. Levere, 'Dr Thomas Beddoes at Oxford: radical politics in 1788-1793 and the fate of the regius chair of chemistry', *Ambix* xxviii (1981).
[5] The chair was founded by the will of George Aldrich (1722-98, m. Merton 1739, DM 1755) proved in 1798, but it was not filled for five years. John Kidd (1775-1851), m. Ch.Ch. 1793; Aldrichian prof. of chemistry 1803-22, regius prof. medicine 1822-51, Radcliffe Librarian 1834-51.

reader, or professor is thus immaterial, for none of these terms appears to have had any precise significance in relation to Beddoes.[1]

The last of the 'chemical readers' in the university was Robert Bourne who succeeded Beddoes in 1794. It has now become reasonably clear that, though the readership was often referred to as an actual university post, the reader in chemistry was merely invited to read courses of lectures, did not hold an established post and received no stipend. But his courses were charged for, and his income was from fees. Bourne was described by his great-grandson, who held the post of professor of comparative anatomy at Oxford early this century, as 'an eminent medical man of his time, but not... an eminent scientific man'. 'He was of the old type, a good scholar, a Fellow of Worcester, and for some time, before he embarked on the practice of medicine, was a classical tutor.'[2]

Bourne obtained his MRCP in 1790 and subsequently studied medicine in Holland. In 1794 he read the first of a series of courses of chemical lectures in the Ashmolean Museum and published a syllabus.[3] What was described as *An Introductory Lecture to a Course of Chemistry, read at the laboratory in Oxford, on February 7, 1797* was also printed. Bourne's approach to the subject was highly practical: to provide students who would become MPs, landed gentry, manufacturers and physicians with a basic, sound knowledge of the properties of matter. There was to be nothing novel, simply a schoolmasterly presentation of the essentials of the subject, as they were then understood. It is probable that Bourne delivered the courses of chemical lectures until his place was taken by the first Aldrichian professor of chemistry, John Kidd.

The three professorships established by the will of George Aldrich, a Nottinghamshire physician, were filled in 1803 as follows: professor of the practice of medicine, Robert Bourne; professor of anatomy, Christopher Pegge;[4] professor of chemistry, John Kidd. It is interesting to note that in 1817 the salary of the professor of chemistry was augmented by a grant from the crown. In 1813 the crown also gave grants to the recently established readers in experimental philosophy (1810) and mineralogy (1813). In 1824 Bourne was appointed to the professorship for reading clinical lectures in the Radcliffe Infirmary.[5] He had a large practice in Oxfordshire and, according to his great-grandson, 'belonged to the school

[1] F. W. Gibbs and W. A. Smeaton, 'Thomas Beddoes at Oxford', *Ambix* ix (1961).
[2] Gunther, *Early Science* i. 68 ff. Robert Bourne (1762-1829), m. Worc. 1777; reader in chemistry 1794, prof. of the practice of medicine 1803, clinical professor 1824-9. Gilbert Charles Bourne (1861-1933), m. New College 1881; Linacre prof. of comparative anatomy.
[3] *A Syllabus of a Course of Chemical Lectures, read at the Museum, Oxford, in seventeen hundred ninety four* [Oxford 1794].
[4] Sir Christopher Pegge (1765-1822), m. Ch.Ch. 1782; fellow Oriel 1788-90; DM Ch.Ch. 1792; Lee's reader in anatomy 1790-1816, regius prof. of medicine 1801-22.
[5] See the *Oxford University Calendar* for 1815, 1817 and 1825.

of exact and careful clinic', recording every case he attended; unfortunately all his medical papers were destroyed by his son in the year after his death.

It is necessary to be clear about the names of subjects and professorships in the scientific field. In the medieval university the seven liberal arts included a higher division, the *quadrivium*, comprising arithmetic, geometry, astronomy and music. The teaching of the liberal arts was supplemented by the three philosophies, natural, moral and metaphysical. Natural philosophy was the study of natural objects and phenomena, and of all the works the most influential were those of Aristotle, who had provided a foundation for the Greeks, Arabs and, after about 1200, western Europe. Aristotle's *Physics* included far more than the name implies today: the study of plants and animals was included. In the medieval university most of the teaching in these subjects was carried out by men who had just taken the degree of MA, in their period of 'necessary regency'. This allowed a standard body of knowledge to be passed on but did not greatly encourage innovation in teaching or in advanced study. This medieval practice was superseded in the early seventeenth century by the establishment of the Sedleian professorship of natural philosophy in 1618 and by the Savilian professorships of astronomy and geometry in 1619. At about this time other chairs were founded too, those of moral philosophy, history and music.

Sir William Sedley's professor of natural philosophy was to lecture on 'Aristotle's Physics, or the books concerning the heavens of the world, or concerning meteoric bodies, or the small Natural Phenomena of the same author, or the books which treat of the soul, and also those on generation and corruption'. He was to give these lectures 'twice every week in full terms', on Wednesdays and Saturdays at eight in the morning. His audience was to be composed of the bachelors who were also to be 'auditors in astronomy'.[1] The actual content of the course in natural philosophy during the seventeenth century is not easy to establish.[2] The first Sedleian professor was Edward Lapworth, followed by John Edwards, Joshua Crosse and Thomas Willis.[3] Willis was a physician, with interests that included anatomy and fermentation. For his lectures in natural philosophy

[1] *Statutes* IV. i. 9, trans. Ward i. 22.

[2] R. G. Frank jr, 'Science, medicine and the universities of early modern England: background and sources, Part I', *History of Science* xi (1973), 203.

[3] Edward Lapworth (1574-1636), m. Exeter 1589; pensioner of Corpus Christi Coll. Cambridge 1590; BA St Alban Hall 1592, MA 1595; master of Magdalen College School 1598-1610; BM and DM Magd. 1611; Sedleian prof. of natural philosophy 1621-36. John Edwards (1601-c1660), m. St John's 1618, DM 1639; headmaster of Merchant Taylors School 1632-4; Sedleian prof. of natural philosophy 1636-48, deprived 1648. Joshua Crosse (1615-76), m. Magd. Hall 1632; fellow Linc. 1642; fellow Magd. 1648; hon. DCL 1650; Sedleian prof. of natural philosophy 1648-60, deprived 1660.

he ignored the statutory requirement to teach only from Aristotle, preferring neurological topics. His classical work, published in London in
1664, was *Cerebri anatome*.

In the hands of Willis natural philosophy was given a markedly
medical bias, and on his death in 1675 his successor was Thomas
Millington. Millington had been involved in the brain-research of the
group of Willis, Wren and Lower, but he soon moved to London and
became royal physician and president of the Royal College of Physicians.
He kept his professorship until his death in 1704, his duties being undertaken by a series of deputies, the most notable and most important of
whom was the Newtonian John Keill, appointed in 1699.

Keill did not obtain the chair on the death of Millington (he had to
wait until 1712 for the Savilian professorship of astronomy). The professors of natural philosophy who followed Millington in the eighteenth
century were James Fayrer or Farrer (1704-20), Charles Bertie (1720-41),
Joseph Browne (1741-67), Benjamin Wheeler (1767-82) and Thomas
Hornsby (1782-1810).[1] Hornsby's four predecessors were undistinguished as holders of the chair and they did not undertake the kind of
course started by Keill. This was kept going, and was considerably
developed, by a series of men who lectured in experimental philosophy
in the Ashmolean Museum using a great deal of apparatus. This tradition was once again united to the teaching of natural philosophy with
the election of Hornsby to the Sedleian Professorship, for he had been
giving the lectures in the museum since 1763, after he succeeded James
Bradley as Savilian professor of astronomy. After Hornsby's death in 1810
these lectures were perpetuated by the establishment of a separate
readership in experimental philosophy.

The man who began the study of experimental philosophy in Oxford
was David Gregory, who came from Edinburgh to the Savilian chair of
astronomy in 1691. He had the backing of both Flamsteed and Newton,
quite remarkable in view of their antagonism to one another, and this
support must have secured his election in competition with the better
scientist Edmond Halley, who became Savilian professor of geometry in
1703.[2] Of Gregory Newton wrote that he was 'very well skilled in Analysis and Geometry both new and Old'.[3] In the discharge of his duties
Gregory told his friend Samuel Pepys that the undergraduates 'should

[1] James Fayrer or Farrer (1655-1720), m. SEH 1672; demy Magd. 1674-83, DD 1704; Sedleian
prof. of natural philosophy 1704-20. Charles Bertie (c1679-1741), m. Ch.Ch. 1695; fellow All Souls
and BCL 1706, DCL 1711; Sedleian prof. of natural philosophy 1720-41.

[2] Edmond Halley (1656-1742), m. Queen's 1673; FRS 1678; hon. DCL 1710; Savilian prof. of geometry 1703-42; secretary of the Royal Society 1713-20; astronomer royal 1720.

[3] Newton-Charlett, 27 July 1691, *The Correspondence of Isaac Newton*, ed. H. W. Turnbull, J. F. Scott,
A. R. Hall and L. Tilling (7 vols Cambridge 1959-77) iii; *David Gregory, Isaac Newton and their Circle:
extracts from David Gregory's memoranda 1677-1708*, ed. W. G. Hiscock (Oxford 1937).

study some Euclid, trigonometry, mechanics, catoptrics and dioptrics ...
the theory of planets and navigation'.[1] This rather elementary teaching
scheme was published in similar words, and ends with the advice that
any one of the courses required about three months' study, and that the
right number in a class lay between ten and fifteen.

John Keill followed Gregory to Balliol College from Edinburgh in
1694, and by means of apparatus, some of his own invention, he demonstrated experiments to illustrate Newton's philosophy. In 1699 Keill was
employed by Millington to deputize for him. Keill's lecture-course
started in 1700 in the school of natural philosophy,[2] and he published its
substance under the title *Introductio ad veram physicam* at Oxford in 1702.[3]
In the preface Keill was highly critical of the Cartesian philosophy and
stated his case for mechanical philosophy in all its parts.

Keill was an important disciple of Newton and was a vigorous pro-
ponent of the doctrine of universal gravitational attraction. This New-
tonianism was taken up by many British and Dutch scientists in order to
attack the 'atheistic' Cartesian explanation of the structure of matter and
of the universe, which was favoured by most continentals.[4] Keill believed
that geometry, combined with experimental machines to demonstrate
effects such as the parabolic path of a projectile and centrifugal force,
would be far more telling as a counter-argument to the Cartesian theory
of gravity, which depended on assuming vortices in a celestial matter
around the Earth. With Keill there was a predominating theological
motive; with later experimental philosophers this was lessened by
reason of the desire to add more and more experiments, as the 'raree-
show' aspect could draw the audiences, and hence the fees. Keill left
Oxford for New England in 1709, returning in 1712 to the Savilian chair
of astronomy. During the break lectures on experimental philosophy
were given by John Theophilus Desaguliers, who lectured at Hart Hall
until 1713 when he left for London.[5] Desaguliers subsequently became
famous for his lecture-demonstrations, his course-books on experimental science and his translations of French scientific texts. He gave a

[1] D. T. Whiteside, 'David Gregory', *Dictionary of Scientific Biography* (16 vols New York 1970–80) v. 520–2.

[2] 'Mr Keil's Lectures, read when deputy Professor to Mr Millington—in the Natural Philosophy Schoole at Oxford'; Hearne, *Collections* i. 42 (4 Sept. 1705).

[3] An English translation was eventually published as *An Introduction to Natural Philosophy, or philosophical lectures read in the University of Oxford, Anno Dom. 1700, to which are added, the demonstrations of Monsieur Huygens's theorems concerning the centrifugal force and circular motion* (Oxford 1720).

[4] M. C. Jacob, *The Newtonians and the English Revolution 1689-1720* (Hassocks 1976).

[5] J. T. Desaguliers, *A Course of Experimental Philosophy* (2 vols London 1734-44) i, preface. John Theophilus Desaguliers (1683-1744), m. Ch.Ch. 1705; MA Hart Hall 1712, BCL and DCL 1719; incorporated at Cambridge 1726. See also J. Stokes, *The Life of John Theophilus Desaguliers* (Margate 1927) and *Dict. Scientific Biog.* iv. 43-6.

warm acknowledgement to Keill, who, he wrote, '*was the first who publickly taught* Natural Philosophy *by* Experiments *in a mathematical Manner*'.[1]

Neither Edward Lhuyd, who was keeper of the Ashmolean Museum 1690-1709, nor his successor David Parry (keeper 1709-14) lectured on physical science, but it is clear that John Whiteside, keeper 1714-29, gave instruction.[2] In a letter to John Richardson, Charlett wrote:

Our Industrious and Faithfull Keeper of our Musaeum Mr Whiteside, is going to London to visit the Virtuosos, being also a Fellow of the R.S., and to take advice and Instructions particularly from our good freind Dr Sloane, being not more willing to ask Councill, than to Follow it.

He has had lately a Collegium-Mathematicum of a Months course, where he taught the Youth of several colleges, particularly the young most hopefull studious Duke of Queensbery, Marquisse of Hartinton [*sic*], &c. He goes thro all the parts, of Natural Philosophie Experiments, and Mathematics, for which he is very well accomplished, with excellent Instruments well made, at expence of neare 300£. His price is a Giny and a Half, I wish every gentleman and student of the University, were enabled by thyr Freinds, if they have any genius, to go thro a whole course. Those two young Noblemen have been very diligent, attentive and much pleased, with the Operations and Lectures.[3]

Hearne, writing after the death of Whiteside (22 October 1729) said: 'He was a very ingenious, industrious Mathematician and one of the best in England in Experimental Philosophy. He carried on a course of Experiments for many years at the Museum, to the great Advantage of the youth of the University.' This 'he did for himself, and not as Custos Musei, and might therefore have done it elsewhere as well, if he had provided himself of a room'.[4] In 1723 'Mr Whiteside said last Night that he values his Glasses and other Mathematical Instruments, which he keeps at the Ashm. Museum, at four hundred Pounds'.[5] Whiteside's instruments were bought in January 1730 by James Bradley, who had already been Savilian professor of astronomy for eight years. At this time the cost of the apparatus was estimated to have been £800, and Bradley secured them all, the stock in trade as one might say, for a sum variously quoted as £170 or £400.[6] Bradley tried unsuccessfully for the keeper-

---

[1] Desaguliers, *Course* i, p. viii.

[2] MacGregor and Turner, 'Ashmolean Museum', 648-9.

[3] Charlett-Richardson, Lady day [25 Mar.] 1716, quoted by Gunther, *Early Science* i. 199 ff. Charlett was not correct in stating that Whiteside was an FRS: he was not elected until 3 July 1718. Charles Douglas (1698-1778), 3rd d. of Queensbery and Dover; m. Ch.Ch. 1714; hon. DCL 1720. William Cavendish (1698-1755), m. of Hartington, from 1729 3rd d. of Devonshire, m. New College 1715; hon. MA 1717.

[4] Hearne, *Collections* x. 191, 209 (23 Oct. and 5 Dec. 1729).

[5] Ibid. viii. 132 (15 Nov. 1723).

[6] Ibid. x. 230 ff (24 Jan. 1730). On 13 February 1730 (ibid. 242) Hearne wrote: 'Mr Bradley, Savilian Professor of Astronomy, hath bought Mr Whiteside's apparatus, for which Mr Taylor of Univ. Coll.

ship; nevertheless he lectured in the museum on experimental philosophy from 1729 to 1760, when he retired. He was appointed astronomer royal in 1742, and brought to this post one of the most original minds of the century.

Luckily some details of the courses given by Bradley have been preserved.[1] In addition there are printed sets of plates, originally published by William Whiston and Francis Hauksbee, the main headings of which are 'Mechanicks, Opticks, Hydrostaticks and Pneumaticks', on which Whiteside and Bradley based their syllabuses. Whiston's course was given in London with the aid of the instrument-maker Francis Hauksbee senior; in his *Memoirs* Whiston said that its origins dated from 1707 in Cambridge and that an enlarged course was given for many years in London with the co-operation of Hauksbee. A booklet, or syllabus, was issued, costing five shillings, which Whiston said was published in 1714, being printed several times.[2] When Pieter Camper was in Oxford he heard two of Bradley's lectures, one on centripetal force and the other on, as he says, 'the vires centrales, but the machine was deplorable'.[3]

There is extant a register of those who attended the courses in the museum from 1746 to 1760.[4] The average attendance was thirty-seven at a course and the charge three guineas, a revenue of about £116 a course. As two or three courses were given each year, the average income was consequently £233 or £350. During this fifteen-year period 1,221 men attended the lectures given by Bradley on experimental philosophy. Twenty-three colleges and halls are represented, nine of them providing twice the number of the other fourteen (813 against 400); there were eight outsiders, including five Russians. If a table is formed one finds Christ Church at the top with 154, followed by Queen's with 137, Oriel 79 (109 when St Mary Hall is included), Jesus 106, Brasenose 89, Trinity 80, Balliol 72 and Magdalen 66. It is worth noting that this list of nine houses, or eight if Oriel and St Mary Hall are combined, includes the six colleges that had their own chemical laboratories at the beginning of the twentieth century (Oriel and Brasenose are the two that did not have laboratories of their own).[5] The total of 1,221 men in fifteen years is quite

---

told me yesterday that he was assured by Mr Brooke of Brasenose College that he gave only an hundred and seventy pounds, tho' I had been before told that he gave above four hundred lbs. for them. Mr Whiteside several years agoe valued them at five hundred lbs. and at last at eight hundred lbs.'

[1] Bodl. MSS Bradley *passim*. These were originally collected and bound by Stephen Peter Rigaud (1774-1839), m. Exeter 1791, fellow 1794-1810; Savilian prof. of geometry 1810-27 and astronomy 1827-39, lecturer in experimental philosophy 1810-39, Radcliffe's Observer 1827-39. See also *Miscellaneous Works and Correspondence of the Rev. James Bradley*, ed. S. P. Rigaud (Oxford 1832).

[2] W. Whiston, *Memoirs of the Life and Writings of Mr William Whiston, containing memoirs of several of his friends also* (London 1749), 135 ff, 235 ff. The sets of plates are now Bodl. MS Bradley 3.

[3] Camper, *Itinera in Angliam*, 77, 79. [4] Bodl. MS Bradley 3.

[5] A. E. Humphries, 'A history of the college laboratories in Oxford' (Oxford BA thesis 1970) Museum of the History of Science.

remarkable when related to the number matriculating each year: if this was on average 200 (as it was around 1750) then 3,000 men would have entered the university during the fifteen-year period.[1]

Thomas Hornsby continued the courses under one of his many hats, and some of his printed notices have been preserved. In 1790 the experimental apparatus that he used was valued by the London instrument-maker Edward Nairne at £375 14s 6d. If experimental philosophy tended to continue in the Whiston tradition of the beginning of the century, there nevertheless could be innovation, that is in teaching if not in research. As professor of natural philosophy Hornsby advertised in May 1785 a course of philosophical lectures at the museum on 'The different Kinds of Air, Natural and Factitious, in which the principal Discoveries of Dr Priestley and others will be introduced and proved by actual Experiment'.[2] It was carefully pointed out that, as these lectures were distinct from the course of experimental philosophy, those who attended the lectures on air would have to pay a guinea subscription. Five of the eight lectures were accompanied by demonstrations, which included the electrostatic generator to make sparks in the gases and to discharge the hydrogen-filled electric pistol. The lecture on inflammable air, that is hydrogen, included the account of the discovery of balloons, their theory explained, and illustrated by experiment.

Ballooning was of topical interest because the French had made the first flights two years previously. But there was yet another Oxford reason for an interest in balloons. The so-called father of British aeronautics, James Sadler, was born in Oxford and became an assistant in the chemical laboratory in the basement of the Museum. Being a highly practical man, as is evident from his later career, he was in a good position to repeat the exploits of the French. For his first ascent, on 4 October 1784, Sadler used the Montgolfier hot-air method, which meant taking up a stove in the gondola. A barometer was also carried to serve as an altimeter. Sadler went up at 5.30 in the morning and travelled in half an hour a distance of 6 miles, landing upon a small eminence between Islip and Wood Eaton.[3] A second ascent was made on 12 November 1784 from the physic garden in a balloon filled with hydrogen. Because the name of this gas at the time was 'inflammable air' the balloons filled with it were called air balloons to distinguish them from fire balloons, although the latter were filled with hot air and the former contained no air at all, properly speaking. The second journey took twenty minutes and 14 miles were covered towards Ayles-

---

[1] The figure for matriculations c1750 is taken from the calculations of Julian Hill, quoted by Sutherland, *University of Oxford in the Eighteenth Century*, 4.

[2] Preserved at the Museum of the History of Science, Oxford.

[3] *Jackson's Oxford Journal*, 9 Oct. 1784.

bury. It is said that in 1789 Sadler lectured on 'philosophical fireworks' and that while he was assistant to Beddoes it was remarked of him that he was 'a clever, practical, and experimental manipulator in chemistry, and as such was patronised by the University, or rather by the few scientific men then in the University'.[1] Later he started a mineral-water factory in London, working to the specification of Joseph Priestley's *Directions for Impregnating Water with a Fixed Air* (London 1772). He also became a member of the board of naval works and inspector of chemistry to the admiralty at an annual salary of £400, showing that he had made good use of his years in the museum's basement.[2]

Thomas Hornsby, an eighteenth-century pluralist, collected successively the following appointments which he held concurrently: Savilian professor of astronomy 1763; first Radcliffe's Observer 1772; Sedleian professor of natural philosophy 1782; and Radcliffe Librarian 1783. He provides the most striking example of the close connection already referred to between natural philosophy and astronomy, but the links occur throughout the century.

Henry Savile founded the professorships that bear his name in 1619, he himself having lectured on astronomy and geometry for some years. In founding the chair of astronomy he laid down that the professor was to 'lecture publicly for three quarters of an hour twice at least every week' to scholars 'after the completion of the second year from their arrival at the University, down to the first year of their bachelorship'. He was to explain the whole mathematical economy of Ptolemy as well as 'the whole science of optics, gnomonics, geography, and the rules of navigation' in so far as they were dependent on mathematics, but he was 'utterly debarred from professing the doctrine of nativities and all judicial astrology without exception'. Apart from his public lectures the professor was also required 'in every lecture-week' to

employ himself at his own lodgings ... for the space of an hour in instructing young men (who choose to call on him for the purpose of learning) in practical logic or arithmetic of all kinds, which is best communicated without any formality, and in the vulgar tongue if he thinks fit.[3]

The professor of geometry was to lecture twice a week and

publicly to expound the thirteen books of Euclid's Elements, the Conics of Apollonius, and all the books of Archimedes; and to leave in the University

[1] Gunther, *Early Science* i. 67 ff; G. V. Cox, *Recollections of Oxford* (London 1868, 2nd edn London 1870), 3.
[2] G. L'E. Turner, 'James Sadler: Oxford engineer, chemist and aeronaut', *Oxfordshire Roundabout* i (1965), 24–5, 52; J. E. Hodgson, 'James Sadler of Oxford, aeronaut, chemist, engineer and inventor', *Trans. Newcomen Soc.* viii (1927–8).   [3] *Statutes*, trans. Ward i. 274.

archives his notes and observations ... It will, besides, be the business of the Geometry professor, at his own time, (as shall seem convenient to himself, with the consent of the University,) to teach and expound arithmetic of all kinds, both speculative and practical; land-surveying, or practical geometry; canonics or music, and mechanics.

And in explaining the above departments the professor had 'a free choice of the books which he chooses to explain, unless the University think otherwise'.[1]

John Wallis's appointment to the professorship in June 1649 must have come as something of a surprise, since he had had little to show in mathematics, apart from his skill in deciphering coded letters for the parliamentarians. Within twenty years, however, he was acknowledged to be one of the leading mathematicians of the age. In addition he helped to found the Royal Society and studied phonetics and the problems of teaching deaf mutes to speak. He was succeeded by Edmond Halley who, as a young man, showed his keenness for his chosen subject by coming up to Queen's with a valuable collection of astronomical instruments. Wallis died on 28 October 1703 and Halley was elected to the council of the Royal Society on 30 November following, when Newton was elected president. From such a position and with Newton's backing, Halley was appointed to the geometry chair. Hearne wrote:

Mr Halley made his Inaugural Speech on Wednesday May 24. which very much pleased the Generality of the University. After some Complements to the University, he proceeded to the Original and Progress of Geometry, and gave an Account of the most celebrated of the Ancient and Modern Geometricians. Of those of our English Nation, he spoke in particular of Sr. Hen. Savil; but his greatest Encomiums were upon Dr Wallis and Mr Newton, especially the latter, whom he styled his Numen etc. Nor could he pass by Dr Gregory, whom he propos'd as an Example in his Lectures.[2]

John Wallis had acquired the lease of a house in New College Lane, and this was given by his son (John Wallis junior) to the university for the use of the Savilian professors. Halley moved in during 1705, there having been a small observatory constructed in the roof especially for him, which remains to this day.[3]

Halley made some remarkable advances in astronomy, the best remembered by the layman being the computation of cometry orbits which led to the realization that the bright comets of 1531, 1607 and 1682 were the same object. He predicted its return in December 1758

[1] *Statutes*, trans. Ward i. 274.
[2] Hearne–Smith, 8 June 1704, *Correspondence and Papers of Edmond Halley*, ed. E. F. MacPike (Oxford 1932), 251; Bod. Lib. MS Rawlinson, Letters 37, xi.
[3] H. E. Bell, 'The Savilian professors' houses and Halley's observatory at Oxford', *Notes and Records of the Royal Society* xvi no. 2 (Nov. 1961); see p. 181 for John Wallis junior and the gift of the lease; see also the photograph of the house.

and it was indeed observed on the 25th of that month. He contributed to the determination of the distance of the Sun from the Earth by observing a transit of Mercury and by publishing in 1716 detailed plans for more accurate measurements using transits of Venus in 1761 and 1769. In 1720 he succeeded John Flamsteed as astronomer royal and immediately began an eighteen-year programme to establish precisely the Moon's orbit, which would solve the problem of determining longitude at sea. Among other scientific innovations Halley charted magnetic variation during voyages in the North and South Atlantic, for the purpose of which he was commissioned as a naval captain. His chart, published in 1701, used for the first time isogonic lines (called Halleyan lines at the time) to connect points of equal magnetic variation.

Halley's originality of mind and painstaking scholarship were acknowledged abroad when he was elected, in 1729, a foreign member of the Académie des sciences. As his biographer remarks, 'he was one of the most brilliant and respected scientists of the late seventeenth and early eighteenth centuries';

It has been Halley's misfortune to be eclipsed by a man whose work he himself was mainly responsible for publishing. Yet his very ability to grasp the profound significance of Newton's research entailed a mathematical and astronomical knowledge and insight possessed by few men of any age. He was instrumental in confirming Newton's genius by being the first to apply the theories set out in the *Principia*.[1]

Halley was followed as professor of geometry by Nathaniel Bliss, a graduate of Pembroke and at the time of his appointment rector of St Ebbe's. He had received support from Bradley, Robert Smith (professor of astronomy at Cambridge) and the earl of Macclesfield, who had a fine private observatory in Oxfordshire. Bliss helped Bradley on a number of occasions, such as at the transit of Venus in 1761 and on matters connected with John Harrison's marine chronometer trials. Conscious of the need for exceptional stability in observing instruments, Bliss fixed some of them to the Oxford city wall close to his official house in New College Lane. His meridian mark was on the buildings of All Souls College, and observations were made on Jupiter's satellites in 1742 and on the comet of 1745. It cannot be said that Bliss made any significant contribution to scientific knowledge, even though he was to follow Bradley as astronomer royal in 1762; he enjoyed a mere two years at Greenwich.

A broadsheet exists that is, in effect, an 'advertisement' for courses of instruction in mathematics put out by Bliss as Savilian professor of geometry, conducted from the house in New College Lane.[2] These

---

[1] C. A. Ronan, *Edmond Halley: genius in eclipse* (London 1970), 215.
[2] It is now in the Museum of the History of Science.

'Classes', to explain the 'Elements of the most useful Mathematical Sciences', are summarized as follows:

1   Arithmetick, vulgar and decimal
2   Euclid's *Elements*, books 1-6 with 11 and 12
3   Algebra, resolving types of equations
4   Plain trigonometry, the use of logarithmic tables, practical geometry [surveying] and the use of instruments.
5   Spherical trigonometry, projections, the use of the globes
6   Elements of conic sections, eclipses

The notice also states that the number of students should be between six and ten in each class, that they had to attend three times a week, for not less than an hour each day. Finally:

It is computed that any one of these *Classes* or *Courses* will require about *three Months*; and any *Gentleman* may go through any *one* or *all* of them as he pleases, paying *two Guineas* at the Beginning of each Course, and *half a Guinea* more for every *Month* the Course shall continue longer than *three*.

It will be seen that this course matches rather closely the proposals of Sir Henry Savile, and that the professor might expect to collect something like £100 in a session.

Of the subsequent professors of geometry of the eighteenth century very little can be said. Joseph Betts[1] was followed by John Smith; neither found himself elected a fellow of the Royal Society. Abram Robertson was elected to the Royal Society in 1795 on the strength of his *Sectionum conicarum libri* VII (1792) and held the chair of geometry from 1797 to 1810, when he transferred to the chair of astronomy. He was one of the editors of James Bradley's *Astronomical Observations*.[2]

An astronomer has to use instruments for which he needs good visibility, and during the early seventeenth century provision was made by Oxford University for the activities of the Savilian professor of astronomy by giving him the top room in the tower of the Schools for observation. The second professor, John Greaves, was exceptional in acquiring and using a large collection of astronomical instruments, which were listed in Edward Bernard's catalogue of manuscript books of 1698.[3]

There could hardly be clearer confirmation of the virtual identification between the two Savilian professorships than the appointment of David Gregory as professor of astronomy in 1691, in close competition

[1] Joseph Betts (1718-66), m. Univ. 1736; Savilian prof. of geometry 1765-6.
[2] *Astronomical Observations made at the Royal Observatory at Greenwich by . . . J. Bradley . . . N. Bliss*, ed. T. Hornsby and A. Robertson (2 vols Oxford 1798, 1805).
[3] *Catalogus librorum manuscriptorum Angliae et Hiberniae* (Oxford 1697 [*recte* 1698]); cf H. G. Carter, *A History of the Oxford University Press* i (Oxford 1975), 245-6. John Greaves (1602-52), m. Balliol 1617; BA St Mary Hall 1621; fellow Merton 1624; incorporated at Cambridge 1633; Savilian prof. of astronomy 1643-8, deprived 1648.

with Halley. Halley and Gregory worked together on a translation of the *Conics* of Apollonius until Gregory's death in 1708, a mathematical project well suited to one whom Newton had recommended for the Savilian chair, considering him to be 'the greatest mathematician in Scotland'.[1] As an astronomer Gregory's contribution was not important, and Flamsteed's description of him as a 'closet astronomer' is probably a fair assessment.

Gregory's successor as professor of astronomy was John Caswell.[2] He held the chair for only three years, being followed by Keill in 1712. It is very likely that it was through the good offices of Caswell that Desaguliers was able to give his lectures on experimental philosophy at Hart Hall. Keill's contribution to astronomical studies at Oxford was a course of lectures, published at Oxford in 1718 as *Introductio ad veram astronomiam, seu lectiones astronomicae* and at London in 1721 in an English edition as *An Introduction to the True Astronomy, or astronomical lectures*, and also in a translation at Paris in 1746. When Keill died in 1721, Bradley, one of the great positional astronomers of all time, became Savilian professor of astronomy. Bradley's uncle, James Pound, kept his own observatory at Wanstead, where Bradley learnt so much, and where he was to make a great scientific discovery.[3] Pound would have been the first choice for the chair providing he could have agreed to give up his clerical appointments, as required by the Savilian statutes. Bradley was so willing. Of his inaugural lecture on 26 April 1722, Hearne had this to say: 'On Thursday Morning last Mr Bradley, our Savilian Professor of Astronomy, made his Inaugural or first Lecture. But I am told 'twas very mean.'[4]

It was not at Oxford that Bradley carried out his astronomical work, where it would have been quite impossible to house the necessary equipment. He even fitted up his transit telescope in one of the back windows of the Ashmolean Museum.[5] One may suppose that his only use for such instruments in the confines of Oxford was for teaching purposes. Clearly the great scientific successes of Bradley allowed Hornsby to press for a new building which could provide fully adequate research facilities. Bradley was fortunate to be able to use properly equipped observatories at Wanstead and at Kew (Samuel Molyneux's) and from 1742, as astronomer royal, at Greenwich.

It was at Kew that Bradley first observed a phenomenon that he

[1] I. Newton–Charlett, 27 July 1691, *Correspondence of Newton*, ed. Turnbull iii. 155.

[2] John Caswell (c1655-1712), m. Wadham 1671; vice-principal Hart Hall and esquire bedell of divinity; Savilian prof. of astronomy 1709-12.

[3] James Pound (1669-1724), m. St Mary Hall 1687; BA Hart Hall 1694; MA Gloucester Hall 1694; rector of Wanstead (Essex) 1707 and of Burstow (Surrey) 1720; FRS.

[4] Hearne, *Collections* vii. 354 (28 Apr. 1722).

[5] *Misc. Works of Bradley*, ed. Rigaud, p. xxxix; J. Ingram, *Memorials of Oxford* (3 vols Oxford 1837) iii *The Observatory*, 4 (17 Feb. 1741); Gunther, *Early Science* ii. 85 ff.

verified completely at Pound's observatory, namely the aberration of light. The results were published by the Royal Society in 1729. By observing a particular star (at first γ Draconis) near the zenith for a full year he realized that the position varied in a manner which could be explained by connecting the Earth's orbital speed with the speed of light.[1] The next discovery was the nutation of the Earth's axis of rotation, a wobble induced by the act of spinning, as with a top. The results of long years of observing were given to the Royal Society in 1747. Bradley was able to provide experimental proof of the fundamental axioms of Copernicus and of the Newtonian theory of universal gravitation.[2] He proved that the Earth was flattened at the poles, settling a dispute between Newtonians and the French astronomer Jacques Cassini who thought the Earth to be elongated at the poles. Only consummate skill in handling the superb instruments made by George Graham—and great patience—could have led to results that depended on the measurement of very tiny angular shifts. Later progress in the determination of the positions, motions and distances of stars would otherwise not have been possible. Bradley's fame as an astronomer may account, in part, for the popularity of his lectures on experimental science given in the Ashmolean Museum.

Hornsby followed Bradley as the professor of astronomy in 1763. He had already made himself a small observatory in Corpus Christi College, which he had equipped at his own expense, paying £80 for a 32-inch mural quadrant made by the renowned John Bird.[3] He also continued Bradley's lectures on experimental philosophy in the museum. For teaching astronomy he had to use the room in the tower of the schools quadrangle, from which he observed the transit of Venus on 3 June 1769.[4] The 1761 transit he had watched from the observatory in Shirburn castle, the home of his friend the earl of Macclesfield. One might assume that as the earl was president of the Royal Society from 1752 until his death in March 1764, Hornsby's election to the Savilian chair was almost a foregone conclusion.

A petition for a new building and proper instruments was put forward by Hornsby in the summer of 1768 to the earl of Lichfield and the Radcliffe trustees. A crucial point was the health of John Bird, the only 'one Person living, who is capable of making them [the instruments] with that Precision and Accuracy on which the Goodness of the Observations essentially depends'. Hornsby continued:

[1] E. G. Forbes, *Greenwich Observatory: the Royal Observatory at Hurstmonceux 1675-1975* (3 vols London 1975) i *Origins and Early History (1675-1835)*, 92-5.   [2] Ibid. 95-7.

[3] The instrument, dated 1767, is preserved in the Museum of the History of Science.

[4] On 24 May 1769 Hornsby began a series of special lectures in the museum on the transit of Venus, for which he charged one guinea. A printed notice is in the Museum of the History of Science.

The Instruments which are essential to an Observatory, are a Transit Instrument, two Mural Quadrants, a Zenith Sector, and an Equatorial Sector: The Price of which, as nearly as can now be computed, will be Thirteen Hundred Pounds. The three former cannot be finished before *September* 1773, and the two latter may probably be finished by the End of the following Year ... The Professor of Astronomy is desirous that the Members of Convocation should be acquainted with the proposed Application of the said Instruments, as set forth in the Petition presented to the *Radcliffe* Trustees in the following manner:

I. That as soon as the Observatory is finished, the Professor be employed in making a continued series of Observations ...

II. That a Course of Lectures in Practical Astronomy be read by the Professor twice in every Year, and proper Assistance given by him to all such Members of the University, as are desirous to improve themselves in that branch of Science.[1]

The proposals were accepted; the duke of Marlborough contributed a lease of about 9 acres of land that he held from St John's College, Hornsby was appointed Radcliffe's Observer in 1772 and in the same year work started to the design of the architect Henry Keene. In 1773 'another elevation' was adopted which was by James Wyatt, and it was this that Keene, and later his son, had to see through. A great part was completed by 1776, but the final flourishes inside and out were not done until 1794. The cost of the building and the instruments, which Bird had supplied by 1774, amounted to £28,000.[2]

Unlike Bradley, Hornsby does not have any astronomical discovery to his credit; his achievement rests in the Radcliffe Observatory. In October 1777 the Danish astronomer Thomas Bugge visited Oxford and naturally made a point of seeing Hornsby. Bugge made copious notes and drawings of the Observatory and its instruments, and even attended one of Hornsby's lectures on physics in the museum, giving incidentally the only known description of the seating arrangement in that place. The final word may be left to the Dane:

Not without regret did I leave the Oxford Observatory which is no doubt the best in Europe, both as regards the arrangement and the instruments. Professor Hornsby most courteously assured me of his friendship and his correspondence.[3]

---

[1] See Hornsby's printed proposal (1771) to convocation beginning 'In the summer of the year 1768', copy in Bodl. Gough Oxf. 90 (9). A printed, two-page outline of *A Course of Astronomical Lectures* is in the Museum of the History of Science.

[2] H. M. Colvin, *A Biographical dictionary of British Architects 1600–1840* (London 1978), 484; see also Bodl. MS minute books of the Radcliffe trustees. The instruments are in the Museum of the History of Science.

[3] Copenhagen, Kongelige Bibliotek, MS Ny kgl. Saml. 377e, Thomas Bugge's travel-diary August–December 1777, p. 67 right, p. 71 left. A copy of Bugge's plan of the seating is in the Museum of the History of Science.

25

The Medical Faculty and the Physic Garden

C. WEBSTER

NOT the least of the many paradoxes in the history of Oxford University in the eighteenth century is the contrast between the fortunes of the medical faculty and the physic garden. Having only recently emerged as a major centre of medical education, the medical faculty entered into a dramatic decline. The physic garden, which at best was an adventitious institution of the university with no clearly defined educational role, survived fluctuations in its fortunes to preserve its place as one of the major botanical gardens in Europe. As the medical faculty virtually faded out of existence as an effective teaching and research agency, the physic garden preserved its importance among taxonomists, and was generally regarded as a splendid ornament to the university.

Little has been written about the medical faculty in the eighteenth century. General surveys of medicine in Oxford tend to pass over this period with a few discreet comments. On the positive side, it has been suggested that in the field of anatomy at least the record is not as dismal as might have been expected.[1] The only other major investigation concluded that 'during the eighteenth century the Medical School at Oxford had reached its lowest point, and its condition was deplorable'.[2] The sister medical faculty at Cambridge experienced precisely the same fate.

Notwithstanding such strictures, the history of the medical faculty should not be regarded as a featureless plateau unmarked by surface

---

[1] H. M. Sinclair and A. H. T. Robb-Smith, *A Short History of Anatomical Teaching in Oxford* (Oxford 1950), 18.
[2] A. Chaplain, 'The history of medical education in the Universities of Oxford and Cambridge 1500-1850' (typescript), London, Royal College of Physicians, MS 663, p. 12. See also A. Chaplain, 'The Oxford medical school in the eighteenth century' in *Contributions to Medical and Biological Research dedicated to Sir William Osler* (2 vols New York 1919) i; M. Davidson, *Medicine in Oxford* (Oxford 1953); A. H. T. Robb-Smith, 'Medical education at Oxford and Cambridge prior to 1850' in F. N. L. Poynter (ed.), *The Evolution of Medical Education in Britain* (London 1966); R. T. Gunther, *Early Science in Oxford* (14 vols Oxford 1923-45), esp. iii *Biological Sciences* and xi *Oxford Colleges and their Men of Science*; R. T. Gunther, *Early Medical and Biological Science* (London 1937); Hearne, *Collections*; W. Munk, *The Roll of the Royal College of Physicians of London* (2 vols London 1861, 2nd edn 3 vols London 1878); H. Rolleston, 'The personalities of the Oxford medical school', *Annals of Medical History* new ser. viii (1936); R. G. Frank jr, *Harvey and the Oxford Physiologists: a study of scientific ideas* (Berkeley, Los Angeles etc. 1980).

irregularities or points worthy of notice. In the course of the eighteenth century it is not only possible to detect clearly defined trends, but also to uncover features of significant historical interest. But it is not possible to make out a case for Oxford being a major teaching centre for medicine in the eighteenth century. Medical education became the function of a haphazard assembly of competing private medical establishments which sprang up in London, and of the more orderly medical school which evolved at Edinburgh University. The University of Oxford offered no competition to these agencies. Its medical faculty surrendered the useful role which it had occupied in medical education in the latter part of the seventeenth century.[1]

Increasingly in the course of the eighteenth century medicine in Britain became dominated by nonconformists who, being debarred from education at the English universities, were naturally attracted to a high-status profession which could be effectively pursued without academic qualifications from these universities. Such physicians as Thomas Dimsdale, John Ferriar, John Fothergill, J. C. Lettsom, Thomas Percival and Benjamin Waterhouse suffered little professional embarrassment at not possessing medical degrees from Oxford or Cambridge, or by being thereby debarred from fellowship of the Royal College of Physicians. There is also no evidence that medical degrees from either of the English universities were regarded as indispensable assets for preferment in the rapidly expanding voluntary hospital system, success in private practice or distinction in scientific circles.

Nevertheless, many medical practitioners, at all levels within the profession, continued to qualify from Oxford or Cambridge. Such practitioners had usually been undergraduates at the university; thereafter they pursued medical studies by a variety of mechanisms, returning to Oxford or Cambridge after a suitable lapse of time to take whatever medical degree was appropriate.

A major and continuing responsibility of the medical faculty was that of examining candidates and awarding medical degrees and licences permitting practice in some branch of medicine. This is the function about which the greatest bulk of reliable evidence survives. Upon investigation it gradually becomes apparent that the granting of degrees and licences was the primary function of the faculty and that all other activities were subsidiary to this purpose. Since the degree-granting machinery was more continuous and better regulated than other aspects

---

[1] For the general state of medical education see C. Newman, *The Evolution of Medical Education in the Nineteenth Century* (London 1957), 4-16. For Edinburgh, A. Grant, *The Story of the University of Edinburgh* (London 1884); J. B. Morrell, 'The University of Edinburgh in the late eighteenth century', *Isis* lxii (1971); R. G. W. Anderson and A. D. C. Simpson (eds), *The Early Years of the Edinburgh Medical School* (Edinburgh 1976). For Leiden, E. A. Underwood, *Boerhaave's Men at Leyden and After* (Edinburgh 1977).

of the work of the faculty it may be regarded as the most reliable barometer of change.[1]

At first sight the degree-granting records seem to be impressive. Table
25.1 indicates that between 1661 and 1800 the faculty granted approximately 450 BMs and 350 DMs, numerous licences (MLs) and a much
lesser number of incorporations and creations. These figures suggest
that the remarkable revival in medical education which occurred as an
aftermath of the civil war generated a sustained momentum within the
medical faculty. Grants of BMs increased in the later seventeenth
century until this previously less favoured option became the more
popular of the two medical degrees. After a brief setback after 1660
(possibly associated with the exceptionally large number of incorporations and creations) the DM gained in popularity until the high totals
appertaining during the Commonwealth were consistently surpassed
during each decade between 1691 and 1730.

TABLE 25.1

DECENNIAL TOTALS FOR MEDICAL DEGREES AND LICENCES
GRANTED AT OXFORD 1651-1800

	BM	DM	incorpora- tions	creations	SL[1]	ML	Number of individuals granted qualifica- tion
1651-60	9	30	43	29	—	21	112
1661-70	21	18	32	22	2	16	74
1671-80	27	16	7	10	1	22	48
1681-90	54	27	3	3	5	54	74
1691-1700	44	41	2	1	5	37	73
1701-10	49	34	4	2	—	32	69
1711-20	41	30	2	—	—	29	55
1721-30	59	32	—	3	—	43	73
1731-40	41	24	2	4	—	34	59
1741-50	33	19	—	3	—	33	47
1751-60	23	18	3	1	—	20	35
1761-70	17	6	1	1	—	11	23
1771-80	10	8	—	1	—	6	16
1781-90	28	19	—	1	—	—	31
1791-1800	25	16	—	—	—	7	31

[1] SL: licence to practise surgery.

[1] Information in the following section is derived from OUA registers of convocation and congregation.

Medical licences followed the same course as the BM although peaking at a lower level. Thus between 1680 and 1730 the university never granted in any decade fewer than an average of 4 BMs, 3 DMs and 3 MLs per annum. Initially such statistics suggest a healthy level of academic activity within the medical faculty. Given the long statutory period of medical studies, the student body might have attained substantial proportions. However, this impression is dispelled when the factor of non-residence is taken into account, and when it is appreciated that it was common for any one individual to take more than one qualification.

It was common practice for a BM and ML to be taken simultaneously, and the DM shortly afterwards. Thus, between 1691 and 1700, 130 licences and degrees were taken by only 73 individuals; and in another peak decade, 1721–30, 137 licences and degrees were taken by 73 individuals. During its most active phase the faculty was granting degrees and licences to an average of approximately 7 individuals per annum.

Medical studies were commenced only after the full course of arts studies had been at least nominally completed. After obtaining the degree of MA, medical students (other than those obtaining degrees by creation or incorporation) fall into three major categories: those qualifying with a BM and ML (32 per cent) those with BM and DM (25 per cent) and finally the largest category, possessing the BM, DM and ML (43 per cent). It was virtually unknown for a candidate to take only a BM, since this did not constitute in itself a licence to practise medicine. Those possessing the DM alone almost invariably obtained this degree by creation or incorporation.

The degree-pattern changed considerably in the course of the eighteenth century. At the beginning of the century the BM–DM–ML combination was clearly the most popular, being favoured by more than half of the candidates, the other two combinations (BM–DM or BM–ML) occurring with about equal frequency. Thereafter the BM–DM–ML and the BM–ML options declined rapidly in relative popularity, while in the latter decades of the eighteenth century the BM–DM combination emerged as the most popular option until, in the last decade, it was chosen by twenty-one out of twenty-eight individuals taking medical degrees. By 1800 medical graduates had virtually dispensed with the medical licence, a qualification hitherto required by the ecclesiastical authorities from any practitioner lacking a DM as a condition of practising medicine in the provinces.[1] Before 1750 the ML was useful for those medical students wishing to begin practising medicine before taking their DMs. The medical licence was thus professionally useful and its effect was to promote a long pause between the BM and DM, or com-

[1] R. S. Roberts, 'The personnel and practice of medicine in Tudor and Stuart England', *Medical History* vi (1962) and vii (1964).

plete omission of the DM. With the telescoping of medical studies in the later eighteenth century, the medical licence was abandoned while the BM became a short step to the DM.

Other notable changes occurred in the degree- and licence-granting mechanism between the Restoration and 1800. Between 1650 and 1670 incorporations of degrees, mainly from foreign medical schools, were granted on a scale unknown before or since. This temporary fashion resulted from foreign travel, largely occasioned by political and religious factors. After 1670 incorporations were a relatively rare occurrence. Of the handful of DMs incorporating at Oxford between 1691 and 1800, four were qualified at Cambridge, four at Dublin, three at Padua and one at Frankfurt. The decline in incorporations at Oxford is not a function of the decline in the popularity of continental medical education. It merely indicates that the swelling ranks of English doctors qualifying at Edinburgh, Leiden or some other continental school were either disinclined, or debarred by the religious tests, from incorporating their degrees at Oxford and Cambridge.

A brief visit to a foreign university, where an MD might be granted with the minimum of formality in the course of a few months, followed by incorporation at an English university, provided the most painless means of obtaining the credentials required for a fellowship of the Royal College of Physicians. This gateway to dilution of standards caused acute annoyance to the College of Physicians from the early seventeenth century onward. The figures already cited suggest that in the eighteenth century the college was being unduly sensitive about an abuse which no longer existed to any meaningful extent.[1]

The granting of doctorates by royal mandate reached a peak at the Restoration, but this practice was not continued on a significant scale after 1670. Creations at the wish of the monarch or grants of medical degrees upon the chancellor's recommendation after this date were usually justified on grounds of academic merit, prudence or university politics. One such case was aptly summarized:

Dr James Sherard of St Marks Lane London. Was younger Brother to Consul Sherard. He was one of Dr Radcliffs Apothecaries and ammas'd a Fortune of £70,000. He was a Botanist, and had a Country House at Eltham in Kent and The University of Oxford gave him a Doctors Degree, and expected a Legacy from him, but were disappointed by his Dieing without Will.[2]

The grant of a DM upon the chancellor's recommendation to the Scottish physician William Fullerton in 1728 was opposed by Richard

---

[1] G. N. Clark, *A History of the Royal College of Physicians* (2 vols Oxford 1964) ii. 509–10. OUA register of convocation 1703–30, fo 188, 14 Feb. 1772; Royal College of Physicians–the university, 16 May 1722; Bodl. G.A. Oxon b. 19, reply from the university.

[2] Endorsement on letter from J. Sherard to R. Richardson, 4 Aug. 1716, Bodl. MS Radcliffe Trust c. 3, fo 37.

Frewin and Matthew Lee, two leading members of the Oxford medical establishment, on account of the suspicion that this exercise was intended as a sign of favour to the non-juring faction of the university. Not surprisingly Fullerton was in league with Hearne. As a retaliation the supporters of Fullerton opposed the grant of a dispensation to enable James Stephens, one of the Radcliffe travelling fellows, to take his DM after a long period of study abroad. Stephens was known as a favourite of the duchess of Marlborough, as 'an Hanoverian, a Latitudinarian, and a bitter enemy to the rightfull heir to the Crown'.[1]

The effect of the above animosities was to induce a rigid clampdown on the award of Oxford medical degrees either by creation or incorporation. This zealous protectionism exposes the existence in Oxford of a small but powerful group of resident physicians. These physicians, though few in number, exercised a powerful influence in the university. In 1773 even the incorporation of a Cambridge DM which slipped through by accident was frowned upon.[2] When the Radcliffe Camera was officially opened in 1749 the trustees had the greatest difficulty in forcing through convocation (against the wishes of the medical faculty) the claims of three distinguished physicians with foreign qualifications whom they wished to honour in commemoration of the benefactor. In 1741 Nathan Alcock, a successful private lecturer in the university who had gained an MD at Leiden and who claimed to have taught there for four years, refused as an indignity an Oxford BA on incorporation for the Leiden MD, and though finally (after an almost unprecedented revolt among the 'young masters' of convocation) he was incorporated MA he did not receive the DM, to which he might reasonably have had a claim, until eight years after his incorporation.[3] At the very end of the century the hebdomadal board thought it wise to present a distinguished physician with a foreign qualification to a DCL instead of the DM appropriate to him to obviate the risk of opposition in convocation.[4]

These 'resident physicians' who exercised so close a guard over the awarding of Oxford's medical degrees were an informal group usually engaged in lucrative private practice in the university, city and county,

[1] OUA register of convocation 1703–30, fos 255, 257, 261, 12 April, 17 May, 16 August 1728; Hearne, *Collections* x. 5–6, 40. William Fullerton (1692–1737), m. Balliol 1710, BM and DM by diploma 1728; FRCP, FRS. Matthew Lee (1695–1755), m. Ch.Ch. 1713, BA 1717, MA 1720, BM 1723, DM 1726; physician to Frederick, prince of Wales 1739; FRCP 1732; see Munk, *Roll of RCP* ii. 119–21. James Stephens (b. 1695) m. CCC 1709, BA 1713, MA 1717, DM by diploma 1728; Radcliffe fellow Univ.

[2] *The Oxford Act A.D. 1733* (London 1735), 44.

[3] See G. l'E. Turner, 'The physical sciences', pp. 663–5 above.

[4] On 8 June 1792, the vice-chancellor having been requested to propose an hon. DM for Daniel Peter Layard (MD Rheims 1742; FRS, licentiate of the Royal College of Physicians 1752) the hebdomadal board had no objection unless one should be raised in convocation. But as a similar case was strongly opposed it was decided to change the grant to a DCL. Layard, being a very well qualified and well known doctor, was admitted on 20 June 1972: OUA, WPα/57/7, minutes of the hebdomadal board 1788–1806, p. 6.

who also often held college fellowships and university appointments. Even if they did not enjoy the privileges of membership of convocation in one of these capacities they could do so by a prescriptive right which they enjoyed as *doctores alentes*, doctors living within the university precincts. For many years before 1761 Richard Frewin, holder of the Camden professorship of history—a sinecure—was the acknowledged leader of this group. When the Radcliffe Infirmary opened in 1770 and when the Lichfield chair of clinical medicine was founded in 1780 the professional solidarity of the DMs in Oxford was yet again strengthened, with results both good and bad. The virtual ban on incorporations still further weakened the small Oxford medical faculty by isolating it from the vigorous elements of the profession. On the other hand, the care taken to check the qualifications of those admitted to the doctorate was helpful in preserving professional standards.

The eighteenth century marked the lapse of the traditional function of the medical faculty of granting medical and surgical licences to those not intending to take a medical degree. Traditionally the universities had granted medical licences to arts graduates and surgical licences to non-graduates. Before 1700 medical licences were frequently granted to clergymen, and surgical licences to experienced practitioners. The rapid extinction of licensing after 1700 may reflect the increasing operation among non-graduates of the alternative system of ecclesiastical licensing, and also the decline in the general prestige of medical licences granted by the university to arts graduates.

Table 25.1 vividly illustrates the contrasts between the stability and relative prosperity of the earlier years of the period and the subsequent decline. This decline was continuous in the decennial totals between 1731 and 1780, and even the marked up-turn in the last two decades of the century left the numbers well below those of the years before 1730. The figures were particularly low between 1746 and 1754. In some years not a single medical degree was awarded, and commonly no more than one or two. The beginning of this collapse correlates very closely with the general decline in numbers within the university, the gradual decline of the arts faculty having its inevitable effect on recruitment to the higher faculties.[1]

As indicated above, the medical faculties at Oxford and Cambridge were in competition with faculties elsewhere, few of which required a long period of residence, and at which degrees were granted with a minimum of formality. As the cases of Leiden and Edinburgh in the eighteenth century prove, the relaxation of traditional rules of academic practice was not an inevitable prelude to a decline in educational

[1] L. Stone, 'The size and composition of the Oxford student body 1580–1909' in L. Stone (ed.), *The University in Society* (2 vols Princeton 1974) i. 37–59.

standards. Both of these medical schools offered short-term English visitors an intensive medical education of the highest academic standard and practical relevance, and furnished them with a medical qualification which was universally esteemed within the profession.[1]

Notwithstanding minor changes introduced after 1760, the medical faculty at Oxford remained bound by the framework of the Laudian code of 1636. Entrants into medical studies were required to have passed through the whole course of arts studies and to have qualified as an MA. An MA of three years' standing could proceed to a BM, and after a further four years he was entitled to qualify as a DM. In the course of this time he was statutorily required to attend regularly lectures given by public teachers in the faculty and to take part in disputations in the schools. Finally in connection with inception for a doctorate the candidate was required to participate in the statutory degree-disputation in the annual Act (the annual conferment of degrees) and to deliver either six solemn lectures or at least three cursory lectures.[2]

The fact that the obligatory lectures were not for the most part delivered, and that even the Act itself was abandoned after 1733 in favour of the Encaenia, where there was no place for disputations, did not affect the candidate's notional obligations, most of which were however annually excused by blanket dispensations. But it meant that, apart from some informal instruction which from time to time became available, he had no fixed academic duties and (unless the rules of his college prevented him) he could avoid the expense and uneconomical use of time involved—up to seven years continuous private study of medicine at the university. The student in a higher faculty (as indeed also the person preparing for an MA) could benefit from what would seem to be an ambiguity in the statutes. He was obliged to attend courses of lectures which (if they existed and he carried out his obligations) would entail residence in the university during considerable periods, but the obligation to reside within college walls applied only to undergraduates so far as university regulations were concerned and no other obligation as to residence was specifically laid down.

There were three main types of dispensation from the provisions about courses. The first dispensed candidates from attendance at lectures (mostly no longer given) and from participation in the Act; these were treated as pure formalities. The second permitted candidates to transfer from one degree course to another terms that were in excess of the statutory minimum required for the first course. Should a candidate

---

[1] See p. 684 above. For Leiden, see also G. A. Lindeboom, *Hermann Boerhaave: the man and his work* (London 1968); G. A. Lindeboom, *Boerhaave and Great Britain* (London 1974); G. C. B. Suringar, 'De Leidsche geneeskundige faculteit in het begin der achttiende eeuw', *Nederlandsch Tijdschrift voor Geneeskunde* ii (1886).

[2] *Laudian Code* VI.v, ed. Griffiths, pp. 62-3.

reading for the BM leave his name on the university books, either for lack of funds to pay the fairly expensive degree fees or for other reasons, for more than the statutory three years, he could obtain permission to transfer any surplus towards the DM, thereby saving himself both time and money, and being especially helpful if, as was common in the medical faculty, he sought to obtain his final qualification by accumulation. Such dispensations by the transfer of surplus terms would seem to have been readily granted as being within the intention of the letter of the Laudian Code. The third and most contentious of the types of dispensation was that which curtailed the length of time spent in obtaining the various qualifications. Such dispensations were granted—and with increasing frequency—as the century wore on. But, in theory at least, a case for each one had to be made out and be subjected to scrutiny.

Examination of the record of the three main categories of medical graduate (table 25.2) indicates that the Laudian intentions with respect to the length of studies were observed with reasonable fidelity. The modal value for the BM was three years. More candidates exceeded this period than fell short of it. Most of those taking the BM in less than three years fall into the last two decades of the century, indicating that they were taking advantage of the terms of a statute of 1781 having the effect of bringing Oxford into line with Cambridge.[1]

TABLE 25.2

DURATION OF MEDICAL STUDIES 1691-1800

qualifications	years of medical study*										
	1	2	3	4	5	6	7	8	9	10	11+
BM, ML	1	14	58	16	10	2	4	2	4		
BM, DM	2	2	11	12	10	12	13	8	5	5	24
BM, DM, ML			1	4	8	30	36	20	12	8	27

* Medical studies are taken as commencing after graduation in arts.

Seven years was the modal value for the two categories of candidate incepting as DM. Again, far more candidates exceeded this period than fell short of it. Indeed it emerges that while 49 candidates studied for seven years, 51 exceeded eleven years. Relatively few candidates sought dispensations to reduce the length of their studies to a major extent, and only in isolated cases are candidates recorded as having obtained a DM

[1] The original Laudian statute of 1636 insisted on three years of attendance on the professor of medicine after taking the MA before taking the BM, and four full years between BM and DM: *Laudian Code* VI.v. ed. Griffiths, pp. 62-3. By the statute finally agreed on 12 November 1781 only one year was required between MA and BM and three years between BM and DM: *Statutes*, trans. Ward ii. 16-17.

in as little as one or two years. Such periods would have been regarded as ample for a medical degree at medical faculties elsewhere.

Over the period 1690-1800 the relatively minor changes occurring in the length of preparation for medical degrees are illustrated in table 25.3.

TABLE 25.3

VARIATIONS IN THE DURATION OF MEDICAL STUDIES
1690-1790*

qualifications		years of medical study										
		1	2	3	4	5	6	7	8	9	10	11+
1690	A	1		1								
	B			1	2	1	2	1		1		
1700	A		1	2		1				1		
	B				1	1	1	1	1			
1710	A	1		1								
	B				1		2	1	1	2		1
1720	A			3								
	B						1	1		1	1	3
1730	A	1		3								
	B						2	1	1	2		
1740	A			1	1	2						
	B					1	1	1	2	1		
1750	A			2	1	1	1					
	B						1	1	1	1		1
1760	A			3	1	1						
	B						2	1		1		1
1770	A		1	4								
	B							4		1		
1780	A		1									
	B			2	3	1	1				1	1
1790	BM	3										
	BM, DM	2		1	4							

A: BM, ML
B: BM, DM, ML *or* BM, DM

* The table is based on samples of the first ten individuals graduating in medicine from January onward in each year given. Medical studies are taken to have commenced after graduation in arts.

Before 1780 those candidates taking only the BM occasionally sought dispensations to obtain their degree in one or two years. Commonly much longer was spent before taking this degree. After 1780 one year became the norm for the BM. With each successive decade before 1780 those preparing for the DM tended, if anything, to extend the length of their studies. There was great diversity of practice within any age cohort.

By contrast after 1780 lengths of preparation for the DM above four years became uncommon. Thus something of a contrast emerges in the degree-profile of candidates between the active period of the faculty at the beginning of the century and its reactivation towards the end. The year 1740 may be taken as typical of the earlier phase. Of the sample of ten, four took a BM and licence. The degree and licence were granted simultaneously. These candidates studied for between three and five years and were awarded their degrees at ages ranging from 26 to 28. The six candidates who proceeded to a DM studied for between five and nine years; only two fell slightly short of the overall statutory period for the DM. The time spent on the BM and DM sections of studies showed wide variation, exposing many departures from the pattern envisaged in the Laudian statutes. Thus the six candidates spent 6:3, 3:4, 8:0, 1:4, 4:4 and 2:4 years on their studies for the degrees of BM and DM respectively. None followed the prescribed pattern precisely; longer periods on the BM tended to be compensated for by lesser time spent on the DM. An extreme case is marked by William Roundell who was granted his BM and DM simultaneously eight years after taking his MA.[1] The candidates incepting as DM ranged in age from 29 to 33, the average being 31.

The one candidate going no further than the BM in the 1780 sample incepted two years after his MA at the age of 26. The DM candidates showed a wide range of variation, taking respectively 2:2, 3:11, 2:1, 5:0, 3:3, 2:1, 1:9, 2:2 and 4:0 years over their BM and DM degrees. Seven of these individuals were departing widely from the practice envisaged by the Laudian statutes. It is clear from these figures that the 1781 statute was merely ratifying a state of affairs which already existed by sanctioning a shorter length of preparation for the BM. However, there was also as much tendency to shorten the period between the BM and DM as to reduce that between the MA and BM, as also envisaged in the statute. As a result of the telescoping of the period of preparation for the DM, this degree was now granted to much younger candidates than was the case earlier in the century. Thus John Matthews was granted his DM at the age of 26, after three years of preparation.[2] Three other candidates obtained their DM at the age of 28, which was also the average age for the entire group granted DMs in the 1780 sample. The DMs of the 1790 sample had an average age of just above 27. They were of similar age to the BMs of the 1740 sample. In the latter years of the century it became increasingly common for a young medical man to accumulate his BM

---

[1] William Roundell (1709-62), m. Ch.Ch. 1726, BA 1729, MA 1732, BM and DM 1740.

[2] John Matthews (1756-1826), m. Merton 1772, BA 1778, MA 1779, BM 1781, DM 1782; FRCP 1783; physician St George's Hospital.

and DM less than five years from graduating in arts. Between 1786 and 1790 such well-known Oxford figures as Matthew Baillie, Thomas Beddoes, Robert Bourne, John Mayo, Christopher Pegge, and Henry Vaughan obtained the BM and DM within three years of graduating in arts.[1]

Despite the trend towards shorter periods of preparation for a medical degree, the faculty at no stage in the eighteenth century sanctioned preemptive grants of degrees to those who were too briefly prepared. If anything Oxford candidates for medical degrees erred on the side of maturity, spending much longer waiting for their medical degrees than was strictly necessary. In the case of the regius professors William Woodforde and William Vivian, eighteen and eleven years respectively elapsed between their arts and higher medical degrees.[2] In the case of Philip Dodwell, a prominent figure in Magdalen College, this period was sixteen years.[3] For the Radcliffe travelling fellows George Dowdswell and James Stephens it was twelve and eleven years respectively.[4] It was envisaged by the founder that these fellows would study medicine for ten years.

The accumulated evidence suggests that Oxford medical graduates allowed ample time to elapse between their arts and medical degrees. What is not clear is the proportion of this time devoted to the study and practice of medicine in Oxford. For those medical graduates for whom biographical evidence survives it is evident that, for the more ambitious student and country practitioner alike, it was rare for more than a brief period to be spent in residence at Oxford.

In a family of distinguished anatomists William Hunter studied only in London and his young brother John Hunter lost patience with St Mary's Hall, Oxford, after two months. Upon William's recommendation their nephew Matthew Baillie in 1779 took up one of the five exhibitions reserved for Scotsmen at Balliol College. By 1780 he was studying medicine in London, where he registered as a surgeon's pupil at St George's Hospital. In 1782, one year before his BA, he began giving anatomical lectures in London. William Hunter's teacher Francis Nicholls had likewise probably lectured on anatomy in London as early as two years before taking his MA. Baillie's MA was taken simultaneously with his

---

[1] Matthew Baillie (1761-1823), m. Balliol 1779, BA 1783, MA 1786, BM 1786, DM 1789; FRCP, FRS. John Mayo (1762-1818), m. BNC 1778, BA 1782; fellow Oriel, MA 1785 BM 1787, DM 1788; FRCP 1789. Henry Vaughan (1766-1844), m. Ch.Ch. 1781, BA and MA 1788, BM 1790, DM 1791; physician to George III, George IV, William IV and Victoria; president of the Royal College of Physicians 1820-44.

[2] William Vivian (1728-1801), m. CCC 1742, BA 1746, MA 1750, BM 1757, DM 1761, fellow; regius prof. of medicine 1772-1801.

[3] Philip Dodwell (b. 1703), m. Ch.Ch. 1719; demy Magd. 1721-8, BA 1723, MA 1726, BM and DM 1742, fellow 1728-70, vice-president 1743.

[4] George Dowdswell (1722-73), m. Ch.Ch. 1738, BA 1742, MA 1745; BM and DM Univ. 1757.

BM in 1786, and his DM in 1789. In securing a dispensation, Baillie claimed that his lectures on anatomy in London had made it inconvenient to take his MA until 1786. Two years before taking his DM Baillie was appointed physician at St George's Hospital. He reported that a few weeks were spent in Oxford each year in order to 'keep up my terms'.[1]

The relatively remote contact with Oxford exhibited by Baillie was more representative than cases of continuous medical study in Oxford. The Radcliffe travelling fellows of necessity spent long periods studying medicine while travelling in Europe. Another typical pattern was exemplified by George Shaw, who obtained his MA in 1772; he entered the church but abandoned a clerical career in favour of medicine, studying at Edinburgh before returning to Oxford to accumulate his medical degrees in 1787. Like many others Shaw was allowed to accumulate his BM and DM, providing that fees were paid for both degrees and exercises performed for the DM.[2]

John Latham was also deflected from the church into medicine. In 1784, the year in which he took his MA, Latham was appointed honorary physician to the Manchester Infirmary; his BM was taken in 1786 upon his transfer to a similar post at the Radcliffe Infirmary in Oxford, and his DM upon his removal to London in 1788.[3]

James Stonehouse represents a less common pattern, involving medical studies abroad. After graduating MA in 1739 he studied medicine at St Thomas's Hospital in London and then in Paris, Lyons, Montpellier and Marseilles, returning to practise medicine in Coventry in 1742 and Northampton in 1743. His BM was taken in 1742 and his DM in 1746.[4]

After taking his BA Thomas Beddoes left Oxford to study medicine in London. Having obtained his MA he transferred to Edinburgh, returning to accumulate his BM and DM in 1786, at the beginning of his short but meteoric career as a non-stipendiary reader in chemistry at Oxford. The habit of studying at both Edinburgh and London between taking arts and medical degrees at Oxford was increasingly common in the later eighteenth century.

Even cases which seem to suggest continuous study in Oxford may turn out to be problematical. William Austin obtained his MA in 1780,

[1] G. C. Peachy, *A Memoir of William and John Hunter* (Plymouth 1924), 53-68; M. Baillie, 'A short memoir of my life', *The Practitioner* lvii (1896); for Nicholls see Peachy, 31.

[2] George Shaw (1753-1813), m. Magd. Hall 1765, BA 1769, MA 1772, BM and DM 1787; FRS; keeper of the Natural History Museum 1807-13.

[3] John Latham (1761-1843), m. BNC 1778, BA 1782, MA 1784, BM 1786, DM 1788; FRS, FLS, president of the Royal College of Physicians 1813-19; physician to Middlesex Hospital 1780-93, St Bartholomew's Hospital 1793-1802.

[4] Sir James Stonehouse (1716-95), 7th bt; m. St John's 1733, BA 1736, MA 1739, BM 1742, DM 1746.

BM in 1782 and DM in 1783, the year of his election as physician to the Radcliffe Infirmary.[1] It may be presumed that he studied medicine at Oxford, but he was also bursar and humanity lecturer at Wadham in 1780 and 1781. He displayed a long-standing interest in oriental studies and had given lectures in Arabic on behalf of the Laudian professor of Arabic. In 1781 he also deputized for the Savilian professor of geometry. This many-sided figure was also studying medicine at St Bartholomew's Hospital in London from 1779 onward, and it was at this hospital that he spent the major part of his career.

The evidence from the registers of convocation relating to the granting of dispensations also suggests that Oxford medical students were generally resident elsewhere, and were merely visiting Oxford for the sake of performing essential degree-exercises. Typically, in 1698 Richard Hale was granted a BM, two years after taking his MA, having a future prospect of settling in the country to his advantage. He was in 1701 granted a dispensation to take his DM prematurely. John Osmond of Wadham and Corpus was granted a dispensation because a 'long stay in the University' would 'prejudice' his affairs in the country. William Cole of Lincoln College was excused from taking his MA and BM and was granted a DM in 1726, on account of the need for 'constant attendance in the business of his profession'. Henry Costard was excused coming to Oxford to perform the exercises for his DM by virtue of the inconvenience of travelling from his practice, 150 miles away.[2]

Reference by Oxford arts graduates to the need for a medical degree as a condition for their acceptance by the Royal College of Physicians, mention of a promise of career advantages away from Oxford, either in the country or abroad, were generally guaranteed to procure a dispensation, providing that necessary fees were paid and a substantial bond given that certain required exercises would be performed.

In other cases evidence of medical studies elsewhere was readily accepted as the basis for dispensation. In 1768 John Breedon of Queen's was given a dispensation for omitting his full term of MA residence because of absence in Edinburgh attending lectures in medicine. John Cockman's travels in Italy were invoked as the basis for the accumulation of his BM and DM in 1715.[3]

[1] William Austin (1755-93), m. Wadham 1773, BA 1776, MA 1780, BM 1782, DM 1783; FRCP 1786; physician St Bartholomew's Hospital 1786-93.

[2] OUA register of congregation 1692-1703, fos 49ᵛ, 133ᵛ, 29 Jan. and 8 Feb. 1698, (Hale); register of convocation 1683-93, p. 234, 27 June 1698 (Osmond); register of convocation 1703-30, fo 241ʳ, 8 Dec. 1726 (Cole); register of convocation 1730-41, fo 62ᵛ, 19 July 1736 (Costard). Richard Hale (1670-1729), m. Trin. 1689, BA 1693, MA 1696, BM 1698, DM 1701; FRCP 1708. Henry Costard (b. 1693), m. Wadham 1709, BA 1713, MA 1717, fellow 1718, BM 1720, DM 1736.

[3] OUA register of convocation 1766-76, p. 56, 3 May 1768 (Breedon); register of convocation 1703-30, fo 128ᵛ, 31 Oct. 1715 (Cockman). John Cockman (1681-1734), m. Univ. 1699, BA 1703, MA 1705, BM and DM 1715; incorporated at Cambridge 1719.

Although the intellectual debt of its medical students to the Oxford medical school was not great, the survival of the degree-granting mechanism indicates that there was an incentive to maintain this point of attachment to the academic institution, with the result that the university's records provide an invaluable index to a substantial body of country doctors.

It is informative to take account of the county of origin of medical students, because in the majority of cases this information also provides an approximate guide to their ultimate place of residence and medical practice. When this pattern was broken it was generally because of the attractions of practice in London or the expanding spa resorts, or perhaps because of foreign travel in a civilian or military medical capacity.

TABLE 25.4

COUNTY OF ORIGIN OF MEDICAL GRADUATES 1691-1800

number of medical graduates	county
1	Anglesey, Bedford, Brecon, Cambridge, Cumberland, Durham, Hertford, Norfolk, Northumberland, Rutland, Sussex
2	Carmarthen, Denbigh, Derby, Essex, Glamorgan, Nottingham
3	Merioneth, Montgomery, York
4	Leicester, Pembroke
5	Monmouth, Surrey
6	Lincoln
7	Buckingham
9	Dorset, Hereford, Northampton
10	Berkshire, Cheshire, Lancashire, Stafford, Warwick
11	Shropshire
14	Worcester
15	Cornwall, Kent
17	Somerset
18	Gloucester, Hampshire
19	Oxford
22	Wiltshire
27	Devon
66	London and Middlesex
others:	Scotland (8), Ireland (2), Channel Islands (1), Antigua (1), Florida (1)

From the details presented in table 25.4 it is evident that Oxford drew the great majority of its medical candidates from a relatively limited number of counties. London is particularly well represented, partly because students of London origin appreciated the many lucrative openings offered to medical practitioners in the rapidly expanding capital, partly because of the residual pressures for association with the Royal College of Physicians. For a full fellowship of the college a candidate required a DM from an English university, while a BM rendered him eligible to become a licentiate.

Apart from London, Oxford drew the majority of its medical students from the west midlands, the western counties of England and from Wales. Lancashire is the only northern county at all well represented. It is notable that few students came from the northern or eastern counties, most of which maintained traditional associations with Cambridge. Thus in medicine, as in arts, Oxford and its constituent colleges maintained strong regional associations.

In view of the above evidence relating to the non-residence of medical students it would be misleading to attach too much importance to college affiliation. Few colleges at Oxford had established lectureships or fellowships in medicine, with the result that none had by 1690 developed into a particular centre for medical studies, although colleges such as Christ Church, University College and Wadham had at times become important meeting points for groups of scientific enthusiasts, many of whom were interested in medicine.

Table 25.5, showing the college attachments of Oxford's medical graduates, includes information relating to the majority of students. Of the twenty-six for whom there is no information, almost all obtained their degrees by incorporation or creation. The pattern which emerges shows little constancy over the period 1691–1800. Most colleges produced a thin trickle of medical graduates; about half the colleges (13) providing two or less per decade. In such cases there were long periods when no medical student was associated with the college. No college displayed a consistently good record, although Christ Church and Balliol score well according to various criteria. These were the only colleges in which the number of graduates ever reached double figures within any one decade, and then only in the decade 1721–30. It is interesting to note that the totals for both of these colleges fell sharply after 1730. Thus the establishment of Dr Lee's readership and the anatomy school at Christ Church in 1765 did nothing to revive the numbers at this college, and little immediately to arrest the general decline in the number of graduates produced by the medical school. In view of the very small numbers involved and the general tendency to non-residence, it is doubtful whether any college can be said to have developed a substantial body of medical students in the course of the eighteenth century. Even a college such as Merton, which was exceptional in having an almost continuous series of medical wardens, failed to establish a viable tradition of medical

TABLE 25.5

COLLEGE AFFILIATION OF MEDICAL GRADUATES 1691-1800

	1691-1700	1701-1710	1711-1720	1721-1730	1731-1740	1741-1750	1751-1760	1761-1770	1771-1780	1781-1790	1791-1800	total
All Souls	2	3	4	1	4	2	1	1			1	19
Balliol	5	3	7	10	2	1	2	1	1	1	4	37
Brasenose	3	1	2	3		1	2			1	1	16
Christ Church	2	5	5	13	3	4	4	3	2	3	3	47
Corpus	3			3	1	1	1			1		10
Exeter	3	5	6	5	2	2		1	2			26
Jesus	2	1		5	3	4		2	2	1		18
Lincoln	3	2	1	1	1		1					9
Magdalen College	4	3				4	1			1	1	14
Magdalen Hall	5	3	2	1	1		1			2	1	15
Merton	5	6	2	2	3	1	2	2	1	1	5	30
New College	5	4	1	4	3	2	1		1			21
Oriel	1	1	1	1	4		2	3		5	1	19
Pembroke	2	1	1	1	1	1				6	2	13
Queen's			1	2	1	1	1	1	2		1	10
St John's	5	2	1	1	4	4	2				1	20
Trinity	5	4	1	6	6	3		1			1	27
University College	1	5	2	2	3	3	1	2	2	4	3	28
Wadham	9	3	2	2	2	1				1		20
Worcester	1	3			2			1		1	1	8
total	66	55	38	62	46	35	21	19	11	28	26	407

Where a student attended more than one college the table records only that college with which he was associated during his medical studies. Entries in the table are according to the date of the student's first medical degree. The colleges are taken to include their associated halls.

education. Indeed when the affairs of the college reached such disorder that the archbishop of Canterbury in 1737 conducted a visitation it was found that out of the four medically qualified fellows only one was contributing to medical education.

An element of continuity was provided by medical graduates who held college fellowships at some time during their medical studies. Almost one hundred medical graduates held fellowships at some stage. These fellowships rarely related directly to medicine. All Souls College was exceptional in establishing in 1704 four fellowships tenable by laymen formally studying law, but with a view to qualifying in medicine. Magdalen was also exceptional in reserving one fellowship specifically for a medical student, and there were two Radcliffe travelling fellowships for medical students at University College. At both Christ Church and Exeter a fellowship was tenable either by a lawyer or medical man. Corpus maintained the office of *medicinae deputatus* which was occupied by a student of medicine. Colleges which had ten or more future medical graduates as fellows between 1690 and 1800 include Wadham (11), Merton (12), Exeter (13), University College (16) and All Souls (18).

All Souls is an anomalous case in which all the intending medical graduates were fellows. In the other four colleges having substantial numbers of medical fellows, about half the medical graduates were fellows at some time. However, this statistic in itself need not be particularly meaningful with respect to medical studies, in view of the complexities and idiosyncrasies of the fellowship system. Some examples from Exeter College indicate the difficulties in interpreting data relating to fellowships. John Tapson, William Furneaux and Samuel Trelawney were fellows for brief periods before the beginning of their medical studies. William Salkeld, William Williams and Christopher Furneaux were fellows during the period of preparation for both their MA and medical degrees, and for a period subsequently. John Andrew and Francis Milman were permitted by the Sir William Petre fellowship (founded 1636) to vacate their fellowships in order to travel abroad for periods of three and four years respectively.[1] Andrew studied medicine at Leiden before returning to Oxford for a further five years in preparation for his BM and DM while still supported by his fellowship. Milman

---

[1] John Tapson (1714-47), m. Exeter 1731, fellow 1733, BA and MA 1737, BM 1741. William Furneaux (1692-1722), m. Exeter 1708, fellow 1710, BA 1713, MA 1716, BM and DM 1721. Samuel Trelawney (b. 1685), m. Exeter 1702, fellow 1706-11, BA 1707, MA 1710, BM 1711. William Salkeld (1749-1812), m. Exeter 1767, BA 1771, fellow 1771-81, MA 1774, BM 1777. William Williams (b. 1681), m. Exeter 1697, fellow 1700-19, BA 1703, MA 1706, BM and DM 1711. Christopher Furneaux (1683-1730), m. Exeter 1710, fellow 1713-29, BA 1715, MA 1718, BM 1719. John Andrew (1710-72), m. Queen's 1727, BA 1731, MA Exeter 1734, BM 1740, DM 1742. Francis Milman (1746-1821), from 1800 1st bt; m. Exeter 1760, BA 1764, fellow 1765-80, MA 1767, BM 1770, DM 1776, BD 1778; FRCP 1778, president 1811-13; physician to George III 1806; FRS.

used his absence for taking up a Radcliffe travelling fellowship, enabling him to travel widely on the continent.

In the case of Milman and William Tonkin their fellowships were tenable on the understanding that they were proceeding to take a degree in divinity. Both instead entered upon the 'physic line'; in order to retain their fellowship each was forced to obtain special permission to take a degree in divinity.[1] In the case of fellowships at All Souls College it was only the legist fellows who could transfer to the medical line. Thus intending medical graduates in the university may well not have been studying medicine during the whole tenure of their fellowships, while fellows registered on the law or theology lines may in fact have been preparing for medical degrees.

The most important medical fellowships in Oxford were the two travelling fellowships established at University College under the terms of a generous bequest made by the wealthy Oxford medical graduate John Radcliffe.[2] These fellowships were worth £300 per annum and were intended to support the travels of the fellow for up to five years in Britain and five years on the continent. The seemingly excessively generous terms of this desirable fellowship caused some consternation at the time of its establishment.[3] Opinions were also mixed about the calibre of the first fellows to be elected in 1715. Hearne regarded Noel Broxholme as 'a very ingenuous, honest, good-natured man', while Robert Wintle he epitomized as 'a violent, proud, ill-natured Whig'.[4] Neither evinced in his medical capacity any particular benefit from foreign travel. Many of the later fellows made better use of their travelling fellowships, and subsequently many attained distinction in science or in the medical profession. Among the better known travelling fellows were John Monroe, Samuel Musgrave, John Sibthorp and William Turton.[5]

Oxford and Cambridge were much slower than Edinburgh to develop a system of public teaching appropriate to the needs of the eighteenth-century medical student. In the course of this century Edinburgh emerged as a non-collegiate, non-residential university, conducting its teaching on a professorial basis. The seven specialist professors of medicine were sufficient to cover every major branch of medical science; they were encouraged to conduct their teaching in a framework of modern

---

[1] Cf *Reg. Exeter Coll.* 149-50, 142. William Tonkin (1718-98), m. Exeter 1735, BA 1738, fellow 1739-71, MA 1741, BM 1748, BD 1749.

[2] For the Radcliffe fellowships and biographies of the fellows see J. B. Nias, *Dr John Radcliffe* (Oxford 1918).

[3] R. Richardson-Charlett, 11 June 1716, MS Ballard 17, fo 141.

[4] Hearne, *Collections* v. 80.

[5] John Monroe (1716-91), m. St John's 1733, BA 1737, MA 1740, BM 1743, DM by diploma 1747; FRCP 1753; physician Bethlehem Hospital. John Sibthorp (1758-96), m. Linc. 1773, BA 1777, MA 1780; BM and DM Univ. 1784; Sherardian prof. of botany 1784-96. William Turton (1762-1835), m. Oriel 1781, BA 1785, MA and BM 1791; fellow of the Linnean Society.

ideas, and ultimately they developed facilities for clinical training. The Edinburgh professors were active, prosperous and successful.[1]

Oxford continued to rely on its regius professor of medicine, whose primary duties under the terms of the Laudian statutes—which remained in operation until the mid-nineteenth century—were to lecture on texts of Hippocrates or Galen twice a week during term time at 8 a.m.[2]

In the seventeenth century the Tomlins readership in anatomy had been established to provide for the regular teaching of anatomy.[3] The emoluments of this post were absorbed by the regius professor, and the rule that either he or his deputy should perform regular anatomies had lapsed long before 1690.

Although not university appointees, the two Linacre lecturers established at Merton College in the sixteenth century were intended to provide public instruction on the classical medical authors. These lectureships had lapsed by the Restoration.[4] By this date the regius professor or his deputy carried the entire responsibility for the official teaching of medicine. The holders of this office between 1690 and 1800, with minor exceptions, performed their duties with so little commitment or distinction that they merit no more than passing mention.[5] John Luffe, an implacable enemy of John Radcliffe, was replaced by a whig nominee, Thomas Hoy, who was released from his office by royal dispensation in 1717. Luffe had been negligent; Hoy was an absentee who lived in Jamaica. Hoy was succeeded by his deputy Thomas Lasher, also a notorious whig, who was over 70 before assuming office.[6] Upon his death at the age of 82 in 1729 he was succeeded by William Beauvoir, whom Hearne referred to disparagingly as a wine-merchant.[7] Beauvoir died within the year, to be succeeded by William Woodforde, a fellow of New College, whose few distinctions included a fellowship of the Royal College of Physicians. Alcock was probably correct in charging Woodforde with treating his post as a sinecure.[8] After Woodforde's death at Bath in 1758 his successor, Evan Pitt, died before taking up his post.[9] John

[1] See p. 684 n. 1 above.
[2] *Laudian Code* IV.i.16, ed. Griffiths, p. 39.
[3] *Statuta antiqua universitatis oxoniensis*, ed. S. Gibson (Oxford 1931), 551-5.
[4] A. Wood, *The History and Antiquities of the University of Oxford*, ed. J. Gutch (2 vols in 3 Oxford 1792-6) ii. 862-3; R. G. Lewis, 'The Linacre lectureships subsequent to their foundation' in F. R. Maddison, M. Pelling and C. Webster (eds), *Linacre Studies* (Oxford 1977).
[5] Cf Wood ii. 859-61.
[6] John Luffe (1647-98), m. Magd. Hall 1661; BA Trin. 1665; MA St Mary Hall 1665, BM and DM 1673; regius prof. of medicine 1681-98. Thomas Hoy (1659-1718),m. St John's 1676, BA 1680, MA 1684, BM 1686, DM 1689; regius prof. of medicine 1698-1718. Thomas Lasher (1647-1729), m. St John's 1665, BA 1668, MA and fellow 1673, BM 1676, DM 1679; regius prof. of medicine 1718-29.
[7] Hearne, *Collections* x. 246. William Beauvoir (1669-1730), m. Pemb. 1697, BA 1701, fellow and MA 1704, BM and DM 1710; regius prof. of medicine 1729-30.
[8] [Thomas Alcock,] *Some Memoirs of the life of Dr Nathan Alcock, lately Deceased* (London 1780), 8-9.
[9] Evan Pitt (c1703-c1758), m. Ch.Ch. 1719, BA 1723, MA 1726, BM 1729, DM 1733.

Kelly, who served from 1759 to 1772, seems to have spent most of his time in Bristol and Bath. William Vivian was the last regius professor of the century;[1] he was a figure of minor local distinction as a physician, and he was one of the first honorary physicians of the Radcliffe Infirmary. Not only were the regius professors inactive as teachers, but also the system of appointing deputies seems not to have functioned efficiently. A minor scandal erupted when it was discovered that Charles Tadlow, the deputy to Hoy, was himself appointing a deputy—in this case the able James Monro of Balliol College, founder of the Monro dynasty at Bethlehem (Bethlam) Hospital.[2] Very soon Tadlow died, to be replaced in 1717 as deputy by Philip Code, who annoyed Hearne by defending the general practice of 'Professors . . . not reading in the Schools'.[3] The negligence of the professors of medicine was a particular cause of concern, since it was their lectures which most interested the many foreign visitors to Oxford. After Code's death in 1718 the only deputies so far identified are Gilbert Trowe and Humphrey Sibthorp, who served as deputies for Woodforde.[4]

The deficiencies of the regius professors were to a limited extent compensated for by informal mechanisms of education developed among the medical students themselves, or by private teachers. The former had been particularly important in the much larger student body in the second part of the seventeenth century. The demand for private teachers, usually operating on a temporary, peripatetic basis, continued into the eighteenth century. As in London, there was a particular demand for lectures and demonstrations in anatomy, intended both for medical students and curious laymen. For the period between 1685 and 1721 evidence has been uncovered relating to occasional anatomical lectures given by eight different individuals—including visitors from Italy, Switzerland, Scotland and London, as well as Christopher Furneaux, William Musgrave, Edward Hannes and James Monro of Oxford.[5] Anatomical observations were also recorded at meetings of the Philosophical Society which was active from 1683 to 1697.[6] Further evidence for anatomies is provided by outbursts of publicity attracted when bodies were procured for dissection according to the provision of a royal charter of

[1] The dates of appointment of the regius professors were: Luffe 23 June 1681; Hoy 14 Oct. 1698; Lasher 1718 (exact date not recorded); Beauvoir 22 Apr. 1729; Woodforde 2 Apr. 1730; Kelly 16 Apr. 1759; Vivian 20 Nov. 1772.

[2] Hearne, *Collections* ii. 379-82. Charles Tadlow (1660-1716), m. St John's 1678, BA 1682, MA 1686, BM 1691, DM 1693. James Monro (1680-1752), m. Balliol 1699, BA 1703, MA 1708, BM 1709, DM 1722; FRCP.

[3] Hearne, *Collections* vi. 74, 200, 224; Sinclair and Robb-Smith, *Anatomical Teaching*, 25. Philip Code (*c*1663-1718), m. Queen's 1691, BA 1694; fellow All Souls and MA 1698, BM 1703, DM 1707.

[4] See L. S. Sutherland, 'Political respectability 1751-71' p. 146 above.

[5] Sinclair and Robb-Smith, 18-26.

[6] For the minute-books of the Philosophical Society see Gunther, *Early Science* iv.

1636. These events were often associated with bawdy scenes among the gownsmen.[1]

Visiting anatomists were allowed access to the anatomy school in the schools quadrangle, which was a hall rather than a purpose-built anatomical theatre of the type established by the Barber-Surgeons' Company in London or at the medical school in Padua. The Oxford anatomy school gradually assumed the role of a minor anatomical museum. In the early eighteenth century the anatomy school came under the auspices of Hearne, whose watchful eye recorded the manifold defects in the characters of the regius professors. When Uffenbach visited Oxford in 1710 he noted the general disorder and dirtiness of the anatomical school, which struck him as being something like a natural history museum or art gallery. He witnessed an anatomical lecture by a visitor from Zurich, but this was given in a more appropriate small vaulted basement room of the Ashmolean Museum, rather than in the uncongenial anatomy school.[2]

In 1700 the aged John Wallis argued that the private anatomical lectures recently introduced at Oxford and Cambridge by James Keill were perpetuating the tradition of expert anatomical teaching established by Thomas Willis and Richard Lower four decades earlier.[3] These lectures were just one manifestation of the debt which Oxford owed to the group formed around David Gregory after his departure from Edinburgh to become Savilian professor of astronomy at Oxford in 1691. Gregory's circle, operating under the patronage of Henry Aldrich, dean of Christ Church, pursued all aspects of science. Gregory, along with his Scottish disciples, the brothers John and James Keill, and the Englishmen Edward Hannes and John Freind, imaginatively applied mathematical and Newtonian principles in the fields of physiology and medicine.[4] Their ideas were developed initially in private discussions and public lectures, and thereafter expressed in publications which attracted widespread attention and comment, drawing the attention of Europe to the residual vitality of the well established tradition of Oxford iatromechanism. The premature deaths of Gregory in 1708 and Hannes in 1710 and the departure of Freind from Oxford left only John Keill in Oxford, undermining

---

[1] Sinclair and Robb-Smith, 16, 24, 26, 28; *Grub Street Journal*, 8 Jan. 1730–16 Sept. 1731, no. 31, copy in Bodl. MS Top. Oxon. d. 174, fo 263.

[2] *Oxford in 1710 being the Travels of Zacharias Conrad von Uffenbach*, ed. W. H. and W. J. C. Quarrell (Oxford 1928), 19–21; see also Turner, 'Physical sciences', 662.

[3] T. W. Jackson, 'Dr. Wallis' Letter against Mr. Maidwell, 1700', *Collectanea* i. 269, 337, 316.

[4] *David Gregory, Isaac Newton and their Circle: extracts from David Gregory's memoranda 1677–1708*, ed. W. G. Hiscock (Oxford 1937); A. Thackray, *Atoms and Powers* (Cambridge Mass. and London 1970); A. Kippis (ed.), *Biographia britannica* (6 vols London 1747–66), iii. 2026–37 (John Freind), iii. 2801–11 (John and James Keill). Relevant publications of this group include James Keill, *An Account of Animal Secretion* (London 1708); J. Freind, *Emmenologia* (Oxford 1703) and *Praelectiones chymicae* (London 1709). Gregory was admitted BM and DM in 1692. The texts of his three cursory lectures on Galen, *De usu partium* and *De locis affectis* given on 9, 10 and 11 March 1692 are preserved in Aberdeen Univ. Library, MS 2206/8. John Freind was granted a ML and BM in 1703 and DM (by diploma) in 1707.

the chances of consolidating the initial work of Gregory's circle into a viable school of medical and physiological research capable of rivalling that which had flourished between 1640 and 1680.[1] Such a movement might well have arrested the decline of the medical school.

Anatomical lectures and demonstrations continued to be in demand. It was worth the while of Christopher Furneaux to advertise his course of lectures at the Oxford anatomy school on human and comparative anatomy in a London newspaper, announcing that he had already attracted forty-two subscribers.[2] Furneaux's anatomical lectures were eclipsed by those given by Francis Nicholls, who began lecturing in Oxford probably some time between 1719 and 1721. Nicholls may have been responsible for wresting the Tomlins readership in anatomy out of the hands of the regius professor and his deputy. He was styled 'praelector in anatomy' in his published works. Nicholls soon established a major reputation as an anatomist and anatomy lecturer, but by 1727 had transferred his lectures to London, where he continued to lecture until 1741. His initial 'complete syllabus of anatomy' and his famous *Compendium anatomico-oeconomicum* were announced as having been prepared for use in the University of Oxford. Nicholls's textbook continued in use at Oxford until nearly the end of the century in the hands of Thomas Lawrence, John Smith and John Parsons.[3]

It is doubtful whether Nicholls continued to perform his duties in Oxford as praelector in anatomy once he was established in London as a successful lecturer, and even this lecturing ceased when he took over the lucrative medical practice of his father-in-law Richard Mead, himself inheritor of Radcliffe's practice.[4] The appointment of a successor to Nicholls was delayed until 1743, when Thomas Lawrence was precipitately called in from London to re-establish official university lectures in anatomy, in the hope of subverting the successful private lectures recently established at Jesus College by Nathan Alcock.[5] In Alcock's

[1] See Frank, *Harvey and the Oxford Physiologists*.

[2] *Daily Courant*, 3 Mar. 1719. For an excellent account of the rise of anatomical lecturing in London see Peachy, *William and John Hunter*, 1-52.

[3] F. Nicholls, *Syllabus anatomicus, et omnia complectens quae ad generalem corporis oeconomiam attinent, in usu academiae oxoniensis compositus et praelectionibus ibi annuatim habitas adaptus* (London 1727); *Compendium anatomicum, et omnia complectens quae ad cognitam humani corporis oeconomiam spectant* (London 1733). On the editions of the *Compendium* see K. F. Russell, *British Anatomy* (Melbourne 1963), 172-4. An interleaved, annotated copy of the 1746 edition which belonged to Francis Henry Egerton (1756-1829, from 1823 8th e. of Bridgewater; m. Ch.Ch. 1773, BA 1776; fellow All Souls 1776; FRS) is now in the library of Magdalen College. For Nicholls's anatomical work see Sinclair and Robb-Smith, *Anatomical Teaching*, 28-31; F. J. Cole, 'History of anatomical injections' in C. Singer (ed.), *Studies in the History and Method of Science* (2 vols Oxford 1921) ii. John Parsons (1742-85), m. Ch.Ch. 1759, BA 1763, MA 1766, BM 1769, DM 1772; reader in anatomy 1769, clinical professor 1780-5; FRCP 1775.

[4] Peachy, 31-3, 88-9; Sinclair and Robb-Smith, 27; T. Lawrence, *Francis Nichollsii MD vita* (London 1780).   [5] Peachy, 33-4; Turner, 'Physical sciences', 664.

estimate, an opportunity for him to succeed as a private lecturer was provided because the regius professor, Woodforde, 'made a sinecure of his place . . . Dr Nicholls had left the anatomy, and was settled in London . . . the readers in this and in chemistry, either were not qualified, or not disposed to prosecute those sciences with any effect'.[1] Thomas Hughes of Trinity was employed to compete with Alcock's chemistry lectures. The official lectures of Lawrence and Hughes collapsed ingloriously. Their supporters proved unable to prevent Alcock being granted an MA, and thenceforth consolidating his position as official praelector in anatomy and chemistry, lecturing in the Ashmolean Museum.[2]

It was inevitable that sooner or later a figure like Alcock would arrive in Oxford to expose the need for more effective teaching in such basic aspects of medicine as anatomy and chemistry. Alcock, who had studied at both Edinburgh and Leiden when the latter was at the height of its fame as a teaching centre, was well placed to experiment in modern medical teaching at Oxford. It was almost predictable that the Oxford medical establishment, headed by Richard Frewin, should resist the overtures of this intruder, whose modern medicine was thought to be tinged with unpalatable and modern theological beliefs.

Alcock was succeeded in 1758 by John Smith, who continued lecturing effectively in anatomy and chemistry until appointed Savilian professor of geometry. Whereas Alcock had been reticent to publish the results of his scientific enquiries, Smith established a minor reputation as a medical writer.[3] Smith's tenure of the Tomlins readership extended until 1766, the eve of the establishment of Dr Lee's readership in anatomy at Christ Church.

The new readership marked the onset of an institutional revival in medicine at Oxford. Lee's benefactions to Christ Church were followed by the establishment of the Radcliffe Infirmary, the Lichfield clinical professorship, and the Aldrichian praelectorship in anatomy, all dating from between 1767 and 1797. The idea of establishing an anatomy school had originated with John Freind, in connection with the work of the Gregory circle. However, it was left for Freind's admirer Matthew Lee to bequeath sufficient funds for the endowment of a lectureship in anatomy and for the building of a substantial anatomy school at Christ Church.[4] This was designed by Henry Keene; its foundation-stone was laid in 1766, and it

[1] *Memoirs of Alcock*, 8-9.

[2] Ibid. 10-19. Alcock obtained his MD at Leiden in 1741, according to the register of convocation, or in 1742, according to R. W. I. Smith, *English Speaking Students of Medicine at Leyden* (Edinburgh, 1932), 3. See also Turner, 664-5.

[3] Smith's first series of lectures on anatomy and animal economy were advertised in *Jackson's Oxford Journal*, 17 Feb. 1758. For lecture-notes of the Merton undergraduate George Wingfield based on Smith's 1759 lectures in anatomy and chemistry see Turner, 665.

[4] Sinclair and Robb-Smith, *Anatomical Teaching*, 86-8.

was built at a cost of £1,200.[1] This building supplanted the old university anatomy school. It housed a lecture-room and a basement used for dissections. Stringent conditions were laid down for the lectureship, designed to disqualify those in holy orders, discourage absenteeism and encourage the effective teaching of anatomy, medicine and botany.[2] Lee's readership was established with very much the same purpose as the defunct Tomlins readership, which it supplanted. Consistent with this development, in 1767 all medical students were required to attend anatomy lectures.[3]

The first incumbent of Lee's readership in 1767 was John Parsons, one of the most enterprising young physicians in Oxford. In his anatomical lectures he was assisted by an officially appointed anatomical surgeon, the first of whom was John Grosvenor[4] who served until 1795, by which time he had married Parsons's widow. Parsons lectured broadly in the tradition of Alcock and Smith, by no means confining himself to the subjects specified in the decrees.[5] He also accumulated a large collection of specimens to illustrate his lectures, which provided the basis for a museum which was augmented subsequently by minor additions bought by the Lee trustees at the request of the readers.[6]

Parsons's successor as Lee's reader and university reader in anatomy was William Thomson who resigned under a shadow in 1790, to be replaced by Christopher Pegge.[7] Both were competent anatomists and scientists; Pegge was to become regius professor. As Sinclair and Robb-Smith point out, Pegge was probably the first regius professor of medicine since the elder Thomas Clayton in the early seventeenth century actually to teach anatomy and thereby fulfil the conditions of the Tomlins readership.[8]

The Radcliffe Infirmary was a relative late-comer to the voluntary hospital movement of the eighteenth century. However, plans for a hospital had been under discussion for more than two decades before

[1] *Jackson's Oxford Journal*, 25 Aug. 1766; Gunther, *Early Science* iii. 114-16.

[2] Gunther, *Early Medical Science*, 114-17, 217-18.

[3] OUA register of congregation 1758-69, 10 Oct. 1767.

[4] John Grosvenor, *chirurgus*, priv. 24 Feb. 1768.

[5] Parsons's first course of lectures on philosophy and medical chemistry was advertised in *Jackson's Oxford Journal*, 22 May 1770. See also J. Parsons, *The Plan of a Course of Lectures in Philosophical and Practical Chemistry* (Oxford [1770]); 'A short account of Dr J. Parsons', *Edinburgh Medical Commentaries* x (1786), 322-5.

[6] Christ Church library, MS lii.b.i, 'Annual visitations of Dr M. Lee's anatomical theatre, accounts etc. 1796-1860'; Gunther, *Early Medical Science*, 191-5.

[7] William Thomson (1761-1803), m. Queen's 1776; Student Ch.Ch. 1779, BA 1780, MA 1783, BM 1785, DM 1786.

[8] Sinclair and Robb-Smith, *Anatomical Teaching*, 39-41. Thomas Clayton (1575-1647), m. Balliol 1591, BA 1594; MA Gloucester Hall 1599, BM and DM 1611; regius prof. of medicine 1612-47; principal of Broadgates Hall 1620-4; first master of Pembroke College 1624-47.

the Infirmary was eventually opened in 1770.[1] Shortly after its opening it was described as one of the finest hospitals in Europe by one seasoned continental medical expert.[2] The Infirmary had no institutional connection with the medical faculty of the university, but it was an indispensable asset in providing clinical experience for university teachers and members of the faculty. Of the longer-serving honorary physicians at the Infirmary, William Vivian (1770–95) became regius professor in 1772; John Smith (1770–96) succeeded Alcock as praelector in anatomy and chemistry in 1758; John Parsons (1772–85) served as Lee's reader between 1767 and 1785; Martin Wall (1775-1824) was reader in chemistry from 1781, and John Sibthorp (1787–94) served as Sherardian professor of botany. Robert Bourne (1787-1829), George Williams (1789-1834), and Christopher Pegge (1790-1808) held between them the appointments in the medical sciences at the turn of the century.

The honorary physicians of the Radcliffe Infirmary were academically better qualified than their equivalents in other provincial infirmaries. As clinicians and teachers they also bear favourable comparison with the physicians at major hospitals in London and the provinces. John Latham (1787-9) was relatively unusual in using the Radcliffe Infirmary as a stepping-stone to preferment in London. Most of the physicians attached to the Infirmary remained in Oxford for the rest of their careers. This hospital therefore exerted a stabilizing influence and acted as a centre for senior members of the medical faculty, between whom were shared out the various teaching offices in medicine and related subjects. The relationship between hospital and university was consolidated by the bequest of Lord Lichfield, one of the original trustees, who established a university professorship for the reading of clinical lectures in the Radcliffe Infirmary.

Under the terms of the Lichfield bequest the clinical professor was required to reside in Oxford during the five winter months, and in the presence of his 'auditors'

once every day, visit, and where it shall seem necessary, prescribe for such Patients in the Radcliffe Infirmary as shall come under his Care: the Prescriptions, together with a Report of the Symptoms and the effects of Remedies, to be enter'd in a Book, which shall, at all times, be open for the Inspection and Use of the Pupils.[3]

---

[1] For general histories of the Infirmary see A. G. Gibson, *The Radcliffe Infirmary* (Oxford 1926); A. H. T. Robb-Smith, *A Short History of the Radcliffe Infirmary* (Oxford 1970).

[2] J. F. C. Grimm, *Bemerkungen eines Reisenden durch Deutschland, Frankreich, England und Holland in Briefen an seine Freunde* (Altenburg 1775), quoted by W. D. Robson-Scott, *German Travellers in England 1400-1800* (Oxford 1953), 153.

[3] OUA WPß/6/5, 20 May 1780. For a meeting of the Radcliffe governors to amend the admission rules in line with the Lichfield benefaction see *Jackson's Oxford Journal*, 7 Feb. 1780.

He was also required to lecture during the same months twice a week 'on the Nature and Circumstances of the particular Cases which shall have been before him, the several Methods of Treatment, and such Medical Topics as they shall lead to'. Like the Edinburgh professors, the clinical professor was to collect a standard fee from those medical students attending each course of tuition.

The first two Lichfield lecturers were competent professionally, and they were effective scholars and teachers. The first was John Parsons (1780-5), who had an already established reputation as Dr Lee's reader.[1] The second Lichfield professor was Martin Wall (1785-1824), who was primarily known as a lecturer and writer on chemistry. Wall's high standing was confirmed when, as a relative outsider, he was elected, albeit by a narrow margin, to the Lichfield chair in competition with William Vivian, the elderly regius professor of medicine. Wall was no doubt assisted by the vigorous defence of the Radcliffe Infirmary which he had written in reply to the accusations of John Howard, the hospital and prison reformer.[2] Wall served as treasurer of the Infirmary from 1801 until 1824. According to the keen student Davies Giddy, Wall's election was regrettable since he neglected his clinical classes; but this view seems to be contradicted by the evidence of regular advertisements for Wall's clinical classes in the Oxford newspaper.[3]

The last medical foundations of the eighteenth century were the Aldrichian praelectorships, the creation of George Aldrich, a Nottingham medical practitioner, who endowed praelectorships in medicine, anatomy and chemistry by the terms of his will of 1797.

The praelectorship in medicine was to be taken up by the regius professor, his deputy or another suitably qualified doctor of medicine in the university.[4] The regius professor was not to be given any particular priority. The medical praelector's duties were to 'read a complete Course of Lectures on the Practise of Physic, to begin each year at the commencement of the latter half of the Lent Term'. The lectures in anatomy were to be held in the winter or spring and were to comprise 'one entire course of Physiology, accompanied with the completed dissection ... explaining ... the figure, situation, connection, nature, function and uses of the several parts and organs'. The anatomy praelector was also

---

[1] His first course of clinical lectures was announced in *Jackson's Oxford Journal*, 13 Oct. 1781.

[2] *A Letter to John Howard Esq., FRS, by Martin Wall, MD* (Oxford 1784). Martin Wall was the son of John Wall MD, the well known physician to the Worcester Infirmary and inventor of Worcester porcelain. His *Syllabus of a Course of Lectures in Chemistry and Medicine* announced his first course of lectures; see Turner, 'Physical sciences', 666. Wall's chemistry lectures were first announced in *Jackson's Oxford Journal*, 7 May and 29 Oct. 1781.

[3] Wall's clinical lectures were advertised from 1 Oct. 1785. Davies Giddy, later Davies Gilbert (1767-1839), m. Pemb. 1785; hon. MA 1789; DCL by diploma and president of the Royal Society 1832; MP Helston 1804-6, Bodmin 1806-33.

[4] OUA WPß/4/1.

required during the Michaelmas or Lent term to deliver a separate public lecture 'on some detached subject in Anatomy, or Physiology'.[1] The praelector in chemistry was expected to give a course on 'Medicinal and Philosophical Chemistry'.

It is notable that the Aldrich will and related schedule of rules devoted the greatest attention to the praelectorship in anatomy. For the first time in the teaching of medicine at Oxford provision was specifically made for the teaching of physiology. After a short delay the first Aldrichian praelectors were appointed in 1803.

If all of the teaching posts in medicine established at university and college level had become fully and continuously effective Oxford would by 1800 have possessed more than an adequate basis for the operation of the medical school. In addition to the posts in medicine and anatomy discussed above, there had been provision for a chair of botany since 1669 and a readership in chemistry since 1683. These posts, although relevant to the teaching of medicine, will be discussed separately with respect to the physic garden and science. Needless to say, the full phalanx of medical teachers failed to materialize. Of the pre-1660 foundations, all lapsed but the regius professorship. Of the foundations surviving into the eighteenth century, some failed to maintain continuity; others were held as sinecures; and the various posts tended to accumulate in a few hands. Thus Christopher Pegge was from 1790 Dr Lee's reader in anatomy and physician to the Radcliffe Infirmary, from 1801 also regius professor and from 1803 Aldrichian praelector in anatomy. His friend Robert Bourne was from 1787 physician to the Radcliffe Infirmary, from 1794 reader in chemistry, from 1803 Aldrichian praelector in medicine and from 1824 Lord Lichfield's professor of clinical medicine. Munk sanguinely reflected that for many years Pegge and Bourne shared 'the medical emoluments of the university and neighbourhood'.[2] As the career of Pegge amply testifies, there was no real incentive for the professor to perform the full range of duties attached to such offices. There was no compulsion for him even to abide by the spirit of the original bequests and their not infrequently prolix schedules of regulations. There was a tendency to neglect one, and then another duty; an inclination to fall victim to the attractions of absenteeism. Eventually responsibilities became confined to duties which could be conveniently accomplished in the course of ritual visits to Oxford.[3] Ultimately emoluments provided the only meaningful bond with the university. Thus

[1] Physiology (but not under that name) had been lectured on since the seventeenth century by various lecturers in other branches of medicine. In 1753 Malcolm Fleming of Edinburgh suggested that it might be taught as a specialist subject at Oxford: Gunther, *Early Medical Science*, 144.

[2] Munk, *Roll of the RCP* ii. 450.

[3] G. V. Cox, *Recollections of Oxford* (London 1868, 2nd edn London 1870), 141; Gunther, *Early Science* xi. 118-19; H. V. Fox, *Further Memoirs of the Whig Party* (London 1905), 339-40.

although the faculty of medicine was stronger in 1800 than in mid-century, organic weaknesses long displayed at the teaching level remained fundamentally unchecked. In this situation any improvements rested on individual initiative, and they tended to be short-lived. It proved impossible to raise the faculty to a level where it could compete with the well-entrenched medical schools elsewhere. At the turn of the century only five graduate students were shown as being registered on the 'physic line'.[1]

Nevertheless, for the moment, it seemed to one often quoted observer that the lectures of Thomas Beddoes, Thomson and Sibthorp had achieved such success that the medical sciences were being more successfully cultivated in Oxford at this time than at any time before or since.[2] In the heat of the moment the reformers developed grandiose notions. Beddoes produced a devastating critique of the Bodleian Library.[3] Proposals were made to modify the exercises performed by medical students. The hebdomadal board expressed no objection to additions being made to the currently required exercises.[4] It may well have been envisaged that more precise knowledge of traditional subjects like anatomy should be required, or that 'new' subjects such as chemistry should be recognized for examination purposes. Whatever the intention, nothing further was heard of this proposal. The initiative collapsed. There was no continuing encouragement for a modernized and more disciplined regime of teaching and examining in the medical sciences. It was a cause of understandable irritation to Beddoes that Oxford's medical men treated their well remunerated professorships as 'perfect sinecures', while his own readership in chemistry was non-stipendiary. Beddoes, under the patronage of Cyril Jackson, dean of Christ Church, aimed to modernize the teaching of medicine and to consolidate the work of Alcock, Smith, Parsons and Wall. He lectured to 'a full and overflowing audience'. His attempt to secure from the crown a stipend was sabotaged by his critics on the grounds of his alleged radical political sympathies at the time of the French Revolution. He resigned his post after the ignominy of witnessing his proposed stipend being deflected to augment the emoluments of his rival, the professor of botany.

The first physic gardens conceived as adjuncts to university medical faculties were founded at Padua and Pisa in the mid-sixteenth

[1] OUA WPß/2/5, official returns of members of colleges and halls on the books (1804).
[2] For Beddoes's career in Oxford see J. E. Stock, *Memoirs of Thomas Beddoes* (London 1811) 18-70; E. Robinson, 'Thomas Beddoes MD and the reform of science teaching in Oxford', *Annals of Science* xi (1955); F. W. Gibbs and W. A. Smeaton, 'Thomas Beddoes at Oxford', *Ambix* ix (1961); T. H. Levere, 'Dr Thomas Beddoes at Oxford: radical politics in 1788-1793 and the fate of the regius chair of chemistry', *Ambix* xxviii (1981); Turner, 'Physical sciences', 666-8.
[3] See I. G. Philip, 'Libraries and the University Press', 742-3 below.
[4] OUA hebdomadal board minutes 1788-1803, 57, 59, 23 May, 27 June 1791.

century.[1] The relevance of such gardens to the teaching of medicine was widely appreciated, and botanical gardens were founded at many of the European medical schools in the course of the sixteenth and seventeenth centuries. English medical students would have been particularly familiar with the garden at Leiden University. At first sight it would seem obvious that the Oxford physic garden, established in 1621, simply represented an implementation of an innovation in medical education which was proving so attractive and successful elsewhere in Europe.[2] However, there is no direct evidence to suggest that the plan to establish the Oxford physic garden originated within the medical faculty, or that the garden was established with primary medical aims in mind. The rudimentary medical teaching structure which existed at Oxford was far from being able to take advantage of such extreme refinements as physic gardens. The Oxford garden should be seen partly, if not primarily, as a reflection of the aristocratic taste for gardening which became manifest at the end of the sixteenth century, and which was fuelled by enthusiasm for accumulating collections of plants emanating from the voyages of explorers and colonists. In the celebrated gardens established by aristocrats and gentlemen medicine was not ignored, but it was subservient to the botanical, culinary and aesthetic aspects of gardening.[3]

Henry Danvers, earl of Danby, the founder of the Oxford garden, might be regarded as having established a permanent and prestigious monument to the botanical passion of his generation. There was no sounder way of guaranteeing permanence than by establishing the garden at one of the ancient universities. Oxford was an obvious choice in view of institutional innovations occurring in the sciences during the Jacobean period, the most important of which were the Savilian chairs of astronomy and geometry established in 1619.[4]

The above factors are important for appreciating problems in the longer-term history of the physic garden. It had no clear academic function and was not organized with respect to a set of well-defined decrees or rules. There was no clear division of authority between the university and the patron with respect to its financial affairs and staff. Hence the

[1] A. W. Hill, 'The history and functions of botanic gardens', *Annals of the Missouri Botanical Garden* ii (1915); K. M. Reeds, 'Renaissance humanism and botany', *Annals of Science* xxxiii (1976); F. H. Stafleu, 'Botanical Gardens before 1818', *Boissiera* xiv (1969).

[2] For general reviews of the history of the physic garden see C. Daubeny, *The Oxford Botanic Garden* (Oxford 1850); G. C. Druce, 'The foundation of the Oxford botanic garden', Botanical Society and Exchange Club of the British Isles, *Report* vii (1923). In this chapter the garden will be called by its more traditional name of 'physic garden', rather than by the term 'botanic garden', which became current in the nineteenth century.

[3] R. W. T. Gunther, *Early British Botanists and their Gardens* (Oxford 1922); A. Amherst, *A History of Gardening in England* (London 1895).

[4] C. Webster, *The Great Instauration: science, medicine and reform 1626-1660* (London 1975), 122-9. See also Turner, 'Physical sciences', *passim*.

officers occupied an anomalous position relative to the university. It is above all uncertain whether it was ever intended to be more than a botanical garden. Periodically the medical interest was asserted, but its primary object was to remain botanical rather than medical.

The early history of the garden illustrates the primacy of the decorative and botanical function.[1] First place was given to architectural construction—three gateways including the massive decorative gateway by Nicholas Stone (1631) and the substantial wall surrounding the five-acre site to the south of Magdalen College.[2] The land was leased from Magdalen College by Danby, and the lease was subsequently renewed by the university. The garden was recognized as a strategically important beautifying element at the entrance to the university from London. The first superintendent was the gardener Jacob Bobart the elder who in 1641 was granted by Danby a ninety-nine-year lease of the site, with the 'benefit of fees and fruits', and, subject to good behaviour, promised him an annuity of £40 for life for caring for the garden.[3] It was not until 1669 that Danby's intention of appointing a professor of botany was honoured. Robert Morison,[4] the first incumbent, although medically qualified, devoted himself exclusively to taxonomic botany. The profits from the rectory of Kirkdale in Yorkshire, set aside by Danby to finance the garden and to provide for the emoluments of its officers, were never adequate for the purpose, with the result that from the civil war onward the garden was supported by subventions from the university, by the private resources of its officers and by various *ad hoc* acts of charity.

Despite the virtual extinction of the bequest the garden was as successful as any of its competitors in Europe. Moves to establish a comparable garden at Cambridge were abortive. The Edinburgh garden, which dates from 1675, was the only other public physic garden to be established in Britain before the mid-eighteenth century.[4] The high reputation of the Oxford garden was largely due to the success of the practical management of the Bobart family and to the ambitious scale of the botanical publications planned by Robert Morison.[5] The fame of the garden rested as much on its herbaria as on the plants themselves. The herbarium kept by the Bobarts reached substantial proportions by the

---

[1] See S. H. Vines and G. C. Druce, *An Account of the Morisonian Herbarium* (Oxford 1914).

[2] J. Sherwood and N. Pevsner, *Buildings of England, Oxfordshire* (London 1974), 267. *In usu Acad. & Reipub.* inscribed over the main gateway emphasizes the garden's more general function.

[3] OUA SEP/2/15. Robert Morison (1620-83), incorp. BM from Angers 1669; prof. of botany 1669-84; physician to Charles II. See R. Pulteney, *Historical and Biographical Sketches of the Progress of Botany in England* (2 vols London 1790) ii. 289-327; S. H. Vines, 'Robert Morison and John Ray' in F. W. Oliver (ed.), *Makers of British Botany* (Cambridge 1913), 8-43; R. Desmond, *Dictionary of British and Irish Botanists* (London 1977), 450.

[4] Hill, 'Botanic gardens', 201-5. The Cambridge botanical garden was not established until 1762.

[5] H. T. Bobart, *A Biographical Sketch of Jacob Bobart, with an account of his two sons, Jacob and Tilleman* (Leicester 1884); Desmond, 72.

end of the seventeenth century, and it was to receive further substantial additions in the course of the next century.[1]

Jacob Bobart the elder remained in charge of the garden until 1679 when he died at the age of 84. He was succeeded by his son Jacob Bobart the younger, who was skilled both as a gardener and botanist. Although criticized in certain quarters for the barbarism of his Latin,[2] Bobart was competent to work as an equal with the leading botanists of his age. His expertise was respected by such eminent figures as John Ray and William Sherard.[3]

When Morison died after a street accident in 1683 Bobart was entrusted by John Fell on behalf of the delegates of the Press with the completion of Morison's *Plantarum historia universalis oxoniensis*.[4] The delegates had already incurred a substantial financial commitment in connection with the publication of this work (the second part had been published in 1680 but the first was never written) which they regarded as a prestige project. A specimen of the second part of Morison's work published in 1672 was only the second book to be undertaken at the Sheldonian Theatre. Vice-Chancellor Aldrich backed the publication of the *Plantarum historia* and Jacob Bobart was paid a fee of £400 for the completion of the third part, which was published between 1696 and 1699. Morison's massive work proved to be a crushing burden on the Press, which by 1703 had spent no less than £2,153 on its production.[5] Morison's *Historia* was poorly received; botanical experts were more impressed by the rival work by John Ray, and Morison's tomes were insufficiently attractive to the lay public. In 1705 almost half the volumes of the *Plantarum historia* remained unsold. It is upon the engravings rather than the text that its long-term reputation rests. However, this work confirmed Bobart's reputation as a botanist. Of permanent value was the substantial collection of approximately two thousand type specimens (known as the Morisonian herbarium), assembled by Bobart from his garden, explorations in the Oxford vicinity, or obtained from his numerous correspondents and visitors.[6]

No successor to Morison was formally appointed by the university. The physic garden now rested in the sole care of Bobart. In the third volume of the *Plantarum historia* Bobart referred to himself simply as *horti praefectus* whereas Morison was described as *professor botanices et*

[1] H. N. Clokie, *An Account of the Herbarium of the Department of Botany in the University of Oxford* (London 1964).

[2] Hearne, *Collections* i. 66, ii. 200.

[3] William Sherard (1659-1728), m. St John's 1677.

[4] For this project see H. G. Carter, *A History of the Oxford University Press* i (Oxford 1975), 236-9.

[5] This does not represent the complete cost, since many of the engraved plates were subscribed by a variety of patrons: ibid. 237.

[6] Clokie, 7-17, 54-8. This herbarium is described in detail by Vines and Druce, *Morisonian Herbarium*.

horti praefectus primus. The memorial to Bobart in St Peter in the East refers to him as *praefectus* rather than *professor*. However, regardless of the formal position, Bobart was regarded by his contemporaries as both professor and keeper of the garden.[1]

Although the garden was nominally superintended by the vice-chancellor and a committee of delegates, little interest was shown in its active management, no doubt with a view to avoiding more than minimal financial commitment beyond returns from the Kirkdale estate.[2]

Bobart was annoyed about this neglect of the garden which he regarded as an institution bearing comparison with the Bodleian Library for 'great and constant use and Ornament' among members of the university and visitors alike. He pointed out that this was the 'only Publick-Garden of Europe, that hitherto maintain'd itself'. The university was reminded that the stipend of £40 a year paid to his father had long since lapsed. Subsequently the garden had been supported by the profits on the sale of its produce. The development of rival market-gardens had removed this source of income. It was now impossible to maintain any garden, especially one so well stocked with exotic plants, without more adequate and stable financial backing.[3] Bobart even considered leaving Oxford, should a suitable alternative employment arise.[4] Despite his pessimism his garden was a success.

Bobart's garden was divided into four quarters by broad walks. Each quarter was surrounded by a tall yew hedge. Visitors usually commented on the topiary work, the most spectacular feature of which was the figures of giants, probably the work of the elder Bobart.[5] According to one contemporary observer the garden contained three thousand species of plants. The younger Bobart's catalogues include some two thousand.[6]

Some improvements were made during the time of the younger Bobart. Substantial construction work was undertaken; the main gateway was completed by the addition of statues of Charles I and Charles II and a bust of Danby, the latter being executed by John Vanderstein.[7] A large stone conservatory for exotic plants and trees had been built in time to be depicted prominently in Loggan's plan of the physic garden

[1] Cf A. Evans, *Vertumnus* (Oxford 1713), dedicated to Bobart as 'Botany Professor to the University of Oxford and Keeper of the Physick Garden'.

[2] It was calculated in 1813 that the income from Kirkdale 1650-1754 amounted to £4,115. During this period the university spent £5,276 on the physic garden. Bodl. MS Sherard 5, fo 116ᵛ.

[3] OUA WPß/60/3, undated petition from Bobart to the university (probably c1690).

[4] W. Sherard-R. Richardson, 6 June 1691, Bodl. MS Radcliffe Trust c. 1, fo 6, printed in *Extracts from the Literary and Scientific Correspondence of Richard Richardson*, ed. D. Turner (London 1835), 7-12. Richard Richardson (1663-1741), m. Univ. 1681; student at Gray's Inn 1681; DM.

[5] The topiary work figures prominently in the engraved frontispiece to Evans, *Vertumnus*.

[6] 'Thomas Baskerville's account of Oxford c. 1670-1700', ed. H. Baskerville, *Collectanea* iv.

[7] OUA vice-chancellor's accounts 1686-7, 1687-8, 1692-3, 1694-5, 1695-6, 1696-7.

dating from 1675.[1] The conservatory was heated in severe weather by a wheeled fire-basket containing glowing charcoal which was moved from place to place by the gardener. The expense of this operation was of concern to the younger Bobart, and the accounts show that fuel represented a continuing notable item in the budget. Perhaps in reaction to Bobart's complaints the university built to the north of the garden a new house for the keeper at one side of the main gate and planned to erect a library at the other side.

Towards the end of Bobart's career the garden seemed to be enjoying better favour. He commented in 1703 that the delegates were

all better minded for the good of the Garden, then I ever knew them before; I think now we shall have an house to live in, and a Repository for Books, and other such standing furniture as is rightly proper to the best Hortulane foundation in England, or perhaps Europe.

Just over a year later the house was completed, and found 'very convenient'. In 1710 Bobart still felt that the 'Academicall Curators respect our Botanick Garden more than formerly, apprehending it considerably to contribute to the Honour of the Universitie'. On behalf of the delegates Charlett expressed his continuing satisfaction with Bobart's work. He reported Bobart's intention of leaving an estate worth £50 a year to provide for the future stipend of the professor of botany.[2]

Two foreign visitors to the garden at this time recorded rather different impressions. Uffenbach stressed its wild and overgrown state, whereas Erndtel was favourably impressed by the collections of rare plants. Uffenbach was indignant that Bobart's hands and face were 'as black and coarse as those of the meanest gardener or labourer'; he would be taken more for a gardener than a professor, since 'he does nothing but continually work in the garden, and botanically speaking is a better gardener than herborist'.[3]

Bobart's career ended in disappointment. In 1717 his work was affected by illness. He vested the care of the garden in his younger brother Tilleman Bobart, who imprudently ran up debts of a hundred pounds in the course of the first year. Jacob had no recourse but to beg assistance from the vice-chancellor and delegates, who adopted an uncompromising position, refusing to countenance such a level of expenditure.[4] After a brief interval

[1] Vice-chancellor's accounts 1670-1; 'Baskerville's account of Oxford', 187; *Gardeners Chronicle* new ser. xxiii (1885), 732.
[2] Bobart-W. Sherard, 18 June, 2 Aug. 1703, 5 Oct. 1704, 28 Sept. 1710, London, Royal Society, MS Sherard correspondence, nos. 105, 106, 108, 110. Charlett-Sherard, 26 Apr. 1715, ibid. no. 567. Charlett-Sloane, 14 Mar. 1707, BL Sloane MS 4040, fo 325.
[3] *Oxford in 1710*, ed. Quarrell, 54-6; C. H. Erndtel, *The Relation of a Journey into England and Holland* (London 1711), 49.
[4] T. Bobart-W. Sherard, 23 Nov. 1718, Sherard corr. no. 112; Hearne, *Collections* vii. 29. Hearne believed that Bobart had 'quitted the Place' on account of age and infirmity.

Vice-Chancellor Shippen dismissed Jacob Bobart from his post, ignored the claims of Tilleman and appointed Edwin Sandys both as professor of botany and keeper of the garden.[1] Bobart's dismissal was seen as a callous act by his family and friends.[2] However, on his death Jacob Bobart, in an act of generosity undeserved by the university, bequeathed to Oxford his herbarium and his library of more than two hundred volumes.[3]

Sandys served as professor of botany until 1724, retaining his fellowship at Wadham until 1731. He vacated his botanical offices in favour of Gilbert Trowe, who in turn resigned in 1734, although continuing as a delegate of the garden for a further two decades in his capacity as deputy to the regius professor of medicine.[4] Neither Sandys nor Trowe is known as a botanist or gardener, although the latter entered a minor bill for expenses in connection with his term of office.[5] It is likely that during the Sandys-Trowe phase Tilleman served as their deputy as keeper of the garden, hence continuing in a subsidiary capacity the arrangement envisaged by Jacob Bobart.[6] At the time of his death Tilleman Bobart was described as 'Gardiner or Keeper of Public Garden'.

Events following the dismissal of Jacob Bobart suggest the onset of a decline in the garden. Nevertheless, complacency or neglect were precluded owing to skilful pressure applied by William Sherard in connection with his plan to leave his library and herbarium to the university and to establish a chair of botany on a sound financial footing. Sherard aimed to obtain a permanent home for his collections, to provide his protégé Dillenius[7] with an academic position from which he could complete Sherard's projected massive *Pinax botannicum*, and impose on the university responsibility for the better management of the garden. The university fell in with this arrangement, no doubt encouraged by the hope of substantial endowments from Sherard or his wealthy apothecary brother James.[8] During negotiations the university undertook immediately to

[1] Edwin Sandys, m. Wadham 1704, BA 1708, MA 1710, fellow 1713-31, BM 1716, DM 1718; prof. of botany 1720-4.

[2] W. Sherard-R. Richardson, 8 July 1719, Bodl. MS Radcliffe Trust c. 3, fo 85.

[3] Will dated 29 Apr. 1719: OUA chancellor's court wills.

[4] Trowe signed the Garden accounts from 1741 to 1756: Bodl. MS Sherard 2, fos 7-21. Richard Bradley (d. 1732; prof. of botany at Cambridge 1728) sought Sloane's support for securing the succession to the physic garden after Sandys's resignation: letter to Sloane, 17 Oct. 1723, BL Sloane MS 4047, fo 73.   [5] OUA WPß/21/6, vice-chancellor's accounts 1697-1735.

[6] Bills and payment of stipend were recorded in T. Bobart's name in 1732-3 and 1735: ibid. 1732-3; Bodl. MS Sherard 2, fo 3ʳ, physic garden accounts; MS Sherard 1, fos 4-5,meeting of the garden committee 1735. Dillenius mentioned in 1734 that the garden was being maintained by Bobart and an interim gardener: letter to Richardson, 28 Sept. 1734, Bodl. MS Radcliffe Trust c. 9, fos 21-3.

[7] Johann Jacob Dillenius (1687-1747), St John's College; privileged person and hon. DM 1735; Sherardian prof. of botany 1734-47.

[8] James Sherard (1666-1738), hon. DM 1731.

improve the conservatory building[1] and it promised for the future a much greater financial obligation to the garden than ever before had been countenanced. In 1718 the vice-chancellor had declared that the university would rather have no garden than pay £100 a year for its upkeep.[2] After the death of William Sherard in 1728 the university was driven by his executors, headed by James Sherard under the terms of a chancery settlement agreed in 1734, to pay £200 for the renovation of the garden, to find whatever funds were needed in future for its modernization, to pay £150 a year for the wages of a gardener and the upkeep of the garden and finally to establish a new delegacy comprising the vice-chancellor, the two proctors, the regius professor of medicine and seven senior residents on the physic line for its management. In return a legacy of £3,000 was settled on the university to provide for the stipend of the professor, who was required to be an MA, not in holy orders, and at least registered on the physic line. The first Sherardian professor would be Sherard's nominee; thereafter he would be selected not by convocation but by the Royal College of Physicians, the body which would also act as Visitor. The above arrangements firmly established the medical interest in the management of the garden.[3] No further legacy from the Sherard family was forthcoming.

In an unprecedented wave of modernization no less than £2,698 was recorded as having been spent on the garden during the first four years of operation of the new delegates. This expenditure was mainly devoted to the building of two architectural conservatories, with attached wooden greenhouses, to the east and west of the main gateway. These buildings were completed by William Townesend between 1733 and 1735. They were a main feature of the engraving of the garden included in the 1766 Oxford almanac.[4] They were highly controversial since they involved breaking the line of Danby's famous wall, and also the demolition of the house built for Bobart without any effective substitute being provided.

[1] This work, completed in 1727, cost £600, almost all of which was donated by Sherard: W. Sherard-Richardson, 14 Mar. 1727, Bodl. MS Radcliffe Trust c. 6, fos 54-5, printed in *Correspondence of Richardson*, ed. Turner, pp. 268-71.

[2] T. Bobart-W. Sherard, 23 Nov. 1718, Sherard corr. no. 112.

[3] The terms were outlined in very different terms in letters from James Sherard and Dillenius to Richardson of 13 and 20 August 1728: Bodl. MS Radcliffe Trust c.7, fos 13-14, 62-3. For the decree in chancery between the university and William Sherard's executors of 11 June 1734 see OUA SEP/2/7 and Bodl. MS Sherard 2, fos 70-91. In their correspondence Dillenius blamed James Sherard, whereas James blamed the university for the delays which occurred between 1728 and 1734. For the orders of the new garden committee see OUA SEP/4/1 and SEP/4/2.

[4] Bodl. MS Sherard 2, fo 3ᵛ. Bills were paid to Townesend for £780 in 1734-5 and 1735-6: ibid. fos 2-4. James Sherard complained that the conservatories had been spread too far apart in the interests of preserving the view of the portal building. This he regarded as an unmerited departure from the plan agreed with the university: letter to Richardson, 4 Nov. 1734, Bodl. MS Radcliffe Trust c.9, fo 323; Clokie, *Herbarium*, 58-81.

Sherard's library of six hundred volumes and his herbarium were installed, under the supervision of Dillenius, in the restored and enlarged conservatory building. Temporary quarters for Dillenius were provided at one end of this building. He and his successors used the Sherardian herbarium as the nucleus for the main herbarium of the university.

Dillenius had come to the attention of William Sherard through the expertise on cryptogams exhibited in his *Catalogus plantarum*.[1] He was brought to England to work on Sherard's *Pinax*, a project which was never completed either in London or at Oxford, the sixteen volumes of the manuscript remaining in the Sherard manuscripts.

After William Sherard's death work on the *Pinax* was interrupted by competing commitments, such as the compilation for James Sherard of the *Hortus elthamensis* (London 1732) or Dillenius's own pioneer work on cryptogams. Dillenius shared Jacob Bobart's interest in mosses. His *Historia muscorum* (Oxford 1741) was regarded by contemporaries as a work unsurpassed in any field of botany.[2] Dillenius found his association with Oxford almost as frustrating as had Bobart forty years earlier.[3] Dillenius expected to take up his appointment during William Sherard's lifetime. Eventually he was kept waiting for at least seven years after the latter's death, during wrangling between the executors and the university in chancery.

Before 1734 Dillenius visited Oxford periodically to arrange for planting and to supervise building operations.[4] Having settled in Oxford, probably in the spring of 1735, as the first Sherardian professor of botany he found that the unwise investment of Sherard's legacy had both reduced the value of the stipend and placed it in arrears. He also complained that 'the garden and other avocations takes away all my time in spring, summer and autumn'.[5]

Dillenius also contended with the problems of worsening relations with James Sherard, who expected to be able to dictate policy to his brother's erstwhile servant. At least through James, Dillenius had the services of James Smith, a gardener expert on exotics. Perhaps the most notable single event during his tenure of the chair of botany was the visit

[1] J. Dillenius, *Catalogus plantarum circa Gissam sponte nascentium* (Frankfurt 1718, 1719); G. C. Druce and S. H. Vines, *The Dillenian Herbarium* (Oxford 1907); L. Spilger, 'Dillenius als Erforscher hessischen Pflanzenwelt', *Bericht der Oberhessischen Gesellschaft für Natur und Heilkunde zu Geissen* xv (1932); Clokie, 30-6; Pulteney, *Historical Sketches* ii. 153-84; Desmond, *British and Irish Botanists*, 186; D. E. Allen, 'John Martin's botanical society', *Proc. Bot. Soc. Brit. Isles* vi (1967) (Dillenius was the inactive president of this society).

[2] J. E. Smith, 'Introductory discourse' (1788), *Trans. Linnean Soc.* i (1791), 34.

[3] For Dillenius's first complaint at delay see his letter to William Brewer of 16 December 1727: Druce and Vines, *Dillenian Herbarium*, pp. lxiv-lxv. In 1731, somewhat prematurely, he expressed joy at having reached an agreement with Oxford: ibid. p. lxxiv.

[4] Dillenius-Richardson, 27 Apr. 1727 and nd, Bodl. MS Radcliffe Trust c.6, fos 60-1, c.9, fos 15-16.

[5] Dillenius-Richardson, 8 Sept. 1737, Bodl. MS Radcliffe Trust c.9, fos 116-17, printed in *Correspondence of Richardson*, ed. Turner, pp. 362-4.

to Oxford in 1736 of Linnaeus. The great botanist spoke highly of Dillenius's work. Another contemporary commentator found that the physic garden had become an important centre for advice 'where all curious persons have an easy access, through the great affability and communicative temper' of Dillenius.[1]

After the brief period of extravagant spending between 1734 and 1738 the university quickly settled down to not exceeding the pledged expenditure. Nevertheless, the annual costs tended to rise above £150 until after 1754. Thereafter the university hardly ever paid out the full sum. But even after 1754 annual expenditure rarely fell drastically short of £150. This was sufficient to maintain the garden, but it precluded any major improvement or attention to basic renovation.

This period of economy coincided with the tenure of Humphrey Sibthorp, who succeeded his teacher Dillenius in 1747. His poor reputation rests largely on the adverse biography written by James Edward Smith, by whom he was apostrophized as an idle nonentity who neglected his lectures and published nothing. According to Smith, botany 'slept' for forty years at Oxford during Sibthorp's term of office.[2] Permanent bad publicity for him was generated when Joseph Banks was given leave by the professor to bring in a private lecturer in botany to satisfy the demand for teaching in this subject. Banks recruited Israel Lyons from Cambridge, who gave a lecture-course in Oxford in 1774.[3] Although Sibthorp was no match for his predecessor in distinction as a botanist, he shows evidence of some minor initiatives, adding a new set of plants from the garden to the herbarium, annotating the existing herbarium and beginning a new catalogue of the garden.[4]

The accounts indicate nothing more than unexceptional low-level expenditure, particularly after 1757. Accountancy was done in a routine and stereotyped manner and the delegates lost interest. Between 1766 and 1775 the accounts were largely unsigned, whereas hitherto they had been signed by a substantial group of the garden committee. The latter was revitalized by events connected with the improvement act of 1771 for the widening of Magdalen Bridge. Sibthorp mounted a vigorous campaign to prevent the demolition of the library building and other out-

[1] T. Shaw, *Travels or Observations... of Barbary and the Levant* (Oxford 1738), pp. xii-xiii; Druce and Vines, *Dillenian Herbarium*, pp. xxiv-xxv. According to Richardson, Dillenius was irascible and likely to fall out with anyone: *Correspondence of Richardson* ed. Turner, pp. 286, 313. See also W. Blunt, *The Compleat Naturalist: a life of Linnaeus* (London 1971), 114-15.

[2] J. E. Smith, 'Sibthorpia' in A. Rees *et al*, *The Cyclopaedia* (39 vols London 1819, 6 vols of plates London 1820) xxxii; *Memoir and Correspondence of the late Sir James Edward Smith, M.D.* ed. P. Smith (2 vols London 1832) ii. 475-6; Desmond, *British and Irish Botanists*, 558.

[3] *The Endeavour Journal of Joseph Banks 1768-1771*, ed. J. C. Beaglehole (2 vols Sydney 1962) i. 8. Sir Joseph Banks (1743-1820), 1st bt; m. Ch.Ch. 1760; hon. DCL 1771; president of the Royal Society 1779.

[4] Clokie, *Herbarium*, 36-7; Bodl. MS Sherard 213.

buildings lying in the path of the new roadway. He fought against the erosion of the site from road and river. It was feared that, as in the case of the professor's house, the library building might never be replaced by a building of equal quality.[1]

Adverse publicity raised by Sibthorp may have created the impression that the university had indulged in an act of bad faith with respect to the garden. The Royal College of Physicians was alerted to protect it, and the university duly promised to restore the library, greenhouse and garden. It was also promised that the mounting surplus in the garden fund would be used to rebuild the library.[2] Sibthorp also hopefully, but unsuccessfully, petitioned for a new house.[3] In the event, having contracted a second marriage to a wealthy wife, he retired to Devon in 1783, seven years before the demolition of the buildings in the physic garden.

Sibthorp's first gardener, James Smith, had served under Dillenius. Upon his death the wages for the gardener were reduced from £50 to £40 yearly, an economy which led to antagonism and evasion on the part of the gardeners. There followed a period of instability when four gardeners served in a period of five years. One of these, Georg Dionysius Ehret, had achieved distinction as a botanical artist.[4] Stabilization returned with the appointment of John Foreman and then the succession of his son John. The wages of the gardener were restored to their former level in 1788.[5]

Intellectual distinction returned to the garden with the appointment of John Sibthorp to succeed his father.[6] He was as cosmopolitan and erudite as William Sherard, whose interest in the flora of the middle east he shared. He had studied medicine at Edinburgh and visited various continental medical schools. For much of his tenure as professor of botany he was travelling abroad in connection with the compilation of his *Flora graeca*. During Sibthorp's absence between 1784 and 1787 George Shaw served as his deputy.[7] John Sibthorp was successful in both

[1] There is a copy of an undated twenty-five-page printed tract, without title, in defence of the physic garden in Bodl. MS Sherard 5, fos 1-13. A broadsheet in reply (ibid. fo 21) suggests that Sibthorp's tract was dated 12 March 1777.

[2] Letter from the university to the Royal College of Physicians, 8 May 1776, Bodl. MS Sherard 2, fos 40^v-1^r.

[3] Bodl. MS Sherard 5, fo 15, proposals for building a house for the professor of botany, May 1776.

[4] W. Blunt, *The Art of Botanical Illustration* (London 1950), 143-50. Ehret was presumably employed as a draughtsman.

[5] John Foreman (1756-79) and his son (1773-1812). John Foreman junior was a gardener to Wadham and was granted privileged status 18 May 1788. Information about the gardeners is derived from the accounts in Bodl. MS Sherard 2.

[6] See J. E. Smith's preface to J. Sibthorp, *Flora graeca* (2 vols London 1806, 1813); Clokie, *Herbarium*, 38-42; Desmond, *British and Irish Botanists*, 558. For his course of thirty lectures on botany see Bodl. MS Sherard 219.

[7] Like Sibthorp Shaw had studied medicine at Edinburgh before taking his BM and DM at Oxford (from Magdalen Hall in 1787). He was disqualified from candidature for the chair of botany

research and lecturing at Oxford from 1787 to 1794. He completed a
Flora oxoniensis (Oxford 1794), added a large number of specimens to the
Sherardian herbarium and completed his father's catalogue of the
garden.[1] In 1788, along with Shaw and others, Sibthorp became a founder of the Linnean Society. He not only lectured according to the advanced taxonomic principles of Linnaeus, but he was also keenly concerned with applied aspects of botany, an interest which led ultimately to his foundation of the Sibthorpian chair of rural economy.

John Sibthorp, like his father, was unable to solve the financial problems of the physic garden. He and his committee needed to seek support
from the Royal College of Physicians to secure adequate funds for the
rebuilding of the library after its demolition for road widening in 1790.
Also like his father, he appealed unsuccessfully for a new house.[2] On the
other hand, he was successful in securing £100 a year from the crown to
supplement his stipend. Furthermore, when Beddoes ran into political
difficulties Sibthorp successfully petitioned to annex the £100 a year
from the crown intended for the chemistry reader. He also then effectively resisted moves by the university to require him to assign half of his
augmented crown income to the running and maintenance of the greenhouses.[3]

John Sibthorp contracted tuberculosis and died before the completion
of his *Flora graeca*. Under the terms of his will arrangements were made
for the completion of the Greek flora, which was entrusted to James
Edward Smith. The residue of his estate was mainly set aside for the
establishment of

a Professor of Rural Economy who shall be the Sherardian Professor of Botany,
conditionally viz. that he ... shall read each Term a publick Lecture on Rural
Economy and shall appropriate some part of his Garden to the Cultivation of
such Plants as are used more particularly in agriculture and the Arts.[4]

John Sibthorp was succeeded by George Williams who, following the
terms of Sibthorp's will, duly became the first Sibthorpian professor of
rural economy. This choice was not altogether surprising. He had been
an active member of the garden committee at least since 1788 and was
known to be a keen botanist. He was probably a more successful lecturer
than any of his predecessors.[5] Like other leading Oxford physicians he

by virtue of being in holy orders. He had also deputized for the elder Sibthorp. His courses of lectures were advertised in 1778, 1781, 1782 and 1784 in *Jackson's Oxford Journal*.

[1] See Bodl. MS Sherard 229.
[2] Bodl. MS Sherard 5, fos 27-37, papers relating to the library and professor's house 1789-1792.
[3] For details of this manœuvre see Balliol College library, Jenkyns papers, VI. A (2), letterbook of
John Wills.
[4] Bodl. MS Sherard 2, fo 69 and MS Sherard 5, fos 124-5, copy of the will of John Sibthorp, 12 Jan.
1796.
[5] See *Gentleman's Magazine* new ser. i (1834), 334-6; Munk, *Roll of the RCP* ii. 467-9; Desmond,

held various other posts, having been physician to the Radcliffe Infirmary since 1789. In 1810 he became the first medically qualified keeper of the Radcliffe Library, whereupon he pursued an active policy of modernization and of developing this library as a major specialist collection in the fields of medicine and natural history.[1] He was primarily an administrator, and in this capacity he was as successful for the longer-term rehabilitation of the garden as he was at the library. He appreciated that all attempts by the garden committee to secure an adequate income for it were handicapped by lack of precise knowledge about the rights and duties of the professor under the terms of the various endowments. He undertook the onerous task of exhaustively surveying the official documents relating to the garden since its foundation, with a view to establishing the precise record of the university with respect to its financial commitments, and so sorting out anomalies and ambiguities relating to the terms of appointment and duties of the professor. As a result of this meticulous investigation he demonstrated that the university's claim to have honoured its obligation by allowing £150 per annum to the garden took no account of the substantial and increasing income available from the Kirkdale estates bequeathed by Danby. Williams proved that that income alone would have been nearly sufficient to have covered the revenue of the garden over the previous one hundred and fifty years.[2] Thus Williams, although undistinguished as a botanist, was more important than his predecessors in preparing the ground for the major investigations into the finances of university institutions which were shortly to be undertaken by the royal commissions, which shared his aim of securing once and for all a stable basis for the support of the medical and scientific foundations of the university.

British and Irish Botanists, 662; E. Tatham, *A New Address to the Free and Independent Members of Convocation* (Oxford 1810), 16-18.

[1] *Bibliotheca radcliviana*, 18-19.
[2] Bodl. MS Sherard 5, fo 87, case of the botanic garden, etc.

26

Libraries and the University Press

I. G. PHILIP

On 19 March 1701 Thomas Hyde, Bodley's Librarian, wrote to the pro-vice-chancellor giving his reasons for his intended resignation. He was 'weary of the toil and drudgery of daily attendance all times and weathers', he was anxious to publish some of his own works on 'hard places of Scripture', but above all he felt frustrated by the lack of money for the library and by the too rigid control exercised by the curators.

I should have left the Library more compleat and better furnish'd but that the building of the Elaboratory did so exhaust the University mony, that no books were bought in severall years after it. And at other times when Books were sometimes bought, it was (as you well know) never left to me to buy them, the Vice Chancellor not allowing me to lay out any University mony. And therefore some have blamed me without cause for not getting all sorts of Books.[1]

Hyde went on to explain that before the annual visitation of the library it had been his custom to prepare lists of books which the curators should buy.

but I could seldom get them bought, being commongly [sic] answered in Short, that they had no mony. Nay, I have been chid and reproved by the Vice-Chancellor for offering to put them to so much charge in buying Books. These things at last discouraged me from medling in it.

Hyde was indeed tired of the office which he had held for thirty-five years. Gout had made the long ascent of the library's staircase painful to him; he had been overburdened by the labour of preparing the library's catalogue of printed books published in 1674; his work on the religion of the Persians had given him a deservedly wide reputation and by contrast the petty frustrations of office had become insupportable. His complaint about finance was justified. The library, which had been so well endowed by its founder[2] and made independent of university funds, had suffered

---

[1] Copy in Wake MS 16, fo 50, printed in W. D. Macray, *Annals of the Bodleian Library* (London etc 1868, 2nd edn, enlarged, Oxford 1890), 170-1. The 'elaboratory' was the (Old) Ashmolean Museum, built 1679-83; see A. MacGregor, 'The Ashmolean Museum'.
[2] Sir Thomas Bodley (1545-1613), joined Magd. Hall 1559; fellow Merton 1563, MA 1566.

financially in the civil war and had never really recovered. Rents, unpaid during the war, had not been fully collected thereafter, and in addition £500 of the library's capital had been lent to King Charles I in 1642. This sum was never repaid and was carried in the library's accounts as a bad debt up to 1782, together with the sum of £450 which the library had lost by the defalcation of John Bennet, one of Thomas Bodley's friends and executors.[1] The reduction of the library's endowments by £950 was a serious matter, and by the end of the seventeenth century the annual library account was often in deficit. In the 1690s the money available for book-purchase amounted on average to about £10 a year. Occasionally large sums were spent on the purchase of outstandingly important collections like the Pococke and Huntington collections of oriental manuscripts bought in 1692-3, and the library of Edward Bernard bought in 1697;[2] but these major purchases were financed in whole or in large part from university resources and were not supplemented by a reasonable level of book-purchase from library funds. In 1692, when £800 of university money was spent on Pococke's manuscripts, the library bought only one book from its own funds, a copy of Furetière's *Dictionnaire universel*, and in the following year, when the final instalment was paid of the £1,118 spent on Huntington's manuscripts, the library bought only one more book, the three-volume set of Zeiller's *Topographia Galliae*.[3] It appears, then, that any attempt to keep the library up to date by the purchase of current scholarly publications from library funds had been virtually abandoned.[4]

To some extent this state of affairs may have been influenced, as Hyde believed, by the foundation of the Ashmolean Museum. Just over £300 had been borrowed from the Bodleian chest in 1678 and this loan, though repaid in full by 1699, would certainly have depressed normal library expenditure in the 1680s and 1690s. And the clash of interest was not merely financial. In 1683 when the new building was nearing completion the Vice-Chancellor praised the new foundation in significant terms: 'Our University having design'd a new Library which may containe the most conspicuous parts of the great Book of Nature, and rival the Bodleian Collection of Mss and printed volumes, in whose neigh-

[1] Sir John Bennet (d. 1627), Student Ch.Ch. 1573; MP Oxford Univ. 1614, 1621; impeached 1621.

[2] Robert Huntington (1637-1701), m. Merton 1654; chaplain to the Levant Company at Aleppo 1671-81 (when he visited Palestine, Cyprus and Egypt acquiring valuable oriental manuscripts); provost of Trinity College, Dublin, 1683-92; bp of Raphoe July-Sept. 1701. Edward Bernard (1638-96), m. St John's 1655; Savilian prof. of astronomy 1673-91.

[3] A. Furetière, *Dictionnaire universel* (3 vols The Hague and Rotterdam 1690); M. Zeiller, *Topographia Galliae* (3 vols Frankfurt 1655-61).

[4] But there were other occasional channels of acquisition not noted in library records. The University Press accounts show that 55 volumes from the Press's warehouse were sent to the Amsterdam bookseller J. H. Wetstein in 1691-2 'in exchange for Bookes which he sent to the publique Library': H. G. Carter, *A History of the Oxford University Press* i (Oxford 1975), 181.

bourhood it is plac'd'.[1] The great book of nature was not over-well represented in the Bodleian Library, but Ashmole's historical collections,
which overlapped the Bodleian collection, the respect which his benefaction inspired and his personal contacts with fellow antiquarians
ensured that, for a time, this new library ranked as a more appropriate
repository for benefactions. The manuscript collections of Dugdale,
Wood and Aubrey made the Ashmolean Museum a rival centre for
English antiquarian studies in the early eighteenth century, particularly
for those nonjurors like Hearne who identified the Bodleian Library with
that political establishment from which they excluded themselves with
pertinacity and passion.

The Bodleian authorities, meanwhile, had to struggle with a growing
diversity of problems. The press licensing acts under which the Bodleian
Library had received free copies of books registered at the Stationers'
Company had lapsed in 1695, and between that date and the implementation of the copyright act of 1709 there was no automatic deposit of
English publications even in theory. For its acquisitions the library had
to rely on donations, but these, though frequent and generous, were by
their very nature haphazard and unpredictable, and some brought their
own special problems. The legacy of Thomas Barlow, bishop of Lincoln
and formerly Bodley's Librarian, whose library was to be shared between
the Bodleian Library and Queen's College, took effect in 1693-4. Of the
Bodleian share the larger books were shelved in the old presses in Duke
Humfrey's Library, but the great number of books in the smaller sizes
were shelved in a newly built gallery over the stalls on the south side of
the library. Within a few years the weight of books in this gallery caused
serious structural weakness in the south wall of the library and in the
vault of the Divinity School below for which Christopher Wren was
called upon to devise remedies, and the rearrangement of many books to
make way for those of Barlow's gift caused great confusion. By 1697 the
failure to keep library records up to date, evidence of a general slackness
of administration, prompted the Bodleian curators to ask the staff for
suggestions for reform, and Humfrey Wanley, who had become a special
assistant late in 1695, seized the opportunity to submit a searching
criticism of the whole management of the library. Not all his suggestions
were acceptable, but any energy infused into the library's affairs in the
last years of the seventeenth century was in large measure due to Wanley. His hard work and perseverance made possible the library's acquisition of Bernard's library and many of the series of gifts from Hans Sloane.
But for Wanley this was only the beginning. He urged that the university
should try to get John Cotton's library and the earl of Clarendon's

_____

[1] J. Lloyd-M. Lister, 10 Apr. 1683, Bodl. MS Lister 35, fo 94. John Lloyd (1638-87), m. Merton
1657; fellow Jesus 1662, principal 1673-87; vice-chancellor 1682-5; bp of St David's 1686-7.

manuscripts for the Bodleian, and with the encouragement of Arthur
Charlett he directly approached a wide range of possible benefactors
ranging from the mayor of Coventry, his native place, to Samuel Pepys,
whose judgement he greatly respected. Wanley asked John Bagford in
1696 to send him word

of any noble spirited and Worthy Gentlemen, who are Masters of any Curiosi-
ties which we want, and are or may be willing to part with them to our Library.
The things we want are these, Books, either MSS or Printed. Medells and
Coins, Antient or Modern. Pictures and Prints or Maps &c.[1]

Such seemed the needs of the library when there were neither funds to
buy books nor any machinery for the automatic deposit of free copies.

Despite his outstanding scholarly expertise, Wanley could not succeed
to Hyde's office in 1701 for he lacked formal academic qualifications, but
fortunately for the university John Hudson, the successful candidate, was
also a man of considerable energy and useful contacts. As a fellow and
tutor of University College he had done much to secure the election to
the college mastership in 1692 of Arthur Charlett who in the early eighteenth century was the most influential and busiest promoter of all
bookish projects in the university. Hudson himself might have been
elected regius professor of Greek in 1698 had his tory sympathies been
less apparent, but though he failed to get other academic or ecclesiastical preferment he was elected to succeed Hyde at the Bodleian Library
in April 1701. Hudson was in every sense a considerable bookman. When
elected he had already edited and published five works and from then on
the University Press always had some work of his editing on hand.[2]
Hearne also noted in 1706 that Hudson 'assisted in most of the things
which have of late years come from the Theatre Press'.[3] It has been said
that Hudson 'paid too much attention to the pecuniary potentialities of
scholarship' and that his librarianship appears to have been remarkable
for its 'inadequacy';[4] but undoubtedly his was the kind of energy which
was then required. Between 1705 and 1710 he gave nearly six hundred
books from his own collection to the library and took all possible steps to
persuade others to follow his example.

By November 1704 Charlett bore witness that: 'Our Public Library,
which for some years had stood still, is now in a thriving condition by the
active diligence and curiosity of Dr Hudson, who spares no author, no
bookseller, but solicits all to augment that vast treasure.'[5] On 17 January

[1] Quoted by P. L. Heyworth, 'Humfrey Wanley and "Friends" of the Bodleian, 1695-98', *Bodleian Lib. Record* ix (1973-8), 219-30.
[2] Carter, *History of the Press* i. 151.
[3] Hearne, *Collections* i. 240.
[4] *The First Minute Book of the Delegates of the Oxford University Press, 1668-1756*, ed. S. Gibson and J. Johnson (Oxford Bibliog. Soc. extra publ. 1943), 75.   [5] Macray, *Annals*, 173-4.

1705 Hudson, commending the example of John Locke, who had presented some of his own works to the library, sent Charlett a list of names of authors and publishers who 'have been very much oblig'd to the publick Library: but yet none of them have yet learn'd so much gratitude as to make any manner of return'.[1] Entries in the library's register show that in the years 1701 to 1709 four London booksellers with close Oxford connections occasionally sent publications as gifts to the library.[2] These were presumably in response to requests from the librarian, but for some time most donations continued to be personal gifts of very varying size and value. Donations of this kind remained the constant element in the library's growth and at no time did the flow dry up completely. Hearne noted in November 1706 'Not any Accession made to the Register for the whole last year, but this was, for once, an error, for even in that barren year (1706) six books were received by gift.[3] By contrast, at intervals from 1700 to 1738, Hans Sloane sent hundreds of duplicate books from his own collection, and gifts of this order still gave the general impression of expansion and activity despite an apparently crippling financial situation. 'I Heare the Bodleian Library fills apace and Dr Sloane tells me there will be no room for benefactions if you goe on as you've begun', a correspondent wrote to Hudson on 5 August 1706, and went on to add the advice 'Methinks Dr soe wise a man as you are should not take soe much pains for soe little profit, but rather like some of your neighbours come to London, turn whig and get preferment'.[4] Hudson had to wait another two years for minor preferment, his succession to the principalship of the almost empty St Mary Hall. Meanwhile he had to contend with the financial problem.

For the years 1700-3 there is no record in the library accounts of any expenditure on books. In 1703-4 £7 5s was spent on the purchase of an eight-volume set of Raynaldus[5] and thereafter for the next few years the expenditure on books was about £9 a year. In the second decade of the century the average expenditure on books was just under £40 a year, an increase made possible partly by increased fines raised on library estates in London and Cookham and more directly by a legacy of £100 from Robert South,. canon of Christ Church, for the purchase of modern books, and a gift of £100 from Lord Crewe, both of which became available in 1716-17.[6] The library's accounts for 1714-15 include payment of

[1] Hudson-Charlett, 17 Jan. 1705, MS Ballard 17, fo 91.

[2] Bodl. register B, pp. 42 ff.

[3] Hearne, *Collections* i. 303. Cf Bodl. register B, p. 49; the donations included dean Aldrich's gift of a copy of [Roger] de Piles, *Art of Painting* (London 1706).

[4] Bodl. MS Rawl. D. 316, fo 39. The correspondent was Sir Andrew Fountaine (1676-1753), m. Ch.Ch. 1693.

[5] The *Annales ecclesiastici* (Rome 1646-63). The lack of this important work for forty years illustrates all too well the results of financial poverty in the late seventeenth century.

[6] For South's legacy see Macray, *Annals*, 196.

£32 14*s* 8*d* to George Clarke 'for books bought in France for the
Library'; and in the following year £70 was paid to the librarian 'for
books bought in Paris'.[1] Again in 1717-18 the sum of £47 5*s* spent on
books included payment to the librarian of £27 for Jean Hardouin, *Con-
ciliorum collectio regia maxima*, published in eleven volumes in Paris in
1715, and Anselmo Bandarius, *Numismata imperatorum romanorum* (Paris
1718). These purchases from Paris indicate a concerted effort to make up
for the deficiencies of the war-years, but the evidence of surviving
correspondence seems to show that all negotiations and financial transactions with foreign booksellers and English agents were conducted not
by the librarian, nor by the curators, but by George Clarke, by his friend
John Savage of Christ Church who bargained for books in Paris and by
Arthur Charlett to whom these negotiations were reported by letter.[2]
For a few years thereafter annual expenditure on books remained relatively high, with a strong emphasis on expensive foreign publications
and a noticeable interest in architecture, probably through the influence
of George Clarke. In the years 1720-2 the library bought the five-volume
Dictionnaire de Trévoux (Paris 1720); Louis Feuillée, *Journal des observations
physiques, mathématiques et botaniques* (Paris 1714); M. de Cordemoy, *Nou-
veau traité de toute l'architecture* (Paris 1714); Sebastian le Clerc, *Traité
d'architecture* (Paris 1719), *Britannia illustrata* (three volumes, London
1709-16); two volumes of Colin Campbell's *Vitruvius britannicus* (three
volumes, London 1715-25), and Giacomo Leoni's edition of Palladio. In
another field J. J. Manget's *Bibliotheca pharmaceutica-medica* (two volumes,
Geneva 1703) and his *Bibliotheca chemica curiosa* (two volumes, Geneva
1702) were bought in 1722 together with Eleazar Albin, *Natural History of
English Insects*, published in London in 1720.[3] By the 1730s expenditure
on books was falling to about £7 a year, and there was no significant
change until in 1750 the library began to receive an annual sum of £10
by bequest from Lord Crewe which was specifically set aside for books.
For the next thirty years this small sum constituted, if not all, certainly
the major part of the annual expenditure on books.

These generalizations on the level of Bodleian book-purchasing are
based on the evidence of the library account books and surviving bills,
but casual references from other sources suggest that other funds were
occasionally available which do not appear in the accounts. There are
several lists of duplicates made in the early eighteenth century, some of
them priced and accompanied by notes of purchasers, but the proceeds
of such sales do not appear in the library accounts, though one would

[1] Bodl. library account book 1676-1813, fos 46ᵛ, 47ᵛ.
[2] MS Ballard 20, fos 83, 102, 106, 120. John Savage (1673-1747), incorporated from Cambridge
1705; BD and DD Ch.Ch. 1707; incorporated at Cambridge 1730.
[3] Bodl. register C.

expect income from this source to be declared and used for further book purchases.[1] Uffenbach, who visited the library in 1710, described a study in the gallery with about four hundred books lying about 'in terrible confusion', which visitors were allowed to pick over and purchase; and Nathaniel Crynes, whose very valuable collection of books came by bequest to the Bodleian Library in 1745, had been allowed to buy duplicates from the library in 1727.[2] Sales of duplicates seem to have been general library policy; such sales were noted in 1790, 1793 and 1794, but only in 1790 is there any surviving reference to receipts in the main account book, where £120 is noted as being received from such a sale. The situation in this respect was no doubt very complicated early in the century when Hudson not only set aside library duplicates for sale, but also kept stocks of his own numerous publications in the library for sale to customers, and possibly also housed there the stock of the University Press's warehouse which, with two friends, he bought in 1713.[3] Those who referred to Bodley's Librarian as 'the bookseller' were not wildly exaggerating.

From 1662 to 1695 the series of press licensing acts designed to prevent the distribution of seditious literature had included provision for the compulsory deposit of all English publications at Stationers' Hall to be forwarded to the royal library and the libraries of Oxford and Cambridge Universities. This provision for deposit was incorporated in the copyright act of 1709, but the main purpose of this new legislation was the protection of publisher copyright, and owing to the vague phrasing of the act it seemed that a publisher not seeking the protection of the act need not register his books with the Stationers' Company. Only books so registered had to be deposited. This was the position throughout the eighteenth century and although the Bodleian Library appointed two London booksellers in 1726 to collect all published works (registered or not) there is no evidence that such a wider scheme operated.[4] In effect only about 10 per cent of all English publications in any one year were registered and deposited in the period 1710-26,[5] but even this seems to have produced a higher annual intake than was achieved in mid-century,

[1] The lists are in Bodl. MS Rawl. D. 732, fos 5-12.

[2] *Oxford in 1710 being the travels of Zacharias Conrad von Uffenbach*, ed. W. H. and W. T. C. Quarrell (Oxford 1928), 26. Macray, *Annals*, 220-1 (Crynes). Nathaniel Crynes (1686-1745), m. St John's 1704; esquire bedel of arts and physic.

[3] Carter, *History of the Press* i. 151.

[4] Macray, *Annals*, 205. For comment on this proposal by the clerk to the stationers see letters of T. Simpson to J. Bowles, 27 Oct. and 24 Nov. 1726, Bodl. library records, library file of copyright correspondence 1726-1912. An ineffectual attempt was made to introduce legislation incorporating more effective measures for registration and deposit in 1731: see R. C. B. Partridge, *History of the Legal Deposit of Books* (London 1938), 39.

[5] J. P. Chalmers, 'Bodleian deposit survivors of the first 16 years of the copyright act of Queen Anne' (Oxford B.Litt. thesis 1974).

and towards the end of the century the number of books actually registered declined still further. From the library's point of view the weakness of this very partial system of registration and deposit was not just a matter of quantity. The lack of quality was even more noticeable. Throughout this period books deposited included plays, poems and other small pieces which could be readily reprinted and for which the proprietors therefore claimed protection under the act. The number of larger books registered was comparatively small: their very bulk and expense protected them from the pirates, and smaller works on weightier topics for which there was no easy or wide market were frequently treated in the same way. This meant that many of the seminal books of the eighteenth century were not registered and not received by the library under the copyright act; Burke's *Inquiry into the Sublime and the Beautiful* (London 1757), Hume's *Treatise on Human Nature* (three volumes, London 1739-40), his *Philosophical Essays concerning Human Understanding* (London 1748), and *Principles of Morals* (London 1751), are instances of important works which were not deposited under copyright and of which there was no copy in the Bodleian Library until the library of Charles Godwyn of Balliol was received by bequest in 1770. It is not altogether surprising, therefore, that the curators had no very high opinion of the copyright deposit system as it affected the library. On 28 November 1788 they resolved that the books sent by the Stationers' Company should in future be examined by a committee of two Curators 'for the purpose of setting aside such as are useless to be dispos'd [of]', and they repeated their resolution in the same terms on 19 May 1790.[1] That this was all too effective is manifest from a memorandum made by John Price, the librarian, in 1794:

all the rejected Books &c. from the Parcels received from the Stationers' Co. which are [in] my study in the Gallery and the enclosed end of the Law School are my own, having paid ten guineas for them—and also promis'd Mr Cooke the Bookseller the refusal when I dispose of them.[2]

The mistaken belief that under the copyright act the Bodleian Library received a free copy of all English publications seems to have influenced one of the great university benefactors of the eighteenth century and diverted from the library funds which would have made the Bodleian collections of more significance in the life of the university much earlier in the century. During his lifetime it was known that John Radcliffe had a 'noble design for enlarging the Bodley library', but in his last years he changed his mind and by his will dated 13 September 1714 bequeathed

---

[1] Bodl. library records, curators' minute-book.
[2] Bodl. library records, day-book 1787-1856. John Price (1735-1813), m. Jesus 1754; Bodley's Librarian 1768-1813.

£40,000 for buying the houses between St Mary's church and the schools and building a new separate library on that site, together with provision for paying £150 per annum to the library's keeper and £100 per annum for buying books.[1] In 1715 Charlett, master of Radcliffe's own college and well informed of the benefactor's intentions, described this new library as being 'chiefly intended for the Purchase of Foreign Books, Dr Radcliff imagining, the Act of Parliament had already given us a Title to all printed in England'. This intention persisted for some years; in 1720 Charlett urged the trustees to increase the allowance for buying books from £100 to at least £200 a year, since the smaller sum 'will not be suffi- cient to buy all the foreign books as they come out'.[2] But by 1749, when Radcliffe's library building was completed, the general idea or expecta- tion of its purpose had changed, and indeed there were very confused ideas as to the outcome. According to John Pointer in his *Oxoniensis aca- demia*, published in that year: 'It is call'd the Physic Library, being to con- sist of all Sorts of Books belonging to the Science of Physic, as Anatomy, Botany, Surgery and Philosophy. In Time it may be the compleatest Physic Library in the World.'[3] Richard Rawlinson had another account and reported to a correspondent that 'Mr Carte's History will be [the] first book placed in it. I am told it is designed for the most modern books in all faculties and languages, not in the Bodleian Library.'[4] This again was mere wishful thinking; the first significant accession was the Bar- tholomew collection of fifty thousand pamphlets given in 1749.[5] Even Rawlinson, omnivorous collector as he was, hopefully supposed that 'the Trustees will not accept of such trash'.[6] Subsequently some important oriental books were acquired, but the collection remained hetero- geneous and without apparent purpose throughout the eighteenth cen- tury. The first Radcliffe Librarian, Francis Wise, had been sub-librarian of the Bodleian from 1719.[7] He largely exercised this office from the

---

[1] Atterbury-Trelawny, 30 Dec. 1712, *The Epistolary Correspondence, Visitation Charges, Speeches, and Miscellanies, of the Right Reverend Francis Atterbury, D.D., Lord Bishop of Rochester, with historical notes, and brief memoirs of the author*, ed. J. Nichols (4 vols London 1783-7, 2nd edn 2 vols London 1799, i–iv printed and dated 1789-90, v 1798), i. 457; *Building Accounts of the Radcliffe Camera*, p. vii; see also H. M. Colvin, 'Architecture', pp. 845-6 below. John Radcliffe (1652-1714), m. Univ. 1666; fellow Linc. 1677; physician to William III and Anne.

[2] Charlett-R. Richardson, 17 Jan. 1715, Bodl. MS Radcliffe Trust. c.3 (9); *Building Accounts of the Radcliffe Camera*, pp. ix, 99.   [3] J. Pointer, *Oxoniensis academia* (London 1749), 145.

[4] R. Rawlinson-T. Rawlinson [1 Apr. 1749], MS Ballard 2, fo 185. Thomas Carte (1686-1754), m. Univ. 1698; BA BNC 1702; incorporated at Cambridge 1706; nonjuror.

[5] This collection, now in the Bodleian Library, is especially important for its seventeenth-century material. It was not catalogued until 1794 and in the early years was probably just stored in the Rad- cliffe Library, for when Vertue visited the library in August 1750 he found 'all presses and shelves, but not one book yet in it'; *The Note-Books of George Vertue relating to Artists and Collections in England*, ed. K. A. Esdaile, G. S. H. F. Strangways and H. M. Hake (6 vols and index to vols i–v Walpole Soc. xviii, xx, xxii, xxiv, xxvi, xxix, xxx 1930-55) v. 81.   [6] Quoted by Macray, *Annals*, 276.

[7] Francis Wise (c1685-1767), m. Trin. 1711; keeper of the archives 1726-67; Radcliffe's Librarian 1748-67.

village of Elsfield, with its charming but distant view of the Radcliffe Camera. He dealt with the inconvenience of admitting readers by putting a padlock on the library's doors and was supported in his protest by the trustees until the vice-chancellor removed the lock.[1] Wise was succeeded by Benjamin Kennicott who was Radcliffe Librarian for sixteen years (1767-83) while he continued his unabating labours on the collation of biblical texts, and he in turn was succeeded by Thomas Hornsby, who was simultaneously Radcliffe Librarian, Radcliffe's Observer, Savilian professor of astronomy and Sedleian professor of natural philosophy. Hornsby remained librarian for twenty-seven years (1783-1810), during which period there is no evidence that any Radcliffe money was spent on books for the Radcliffe Library. The trustees had financed a magnificent building, but the collection which it contained in the eighteenth century was neither planned nor administered for any public good.

There is more evidence for the use of the Bodleian Library by readers in the eighteenth century. A series of day-books records orders for manuscripts and for those printed books which were not, like the chained folio books in Duke Humfrey's Library and Arts End, immediately available to readers. The series starts in November 1708 and in the early years the most notable feature is the influx of foreign scholars.[2] In the month of December 1708, for instance, 317 volumes were ordered by readers and 279 (88 per cent) of these were for seven foreign scholars: J. C. Wolf from Saxony, C. M. Pfaff from Tübingen, A. C. Zeller from Würtemburg, J. H. Lochner from Weimar, J. Ritter from Lübeck and one Frenchman, P. M. Daumesnil. The German scholars each stayed in Oxford for about six months and thereafter for some years kept in touch with Oxford affairs by correspondence with Hearne, who reported their subsequent activities and promotions to those who had befriended and encouraged the visitors, particularly Henry Dodwell and Francis Cherry.[3] The results of Wolf's labours in Oxford can be seen in the references to Bodleian material in his *Bibliotheca hebraea* (Hamburg 1715-33) and his *Anecdota graeca* (Hamburg 1722-4), and Pfaff's Oxford visit contributed to the immense array of sources listed in his *Institutiones theologiae* (Tübingen 1720) and *Introductio in historiam theologiae literariam* (Tübingen 1724-6). When, in 1709, these particular scholars had left Oxford, book-orders in the library sharply declined, and indeed the decline in numbers both of foreign scholars and book-orders continued. In

---

[1] S. Gibson, 'Francis Wise', *Oxoniensia* i (1936), 191.

[2] Bodl. library records, day-books. The first extant day-book starts too late to record the reading of Ludwig Holberg, founder of Danish literature, who was admitted as a Bodleian reader on 18 April 1706, and in later years expressed his gratitude to the libraries of Oxford which had inspired him with the thought of 'how splendid and glorious a thing it would be to take a place among the authors': *The Encylopaedia Britannica* (11th edn Cambridge 1910), 580-1.

[3] Francis Cherry (*c*1665-1713), m. SEH 1682; nonjuror.

the first decade of the century 143 *extranei* signed the Bodleian register, and by far the great majority of these were visitors from Europe. In the decade 1741-50 only 34 *extranei* subscribed, and only 9 of these were visitors from Europe. The drop in book-orders was even more dramatic; the total number of orders for the whole year 1742 was 257 compared with 317 for the month of December 1708. Throughout the 1740s there were many days on which no book-order was recorded, although some readers may of course have used the library to consult the folio works on the open shelves.

The partial evidence of recorded book-orders cannot be taken as a picture of Oxford scholarship, but in addition to the record of intensive work by foreign scholars they do throw occasional light on the studies of some Oxford men like Edmond Halley, who was a regular reader in the Bodleian Library from 1709 to 1712, and William Blackstone, whose book-orders are recorded from 1743 to 1762. The most constant and diligent readers at this time were, however, the orientalist Thomas Hunt, Benjamin Kennicott and Thomas Warton the younger. In July 1746 Hunt, then Laudian professor of Arabic, and soon to be also regius professor of Hebrew, was allowed to borrow oriental manuscripts for use in the Savilian study, a privilege later granted also to his friend Kennicott.[1] Kennicott pursued his vigorous research into Old Testament commentaries and texts, and by 1760 was not only ordering manuscripts for use in the Savilian study but was on occasion allowed to have Laudian manuscripts delivered to his rooms in Exeter College by order of the vice-chancellor and proctors.[2] Thomas Warton was also given special facilities both in 1760 when books needed for his edition of Theocritus were delivered to him in the study in the gallery, a privilege formerly granted to Richard Bentley while collating manuscripts of Horace in 1707, and again in 1766 when the curators gave Warton permission to take out of the library for transcription and printing St Amand's index to Theocritus.[3]

These instances show that some reputable and determined scholars were encouraged by special facilities and had access to collections, including collections of manuscripts, which were comparatively new acquisitions. The fact that no official printed catalogue of any Bodleian

---

[1] The Savilian study, immediately over the arch of the Tower of the Five Orders, set between the Schools of Astronomy and Geometry, was also used as an armoury for the university's muskets, pikes and drums, relics of the troubled times of Charles I and James II: J. Walter, *Poems* (Oxford 1780), 57.

[2] Bodl. library records, day-book, 15 Apr. 1760. On 10 December 1768 the curators supported Kennicott's application to convocation for a dispensation to allow them to lend manuscripts to him 'under the Penalty of £20 for the restoring each Volume so lent': Bodl. library records, curators' minute-book.

[3] Bodl. library records, entry-book 1758-65 (Warton 1760); Hearne, *Collections* ii. 45 (Bentley); Bodl. library records, curators' minute-book, 6 May 1766 (Warton).

collection of western manuscripts was issued in the eighteenth century would suggest grave obstacles in the way of research.[1] Certainly the great collections of Tanner (1736), Carte (1753-4) and Rawlinson (1756) together with the Clarendon papers deposited at various dates from 1753 must often have overwhelmed by their sheer bulk the exiguous library staff, but with outside help much of the most important material was made accessible in reasonable time. Bishop Tanner's collection of manuscripts, now numbering 473 volumes, and particularly valuable for Archbishop Sancroft's papers and part of the Nalson collection of civil-war documents, was received by the library in 1736, and though the arrangement left much to be desired, bundles of papers were being sent out for binding in 1737-8 and Thomas Toynbee of Balliol was paid in 1744 for writing a catalogue of the collection.[2] The first instalment of state papers collected by Thomas Carte for his life of Ormonde and history of England came to the library in 1753-7 already bound and accompanied by Carte's own brief catalogue and index which helped to make · the collection usable. One of the greatest collections in the history of the library came in 1756 as a bequest from Richard Rawlinson, fellow of St Johns, a bishop among the nonjurors and regular benefactor to the library from 1733. Rawlinson was a collector of all-encompassing taste and at his death his collections, 'formed abroad and at home, the choice of book-auctions, the pickings of chandlers' and grocers' waste-paper', came to the library in one heterogeneous mass.[3] When eventually sorted and finally numbered in the nineteenth century the collection was seen to comprise about 1,900 printed books and some 5,000 volumes of manuscripts. Such a collection is impossible to describe briefly but the important point in this context is that volumes from the collection were being used by readers as early as 1757. Humphrey Owen, Librarian from 1747 to 1768, drew up a scheme of classification for most of the manuscripts and by 1764 William Huddesford of Trinity was writing to explain that he had been 'employd by the University, for some Time, in examining and cataloguing the MSS left us by Dr Rawlinson'.[4]

For access to the great collections of manuscripts received by the

[1] R. W. Hunt, *Summary Catalogue of Western Manuscripts in the Bodleian Library* i (Oxford 1953), p. xl.

[2] The Tanner manuscripts were, with those in the Rawlinson collection, the first manuscripts to be placed in the picture gallery. The Tanner printed books were less well treated. Thomas Warton described them in a letter of 22 June 1781 as: 'squeezed into a most incommodious room, covered with dust, unclassed, and without a catalogue. Such is the confused and impracticable State of this Collection, that I have often been unable to find a book a second time which I have seen not half a year before.' BL MS Add. 30375, fo 1, printed in *Jl English and German Philology* xiv (1915), 107-8.

[3] Macray, *Annals*, 233-4.

[4] Hunt, *Summary Catalogue* i, p. xxxvii. Humphrey Owen (1702-68), m. Jesus 1718, principal 1763-8; Bodley's Librarian 1747-68. W. Huddesford-S. Pegge junior, 12 Apr. 1764, Bodl. Eng. lett. d. 45, fo 349. On 10 November 1779 the librarian, John Price, wrote to Richard Gough: 'We have a MS Catalogue of most of his [Rawlinson's] MSS &c., but when it will be printed, I cannot say.' J. Nichols, *Literary Anecdotes of the Eighteenth Century* (9 vols London 1812-15) v. 494.

library in the seventeenth century readers relied on Bernard's catalogue published in 1698, and for printed books Hyde's catalogue of 1674 was in general use up to 1738.[1] Talk of a new catalogue of printed books began early in the century and when in 1703 Thomas Smith, Cottonian Librarian, lent Hudson a copy of Garnerius, *Systema bibliothecae collegii parisiensis societatis Jesu* (Paris 1678) the librarian replied:

I cannot but approve of the Jesuite's ingenuity in the model of the Library; tho tis not practicable with us. I think a catalogue of our books according to his method would be of great use, and not very difficult to be made ... The only thing that discourages me from attempting it you may easily imagine: which is the great expence of printing it, and the inconsiderable recompense I should have for my paines.[2]

Such discouragement was not a novel experience but perhaps Hudson was too energetic an editor and book-collector ever to commit himself to the drudgery which his assistant Thomas Hearne undertook with complete devotion and admirable care. Soon after his appointment as library janitor in 1702 Hearne set to work to compare every book in the library with the entry in Hyde's catalogue of 1674 and made many corrections and additions which were to be issued as a supplement to the main catalogue.[3] This plan was then revised by Hudson who wanted an amalgamated catalogue, and in 1714 he produced a proposal and specimen for a new catalogue which was accepted by the delegates of the press.[4] But Hudson does not appear to have taken any further action, and in January 1716 Charlett wrote to Wanley asking for his advice about reprinting the catalogue of 1674, and commending Joseph Bowles, 'a most excellent youth ... who must do the Drudgery and let others have the credit'.[5]

Bowles succeeded Hudson as librarian in 1719 and in the following year presented to the delegates of the press, 'not at a Solemn meeting but rather in a private way', new proposals for publishing a catalogue of printed books in the Bodleian Library.[6] Bowles's detailed proposals were presumably accepted, although no mention is made of the fact in the delegates' formal minutes. In 1725 he received from the curators a special payment of just over £50 which must relate to work on the catalogue, and by 1727 he was excusing himself from other calls on his time by 'my constant Business in the Bodleian Library, and my attendance on the Press, during my publishing a Catalogue of all the Bodleian-printed

[1] *Catalogi librorum manuscriptorum Angliae et Hiberniae* (Oxford 1697 [recte 1698]); *Catalogus impressorum librorum bibliothecae bodleianae, in academia oxoniensi* (Oxford 1674). See Carter, *History of the Press* i. 245-7, 76-8.

[2] J. Hudson–T. Smith, 6 Oct. 1703, Bodl. MS Smith 50, fo 143.

[3] Macray, *Annals*, 213.

[4] *First Minute Book*, ed. Gibson and Johnson, p. 41.

[5] BL MS Harl. 3778, fo 33.

[6] *First Minute Book*, ed. Gibson and Johnson, pp. 83-4.

Books'.[1] After Bowles's death in 1729 the work was carried on by his successor as librarian, Robert Fysher, and eventually the catalogue was published in two volumes in 1738.[2] For its remarkable 'accuracy' and 'abundance and minuteness of its cross-references' the catalogue probably owed much to Hearne.[3] Throughout the eighteenth century the library was hopelessly understaffed and cataloguing could not keep pace with the flood of generous donations. So the 1738 catalogue remained in use in the library for another hundred years in an interleaved copy annotated with addenda in a variety of hands, one of them being that of Samuel Johnson, who on a visit to the Library in 1756 presented Zachariah Williams's *Account of an Attempt to Ascertain the Longitude at Sea* and, as Warton noted, 'for fear of any omission or mistake, he entered in the great Catalogue, the title-page of it with his own hand'.[4] Unfortunately not all donors could add their benefactions to the catalogue in this peremptory way. Richard Rawlinson proposed in a letter to the librarian of 15 April 1751 that 'large benefactors should pay the expense of entries into the Bodleian, as their books are useless till so entered';[5] but generous benefactor as he was, he paid no further heed to his own suggestion. Rawlinson's gifts of printed books, covering a wide field of history and topography, came to the library in instalments from 1730, and the care with which the librarian acknowledged and shelfmarked the steady stream of minor benefactions contributed to Rawlinson's final decision to leave his manuscripts to Oxford. But meanwhile these generous gifts, together with Tanner's bequest which included over nine hundred printed books rich in 'black-letter divinity', merely emphasized the speed with which the 1738 catalogue was becoming out of date as a true record of the library's holdings of printed books.

On his visit to the Bodleian Library in 1756 Dr Johnson would have seen the last stages of a refurbishing of the library which began in 1746 as a reflection of the new splendour of the Radcliffe Camera. The view from the south range of the schools gallery had been transformed by the clearing away of the huddle of old houses in Catte Street and the building of the Camera which, in 1746, was almost complete. Humphrey Owen, the librarian, first commissioned a fine range of bookcases for the south range of the gallery, bookcases in the new style, with carved pediments and wiremesh doors.[6] Then, in 1749, the Arundel marbles were

---

[1] Bodl. MS Rawl. D. 376, fo 202ᵛ.

[2] *Catalogus impressorum librorum bibliothecae bodleianae in academica oxoniensi* (2 vols Oxford 1738). See Carter, *History of the Press* i. 294-6. Robert Fysher (1699-1747), m. Ch.Ch. 1715; fellow Oriel; Bodley's Librarian 1729-47. [3] Macray, *Annals*, 213.

[4] *Boswell's Life of Johnson*, ed. G. B. Hill (6 vols Oxford 1887), rev. L. F. Powell (6 vols Oxford 1934-50) i. 275n. [5] Macray, 235n.

[6] I. G. Philip, 'Reconstruction in the Bodleian Library and convocation house in the eighteenth century', *Bodleian Library Record* vi (1957-61). The centre portion of these cases has been re-erected in the basement library of the Museum of the History of Science, Oxford.

moved to a ground-floor school in order that the gallery might be wain-scotted 'in a regular manner'. The gallery had been wainscotted, at least in part, in the mid-seventeenth century, but Edward Butler (president of Magdalen 1722-45) contributed £200 towards the re-wainscotting and the duke of Beaufort,[1] a Radcliffe trustee, paid for the completion of the new work in 1749.[1] In 1753 the tower room was transformed with elaborate plaster decoration, echoing that in the Radcliffe Camera, an embellishment which must have been the occasion for the move of the library's coin collection from the tower room to the coin room in the south range of the gallery.[1] In the eighteenth century many libraries possessed collections of coins and medals, but the Bodleian collection, inaugurated by a gift from Archbishop Laud, was the first in time and in the mid-eighteenth century was rapidly growing in importance. Francis Wise's catalogue of the collection, published in 1750, preceded a series of bene-factions which modified the character of the collection and greatly increased its importance. Browne Willis, the historian of Buckingham-shire, who had given coins on various occasions since 1739, completed the series of English silver coinage by his gift in 1750;[2] Richard Rawlin-son gave many coins and medals in 1755 and Francis Wise added to the collection in 1760.

The university was fortunate in that the librarian Humphrey Owen shared the enthusiasms of men like Browne Willis and Rawlinson. He bought the essential numismatic books and encouraged his antiquarian friends to build up a great numismatic collection, and his flair for the physical embellishment of the library provided just that environment which encouraged further benefactions, like the bequest of Charles God-wyn, who died in 1770 and whose collection made him the real founder of the Bodleian collection of Greek coinage.

By 1753 Owen had also turned his attention to Selden End, where two of the west windows were blocked up, and then in 1756, the 'pre-vailing Spirit of Improvement' still running strongly, the old benches between the bookstalls in Duke Humfrey's Library were removed and replaced with Windsor chairs, of a type still in use. Between 1757 and 1761 all the chains were removed from the folio books and to all appear-ances the age of enlightenment had dawned, quietly and placidly, with the first considerable concession to reader-comfort in those Windsor chairs 'so admirably calculated for Ornament and Repose'.[3] There

[1] Charles Noël Somerset (1710-56), 4th d. of Beaufort; m. Univ. 1725; hon. MA 1727, hon. DCL 1736; MP Monmouth 1731-4, 1734-45. See J. N. L. Myres, 'The Bodleian coin cabinets', *BLR*, iii. (1950-1), 45 ff. For the history of the coin collection, which was transferred to the Ashmolean Museum in 1920, see H. H. E. Craster, *History of the Bodleian Library 1845-1945* (Oxford 1952) 116-19.

[2] By his will Willis enabled the university to acquire on preferential terms his very important collection of English gold coins.

[3] The phrase is Thomas Warton's, writing as 'Thomas Hearne Junior' in *Jackson's Oxford Journal*, 29 Nov. 1766.

followed new provisions for the convenience of readers in revised opening hours:

The hours of being admitted into the public library being suited to the dinner-hour of our ancestors, are now become so unseasonable that we have alter'd them. During the winter half-year the library is to be open from nine in the morning to three in the afternoon. During the summer half-year from eight in the morning till two in the afternoon, and from three in the afternoon till five.[1]

Owen's work in refurbishing the gallery had begun before the library received, in the 1750s, the three great manuscript collections of Carte, Rawlinson and Clarendon, and when the scale of library activities was still, in general, on a very small scale. In Owen's first year of office, for instance, the general use of the library can be gauged from the figures for one month in full term; on only twelve days in May 1748 were any orders placed for books and on those twelve days no more than two or three readers ordered books.

In the financial year 1747-8 less than £100 was spent on books and the purchases were almost entirely current numbers of a few reference works: two volumes each of the *Journal des sçavans* and of the *Philosophical Transactions*, the current *Acta eruditorum Lipsiae*, the first ten volumes of *Histoire et mémoires de l'Académie des Inscriptions et Belles Lettres* and two volumes of *Histoire et mémoires de l'Académie Royale des Sciences*. Fifty items were received from the Stationers' Company and eighteen books were received as donations.[2] This amounts to a total annual intake of eighty to ninety items, and many of those received under copyright were slight pamphlets. Of the eighteen books received from personal donors ten were the gifts of authors or editors, illustrating that wish to be represented in the library where, as Alexander Pope said on an earlier occasion, 'it is always an Honour to be read'.[3] But it remained true that though the library never lacked friends their gifts often represented the interests of the donors more clearly than they fulfilled the needs of the library, and so far there had been little opportunity for planned or consistent growth.

From 1750 the annual expenditure on books was normally no more than the £10 received from Lord Crewe's benefaction, and in addition to the few books so purchased the library could only count on those books which the Stationers' Company was obliged to deposit, 'an obligation, which has been frequently disregarded with Impunity, and which indeed has seldom been observed with `that Punctuality which the Necessities

---

[1] C. Godwyn-J. Hutchins, 27 Nov. 1768, Bodl. MS Top. Gen. d.2, fo 135.

[2] The volumes received from the Stationers did not include the year's most notable publication, Hume's *Philosophical Essays concerning Human Understanding*.

[3] A. Pope-J. Bowles, 26 Sept. [1721], Bodl. MS Rawl. lett. 90, fos 47-8. This letter was accompanied by a gift of the last two vols of his translation of Homer.

of the University require'. This trenchant view of the necessities of the university, a new note in Bodleian documentation, was expressed by William Scott in a printed sheet circulated in the autumn of 1779 when he was Camden professor of history. Scott had resigned his tutorship at University College in 1777 and taken chambers in the Temple, but he resided in Oxford from time to time and as he was a fairly regular reader in the Bodleian Library from the beginning of August to early October 1779 it is likely that his plea for a new consideration of library resources was written then. For the first time in the eighteenth century an influential member of the university considered the Bodleian Library in relation to contemporary needs of scholarship and published his findings with a reasoned and practical solution. Scott's style was magisterial:

No Member of a learned Society it is presumed will be inclined to deny, that the Support and Improvement of its public Repositories of Learning, is one of the first and most natural Objects of its Attention.

The University of Oxford owes the most important Obligations to the Munificence of Sir Thomas Bodley, of Archbishop Laud, of Mr Selden's Executors, and of other eminent Persons, who established, or by subsequent Benefactions have enriched the inestimable collection of the Bodleian Library. If any Circumstance, however, may be thought to detract from the Merit of that Gratitude which the University has been always studious to express, it may perhaps be this, that content with enjoying the Benefits of their Liberality, it has never attempted to enlarge them by any Efforts of its own, and has seen, without making any Provision for a growing Deficiency, a Fund which was originally small, become at last totally inadequate to the Purposes of its Establishment.[1]

Then, having considered the inadequacies of Lord Crewe's benefaction and the Stationers' deposits, Scott continued:

When it is considered to what Sources the University is thus indebted for all the Additions which it regularly receives to its original Stock of Books, it will not appear surprising, that in the present State of Learning its Collection should become more inconveniently defective every Day, and that every Gentleman who has Occasion to make Literary Researches in it, has Reason to lament, that its Modern Utility falls considerably short of its Ancient Reputation. Several of the most valuable Productions of our eminent *Divines* are not to be found in it; its Catalogue of *Law*, both *Civil* and *Common*, is extremely imperfect; in the various Articles of *Natural History*, of *Chemistry*, of *Botany*, and of other Sciences which have been cultivated with great Diligence during the present Century, many Works of great Merit and Expence have been published, both at Home and Abroad, which are far beyond the reach of its present Fund; and in the Class of *History* and *Antiquities* many Volumes might be mentioned, which a private Enquirer can only expect to find in public Collections, but which he will

[1] There is a copy of Scott's proposals in Bodl. Bliss B.417 (1). 'Mr Selden' refers to John Selden (1584-1654), m. Hart Hall 1600; MP Oxford Univ. 1640-53.

look for in vain in the Collection of the University. These Defects would have been still more inconveniently felt, if the Kindness of some private Benefactors had not occasionally stept in, and assisted it with a Liberality, which tho' extremely beneficial for the present, cannot be depended upon as the Source of a Constant and regular Supply.

The solution put forward for a rectification of this situation was that the library should receive annual fees from all persons entitled to read in the library and a share of the matriculation fees. The time was ripe and the argument unanswerable. For the first time members of the university realized that they must pay for the support of the library, which was essential to scholarship. In less than three months discussion was concluded; a new statute incorporating the suggested payments to the library was considered by the heads of houses in December 1779 and confirmed by convocation on 22 January 1780. As a result, from 1780 to 1800 the average income to the library from fees amounted to about £450 a year, and the library was transformed.[1] The bulk of this new money was spent on books, and new standards were at once apparent: the first annual list of purchases included the five-volume supplement to the French *Encyclopédie*, the sixteen-volume set of Somers's *Collection of Tracts*, the *Harleian Miscellany*, the six volumes of John Comyns's *Digest of the Laws of England* and five of Albrecht von Haller's works on botany and anatomy.[2]

At their meeting on 4 May 1786 the curators directed the librarian to purchase law books according to the list delivered to him, and thus 'to complete the Collection of Law Books now in the Library'. Since 1780 the curators had issued an annual printed list of new accessions, but this was clearly not good enough and now they instructed the librarian to 'make a Catalogue of the new books as they come in that they may be accessible for immediate use'.[3] In 1787 they had to consider wider aspects of library administration when they received a printed *Memorial concerning the State of the Bodleian Library* from Thomas Beddoes, 'chemical reader' in the university. Beddoes had returned to Oxford to take up this post in 1787; he was energetic, gifted and volatile. His *Memorial*, written within a few months of his return to Oxford, began with a stirring denunciation of the whole Bodleian organization. He criticized the librarian for inattention and non-attendance, complained of the library

---

[1] The new money was separately accounted; the main library account continued to show only book purchases made from the annual £10 of Lord Crewe's benefaction.

[2] J. Somers, *A Collection of Scarce and Valuable Tracts* (with the second, third and fourth collections, 16 vols London 1748-52); *The Harleian Miscellany* (8 vols London 1744-6); J. Comyns, *A Digest of the Laws of England* (6 vols London 1762-76). Haller's works ranged from the *Icones anatomicae* (Göttingen 1743) to the London editions of *Bibliotheca botanica* and *Bibliotheca anatomica* (1771 and 1774), neither of which was registered under copyright.

[3] Bodl. library records, curators' minute-book, 4 May 1786, 4 May 1780.

being open for insufficient hours and closed without statutory warrant and criticized at length and in detail the choice of books and the methods of acquisition. There is little doubt that his criticism of the librarian for non-attendance was justified. Price had a curacy at Wilcote in Oxfordshire and devoted his Saturdays and Mondays to leisurely travel to and fro; but 'it unfortunately happens', Beddoes complained, 'from the disposition of the Chemical Lectures, that I have scarce any leisure, but on Saturdays and Mondays, to consult such books as may assist me'.[1] Beddoes's complaints about the inadequate supply of books covered a wide field: there were delays; he himself could buy more cheaply and more expeditiously; the library's sets of periodicals were not always up to date and some, when wanted by readers, were at the bookbinders; more subject specialization was needed, and too much had been left to the discretion of the booksellers who imported foreign material. As for the library suggestion-book of *libri desiderati*, this was of no use since suggestions were not acted upon. In many ways Beddoes's *Memorial* is a classic of library criticism. He was no doubt opinionated and irascible; his references to English books lacking in the library showed that in the haste of his critical zeal he overlooked those helpful cross-references which the Bodleian catalogue provided, but his serious charges made a great impression. For the first time the curators of the library were forced to consider what reforms were necessary in the general administration of the library in order to satisfy the needs of scholarship which was no longer confined to theology and classical literature, and to meet the demands of teachers whose activities had begun to range far beyond college tutorials and the formal exercises of the traditional curriculum.

The curator's immediate reaction to Beddoes's *Memorial* was to resolve to increase the staff of the library by an under-librarian and two assistants (undergraduates or BAs) in order to give attendance during the library's opening hours, and the curators themselves were to meet more regularly and frequently if necessary 'for giving orders about purchases of books'. They therefore asked to have available all useful catalogues, including those of the Leipzig book-fairs, and the librarian was to attend their meetings with the readers' suggestion-book.[2] Further

---

[1] Beddoes, *Memorial*, 6-7. There is a copy of the *Memorial* in Bodl. library records. Price was severely criticized at this time and there is no doubt that he took little interest in science (except for botany) and German academic publications. But Price went to great lengths to help those whose interests he understood and shared. Michael Tyson, antiquary, botanist and book-collector, recommended Richard Gough to get in touch with Price, who was 'the most civil man I ever met with': letter of 5 Nov. 1772, Nichols, *Literary Anecdotes*, viii. 600. Price's helpfulness resulted in the library's acquisition of that most valuable topographical collection which Richard Gough bequeathed to it in 1809.

[2] Bodl. library records, curators' minute-book, 15 Nov. 1787. The book of *libri desiderati* to which Beddoes referred no longer exists; a new book started in 1788 shows that from that date with few exceptions all books suggested, and not already in the library, were ordered without delay.

consideration of book-purchasing policy was deferred for a year while the question of staffing the library degenerated into a long wrangle with the heads of houses who could not agree with the curators' proposals and insisted that not one but two under-librarians should be appointed. This, the curators maintained, would be too expensive; it would tend to make the office of librarian a sinecure. 'Confusion would be apt to arise amongst so many from the difficulty of adjusting their respective times of attendance; and there would always be a temptation to neglect.' The heads' further proposal for increasing the librarian's salary was equally unacceptable, the curators being now apprehensive that making the salary too large 'might be a temptation to improper persons to become candidates for the place'. In December 1788 the curators resolved to give public notice that they were unable to provide the establishment which the library required, and the existing staff struggled on.[1] Meanwhile the curators had increased their own activity. In January 1788 they agreed that all new books should be examined by them each term, and 'immediately given out for the purpose of cataloguing them and placing them in the Library', and that all catalogues and book-lists sent by Elmsley, their bookseller, should be immediately circulated among the curators.[2]

In December 1788 the curators resolved that John Randolph, regius professor of divinity, and Cyril Jackson, regius professor of Greek, should consider purchases from the sale of the Pinelli library, and be empowered to give commissions to bid. This was not an area in which the 'chemical reader' had any interest, but it was the beginning of a quite remarkable book-buying operation. Desiring to acquire as many as possible of the first printed editions of classical authors, the curators bought heavily at the sale of the library of Mapheo Pinelli and then issued an appeal to the university because 'by reason of their Purchases at the Pinelli Sale, and the great importation of Foreign books within the last two years, they have so far exhausted the Fund as not to be able to pay the Bills now due without borrowing a considerable sum of money'.[3] At the same time they pointed out that the sale of the Crevenna library in Holland in the following year would also afford 'uncommon opportunities of purchasing Books, and of making up the deficiencies of the Library'. They therefore appealed for loans from colleges and individuals so that they might settle their present business and 'reserve a sufficient sum out of the Annual Receipts for the continuing the Philosophical Acts and

[1] The curators insisted that the money accruing under the terms of the 1780 statute was meant for the purchase of books, not the payment of staff.

[2] The London bookseller Peter Elmsley was appointed bookseller to the curators, but this should 'not preclude the Oxford Booksellers from offering . . . such Articles as they may have in their shops': curators' minute-book, 29 Jan. 1788. Elmsley had been acting as London wholesaler for the University Press since 1774: Carter, *History of the Press* i. 370.

[3] Printed proposal, dated 1 Dec. 1789, in curators' minute-book.

Transactions, and buying other new and modern Books more immediately wanted'. This campaign to build up the library's collection of *editiones principes* of the classics was supported by a number of colleges; promises of substantial loans were soon received from Magdalen, All Souls, Queen's, Christ Church and Pembroke, and these were followed by gifts from twelve individual donors including the duke of Marlborough, the two archbishops and the bishops of Salisbury, Chester and Oxford, ten of the twelve donors being Christ Church men, past or present.[1] A total of £281 10*s* in gifts and over £1,550 in loans was received and all the latter were paid off by 1795, an operation which reflected a quite different spirit from that of a library management which for forty years before 1780 had been quietly content with an expenditure of £10 a year on books.

The early printed books which were gathered together at this time were then incorporated in a select collection of Bibles and Greek and Latin classics, printed and manuscript, which was installed in a newly furnished room with elegant bookcases designed by Wyatt, which the curators had had in hand since 1787. 'It was a fine piece of librarianship in the spirit of the eighteenth-century enlightenment' and it was to serve a particular practical purpose too, for the curators agreed that it should 'be also consider'd as a collating room to be reserv'd for the constant use only of persons employ'd in any considerable collation'.[2] The choice and arrangement of books in this room was in the hands of the curators. The Oxford bookseller Daniel Prince reported on these activities in a letter of 2 July 1789: 'Our Bodleian Library is putting into good order. It has been already one year in hand. Some one, two or three of the Curators work at it daily, and several assistants.' Prince went on to comment on the increased intake of books, particularly expensive foreign publications, which made the provision of a new catalogue an urgent necessity.[3] Not only the *editiones principes* bought in 1789-90, a brief list of which was printed in 1795,[4] but still more the forty-fold increase in book-purchases from 1780 onward and donations of extensive collections of modern printed books, like the bequest of Charles Godwyn in 1770, made the 1738 catalogue increasingly inadequate as a guide to the library's resources. The curators tried to make new acquisitions more widely known by deciding on 28 November 1788[5] that the annual printed list of

---

[1] A list is printed in Anthony Wood, *The History and Antiquities of the University of Oxford*, ed. J. Gutch (2 vols in 3 Oxford 1792-6) ii. 949-50. For further details see I. G. Philip, 'The background to Bodleian purchases of incunabula . . . 1788-90', *Trans. Cambridge Bibliographical Soc.* vii (1979).

[2] Hunt, *Summary Catalogue* i, p. xxxix; curators' minute-book, 21 Jan. 1789. The room, at the south-west of the first floor of the schools quadrangle, was then known as the *auctarium*.

[3] Macray, *Annals*, 272-3; Nichols, *Literary Anecdotes* iii. 699.

[4] Macray, 276-7.

[5] A decision repeated in their minutes of 27 Oct. 1789.

books purchased should be sent each year to college libraries and common rooms, and then in the 1794 annual list they asked for returns of such books in college libraries as were not in the Bodleian Library, in order to undertake a general catalogue of all the books in Oxford.

The concept of a union catalogue of books in the Bodleian Library and Oxford colleges reappears from time to time in the eighteenth century. Edmund Gibson, then librarian at Lambeth, advised Charlett as early as 1711 that any new catalogue of books in the Bodleian Library should be 'first collated with the Catalogues of the private Libraries of Colleges: and such books and editions inserted as are not in the publick library'.[1] As soon as he heard that Joseph Bowles had been appointed librarian in November 1719, Gibson, by then bishop of Lincoln, reiterated to Charlett his concern for the inclusion of college holdings in the Bodleian catalogue.[2] By December 1720 a proposal on these lines was incorporated in the plan for publishing a new catalogue of Bodleian printed books. 'That this Catalogue may be render'd more useful and *compleate*', Bowles explained to Charlett,

tis farther propos'd that the Heads of Houses would communicate this Design to their Respective Societys, in order to procure from them an account of those Books which are in *Their* Librarys, and not in the Bodleian ... By this means our new Catalogue will be a sort of universal Index to the most considerable Library's in England.[3]

In the following year All Souls College lent Bowles its three catalogues of Codrington's library in order that he might note the books that were not in the Bodleian Library and with such encouragement Bowles, in 1728, included in his plan for a new Bodleian catalogue proposals for a supplement containing college holdings.[4] But no further action was then taken. Again in 1748 All Souls resolved to pay ten guineas to Messrs Bisse and Hall 'who were employed to take a catalogue of the books in the College Library which were not in the Bodleian'.[5] In response to the 1794 appeal four colleges—Balliol, Exeter, Jesus and Magdalen—had sent in lists by 1801,[6] but libraries like those of All Souls and Christ Church were already far too large for any project of a union catalogue to be undertaken with the limited staff available.

These two latter colleges had established new standards of library

[1] Gibson-Charlett, 27 Jan. 1711, MS Ballard 6, fo 110.
[2] Letter of 2 Jan. 1720, ibid. fo 139, printed in J. Aubrey, *Letters Written by Eminent Persons... and Lives of Eminent Men* [ed. J. Walker] (2 vols London 1813) ii. 54.
[3] Bowles-Charlett, 13 Dec. 1720, MS Ballard 18, fo 39.
[4] H. H. E. Craster, *The History of All Souls College Library*, ed. E. F. Jacob (London 1971), 71; S. Gibson, 'Library co-operation in Oxford', *Proc. and Papers of the Oxford Bibliographical Soc.* ii (1927-30).
[5] All Souls, Warden's MS 35.
[6] Macray, *Annals*, 277.

provision in Oxford, both in the splendour of their buildings and the richness of their collections.[1] All Souls had started a building fund for a new library before it learned, in 1710, of the bequest made by one of its fellows, Christopher Codrington, governor of the Leeward Islands.[2] It was known that Codrington intended that his library should come to Oxford, for as early as 1702 he had written to Charlett that he hoped to make it 'as curious as any private one in Europe, particularly in some sort of books which I believe are not known in Oxford'.[3] When in February 1703 Codrington bequeathed his books to All Souls with £6,000 to be spent on library buildings and £4,000 on books, he was preceding, if he did not at all points rival, the munificence of John Radcliffe. It seems likely that Codrington, again like Radcliffe, thought of the Bodleian Library as a collection largely of English books to which his collection of French and Italian history and literature would be a novel and important supplement. But Codrington's own books were not the important part of his benefaction. Hearne's dismissal of them as 'some scarce, but the greatest part Riff-Raff' lacked judgement as well as charity, but they were certainly eclipsed in importance by the purchases made with Codrington's endowment.[4] After the new library building was completed, and the two libraries, Chichele's and Codrington's, were amalgamated in 1751, a consistent purchasing policy was followed under Blackstone's impetus and inspiration to make the joint library what has been called 'as fine an instrument as possible for legal and humane studies'.[5] Starting with orders of 1757 for the completion of a collection of ancient historians, the library committee went on to buy English, French and Italian literature as well as completing their collection of English history and law.[6] Under this policy the composition of the library changed: no longer a library for vocational training in theology and civil and canon law, it became a general reference library 'resembling the many others that were being formed in the eighteenth century by men of means with literary tastes'.[7]

[1] When Boswell observed to Johnson 'that some of the modern libraries of the University were more commodious and pleasant for study, as being more spacious and airey', Johnson replied, 'Sir, if a man has a mind to *prance*, he must study at Christ-Church and All-Souls'. *Boswell's Life of Johnson*, ed. Hill, rev. Powell ii. 67-8.

[2] This brief account of the Codrington Library is based on Craster, *All Souls Library*; see also J. S. G. Simmons, *A Note on the Codrington Library, All Souls College, Oxford* (Oxford 1982). For the history and holdings of all college libraries see P. Morgan, *Oxford Libraries outside the Bodleian* (Oxford 1973, 2nd edn Oxford 1980).

[3] Craster, 68.

[4] Hearne, *Collections* i. 303.

[5] *VCH Oxon.* iii. 181. Henry Chichele (1362-1443), abp of Canterbury 1414-43, was the founder of the college.

[6] On the French acquisitions see J. S. G. Simmons, *French Publications acquired by the Codrington Library, 1762-1800* (Oxford 1978).

[7] Craster, 86.

748 I. G. PHILIP

Three months after the foundation stone of the Codrington Library was laid, William Stratford, treasurer of Christ Church, wrote to Edward Harley about a plan to rebuild the south side of Peckwater quad: 'we design to turn the inside into a library, and to make it the finest library that belongs to any society in Europe.'[1] by then the college had received by bequest the libraries of deans Henry Aldrich and Francis Atterbury, the former famous not only for its mathematical and architectural books but also for its collection of music and engravings. The new library building, started in 1717 and modified by many changes in plan in the next forty or fifty years, was designed to house these benefactions and those which shortly followed, the library of Stratford and, after his death in 1737, that of William Wake, archbishop of Canterbury. Benefactions on this scale, adding about eighteen thousand volumes to the old library, went far towards substantiating Stratford's proud expectations.

All Souls and Christ Church were also notable for new buildings planned initially under the influence of George Clarke and Henry Aldrich on classical lines which broke away from the traditional Oxford library plan of a first-floor room with folio books chained to stalls between which were fixed benches for those who wished to sit and read. Queen's College had built the most splendid example of a library in this style to house the great collection of Bishop Barlow's books which the college received in 1693.[2] In 1739 Lincoln College library was the last to be refitted with stalls for chained books, but those colleges which had to house great benefactions adopted a less restrictive plan. The large collection bequeathed to Brasenose College by Francis Yarborough in 1770 led to the old library being refitted by James Wyatt in 1780, and Oriel College built a new 'senior library' when its collections were doubled in size by the bequest from Lord Leigh in 1786.[3]

As with the Bodleian Library, college libraries were growing spasmodically through benefactions of very different size and interest. The range of their development and effectiveness therefore varied widely and no one generalization could cover a period of library history which included Blackstone's work for the Codrington Library and the situation at Merton where the library was 'an old ruinous place that lies in neglect' and where a college librarian spent the library income on junior fellows to 'keep up his faction' and hurled works of logic out into the quadrangle to spite the Warden.[4]

[1] HMC *Portland MSS* vii. 217, letter of 20 Sept. 1716.
[2] For discussion of library plans see J. N. L. Myres, 'Oxford libraries in the seventeenth and eighteenth centuries' in F. Wormald and C. E. Wright (eds), *The English Library before 1700* (London 1958) 236-52.
[3] A. Dale, 'The building of the library', *Oriel Record* (1951). The library building was completed in 1796. Francis Yarborough (1695-1770), m. Univ. 1713; MA BNC, principal 1745-70. Edward Leigh (1743-86), 5th bn Leigh; m. Oriel 1761; hon. MA 1764, hon. DCL 1767; high steward of the university 1767-86. [4] B. W. Henderson, *Merton College* (London 1899), 241.

When in 1780 William Scott made his plea for a better endowment of the Bodleian Library he contrasted the university library, 'declining in Point of extensive Utility', with 'some Collegiate Libraries ... (particularly Two) which are much more completely furnished with the learned Productions of later Times, and one of them in particular is endowed with a very ample Revenue'.[1] This was, perhaps, taking too narrow a view. It is true that most notable increases in the collections of college libraries were the result of benefactions whereas planned purchases were inadequate, but most colleges, starting in the seventeenth or early eighteenth century had, for the benefit of their college libraries, levied some fees on their members, on admission or graduation or other occasion such as moving to a higher table in hall.[2] Again the results varied very greatly but some, such as New College, had by mid-century reasonable book-funds derived from fees and were building up considerable collections.

Gradually during the century the practice of chaining books in college libraries was abandoned, but most colleges had maintained some sort of lending collection for fellows in addition to the chained collection. Yet even in such small societies the problem of recovering borrowed books seems to have been considerable. In 1702 Edward Thwaites wrote from Queen's to Hickes regretting that he could not get a book for him from the college library because 'we have made an order that noe book shal goe out of the library for the future, having lost many books borrowed by fellows out of our old library'.[3] In 1729 the fellows of St John's agreed that all library books should be immediately called in, and none lent out for the future; but seven years later, though the great inconvenience arising 'from permitting books to be lent out of the library for the use of particular persons in their private chambers' was still recognized, it was agreed that borrowing by members of the college of master's standing should be restored, but only in accordance with strict conditions of control.[4] Other colleges had similar problems, and the difficulties may have arisen partly from tutors borrowing books for students who were not permitted to use the college library.

All undergraduates were generally excluded from the main college library, and only a few colleges seem to have made any attempt to make special provision for them. Such records as still exist suggest that the undergraduate library, where it existed, provided some commentaries on classical texts and a small selection of works of philosophy and mathematics. There is some evidence of collections maintained for

[1] See pp. 741-2 above.
[2] Costin, *St John's* 177.
[3] Bodl. MS Eng. hist. c.6, fo 103.
[4] Costin, *St John's*, 191; SJM register 1712-30, p. 604, 25 Nov. 1729, register 1731-94, 10 Apr. 1736.

undergraduates or junior bachelors in Balliol, Exeter, Magdalen, Merton, Queen's, Trinity, University and Wadham.[1] An undergraduate library existed in Trinity as early as the 1680s, for John Harris recalled:

There was also in this College a very Good collection of Philos: and Mathem: Books of all kinds as also of the Classicks placed in a room which we called the *Lower Library*, where every undergraduate had the liberty to go and study as long as he pleased, which was a mighty advantage to the House, and ought to be imitated by other Colleges.[2]

Balliol had an undergraduate library which was in existence in 1700.[3] Accessions to this library were very spasmodic but from 1725 to 1728 substantial sums were spent in what was clearly an attempt to form a good general library. Purchases then included, in addition to some classical commentaries and theology, Saunderson's *Algebra*, Ozanam's *Cursus mathematicus*, Gregory and Keill on astronomy, Hobbes on mathematics and the earl of Clarendon on Hobbes (*Leviathan*), philosophical pieces by Kenelm Digby[4] and Boyle, Grotius, *De jure belli et pacis*, Pope's *Iliad*, Dryden's *Virgil* and Addison's works. It did not last. In the second half of the century the funds for the 'minor library' became one with the chapel account, and expenditure on books had decreased to vanishing point when in 1799 the undergraduate library books were apparently absorbed into the senior library and at the same time the fellows agreed that 'no Person having a Key to the Library shall introduce any Bachelor of Arts, Civilian or Undergraduate into the Library on any account whatever'.[5] Other undergraduate libraries disappeared after an uncertain existence. At Exeter the library, which had its own librarian up to 1715-16, seems, according to the accounts, to have faded away by 1746-7. Undergraduates were allowed in the main library before 1739, but were then restricted on account of fire-risk. The taberdars' library at Queen's, a seventeenth-century creation for the use of senior scholars, was by 1785 threatened by the ravages of time (*injuria temporis peritura*).[6]

But the most striking instance of neglect leading to preservation was at Trinity where the undergraduate library, which had been the pride of the college in the 1680s, was removed in the 1780s by an undergraduate whose abstraction of a great part of the library seems to have escaped

[1] For further references see Morgan, *Oxford Libraries* and P. Morgan, 'Books for the younger sort; Oxford undergraduates and their books from Stuart to modern times', *Antiquarian Book Monthly Rev.* (April–May 1976).
[2] Quoted by M. Maclagan, *Trinity College, a short guide* (Oxford 1955, 2nd edn Oxford 1963). 22. John Harris (1666-1719), m. Trin. 1683; MA Hart Hall 1689.
[3] J. Jones, 'The eighteenth century undergraduates' library', *Balliol College Annual Record* (1980).
[4] Kenelm Digby (1603-65), of Gloucester Hall 1618.
[5] BCA register 1794-1875, fo 11, 21 Oct. 1799.
[6] J. R. Magrath, *The Queen's College* (2 vols Oxford 1921) ii. 260; *Letters of Radcliffe and James*, 86 n.

the notice of his seniors until he himself offered explanation and expia-
tion. William Mills, who matriculated at Trinity in 1785, wrote to the
president in 1804 that he 'was so sinfull and ungrateful as to despoil the
upper Library Room, above the College Library, and which upper Reading Room was, as I heard, originally intended for the Use of the Younger
Students, of many books and take them away into his own keeping . . .
an awakened conscience now strikes him with remorse' and he now
offered to return the books 'with the additional surrender of one or two
articles of his own property, in the book-line, such as he judges may be
acceptable to the College Library, belonging to the Fellows'. With this
letter Mills sent a list of 151 books, of which just over a hundred are
seventeenth-century publications and only a dozen are of the eighteenth.[1] Some of these books may have been those which Mills gave as
'articles of his own property' but the general list is probably the best
evidence we have of a good undergraduate library built up in the late
seventeenth and early eighteenth century. There is a limited range of
classics, philosophy and mathematics, and an interesting selection of
scientific books published between 1660 and 1683, including Hooke's
Micrographia and his *Posthumous Works*, Molyneux's *Dioptrica nova*,
Willis's *De anima brutorum*, and *Pathologiae cerebri*, eight volumes of
Boyle's experimental works, Sprat's *History of the Royal Society* and an
abridgement of 1705 of the *Philosophical Transactions*.[2] These last two
were popular reading with young students who had cultivated an extra-
curricular interest in chemistry. In some colleges such students could
find what they wanted in the fellows' library. In Queen's College for
instance, although undergraduates were as usual excluded from using
the senior library, they could obtain limited access on payment of a
special fee. John James, for example, wrote to his father in 1781:

The honour of [a] key of the library was in consequence of my application to
the Doctor. It has however many inconveniences, whenever I want to go in, I
am forced to get the *butler's* keys, there being two locks on the door to prevent
a subscriber's entering without leave. The chief use I have made of my privilege
is consulting lexicons, and Bayle's Dictionary. The Memoirs of the Royal
Society afford me many opportunities of better understanding some passages
in the chemical lectures.[3]

In a further letter James, precocious and severe, expatiated further:

If the library at Queen's contains some rubbish, it has also much useful, or at
least curious learning. The collection of books in medicine is large, from the
works of Hippocrates and Galen (which I find is *Greek*) to Boerhaave and

---

[1] TCA misc. iii. The last publication-date in the list is 1727.
[2] See J. Yolton, 'Schoolmen, logic and philosophy', above.
[3] *Letters of Radcliffe and James*, 165 (31 Oct. 1781).

Mackenzie ... We have also some good things in philosophy; the best perhaps are the Transactions of the Royal Soceity ... The articles in which we are most deficient are the classics, the Belles Lettres, history, travel, &c.

But even with James the physical difficulties overcame his enthusiasm for learning and he regretted that

I have not been able to make either frequent or long visits to the library, being obliged to have the keys from a servant of the college, who is often out of the way, and sometimes cannot spare them; while the unwholesomeness of the air makes it very disagreeable and even dangerous to remain long.[1]

When John James criticized the weakness of his college library for its inadequate holdings of the classics, the Bodleian Library was beginning to build up that collection of classical texts which, greatly strengthened by purchases at the Pinelli and Crevenna sales, had important results both for the university library and the University Press. For the policy of the curators of the Bodleian Library in building up such a collection was at one with the desire of the delegates of the press to publish and encourage the production of new editions of classical authors. It was a tradition which dated back to the plans of Archbishop Laud who had hoped to see a university press which would be capable of printing the treasures, particularly the Greek and Arabic manuscripts, in the Bodleian Library. In the 1670s Bishop Fell for a few years gave practical shape to Laud's ideal, and when in 1690 Fell's executors made over to the university his interest in the press and its equipment, the university had at last under its own control a well equipped printing house with a scholarly publishing tradition. The debt of this press in the eighteenth century to the example of Fell is made very clear in a letter written in 1715 by Arthur Charlett, one of the busiest delegates of the press, as he tried to explain what he thought the policy of the press should be:

Bishop Fell's design of printing all the Classic Authors with few or no notes was principally firstly to attest our *Right* to those *Copys*, secondly to establish the manufacture of printing by publishing books of a quick sale and that would be ready always to employ many hands, thirdly to furnish the youth of better quality and to accustom them to a respect and preference of Oxford, to which purpose I have always wisht and designed to print every one of the Classic Poets ... leaving the Honor and glory of the University to be promoted and spread, by the greater volumes of Fathers, Mathematicians, Historians &c, but principally by the Collation and Publication of our MSS, as more peculiarly to our own Honor, and the Public Improvement of knowledge.[2]

[1] J. James junior-J. Boucher, 18 Nov. 1781, ibid. 168-9.
[2] A. Charlett-T. Hearne, Michaelmas 1715, Bodl. MS Rawl. 14, fo 64.

This was the ideal, but performance lagged behind, and much of the work which issued from the press to the honour of the university owed very little to the delegates. In the early years they did indeed issue important works, John Wallis's *Opera mathematica* (1693-9), Bernard's *Catalogi librorum manuscriptorum* (1698), and the first edition of Clarendon's *History* (1702) but the output was small. From 1690 to 1712 the press published twenty-three new titles, and then output fell still further. From 1713 to 1755 fourteen new titles were published, one new work every three years. It was this which aroused and justified the criticism levelled at the press in the first half of the eighteenth century. In 1712 Hearne complained 'there is hardly any thing that the University print', and again twenty years later he asserted that 'the University prints nothing of Learning, indeed nothing at all hardly but a sheet Almanack'.[1]

There were indeed great works issued with the imprint of the University Press, but these, George Hickes's *Thesaurus* (1703-5), John Mill's edition of the Greek New Testament (1707), Ernst Grabe's work on the Greek Septuagint (1707-20), were not published by the delegates. They were financed by subscription organized by the authors, printed at the press and marketed by the authors and their friends. The success and reputation of these publications were in marked contrast to the procedures of the delegates, who sought works that would be 'Vendible as well as Useful' but failed as salesmen. In 1712, when the press moved to the newly built Clarendon Building, there were eight thousand volumes in the warehouse, valuable but slow-moving stock which the delegates sold off in bulk.

The importance of the press in the early years of the eighteenth century lay in its possessing a wide range of type which the delegates never failed to make available to any scholar who had a real contribution to make to the established forms of scholarship, however out of fashion or favour the author's political or ecclesiastical background may have been. The nonjurors who were excluded from teaching or advancement in the university were never prevented from employing the press's printers, and so it was possible for men like Hickes and Hearne to continue to make their contribution to scholarship with, for the most part, the tacit approval of the university. Still more important, these scholars who employed the university's printers on their own account showed how it was possible to foster that wider market which eluded the delegates. When preparing his *Thesaurus* for publication before it was issued by subscription in three great volumes in 1703-5, Hickes distributed a prospectus in which he explained how

[1] Hearne, *Collections* iii. 288, xi. 229.

The Booksellers, whom the dearness of Paper obligeth to print no Books, but of quick and common Sale at home, having refused to undertake the Impression of this great Work; the Author hath adventur'd to undertake it himself, upon the encouragement of many Learned Gentlemen, especially among the Learned Clergy, who, in many parts of the Kingdom, have generously contributed towards the Printing thereof.[1]

Hearne too drew upon the encouragement of many learned gentlemen, and from 1703 to 1735 issued from the University Press thirty-seven editions. Among the learned gentry who were becoming an increasingly important element in English life there were many lovers of antiquity for whom the reputation of Oxford was maintained in part by Hearne's publications, which, despite all the animosities which he engendered, continued to bear the imprint of the University Press.

The continued publication by individual scholars backed by the private encouragement of the clergy and gentry is in complete contrast with the inertia of the delegates in the first half of the eighteenth century. By tradition the delegates were drawn from a small group of heads of colleges who were appointed primarily to be delegates of accounts, for whom the affairs of the press tended to be of subordinate interest. There were notable exceptions like Dean Aldrich of Christ Church, who carried on the Fell tradition until his death in 1710, and Arthur Charlett, who generated a quite unusual enthusiasm for publicity and the marketing of the press's publications until his death in 1722; but the delegates in general do not seem to have concerned themselves very energetically with any publishing policy or any direct attempt to promote scholarly publications. The decline in the affairs of the press was dramatically halted by the vigorous campaign conducted by William Blackstone in 1756-8, a direct attack on the ignorance and ineptitude of the delegates which resulted in a complete reorganization of the learned press and radical reforms in the control of printing which prepared the way for more responsible and successful publishing in the latter half of the century.[2]

Blackstone's own views on publishing were conventional and conservative, but he persuaded the delegates to consult others and there followed the publication of scholarly works more worthy of the press. Twenty years later Blackstone looked back with satisfaction on works the delegates had published since he reformed them: the *Life of Lord Clarendon* (1759), a second edition of Thomas Hyde's *Religion of the Persians* (1760), a second edition of Edmund Gibson's *Codex* of English

---

[1] J. A. W. Bennett, 'Hickes's "Thesaurus": a study in Oxford book-production', *Essays and Studies* new ser. i (1948: new ser. i–ii only entitled *English Studies*), 39–40.

[2] I. G. Philip, *William Blackstone and the Reform of the Oxford University Press in the Eighteenth Century* (Oxford Bibliog. Soc. new ser. vii 1957).

ecclesiastical law (1761), a new edition of *Marmora oxoniensia* (1763), the Greek New Testament in Baskerville type (1763) and Warton's edition of Theocritus (1770)—a worthy list, many of the volumes, spendidly produced, but basically a conservative selection of work offered to the delegates many years before. And Blackstone's own suggestion for publication was pre-eminently conservative. In 1760 he persuaded the delegates to put in hand an edition of Cicero which was intended to be 'part of a great Plan for publishing an intire edition of all the Classics in an elegant manner and at a very cheap Rate for the benefit of Students'.[1] Years later he complained that this plan had been frustrated when the delegates allowed editors to consider elaborate collations—and the final edition, published in 1783, was indeed far removed from Blackstone's own brain-child. But a new generation of delegates had moved on to other worthy and more taxing projects, which showed no possibility of profit, like the first edition of the Philoxenian Syrian gospels (1778), or which called for extraordinary pains in compositorial work, like James Bradley's *Astronomical Observations* which were issued from 1798. But for the majority of scholars one of the greatest achievements of the press in the eighteenth century was probably the long series of Greek texts which showed Oxford work at its best. In his *View of the Various Editions of the Greek and Roman Classics* Edward Harwood declared 'the University of Oxford has produced more splendid and accurate Editions of the Greek Classics, than all the other Universities in Europe', and he enumerated Oxford editions conspicuous for their 'correctness of text, splendour of execution, and sagacity of criticism'.[2] Some of these editions made no great claim to textual innovation, but standards were steadily rising. When in 1780 the press resumed its privilege of bible-printing in partnership with London printers the profits of the new venture financed a wider range of learned publications, and in the last decade of the century the delegates were able to attract editors of the stature of Daniel Wyttenbach of Leiden to produce texts which gave the press a growing European reputation presaging its achievements under the inspiration of Thomas Gaisford in the first half of the nineteenth century.

[1] Ibid. 115.
[2] E. Harwood, *View of the Various Editions of the Greek and Roman Classics* (London 1775, 2nd edn London 1778), p. xiv.

27

Antiquarian Studies

S. PIGGOTT

'What did the man talk about?' 'About stones! about stones! he answered, with a down-cast look and in a melancholy tone, as if about to say something excessively profound. 'About stones!—stones, stones, stones! nothing but stones! and so drily. It was wonderfully tiresome—and stones are not interesting things in themselves!'[1]

THE *New Dictionary of the Canting Crew* of 1699 felt it worth while devoting an entry to a contemporary phenomenon, 'The Antiquary', defining him as 'curious Critick in old Coins, Stones and Inscriptions, in Worm-eaten Records and ancient Manuscripts; also one that affects and blindly doats, on Relicks, Ruins, old Customs, Phrases and Fashions'.[2] Antiquaries were being talked about from the sixteenth century if not before, and John Earle included one as a character in his *Microcosmographie* of 1628.[3] By the end of the century the antiquary was a well-known figure, seen as interested not only in the documentary sources which were then becoming more and more the province of historians recognized as such, but also, and perhaps primarily, thought of as being concerned with ancient material culture as evidence of the past, the prototype of an archaeologist. While the two approaches are rarely separable in any one individual until the end of the eighteenth century, for convenience anti-quarianism will be taken here to be concerned with the 'old Coins, Stones and Inscriptions . . . Relicks, Ruins' rather than the 'Worm-eaten Records and ancient Manuscripts'.

The background of such inquiries in Britain lies in the impact of re-naissance studies of the classical past and the first great topographer-antiquary, William Camden. By the middle of the seventeenth century the decisive change in the climate of antiquarian thought had been its incorporation in the early development of classificatory systems, ulti-mately within the Baconian tradition, of natural phenomena by the

---

[1] Shelley in *Reminiscences of Oxford*, 258.

[2] B. E. *A New Dictionary of the Terms Ancient and Modern of the Canting Crew, in its Several Tribes, of Gypsies, Beggers, Thieves, Cheats &c* (London 1699).

[3] [J. Earle,] *Microcosmographie* (London 1628). John Earle (*c*1601-65), m. Ch.Ch. 1619; fellow Merton 1624; bp of Salisbury 1663-5.

new men of experiment, the moderns as against the ancients and Aristotelian authority. This took the form of actual classified collections of natural history, ethnographic and non-classical antiquities, of which the Tradescant collection installed in Oxford in the original Ashmolean Museum in 1683 is the most famous example, or of written studies attempting a new taxonomy such as those in natural history by John Ray, Francis Willughby, Martin Lister and Edward Lhuyd.[1] 'Soon antiquities, as part of the earth and landscape, followed fossils as subjects for investigation within the same scheme', coming within the purview of the topographers such as John Aubrey or Robert Plot—and again Lhuyd—and representing what may be called the Royal Society tradition.[2] Early science and nascent archaeology were both part of the intellectual revolution of the seventeenth century. Antiquities were seen to be susceptible to ordered classification as much as plants and animals; a prehistoric past of stone-using peoples comparable to American Indians was envisaged, with some hint of their later working in bronze and iron; their burials and field monuments, defensive or ceremonial, were recognized and surveyed; a pre-Roman coinage defined. Roman antiquities were seen as potential historical documents and John Aubrey even applied taxonomy to medieval architecture. The rudiments of a recognizably modern discipline are clearly perceptible.

It was not to last. The Royal Society and its distinctive viewpoint was soon under attack and the universities were accusing it of replacing humanistic by materialist education. By the 1690s 'the Humour of the Age, as to those things, is visibly altered from what it was Twenty or Thirty Years ago'; and while the Royal Society had 'weathered the rude Attacks' of its critics, 'yet the sly Insinuations of the *Men of Wit*, That no great things have ever, or are ever like to be performed by the *Men of Gresham*, and, That every Man whom they call a *Virtuoso*, must needs be a *Sir Nicholas Gim-crack*' had discredited science.[3] Sir Nicholas plays the title role in Thomas Shadwell's comedy *The Vertuoso* of 1676. Modern historians have commented on 'the general lethargy which overtook European science soon after 1700' and the particular relapse in England of the study of palaeontology and the earth sciences, but the end of the great tradition of Restoration historiography as its last exponents died between 1710 and 1740 is well known.[4]

The history of the Ashmolean Museum and its keepers over the

---

[1] On the Tradescant collection see A. MacGregor, 'The Ashmolean Museum' above.
[2] S. Piggott, *Ruins in a Landscape* (Edinburgh 1976), 102.
[3] W. Wotton, *Reflections upon Ancient and Modern Learning* (London 1694), 356-7. See R. F. Jones, 'The background of *The Battle of the Books*' and 'Science and criticism in the neo-classical age of English literature' in R. F. Jones *et al. The Seventeenth Century* (Stanford 1951).
[4] See Piggott, *Ruins in a Landscape*, 117.

eighteenth century is a melancholy epitome of the general decline of scientific and historical studies in Oxford as elsewhere. Other collections of curiosities natural and artificial, which might well include antiquities, could be seen in more than one place in Oxford, notably the Bodleian Library (which held the university's coin collections until 1922), the '*Physick* or Anatomie Schoole', where John Evelyn in 1654 had seen 'some rarities of natural things', and St John's College, also visited by Evelyn, and by Celia Fiennes twenty years later.[1] This by 1749 had been augmented by the collections of John Pointer, who had published an account of the Stonesfield Roman pavement and in 1724 a *Britannia Romana or Roman Antiquities in Britain*, 'a little Thing about Roman Coyns, Highways, &c., which is', wrote Hearne, 'as silly as, if not sillier than, any thing he hath done yet'—and the pamphlet of fifty odd pages is certainly a trifling performance.[2] The combined collections at St John's contained not only the Baptist's thigh-bone but fragments of Roman mosaic pavements, urns, specimens of the stones of Stonehenge and 'A Fragment of the Walls of TROY'. It also included a polished flint axe from a hoard found at the Oldbury hill-fort in Warwickshire published in 1656, by Sir William Dugdale, who for the first time recognized such tools, by analogy with American Indian artifacts, as 'weapons used by the Britons before the art of making arms of brass or iron was known';[3] another from the same find was in Plot's collection in the Ashmolean Museum; neither survives. Hearne recorded in 1707 that Arthur Charlett had in his private collection another famous flint implement, the first palaeolithic hand-axe to be identified as 'a British weapon', found in the London gravels of Gray's Inn Lane in the late seventeenth century and published by Hearne in 1715. This has survived, eventually finding its way, *via* Sir Hans Sloane's collection, to the British Museum, but it is interesting to note that all these classic instances of early archaeological identification were at one time in Oxford.[4]

The coin collections had been formed since the sixteenth century, and by the seventeenth more than one college had its coin cabinet.[5] The Bodleian Library, however, with the important collections of Archbishop

[1] *The Diary of John Evelyn*, ed. E. S. de Beer (6 vols Oxford 1955) iii. 108 (11 July 1654); *The Illustrated Journeys of Celia Fiennes 1685-c.1712*, ed. C. Morris (London 1982), 57.
[2] J. Pointer, *An Account of a Roman Pavement lately found at Stunsfield in Oxford-shire* (Oxford 1713); J. Pointer, *Britannia Romana or Roman Antiquities in Britain* (Oxford 1724); Hearne, *Collections* viii. 217.
[3] W. Dugdale, *Warwick-shire* (London 1656), 788.
[4] Hearne, *Collections* ii. 59; J. Leland, *Collectanea*, ed. T. Hearne (6 vols Oxford 1715) i, p. lxiv; J. Evans, *The Ancient Stone Implements, Weapons and Ornaments of Great Britain* (London 1872, 2nd edn London 1897), 581; R. T. Gunther, *Early Science in Oxford* (14 vols Oxford 1923-45) iii. 336.
[5] C. H. V. Sutherland, 'The coin collection of Christ Church, Oxford', *Oxoniensia* v (1940); J. G. Milne, 'Oxford coin-collectors of the seventeenth and eighteenth centuries', ibid. xiv (1949); J. D. A. Thompson, 'The Merton College coin collection', ibid. xvii-xviii (1952-3).

Laud and Thomas Roe,[1] acquired in 1636 and 1644, became the main university repository. Its coins were catalogued first by Ashmole in 1668, then by Hearne up to 1715, and by Francis Wise, whose printed catalogue, 'a meritorious work, carefully executed and furnished with a good commentary', was published in 1750.[2] A notable accession of the eighteenth century was the collection of seventeenth-century tradesmens' tokens, and of English, Scottish and Irish coinage (with an outstanding series of English gold pieces) given between 1742 and 1746 by the antiquary Browne Willis of Whaddon Hall near Bletchley. The Christ Church coin collections were greatly augmented by the bequest in 1737 of the coins collected by Archbishop Wake, remarkable as being formed deliberately as a representative teaching collection rather than as a cabinet of rarities. In 1727 he wrote to William Stukeley of 'the desire I have to finish a collection intended for the use of the public when I myself must have done with it', showing a perceptive appreciation of the purpose of numismatics in advance of most of his contemporaries.[3]

During the eighteenth century William Camden's chair of history fared no better than the Ashmolean Museum. Stuart-Jones, chronicling its history, laconically remarked that after the 1690s the 'four score years which follow ... are the Dark Age of the Camden Chair'.[4] Antiquarianism, however, was pursued outside the ambit of the traditional university curriculum, and its development at Oxford during the period was due to individuals rather than to institutions. Three representative figures span the century with its changing modes of taste and scholarship: Hearne, Francis Wise and Thomas Warton. Hearne, a friend of Edward Lhuyd, is a link with the Royal Society tradition of the end of the previous century; Wise all too well exemplifies the intellectual doldrums of the decades 1740-60; Warton leads into the rediscovery of medieval England by the early Romantics among whom he was so important a figure. In their social status and personalities they again provide a cross-section of the Oxford of the day; Hearne the learned rustic, selflessly devoted to scholarship, prickly and suspicious; Wise the shopkeeper's clever son, a smart townee with an eye to his own advancement; Warton the son of a fellow of Magdalen in a comfortable Hampshire living, a gentleman of taste and original scholarship who, careless of appearances, enjoyed his evenings in the ale-house. All three are fortunately well documented, and each has his interest in his own right no less than in the history of antiquarianism.

[1] Sir Thomas Roe (c1581-1644), m. Magd. 1593; MP Oxford Univ. 1640-4.
[2] Milne, 60 ('meritorious work'); see also W. D. Macray, Annals of the Bodleian Library (London etc. 1868, 2nd edn Oxford 1890), 483-4.
[3] Sutherland, 'Coin collection of Christ Church', 141.
[4] H. S. Jones, 'The foundation and history of the Camden chair', Oxoniensia viii-ix (1943-4), 182; see also L. S. Sutherland, 'The curriculum'.

The story of Hearne is well known. He became the contemporary stereotype of the futile antiquary, crabbed and credulous and beneath the notice of a gentleman of taste, but in his own epitaph he modestly claimed no more than that he had 'studied and preserved antiquities'. A portrait of Hearne as a historian has been presented with sympathy and perception by David Douglas.[1] He was born in 1678 in White Waltham in Berkshire, son of the literate but impoverished parish clerk; a farmworker until 15, his talent was noticed by a local squire who saw to it that he was educated at Bray school, and thereafter in Oxford at St Edmund Hall. He obtained a position in the Bodleian Library and was underkeeper when in 1715, at the age of 37, he declared himself a nonjuror and refused to take the oaths of allegiance. Dismissed from his post, and debarred access to the library and from all hope of a university post, he retreated to his hall and set up an independent, self-financing, editing and publishing enterprise, which resulted in those 'whole shelves of medieval writers whom he accurately edited with notes and prefaces of his own', making 'properly available to scholars, as the basis of English medieval history, the great chronicles of England'.[2] Some forty such volumes were produced personally by an elaborate system of subscriptions, financial arrangements with printers and binders, proof-reading and eventually distribution, side by side with a voluminous correspondence and virtually daily entries in a combined personal journal and commonplace book which ultimately extended to 145 volumes of manuscript. An Oxford misfit, withdrawn into himself, he had the peasant's hoarding instinct, incurious too often of the real value of this or that scrap of knowledge that might one day be useful, the worth of the bric-à-brac with which he crowded his mind. Thomas Hardy would have understood Hearne. When his antiquarian rather than historical contributions are sought, they reveal a limited and pedantic mind, even though, as Douglas saw, he 'belonged in spirit to the century preceding that in which he died'.[3]

While notes on Roman coins and other finds crop up sporadically in Hearne's manuscript collections throughout the thirty years of their compilation, from 1705 until his death, his main period of interest in non-documentary antiquities seems understandably enough to have been while he was mainly concerned with editing the *Itineraries* of the sixteenth-century antiquary John Leland, published at Oxford in nine volumes from 1709 to 1714, and Leland's *Collectanea*, which appeared in six volumes in 1715. It may not be coincidence that his friend Edward

---

[1] D. C. Douglas, *English Scholars 1660–1730* (London 1939, 2nd edn London 1951), ch. 9; see also [W. Huddesford,] *The Lives of those Eminent Antiquaries John Leland, Thomas Hearne, and Anthony a Wood* (vol i only, Oxford 1772), p. ii.

[2] Douglas, 184, 188.

[3] Ibid. 194.

Lhuyd lived until 1709, and another friend and correspondent, Ralph Thoresby of Leeds, died in 1725, both of them links with the Restoration traditions of antiquarian learning. In 1712 a large and spectacular Roman mosaic pavement was found at Stonesfield, 10 miles north-west of Oxford, and Hearne was directly concerned with having it drawn and published. It was his practice to add to the main texts he printed one or more shorter antiquarian or historical pieces: the second volume of Leland's *Itinerary* (1711) contained four, the historical texts even more, such as the fifteen appended to Robert of Gloucester's chronicle (1724) or the twenty-five to Adam of Domerham (1727). It was not as inconsequent as might appear at first sight, for Hearne could include pieces by or of special interest to his subscribers and so promote sales, and in the absence of any periodical of historical and antiquarian studies ensure prompt publication of minor as well as major documents in his almost annual volumes.

So far as prehistoric antiquities were concerned he was 'intirely of Sir William Dugdale's opinion that the Flints he tells us to be found at Old-bury are British Axes'; it has already been noted that some of these neolithic axe-blades were then in Oxford. 'There have been [many] of them found at other places, and the other Intruments of Flint, as their Arrow and Spear Heads, sufficiently show that they made use of Flint, the way of working in Iron being quite unknown to them.' 'I have seen of their Arrow Heads my self, we having several of them in our Repositories', and he knew of the Scottish legend of their being 'Elf-Arrows', almost certainly from Lhuyd, who recorded this with amusement on his visit to Robert Sibbald in Edinburgh in 1699.[1] But when Thoresby in 1710 sent him an admirable and concise account with sketches of an immediately recognizable grave-assemblage of the middle of the second millennium BC from Broughton-in-Craven, published in the fourth volume of Leland's *Collectanea*, Hearne was less fortunate in his comments. Thoresby thought it Roman, but Hearne began sensibly enough by saying that with neither coins nor an inscription a Roman attribution was improbable and then less happily that the inverted cinerary urn and stone shaft-hole battle-axe bespoke a later, Danish, origin. It was the result of an excellent foreign book unintentionally misleading its English readers, the *Danicorum monumentorum libri sex* (Copenhagen 1643) by the Danish antiquary Ole Worm, where inverted cinerary urns of the local bronze age, and stone battle-axes of the late neolithic, were in fact illustrated and described, as were many other antiquities, such as megalithic tombs, likely to interest English antiquaries. With no concept of a prehistoric perspective many, like Hearne, equated these with the historically documented Danes in England, and so attributed them to this period. And

---

[1] Hearne, *Collections* ii. 146-7; Piggott, *Ruins in a Landscape*, 138-9.

the Latinized name *Wormius* may have been in Pope's mind as much as book-worms when he wrote the *Dunciad* verses.

The Broughton-in-Craven grave-group included a small bronze blade, and bronze (or 'brass') tools and weapons were still an archaeological problem in the eighteenth century, both in function and date. Ethnographic parallels among American Indians existed for stone tools, and the general conceptual model for ancient Britons was one of savagery, with which an accomplished bronze technology would be incompatible. Thoresby in 1709 had written to Hearne about a hoard of late bronze-age socketed axes found in Yorkshire, thinking they were the 'heads of spears or walking staves of the civilised *Britains*'.[1] Hearne argued at length for a Roman origin, as they did not accord with any tool or weapon assigned to the Gauls, ancestors of the Britons, by classical writers; nor were they Danish, for nothing like them was illustrated by Worm; nor Saxon, for they were not shown in the wholly imaginative and anachronistic scenes depicting Hengest and Horsa in Richard Verstegan's *Antiquities* (where one of them incidentally holds a cross-bow).[2] It is hardly an impressive use of sources. On Stonehenge he changed his mind from time to time, originally accepting its attribution to the Romans by Inigo Jones, but later feeling he 'can hardly differ from those who make it to be British'. As for Avebury, however, 'I take it to have been rather Roman'.[3]

The Stonesfield Roman pavement was found in ploughing on 25 January 1712, and Hearne was out there on 2 February, starting his walk at 5 a.m.—'but cannot find that 'tis Roman, but rather modern, perhaps about the time of Edw. I. or later'.[4] He made nine visits in the next six months, constantly changing his mind, until 'upon a more mature Consideration I am perswaded 'twas a Roman Praetorium'.[5] Great interest was aroused in Oxford: Bernard Gardiner went out and made a drawing, as did others; Vanbrugh, then working on Blenheim palace, visited it and carried off a tile. Hearne took out Michael Burghers, the university engraver, to make what appears to have been a very accurate drawing, which he published under the title 'A Discourse concerning the Stuns-field Tessellated Pavement' in the eighth volume of Leland's *Itinerary* (1712) where he considered it to have belonged to 'a considerable *Hall* or *Palace*' built for a Roman general subordinate to the Emperor Theodosius in 367, and spent much time in a rambling discussion of the

---

[1] See S. Briggs, 'Thomas Hearne, Richard Richardson, and the Osmondthick hoard', *The Antiquaries Journal* lviii (1978), 249.

[2] R. Verstegan, *Restitution of Decayed Intelligence in Antiquities* (Amsterdam 1605, London 1673 edn).

[3] Hearne, *Collections* viii. 89–90, x. 187.

[4] M. V. Taylor, 'The Roman tessellated pavement at Stonesfield, Oxon.', *Oxoniensia* vi (1941); Hearne, *Collections* iii. 297.

[5] Taylor, 'Pavement'.

subject-matter of one panel (a figure of Bacchus). John Pointer also published an account in the following year.[1] New pavements were found in 1779–80, but all were destroyed by the end of the century and drawings alone remain as records.

From these it can be seen that the pavements belong to the fourth-century 'Corinian' school of mosaicists, probably by the same craftsmen who worked at Woodchester and elsewhere in the area.[2] Roman tessellated pavements in Britain were recognized antiquities from the seventeenth century onward, and John Aubrey devoted a section to them in his unpublished *Monumenta Britannica*, while Plot in 1677 recorded pavements in Oxfordshire at Great Tew and Steeple Aston. During the eighteenth century a large number was discovered and put on record, often in accurate and beautiful drawings, for example the drawing by Burghers of Stonesfield or those made later in the century of the same site by William Levington, a Woodstock painter. Other drawings were in circulation, and the study of the Roman empire being of international concern, just as inscriptions from Britain had been known to foreign scholars since the sixteenth century, so drawings of the Stonesfield pavement appeared in publications printed in Holland and Venice in 1713 and 1719, as well as in several English versions.

The conceptual framework within which Hearne and his contemporaries saw the Roman province of Britain was essentially a military one. The classical texts related to conquest and military operations, and the epigraphic evidence supplementing them came predominantly from the northern military zone and from those most dramatic military frontier monuments, Hadrian's and the Antonine walls. Plot and many others quoted Suetonius to support the view that tesserae for mosaic pavements were portable military stores 'whereof the *Roman* Generals, amongst their other Baggage, were used to carry a Quantity sufficient to pave the Place, where they set the *Praetorium* or *Generals* Tent'.[3] Hearne wisely perceived that Stonesfield had been no tent, but a substantial building, and correctly interpreted the wall flues by reference to Palladio's *Antiquitates urbis Romae*, published in Oxford in 1709, and saw that the presence of tiles implied a permanent roof. But it had to belong to a general, and the appreciation of the farms and country houses of the civil province of Roman Britain had to wait, though antiquaries such as William Stukeley in the 1720s were interpreting pavements as belonging to 'a villa of some great *Roman*' or saying of another site, 'probably it was a *roman villa*'.[4]

    [1] Pointer, *Roman Pavement at Stunsfield*.
    [2] D. J. Smith, 'The Mosaic Pavements' in A. L. F. Rivet (ed.), *The Roman Villa in Britain* (London 1969).
    [3] R. Plot, *The Natural History of Oxford-shire* (Oxford 1677), ch. 10, p. 54; cf MacGregor, 'Ashmolean Museum', 640.
    [4] W. Stukeley, *Itinerarium curiosum* (London 1724), 79, 107.

Hearne interested himself in Roman finds in and around White Waltham, at Berry Grove or Weycock for instance, and visited the Roman town of Silchester, where in 1714 and again in 1722 at Dorchester-on-Thames he recorded 'crop marks' in the growing corn as evidence of buried structures. But unfortunately at Silchester he accepted Geoffrey of Monmouth and Nennius as credulously as he believed in the legends of the high antiquity of the University of Oxford, and when ridiculing Stukeley's identification of the amphitheatre as such (where Stukeley was correct) did not notice that his plan of the town walls is grotesquely wrong. He once met Stukeley and took a dislike to him, and thought Stukeley's friend Roger Gale 'but a poor, stingy man'.[1] Never a fieldworker, his increasing self-imposed confinement to Oxford removed him from this kind of antiquarianism; and as for the middle ages, for him they began and ended in the documents by the publication of which he made his enduring contribution to English historical studies. As Douglas observed, Hearne 'never became a "Saxonist" either in competence or in appreciation', despite George Hickes, one of the greatest Old English scholars, being a fellow nonjuror. But Hearne did print in 1726 an accurate text of the poem on the battle of Maldon of *circa* 991 from a manuscript which was later destroyed in the Cottonian Library fire of 1731; and his version of Robert of Gloucester, published in 1724, was 'the first workmanlike edition of a Middle-English text'.[2]

In 1719, Hearne recorded, Bodley's Librarian, Joseph Bowles, 'that impudent, saucy, brazen-faced Rascall . . . a most vile wicked wretch . . . a Breaker of his Word, and a whiffling silly, unfaithfull Coxcombe . . . put in one Mr Wise, A.M. of Trin. Coll. (a Pretender to Antiquities)' as sublibrarian following the resignation of John Fletcher, appointed in 1716 when Hearne as a nonjuror was removed from his post.[3] Bowles became the obvious target for Hearne's invective, and in the sensitive circumstances of an appointment to a post of which Hearne believed himself still to be the rightful holder Francis Wise escaped comparatively lightly in being styled 'a Pretender to Antiquities'. Son of an Oxford mercer he was an unashamed place-seeker eager for personal advancement, getting himself elected keeper of the university archives for his lifetime in 1726 and unsuccessfully intriguing first for the post of Bodley's Librarian in 1729 and two years later for that of president of Trinity, when he was outwitted by Huddesford. Undeterred, on the foundation of the Radcliffe Library in 1737 Wise turned to, in his own words, 'the pursuit of an affair, having more interest and profit in it than learning', and continued

---

[1] Hearne, *Collections* ix. 25. Roger Gale (1672-1744), incorporated at Oxford from Trinity Coll. Cambridge in 1699; first vice-president of the Society of Antiquaries.

[2] Douglas, *English Scholars*, 188.

[3] Hearne, *Collections* vii. 81. John Fletcher, m. Queen's 1706.

assiduously to advance his interests for a decade until in 1749 he left the
Bodleian Library to become the first Radcliffe Librarian at £150 a year.
He found himself, it has been remarked, 'the custodian of a magnificent
Library which for some years was little cumbered by books and almost
entirely unencumbered by readers'.[1] He had accepted a living at Elsfield
outside Oxford, where he created a romantic garden full of follies and
eye-catchers (including a druid temple, a Chinese pagoda and an Egyptian pyramid) from which he could at least keep an eye on the dome of
James Gibbs's Camera, completed in 1749. He formed friendships with
Thomas Warton and Samuel Johnson in the mid-1750s and died in 1767
aged 72.

The half-dozen books and pamphlets published by Wise show that he
was hardly more than second rate, but he spanned an age of second-rate
scholarship, and as an Oxford figure sneered at by Hearne in his youth
who in later life helped to arrange Johnson's honorary degree he admirably links one world with another. He was also caught up in an antiquarian dispute not without interest today. His least superficial studies
were in numismatics: his catalogue of 1750 entitled *Nummorum anti-
quorum*, a list of the Bodleian coin collection, has been estimated as
'Wise's main contribution to numismatic knowledge: and it justifies us in
ranking him high among his contemporaries'.[2] His first published work,
an edition of Asser's *Life of Alfred* in 1722, before he obtained his Bodleian post, is condemned rather than commended by modern scholars. It
was based on the Camden edition of 1603 which contained the well
known forged interpolation taking the antiquity of the university back to
Alfred's time, so piously and misguidedly accepted by Hearne. Wise did
draw attention to the fact that the passage did not occur in the oldest
manuscript, burnt in the Cottonian Library fire, but although his text
purported to be collated with the manuscripts, it seems unlikely that he
ever saw the originals.[3] His interest in Anglo-Saxon England centred on
the coinage, and he openly deplored the low state of Saxon scholarship
in the mid-century. While with almost alarming honesty he confessed in
correspondence with Charles Lyttelton,[4] that his own knowledge was
'very superficial' and that he 'was in too great an hurry to study it grammatically', this did not deter him from criticizing George Hickes and
proposing to write a 'Critique upon the Saxon Poetry'.[4] His last two
books are in subject characteristic of the times and in content typical of
the low standards of contemporary speculative antiquarianism: *The
History and Chronology of the Fabulous Ages Considered* (Oxford 1764)

---

[1] S. Gibson, 'Francis Wise, B.D.', *Oxoniensia* i (1936); see also I. G. Philip, 'Libraries and the University Press', above.
[2] Gibson, 183n.
[3] Ibid. 174.
[4] Ibid. 187. Charles Lyttelton (1714-68), m. Univ. 1732; dean of Exeter 1747, bp of Carlisle 1762-8.

preceded by *Some Enquiries concerning the First Inhabitants, Languages, Religion, Learning, and Letters of Europe* (Oxford 1758). The latter adopts many earlier fantasies of origin-myths and folk movements involving Scythia, Cimmerians and the enigmatic Cabiri: the Gothic language was Cimmerian, and Wise repeats with approval the claim of 1738 of David Malcolme to have demonstrated a relationship between the languages of China, the isthmus of Darien and the island of St Kilda.[1] We are a long way from the exacting philological scholarship of Lhuyd or Hickes half a century earlier.

Before 1738 Wise, unexpectedly for a Bodleian sub-librarian then in his forties, undertook a piece of original archaeological field-work on the Berkshire downs apparently prompted by his interest in King Alfred, for its outcome was the publication at Oxford in 1738 of his *Letter to Dr. Mead concerning some Antiquities in Berkshire*, claiming the White Horse of Uffington as commemorative of Alfred's victory on Ashdown in 871. He visited the Horse and the area around, including in his pamphlet descriptions of the semi-artificial Dragon's Hill below the figure and of the neolithic chambered long barrow of Wayland's Smithy to the west; while commenting on the Lambourn Seven Barrows he noted another long barrow there, forgotten until recorded anew in 1935. He also collected for the first time the folklore associated with Dragon's Hill (the slain dragon's blood inhibiting the growth of grass) and Wayland's Smithy (of the invisible smith who shod travellers' horses). We have an unexpected record of his expenses: field-work about £22, two engraved plates £5 each, paper and printing eight hundred copies of fifty-eight pages, small quarto, £20. The plates were in the event dedicated to and so paid for by Lord Craven and Richard Mead, the fashionable London physician and man of taste to whom the essay was addressed.[2]

This mild piece of antiquarianism unexpectedly prompted the publication in London in 1739 of an anonymous and acrimonious rejoinder with a lengthy and vigorous title beginning *The Impertinence and Imposture of Modern Antiquaries Displayed*, by 'Philalethes Rusticus'. Various authors have been suggested at the time and since, but William Asplin, a Trinity man and vicar of Banbury, seems likely to have been mainly responsible.[3] The pamphlet, today partly tedious, partly still entertaining, is clearly motivated by personal spite and political rancour, and in the discursive diatribe Philalethes scorns an Anglo-Saxon date for the White Horse and favours an ancient British origin. In 1741 George North took up the cudgels on Wise's behalf to a certain extent in *An Answer to a Scandalous Libel*, arguing that any British horse would have

---

[1] S. Piggott, *William Stukeley* (Oxford 1950), 34.
[2] Gibson, 178. Richard Mead (1673-1754), hon. MD Oxford 1707.
[3] William Asplin (1687-1758), m. Trin. 1704; degrees St Alban Hall, vice-principal 1710.

been destroyed by the Romans and that, though he could not accept the Alfredian attribution, he nevertheless thought it Saxon. Wise reaffirmed his views in *Further Observations on the White Horse* (Oxford 1742) adding an account of the turf-cut crosses at Bledlow and Whiteleaf on the Chilterns.

The dusty little pamphlet-war might well be ignored and forgotten were it not for the fact that modern archaeological opinion has favoured a pre-Roman iron-age date for the Horse on stylistic grounds which at first sight seem to have been anticipated by Philalethes Rusticus, but which a modern critic has called into question. Wise stated (rather than argued) that 'No one can be ignorant, that the Horse was the Standard which the Saxons used, both before and after their coming hither', quoting Tacitus on the ancient Germans' veneration of white horses, the white colt emblem attributed to Widukind in 785 and, appropriately in George II's reign, the modern arms of Saxony and Brunswick.[1] He did not know that in his unpublished *Monumenta* John Aubrey had noted as possible that the Horse might be 'made by Hengist, who bore one on his arms or standard', still less that he had also considered an alternative British origin.[2] Both Aubrey and Wise are in fact likely to have obtained the idea, direct or at second hand, from Verstegan's *Restitution of Decayed Intelligence in Antiquities*, whose delightful but wholly fanciful illustration showing the arrival of Hengest and Horsa with a flag bearing a white horse is 'a timely reminder', it has been remarked, 'that its author was the first to attribute a badge of a White Horse to the leaders of the Saxons'.[3] Hearne was also deceived by the same illustration, and Wise's case rests on no more than a seventeenth-century invention.

Wise was absurdly at pains to praise the consummate naturalism of the White Horse ('being designed in so masterlike a manner, that it may defy the painter's skill, to give a more exact description of that animal') and his engraved view from above Faringdon indeed shows a very lifelike Hanoverian horse.[4] But whatever his enthusiastic words, the standards of topographical and antiquarian draughtsmanship of his day were almost invariably sketchy and unreliable, and his plate of Wayland's Smithy bears little resemblance to the monument, showing many stones and other features impossible to reconcile with those visible in modern times or recovered in the excavations of the 1960s.

Philalethes ridiculed Wise on the subject of naturalism, and at some length. As to the plump stallion of the engraving: 'he is quite a *light-bodied one*: I may say, for a Horse that has lain so long at Grass, carries no *Body at all*; insomuch that, should he take up Hill, were I upon the Back

---

[1] *Letter to Dr. Mead*, 27; see Gibson, 'Francis Wise', 177.
[2] M. Hunter, *John Aubrey and the World of Learning* (London 1975), 189.
[3] R. Jessup, *Anglo-Saxon Jewellery* (London 1950), 23.
[4] Gibson, 177.

of him, I should be under terrible Apprehensions he would slip thro' his Girth'.[1] There is more to this effect, making the point that Philalethes saw the Horse as lean and linear, and quite unlike Wise's concept. He goes on to abuses of the 'Tory-Priest' and laughs at the collection of folklore as 'wretched, low, Chimney-corner Stuff', much 'fitter for a *Nurse* than a *Doctor*'—an interesting example of a contemporary attitude recalling the satire of Amhurst's *Terrae-Filius* and anticipating the reception given to Warton and others studying the romances and ballads in the 1760s. As to the date of the Horse, Dragon's Hill is a barrow, and Philalethes knows barrows to be British:

Might I therefore put in my Fancy amongst the rest, I should imagine that if the *Horse* were a *Standard* or *Banner*, it was a *British* one ... And this Conjecture would be strengthened also by the *Figure* and *Posture* of the *Horse* in every Circumstance; which are exactly the same with what we may observe upon some *British Coins* in *Speed*.[2]

George North dismissed this, finding no similitude of posture either on the coins in John Speed's *History of Great Britaine* (London 1611 and subsequent editions) or in other originals or illustrations he knew. Wise in his rejoinder took no notice of the coin argument, but reiterated his conviction of an Alfredian origin, attributing to the Saxons as well the chalk-cut crosses on the Chilterns. Aubrey had offered an alternative to his Hengest identification, for he compared the Horse with that on a British coin from Colchester he had seen; and again and independently, William Stukeley's daughter Anna, visiting friends in Berkshire in 1758, wrote to her father that the Uffington figure was 'very much in the scheme of the British horses on the reverse of their coins'.[3]

In a modern archaeological context explicit comparison between the Uffington White Horse and those on early British coins seems first to have been made, without mention of antecedent ideas, at the end of the nineteenth century, when the Uffington Horse was compared with coins on which the horse on the reverse has departed far from the naturalistic prototype on the Macedonian staters which ultimately inspired these coin types in Europe from the second century BC. Such elongated and disjointed representations appear in Britain on, for instance, the 'early uninscribed' series or again those of the Dobuni, and the White Horse has since that time been assigned to a context within the stylistic conventions of early Celtic art.[4] This view of a late pre-Roman iron age date became accepted and re-emphasized in British archaeology, with

---

[1] *Impertinence and Imposture of Modern Antiquaries*, 13.
[2] Ibid. 21, 20, 22.
[3] Piggott, *Ruins in a Landscape*, 168.
[4] M. Marples, *White Horses and other Hill Figures* (London 1949), 28-66; R. P. Mack, *The Coinage of Ancient Britain* (London 1952).

Aubrey, 'Philalethes' and Anna Stukeley commended as having pres-
ciently anticipated modern studies in numismatics and Celtic art. However, it has recently been pointed out in the course of a more
far-reaching argument that whatever may be said of horses on British
coins in general, those quoted by Philalethes as illustrated by Speed
show not the disintegrated and attenuated animal required for the stylistic argument, but the naturalistic reclassicizing types associated with the
normally inscribed coins of the Belgic dynasties of south-eastern
Britain.[1] Furthermore, practically all the published British coins readily
available for comparison in the mid-eighteenth century were of these
same naturalistic types. There are for instance the seventy or so illustrated in Gibson's 1695 edition of Camden (including specimens from
Cotton, Thoresby and Plot as well as Speed) or those scattered in smaller
numbers through many antiquarian publications by such as Obadiah
Walker. Philalethes, and probably Aubrey, were not making true stylistic
comparisons at all, but merely finding alternative ancient equine insignia
in a context other than Saxon, and Anna Stukeley alone might have
known the relevant types from her father's notes. Stylistic analysis of art-
forms as we know it was a concept practically unknown in Wise's day,
more especially in a context other than classical, and outside this limited
canon any barbarian mode, British or Saxon, would not be art at all, and
unacceptable to the man of taste. There have been recent arguments for
a date later than the iron age for the White Horse, and indeed a possible
pagan Saxon origin, but the high antiquity attributed by Wise to the
Bledlow and Whiteleaf crosses has seriously been called in question.

Neither Hearne nor Wise, nor any of their contemporaries, had visual-
ized an antiquarian approach to the middle ages by any means other
than by documents, and to some extent coins. John Aubrey seems to
have been alone in his application of the taxonomic principles first being
explored in the natural sciences to medieval architecture, for which he
had a personal affection and to which he brought a disinterested
approach. In the debate between the ancients and moderns the arts were
usually excepted and protagonists of both sides were united: like Glanvill
they did 'not believe, that the Moderns surpass the Antients in Architecture, Sculpture, Picture, or the Arts of Ingenious Luxury'.[2] Architecture
here is of course that of Greece and Rome, and the Goths were its barbarian destroyers; to the moderns, too, they represented medieval Aristotelianism. The Restoration scholars established the history of the
middle ages as a valid discipline on a majestic scale, but its buildings

[1] D. Woolner, 'The White Horse, Uffington', *Trans. Newbury District Field Club* xi (1965); J. V. S.
Megaw, *Art of the European Iron Age* (Bath 1970), no. 184.

[2] J. Glanvill, *A Praefatory Answer to Mr. Stubbe* (London 1671), 165, cited by Jones, 'Background of
The Battle of the Books', 19. Joseph Glanvill (1636–80), m. Exeter 1652; MA Linc. 1658; prebendary of
Worcester 1678–80.

were under a cloud, unappreciated for their aesthetic qualities and with their formal architectural content wholly misunderstood.

The circumstances of the decline in many branches of learning by about 1730, involving not only the collapse of a great historical tradition but a falling-off of standards in the earth and life sciences, is illustrated in Oxford by the history of the Ashmolean Museum and of the Camden chair. In Anglo-Saxon studies, however, some attention had been paid to antiquities and art, especially when associated with inscriptions.[1] The Alfred jewel was found in 1693 near Athelney and was published in 1698 by William Musgrave and in 1700 by Hickes, on both occasions in the *Philosophical Transactions* of the Royal Society, at that date still concerned with antiquities.[2] In 1711 Hearne included reference to it in a short Latin essay on Alfred's use of the word *aestel*, glossed as a pointer. In 1698 Musgrave commented appreciatively on the jewel's workmanship—'the Work very fine; so as to make some Men question its true Age: But in all probability it did belong to that great King'—whereas Wise in 1738 could only see 'to how low a level the art of drawing was sunk at that time; as appears from the works of the best masters, the Saxon coins, and the jewel of King Alfred, described by Dr Hickes and others, and now preserved in the Museum at Oxford'.[3]

In 1705 Hickes contributed an appendix to Andrew Fountaine's *Numismata anglo-saxonica et anglo-danica breviter illustrata* on a remarkable silver disc-brooch with inscriptions in Old English and Runic, found with coins of William the Conqueror and other treasure at Sutton in the Isle of Ely in 1694. The account and full-size engraving were available to be published with Hickes's *Thesaurus*.[4] The drawing also appeared in the second edition of Gibson's Camden in 1722. The brooch disappeared until 1950 when it was brought to the British Museum without a provenance, and can now be seen to date from about 1025 to 1050 and to be the latest and largest of a series of such late Saxon pieces, and the only one ornamented in Viking style. 'Study of the original shows that Hickes's engravings were exactly full-scale and of an extremely high degree of accuracy.'[5] Fountaine was a virtuoso interested in early English coins, which also interested Thoresby, Archbishop Wake and Wise. In an age dominated by a single aesthetic canon, that of Greece and Rome, alternatives were impossible to accept. All else was barbarous; there was no

---

[1] See D. Fairer, 'Anglo-Saxon studies' below.

[2] See J. R. Clarke and D. A. Hinton, *The Alfred and Minster Lovell Jewels* (Oxford, 1971); and MacGregor, 'Ashmolean Museum', 649.   [3] Wise, *Letter to Dr. Mead*, 25.

[4] G. Hickes *et al. Linguarum veterum septentrionalium thesaurus grammatico-criticus et archaeologicus* (2 vols Oxford 1703–5). On the *Thesaurus* see Douglas, *English Scholars*, ch. 4, esp. 88 and n. 5; H. G. Carter, *A History of the Oxford University Press* i (Oxford 1975), 261, 446; and D. Fairer, 'Anglo-Saxon Studies', pp. 816–19 below.

[5] R. L. S. Bruce-Mitford, 'Late Saxon disc-brooches' in D. B. Harden (ed.), *Dark-Age Britain* (London 1956).

other art. In such a climate of thought there was clearly no place for the art and architecture of the post-Roman middle ages, even at a later stage than that of the Alfred jewel.

The whole subject of the middle ages was entangled in a web of prejudice and misunderstanding. The emotive overtones of the word 'Gothic' could not be evaded; the Goths were the barbarian northern nations, derived, it was widely thought, from those other irredeemably savage peoples of antiquity, the Cimmerians and Scythians. That their architecture was non-Roman precluded it from being civilized and so worthy of study; the barbarians were inchoate and therefore their buildings must be inchoate and devoid of system; the Goths were the destroyers of order and so order was impossible in their products. These, moreover, were not only aesthetically unacceptable but religiously and politically suspect; the outcome of monkish superstition and feudal tyranny. Aubrey, in his investigation into the sequence of medieval building styles, had avoided these difficulties because they did not appear to him as such; he had an unashamedly sentimental love for the medieval past as he saw it, was indifferent to any religious or political emotions it might evoke and was unconcerned by questions of aesthetic judgement. To him old buildings could be classified just as plants and fossils, stone circles and barrows, and with the added advantage that by using written records of their date of construction their distinctive architectural features ('the windows the most remarkqueable') could be arranged chronologically, and such a sequence could then be extended to undocumented buildings ('hence one may give a guess about what Time the Building was').[1] But Aubrey's ideas were never published, and when the sequence of English medieval building styles was first put into published form in Oxford in the 1760s it appeared to be something completely new and came from a remarkable character, Thomas Warton.[2]

Brought up in an academic and scholastic household, Warton was basically a classicist, and had been increasingly concerned with the historical study of English literature. It was as an incidental by-product of these studies that he produced his remarkable contribution to the understanding of medieval architecture and its historical sequence. In 1802 Richard Mant, his biographer, recorded that Warton 'always committed to journals, kept for the purpose, his remarks on the different Saxon and Gothic buildings which he visited' and that he intended communicating a history of ecclesiastical architecture in England to the Society of Antiquaries (to which he was elected in 1771).[3] In his *History*

[1] H. M. Colvin, 'Aubrey's *chronologia architectonica*' in J. Summerson (ed.), *Concerning Architecture* (London 1968); Hunter, *Aubrey*, 162.

[2] *The Poetical Works of the late Thomas Warton, B.D.* ed. R. Mant (2 vols Oxford 1802); A. Johnston, *Enchanted Ground* (London 1964); J. Pittock, *The Ascendancy of Taste* (London 1973).

[3] *Poetical Works of Warton*, ed. Mant i, p. xxxi.

of English Poetry he twice mentioned his intention to publish a history of gothic architecture with 'Observations, Critical and Historical, on Castles, Churches, Monasteries and other Monuments of Antiquity'—the precise title of his surviving notebooks now in Winchester College library.[1]

The notebooks, mainly dating from around 1759 to 1760, do not appear to show any surprising insights and are comparable with what became common form in the many journals of antiquarian tourists in the later eighteenth century. They include records of not only obvious medieval buildings (Gloucester and Llandaff cathedrals, St Albans abbey and St Nicholas, Abingdon, for instance) but of sites associated with the early romances such as Tintagel, Roman towns such as Caerwent, or, in a later notebook, a Roman road near Horsham. Warton was looking at antiquities at first hand, and though he may not have seen all the buildings he mentions in the *Faerie Queene*, these total nearly twenty, from Canterbury and Rochester cathedrals to those of Salisbury and Exeter, and from Lincoln cathedral to King's College, Cambridge. They are chosen, as Aubrey chose his architectural details, because they exemplified styles dated by documentary evidence. 'The beginning and progressive state of architecture' was Warton's concern; his idea of a history of English poetry implies that he felt strongly that the middle ages had a coherent sequence in language and literature as well as in its dynastic and constitutional history, just as Percy hoped that the poems he published would 'shew the gradation of our language, exhibit the progress of popular opinions'.[2] Palaeographers such as Humfrey Wanley and others had shown how the sequence of styles of handwriting could establish a chronology of manuscripts, though it seems to have been left to Joseph Strutt to set out the first short but comprehensive account of the sequence of medieval art as illustrated by manuscript illumination from the Lindisfarne Gospels onwards.[3] The middle ages were now being seen as dynamic rather than static, though understanding of the language had to wait longer: Anglo-Norman was not distinguished from French, and after Anglo-Saxon all was seen as ruin and confusion until the emergence of modern English, and 'Semi-Saxon' was the only phrase to hand. The term 'Middle English' seems first to have been used by the German philologists, for example, Jacob Grimm in the 1820s, while 'Old English' rather than 'Anglo-Saxon' is hardly to be found before Henry Sweet in the 1870s.[4]

[1] T. Warton, *The History of English Poetry* (3 vols London 1774-81).

[2] T. Warton, *Observations on the Faerie Queene of Spenser* (London 1754, 2nd edn 2 vols London 1762) IV. x. 6; T. Percy, *Reliques of Ancient English Poetry* (2 vols London 1765) i, p. ix.

[3] J. Strutt, *A Complete View of the Dress and Habits of the People of England* (2 vols London 1774-6). See J. D. Macmillan's review of D. V. Erdman, *The Illuminated Blake* (London and Oxford 1975), *Apollo* (Aug. 1976), 142-3.   [4] Henry Sweet (1845-1912), m. Balliol 1869.

The Normans, said Warton, 'introduced arts and civility' to England, including the architecture which 'has been named the *Saxon Stile*, being the national architecture of our Saxon ancestors, before the Conquest: for the Normans only extended its proportions and enlarged its scale'.[1] The nomenclature is confusing, but his half-dozen examples seem, by using such sources as William of Malmesbury for instance, to date the south transept of Winchester cathedral to the later eleventh and Christ Church, Oxford, to the end of the twelfth century. 'The style which succeeded to this', he went on, 'was not the absolute *Gothic*, or *Gothic* simply so called, but a sort of *Gothic Saxon*, in which the pure *Saxon* began to receive some tincture of the *Saracen* fashion', with clustered shafts and pointed windows 'much in the shape of a lancet' (this well-known simile may have arisen with Warton). There was much speculation on the origins of gothic in the late eighteenth century (sixty-six theories have been listed) and a derivation from the Saracens through the crusades was much favoured, a source to which Warton and others also looked for the marvellous and magical elements in the romances. Architecturally, Warton placed the beginning of this style around 1200, as in the cathedrals of Lincoln and Rochester; Salisbury (consecrated 1258) he regarded as more advanced, though it did not have the 'ramified window' which he saw as distinguishing, after about 1300, 'Absolute Gothic' from its predecessor 'Saxon Gothic'. With window-tracery came elaborated capitals and increased ornament, and Warton moved on to William of Wykeham and quotations from Langland and Chaucer. By the beginning of the fifteenth century he discerned the phase of 'Ornamental Gothic', running on through the Divinity School at Oxford and culminating in King's College chapel, Cambridge, to be followed by the final phase of 'Florid Gothic' as in St George's chapel, Windsor. The last buildings mentioned were Hampton Court and Nonsuch palace.

Apart from the odd nomenclature of the earlier periods it was not too bad a scheme, and something completely new to the reader of 1762. In addition to the documentary sources, Warton drew attention to the dated architectural sequence evinced by the changing details of the aedicular setting of the monarch on successive great seals from Henry III, and added notes on the relationship of stained glass to tracery, the use of statuary and of towers and spires. Elsewhere in the *Observations* he commented on ceilings, tapestry and other wall-decorations. He apologizes for his inadequacies: 'the hasty remarks are submitted to the candour of the curious, by One, who besides other defects which render him disqualified for such a disquisition, is but little acquainted with the terms and principles of architecture.'[2] But whatever the faults and inaccuracies of his scheme, he had been further than his contemporaries and had

[1] Warton, *Faerie Queene* IV. x. 6. [2] Ibid. VII. vii.10.

found intuitively a way to bring order into buildings which they, steeped in the classical tradition, found hard to understand or in which, like Batty Langley in 1742, they could only seek for rules and orders from a Vitruvian standpoint. It was not until 1817 that the architect Thomas Rickman published the classification that was to endure through the nineteenth century and beyond and gave us the 'early English', 'perpendicular', and 'decorated' of the guidebooks. But to Warton must go the credit of the pioneer. There is truth as well as humour in his remark that 'taste and imagination make more antiquaries than the world is willing to allow'.[1]

By the 1760s misunderstood gothic, as a decorative style rather than a part of medieval archaeology, had of course found firm favour. This new world of antiquarianism had its origins in the same changes in thought and mood that had led Warton, like Percy, Hurd and others, to find intellectual satisfaction and aesthetic enjoyment in the early ballads and romances; a new sensibility that found pleasure in landscape and, increasingly, mountains; a new appreciation of rocks and ruins. All this required a vocabulary in which above all words like romantic and picturesque were found indispensable, and was concerned with that complex mood summed up as the Romantic movement. Enjoyment and exploitation of this mood were made possible by improvements in roads and transport in the later decades of the century, and the 'tour' in search of the picturesque and ruinous could be enjoyed by increasing numbers of the public either directly on horseback or by coach, or vicariously in the illustrated publications which often utilized novel printing techniques such as aquatint. Taste and imagination could now make at least amateur antiquaries out of many. But side by side with this aesthetic experience the later eighteenth century also saw a return to better standards, lost in the generations between about 1720 and 1770, once again concerned with local and topographical studies, themselves bound up with the new facilities for travel and the tours themselves. This phase of antiquarianism can be glimpsed not so much within the university as peripherally in persons with Oxford origins and affiliations.

Just such a person was Browne Willis, the squire of Whaddon Hall. Hearne, a highly critical friend, thought little of his works on English and Welsh cathedrals: 'a poor Writer of History and Antiquities, unless he get somebody to do it for him, at least to cook and adjust his Papers'.[2] Unfortunately Hearne's criticism was justified.

Another Warton connection was Gilbert White, who had been educated by Thomas Warton the elder at his Basingstoke school. White is hardly thought of as an antiquary today, but his famous book *The Natural*

[1] Ibid.
[2] Hearne, *Collections* ix. 42. On Willis see J. G. Jenkins, *The Dragon of Whaddon* (High Wycombe 1953).

History and Antiquities of Selborne (London 1789) has 220 pages on antiquities, exclusive of 36 of medieval documents, out of a total of 468. White's approach was very much that of the earlier topographers such as Plot, and it is hard to see whether this was conscious or not, but it also looked forward to what at the end of the century was to become a revival of sound historical and antiquarian studies on a parish or county level (in 1782 the young Warton had produced his *History of Kiddington* 'as a specimen of a parochial History of Oxfordshire').[1]

White's book was cast in the form of letters to two correspondents, Daines Barrington and Thomas Pennant. The former, who was said to have persuaded White to publish, was a lawyer and antiquary who had produced an edition of Alfred's *Orosius* in 1773; the latter a Welsh country gentleman from Flintshire whose first interest was natural history. Pennant's zoological books of 1766 and 1781 long remained standard works and his published *Tours* in Wales and Snowdonia (1778 and 1781) and in Scotland and the Hebrides (1769, 1774) in which antiquities and romantic landscape were combined were at once the outcome of the new enthusiasm for ruins and rude nature and an important contribution to the popularity of this mood. In 1758 he presented collections of minerals and antiquities to the Ashmolean Museum.

There were of course others such as William Borlase, whose *Antiquities of the County of Cornwall* constitutes a valuable record of antiquities, even though a large number of natural rock features are included with these and all are interpreted in druidic terms.[2]

There were parsons up and down the country who had been at Oxford and had an amateur interest in antiquities, writing if not always publishing their observations. But the amateur studies of an earlier age were now beginning to tighten their disciplines. New students of natural history had by the early nineteenth century 'turned that genial pursuit into the sciences of geology, biology, palaeontology, zoology' and others. Geology in particular had become commercially acceptable: 'it has also its cash value' as Hugh Miller observed.[3] As with the sciences, so medieval architectural history was soon to emerge from the religious movements of the early nineteenth century, if more in Cambridge than in Oxford. Archaeology was adopting Richard Colt Hoare's proud phrase, 'we speak from facts, not theory'.[4] 'When archaeology is made part of the system of Education in Oxford, as I trust it will be ... any educated man will feel it a disgrace to be ignorant of it', said J. H. Parker, lecturing as

[1] *Poetical Works of Warton*, ed. Mant i, p. lxxviii.
[2] W. Borlase, *Observations on the Antiquities, Historical and Monumental of the County of Cornwall* (Oxford 1754, 2nd edn London 1769).
[3] Quoted by Piggott, *Ruins in a Landscape*, 173.
[4] R. C. Hoare, *The Ancient History of Wiltshire* (2 vols London 1812) i. 7.

keeper of the Ashmolean Museum in 1870.[1] But none had felt this for a century before he spoke and hardly any were to feel it for many decades to come.

---

[1] J. H. Parker, 'The Ashmolean Museum: its history, present state, and prospects' (1870) quoted by G. Daniel, *The Origins and Growth of Archaeology* (Harmondsworth 1967), 141.

28

Oxford and the Literary World

DAVID FAIRER

OXFORD has often felt uneasy, even guilty, about its relationship with the outside world; and for its literary men during the eighteenth century this uneasiness, whether atoned for by service to truth and society, or defied by waggery and romance, was a major preoccupation. Seen through the eyes of a modern literary historian this relationship is a fascinating exemplar of the wider eighteenth-century debate about the function of literature in general. The shift from Addisonian poise and responsibility towards the nostalgic delights of Warton and his followers is not merely a shift in Oxford's relationship with the 'world',[1] but part of the wider movement from Augustan to Romantic. To the literary world of the eighteenth century Oxford represented primarily two things: the past and the fancy, each in its own way unconnected with the world—one in the realm of dead facts and customs, the other in the equally remote realm of the imagination. The literary trends of the period were drawing inevitably towards both, so that by the end of the century Oxford had grown more confident in the claims of what it represented. The increased political respectability of the university during the last three decades thus appears to be paralleled by the establishment of Oxford's twin image at the heart of the nation's literary consciousness.

The stereotype is Alexander Pope's description of his stay in Oxford during September 1717. He describes his journey to the city as a dream-voyage haunted by things unseen, and he continues:

All this was no ill preparation to the life I have led since; among those old walls, venerable Galleries, Stone Portico's, studious walks and solitary Scenes of the University. I wanted nothing but a black Gown and a Salary, to be as meer a Bookworm as any there. I conform'd myself to the College hours, was rolld up in books and wrapt in meditation, lay in one of the most ancient, dusky parts of the University, and was as dead to the world as any Hermite of the desart . . . I found my self receivd with a sort of respect, which this idle part

---

[1] 'Human society considered in relation to its activities, difficulties, temptations, and the like ... the occupations and interests of society at large': *OED* under *world* (17).

of mankind, the Learned, pay to their own Species; who are as considerable here, as the Busy the Gay and the Ambitious are in your World.[1]

Pope is playing around in literary fashion with the image of an Oxford totally removed from the normal world; it is the equivalent of the world of the poet's own fancy, to which he has temporarily succumbed. It is delightful and romantic, but the tone of urbane amusement betrays an awareness that the claims of reality must eventually prevail.

Pope (disqualified by his Catholicism from formal study at either university) came to Oxford as the new literary giant of his day. Three months previously had seen the publication, both in quarto and magnificent folio, of his *Works* (1717),[2] and though still in his twenties he came to a university eager to do him honour. He had made his name there two years before with the first volume of his translation of Homer (*Iliad* I–IV). On that occasion Oxford itself had a rival candidate for the laurels in Thomas Tickell who had thrown down the gauntlet before Pope by issuing simultaneously his own version of *Iliad* I. Tickell's translation was backed by the great Joseph Addison, but Oxford declared for Pope. Edward Young ruefully reported to Tickell: 'To be very plain, the University almost in General gives the preference to Popes Translation; they say his is written with more Spirit, Ornament, and Freedom and has more the Air of an Original'.[3] There was nothing parochial in this judgement and no sense on the part of the university that Pope was an outsider. Indeed the admiration of the Oxford establishment was to be confirmed in 1741, when the university made moves to award him, along with the critic and divine William Warburton, an honorary degree as a formal mark of its favour; but Pope's colours had been firmly nailed to his friend's mast, and when the university began to hesitate about Warburton's degree Pope took these scruples as a personal affront. 'I will be

---

[1] Pope–Teresa and Martha Blount, [Sept. 1717,] *The Correspondence of Alexander Pope*, ed. G. Sherburn (5 vols Oxford 1956) i. 430. The gothic other-worldliness of Oxford is suggested by Horace Walpole: 'the moon rose as I was wandering among the colleges, and gave me a charming venerable Gothic scene, which was not lessened by the monkish appearance of the old fellows stealing to their pleasures.' H. Walpole–R. Bentley, Sept. 1753, *Horace Walpole's Correspondence*, ed. W. S. Lewis *et al.* (48 vols New Haven, London and Oxford 1937-83) xxxv. 147. Some seventy years later William Hazlitt brought the idea to its romantic climax: 'Let him then who is fond of indulging in a dreamlike existence go to Oxford and stay there; let him study this magnificent spectacle, the same under all aspects, with its mental twilight tempering the glare of noon, or mellowing the silver moonlight ... but let him not ... speak a word to any of the privileged inhabitants; for if he does, the spell will be broken, the poetry and the religion gone, and the palace of enchantment will melt from his embrace into thin air!' *Sketches of the Principal Picture Galleries in England* (1824) in *The Complete Works of William Hazlitt*, ed. P. P. Howe (21 vols London 1930-3) x. 70.

[2] *The Works of Mr. Alexander Pope* (London 1717).

[3] Young–Tickell, 28 June 1715, *The Correspondence of Edward Young 1683-1765*, ed. H. Pettit (Oxford 1971), 5. Thomas Tickell (1686-1740), m. Queen's 1701, fellow 1709. Joseph Addison (1672-1719), m. Queen's; demy Magd. 1689, fellow 1697-1711. Edward Young (1683-1765), m. New College 1702; migrated CCC 1704; fellow All Souls 1706; chaplain to George II; author of *Night Thoughts* (London 1742-5).

Doctor'd with you, or not at all', he told Warburton; and so Oxford's move to claim Pope as its own came to nothing.[1]

The civilized and generous view of Pope taken by the university establishment was not shared by the antiquary Thomas Hearne, to whom Pope was 'a very ill-natured man, and covetous and excessively proud'[2]— an understandable reaction from Oxford's most notable representative in *The Dunciad*. In a context in which a work's 'solidity' is a mark of its impenetrable dullness, Hearne's solid achievements make him an ideal dunce ('Wormius'), to be approached warily, with mocking Spenserian jargon:

> But who is he, in closet close y-pent,
> With visage from his shelves with dust besprent?
> Right well mine eyes arede that myster wight,
> That wonnes in haulkes and hernes, and *H*— he hight.[3]

Oxford has again provided Pope with an image, here of a remote curiosity digging around in the rubbish of the past, cut off from society, losing sight of true human values in an indiscriminate fascination with the past.

This indictment of irrelevance, however quaint and beautiful its image, haunted the conscience of Oxford's literary men. It was partly in response to this that the university made so much of its great representative in the 'world', Joseph Addison, who for it was the ideal example of how the allurements of the cloister could give way before the nobler responsibilities of the state. Polite letters were at this time a means of courting the world, and Addison's literary career between 1687 and 1705 is a model of how a rising poetical star could be welcomed into the political firmament. Addison came up to Queen's at a time when a young man's literary accomplishments provided easy access to the great, and by a stroke of good fortune William Lancaster, then a fellow of Queen's, was eager to encourage literary talent, and he admired one of the young undergraduate's poems, 'Tityrus et Mopsus'. Addison had been at Queen's for about two years 'when the accidental sight of a paper of his verses, in the hands of Dr *Lancaster*... occasioned his being elected into *Magdalen* college'.[4] As a demy of Magdalen his talents were cultivated by his tutor, and his Oxford reputation soared with various English and Latin poems: *A Poem to His Majesty* (1695) was presented to Lord Keeper Somers; *Pax Gulielmi*, on the peace of Ryswick (1697), was dedicated to another powerful patron, Charles Montagu, first earl of

---

[1] Pope-Warburton, 12 Aug. [1741], *Correspondence of Pope*, ed. Sherburn iv. 357.
[2] Hearne, *Collections* x. 158 (18 July 1729).
[3] A. Pope, *The Dunciad* (Dublin, 1728) bk III, lines 177–80.
[4] *The Works of the Right Honourable Joseph Addison* [ed. T. Tickell] (4 vols London 1721) i, p. v.

Halifax.[1] Such a combination of literary skill, well directed flattery and a distinctive social charm had the desired results. Addison was subsidized to travel abroad for five years, taking with him copies of the Oxford volume *Musarum anglicanarum analecta* (1699) containing eight of his best Latin poems to distribute to the great as a badge of his intellectual accomplishment. In Oxford Hearne and his scholarly friends were not to be won over by Augustan urbanity; to him Addison's *Remarks on Italy* (published in London on his return in 1705) were 'very trite . . . tho' it must be acknowledg'd, that the Book is written in a clean stile, and for that reason will please Novices, and superficial Readers'.[2] If the world could laugh at the isolation of Oxford scholars, they in turn regarded the productions of the world as trite and superficial. At the government's request Addison celebrated the victory of Blenheim in *The Campaign* (London 1704), a poem praised by Dr Johnson for the experience of the world that it contained, but the stiff, portentous couplets have not fulfilled Voltaire's prediction that they would be a monument more lasting than Blenheim Palace.[3]

Although Addison held his Magdalen fellowship until 1711 he ceased to reside after 1699 and returned from the continent to begin a career of service to the nation, culminating in his appointment as secretary of state (1717-18). Addison was always aware that he had escaped the cloister; his norm was social, Augustan. In 1711 he remarked in the *Spectator*: 'I shall be ambitious to have it said of me, that I have brought Philosophy out of Closets and Libraries, Schools and Colleges, to dwell in Clubs and Assemblies, at Tea-Tables, and in Coffee-Houses.' For Addison this was a triumph over those who remained in Oxford to pore over dusty books. In 1714 he could not resist poking fun at his university by including a fictitious letter from two dons, asking Mr Spectator for a copy of the magazine for deposit 'near an old Manuscript of *Tully*'s Orations, among the Archives of the University'—obviously with the vicious intention of removing philosophy from the coffee-house back into the closet. In 1711 Addison's friend and collaborator Richard Steele had made a similar jibe with his satire on the 'Hebdomadal Meeting' club. The minutes are headed '*Four a Clock in the Morning*', and there is some consternation because news from the outside world of politics has broken into their sociable cocoon:

[1] The orator at the funeral of Addison's tutor James Fayrer described 'his being a means of discovering Mr Addisons Genius and Improving it by Exercises Imposed on Him': Young-Tickell, 1 Mar. 1720, *Correspondence of Young*, ed. Pettit, p. 21. John Somers (1651-1716), 1st bn; m. Trin. 1667; lord keeper 1693; lord high chancellor 1697-1700.

[2] Hearne, *Collections* i. 105 (28 Nov. 1705).

[3] 'His poem is the work of a man not blinded by the dust of learning: his images are not borrowed merely from books.' S. Johnson, *The Lives of the English Poets* (1779-81), ed. G. B. Hill (3 vols Oxford 1905) ii. 129. F. M. A. de Voltaire, *Le Siècle de Louis XIV* (2 vols Berlin 1751), ch. 19.

... some Letters from other People, who had talk'd with some who had it from those who should know, giving some Countenance to it, the Chairman reported from the Committee ... That 'twas Possible, there might be something in't ...

Such were the kinds of satirical thrust that Oxford had to endure even before 1714, when the university began its long period of isolation from the political establishment.[1]

It was chiefly as an idealistic gesture for the times that Addison took up a literary project which had germinated during his early Oxford days. The heroic tragedy *Cato* opened in April 1713 as a great popular success. Its patriot-hero spoke for the times, and for much of the century was to speak for Oxford too:

> The soul, secured in her existence, smiles
> At the drawn dagger, and defies its point.
> The stars shall fade away, the sun himself
> Grow dim with age, and nature sink in years,
> But thou shalt flourish in immortal youth,
> Unhurt amidst the war of elements,
> The wrecks of matter, and the crush of worlds.[2]

Cato's soul might have been Oxford herself. In the following decades this suicidal hero was used to proclaim Oxford's determination to maintain its independence. (Luckily, perhaps, Addison did not live to see the ironic outcome of his appeal to patriotism and virtue.) The play's popularity was immediate, and Pope reported from town soon after the first performance:

of all the world none have been in so peculiar a manner enamoured with *Cato*, as a young gentleman of Oxford, who makes it the sole guide of all his actions, and subject of all his discourse; he dates everything from the first or third night, &c., of *Cato*.[3]

This enthusiasm was soon caught in Oxford. The players brought *Cato* to the city that summer, and Colley Cibber reported how their high expectations were fulfilled, at the same time giving an interesting view of the university's conservative theatrical tastes at this time:

A great deal of that false, flashy Wit, and forc'd Humour, which had been the Delight of our Metropolitan Multitude, was only rated there at its bare, intrinsick Value ... *Shakespear* and *Johnson* had, there, a sort of classical Authority; for whose masterly Scenes they seem'd to have as implicit a Reverence, as formerly, for the Ethicks of *Aristotle*; and were as incapable of allowing Moderns

---

[1] *The Spectator* nos. 10 (12 Mar. 1711), 560 (28 June 1714), 43 (19 Apr. 1711). Richard Steele (1672-1729), m. Ch.Ch. 1690; postmaster Merton 1691-4; knighted 1715.

[2] J. Addison, *Cato* (London 1713) V. i. 25-31.

[3] Pope-Caryll, 30 Apr. 1713, *Correspondence of Pope*, ed. Sherburn i. 175.

to be their Competitors, as of changing their Academical Habits for gaudy Colours, or Embroidery . . . The only distinguish'd Merit, allow'd to any modern Writer, was to the Author of *Cato*.[1]

Cibber admired the way Oxford had resisted the more flippant tastes of the capital. Addison himself had been established in his native university as a classic; an influential section of Oxford respected him and valued the gesture that he had made on her behalf. But Addison did not return this admiration. After 1714 he saw that Oxford's isolation was becoming increasingly political in character, and after 1715 Jacobitism could not be regarded as harmless nostalgia. His potent message to the university at this time was number 33 of his periodical *The Freeholder* (13 April 1716). It is a superb example of the regal ticking-off, embodying the very qualities of dignity and self-command that it recommends:

When Men of Learning are acted thus by a Knowledge of the World as well as of Books, and shew that their Studies naturally inspire them with a Love to their King and Country; they give a Reputation to Literature, and convince the World of its Usefulness. But when Arts and Sciences are so perverted as to dispose Men to act in Contradiction to the rest of the Community, and to set up for a kind of separate Republick among themselves, they draw upon them the Indignation of the Wise, and the Contempt of the Ignorant.

If Addison felt himself in aloof estrangement from his university, that does not mean that he was without disciples. Just as he had been helped towards a career through his Oxford verse-writing, so other poetically minded students, ambitious for patronage from the outside world, paid court to him. One of these was Thomas Tickell, his close friend and obviously from the same mould.[2] Tickell attracted attention in 1709 with some verses on Addison's *Rosamond* (an unsuccessful opera), but his major literary work was *The Prospect of Peace* (1712), an ambitious poem in anticipation of the peace of Utrecht, generously puffed in the *Spectator*.[3] It was he also who wrote the prologue when *Cato* was performed in Oxford. Through such literary gestures he and Addison became friends, and when his patron became secretary of state he made Tickell his under-secretary. At this Tickell proudly exclaimed:

[1] *An Apology for the Life of Colley Cibber*, ed. B. R. S. Fone (Ann Arbor 1968), 254-5. The players made only two visits to Oxford (1703 and 1713) before the 1737 licensing act prohibited acting within 5 miles of the city. They were not to return until 1799: see S. Rosenfeld, 'Some notes on the players in Oxford 1661-1713', *Review of English Studies* xix (1943). See also F. S. Boas, *Shakespeare and the Universities* (Oxford 1923), 36: 'with powerful sections of the University keeping up the traditional hostility to professional actors, and with the patronage of the City authorities withdrawn, is it wonderful that the theatre at Oxford in the eighteenth century sank into the lowest depths?'
[2] Johnson characterized Tickell as 'not one of those scholars who wear away their lives in closets': *Lives of the English Poets*, ed. Hill ii. 304.
[3] 'A Poem . . . which, I hope, will meet with such a Reward from its Patrons, as so noble a Performance deserves': *Spectator* no. 523 (30 Oct. 1712).

> Far other Labours now demand my Time
> Who from the Cock-pit ever writ in Rhyme?
> Here while my Mind more useful Paths pursues,
> No Gods I call on, and invoke no Muse[1]

Obviously he had gleefully left behind both the closet and the poetic fancy.

Tickell's closest Oxford friend was Edward Young, whose career at this time neatly paralleled his own: Young similarly addressed Addison in verse, celebrated *Cato* and wrote an ambitious poem on the peace of Utrecht; once more like his friend he became one of Addison's secretaries, and at Button's coffee-house in London both men sat at Addison's feet; in 1719 both wrote poems on his death.[2] In these early years by such networks of patronage young Oxford men might still hope for public office, and their poetry sat easily with such ambitions. John Wallis, a member of Addison's own college, Magdalen, and a young man with a considerable reputation for his English poetry, summed up the situation in a letter to a friend:

Since the publishing of the Musae Anglicanae and the English Miscellanies Poetry is grown so much the Humour of the University that a young Man can't pretend to a character without some handsome Performance in this kind, nor will any Thing better recommend a Person who intends to appear at an Election.[3]

Addison's achievements reflected considerable glory on his two colleges, Queen's and Magdalen. The reputation of a society could be boosted by such a literary figurehead or by the activities of a small group of poetical friends within it, and heads of houses recognized the value of encouraging young men with literary talent. William Lancaster of Queen's was hailed without embarrassment by Tickell as 'patron of our song'; at Magdalen John Hough was anxious to encourage literary talent; Richard Newton was another enlightened spirit who saw the value of English verse composition; Arthur Charlett of University College was regarded as a patron of letters who at first 'laboured with a fair measure of success to improve the literary reputation of the College'; Christ

---

[1] R. E. Tickell, *Thomas Tickell and the Eighteenth Century Poets* (London 1931), 61.

[2] Joseph Spence wrote that Tickell and Young 'were so intimately acquainted at Oxford that each used to communicate to the other whatever verses they wrote, even to the least things': J. Spence, *Observations, Anecdotes, and Characters of Books and Men*, ed. J. M. Osborn (Oxford 1966), 69. Young wrote poems *On the Late Queen's Death, and His Majesty's Accession* (addressed to Addison; London 1714), 'To Mr Addison on the Tragedy of Cato' (published with the play, 1713) and on the peace of Utrecht, his *Epistle to ... Lord Lansdown* (London 1713). Tickell's noble elegy 'To the Right Honourable the Earl of Warwick' was prefixed to his edition of Addison's *Works* (1721) which he undertook as literary executor. Young's poem was *A Letter to Mr Tickell, Occasioned by the Death of ... Joseph Addison* (London 1719).

[3] J. Wallis-J. Postlethwayt, July 1695, *The Oxford Magazine* xxix (3 Nov. 1910), 43-4.

Church could boast the accomplished George Smalridge, another of Addison's intimates and the 'Favonius' of *Tatler*s numbers 72 and 114.[1]

Under the rule of such men literary friendships might flourish. At Magdalen Addison had two close friends in Thomas Yalden and Henry Sacheverell. Yalden, author of the 'Hymn to Darkness' admired by Dr Johnson, gained the favour of President Hough by his skill in composition and was elected fellow of Magdalen in 1698, the year after Addison.[2] Sacheverell wrote verses in Latin and English and translations from the *Georgics*. Johnson also admired the work of two poetical friends at Christ Church: John Philips, who achieved fame with his Miltonic parody *The Splendid Shilling* (London 1701), *Blenheim* (London 1705) the tory counterpart of Addison's poem, and *Cyder* (London 1708) 'an imitation of Virgil's *Georgick*, which needed not shun the presence of the original';   . and Edmund Smith (later Neale) who wrote *Phaedra and Hippolitus* in imitation of Racine and elegized Philips in a poem 'which justice must place among the best elegies which our language can shew'.[3]

Another group of friends raised the literary reputation of Pembroke in the 1730s: Richard Graves, Anthony Whistler and William Shenstone, known to themselves as 'the triumvirate'. As undergraduates they held regular literary debates 'almost every evening, at each other's chambers the whole summer; where we read plays and poetry, Spectators or Tatlers, and other works of easy digestion'.[4] One of their favourite topics was Pope's *The Rape of the Lock*, of which Whistler wrote an imitation, 'The Shuttle-cock'.[5] Graves eventually gained fame as a novelist with *The Spiritual Quixote* (three volumes, London 1773) which satirized the Methodism of their Pembroke contemporary George Whitefield. In 1737 Shenstone printed at Oxford his *Poems upon Various Occasions*—not as as a bid for worldly preferment but merely 'for the Amusement Of a few Friends'.[6] The volume has a core of witty compliment and polite

[1] [T. Tickell], *Oxford* (London [1706]), line 208. R. Newton, *Rules and Statutes for the Government of Hertford College* (London 1747), 26: 'If any Undergraduate, having a *Genius* to *Poetry*, shall choose to make *Verses*, instead of the *Theme* or *Translation* required of him, he may be indulged this Liberty, if ... it shall not be found to draw off his Mind from serious Studies.' W. Carr, *University College* (London 1902), 159.

[2] Johnson recounts the story in his *Lives of the English Poets*, ed. Hill ii. 297-8. He considered the Hymn 'for the most part imagined with great vigour and expressed with great propriety': ibid. 301.

[3] Ibid. i. 313 (Philips), ii. 16 (Smith). John Philips (1676-1709), m. Ch.Ch. 1697. E. Smith, *Phaedra and Hippolitus* (London [1709]).

[4] R. Graves, *Recollections of William Shenstone, Esq.* (London 1788), 20. On Whistler see W. P. Courtney, *Dodsley's Collection of Poetry: its contents and contributors* (London 1910), 141-5. Anthony Whistler (1714-54), m. Pemb. 1732.

[5] A. Pope, *The Rape of the Lock* (London 1714). Pope's poem was apparently a popular model among Oxford poets. Another well-known imitation was *The Kite* (Oxford 1722), a three-canto 'heroi-comical' poem by Phanuel Bacon (1700-83, m. St John's 1715; degrees Magd.). Yet another was *The Thimble: an heroi-comical poem in four cantos ... by a gentleman of Oxford* (London 1743)—later expanded to five cantos; This was by William Hawkins, professor of poetry 1751-6.

[6] W. Shenstone, *Poems upon Various Occasions* (Oxford 1737), title-page.

love-verse, some clever undergraduate imitations, good parodies (especi-ally 'Colemira: a culinary eclogue') and is obviously the work of a young man anxious to display his all-round abilities, with little attempt to be original. It also contained an early version of *The School-Mistress* (separ-ately published at London in 1742) which became Shenstone's most pop-ular poem during the century. When his *Judgment of Hercules* was published in 1741 the master of Pembroke, John Ratcliff, acknowledged his presentation copy in an admiring letter, but, as Shenstone wrily reported to Graves, 'he expects to hear, since my pen has so well adorned the fable, that my conduct will, with equal propriety and elegance, illustrate the moral'.[1]

Pembroke's most famous son was undoubtedly Samuel Johnson, who matriculated there as a commoner in 1728. His Oxford career was brief— he left in December 1729 without taking a degree—and handicapped by miserable poverty, but his stay there set him on the literary road.[2] As a Christmas exercise his tutor William Jorden, perhaps with an awareness of his pupil's poetical interests, set him to adapt Pope's *Messiah* into Latin verse. Copies were handed round, Pope himself praised it, and among the Oxford literati Johnson gained great applause 'which ever after kept him high in the estimation of his College, and indeed, of all the Univers-ity'.[3] When John Husbands came to edit *A Miscellany of Poems by Several Hands* (Oxford 1731) Johnson's verse reached a wider audience.[4] In 1738 Johnson once again caused a stir in the university with his poem *London*: John Douglas recollected that in Oxford 'every body was delighted with it; and there being no name to it, the first buz of the literary circles was "here is an unknown poet, greater even than Pope" '.[5] But for Johnson the years of hack-work and struggle in London went on, and he did not revisit Oxford until 1754, when he returned as the famous *Rambler* essayist and the man from whom a great dictionary of the language was expected. Significantly, he spent his five weeks not in Pembroke, but as the guest of his new friend Thomas Warton. John Ratcliff remained

---

[1] [W. Shenstone,] *The Judgment of Hercules* (London 1741); Shenstone-Graves [30 Apr. 1741], *The Letters of William Shenstone*, ed. M. Williams (Oxford 1939), 23.

[2] Boswell's statement that Johnson did not leave Oxford until autumn 1731 has caused some con-fusion; his name remained on the college books until that date but he was no longer resident: see *Boswell's Life of Johnson*, ed. G. B. Hill (6 vols Oxford 1887), rev. L. F. Powell (6 vols Oxford 1934-50) i. 78n; J. L. Clifford, *Young Samuel Johnson* (London 1955), 123. It is typical of Johnson's strength of character that he could generalize from his own experience and see poverty as a handicap to the uni-versity itself. In 1776 he told Boswell: 'Our Universities are impoverished of learning, by the penury of their provisions. I wish there were many places of a thousand a-year at Oxford, to keep first-rate men of learning from quitting the University.' *Boswell's Life of Johnson*, ed. Hill, rev. Powell iii. 14.

[3] *Boswell's Life of Johnson*, ed. Hill, rev. Powell i. 61. William Jorden (*c*.1686-1739), m. CCC 1702; degrees Pemb.

[4] John Husbands (1706-32), m. Pemb. 1721

[5] *Boswell's Life of Johnson*, ed. Hill, rev. Powell i. 127. John Douglas (1721-1807), m. St. Mary Hall 1737; degrees Balliol; bp of Salisbury 1791-1807.

unimpressed by literary reputations and did not even invite him to dinner. Warton recalled that the master 'received him very coldly' and did not offer to order a copy of the forthcoming *Dictionary*. Johnson was disgusted: '*There* lives a man, who lives by the revenues of literature, and will not move a finger to support it. If I come to live at Oxford, I shall take up my abode at Trinity.' The two friends walked to Elsfield to visit Francis Wise 'with whom Johnson was much pleased' and in whose library he was often busy during his stay.[1] When his visit was over Wise and Warton between them set about gaining from the university some recognition for him, with the result that the *Dictionary* was published on 15 April 1755 as by Samuel Johnson MA. As Wise confessed to Warton: 'It is in truth doing ourselves more honour than him, to have such a work done by an Oxford hand, and so able a one too, and will shew that we have not lost all regard for good letters, as has been too often imputed to us by our enemies.'[2] The response in Oxford was generally very favourable, as Thomas Warton told his brother Joseph: 'Johnson's Dictionary is mightily liked here, but Men who don't know what it is to *write*, and yet think they have a right to *judge*, pretend to carp.'[3]

Though Johnson seems to have had thoughts of settling in Oxford he never did so.[4] He was too committed, as a man and a moralist, to the business of living, and, after all, 'he that lives well in the world is better than he that lives well in a monastery'.[5] There was always that side of Johnson which disdained mere bookishness; he disliked poetry that smelt of the dust of college libraries.[6] But for the rest of his life he enjoyed making regular visits, would wear his gown 'ostentatiously' and was an honoured guest in several colleges. He told the king that 'he was indeed fond of going to Oxford sometimes, but was likewise glad to come back again'.[7] One reason was that only on leaving the place did he

---

[1] *Boswell's Life of Johnson*, ed. Hill, rev. Powell i. 271-3.

[2] Wise-T. Warton, 14 Dec. 1754, *Biographical Memoirs of . . . Joseph Warton, D.D.* ed. J. Wooll (London 1806), 228.

[3] T. Warton-J. Warton, 9 May 1755, BL Add. MS 42560, fo 40. Joseph Warton (1722-1800), m. Oriel 1740; BD and DD New College 1768; headmaster of Winchester College 1766-93.

[4] On 28 November 1754 he told Warton: 'if you can accomplish your kind design [for the MA], I shall certainly take me a little habitation among you.' *Boswell's Life of Johnson*, ed. Hill, rev. Powell i. 275.

[5] [S. Johnson,] *The Prince of Abissinia [Rasselas]* (2 vols London 1759), ch. 47. The words are Imlac's.

[6] He censured John Philips's *Blenheim* as the poem 'of a man who writes books from books, and studies the world in a college' and he felt distaste for Milton's *Lycidas* with its 'long train of mythological imagery, such as a College easily supplies'. Johnson, *Lives of the English Poets*, ed. Hill i. 317, 164.

[7] *Boswell's Life of Johnson*, ed. Hill, rev. Powell ii. 35. For a list of Johnson's visits see ibid. iii. 450-5; on his academic punctiliousness see ibid. i. 347. He was at different times entertained at or accommodated by All Souls, Magdalen, New Inn Hall, Pembroke, Trinity and University College. At Pembroke Johnson's long-standing friend William Adams (1706-89, m. Pemb. 1720, master 1775-89) more than compensated for his predecessor's coldness.

'come into a region where any thing necessary to life is understood'.[1] It was fitting that in 1775 Johnson received the culminating honour from his university of the degree of doctor of laws for his contribution 'to the advancement of literature and the benefit of the community'—an aptly Johnsonian ideal.[2]

But Johnson, though Oxford's most eminent literary son, cannot claim to be the university's representative literary figure. That honour belongs to Thomas Warton, poet, humorist, classical scholar, historian, editor, biographer, Gothic enthusiast and resident fellow of Trinity from 1752 until his death in 1790. Warton's career is a suitable medium through which to view different aspects of Oxford's literary life during the latter half of the century.

As a poetically minded undergraduate Warton was lucky to be in a college whose president, George Huddesford, encouraged the pursuit of literature. Warton's popular humorous poem 'The Progress of Discontent' was in fact written at Huddesford's suggestion as an English version of a Latin verse exercise. Having already published some of his undergraduate literary efforts, Warton was elected 'laureate' of the bachelors' common room at Trinity, a post which carried the annual duty of poeticizing on the merits of a lady patroness, and his verses for 1747 and 1748 were published as *Verses on Miss C[ote]s and Miss W[ilmo]t* in 1749. In such ways a budding poetic talent could attract notice, and there were also opportunities at university level. The annual commemoration in the Sheldonian Theatre allowed a promising student to hear his verses sounded out by orchestra, chorus and soloists before the assembled dignitaries: William Collins's ode, *The Passions*, was performed at the 1750 commemoration; and his friend Warton's *Ode for Music* the following year, both to settings by William Hayes, professor of music.[3]

In January 1750 an ambitious and enterprising periodical was launched which specialized in publishing original poems and articles by younger university contributors. This was *The Student, or the Oxford Monthly Miscellany* (1750-1)—'Cambridge' was added to the title for the sixth issue. Thomas Warton became its Oxford editor and several of his humorous pieces (including 'The Progress of Discontent') first appeared there. The magazine set out to 'comprehend all the branches of *polite Literature*',[4] and as well as homorous items it included Latin verses,

---

[1] Johnson-Mrs Thrale, 4 Aug. 1777, *Letters of Samuel Johnson*, ed. R. W. Chapman (3 vols Oxford 1952) ii. 189.

[2] *Boswell's Life of Johnson*, ed. Hill, rev. Powell ii. 331. The words are those of Lord North, chancellor of the university.

[3] Bodl. MS Mus. d. 120-1 (Collins) and MS Mus. d. 70 (Warton); see also S. L. F. Wollenberg, 'Music and musicians', pp. 872-3 below. William Collins (1721-59), m. Queen's 1740; demy Magd. 1741.

[4] *The Student* i, p. iii ('To the Reader').

essays on religious and moral subjects, textual emendations and historical anecdotes. Pieces of historical interest included an unpublished letter
from William Laud and verses by Walter Raleigh (carefully printed from
manuscript). Contributions also came from Christopher Smart, the
Cambridge-based editor, and from Samuel Johnson (his 'Life of Dr
Francis Cheynel').

The age of Somers and Addison was no more; young Oxford poets of
1750 saw that patronage from men at the centre of power had greatly
diminished. But one *Student* contributor could declare that in spite of this
poetry was flourishing as never before, and he instanced 'The FIELDING's,
the JOHNSON's, the AKINSIDE's, the ARMSTRONG's, the COLLINS's, the
WARTON's ... and not a few concern'd in the STUDENT'. In his view these
were 'clever men in the poetical way ... more so than there ever were at
any given time together'.[1] The 1740s had indeed marked a decisive shift
in poetic trends, and several Oxford figures played major roles in this,
particularly the younger generation of Joseph Warton, his brother
Thomas and their close friend William Collins. All three asserted the
pre-eminence of the fancy in poetry, and Joseph Warton spoke on their
behalf in the advertisement to his *Odes* (1746): 'The author ... as he
looks upon Invention and Imagination to be the chief faculties of a Poet,
so he will be happy if the following Odes may be look'd upon as an
attempt to bring back Poetry into its right channel.'[2] Such ambitions
were purely poetic ones, and the friends saw themselves as pioneers in
works such as Joseph Warton's *The Enthusiast, or the Lover of Nature*
(London 1744), William Collins's *Odes on Several Descriptive and Allegoric
Subjects* (London 1747) and Thomas Warton's *The Pleasures of Melancholy*
(London 1747). Thomas Warton's poem had been written in 1745 during
his first year as an undergraduate; this blank-verse contemplation with
its imaginative cameos, gothic 'horror' passage and its landscapes
suffused with the atmosphere of the early Milton was not merely in line
with the new trend but helped to shape it. The well of patronage may
have failed, but publications such as these placed little value upon
society, politics or current affairs (significantly, none had a dedicatee);
their concern was with the colourful world of the poet's own fancy, and
through William Collins and the Warton brothers the university could
claim to be represented in the vanguard of literary taste during the
middle years of the century.[3] The *Student* essayist went on to declare that
true poetry relished its exile from the world:

[1] *The Student* ii. 7.
[2] J. Warton, *Odes on Various Subjects* (London 1746).
[3] To Joseph Warton the virtues of Addison were now prosaic and dated:

What are the lays of artful Addison,
Coldly correct, to Shakespear's warblings wild?

The Enthusiast, lines 168–9.

The patriot Muses have been banished the C[ou]rt ever since the auspicious days of the ever-blessed Queen ANNE, and being kick'd out of all *good company*, and forced into their original woods and groves, they sing with the same native wildness and unrestrained vivacity as they did in the *other golden age*.[1]

It is an attractive idea (the poet discovers the original sources of inspiration within himself, without needing support from the outside world) and one especially congenial at this time to Oxford, kicked out of good company in the political sense. By such a parallel the university's isolation could be seen as a supremely poetic gesture, and it was exactly this tactic that Thomas Warton adopted in perhaps the most significant 'Oxford' poem of the century, published in the wake of the attacks launched by the government in 1747-8 upon the university's alleged Jacobite sympathies.

The poet William Mason, from a Cambridge basking in the sunlight of government favour, had published *Isis: an elegy* (written in 1748) accusing the University of Oxford of irresponsibility and sedition and lamenting her fall from grace. President Huddesford encouraged the twenty-one-year-old Thomas Warton to write *The Triumph of Isis* in reply—a poem which made his own reputation in the university and gave Oxford new heart.[2] The literary tactics behind attack and counter-attack are interesting. Mason's *Isis* sits like a distressed Roman matron contemplating her vase, her fancy leading a succession of images across the plain of memory: formerly Oxford had represented solidly real virtues, but only the idea and the memory remain. She remembers her great representatives of truth (Addison and Locke) and laments that Oxford has slipped from a classical age to one of 'gothic licence'; the clear light of truth is extinguished, and the enemies of freedom, like the rabble in Milton's *Comus*, celebrate with 'infernal orgies'. For Mason this was not merely a perversion of Oxford but a neglect of the responsibilities that poetry owed to truth and reality. Oxford had sunk into the anarchic world of the imagination. To Thomas Warton, an enthusiast for gothic architecture and the early Milton, this was both a political and poetic challenge, setting up as it did the clear light of truth and reason as good, and the alluring half-light of the imagination as evil. Mason had sneered at Oxford's 'gothic licence', and so Warton's *Isis* proclaims, in a suitably daring phrase, the grandeur of her true gothic architecture:

My Gothic spires in ancient glory rise,
And dare with wonted pride to rush into the skies

---

[1] *The Student* ii. 7.

[2] W. Mason, *Isis: an elegy* (London 1749); [T. Warton,] *The Triumph of Isis* (London [1750],). King called on Prince the bookseller with five guineas for the anonymous author: *The Poetical Works of the late Thomas Warton, B.D.* ed. R. Mant (2 vols Oxford 1802) i, p. xv. For such a work, however, patronage did not extend beyond the university.

Warton triumphantly picks up Mason's *Comus* image and declares that
Oxford's allegiance, though to the world of the spirit, is not to Comus
and his crew but to Sabrina, the 'silver-slipper'd virgin' who protects the
chaste and virtuous. In Warton's poem her Miltonic 'rushy-fringed banks'
become the 'willow-fringed banks' of Isis, who similarly rose from the
waters with her message of grace. The tribute poetry pays to the outside
world becomes the base tribute of flattery to a whig political establishment: a corrupt state can only be served by those without purity or
principle. Oxford triumphs in its lack of preferment, but Cambridge has
sold out to the world:

> Still of preferment let her shine the queen,
> Prolific parent of each bowing dean:
> Be hers each prelate of the pamper'd cheek,
> Each courtly chaplain, sanctified and sleek.

For Warton Oxford's commitment is to a higher reality: she is the home
not only of knowledge, but of the poetic imagination—and the Muse
scorns political power. In proclaiming *The Triumph of Isis* Warton
challenges not merely Mason's political principles but his assumptions
about the allegiance that poetry, and Oxford, should give to the world
outside.

The aspect of Warton's career which appears most significant today is
his achievement as a literary historian in three important works of
scholarship: *Observations on The Faerie Queene of Spenser, The History of
English Poetry* and his edition of the early poems of Milton.[1] The *Observations* were a landmark in the writing of English literary history: Johnson
told him that he had shown the way 'to all who shall hereafter attempt
the study of our ancient authours . . . by directing them to the perusal of
the books which those authours had read'.[2] Such a task of exploration
among old books and manuscripts was no longer to be regarded as mere
antiquarian rummaging among 'all such reading as was never read'.[3]
Both this book and his brother Joseph's *Essay on the Writings and Genius of
Pope*[4] were instrumental in bringing such pursuits within the realm of
literary taste.

Thomas Warton automatically saw the historical perspective of any
context he was in, and his lifelong attachment to Trinity found expression in two works of piety, the lives of President Bathurst and of the
college's founder, Thomas Pope.[5] As senior fellow and the most eminent

---

[1] T. Warton, *Observations on the Faerie Queene of Spenser* (London 1754, 2nd edn 2 vols London
1762); T. Warton, *The History of English Poetry* (3 vols London 1774-81); J. Milton, *Poems upon Several
Occasions*, ed. T. Warton (London 1785).
[2] Johnson-T. Warton, 16 July 1754, *Letters of Johnson*, ed. Chapman i. 56.
[3] Pope, *Dunciad* (London 1743 edn) bk IV, line 250.
[4] [J. Warton,] *An Essay on the Writings and Genius of Pope* (2 vols London 1756, 1782).
[5] T. Warton, *The Life and Literary Remains of Ralph Bathurst, M.D.* (London 1761): T. Warton, *The*

figure in Trinity Warton might have expected to succeed to the college headship in 1776 on the death of George Huddesford, but a cabal was formed against him and he failed.[1] He would not have been a conventional choice for president, with his reputation as a punster and keeper of 'low drunken company'.[2] Warton was at home not just in the common room of Trinity but at Captain Jolly's Tavern, where porter was fourpence a quart and Ben Tyrrell's mutton-pies could be had for threepence.

The side of Oxford's literary life represented by tavern, bench and bowling alley (easily lost sight of in official publications) must not be forgotten. Warton himself made an important contribution to this sub-culture with his *Companion to the Guide* (1760). This had appeared ten years earlier as a humorous essay in *The Student* and was expanded into a full-scale burlesque upon, and supplement to, the official guide to Oxford. It provides a tour of neglected places of interest—the tennis courts, race-tracks, the unofficial university 'libraries' run by coffee-house proprietors, where 'Learning remains no longer a *dry* pursuit'.[3] It is an interesting fusion of ridiculous humour and affectionate detail: he describes the old Cornmarket pillory, the down-and-outs' bench under Carfax clock-tower and the two-faced pump in the High Street; he records amusing epitaphs, gives a woodcut of Carfax clock and prints the Bodleian manuscript of the boar's head carol sung at Queen's. The book's message is drawn from a particular grotesque statue laughing above Magdalen cloisters—'to admonish Strangers, and particularly the Young Student, that Science is not inconsistent with Good-Humour, and that Scholars are a *merrier* Sett of People than the World is apt to imagine'.[4]

The literary life of tavern and coffee-house was well represented during the earlier years of the century by the Poetical Club, which met regularly at the Tuns to drink, gossip and write witty verses. The diary

---

Life of Sir Thomas Pope (London 1772, expanded edn London 1780). Warton's life of Pope (1507–59) had been contributed in its earliest form to volume five (1760) of *Biographia britannica* (6 vols London 1747–66). His enthusiasm for medieval buildings led him to begin a 'History of gothic architecture' (never completed); his attachment to Winchester brought *A Description of the City, College, and Cathedral of Winchester* (London [1760]); when the chancellor of the university, Lord Lichfield, presented him to the rectory of Kiddington, near Woodstock, he set about writing the history of the parish, published as *Specimen of a History of Oxfordshire* (London 1782); his odes as poet laureate also explored the history of the office.

[1] T. Warton–Jane Warton, 14 May 1776, Bodl. MS Don. c. 75, fo 78.
[2] Boswell records this gossip in his diary: *Boswell: the ominous years 1774–1776*, ed. C. Ryskamp and F. A. Pottle (London 1963), 281. See also *Poetical Works of Warton*, ed. Mant i, p. ciii: 'a smile may perhaps be excited at the information, that the Historian of English Poetry was fond of drinking his ale and smoking his pipe with persons of mean rank and education.'
[3] [T. Warton,] *A Companion to the Guide* (London etc. [1760]), 10. It had appeared as 'An account [of] several public buildings in Oxford, never before described', under the signature of 'Pointer Junior' in *The Student* ii. 372–6.
[4] *Companion to the Guide*, 32.

of Erasmus Philipps gives a characteristic glimpse of this poetical society in 1721:

Went with Mr Tristram to the Poetical Club ... at the Tuns (kept by Mr Broadgate), where met Dr Evans, Fellow of St John's, and Mr Jno Jones, Fellow of Baliol, Members of the Club. Subscribed 5s to Dr Evans's *Hymen and Juno* (which one merrily call'd Evans's Bubble, it being now South Sea Time). Drank Gallicia Wine, and was entertained with two Fables of the Doctor's Composition, which were indeed Masterly in their kind: But the Dr is allowed to have a peculiar knack, and to excell all Mankind at a Fable.[1]

One of the successors of the Poetical Club in mid-century was the Jelly-Bag Society, whose members wore jelly-bag caps at meetings and gave vent to ever more witty inspirations as the candles and port ran low.[2] *The Oxford Sausage*, a miscellany published in 1764, grew out of these Jelly-Bag proceedings and included pieces by some of its members, such as Thomas Warton (the editor) and John Newbery (1713-67) the children's book publisher. The collection included 'Verses occasioned by Ben Tyrrell's mutton pies', 'Ode to a grizzle wig' and 'A panegyric on Oxford ale' (all by Warton). The *Sausage* was intended as a burlesque of Taste, 'which All will allow to be *highly seasoned* ... and happily blended'.[3] Good-humoured mockery of the university establishment was one vital ingredient. It printed 'Verses on the expected arrival of Queen Charlotte' ('containing the *Sentiments, Images, Metaphors, Machinery, Similies, Allusions*, and all other Poetical *Decorations*, of the OXFORD VERSES'); and Warton even found a place for Wodhull's 'Ode to criticism' with its parody of his own *Triumph of Isis* ('Thou, a *Silver-slipper'd*Nymph, Lightly tread'st the *dimply*Lymph ...'). There were always Oxford men willing to laugh at themselves and their university—as in two theatrical burlesques of Oxford manners and customs, *The Humours of Oxford* by 'a gentleman of Wadham-College' (acted at Drury Lane) and *The Oxford Act* 'a new ballad-opera, as it was perform'd by a company of students at Oxford'.[4] Even an establishment figure like Benjamin Buckler could gain a reputation as a master of mock-heroic with his *Complete Vindication of the*

---

[1] *Notes and Queries* 2nd ser. x (1860), 443. Abel Evans (1679-1737), m. St John's 1692, friend and correspondent of Pope. His best-known poem was *The Apparition* (London 1710), describing the visit of Satan to All Souls, where he meets his ally, Matthew Tindal. In Evans's poem *Vertumnus* (London 1713) he tried his hand at a poem in praise of the peace of Utrecht, but in a rather provincial manner he addressed it to Jacob Bobart, superintendent of the physic garden. Jones, the fellow of Balliol, was probably John Jones, m. Balliol 1714, MA 1720.

[2] See F. Newbery's account in C. Welsh, *A Bookseller of the Last Century* (London 1885), 67-8.

[3] *The Oxford Sausage* [ed. T. Warton] (London 1764), preface, p. iv. In 1830 George Colman the younger was still recommending *The Oxford Sausage* to visitors as 'very amusing; particularly if you read it on the spot, and wish to surrender your mind to the *genius loci*': G. Colman, *Random Records* (2 vols London 1830) i. 136.

[4] [James Miller,] *The Humours of Oxford* (London 1730); *The Oxford Act, a new ballad-opera, as it was perform'd by a company of students at Oxford* (London 1733).

Mallard of All-Souls College or with his humorous sermon (preached at All Souls on 2 November 1759) *Elisha's Visit to Gilgal, and his healing the Pot of Pottage, symbolically explain'd.*[1]

Groups like the Poetical Club and the Jelly-Bag Society, with a ready delight in the mockery of their own institutions, are examples of Oxford 'waggery'. These secret literary clubs (and great emphasis was put on their secrecy[2]) had for one of their chief delights the conscious self-mockery of their members, who were intentionally 'wags' and revelled in not taking each other seriously. True satire demands the inviolability and righteousness of truth against which aberration is measured, and such masterly satire was produced during the Augustan age of Dryden, Swift and Pope because Augustanism assumed such a reference to truth and objective reality; it assumed that a man had social duties and was responsible for his actions. Oxford waggery was un-Augustan for the same reasons that it was not satire—its burlesque tended to be too endearing, written out of shared fun rather than individual indignation. Waggery was Oxford's amusing way of accepting itself as a literary target and revelling in the anarchy that resulted from a self-conscious indulgence in fancy and the ridiculous. Oxford wags could throw custard pies haphazardly around, in the safe knowledge that they were already well splattered themselves.

One well-splattered individual was 'Poet Harding' who lived on the money he could extract from undergraduates for engaging to find, instantaneously, a rhyme for any word in the English language:

To this *improvisare* talent, he added that of personification;—sometimes he walk'd about with a scythe in his hand as Time; sometimes with an anchor, as Hope.–One day, I met him with a huge broken brick, and some bits of thatch, upon the crown of his hat; on my asking him for a solution of this *prosopopoeia*,– 'Sir', said he, 'to-day is the anniversary of the celebrated Doctor Goldsmith's death, and I am now in the character of his '*Deserted Village*'.[3]

Harding turns poetry into pure fantasy, and his waggish irresponsibility (mocking himself as much as he mocks literature) made him the kind of character that Oxford could take to its heart.

A piece of Oxford waggery with a national influence was the popular periodical *The Connoisseur* (1754-6) run by the two Oxford friends

---

[1] [B. Buckler,] *A Complete Vindication of the Mallard of All-Souls College* (London 1750, 2nd edn, expanded, London 1751). B. Buckler, *Elisha's Visit to Gilgal, and his healing the Pot of Pottage, symbolically explain'd* (Oxford 1759); see L. S. Sutherland, 'Political respectability 1751-71', pp. 140-2 above.

[2] According to Nicholas Amhurst the third rule of the Poetical Club was: 'That no Member do presume to discover the Secrets of this Society to any Body whatsoever, upon Pain of Expulsion.' [N. Amhurst,] *Terrae-Filius* (52 nos. London Jan.-July 1721) xix (15-18 Mar. 1721). Daniel Prince told how the secret venue of the Jelly-Bag Society was discovered: J. Nichols, *Literary Anecdotes of the Eighteenth Century* (9 vols London 1812-15) iii. 702.

[3] Colman, *Random Records* i. 307.

George Colman (the elder) and Bonnell Thornton.[1] Johnson said that it 'wanted matter' but Boswell praised it for having 'just views of the surface of life, and a very sprightly manner'.[2] Its persona of 'Mr Town' was that of a dreamer and fantasist, unable to take anything solemnly; even on the most serious subjects his fancy soon got to work:

I have resolved not to disturb the tranquility of the polite world by railing at their darling vices. A CENSOR may endeavour to new-cock a hat, to raise the stays, or write down the short petticoat, at his pleasure. Persons of quality will vary fashions of themselves, but will always adhere steadily to their vices.[3]

In the face of this fact 'Mr Town' could allow his fancy to play over the most serious subjects—gaming, prostitution, duelling and suicide. Typical items are a 'Letter from a mind-and-body clothier', an 'Account of the female thermometer', 'Cramwell and his eating club' and 'On keeping low company'. In paper 71 'Mr Town' declares that he has deliberately avoided modelling himself on the *Spectator* since 'in the high road of life there are several extensive walks, as well as bye-paths, which we may strike into, without the necessity of keeping the same beaten track with those that have gone before us'. This ambulatory imagery, with its light-hearted acceptance of 'characters of fancy', clearly prefigures Sterne's *Tristram Shandy* (1759-67) with its memorable portraits of Walter Shandy and Uncle Toby. The anti-Augustan move away from satire towards a more generous, accepting humour was clearly in line with a national bias. By the 1760s literary trends were moving towards the fanciful, in humour as in poetry.

This change is evident in the contrast between two of the *Terrae-Filius* publications of the eighteenth century. The ancient tradition of the licensed castigator of the university had fallen off by the eighteenth century, but Nicholas Amhurst was determined to revive the custom in 1721 as a weekly half-sheet. He attacked Oxford as a nursery of bigotry, treason and incompetence. Many eminent figures came under the lash,

---

[1] Bonnell Thornton (1724-68), m. Ch.Ch. 1743. Colman and Thornton became members of the Nonsense Club, and proprietors of the *St. James's Chronicle*. Thornton's talent for burlesque comes across in the eight papers he wrote (signed 'A') for *The Adventurer* (1752-4) and in his parody *An Ode on Saint Caecilia's Day, adapted to the ancient British musick* (London 1749) by 'Fustian Sackbut'—the instruments being the salt-box, jew's harp, marrow-bones, cleaver and hurdy-gurdy. Colman became manager of Covent Garden Theatre and a successful dramatist; his farce *The Oxonian in Town* (London 1767) described the distractions that London offered an undergraduate. Both men were Warton's close friends.

[2] *Boswell's Life of Johnson*, ed. Hill, rev. Powell, i. 420.

[3] *The Connoisseur* no. 31 (29 Aug. 1754). 'Mr Town' declared that he 'purposely avoided the worn out practice of retailing scraps of morality, and affecting to dogmatize on the common duties of life . . . I have endeavoured to laugh people into a better behaviour': ibid. no. 71 (5 June 1755). This was a glance at Johnson's *The Rambler* (1750-2, 6 vols London 1752) of which Thornton published a parody in his *Have At You All: or, the Drury-Lane Journal* (London 1752) as 'A Rambler. Number 99999' (30 Jan. 1752).

one of whom was Thomas Warton the elder, a well-known Oxford wag, Jacobite and president of the Poetical Club.[1] Amhurst mocks his appearance, accuses him of preaching a treasonable sermon and pours scorn on his humorous writings: 'To publish them, would be to throw Filth and Ordure in the Face of the King . . . I know nothing that he is fit for, but *Billingsgate Sermons*, and Inscriptions for Bog-House Walls'.[2] Whatever its literary merit, the paper was written with the genuine acerbic spirit of the licensed 'truth-teller' and with a fervent desire for reform. Over forty years later, on the eve of the great Encaenia in celebration of the peace of Paris (July 1763) Oxford was jolted by the reappearance of its castigator, 'the great TERRAE-FILIUS, the redoubted Academical Satyrist, the Terror of Old and Young, Male and Female, Graduates and Undergraduates'.[3] But for George Colman the elder (the man behind the venture) this was to be an exercise in anti-climax. The six *Terrae-Filius* papers published daily during the Act never went further than good-humoured raillery, and people soon realized that the lion had 'filed his Teeth, and pared his Claws'.[4] There was some laughter at 'Mr Folio' and his wife as eighteenth-century naïve tourists, and an amused wink at 'that merry *Fellow*' Thomas Warton.[5] But Oxford waggery did not belong in the tradition of the satirical *Terrae-Filius*. Colman declared in the final issue 'I am resolved to take my Leave in good Humour', and he did so.[6]

Part of Thomas Warton's contemporary fame was as a classical scholar, and in this he represented the Oxford establishment far more closely. He published a collection of Latin inscriptions, edited part of the Greek anthology of Constantine Cephalas, and as a hardworking delegate of the Clarendon Press produced a two-volume edition of Theocritus.[7] He also acted as one of the inspectors for the Oxford verses on the king's marriage of 1761, one of several printed tributes from the university in the early 1760s which show a new atmosphere of reconciliation with the central government.[8] Such collections gave students and

---

[1] Warton's *Poems on Several Occasions* (London 1748) were published after his death by his two sons, Joseph and Thomas.

[2] *Terrae-Filius* xi (15 Feb. 1721). In 1713 Hearne recorded some anonymous verses 'written in the Boghouse of Mother Gordon's at Heddington':

Alma novem claros peperit Rhedi[ci]na [= Oxford] Poëtas,
Trap, Young, Bub, Stubb, Crab, Fog, Cary, Tickel, Evans.

'All bad Poets', he commented. Hearne, *Collections* iv. 151 (6 Apr. 1713).

[3] [G. Colman the elder,] *Terrae-Filius* 4 nos. (London July 1763) no. 1, p. 3.   [4] Ibid. p. 7.
[5] Ibid. no. 2, p. 26 (6 July 1763).   [6] Ibid. no. 3, p. 62 (7 July 1763).

[7] *Inscriptionum romanorum metricarum delectus* [ed. T. Warton] (London 1758); *Anthologiae graecae a Constantino Cephala conditae libri tres* [ed. T. Warton] (Oxford 1766); *Theocriti syracusii quae supersunt*, ed. T. Warton (2 vols Oxford 1770).

[8] These were *Pietas universitatis oxoniensis* (Oxford 1761) on the death of George II, *Epithalamia oxoniensia* (Oxford 1761) on the marriage of King George III and *Gratulatio solennis universitatis oxoniensis* (Oxford 1762) on the birth of the prince of Wales.

fellows an opportunity to obtain kudos with a poem in English or
another language. There was hot competition with the equivalent publication from Cambridge, and colleges were eager to see their notable
members included—their names often attached to poems written on
their behalf by the inspectors and their friends. In the collection *Pietas
universitatis oxoniensis* Thomas Warton had provided (as well as his own
contribution) 'The Complaint of Cherwell' above the name of his pupil,
John Chichester, brother to the marquess of Donegall, and in the
Epithalamia Joseph Warton had contributed verses 'To His Royal High-
ness the Duke of York' on behalf of the Wykehamist Richard Phelps,
then serving with the militia. The presentation copies, dressed up in
'velvet and gold fringe', were eagerly awaited and discussed.[1]

The foundation of the chair of poetry in 1708 provided the university
with an official literary mouthpiece.[2] The first professor, Joseph Trapp,
gave his students an Aristotelian 'art of poetry' soundly based on the
classical critics, but with an enthusiasm for Milton, whom he urged as a
model for modern writers.[3] These *Praelectiones poeticae* were published in
three volumes.[4] His successor, Thomas Warton the elder (1718-28) did
not publish his lectures and there was a good deal of irony behind
Amhurst's invocation:

> TRAP and WHARTON melt upon the tongue,
> Egregious wits! and criticks both sublime,
> Whose kindred talents so exactly chime,
> That hard it is to say, in verse or prose
> Which happy genius more divinely flows;
> In this alone the former does excel,
> That TRAP writes most, but WHARTON writes as well.[5]

---

[1] 'The Complaint of Cherwell' is printed in *Poetical Works of Thomas Warton*, ed. Mant i. 171-6. John Chichester (1741-83), m. Trin. 1759. 'I send you Phelps' Verses, which I hope and am apt to think you will like ... Phelps went up to London to be reviewd before I had finished them': J. Warton-T. Warton, 29 Oct. 1761, BL Add. MS 42560, fo 83. The Clarendon Press account for 1762 records £24 4s 6d spent on 'velvet and gold fringe' for presentation copies. Joseph Warton wrote to his brother with the critical reaction at Winchester School: 'I received the Oxford verses ... many of them good. Above all, is not *Spence*'s a noble copy ... They were written and indeed owned by Dr Lowth, so says Sturges ... Phelps's verses are much talked of here. Guess how much I enjoy what is said of them. The Warden, &c. don't seem to suspect any thing ... Who made Penruddocke's—truly the Warden says you did. Dr Fanshaw's are something well—Williams's the Doctor likes.' *Memoirs of Joseph Warton*, ed. Wooll, pp. 279-80.

[2] The professorship was established under the will of Henry Birkhead with revenues from his lands in Berkshire and Durham: see J. W. Mackail, *Henry Birkhead and the Foundation of the Oxford Chair of Poetry* (Oxford 1908).

[3] See M. T. Herrick, *The Poetics of Aristotle in England* (New Haven 1930), 109-10. Thomas Tickell lectured as Trapp's deputy in 1711; see Hearne, *Collections* III.III (23 Jan. 1711). A lecture Tickell delivered in Easter Term 1711 'De poesi didactica' is printed by Tickell, *Thomas Tickell*, 198-209.

[4] J. Trapp, *Praelectiones poeticae* (3 vols Oxford and London 1711-19, 2nd edn London 1722, 3rd edn London 1736, trans. W. Clarke and W. Bowyer London 1742).

[5] N. Amhurst, *Oculus Britanniae: an heroi-panegyrical poem on the University of Oxford* (London 1724),

During his tenure of the office (1728-38) Joseph Spence spent three years travelling abroad, and Edward Rolle gave several lectures as his deputy. But the travels bore fruit in Spence's *Polymetis*, a handsomely printed folio volume which fused his love for ancient art and for 'poetical criticism' in a series of dialogues on the allegorical nature of the arts.[1] Spence was succeeded by John Whitfeld, who after three years vacated the professorship for a living in Devon, leaving behind him a reputation for having 'a ready wit and a knack of writing epigrams'.[2] By far the most important poetry lectures of the century were those by Robert Lowth (professor 1741-51) who gave an influential series on the sacred poetry of the Hebrews, which he considered 'the only specimens of the primeval and genuine poetry'.[3] These lectures were a breakthrough in critical thinking, and by contrast the work of Trapp and Spence seems to belong to a former age. Lowth looked beyond the classical tradition to the Hebraic, and for him the most ancient form of poetical expression was not the epic but the lyrical effusion of the ode—and it was this literary form which rose in popularity during the 1740s. William Collins and the Warton brothers may have been among Lowth's original audience, and one critic has described some of Collins's odes as 'secular versions of what Lowth was describing'.[4] His enthusiasm for Hebrew poetry and his analysis of its metrical structure were an important influence on his friend Christopher Smart,[5] and his remarks on the necessity of understanding a poem's context prefigure the principles of Thomas Warton's *Observations on the Faerie Queene* of 1754. Lowth's poetry lectures during the 1740s reinforce the conclusion that Oxford was represented in the forefront of literary trends during this decade.

The professorship next passed to an academic with a strong interest

47-8. Among the Warton papers of Trinity College (on deposit in Bodl.) are the manuscripts of several lectures delivered by Thomas Warton the elder as professor of poetry. They include 'De sacra poesi', numbered '5' and bearing the dates '1719, Michaelmas Term' and 'April 27, 1721 Easter Term' (apparently delivered twice!). Other titles are 'De orationibus poeticis', 'De poesi epica' (Easter 1725) and 'De machinis epopoeiae'. See J. Pittock, 'Thomas Warton and the Oxford chair of poetry', *English Studies* lxii (1981).

[1] J. Spence, *Polymetis* (London 1747). The *DNB* states that Spence did not lecture, but his ninth and tenth lectures, on the *Aeneid* (the former 'Read Oct. 14, 1730') are in BL Add. MS 17281. 'Mr Spence's Lectures on the Iliad, &c., as Poetry Professor' were sold by Sotheby and Wilkinson, 3 Aug. 1858 (lot 197); see also A. Wright, *Joseph Spence, A Critical Biography* (Chicago 1950), 34-5. Joseph Spence (1699-1768), m. Magdalen Hall 1717; fellow New College 1724; prof. of poetry 1728-38, regius prof. of modern history 1742-8. Edward Rolle (*c*.1705-91), m. New College 1723.

[2] G. F. Russell Barker and A. H. Stenning, *The Record of Old Westminsters* (London 1928), 989. John Whitfeld (*c*.1705-83), m. Ch.Ch. 1722; prof. of poetry 1738-41.

[3] R. Lowth, *De sacra poesi Hebraeorum* (Oxford 1753), trans. G. Gregory as *Lectures on the Sacred Poetry of the Hebrews* (2 vols London 1787) i. 50.

[4] A. Johnston, 'Poetry and criticism after 1740' in R. Lonsdale (ed.), *Dryden to Johnson* (London 1971), 363.

[5] See C. Smart, *Jubilate agno*, ed. W. H. Bond (London 1954), 20.

in the theatre, William Hawkins, who chose to deliver his lectures on classical and English drama.[1] Some of the more entertaining moments in this course must have come in lectures ten and eleven when Hawkins declaimed lengthy versions (in Latin verse) of his favourite passages from Shakespeare. Thomas Warton, following the steps of his father, succeeded Hawkins in the chair of poetry in 1756, and for the next decade he delivered four lectures annually on 'The poetry of the Greeks'. Though one of them ('De poesi bucolica') formed the basis of the essay prefixed to his edition of Theocritus, the lectures as a whole were never printed. Warton's successors in the office were Benjamin Wheeler (1766–76), John Randolph (1776–83) whose lectures on Homer were edited by his son Thomas Randolph, Robert Holmes (1783–93) and James Hurdis (1793–1801).[2] Hurdis declared to his audience that his lectures would 'not be obscured by quotation from any dead language', and so he delivered them in English. The first twenty-one, consisting of readings from his favourite descriptive passages in English poetry, were printed at his own private press at Bishopstone in 1797 under the pretentious title, *Lectures shewing the Several Sources of that Pleasure which the Human Mind receives from Poetry*. In Hurdis, the scholar had clearly given place to the 'man of sensibility'.

During the 1770s 'reconciliation' was the order of the day between government and university, and in Thomas Warton's writings after 1770 this becomes an almost obsessive theme, transposed into literary terms. The organizing idea of his *History of English Poetry* is the interplay of fiction and truth, fancy and reality. For him the great age was that of Elizabeth I when fancy and truth held a rewarding mutual relationship— 'that period, propitious to the operations of original and true poetry, when the coyness of fancy was not always proof against the approaches of reason'.[3] Edward Gibbon was one of many writers who understood Warton's aims and praised him for reconciling 'the taste of a poet and the minute diligence of an antiquarian'.[4] Warton wanted to bring the neglected writings of the later middle ages within the area of respectable taste, to discover the facts as a scholar and uncover as a poet the lost beauties and imagery of 'gothic' writers—Wormius was beginning to feel at home in the drawing-room. Reconciliation was likewise the theme of Warton's poem of 1782 which sees Reynolds's classical west window at New College not as an anachronistic intrusion into a medieval building

---

[1] Hawkins's published plays include a rewriting of Shakespeare's *Cymbeline* (London 1759).

[2] J. Randolph, *Praelectiones ac ademicae in Homerum*, ed. T. Randolph (Oxford and London 1870). Robert Holmes (1748–1805) (m. New College 1767) was the author of *Alfred: an ode, with six sonnets* (Oxford 1778).

[3] Warton, *History of English Poetry* iii. 501.

[4] E. Gibbon, *The Decline and Fall of the Roman Empire*, ed. J. B. Bury (7 vols London 1896–1900) iv. 152n.

but as a parallel to his own achievement: the painter had been able 'to reconcile | The willing Graces to the Gothic pile'.[1]

It was one of the signs of Oxford's reconciliation with the government that in 1785, at the prompting of Reynolds, Warton was made poet laureate. Delighting in the tradition (as he saw it) of Spenser, Jonson and Dryden, Warton re-enacted the old relationship between the chosen poet and his monarch. At the regular musical performances of his odes for the new year and the king's birthday, George III and his good queen would listen to Warton's reminders of the courtesy and chivalry of the past. At one point he alludes to the romantic veil of the imagination which his predecessor Spenser had cast over Elizabeth:

> From fabling Fancy's inmost store
> A rich romantic robe he bore;
> A veil with visionary trappings hung,
> And o'er his virgin-queen the fairy texture flung.[2]

It was a robe which George wore awkwardly but uncomplainingly. (Such romantic gestures were closer to the taste of the prince of Wales, eventually to become an enthusiast for Walter Scott.) In another ode the king's official visit to Oxford in 1786 is seen by Warton in terms of the monarch seeking out the timid maiden of knowledge, and viewing from a distance the groves of poetry where the muses play.[3] The literary image of Oxford remains the same, now valued by the outside world largely on its own terms.[4]

As an undergraduate of the 1740s Warton had found in Trinity a congenial climate for his poetry, and in the 1780s it was he who helped create such a climate for the new generation in Oxford. In March 1777 he had published his *Poems*, containing odes and sonnets whose unifying tone was one of nostalgia for loved scenes left or revisited, some recalling the chivalric past and others with detailed descriptions suffused by an

---

[1] T. Warton, *Verses on Sir Joshua Reynolds's Painted Window at New College Oxford* (London 1782), lines 105-6.

[2] T. Warton, *Birthday Ode* (1787), lines 29-32.

[3] George III was one of those kings

> Who seek coy Science in her cloister'd nook,
> Where Thames, yet rural, rolls an artless tide;
> Who love to view the vale divine,
> Where revel Nature and the Nine,
> And clustering towers the tufted grove o'erlook.

T. Warton, *New Year Ode* (1787), lines 45-9.

[4] During the 1780s Oxford's men of letters had no excuse for not keeping up with the literary life of the continent. James Fletcher, the bookseller, set up a reading room for fifty subscribers, and it is possibly this which John Parsons described to Ralph Griffiths on 14 March 1788: 'There is such a Society established in Oxford as you mention—It is limited to fifty Members—I am not a Member—but I find upon enquiry that there is one or two Vacancies . . . They take in twelve French, German, and Italian Reviews, Journals, Gazettes &c—besides the English things of that kind.' Bodl. MS Add. C. 89, fo 276.

elegiac atmosphere.[1] Two of the most effective are 'Ode Written at Vale-Royal Abbey', with its shifting of scene between past glory and picturesque decay, and 'Sonnet to the River Lodon' evoking Warton's 'sweet native stream' which he revisits in a mood of mature sadness. Johnson was not in sympathy with Warton's attempts to revive the sonnet form and to associate his poetry with the pre-Dryden tradition. Johnson was out of step with the changing tastes of the age when he characterized Warton's volume as

> Phrase that Time has flung away;
> Uncouth words in disarray,
> Trick'd in antique ruff and bonnet,
> Ode, and elegy, and sonnet.[2]

Warton gathered around him in Oxford a band of enthusiastic young poets who regarded him as their mentor. Herbert Croft remarked in 1786: 'The magnetism of Tom Warton draws many a youth into rhymes and loose stockings, who had better be thinking of prose and propriety.'[3] Two such protégés were Henry Headley and William Lisle Bowles.[4] Headley received much early encouragement from Warton and published several poems in the monthly magazines;[5] *An Invocation to Melancholy* (Oxford and London 1785), strongly influenced by Warton's poem of forty years earlier, was separately printed. In the remainder of his tragically brief life Headley issued his *Poems and Other Pieces* (London 1786), a collection reminiscent of Warton's 1777 volume, with some imitations of Old Welsh poetry and an ode 'written amidst the ruins of Broomholm Priory' (the ancestry of the volume is obvious) and his *Select Beauties of Ancient English Poetry* (1787) an anthology compiled with a Wartonian fusion of taste and scholarliness which aimed to popularize medieval and Elizabethan poetry.[6] His skill and good sense as a critic

---

[1] T. Warton, *Poems* (London March 1777, 2nd edn July 1777, 3rd edn 1779).

[2] H. L. Piozzi, *Anecdotes of the Late Samuel Johnson, LL.D.* (London 1786), 64. Interestingly, Robert Southey's first collection was subtitled 'odes, elegies, sonnets': R. Lovell and R. Southey, *Poems: containing The Retrospect, odes, elegies, sonnets &c* (Bath 1795).

[3] J. Nichols, *Illustrations of Literary History* (8 vols London 1817-58) v. 210. Sir Herbert Croft (1751-1816), 5th bt; m. Univ. 1771.

[4] Henry Headley (1765-88), m. Trin. 1782. William Lisle Bowles (1762-1850), m. Trin. 1781.

[5] On 14 September 1785 Warton sent a copy of Headley's 'The beggar's dog' to John Nichols, manager of the *Gentleman's Magazine*, asking him to print 'the production of an ingenious young friend': Nichols, *Literary Anecdotes* vi. 641. It was duly printed in *Gentleman's Magazine* lv (1785), 734. A damaging review of his poems appeared, however, in the *Magazine* in the next year: ibid. lvi (1786), 413.

[6] H. Headley, *Select Beauties of Ancient English Poetry* (2 vols London 1787), edited in two volumes with a memoir by Henry Kett (London 1810). In October 1793 Kett was narrowly defeated for the poetry professorship by Hurdis, in spite of the publication of his *Juvenile Poems* (Oxford 1793). These contain his elegiac 'Verses on the Death of Mr Headley' and twelve Wartonian sonnets, one of which, 'To a Welch Harper', is good.

comes across in the single paper he wrote for the Oxford magazine *Olla Podrida* (1787-8).[1]

William Lisle Bowles's discreet volume of sonnets published in 1789 clearly shows the influence of Warton, whose 'River Lodon' sonnet lies behind Bowles's 'To the River Itchin, near Winchester'. They were a decisive influence on the young Coleridge and Southey.[2] Both men imitated them, and Coleridge transcribed more than forty copies of the scarce volume for his friends. Wartonian nostalgia was now in full fashion: 'There is something in the recollection of scenes of child hood that give a pleasing melancholy to the mind' wrote Southey before going on to quote Bowles's 'so very beautiful' sonnet to the Itchin.[3] For Coleridge, Bowles was 'a poet by whose works, year after year, I was so enthusiastically delighted and inspired'. Though this admiration was to wane, Bowles had awakened the young man from a gloomy obsession with metaphysics 'by the genial influence of a style of poetry so tender and yet so manly, so natural and real, and yet so dignified and harmonious'.[4]

Loose stockings could perhaps be forgiven, but during the 1790s, when revolutionary ideas were in the air, tutors and heads of houses had to remain vigilant. At the weekly meetings of the Literary Society religious and political subjects were excluded from the debates.[5] In February 1794 the newly elected John Skinner gave a solemn paper on emulation and truth; his later essay 'On the pleasure which men take in horrid spectacles' dealt with the slightly more dangerous topic of public

[1] *The Olla Podrida, a periodical work, complete in forty-four numbers*, ed. T. Monro (Oxford 1788). Headley's paper (no. 16, 30 June 1787) was a scholarly and well-argued criticism of modern dramatists' 'indiscriminate recourse to the bowl and the dagger'. Munro had some notable helpers: Richard Graves contributed a paper (no. 30) and Kett six. Some of the best are the nine written by president George Horne of Magdalen, Monro's college; they are genial and light-hearted (Horne was obviously good company) and no. 13 is noteworthy for being a genuine and glowing tribute to Johnson. A successor to *Olla Podrida* was *The Loiterer* (6 issues 1789-90) written by James Austen.

[2] W. L. Bowles, *Fourteen Sonnets, Elegiac and Descriptive, written during a Tour* (Bath 1789). For the influence of Warton and Bowles on the 'first generation' of Romantics see J. B. Bamborough, 'William Lisle Bowles and the riparian muse' in W. W. Robson (ed.), *Essays and Poems Presented to Lord David Cecil* (London 1970). Wordsworth's 'Lines written a few miles above Tintern Abbey, on re-visiting the banks of the Wye during a tour' belong to this tradition.

[3] Southey—G. C. Bedford, 13 Apr. 1794, *New Letters of Robert Southey*, ed. K. Curry (2 vols New York and London 1965) i. 52-3. In 1824 Southey wrote of the poetic scene 'if any man may be called the father of the present race, it is Thomas Warton', and he talked of the 'school' of Warton as 'the true English school': *The Quarterly Record* xxxi (1824), 289. Coleridge remarked that 'in his taste and estimation of writers Mr Southey agreed far more with Warton than with Johnson': *Biographia literaria*, ed. G. Watson (London and New York 1965) ch. 3.

[4] *Biographia literaria*, ed. Watson, ch. 1.

[5] John Skinner's diary records: 'At this period there were sixteen members, chiefly under-graduates, who used to meet every Thursday during term at each others rooms to debate on any literary question, religious and political subjects being expressly excluded.' H. H. E. Craster, 'Oxford literary societies of the eighteenth century', *Bodleian Quarterly Record* iii (1920-2), 101.

executions.[1] Skinner, however, was more concerned with the effects on a spectator's sensibility than with commenting on the Parisian 'terror'. But the activities of the Literary Society had aroused the suspicions of the president of Trinity, and Skinner was obliged to resign. His diary records ruefully: 'I had the satisfaction of attending only two terms, as Dr Chapman, the head of Trinity, being apprehensive of the debates taking a different turn from what was proposed, requested me to withdraw my name.'[2]

A more independent spirit was Robert Southey, who came up to Balliol in 1792. Fortunately for him his tutor, Thomas How, had an enlightened attitude to academic matters: 'Mr Southey, you wont learn any thing by my lectures Sir, so if you have any studies of your own you had better pursue them.'[3] Southey thankfully accepted the offer. He brought out his first volume of *Poems* in 1795 jointly with his friend Robert Lovell under the names of 'Bion' and 'Moschus'.[4] But his main absorption as an undergraduate was *Joan of Arc* (1796), an ambitious epic full of youthful libertarian idealism: 'twill be my legacy to this country, and may perhaps preserve my memory in it.'[5] He even anticipated some pleasure in the publication from How, whom he considered to be 'half a democrat'. But most significantly for young Southey it was in Oxford in June 1794 that he met Coleridge, who was visiting his friend Robert Allen at University College. He and Southey became immediate friends—a meeting with obvious significance for English literature and one which Coleridge later remembered as another turning-point in his life.[6] Southey left Oxford for good that summer, full of plans: he and Coleridge would embark for America to set up a 'pantisocracy', a communal society based on the twin ideals of tolerance and equality.

Oxford's literary men at the beginning of the century had, under the guidance of Addison, felt drawn to the world of public affairs; serious poetry had been a preparation for a career and a bid for patronage. As the century progressed the university's isolation from the seat of power and its suspicion of whig politics went along with an acceptance of its literary image and a growing confidence in its own virtue. Its typical waggery merged quite naturally into the benevolent humour popular

---

[1] Bodl. MS Eng. Misc. f. 34, fos 52–7, read 'in the Literary Society at Oxford. Anno 1794'. John Skinner (c 1772–1839), m. Trin. 1790.

[2] Craster, 'Literary societies', 101–2.

[3] Southey–G. C. Bedford, 20 July 1794, *New Letters of Southey*, ed. Curry i. 64. Thomas How (1758–1819), m. Balliol 1776, fellow 1784.

[4] Like Bowles's *Sonnets* it was printed by Cruttwell at Bath.

[5] Southey–Bedford, 20 July 1794, *New Letters of Southey*, ed. Curry i. 63. 'I shall not reside next Michaelmas at Oxford, because the time will be better employed in correcting *Joan* and overlooking the press': ibid. 61.

[6] 'I dwell with unabated pleasure on the strong and sudden, yet I trust not fleeting influence, which my moral being underwent on my acquaintance with him at Oxford': *Biographia literaria*, ed. Watson, ch. 3, p. 40n.

6 of the muses' was secure.[1]

during the latter half of the century; its younger poets were among the leaders of the nation's tastes, as a delight in the fancy and the gothic past came into fashion; and at the end of the century an undergraduate poet could regard 'the world' not as the established system of values and responsibilities, but as something which could be created by an individual—whether in the poetic imagination or in America. The shift from Augustan to Romantic during the eighteenth century was in these ways reflected in the university's literary life. The important conclusion is that Oxford was not cut off from the literary trends of the age, but played its part in shaping them, particularly in the 1740s and 1780s. It fostered productive literary friendships, gave young men opportunities and a congenial atmosphere in which to write; in Oxford the indulgence of the fancy, in humour or poetry, was a respectable pastime; the past was cherished, nostalgia was an acceptable emotion and literary studies were generally welcomed as a valuable accomplishment; the encouragement of tutors (or even their laziness) could further the writing of poetry. In all these ways Oxford found that by 1800, far from being a literary backwater, its reputation as 'the seat of the muses' was secure.[1]

---

[1] So called by Pope (Pope-Caryll, June 1718, *Correspondence of Pope*, i. 475). J. Heany published *Oxford, the Seat of the Muses* at Oxford in 1738.

29

Anglo-Saxon Studies

DAVID FAIRER

IT IS a tribute to the learning of the university to say that the history of Anglo-Saxon scholarship between 1688 and 1715 is the history of its development at Oxford. Thereafter the marked decline of such studies over the remainder of the century is partly to be explained by the weakening of its position within the university. Between the Glorious Revolution and the death of George Hickes the University of Oxford made a remarkably concerted attempt to advance the study of the Saxon ancestors of the English to the extent that this community of effort deserves the name of a 'school'. It is important to understand the communal nature of these studies, that projects were often shared or inherited and that no scholar during the early period felt that he was working alone. The aims of this present chapter are to examine why and how this school of Anglo-Saxon studies arose, what were its aims and achievements and why it should finally have declined.

Towards the end of the seventeenth century the University of Oxford felt proud of its own supposed Anglo-Saxon origins. King Alfred himself was believed by many to have been the founder of University College, and this house paid its own tribute with the publication in 1678 of John Spelman's life of Alfred. The master of the college, Obadiah Walker, translated the life into Latin and added several significant appendices, including translations of Alfred's preface to the *Cura pastoralis*, the voyages of Ohthere and Wulfstan and other Anglo-Saxon remains.[1] In 1709 the scholar William Elstob declared that 'being a University college man, [he] would willingly publish all that King Alfred did'.[2] During the 1690s there appears to have been a conscious effort to publicize Alfred's scholarly work; Humfrey Wanley wrote to Hickes in 1698 from the master's lodgings in University College:

[1] For the belief in the foundation by Alfred see Parker, *Early History of Oxford*, 39-47. J. Spelman, *Aelfredi magni Anglorum regis vita* (Oxford 1678). According to Madan the translation may have been by Christopher Wase (*c*1625-90), supervisor of the University Press; F. Madan, *Oxford Books* (3 vols Oxford 1895-1931) iii. 365.

[2] E. Elstob-R. Thoresby, 6 May 1709, *Letters of Eminent Men Addressed to Ralph Thoresby* (2 vols London 1832) ii. 163. William Elstob (1673-1715), m. Queen's 1691; fellow Univ. 1696; incorporated at Cambridge 1698.

we expect K. Aelfreds Boethius by Easter, after which Mr Thwaites will put P. Gregories Pastoral into the Press; and for ought I know, when that comes out, an honest Gentleman of this College [Elstob], may publish Orosius, and so compleat our Royal Founders works.[1]

The Oxford Saxonists were concerned to stress the continuity between the language, laws and religion of the Saxons and those of their own day. Elizabeth Elstob (sister of William) believed that the laconic simplicity of the Anglo-Saxon language showed the true native tradition of English; the author of the *Historical Collections* held that the Saxon laws had withstood the Viking and Norman invasions, 'so that though the several Revolutions broke in upon the present Government of *Britain*, yet every one found it their Interest to continue the same Incomparable Constitution'; George Hickes used his Anglo-Saxon learning as a weapon in religious controversy; and Edmund Gibson wrote to Edward Thwaites in 1697 'if you should run over the Homilies ... I hope you'll have an eye to all the passages against Popery ... a collection of that kind ... would be undeniable evidence to all posterity, that the belief of our Papists at this day is a very different thing from that of our Saxon ancestors'.[2] To many Oxford scholars, therefore, the study of the native English line of King Alfred, with its simple and dignified language, its constitutional laws and its purity of religion, held an essential virtue. This is why, in the rebirth of interest in Oxford in the old northern ('septentrional') tongues it was the Anglo-Saxon which took precedence.

In the earlier years of the seventeenth century Cambridge had been the home of Saxon studies, and its greatest achievement had been William Somner's dictionary, published in 1659.[3] The revival of Saxon studies in Oxford was due to a combination of enlightened leadership by powerful university figures and the vital impetus given by the arrival in Oxford of the great continental scholar, Francis Junius.[4]

[1] Wanley-Hickes, 18 Feb. 1698, Bodl. MS Eng. Hist. c.6, fo 20.

[2] E. Elstob, *The Rudiments of Grammar for the English-Saxon Tongue, first given in English, with an apology for the study of northern antiquities* (London 1715); R. Tuve, 'Ancients, moderns, and Saxons', *English Literary History* vi (1939) argues that this belief reflected the view of the moderns in the 'ancients v. moderns' controversy. On Elizabeth Elstob see M. Ashdown, 'Elizabeth Elstob, the learned Saxonist', *Modern Language Rev.* xx (1925); also A. Wallas, *Before the Bluestockings* (London 1929), 133–89. [T. Salmon,] *Historical Collections, relating the originals, conversions, and revolutions of the inhabitants of Great Britain to the Norman Conquest* (London 1706), 450. G. Hickes, *Several Letters which passed between Dr. George Hickes, and a Popish Priest* (London 1705), preface and p. 70 argued that the 'purity' of Saxon worship gave no popish titles to the Virgin Mary, had no adoration of saints' images and no doctrine of the real presence. On Hickes see D. C. Douglas, *English Scholars 1660–1730* (London 1939, 2nd edn London 1951), ch. 4. Tuve, 165–71 shows that in the sixteenth century Matthew Parker, John Foxe and others had used Anglo-Saxon religious texts to support anti-Catholic doctrine. Gibson-Thwaites, 20 May 1697, quoted by J. Nichols, *Literary Anecdotes of the Eighteenth Century* (9 vols London 1812–15) iv. 143.

[3] W. Somner, *Dictionarium saxonico-latino-anglicum* (Oxford 1659).

[4] Francis Junius (1589–1677), B. Heidelberg; librarian to Thomas Howard, 2nd e. of Arundel, 1621–51.

Fortunately for the university, a favourite pupil of Junius was Thomas Marshall, who had collaborated with his friend during their residence together in Holland and had included Junius's extensive Gothic glossary with his 'Observations' on the Anglo-Saxon and Gothic Gospels in 1665.[1] Marshall's 'Observations' were a pioneering work in applying a rigorous comparative method to an Anglo-Saxon text and they brought him, apparently unsolicited, a fellowship at Lincoln in 1668.[2] Four years later this enthusiastic Saxonist found himself rector of his college, and in 1674 Junius, now in his mid-eighties, returned to settle in Oxford near his friend, where students evidently found him kindly and approachable. William Nicolson recalled: 'I was indeed frequently with him, dureing his stay there: But (alass!) I can remember little more of him then that he was very kind and communicative, very good and very old.'[3] At Junius's death in 1677 the university gained possession of his impressive collection of Anglo-Saxon and 'septentrional' type (punches and matrices) and this, together with the old man's invaluable manuscripts, gave Oxford an unparalleled opportunity.[4] John Fell, taking the initiative in this as in so many other scholarly matters of his day, realized that Anglo-Saxon study needed to establish its priorities before genuine advances could be made. There were three things necessary: a new dictionary which would be helpful to students as well as scholars (Somner's was becoming scarce and expensive),[5] an authoritative grammar (so that Anglo-Saxon could take its place as a respectable learned language) and a comprehensive catalogue of Anglo-Saxon manuscripts. During the next twenty-five years these projects remained, along with the editing of important texts, the chief priorities of the Oxford Saxonists.

It was necessary, too, to have some kind of formal teaching of the subject within the university. This was first provided by William Nicolson, who had entered Queen's as a batteler in 1670 and made such progress in his studies as to recommend himself to Joseph Williamson, Secretary of State, the college's influential patron.[6] In 1678 Williamson paid for Nicolson to travel abroad, where he studied at the University of Leipzig and returned to a fellowship at Queen's in 1679. Williamson, like Fell,

[1] T. Marshall, *In quatuor d.n. Jesu Christi evangeliorum versiones perantiquae duae, gothica scil. et anglo-saxonica* (Dordrecht 1665).

[2] *DNB*.

[3] Nicolson-Thwaites, 11 Mar. 1698, Bodl. MS Rawl. d. 377, fo 81.

[4] On Junius's punches and matrices see S. Morison, *John Fell, the University Press, and the 'Fell' Types* (Oxford 1967), 244-5.

[5] Somner's dictionary 'had not been re-published after its first appearance in 1659, and could not now be bought for less than 30/- a copy': J. A. W. Bennett, 'The history of Old English and Old Norse studies in England from the time of Francis Junius till the end of the eighteenth century' (Oxford D.Phil. thesis 1938), 79.

[6] On Nicolson see F. G. James, *North Country Bishop: a biography of William Nicolson* (New Haven and London 1956). Sir Joseph Williamson (1633-1701), m. Queen's 1650; incorporated at Cambridge 1659; secretary of state 1660-1, 1674; president of the Royal Society 1677-80.

was eager to further Anglo-Saxon studies, and so, as well as giving Nicolson financial assistance, he founded a Saxon lectureship at Queen's and appointed his protégé to the post.[1] Thomas Dixon wrote to Daniel Fleming:

wee have admitted one Mr Nicholson (whom Sir Joseph has sent both into Germany and France) into our Society ... hee's so well skill'd in the Saxon Language that Sir Joseph has founded a Saxon Lecture in our Colledge which he reades every Wednesday in Terme time.[2]

The first task Nicolson engaged in proved to be abortive. Junius's great work, still in manuscript, was the 'Dictionarium saxonicum', and as part of his great scheme for Anglo-Saxon studies Fell determined that his Oxford press should publish it. Nicolson embarked on the task of its transcription, which he completed in eleven folio volumes; but the project ran into financial difficulties and at Fell's death in 1686 the unpublished manuscript was bequeathed to the Bodleian Library. A specimen of the dictionary had, however, appeared, and Nicolson himself was still sanguine about its publication in 1696.[3]

If work on the dictionary was disappointing, the enterprise of the grammar, in spite of setbacks, proved an unqualified success. Fell intended that this should be a companion to Junius's dictionary, and Thomas Marshall began work on it.[4] At Marshall's death in 1685 the task devolved upon Nicolson, whose ecclesiastical career intervened. Fell then astutely settled the inheritance on Marshall's own promising protégé at Lincoln College, George Hickes, who was given encouragement and assistance after Fell's death by John Mill, principal of St Edmund Hall, and Arthur Charlett, who superintended the printing of the work—more evidence of the importance leading university figures gave to the study of Anglo-Saxon. Hitherto scholars had had to rely upon the venerable grammar of Aelfric, printed in Somner's dictionary; the appearance at Oxford in 1689 of Hickes's *Institutiones grammaticae anglo-saxonicae et moeso-gothicae* was a great leap forward; its impressive accuracy and clarity of presentation raised the stature of the Anglo-Saxon language and gave invaluable assistance to a new generation of

---

[1] *CSPD 1679-80*, 92, 157.

[2] Dixon-Fleming, 27 Nov. 1679, *The Flemings in Oxford* i. 302.

[3] Junius's manuscript of his dictionary is now Bodl. MSS Junius 2 and 3; Nicolson's transcript is now Bodl. MSS Fell 8-18. 'Dr Wallis has undertaken the management of the Saxon Dictionary, and printed a Specimen which I shall send you': H. Todd-D. Fleming, 11 Apr. 1682, *The Flemings in Oxford* ii. 50. For Nicolson's view see W. Nicolson, *The English Historical Library* (London 1696), 104: 'His large Glossary or Lexicon of the five old Northern Languages (whereof the *Saxon* has the preference) may be seen in the Author's own MS in *Bodley*'s Library; and a fair Transcript of it (in Eleven volumes, at the charge of the late pious Bishop *Fell*) in the *Musaeum Ashmoleanum*. It was design'd for the Press by that most excellent Prelate; and may be yet hoped for.'

[4] Rough outlines of Marshall's work are in Bodl. MS Marshall 78.

students. It is typical of the generosity of these scholars that William Nicolson later admitted that Hickes had been better equipped than he for the work, and he praised his friend's 'excellent performance', adding that the grammar

discovers an Accuracy in this Language beyond the Attainments of any that had gone before him in that Study; and will be of most necessary use to such as shall apply themselves to the right understanding of the ancient History and Laws of this Kingdom.[1]

As well as the grammar the volume contained the 'Rudiments of Icelandic grammar' and an Icelandic glossary (both by Runólfur Jónsson);[2] a handy, though far from exhaustive, catalogue of books and manuscripts; and Edward Bernard's 'Etymologicon britannicum'.

While Hickes's grammar was being printed a precocious undergraduate at Queen's, Edmund Gibson, was engaged on a complete transcription of one of the Bodleian Library's Old English manuscripts.[3] John Mill, who had encouraged Gibson, was clearly impressed by the young man's knowledge and accuracy, to the extent that he now enlisted him to prepare a new and full edition of the Anglo-Saxon chronicles, a project long accepted as a *desideratum* by Marshall, Junius and Fell, and one of the tasks which had fallen to William Nicolson, now resident in the north of England. The most recent edition by Abraham Wheloc of Cambridge (1643) had been based on two of the existing manuscripts, but in spite of valuable notes it was inadequate as a critical edition.[4] Gibson's *Chronicon saxonicum*, published at Oxford in 1692, had the advantage of being able to make use of three further manuscripts (including the 'Peterborough' chronicle and Junius's transcription from another recension) though this led him to print the chronicle to the year 1154 as one continuous narrative—an unfortunate and influential error. The text, split vertically into two columns to allow parallel printing of the Anglo-Saxon with Gibson's 'elegant and proper Translation'[5] was followed by extensive notes on textual variants, a fifty-page explanatory study of place-names, an index of personal names and a full chronological index. It was a remarkable piece of work for a twenty-three-year-old, and it remained the standard edition until 1823.

[1] Nicolson, *English Historical Library*, 101-2.
[2] The Icelandic scholar Runólfur Jónsson (d. 1654) had published his grammar, the first modern grammar of Icelandic, at Copenhagen in 1651.
[3] Bodl. MS Junius 121, containing Old English canons and constitutions. Gibson's transcript is now BL MS Harl. 441. The text itself was probably presented by Fell and therefore not part of the original Junius bequest: see *A Summary Catalogue of Western Manuscripts in the Bodleian Library at Oxford* (7 vols in 13 Oxford 1895-1953) ii (by F. Madan, H. H. E. Craster and N. Denholm-Young), p. 990.
[4] Wheloc's edition of the *Chronologia saxonica* appeared with his edition of Bede, *Historiae ecclesiasticae gentis Anglorum libri V* (Cambridge 1643).
[5] Nicolson, *English Historical Library*, 115.

Like Nicolson before him, however, Gibson felt called to an ecclesiastical career, and though he remained attached to Anglo-Saxon studies his
strenuous activities as bishop of Lincoln and bishop of London robbed
Queen's of an important member of its 'school'. The greatest days of the
college's 'nest of Saxonists' were, however, still to come with the arrival
there in 1689 of Edward Thwaites.[1] Thwaites was by all accounts a man of
enormous charm, handsome, good-humoured, lively in conversation and
tirelessly devoted to his work and his pupils. Not only did he produce valuable work under his own name, but he unselfishly assisted and encouraged
others. With Hickes—as a nonjuror—unable to play a full part in the studies
of the university it was Thwaites who became the Oxford leader of the
Saxonists at the height of their importance.

Thwaites's first project was an edition of parts of the Anglo-Saxon Old
Testament, consisting of the 'Heptateuch' (Genesis, Exodus, Leviticus,
Numbers, Deuteronomy, Joshua, Judges) and the Book of Job, with the
gospel of Nicodemus and the fragment of Judith.[2] Some of this material
had not been published before, and the volume marked an important
advance in the reputation of Aelfric, whose preface to Genesis it contained. William Nicolson, thanking Thwaites for his present of the
volume, regretted that the Latin texts had not been included, and in
doing so he made a significant point about the limited readership the
book would have:

I wish you had given us the Vulgar Latin with it. It looks indeed more masterly
and more becoming an University edition, to have a book sent abroad that supposes it shall meet with plenty of readers that shall understand it as well as the
publisher does ... the world is not yet so well stocked with men skilled in our
Saxon language and antiquities as we may hope to see it.[3]

In the same year (1698) Thwaites was admitted to a fellowship at
Queen's, and on 28 July he called upon his friend Hickes, 'the great
restorer of our Saxon learning' (to whom the *Heptateuchus* was dedicated) and the two men discussed another project:

he thought fit to mention his having heard that I design'd an edition of King
Alfred's Saxon translation of Orosius. I told him I knew not whether such a thing
would be tolerably well receiv'd. He said it was certainly worthy of the publick,
because it would enrich us with a store of words in that language, and acquaint us
with the terms they made use of in those days, both in History and Geography.[4]

[1] See M. Murphy, 'Edward Thwaites, pioneer teacher of Old English', *Durham Univ. Jl* lxxiii
(1980-1).
[2] *Heptateuchus, liber Job, et evangelium Nicodemi; anglo-saxonice; historiae Judith fragmentum, dano-
saxonice*, ed. E. Thwaites (Oxford 1698). There was no further edition of the Heptateuch until 1922.
[3] Nicolson-Thwaites (nd), quoted by Nichols, *Literary Anecdotes* iv. 145.
[4] Note by Thwaites, 28 July 1698, in 'Memoranda of Thwaites the Saxonist', *Gentleman's Magazine*
new ser. ii (1834), 260-3.

(It is significant that these men thought of themselves as historians rather than literary scholars.) Hickes might have added that years earlier Thomas Marshall had begun work on such an edition, and for this purpose had collated Junius's transcript of Cotton Manuscript Tiberius B.i with the Lauderdale manuscript.[1] This project, however, and Thwaites's own, were laid aside, and it was not until 1773 that the design was carried into execution.[2]

Thwaites was kept busy by his new post as 'Anglo-Saxon praeceptor' and devoted much of his energies to teaching. On 14 January 1699 he wrote hurriedly to Hickes: 'I have a class of young Saxons. A gentleman Commoner, and three Commoner[s]. All men of parts. 2 of them are my own pupils, and 2 of Edmund Hall. If I write not soe often as formerlie you must excuse me.'[3] And two months later he told Humfrey Wanley about one of the difficulties which his pupils faced: 'I have 15 young Students in that Language and but one Somner for them all.'[4] It was obviously becoming a priority to have a handy and easily accessible dictionary: in 1692 Wanley himself had been forced to make one for his own use and that of his friends and it was obviously becoming something of a sore point between them.[5]

It was to rectify this deficiency that one of Thwaites's 'young Saxons' at Queen's, Thomas Benson, began to prepare an epitome of Somner's dictionary; but this scheme was set aside, and only a specimen title-page and first leaf appear to have been printed in 1699.[6] But the English 'school' at Queen's pressed on with the task, and it was over the name of Benson that the *Vocabularium anglo-saxonicum* (or Anglo-Saxon/Latin word-list) was published in 1701. Thomas Hearne, his ear close to the ground as always, reveals how much of a common enterprise it was:

The Saxon Dictionary printed at Oxon which bears the Name of Mr Thomas Benson then B. of Arts, afterwards Master in that Faculty, of Queen's College was done chiefly by Mr Thwaites. Mr Todhunter of the same College had some hand in it, as had also two or three more Young Gentlemen of the same College tho' not mention'd in the Preface which was writ by Mr Thwaites, or rather Dr Mill. 'Tis a Compendium of Mr Somner. The Additions taken from Mr Junius's Papers in the Bodlejan Library.[7]

Another precocious student of Queen's, Christopher Rawlinson, made use of Junius's transcripts to produce a valuable edition of Alfred's

[1] See Bennett, 'Old English and Old Norse studies', 35.
[2] See p. 823 below.
[3] Bodl. MS Eng. Hist. c.6, fos 100-1.
[4] Letter of 24 Mar. 1699, BL MS Harl. 3781, fo 188.
[5] Wanley's dictionary, 'Liber Humfredi Wanley et amicorum', is now BL MS Harl. 3317.
[6] Bodl. MS Rawl. d.377, fos 80-1. H. G. Carter, *A History of the Oxford University Press* i (Oxford 1975), 414 and 438, misled by the unevenly inked imprint, assigns the specimen to 1690.
[7] Hearne, *Collections* i. 248 (21 May 1706). Joseph Todhunter (1679-1732), m. Queen's 1695.

translation of Boethius. It was dedicated to Thwaites and was note-worthy in that Rawlinson recognized parts of the text (translating Boeth-ius's metrical sections) to be in fact Anglo-Saxon verse and not the continuous prose that they appeared.[1] This difficulty in the printing of some Anglo-Saxon texts was to recur, and it is to Rawlinson's credit that he set the verse in the correct metrical half-lines. Two hundred and fifty copies were printed, at Rawlinson's own expense, and many were distri-buted as presents to other scholars and friends.[2]

William Nicolson too, although many miles away in Cumberland, kept in regular touch with his Oxford friends. He confessed to Benson that Anglo-Saxon studies still exercised a fatal fascination for him:

It has been lately said that I *have no Luck in Saxon*; and perhaps I am here as unfortunate as in any other Conjectures: But the Fate of many Unfortunate Lovers attends me. I am not easily to be brow-beaten into a discontinuance of my Suit; even when I know I serve a Coy Mistress.[3]

He had certainly seen his own earlier projects (Junius's dictionary, the Saxon grammar and the chronicles) pass into different hands; but if he could not serve his mistress personally he would encourage the wooing of others. The fourth chapter of his *English Historical Library* is both a helpful guide to the materials available to prospective pre-conquest his-torians and a review of the progress up to his own day of Anglo-Saxon scholarship. Writing in the thick of the 'ancients v. moderns' controversy he was eager to justify such studies by challenging Swift's patron and champion of the 'classics', William Temple:

The times [of the Saxons and Danes] were not so *lawless*, nor the Authors so *few* and *mean*, as he imagines . . . we have a pretty good stock of their Laws and His-torical Treatises; and those that have been conversant in 'em do not think they have thrown away their time upon so *ignoble a Subject* as some may fansie it.[4]

---

[1] *An. Manl. Sever. Boethii consolationis philosophiae libri V. anglo-saxonice redditi ab Alfredo inclyto Anglo-Saxonum rege*, ed. C. Rawlinson (Oxford 1698). Christopher Rawlinson (1677-1733), m. Queen's 1695. 'Much of the care with which it was edited must be ascribed to Mr Thwaites; and, if I am not very much mistaken, the Latin Preface was written by the same hand as Thwaites's Grammar was': H. Ellis in Nichols, *Literary Anecdotes* iv. 146. Rawlinson's text is based on Bodl. MS Junius 12, Junius's transcript of Bodl. MS Bodley 180 with variants from the Cotton MS Otho A.vi. Junius also tran-scribed into this manuscript the passages in Old English verse (translating Boethius's metrical sec-tions) which are unique to the Cotton manuscript (the other manuscripts being in prose throughout) but he did not set these out as verse. In his preface (sig. a2ᵛ) Rawlinson noted that he had decided to set them out as such at the end of his volume as a specimen of Anglo-Saxon poetry: 'sepositis in finem libri metris codicis *Cottoniani*; ita quidem, ut Anglo-Saxonicae poeseos ratio, ut ita dicam, ac forma, quoad ejus fieri poterat, exhiberetur; divisis scilicet ac distinctis singulis versibus, qui in exemplari MS continuâ scripturâ, posita licet ad singulos versus interpunctione, repraesen-tantur'.

[2] Bennett, 78.

[3] Nicolson-Benson, 2 Oct. 1701, Bodl. MS Rawl. d.377, fo 27ᵛ.

[4] Nicolson, *English Historical Library*, 99-100. Temple's 'Essay upon the ancient and modern learning' had appeared in his *Miscellanea* pt 2 (London 1690).

It must not be forgotten that throughout this period the Oxford Saxonists were faced with justifying their subject before the outside world.

By the turn of the century, however, Anglo-Saxon studies in Oxford were thriving as never before. The Oxford press was publishing major editions and works of reference; the university's teaching in the subject was in the hands of Edward Thwaites, a capable and charismatic figure; young students were actively contributing to the new knowledge and some of the university's leading figures (notably Mill and Charlett) were continuing the patronage of the previous generation of Fell and Marshall. The Junius type had been put to official use when Anglo-Saxon contributions appeared in the Oxford verses, and at the 1693 commemoration Thomas Hooper of University College delivered a Latin oration on the old northern languages.[1] Humfrey Wanley was by no means exaggerating when he declared to Hickes in 1698: 'The Saxon we see flourishes here, more than in all the world besides.'[2] This does not mean that Anglo-Saxon studies proceeded without opposition: Hooper's speech (for which Edmund Gibson appears to have been at least partly responsible) included a rhetorical onslaught against the anti-Saxonists within and outside the university:

Those who are fastidious and arrogant, possessed with a high opinion of themselves ... These are the people who permit themselves to think that their ancestors were not endowed with the same judgement as themselves, or provided with the same penetration, or scarcely even animated by the same common breath ... Those hands are so delicate that they dare not handle parchments covered with dirt and dust; those minds are too tender to be able to bear the more repulsive sight of Saxon, Gothic or Runic script. The result is that their mental powers are stunted ...[3]

It was in this context of aggressive confidence that work was set in hand on what was to be the most ambitious monument to Oxford's Anglo-Saxon scholarship, and indeed it was Hickes, the renegade and wanted man for whom settled scholarly work was proving virtually

[1] William Elstob contributed a 'Carmen anglo-saxonicum' to the *Exequiae* (Oxford 1700), *Pietas universitatis oxoniensis* (Oxford 1702), *Exequiae* (Oxford 1708) and *Pietas universitatis oxoniensis* (Oxford 1714); Humfrey Wanley also contributed one to the first collection. See also D. Patterson, 'Hebrew studies', above. Two of Elstob's are printed (with translations) by M. Murphy, 'Scholars at play: a short history of composing in Old English', *Old English Newsletter* xv (1981-2). Hooper's oration 'Linguae avitae septentrionales postliminio recuperatae' is in *Theatri oxoniensis encaenia, sive comitia philologica* (Oxford 1693), sigs. E1ᵛ-E2ᵛ. Bennett, 58 states that a similar address was given the following year for which Edmund Gibson was 'partly responsible', but there was no commemoration in 1694.

[2] Wanley-Hickes, 18 Feb. 1698, Bodl. MS Eng. Hist. c.6, fo 20.

[3] This passage has been kindly translated from the Latin by R. L. Thomson of the School of English, University of Leeds. In a letter to Charlett of 20 April 1694 Gibson admitted his part in a 'declamation upon the *Septentrional* tongues', probably Hooper's speech of 1693: MS Ballard 5, fo 30. Hickes apparently disapproved of its tactics and had hoped for a more scholarly account of the subject.

impossible, who took this study to a new level of achievement. The story of his massive *Thesaurus* is once again that of a genuinely co-operative venture, but it was the energy and dedication of Hickes himself, labouring under enormous personal difficulties, which informed the whole enterprise.[1]

Hickes had been installed as dean of Worcester in 1683, during a decade when religious and constitutional principles were being strained to breaking point. The year of the Revolution settlement (1689) saw the publication of Hickes's *Institutiones grammaticae*, and it was no mere scholarly interest which caused him to include in his preface the ancient coronation oath of the Saxon kings.[2] Refusing the oath of allegiance to William, Hickes was ejected in 1690 from his deanery and for the next nine years he was a man on the run, hidden by his friends and in danger from the mob.[3] Negotiating as a nonjuring 'bishop' with the exiled King James he put his very life in danger and it was against this turbulent and uneasy background that he began his great work.

Hickes's original plan was for a second edition of his grammar;[4] but as the work progressed and as his helpers increased in number the scope of the book widened. Evidence from the correspondence of Árni Magnússon, the Icelandic manuscript-collector, shows that Hickes was in contact with Scandinavian scholars and was eager to draw on their help to expand his work.[5] William Nicolson, working tirelessly from Cumberland to secure subscriptions for the volume, was delighted at its progress: 'the Doctor meets with far more encouragement than his own

[1] G. Hickes *et al. Linguarum veterum septentrionalium thesaurus grammatico-criticus et archaeologicus* (2 vols Oxford 1703–5); the work bears the general title *Antiquae literaturae septentrionalis libri duo*, but is known by the title of its first part, Hickes's *Thesaurus*. On the development of the *Thesaurus* see J. A. W. Bennett, 'Hickes's "Thesaurus": a study in Oxford book-production', *Essays and Studies* new ser. i (1948: new ser. i–ii only entitled *English Studies*); and R. L. Harris, 'George Hickes, White Kennett, and the inception of the *Thesaurus linguarum septentrionalium*', *Bodleian Library Record* xi, no. 3 (Nov. 1983).

[2] Hickes, *Institutiones grammaticae*, sigs. C1ᵛ-C2.

[3] A graphic description of Hickes's struggles is given by Douglas, *English Scholars*, 80–3.

[4] He wrote to Charlett on 20 April 1698 asking if the University Press would once again print the work: 'I have found good encouragement from severall learned men, who have desired me to reprint this work'. MS Ballard 12, fo 132.

[5] 'A good friend has written to me, to the effect that Hickes wishes to edit and have printed his Grammar, and improve it with a list of more Icelandic and Scandinavian writings': Peder Syv-Magnússon, 9 Dec. 1696, *Arne Magnússons Private Brevveksling* (Copenhagen and Christiania 1920), 504. P. Poulsen wrote to Magnússon from Oxford on 25 August 1699: 'The reason for my writing is a request from a learned Englishman, George Hickes, who has had published a book with this title: Institutiones Grammaticae . . . and since he now plans to have published a new edition of this same work, and needs help in increasing the Catalogus librorum Septentrionalium he has not merely written to me, but actually spoken to me, requesting that, since I knew you, I would write to you asking if you would send him a Catalogue 'veterum Danorum, Suecorum, Islandorum, tam eorum, qui in Archivis adhuc delitescunt, quam qui Doctorum cura in publicum prodiere', since he was convinced that you could best help him in this respect; your name has long been known to him . . .' Ibid. 363–4. These passages have been kindly translated from the Danish by R. W. McTurk of the School of English, University of Leeds.

circumstances, and those of the times, seemed to allow him to hope for'.[1] The subscriptions flowed in, and by November 1698 Edmund Gibson reported that he had seen fifteen sheets of the book already in print; a little later he rejoiced that it would be 'as much a book of criticisms as grammar rules' and would 'give us an insight into many customs, &c. about which we were wholly in the dark before'.[2] Fifty-five sheets were in print by August of the following year and there were hopes that its publication was imminent.[3] Delays increased, however, as Hickes and his collaborators worked on. Nicolson began to worry about the postponements: 'I am (I assure you) already call'd on by the Subscribers in this and the Neighbouring Counties; and I know not what Apology to make for my self.'[4]

In Oxford Thwaites took on the responsibility for the printing of the volume: he dealt with the financial details and the layout and supply of paper, as well as the mammoth task of proof-reading. Hickes acknowledged in his preface the assistance of this 'auctor adjutor maximus', who 'used his utmost Application in Revising and Correcting, with constant Care and Pains, the Sheets, as well those that were to go to the Press, as those that were already printed'.[5] Hickes clearly felt that the work was in good hands and that his own presence on the scene was unnecessary. On 5 January 1699 he told Arthur Charlett: 'I thank you most heartily for your affectionate invitation to Oxford; but Mr. Thwaites's skill, care, and diligence, makes it needless for me to be there.'[6]

The *Thesaurus* certainly was a 'treasure-house'. An example of its scope, and the way in which it drew help from the most unexpected quarters, was the catalogue of coins contributed by Sir Andrew Fountaine, virtuoso, diplomat and friend of Swift, who had studied Anglo-Saxon under Hickes. His 'Numismata anglo-saxonica & anglo-danica' was illustrated by plates and demonstrated how the study of coins could be an important source of historical evidence. During 1701–2 Fountaine travelled through Europe, and he reported regularly to his 'Dearest Ned' on his search for antiquities. On 23 February 1702 he wrote from Venice:

I have done at Vienna as much as was possible to get a sight of the MSS there, but the Library keeper being dead, I could by no means get a sight of 'em . . . As soon as the Carnivall is ended at this place, I will search the Librarys Here . . . I shall, if it please God I return safe, have one of the best collections of silver coins in England . . . they frequently meet with coins of our Saxon Ethelred in Germany.[7]

[1] Nicolson-Thoresby, 22 Oct. 1698, *Letters to Thoresby* i. 331.
[2] Gibson-Thoresby, 11 Nov. 1698, 23 Jan. 1699, ibid. 341, 357.
[3] Bennett, 'Hickes's "Thesaurus" ', 32–3.
[4] Nicolson-Thwaites, 10 July 1699, Bodl. MS Rawl. d.377, fos 46ᵛ-7.
[5] *Wotton's Short View of George Hickes's Grammatico-Critico and Archaeological Treasure of the Ancient Northern-Languages*, trans. M. Shelton (London 1735), 4.
[6] Nichols, *Literary Anecdotes* iv. 147.
[7] Bodl. MS Rawl. d.377, fo 61.

This roving unofficial ambassador for the Oxford Saxonists did return safe, and his illustrated catalogue proved one of the most praised sections of the *Thesaurus*.

Other helpers included Edmund Gibson, who provided transcripts from the Saxon laws, and Thomas Tanner (another former student of Queen's) who sent the texts of a Norwich charter and the *Land of Cockayne*; William Hopkins, prebendary of Worcester, supplied an annotated Anglo-Saxon commentary on the saints buried in England;[1] William Elstob gave a Latin translation, with notes, of Wulfstan's *Sermo Lupi ad Anglos*; Nicolson provided the inscription from the Ruthwell cross, and Thwaites made selections from the *Ormulum*. The scope of the work encompassed other northern tongues: Hickes included a comprehensive Frankish grammar and reprinted Runólfur Jónsson's Icelandic grammar and glossary.

The outstanding contribution, however, was Humfrey Wanley's 'Critical and historical catalogue of Anglo-Saxon manuscripts', generally recognized (then and now) as a landmark of Old English scholarship. Wanley's first patron had been Arthur Charlett, who found the young man an assistantship in the Bodleian Library, where he worked at the index to Bernard's catalogue, and then recommended him to Hickes.[2] It seems that Wanley's original aim was to make an enlarged revision of Hickes's own catalogue (appended to the *Institutiones grammaticae* of 1689). Wanley spread his search for Anglo-Saxon manuscripts through various parts of England and in 1699 he obtained leave from his Bodleian duties to make a two-month visit to Cambridge to inspect the libraries there. Hickes encouraged his enterprise and allowed him a free hand, with the result that the catalogue swelled to a separate folio volume of over three hundred pages. It was no mere list, but a detailed work of palaeography, within which for the first time the rich remains of the Anglo-Saxon heritage were displayed and examined. For succeeding generations 'Wanley's catalogue' was the key to any study of the period. Oxford, however, made little effort to keep him; he was frustrated in his aim to become Bodley's Librarian, and it was left to Robert Harley to provide him with an ideal situation as keeper of his own magnificent collection of manuscripts.

Hickes worked indefatigably at his *magnum opus*, and for the new work

---

[1] William Hopkins (1647-1700), m. Trin. 1661; MA St Mary Hall 1668, DD 1692.

[2] By 1698 Wanley was in great demand as a transcriber, and he was not slow to exploit this. Thwaites complained to Hickes: 'I cannot much use him, because he values his labours soe high. They must all be sold by weight and measure. And you will find, he must lose his interest in this place by that very means. I tell him plainly of it, but I find he will not write a sheet under a Guinnea. Tis more than an author expects for composing. A friend of mine offer'd him a Guinnea, for what he might have done in a day, but he would not accept it.' Letter of 19 Sept. 1698, Bodl. MS Eng. Hist. c.6, fo 70. On the *Catalogi librorum manuscriptorum Angliae et Hiberniae* (Oxford 1697 [*recte* 1698]) see Carter, *History of the Press* i. 245-7.

expanded his own *Institutiones grammaticae* by six chapters which were a breakthrough in comparative philology. One twentieth-century Saxonist has commented: 'he is as good as any modern grammarian on the disintegration and confusion of Late Old English in spelling, syntax, inflexional forms, gender, and number.'[1] Hickes was the first to use dated charters in order to trace the development of language, and his final chapters inaugurated the critical discussion of Old English poetry.[2] Of special significance for the study of Saxon laws was the *dissertatio epistolaris*, which investigated the source-materials for pre-conquest history and analysed the Anglo-Saxon system of government. 'After the *Thesaurus*, Anglo-Saxon studies were to make no appreciable advance until the development of the new philology in the nineteenth century.'[3]

Linguarum veterum septentrionalium thesaurus grammatico-criticus et archaeologicus duly appeared (1703-5) and was welcomed throughout Europe as a remarkable achievement. It did not, however, have a very large numerical circulation, and it neither intended to be, nor was, a financial success. Its influence, however, was far-reaching, and it stands as the fitting culmination of two decades of scholarly enterprise and cooperation within the university.

Now that the glorious work had been achieved, there was felt the need to make its contents more accessible to students and general readers. William Wotton, with Hickes's agreement and co-operation, produced in 1708 his *Conspectus*, an epitome of the larger work, branded by Hearne as 'a trivial, mean, Performance'.[4] In contrast with the massive *Thesaurus* no doubt it was, but Hickes himself had been concerned in it: 'Dr Hickes took care of the impression; and the notes (which I believe is a secret) are all his, except those upon the Saxon coins by Mr Thwaites.'[5] Thwaites's contribution was *Notae in Anglo-Saxonum nummos*, published separately at Oxford in that year and included in the *Conspectus* at Wotton's request; the coins in question were those of Thwaites's friend Fountaine. The *Thesaurus* became even more accessible with Maurice Shelton's translation of Wotton's *Conspectus* (London 1735). Shelton declared in his preface:

I make no doubt but a great many who may understand it better are discouraged from Reading either of them by a Sight of the *Saxon* and other

[1] Bennett, 'Old English and Old Norse studies', 96-7.
[2] It is to Hickes that we owe the survival of the 'Finnsburh fragment', which he discovered in a manuscript in the Lambeth library and printed in the first volume of the *Thesaurus*. The manuscript disappeared soon afterwards.
[3] Douglas, *English Scholars*, 89.
[4] W. Wotton, *Linguarum veterum septentrionalium thesauri grammatico-critici & archaeologici, auctore Georgio Hickesio, conspectus brevis* (London 1708). Hearne, *Collections* ii. 92 (8 Feb. 1708). Wotton had written *Reflections upon Ancient and Modern Learning* (London 1694) in support of the 'moderns' against Temple. [5] W. Clarke-W. Bowyer, Nichols, *Literary Anecdotes* ii. 110.

Characters in them, and by the Apprehensions they labour under besides that they contain nothing else but old dry Stuff.[1]

Such justifications were nothing new, and were to be repeated throughout the century. Thwaites, as always, showed concern for the inexperienced students of Anglo-Saxon, when he produced a useful small version of Hickes's grammar. His *Grammatica anglo-saxonica ex Hickesiano Linguarum Septentrionalium thesauro excerpta* (Oxford 1711) was to receive proper tribute from a later leader of Old English studies:

This little work only extends to 48 octavo pages; but being closely printed, it contains most of what is necessary for the young Saxon student; and, for the alphabetical arrangement of the irregular verbs, and some other particulars, it is a more practical and convenient work for a learner than Dr. Hickes's large Thesaurus.[2]

It is through Thwaites that Oxford can claim a minor share in one of the finest works of eighteenth-century scholarship, John Smith's Cambridge edition of Bede's *Ecclesiastical History*. His son, George Smith, left Cambridge for Oxford in 1711 to be Thwaites's pupil at Queen's, and when the Bede was left unfinished at his father's death in 1715 George took on the task of completing it, adding some valuable notes in the process.[3]

A severe blow to the Anglo-Saxon 'school' came when Thwaites died in 1711 after a heroic fight against illness. In his devotion to his students and his tireless encouragement of fellow scholars he had been an inspiration to many, the mainstay of Oxford's achievement in Saxon scholarship, and he could not be replaced.

Two committed Saxonists who owed a lot to Thwaites were William and Elizabeth Elstob, the brother and sister whose careers illustrate the struggle and frustration that Anglo-Saxon scholarship could involve. According to Hickes, William Elstob was 'extremely well versed in the Saxon tongue'[4] and at Hickes's request he contributed a Latin translation of *Sermo Lupi* to the *Thesaurus*. But William had an equally talented sister, who had settled with him in Oxford and taught herself Anglo-Saxon;

---

[1] *Wotton's Short View*, trans. Shelton, sig. A4ᵛ. Mores commented that the *Conspectus* had been 'translated into *Engl.* by *Mr Shelton* for his own improvement, and published to shew that one of his Majesty's justices of the peace may have sense and a taste for learning. Further use of the publication we know not: for those who seek after this or any other sort of knowledge will have recourse to the originals.' E. R. Mores, *A Dissertation upon English Typographical Founders* ([London] 1778), 27; Mores's *Dissertation* has been edited by H. G. Carter and C. Ricks for the Oxford Bibliographical Society (new ser. ix 1961).

[2] J. Bosworth, *The Elements of Anglo-Saxon Grammar* (London 1823), p. xxviii. Joseph Bosworth was Rawlinson prof. of Anglo-Saxon 1858-76.

[3] *Historiae ecclesiasticae gentis Anglorum libri quinque, auctore sancto ac venerabili Baeda* (Cambridge 1722). John Smith (1659-1715); George Smith (1693-1756), incorporated from Cambridge at Queen's 1711 where his uncle, Joseph Smith, was fellow and later provost.

[4] Nichols, *Literary Anecdotes* iv. 115.

besides this she was 'not only mistress of her own and the Latin tongue, but also of seven other languages'.[1] To a later scholar she was 'the *indefessa comes* of [her brother's] studies; a female student in the *Univ.*'.[2] Elizabeth Elstob had to endure during her lifetime the patronizing sobriquet of 'the Saxon nymph', but she refused to play the role expected of her. The long preface to her edition of Aelfric's homily for St Gregory's day, boldly dedicated to Queen Anne, was a powerful and direct piece of writing, being at the same time a justification of female education ('Where is the Fault in Womens seeking after Learning?') a defence of the 'primitive purity' of English religion and an attack on those who were 'ignorant, even to barbarity, of the Faith, Religion, the Laws and Customs, and Language of their Ancestors'.[3] As a propagandist for Anglo-Saxon studies she showed considerable boldness, particularly when she took up her cudgels against the great Dr Swift at the height of his career. Swift lamented that English was 'overstocked with Monosyllables' and he placed the blame squarely on the Germanic languages: 'This perpetual Disposition to shorten our Words, by retrenching the Vowels, is nothing else but a Tendency to lapse into the Barbarity of those *Northern* Nations from whom we are descended, and whose Languages labour all under the same Defect.'[4] This Augustan myth of progress from barbarity to civilization was a commonplace of the literary establishment, and it challenged the Saxonists' equally powerful myth of the virtuous native tradition. The preface (addressed to Hickes) of Elizabeth Elstob's Anglo-Saxon grammar of 1715 was no glib satirical response but a carefully argued justification of Anglo-Saxon studies, and also a cogent defence of monosyllables. She stressed the seriousness of the documents on which the Saxonists worked: 'The *Gospels*, the *Psalms*, and a great part of the *Bible* are in *Saxon*, so are the *Laws* and *Ecclesiastical Canons*, and *Charters* of most of our *Saxon Kings*; these one wou'd think might deserve their Credit.'[5] (Perhaps she remembered the *Tatler*'s sketch of her as a professor in 'a college for young damsels . . . who is now publishing two of the choicest Saxon novels'.[6]) In its informal, pointed style it struck a new note among scholarly works, and in presenting 'the Rudiments of that Language in an English Dress' she obviously hoped to make Old English studies accessible to as wide an audience as possible.

The reception of Elizabeth's edition of Aelfric's homily encouraged

[1] Ibid. 129.

[2] Mores, *Dissertation*, 28.

[3] Aelfric, *Homily on the Birth-Day of St. Gregory*, ed. E. Elstob with Latin trans. by W. Elstob (London 1709), pp. ii, vi, xiii.

[4] J. Swift, *A Proposal for Correcting, Improving and Ascertaining the English Tongue* (London 1712), ed. H. Davis and L. Landa (Oxford 1957), 12.

[5] Elstob, *Rudiments of Grammar for the English-Saxon Tongue*, p. vi.

[6] Letter from 'Tobiah Greenhat', *Tatler* no. 63 (3 Sept. 1709).

the Elstobs to begin work on an ambitious enterprise for an Anglo-Saxon *homilarium*, to include most of the homilies of Aelfric. Hickes was in no doubt of the value of such a work, as he told Charlett:

I suppose you may have seen Mrs Elstob, sister to Mr Elstob formerly fellow of your Coll., and the MSS she hath brought to be printed at your presse. The university hath acquired much reputation and honour at home, and abroad by the Saxon books printed there ... the publication of the MSS she hath brought (the most correct I ever saw or read) will be of great advantage to the Church of England against the papists ... and the credit of our country, to which Mrs Elstob will be counted abroad, as great an ornament in her way, as Madame Dacire is to France.[1]

Aware of how important financial support was to the enterprise, Elizabeth Elstob issued from London in 1713 a small pamphlet, *Some testimonies of learned men in favour of the intended edition of the Saxon homilies, concerning the learning of the author of those homilies; and the advantages to be hoped for from an edition of them*. Royal support was obtained through Robert Harley, proposals were published and a two-page specimen issued to encourage subscriptions. But after the printing of thirty-six folio pages, 'for reasons now unknown the Press was stopped'. Their transcripts and notes for this ambitious enterprise remain unpublished.[2]

William Elstob was no more fortunate with his own plans. As early as 1699 he had issued a specimen of an edition of Alfred's Orosius[3] and he later embarked on a project which, to judge from one account, would have been a considerable achievement: 'an edition of the Saxon Laws, with great additions, and a new Latin Version by Somner, notes of various learned men, and a prefatory history of the origin and progress of the English Laws down to the Conqueror, and to Magna Charta.'[4] His sister told Ralph Thoresby in 1709: 'My brother ... has many things to do, if he had leisure and encouragement; King Alfred's translation of Orosius, he has ready for the press, and a great many materials towards the Saxon Laws, and a promise of more.'[5] Both works, however, were left unpublished at his death in 1715. Perhaps things might have been different if he had been successful in his many applications for ecclesiastical patronage, which would have given him more leisure and financial

---

[1] Hickes-Charlett, 23 Dec. 1712, MS Ballard 12, fo 203.

[2] Their five volumes of transcripts are now BL Lansdowne MSS 370-4: see *Catalogue of the Stowe Manuscripts in the British Museum* (London 1895) i. 653-4 and Ashdown, 'Elizabeth Elstob', 132-3. The quotation is a manuscript note on a copy of the proofs: Ashdown, 133.

[3] *Hormesta Pauli Orosii quam olim patrio sermone donavit Aelfredus magnus* (Oxford 1699). Only the title and two leaves were printed; according to Carter, *History of the Press* i. 432 these are now to be found in BL Lansdowne MS 373, fos 86-7.

[4] Nichols, *Literary Anecdotes* iv. 119-20.

[5] E. Elstob-Thoresby, 6 May 1709, *Letters to Thoresby* ii. 163.

security. It was left to Daines Barrington (a man with both) to rescue Elstob's Orosius manuscript and publish it with his own translation in 1773, 'for my own amusement and that of a few antiquarian friends'.[1]

With the deaths of Thwaites (1711) and Hickes (1715) Anglo-Saxon scholarship in Oxford lost its driving force. Young Saxonists had left the university for the grand tour or the vicarage, and there was no one to fill the roles of inspired teacher and heroic leader as those two had done. Thomas Benson, for example, after the publication of his dictionary in 1701, went north to become resident chaplain to his patron, William Nicolson, then bishop of Carlisle; and having married Nicolson's daughter in 1714 his career as a pluralist in the church was assured.[2] In his absence from Oxford Nicolson worked hard in soliciting subscriptions for scholarly works, and had lent his financial support too. In 1706 he was giving assistance to Thwaites's brother James: 'Mr Thwaites has a Brother, now Taberder of Queen's College, an ingenious man. He studys the Saxon Language, and receives an Annual Pension (as I heard Mr Thwaites say) from the said Bp of Carlisle to incourage him in the said studies.'[3] Nicolson apparently realized the need for an established university post, and when he became lord high almoner in 1716 he was in a position to do something positive in that direction. Moves had already been made in the university towards the endowment of a lectureship. In 1714 Hickes had welcomed Charlett's support for such a scheme: 'I am glad you intend to move for a Saxon lecture, by which you must let them understand, that you mean a Lecture for the ancient Septentrional tongues, and literature contained in them.'[4] Nicolson's 1716 plan was to endow lectureships at both universities, and for this purpose to reallocate two £50 pensions reserved for students of Arabic at Oxford and Cambridge.[5] Royal agreement was obtained, and in August Nicolson broached the subject to the vice-chancellor, John Baron:

I humbly pray'd, That (whereas there were establish'd professours of Arabic in both Universities) the King would please to order the payment of these Salaries, for the future, to two Readers of the antient Septentrional (and particularly the Anglo-Saxonic and Gothic) Languages; for the benefit (chiefly) of such young Gentlemen as are design'd for the Study and Profession of our Municipal Laws. His Majesty very Graciously and Readily agreed to the proposal; and commanded me to take such measures herein as I thought most proper.

[1] *The Anglo-Saxon Version, from the Historian Orosius, by Ælfred the Great* (London 1773), preface. Barrington's interest in the work is clear from his correspondence with Richard Gough: *Illustrations of the Literary History of the Eighteenth Century*, ed. J. Nichols (8 vols London 1817-58) v. 589-98.
[2] James, *North Country Bishop*, 208-9.
[3] Hearne, *Collections* i. 248 (21 May 1706). James Thwaites (c1684-1755), m. Queen's 1699, MA 1708. [4] Hickes-Charlett, 15 Dec. 1714, MS Ballard 12, fo 217.
[5] See L. S. Sutherland, 'The origin and early history of the lord almoner's professorship in Arabic at Oxford', *Bodleian Lib. Record* x (1978-82).

Now, Sir, the Bishop of Oxford and others have given me such an Advantageous
Character of Mr Gagnier that I am willing to continue his pension; provided
that (in such manner, and at such times, as you shall appoint) he Reads Eighteen lectures yearly on the foremention'd subject: Which, 'tis to be hoped, will
not be difficult for one of his Application to do.[1]

By the end of the month Nicolson had appointed David Wilkins to
receive one of the pensions, but a permanent endowment had still to be
achieved, as Wilkins wrote to his patron:

The sum of the Saxon Pension may be what it will, I am infinitely obliged to
your Lordship for bestowing it upon me, and shall strive to deserve it by
publishing what your Lordship shall approve of. I do not question, if in progress
of time I could print something in that study worth his Majesty's Dedication, a
grant for a perpetual establishment of a Royal Lecturer in both Universities
might easier be obtained, than it seems it can now.[2]

Nicolson's temporary expedient can be said to have had mixed success:
Wilkins went on to make an invaluable contribution to the study of the
history of the English church and of English law, but in Oxford the inexperienced Jean Gagnier (who retained his pension until 1740) did 'but
little in Saxon'[3] and was not the man to sustain the tradition of Hickes
and Thwaites.

Oxford's achievements in Anglo-Saxon studies had rested on three
foundations and each was now weakened: organized teaching of the language in the university had faltered; the sense of communal effort, by
which individual scholars supported and assisted each other, had been
lost; and there was no one to inherit Hickes's mantle as an inspiring
leader. Also, in spite of all their efforts, the Oxford Saxonists had never
won the propaganda battle with the cultural establishment outside the
university, and over the remaining decades of the century the story is at
best sketchy and episodic.

A great scholar who could have played an important role in continuing the work of the Oxford 'school' was Thomas Hearne. But so much
conspired against this. Hearne himself had never mastered the Anglo-
Saxon language, and though he admired Hickes and Thwaites he was
temperamentally unsuited to scholarly teamwork (his remarkable contribution to medieval historiography was a solo effort).[4] In addition to
this, his refusal to take the oaths in 1715 brought the loss of his Bodleian
post and a lifelong ban from the university libraries. Hearne, however,

[1] Nicolson-Baron, 2 Aug. 1716, Bodl. Add. MS c.217, fo 48 (Nicolson's copy).
[2] Wilkins-Nicolson, 29 Aug. 1716, *Letters on Various Subjects … to and from William Nicolson*, ed.
J. Nichols (2 vols London 1809) ii. 447. Wilkins's great achievement was to be his *Concilia Magnae
Britanniae et Hiberniae* (4 vols London 1737).
[3] Wilkins–Nicolson, *Letters to and from Nicolson* ii. 470.
[4] Hearne considered Elizabeth Elstob's edition of Aelfric's *Homily on the Birth-Day of St. Gregory* a
'Farrago of Vanity': *Collections* ii. 290 (20 Oct. 1709).

did leave his mark on Anglo-Saxon studies with his editions of the *Textus roffensis* and Heming's cartulary, and it is partly to him that we owe the survival of *The Battle of Maldon*. This poem in the Cottonian collection had been noted in Wanley's catalogue and was included by Hearne as an appendix to his edition of the chronicle of John of Glastonbury; Hearne worked not from the original manuscript but from a transcript by John Elphinston, and lacking technical knowledge of Old English verse he printed it as prose.[1] Nevertheless, after the disastrous Cottonian Library fire in 1731 in which the manuscript perished, Hearne's text was for two centuries the only extant version until Elphinston's transcript came to light earlier this century.

The one notable exception to the dearth of Anglo-Saxon scholarship during the middle and later years of the century is the work of Edward Lye; but, though he studied at Oxford, he does not appear to have begun learning the language until he settled at his Northamptonshire vicarage in 1721.[2] His works therefore did not issue from the university, but they did take further the plans of the Oxford Saxonists of the previous two generations. His edition of Junius's manuscript etymology of the English language in the Bodleian Library contains also Graevius's life of Junius and an Anglo-Saxon grammar by the editor. As a result of this publication Johnson was able to make extensive use of Junius's etymologies (though not uncritically) in his *Dictionary*.[3] Lye's next task was an edition of the Gothic Gospels, again including a grammar of the language.[4] The climax of his studies, though, was the long-wished-for Anglo-Saxon dictionary on which he had begun work in 1737. A two-leaf specimen was issued in 1763 and encouraging subscriptions began to come in.[5] But at Lye's death only about thirty sheets were in print, and the *Dictionarium saxonico et gothico-latinum* appeared posthumously at London in 1772 in two volumes under the editorship of his friend Owen Manning (the historian of Surrey) who made some additions of his own and included Lye's Anglo-Saxon and Gothic grammars.

---

[1] *Textus roffensis*, ed. T. Hearne (Oxford 1720); *Hemingi chartularium ecclesiae wigorniensis*, ed. T. Hearne (2 vols Oxford 1723); *Johannis glastoniensis chronica*, ed. T. Hearne (2 vols Oxford 1726). Elphinston's transcript of Cotton MS Otho A xii, fos 57-62ᵛ is now Bodl. MS Rawl. b.203, fos 7-12ᵛ: see *The Battle of Maldon*, ed. D. G. Scragg (Manchester 1981), 1-8.

[2] 'In this retreat he laid the foundation of his great proficiency in the Anglo-Saxon language': A. Chalmers (ed.), *The General Biographical Dictionary* (32 vols London 1812-17) xxi. 10.

[3] Francis Junius, *Etymologicum anglicanum*, ed. E. Lye (Oxford 1743). In 1696 Nicolson had looked forward to the printing of Junius's etymology, 'a work completely finish'd in two Volumes; which will be also of singular use to our *English* Antiquary': *English Historical Library*, 105. Cf S. Johnson, *A Dictionary of the English Language* (2 vols London 1755), preface, sig. B1: 'For the *Teutonick* etymologies I am commonly indebted to *Junius* and *Skinner*... *Junius* is always full of knowledge; but his variety distracts his judgment, and his learning is very frequently disgraced by his absurdities.'

[4] *Sacrorum evangeliorum versio gothica*, ed. E. Lye (Oxford 1750).

[5] *Specimen dictionarii anglo-saxonico-gothico-latini*, Bodl. MS Add. c.244, fos 407-8. This contains entries for Aa-Ad.

Within the university Francis Wise and George Ballard were Oxford's representative Saxonists, but in each of them a knowledge of the Old English language shaded into antiquarianism and numismatics, and neither made a significant contribution to Anglo-Saxon studies.[1] In 1754, when Ballard left Oxford for the last time, there was still interest in the subject among some of the students, but Wise lamented to Edward Lye that they lacked someone to inspire and organize them:

[Ballard] told me at parting, that there is a good disposition in some of the young people in the place towards the Northern languages: though they have as yet made but little progress in them, but without doubt would make a great deal, if they had but the countenance of two or three leaders here, to keep them from being laughed out of the study. As you are at the head of this sort of learning, it would be but kind in you to spend a few weeks among us now and then, and set us forward by your example. It is a duty you owe to the commonwealth of learning, and to your friend Junius, whose labours are likely to continue neglected, unless a spirit and taste for these things can be revived among us.[2]

Lye does not appear to have responded to this invocation of the spirit of Junius, and young Oxford Saxonists remained in danger of being 'laughed out of the study'.

During the second half of the century it proved impossible to break out of the view that linguistic and cultural history since Saxon times had been a growth from barbarity to civilization; Anglo-Saxon studies were seen as matter for antiquarians. Even the gothic enthusiasts were led to undervalue it. Horace Walpole remarked dismissively: 'never did exist a more barbarous jargon than the dialect, still venerated by antiquaries, and called *Saxon*'; and Thomas Warton, who could so easily have inherited the tradition of Hickes and Thwaites, opened his *History of English Poetry* with the Norman conquest.[3] The great Dr Johnson gave an

---

[1] At his house in Elsfield Wise collected a library rich in works of 'northern' literature. He produced an edition of Asser's life of Alfred (Oxford 1722) and several works on coins and antiquities. Originally a stay-maker at Chipping Campden, Gloucestershire, Ballard developed a taste for Anglo-Saxon and coin-collecting. He visited Oxford several times and made the acquaintance of Hearne. In 1750 he settled in Oxford on £60 a year from his patrons in Gloucestershire and was made one of the eight clerks of Magdalen College. He transcribed Somner's dictionary (his transcript is now MS Ballard 51) and Alfred's Orosius (London, Society of Antiquaries Library, MS 64) but his only separate publication was *Memoirs of Several Ladies of Great Britain who have been Celebrated for their Writings or Skill in the Learned Languages, Arts and Sciences* (Oxford 1752).

[2] Wise-Lye, 10 Sept. 1754, BL Add. MS 32325, fo 117.

[3] H. Walpole, *Historic Doubts on the Life and Reign of King Richard the Third* (London 1768), p. x. T. Warton, *The History of English Poetry* (3 vols London 1774-81) i, p. vi: 'Some perhaps will be of opinion, that these annals ought to have commenced with a view of the Saxon poetry. But besides that a legitimate illustration of that jejune and intricate subject would have almost doubled my labour, that the Saxon language is familiar only to a few learned antiquaries, that our Saxon poems are for the most part little more than religious rhapsodies, and that scarce any compositions remain marked with the native images of that people in their pagan state, every reader that reflects but for a moment on our political establishment must perceive, that the Saxon poetry has no connection with the nature and purpose of my present undertaking. Before the Norman accession ... we were an

extremely brief and sketchy account of Anglo-Saxon in the 'History of the English Language' which was prefixed to his *Dictionary*, and though he printed a specimen of Alfred's Boethius ('the *Saxon* in its highest state of purity') the 'Land of Cockayne' and a passage from the chronicles (1135-40) he chose his extracts from the English language between Alfred and the Tudors 'in such a manner that its progress may be easily traced, and the gradations observed, by which it advanced from its first rudeness to its present elegance'.[1]

The one hope for the future lay in the bequest made to the university in 1755 under the will of Richard Rawlinson, which made an endowment for 'an Anglo-Saxon lecture'. The terms of the will, however, were hedged about with so many complications and idiosyncratic conditions that no action was taken until 1795.[2] It says little for the university's enthusiasm for Anglo-Saxon studies that such a long delay was allowed. The situation in 1795 does appear to have been serious. The old Oxford bookseller Daniel Prince (then in his eighties) lamented: 'Since the deaths of Mr. Lye, Rowe Mores, and two or three of Bishop Gibson's encouragers at Queen's College, I cannot hear of a buyer of Saxon Books.'[3] The professorship therefore seems to have been inaugurated at a time when Anglo-Saxon studies were languishing. The first professor (a St John's man as laid down in Rawlinson's will) was Charles Mayo,[4] whose lectures were apparently 'much applauded', but who published no scholarly work.[4] It may be, however, a slight exaggeration to say that

---

unformed and an unsettled race. That mighty revolution obliterated almost all relation to the former inhabitants of this island; and produced that signal change in our policy, constitution, and public manners, the effects of which have reached modern times.' By 1774 the Saxonists had lost the 'continuity' argument. But it would be wrong to think that Warton ignored Anglo-Saxon literature. In the two dissertations prefixed to his first volume he gave an English translation of *Brunanburh* and an account of Alfred, Aldhelm, Alcuin, Coelfrid and Bede, and in his opening chapter he mentioned *Beowulf, The Battle of Maldon* and *Genesis*: Warton, *History* i, diss. I, 'Of the origin of romantic fiction in Europe', sigs E3^v-4^v, diss. II, 'On the introduction of learning into England', sigs D1-F1, ch. 1, p. 2. Warton made use particularly of Hickes's *Thesaurus* and Wanley's catalogue.

[1] *Dictionary of the English Language*, sig. K2.

[2] See *The Deed of Trust and Will of Richard Rawlinson, of St. John Baptist College, Oxford, Doctor of Laws, containing his endowment of an Anglo-Saxon lecture, and other benefactions to the college and university* (London 1755). The professor was to be appointed for five years only and the first occupant (and every fifth succeeding occupant) was to be a St John's man. Rawlinson also excluded Scotsmen, married men and fellows of the Royal Society or the Society of Antiquaries.

[3] Prince-Gough, 18 Mar. 1795, Nichols, *Literary Anecdotes* iii. 707. Edward Rowe Mores (1731-78), m. Queen's 1746; one of the founders of the Society of Antiquaries.

[4] Charles Mayo (1767-1858), m. St John's 1785, fellow 1788; Rawlinson prof. of Anglo-Saxon 1795-1800. Mayo was apparently little known among Anglo-Saxon scholars. In 1796 Owen Manning wrote to Thomas Percy: 'I hope the new Saxon Professor is qualified to answer the intention of his founder, as well as to receive his salary. If the young students of Oxford knew but how much a knowledge of this our ancient language contributes to the perfect understanding of the modern English, he would not long want pupils.' Nichols, *Illustrations of Literary History* viii. 286 (1 June 1796). The rival candidate for the professorship in 1795 had been William Finch (1748-1810, m. St John's 1764; Bampton lecturer 1797): Nichols, *Literary Anecdotes* iii. 707.

828 D. FAIRER

'there is no evidence that he or anyone else in Oxford at that time knew
much Anglo-Saxon',[1] since in 1798 Mayo was provoked into defending in
print the great tradition of the university Saxonists against attack by an
Oxford man, Samuel Henshall.[2] Henshall's *Saxon and English Languages*
was a horrifying reversal of the work of Hickes and Lye, whom he considered to have been 'grossly wrong'. He overturned traditional Anglo-
Saxon grammar by declaring that all came naturally and easily so long as
the consonants were strongly pronounced and the vowels largely ignored. (He castigated Lye for paying 'too much attention to Vowels'.) All
formal grammar, conjugations, cases, gender and so on disappeared, to
be replaced by a totally fanciful etymology based on no other rule than
similarity of sound (*drighten*, 'lord', from *do-right*; *taken, broken* and the
like from an original *take-end, break-end*) and by the advice that students
should use Lye's grammar only as 'the last resource'; an aggressive Lan-
castrian pronunciation and a plentiful use of the imagination would do
all that was necessary. Henshall's illustrative translations, if that is the
word, revealed the scope of his achievement:

and lo thou thee the that, thou that Think in that Judaish folk hast sent, that
they this Healing one high-hang, that thou him none guilt on never once knew,
and thou now thorough that true *one*, and thorough that Rood havest all thine
Bliss fore-spoiled.[3]

In response to Henshall's wild onslaught on all that Oxford had built
up over more than a century, Mayo collaborated with Richard Gough to
publish a scholarly and uncompromising review, and though Henshall
counter-attacked he failed to answer their criticisms.[4] Perhaps Henshall's
publication may be allowed to represent Oxford's Anglo-Saxon studies at
their lowest ebb: in 1800, when Mayo's term of office ended, Henshall
stood as his successor in the professorship but was defeated by Thomas
Hardcastle, a man about whom little is known but who was probably a
sounder candidate.[5]

[1] Bennett, 'Old English and Old Norse studies', 206.
[2] S. Henshall, *The Saxon and English Languages Reciprocally Illustrative of Each Other* (London 1798).
Samuel Henshall (c1764-1807), m. BNC 1782.
[3] Henshall, 17, 58.
[4] The review appeared in the *Gentleman's Magazine* lxviii (1798), 1861-5. A sheet of notes for the
review, sent by Mayo to Gough, is in Bodl. MS Eng. lett. c.359, fo 78. The notes are undated but
clearly form part of the 1798 review, and they demonstrate Mayo's knowledge of Anglo-Saxon.
Gough sent Henshall's pamphlet-reply to Mayo, commenting: 'the man is confounded sore: his
views are blasted and he goes on like a desperado floundering before he finally sinks': Gough-Mayo,
20 Dec. 1798, Bodl. MS Eng. lett. b.4, fo 157[r-v]. Mayo replied on 17 February 1799: 'the author of it
excites my contempt and not my resentment . . . he has not attempted to confute any of the charges
brought against him in the Gent. Mag:' Bodl. MS Eng. lett. c. 359, fo 76.
[5] Thomas Hardcastle (c1751-1814), m. Queen's 1769; MA and fellow Merton 1776; Rawlinson
prof. of Anglo-Saxon 1800-3. His death-notice recorded that 'it would be difficult to describe a
character, in the several relations of life, more perfect, or more excellent': *Gentleman's Magazine*
lxxxiv (1814), 204.

The story of the Oxford Saxonists over the period is therefore one of triumph and decline. Between 1688 and 1715, the span of a single generation, the university achieved remarkable results thanks to a group of energetic and dedicated men (and one woman). Many elements, besides individual genius, played their part: ancestral piety, protestant zeal, patronage by the heads of houses, the availability of Anglo-Saxon manuscripts and the type with which to print them. But most important was a sense of joint endeavour, so vital when the polite world was eager to sneer at native antiquity. It was the loss of this continuity of effort, and a leader to inspire it, which did most to hasten the decline, and it was not until the new century opened that the subject began to make any advance. Thomas Hardcastle's successor in the Rawlinson chair, James Ingram, showed the way with an edition of the Anglo-Saxon chronicle which finally supplanted Gibson's *Chronicon* of 1692.[1] The path was now open for the Oxford 'school' to continue its progress.

[1] James Ingram (1774-1850), m. Trin. 1793, president 1824-50; prof. of Anglo-Saxon 1803-8; keeper of the archives 1815-18. He published *An Inaugural Lecture on the Utility of Anglo-Saxon Literature, to which is added the geography of Europe by King Alfred* (Oxford 1807) and *The Saxon Chronicle, with an English translation, and notes, critical and explanatory* (London 1823).

30

Architecture

H. M. COLVIN

IN 1689 a young man coming into residence at Oxford would have found himself in an architectural environment that was essentially medieval in its planning and predominantly gothic in its style. The layout established by William of Wykeham at New College in the fourteenth century[1] was still influential when colleges were built or rebuilt in the seventeenth century; hall and chapel continued to be built end to end (or side by side) on one side of the quadrangle, and the Reformation had not made the T-shaped chapel seem any less appropriate to Anglican fellows than it had to their Catholic predecessors. To some extent this architectural conservatism no doubt reflected the innate conservatism of academic society. But it also reflected a lack of intellectual interest in architecture as an art. For architecture (unlike music) formed no part of the curriculum, and men deeply versed in the niceties of Latin and Greek literature were largely ignorant of the classical language of architecture. Architecture, indeed, was something outside the ken of the average Oxford don. So was science, but the processes of scientific inquiry had attractions for minds that were also inclined to the study and even practice of architecture. It was in fact a scientific mind that gave Oxford its first major building to be consistently classical in style. This was the Sheldonian Theatre (1664–9), designed by the Savilian professor of astronomy, Christopher Wren. By 1675, when Loggan published his *Oxonia illustrata*, two colleges could show examples of Wren's architecture, both commissioned by fellows of the Royal Society, Ralph Bathurst at Trinity and Joseph Williamson at Queen's. These simple pedimented blocks were buildings of no great pretensions. But their very simplicity indicated their classical affinities. They showed that there was an alternative to gothic windows and curved gables, and as the first wing of an open court looking out onto the garden the Trinity block opened out the closed medieval quadrangle and pointed the way to the spatial innovations of New College, Queen's and All Souls.

[1] See R. L. Storey, 'The foundation and the medieval college 1379–1530' and G. Jackson-Stops, 'The building of the medieval college' in J. Buxton and P. Williams (eds), *New College, Oxford, 1379–1979* (Oxford 1979).

If Oxford's emancipation from its gothic past owed much to Wren's early connection with the university, the continuance of a sophisticated classical architecture (as opposed to the vernacular variety) was due largely to two talented amateurs, Dean Aldrich of Christ Church and George Clarke of All Souls. For Aldrich architecture was only one of many accomplishments. He had a reputation for learning in many fields and his writings included editions of Greek and Latin texts, ecclesiastical tracts, a treatise on geometry and a well-known textbook on logic. His library contained many books on antiquities and a large collection of architectural and other engravings.[1] From 1676 until his death in 1710 most of the university almanacks were engraved to designs either made or suggested by him, and many of them included allegorical scenes with elaborate architectural settings derived from French and Italian engravings in his collection.[2] When in 1709 the University Press produced its first architectural book, a translation (into Latin) of Palladio's *Antichità di Roma* (1554), it was the work of Charles Fairfax, one of Aldrich's pupils, and he himself had in hand a systematic treatise on architecture written and illustrated by himself. It was intended to have been divided into two parts treating respectively of 'civil' and 'military' architecture, each consisting of three books, but only book one and part of book two of the civil section were completed. A few copies of the first forty-four pages of the text were printed at the University Press during the author's lifetime,[3] but it was not until long after his death that the first edition (in Latin and English) was published at Oxford in 1789 as *Elementa architecturae civilis*. Based largely on Vitruvius and Palladio, it was a theoretical rather than a practical work, but Aldrich was more than just an academic student of architecture. In fact he was an accomplished draughtsman, and when a bequest of £3,000 enabled Christ Church to rebuild the Peckwater Quadrangle the dean designed the new building himself. On the foundation-stone laid by the earl of Salisbury on 25 January 1706 he was formally described as its 'architect'.[4] It consists of three ranges of rooms, forming three sides of a large quadrangle. For the first time in Oxford collegiate architecture each elevation is controlled by an order (of Ionic pilasters). The three façades are identical, so there is no subordination of wings to centre, and the effect, though grandly classical, is that of an unresolved triality. For reasons of circulation the fourth side could not be closed, and here Aldrich planned a free-standing building containing more rooms,

---

[1] W. G. Hiscock, *Henry Aldrich of Christ Church, 1648-1710* (Oxford 1960).

[2] H. M. Petter, *The Oxford Almanacks* (Oxford 1974), 4-10.

[3] Copies are to be found in Bodl. 8° Rawl. 1068 and Worcester College library, B.n.9. According to a note in the sale catalogue of James West's library (1773) only ten copies were printed 'and these never perfected, the author's death preventing' (information supplied by Mr Paul Quarrie). James West (c1704-1772), m. Balliol 1720.

[4] See Bodl. MS Tanner 338, fo 315.

but distinguished from the remainder of the quadrangle by a monumental Corinthian order.[1] In the event this was never built, and its place was taken by George Clarke's library. At a time when English architecture was at its most baroque, Peckwater was remarkable as an essay in an academic classical style that was almost Palladian in character. In the preface to his edition of Palladio's *Antichità di Roma* Charles Fairfax stated that Aldrich acknowledged Palladio as his professed master in architecture, and Peckwater entitles him to be regarded as a forerunner of the Palladian revival which he did not live to see.

Important though Aldrich was as Oxford's architectural mentor, he himself appears to have had few opportunities to practise architecture. All Saints church (1701-10) is the only other building for which his authorship is well established.[2] In the case of Trinity College chapel (1691-4) all that is definitely known is that he was one of the 'able judges in architecture' whose advice the college took before deciding to rebuild 'wholly upon new foundations'.[3] Wren was also consulted, though apparently too late to make any major alteration to the design, the responsibility for which remains in doubt.[4] An early version of the design that survives in the form of an engraving exhibits crudities that make it difficult to believe that it was due to Aldrich, but (like Wren) he may well have helped to improve the elevations and the richly decorated interior may also have benefited from his advice. The pierced screen in particular suggests the influence of engravings by the French architect le Pautre that were known to Aldrich. The incomplete building accounts show that the carpentry and joinery were the work of the Oxford craftsman Arthur Frogley, but a small payment indicates that the accomplished London carver Jonathan Maine was also employed, and the brilliant carving over the altar is clearly by Grinling Gibbons, as reported by the traveller Celia Fiennes, who saw the chapel soon after its completion.[5]

At Queen's College the documentation of the new library built in 1693-6 is unfortunately incomplete. It was, as Celia Fiennes noted, 'a stately building emulating that of Christ Church [she meant Trinity College] in Cambridge',[6] but neither she nor any other contemporary

[1] Aldrich's design was published in the form of a pair of engravings, reproduced by Hiscock, plates 30, 31. The ground plan (pl 30) clearly shows the intended arrangement of staircases and rooms in the interior of the building.

[2] H. M. Colvin, 'The architects of All Saints Church, Oxford', *Oxoniensia* xix (1954). The steeple was completed in 1718-20 to a different design.

[3] T. Warton, *The Life and Literary Remains of Ralph Bathurst, M.D.* (London 1761), 68n.

[4] For the correspondence between Wren and President Bathurst of Trinity see *Designs of Sir Chr. Wren for Oxford, Cambridge, London, Windsor, etc.* ed. A. T. Bolton and H. D. Hendry (Wren Soc. v), 14-16. The bursar's account for 1692 includes payments to the master-mason Christopher Kempster of Burford (who was evidently among those consulted) and to Wren's servant: BL Lansdowne MS 718, fo 64. Incomplete accounts at Trinity show that Bartholomew Peisley was the master-mason employed.

[5] *The Illustrated Journeys of Celia Fiennes 1685-c.1712*, ed. C. Morris (London 1982), 59.

[6] Ibid.

source records the authorship of the design. Internally its arrangement is conservative, but the principal elevation bears some resemblance to one of the lateral façades of Wren's grand design for rebuilding Whitehall Palace after the fire of 1698. This might suggest that the design had originated in Wren's office, but for the existence (in Aldrich's collection) of an engraving dated 1693 showing that in its original form it was a somewhat clumsy composition whose pediment stood awkwardly against the attic unsupported by either entablature or pilasters. Neither Wren nor Aldrich is likely to have committed this solecism, but as the fault was remedied in execution someone must clearly have criticized and perhaps corrected the design, and in the circumstances that person is most likely to have been Aldrich.

One other Oxford building has been attributed to Aldrich. This is the Fellows' Building at Corpus (1706-12) which was said by Dallaway in 1827 in his edition of Walpole's *Anecdotes of Painting* to 'present a specimen of his architecture, which, for correctness and a graceful simplicity, is not excelled by any edifice in Oxford'.[1] Here again documentary evidence is lacking, and the design may have been due to William Townesend, the contracting mason, but the character of the principal façade is sufficiently akin to the restrained classicism of Peckwater for Dallaway's attribution to be taken seriously.

Aldrich's successor as Oxford's leading architectural authority was George Clarke. That he was a close friend of Aldrich is evident from the inscription on the monument which he erected to the latter's memory in the nave of the cathedral, and his architectural activity, like Aldrich's, had a strong scholarly basis. His library (now at Worcester College) was rich in architectural books and he acquired and studied many of the surviving drawings of Inigo Jones and his pupil John Webb. Although he lacked Aldrich's skill as a draughtsman Clarke could express an architectural concept on paper and his sketches were often developed by the various architects with whom he was associated.[2] His most regular collaborator was Nicholas Hawksmoor, but he had contacts with nearly all the leading architects of his day. Like Aldrich, Clarke was closely associated with the design and production of the university almanacks, which from 1714 onwards became a regular vehicle for the illustration of new or projected buildings. This practice continued for some time after Clarke's death, until in the 1750s the illustrations began to take the purely topographical form that has persisted to the present day.

Clarke's long association with Oxford (he held his fellowship at All

---

[1] *Anecdotes of Painting in England... collected by... George Vertue*, ed. H. Walpole (4 vols Strawberry Hill 1762-7, enlarged edn by J. Dallaway 5 vols London 1826-8) iv. 75n.

[2] For Clarke's architectural drawings see H. M. Colvin, *A Catalogue of Architectural Drawings of the 18th and 19th centuries in the Library of Worcester College, Oxford* (Oxford 1964).

Souls for fifty-six years) coincided with a period of intensive building activity. Out of the nineteen colleges then in existence two were completely rebuilt and eleven were enlarged or partly rebuilt, while nearly all underwent considerable internal alterations. Two important additions—the Clarendon Building and the Radcliffe Library—were made to the public buildings of the university. Almost every year saw the beginning of some new architectural project, and during the 1720s major works were simultaneously in progress at All Souls, Christ Church, Queen's and Worcester Colleges. In addition Pembroke was building a new chapel (1728-32), Trinity completing the Garden Quadrangle (1728), and Oriel extending northwards (Robinson Building 1719-20, Carter Building 1729-34). The total outlay on building in Oxford during the first half of the eighteenth century must have been at least £120,000.[1] Much of this came from private benefaction. Towards the cost of the library at Queen's Provost Halton contributed nearly £2,000. At Christ Church the Peckwater quadrangle was paid for largely by a bequest of £3,000 from one of the canons. At All Souls the Codrington Library commemorates the name of Christopher Codrington, the West Indian magnate who left £6,000 for its erection. The munificence of Dr Radcliffe paid not only for the library which bears his name but also for a substantial addition to University College. And at Worcester College the new buildings benefited from a legacy of £3,000 from Clarke himself. But the raising of money was often a slow and painful task, involving economies such as the temporary giving up of gaudies or even the suspension of a fellowship.[2] Queen's and Worcester both took half a century to complete, at Magdalen the New Building represents only the first stage of an over-ambitious scheme for rebuilding the entire college, and all that Balliol ever realized of a comprehensive design illustrated in the almanack of 1742 was the rebuilding, in 1738-43, of the eastern half of the Broad Street front, which for over a century remained in awkward proximity to the surviving medieval gate-tower.

The chief beneficiaries of all this expenditure were successive members of the Townesend family of master-masons. In Oxford brick was little used in the eighteenth century, a plentiful supply of good building stone having long been available from the quarries at Headington. By the middle of the century the quality of the freestone being extracted from the Headington quarries was beginning to deteriorate, and from about 1820 onwards Bath stone (brought along the Kennet and Avon canal) took its place as the favourite facing material. But throughout the

---

[1] See the appendix to this chapter, pp. 854-60 below.
[2] At Balliol a fellowship and a scholarship were (with the visitor's sanction) suspended from 1775 onwards in order to pay a debt incurred in repairing the college buildings: BCA minutes of college meetings 1794-1875, 21 Oct. 1802.

greater part of the eighteenth century Headington stone remained the normal material for buildings in Oxford of all kinds.[1] The principal quarries were in the hands of the Townesends, three generations of whom dominated the building trades in eighteenth-century Oxford. John Townesend I (1648-1728) was the founder of the firm. Twice mayor of Oxford, he is commemorated by a handsome tomb in St Giles's churchyard. According to the inscription he was *in re architectonica magister peritissimus, exactis demum pluribus et ad scientiam et ad universitatis hujusce ornamentum aedificiis*. Of his activity as an architect (as opposed to that of a contracting mason) there is little evidence, but his son William (died 1739) had some skill as an architectural designer, so much so that in the accounts of Queen's College, where his father appears as *Lapicida Townesend*, he is distinguished as *architectus Townesend*. From the appendix to this chapter it will be apparent that Hearne was not exaggerating when he stated that William Townesend 'hath a hand in all the Buildings in Oxford, and gets a vast deal of Money that way',[2] for it includes nearly every important building erected in the university between 1710 and 1740. After his death the business was continued by his son John Townesend II (died 1746) and then by another John (died 1784) whose son Stephen (died 1800) was the last of the dynasty.[3] The Townesends' only serious rivals in the masonry business were the Peisleys, one of whom built for himself the handsome house in what is now St Michael's Street that is known as 'Vanbrugh House'.[4] The Peisleys, like the Townesends, had a stake in the Headington quarries and in the 1680s and 1690s were supplying stone from there for the building of St Paul's cathedral.[5] They did a good deal of work in Oxford in the last decade of the seventeenth century, and early in the eighteenth they often joined forces with the Townesends as joint contractors, so much so that in 1727 Hearne wrote that Peisley and Townesend 'carried (as it were) all the business in masonry before them, both in Oxford and all the Parts about it'.[6] But the death in 1727 of the third and last Bartholomew Peisley left the field clear for the Townesends. Only for the major task of building the Radcliffe Library was it found expedient to bring in a second mason-contractor in the person of Francis Smith of Warwick. The carpentry trade was less susceptible to monopoly than the mason's, but Jeremiah Franklin in the reign of George II and Henry Tawney (died 1798) and James Pears (died 1804) in that of George III all enjoyed a large measure

[1] W. J. Arkell, *Oxford Stone* (London 1947).

[2] Hearne, *Collections* vii. 171.

[3] For the Townesends see H. M. Colvin, *A Biographical Dictionary of British Architects 1600-1840* (London 1978), 830-5.

[4] *VCH Oxon* iv. 99.

[5] Colvin, *British Architects*, 629-30.

[6] Hearne, *Collections* ix. 343.

of university patronage. Indeed in the 1790s it was Pears rather than the last of the Townesends who was Oxford's leading master-builder. For more specialized craftsmen such as stone- and wood-carvers and ornamental smiths it might be necessary to go outside Oxford, usually to London, but Oxford was the home of an outstanding plasterer named Thomas Roberts (died 1771) whose exquisite workmanship can be seen in Christ Church library, the Radcliffe Camera, the senior common room at St John's and elsewhere in Oxford.[1]

The first Oxford building with which George Clarke was concerned was his own college of All Souls. Here in 1703 he proposed to build a house for his own use, to revert to the college on his death. This eventually resulted in the building of the existing warden's lodging facing the High Street,[2] but a site adjoining the cloister which then ran along Catte Street was also considered and this developed into a scheme for a new north quadrangle for which Clarke made a basic plan showing a pedimented block containing twelve sets of rooms for fellows, linked to a regularized old quadrangle by colonnades. For this new block different elevational treatments were made by Aldrich, Nicholas Hawksmoor, William Townesend, a London builder-architect called Wilcox, the connoisseur John Talman and Clarke himself.[3] For want of money nothing had been decided when in 1710 the situation was transformed by Christopher Codrington's legacy of £6,000 to build a library. By 1714 it had been decided to substitute the library for the 'Grand Dormitory' or residential building and to create a three-sided quadrangle facing west towards Catte Street instead of south towards the old quadrangle. This change of axis was crucial, for now the library would balance the chapel, and symmetry demanded that, like the chapel, it should be gothic in style. Hawskmoor accordingly produced a series of gothic designs, accompanied by an 'Explanation', and in February 1715 the warden and fellows resolved that 'the Library of Coll Codrington should be built as the Coll. Chappell was, according to the Model [design] that was then showne to the Society, and that Dr Clarke and Sir Nat Lloyd be desired, to be inspectors, and take care of the said buildings'. Many more variant designs were produced by Hawksmoor's prolific pen before—and even after—building began in 1716, and as late as the 1730s some members of

---

[1] G. Beard, *Decorative Plasterwork in Britain* (London 1975), 235-6.

[2] This has been surprisingly singled out as 'the first Palladian building in Oxford' by J. Sherwood and N. Pevsner, *Oxfordshire* (Harmondsworth 1974), 45. The engraving of All Souls in William Williams's *Oxonia depicta* (1732-3) shows it as a simple and unassertive building of indeterminate architectural character crowned by a gothic stringcourse and battlements uniform with those of the college. Its present 'Palladian' front dates from Daniel Robertson's refronting of 1827.

[3] Colvin, *Catalogue of Architectural Drawings in Worcester College*, plates 45-53, 55-6. The drawing illustrated in pl 49 can now be attributed to Aldrich, as the draughtsmanship corresponds to drawings by him at Christ Church and the perspective presentation is identical with the engravings of his design for the Peckwater Quadrangle. Plate 50 is a plan and elevation of Aldrich's design drawn out by the architect John James.

the college still hoped to complete the grand scheme by rebuilding the old quadrangle on lines indicated by their architect. But money was lacking, and when Hawksmoor died in 1736 Sir Nathaniel Lloyd correctly concluded that 'Hawksmooring and Townsending, is all out for this century'.[1] The college had nevertheless acquired a noble hall and library, a vaulted buttery worthy of Borromini (whose architecture it emulates), some much needed accommodation for its fellows and a quadrangle whose spectacular skyline demonstrates Hawksmoor's genius for using gothic forms for baroque ends.

The next building to claim Clarke's attention was a new home for the University Press, which hitherto had been inconveniently accommodated in and about the Sheldonian Theatre. Nothing better could be provided until the publication in 1702-4 of Clarendon's *History of the Rebellion* brought a substantial increase in the delegates' income. It was the profits derived from the sale of this celebrated work which, together with the sum of £2,000 paid by John Baskett, the king's printer, for the lease of the University Press, made possible the erection of a new printing house designed for the purpose. A site for the building was found in Broad Street and designs were obtained from at least three architects, including Hawksmoor, John James and William Townesend. The original drawings are all in Clarke's collection and it is evident that he was closely involved in an advisory capacity. The design chosen was one of several submitted by Hawksmoor, in all of which he sought to use the Roman Doric order to monumental effect. Internally the building was deliberately divided into two by a central passageway because, as Hawksmoor noted on one of his drawings, there were '2 distinct companys' of printers—the learned press under the direct control of the delegates, and the 'Bible press' conducted by Baskett. Externally its roofline was enlivened by lead statues of the muses designed, probably at Clarke's behest, by Sir James Thornhill.[2]

Drawings in Clarke's collection make it clear that he also played an important part in the rebuilding of Queen's College, projected in 1708 or 1709, the first stage of which was carried out by William Townesend between 1710 and 1721. Here, as in the case of other contemporary Oxford buildings, the ultimate design cannot be regarded as the exclusive work of any one individual. Hawksmoor produced a series of brilliant but over-ambitious proposals, none of which was accepted, though some of them were not without influence; Clarke drew outline plans and

---

[1] For further details see K. Downes, *Hawksmoor* (London 1959), ch. 9. For the drawings see Colvin, *Catalogue*, plates 59-81. Sir Nathaniel Lloyd (1669-1745), m. Trin. 1685; fellow All Souls 1689; incorporated at Cambridge 1710; master of Trinity Hall, Cambridge, 1710-35.

[2] The drawings are all reproduced by Colvin, *Catalogue*, plates 103-12. For the building see also *VCH Oxon*. iii. 54 and Downes, 107-9.

elevations which form the basis of the existing hall, chapel and front quadrangle, and Townesend carried them out with modifications of his own. Whether it was Hawksmoor or Clarke who first suggested an elevation derived from that of Chelsea Hospital we cannot tell, but Clarke certainly worked out a façade very like the one finally adopted. In this particular drawing Clarke envisaged the hall and chapel forming the street front, but another of his drawings indicated the plan ultimately adopted, with the hall and chapel set back and a screen wall to the street. Here again it was probably due to Clarke that the decorative sculpture in the pediment, intended to represent Queen Anne holding the balance of power, was designed by his friend Sir James Thornhill.[1] In the 1720s work was suspended while the college recouped its finances and it was not until 1733-6 that Townesend built the entrance screen and cupola on lines indicated by Hawksmoor, though modified in execution to accommodate a statue of Queen Caroline by Henry Cheere. Still the east side of the front quadrangle was not completed, and it was only in 1760 that the college could at last congratulate itself on having exchanged a ramshackle collection of medieval buildings for the handsome and unified design that has ever since been one of the great ornaments of the High Street.[2]

At University College Clarke was concerned with the building of the Radcliffe Quadrangle (1717-19) and with an unfulfilled project for new master's lodgings. In accordance with Radcliffe's wishes the quadrangle was built in the same Jacobean style as the rest of the college, and it appears to have been designed and built by Townesend under Clarke's direction. Externally it is almost indistinguishable from the adjoining quadrangle begun in the reign of Charles I, and the fan-vaulted ceiling of the gateway is a striking demonstration of the continuity of gothic masoncraft in Oxford. Nevertheless in leaving the south side of the quadrangle open the college was following the precedent established by Wren at Trinity, and drawings in Clarke's collection show that the projected master's lodgings (axially sited opposite the new gateway) were to have been a classical building somewhat similar in character to the gentlemen commoners' building which Townesend built for Corpus in 1737.[3]

Simultaneously Clarke and Townesend were engaged in building a new library at Christ Church. This took the place of the detached residential block envisaged by Aldrich and was at first intended to conform

---

[1] Thornhill's annotated designs for the sculpture are in the Huntington Library, San Marino, California. One of them is dated 1716.

[2] For the rebuilding of Queen's College see *VCH Oxon*. iii. 138-43 and Downes, *Hawksmoor*, 102-6.

[3] For the Radcliffe Quadrangle see *VCH Oxon*. iii. 78. The designs for the master's house are reproduced by Colvin, *Catalogue*, plates 99-102.

externally to his design. A legacy from Robert South enabled the work to start. 'We have got the £500 which Dr South left us to our building, and shall pull down the last side of Peckwater next spring', wrote Canon Stratford to Edward Harley in September 1716, '... we shall observe Dr. Aldrich's model as to the case, but we design to turn the inside into a library, and to make it the finest library that belongs to any society, in Europe'.[1] Although Clarke retained Aldrich's giant Corinthian order, the change of use enabled him to eliminate the attic windows and to reduce the number of bays from nine to seven. After several experiments he finally worked out a monumental façade in which a subordinate Doric order is threaded through giant Corinthian columns in a manner clearly suggested by Michelangelo's Capitoline palace in Rome. The interior, with its fine joinery by George Shakespear and John Phillips and its splendid plasterwork by Thomas Roberts, was not completed until 1762. In 1769 the ground floor, hitherto open on three sides, was enclosed in order to house the collection of pictures bequeathed by General John Guise. Altogether the building had cost the college some £15,000.[2]

Magdalen was the next society to be infected with the urge to build. It was one of the few medieval foundations whose original buildings had not been enlarged (except by the addition of 'cock-lofts') in the seventeenth century, and the cloistered quadrangle, standing to the north of the hall and chapel, must always have been somewhat dark and damp. It may also have been in bad repair, for in 1724 Hawksmoor wrote to Clarke that Magdalen was 'a College soe decriped that Repairing any part (except the hall and chapell) signifys but little, so that the whole must (or ought to be) new'.[3] In 1720 Hearne was told that 'they unanimously agreed at Magdalen-College to pull down and rebuild the East Side of that College', and it was in that year that one of the fellows, *aedificiis de novo extruendis prospiciens*, gave one hundred guineas to start a building fund.[4] For the basic design the college was indebted to Edward Holdsworth, a talented classical scholar and connoisseur of the arts who had renounced his fellowship as a nonjuror in 1715 but remained in close touch with his former colleagues.[5] In 1720 a survey of the college

[1] HMC *Portland MSS* vii. 217.
[2] W. G. Hiscock, *A Christ Church Miscellany* (Oxford 1946), chaps 4, 6 and plates 17-23, illustrating drawings by Clarke and Townesend.
[3] Letter in Worcester College library accompanying drawing no. 85.
[4] Hearne, *Collections* vii. 103-4. For the names of the principal benefactors, who between them contributed some £7,500, see A. Wood, *The History and Antiquities of the Colleges and Halls in the University of Oxford*, ed. and cont. J. Gutch (Oxford 1786), 322, n. 65.
[5] Edward Holdsworth (1684-1746), m. CCC 1704; demy Magd. 1705-15. Holdsworth's responsibility for the design, affirmed by J. C. Buckler in his *Observations on the Original Architecture of Magdalen College* (London 1823), 98 but rejected in *VCH Oxon*. iii. 206n and by the present writer in *Catalogue*, p. xxi has now been fully established by letters and other documents recently discovered among the archives of Magdalen.

was made for his use, but it was not until 1729 that the fellows were in a position to contemplate building. Early in that year Holdsworth, then in London, consulted the architect James Gibbs, who undertook to 'revise' his plans and was paid twenty guineas by the college for his help. George Clarke may also have been involved.[1] The entire scheme was illustrated in the 1731 almanack, as well as in Williams's *Oxonia depicta* of 1732-3. It consisted of an extensive new quadrangle sited to the north of the old buildings, with a T-shaped library-wing projecting from it on the west side. In front of the library there was to be a curved forecourt with access to Longwall, flanked on one side by new lodgings for the president and on the other by a smaller house for the divinity reader. This forecourt would have encroached on the territory of Magdalen Hall, and a sketch-plan exists in Holdsworth's hand showing the area that it would be necessary to purchase from the hall.

With some modifications by William Townesend and further advice from James Gibbs and others, the first range of the New Building was begun in 1733 by two Oxford masons, William King and Richard Piddington. Though conforming in general to the original design, it incorporated various modifications, of which the most important was the introduction of a continuous architrave and frieze under the cornice on the south side. At each end the returns were left unfinished in preparation for the next phase of building, but the New Building had hardly been completed before the layout of the quadrangle once more came into question. Holdsworth was again consulted and submitted a new plan placing the library on the south instead of the west side of the quadrangle. But nothing was done until, in the 1790s, the idea of completing the quadrangle was revived, resulting in the submission of a bewildering variety of designs, some classical, some gothic.[2] In the end none of them was adopted, and in 1824 the facing up of the unfinished returns of the New Building marked the final abandonment of the great scheme launched a hundred years earlier.

At Magdalen the New Building remained an isolated fragment of a grand design that was never to be completed. But at Worcester College a master-plan for replacing the medieval buildings of Gloucester Hall was largely realized in the course of the eighteenth century. Here George Clarke was both architect and benefactor. For, in disgust at the quarrels which divided his own college, it was to Worcester that he eventually left not only his library and his collection of architectural drawings, but also the bulk of his fortune, which was to be devoted to the endowment of additional fellowships and the completion of its buildings. The new hall,

[1] For the evidence of Clarke's involvement in the design see Colvin, *Catalogue*, pp. xxi-xxiii.
[2] See T. S. R. Boase, 'An Oxford college and the gothic revival', *Jl Warburg and Courtauld Institutes* xviii (1955).

chapel and library were begun in his lifetime, and the basic designs appear to have been his. Though the elevations were unadventurous, the placing of hall and chapel on either side of the recessed entrance and the prominence given to the library were well-conceived innovations in planning that were without precedent in Oxford's collegiate architecture. Here Hawksmoor was once more Clarke's architectural adjutant, and to him were probably due such important details as the arched windows with pilastered jambs which form the central feature of the library and therefore of the whole college. These (as an annotation of Hawksmoor's shows) were derived from the Roman arch at Saintes, depicted in Blondel's *Cours d'architecture* of 1698. To complete the college Clarke envisaged two wings projecting westwards to the north and south of the library with new lodgings for the provost at the west end of the north wing. This proposal was illustrated by Williams in his *Oxonia depicta*, and in his will Clarke directed that the new north range should be built in accordance with the engraving. But finding that there was not sufficient room for the building as originally envisaged between the library and the old provost's lodgings he left instructions in a codicil that an alternative plan and elevation, which he had initialled, should be followed instead. This drawing has not survived, but appears to have provided for the thickening of the residential ranges from 'single' to 'double pile', thus enabling the smaller rooms to be placed at the rear. In this form the three easternmost staircases on the north side were duly erected by Clarke's trustees between 1753 and 1759. The remainder of the north range, including the provost's lodgings, was built between 1773 and 1776 to modified designs by Henry Keene. The corresponding range on the south side was never built, and it was not until 1783-4 that the interiors of the hall and chapel were decorated in an elegant neo-classical style by James Wyatt.[1]

What was remarkable about much of the Georgian building activity in Oxford was its conscious striving after architectural effect. In the past grandeur had always been at the command of the wealthy benefactor (for example William of Wykeham at New College in the fourteenth century and Archbishop Laud at St John's in the seventeenth) but most collegiate building had been relatively modest in character. But in Georgian Oxford, colleges like Christ Church, All Souls, Queen's and Magdalen were all determined to erect large and monumental buildings and did so despite considerable financial difficulties. The result was to put Oxford, for the first time since the Reformation, in the forefront of English architecture. For this change of attitude Aldrich and Clarke must be given much of the credit, but in an age when a knowledge of

---

[1] *VCH Oxon.* iii. 307-9 (with plan). Nearly all the surviving drawings are reproduced by Colvin, *Catalogue*, plates 1-34.

architecture was fashionable among the aristocracy and gentry, colleges whose membership was increasingly being drawn from those ranks of society would naturally share the tastes of their class.

It is certain that, despite an overall decline in numbers of both senior and junior members until about 1760, the new element of upper-class fellows and undergraduates—above all the gentlemen-commoners—set a higher standard in accommodation which lies behind much of the new building in Oxford.[1] In many colleges the medieval system of sharing rooms—known as 'chumming'—had persisted throughout the seventeenth century. But to gentlemen accustomed to living in a spacious town or country house chumming was no longer acceptable. At Wadham, a college whose statutes envisaged scholars living three to a room, chumming had by the reign of George III 'almost grown totally into Disuse'. Accordingly in 1773 the college decided to bring back into use its empty garrets, hitherto 'looked on as lumber holes', in order to provide each scholar with a single room.[2] As early as 1664 the visitor had dispensed New College from obeying a statute which required as many as four fellows to occupy each of the lower chambers. He did so on the ground that, since the invention of printing, the medieval studies in the corners of the common living rooms had become too small to accommodate fellows' libraries, and that the multiple occupation of rooms encouraged the spread of contagious diseases.[3] When in 1682-3 the Garden Quadrangle was built its planning still provided for the sharing of rooms, for each consisted of a common chamber with two studies and two bedrooms, but when two further blocks were added in 1700-7 they contained twelve 'sets', each of which consisted of a spacious sitting room with a study and a bedroom to the rear (figure 1). 'A very pretty appartment of dineing roome bed chamber and studdy' was how Celia Fiennes described the accommodation provided for fellows at New College in the reign of William III, and it was in fact the equivalent of the individual 'apartments' in a large country house.[4] This became the standard arrangement in eighteenth-century Oxford. It was provided for whenever a new building was planned, and in the course of the period covered by this volume every college rearranged its existing medieval or Tudor accommodation to conform as far as possible to this pattern.[5] What had originally been individual studies clustered round a common

---

[1] Cf V. H. H. Green, 'The university and social life' above, esp. 330-1; G. V. Bennett, 'University, society and church 1688-1714' above *passim*.

[2] WCM convention book III, 8 July 1773.

[3] *VCH Oxon*. iii. 151.

[4] *Journeys of Celia Fiennes*, ed. Morris, p. 59.

[5] The very lavish accommodation envisaged by the fellows of All Souls in the first decade of the century comprised four rooms, namely 'outward room', 'entertaining room', 'library' and 'bedchamber': see Colvin, *Catalogue*, pl. 56.

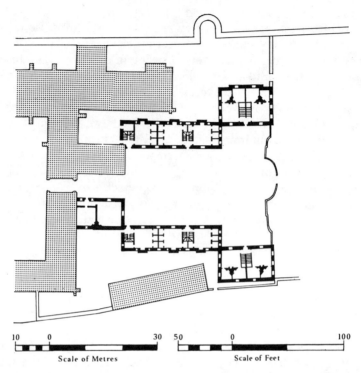

10   0   30 50   0   100

Scale of Metres   Scale of Feet

Fig. 1. Plan of the Garden Quadrangle at New College, showing on the left the two inner blocks built in 1682–3, with shared rooms, and on the right the two outer blocks built in 1700–7, each containing two sets with a dining-room, bedchamber and study.

living room were converted into bedrooms or closets for the use of a single fellow or commoner in exclusive occupation of the whole unit. Wainscoting with fielded panels was introduced, doors with classical architraves took the place of the ancient framed openings and the stone mullions and transoms of the windows were often removed to make way for wooden sashes. At Brasenose some of the small bedrooms in the old quadrangle were provided with large folding doors, so that at night when the doors were folded back 'the sitting room was transformed into a spacious bedchamber, with the bed in a recess in one corner'.[1] These internal alterations were sometimes due to private initiative on the part of the occupants, thus accounting for variations in the details of chimney-pieces and panelling. At St John's, for instance, it was formally resolved in 1742 that

for the encouragement of all such persons as shall be inclined to finish and fit up Chambers within the College in an handsome and durable manner ...

[1] E. W. Allfrey, 'The architectural history of the college' in *Brasenose Monographs* i, no. 3, p. 38.

whosoever shall be at the expense of wainscotting a College Chamber in such sort, and fashion, as shall be approved of by the Convention, shall be empower'd to demand, and receive, four fifth parts of his said expence from the person who immediately succeeds him in the said chamber . . .[1]

To judge by the architectural evidence this 'alteration in the manner of living' had been generally accomplished throughout the university by the end of the eighteenth century, and in many colleges sets can still be seen which retain their Georgian fittings intact.

Although it was in the colleges that most of the new building in Georgian Oxford took place, the greatest architectural event of the eighteenth century was the construction by private trustees of the Radcliffe Library. Not only was it the building in which purely aesthetic considerations were least constrained by those of cost or utility; it was also the central feature of a town-planning scheme which at its most ambitious would have transformed Oxford and which did in fact give the town the only formally planned open space that it has ever possessed.

John Radcliffe was the most fashionable doctor of his age and made a large fortune by his practice. He died unmarried, and the university was the principal object of his benefactions. At least two years before his death in 1714 he expressed the intention of enlarging the Bodleian Library, and in his will he left ample funds for the purpose. His original idea, as described in a letter of 30 December 1712 from Francis Atterbury to Bishop Trelawny of Winchester, was to build out from the Selden End of the Bodleian Library into the garden of Exeter College. The new building was to be 90 feet long and two storeys high. The upper floor was to be on the level of Duke Humfrey's Library. The ground floor was to be given to Exeter as a library in order to compensate that college for the loss of its ground.[2] For such a building several alternative designs were drawn by Hawksmoor, but it appears that the fellows of Exeter 'insisted upon such terms, as evinced their great unwillingness to lose the benefit of a good part of their garden', and when Radcliffe made his will in September 1714 he directed that (subject to the life-interest of his two sisters) £40,000 should be devoted to 'building a library in Oxford and the purchasing the houses between St Maries and the scholes in Catstreet where I intend the Library to be built'.[3] Besides leaving Exeter in possession of its garden this would give the library a much more prominent site, a consideration which may have weighed with a benefactor who (according to Hearne) was 'very

[1] SJM register 1731–94, p. 137. Estimates were made in 1745 for wainscoting fourteen rooms in the Front Quadrangle and eight in the Canterbury Quadrangle: SJM lxxxi. 13, 14.
[2] *The Epistolary Correspondence, Visitation Charges, Speeches, and Miscellanies, of the Right Reverend Francis Atterbury, D.D., Lord Bishop of Rochester, with historical notes, and brief memoirs of the author*, ed. J. Nichols (2nd edn 5 vols London 1799, i–iv printed and dated 1789–90, v 1798) i. 457.
[3] *Building Accounts of the Radcliffe Camera*, ed. S. G. Gillam (O.H.S. 1958) p. viii note.

ambitious of Glory'.[1] The buying up of property to obtain the site was a slow process, necessitating an act of parliament for which Clarke and William Bromley, the two members for the university, made themselves responsible, and it was not until 1737 that work could actually begin.[2]

Meanwhile Hawksmoor had made fresh designs for an insulated building on the new site. In addition he had devoted some thoughts to possible improvements in the town-plan of Oxford. Here, as at Cambridge, his aim was to transform what was essentially a medieval street-system by the opening up of new vistas and the construction of new public buildings. At Cambridge he had in mind the baroque replanning of Rome by Domenico Fontana in the time of Sixtus V, but at Oxford the approximately rectilinear pattern of streets encouraged him to think in terms of a Roman city, with a *forum universitatis* between the schools and St Mary's church, a *forum civitatis* at Carfax and triumphal gateways at the north end of the Cornmarket and the east end of the High Street. On the west side of the university forum a rebuilt Brasenose would answer to a rebuilt All Souls, and on the site of Hart Hall a vast classical temple would serve as a *capella universitatis*. There is no evidence that any of these ideas was ever considered by the university, let alone the civic authorities, and over fifty years were to elapse before town and university were to unite in achieving the much more modest improvements effected by the Oxford paving commissioners.[3]

By 1734 Radcliffe's trustees were ready to contemplate the implementation of his wishes, and early in the following year they had before them plans submitted by Nicholas Hawksmoor and James Gibbs. Hawksmoor had by now been associated with the scheme for over twenty years. Gibbs had not previously been employed in Oxford, but at Cambridge he had designed both the senate house and the New Building at King's College. Moreover, his great patron Edward Harley had recently become one of the Radcliffe trustees. The two architects submitted quite different designs. Hawksmoor envisaged a circular building crowned by a dome, Gibbs a long rectangular one occupying the greater part of the new square. As a working library there can be no doubt that Gibbs's proposal was much the more practical. But at the time there was no urgent need for more library space. And as an embellishment to Oxford—above all as a monument to Radcliffe—Hawksmoor's domed building was obviously to be preferred. The antecedents of this type of

[1] Hearne, *Collections* v. 2. See also the remarks of Thomas Salmon in his *Present State of the Universities* (London 1744), 42–3 about 'Ratcliff's Mausolaeum'.

[2] *Building Accounts of the Radcliffe Camera*, p. xiv.

[3] For Hawksmoor's town-planning schemes see S. Lang, 'Oxford and Cambridge reformed: Hawksmoor as town planner', *Architectural Rev.* ciii (March–June 1948) and Downes, *Hawksmoor*, ch. 8.

building were in fact ornamental and commemorative rather than utilitarian in character. The learned would recognize its affinity with a tomb like that of Cecilia Metella in Rome, while others might recollect the similar structure intended by Wren as a mausoleum for Charles I.

It was Hawksmoor's design that appears to have been favoured by the trustees, but his death in March 1736 left the commission in Gibbs's hands, and it was under the latter's direction that the library was built between 1737 and 1748. What he did—presumably at the trustees' bidding—was to accept the theme of a circular domed building but to interpret it in his own way. As an architect trained in Rome by the baroque master Carlo Fontana, Gibbs was well acquainted with the many domed churches of Italy, and the result was more like a baroque church and less like an antique mausoleum than Hawksmoor had intended. In Oxford it stands out amid its gothic neighbours as the visual centre of the university, as prominent in its setting as S. Maria della Salute at the entrance to the Grand Canal in Venice or as Brunelleschi's dome in the middle of Florence. Its only weakness lies in the lantern crowning the cupola, which is simpler and less prominent than the one originally intended by the architect. This followed the decision in 1741 to substitute a timber dome for the one of stone shown in Gibbs's original designs. There is no suggestion in the trustees' minutes that this was due to any shortage of money, but no stone dome of such size had ever been built in England and Gibbs may have feared that the task would prove to be beyond his masons' skill. A scale model of the stone dome was, however, made, and survives as part of a garden building at St Giles' House, then the residence of Thomas Rowney, MP for the city of Oxford.

The masonry contracts were shared between William Townesend and Francis Smith of Warwick, both builders of great experience and repute. Both, however, died in the course of the year 1738-9, so it was their sons John and William who were responsible for much of the fabric. The interior is a showpiece of Georgian craftsmanship, with carpentry and joinery by John Phillips of London, ironwork by Robert Bakewell of Derby and elegant plasterwork by Joseph Artari, Charles Stanley and Thomas Roberts. The total cost, including the site, amounted to £43,226.[1]

The completion of the Radcliffe Library in 1748 marked the end of the early eighteenth-century building boom in Oxford. The long delay in starting work on the library and the slow continuance of buildings begun long before at Worcester and Queen's meant that, while elsewhere

[1] For the design see S. Lang, 'By Hawksmoor out of Gibbs', *Architectural Rev.* cv (Jan.-June 1949) and Downes, 126-31. The drawings are reproduced and the accounts printed in *Building Accounts of the Radcliffe Camera*. The vaulted ground floor, though protected by Bakewell's iron grilles and gates, was open to the air and was not enclosed for library purposes until 1863. In 1751 the square was embellished with Portland stone obelisks carrying lamps.

Palladianism was in fashion between the Anglo-baroque of the early eighteenth century and the neo-classical architecture of the reign of George III, in Oxford the latter followed close on the heels of the former without any intervening Palladian phase. The conduct of architecture in the university was, moreover, changing. Aldrich and Clarke had no successor in the reign of George III. A fellow of New College named William Crowe did, it is true, lecture occasionally on architecture, and in 1789 Aldrich's book was belatedly published by the Clarendon Press.[1] But in Oxford the age of the amateur architect was over and that of the professional had arrived. As each college was an autonomous society it was open to its fellows to employ any architect of their choice, but one college tended to follow the example of another, and in practice two architects monopolized commissions in the university: first Henry Keene from 1766 until his death in 1776 and then James Wyatt from 1776 until the end of the century.

Henry Keene, who was surveyor to Westminster Abbey, owed his introduction to the university to Roger Newdigate, who was himself something of an amateur architect, and an early enthusiast for the revival of gothic architecture. From about 1750 onwards he was re-modelling his country house at Arbury in Warwickshire in the gothic style, incidentally copying the windows of the proscholium in his dining room, and Keene was one of his architectural assistants.[2] In 1766 the interior of the hall of University College, of which Newdigate was a member, was remodelled in the gothic style, and Keene was employed to make the designs. He concealed the Caroline hammer-beam roof with a plaster vault, wainscoted the walls in similar style and introduced a marble chimney-piece with a relief of King Alfred (the legendary founder of the college) framed in gothic tracery. This chimney-piece was paid for by Newdigate, and was based on the canopy over the tomb of Aymer de Valence in Westminster Abbey. The result, as the aquatint published by Ackermann shows (plate X) was a charming example of the Georgian rediscovery of gothic as a decorative style. Unfortunately it did not satisfy the more scholarly taste of a later age and was destroyed in 1904.[3]

The remodelling of the hall of University College was not the first manifestation of the gothic revival in Oxford, for in 1750-1 the old library at All Souls had been converted into rooms for one of the fellows, Robert Vansittart, and he had asked the amateur architect Sanderson

[1] William Crowe m. New College 1765; public orator 1784-1829. Aldrich, *Elementa architecturae civilis*.

[2] For Newdigate's architectural activities see Colvin, *British Architects* and references there cited. In 1776 he presented to the university the two candelabra (now in the Ashmolean Museum) constructed by Piranesi out of antique fragments. He was MP for the university 1750-80.

[3] A. Wood, *Appendix to the History and Antiquities of the Colleges and Halls in the University of Oxford, containing fasti oxonienses*, ed. and cont. J. Gutch (Oxford 1790), 236; *VCH Oxon.* iii. 80.

Miller to design Gothic partitions and doorways, some of which survived the restoration of the library in the nineteenth century.[1] Miller was one of the pioneers of the gothic revival, and his work at All Souls actually preceded the last example of traditional mason's gothic in Oxford. This was the fan-vault which John Townesend inserted in the convocation house in 1758-9 in place of a plaster one dating from the seventeenth century.[2] Townesend's vault is a straightforward fan-vault of traditional gothic character quite unaffected by the self-conscious gothic taste of men like Newdigate and Miller, so much so that the Royal Commission on Historical Monuments assumed it to be a work of the 1630s.[3] It is in fact a more or less straightforward copy in stone of its plaster predecessor. It is of some importance as the last gothic vault to be built in stone anywhere in England until the nineteenth century. In Oxford, as elsewhere, the gothic enthusiasts of the 1750s and 1760s showed no interest in the surviving traditions of medieval craftsmanship that were still alive in their midst and preferred to employ plasterers and joiners to simulate the more elaborate decorative features of late gothic design. This was what Keene did at University College and what Wyatt was later to do at New College, Merton, Magdalen and Balliol.

Keene's other works in the university were all in a late Georgian classical style of considerable elegance but of no special distinction. They comprise the plain anatomy school (now the senior common room) at Christ Church (1766-7) the interior of what is now the lower library at the same place (1769-72), the Fisher building at Balliol (1768-9, but mischievously altered by Waterhouse in 1870) the provost's lodgings and part of the north range of Worcester College (1773-6) and at least the plan of Radcliffe Observatory.

The Radcliffe Observatory was commissioned by the Radcliffe trustees for the use of the Savilian professor of astronomy. Keene was appointed architect and also contracted to erect the building to his own designs. The foundation-stone was laid in June 1772 on a site in the northern outskirts of the town. But in March 1773 the trustees ordered Keene to suspend work and to follow 'another elevation' which had been laid before them 'in consequence of an order from Lord Lichfield'. Many years later Edward Tatham, by then rector of Lincoln College, claimed that this decision had followed the animadversions on Keene's design in

[1] This work is documented by letters from Vansittart among Miller's correspondence in the Warwickshire Record Office, CR125B/715, 718, 719. Some of Miller's panelling is visible in plate 67 of *An Inventory of the Historical Monuments in the City of Oxford* (Royal Commission on Historical Monuments, England: London 1939). Robert Vansittart (1728-89), m. Trin. 1745; fellow All Souls 1748; prof. of civil law 1767-89.
[2] I. G. Philip, 'Reconstruction in the Bodleian Library and convocation house in the eighteenth century', *Bodleian Library Record* vi (1957-61).
[3] *Inventory of Historical Monuments*, 9 and pl. 4(1).

his pamphlet *Oxonia explicata et ornata*, published in 1773. However, as Lord Lichfield (the senior trustee) had died in September 1772, the decision to obtain a new elevation must have preceded the publication of Tatham's pamphlet, though its adoption may possibly have been influenced by this and other expressions of public disapproval. Of this new elevation Keene was evidently not the author, and it was almost certainly the work of James Wyatt, then the rising star of British neo-classical architecture, to whom the trustees made a payment of £100 in 1774. When Keene died in 1776 the trustees directed that the building should be completed by his son 'under the direction of Mr Wyatt'. None of Keene's original designs have survived, but drawings made by J. B. Malchair in 1773-4 show that by then the professor's house, the linking quadrant and much of the lower storey of the main building had been erected. But the tower had not yet been started, and this striking and original piece of neo-classical design, based on the Temple of the Winds at Athens (then recently published in Stuart and Revett's *Antiquities of Athens*[1]) must have been wholly Wyatt's work. The exquisitely detailed interior (now the senior common room of Green College) shows Wyatt at his best as a decorative designer, though his characteristic dilatoriness in completing it cannot have endeared him to the trustees.[2]

Wyatt's intervention in the design of the Radcliffe Observatory was followed almost immediately by his employment as architect of the new Canterbury Quadrangle at Christ Church. This was built partly at the expense of Richard Robinson, archbishop of Armagh. It was begun in 1775 and completed in 1778.[3] Its principal architectural feature is a beautifully detailed Doric gateway giving access to Peckwater Quadrangle from Merton Street. This commission may simply have been due to Wyatt's growing reputation as a brilliant young architectural designer, but it is worth pointing out that Lewis Bagot, then a canon of Christ Church and soon to be its dean, was the younger brother of Sir William (later Lord) Bagot, who was one of the four Radcliffe trustees. Moreover, the Bagots were landowners in Staffordshire, Wyatt's native county, and it was another member of the family who in the 1760s had been instrumental in enabling him to visit Rome as a student.[4] It is therefore very

[1] J. Stuart and N. Revett, *The Antiquities of Athens* (4 vols London 1762-1816).
[2] Minutes and accounts of the Radcliffe trustees, Bodl. MS dd. Radcliffe c.51 (minute-book 1752-91), c.58 (account-book 1727-74).
[3] The date of commencement has generally been stated as 1773, but it was not until May 1775 that *Jackson's Oxford Journal* reported the demolition of the old quadrangle preparatory to the erection of the new one, and the first entry in the building accounts is dated 9 June 1775: CA xxxiii.b.3. A drawing by J. B. Malchair, dated 4 May 1774, showing the old Canterbury Gateway still standing is reproduced in *Oxoniensia* viii-ix (1943-4), as plate xvi.B. Richard Robinson (1709-94), 1st bn Rokeby m. Ch.Ch. 1726; abp of Armagh 1765-94.
[4] A. Dale, *James Wyatt* (Oxford 1956), 3-4.

likely that the Bagot brothers played some part in getting Wyatt his first two commissions in Oxford. After Keene's death in 1776 Wyatt immediately took his place as the established Oxford architect, enjoying almost a complete monopoly of university work, and totally excluding his great rival Robert Adam.

Apart from the Radcliffe Observatory and the Canterbury gateway Wyatt's principal works in Oxford in the classical style were the remodelling of the interiors of the libraries at New College (1778) and Brasenose (1779-80) the rearrangement of the interior of the music room in Holywell (1780) the completion of the hall and chapel at Worcester College (1783 onward) and the building of a new library at Oriel (1788-9).[1] The interiors, though elegantly enough designed, were standard products of Wyatt's office. Only at Oriel did he have the opportunity to design an entirely new building. Here his new library, with its Ionic order standing on an arched and rusticated basement, uses a formula familiar from the Strand front of William Chambers's Somerset House, and simplifies it in accordance with the taste of the 1780s. As a gothic architect Wyatt demonstrated his skill by altering or remodelling the interiors of the halls of Merton (1790-1) Magdalen (1790-5) and Balliol (1792).[2] The chapels at Magdalen and New College and the library at Balliol were also re-gothicized under his direction, and at Christ Church he designed the stone staircase that leads up to the hall and the panelling and fireplaces in the hall itself. Of these gothic works relatively little has survived the restorations of the nineteenth century, but some of Wyatt's designs for Magdalen, and photographs of the interior of the chapel at New College (plate IX) with the organ cleverly divided to provide a view of the Reynolds window, demonstrate that capacity for romantic composition which, allied to a superior knowledge of medieval detail, made his reputation as a gothic architect.[3]

The taste which favoured a gothic dress for the interiors of college halls and chapels rather than the classical décor of the recent past was one which also looked with disfavour on the formal gardens of the seventeenth and eighteenth centuries. Williams's *Oxonia depicta* of 1732-3 shows that in the reign of George II formality was still the rule in college gardens, even more so than it had been when Loggan depicted them in his *Oxonia illustrata* of 1675. Some gardens had changed little between 1675 and 1732: at Balliol, for instance, neither the master nor

[1] For the upper library of New College see G. Jackson-Stops, 'Restoration and expansion: the buildings since 1750'; in Buxton and Williams, *New College*, 238-40. For Brasenose library see Allfrey, 'Architectural history', 34-6.
[2] For Wyatt's works at Magdalen and New College see Boase, 'An Oxford college and the gothic revival' and Jackson-Stops, 238-44.
[3] For further details of Wyatt's works in Oxford see *VCH Oxon.* iii, *passim* and Colvin, *British Architects*, 943-4.

the fellows had significantly altered the layout of their respective areas, while at New College the heraldic parterre (exhibiting the arms of Charles II and William of Wykeham) and the large sundial cut in box still surprised and amused like the floral clocks of more recent times. Other gardens had become even more elaborately formal with the aid of topiary and pleached alleys, notably the botanic garden itself, and those of Corpus, Wadham and St John's. At Trinity the 'grove', shown by Loggan as an irregular plantation of trees, had in the reign of Queen Anne been transformed into the most ambitious of all Oxford college gardens, with a profusion of topiary obelisks, pillars and balls, all surrounded by a wall of yew, 'cut in to regular pilasters and compartments', and aligned on the west with the Garden Quadrangle and on the east with a *clairvoyée* grille framed by baroque piers. In addition there were to the south a lime walk and an intricate plantation of the kind known as a 'wilderness'.[1] Unfortunately there is no comparable record of Oxford gardens in the latter part of the eighteenth century, but by the early years of the nineteenth clipped yews, box hedges and axial paths had everywhere given way to planting of a less formal character. New College appears to have been the first college to naturalize its garden, for it was in or about 1762 that the parterres were grassed, though the mount survived to be transformed later into the present wooded hillock.[2] St John's followed suit in 1777-8, doing away with its topiary and pleached alleys in order to create an informal landscape garden of green lawns framed by carefully composed trees and flowering shrubs.[3] At Wadham the change took place in 1796 under the direction of the duke of Marlborough's gardener Shipley.[4] Trinity's garden layout was still mainly if not wholly formal in 1794, when the 'order and symmetry' of its 'clipped hedges and straight walks' were commended by no less a person than the landscape gardener Humphry Repton, and it was not until the 1820s that Worcester took advantage of its site on the western edge of the town to create a well-planned landscape garden which gives its

[1] According to John Pointer's 'Chronology of Oxford University' (Bodl. MSS Rawl. Q. f. 5-6) Trinity's garden was 'altered' in 1706. TCA misc. i, fo 105 shows that the stone piers (built by B. Peisley) the 'iron gate' (made by Thomas Robinson) and the planting of limes, elms and yews were all paid for in 1714. At St John's the building in 1697-8 of a similar grille or iron gate may indicate the date of the formal layout which lasted until 1777.

[2] *VCH Oxon.* iii. 154. But in his *Letters from England*, published in 1807, Southey stated that one relic of the formal garden—a row of trees 'every one of which has its lower branches grafted into its next neighbour'—had been retained: R. Southey, *Letters from England*, ed. J. Simmons (London 1951), 177.

[3] Though often said (without any contemporary authority) to have been the work of 'Capability' Brown, this transformation was probably due to the Oxford gardener Robert Penson, who not only supplied the new trees and shrubs but also made an alternative design for the layout, signed and dated 1774, which has survived among the college's archives. For the date see Costin, *St John's*, 216.

[4] T. G. Jackson, *Wadham College* (Oxford 1893), 216. In 1794 Balliol spent £154 in 'laying out and adorning grove garden and quad' in the form shown in Hoggar's map of 1850.

provost's lodgings an arcadian setting like that of a Georgian country house.[1] The only other colleges which enjoyed sufficient space to think in similar terms were Magdalen and Christ Church. Magdalen's 'water-walk', celebrated by its association with Addison, was a popular place of resort throughout the eighteenth century. Its attractions lay in the shady tree-lined walk enlivened by the proximity of running water rather than in any conscious display of the gardener's art. In 1801 Repton submitted to the fellows of Magdalen an enticing scheme for the conversion of the walk into a picturesque landscape of trees and water, but it shared the fate of the designs for new buildings in the gothic style with which it was linked.[2] As for Christ Church, its governing body seems never to have considered the capabilities, in landscape terms, of its Meadow, then as now a swampy field in a state of unimproved nature calculated to appeal more to the taste of the twentieth century than to that of the eighteenth.

[1] *The Landscape Gardening and Landscape Architecture of the late Humphry Repton*, ed. J. C. Loudon (London 1840), 112. The formal layout at Trinity seems to have been done away with some time between 1808 and 1829: see J. D. U. Ward, 'Landscape comes to Oxford', *Architectural Rev.* ciii (March-June 1948). For Worcester see C. H. Daniel and W. R. Barker, *Worcester College* (London 1900), 221.

[2] Boase, 'An Oxford college and the gothic revival', 152-5.

Appendix

PRINCIPAL ARCHITECTURAL WORKS AT
OXFORD UNIVERSITY 1689-1800

building	date	architect	mason or principal building contractor	cost[1]
University				
Bodleian Library:				
buttressing	1701-3	C. Wren	T. Robinson	
botanic garden:				
greenhouse	1727	–	W. Townesend	£319[2]
Clarendon Building	1712-15	N. Hawksmoor	W. Townesend	£6,185
Radcliffe Library	1737-48	J. Gibbs	W. and J. Townesend, F. and W. Smith	£43,226[3]
Radcliffe Observatory	1772-9	H. Keene and J. Wyatt	J. Pears	£23,527[4]
All Souls:				
Codrington Library	1716-56	N. Hawksmoor	W. Townesend	£12;101
N. Quadrangle	1720-48	N. Hawksmoor	W. Townesend	£4,000 (approx.)
hall	1730-3	N. Hawksmoor	W. Townesend	£3,138
Balliol:				
Bristol Buildings	1716-20	–	W. Townesend	
Front Quad (E side)	1738-43	–	W. Townesend	£1,867[5]
Fisher Building	1768-9	H. Keene		£3,000 (approx.)
Brasenose:				
library remodelled	1779-80	J. Wyatt		£732[6]
Christ Church:				
Peckwater Quad	1707-14	H. Aldrich	W. Townesend	£3,000+
library	1717-72	G. Clarke	W. Townesend	£15,000 (approx)
anatomy school	1766-7	H. Keene		
Canterbury Quad	1775-8	J. Wyatt	W. Osborn	£7,438[7]

[1] Derived from *VCH Oxon.* iii unless otherwise stated.
[2] Hiscock, *Christ Church Miscellany*, 55 n. 3.
[3] *Building Accounts of the Radcliffe Camera*, appx II.
[4] Bodl. MS dd. Radcliffe Trust c. 51 (minute-book of the Radcliffe trustees 1752-91).
[5] H. W. C. Davis, *A History of Balliol College* (Oxford 1899), rev. edn by R. H. C. Davis and R. W. Hunt (Oxford 1963). [6] Allfrey, 'Architectural history', 35.
[7] CA xxxiii. b.3.

building	date	architect	mason or principal building contractor	cost
Corpus:				
Fellows' Building	1706-12	H. Aldrich(?)	W. Townesend	£4,000(?)[1]
Gentlemen-Commoners' Building	1737	—	W. Townesend	£1,768
Exeter:				
gateway	1702-3	—	W. Townesend	
library	1778		J. Townesend	
Jesus:				
Inner Quad (completion)	1699-1713	—		£1,175
Lincoln:				
6 chambers	1739	—		£365[2]
Magdalen:				
New Buildings	1733-4	G. Clarke and W. Townesend	R. Piddington, W. King	£5,091[3]
hall and chapel (altered)	1790-5	J. Wyatt	J. Pears	£4,360
Merton:				
hall (altered)	1790-1	J. Wyatt	J. Pears	
New:				
Garden Quad (SE block)	1700	—	R. Piddington, G. Smith	£800[4] (approx.)
Garden Quad (NE block)	1707	—	W. Townesend, G. Smith	£800[5] (approx.)
libraries (refitted)	1778-80	J. Wyatt (advice)	J. Pears	£621
hall (new roof)	1786	—	J. Pears	£578[6]
chapel (remodelled)	1788-94	J. Wyatt	J. Pears	£9,694[7]
Oriel:				
Robinson Building	1719-20	—	W. Townesend	£750[8] (approx.)
Carter Building	1729-34	—		£1,059
library	1788-9	J. Wyatt	E. Edge	£5,000[9] (approx.)
Pembroke:				
chapel	1728-32	—	W. Townesend	£730 (approx.)
Queen's:				
library	1692-5		J. Townesend	£5,247[10]
rebuilding of college	1710-70	N. Hawksmoor	W. and J. Townesend, E. King	£27,300 (approx.)

[1] Townesend was paid £1,223 for masonry: Bodl. MS Rawl. lett. 98, fo 232.

[2] LCM.

[3] Macray, *Reg. Magdalen* v. 11-12.

[4] G. Jackson-Stops, 'Gains and losses: the college buildings, 1404-1750' in Buxton and Williams, *New College*, 223.   [5] Ibid.

[6] Jackson-Stops, 'Restoration and expansion', 240.

[7] Ibid. 241.   [8] Hiscock, 52.

[9] Dale, *Wyatt*, 84-5 gives the architect's fee, which (if charged at the usual 5 per cent) would indicate a total expenditure of about £5,000. The mason's contract amounted to about £1,800: Arkell, *Oxford Stone*, 25, 80.

[10] J. R. Magrath, *The Queen's College* (2 vols Oxford 1921) ii. 70-1.

building	date	architect	mason or principal building contractor	cost
St John's:				
hall screen	1742	J. Gibbs	J. Townesend	£120[1]
Holmer Building	1794-5	—	J. Pears	£2,000[2] (approx.)
Trinity:				
chapel	1691-4		B. Peisley	
Garden Quad (S side)	1728	—	W. Townesend	
University College:				
Radcliffe Quad	1717-19	—	B. Peisley, W. Townesend	£4,695[3]
hall (remodelled)	1766	H. Keene	W. Townesend	£1,200
Wadham:				
SW block	1693-4	—	B. Peisley	£450 (approx.)
Worcester:				
rebuilding of college	1720-76	G. Clarke, H. Keene	W. Townesend, J. Townesend	£13,000 (approx.)

[1] SJM. computus annus 1743, fo 45.
[2] Costin, *St. John's*, 235.
[3] Bodl. MS dd. Radcliffe Trust c.48 (minute-book of the Radcliffe trustees 1717-20).

31

Paintings and Painted Glass

E. WATERHOUSE

UNLIKE the University of Cambridge, which in about 1790 owned only some twenty-four paintings and three statues,[1] the University of Oxford already owned two considerable collections of portraits at the beginning of the eighteenth century: that in the Ashmolean Museum, which included about nine paintings other than portraits and was made up of the portraits which had originally belonged to the Tradescant family and of those added by Elias Ashmole, who had presented the collection to the university in 1683; and the collection which had accumulated in the Bodleian Library. A manuscript catalogue of the portraits in the Ashmolean Museum had been transcribed in 1697 for the use of the vice-chancellor, and some inscriptions and dates seem to have been painted on to some of the pictures during the keepership of John Whiteside, between 1714 and 1729.[2] No doubt this formed the basis of the rather summary account published in 1759 in the first edition of *The New Oxford Guide* and the full list in *The English Connoisseur* in 1766, when the pictures seem to have been, to some extent, accessible to the public;[3] but George Vertue, who visited the university in 1721 and 1743 specifically to look at portraits, appears not have noticed them, although the Tradescant portraits seem today to be among the most interesting possessed by the university. They may well have not been very visible as they were hung in the old Ashmolean building, whose display methods can be glimpsed from Hearne's sour comment of 1729.[4]

The Ashmolean collection did not receive any addition during the eighteenth century, but it was otherwise with the collections which belonged to the Bodleian Library. This has good claims to be considered the oldest public picture-gallery in England. A few pictures were in the library proper, or on the staircase, but most of them were in 'the

---

[1] J. W. Goodison, *Catalogue of Cambridge Portraits* i *The University Collection* (Cambridge 1955), p. xvii.

[2] *Catalogue of Portraits* i. 166.

[3] *The English Connoisseur* (2 vols London 1766), said to be by Thomas Martyn.

[4] Hearne, *Collections* x. 209 (5 Dec. 1729); see A. MacGregor, 'The Ashmolean Museum' above, *passim*.

School-Gallery adjoyning the Bodleian Library', and of these Hearne had in 1705 drawn up a catalogue which was first printed in 1708/9.[1] We learn from *The English Connoisseur* (1766) that 'the *Bodleian Library* and Picture Gallery are to be seen from 8 to 11 in the morning, and in the afternoon between 1 and 4, from Michaelmas to Lady-day, and between 2 and 5 from Lady-day to Michaelmas'.[2] Lists of the pictures appeared in a separate pamphlet, *A Catalogue of the several Pictures, Statutes and Busto's in the Picture Gallery at Oxford* (Oxford 1759). By 1763 'a new edition' of this latter appeared with the title extended ... *the Picture Gallery, Bodleian Library, and Ashmolean Museum*. In these lists about a dozen pictures which can be called 'Old Masters' appear as well as portraits. Most of these came from the bequest in 1739 of John King DD and are Dutch seventeenth-century paintings (mainly of maritime subjects). They were transferred to the new Ashmolean Museum in 1845 and most of the attributions have been altered.

The excellent modern catalogue by Mrs Reginald Lane Poole of the portrait holdings in the Bodleian collection makes any detailed account unnecessary here, but some comment may be made on the character the collection was thought to have, on the prestige which may have been associated with the collection and on the additions made to it during the eighteenth century.[3]

Although portraits of a few eminent foreigners (Sarpi, Galileo and Grotius) were presented in the seventeenth century—and the Polish astronomer Hevelius presented his own portrait in 1679—by the mid-eighteenth century the Bodleian collection was regarded as a sort of national portrait gallery, and a friend in 1739 congratulated Swift on his portrait being 'placed in the Gallery among the most renowned and distinguished personages this island has produced';[4] and, in 1735, Humphrey Bartholomew of University College, had a series of portraits of eight eminent doctors copied by John Wollaston, and he presented the copies to the collection. In 1730 Sarah, duchess of Marlborough, presented a Rysbrack bust of the great duke to the university; and in 1721 Sir Godfrey Kneller saw fit to give a portrait of himself.

Kneller may also have presented a portrait of the duke of Ormonde, as a letter from Charlett to Pepys dated 1700 mentions that 'Kneller is desirous to have some of his art visible in the Gallery', which may have

[1] Hearne's list was published in *Memoirs for the Curious or The Monthly Miscellany* (Dec. 1708-Jan. 1709) and reprinted in his *Letter, containing an Account of some Antiquities between Windsor and Oxford, with a list of the several pictures in the school-gallery adjoining the Bodlejan Library* (np 1725).
[2] *English Connoisseur* ii. 42.
[3] Mrs Poole's *Catalogue of Portraits* includes all the portraits now in the Bodleian Library, the Sheldonian Theatre, the Examination Schools, the Ashmolean Museum and elsewhere in university possession.
[4] *Catalogue of Portraits* i. 99.

encouraged Pepys to commission Kneller in 1701 to paint a portrait of John Wallis, which was also for the Bodleian collection.[1] Other painters felt the same, and Thomas Wright in 1730 presented a portrait of Bodley's recently deceased Librarian, Joseph Bowles, while Thomas Gibson in 1733 presented a portrait of John Locke. It is worth recalling that until the foundation in 1760 of the Foundling Hospital, whose offices became the first accessible public picture-gallery in London, to which painters presented pictures, portraits or otherwise, of the sort that they wished to have commissioned from them, there was nowhere outside their own studios where painters could exhibit their works. In 1787 the painter Edward Penny (1714-91) presented to the gallery two pictures (*The Death of General Wolfe* and the *Marquis of Granby giving Alms*) which he had painted twenty years earlier, presumably to ensure that his name would not be forgotten.

Very occasionally the university bought a portrait for the Gallery, but most acquisitions were gifts from the sitter, or from a descendant or friend. Two considerable benefactors, who had a sense of the collection as a historical portrait-gallery, were George Clarke and, above all, Richard Rawlinson, the antiquary to whom the collection may owe as many as fifty pictures by gift or bequest. Unfortunately Rawlinson was much more interested in the sitters than in the artist, and he made his purchases as inexpensively as possible. Some of his marked catalogues survive in the Bodleian Library and make curious, and rather sad, reading.[2]

A small number of Old Masters, other than portraits, were given or bequeathed to the Bodleian gallery during the eighteenth century, and these were transferred to the new Ashmolean Museum between 1845 and 1847. Apart from the two pictures by Penny already mentioned, which were the gift of the artist, not many find a place in the current catalogue of the Ashmolean Museum. There were five of the *Cardinal Virtues* and all seven *Deadly Sins* by unidentifiable Netherlandish painters, and a small group of Dutch pictures bequeathed in 1739 by John King. Two or three of these were cleaned for an exhibition of 'Dutch pictures in Oxford' in 1975 and proved of considerable interest, notably *Two Children Stealing an Apple from a Man with a Basket* which had been ascribed to Frans Hals in the eighteenth century but is now given to Moeyaert.[3] A picture of *Noah's Sacrifice* ascribed to Sebastien Bourdon was given by a J. Cornish in 1759;[4] and one or two of Richard Rawlinson's gifts of portraits fell more or less into the category of Old Masters.

---

[1] For Charlett's letter see ibid. 141.
[2] Ibid. p. xiii and note.
[3] See *Dutch Pictures in Oxford, 10 May to 27 July 1975* (Ashmolean Museum exhibition catalogue).
[4] It is not in fact by Bourdon; it is perhaps Genoese and by, or after, A. M. Vassallo.

But it is likely that Rawlinson's most interesting acquisitions in this field found their way to his own college, St John's. Although a number of inventories in the archives of the university reveal that dons sometimes owned a considerable number of pictures,[1] the only college which owned a group of Old Masters in the eighteenth century (apart from General Guise's great gift to Christ Church) was St John's. Five inventories, ranging from 1728 to 1767, survive.[2] Although several pictures listed as in the president's lodgings have disappeared, and it is by no means clear whether Rawlinson, Holmes or his successor William Derham was responsible for certain of the pictures, half a dozen Dutch pictures of good quality survive.

But the most remarkable accretion of Old Masters to the Oxford scene was the bequest to Christ Church in 1765 by General John Guise of his considerable collection of Old Masters and his much more considerable collection of Old Master drawings.[3] Christ Church had received in 1729 the bequest from William Stratford of a pair of portraits (now ascribed to Scorel) which had been relegated in 1760 to an 'old buttery';[4] but the Guise collection, the bulk of which was installed in the library, had previously been considered as one of the sights of London. In 1766 The English Connoisseur rather hopefully stated after listing the pictures in the hall that 'the fine collection of Pictures lately left to the College by General Guise, will make these trifles overlooked', and it issued the somewhat over-optimistic catalogue which had been printed in London.[5] Christ Church did in fact print a small catalogue of its own in 1776, and the pictures were latterly shown to visitors by a rather witch-like lady improbably named Mrs Showell.[6] They were not seen at their best, owing to unfortunate restorations by a certain 'Old Bonus', and the full distinction of the collection has only become apparent in the present century, when the important pictures have been cleaned and

[1] See Catalogue of Portraits i, pp. xvi-xvii.

[2] A note ibid. iii. 147-50 gives an account of the reasons why uncertainty prevails about the sources from which some pictures from St John's derive, and also gives extracts from Rawlinson's correspondence with the president, William Holmes.

[3] Further detail is rendered unnecessary by the two admirable catalogues by J. B. Shaw: Paintings by Old Masters at Christ Church, Oxford (London 1967) and Drawings by Old Masters at Christ Church, Oxford (2 vols Oxford 1976).

[4] H. Walpole-G. Montague, 19 July 1760, Horace Walpole's Correspondence, ed. W. S. Lewis et al. (48 vols New Haven, London and Oxford 1937-83) ix. 288-90.

[5] The English Connoisseur ii. 48 ('fine collection'). A 'list of the pictures belonging to General Guise, at his house in George Street, Hanover Square', is given in London and its Environs Described (6 vols London 1761), iii. 18-36, which is said to be by Samuel Gurney. This catalogue was copied bodily into The English Connoisseur ii. 49-67, as was first pointed out by F. Simpson, 'The English Connoisseur and its sources', The Burlington Magazine xciii (1951), 356.

[6] A caricature of her by T. Newton as Mrs Showell, published in 1807, is illustrated in W. G. Hiscock, A Christ Church Miscellany (Oxford 1946), 95; Hiscock states that her name occurs in the college accounts.

both pictures and Old Master drawings have been meticulously cata-logued. The pictures by Annibale Carracci are especially remarkable.

The ceiling of the new chapel of Trinity College, which was under construction from 1691 to 1694, was painted by Pierre Berchet, a French-man who had originally come over to work for Verrio. In the main field is the *Ascension* and there are also two separate strips of painting contain-ing *Angels*. This is Berchet's only surviving work and is of some distinction. About 1700 Henry Cook painted an altarpiece for New Col-lege chapel which 'consists of a Salutation Piece, behind which the pain-ter has artfully thrown the concave of a well ornamented dome, in which the Chapel appears to terminate'.[1] This disappeared in the last quarter of the century.

The final outcrop of the baroque in college chapels was due to James Thornhill at All Souls. About 1714 he covered the east wall of the chapel, above the altarpiece, with a huge fresco which rather surprisingly showed the reception of the founder, Archbishop Chichele, into heaven, described in the eighteenth-century guidebooks as a 'fine Assumption piece of the Founder'.[2] This survived until 1872. In 1716 Thornhill also painted in fresco a circular *Ascension* in the apse ceiling of the chapel at Queen's, which survives today but makes very little impact. There was then a lull of some thirty years, during which the east ends of college chapels remained unaltered.

The taste for a painted altarpiece in the manner of the Roman Catholic church was begun by Magdalen. In 1745 the college received as a gift an altarpiece of *Christ bearing the Cross*, which was then ascribed to Guido Reni and has later been called Valdés Leal.[3] The picture was said originally to have been captured by the attainted duke of Ormonde at Vigo, and the year and the decidedly mediocre qualities of the painting make one wonder if 'taste' alone was a sufficient explanation for this new venture in college altarpieces. It was not followed for nearly a quarter of a century, until in 1769 All Souls took the unprecedented step of commis-sioning a new altarpiece from a foreign painter, Raphael Mengs, who had some claims, at any rate in learned circles, to being the most famous painter in Europe.[4] This handsome picture, a *Noli me tangere*, remained

[1] *New Oxford Guide* (1759 edn), 37.

[2] Ibid. 34. Only some battered fragments remain, but a small copy now belongs to the college and four drawings are known, as well as an engraving showing the east end in 1814. All of these are reproduced by J. Sparrow, 'An Oxford altar-piece', *The Burlington Magazine* cii (Jan. and Oct. 1960), 7, 453.

[3] T. S. R. Boase, *Christ bearing the Cross, attributed to Valdés Leal, at Magdalen College: a study in taste* (Oxford 1955); on p. 7 is a list of the subsequent modifications to the altar-ends of college chapels during the eighteenth century. The attribution to Valdés Leal is not satisfactory.

[4] In Johann Winckelmann's *Geschichte der Kunst des Alterthums* (Dresden 1764), 184 Mengs was proclaimed as the greatest painter 'of his own and perhaps of the next age', and the book was dedi-cated to him.

one of the sights of Oxford for nearly a century.[1] After narrowly escaping from the risk of being sold, it is now on loan to the Ashmolean Museum. It was the one remarkable example of the exercise of patronage in the field of painting achieved by the university in the eighteenth century.

In 1773 Lord Radnor, who had been at Winchester College but was not otherwise connected with New College, presented a large *Adoration of the Shepherds* which served as the altarpiece in New College chapel, with an attribution to Annibale Carracci, for a number of years, but it had been transferred to the hall before the end of the century.[2] In 1779 Merton received the gift of a *Crucifixion*, perhaps by Domenico Tintoretto, which still serves as the altarpiece in the chapel; and at an unspecified date Corpus received for its chapel a copy, quite plausibly ascribed to Pompeo Batoni, of Guido Reni's *Annunciation* in the Quirinal chapel, which was withdrawn and presented in 1794 by Christopher Willoughby to his parish church at Marsh Baldon. This was later replaced by a Rubens-school piece. A copy by James Cranke of Correggio's *Notte* still survives as an altarpiece at Queen's.

Although there was always some demand for heraldic glass, the art of historiated glass windows almost died out in Europe during the eighteenth century and there was little enough during the seventeenth. Under the impulse of the Laudian movement Oxford college chapels had been among the best patrons for stained glass up to the time of the civil war. As they had lost surprisingly little of it, a taste for it still lingered, and Oxford remains one of the few places where good eighteenth-century historiated glass survives. There were first three members of the Price family: Joshua (died 1717) who repaired and adapted the van Linge glass in Queen's chapel between 1715 and 1717 and made a new east window himself in the latter year, with the *Rest on the Flight into Egypt*, rather vaguely derived from a design of Carlo Maratta; his brother, the elder William Price (died 1722) made a window for Merton chapel in 1712 which has survived but is now in store; and Joshua's son, William Price the younger (died 1765) who made the windows on the south side of New College chapel in 1735-40.[3] These latter are more distinguished in drawing than those on the north side which are mainly by William Peckitt (1731-95), who made considerable technical improvement in the preparation and use of coloured glass, but was not a distinguished draughtsman.[4] In 1767 he did the east window of Oriel chapel (which

---

[1] For a full account of the commissioning of the picture and its subsequent peripeties see Sparrow, 'An Oxford altar-piece', where it is published for the first time.

[2] For its use as an altarpiece see the 1785 edition of the *New Oxford Guide*.

[3] The fairly full documentation for all the eighteenth-century windows in New College chapel is published by C. Woodforde, *The Stained Glass of New College, Oxford* (Oxford 1951).

[4] See J. A. Knowles, 'William Peckitt, glass-painter' (in Walpole Soc. xvii. 1929).

has now been transferred to the south side) as *Presentation in the Temple*; and between 1772 and 1774 he did the three western windows on the south side of New College chapel, the designs for the figures being by Biagio Rebecca. Peckitt had previously completed the great west window in the antechapel in 1765. But the college was not pleased with his work and, with more money and more ambitions, they at first planned in 1777 that the two remaining windows on the north side should be by Thomas Jervais after designs by Joshua Reynolds. However, by the end of 1777 it had been decided to break up Peckitt's west window and adapt it to the remaining two windows on the north side,[1] and to allow Jervais and Reynolds a free hand in the antechapel to design an enormous *Nativity* above full-length figures of the *Cardinal Virtues*. The tracery was modified to give greater scope for Reynolds's design, and the window was revealed to, in general, a very admiring public in 1785.[2] After the *Nativity* had been first set up in 1783, the *Reading Mercury and Oxford Gazette* (13 September 1783) voiced what was a widely held view that 'when this window is completed it will perhaps exhibit the finest specimen of Enamel painting in Europe'. Unfortunately the new kind of painting on glass was more or less opaque and required, to be seen at its best, conditions of lighting which were not available. It was extremely expensive and has, rather mysteriously, always remained one of the artistic sights of Oxford, although it has often been considered an aesthetic disaster.

The only other window which deserves mention is that by James Pearson who executed in 1776 the figures of *Christ and the Evangelists*, from John Hamilton Mortimer's design, in the west window of Brasenose chapel. This has been incorporated into a Victorian setting—with misleading effect.

Colleges were at least concerned to have portraits of their founders by the eighteenth century, and Pembroke College commissioned posthumous portraits of its two co-founders in 1712 from Enoch Seeman;[3] but, with the notable exception of Christ Church, most colleges were content that their collections of portraits should build up more or less accidentally. No general notion seems to have prevailed that it was desirable that a college should have a series of portraits of successive heads of the house and it was altogether eccentric to find the statement in Pointer's *Oxoniensis academia* that at Christ Church in the 'Audit-Room

---

[1] There was not quite enough of Peckitt's glass to fill the two windows and the two main lights on the western side of the window nearest the altar were executed by W. R. Eginton in 1821.

[2] Contemporary and later views are given by Woodforde.

[3] W. G. Hiscock, 'Notes on some Christ Church portraits, including one of Oriel and two of Pembroke', *Oxoniensia* xi-xii (1946-7), 151.

... are preserv'd the Pictures of most, if not all, the Deans of this College'.[1] This was in 1749, and by 1766, when *The English Connoisseur* was published, these portraits had been transferred to the hall. Except for three portraits in the hall at All Souls, these are the only college portraits thought fit to be listed in 1766, and the names only of the sitters, never of the painters, were thought worth mentioning. New College has portraits of a number of its eighteenth-century wardens (one at least by Romney). Magdalen has a few portraits; George Clarke bequeathed a number of portraits to All Souls, and William Derham left some to St John's, but in general it was not until the nineteenth century that most colleges made any serious attempt to preserve the likenesses of their more eminent members. Academic persons in the main were not painted by artists of distinction. The rather dreary Thomas Gibson, who lived in Oxford for a time, was perhaps employed, but his portraits are not often signed. The colleges contain only a very small number of portraits by named artists which were in their possession before 1800.

But Christ Church in this matter is altogether exceptional. By 1800 there were portraits by Kneller, Dahl, Richardson, Vanderbank, Hudson, Highmore, Wills, Hoare, Reynolds, Gainsborough, Romney and the young Lawrence. The collection of portraits, specifically in the hall, was deliberately built up and a formula of application had become standard by the beginning of the nineteenth century. A request was sent to the desired sitter that 'he would enable the Chapter to place his portrait in the Hall', and he usually responded by presenting the portrait. The anxious and sometimes controversial decisions of today concerning who the painter should be were quite unknown.

During the last quarter of the eighteenth century occasional travelling painters, especially in crayons, put in an appearance at Oxford. In 1779 the precocious 'Master Lawrence' (eventually to be Sir Thomas Lawrence, president of the Royal Academy) at the age of ten had spent a week in Oxford and 'done over 50 portraits of University men', but none of these has so far been traced.[2] Perhaps in emulation of Downman, who had some success at Cambridge in 1777 doing small portraits, the attractive crayons portraitist Lewis Vaslet spent at least two periods in Oxford, first in 1780 and latterly for a period of four months ending in May 1790.[3] The chief surviving outcome of these visits consists of a group of fifteen charming crayons, portraits of the warden and fellows of Merton which anticipate the spirit and scale of the pencil portraits commissioned by a number of colleges today.

---

[1] J. Pointer, *Oxoniensis academia* (London 1749), 82.

[2] *Jackson's Oxford Journal*, 13 Nov. 1779.

[3] *Catalogue of Portraits* ii. 52–3, 62–3 (1780). *Jackson's Oxford Journal* 8 May 1790: 'Mr Vaslet artist in crayons (miniatures and likenesses) intends shortly to end his 4 months stay in Oxford. Staying at Glover Haynes's High St.'

32

Music and Musicians

S. L. F. WOLLENBERG

To calm the boisterous passions. To relieve the anxieties of the world—To inspire cheerfulness—To appease the nerves when irritated . . . to kindle in our Souls the bright flame of Devotion; and to raise the Mind to a sensibility, and love of order. Those will not surely have mispent their time, in acquiring the knowledge of Musick, who apply it to these Purposes . . . contributing its powerful influence to the support of Charities; the Relief of the sick; and the distresses of the decay'd professors in this science.[1]

THE versatility which characterizes the role of music in a university community was established in the eighteenth century as a feature of Oxford music.[2] During the period 1688-1800 musical activity in the university was richly cultivated in a variety of settings. Only to a limited extent did it appear as an academic pursuit connected with lectures, examinations and degrees. Music was involved in academic affairs more as an ornament, enhancing the splendour of annual ceremonies (the Act, Encaenia and commemoration of benefactors) and special occasions such as the opening of new buildings. The university and the colleges also depended on music for the proper observance of religious ritual; college choirs and chapel organs, secure again after the uncertainties of the seventeenth century, formed another of the strands in the musical life of Oxford. Secular music meetings occurred regularly, and Oxford concerts gained a permanent location with the opening of the Holywell Music Room in 1748. A wide range of music-lovers formed the membership of choirs and orchestras, appeared as soloists, came to take degrees or stayed to work as composers and teachers; the continuity provided by the Heather professorship and later by the Music Room encouraged a constant presence of resident musicians and attracted distinguished visitors. Among these latter were Handel during the earlier part of the century and Haydn towards its close.

A reading of eighteenth-century sources and more recent secondary

[1] Jeremiah Milles, *Ars musica* (an essay spoken in The Sheldonian Theatre on Wednesday, 7 July 1773), Bodl. MS Top. Oxon. e. 375.
[2] S. Wollenberg, 'Music in 18-Century Oxford', *Proceedings of the Royal Musical Association*, cviii (1981-2), 69-99.

works[1] suggests that the purely academic study of music was less important at this period than it had been traditionally in connection with the
quadrivium, or than it was to become in the nineteenth and twentieth
centuries, stimulated by a growing interest in the history of the arts and
in systematic analytical techniques.[2] Williams remarks that 'when the *art*
of music began to be more cultivated, its *science*, as taught in the Universities, fell into disrepute, and students found it merely a waste of time to
study it for the arts degree'.[3] By the eighteenth century the traditional
scientific and philosophical approach to musical education had lost its
place (although it was still echoed in general expressions of ideas about
music[4]) and not until later in the next century was there a move to
replace it with other curricular musical instruction. The two degrees in
music—those of bachelor and doctor of music—were not awarded as the
culmination of a course of formal instruction in the subject; candidates
need not have attended regularly at the university, but could merely
matriculate under the aegis of an Oxford college (usually Magdalen in
the eighteenth century) in order to take the degrees.

Unlike other subjects music was largely detached from the main
academic activities of tutorials and lectures during the eighteenth
century.[5] The requirements for the degrees of bachelor and doctor of
music consisted of the traditional exercises in composition:

By the statutes of the university of Oxford, it is required of every proceeder to
the degree in music, that he employs seven years in the study or practice of that
faculty, and at the end of that term produce a testimonial of his having so done,
under the hands of credible witnesses; and that previous to the supplication for
his grace towards this degree, he compose a song of five parts, and perform the
same publicly in the music-school, with vocal and instrumental music, first
causing to be affixed on each of the doors of the great gates of the schools a
Programme . . .
Of a bachelor, proceeding to the degree of doctor, it is required that he shall
study five years after the taking his bachelor's degree; and produce the like
proof of his having so done . . . and farther, shall compose a song in six or eight
parts, and publicly perform the same 'tam vocibus quam instrumentis etiam
musicis' . . . in the presence of Dr Heyther's professor of music.[6]

---

[1] Particularly informative are Hearne, *Collections* (all 11 vols); J. Hawkins, *A General History of the
Science and Practice of Music* (5 vols London 1776); and C. F. A. Williams, *Degrees in Music* (London
1893). Little however has been written specifically on music in eighteenth-century Oxford.
[2] The medieval association of music with mathematics and philosophy was retained during the
sixteenth and seventeenth centuries. The *nova statuta* of 1564-5 still referred to two terms' study of
Boethius for music: *Statuta antiqua universitatis oxoniensis*, ed. S. Gibson (Oxford 1931), pp. xcii, 390.
The demand for such study was still evident in the Laudian code of 1636.   [3] Williams, 30.
[4] Milles's essay *Ars musica*, 'to which the Chancellor's Prize was adjudged', begins with references
to the harmony of the spheres and the system of creation drawn from the ancient philosophers.
[5] The music lectures originally endowed by Heather were not designed to instruct candidates for
degrees; already in the seventeenth century they had become absorbed as a form of entertainment
into the Act. See Wood, *Life and Times* ii. 564; pp. 869-70 below.
[6] Cited by Hawkins, *Science and Practice of Music* ii. 349.

Doctors of Music were set apart from 'Doctors of Divinity, Physick, and Law'; Hearne stated that they were not to be regarded as 'Doctors of a Faculty', nor were they entitled to vote in convocation 'unless they were first Masters of Arts'.[1] The statutes governing the award of the DMus were, moreover, loosely interpreted in the eighteenth century, especially with regard to the interval between the bachelor's and doctor's degree; the BMus and DMus were often awarded jointly on production of an exercise.[2] In 1799 William Crotch warned that a doctor's degree

cannot in future be taken without previously taking a Bachelor's and afterwards a space of 5 years intervening between the two degrees. Such things have been permitted but the Vice-Chancellor looks upon it as degrading to the honour of the Profession, and desires me never to permit any more.[3]

Degrees in music were awarded primarily to practitioners of the art although some, such as Burney and Callcott, combined an interest in composing with theoretical, historical and antiquarian work. The majority of supplicants for the degree of bachelor or doctor of music were church and cathedral organists and choirmasters: John Alcock (BMus 1755, DMus 1766) at Lichfield; his son John (BMus 1766) at Newark and Walsall; John Wall Callcott (BMus 1785, DMus 1800) at St Paul's; George Drummond (BMus *circa* 1818) at Paddington; Joseph Harris (BMus 1773) at Birmingham; Richard Langdon (BMus 1761) at Exeter cathedral, later at Bristol and Armagh; and others in similar posts. For most, the Oxford BMus represented the summit of their aspirations; the DMus was awarded much less frequently, and usually to notably distinguished men such as Burney, William Croft (1713) and Crotch. Several recipients of degrees were connected with the Chapel Royal, including the celebrated Samuel Arnold whose oratorio *The Prodigal Son* was in unusual circumstances accepted as an exercise when the university offered him the degrees of BMus and DMus and requested permission to use the oratorio at the installation of Lord North as Chancellor in 1773. Although Arnold had brought with him a formal exercise, the professor apparently deemed it unnecessary to judge this.[4] Some recipients of degrees were resident in Oxford, among them the successive professors of music: Richard Goodson senior (BMus *circa* 1682); Richard Goodson junior (BMus 1717); William Hayes (BMus 1735, DMus 1749); his son Philip (BMus 1763, DMus 1777); and William Crotch (BMus 1794, DMus 1799); all these held appointments as college

---

[1] Hearne, *Collections* vi. 298.

[2] William Heather was the first to accumulate both degrees, in 1622.

[3] W. Crotch–T. Busby, 15 Aug. 1799, CA MS 347/2. William Crotch (1775-1847), m. St Mary Hall 1791; prof. of music 1797-1847; organist Ch.Ch. and St John's.

[4] R. Fiske, 'Samuel Arnold' in *The New Grove Dictionary of Music and Musicians* (London 1980) i. 616.

and church organists, as did others such as William Walond (BMus 1757, organist at Christ Church from that year).[1] Ages of candidates and time-lapses between the degrees of bachelor and doctor varied widely, from Crotch and Callcott (both awarded the BMus at the age of 18) to Theodore Aylward (who took both degrees at the age of about 60) with fifteen years between Callcott's BMus and DMus and five between Crotch's. Oxford's youngest bachelor of music of the century seems to have been the blind organist and composer John Stanley, who matriculated at Magdalen and graduated BMus in 1729 at the age of 17.

In keeping with their employment, and following the fashion in English church music, most candidates submitted sacred anthems for solo voices and chorus with orchestra (usually to English, occasionally to Latin, psalm-texts).[2] Some exercises were secular odes (to texts by Addison, Pope and Milton among others) representing another popular form of English composition. The old specification of a five-, six- or eight-part song with instruments was absorbed into these forms of exercise (choruses were often written in five or eight parts) together with certain unwritten but generally accepted rules, for example that there should be some demonstration of fugal writing and perhaps also canon. The weakest composers sometimes attempted the most ambitious technical feats, as with Callcott's eight-part choral canon in the anthem 'Propter Sion' (1800) while some of the more pleasantly unambitious pieces such as Harris's pastoral evocation of Milton's 'Ode to May' (1773) lacked any appropriate display of technique; others were technically incompetent.[3] These were all minor composers; their exercises confirm the impression of a fall in standards in English music after Handel, for which his own dominating influence has traditionally been blamed. Those Handelian (sometimes also Purcellian) settings which worked successfully enough in the 1760s had taken on a faded air by the 1790s,[4] though some later pieces such as Crotch's anthem 'O Sing unto the

---

[1] Richard Goodson senior (d. 1718), prof. of music 1682-1718. Richard Goodson junior (d.1741), prof. of music 1718-41. William Hayes (a1708-77), priv. Magd. 1735; prof. of Music 1742-77. Philip Hayes (1738-97), m. Magd. 1763; prof. of music 1777-97. William Walond (c1725-70), priv. 1757.

[2] Charles Burney asked the reader to excuse his 'egotism' in citing his own exercise in answer to 'occasional and sinister assertions, "that I neither liked nor had studied Church Music" ': C. Burney, A General History of Music (4 vols London 1776-89) iii. 329. The possession of an Oxford BMus or DMus was generally taken to indicate an interest in church and choral composition.

[3] Bodl. MS Mus. Sch. Ex. d.25 (Callcott, DMus 1800), b.11 (Harris, BMus 1773). For an example of technical incompetence see Aylward's anthem 'I will cry unto God with my voice', ibid. d.7 (BMus and DMus 1791). Pencilled corrections (presumably by the examiner) throughout the manuscript refer to a variety of faults including the most elementary (pairs of consecutive fifths). Aylward had been elected professor of music at Gresham College in 1771.

[4] See Langdon's anthem 'O be joyful', Bodl. MS Mus. Sch. Ex. d.70 (BMus 1761) and John Alcock junior's 'Messiah, a sacred pastoral' (to a text by Pope), ibid. d.2 (BMus 1766); cf Callcott's 'Propter Sion' of 1800 and William Parsons's anthem 'Great is the Lord', ibid. d.101 (BMus and DMus 1790) with their uninspired repetitions of worn baroque formulae.

Lord' (1794) and his 'Ode to Fancy' (1799) were neatly turned and elegantly competent within conventional limits.[1] Only occasionally did an Oxford exercise go beyond the traditional Handelian counterpoint and routine choral style to take in more progressive ideas: Burney's anthem, 'I will love Thee, O Lord my Strength' (1769), the finest exercise extant, was more akin in its imaginative power and modern symphonic style to C. P. E. Bach and Haydn than to Handel, reflecting Burney's up-to-date and cosmopolitan taste.[2] Altogether, exercises for the bachelor's and doctor's degrees extant from this period covered such a diverse range of quality that it was clearly impossible to establish and maintain consistent standards in a discipline which was neither taught as an undergraduate degree course nor examined regularly by the university in the same manner as were the other arts subjects.

Because the Act, incorporating among its degree-ceremonies the statutory public performance of musical exercises (the Music-Act) occurred only sporadically during the eighteenth century, musical exercises were often performed at other times of the year.[3]

The Act, Encaenia and commemoration celebrations during the summer months were traditionally associated with musical (and other) entertainment as well as with academic ceremonial.[4] When the Act ceased to be held annually the Encaenia and commemoration retained the character of a music festival. The initiation of regular concerts at the Holywell music room and of a resident orchestra with excellent visiting soloists later added to the popularity of these annual festivals. Contemporary observations suggest that music at Act-time was thoroughly appreciated: Wood's 'all well done and gave good content' was a typical comment, although, especially in the eighteenth century, an often

[1] Bodl. MS Mus. Sch. Ex. d.37 (BMus 1794), b.4 (DMus 1799); the latter was to a text by the Oxford poet Thomas Warton which was set by several composers including William Hayes (Bodl. MS Mus. d.70.1).

[2] Bodl. MS Mus. Sch. Ex. c.15 (DMus 1769). This work was performed at Hamburg under the direction of C. P. E. Bach in 1773, as well as 'repeatedly performed at Oxford, after it had fulfilled its original destination': Burney, History of Music iii. 329. Among its virtues are the skilled and interesting string parts, subtle phrasing of the vocal line and sensitive word-setting; individual numbers are vividly characterized, and incidental delights include the obbligato use of clarinets in the aria 'The Voice of Joy' (fo 105ʳ). The variety of scoring in Oxford exercises generally was dictated to some extent by the forces available, and distinctive solo parts may (as in the case of the clarinets) have been designed for specific Oxford performers.

[3] Cf. Bodl. MS Hearne's diaries 175, p. 124: 'After the Exercise of the Artists on Act Monday is over, there is to be a Musick Act, provided there be anyone to take a degree in Musick, for which he is then to perform one Consort ... vocal and instrumental.' A similar process of detachment from the public ceremonies affected the performance of musical exercises at Cambridge, where the location changed from a central hall such as the senate house to individual colleges: Williams, Degrees in Music, 30.

[4] For the original Encaenia (1669) an organ was borrowed from Gloucester Hall; thereafter 'music in the theatre' formed an integral part of the ceremony (in 1671 the Sheldonian acquired its own organ).

overcrowded and overexcited audience was sometimes provoked to disruptive behaviour.[1]

A traditional musical feature of the Act was the music lecture or music speech, originally endowed by Heather as part of the duties of the music professor or lecturer.[2] This 'solemn lecture in English ... with intervals of instrumental music' was intended to be given 'on the vespers of the Act every year' (that is on the Saturday before the Act) at the music school, but in 1669 it was removed to the Sheldonian Theatre.[3] It became, like the Act itself, a haphazard occurrence. The professor of music was generally involved in composing ceremonial works for university events, rather as a court *Kapellmeister* would furnish occasional pieces for his employers, and several Heather professors contributed to the composition of Act-music (incidental music for performance during degree ceremonies, as distinct from the formal exercises in composition submitted by candidates for degrees). The patchy survival of the sources is linked with the ephemeral nature of these works (the exercises were, naturally, more carefully named and dated). Most surviving Act-music dates from the period 1669-1710, when the Act flourished.[4] One of its enthusiastic supporters during this period was Henry Aldrich, who provided Act-Music in various years. The music usually took the fashionable form of an ode for solo voices, chorus and instruments, often to Latin texts as in the elder Goodson's 'O qui potenti' (about 1700) and 'Carminum praeses' (about 1706) mixing instrumental overtures, symphonies and dances with songs, vocal ensembles and choruses.[5]

After the heyday of the Act in Aldrich's and Goodson's time its disappearance (by order of special decrees passed each year) during the early eighteenth century was followed by a dramatic revival in 1733.[6]

---

[1] Wood, *Life and Times* ii. 248, referring to the 1672 Encaenia, with verses by Fell set to music by Aldrich. In 1793 Philip Hayes's 'Ode for the Encaenia' was interrupted and only half of it performed: see Bodl. MS Top. Oxon. d.174, fo 238. In 1785 the celebrated Madame Mara was at the centre of a riot in the Theatre: see V. H. H. Green, 'The university and social life', pp. 350-4 above.

[2] *Laudian Code* IV.i.8, ed. Griffiths, p. 36. The lecture later became a separate responsibility, and the lecturer who was to deliver it was elected annually by the proctors and vice-chancellor: Williams, 35. These lecturers seem to have attracted a good audience: Wood, *Life and Times* ii. 490, iii. 427.

[3] In 1733, when the Act was revived, the music speech was again 'remov'd from the Musick-School to the *Theatre* by Act of Convocation': Bodl. MS Top. Oxon. e.214. It seems to have been designed partly to please the ladies in the audience, for whom special provision was made at the Sheldonian in 1733 ('and then the Enclosure within the Rail will be for the Ladies'): ibid. A music speech of about 1680 was addressed especially to the ladies who had come 'to honour [the university] with your Company': Bodl. MS Eng. poet. e.4, p. 206.

[4] See *A Summary Catalogue of Western Manuscripts in the Bodleian Library at Oxford* (7 vols in 13 Oxford 1895-1953) v (by F. Madan), pp. 251-5. It was only in the second half of the century that exercises were systematically deposited in the music-school collection.

[5] R. Goodson (senior), 'O qui potenti' and 'Carminum praeses', Bodl. MS Mus. Sch. c.127-8. Similar *pièces d'occasion* survive from special events such as royal visits to Oxford; Goodson's 'Ode for the visit of William III' in 1695 includes a choral setting of the words 'Plaudite regi, plaudite Gulielmo'.

[6] For the disappearance of the Act early in the century see the remarks in Hearne, *Collections, passim*.

Like that of any discontinued tradition, this revival caused problems as well as exciting considerable attention, as Hearne noted in 1733, since 'Acts have been discontinued so long, that few are living in Oxford, that know the old method of proceeding'.[1] The 1733 Act was an attempt to re-establish the ceremony on a grand scale. Musically its grandeur was to be derived from the visit of 'Mr Handel', at the request of the vice-chancellor, William Holmes, a visit well documented in numerous sources.[2] Although Handel's music secured the devotion of Oxford audiences throughout the later eighteenth century, and subsequent Encaenia celebrations were marked by performances of favourite Handel oratorios, the composer's presence at Oxford in 1733 was regarded with some disfavour, especially as he seized the opportunity to hold the maximum number of benefit-concerts during his stay and made an excellent profit from these but declined the university's offer of the honorary degree of doctor of music.[3] Hearne's reactions reflected the mixed feelings with which some supporters of the Act viewed the festivities of 1733: besides objecting to the high cost of tickets and programme-books for Handel's benefit-performances at the Sheldonian, he complained sourly of other aspects, for example that the music performed at the music-school on Saturday morning was 'very poor' and 'there was no Music Speech as used formerly to be, tho' none hath been since 1693'. He agreed with Cockman, master of University College, that the 1733 Act was 'an imperfect one' though 'better than none'. Yet after all he thought that 'the Vice-Chancellor . . . is to be commended for reviving our Acts, which ought to be annual . . . provided the statutes were strictly followed'.[4] Further reaction to the 1733 Act was expressed, in the current satirical form of ballad-opera, in *The Oxford Act* (1733).[5] Certainly this Act achieved its aim of re-creating public interest in the event.

[1] Hearne, *Collections* xi. 231.

[2] See particularly Hearne, *Collections, passim*; J. H. Mee, *The Oldest Music Room in Europe* (London 1911); and standard biographies of Handel such as O. E. Deutsch, *Handel: a documentary biography* (London 1955).

[3] Handel's music was often chosen to grace special ceremonies, as with the opening of the Radcliffe Library in 1749, when *Esther, Samson, Messiah* and some anthems were heard on three afternoons, under the direction of William Hayes: see Bodl. MS Top. Oxon. b.43, fo 21, printed in *Bodleian Quarterly Record* i (1914-16), 165. This seems to have been an occasion full of political complications: the phrase 'Mercy to Jacob's Race God Save the King' was taken to be particularly inflammatory. In 1733, apart from his Utrecht *Te Deum* and *Jubilate* and coronation anthems at St Mary's church on the Sunday morning, Handel's benefit-performances were: *Esther* on the evenings of Thursday 5 and Saturday 7 July; *Athalia* (in its first performance) on the Tuesday and Wednesday evenings 10 and 11 July; *Deborah* on Thursday evening 12 July; and *Acis and Galatea* at Christ Church, on the morning of 11 July. Handel considered other holders of honorary degrees to be inferior; but possibly his main reason for declining such a degree was his reluctance to pay the fee!   [4] Hearne, *Collections* xi. 232, 235, 224.

[5] *The Oxford Act, a new ballad opera, as it was perform'd by a company of students at Oxford* (London 1733). The cast included a don 'Haughty' and a scholar 'Thoughtless' who had to sell his furniture in order to afford tickets for Handel. *The Oxford Act, A.D. 1733, a particular and exact account of that solemnity* (London 1734) is a corrective in the form of a straightforward account of events more favourably viewed.

In the period after 1733 the main musical events during the summer months were connected with the Creweian Commemoration and the Encaenia, and from 1770 the annual Radcliffe Infirmary meeting.[1] A typical pattern of proceedings is illustrated in the summers of 1787-9, reported in *Jackson's Oxford Journal*. In 1787 on the evening of Monday 18 June there was a 'grand miscellaneous concert' in the Holywell Music Room to mark the beginning of the festivities: Mrs Billington sang and Mr Cramer played. On Tuesday, 19 June there was a second concert for the Infirmary meeting and on Wednesday, 20 June the Creweian Commemoration was rounded off by a third concert in the evening. It was usual to have three successive days of concerts: in 1788 they were held on Wednesday, Thursday and Friday, 25, 26 and 27 June, with *Acis and Galatea* at the Sheldonian on Wednesday, *Messiah* for the anniversary of the Radcliffe Infirmary on Thursday and a grand miscellaneous concert at the Sheldonian on Friday 'to commemorate the Founders and Benefactors of the University'.[2] Richard Paget, a demy at Magdalen, was full of praise for these performances: 'three very capital concerts at the Theatre for the benefit of Dr Hayes ... A great deal of Company in Oxford this music meeting, and of the 1st Rank. Many foreigners.'[3] By this time the Holywell band and the soloists engaged to perform with it had become essential to the success of the occasion. During the 1789 festival (Wednesday to Friday 24-6 June) the commemoration concerts were particularly enhanced by the singing of the Mozartian stars Signora Storace and Signor Benucci, enthusiastically received by a large audience and favourably reviewed in the press.[4] In 1793, when the duke of Portland was installed as chancellor, a commentator remarked of an evening concert on 2 July that 'Mrs Billington, by her angellic strains proved herself worthy of the popularity she has obtained at Oxford'.[5]

Musically the most distinguished of all commemoration celebrations in the second half of the century were those of 1791, when the customary 'three grand concerts in the Theatre' (on Wednesday, Thursday and Friday 6-8 July) and the honorary-degree ceremony of 8 July were graced by the presence of Joseph Haydn.[6] Haydn's music had already won

[1] Cambridge similarly commemorated with an annual concert the founding of Addenbrooke's hospital in 1766: *VCH Camb*. iii. 160 ff.

[2] As suggested above, the commemoration concerts often became in effect 'Handel festivals', for example in 1754 when 'a Convocation was held in the Theatre to commemorate the Benefactors to the University and to receive ... the Earl of Westmorland as its High Steward', and the following three days from 3 to 5 July were used for performances of *L'Allegro, Judas Maccabaeus* and *Messiah* in the Sheldonian: Bodl. MS Top. Oxon. d.247, p. 114, 2 July 1754.

[3] Bristol University Library, Paget collection, DM 106/419, Richard Paget's diary, June 1788.

[4] *Jackson's Oxford Journal*, 26 June 1789; Paget's diary, June 1789.

[5] Bodl. MS Top. Oxon. d.174, fo 238ᵛ.

[6] Reported in Paget's diary and *Jackson's Oxford Journal*. Among modern documentary compilations see particularly H. C. R. Landon, *Haydn: Chronicle and Works* (5 vols London 1976-80) iii, *Haydn in England 1791-1795* esp. 88-95, from which the information presented here is mainly derived.

recognition in Oxford, and after his arrival in January 1791 to begin the English visit organized by his friend Salomon he became associated through Salomon with many of the musicians who performed regularly in London and Oxford.[1] Early in 1791 Salomon introduced Haydn to Burney, who presented Haydn with a copy of his history of music, wrote a poem welcoming him to England and suggested that he should take an honorary degree at Oxford. Burney's enthusiasm for Haydn's character and talents reflected the feeling expressed in numerous contemporary reviews and summed up by an Oxford correspondent writing in the *European Magazine* on 15 July 1791:

Music [at Oxford] has still made farther strides towards perfection ... Can any thing exhibit the improved taste in that divine science so justly, as the degree just given to the modest Haydn by the University—this musical Shakespeare ... indeed such transcendant merit deserves the liberal compliment in the way it was conferred.[2]

Haydn's modesty led him to attribute his success in England to this honorary doctorate; unlike Handel, he greatly valued the Oxford degree, for which he had to pay '$1\frac{1}{2}$ guineas for having the bell rung ... and $\frac{1}{2}$ guinea for the robe'. 'The trip cost 6 guineas', and he believed that it had brought him 'the acquaintanceship of the most prominent men and the entree into the greatest houses.'[3] Oxford was equally conscious of the great honour accorded it by Haydn's appearing at the university in 1791: 'Haydn was introduced to the audience by Dr. Hayes, and received with a degree of respect and attention worthy [of] his genius'.[4]

Haydn's first appearance in Oxford was scheduled for Wednesday 18 May, when he was due to perform at a benefit-concert for Mr Hayward (a member of the Holywell band). This event was announced with great enthusiasm and was 'most numerously attended', so that when Haydn was prevented by an opera-rehearsal in London from coming to Oxford that evening the audience broke into a riot. Both Hayward and Haydn printed an apology in *Jackson's Oxford Journal* in which Haydn humbly expressed the hope that 'as the University of Oxford, whose great Reputation I heard abroad, is too great an Object for me not to see before I leave England, I shall take the earliest Opportunity of paying it a Visit'.[5] This hope was duly realized to everyone's satisfaction when

[1] Johann Peter Salomon was actively involved in Oxford concerts from 1781 (the year of his London debut) and promoted Haydn's music in England during the 1780s. There were other connections, for example through Andreas Lidl, baryton player in Haydn's orchestra at Eszterháza, who appeared in Oxford in 1776, and Haydn's friend Philippe Jung, violinist, originally of Vienna, who settled in Oxford and played an active and varied part in its musical life.

[2] Quoted by Landon, *Haydn* iii. 93.

[3] Ibid. 92; R. Hughes, 'Haydn at Oxford', *Music and Letters* xx (1939), 248.

[4] Landon iii. 89.

[5] Landon, op. cit. 80.

when Haydn personally took part in the July commemoration concerts. Although the honorary degree awarded him on 8 July did not depend on the production of an exercise, two compositions by Haydn became specially connected with his visit to Oxford: the 'Oxford' symphony (no. 92 in G major) and the canon 'Thy voice O harmony' (later absorbed into his setting of the Ten Commandments). Some confusion surrounding the history of the 'Oxford' symphony has been clarified by recent writers, and Landon's account shows that the work listed as Haydn's 'Sinfonia MS in G' in Hayward's programme for 18 May 1791 was to be number 92, conducted by the composer; this was not a new work but was probably introduced to London audiences as a 'new' symphony in the first concert of Salomon's series, and later received its first Oxford performance on 7 July 1791.[1] It represented Haydn at the height of his technical powers. The canon 'Thy voice O harmony' which he sent to the university conceals beneath its apparently simple exterior a highly concentrated demonstration of technical skills: it works in both inverted and retrograde form, and its realization can be derived from a notational trick (using both C and G clefs).[2] The visit to Oxford, like other events and travels, stimulated Haydn's genius.

The three grand concerts of July 1791 included, besides Haydn's music, a typical miscellany of vocal and instrumental pieces by a variety of composers, among them Purcell, Handel and the more modern Italians (Sarti) and the popular Pleyel; the performers included equally popular figures such as the violinist Cramer (who led the orchestral band) and the singer Nancy Storace. Haydn was delighted with the excellence of these Oxford performances.

Such concerts marked a climax in a continuous round of performances organized throughout the academic year. A well-established concert-tradition existed long before: from the seventeenth century there had been flourishing music-meetings in college rooms and in taverns, such as the Mermaid at Carfax to 1709 and the King's Head in the High Street, reflecting the English love of concerts as well as the sociability of university life.[3] In the seventeenth century such meetings had a special

[1] Ibid. 53-4, 85-95, 504 etc.
[2] Landon prints a facsimile of the autograph, with a correct realization: ibid. 94. When Haydn was elected to the English Society of Musical Graduates he presented this canon to the Society.
[3] For similar meetings held at various rooms and taverns in London, Cambridge and elsewhere see E. Walker, *A History of Music in England* (Oxford 1907, 3rd edn, rev. J. Westrup, Oxford 1952) and other standard books on English music and concert-life. Williams, *Degrees in Music*, 53 mentions a concert club at Christ's College, Cambridge, in 1710; see also C. Wordsworth, *Scholae academicae* (Cambridge 1877), 315 and C. Wordsworth, *Social Life at the English Universities* (Cambridge 1874), 202. Mallet illustrates with a Latin quotation the eighteenth-century idea that 'the civilising influence of music would tempt gentlemen from "midnight Drinkings" ': C. E. Mallet, *A History of the University of Oxford* (3 vols London 1924-7) iii. 145. The 'new sociability' of the time was enthusiastically channelled into the co-operative production and enjoyment of music (that most sociable of arts) in the universities. See also Green, 'Social Life', 342.

in maintaining a seriously threatened musical culture, and Hawkins later noted that after the Restoration 'meetings of such as delighted in the practice of music began now to multiply, and that at Oxford, which had subsisted at a time when it was almost the only entertainment of the kind in the kingdom, flourished at this time more than ever'.[1] There is evidence that Oxford music-meetings were formally organized, with a rota of stewards and formal orders governing their conduct. A set of *Orders to be observed at the Musick-Meeting* dating from the 1680s gives details of the arrangements: 'That it be kept every last Thursday in the Month at Mr HALL's Tavern at five of the Clock precisely in the Evening, and continue till Ten.'[2] The club's seventh rule was that 'Whoever does not come before Seven a Clock is to forfeit Six Pence, besides his Club [money]' and the twelfth that 'The Steward is obliged to sconce any that makes a noise in time of performance, or to be sconced himself'. The number of members must not exceed forty-one; forty members were listed, including Richard Goodson (senior) and Simon Child (organist of New College from 1702).

In the early eighteenth century Oxford musicians continued to meet regularly: the records of the Musical Society from 1712 to 1719 show that the weekly meetings on Monday evenings were well supported and the stewards (elected from among performing members to serve for a month each) were kept busy with the accounts and organization of the Society.[3] Domestic expenses, such as those noted by the steward for November 1712, Mr Lee, included tobacco, ale, pipes, bread and butter, 'more ale', candles and fire; among other expenses incurred were rent of rooms, binding, strings, repairs to the harpsichord and music-copying. Lee's list of members for November 1712, headed as was customary by 'Mr Professor' (that is Goodson) contained the names of sixteen performers and a similar number of non-performing members. The society also owned and lent instruments and music-books. By the mid-eighteenth century its activities and resources could no longer be contained adequately in tavern or college rooms. William Hayes, describing weekly concerts at the King's Head tavern and benefit-concerts in college halls, specified the unsatisfactory nature of this accommodation as the main reason for the launching of a new scheme during the 1740s.[4] By 1748, when the Holywell concerts began, the Musical Society had already

---

[1] Hawkins, *Science and Practice of Music* iv. 374.

[2] Bodl. MS Top. Oxon. a.76. Mr Hall's tavern was the Mermaid at Carfax.

[3] MCR 4.33 (discovered by Dr J. R. L. Highfield). See M. Crum, 'An Oxford music club, 1690–1719', *Bodleian Library Record* ix (1973–8).

[4] Bodl. MS Top. Oxon. d.337. Hayes's manuscript 'History of the Music Room', including details of financial arrangements for the original building, is printed in fuller form in [J.Peshall,] *The History of the University of Oxford, from the death of William the Conqueror to the demise of queen Elizabeth* (Oxford 1773), 247–8. See also Bodl. Gough Maps xxvii, fo 95 for an architectural sketch of the Music Room (front view and interior); and for its history Mee, *Oldest Music Room in Europe*, from which the main points

created successful models of organization: the formal orders exemplified by a set of *Articles of the Musical Society in Oxford* of 1757 have a strong resemblance to earlier documents, with stewards to be elected in rotation, committee-members to be fined for non-attendance at meetings, and borrowers fined for non-return of books and instruments.[1] There is more precise specification of conditions for membership of the committee: 'the Person to be chosen' (one from each college) must be 'a Fellow, Scholar, Exhibitioner, or Chaplain of some College, a Vice-Principal of an Hall, or one who bears some public Office in the University', and must be 'a Graduate, or at least four full Years standing'. These articles have a more formal, legalistic character than those of the pre-Holywell society.

The main difference was of course that from 1748 the Holywell Music Room provided, uniquely for its time, a purpose-built public room (rather than merely an adaptation of a pre-existing one) with a permanent orchestra and singers. Its effect was to involve Oxford in the progressive growth of democratically organized concerts, choirs and orchestras during the eighteenth century, presenting a challenge to the tradition of court establishments with resident musicians subject to the whims and tastes of their patrons and performing for a socially exclusive audience in often highly artificial conditions.

The series of Monday evening subscription concerts held at the Holywell Music Room had its parallel in metropolitan ventures such as the Bach-Abel concerts (from 1765) Antient Music (from 1776) Professional (from 1783) and Salomon concerts (1791 and 1794). Many of the performers associated with these, and with the fashionable pleasure-gardens at Vauxhall and Ranelagh, the grand annual Handel commemoration festivals, and the three choirs festivals, appeared also at Holywell: the remark that 'English music lovers could hear a great deal of admirable vocal and instrumental performance'[2] is applicable to Oxford as well as London. A wave of foreign musicians passing through or settling in London, attracted by the opportunities it afforded for a concert or stage career, spilled over into Oxford and enriched the cultivation of music there. Among these visitors from London and abroad

are extracted and co-ordinated here with additional material from a variety of original sources in the Bodleian Library, supplemented by more recent works of reference such as *New Grove Dictionary* and F. Blume (ed.), *Die Musik in Geschichte und Gegenwart* (14 vols and 2 supplementary vols Kassel 1949-68, 1973, 1979) for biographical information on individual performers.

[1] There is a copy of the *Articles* in Oxford, Music Faculty Library, rare books, 1757; printed by Mee, 45-53.
[2] Walker, *Music in England*, 273. The conglomeration of concerts into a festival was another popular feature of English music-making reflected in Oxford. Music at Act-time assumed the character of a festival and was described as such in contemporary records: see Bodl. MS Top. Oxon. d.174, fo 239ʳ (1793). Oxford musicians took an interest in festivals elsewhere; William Hayes conducted for the three choirs and William Matthews and Thomas Norris (see below) sang in the Handel commemorations at Westminster Abbey, with which Philip Hayes was also connected.

were the gamba-player Carl Friedrich Abel; the cellist John Crosdill; the violinists Wilhelm Cramer and D. P. Pieltain; the oboists J. C. Fischer, John Parke and Gaetano Besozzi; the bassoonist Miller; and singers, including equally famous virtuosi such as Mrs Billington (née Weichsel), Miss Cantelo (Mrs Harrison), Signora Davies (*l'Inglesina*), Miss Linley (Mrs Sheridan), Madame Mara, Miss Poole (Mrs Dickons), Signora Sales, Signora (Nancy) Storace, the original Susanna in Mozart's *Figaro*, Francesco Benucci (also in *Figaro* and the first Guglielmo in *Così fan tutte*) and the castrato Giusto Ferdinando Tenducci, idol of London society.[1] Their 'star' quality obviously prevented them from contributing more than occasionally to Oxford concerts—they were so much in demand everywhere—but the formation of a permanent band of resident musicians on long-term contracts and with regular employment throughout the year ensured that a good standard was maintained at the Music Room.

The responsibility for organizing all this rested on the stewards of the Music Room. Their duties included drawing up programmes, supervising the orchestra, its instruments and its music, dealing with subscriptions and accounts and engaging performers.[2] The professor of music was generally on the management committee and directed performances. The stewards faced many problems, ranging from failure to return music borrowed from the society, quarrels among members provoked by the 'irrascible' Philip Hayes and poor decorum at concerts, to periodic falls in subscriptions which seriously threatened the future of the Society.[3] Through the most difficult periods the resilience and determination of the stewards were evident in their efforts to preserve the concerts: in 1800 financial circumstances forced them to beg their subscribers, and 'the University and City at large', to consider

whether after a commodious Room has been built and furnished at a great expence, and the Orchestra has been provided with a complete set of Instruments and Books; and after a Band of Instrumental Performers, of acknowledged Abilities in their Profession has been collected; they will suffer the Room and its Furniture to be rendered useless, and the Performers to be dispersed, by withdrawing their support from an Institution which has been

[1] All these were generally recognized at the time as outstanding exponents of their art and their names occur throughout works of reference and memoirs: for example Burney, *History of Music* iv. 681-2; W. Parke, *Musical Memoirs* (2 vols London 1830), *passim*.

[2] Much of their activity can be deduced from announcements in *Jackson's Oxford Journal*; the articles of subscription for the Musical Society were printed regularly in the *Journal*, for example 23 Mar. 1782.

[3] For an account of the quarrel between the cellist Monro and Hayes (popularly referred to as 'Fillchaise' on account of his size) see Mee, *Oldest Music Room in Europe*, 88-106. Crotch related how the 'fine Cremona' violin 'on which he [J. B. Malchair] used to lead . . . was broken by an Orange thrown at the Orchestra during a tumult of young men about the year 1792 after which he never lead': Bodl. MS Mus. d.32, facing p. 1. On the 'riotous conduct of the students' at musical events see also Bodl. MS Top. Oxon. f.296, fos 16-19, extracts from 'The musical tour of Mr Dibdin . . . 4 Oct. 1767'.

established upwards of 50 years, and which provides so much rational and elegant Amusement at an Expence comparatively inconsiderable.[1]

Such appeals usually elicited a satisfactory response, and by reorganizing the concerts to draw in audiences and arranging numerous benefit-concerts to keep up funds the stewards succeeding in guiding the society into a period of 'tranquil prosperity for the concerts in the Music Room' at the beginning of the nineteenth century: 'the stewards had completely vindicated their authority to determine what should be performed and who should perform it'.[2] Among the most successful aspects of their work must be counted their ability to recognize and locate talent; they engaged foreign virtuosi soon after their arrival in England, and several young prodigies had their debuts at Holywell before emerging in London.[3]

Thus the stewards constantly secured the services of the finest solo-ists. Their receptiveness to talent similarly informed their choice of per-formers for the indigenous band at Holywell. Several distinguished foreigners were welcomed into it: Paul Alday, Parisian pupil of Viotti, became leader of the orchestra in 1793 and his wife joined as harpist shortly after; previously, from 1760, the leader had been John Baptist Malchair, originally of Cologne, and a talented artist;[4] the leader of the cellos from about 1768 was E. C. Orthmann, also of German birth. Among other notable members were the cellist Joseph Reinagle junior and the singers William Matthews and Thomas Norris, whose reputa-tions spread well beyond Oxford. Members were required to reside in Oxford on appointment to the band and to abide by the rules of the Society: 'All Performers who receive Pay are expected to attend all Rehearsals.'[5] They supplemented their income not only by the benefit-concerts permitted under the Society's rules, but also by college choris-terships and organists' posts, by bookselling, musical instrument-making and teaching (perhaps giving instrumental tuition to undergraduates and townspeople, or, like Jung, teaching foreign languages; Monroe was

[1] Quoted by Mee, 148.

[2] Ibid. 146; see also preface to P. Jung, *Concerts of Vocal and Instrumental Music, as Performed at the Music Room, Oxford* (Oxford 1808) for an expression of the sense of loyalty and dedication felt by the stewards and performers. Richard Paget described the audience in 1793 as 'in high good humour, and as loyal as ever': Paget's diary, 19 Nov. 1793. From 1789 to 1792 it proved impossible, due to lack of support, to continue the weekly subscription concerts; meanwhile the stewards energetically pro-duced various special concerts (such as commemoration events and benefits at the town hall) thus keeping the orchestra together in spite of changes in personnel, and raising money, so that by 1793 they were able to revive the traditional Monday evenings with a new list of performers.

[3] Crosdill was playing in Oxford from 1768, aged seventeen; Hummel in 1788 at the age of 9; and Miss Poole (later a favourite at Covent Garden and Drury Lane) sang in a benefit concert at the Music Room in 1785, 'not eleven years of age'. Unlike Handel, many of these visiting performers were content with modest remuneration.

[4] Malchair was president of the School of Art in Oxford and was succeeded in this post by his friend Crotch. See also H. Minn, 'Letters of J. B. Malchair, the eighteenth-century Oxford artist', *Oxoniensia* xxii (1957).

[5] Rule 32 of the *Articles* of 1757: Mee, 51.

a dancing master). Several members evidently filled more than one musical function: William Woodcock, 'Organist and Singing Man of New College' and Singing Man of Magdalen, was also a viola-player in the Holywell band,[1] and Paul Jackson played both flute and horn during a lifelong career in the band; many of the performers, as was then customary, also composed works for their own performance. Some belonged to musical families: the Jackson and Hatton brothers and the various Mahons for example.[2] In 1800 Jung listed as regular performers, in addition to the conductor Walter Vicary, 4 instrumental soloists (2 keyboard players, including Crotch, a harpist and a violinist) 17 vocal soloists; 22 members of the vocal chorus (8 sopranos, 4 altos, 4 tenors, 6 basses) 3 first violins, 3 second violins (led by Jung) 1 viola, 1 cello, 1 flute, 2 clarinets, 2 horns, 1 trumpet, 1 double bass and 3 bassoons (one bassoonist doubling on timpani).[3] The chamber size of the orchestra was obviously intended to be commensurate with the size of the room and the scale of the concerts.[4] In constitution it was progressive, regularly employing clarinettists at a relatively early stage in the history of the orchestral use of the clarinet,[5] and in spite of some doubling evidently following the more modern practice of encouraging players to specialize.

The music performed by the Holywell band at subscription and benefit-concerts, quarterly choral nights, 'grand miscellaneous concerts', commemoration concerts in the Sheldonian Theatre and on other ceremonial and festive occasions, shows an up-to-date taste as well as a predictably Handelian traditionalism among Oxford musicians and their audiences.[6] A wide range of composers was represented, with certain favourites (and favourite works) recurring often.[7] There was much Handel, both individual items (especially popular sources were *Acis and Galatea* and *Messiah*) and complete works (performed for example on choral nights and at festival concerts, with *L'allegro ed il penseroso* another prime favourite). Eighteenth-century English composers included Arne, Avison, Boyce and the two Hayeses; among sixteenth- and seventeenth-century composers were Dowland, Locke, Morley and Purcell. Music by foreigners resident in England—Abel, J. C. Bach, Geminiani—appeared

[1] William Woodcock (1754-1825), m. New College 1806; lay clerk Magd. 1784-1818, 1819-25.

[2] See B. Matthews, 'The musical Mahons', *The Musical Times* cxx (1979).

[3] Jung, *Concerts at the Music Room*, pp. xiii-xiv.

[4] It was augmented when necessary (as was the chorus) by outsiders. Clearly it should not be compared with other famous eighteenth-century orchestras such as those at Mannheim, Paris or London, which kept their numbers of instrumentalists at 40 or 50.

[5] William Mahon, clarinettist, pioneered the use of this instrument in Oxford.

[6] Quarterly choral nights replaced one of the Monday evening concerts in each of the four terms, and usually consisted of an oratorio. From 1776 'grand miscellaneous concerts' replaced choral nights in Easter and Michaelmas terms.

[7] Informative catalogues of music owned by the Music Society are extant in Bodl. MS. Eng. misc. c. 314 (the pre-1830 entries are distinguishable) and in Oxford, Music Faculty Lib. rare books, 1757. See also printed lists by Mee, *Oldest Music Room in Europe*, 54-62.

alongside contemporary music from abroad, by Italians (Cimarosa, Gazzaniga, Sarti) Germans, particularly Mannheimers (Filtz, Richter, Stamitz) presumably appreciated for their idiomatic orchestral style, and Austrians (Vanhal, Dittersdorf, Haydn). Gluck featured occasionally, Pleyel frequently, and works by Haydn regularly appeared in manuscript long before his visits to England in the 1790s. These names form only a sample of the total repertoire. Members of the Holywell band (Alday, Norris and others) contributed their own compositions. Types of composition included solo songs and duets, concertos (organ, flute, clarinet, violin, cello) chamber works, symphonies, overtures and choruses. Sometimes a lighter piece—a glee perhaps—might be inserted between the 'acts': sometimes a sacred anthem or chorus appeared in an otherwise secular programme. The arrangement of items followed a set pattern in two halves ('acts') with a varied selection of vocal and instrumental pieces in each half, usually beginning and ending with an overture, symphony or concerto, or perhaps ending with a chorus, and with smaller works in between.[1] Two programmes are given in full below, to illustrate the characteristic mixture:

MUSIC ROOM [Monday] October 20, 1788[2]

ACT I

Overture. Rodelinda . . . . [Handel]
Song. Mr Mathews.
    'Shall I in Mamre's fertile Plain.' . . . . Handel
Sinfonia . . . . Abel
Song. Mr Norris.
    'Here amid the shady woods.' . . . . Handel
Concerto . . . . Corelli

ACT II

Overture . . . . [J. C.] Bach
Song. Mr Mathews.
    'Ye Men of Judah.' . . . . Handel
Sinfonia . . . . Ditters
Song. Mr Norris.
    'Donne donne.' . . . . Galluppi [*sic*]
Concerto 1st, Grand [concerto grosso] . . . . Handel

---

[1] Programmes still extant are in Bodl. MS Mus. 1. d.64, MS Top. Oxon. d.281 (160-70), Gough Oxf. 90 (5.29-34). A list of subscribers for 1800 in MS Mus. 1. d.64 includes the chancellor (the duke of Portland), the vice-chancellor (M. Marlow), heads of houses, fellows of colleges, city people and some ladies. MS Mus. 1. d.64 (item 5b) is a 'Lady's Ticket' for the 'Musical Society at Oxford' (25 Mar. 1785); a 'Gentleman's Ticket' dated '25 March 17[—]' is included with the material in Oxford, Music Faculty Lib. rare books. An evening performance-time of 6 or 6.30 seems to have been usual.

[2] Bodl. MS Mus. 1. d.64, item 6. The texts of the songs are printed on the programme, and a note

GRAND MISCELLANEOUS CONCERT [Thursday] 25 June, 1789[1]

ACT I

Overture	Ditters
Song. Signor Bunucci [*sic*]:	
'Quando vedrai che sono.'	Gazzaniga
Sinfonia	Borghi
Song. Signora Storace.	
'Mia Speranza.'	Sarti
Concerto 1st	Corelli
Chorus. 'Sing unto God.'	Handel
With Trumpets and Drums	

'Between the Acts, (by Particular Request)
GLEE. (Three Voices, by Dr Hayes.)
Messrs. Walton and Radcliffes'
'Hark! how the jolly Huntsman's Cries.'

ACT II

Overture. Occasional Oratorio	[Handel]
Duett. Signora Storace, and Signor Benucci.	
'Piche, Cornacchie e Nottole.' (From the	
celebrated Opera of Gli Schiavi per Amore)—	
Paisellò [*sic*].	
Solo, Violoncello	Mr Reinagle
Sinfonia	Vanhal
Song. Signora Storace. 'The Prince unable to	
conceal his Pain, &c.'	
Chorus. 'Let their coelestial Concerts all unite.'	
with Trumpets and Drums	Handel

Apart from the regular concerts and festivals, particular occasions in the city and university were often celebrated by musical performances. The professor of music, traditionally a practitioner of the art, was involved as composer and performer in many of these events. In 1769, for example, William Hayes 'opened' the new organs built by Byfield and Green for Jesus College (18 May) and St John's College (24 May).[2] For the visit of George III, Queen Charlotte and their children to Nuneham and Oxford

---

is appended: 'N.B. By the ARTICLES OF SUBSCRIPTION, no *Performance*, whether *Vocal* or *Instrumental*, is to be *repeated*.' This appears on other weekly concert programmes. A note of rather different character occurs at the end of a programme for Monday, 20 December 1779: 'The Committee will readily hearken to Complaints against any of the Performers; and will be careful, on all Occasions, to give due Redress', MS Top. Oxon. d.281 (165).

[1] Bodl. MS Mus 1. d.64, item 26.
[2] The examples given here are reported in *Jackson's Oxford Journal* and in sources such as the calendar of Oxford events contained in Bodl. MS Top. Oxon. d. 247.

in 1785, Philip Hayes 'at their entrance into the Theatre and during the Ceremony entertained their Majesties with overtures on the organ'.[1] In April of that year Hayes had directed a performance of *Judas Maccabaeus* at St Martin's church: the charity children sang and Mr Cross (owner of Cross's music shop) played the new organ. Benefit-performances were frequently arranged, and in 1786 and 1787 Handel's *Messiah* was given under Philip Hayes's direction for Cross at St Martin's. Ceremonial anthems were often required: when the duke of Portland and his procession attended choral service at St Mary's in the year of his installation, 1793, they heard an anthem composed by Philip Hayes.[2] The professor might also compose music for the use of the choir at his own college. Crotch's *Ten Anthems* were 'respectfully Dedicated (by Permission) to the Reverend The Dean and Chapter of Christ Church and composed for the Use of that Cathedral'.[3]

Partly due to the greater quantity of surviving documentary material relating to the professors in the second half of the eighteenth century, and partly due to the strength of their personalities, the impression emerges that the two Hayeses and Crotch made a considerable personal impact on their musical surroundings. William Hayes (*circa* 1708-77, professor from 1742) came to Oxford in 1734 as organist and master of the choristers at Magdalen, having already acquired a thorough experience of choral music, first as a chorister at Gloucester cathedral (from 1717) and then as organist at Gloucester, Shrewsbury and Worcester: 'he became excellent in playing Church Music (on the organ) and extempore Voluntaries' but 'his genius was not designed for so narrow a sphere: Oxford was the place ... he wished to settle in'.[4] Hayes's contribution to Oxford music was influenced by his championship of Handel, his connections with the three choirs festival, which may initially have encouraged soloists from the festival to come to Oxford, and his enthusiasm for the project of building the Holywell Music Room. His published work included academic writings on music as well as numerous compositions in popular forms and a quantity of sacred music.[5]

---

[1] Bodl. MS Top. Oxon. d.247, p. 162, 12 Sept.

[2] Ibid. p. 185, 1 July.

[3] W. Crotch, *Ten Anthems* (Cambridge 1798).

[4] *Cathedral Music in Score composed by Dr William Hayes* [ed. P. Hayes, Oxford 1795], preface, 'Life of W. Hayes'.

[5] Notable among his academic writings are his anonymous *Remarks on Mr Avison's Essay on Musical Expression* (London 1753). A contentious streak in the elder Hayes's nature was further illustrated by the anonymous satirical pamphlet he directed against the Gloucester organist Barnabas Gunn: see O. E. Deutsch, ' "Ink-pot and squirt-gun", or "The art of composing music in the new style" ', *The Musical Times* xciii (1952). Hayes's popular compositions included his *Catches, Glees, and Canons* (4 vols and supplement Oxford and London 1763-[85]). Composing and singing light unaccompanied part-songs of this kind formed a favourite occupation of academic musicians: see D. Johnson, 'The 18th-century glee', *The Musical Times* cxx (1979). The fashion is illustrated at an earlier period by Aldrich's 'Smoking Catch', to be sung by four men smoking their pipes.

Philip Hayes commented in his 'Life of W. Hayes' on his father's 'sweetness of Temper'; he himself was renowned for his irascibility as well as for his enormous girth (the story of his nickname 'Fill-chaise' recurs throughout the sources). He became notoriously involved in personal quarrels with Oxford colleagues.[1] His potentially disruptive effect on Oxford music was counterbalanced by his efforts on behalf of the Music Room, the music school and various individuals for whom he raised money by organizing benefit-concerts. He too was active, though not greatly distinguished, as a composer; his song style was more akin to that of his contemporary Joseph Haydn than to that of his father's idol, Handel.[2] Performances of works by the two Hayeses were not confined to Oxford churches and concert rooms: Philip Hayes's setting of Smollett's 'When Sappho tun'd the raptur'd strain'[3] was inscribed 'Sung by Mr Webb in the Concert for the New Musical Fund at the King's Theatre Haymarket'. Philip Hayes's successor, William Crotch, was the best-known composer among these Oxford professors, and the most distinguished musician generally. From his infancy he was famed as a musical prodigy, touring the country with his mother and appearing several times at Oxford from 1779.[4] Crotch continued his association with Oxford concerts throughout the remainder of the century. In 1796 he founded the Oxford Harmonic Society[5] and in 1797 he was appointed Heather professor of music. In 1822 he became the first principal of the Royal Academy of Music; although he retained the Oxford professorship, by 1806 he had established his home in London, initiating the nineteenth-century trend whereby the professors of music lived and worked out of Oxford.

The professor of music traditionally presided over the music school.[6] Williams describes this as having no connection with the 'teaching of candidates for musical degrees, as its name would seem to imply. It was merely one among the schools of the seven liberal arts. Dr Heather

[1] See p. 877 above.

[2] See the opening of his setting of Smollett's 'Thy fatal shafts': Bodl. MS Mus. Voc. I.26, no. 65.

[3] Ibid. no. 69.

[4] Bodl. MS Top. Oxon. d.247 describes how 'Master Crotch, a Child in a Frock on his Mother's Knee, performed on the organ in the Music Room, to the great astonishment of a large Audience' (p. 147, 3 July 1779) and on another occasion 'performed at the Music Room on the Organ, Harpsichord and Violin' (p. 155, 5 July 1783). For details of Crotch's life and work see J. Rennert, *William Crotch 1775–1847: composer, artist, teacher* (Lavenham 1975). Burney wrote an essay on Crotch's life as a prodigy comparing him with Mozart: C. Burney, *Account of an Infant Musician* (London 1779). An amusing verse account of Crotch as 'director of the band' at an Oxford music-meeting is quoted in *Reminiscences of Oxford*, 195–6.   [5] Rennert, 37–8.

[6] The professor was referred to as 'choragus' under the terms of Heather's benefaction, but by the eighteenth century was known as 'professor'. The duties and posts of choragus and professor were not separated until the nineteenth century. The history of the Heather professorship is outlined in the Bodleian Library pamphlet *The Heather Professor of Music, 1626–1976: exhibition in the divinity school October 1976*; cf. p. 870 above.

supplied it with music and instruments . . . and it was afterwards used for the performance of degree exercises.'[1] But the music school did not remain unchanged during the eighteenth century:

In 1780, DR PHILIP HAYES, Professor of Music, anxiously wishing to have the Music School made more commodious, consulted Mr Wyatt about a plan for that purpose. The design furnished by this ingenious architect . . . [was] approved . . . and the School was opened in December with a Lecture for Michaelmas Term.[2]

Hayes's oratorio *Prophecy* was produced for one of the benefit-concerts in aid of the alterations to the music school; Hayes himself donated some of the furnishings, and donations were received from other sources, including Burney. By the end of the eighteenth century the music school had acquired the character of an archive: 'The Bookcases . . . contain the FOUNDER's collection, and subsequent donations, as well as the Exercises of Proceeders to Musical Degrees.'[3] Hawkins worked there when preparing his history of music; 'recourse has been had to the Bodleian library and the college libraries in both universities; to that in the music-school at Oxford', and so it was from direct experience that he described the last-named as 'the repository of a great number of books containing compositions of various kinds, some of them of great antiquity'.[4] Burney studied, among other sources, the Christ Church collection for the purposes of his history: '[Aldrich] bequeathed to his college, at his decease in 1710, an admirable collection of Music, to which, by the indulgence of the dean and canons, I have not only been honoured with frequent access, but been liberally allowed to transcribe and make extracts'.[5]

   In an age which saw the production of Burney's and Hawkins's great histories of music and the formation of societies devoted to music of the past, Oxford, with its music-school archive, Bodleian collections and the

---

[1] Williams, *Degrees in Music*, 32. For details of the holdings of the music school see M. Crum, 'Early lists of the Oxford music school collection', *Music and Letters* xlviii (1967) and W. K. Ford, 'The Oxford music school in the late 17th century', *Jl American Musicological Soc.* xvii (1964). A list of portraits at the Music School is in A. Wood, *The History and Antiquities of the University of Oxford*, ed. J. Gutch (2 vols in 3 Oxford 1792-6) ii. 889 ff; see also *Catalogue of Portraits* i, pp. xii, 151-65.

[2] Wood, 888.   [3] Wood, 889.

[4] Hawkins, *Science and Practice of Music* i, preface, ii. 522.

[5] Burney, *History of Music* iii. 602. See also A. Hiff, *Catalogue of Printed Music Published prior to 1801, now in the Library of Christ Church, Oxford* (Oxford 1919); G. E. P. Arkwright, *Catalogue of Music in the Library of Christ Church Oxford* (Oxford 1915, repr. with corrections and additions (Oxford 1971); Christ Church, library record 12, catalogue of the Aldrich collection, a list in two sections (the first dated 1778, the second inscribed by P. Hayes and dated 1779) which ranges over secular and sacred vocal and instrumental music by sixteenth- and seventeenth-century English and continental composers, including Byrd, Tallis, Gibbons, Blow, Purcell, Marenzio, Monteverdi and Lully, and Aldrich himself, together with some eighteenth-century additions. Also in Christ Church Library (Music MS 1187) are voluminous papers for a learned treatise on music, attributed to Aldrich but now known to be only partly his work.

resources of college libraries, both reflected and stimulated awareness of the historical approach to music, based on scholarly study, editing and performance.[1] Among evidence of scholarly interests pursued by the professors of music (in addition to but partly connected with their performing and conducting activities) are Philip Hayes's editions of sixteenth-, seventeenth- and eighteenth-century composers including Purcell, William Hayes and William Boyce. Hayes's successor, Crotch, produced in his *Syllabus of a Course of Lectures on Music* together with his *Specimens of Various Styles of Music* the most substantial indication of academic teaching interests.[2] Inevitably Crotch's choice of illustration, with its considerable emphasis on 'folk' and 'national' music of dubious origin, was limited by the state of knowledge and taste of his time.[3] But his collection of examples reveals an imaginative attempt to seek beyond the immediate and accessible, and his thoughtful approach to teaching is expressed in his avowed aim of combining academic example with practical purpose in selecting his material from different countries and periods:

The intention ...
  i. To improve the taste, by introducing the performer to every kind of excellence.
  ii. To give a *practical* History of the progress of the Science.
  iii. To present in one work to the Student in Composition a great variety of matter for his study and imitation.
  iv. To furnish performers in general with good subjects for practice, calculated for all stages of their progress.[4]

The concept of a lecture covering a historical topic such as the early development of opera contrasts strongly with those previously fashionable music-lectures in which scientific and philosophical considerations

[1] Among the societies was the Madrigal Society (1741) whose members included Callcott and Hawkins. Printed music was among books given by Wood and others to the Bodleian Library; music in manuscript was not acquired by the Library in any quantity until 1801, when Osborne Wight bequeathed music derived from sources including Philip Hayes and covering seventeenth- and eighteenth-century English and Italian music: *Summary Catalogue of Western Manuscripts in the Bodleian Library* iv (by F. Madan), nos. 16670-878.

[2] *Syllabus of a Course of Lectures on Music* ([Oxford] nd), copies in Bodl. Top. Oxon. d.22 (11), G. A. Oxon. b.19 (265); the lectures were given 1800-4. Lectures I-IV cover general considerations, ancient and national music ('National Music probably the remains of the Music of the Ancients') while lectures V-XII go through from early church music, renaissance polyphony, the invention of opera, seventeenth- and early eighteenth-century composers including the Scarlattis, Bach and Handel, to the invention of the symphony, Gluck, Piccinni, Mozart, Haydn and Clementi. W. Crotch, *Specimens of Various Styles in Music* (3 vols London [*c*1808-15]); the original of the lectures manuscript is now in Norwich, Norfolk and Norwich Record Office, MSS 11063-7, 11228-33, 1806-32, later excerpted in *The Substance of Several Courses of Lectures on Music* (London 1831).

[3] 'East Indian' tunes are given with eighteenth-century Italian-Viennese *galant* cadences, for example. Crotch shared his enthusiasm for national song with his friend Malchair; Bodl. MS Mus. d.32 contains Crotch's arrangements of 'Malchair's tunes', mainly folk melodies and dances.

[4] Crotch, *Specimens*, introduction.

were explored with reference to classical authors.[1] Although it was not until later in the nineteenth century, with the reforms of Gore Ouseley in 1862, that the history of music was specified together with other elements (such as critical analysis of musical scores) as part of a set syllabus, Crotch's lectures show that the eighteenth-century movement towards the historical study of music had begun to influence Oxford musical teaching by about 1800.

Crotch's Oxford career was a fitting monument to the versatility of the eighteenth-century professors. Apart from lecturing, composing and performing in concerts, he continued the tradition of combining the Heather professorship with posts as college and university organist. The professor was customarily organist of the university church of St Mary. Crotch acted as organist at Christ Church from 1790 and at St John's from 1797; Richard Goodson senior had been organist at New College from 1682 and at Christ Church from 1692; Philip Hayes at Christ Church 1763-5, Magdalen 1777-97 and St John's 1790-7. The series of distinguished organists at various colleges during the period 1688-1800 was one factor in the continuation of the choral tradition.[2] At New College Simon Child served as organist for thirty years from 1702, and Richard Church for forty-four years from 1732;[3] this long-serving personnel ensured a basic continuity amid the changing constituents of college choirs. Wykeham's original benefaction had stipulated that the ten chaplains, three clerks and sixteen choristers attached to New College were to be retained at all costs. Several colleges had similarly specific provision of endowments to cover chapel-clerks, choristers, chaplains and organists as well as the upkeep of chapel instruments, music and books. Although, prior to the period under consideration, the Puritan proscription of music had disrupted the choral tradition in Oxford as elsewhere, some resources remained, and much was restored, after 1660. The organ in use at St John's until 1768 was the same as before the Restoration.[4] At New College, where the organ had been dismantled in 1649, a new instrument was built in 1663.[5] Cromwell's act of mercy, whereby the organ from Magdalen was removed for his entertainment to Hampton Court, enabled the college to retrieve it safely after the Restoration and return it to its proper place in the chapel.[6]

[1] Cf Milles, *Ars musica*.
[2] The basic training of musicians was still very often rooted in the church, for example the early career of William Hayes as chorister and organist.
[3] P. H. Hale, 'Music and musicians' in J. Buxton and P. H. Williams (eds), *New College, Oxford, 1379-1979* (Oxford 1979), 272-3.
[4] A. Wood, *The History and Antiquities of the Colleges and Halls in the University of Oxford*, ed. J. Gutch (Oxford 1786), 3.
[5] For the history of New College's organ see Hale, 270-3.
[6] A. Wood, *Appendix to the History and Antiquities of the Colleges and Halls in the University of Oxford, containing fasti oxonienses*, ed. and cont. J. Gutch (Oxford 1790), 271.

Throughout the eighteenth century the colleges continued to devote money to the upkeep of choral establishments and choir-schools (such as those at Magdalen and New College). Organists could influence the facilities available, so that Philip Hayes arranged for much work to be done on the organ of New College (rebuilt by Byfield and Green in 1794) and for improvements in the training of choristers. The regular employment of organists and choristers was recorded in a series of documents, as at New College, where chapel employees are listed and payments made and expenses incurred are recorded.[1] Examples of expenditure at New College include repairs to the organ, music-copying (for example £5 7s 9½d to one Kelway in 1729) extra singing and teaching the choristers. There are also extant manuscript records of music used in chapels, such as the service books from New College and Christ Church.[2] These contain sixteenth- and seventeenth-century English music, for example by Byrd and Tallis, Gibbons, Aldrich and Purcell, besides music by eighteenth-century composers (Alcock, Crotch, Dupuis, William and Philip Hayes—all Oxford graduates—as well as some more internationally known names). Chapel music was composed and copied throughout the eighteenth century in Oxford; in this seemingly more secular age the provision of music for church use was still a vital concern. Oxford chapels created a strong link in the English choral tradition. In this respect, as with the Holywell concerts on the secular side, Oxford was an important musical centre, connected in the eighteenth century with some of the most significant traditions and innovations in the history of English music.

[1] NCA 9857-9 increment books 1793-1801; 9655, great register 1652-1773; 976 (includes applications for choristerships etc. 1759-1802). I am grateful to Miss M. Crum, formerly of the Bodleian Library, for the loan of her notes on some New College account-books.

[2] See, for example, Bodl. MS 1 Mus. c.46 (New College partbooks, copyists including Philip Hayes) and MS Mus. d. 169 (inscribed 'Chants/Basso/Fellows' copy'); New College Library, G. Heathcote, 'Catalogue of the music books in New College chapel, November 1794'; and the catalogues of music at Christ Church cited in p. 884 n. 5 above.

Appendix

Selected Officers of the University and Professors and Readers

OFFICERS

CHANCELLORS

1669–88	James Butler (1610–88), first duke of Ormonde
1688–1715	James Butler (1665–1745), second duke of Ormonde
1715–58	Charles Butler, earl of Arran
1758–62	John Fane, earl of Westmorland
1762–72	George Henry Lee, earl of Lichfield
1772–92	Frederick North, Lord North
1792–1809	William Henry Cavendish Bentinck, duke of Portland

VICE-CHANCELLORS

1666–9	John Fell
1669–73	Peter Mews
1673–6	Ralph Bathurst
1676–7	Henry Clerke
1677–9	John Nicholas
1679–82	Timothy Halton
1682–5	John Lloyd
1685–6	Timothy Halton (again)
1686–7	John Venn
1687–9	Gilbert Ironside
1689–92	Jonathan Edwards
1692–5	Henry Aldrich
1695–7	Fitzherbert Adams
1697–8	John Meare
1698–1700	William Paynter
1700–2	Roger Mander
1702–6	William Delaune
1706–10	William Lancaster
1710–12	Thomas Braithwaite
1712–15	Bernard Gardiner
1715–18	John Baron
1718–23	Robert Shippen
1723–8	John Mather
1728–32	Edward Butler
1732–5	William Holmes
1735–8	Stephen Niblett
1738–41	Theophilus Leigh
1741–4	Walter Hodges
1744–7	Euseby Isham
1747–50	John Purnell
1750–3	John Brown
1753–6	George Huddesford
1756–9	Thomas Randolph
1759–65	Joseph Browne
1765–8	David Durell
1768–72	Nathan Wetherell
1772–6	Thomas Fothergill
1776–80	George Horne
1780–4	Samuel Dennis
1784–8	Joseph Chapman
1788–92	John Cooke
1792–6	John Wills
1796–7	Scrope Berdmore
1797–8	Edmund Isham
1798–1802	Michael Marlow

HIGH STEWARDS

1686–1709	Henry Hyde (1638–1709)
1709–11	Laurence Hyde
1711–53	Henry Hyde (1672–1753)
1754–60	John Fane

ANGLO-SAXON, RAWLINSON'S PRO-
FESSORS OF

1795–1800 Charles Mayo
1800–3 Thomas Hardcastle

ARABIC, LAUDIAN PROFESSORS OF

1636–91 Edward Pococke
1691–1703 Thomas Hyde
1703–38 John Wallis
1738–74 Thomas Hunt
1774–1814 Joseph White

ARABIC, THE LORD ALMONER'S
PROFESSORS OF

1724–40 Jean Gagnier
1741–8 Thomas Hunt
1748–80 Richard Browne
1780–1813 Henry Ford

ASTRONOMY, SAVILIAN PROFESSORS
OF

1673–91 Edward Bernard
1691–1708 David Gregory
1709–12 John Caswell
1712–21 John Keill
1721–62 James Bradley
1763–1810 Thomas Hornsby

BOTANY, PROFESSORS OF

1684–c1719 Jacob Bobart
1720–4 Edwin Sandys
1724–34 Gilbert Trowe

BOTANY, SHERARDIAN PROFESSORS
OF

1734–47 Johann Jacob Dillenius
1747–84 Humphrey Sibthorp
1784–96 John Sibthorp
1796–1834 George Williams

CHEMISTRY, PROFESSORS OF

1683–90 Robert Plot
1690–1704 Edward Hannes

CHEMISTRY, READERS IN

1781–5 Martin Wall
1785–6 William Austin
1787–92 Thomas Beddoes
1793–1801 Robert Bourne

DIVINITY, REGIUS PROFESSORS OF

1680–1707 William Jane
1707–37 John Potter
1737–41 George Rye
1741–63 John Fanshawe
1763–76 Edward Bentham
1776–83 Benjamin Wheeler
1783–1807 John Randolph

DIVINITY, LADY MARGARET PRO-
FESSORS OF

1648–52 Francis Cheynell
1652–60 Henry Wilkinson
1660–76 Thomas Barlow
1676–91 John Hall
1691 Henry Maurice
1691–1705 Thomas Sykes
1705–15 John Wynne
1715–28 William Delaune
1728–68 Thomas Jenner
1768–83 Thomas Randolph
1783–98 Timothy Neve
1798–1827 Septimus Collinson

EXPERIMENTAL PHILOSOPHY,
READERS OR PROFESSORS

1749–60 James Bradley
1763–1810 Thomas Hornsby

GEOMETRY, SAVILIAN PROFESSORS OF

1649–1703	John Wallis
1703–42	Edmond Halley
1742–64	Nathaniel Bliss
1765–6	Joseph Betts
1766–96	John Smith
1797–1810	Abraham Robertson

GREEK, REGIUS PROFESSORS OF

1665–98	William Levinz
1698–1705	Humphrey Hody
1705–7	Thomas Milles
1707–11	Edward Thwaites
1712–35	Thomas Terry
173–47	John Fanshawe
1747–51	Thomas Shaw
1751–63	Samuel Dickens
1763–82	William Sharpe
1782–3	John Randolph
1783–1811	William Jackson

HEBREW, REGIUS PROFESSORS OF

1648–51 and 1660–91	Edward Pococke
1691–7	Roger Altham
1697–1703	Thomas Hyde
1703–14	Roger Altham (again)
1715–47	Robert Clavering
1747–74	Thomas Hunt
1774–80	Richard Browne
1780–7	George Jubb
1787–1801	Benjamin Blayney

HISTORY, CAMDEN PROFESSORS OF ANCIENT

1688–91	Henry Dodwell
1691–1720	Charles Aldworth
1720–7	Sedgwick Harrison
1727–61	Richard Frewin
1761–73	John Warneford
1773–85	William Scott
1785–90	Thomas Warton the younger
1790–1823	Thomas Winstanley

HISTORY, REGIUS PROFESSORS OF MODERN

1724–36	David Gregory (1696–1767)
1736–42	William Holmes
1742–68	Joseph Spence
1768–71	John Vivian
1771–1801	Thomas Nowell

LAW, PROFESSORS OF CIVIL

1672–1712	Thomas Bouchier
1712–36	James Bouchier
1736–52	Henry Brooke
1754–67	Robert Jenner
1767–89	Robert Vansittart
1789–96	Thomas Francis Wenman
1796–1809	French Laurence

LAW, VINERIAN PROFESSORS OF

1758–62	William Blackstone
1762–77	Robert Chambers
1777–93	Richard Wooddeson
1793–1824	James Blackstone

MEDICINE, REGIUS PROFESSORS OF

1681–98	John Luffe
1698–1718	Thomas Hoy
1718–29	Thomas Lasher
1729–30	William Beauvoir
1730–58	William Woodford
1759–72	John Kelly
1772–1801	William Vivian

MUSIC, PROFESSORS OF (WITH OFFICES OF CHORAGUS AND PRAECENTOR)

1682–1718	Richard Goodson the elder
1718–41	Richard Goodson the younger
1741–77	William Hayes
1777–97	Philip Hayes
1797–1847	William Crotch

NATURAL PHILOSOPHY, SEDLEIAN PROFESSORS OF

1675–1704	Thomas Millington
1704–20	James Fayrer
1720–41	Charles Bertie
1741–67	Joseph Browne
1767–82	Benjamin Wheeler
1782–1810	Thomas Hornsby

POETRY, PROFESSORS OF

1708–18	Joseph Trapp
1718–28	Thomas Warton the elder
1728–38	Joseph Spence
1738–41	John Whitfield
1741–51	Robert Lowth
1751–6	William Hawkins
1756–66	Thomas Warton the younger
1766–76	Benjamin Wheeler
1776–83	John Randolph
1783–93	Robert Holmes
1793–1801	James Hurdis

Index

For full lists of the holders of posts readers are referred to the appendix (pp. 888–92). Page references in *italics* below refer to whole chapters in the volume.